VIRTUAL REALITY

Edited by **Jae-Jin Kim**

Virtual Reality
Edited by Jae-Jin Kim

Published by InTech

Janeza Trdine 9, 51000 Rijeka, Croatia

Publishing Process Manager Iva Lipovic

Technical Editor Teodora Smiljanic

Cover Designer InTech Design Team

Additional hard copies can be obtained from orders@intechopen.com

Virtual Reality, Edited by Jae-Jin Kim
p. cm.
ISBN 978-953-307-518-1

For EU product safety concerns:
IN TECH d.o.o., Prolaz Marije Krucifikse Kozulić 3, 51000 Rijeka, Croatia,
info@intechopen.com or visit our website at intechopen.com.

Meet the editor

Jae-Jin Kim received the M.D. (1987) and Ph.D. (2002) degrees in psychiatry from Seoul National University, Seoul, Korea. He currently works as a professor and a chair at the Department of Psychiatry, Yonsei University Gangnam Severance Hospital, and as s director at the Institute of Behavioral Science in Medicine, Yonsei University College of Medicine, Seoul, Korea. His research interests are to develop the virtual reality programs for improving social functions in psychiatric patients such as schizophrenia and social phobia, and to investigate the pathophysiology of social deficits using the fMRI and PET. He has published a lot of papers about virtual reality and neuroimaging, and recently won the best researcher award, Yonsei University Gangnam Severance Hospital (Oct, 2010).

Contents

Preface XIII

Part 1 Human-computer Interaction 1

Chapter 1 **Brain-Computer Interface Systems used for Virtual Reality Control 3**
Gert Pfurtscheller, Robert Leeb, Josef Faller and Christa Neuper

Chapter 2 **Hapto-Acoustic Interaction Metaphors in 3D Virtual Environments for Non-Visual Settings 21**
Fabio De Felice, Floriana Renna, Giovanni Attolico and Arcangelo Distante

Chapter 3 **Collaborative 3D Interaction in Virtual Environments: a Workflow-Based Approach 49**
Samir Otmane, Christophe Domingues, Frédéric Davesne and Malik Mallem

Part 2 Advanced Virtual Reality Technologies 69

Chapter 4 **Virtual Reality to Simulate Visual Tasks for Robotic Systems 71**
Manuela Chessa, Fabio Solari and Silvio P. Sabatini

Chapter 5 **Development of a Finger Pad Force Display for a Hand Haptic Interface 93**
Haruhisa Kawasaki, Shinya Koide, Tetuya Mouri and Takahiro Endo

Chapter 6 **Face-Touch: An Emotional Facial Expression Technique of Avatar Based on Tactile Vibration in Virtual Reality Game 107**
Ahmad Hoirul Basori, Abdullah Bade, Mohd. Shahrizal Sunar and Daut Daman

Chapter 7 **VR Development with InTml 127**
Pablo Figueroa

Part 3 Evaluation of Cognition and Behavior 147

Chapter 8 **Compelling Self-Motion Through Virtual Environments without Actual Self-Motion – Using Self-Motion Illusions ("Vection") to Improve User Experience in VR 149**
Bernhard E. Riecke

Chapter 9 **Neck Motion Analysis Using a Virtual Environment 177**
Sarig Bahat Hilla

Chapter 10 **Handedness and Dexterity Evaluation System Using Haptic Virtual Reality Technology 203**
Masanao Koeda, Mako Matsuyama, Munetaka Sugihashi and Tsuneo Yoshikawa

Chapter 11 **An Exploratory Study on the Relationship between Orientation Map Reading and Way-finding in Unfamiliar Environments 223**
Chieh-Hsin Tang, Chin-Wei Chang, Ying-Ji Chuang and Ching-Yuan Lin

Part 4 VR as a Therapeutic Tool 245

Chapter 12 **Virtuality Supports Reality for e-Health Applications 247**
Giovanni Saggio and Carlo Alberto Pinto

Chapter 13 **Simulation of Subject Specific Bone Remodeling and Virtual Reality Visualization 273**
Ajay Sonar and James Carroll

Chapter 14 **Application of Advanced Virtual Reality and 3D Computer Assisted Technologies in Computer Assisted Surgery and Tele-3D-computer Assisted Surgery in Rhinology 291**
Ivica Klapan, Pero Raos, Tomislav Galeta, Ljubimko Šimičić, Juraj Lukinović, Željko Vranješ, Josip Maleš, Stanko Belina and Višeslav Ćuk

Chapter 15 **Development of a Medical Training System with Integration of Users' Skills Assessment 325**
Ronei M. Moraes and Liliane S. Machado

Chapter 16 **Virtual Reality Simulators for Objective Evaluation on Laparoscopic Surgery: Current Trends and Benefits. 349**
Ignacio Oropesa, Pablo Lamata, Patricia Sánchez-González, José B. Pagador, María E. García, Francisco M. Sánchez-Margallo and Enrique J. Gómez

Part 5 **Neuroscience and Neuro-rehabilitation 375**

Chapter 17 **Research in Neuroscience and Virtual Reality 377**
Beatriz Rey and Mariano Alcañiz

Chapter 18 **Exploring the Potential of Virtual Reality for the Elderly and People with Disabilities 395**
Felix Kamieth, Patrick Dähne, Reiner Wichert, Juan Luis Villalar, Viveca Jimenez-Mixco, Antonella Arca and Maria Teresa Arredondo

Chapter 19 **Common Issues of Virtual Reality in Neuro-Rehabilitation 419**
Man, D.W.K.

Chapter 20 **Application of Virtual Reality in Neuro-Rehabilitation: an Overview 429**
Lucia F Lucca, Antonio Candelieri and Loris Pignolo

Part 6 **Psychiatric Evaluation and Therapy 443**

Chapter 21 **Virtual Reality in Evidence - Based Psychotherapy 445**
Aurora Szentágotai, David Opriş and Daniel David

Chapter 22 **Application of "Virtual Realities" in Psychotherapy: Possibilities, Limitations and Effectiveness 469**
Christiane Eichenberg

Chapter 23 **Virtual Reality-Based Assessment of Social Skills and Its Application to Mental Illnesses 485**
Jae-Jin Kim, Joseph Kim

Chapter 24 **Emotions and the Emotional Valence Afforded by the Virtual Environment 501**
Stéphane Bouchard

Chapter 25 **Serious Games for Serious Problems: from *Ludicus* to Therapeuticus 515**
Pedro Gamito, Jorge Oliveira, Diogo Morais, Pedro Rosa and Tomaz Saraiva

Part 7 **Educational and Industrial Applications 537**

Chapter 26 **Integrating Low-Cost Virtual Reality into Engineering Design Curricula 539**
Shana Smith

Chapter 27 **Virtual Reality and Computational Design 547**
Michael S. Bittermann and I. Sevil Sariyildiz

Chapter 28 **Didactic Models in Civil Engineering Education: Virtual Simulation of Construction Works 579**
Alcínia Z. Sampaio, Carlos O. Cruz and Octávio P. Martins

Chapter 29 **Application of Augmented Reality to Evaluate Invisible Height for Landscape Preservation 599**
Nobuyoshi Yabuki

Chapter 30 **Virtual Reality Simulation System for Underground Mining Project 615**
Keping Zhou and Mingming Guo

Part 8 Virtual Worlds and Human Society 633

Chapter 31 **The Otherness of Cyberspace, Virtual Reality and Hypertext 635**
Tuğrul İlter

Chapter 32 **Actual Policing in Virtual Reality – A Cause of Moral Panic or a Justified Need? 647**
Katalin Parti

Preface

Even though virtual reality techniques and their applications have been present for only two decades, a lot of various interactive methods and applications have been introduced. In its inception, button boxes or joysticks were used as virtual reality's sole interface mechanism. However, input devices have increasingly become more multifaceted and intuitive by taking advantage of numerous developing technologies such as haptic interface, motion capture, eye-gaze tracking, camera marker tracking, and position tracking. Moreover, enhancement of visual display qualities and increased computational capacity and efficiency of personal computers have contributed to dramatic improvement in providing a realistic and interactive experience of virtual environments. Research in virtual reality have gradually broadened its scope from primarily focusing on the hardware and technology itself to including more functional aspects of various possible virtual reality applications. Recently, virtual reality applications have widely expanded to accommodate their usage in scientific research, manufacturing, business, medicine, education, sports, video games, art, and military training and operations.

Our goals in writing this book were to provide a comprehensive volume on the medium of virtual reality, introduce how it can be used, and how compelling virtual reality applications can be created. In this book we mainly introduce rapidly developing technology of virtual reality which includes new developments in hardware, software and applications, particularly in the field of medicine and engineering. We additionally address relevant ethical concerns in the community regarding the current trend in scientific research that utilize virtual reality. First two sections – "Human-computer interaction" and "Advanced virtual reality technologies" - discuss software and hardware. Various interaction techniques and their simple applications are presented. Next four sections – "Evaluation of cognition and behavior", "VR as a therapeutic tool", "Neuroscience and neuro-rehabilitation", and "Psychiatric evaluation and therapy"– are about the-state-of-the-art virtual reality applications in medicine. Moreover, applications in other fields - "Educational and Industrial applications" - are also illustrated in the next section. Last section – "Virtual worlds and human society" – is about intention in virtual reality and ethical issues in virtual communities.

Our reviews regarding virtual reality as an important medium ranges from discussion of its design and implementation of the hardware that enables virtual reality systems to be built, to how the medium can be used as a new tool, and also on how to provide better understanding and interest in virtual reality. For the latter of aforementioned goals, we briefly discuss the types of virtual reality systems and their differences without going into in-depth technical details on the hardware technology. While new advances in the field of virtual reality technology may be too vast and rapid to be covered exhaustively in this volume - and other additional resources may supplement information provided here - we hope this book will help readers understand and appreciate the utility of VR systems and their applications.

JAE-JIN KIM, MD, PhD
KIWAN HAN, PhD

Part 1

Human-computer Interaction

1

Brain-Computer Interface Systems used for Virtual Reality Control

Gert Pfurtscheller[1], Robert Leeb[2], Josef Faller[1] and Christa Neuper[1]
[1]Laboratory of Brain-Computer Interfaces (BCI-Lab), Institute for Knowledge Discovery, Graz University of Technology,
[2]Chair on Non-Invasive Brain-Machine Interface, School of Engineering, Ecole Polytechnique Fédérale de Lausanne,
[1]Austria
[2]Switzerland

1. Introduction

A Brain-Computer Interface (BCI) is a non-muscular communication channel for connecting the brain to a computer or another device. Currently, non-invasive BCIs transform thought-related changes in the electroencephalogram (EEG) online and in real time into control signals. In such an EEG-based BCI, specific features are extracted from brain-signals, transformed into a control signal, and used to restore communication to patients with locked-in-syndrome or to control neuroprosthesis in patients with spinal cord injuries (Birbaumer et al., 1999; Pfurtscheller et al., 2008b; Wolpaw et al., 2002). In addition to these applications, which focus on communication and control, the related field of neurofeedback supports feedback training in people suffering from epilepsy, autism, stroke, and emotional or attentional disorders (Birbaumer & Cohen, 2007).

Today the world of BCI applications is expanding and new fields are opening. One new direction involves BCIs to control virtual reality (VR), including BCIs for games, or using VR as a powerful feedback medium to reduce the need for BCI training (Leeb et al., 2007b; Scherer et al., 2008). Virtual environments (VE) can provide an excellent testing ground for procedures that could be adapted to real world scenarios, especially for patients with disabilities. If people can learn to control their movements or perform specific tasks in a VE, this could justify the much greater expense of building physical devices such as a wheelchair or robot arm that is controlled by a BCI. BCIs are more and more moving out of the laboratory and becoming also useful for healthy users in certain situations (Nijholt et al., 2008).

One of the first efforts to combine VR and BCI technologies was Bayliss and Ballard (2000) and Bayliss (2003). They introduced a VR smart home in which users could control different appliances using a P300-based BCI. Pineda et al. (2003) showed that immersive feedback based on a computer game can help people learn to control a BCI based on imagined movement more quickly than mundane feedback, a finding we later validated with other immersive feedback (Leeb et al., 2006; 2007b). Lalor et al. (2005) used a steady-state visual evoked potential (SSVEP)-based BCI to control a character in an immersive 3-D gaming environment. Recently, Leeb et al. (2007b) have reported on exploring a smart virtual apartment using a motor imagery-based BCI, and Holzner et al. (2009) in an experiment for P300-based BCI for smart home control.

This short overview about BCI applications in VR shows that there are many different types of BCIs. The next section provides a short introduction to BCIs.

2. Definition and basic principles of a BCI

Wolpaw et al. (2002) defined a BCI as a "...new non-muscular channel for sending messages and commands to the external world". Here, we clarify this definition to emphasize that any BCI must have the 4 following components (Pfurtscheller et al., 2010a):

1. Direct recording: The BCI must rely at least partly on direct measures of brain activity, such as through electrical potentials, magnetic fields, or hemodynamic changes.
2. Real time processing: The signal processing must occur online and yield a communication or control signal.
3. Feedback: Goal-directed feedback, about the success or failure of the control, must be provided to the user.
4. Intentional control: The user must perform an intentional, goal-directed mental action to control, such as imagining movement or focusing on a stimulus.

These definitions implicate that each BCI is a closed-loop system with two adaptive controllers: the user's brain, which produces the signals and provides the input to the BCI; and the BCI itself, which analyses the brain signals and transforms them to a control signal as the BCI output (Figure 1).

The EEG is the most widely used brain signal in BCIs (Mason et al., 2007), and is also the most common signal when using a BCI system for VR control. Two types of changes can be extracted from the ongoing EEG signals: one change is time and phase-locked (evoked) to an externally or internally-paced event, the other is non-phase-locked (induced). Evoked signals include event-related potentials (ERPs), including the P300 and SSVEPs (Allison et al., 2008). Induced signals include the dynamic amplitude changes of oscillations in different frequency bands (Pfurtscheller & Lopes da Silva, 1999; Pfurtscheller & Neuper, 2010). Thus, we can differentiate between 2 types of BCI systems. One is based on predefined mental

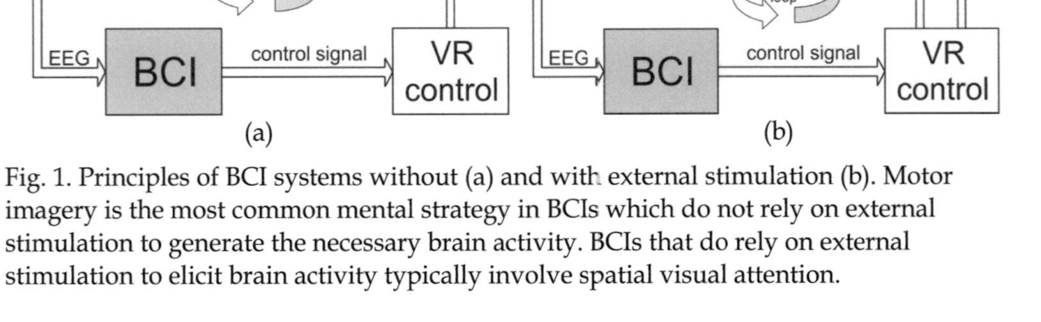

Fig. 1. Principles of BCI systems without (a) and with external stimulation (b). Motor imagery is the most common mental strategy in BCIs which do not rely on external stimulation to generate the necessary brain activity. BCIs that do rely on external stimulation to elicit brain activity typically involve spatial visual attention.

tasks and classifying induced brain activities (Figure 1a), while the other is based on sensory stimulation (e.g. visual) and classifying evoked potential changes (Figure 1b).

Three different BCI approaches have received the most attention in recent years:

P300-based BCI (P300 BCI): The P300 is the positive component of the evoked potential that may develop about 300 ms after an item is flashed. The user focuses on one flashing item while ignoring other stimuli. Whenever the target stimulus flashes, it yields a larger P300 than the other possible choices. P300 BCIs are typically used to spell (Allison & Pineda, 2006; Donchin et al., 2000; Farwell & Donchin, 1988), but have been validated with other tasks such as control of a mobile robot (Bell et al., 2008) or a smart home control (Holzner et al., 2009).

SSVEP-based BCI (SSVEP BCI): Steady-state evoked potentials (SSEPs) occur when sensory stimuli are repetitively delivered rapidly enough that the relevant neuronal structures do not return to their resting states. In a BCI application, the user focuses on one of several stimuli, each of which flicker at a different rate and/or phase. Flickering light sources are typically used to trigger steady-state visual evoked potentials. Gao et al. (2003) described a BCI with 48 flickering lights and a high information transfer rate of 68 bits/min. This was the fastest BCI reported in the published literature until recently, when the same group described some improved approaches (Bin et al., 2009). Like P300 BCIs, SSVEP BCIs require no training and can facilitate rapid communication (Allison et al., 2008; Krusienski et al., 2006). SSVEP BCIs have also recently expanded to tasks beyond spelling, such as controlling a virtual character (avatar) in a computer game (Faller et al., 2010; Lalor et al., 2005; Martinez et al., 2007) or controlling an orthosis (Pfurtscheller et al., 2010b).

ERD-based BCI (ERD BCI, SMR BCI): Brain rhythms can either display an event-related amplitude decrease or desynchronization (ERD) or an event-related amplitude increase or synchronization (ERS) (Pfurtscheller & Lopes da Silva, 1999). The term ERD BCI describes any BCI system that relies on the detection of amplitude changes in sensorimotor rhythms (mu and central beta rhythms) and/or other brain oscillations, also including short-lasting post-imagery beta bursts (beta ERS, beta rebound) (Blankertz et al., 2007; Pfurtscheller et al., 2006a; 2008b; Pfurtscheller & Solis- Escalante, 2009). The term SMR BCI is frequently used when only sensorimotor rhythms are classified (Birbaumer & Cohen, 2007). In the standard protocol, the user performs a motor imagery task to consciously modify brain rhythms. Motor imagery results in a somatotopically organised activation pattern, similar to that observed when the same movement is really executed (Lotze et al., 1999; Pfurtscheller & Neuper, 2010). In particular, hand and feet motor imagery affect sensorimotor EEG rhythms in ways that allow a BCI to detect such changes online and generate a reliable control signal.

The ERD BCI can operate in two different modes: the input data are either processed in a predefined time windows of a few seconds each following cue stimuli (synchronous or cue-based BCI), or continuously sample-by-sample (asynchronous or self-paced BCI). In a synchronous protocol, the user performs a mental task after each cue; the EEG processing is time-locked to externally-paced cues that are repeated in intervals of several seconds because the onset of motor imagery is precisely known. No cue is presented in the asynchronous mode. Hence, the system is continuously available for control, allowing users to freely decide when they wish to generate a control signal. The output (control) signal of a BCI can be either the result of the user's intended control (IC) or intended non-control (INC). In the latter case, during the resting state, undefined mental tasks (thoughts) or artifacts may be erroneously classified as control signals. Such an asynchronous BCI is more complex and demanding for developers, even though it may be easier for the user.

However, asynchronous BCIs have been validated even in advanced situations, such as navigating in a virtual environment (Leeb et al., 2007a; 2007d; Scherer et al., 2008).

3. Virtual Reality system

In order to carry out the VE experiments, two different and complex systems had to be integrated: the BCI and the VR system. Figure 2 shows that both systems run on two different machines (hardware) and different platforms (software). The interaction between them is realized via a network connection (usually TCP/IP).
The participant is placed in the middle of a multi-projection based stereo and head-tracked VR system commonly known as a "CAVE" (Cruz-Neira et al., 1993). The surround projection system consists of three rear-projected active stereo screens (left, right and front wall on which the images are projected from outside) and a front-projected screen on the floor (image for the floor is projected from above), as shown in the right part of Figure 2. It generates three-dimensional stereoscopic representations of computer animated worlds, depending on the current viewing position and direction of the visitor.
The projections on the screens are continuously adapted to the movements of the visitor by re-computing the projected images for the respective current viewing position and direction (update rate of 30 – 50 times per second). The position of the subject is determined using four infrared cameras that keep track of a number of highly retro-reflective balls that are attached to the shutter glasses. This makes it possible to compute images for every screen that accurately fit the visitor's view on the simulated scene.
A special feature of any multi-wall VR system is that the images on the adjacent walls are seamlessly joined together, so that participants do not see the physical corners but the continuous virtual world that is projected with active stereo (Slater et al., 2002). The basic idea is to let a user become immersed in a 3-D scene (Slater & Usoh, 1993). Therefore, the subject has to wear shutter glasses (CrystalEyes, StereoGraphics Corporation, San Rafael, USA) to see the two separate stereoscopic images generated for each eye of the observer. The creation of the 3-D virtual environment entails two consecutive steps: first, the creation of a 3-D model of the scene; and second, the generation of a VR-application that controls and animates the modeled scene.

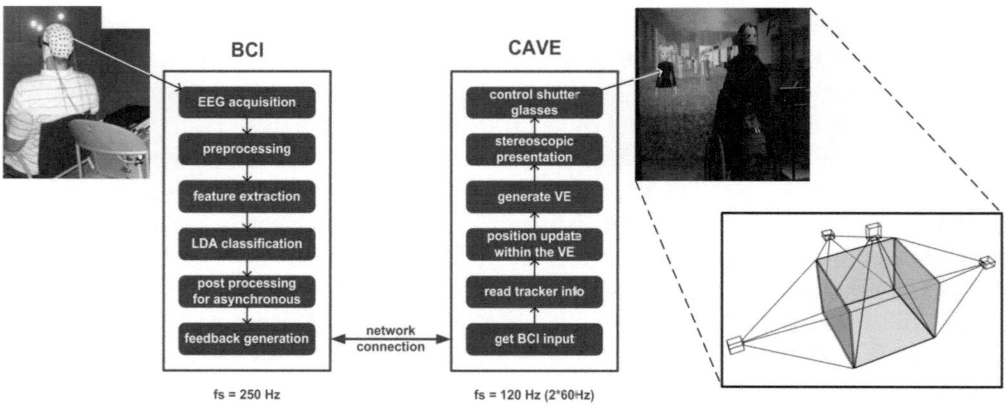

Fig. 2. System diagram of the hardware setup. The BCI system on the left analyses the EEG signals, and the extracted control commands are transferred into movements with the VE projected in the CAVE system. On the right bottom side is the physical CAVE installation with indicated projection screens. Modified from Leeb (2008).

4. Setup of an EEG-based BCI

The first step is always the same. The computer (classifier) has to learn how subject-specific EEG data (trials) look during execution of a predefined mental task. In general, each trial starts with a warning stimulus followed by a cue stimulus, indicating the type of mental task. The task depends on whether the BCI requires external stimulation to generate the necessary brain signals. P300 BCI and SSVEP BCIs do require such stimuli, while ERD BCIs do not. In the former BCI approaches, the user typically must pay attention to one out of 2 or more flickering lights or to flashing letters, numbers, and/or other symbols or commands. In the latter case the user has to perform a motor imagery task (e.g. hand or foot movement imagery) as indicated by the cue stimulus. During this training, about 80 trials of EEG data (each lasting several seconds) are recorded without any feedback to the user and used to set up the classifier. In a second step, the user has to perform the cue-paced mental task, and real-time feedback informs the user about success or failure of the online classification. P300-based and SSVEP-based BCIs have an apparent advantage in that both require no or only minimal user training. In contrast, ERD-based BCIs often need extensive user training, sometimes lasting many weeks (for details see Pfurtscheller et al., 2000; 2006a).

The experimental procedure commonly used with ERD-based BCI research can be divided into the following steps:

1. The (new, naive) subject must be instructed on what exactly is going to be done. It is crucial that the subject performs kinesthetic motor imagery (Neuper et al., 2005).
2. Training without feedback is done to acquire subject specific data for the imagery task used.
3. The most discriminative features (e. g., frequency bands) are extracted from this data.
4. The classifier is set up based on the features from step 3. If the classification accuracy is above 70 %, move on the next step, otherwise continue with step 2. This involves the selection of the best mental strategy, the localization of the best electrode recording sites and the optimal frequency bands.
5. Training with feedback; that is, online processing of EEG signals.
6. Classifier update, if the frequency bands have been modified or the EEG patterns have been changed.
7. Online applications like virtual environments can be controlled.

In general, multi-EEG channel recordings using various mental strategies can be performed at the beginning of step 2. Furthermore, offline optimization can be applied to determine the best mental strategies, electrode positions and frequency bands.

A BCI-system is, in general, composed of the following components: Signal acquisition, signal processing (which includes preprocessing, feature extraction, classification / detection, and post processing), application interface and an output device or application (left part of Figure 2; see also Wolpaw et al., 2002). For the experiments reported here, the Graz-BCI system was used (for details see Pfurtscheller et al., 2006c). It consisted of a biosignal amplifier (gBSamp, g.tec medical engineering, Graz, Austria), one data acquisition card (E-Series, National Instruments Corporation, Austin, USA), and a standard personal computer running Windows XP operating system (Microsoft Corporation, Redmond, USA) The recording was handled by rtsBCI (Scherer, 2004), based on MATLAB 7.0.4 (MathWorks, Inc., Natick, USA) in combination with Simulink 6.2, Real-Time Workshop 6.2 and the open source package BIOSIG (BioSig, 2010). In the case of an ERD BCI band power (BP) features were estimated from the ongoing EEG by digitally band-pass filtering the EEG recordings

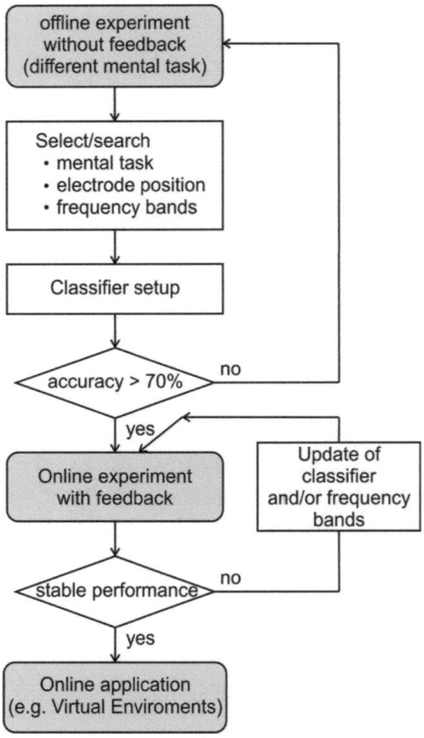

Fig. 3. General workflow of an experiment with a motor imagery-based BCI.

(Butterworth IIR filter of order 5) and squaring and averaging the samples over the past second. Finally, the logarithm was computed from this time series. To distinguish between the two motor imagery tasks, Fisher's linear discriminant analysis (LDA, Bishop, 1995) was applied to the BP estimates (sample-by-sample).

In the case of a SSVEP BCI, after calculation of the power spectrum, the first, second and third harmonic components are individually defined for each target frequency. For selecting one class, the sum of all its harmonic frequency components need to be larger than that of the other classes (for details see Müller-Putz et al., 2005).

The philosophy of the Graz-BCI is to use as few electrodes as possible for online experiments, which makes the BCI both, more comfortable and easier to apply, especially for subjects out of laboratory (e.g. at home or in working space). In all of the 4 experiments reported, EEG was recorded with an electrode cap (Easycap, Germany) fitted to the subject's head. EEG electrodes were mounted bipolarly over the sensorimotor cortex (ERD BCI) or over the occipital cortex (SSVEP BCI). The EEG was amplified (power-line notch filter was activated), band pass filtered between 0.5 and 100 Hz (EEG acquisition and preprocessing block, see Figure 2, left part) and recorded with a sampling frequency of 250 Hz.

5. Walking from thought - impact of immersive environments

The goals of the first study were: (i) to demonstrate that it is possible to move forward - "to walk" - within a VE (e.g. a virtual street) without any muscular activity, using only the imagination of movements recorded with a BCI and (ii) to compare the influences of different feedback types (common BCI feedback versus VE feedback (HMD and CAVE)) on the BCI performance. Therefore, the results from three different feedback (FB) conditions were compared: First, the results of the standard BCI with a simple bar graph; second, using a head-mounted display (HMD) as a FB device; and finally, using a highly immersive "CAVE" projection environment (see Figure 4a). In case of the HMD and CAVE conditions, the idea was to use the imagination of foot movement to walk through the VE, based on a synchronous BCI paradigm. The subject was instructed by a cue to imagine a right hand movement (single beep) or a foot movement (double beep). Three healthy volunteers participated several times over 5 months in this study. The task given to each participant was to walk to the end of a virtual street (see Figure 4a), and only in the case of successful foot motor imagery would a motion occur (for further details see Leeb et al., 2006; Pfurtscheller et al., 2006a). Correct classification of foot motor imagery was accompanied by forward movement at a constant speed in the virtual street, whereas a correct classification of hand motor imagery stopped the motion. Incorrect classification of foot motor imagery resulted in halting, and incorrect classification of hand motor imagery in backward motion (same speed). The walking distance was scored as "cumulative achieved mileage" (CAM, Leeb & Pfurtscheller, 2004; Leeb et al., 2006), which was the integrated forward/backward distance covered during foot movement imagination and was used as the performance measurement. So the BCI output of the online classification was either used to control the length and orientation of the bar graph feedback (control condition) or to move through a virtual street (HMD or CAVE condition). The CAM performances of the bar graph feedback experiments were simulated offline to enable comparison.

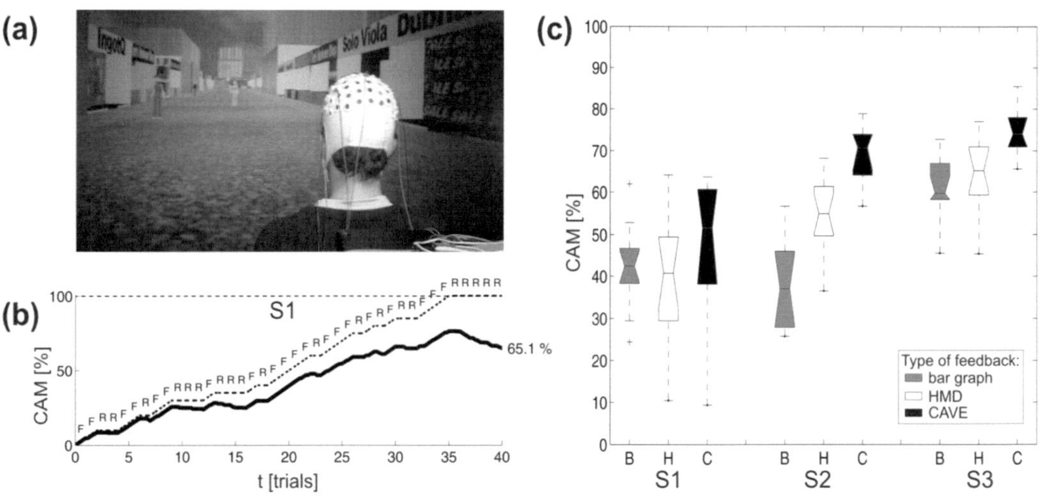

Fig. 4. (a) Participant in the virtual main street with shops and animated avatars. The subject wears an electrode cap and shutter glasses. (b) Examples of task performances displayed in the theoretical possible CAM (dashed line) and the real CAM (full line) of one run of one subject. The cue class indicated is written above the line. Due to the random cue sequence, each participant had a different theoretical pathway (dashed line). (c) Boxplot of all achieved CAMs of all subjects and feedback types. The diagram consists of 3 groups, each corresponding to a subject. Within these groups the left plots corresponds to standard bar-graph feedback (B), the middle to HMD feedback (H) and the right one to CAVE feedback (C). Modified from Leeb et al. (2007c).

The CAM of an example result of subject S1 (session 2, run 4) is plotted in Figure 4b. Both the theoretically possible CAM (dashed line) and the real achieved CAM (full line) are plotted. A CAM of 100 % corresponds to a correct classification of all 40 imagery tasks over the entire feedback time. A random classification would result in an expected CAM of 0 %. It is almost impossible to achieve the maximum attainable CAM of 100 %, because even a small procrastination or hesitation reduces mileage.

All the subjects were able to walk through the virtual street, and the resulting BCI performance in the VR tasks was comparable to standard BCI recordings. The use of VR as feedback stimulated the participant's performances and provided motivation. All the subjects achieved their best results within the CAVE and the worst in the standard BCI conditions. The mean achieved CAM of all participants and condition is plotted in Figure 4c. Two participants showed an increase over the condition, but participant S1 achieved worse results with the HMD (for further details see Leeb et al., 2006).

These data indicate that foot motor imagery is a suitable mental strategy to control events within the VEs. Imagination of feet movement is a mental task which comes very close to that of natural walking. In the CAVE condition (highest immersion) the performance of two participants was especially outstanding (up to 100 % BCI classification accuracy of single trials), although we observed a variability in the classification results between individual runs.

6. Exploring a virtual apartment using an ERD-based BCI

The second study shows that ten naive subjects can be trained in a synchronous paradigm within 3 sessions to navigate freely through a virtual apartment (see Figure 5a), whereby, at every junction, the subjects could decide on their own how they wanted to explore the VE. The very important and crucial step away from a synchronized or cue-based BCI and from laboratory conditions towards real world applications is performed in this experiment. The virtual apartment was similarly designed to a real world application, with a goal-oriented task, a high mental workload and a variable decision period for the subject. All the subjects were able to perform long and stable motor imagery over a minimum time of two seconds (for further details see Leeb et al., 2007b).

In this paradigm, only the start of the decision period was indicated with a "neutral" cue consisting of two arrows (see Figure 5b). The subject could decide for him/herself which motor imagery he/she wanted to perform and therefore which direction he/she wanted to select, but walking was only possible along predefined pathways through the corridors or rooms. The subject received feedback by viewing the size of the arrows, which were modulated depending on the BCI classification output. In this case, the corresponding arrow was huge and the subject was turned to the right/left/straight. Afterwards, the system automatically guided the subject to the next junction. As stated above, a "neutral cue" was used to indicate the starting point of the decision period (similar to the cue-based BCI), but the neutral cues were completely embedded in the given task and the duration of the decision periods (similar to trials) was variable, depending only on the performance of the subject. The subjects were instructed to go to a predefined target room. A small flag pole on the map indicated the destination which should be reached by using the shortest route through the maze-like apartment (see Figure 5a). The performance error was calculated by dividing the number of wrong decisions by the total number of junctions.

Each of the ten participating subjects performed 12 runs of variable duration in the virtual apartment. All the runs started at the same point (entrance door). During the first run, no instructions were given to the subjects, so they could walk freely through the apartment for 5 minutes to become familiar with the VE. In all the other runs, the subjects were instructed to go to a predefined target room. A small flag pole on the map indicated the destination which should be reached by using the shortest route through the maze-like apartment (see Figure 5a). Only one target was given in the first two runs, but in further runs, the number of targets was increased and only one target was visible each time. If this target was reached, either the follow-up target was inserted or the run was finished. Each run was limited to 5 minutes in total.

For comparison, synchronous BCI sessions with a standard bar-graph feedback were performed before and after the sessions with the virtual apartment, whereby the experiments with the virtual apartment were performed in front of a normal TFT monitor (TFT) and within an immersive virtual environment (iVE). In Figure 5c, the mean and standard error over all subjects is given and the statistical differences between the sessions are marked. All the subjects were able to deal with the variable trial length (the duration of the trial depended on how fast or slow the subject could perform a decision) and the variable inter-trial interval. The subjects noted that the task in the virtual apartment was much harder compared to the prior feedback training, because it was not only necessary to perform the "correct" imagination, but also the shortest way through the apartment had to be found. Therefore, the cognitive load was much higher compared to the standard BCI paradigm (for further details see Leeb et al., 2007b). According to our hypothesis, we found that the performance improves (that is, reduced error) over the sessions, and the lowest error was found during the sessions with virtual feedback. The slight but stable performance improvement of all subjects is very well known as the training effect (Pfurtscheller & Neuper, 2001; Wolpaw et al., 2002).

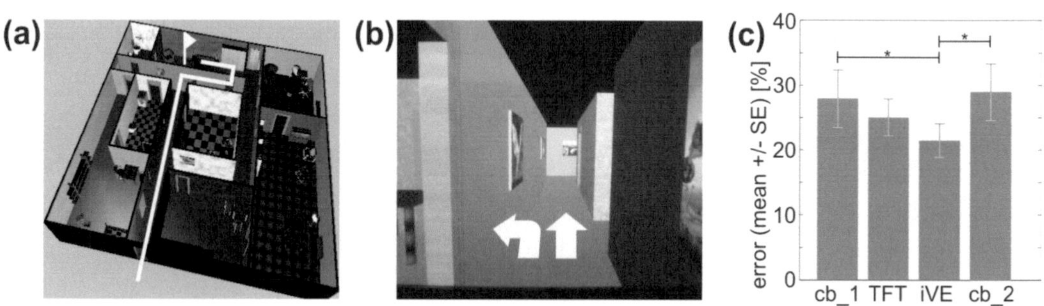

Fig. 5. (a) View into the virtual apartment, with one possible pathway plotted in white. The target room is marked with a small flag pole (in this example, the room at the upper end of the apartment). (b) First-person view of the virtual apartment with two arrows indicating the possible directions to go ("neutral cue"). (c) Mean ± standard error (SE) over all subjects of the integrated classification error and performance error. The asterisk (* $p<0.05$) shows statistically significant post-hoc differences. Cb_1 and cb_2 are the two sessions with standard BCI feedback before and after the VR sessions. TFT is the session with VR feedback presented on a normal TFT monitor and iVE in an immersive environment. Modified from Leeb (2008).

7. Exploring a virtual apartment using an SSVEP-based BCI

Another study involving seven healthy participants (see Faller et al., 2010) presented an even more flexible, asynchronous navigation paradigm within the same apartment scenario as in Leeb et al. (2007b) using an SSVEP-based BCI. The participants were instructed to navigate an avatar to two waypoints (see Figure 6a) along a given path in two runs, by alternately focusing attention on one of three visual stimuli that were flickering at the different frequencies 12, 15 and 20 Hz. Successful classifications of the according classes triggered the associated commands (i) turn 45° left (ii) turn 45° right and (iii) walk one step ahead.

In contrast to the work presented in Chapter 6, this system requires minimal setup and training time and offers faster, more accurate control, with the trade-off that it requires the user to visually fixate certain stimuli in order to communicate a control signal. The stimuli were presented directly within the 3D environment (see Figure 6b). Compared to systems that rely on external stimuli (e.g. LEDs), this approach is more dynamic and allows the user to better focus on goal-directed interactions and deal with a higher mental workload in the task.

Six out of seven subjects were able to navigate to the first waypoint in the first run halfway through the apartment. Five participants successfully reached the second waypoint in the second run. The average positive predictive value (precision, PPV = TP/(TP+FP), whereby TP stands for true positive and FP for false positive detections) over all participants was 91.7 ± 9.9 %, which resulted in an average of 6.5 ± 2.3 TP and 0.4 ± 0.4 FP activations per minute given a dwell-time of 1.5 s and a refractory period of 4s. These fixed temporal restrictions do of course limit the number of possible control commands per minute. However, some factors other than speed may be more important for the user. For instance, choosing a higher refractory period (Townsend et al., 2004) makes the SSVEP BCI easier to use, more likely to provide effective communication for a broader population of users, more reliable, and less fatiguing. This system demonstrates a virtual feedback environment that allows both disabled and healthy users to seamlessly communicate and interact through an intuitive, natural and friendly interface.

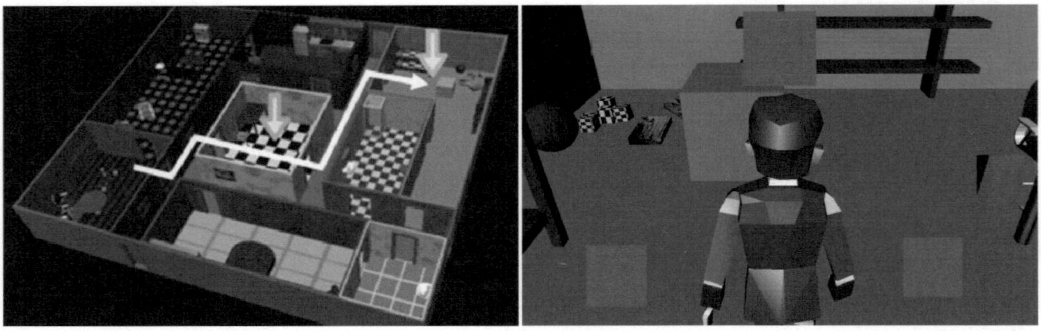

(a) (b)

Fig. 6. (a) Overview of the apartment showing the path along the two waypoints (marked by the arrows) that the participants are supposed to reach in the runs 1 and 2 respectively. (b) Screenshot of an in-game scene, showing the avatar in third person perspective along with the three navigation stimuli on the left, the right and over the avatar's head.

8. Moving a wheelchair in VR

Finally, we report on a 35 year old male tetraplegic subject. After a traumatic injury of the spinal cord in 1998, he has a complete motor and sensory lesion below C5 and an incomplete lesion below C4. During an intensive training period of approximately 4 months, he learned to control the cue-based Graz-BCI (details about this training are reported elsewhere (Pfurtscheller et al., 2000). Specifically, the midcentral focused beta oscillations with a dominant frequency of approximately 17 Hz allowed a brain-switch like application and control of a VE (recorded close to Cz, foot representation area). Only one single EEG channel was recorded bipolarly at Cz (foot representation area). One single logarithmic band power feature was estimated from the ongoing EEG (see Figure 7b-c). A simple threshold (TH) was used to distinguish between foot movement imagination (IC) and rest (INC). For further details see Leeb et al. (2007a).

The tetraplegic participant was placed with his wheelchair in the middle of a multi-projection based stereo VR system ("CAVE"). The VE used was a virtual street with shops on both sides (Leeb et al., 2006) and populated with 15 avatars, who were lined up along the street (see Figure 7a). The participant was instructed to "move" from avatar to avatar towards the end of the virtual street (65 length units) by movement imagination of his paralyzed feet. Only when foot MI was detected (IC) did the subject move forward (see Figure 7d, walking speed 1.25 units/second). Every time he was about to pass an avatar, he had to stop very close to it. The avatar started talking to the subject if he was standing close and still to it for one second. Each avatar was surrounded by an invisible communication

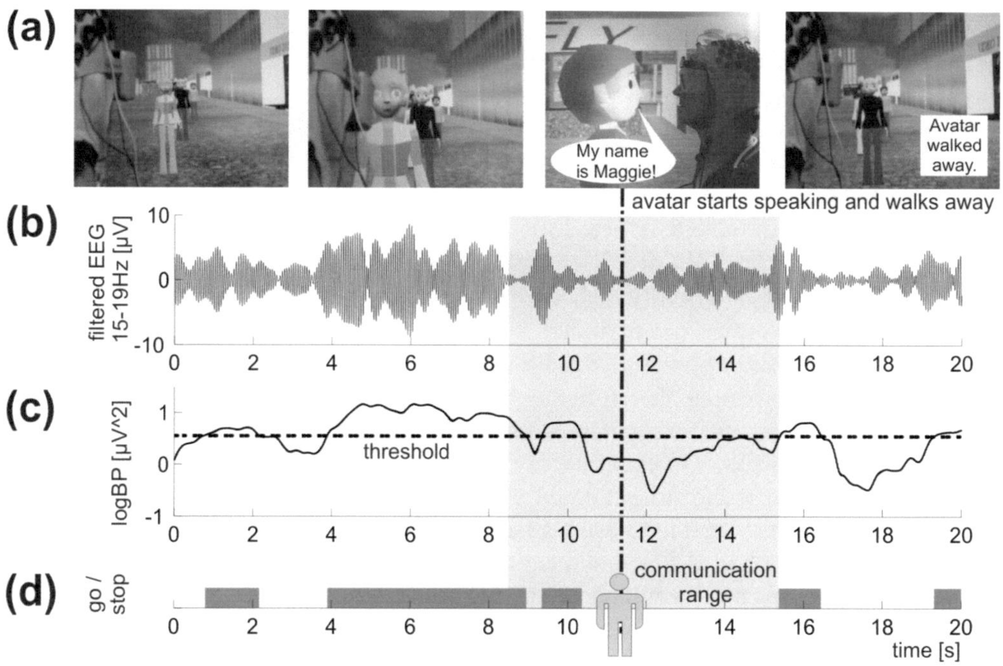

Fig. 7. (a) Picture sequence before, during and after the contact with an avatar. (b) Band-pass filtered (15–19 Hz) EEG and (c) logarithmic band power time course with threshold. (d) Indicated periods of moving and stopping. The contact with the avatar occurred at second 11.4. Modified from Leeb (2008).

sphere (0.5 – 2.5 units) and the subject had to stop within this sphere. The size of the sphere approximated the distance for a conversation in the real world. The avatar started talking to the subject if he was standing still for one second within this sphere. After finishing a randomly chosen short statement (like: "Hi", "My name is Maggie", "It was good to meet you"...), the avatar walked away. Communication was only possible within the sphere; if the subject stopped too early or stopped too close to the avatar, nothing happened. After a while, and with his own free will, the subject could imagine another foot movement and started moving again towards the next avatar, until the end of the street was reached.

The tetraplegic subject performed ten runs on two days, and he was able to stop at 90 % of the 150 avatars and talk to them. In four runs, he achieved a performance of 100 %. In 11 of the 15 missed avatars (of all runs), the subject stopped within the communication range, but the stopping time was too short (between 0.08 to 0.88 s mean ± SD = 0.47 s ± 0.27 s).

In an interview after the experiment, the patient confirmed that "moving" occurred only during periods of foot motor imagery, but he reported that it was hard to stop precisely. When the avatars were placed very laterally, it was especially hard to find the correct distance to the avatar. Concerning the experience with the interaction, he mentioned that "*It has never happened before, in the sense of success and interaction. I thought that I was on the street and I had the chance to walk up to the people. I just imagined the movement and walked up to them. However, I had the sensation that they were just speaking but not talking to me...*" He said that he had the feeling of being in that street and forgot that he was in the lab and people were around him. "*Of course the image on the CAVE wall didn't look like you or me, but it still felt as if I was moving in a real street, not realistic, but real. I checked the people (avatars). We had 14 ladies and 1 man.*" The subject stated that he felt surprised as one avatar walked through him; he wanted to get out of the way, to go backwards. This suggests that the subject felt very absorbed in the virtual reality environment.

This work demonstrated for the first time that a tetraplegic subject, sitting in a wheel chair, could control his movements in a VE by the usage of a self-paced (asynchronous) BCI based on one single EEG recording (for further details see Leeb et al., 2007a). The mentally induced beta oscillation in our patient is a unique phenomenon and probably the result of the intensive and long-lasting BCI feedback training with the goal of achieving control over brain waves. The use of visually rich and stimulating VE, involving avatars that were interacting with the subject, accounted for a diverse and challenging experimental paradigm. The simulation power of the VE ensured that he had the sense of being in the street and going to the people; therefore the experiment was similar to a task in a real street.

VEs are especially attractive for a person who is wheelchair-bound. First, simply using a VE can give such persons access to experiences that may be long forgotten (or which they have never had). The fact that the subject could still perform feet motor imagery, years after an injury that rendered him unable to use his feet, is a testament to the plasticity of the human brain (see also Kübler et al., 2005). Another advantage here is that VEs can be used to create virtual prototypes of new navigation or control methods, and give potential users experience of them in a safe environment before they are ever physically built.

9. Importance of VR feedback in BCI research

The increasing availability of VR technology has generated a high interest in studying BCI interaction with VEs.

Compared to traditional, abstract interfaces like mouse or keypad, BCI systems could potentially promise a more direct and intuitive way of interacting and thereby overcome some limitations of navigating within VEs (Usoh & Slater, 1995). This is especially obvious for *stimulus-dependent* BCI-VR systems (Figure 1b), where users can control appliances in the VE by simply directing their eye gaze and/or focus of attention towards the desired element (e.g., looking at the TV to switch it on, looking at the door to open it; Allison et al., 2008). In a typical *independent* BCI paradigm (Figure 1a) as described above, users learn to direct, e.g., a computer cursor towards a highlighted target via certain changes of specific EEG features. To accomplish this task, each participant develops a specific mental strategy to modify the relevant brain signals and use a BCI effectively. As ERD BCIs mostly rely on motor imagery, the mental process of imagining different types of movements offers an intuitive way of VE control like, for example, imagining foot movements for moving forward in a VE (Leeb et al., 2007a; Pfurtscheller et al., 2006a). A further advantage of using sensorimotor rhythms in BCI-based VE control is that they are typically modulated by motor activity (including both actual and imagined movements), but unaffected by changes in visual stimulation. Therefore people can use an ERD BCI while performing other visual tasks. Indeed, we have successfully shown that people can use an ERD BCI (based on motor imagery) at the same time as an SSVEP BCI (based on visual attention) (Allison et al., 2010; Brunner et al., 2010; Pfurtscheller et al., 2010a; 2010b).

Furthermore, research that explores BCI training in VEs is important for many reasons. VEs can help focus the training on the specific target application. For example, different training settings and paradigms may be more or less efficient, depending on whether the user's task is to select certain characters or icons for communication, control a neuroprosthesis to restore grasping, or navigate a wheelchair in a realistic environment. Moreover, it is a matter of ongoing research whether BCI training in stimulus-rich virtual environments is more effective than the standard training procedure using simple, more or less abstract, visual cues and feedback stimuli. The literature suggests that a realistic VE enhances the feeling of presence, task performance and also cortical activation (Jäncke et al., 2009; Lee and Kim, 2008; Slater et al., 2002). Combining BCI and VR technologies can lead to highly realistic and immersive BCI feedback scenarios that make participants more engaged and motivated. Thus, it is not unexpected that a rich visual representation of the feedback signal, such as a 3-dimensional video game or VE, may facilitate learning to use a BCI (Leeb, 2008; Pineda et al., 2003; Ron-Angevin et al., 2005).

The feedback is a very important component of the BCI as it provides the user with information about the efficiency of his/her strategy and enables learning. The studies mentioned above support realistic and engaging feedback scenarios which are closely related to the specific target application. However, the processing of such a realistic feedback stimulus may also interfere with the mental motor imagery task, and thus might impair the development of BCI control (Neuper et al., 2009). This could be the case when the realistic feedback presentation showing (for instance) a moving visual scene is not compatible with the specific mental action the user creates to induce the relevant brain signals. Therefore, the mutual interaction between a mentally simulated movement (for BCI control) and simultaneous watching of a moving scene should be further investigated in future studies.

Another interesting aspect is that mental simulation of movement (motor imagery) results in cardiovascular changes explained by two factors, i.e. function of anticipation of movement and central preparation of movement (Damen & Brunia, 1987; Oishi et al., 2000). The heart rate (HR) generally decreases during motor imagery in laboratory conditions without VR feedback (Leeb, 2008; Pfurtscheller et al., 2006b), but can be increased during effortful imagery and/or enhanced mental effort (Decety et al., 1991), such as during VR feedback in BCI experiments (Pfurtscheller et al., 2006b; 2008a). This underlines the importance of VR feedback in modifying emotional experiences and enhances autonomic and visceral responses. The HR changes can be in the order of several beats per minute and therewith used to increase the classification accuracy of an ERD-based BCI when both the EEG and the HR are analyzed simultaneously.

10. Concluding remarks

One important component of a BCI system is feedback. VR offers a powerful possibility not only to rehearse scenarios that are otherwise too dangerous or expensive to set up, such as simulation of wheel chair movement, but also to modify emotional experiences and enhance therewith autonomic responses as e.g. heart rate changes. This opens a new way to improve the performance of a BCI by simultaneously analyzing and classifying brain and heart rate changes and to realize a "hybrid BCI" (Pfurtscheller et al., 2010a). Furthermore, VR environments may offer numerous other benefits, such as reduced training time, improved classification accuracy, increased sense of immersion/presence in an artificial setting, and reduced boredom or fatigue.

11. Acknowledgment

This work was carried out as part of the "PresenCCia" project, an EU funded Integrated Project under the IST program (project no. 27731) and the EU funded project "BrainAble" (project no. ICT-2010-247447). The authors are grateful to Brendan Allison for proofreading the manuscript.

12. References

Allison, B. Z.; Brunner, C.; Kaiser, V.; Müller-Putz, G. R.; Neuper, C. & Pfurtscheller, G. (2010). Toward a Hybrid Brain-Computer Interface Based on Imagined Movement and Visual Attention, *J Neural Eng*, Vol. 7, No. 2, 26007

Allison, B. Z.; McFarland, D. J.; Schalk, G.; Zheng, S. D.; Jackson, M. M. & Wolpaw, J. R. (2008). Towards an Independent Brain-Computer Interface Using Steady State Visual Evoked Potentials, *Clin Neurophysiol*, Vol. 119, No. 2, 399-408

Allison, B. Z. & Pineda, J. A. (2006). Effects of SOA and Flash Pattern Manipulations on ERPs, Performance, and Preference: Implications for a BCI System, *Int J Psychophysiol*, Vol. 59, No. 2, 127-40

Bayliss, J. D. (2003). Use of the Evoked Potential P3 Component for Control in a Virtual Apartment, *IEEE Trans Neural Syst Rehabil Eng*, Vol. 11, No. 2, 113-6

Bayliss, J. D. & Ballard, D. H. (2000). A Virtual Reality Testbed for Brain-Computer Interface Research, *IEEE Trans Rehabil Eng*, Vol. 8, No. 2, 188-90

Bell, C. J.; Shenoy, P.; Chalodhorn, R. & Rao, R. P. (2008). Control of a Humanoid Robot by a Noninvasive Brain-Computer Interface in Humans, *J Neural Eng*, Vol. 5, No. 2, 214-20

Bin, G.; Gao, X.; Yan, Z.; Hong, B. & Gao, S. (2009). An Online Multi-Channel SSVEP-Based Brain-Computer Interface Using a Canonical Correlation Analysis Method, *J Neural Eng*, Vol. 6, No. 4, 046002

BioSig (2003-2010). An Open Source Software Package for Biomedical Signal Processing under Matlab, *Available online at http://biosig.sf.net/*

Birbaumer, N. & Cohen, L. G. (2007). Brain-Computer Interfaces: Communication and Restoration of Movement in Paralysis, *J Physiol*, Vol. 579, No. Pt 3, 621-36

Birbaumer, N.; Ghanayim, N.; Hinterberger, T.; Iversen, I.; Kotchoubey, B.; Kübler, A.; Perelmouter, J.; Taub, E. & Flor, H. (1999). A Spelling Device for the Paralysed, *Nature*, Vol. 398, No. 6725, 297-8

Bishop, C. M. (1995). *Neural Networks for Pattern Recognition*. Clarendon Press, Oxford, UK

Blankertz, B.; Dornhege, G.; Krauledat, M.; Müller, K. R. & Curio, G. (2007). The Non-Invasive Berlin Brain-Computer Interface: Fast Acquisition of Effective Performance in Untrained Subjects, *Neuroimage*, Vol. 37, No. 2, 539-50

Brunner, C.; Allison, B. Z.; Krusienski, D. J.; Kaiser, V.; Müller-Putz, G. R.; Pfurtscheller, G. & Neuper, C. (2010). Improved Signal Processing Approaches in an Offline Simulation of a Hybrid Brain-Computer Interface, *J Neurosci Methods*, Vol. 188, No. 1, 165-73

Cruz-Neira, C.; Sandin, D. J. & DeFanti, T. A. (1993). Surround-Screen Projection-Based Virtual Reality: The Design and Implementation of the Cave, *Proceedings of the 20th annual conference on Computer graphics and interactive techniques*, 135-42

Damen, E. J. & Brunia, C. H. (1987). Changes in Heart Rate and Slow Brain Potentials Related to Motor Preparation and Stimulus Anticipation in a Time Estimation Task, *Psychophysiology*, Vol. 24, No. 6, 700-13

Decety, J.; Jeannerod, M.; Germain, M. & Pastene, J. (1991). Vegetative Response During Imagined Movement Is Proportional to Mental Effort, *Behav Brain Res*, Vol. 42, No. 1, 1-5

Donchin, E.; Spencer, K. M. & Wijesinghe, R. (2000). The Mental Prosthesis: Assessing the Speed of a P300-Based Brain-Computer Interface, *IEEE Trans Rehabil Eng*, Vol. 8, No. 2, 174-9

Faller, J.; Müller-Putz, G. R.; Schmalstieg, D. & Pfurtscheller, G. (2010). An Application Framework for Controlling an Avatar in a Desktop Based Virtual Environment via a Software SSVEP Brain-Computer Interface, *PRESENCE Special Issue, "Brain-Computer Interface (BCI) Systems in Virtual Reality Environments."* Vol. 19, No. 1, 25-34

Farwell, L. A. & Donchin, E. (1988). Talking Off the Top of Your Head: Toward a Mental Prosthesis Utilizing Event-Related Brain Potentials, *Electroencephalogr Clin Neurophysiol*, Vol. 70, No. 6, 510-23

Gao, X.; Xu, D.; Cheng, M. & Gao, S. (2003). A BCI -Based Environmental Controller for the Motion-Disabled, *IEEE Trans Neural Syst Rehabil Eng*, Vol. 11, No. 2, 137-40

Holzner, C.; Guger, C.; Edlinger, G.; Gronegress, C. & Slater, M. (2009). Virtual Smart Home Controlled by Thoughts, *Proc. of the 2009 18th IEEE International Workshops on Enabling Technologies: Infrastructures for Collaborative Enterprises - Volume 00*, 236-39

Jäncke, L.; Cheetham, M. & Baumgartner, T. (2009). Virtual Reality and the Role of the Prefrontal Cortex in Adults and Children., *Front Neurosci.*, Vol. 3, No. 1, 52-59

Krusienski, D. J.; Sellers, E. W.; Cabestaing, F.; Bayoudh, S.; McFarland, D. J.; Vaughan, T. M. & Wolpaw, J. R. (2006). A Comparison of Classification Techniques for the P300 Speller, *J Neural Eng*, Vol. 3, No. 4, 299-305

Kübler, A.; Nijboer, F.; Mellinger, J.; Vaughan, T. M.; Pawelzik, H.; Schalk, G.; McFarland, D. J.; Birbaumer, N. & Wolpaw, J. R. (2005). Patients with Als Can Use Sensorimotor Rhythms to Operate a Brain-Computer Interface, *Neurology*, Vol. 64, No. 10, 1775-7

Lalor, E.; Kelly, S.; Finucane, C.; Burke, R.; Smith, R.; Reilly, R. B. & McDarby, G. (2005). Steady-State Vep-Based Brain-Computer Interface Control in an Immersive 3-D Gaming Environment, *EURASIP J on Appl Sig Proc*, Vol. 19, 3156-64

Lee, S. & Kim, G. J. (2008). Effects of Visual Cues and Sustained Attention on Spatial Presence in Virtual Environments Based on Spatial and Object Distinction, *Interact. Comput.*, Vol. 20, No. 4-5, 491-502

Leeb, R. (2008). *Brain-Computer Communication: The Motivation, Aim, and Impact of Virtual Feedback*. Graz University of Technology, PhD thesis

Leeb, R.; Friedman, D.; Müller-Putz, G. R.; Scherer, R.; Slater, M. & Pfurtscheller, G. (2007a). Self-Paced (Asynchronous) BCI Control of a Wheelchair in Virtual Environments: A Case Study with a Tetraplegic, *Computational Intelligence and Neuroscience, special issue: "Brain-Computer Interfaces: Towards Practical Implementations and Potential Applications"*, Vol. 2007, No. Article ID 79642, 1-8

Leeb, R.; Keinrath, C.; Friedman, D.; Guger, C.; Scherer, R.; Neuper, C.; Garau, M.; Antley, A.; Steed, A.; Slater, M. & Pfurtscheller, G. (2006). Walking by Thinking: The Brainwaves Are Crucial, Not the Muscles! *Presence Teleoper Virtual Environ.*, Vol. 15, No. 5, 500-14

Leeb, R.; Lee, F.; Keinrath, C.; Scherer, R.; Bischof, H. & Pfurtscheller, G. (2007b). Brain-Computer Communication: Motivation, Aim and Impact of Exploring a Virtual Apartment, *IEEE Trans Neural Syst Rehabil Eng*, Vol. 15, No. 4, 473-82

Leeb, R. & Pfurtscheller, G. (2004). Walking through a Virtual City by Thought, *Proc. of the 26th A Int Conf IEEE EMBS - EMBC 2004, San Francisco, USA*, 4503-6

Leeb, R.; Scherer, R.; Friedman, D.; Lee, F.; Keinrath, C.; Bischof, H.; Slater, M. & Pfurtscheller, G. (2007c). Combining BCI and Virtual Reality: Scouting Virtual Worlds, In: *Toward Brain-Computer Interfacing*, edited by G. Dornhege, J. del R. Millan, T. Hinterberger, D. J. McFarland & K.-R. Müller, 393-408. MIT Press, Cambridge, MA, USA

Leeb, R.; Settgast, V.; Fellner, D. W. & Pfurtscheller, G. (2007d). Self-Paced Exploring of the Austrian National Library through Thought, *Int J Bioelectromagnetism*, Vol. 9, No. 4, 237-44

Lotze, M.; Montoya, P.; Erb, M.; Hulsmann, E.; Flor, H.; Klose, U.; Birbaumer, N. & Grodd, W. (1999). Activation of Cortical and Cerebellar Motor Areas During Executed and Imagined Hand Movements: An Fmri Study, *J Cogn Neurosci*, Vol. 11, No. 5, 491-501

Martinez, P.; Bakardjian, H. & Cichocki, A. (2007). Fully Online Multicommand Brain-Computer Interface with Visual Neurofeedback Using SSVEP Paradigm, *Comput Intell Neurosci*, 94561

Mason, S. G.; Bashashati, A.; Fatourechi, M.; Navarro, K. F. & Birch, G. E. (2007). A Comprehensive Survey of Brain Interface Technology Designs, *Ann Biomed Eng*, Vol. 35, No. 2, 137-69

Müller-Putz, G. R.; Scherer, R.; Brauneis, C. & Pfurtscheller, G. (2005). Steady-State Visual Evoked Potential (SSVEP)-Based Communication: Impact of Harmonic Frequency Components, *J Neural Eng*, Vol. 2, No. 4, 123-30

Neuper, C.; Scherer, R.; Reiner, M. & Pfurtscheller, G. (2005). Imagery of Motor Actions: Differential Effects of Kinesthetic and Visual-Motor Mode of Imagery in Single-Trial EEG, *Cogn Brain Res*, Vol. 25, No. 3, 668-77

Neuper, C.; Scherer, R.; Wriessnegger, S. & Pfurtscheller, G. (2009). Motor Imagery and Action Observation: Modulation of Sensorimotor Brain Rhythms During Mental Control of a Brain-Computer Interface, *Clin Neurophysiol*, Vol. 120, No. 2, 239-47

Nijholt, A.; Tan, D.; Pfurtscheller, G.; Brunner, C.; Millan Jdel, R.; Allison, B. Z.; Graimann, B.; Popescu, F.; Blankertz, B. & Müller, K. R. (2008). Brain-Computer Interfacing for Intelligent Systems, *IEEE Intelligent Systems*, Vol. 23, No. 3, 72-79

Oishi, K.; Kasai, T. & Maeshima, T. (2000). Autonomic Response Specificity During Motor Imagery, *J Physiol Anthropol Appl Human Sci*, Vol. 19, No. 6, 255-61

Pfurtscheller, G.; Allison, B. Z.; Brunner, C.; Bauernfeind, G.; Solis-Escalante, T.; Scherer, R.; Zander, T. O.; Müller-Putz, G.; Neuper, C. & Birbaumer, N. (2010a). The Hybrid BCI, *Front Neurosci*, Vol. 4, 42

Pfurtscheller, G.; Guger, C.; Müller, G.; Krausz, G. & Neuper, C. (2000). Brain Oscillations Control Hand Orthosis in a Tetraplegic, *Neurosci Lett*, Vol. 292, No. 3, 211-4

Pfurtscheller, G.; Leeb, R.; Friedman, D. & Slater, M. (2008a). Centrally Controlled Heart Rate Changes During Mental Practice in Immersive Virtual Environment: A Case Study with a Tetraplegic, *Int J Psychophysiol*, Vol. 68, No. 1, 1-5

Pfurtscheller, G.; Leeb, R.; Keinrath, C.; Friedman, D.; Neuper, C.; Guger, C. & Slater, M. (2006a). Walking from Thought, *Brain Res*, Vol. 1071, No. 1, 145-52

Pfurtscheller, G.; Leeb, R. & Slater, M. (2006b). Cardiac Responses Induced During Thought-Based Control of Virtual Environments, *Int J Psychophysiol*, Vol. 62, No. 1, 134-40

Pfurtscheller, G. & Lopes da Silva, F. H. (1999). Event-Related EEG /MEG Synchronization and Desynchronization: Basic Principles, *Clin Neurophysiol*, Vol. 110, No. 11, 1842-57

Pfurtscheller, G.; Müller-Putz, G. R.; Scherer, R. & Neuper, C. (2008b). Rehabilitation with Brain-Computer Interface Systems, *Computer*, Vol. 41, No. 10, 58

Pfurtscheller, G.; Müller-Putz, G. R.; Schlögl, A.; Graimann, B.; Scherer, R.; Leeb, R.; Brunner, C.; Keinrath, C.; Lee, F.; Townsend, G.; Vidaurre, C. & Neuper, C. (2006c). 15 Years of BCI Research at Graz University of Technology: Current Projects, *IEEE Trans Neural Syst Rehabil Eng*, Vol. 14, No. 2, 205-10

Pfurtscheller, G. & Neuper, C. (2010). Dynamics of Sensorimotor Oscillations in a Motor Task, In: *Brain Computer Interfaces: Revolutionizing Human-Computer Interaction*, edited by B. Graimann, B. Z. Allison & G. Pfurtscheller. Springer

Pfurtscheller, G. & Neuper, C. (2001). Motor Imagery and Direct Brain-Computer Communication, *Proceedings of the IEEE*, Vol. 89, No. 7, 1123-34

Pfurtscheller, G. & Solis-Escalante, T. (2009). Could the Beta Rebound in the EEG Be Suitable to Realize a "Brain Switch"? *Clin Neurophysiol*, Vol. 120, No. 1, 24-9

Pfurtscheller, G.; Solis-Escalante, T.; Ortner, R.; Linortner, P. & Müller-Putz, G. R. (2010b). Self-Paced Operation of an SSVEP -Based Orthosis with and without an Imagery-Based "Brain Switch": A Feasibility Study Towards a Hybrid BCI., *IEEE Trans Neural Syst Rehabil Eng*

Pineda, J. A.; Silverman, D. S.; Vankov, A. & Hestenes, J. (2003). Learning to Control Brain Rhythms: Making a Brain-Computer Interface Possible, *IEEE Trans Neural Syst Rehabil Eng*, Vol. 11, No. 2, 181-4

Ron Angevin, R.; Diaz-Estrella, A. & Reyes-Lecuona, A. (2005). Development of a Braincomputer Interface Based on Virtual Reality to Improve Training Techniques, *Cyberpsychol Behav*, Vol. 8, No. 4, 353-54

Scherer, R. (2004-2006). RtsBCI: Graz brain-computer interface real-time open source package. Available at http://sourceforge.net/projects/biosig

Scherer, R.; Lee, F.; Schlögl, A.; Leeb, R.; Bischof, H. & Pfurtscheller, G. (2008). Toward Self-Paced Brain–Computer Communication: Navigation through Virtual Worlds, *IEEE Trans Biomed Eng*, Vol. 55, No. 2, 675-82

Slater, M.; Steed, A. & Chrysanthou, Y. (2002). *Computer Graphics and Virtual Environments: From Realism to Real-Time*. Addison-Wesley, Harlow, UK

Slater, M. & Usoh, M. (1993). Presence in Immersive Virtual Environments, *Proc. IEEE Virtual Reality Annual International Symposium, Seattle, WA*, 90-96

Townsend, G.; Graimann, B. & Pfurtscheller, G. (2004). Continuous EEG Classification During Motor Imagery-Simulation of an Asynchronous BCI, *IEEE Trans Neural Syst Rehabil Eng*, Vol. 12, No. 2, 258-65

Usoh, M. & Slater, M. (1995). An Exploration of Immersive Virtual Environments, *Endeavour*, Vol. 19, No. 1, 34-38

Wolpaw, J. R.; Birbaumer, N.; McFarland, D. J.; Pfurtscheller, G. & Vaughan, T. M. (2002). Brain-Computer Interfaces for Communication and Control, *Clin Neurophysiol*, Vol. 113, No. 6, 767-91

2

Hapto-Acoustic Interaction Metaphors in 3D Virtual Environments for Non-Visual Settings

Fabio De Felice[1], Floriana Renna[2],
Giovanni Attolico[2] and Arcangelo Distante[2]
[1]*Computer Science department, Università degli studi di Bari "A. Moro"*
[2]*Institute of Intelligent Systems for Automation, National Research Council*
Italy

1. Introduction

Three-dimensional Virtual Environments (VEs) enable the acquisition of knowledge on a given domain through the interaction with virtual entities. The flexibility of a VE allows to represent only the part of the world that is considered relevant for the final user: the proper choice of the information, representation and rendering included in the virtual world can strongly simplify the perception and interpretation efforts required to the users. Moreover, VE can provide data that would be difficult or impossible to appreciate in the real world in an easily and simply perceivable way: domain experts can communicate specific views and interpretations of the reality in a way accessible to final users. A properly designed virtual experience can significantly improve and simplify several learning tasks.

Organizing information in three dimensions and designing techniques to interact with them require a complex effort: interaction metaphors have been introduced to facilitate the access and interaction with VEs (Bowmann, 2001). A metaphor is the process of mapping a set of correspondences from a source domain to a target domain (Lakoff & Johnson, 1980). Metaphors help designers to map features of the interaction techniques to concepts more immediately accessible to final users. Interaction can be made more immersive and engaging by multi-modality. A multimodal system coordinates the processing of multiple natural input modalities—such as speech, touch, hand gestures, eye gaze and head and body movements—with multimedia system output (Oviat, 1999). The interaction is carried out with advanced input/output devices involving different sensorial channels (sight, hear, touch, etc.) in an integrated way. Spatial input devices (such as trackers, 3D pointing devices, gesture and vocal devices) and multisensory output technologies (head mounted displays, spatial audio and haptic devices) are increasingly being used as common components of Virtual Reality applications. Each device addresses a particular sense and exhibits a different interface: (Bowmann et al., 2004) offers a broad review of multimodal interaction while (Salisbury, 2004) is a good introduction to haptics. A multimodal interaction requires data to be redundant and polymorphous to address different sensorial modalities at the same time (Jacobson, 2002).

Metaphors effectiveness strongly depends on the sensory channels they refer to and on the users characteristics. Therefore this presentation will correlate and compare hapto-acoustic metaphors in visual and non-visual settings, evaluating their relevance when used alone or to support and complement vision. The multimodal interaction allows VE applications to address users with sensorial impairments that can rely on the particular interaction modalities they feel comfortable with. Many researches have proved hapto-acoustic VR applications to represent valid tools for visually impaired users in organizing hapto-acoustic perceptions into a mental schema of reality.

Sight is a parallel sense that allows a top-down approach to perception and cognition: it makes possible to catch a global and coarse idea of the scene in a very fast and easy way leaving to further explorations the detection, interpretation and integration of details in the mental schema of the scene. Blind mainly use touch and hear to perceive the surrounding world. Touch is a serial sense and generates a long spatio-temporal sequence of data that the user mind must integrate to build a globally meaningful mental model through a bottom-up process. Moreover, touch is ineffective or even useless when dealing with objects that are very large or that cannot be touched (far in space, sensible to damages, etc.). Contextualization can be improved by the use of acoustic cues.

Sight allows a multi-resolution approach: by using proper lenses it is easy to perceive details at scales beyond the capacity of the human eye. Touch is tied to a single level of detail (depending on the dimension of the fingertips) and cannot appreciate details that are smaller than a specific threshold. Building several proper physical artifacts (offering different enlarged versions of the objects) is expensive and can be less productive. VEs offer an easier and more effective manipulation and understanding of many kinds of information. Digital models allow the dynamic change of scale and resolution of the context to investigate with a positive impact on the human haptic perception of objects (Klatzky & Lederman, 1995) (Okamura & Cutkosky, 1999). Details of VE can be dynamically highlighted or hidden, to focus visually impaired people attention on the most relevant information.

The design of multimodal rendering must account for current technological limitations: haptic technology does not allow a stable interaction using both hands, the acoustic simulation cannot completely reproduce the richness of sounds occurring during an experience in the real world, smell and taste simulation are still far from being effective. To be preferred to tactile maps or scaled models or to the direct exploration of environment the virtual experience must be complementary with respect to the experience of reality. It must be properly created to make clear the perception and the comprehension of the desired informative content and tailored to the interests and capabilities of the user to enhance his knowledge and comprehension of the world. This poses criticism to haptic and acoustic because the combined display has to make up the lack of visual information. The limited bandwidth of haptic must be compensated by well defined interaction metaphors. This alternative way of perceiving VEs must supply a quick acquisition of the overall meaning of a scene that vision provides at a glance. Computer haptics in VEs for visual impaired is quite a recent research activity but despite to this, many different guidelines have been proposed to make hapto-acoustic interaction more effective. However there are no works reporting a taxonomy of interaction metaphors based on user tasks, as reported in the area of classic VE interaction for sighted users in (Bowmann, 2004) and (De Boeck et al., 2005).

This chapter gives an overview of the current interaction techniques in the field of multimodal VEs for non-visual interaction. The term non-visual will be used throughout the chapter to refer, further than blind users interaction, the possibility that these techniques could be used even by sighted users to support and integrate vision, when visual feedback is not available, or unpractical, or when they cooperate with blind subjects. The proposed overview will correlate the designed non-visual interaction techniques with the well known visual interaction metaphors according to classical users tasks in VEs (navigation, selection and manipulation of virtual entities). This will make more straightforward for the reader to understand each technique and how tasks normally carried out by vision can be completed with sensorial substitution. Some of the metaphors identified as effective, integrated with new features, have been used as a conceptual framework to develop a general-purpose multimodal interaction software framework: this framework has been applied to the development of different applications experimentally verified with several blind users.

The chapter is organized as follows. In the next paragraph some reviews are analysed to better situate the taxonomy used by this presentation; then a survey of non-visual interaction metaphors will be presented and compared to visual interaction metaphors from literature. For each user task the differences between visual and non-visual setting will be outlined and the non-visual metaphors will be motivated. In section four our software interaction metaphors will be presented and in the fifth section several experiences with blind users will be reported with their subjective feedbacks.

2. Related works

In literature there are several works that propose different taxonomies of multimodal interaction techniques. In (Panëels & Roberts, 2010), (Roberts & Panëels, 2007) an overview on Haptic Data Visualization (HDV) based on data representation is presented. HDV represents the virtual model as an abstraction, encoding numerical values or an abstract mathematical concept rather a physical environment. Haptic and audio cues are used to convey analytic information in a non-visual way. This can be useful for blind users but even for sighted users in contexts where the visual feedback is not available. The taxonomy reports the following topics: charts, maps, signs, networks, diagrams, tables and images. This review outlines how most research has been performed to render charts. Other areas intensively investigated are maps, diagrams and signs.

(Nesbitt, 2005) defines a framework to support the design of multimodal displays for HDV and presents the MS Taxonomy divided in spatial, direct and temporal metaphors. Spatial metaphors describe concepts involving our perception of space and are related to spatial features such as position, size and structure. Direct metaphors describe concepts that explain the way our individual senses detect information. Temporal metaphors refer to the way we perceive occurring events in time and influence the other two metaphor types. Despite the paper proposes an articulated taxonomy, it does not go into details about possible interaction techniques.

A broad review on multimodal human-computer interaction can be found in (Jaimes & Sebe, 2007) where an overview of the field is given from a computer vision perspective. The paper focuses on the possibility of creating intelligent systems able to recognize the emotional state of the user analyzing different input sources such as facial expression and vocal recognition. In spite of the fact that haptic is just mentioned but not related systems are described, this work could help in understanding the role of haptics in affective human-computer interaction.

(Coomans & Timmermans, 1997) gives a taxonomy of human-computer communication in VR systems, focused on categorizing multimodal communication channels occurring during user virtual experiences, types of interaction and ways to display retrieved data. No classification of adoptable techniques according to user task is given.

This chapter addresses interactions metaphors according the user tasks and the metaphors proposed to effectively accomplish them. User tasks, in our opinion, are a more general and straightforward way to ground interaction techniques; they can be considered as events occurring in time therefore they can be linked with temporal metaphors (Nesbitt, 2005). In particular navigation metaphors can be applied to maps as described in the works of Panëels and Roberts. We can refer to selection and manipulation as general interaction tasks, with which the user picks up an object and manipulates it both in a physical sense (translating, rotating or scaling it) and in a semantic sense (extracting enclosed information). The latter manipulation technique is particularly related to techniques for data visualization therefore manipulation metaphors can fall inside spatial and direct metaphors and can be connected to techniques used for charts and maps.

3. Hapto-acoustic interaction with Virtual Environments

The classification of users tasks in VEs we refer to comes from the works of Gabbard, (Gabbard, 1997) and Esposito (Esposito, 1996) that organize them in:

- Navigation
- Object Selection
- Object Manipulation, Modification and Querying

Based on this classification many interaction metaphors have been designed and implemented. The majority of them are based on vision as the main feedback channel.
In this section, a survey of the most used metaphors for each task will be given, their hapto-acoustic version, if possible, will be described with their relevance in non-visual settings.

3.1 Navigation metaphors

The navigation task refers to how users move inside the VE. Many works (Bowmann, 2005), (Shermann & Craig, 2003) agree in distinguishing two main components of the navigation task: travel and wayfinding. The former is the navigation physical component: the user moves through a series of locations exploring the environment, investigating its structure and the position of virtual entities. Other travel sub tasks can be the search tasks (moving to a specific target location) or manoeuvring tasks (highly precise small movements place the user viewpoint in the position/attitude most suitable to a specific goal). Wayfinding is the cognitive component of navigation: it involves the synthesis of the information acquired while travelling into a mental representation of the space and its use to plan paths in the VE.

3.1.1 Physical movement based metaphors

A group of travel metaphors is based on user physical movements. These metaphors use the body motion to drive the user movement inside the VE: most of them are intended for immersive VEs (such as CAVE applications). Types of physical metaphors are:

- Walking
- Walking in Place
- Devices Simulating Walking
- Cycles

Walking is the most direct form of travelling in a 3D world. It is a natural technique and provides vestibular cues but technological and spatial limitations make it not always feasible. It can be used when the VE size is smaller than the tracker working area. Other

solutions (Welch et al., 1994) use an optical tracking system that enables the use of a wider area by using a scalable tracking grid on the ceiling. Walking is more important for 3D applications such as mobile Augmented Reality (Höllerer et al., 1999). Walking in place is a natural alternative to walking: users move their feet to simulate walking always remaining in the same place. It does not have spatial limitations and still allows users to drive the movement with their body but it does not provide vestibular cues and gives a lower sense of presence in the VE. Devices Simulating Walking metaphors can be applied in very large VEs: they simulate the real walking with various types of treadmills allowing a more effective walking but they are expensive and do not provide the perception of a natural walking. Rather, user learns how to adapt his walking motion to the device characteristics. Finally, Cycles devices can be applied to simulate walking: they are less effective in providing a real walking sensation but are less complex and expensive than treadmills.
Body based haptic devices, such as vibrotactile gloves, belts or suits (Piateski & Jones, 2005), can be integrated in the walking metaphor and can define useful tactile cues to convey information even for blind users. In particular, vibrotactile solutions for non-visual autonomous mobility are currently investigated inside the (HaptiMap European project).
Ground based haptic devices, such as the PHANToM or the CyberForce, could be suitable for integration with other physical metaphors both in contexts of visual and non-visual feedback. The whole hand haptic interaction can be useful to feel the grasping of virtual objects while stylus based haptic devices can simulate the blind cane. However, to our knowledge, there is no literature in this direction.

3.1.2 Steering based metaphors

Steering is the continuous specification of absolute or relative direction of travel in different ways and with different devices. These metaphors share a direct camera manipulation approach. The techniques we will describe are:

- Gaze-directed
- Pointing
- Flying Vehicle
- Scene in Hand
- Eyeball in Hand

When a head tracker or an eye tracker is available the most natural choice for travelling in the VE is the Gaze-directed steering (Mine, 1995). With this metaphor, the direction the user is looking at specifies the direction of motion. In spite of its simplicity, this solution can become inefficient because whenever the user looks around to explore the environment he changes the motion direction. To avoid this problem the Pointing technique has been introduced in (Mine, 1995). It is based on two separate trackers: one used to look around in the VE while the other one, generally held in the user hand, specifies the direction of travel.
(Lécuyer et al., 2003) presents a system for blind people based on the egocentric navigation: travelling is constrained by a predefined path where the user moves using a wireless gamepad while a haptic device simulates a cane used to feel the VE. The exploration is integrated with auditory and thermal feedbacks (providing a perception of the sun position) besides the visual one, that allows sighted people to follow the navigation. This system can be Considered as using the Pointing Metaphor, where the trackers are respectively the gamepad, used to navigate the VE, and the cane used to look around. Criticisms mainly concern the constraint posed on the route and the constant speed of navigation; moreover the thermal effect needed additional work and the virtual cane was not always perceived.

In (Ware & Osborne, 1990) three metaphors are described and compared. The first is the Flying Vehicle metaphor where the virtual camera is represented as mounted on a virtual vehicle and the user can move the vehicle specifying its direction of motion. This is the most used travel technique applied in immersive and desktop solutions whose major drawback is the time required to travel between two far apart points in large VEs, depending on the maximum allowed speed. In the Scene in Hand metaphor, a virtual object is taken as an anchor around which the user can orbit: the direction of movement is related to the object position. This is useful for manoeuvring tasks while it results less effective for exploration and search tasks. The third metaphor is the Eyeball in Hand: the user holds a 6DOF tracker in his hand as if he would really hold his eyeball in the hand whose movements are directed coupled with the camera motion in the virtual space.

The Flying Vehicle metaphor can be extended to haptic display in the context of visual feedback (Anderson, 1998). Haptic feedback allows feeling objects through vibration and bump, according to the type of haptic device at hand.

In (De Boeck et al., 2001) and (De Boeck et al., 2002) the Camera in Hand metaphor is presented as a hapto-acoustic extension to the Eyeball in Hand technique. This technique uses the PHANToM haptic device to allow the user to combine Pointing and travel tasks in a single device avoiding the use of any further distracting tools. The virtual camera is directly coupled with the stylus of the haptic device and the user can specify camera direction and orientation in an absolute manner by moving the haptic stylus. Further enhancement to this technique (Extended Camera in Hand) allows switching from the absolute mode to a relative mode of direction specification to explore VEs larger than the physical haptic workspace. Acoustic feedback is used to highlight the hardness of pushing and the subsequent navigation velocity.

Although Flying Vehicle and Camera in Hand metaphors allow the use of haptic and acoustic cues in visual setting, they are not effective in non-visual setting. For sighted users, the point of view of the VE is the perspective from the position of the virtual camera. In hapto-acoustic applications addressing blind or eyes busy users, the point of view can be defined as the perspective from the position of the haptic probe. Directly coupling the haptic stylus with the virtual camera enables an egocentric point of view of the VE and a subjective navigation. In this type of navigation, the point of view continuously changes depending on the user hand movements and this can confuse blind users that lack the stable references points provided by vision (Sjöström, 2001). Indeed, this missing visual feedback makes more difficult to match information acquired from different point of views and very hard to construct a global schema of the VE.

Steering metaphors with direct camera manipulation, involving a continuously changing point of view, can be integrated with hapto-acoustic cues to enhance the sense of immersion of sighted users. In case of visually impaired or eye busy users, the use of Steering metaphors with haptics as the main feedback channel can be confusing.

3.1.3 Route planning and Target based metaphors

Another way of travelling is through the specification of a travel route or of the given target. Both these approaches have in common an indirect camera manipulation because the viewpoint is automatically manipulated by the system after the specification of the route or of the final destination made by the user. Route Planning metaphors constraint the navigation along the path specified by the user: the system handles the sequence of movements. The user has a minimum control on the travel and can pay attention to other tasks. Described metaphors are:

- Drawing a Path
- Marking Points

The Drawing a Path metaphor allows the user to draw a 2D path that is then projected into the 3D space. In (Igarashi et al., 1998) the 2D line is specified using the mouse. The Marking Points metaphor requires the placement of markers along a path of the VE: the system is responsible for creating a continuous path through this sequence of points. In (Bowmann et al., 1999) the user places markers using a 3D map of the VE; points marked on the map are then projected on the VE and connected by straight segments. An advantage of this technique is the possibility of changing the precision of the path by placing a greater or lower number of markers.

If the entire route is not relevant, it is possible to directly move the viewpoint to a target specified by the user. Some target based metaphors are:

- Teleportation
- Small Scene Manipulation
- Map-based Specification

With Teleportation users are instantly brought into a given position in the scene. This approach can easily disorient sighted users (Bowmann et al., 1997) because jumping from one place to another significantly decreases spatial orientation. A gradual movement from the starting point to the target is always recommended to reduce this effect. The Small Scene Manipulation metaphor has been introduced in (De Boeck et al., 2004): the camera smoothly zooms in a particular part of the world chosen by the user. Map based specification employs a 2D map depicting the entire world over the 3D VE and users can trace markers everywhere in the scene without being constrained by the viewpoint. The World in Miniature (WIM) metaphor (Mine, 1996) implements this approach allowing the user to place markers by manipulating a 3D miniature version of the VE. This metaphor can be considered more than a navigation metaphor because users can even select and manipulate distant objects through their miniature representation.

Haptic integration in Route Planning and Target based techniques is not well documented for visual settings. Moreover it is judged not useful for indirect camera manipulation in visual feedback context (De Boeck et al., 2005). Something analogue to a haptic route planning approach can be found in (Vidholm et al., 2004). This paper investigates how stereo graphics and haptics can be combined to facilitate the seeding procedure in semi-automatic segmentation of magnetic resonance angiography images. A force feedback based on local gradients and intensity values generates constraint forces allowing users to trace vessels in the image by placing in the 3D data set the seed points that will guide a region based segmentation algorithm.

On the other hand, planning routes and defining targets in VE are very useful techniques that designers can employ to develop hapto-acoustic metaphors for virtual navigation of visual impaired. For this kind of users, the combination of attractive forces and magnetic paths can implement a sort of haptically guided tour through the VE (Sjöström, 2001), very useful to support non-visual wayfinding.

Different solutions are available for the haptic guided exploration. (De Felice et al., 2007) and (Pokluda & Sochor, 2005) propose an exploration based on free movements with guide: the user can freely explore the VE, asking for being guided to a known point whenever he feels lost. Other applications fully constrain user movements to follow a predefined path (Roberts et al., 2002), (Pokluda & Sochor, 2003). In (De Felice et al., 2005), blind can switch from a free exploration of a 3D reconstruction of an ancient pillory to a guided tour through the most interesting features of the model (Figure 1). Whenever to user is brought in a target, a synthetic speech informs him with historical data of that feature. The guiding force must be gently enough not disturbing the user attention but sufficiently strong to be perceived and followed. In this work the following logarithmic force feedback has been used:

$$F_a = \text{Log}(D) - \varepsilon \tag{1}$$

where D is the current distance between the haptic probe and the target, while ε is an offset taking into account the fact that the 3D position of the target is placed inside the object mesh. The force direction is given by the vector connecting the haptic probe to the target. The force decreases as the haptic probe comes closer to the used feature: the user can freely orbit around the target being always haptically advised to come closer to it whenever he moves too far. In non-visual navigation, routes and markers are needed to supply the haptic experience with tools that enhance the construction of the global schema of the VE. These types of planning must be predefined by designers in the non-visual contest while they can be dynamically specified during the navigation by sighted users.

Fig. 1. A haptic guided tour on a 3D model. The sphere is attracted by the salient portions of the model (rectangles) while a synthetic speech gives information on historical data. Black arrows depict the attractive force, while the green arrows describe the contact force.

The World in Miniature metaphor offers an effective starting point to describe the most diffuse approach for navigating VE in application with non-visual display. As stated above, a subjective navigation involving a continuous change of the viewpoint is not suitable for blind navigation, and VE to result effective must overcome the traditional difficulties that blind subjects experience in the real life. For these reasons, many applications propose the entire VE as a world in miniature that fits the workspace of a one-point haptic device. In this way, the blind user has the entire world below his hand and can navigate rapidly and safely from one point to another (Figure 2). The movement of the stylus does not affect the reference system of the VE, that keeps its absolute position and orientation in relation to the desk. The avatar moves in a physical workspace, depending on the haptic device, that the user explores in an exocentric way.

Many works refers to this setting when VE helps blind users to navigate in real environments (Magnusson & Rassmus-Gröhn, 2004), (Lahav & Mioduser, 2008), (De Felice et al., 2007), (Murai, 2006) or to acquire geographical data from virtual maps (De Felice et al., 2007), (Parente & Bishop, 2003), (Moustakas et al., 2007). Experiments with VE representing real environments investigate the possibility that a preliminary virtual exploration can support the construction of an effective cognitive map, helping blind to navigate the real counterpart in a more autonomous and secure way. (Magnusson & Rassmus-Gröhn, 2004) used the PHANToM to virtually navigate a complex traffic VE. The study shows that most of the users were able to understand and navigate the VE and that users with better performances in the VE were very good at moving with a cane. Moreover, it outlines that blind users require detailed and articulated 3D virtual worlds so that it is important to find more automatic ways to create such environments. (Lahav & Mioduser, 2008) developed a 3D multimodal indoor VE that can be navigated with the Microsoft Force Feedback Joystick. They compared the performance in the real environment of people trained on the VE with those of the control group that directly explored the real one. They state that VE allows users to navigate real environments better than people belonging to the control group because virtual navigation allows a comprehension of all the parts, even the inner ones, that is faster and safer. (Murai et al., 2006) used the PHANToM Omni to explore an indoor environment. The use of a virtual simulator can offer some remarkable features such as guidance by using two haptic devices, one for the trainer and one for the user. It also reported that an extended training with the application enhances users performances and the system efficacy compared to traditional media. In (Yu & Brewster, 2002) a system designed to improve visually impaired people access to graphs and tables is presented.

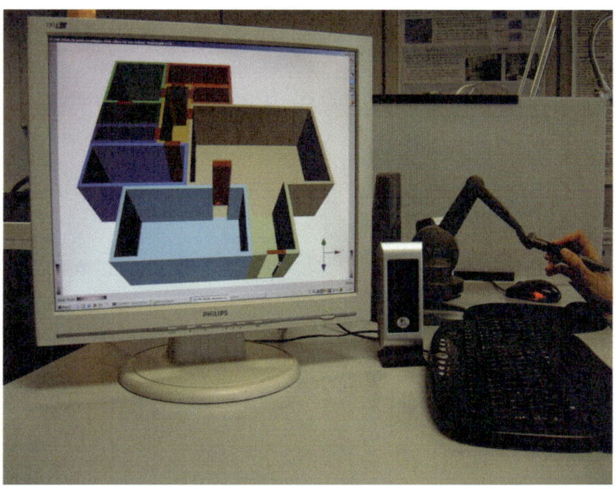

Fig. 2. The hapto-acoustic version of the World in Miniature metaphor used to navigate VE. The user pilots the avatar through the haptic stylus of a PHANToM Desktop

Table 1 reports an overview of the described metaphors highlighting their compatibility with haptics in visual and non-visual setting. Their typologies are reported as pm (Physical Movement), s (Steering), rptb (Route planning and Map Target based).

Metaphors	Metaphor type	Other tasks possible	Compatible with haptic (visual)	Compatible with haptic (non-visual)
Walking in place	pm	no	yes	possible
Treadmills	pm	no	yes	possible
Cycle	pm	no	yes	possible
Gaze Directed	s	no	no	no
Pointing	s	no	no	no
Flying Vehicle	s	no	possible	possible
Scene in Hand	s	no	possible	yes
Eyeball in hand	s	no	no	no
Camera in Hand	s	no	yes	no
Teleportation	rbtb	no	no	no
Small Scene Manipulation	rbtb	no	no	yes
World in Miniature	rbtb	selection/ manipulation	possible	yes

Table 1. Navigation metaphors overview. Compatibility is possible if haptic can be useful but little or no related literature is available.

3.2 Selection metaphors

Selection, also called target acquisition task (Zhai et al., 1994), refers to the acquisition or identification of a particular object in the virtual scene. Selection techniques, that require the indication of a particular object and the confirmation of its selection, can be grouped in:

- Virtual Hand
- Ray-casting
- Aperture-based
- Speech

Virtual Hand, the most intuitive and used selection technique, allows the user to directly select and manipulate an object with his hand. Ray-casting metaphors allow the object selection by pointing a ray at it. These mentioned metaphors have hapto-acoustic extension for visual and non-visual settings, and will be described in the following sub sections.

Aperture-based metaphors (Forsberg et al., 1996) provide users with an aperture cursor sliding over a cone shaped pointer that enables the dynamic control of the cone width whose apex is at the user eye and of the central axis whose direction is specified by the hand tracker movement. At our knowledge, no works have addressed the multimodal enhancement of these metaphors in non-visual settings.

The Speech metaphor (De Boeck et al., 2003) is a very natural and intuitive solution when selectable objects can be univocally named but in complex environments disambiguation can be required and the Automatic Voice Recognition applications are still error-prone. The integration with force feedback is difficult. Sound cues can be used to confirm selections.

3.2.1 Virtual Hand

With the Virtual Hand metaphor, the user moves a virtual cursor by using a tracker such as the Cyber Glove or any 3 DOF input device. The virtual cursor can have different shapes, typically it is a human hand 3D model. The user hand motion is directly mapped to the virtual hand motion by calculating its 3D position $\mathbf{p}_v$ and orientation $\mathbf{R}_v$ in the VE:

$$\mathbf{p}_v = \alpha \mathbf{p}_r \ ; \quad \mathbf{R}_v = \mathbf{R}_r \tag{2}$$

where α is a scaling factor while $\mathbf{p}_r$ and $\mathbf{R}_r$ are position vector and orientation matrix of the user hand respectively. Whenever the virtual hand intersects a virtual object, it becomes selected. The movements of the selected object are directly coupled with the user hand motion, making this metaphor also a useful technique for manipulation tasks (for details see section 3.3). This metaphor results very intuitive and natural because allows a behaviour similar to touch an object in every day life. Its major drawback is the limited workspace into which objects can be selected, due to the limited range of user limb, making a distant object only selectable after a navigation task. To overcome this limitation, in (Poupyrev et al., 1996) the Go-go metaphor has been proposed, which provides to the user a way to interactively and non-linearly change the length of the virtual arm.

3.2.2 Ray-casting

Ray-casting is by far the most popular distant selection metaphor that allows the user to select objects by directing a virtual ray. In immersive solutions the ray can be attached to the user virtual hand, while in desktop solutions can be attached to a 3D widget controlled by a mouse. The basic version of the metaphor allows to select the closest object intersecting the ray, resulting in a very effective and simple local selection technique while its precision significantly decreases selecting far objects (Poupyrev et al., 1998), (Bowmann et al., 1999), (De Boeck et al., 2004). Indeed, when the ray operates over large distances it results in a lower accuracy due to the hand jitter amplification; moreover small angular motion of the input device causes large movements of the ray. Objects occluded or in high dense arrangement are difficult to be selected (Liang & Green, 1994). The Cone-casting enhances the basic technique involving the use of a cone shaped selection volume with the apex placed at the virtual input device 3D position (Liang & Green, 1994), (Zhai et al., 1994). By increasing the activation area, multiple targets can be selected and a more stable pointing is allowed but this approach, due to the need of a disambiguation mechanism, leads to a more complex interaction (Hinkley et al 1994).

(Vanacken et al., 2009) presents and compares the 3D Bubble cursor, Depth ray and Haptic Lock ray techniques trying to overcome the ray-casting metaphor limitations; the visual and multimodal versions of each metaphor are tested in environments with different degrees of density. To highlight selection and confirmation of targets, 3D Bubble cursor and Depth ray multimodal versions introduce short sinusoidal bumps and earcons (Cockburn & Brewster, 2005). The multimodal feedback for Haptic Lock ray is dynamically activated when the user disambiguates multiple selected targets: the haptic probe behaves as a depth marker, haptically constrained along the ray vector and whenever it intersects an object, the user feels a haptic bump and an earcon. Experiments showed that the added multimodal feedback did not provide any real improvement in planning the selection of occluded objects in dense scenes while the advantage of hapto-acoustic cues is in increasing the user awareness of the target capturing operation. The use of haptic with stereo graphics for the

selection task is reported in (Wall et al, 2002). Users had to select targets in a 3D VE in different experimental setups switching from 2D visual feedback to stereo visual feedback, with and without haptic feedback. Results suggested that the haptic feedback provides insignificant benefits in enhancing target selection time especially when stereo graphics is used and are consistent with (Akamatsu et al., 1995), (Cockburn & Brewster, 2005) works.
In non-visual setting, the selection task is a quite passive procedure due to the lack of global knowledge of the whole scene; active non-visual selection techniques should provide both a way to show the user the objects available for the selection and tools to select them and to confirm the choice. (Magnusson & Rassmus-Gröhn, 2005) compares a set of hapto-acoustic tools to help users in selecting objects within a memory game. In particular, attractive forces and Linear Fixture (Prada & Payandeh, 2005) have been compared. Linear Fixture constrains the haptic probe on a magnetic line pointing towards the selected object where the user can move. Results showed no preferences between the two haptic techniques and that user ratings depend on the type of interaction. Moreover, 3D positional sound was preferred chosen among the proposed acoustic designs. In (Ménélas et al., 2010) hapto-acoustic metaphors are used to enhance target selection in non-visual VE with multiple and occluded objects. The Virtual Magnet metaphor is used: an attractive sphere placed around targets attracts the haptic probe with a force decreasing as long as the probe approaches the target. The positional information (via spatialisation) and distance (via repetition rate and level variations) are the two proposed acoustic cues. Comparisons are made between acoustic only, haptic only and multimodal conditions resulting in a lower selection time with haptic only and multimodal conditions.
An approach to increase the activation area allowing multiple selection candidates is presented in (Pokluda & Sochor, 2005): the selection area is a 3D sphere (Navigation Sphere) centred in the user avatar position that limits the haptic device movements to a small radius. Objects in the scene are projected on the sphere surface and the user can perceive distal virtual objects by haptic effects (vibrations). In our opinion, this is a very useful technique for selection in non-visual setting because it allows the acquisition of a global haptic view of the available objects at any distance. Unfortunately the paper lacks detailed blind users feedback. An interesting extension could be obtained integrating the Navigation Sphere technique with a guiding force moving the user hand toward the object.
In table 2 an overview of the selection metaphors is reported highlighting compatibilities with hapto-acoustic cues in visual and non-visual settings.

Metaphors	**Distant action possible**	**Other tasks possible**	**Compatible with haptic (visual)**	**Compatible with haptic (non-visual)**
Virtual Hand	no	Manipulation	yes	possible
Go-go	yes	Manipulation	yes	possible
Ray-casting	yes	Manipulation	yes	yes
Cone-casting	yes	Manipulation	yes	yes
Apertured-based	yes	no	possible	possible
Speech	yes	no	no	no

Table 2. Selection metaphors overview

3.3 Manipulation metaphors

Manipulation in VEs consists in translating, rotating and scaling the selected objects to acquire, through sight, a full knowledge of their shape and geometry for general interaction purposes. According to (Poupyrev et al., 1998), the manipulation task can be divided into exocentric and egocentric manipulation. In the former the user manipulates objects acting from outside the world with a god eye's view while, in the latter, he acts from inside the world and manipulates objects with a subjective point of view. Multimodal manipulation allows an enhanced examination of VE in visual settings because more properties can be acquired: shape and geometry with sight, material and weight with haptic, acoustic properties with hearing. In non-visual settings, touch is the main feedback channel and manipulation must supply features to make effective haptic examination of objects for a complete comprehension of their features. Egocentric manipulation metaphors includes:

- Virtual Hand
- Object in Hand
- HOMER
- Image Plane

while exocentric manipulation are:

- World in Miniature
- Scaled World Grab
- Voodoo Dolls

3.3.1 Egocentric manipulation

Egocentric manipulation metaphors allow to interact with the world from a first person viewpoint. In visual settings, these techniques are well suited for manipulation tasks such as object deformation, texture change and 3D menu interaction. In non-visual settings, egocentric manipulation can help as long as the examined object is not moved, otherwise reference points are missed confusing the user.

Direct manipulation metaphors such as the Virtual Hand and Object in Hand can be integrated with haptics and acoustic feedbacks. HOMER (Hand-centred Object Manipulation Extending Ray Casting) metaphor (Bowmann & Hodges, 1997) allows to select objects as in Ray-casting technique; then the user virtual hand moves to the object position where a direct manipulation can be applied. Despite the lack of works specifically addressing the integration of this technique with hapto-acoustic cues, it is plausible that multimodal versions of this metaphor could be obtained mixing the Ray-casting hapto-acoustic version and the virtual hand metaphor haptic version. Image Plane technique (Pierce et al., 1997) allows the user to select, move or manipulate objects indicating their projection on a 2D screen with a 2D mouse; since this is a 2D interaction technique for a 3D world, it is not possible to have a 6 DOF manipulation so haptic is not an added value.

3.3.1.1 Virtual Hand

As already stated in 3.2, Virtual Hand allows users to directly select and manipulate objects in the VE. Once the object has been selected, virtual hand movements are directly applied to the object in order to move, rotate and scale it.

This metaphor is well suited for the integration with the haptic feedback. It can be used with one-point haptic devices, such as the PHANToM Desktop from the (Sensable), and whole hand devices such as the Haptic Workstation from the (Immersion). Whole hand haptic manipulation in visual environments can be very useful in application of virtual prototyping and CAD design. (Ott et al., 2010) addresses the possibility for the user to interact with objects with both hands and the Haptic Workstation is used. The enhanced realism and effectiveness in VEs allowed by the haptic feedback require a greater complexity in computing forces for one or two whole hands manipulation with respect to a one point interaction. They propose a haptic hand model based on the God-object method of (Zilles & Salisbury, 1995), a proxy-based method largely used for one-point interaction devices. The virtual hand is decomposed in a Tracked Hand, directly coupled to the user real hand data; the Proxy that is a mass-spring-damper system connected to the Tracker hand by a set of viscoelsatic links and, the Visual Hand that is the only visible one. As long as the user moves into free space, the Proxy follows the Tracked Hand and the Visual Hand reflects the Proxy configuration. Whenever a virtual object is intersected, the Tracked Hand is allowed to penetrate its geometry, while the Proxy and consequently the Visual Hand are constrained to remain on the object surface. The viscoelastic links, connecting the Tracked Hand and the Proxy, determine the force feedback magnitude and directions to be applied to the device. Other works addressing the haptic rendering of the whole hand are (Garre & Otadui, 2009) for the manipulation of deformable objects and (Tzafestas, 2003) that also investigates the problem of torques rendering. They do not refer to any acoustic feedback.

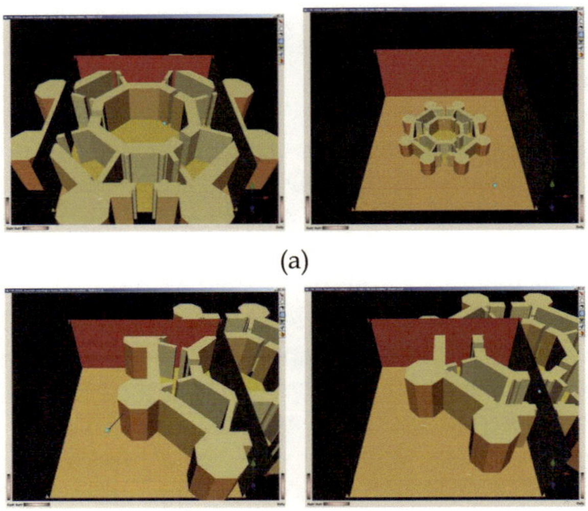

(a)

(b)

Fig. 3 Haptic manipulation techniques: a) zooming in and out, b) PHANToM dragging and Box dragging.

Haptic manipulation in non-visual settings aims at understanding objects rather than moving them around changing their position and orientation. Applications are mainly based on one-point interaction devices, that are more stable and effective if compared to whole hand armatures that resulted still not very effective in contexts where haptic is the only feedback channel. Moreover, one-point devices allow to easily add different haptic effects such as vibration and attraction using SDKs as Chai3D (Conti et al, 2005) or H3D (H3Dapi) while whole hand devices need to program these effects from scratch. Simulating special haptic effects, further than the basic contact force, supplies different ways to acquire knowledge about shape, geometry and details. In (Kolcárek & Sochor, 2005) a velocity driven LOD is introduced to allow blind users to directly manipulate and examine 3D virtual objects at different level of details. The algorithm is based on the assumption that fast movements of the haptic probe correspond to a user intention of acquiring a coarse idea of the object, while slow movements correspond to user intention of obtaining more details. Consequently, the 3D mesh is rendered at a simplified version for fast probe movements, while more detailed versions are dynamically rendered as speed slows down. Seven out of ten subjects participating in the test stated that the method effectively helps to better recognize global shape and details of the virtual objects. Other type of features, that can be added to object in order to better comprehend them, are dragging and scaling techniques. In (Magnusson & Rassmus-Gröhn, 2003) dragging and scaling functionalities are provided to dynamically change the part of a large model to be shown in the workspace and its scale. Three types of dragging are given. The PHANToM dragging technique gives the user the sensation of moving the whole model of the VE (according to the movements of the stylus) with respect to the position of a containment Box. In the box dragging technique the user seems to move the containment box (by pushing on its walls) with respect to the VE. Both these techniques are depicted in Figure 3b. Finally, the keyboard technique allows users moving the world pressing the arrow keys. The scaling functionality, depicted in Figure 3a, dynamically changes the sizes of scene details according to the dimension of the user avatar. All these operations are highlighted by a suitable sound (a sliding rock for dragging, increasing and decreasing sounds for zooming in and out). Users used without preferences the three dragging techniques and judged intuitive the zoom technique.

3.3.1.2 Object in Hand

The Object in Hand metaphor has been developed by (De Boeck et al, 2004) in order to exploit both user hands during the interaction with virtual objects: the non dominant hand can be used to grab and bring directly selected objects into a comfortable position to be better manipulated by the dominant hand. This metaphor is directly implemented with haptics enabled, indeed a CyberGrasp is used to grasp the virtual object. When the manipulated object is released, it comes back to the initial position. The main advantage of this technique is its intuitiveness that allows users to manipulate objects as in every-day life while its main drawback is the duplication of devices with their burden of cables. Its use in a non-visual settings is not documented, although it could be interesting to investigate how blind users can take advantage from this type of interaction taking into account that the returning of the manipulated object to its initial position after the manipulation can confuse them.

3.3.2 Exocentric manipulation

With exocentric manipulation, users are able to manipulate objects from a god-eye viewpoint, selecting and manipulating them everywhere in the VE, without being constrained to the local area as with egocentric techniques.

World in Miniature metaphor can be used for selecting and manipulating tasks further than navigation. Users can reach very quickly any object in the environment without navigation efforts. Haptics and acoustic cues provide direct and intuitive feedback on the accomplished task; this can be especially useful for blind or eye-busy users. The main drawback is the lack of accuracy due to the small scale of the miniature representation.

With the World-scaled grab metaphor (Mine & Brooks, 1997) the user can select and manipulate distant objects by pointing them with the Ray-casting, then the entire VE can be scaled with respect to the user viewpoint in order to make the remote selected object reachable by the user hand. The manipulation is then possible as with the virtual hand metaphor but with the disadvantage of having smaller object dimensions and a less accurate manipulation. The scaling factor α_s is calculated as follows:

$$\alpha_S = \frac{D_V}{D_O} \quad (2)$$

where D_v is the distance between the user viewpoint and the position of the virtual hand and D_o is the distance between the user viewpoint and the selected object.
The Voodoo Dolls metaphor (Pierce et al, 1999) allows manipulating distant objects in an exocentric frame of reference. It is a two hands interaction technique usually implemented with hand trackers such as the Pinch Glove or the CyberGlove. The user can select an object and create a miniature version of it, called doll, with the non-dominant hand. This doll represents a stationary frame of reference, meaning that if the user moves the doll, the corresponding distant object does not move. The user can select another object with his dominant hand while its position and the orientation in the stationary frame of reference are defined by the created doll.
Consideration about hapto-acoustic integration for these techniques are analogue to those reported for the Virtual Hand metaphors because they both allow a direct manipulation. No relevant literature can be found about manipulation techniques in non-visual settings. It is plausible that much work must be done to systematically observe the behaviour of blind or eye-busy users engaged in articulated multimodal manipulation tasks based on these metaphors.

Metaphors	Distant action possible	Other tasks possible	Compatible with haptic (visual)	Compatible with haptic (non-visual)	Taxonomy
Virtual Hand	no	Manipulation	yes	possible	Egocentric
HOMER	yes	Selection	yes	possible	Egocentric
Object in Hand	yes	no	yes	possible	Egocentric
Image Plane	yes	Selection	no	no	Egocentric
World in Miniature	yes	Selection/ Navigation	yes	yes	Exocentric
HOMER	yes	Selection	yes	possible	Exocentric
Voodoo dolls	yes	no	possible	possible	Exocentric

Table 3. Manipulation metaphors overview

4. The OMERO framework

The most effective techniques to accomplish user tasks, taken from literature and experimented in our past works (De Felice et al., 2005) and (De Felice et al., 2007), have been chosen and integrated to develop a multimodal interaction framework called OMERO (Organized Multimodal Experience of Relevant virtual Objects) that supports haptic devices characterized by one-point interaction and kinesthetic feedback and users tasks as navigation, objects selection, objects manipulation and scene querying. We introduced the

Scene Querying as a task to dynamically display the scene informative contents in response to particular user queries. This task is supported by the Scenarios metaphor. Moreover, we defined Active Objects as a metaphor to support object selection and manipulation. A conceptual framework has been developed to integrate the interaction techniques, (Figure 4). Based on this conceptual model a set of multimodal applications, described in the following section, has been developed and tested with groups of blind and low vision subjects.

4.1 The Active Object metaphor

A VE can be defined as a set of virtual objects (Figure 4). A given virtual object is described through its name, geometry and haptic material. A distinction is made between Active and Background objects. The former are objects with which users can interact by means of selection and manipulation while the latter convey to the user only their shape. Active Objects can be associated with simple behaviors (haptic, acoustic or dynamic) or complex behaviors that are combinations of the simple ones. Haptic behaviors are given by haptic

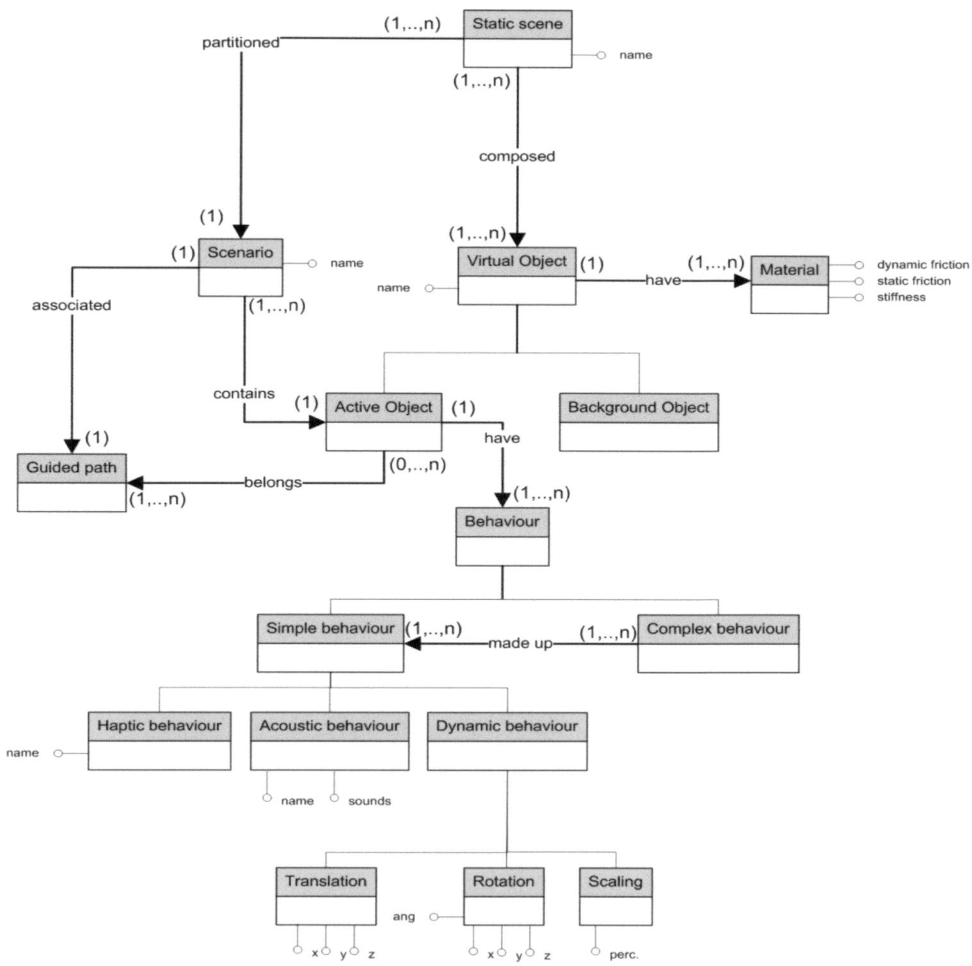

Fig. 4. The OMERO interaction conceptual model

effects such as vibration, attraction, viscosity or any given force field. Acoustic behaviors associate sounds and/or synthetic speech. Dynamics behaviors allow active objects to be manipulated in a strictly physical sense. Active Objects can act as targets in a route planning interaction belonging to a given Guided Path. In non-visual settings (section 3.1.3) targets are predefined by the designer to make easier to acquire particular information enclosed in the scene. Active Objects can be useful metaphors for designer and users. They give to designers an intuitive model to encapsulate selection and manipulation metaphors described in terms of their behavior.

4.2 The scene querying task

A rich in details virtual world generates a long sequence of local perceptions. Integrating all these data into a coherent and meaningful mental schema by means of touch, that does not provide a quick and global perception of the scene as sight does, is often a real challenge for blind. A VE can be seen as a database containing different kinds of information represented in the form of 3D objects shapes, together with their multimodal interface. Therefore, a user can explore a VE querying the scene to display different type of information. To better comprehend this task, we organize the scene using the Scenarios metaphor. Scenarios are sets of semantically related active objects that encapsulate informative contents. The user, at each specific time, can query the scene asking for a particular scenario and can focus his attention only on the information associated with it, temporarily discarding all the other data. This feature can reduce the discomfort that even seeing people may experience when faced with complex environments. Each Scenario of the model can be turned on and off (being touchable and visible or not). In this way, the scene can be tailored to focus on the data of interest having a progressive access to information.

5. Hapto/Acoustic interaction evaluation

Different applications of the OMERO system have been designed and proposed to visually impaired users to navigate VEs with the main aim of acquiring knowledge about particular domains, constructing their cognitive map and to exploit them, when it is possible, in navigating the corresponding real environments. The flexibility of digital models and multimodal interaction have been used to design VEs that allow blind to overcome some of the difficulties they encounter in acquiring spatial information in the every day life. Very different navigation contexts have been proposed to blind in several occasions. Their 3D virtual models, the related multimodal features and some details of the experimentation with blind people will be described in the following paragraphs.

5.1 Navigation task

The navigation of VEs in the applications we have designed for blind users is mainly based on the World in Miniature metaphor. Users first virtually navigate the most simple VE for a given context to construct the mental schema of the whole environment where then they can locate further objects. During the navigation they can interact with active objects, such as door or speaking walls. Experimental results validate the implemented approach.

The proposed approach is especially useful to navigate VEs reproducing sites characterized by large extension, complex topology and a huge amount of information to be conveyed to the user. This is the case of the visitable part of the ground floor of the Norman-Svevian

Castle located in Bari (Italy) whose virtual plant has been constructed from its detailed planimetry. The basic model includes: the entry area and the ticket office, the external and internal courtyards, the gallery of plaster casts, the chapel, the bathrooms and some connecting places (Figure 5a). Some doors can be opened and are defined as haptic-acoustic dynamic objects while doors to inaccessible environments are modelled as static objects with associated vocal explanatory messages. Transit areas without doors are modelled by bumps, defined as haptic-acoustic static objects.

Three sessions of tests have been accomplished on three different groups of users during two different events. The two groups tested during the first event were composed by four visually impaired people each, while the third group tested during the second event was composed by twelve blind. Any of them had previous knowledge of the castle.

The task they had to accomplish during the first two test sessions was to navigate the VE to acquire information on disposition and dimension of the castle environments and on the location of some objects. In the subsequent real visit they exploited knowledge coming from the virtual experience to consciously move in the castle. Models who they interacted with during the two test sessions were different. During the first test session, the model included most of the objects located inside the reproduced environments (trees, hedges, pots, ...) that were represented by simple solid shapes and defined as acoustic active objects (touching them, users automatically received vocal messages clarifying their identity). During the second one, the VE was modified removing any object different from doors and bumps and, after a first navigation of this model, users could explore zoomed models of some environments they required, with all the corresponding objects, to integrate the new pieces of information within the overall schema (Figure 5b).

Fig. 5. (a) The 3D plant of a part of the Swebian castle (b) A blind finds the well in the internal courtyard of the real castle after the exploration of the corresponding zoomed VE.

All the people in the two groups were able to accomplish the proposed tasks in a satisfactory way, but those belonging to the first one had to overcome some difficulties due to the large number of objects placed in the model, the vocal messages frequently activated touching them and the small size of some environments of the castle with respect to the haptic device workspace. Users in the second group could better focus on shape and disposition of the rooms and on the haptic-acoustic interaction with doors and bumps

without being annoyed by the objects and the related vocal messages. The main strategy used to explore the VE was following its borders, in order to understand the related shape.
Both the test sessions with the multimodal system were followed by a real visit; visually impaired people could verify the mental schema of the environments they had constructed during the virtual experience. Each blind person accomplished the real visit assisted by the most congenial support (companion, cane or guide dog) to ensure its safety: in all cases, the blind was able to decide autonomously the path across the castle without any help. Users had some difficulties during the real exploration of the largest areas in the castle due to the fact that in this case it is not simple to recognize references and correctly match real and VEs in a short time. In any case, they outlined that all the implemented features (haptic/vocal synchronization, change of the scale of the model, insertion/removal of details, ...) allowed them to construct an effective mental representation of the real environment and to navigate it in a conscious way. Some users stated to be interested in a new virtual visit, following the real one, to definitely assess their castle mental schema.
During the second test session, users were able to explore the virtual model in a faster and more effective way with respect to those of the first one; also their capacity to recognize the disposition of the environments in the real visits was enhanced. This could be probably due to the more intuitive and direct interaction with a simpler model, characterized by a much smaller amount of details and automatic vocal messages.
The task users had to accomplish during the third test session was to navigate the VE to acquire information not only about the topology of the castle but also about its history. Moreover users could virtually train for a little exhibition dedicated to blind people prepared in the gallery of plaster casts, with the aim of integrating information acquired from virtual and real visit. In this case, the VE presented a guided path (Figure 5a) that by means of 17 attractive target points placed along the predefined route, realized by means a sort of pipe, allowed blind to fast identify the salient portions of the castle. Whenever they remained trapped in a target they could activate a vocal message giving information on the place where they were. Then they could free navigate the virtual plant without objects inside enriched with respect the previous tests by means of on demand messages about dimensions of the environments, materials used for their construction and historical information. Finally they could experience the enlarged model of the gallery of plaster casts where some objects that they could explore during the real visit were located; their presence was highlighted by a suitable attraction effect that was noticeable whenever the avatar was into their neighbourhoods.
Users 1, 2 and 8 started their navigation moving too fast along the path and losing some targets but after few minutes they were able to move with the right speed. User 3, a guy with low vision, was able to reach each target by exploiting his residual sight. User 4 claimed that the experienced guided path should be integrated with vocal messages informing to the next direction to be taken. User 5 paid attention to ask for vocal messages whenever he reached a new target, and stated that this type of functionality can be really useful when exploring unknown environments. User 9 followed the path in a systematic way and he could feel every target; during the free exploration his movements followed the direction dictated by the guided path. He claimed that more experience with the VE could enhance the comprehension of the targets displacement. Users 10 and 12 had analogous results. Users, in spite of some difficulties due to their first approach with multimodal

interaction, judged the system to be very effective in making them able to move in unknown environment and acquiring different kinds of information that can be added as a useful complement to those provided by the real exploration.
Another example of guided path is the support function introduced in the Apulia model that pushes the avatar toward the nearest town when pressing the spacebar on the keyboard, helping the user to find the closest place of interest. This facility proved to be very useful and was intensively used especially during the first phases of the VE exploration.

5.2 Scene querying task

A virtual scene reproducing a complex environment can contain a big amount of information to be conveyed to users. Providing all the contents at the same time can overburden the blind user, making hard an effective navigation and comprehension of the VE. To simplify the user interaction with the virtual scene and organizing information on the basis of their semantic meaning, VEs can be designed exploiting the scenarios metaphor.
Based on this metaphor the virtual model of the Apulia region has been realized and tested with blind users. It has been constructed starting from GIS data to allow visually impaired users to acquire a proper knowledge of the territory from different points of view (Figure 6). It is multi-layered and, simply pressing the function keys on the keyboard, it is possible to navigate among four different scenarios each reproducing data related to a particular semantic view of the region, progressively building a structured and complete mental schema of the territory and its peculiarities.
A first scenario of the region model concerns the shape and the disposition of provinces, their borders and the borders between Apulia, the neighborhood regions and the sea. All the borders and the provincial areas have been defined as acoustic active objects. A second view reports the hydrographic network of the region: rivers and lakes have been respectively realized as canyon and ditches in which the avatar can fall and move to provide perceptions about their course and shape. All these objects have been defined as acoustic active objects associated with vocal messages telling their names. Another level includes the location of the major towns. The last view shows the main connections between towns. Roads are haptically represented as canyons connecting two towns and are acoustically active: on demand, they provide a vocal message about name, kind of the road and connected towns.
The described model has been proposed to twenty visually impaired users. Some of them did not have any previous knowledge of the region features. Users started their test exploring the first view of the model, to construct the cognitive map of the shape of the whole region and of each province, their borders, names and the relative position. Then they went through the next scenarios to increase their knowledge of the VE. The scene querying interaction modality helped them during the VE exploration and it was quite transparent; users were informed on the informative content of the scenario so they were not confused by comparing and disappearing objects in the different scenes but they were able to organize the information in an effective learning. Only a user complained loosing the reference points when changing scenario and suggested the possibility of merging scenarios information. Most of the users were able to correctly locate rivers, lakes and towns with respect to the regional and/or provincial territories and with respect to each other. Almost all the users judged the proposed interaction a valid and more flexible alternative to tactile maps and found the haptic-acoustic interaction really stimulating.

Fig. 6. The hydrographic network (a) and the main road scenarios (b) of the Apulia region

5.3 Selection/Manipulation task

While navigating VEs, users interacted with active objects such as doors, speaking walls or attractive objects. Doors, modeled as hapto-acoustic active objects, have been associated to a vibration effect that allows users to distinguish them from walls; they can be opened on demand by clicking the stylus button while the probe is in touch with them, listening at the same time to the opening/closing sound that makes more realistic the action in the virtual world. Few trials were usually sufficient to allow users to correctly interact with doors and to usefully exploit automatically triggered and on demand messages. Some users had problems in opening doors, due to the fact that sometimes the pressing movement can bring the probe from the modeled door down to the pavement, failing the opening command. Other users, after the door was opened, remained still without going in the other room.

Other type of active objects can be only acoustic: they tell the name of the touched object, the place where the avatar is in the VE or can act as informative points giving the user more structured information about geometrical formulas, definitions, materials, history… Vocal messages can be triggered on touch or on demand. Experiences with blind users suggested that vocal messages triggered on touch can be confusing if the activation is due to an accidental collision between avatar and active object. Sometimes, the pressing movement can influence the right placement of the avatar with respect to the active object to prevent from activating the message. Haptic active objects, exerting an attractive force onto the avatar whenever it comes close, were inserted in some rooms of the castle to highlight the presence of artefacts or were used to easily find towns in the Apulia model. In general the active objects interaction resulted effective for users that moving with slow movements were able to feel the attraction and to correctly interact with them listening to messages on the object nature. Users that moved fast in the VE often failed to feel the attraction and found objects only when accidentally collided with them. Some users outlined that objects located along the borders of the VE can act as effective reference points, while the most central objects are not important to this aim even if they allow a complete comprehension of the site. The most active users were really intrigued by finding them both in the virtual and when possible in the real visit.

Often blind users judged multimodal displays in different ways. For this reason, in (De Felice et al., 2009) a method for a fast multimodal authoring of VE has been proposed based on decoupling the geometric scene representation from its multimodal rendering. Designers can easily change hapto-acoustic cues using a visual editor in order to fit users feedback. A didactical application conveying information on plane geometry has been realized to test this feature. It has been first tested on a visually impaired user that had never used haptic interfaces (PHANToM Omni) before. User feedback highlighted that haptic cues such as vibration and magnetic forces can be hard to appreciate if associated with tiny features such as the circle radius line as in (Yu & Brewster, 2002). The system facility was used to find in real time the configuration of haptic effects that allowed the user a better understanding of the geometrical VE. Moreover, synthetic speeches helped him in integrating information coming from the haptic feedback with higher level information on the related concepts.

To face with the problem of the limited physical workspace that constrains models dimension, Dragging and Scaling functionalities have been implemented as in (Magnusson & Rassmus-Gröhn, 2003). The dragging technique allows to make always available a part of any VE in the workspace for the virtual exploration. To simplify the perception of details that would be too small in a complete view of the environment and simplify the understanding of spatial data, the model can be presented at a larger scale changing the relative size of the models with respect to the avatar. Moreover, in addition to what implemented in (Magnusson & Rassmus-Gröhn, 2003), if the user requires the scaling while touching an object, the VE is scaled according to the position of this contact point, otherwise the scaling is made according to the position of the centre of the scene. This meaningful reference prevents the user from being confused by uncontrolled movements of the VE. A 10% scale factor has been applied for each zoom in/out step. Preliminary experimental tests with blind users showed no preferences between the two dragging techniques: the choice of the most comfortable method seemed to be influenced by subjective user characteristics. However, further studies are needed to better ground these conclusions.

6. Conclusion

In this chapter an overview of interaction techniques in the field of multimodal 3D VEs for non-visual interaction has been presented, based onto classic users tasks in VEs (navigation, selection and manipulation of virtual entities). For each of them and where possible a comparison between hapto-acoustic versions in visual and non-visual settings has been accomplished. This will facilitate the understanding of each technique and the way tasks normally carried out by vision can be completed with sensorial substitution.

Navigation tasks refer to strategies used to move in VEs. Direct camera manipulation techniques for blind or eye busy users should be avoided preferring an exocentric viewpoint with world in miniature metaphors. Guided paths and attractive targets techniques aid blind to compensate the lack of a global glance of the scene.

Selection task refers to the acquisition or identification of an object in the VE. Visual settings propose the integration with hapto-acoustic feedbacks such as bumps, magnetic lines, attractive forces, earcons and spatial sounds. Experimental results show that in visual settings hapto-acoustic cues do not provide significant benefits in improving the selection time and in disambiguating multiple selected and occluded targets. Users heavily rely on the visual feedback while the multimodal feedback helps to highlight the selection confirmation. In non-visual settings, selection is a quite passive procedure and attractive forces can be applied to objects in order to highlight their presence. To realise an active selection, a coarse haptic glance of the virtual scene is necessary. To this aim vibration tips

help locating objects for selection while attractive forces can guide the user to the selected object. Positional sounds highlight the object position and the confirmation of its selection.
Manipulation task allows to acquire the knowledge of selected objects though their translation, rotation and scaling or can refer to a more general concept of interaction. Few works exist for non-visual multimodal manipulation of virtual objects. In non-visual contexts, objects cannot be moved around but must remain fixed to define reference points. Egocentric viewpoint could be investigated to exploit the proprioceptive subsystem.
The most effective techniques for user tasks taken from literature and experimented in our past works have been chosen and integrated to build the OMERO multimodal interaction framework. The Scene Querying user task has been introduced for a gradual access to scene information based on the scenarios metaphor that decomposes the virtual world in sets of semantically related objects. Moreover, the Active Object metaphor has been developed to support selection and manipulation tasks allowing to encapsulate multimodal behaviours to better design selection and manipulation metaphors. Based on these features different applications have been developed and a large number of experiments with blind people have shown the effectiveness of the implemented interaction techniques for user tasks such as Navigation, Object Selection\Manipulation and Scene Querying. Virtual guided tours have proved to help blind users to acquire a first coarse schema of the salient areas of the VE while vocal messages provided useful cues to support way finding. Active Objects have been able to convey information in a effective and compact way. The scenarios mechanism has been well accepted and exploited for acquiring a better knowledge of Ves. Future works aim to develop scenarios mixing information to answer more complex user queries.

7. References

Akamatsu, M., MacKenzie, I.S. & Hasbrouc, T. (1995). A Comparison of Tactile, Auditory, and Visual Feedback in a Pointing Task using a Mouse-type Device, *Ergonomics*, Vol. 38, pp. 816-827

Anderson, T.G., (1998). Flight: An advanced human-computer interface and application development environment, *Master's thesis*, University of Washington, 1998

Bowmann, D.A. & Hodges, L.F. (1997). An evaluation of techniques for grabbing and manipulating remote objects in immersive virtual environments, *Proceeding of the Symposium on Interactive 3D Graphics*, Providence, RI, USA, April 1997

Bowmann, D., Johnson, D. & Hodges, L. (1999). Testbed Evaluation of the VE Interaction Techniques, *Proceeding of the 1999 ACM Symposium on Virtual Reality Software and Technology*, ACM Press, pp. 26-33

Bowmann, D.; Kruijf, E., La Viola, J. & Poupyrev, I. (2001). An Introduction to 3-D User Interface Design. *Presence: Teleoperators and Virtual Environments*, Vol. 10, No. 1, pp. 96-108, February 2001

Bowmann, D.; Kruijf, E., La Viola, J. & Poupyrev, I. (2005). 3D User Interfaces: Theory and Practice. Addison-Wesley

Cockburn, A. & Brewster, S. (2005). Multimodal Feedback for the Acquisition of Small Targets, *Ergonomics*, Vol. 48, pp. 1129-1150

Conti, F., Barbagli, F., Morris, D. & Sewell, C. (2005). CHAI 3D: An Open-Source Library for the Rapid Development of Haptic Scenes, *IEEE Proc. WorldHaptics*, Italy, 2005.

Coomans, M.K.D. & Timmermans, H.J.P. (1997). Towards a Taxonomy of Virtual Reality User Interfaces, *Proc. 4th Int. Conf. on Information Visualisation*, England, Aug. 1997

De Boeck, J., Raymaekers, C. & Coninx, K. (2001). Expanding the haptic experience by using the phantom device to drive a camera metaphor, *Proceedings of the sixth PHANToM User Group Workshop*, Aspen, CO, USA, October 2001

De Boeck, J. & Coninx, K. (2002). Haptic camera manipulation: Extended the camera in hand metaphor, *Proceedings of EuroHaptics 2002*, pp. 36-40, Edinburgh, UK, July 2002

De Boeck, J., Raymaekers, C & Coninx, K. (2003). Blending speech and touch together to facilitate modelling interactions, *Proceedings of HCI International 2003*, Vol. 2, Crete, June 2003, pp. 621-625

De Boeck, J.; Cuppens, E., De Weyer, T., Raymaejers, C. & Coninx, K. (2004). Multisensory interaction metaphors with haptics and propioception in virtual environments, *Proceedings of NordiCHI 2004*, Tampere, FI, October 2004

De Boeck, J.; Raymaekers, C. & Coninx, K. (2005). Are Existing Metaphors in Virtual Environments Suitable for Haptic Interaction, *Proceedings of the 7th International Conference on Virtual Reality*, pp. 261-268

De Felice, F.; Gramegna, T., Renna, F., Attolico, G. & Distante, A. (2005). A Portable System to Build 3D Models of Culturale Heritage and to Allow Their Explorations by Blind People, *IEEE Proc. of HAVE 2005*, Ottawa, Ontario, Canada, October 2005.

De Felice, F.; Renna, F., Attolico, G. & Distante, A. (2007). A haptic/acoustic application to allow blind the access to spatial information, *Proceeding of WorldHaptics 2007*, Tzukuba, Japan, March 2007

De Felice, F., Attolico, G. & Distante, A. (2009). Configurable Design of Multimodal Non-Visual Interfaces for 3D VEs, *Proceedings of HAID 2009 4th International Conference on Haptic and Audio Interaction Design*, Dresden, Germany, September 2009, pp. 71-80

Esposito, C. (1996). User interfaces for virtual reality systems, *Human Factors in Computing Systems, CHI96 Conference Tutorial Notes*, April 1996

Forsberg, A., Herndon, K & Zeleznik, R. (1996). Aperture Based Selection for Immersive Virtual Environments, *Proceeding of the 1996 ACM Symposium on User Interface Software and Technology*, ACM Press, pp. 95-96

Gabbard, J. & Hix, D., (1997). A Taxonomy of Usability Characteristics in Virtual Environments, Virginia Polytechnique Institute and State University, Nov. 1997

Garre, C. & Otadui, M.A. (2009). Toward Haptic Rendering of Full-Hand Touch, *in Proceedings of CEIG'09*, San Sebastian, September 2009

H3DAPI: www.h3d.org, accessed the 5 Agoust 2010.

HaptiMap European project, www.haptimap.org, accessed the 5 Agoust 2010

Hinkley, K., Pausch, R., Goble, J. & Kassell (1994). Passive Real-World Interfaces Props for Neurosurgical Visualization, *Proceeding of the 1994 ACM Symposium on Human Factors in Computing Systems*, ACM Press, pp. 452-458

Höllerer, T., Feiner, S., Terauchi, T., Rashid, G. & Hallaway, D. (1999). Exploring MARS : Developping Indoor and Outdoor User Interfaces to a Mobile Augmented Reality System, *Computer and Graphics*, Vol. 23, No. 6, 1999, pp. 779-785

Igarashi, T., Kadobayahi, R., Mase, K. & Tanaka, H. (1998). Path Drawing for 3D Walktrough, *Proceeding of the 1998 ACM Symposium on User Interface Software and Technology*, ACM Press, pp. 173-174

Immersion: www.immersion.com, accessed the 5 August 2010.

Jacobson, R.D. (2002). Representing spatial information through multimodal interfaces, *Proceedings of Sixth International Conference on Information Visualisation*, 2002

Jaimes, A. & Sebe, N. (2007). Multimodal human-computer interaction: A survey, *Computer vision and image understanding*, Vol. 108, No. 1-2, pp. 116-134

Klatzky, R. & Lederman, S. (1995). Identifying objects from a haptic glance, *Perception and Psychophysics*, 57, 1995, pp. 1111-1123

Kolcárek, P., Sochor, J. (2005). Velocity Driven Haptic Rendering, *Proceedings of the 3rd international conference on Computer graphics and interactive techniques in Australasia and South East Asia*, Dunedin, New Zeland, 2005.

Lahav, O. & Mioduser, D. (2008). Haptic-feedback support for cognitive mapping of unknown spaces by people who are blind, *Int. J. of Human-Computer Studies*, 23-25

Lakoff, G. & Johnson, M. (1980). Metaphors we live by, The Chicago University Press

Lecuyer, A., Mobuchon, P., Megard, C., Perret, J., Andriot, C. & Colinot, J. (2003). Homere: A Multimodel System for Visually Impaired People to Explore Virtual Environments, *Proceedings IEEE Virtual Reality*, pp. 251-258, 2003.

Liang, J. & Green, M. (1994). JDCAD: A Highly Interactive 3D Modeling System, *Computer and Graphics*, Vol. 18, No. 4, pp. 499-506

Magnusson, C. & Rassmus-Gron, K. (2003). Non-visual zoom and scrolling operations in a virtual haptic environment, *in Proc. of EuroHaptics 2003*, Dublin, Ireland, July 2003.

Magnusson, C. & Rassmus-Gron, K. (2004). A Dynamic Haptic-Audio Traffic Environment, *Proceedings of Eurohaptics 2004*, Munich, Germany, June 2004

Magnusson, C. & Rassmus-Gron, K. (2005). Audio haptic tools for navigation in non visual environments, *Proceedings of Enactive05, 2nd International Conference on Enactive Interfaces*, Genoa, Italy, November 2005.

Menelas, B., Picinali, L., Katz, B. & Bourdot, P. (2010). Audio Haptic Feedbacks in a Task of Targets Acquisition, *Proceedings of IEEE Symposium on 3D User Interface*, Waltham, MA, USA, March 2010, pp. 51-54

Mine, M. (1995). ISAAC: A virtual environment tool for the interactive construction of virtual worlds, *Technical Report TR95-020, UNC Chapel Hill Computer Science*

Mine, M.R. (1996). Working in Virtual World: Interaction Techniques Used in the Chapel Hill Immersive Modelling Program, *Technical Report TR96-029*, August 1996

Mine, M.R. & Brooks, F.P. (1997). Moving objects in space: Exploiting proprioception in virtual environment interaction, *Proocedings of the SIGGRAPH 1997 annual conference on Computer Graphics*, Los Angeles, CA, USA, August 1997

Moustakas, K.; Nikolakis, G., Kostopoulos, K., Tzovaras, D. & Strinzis, M. (2007). Haptic Rendering of Visual Data for the Visually Impaired. *IEEE MultiMedia*, 1, pp. 62-72

Murai, Y.; Tatsumi, H., Nagai, N. & Miyakawa, M. (2006). A Haptic Interface for an Indoor-Walk-Guide Simulator, *Proc. of ICCHP 2006,* Lintz, Austria, July 2006, Springer

Nesbitt, K.V. (2005). A Framework to Support the Designers of Haptic, Visual and Auditory Displays, *In Carter and Fourney {3},* pp. 54-64

Okamura, A. & Cutkosky, M. (1999). Haptic exploration of fine surface features, *Proceedings of IEEE Int. Conf. on Robotics and Automation,* pp. 2930-2936, 1999

Ott, R., Vexo, F. & Thalmann, D. (2010). Two-handed Haptic Manipulation for CAD and VR Applications, *Computer-Aided Design & Applications,* Vol. 7, No. 1, pp. 125-138

Oviatt, S.L. (1999). Ten Myths of Multimodal Interaction, *Comm. ACM,* Nov. 1999, pp. 74-81.

Panëels, S., Roberts, J.C. & Rotgers, P.J. (2010). Review of Design for Haptics Data Visualization, *IEEE Transactions on Haptics,* Vol.3, No. 2, pp. 119-137

Parente, P. & Bishop, G. (2003). BATS: The Blind Audio Tactile Mapping System, *Proceedings of the ACM Southeast Regional Conference,* March 2003, ACM

Piateski, E. & Jones, L. (2005). Vibrotactile Pattern Recognition on the Arm and Torso, *Proceedings of the First Joint Eurohaptics Conference and Symposium on Haptic Interfaces for Virtual Environment and Teleoperator Systems,* pp. 90-95.

Pierce, J., Forsberg, A., Conway, M., Hong, S., Zeleznik, R. & Mine, M. (1997). Image Plane Interaction Techniques in 3D Immersive Environments, *Proceeding of the 1997 ACM Symposium on Interactive 3D Graphics,* ACM Press, pp. 39-44

Pierce, J., Stearns, B. & Paush, R., (1999). Voodoo Dolls: Seamless Interaction at the Multiple Scales in Virtual Environments. *Proceeding of the 1999 ACM Symposium on Interactive 3D Graphics,* ACM Press, pp. 141-145

Pokluda, L. & Sochor, J. (2005). Spatial Orientation in Buildings Using Models with Haptic Feedback, *Proceedings of WorldHaptics 2005,* Pisa, Italy, 2005.

Poupyrev, I., Billinghurst, M., Weghorst, S. & Ichikawa, T. (1996). The Go-Go Interaction Technique: Non Linear Mapping for Direct Manipulation in VR, *Proc. of the 1996 ACM Symposium on User Interface Software and Technology,* ACM Press, pp. 79-80

Poupyrev, I., Tomokazu, N. & Weghorst, S. (1998). Virtual Notepad: Handwriting in Immersive VR, *Proceeding of the 1998 IEEE Virtual Reality Annual International Symposium,* IEEE Press, pp. 126-132

Prada, R. & Payandeh, S. (2005). A Study on Design and Analisys of Virtual Fixtures for Cutting in Training Environments, *Proc. of Worldhaptics 2005,* Pisa, Italy, pp. 375-380

Roberts, J.C. & Panëels, S. (2007). Where are we with Haptic Visualization?, *Proceedings of WorldHaptics 2007,* Tzukuba, Japan, March 2007, pp. 316-321

Salisbury, K.; Conti, F., & Barbagli, F. (2004). Haptic Rendering: Introductory Concepts, *IEEE Computer Graphics and Applications,* Vol. 2, 2004, pp. 24-32

Sensable: www.sensable.com, accessed the 5 August 2010

Sjöström, C. (1999) The IT Potential of Haptics - touch access for people with disabilities. Licentiate thesis, available at http://www.certec.lth.se/doc/touchaccess

Sherman, W.R. & Alan, B.C. (2003). Understanding Virtual Reality, Interface, Application, and Design, Morgan Kaufmann

Tzafestas, C.S. (2003). Whole-Hand Kinesthetic Feedback and Haptic Perception in Dextrous Virtual Manipulation, *IEEE Transactions on Systems, Man, and Cybernetics – Part A: Systems and Humans,* Vol. 33, No. 1, January 2003

Vanacken, L., Grossman, T. & Coninx , K. (2009). Multimodal Selection Techniques for Dense and Occluded 3D Virtual Environments, *International Journal of Human-Computer Studies,* Vol. 67, 2009, pp. 237-255

Vidholm, E., Tizon, X., Nyström, I. & Bengtsson, E. (2004). Haptic Guided Seeding of MRA Images for Semi-Automatic Segmentation, *in ISBI,* pp. 288-291

Wall, S.A., Paynter, K., Shillito, A.M., Wright, M. & Scali, S. (2002). The Effect of Haptic Feedback and Stereo Graphics in a 3D Target Acquisition Task, *Proceedings of Eurohaptics 2002,* pp. 23-28

Ware, C. & Osborne, S., (1990). Exploration and Virtual Camera Control in Virtual Three-Dimensional Environments, *Computer Graphics, Vol. 24, No. 2.*

Welch, G., Vicci, L., Brumback, S., Keller, K. & Colucci, D. (2001). High-performance Wide-Area Optical Tracking: The HiBall Tracking System, *Presence: Teleoperators and Virtual Environments,* Vol. 10, No. 1, pp. 1-21

Yu, W. & Brewster, S. (2002). Multimodal Virtual Reality Versus Printed Medium in Visualization for Blind People, *Int. ACM Conf. on Assistive Technologies,* pp. 57-64

Zhai, S., Buxton, W. & Milgram, P. (1994). The "Silk Cursor": Investigating Transparency for 3D Target Acquisition, *Proceedings of the 1994 ACM Conference on Human Factors in Computing Systems,* ACM Press, pp. 459-464

Zilles, C.B. & Salisbury, J.K. (1995). A constraint-based god-object method for haptic display, *Proceedings of the International Conference on Intelligent Robots and Systems,* Vol. 3

3

Collaborative 3D Interaction in Virtual Environments: a Workflow-Based Approach

Samir Otmane, Christophe Domingues,
Frédéric Davesne and Malik Mallem
IBISC Laboratory, University of Evry
France

1. Introduction

Collaborative Virtual Environments (CVEs) are complex environments where multiple users share the same objects to act together. The complexity of these environments is related to the interaction of the user group with shared items. In a shared world, several constraints appear, including those related to coordination and communication of users and user interaction management in virtual world towards objects and other users. The existing single or multiuser 3D interactions in Virtual Reality (VR) are currently far from providing suitable solutions. Indeed, the 3D interaction suffers from a lack of models and formalisms to manage and control the actions and intentions of users in the virtual environment. The interaction of multiple users with the virtual environment is limited and many researches are in progress. The main objective of the research in the field of multiuser 3D interaction is to instruct users to evolve in CVEs, and to interact together efficiently and easily with virtual entities.
Currently, there are two types of synchronous multiuser 3D interaction techniques. A first category separates the degrees of freedom (DoF) for the object to manipulate. In this case, users operate single user techniques by acting on the degrees of freedom which are assigned to them. For the second category, a function will determine the final movement from the position and orientation of the user object in the CVE. This involves using a new technique in multiuser situations. However, all of these techniques do not take into account the constraints of coordination and communication between users and focus exclusively on manipulation tasks with two users. However, the design of a CVE requires considering multiuser interactions from Computer Supported Collaborative Work (CSCW) point of view, as well as the management of group interactions. Another aspect to consider is the heterogeneity of virtual reality platforms used by participants as well as the disparity between users for providing new models and systems supporting efficient collaborative work and enhancing presence in CVEs.
This chapter presents a useful workflow-based approach to manage 3D interactions and enhance presence in CVEs. This approach combines astutely different concepts from two research domains: CSCW and VR. The second section outlines and discusses the background of recent contributions concerning collaborative 3D interaction techniques. Section three presents some fundamental concepts relevant to the management of group interactions in a CVE. Section four describes and details our contribution concerning a workflow-based approach to design collaborative 3D interactions. Experimentations and evaluations are given

and discussed in section five. The last section concludes the chapter and presents some future works.

2. Background and related work within collaborative 3D Interaction

In the literature there are two approaches to describe a collaborative 3D interaction. The first approach, allows a simultaneous action on an object by separating data (for example degrees of freedom: DoF) as rotations and translations to assign them to different users. In this approach, users can act together on the same object but when one user performs translations the other user does only rotations. Pinho and associates Pinho et al. (2002) classified this approach in two sub-categories:

- Homogeneous cooperative metaphors: users manipulate the object by using a unique single-user technique;
- Heterogeneous cooperative metaphors: in this case, users manipulate the object by using different single user techniques.

In the second approach, users have access to all available data (for example DoF). During manipulation the movement of the object is a combination of different movements of all users. Noma and associates Noma & Miyasato (1997) presented work on multiuser manipulation and interact with a shared object via haptic arms. Users are represented by simple virtual hands. The final movement of the object is the result of balance of forces applied by users. However, it may lead to inconsistency between virtual hand position and real hand. Indeed, when a user is going to apply a force to the object to move it, simple virtual hands of other participants attached to the object will also follow the moving object, which may seem inconsistent for users, because they have not activated their haptic arm.
A 3D cursor or SkeweR Duval et al. (2006) is another technique designed to keep the history of interaction and allow the correct representation of simultaneous interactions. It allows the simultaneous manipulation of an object by multiple users. Users control a 3D cursor that acts as a virtual simple hand, except that the selection is carried out automatically when approaching the shared object. If a user is available to manipulate the object, only rotations can be communicated to the object. If two users are available for the manipulation, the object is controlled as a "rod" from the translation and rotation movements.
Duval Duval & Tenier (2004) have proposed a technique that derives from a RayCasting technique Bolt (1980) for manipulating object with two users. This technique is based on the following observation: if a user manipulates its ray to move a shared object, the ray of another user "attached" to the same object will also move. However, the hand of the second user has not moved which creates a mismatch between the real movement and the virtual movement. Authors proposed to change direction of the ray in function of the force that is applied. They proposed three forms of rays (elastic, elbow or deformable).Another similar technique using a virtual ray (Bent Pick Ray technique) is also proposed by Riege and associates Riege et al. (2006).
More recently, the "Three virtual hands" technique Aguerreche et al. (2009) which determines the motion (position and rotation) of an object from three points (position) associated to three virtual hand. In this technique only translations of virtual hands are taken into account.
Duval and associates Duval & Fleury (2009) proposed an asymmetric "2d pointer /3d rays" technique for 3D interaction within CVE. The avatar is represented by a 3D object in the CVE but is controlled via a simple 2D pointing device (for example a mouse). This technique allows an asymmetric collaboration between a user immersed in a virtual reality platform

and another user using a simple PC.
Designing and using of collaborative 3D interaction techniques is not an easy task for developers and users respectively. Indeed, there are no mathematical models and formalisms for easy developing of generic and usable techniques yet. The design approach of most collaborative 3D interaction techniques (selection or manipulation) is considered as *local*. However, this design approach is focussed generally on how objects are to be selected or manipulated and often forget the principal players who are the users. It is necessary to consider a new design approach of collaborative 3D interaction from the *global* point of view by taking into account objects, 3D interaction tasks and users. Indeed a global approach to design collaborative 3D interaction techniques must take into account all of these parameters needed for interacting in CVE.
Therefore, it is necessary to find a way to manage and coordinate all these parameters to provide users with easy and intuitive interactions while enhancing the sensation of presence in a CVE. In the following section we present some fundamental concepts relevant to the management of group interactions in a CVE. These concepts are the basis of our contribution based on the design of a workflow for collaborative 3D interaction presented in section 4.

3. Managing interactions in CVEs

The best-known work performed for the management of interactions in the CVEs includes the spatial model of interactions proposed by Benford & Fahlen (1993). It was developed in the 1990s as a method of data transmission control in the CVEs. This model uses the properties of space as a basis to negotiate interactions and communications between communicating objects. The basic concept of this model is based on a breakdown of the virtual space. A metric space is defined and used to measure the positions and directions of different objects. From the position and orientation settings, objects have the ability to modify their interaction and communication. Objects interact with each other via a combination of media transmission such as audio, text or visual data through specific interfaces.
This model defines a set of interesting concepts such as the aura, the focus, the nimbus and the awareness. These concepts used separately or combined astutely can produce different interactions between objects in the virtual environment. In the following a brief presentation to these concepts is given:

- **Aura:** It represents an area in which an object can interact with another object. Objects are surrounded by their auras and move in the virtual world. When two auras are in collision the interaction becomes possible. Therefore, the aura may be considered as a fundamental interaction technology tool. The aura can take any shape or size. Typically, objects will bring up different auras (size, colour).
- **Focus:** It can be seen as a tool for direct attention and therefore filter information based on the boundaries delimited by the aura. It can be considered in some way as the user point of view.
- **Nimbus:** It represents a subspace in which an object makes many of its aspects available to other objects. These can be its presence, identity, activity, or a combination of these aspects. The Nimbus allows objects to draw attention of other objects to them.
- **Awareness:** It calculates the quality of interaction between two objects. The awareness calculation between two objects is not symmetrical (the awareness of an object A against the object B does not equal to awareness of B against A). This computation is performed by

using the focus and the nimbus. The awareness levels are calculated from a combination of nimbus and focus of the objects.

This model was subjected to numerous extensions during the years. We can cite the Sandor work with the AETHER system Sandor et al. (1997), the Greenhalgh work Greenhalgh (1997) and Greenhalgh & Benford (1999). In AETHER system, authors use focus, nimbus, and awareness concepts on semantic networks objects and relations. This allows building a history of objects and relations between objects that have been updated or deleted. Greenhalgh integrates "third-party objects" that provide support for contextual factors in awareness calculations and that enhance scalability. Third parties can have two effects on awareness: attenuation or amplification of existing awareness relationships, and the introduction of new aggregate awareness relationships.

The model of presence for cooperative applications Rodden (1996) represents an awareness model of interaction for multiuser applications. The main objective of the model of presence is to allow the sharing workspace of a cooperative application based on the notions of awareness and presence. This model is mainly based on the spatial model of interaction Benford & Fahlen (1993). The model of dynamic management of interests Ding & Zhu (2003) deals with the problem of presence management in collaborative virtual environments between different users. This model is focused on a dynamic interaction of environments. The model describes user's behaviours and more specifically the changes of their centre of interest over time.

More recently Bharadwaj et al. (2005) have proposed a model to ensure the awareness in heterogeneous environments, especially in environments with different interfaces. This model is based on the spatial interaction model discussed above. This model allows a user to have more focus to allow an easy choice of sources. Access rules are used to allow or reject certain sources.

An other recent model is proposed by Otmane and associates Otmane et al. (2007). This model is fully dedicated to collaborative 3D interaction. The authors have established a conceptual framework based on the functional aspect of 3D interaction (navigation, selection and manipulation) called "functional clover of 3D interaction". This model gives to users an ability to have knowledge about the system state and on the other hand provides information needed by the system to assist users to interact together. The navigation set contains functions for management of the user's position and orientation in the CVE. Selection and manipulation sets include respectively dedicated functions for selection and manipulation of an object or group of objects. This allows users to be aware of selections and manipulations that are performed in the CVE.

4. A workflow-based approach

In virtual reality the perception/cognition/action loop describes the relationship between a user and the virtual world (Fuchs et al. (2003)). We proposed to disrupt this loop by incorporating the concept of workflow (see figure 1). The workflow manages all the tasks to be performed and all actors involved in the collaboration process. Therefore it can be used on one hand for the coordination of 3D interaction tasks (navigation, selection and manipulation) and on the other hand for the communication of users in the CVE.

This functional framework allows users to have knowledge about the system state and other users activities: who navigates? who interacts? who communicates? who has difficulty?. On the other hand, the system must provide information to assist users to interact (easy selection, intend detection when moving towards an object) and communicate with others and more generally to work together.

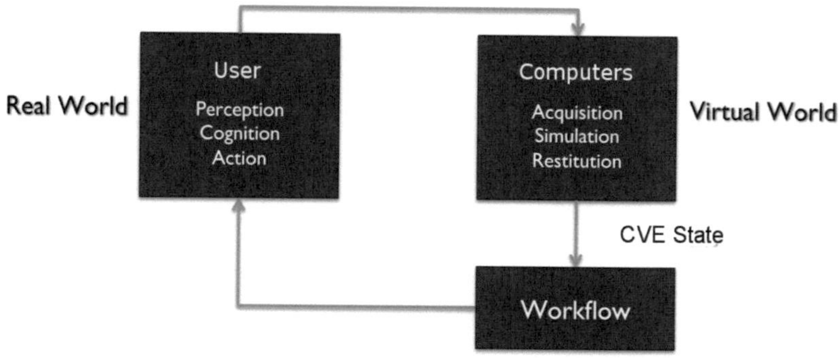

Fig. 1. Integrating the workflow in the perception/cognition/action loop

Workflow is a component ensuring coordination of users that can produce together (manipulate an object by several users, navigate, communicate, etc.). The proposed workflow consists of two components: a shared component and a motor component. The *shared component* represents the shared data space that symbolizes the behaviour of users and sources in the CVE. This component in someway can be considered as a collective memory in the CVE. This collective memory will give information about actions of the users. The second component of the workflow (*motor component*) represents the set of functions that deal with data processing from the shared space and provides tools to assist the users during the collaboration.

4.1 Shared component

The shared component consists of two state matrixes representing respectively the state of all users and all sources in the CVE. These two matrixes define the overall state of the system and are used to characterize the CVE at any time. The figure 2 illustrates this shared component. These state matrixes are constructed from information of users and sources. A *source* is an object that generates sensory information (virtual object and data media) that can be perceived by the users.

4.2 Motor component

The second component of the workflow corresponds to features dedicated to tasks and roles assignment during different interaction processes. It uses the shared data and applies them on *particular sources* in the CVE via *assistance functions*. Particular sources are objects that can be changed during the interaction process by different assistance functions dedicated to 3D interaction tasks. They act as a support tools for 3D interaction tasks coordination. Assistance functions are functions that help manage 3D interaction. They can act on particular sources to provide support to coordination.
The two following sections present particular sources and assistance functions used in the workflow motor component.

4.2.1 Particular sources

Particular sources are associated with functions that can be used by the motor component of the workflow to detect actions of the participants, or inform users about actions performed by other users in the CVE. Based on the spatial interaction model Benford & Fahlen (1993) and the functional clover of 3D interaction model Otmane et al. (2007). These particular sources are used to coordinate 3D interaction tasks in order to predict user's interactions thanks to **aura,**

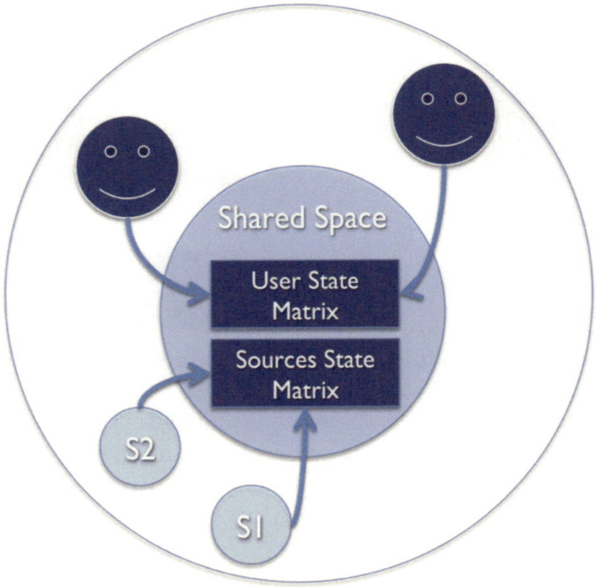

Fig. 2. Illustration of the shared component

focus and nimbus concepts. The coordination process is based on positions and orientations of the users in the CVE.
The workflow engine (motor component/space) receives information from the shared component that contains state vectors of users and sources. It acts on the aura, the focus and the nimbus to change the perception of users in the CVE (see figure 3).
Concretely we defined five particular sources: 3DIFocus, 3DIAura, 3DINimbus, 3DIAssistant and 3DIAvatar. Other sources are virtual objects in the virtual environment. These particular sources are used by the workflow, and they are exclusively dedicated to 3D interaction tasks.

- **3DIFocus:** This particular source corresponds to all other sources (virtual objects) with which the user can interact. They are sources that belong to the user's field of view. The intersection of two focus returns a common viewed sources of two users. This allows for example two users to interact on the same viewed sources. The 3DIFocus source can be considered as a tool for direct intention and will therefore enable filter sources that are not in the user's field of view. For example, the focus of $user3$ (see figure 3) corresponds to the source $S2$.
- **3DINimbus:** This particular source represents all users with the intention to interact on a single source. It represents the group of users who might select the source for possible manipulation in the future. For example the nimbus of the source $S1$ (see figure 3) represents the set $user1, user2$.
- **3DIAura:** It represents a 3D zone that surrounds a virtual object and allows single or multiuser selection. The selection is possible only if the avatars of users are in the aura of the source. This aura determines users who potentially want to select the source. This aura can also be used to surround the user's avatar in order to start conversations between users.
- **3DIAssistant:** This particular source enables a user to be assisted on specific actions that it performs. For example in the case of the selection of a source, the assistant can be activated

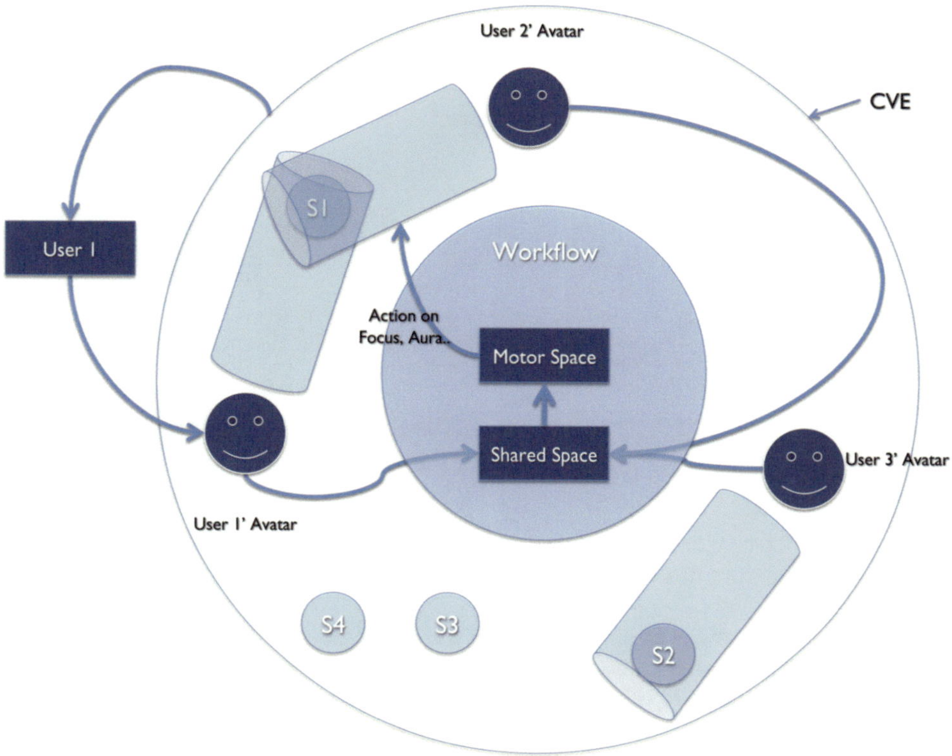

Fig. 3. Illustration of the workflow running in a CVE. Cylinders represent users focus and the nimbus of the source $S1$ represents a set of two users (user 1 and user 2)

as a multimodal (audio, visual and haptic) *virtual guide* Otmane et al. (2000), Ullah et al. (2009), Ullah et al. (2008) and Prada & Payandeh (2009). The assistant source as a virtual guide will enable an easier and precise selection of an object.

- **3DIAvatar:** The avatar source is a virtual representation of the user. It may take the form of a humanoid or a simple recognizable 3D object. It represents the position and orientation of the user in the collaborative virtual environment.

4.2.2 Assistance functions

Assistance functions are functions that operate on particular sources that can be used by the workflow engine. These functions operate with different 3D interaction tasks (navigation, selection and manipulation). By acting on these particular objects, the system is able to provide assistance to users and therefore coordinate their interactions in the CVE.

4.2.2.1 Navigation and selection functions

The navigation function will act on the aura colour using matrixes state data to indicate to the user his position towards the sources (see figure 4). This will inform the local user that he/she is close or away from the sources. For remote users, this function can for instance change the colour of the avatar of the other participants.

In our implementation example, the colour of the aura varies from red to green; red (see figure 5(a)) means a far distance while green (see figure 5(b)) means that the user is near the object.

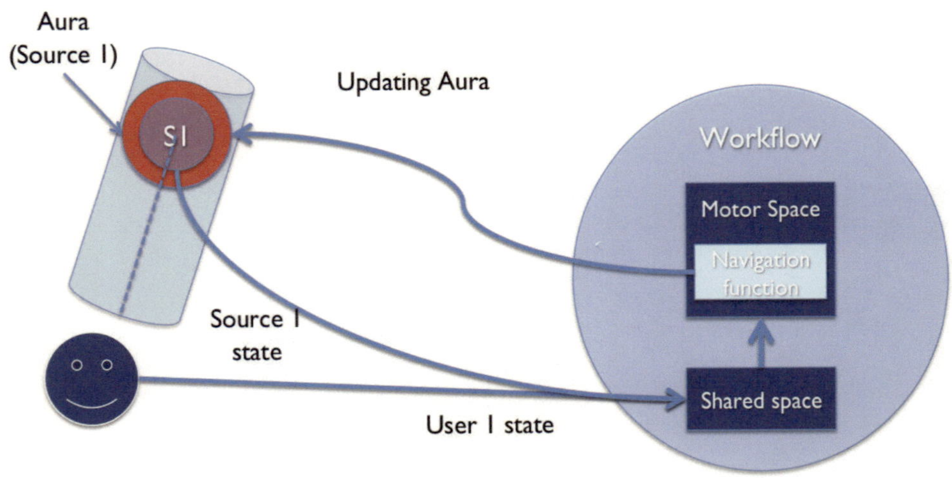

Fig. 4. The assistance function during the navigation task. In this example the navigation function updates the aura of the source $S1$ that is in the focus of the *user*2.

The user will see the changes of the aura colour depending on his movements.
The selection function is dedicated to manage selection of objects by the users. It becomes active when it enters the aura of the source. An assistant appears as a virtual guide (a cone which contains the user's avatar) to help the user in selecting the object (see figure 6). When the selection is validated, the manipulation may be possible.
The selection function acts on the colour of the virtual assistant (see figure 7). Once the user is in the aura of the object, the assistants (virtual guides) appear and guide the user towards the target (attachment point). The virtual guide colour modification is based on the distance between the user position (inside the assistant) and the object attachment point. This function gives the user the capability to know the position of his avatar to correctly validate the selection. Additionally, this function can act on the control of user interaction by prohibiting certain movements when the user's avatar belongs to the geometric shape of the assistant.

4.2.2.2 Manipulation function

As discussed in the related works, multiuser object manipulation is often limited to two users per object. In addition, dedicated techniques are usually proposed in multiuser manipulation making more laborious learning of users. Consequently, the transition from single-user to multiuser manipulation requires the change of technology and/or interaction technique. Indeed, if a user manipulates an object with a simple virtual hand technique, it is not conceivable that when a second user will select the same object, it needs to change his initial manipulation technique.
We want to allow multiuser manipulation of objects through any single-user interaction technique. In this way, the transition from the single-user to multi-user manipulation can be a natural and intuitive way. Indeed, this avoids the learning of a new metaphor and an additional cognitive load for users. Our approach is to integrate concepts of classical mechanics to modelling multiuser manipulation via a mechanical system composed by mechanical joints. In the following section we only presented the concepts of our multiuser manipulation. Technical details are not given in this chapter.

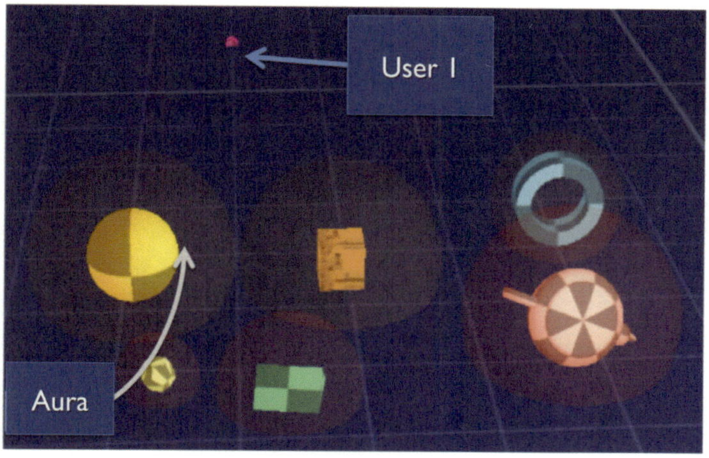

(a) The user is far from the sources, the aura is red

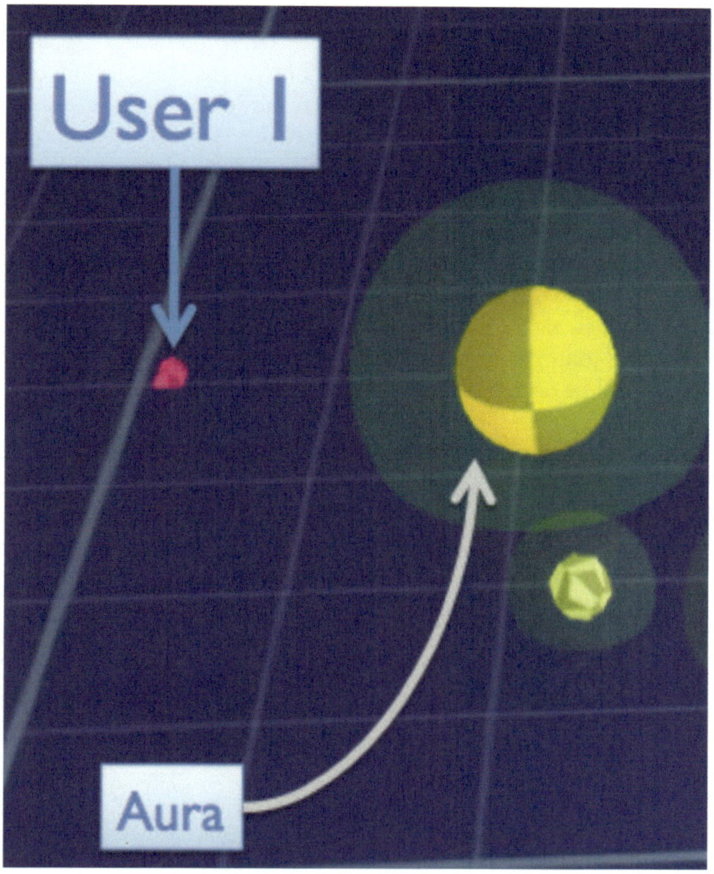

(b) The user is close to the sources, the aura is green

Fig. 5. Implementation example of the influence of the assistance function on the aura during the navigation task

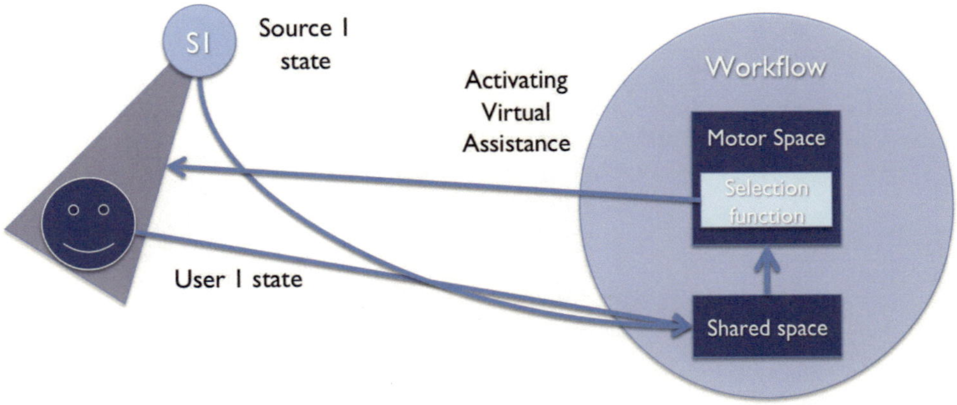

Fig. 6. The assistance function during the selection task. In this case the source $S1$ can be selected by the $user1$.

In the field of mechanics, a mechanism is the combination of several pieces, whereas in our case it will apply to multiple objects and avatars. These elements are linked together by contacts called mechanical joints. A mechanical joint is the description of the relationship between the different elements using mathematical models. When selecting an object via a single-user interaction, the avatar of the user becomes the "parent" item and therefore inherits the movements of the avatar. However, in the multiuser case, this principle may not apply.
For example, in the real world, when two users move a board, the resulting movement dependents on simultaneous users actions (users are related to the board by joints). We can model this by introducing virtual joints between avatars and objects (see figure 8). These joints will act as an *adapter* to allow a transition from single-user to multiuser manipulation.
In our case, joints between users and the object can be modelled by fixed or ball joint (see figure 9) links. This ball joint has three degrees of freedom on its three rotation components. Transmissible efforts will be on translation components.
To determine the object movement, we use forces that users perform on the attachment points of the object. The movement of the object is calculated from forces provided by users. In fact, by solving laws of dynamics relationship, we can determine accelerations in translation and rotation of the object. The figure 10 introduces the principle of the manipulation function when two users manipulate a source together. Figure 11(b) presents implementation of the

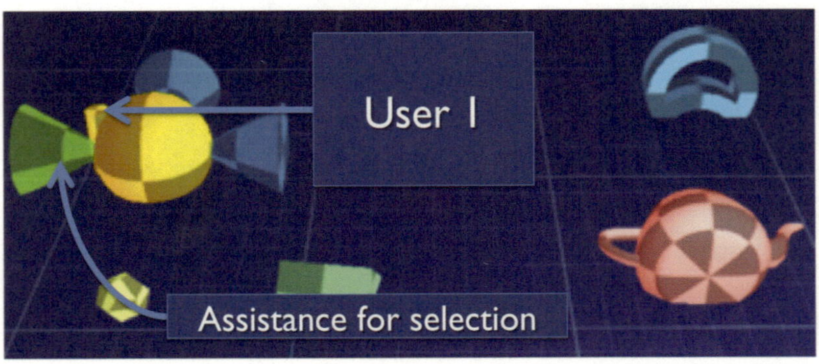

Fig. 7. Implementation example of influence of the assistance function on the assistant during the selection task.

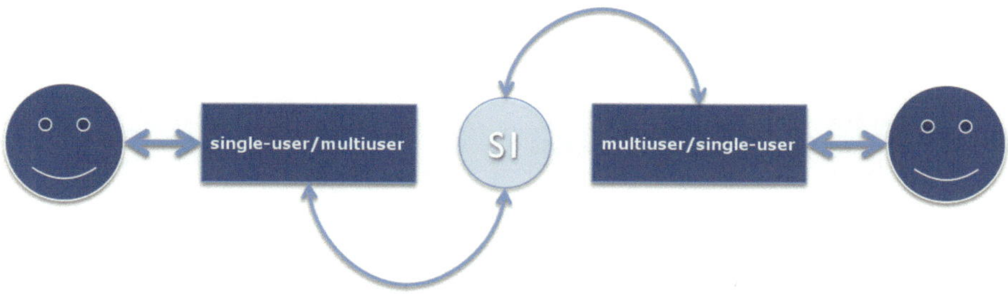

Fig. 8. Principle of our proposal to allow multiuser manipulation (adapters are represented between the user's avatar and the source).

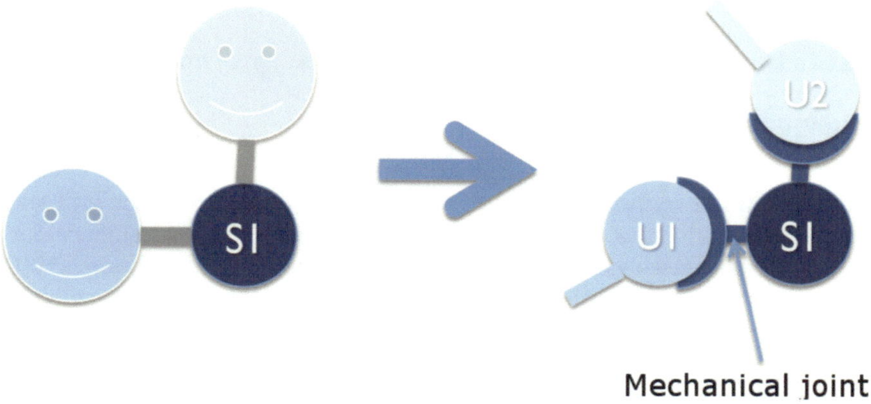

Fig. 9. Kinematic modelling of our cooperative manipulation problem.

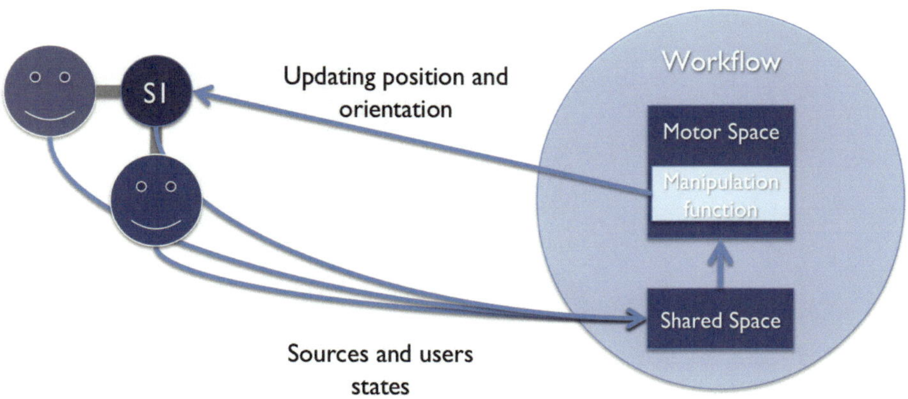

Fig. 10. The assistance function during the manipulation task. In this example a source $S1$ is manipulated by two users.

manipulation assistance function. In this case, the assistance function is activated (the colour of avatars become red).
During the manipulation of the object, the workflow system can also manage other virtual guides (see figure 11(a)) by displaying new directions to the users to enhance the coordination of the manipulation task.

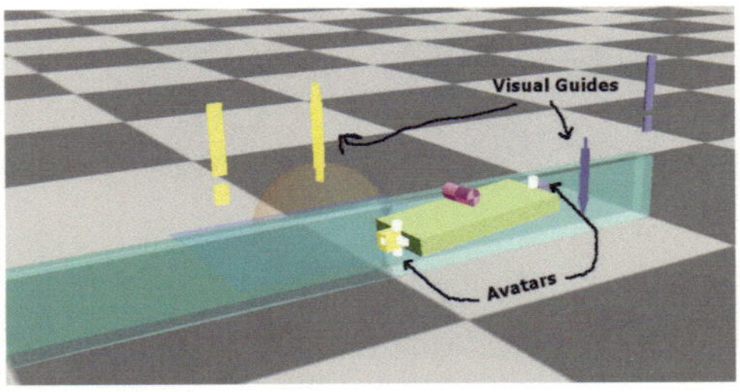

(a) Displaying visual guides during multiuser manipulation

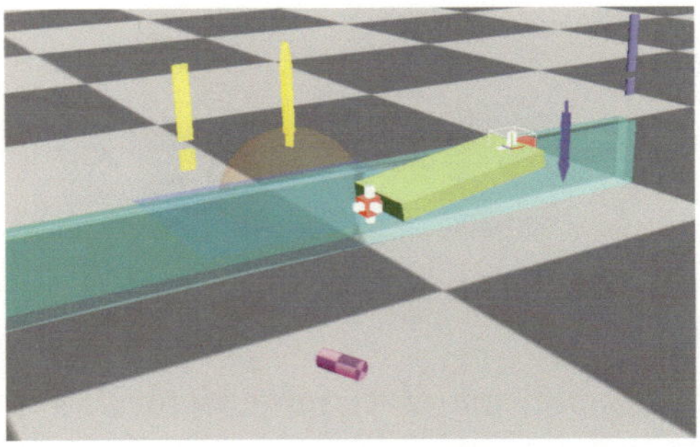

(b) Activation of the manipulation assistance function (avatars become red)

Fig. 11. The two kinds of assistance used to help the coordination of multiuser manipulation.

5. Experimentation and evaluation

In order to investigate the effect of the proposed workflow approach on human performance in a collaborative virtual environment, we developed two experiments. The first one is in a single user mode and tests the effect of assistance function on human performance during the navigation and selection tasks (activation and updating of the aura and the assistant sources). The second experiment is in a multiuser mode and investigates the effect of the manipulation assistance function (activation and updating of visual assistances and the command guide) on human performance during a manipulation task.
For these two experiments we used a human scale virtual reality platform (EVR@ platform[1] see figure 12. It is a large scale semi-immersive environment equipped with a retro-projected large screen (3m x 2.5m) for stereoscopic images, viewed with polarized glasses. In addition we have an ART optical tracking system with two Flysticks devices for 3D interaction.

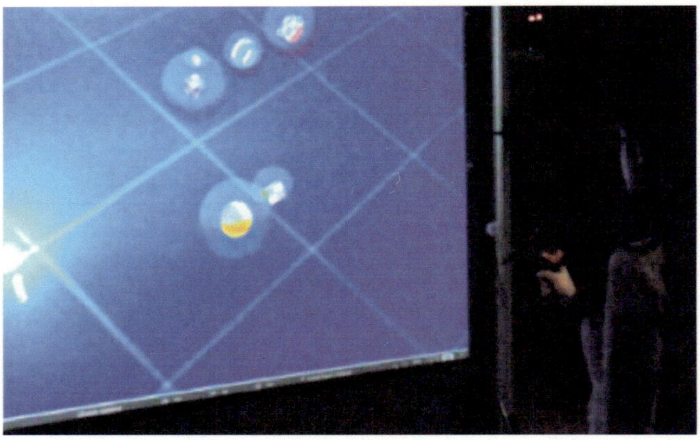

Fig. 12. The EVR@ platform with a user using a Flystick to interact in the virtual environment.

5.1 Experiment I

In this experiment the navigation and selection tasks were carried out in a single user setup. For this purpose one Flystick device and a simple virtual hand interaction technique were used.

[1]http://evra.ibisc.univ-evry.fr

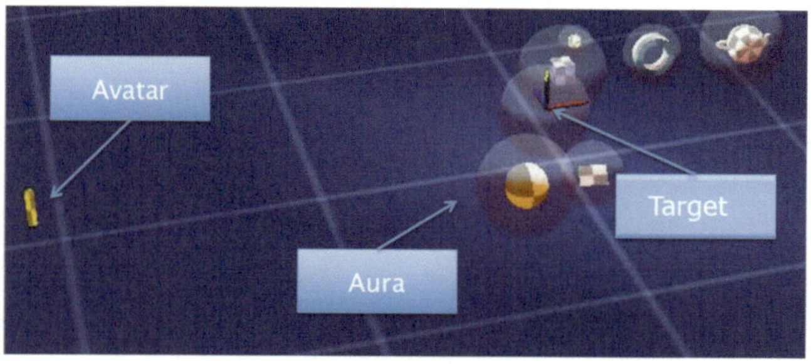

Fig. 13. The virtual environment used to conduct the first experiment.

For this experiment we used a collaborative virtual environment as presented in the figure 13. It is composed of an avatar, and multiple objects (sphere, cube, cylinder, ring, etc.). These objects can be selected and are surrounded by their aura. All objects have the same colour. Users are represented by avatars with cylindrical shape. The colour of the aura varies as explained in the previous section and disappears when the user is inside (to do the selection). Virtual guides are conical shape and have a blue colour.
This experiment was performed by ten volunteers consisting of eight male and two female. Each subject was given a pre-trial along with a short briefing. Here the task for each user was to navigate in the virtual environment following the control points and to select the attachment point of the object cube (see figure 14). The test ends when the user validates the selection of the attachment point. In our model, the attachment points are points used to create mechanical joints described in the previous section that will allow users to manipulate a common object. They also specify the number of participants required for manipulating the selected object (in this case four users can manipulate the object)
For the objective evaluation, we test only the effect of the Selection Assistance Function (SAF) on the selection task performance, while the navigation assistance function is still activated during all the tests. Two conditions A and B are tested. In the Condition A (CA) the SAF is not activated (there is no assistance for the selection) and in the Condition B (CB) the SAF is activated (the selection is still assisted by the activated virtual guide). There were four trials under each condition and the evaluation is based on task completion time, errors and user's response collected through questionnaire.

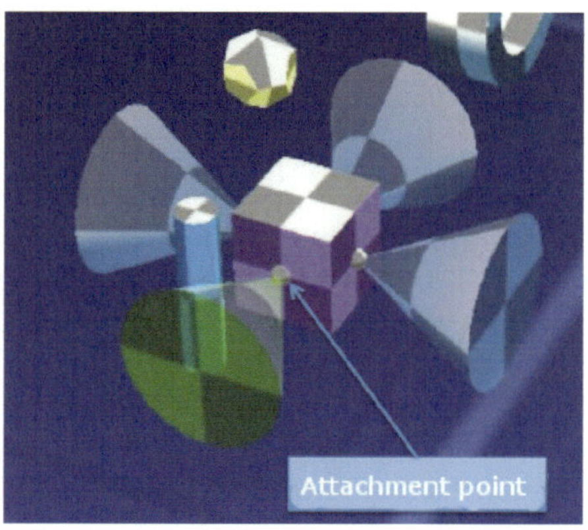

Fig. 14. Attachment points to reach with a simple virtual hand technique to validate the selection.

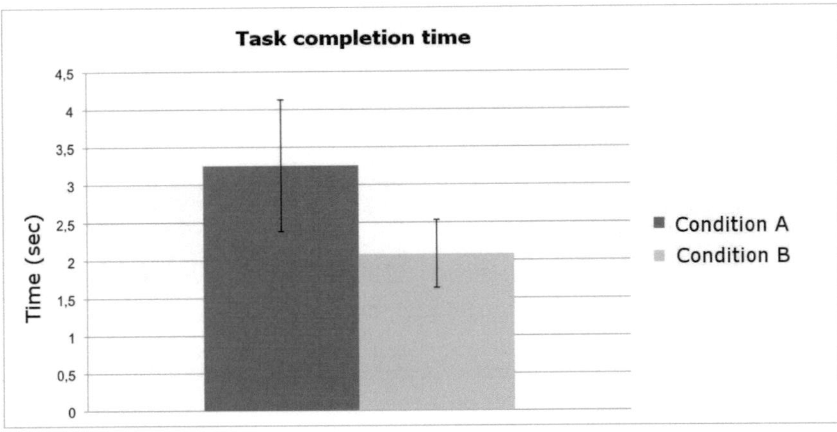

Fig. 15. Task completion time under conditions A and B in the selection task

5.1.1 Task completion time

Figure 15 illustrates the average task completion time for condition CA (SAF is not activated) and CB (SAF is activated) . For task completion time the ANOVA ($F = 14{,}86$, $p < 0.01$) is significant. Comparing the task completion time of CA and CB, we have 3.25 sec and 2 sec respectively with a significant ANOVA. This result shows that the SAF has an influence on task performance in the selection task.

5.1.2 Error in task completion

Figure 16 illustrates the average error rate for condition CA an CB. Here we present a global error analysis for each condition. For errors in task completion, the ANOVA ($F= 4{,}69$, $p < 0.01$) is significant. Tests without assistance (when SAF is not activated) have caused more errors (38%) opposing to tests with assistance (25% when the SAF is activated). The presence of errors made by the subjects is highly dependent on the conditions corresponding to the presence of virtual guides in the selection task.
These results are not surprising as the simple virtual hand technique is difficult to use when the object to select are small, which is the case here for cube attachment points. Virtual guides (in CA) improve significantly the perception of the distance between the avatar and the attachment point, which reduces both the selection error and the selection time comparing to the CB.

5.1.3 Subjective evaluation

For subjective evaluation users responded to the questionnaire after task completion. Here is a summarized result of the analysis of the answers. Users appreciate the presence of the particular source (aura) as well as the colours change according to the proximity of the avatar to the object. This allows users to have a better approach to reach objects.
However some users did not understand the purpose of the aura despite explanations before the beginning of the experience. Thus, for the question *"I think that I understand the role of the aura quickly?"*, we got only 60% *"Yes"*. Indeed, we saw that the use of the aura needs some user learning. However, we got 90% *"Yes"* and 10% of *"Probably Yes"* to the question *"Is the variation of the aura colours useful?"*.
We found that changing colours of the aura helped users to move towards objects and to follow the given path. Users have therefore taken advantage of colours variation and the

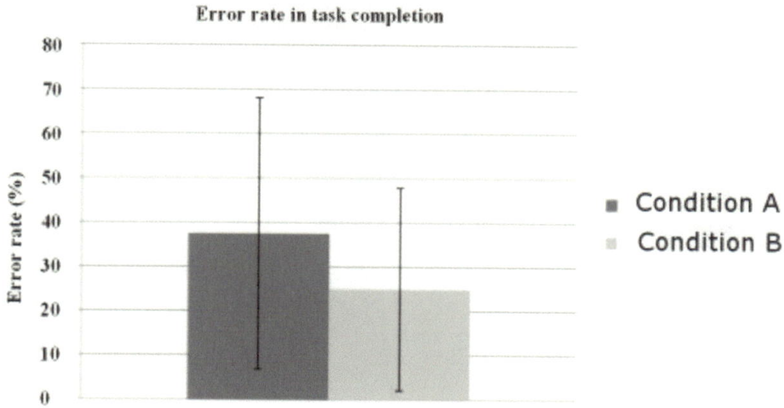

Fig. 16. Influence of the selection assistance function (SAF) on error rate during the selection task

assistance they provide. However, they did not necessarily understand the role of the aura. But, users have quickly understood the role of virtual guides in the selection phase and they found them very helpful and efficient.

5.2 Experiment II

The second experiment is dedicated to cooperative manipulation while in the first experiment the task was performed by users in a single user setup to achieve only navigation and selection. This multiuser experiment enables us to analyze the reaction of participants towards the use of our model and especially to study the influence of the Manipulation Assistance Function (MAF) on a performance of cooperative manipulation task.

In this experiment, a cooperative manipulation task was carried out with a couple of users. For this purpose two Flystick devices and a simple virtual hand interaction technique were used. Figure 17 illustrates this second experiment where two users manipulate a common object (a board) using two Flysticks.

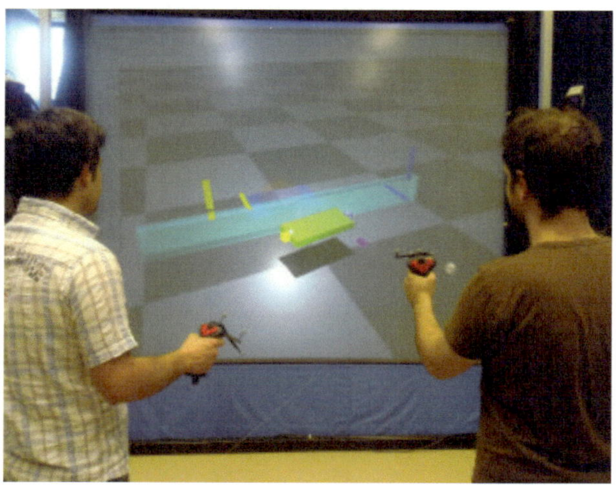

Fig. 17. The EVR@ platform where two users manipulate a virtual board via their Flysticks.

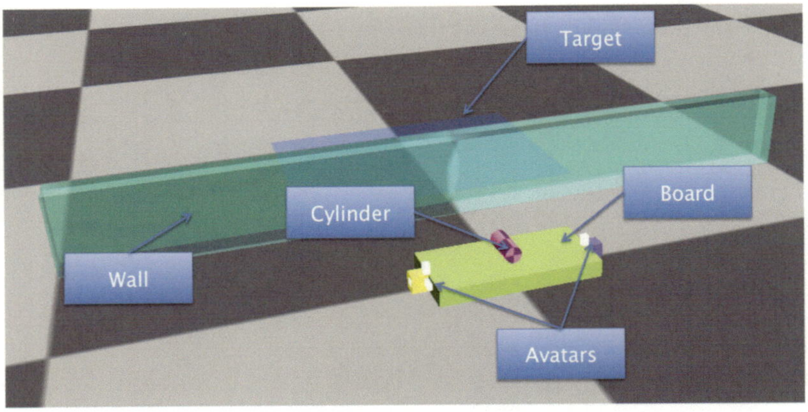

Fig. 18. The virtual environment used to conduct the second experiment

As in the first experiment, we have developed a simple collaborative virtual environment to focus on the study of the influence of the MAF on performance of a cooperative manipulation task. The aim is to compare the performances of multiuser manipulation task when the MTF is not activated (no assistance is given for coordination), partially (only visual aides are used) or fully activated (visual aides and manipulation control aides are used).
The collaborative virtual environment used for this second experiment is illustrated in the figure 18. This CVE consists of two avatars (for both users) and one board which support a free cylinder object. Users must move a board up to a drop area that will be used to validate the end of manipulation, avoiding the fall down of the cylinder that is setting above it. Two avatars (cubic shape) have the same size but with different colours. The yellow colour represents the first user, and the second user is in blue. The drop zone is in a blue colour. Access to the drop zone is located behind a wall.
User avatars are linked to the attachment points of the object board via a fixed (ceiling) mechanical joint (no degrees of freedom). This means that the avatar of each user is still fixed with the board (no translation and rotation are possible) between the avatar and the board as illustrated in figure 19.
This experiment was performed by twenty volunteers (ten couples) consisting of eighteen male and two females. Each couple was given a pre-trial along with a short briefing. For the objective evaluation, we tested the effect of the MAF (Manipulation Assistance Function) on the manipulation task performance. Three conditions A, B and C were tested. In the Condition A (CA) the MAF is not activated (there is no assistance at all), in the Condition B (CB) the MAF is partially activated (only visual aides are given during the manipulation). In the Condition C (CC) the MAF is fully activated (visual aides and manipulation control assistance are used).

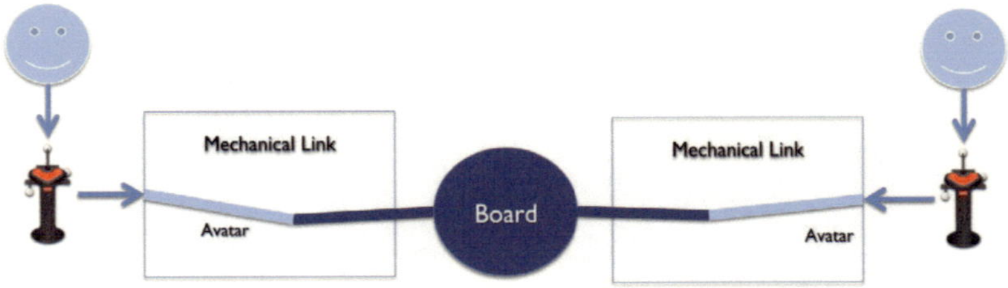

Fig. 19. Illustration of links between two user avatars and the board

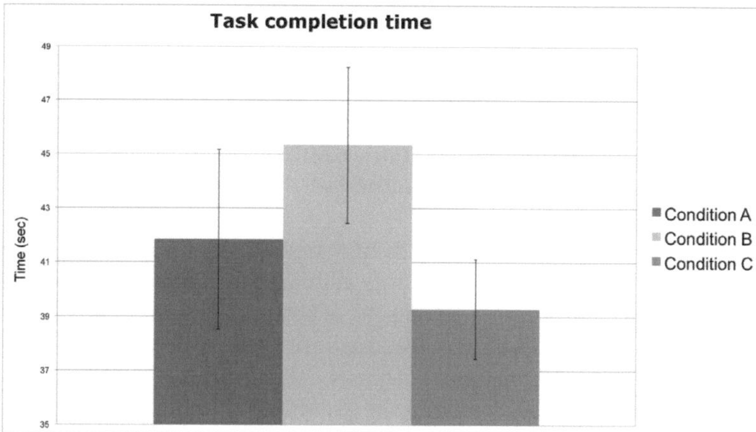

Fig. 20. Task completion time under various conditions in the multiuser manipulation task

There were two trials under each condition and the evaluation is based on task completion time, errors and user's response collected through questionnaires.

5.2.1 Task completion time

Figure 20 illustrates the average task completion time for CA, CB and CC conditions.
On average, tests on condition C are faster than those of the condition B. Indeed, visual assistances can certainly avoid falling objects while viewing how to correct the board movement more easily, but assistance is done at the expense of the manipulation time. Indeed, we observed that in the tests under the condition B when the visual aides appears (which means a future possible fall), users take more time to talk and discuss policy to correct and avoid falling, consequently they spend more time to achieve the task.
Without assistance (in condition A), users are not informed of a possible fall down of the cylinder and discover it only when it starts to roll on the board, which generally causes the fall of the cylinder. However, in the condition A, users do not stop working but try to avoid falling and communicate more.
This result shows that the MAF has an influence on a task performance in the cooperative manipulation setup. The full activation of the MAF (in the condition C) provides a best time performance (a mean of 39,2 sec) comparing to 45,2 sec and 41,4 sec in condition B (MAF is partially activated) and C (MAF is not activated) respectively.

5.2.2 Error in task completion

The CVE is decomposed into three sectors up to the drop zone (see figure 21). Sector 1 corresponds to the taking up step of the board; section 2 corresponds to horizontal movement of board to jump on top of the wall and the sector 3 corresponds to the go down step.
Figure 22 illustrates the error rate for CA, CB and CC conditions. The manipulation error rate corresponds to the average number of falls of cylinder of all users and for all tests.
Generally, we notice that when the MAF is activated, fully or partially (Conditions C and B respectively), thus may limit the number of falls. Indeed, the visual aid is a tool for anticipating the fails; it therefore allows users to correct their manipulation strategy. Besides adding correction movements (full assistance in CC) carried out by two users allows stabilizing the board to avoid as far as possible the fall of the cylinder.

5.2.3 Subjective evaluation

For subjective evaluation users responded to the questionnaire after task completion. Here is a summarized result of the analysis of the answers. Almost a ten couples users have found using the flystick is simple for the requested task (90% *"Yes"*, 5% *"Probably Yes"* and 5% *"No"*). The use of assistant tools doesn't cause additional difficulties for users. Indeed, visual guides are comprehensible for all subjects and are found to help much during the coordination (80% *"Yes"* and *"Probably Yes"* 20%).
Subjective analysis revealed us the preference of users for the condition C in which the two kinds of assistance are available (the MAF is fully activated). This mode of operation facilitates the board movement in sectors 1 and 3. However in sector 2, it produces cylinder falling (this requires a modification of the MFT to take into account the immediate stop of the board).
Concerning involvement and awareness aspects Gerhard et al. (2001), which give us information about the feeling of users during the experience; users were generally all involved during the experience, 90% responded *"Yes"* and 10% *"No"* to the question: *"Do you enjoy working with your partner?"*. This showed that users are involved in the common task. This makes sense because the experiment is quite fun and presents a challenge. For the question: *"I was a very active participant in the dialogue phases?"*, we obtained 80% *"Yes"* and 20% *"Probably Yes"*. This subjective result confirms the involvement of users in the task. However, it also highlights that users of the same couple have probably felt they were involved more than the other partner.

6. Conclusion

In this chapter, we presented a workflow-based approach to assist the coordination of 3D interactions in CVE. Principles as well as main concepts were presented and discussed. The goal was to provide a workflow system that helps users to interact together in a CVE. We highlighted the ability of the system to provide assistance to improve performances as well as in single-user interaction (to navigate and select) and in multiuser setup (in the case of more users manipulate the same object).
The proposed workflow consisted of two components: a shared component and a motor component (component engine). The shared component is presented as the shared data space that symbolizes the behaviour of users and sources in the CVE. The second component is presented as a set of assistance functions that deal with data processing from the shared space and provides tools to assist the users during the 3D interaction process. It uses the shared data

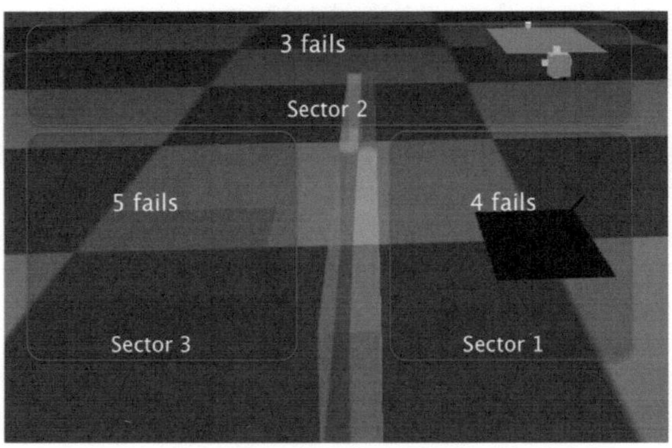

Fig. 21. Three sectors to determine the number of fails during the experiment II

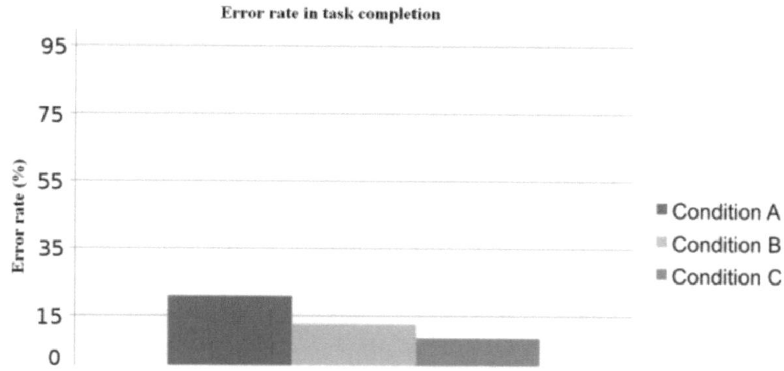

Fig. 22. Influence of the manipulation assistance function (MAF) on error rate during the cooperative manipulation task

and applies them via assistance functions (navigation, selection and manipulation functions) on particular sources (focus, aura, nimbus, assistant and avatar) in the CVE. Particular sources are objects that can be changed during the interaction process by different assistance functions dedicated to 3D interaction tasks. The proposed conceptual model can be used as a basis in many implementations and experimentation by developers of CVE.

In order to assess the relevance of our concept we have developed two CVEs and conducted two experiments. The first experiment (in the single-user setup) was intended to study the influence of the selection assistance function (SAF) when users navigate and select an object. The results are very encouraging because they showed that the presence of particular sources like aura and the assistant (when STF is activated) reduces significantly selection time and errors. The second experiment (with two users) studied the influence of the manipulation assistance function (MAF) when two users manipulate a common object. The obtained results were also encouraged because they highlight the importance of the presence of visual cues and manipulation control assistance (when MAF is fully activated).

Future work will be carried out to integrate the force feedback modality and examine its effects on cooperative task. Furthermore we will evaluate and implement the system on long distance network (i.e internet) and investigate the influence of network delay on it.

7. References

Aguerreche, L., Duval, T. & Lécuyer, A. (2009). Short paper: 3-hand manipulation of virtual objects, *Joint Virtual Reality Conference of EGVE - ICAT - EuroVR (2009)* .

Benford, S. & Fahlen, L. (1993). A spatial model of interaction in large virtual environments, *Proceedings of the third conference on European Conference on Computer-Supported Cooperative Work* pp. 109–124.

Bharadwaj, V., Reddy, Y. & Reddy, S. (2005). Integrating awareness sources in heterogeneous collaboration environments, *Doctoral Consortium Enterprise Information Systems ICEIS 2005* p. 18.

Bolt, R. (1980). "put-that-there": Voice and gesture at the graphics interface, *Proceedings of the 7th annual conference on Computer graphics and interactive techniques* pp. 262–270.

Ding, D. & Zhu, M. (2003). A model of dynamic interest management: interaction analysis in collaborative virtual environment, *Proceedings of the ACM symposium on Virtual reality software and technology* pp. 223–230.

Duval, T. & Fleury, C. (2009). An asymmetric 2d pointer/3d ray for 3d interaction within collaborative virtual environments, *Web3D '09: Proceedings of the 14th International Conference on 3D Web Technology* .

Duval, T., Lecuyer, A. & Thomas, S. (2006). Skewer: a 3d interaction technique for 2-user collaborative manipulation of objects in virtual environments, *Proceedings of the 3D User Interfaces (3DUI'06)* .

Duval, T. & Tenier, C. L. (2004). Interactions 3d coopératives en environnements virtuels avec openmask pour l'exploitation d'objets techniques, *Mécanique & Industries* 5(2): 129–137.

Fuchs, P., Arnaldi, B. & Tisseau, J. (2003). *La ralit virtuelle et ses applications*, Les Presses de l'Ecole des Mines de Paris, chapter 1, pp. 3–52.

Gerhard, M., Moore, D. & Hobbs, D. (2001). Continuous presence in collaborative virtual environments: Towards a hybrid avatar-agent model for user representation, *Lecture notes in computer science* 2190(2001): 137–155.

Greenhalgh, C. (1997). Large scale collaborative virtual environments, *University of Nottingham* .

Greenhalgh, C. & Benford, S. (1999). Supporting rich and dynamic communication in large-scale collaborative virtual environments, *Presence: Teleoperators and Virtual Environments* 8(1): 14–35.

Noma, M. & Miyasato, T. (1997). Cooperative object manipulation in virtual space using virtual physics, *Proceeding of Dynamic System and Control ASME* 61: 101–106.

Otmane, S., Mallem, M., Kheddar, A. & Chavand, F. (2000). Active virtual guides as an apparatus for augmented reality based telemanipulation system on the internet, *Proceedings of the 33rd Annual Simulation Symposium* pp. 185–191.

Otmane, S., Ouramdane-Djerah, N. & Mallem, M. (2007). Towards a collaborative 3d interaction model for cooperative design in virtual environments, *Computer Supported Cooperative Work in Design, IEEE CSCWD* pp. 198–203.

Pinho, M., Bowman, D. & Freitas, C. (2002). Cooperative object manipulation in immersive virtual environments: framework and techniques, *Proceedings of the ACM symposium on Virtual reality software and technology* pp. 171–178.

Prada, R. & Payandeh, S. (2009). On study of design and implementation of virtual fixtures, *Virtual Reality* 13(2): 117–129.

Riege, K., Holtkamper, T., Wesche, G. & Frohlich, B. (2006). The bent pick ray: An extended pointing technique for multi-user interaction, pp. 62–65.

Rodden, T. (1996). Populating the application: a model of awareness for cooperative applications, *Proceedings of the 1996 ACM conference on Computer supported cooperative work* pp. 87–96.

Sandor, O., Bogdan, C. & Bowers, J. (1997). Aether: an awareness engine for cscw, *Proceedings of the fifth conference on European Conference on Supported Collaborative Work, ECSCW'97* pp. 221–236.

Ullah, S., Ouramdane, N., Otmane, S., Davesne, F. & Richard, P. (2008). Augmenting 3d interactions with haptic guide in a large scale virtual environment, *Proceedings of The 7th ACM SIGGRAPH International Conference on Virtual-Reality Continuum and Its Applications in Industry* .

Ullah, S., Richard, P., Otmane, S., Naud, M. & Mallem, M. (2009). Human performance in cooperative virtual environments: the effect of visual aids and oral communication, *The International Journal of Virtual Reality*, Vol. 8, pp. 79–86.

Part 2

Advanced Virtual Reality Technologies

4

Virtual Reality to Simulate Visual Tasks for Robotic Systems

Manuela Chessa, Fabio Solari and Silvio P. Sabatini
Department of Biophysical and Electronic Engineering, University of Genoa
Via all'Opera Pia 11/A - 16145 Genova
Italy

1. Introduction

Virtual reality (VR) can be used as a tool to analyze the interactions between the visual system of a robotic agent and the environment, with the aim of designing the algorithms to solve the visual tasks necessary to properly behave into the 3D world. The novelty of our approach lies in the use of the VR as a tool to simulate the behavior of vision systems. The visual system of a robot (e.g., an autonomous vehicle, an active vision system, or a driving assistance system) and its interplay with the environment can be modeled through the geometrical relationships between the virtual stereo cameras and the virtual 3D world. Differently from conventional applications, where VR is used for the perceptual rendering of the visual information to a human observer, in the proposed approach, a virtual world is rendered to simulate the actual projections on the cameras of a robotic system. In this way, machine vision algorithms can be quantitatively validated by using the ground truth data provided by the knowledge of both the structure of the environment and the vision system.

In computer vision (Trucco & Verri, 1998; Forsyth & Ponce, 2002), in particular for motion analysis and depth reconstruction, it is important to quantitatively assess the progress in the field, but too often the researchers reported only qualitative results on the performance of their algorithms due to the lack of calibrated image database. To overcome this problem, recent works in the literature describe test beds for a quantitative evaluation of the vision algorithms by providing both sequences of images and ground truth disparity and optic flow maps (Scharstein & Szeliski, 2002; Baker et al., 2007). A different approach is to generate image sequences and stereo pairs by using a database of range images collected by a laser range-finder (Yang & Purves, 2003; Liu et al., 2008).

In general, the major drawback of the calibrated data sets is the lack of interactivity: it is not possible to change the scene and the camera point of view. In order to face the limits of these approaches, several authors proposed robot simulators equipped with visual sensors and capable to act in virtual environments. Nevertheless, such software tools are capable of accurately simulating the physics of robots, rather than their visual systems. In many works, the stereo vision is intended for future developments (Jørgensen & Petersen, 2008; Awaad et al., 2008), whereas other robot simulators in the literature have a binocular vision system (Okada et al., 2002; Ulusoy et al., 2004), but they work on stereo image pairs where parallel axis cameras are used. More recently, a commercial application (Michel, 2004) and an open source project for cognitive robotics research (Tikhanoff et al., 2008) have been developed both capable to fixate a target, nevertheless the ground truth data are not provided.

2. The visual system simulator

Figure 1a-b shows the real-world images gathered by a binocular robotic head, for different stereo configurations: the visual axes of the cameras are kept parallel (Fig. 1a) and convergent for fixating an object in the scene (the small tin, see Fig. 1b). It is worth noting that both horizontal and vertical disparities have quite large values in the periphery, while disparities are zero in the fixation point. Analogously, if we look at the motion field generated by an agent moving in the environment (see Fig. 1c), where both still and moving objects are present the resulting optic flow is composed both by ego-motion components, due to motion of the observer, and by the independent movements of the objects in the scene.

(a) (b) (c)

Fig. 1. Binocular snapshots obtained by real-world vision systems. (a)-(b): The stereo image pairs are acquired by a binocular active vision system (http://www.searise.eu/) for different stereo configurations: the visual axes of the cameras are (a) kept parallel, (b) convergent for fixating an object in the scene (the small tin). The anaglyphs are obtained with the left image on the red channel and the right image on the green and blue channels. The interocular distance is 30 cm and the camera resolution is 1392 × 1236 pixels with a focal length of 7.3 mm. The distance between the cameras and the objects is between 4 m and 6 m. It is worth noting that both horizontal and vertical disparities are present. (c): Optic flow superimposed on a snapshot of the relative image sequence, obtained by a car, equipped with a pair of stereo cameras with parallel visual axes , moving in a complex real environment. The resolution of the cameras is 1392 × 1040 pixels with a focal length of 6.5 mm, and the baseline is 33 cm (http://pspc.dibe.unige.it/drivsco/). Different situations are represented: ego-motion (due to the motion of the car) and a translating independent movement of a pedestrian (only the left frame is shown).

The aim of the work described in this chapter is to simulate the active vision system of a robot acting and moving in an environment rather than the mechanical movements of the robot itself. In particular, we aim to precisely simulate the movements (e.g. vergence and version) of the two cameras and of the robot in order to provide the binocular views and the related ground truth data (horizontal and vertical disparities and binocular motion field). Thus, our VR tool can be used for two different purposes (see Fig. 2):

1. to obtain binocular image sequences with related ground truth, to quantitatively assess the performances of computer vision algorithms;
2. to simulate the closed loop interaction between visual perception and action of the robot.

The binocular image sequences provided by the VR engine could be processed by computer vision algorithms in order to obtain the visual features necessary to the control strategy of the robot movements. These control signals act as an input to the VR engine, thus simulating the

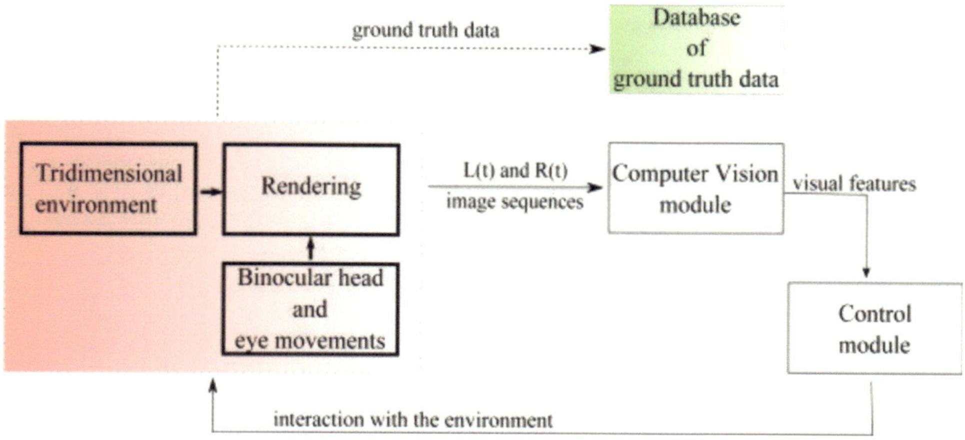

Fig. 2. The proposed active vision system simulator. Mutual interactions between a robot and the environment can be emulated to validate the visual processing modules in a closed perception-action loop and to obtain calibrated ground truth data.

robot movements in the virtual environment, then the updated binocular views are obtained. In the following, a detailed description of the model of a robotic visual system is presented.

2.1 Tridimensional environment

The 3D scene is described by using the VRML format. Together with its successor X3D, VRML has been accepted as an international standard for specifying vertices and edges for 3D polygons, along with the surface color, UV mapped textures, shininess and transparency. Though a large number of VRML models are available, e.g. on the web, they usually have not photorealistic textures and they are often characterized by simple 3D structures. To overcome this problem, a dataset of 3D scenes, acquired in controlled but cluttered laboratory conditions, has been created by using a scanner laser. The results presented in Section 6 are obtained by using the dataset obtained in our laboratory.

It is worth noting that the complex 3D VRML models can be easily replaced by simple geometric figures (cubes, cones, planes) with or without textures at any time, in order to use the simulator as an agile testing platform for the development of complex computer vision algorithms.

2.2 Rendering

The scene is rendered in an on-screen OpenGL context (see Section 5 for details). Moreover, the `SoOffScreenRenderer` class is used for rendering scenes in off-screen buffers and to save to disk the sequence of stereo pairs. The renderer can produce stereo images of different resolution and acquired by cameras with different field of views. In particular, one can set the following parameters :

- resolution of the cameras (the maximum possible resolution depends on the resolution of the textures and on the number of points of the 3D model);
- horizontal and vertical field of view (HFOV and VFOV, respectively);
- distance from camera position to the near clipping plane in the camera's view volume, also referred to as a viewing frustum, (`nearDistance`);

- distance from camera position to the far clipping plane in the camera's view volume (`farDistance`);
- distance from camera position to the point of focus (`focalDistance`).

2.3 Binocular head and eye movements

The visual system, presented in this Section, is able to generate the sequence of stereo image pairs of a binocular head moving in the 3D space and fixating a 3D point (X^F, Y^F, Z^F). The geometry of the system and the parameters that can be set are shown in Figure 3.

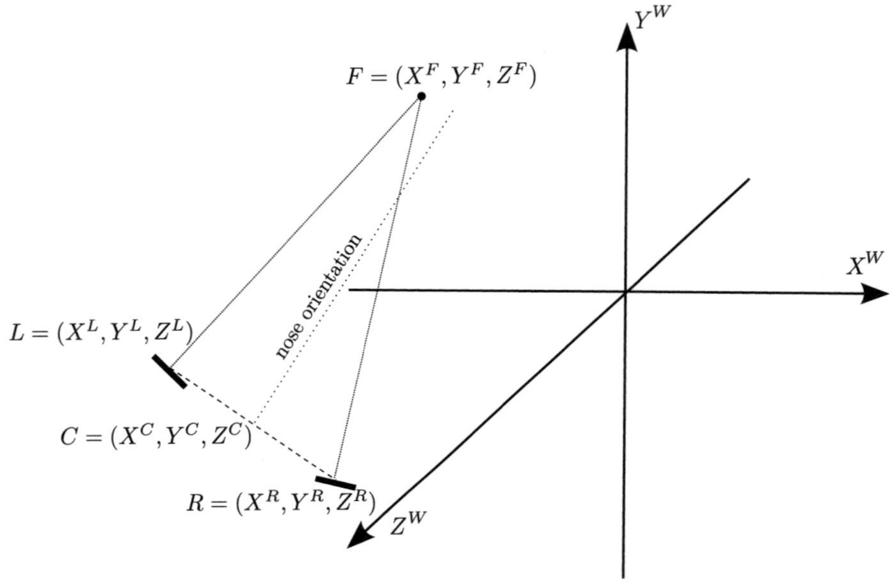

Fig. 3. Schematic representation of the geometry of the binocular active vision system.

The head is characterized by the following parameters (each expressed with respect to the world reference frame (X^W, Y^W, Z^W)):

- cyclopic position $\mathbf{C} = (X^C, Y^C, Z^C)$;
- nose orientation;
- fixation point $\boldsymbol{F} = (X^F, Y^F, Z^F)$.

Once the initial position of the head is fixed, then different behaviours are possible:

- to move the eyes by keeping the head (position and orientation) fixed;
- to change the orientation of the head, thus mimicking the movements of the neck;
- to change both the orientation and the position of the head, thus generating more complex motion patterns.

These situations imply the study of different perceptual problems, from scene exploration to navigation with ego-motion. Thus, in the following (see Section 6), we will present the results obtained in different situations.

For the sake of clarity and simplicity, in the following we will consider the position $\mathbf{C} = (X^C, Y^C, Z^C)$ and the orientation of the head fixed, thus only the ocular movements will be considered. In Section 3.3.1 different stereo systems will be described (e.g. pan-tilt, tilt-pan, etc.), the simulator can switch through all these different behaviours. The results presented in the following consider a situation in which the eyes can rotate around an arbitrary axis, chosen in order to obtain the minimum rotation to make the ocular axis rotate from the initial position to the target position (see Section 3.3.1).

2.4 Database of ground truth data

In the literature several database of ground truth data can be found, to quantitatively assess optic flow and disparity measures.
One of the best known and widely used is the *Yosemite sequence*, that has been used extensively for experimentation and quantitative evaluation of the performances of optical flow computation techniques, camera motion estimation, and structure from motion algorithms. The data was originally generated by Lynn Quam at SRI and David Heeger (Heeger, 1987) was the first to use it for optical flow experimentation. The sequence is generated by taking an aerial image of Yosemite valley and texture mapping it onto a depth map of the valley. A synthetic sequence is generated by flying through the valley.
Other simple, but widely used, image sequences with associated ground truth data are the *Translating tree* and the *Diverging tree* by (Fleet & Jepson, 1990). Moreover, it is possible to find the *Marbled-Block sequence*, recorded and first evaluated by (Otte & Nagel, 1995), a polyhedral scene with a moving marbled block and moving camera.
A large number of algorithms for the estimation of optic flow have been benchmarked, by using these sequences. Unfortunately, it is difficult to know how relevant these results are to real 3D imagery, with all its associated complexities (for example motion discontinuities, complex 3D surfaces, camera noise, specular highlights, shadows, atmospherics, transparency). To this aim (McCane et al., 2001) have used two methods to generate more complex sequences with ground-truth data: a ray-tracer which generates optical flow, and a Tcl/Tk tool which allows them to generate ground truth optical flow from simple (i.e. polygonal) real sequences with a little help from the user.
Nevertheless, these sequences are too simple and the needs of providing more complex situation leads to the creation of databases that include much more complex real and synthetic scenes, with non-rigid motions (Baker et al., 2007). The authors rather than collecting a single benchmark dataset (with its inherent limitations), they collect four different sets, each satisfying a different subset of desirable properties. A proper combination of these datasets could be sufficient to allow a rigorous evaluation of optical flow algorithms.
Analogously, for the estimation of binocular disparity, synthetic images have been used extensively for quantitative comparisons of stereo methods, but they are often restricted to simple geometries and textures (e.g., random-dot stereograms). Furthermore, problems arising with real cameras are seldom modeled, e.g., aliasing, slight misalignment, noise, lens aberrations, and fluctuations in gain and bias. Some well known stereo pairs, with ground truth, are used by researcher to benchmark their algorithms: the *Tsukuba* stereo pair (Nakamura et al., 1996), and *Sawtooth* and *Venus* created by (Scharstein & Szeliski, 2002). Though these sequence are widely used also in recent papers, in the last years the progress in the performances of stereo algorithms is quickly outfacing the ability of these stereo data sets to discriminate among the best-performing algorithms, thus motivating the need for more challenging scenes with accurate ground truth information. To this end, (Scharstein & Szeliski, 2003) describe a method for acquiring high-complexity stereo image pairs with pixel-accurate correspondence information using structured light.

Nevertheless, databases for the evaluation of the performances of *active* stereo systems are still missing. The stereo geometry of the existing database is fixed, and characterized by parallel axis cameras. By using the software environment we developed, it is possible to collect a large number of data in different situations: e.g. vergent stereo cameras with different fixation points and orientation of the eyes, optic flow maps obtained for different ego-motion velocities, or different gaze orientation. The true disparity and optic flow maps can be stored together with the 3D data from which they have been generated and the corresponding image sequences. These data can be used for future algorithm benchmarking also by other researchers in the Computer Vision community. A tool capable of continuously generating ground truth data can be used online together with the visual processing algorithms to have a continuous assessment of their reliability. Moreover, the use of textured 3D models, acquired in real-world conditions, can solve the lack of realism that affects many datasets in the literature.

2.5 Computer vision module

Visual features (e.g. edges, disparity, optic flow) are extracted by the sequence of binocular images by the Computer Vision module. It can implement any kind of computer vision algorithm. The faithful detection of the motion and of the distance of the objects in the visual scene is a desirable feature of any artificial vision system designed to operate in unknown environments characterized by conditions variable in time in an often unpredictable way. In the context of an ongoing research project (EYESHOTS, 2008) we aimed to investigate the potential role of motor information in the early stages of human binocular vision, the computation of disparity and optic flow has been implemented in the simulator by a distributed neuromorphic architecture, described in (Chessa et al., 2009). In such distributed representations, or population codes, the information is encoded by the activity pattern of a network of simple and complex neurons, that are selective for elemental vision attributes: oriented edges, direction of motion, color, texture, and binocular disparity (Adelson & Bergen, 1991). In this way, it is possible to use the simulator to study adaptation mechanisms of the responses of the neural units on the basis of the relative orientation of the eyes.

2.6 Control module

This module generates the control signal that is responsible for the camera/eye movements, in particular for version and vergence, and for the movement of the neck (rotation and position). By considering the neck fixed, and thus focusing on eye movements only, the simulator has been exploited to study a model of vergence control based on a dual-mode paradigm (Gibaldi et al., 2010; Hung et al., 1986). The goal of the vergence control module is to produce the control signals for the eyes to bring and keep the fixation point on the surface of the object of interest without changing the gaze direction. Since the task is to nullify the disparity in fovea, the vergence control module receives inputs from the same disparity detector population response described in Section 2.5 and converts it into the speed rotation of each eye. Other control models can be easily adopted to replace the existing one, in order to achieve different behaviours or to compare different algorithms and approaches.

3. Geometry of the stereo vision

In the literature the most frequently used methods to render stereo image pairs are (Bourke & Morse, 2007; Grinberg et al., 1994): (1) the off-axis technique, usually used to create a perception of depth for a human observer and (2) the toe-in technique that can simulate the actual intensity patterns impinging on the cameras of a robotic head.

3.1 Off-axis technique

In the off-axis technique, the stereo images are generated by projecting the objects in the scene onto the display plane for each camera; such projection plane has the same position and orientation for both camera projections. The model of the virtual setup is shown in Figure 4a: **F** represents the location of the virtual point perceived when looking at the stereo pair composed by $\mathbf{F}^L$ and $\mathbf{F}^R$.

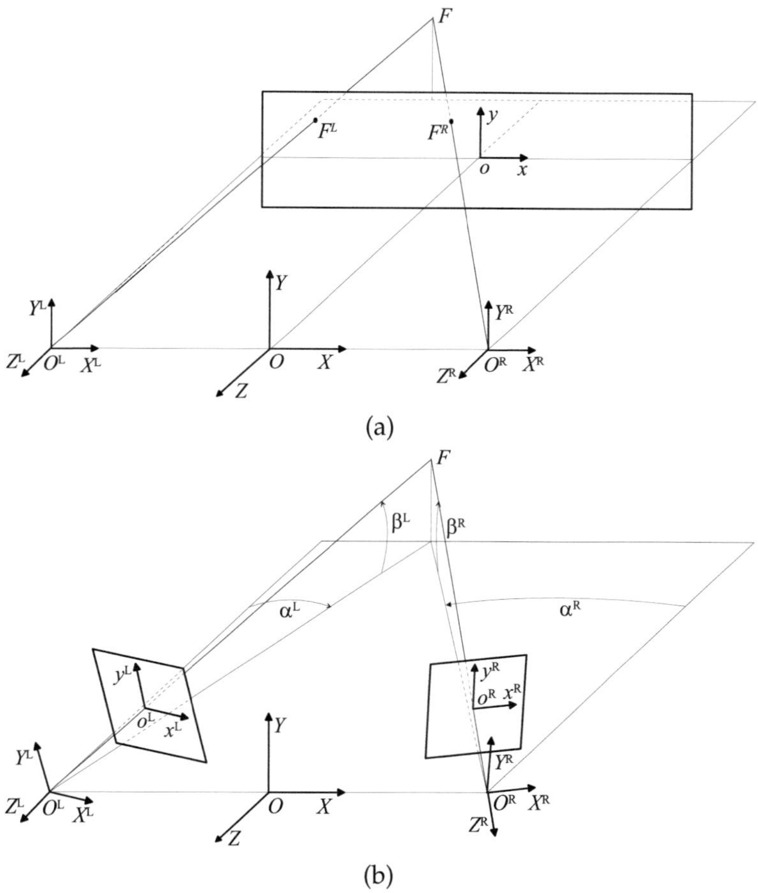

Fig. 4. (a) Geometrical sketch of the off-axis technique. The left and right camera frames: (X^L, Y^L, Z^L) and (X^R, Y^R, Z^R). The image plane (x, o, y) and the focal length Oo. The image points $\mathbf{F}^L$ and $\mathbf{F}^R$ are the stereo projection of the virtual point $\mathbf{F}$. The baseline b is denoted by $O^L O^R$. (b) Geometrical sketch of the toe-in technique. The left and right camera frames: (X^L, Y^L, Z^L) and (X^R, Y^R, Z^R). The left and right image planes: (x^L, o^L, y^L) and (x^R, o^R, y^R). The left and right focal lengths: $O^L o^L = O^R o^R$, named f_0. The camera optical axes $O^L F$ and $O^R F$ are adjusted to fixation point **F**. The baseline b is denoted by $O^L O^R$, the pan angles by α^L and α^R, and the tilt angles by β^L and β^R.

To produce a perception of depth for a human observer, it is necessary to pay attention to some specific geometrical parameters of the stereo acquisition setup (both actual and virtual) (Grinberg et al., 1994):

- the image planes have to be parallel;
- the optical points should be offset relative to the center of the image;
- the distance between the two optical centers have to be equal to the interpupillary distance;
- the field of view of the cameras must be equal to the angle subtended by the display screen;
- the ratio between the focal length of the cameras and the viewing distance of the screen should be equal to the ratio between the width of the screen and of the image plane.

This is the correct way to create stereo pairs that are displayed on stereoscopic devices for human observers. This technique introduces no vertical disparity, thus it does not cause discomfort for the users (Southard, 1992).
However, it is difficult to perceptually render a large interval of 3D space without a visual stress, since the eye of the observer have to maintain accommodation on the display screen (at a fixed distance), thus lacking the natural relationship between accommodation and vergence eye movements, and the distance of the objects (Wann et al., 1995). Moreover, the visual discomfort is also due to spatial imperfections of the stereo image pair (Kooi & Toet, 2004). The main factors yielding visual discomfort are: vertical disparity; crosstalk, that is a transparent overlay of the left image over the right image and vice versa; blur, that is different resolutions of the stereo image pair.

3.2 Toe-in technique

Since our aim is to simulate the actual images acquired by the vergent pan-tilt cameras of a robotic head, the correct way to create the stereo pairs is the toe-in method: each camera is pointed at a single target point (the fixation point) through a proper rotation. The geometrical sketch of the optical setup of an active stereo system and of the related toe-in model is shown in Figure 4b.
It is worth noting that, for specific application fields, the toe-in technique is also used for the perceptual rendering of the stereo image pair to a human observer. In the field of the telerobotic applications (Ferre et al., 2008; Bernardino et al., 2007), it is important to perceive veridical distances in the remote environment, and the toe-in technique allows choosing where the stereo images are properly fused and the optimal remote working area. However, the parallel axes configuration is again effective when a large workspace is necessary, e.g. for exploration vehicles. The toe-in method is also helpful in the field of stereoscopic television (Yamanoue, 2006), since the perception of the 3D scene is more easily manipulated, and the objects can be seen between the observer and the display screen, i.e. it is possible to render the crossed, zero, and uncrossed disparity.
The disparity patterns produced by the off-axis and toe-in techniques are shown in Figure 5a and Figure 5b, respectively.

3.3 Mathematics of the toe-in technique

Our aim is to formally describe the toe-in technique in order to generate stereo image pairs like in a pan-tilt robotic head. To this purpose, the skewed frustum (see Fig. 6a) (necessary to obtain the off-axis stereo technique) is no longer necessary. Accordingly, we introduced the possibility of pointing the left and the right optical axes at a single 3D target point, by rotating two symmetric frustums (see Fig. 6b), in order to obtain the left and the right views both fixating a point **F**.

In general, the two camera frames $\mathbf{X}^L$ and $\mathbf{X}^R$ are related by a rigid-body transformation in the following way:

$$\mathbf{X}^R = \mathcal{R}\mathbf{X}^L + \mathcal{T} \tag{1}$$

where $\mathcal{R}$ and $\mathcal{T}$ denote the rotation matrix and the translation, respectively. The coordinate transformation described by Eq. 1 can be converted to a linear transformation by using homogeneous coordinates (Ma et al., 2004). In the following, we use the homogeneous coordinates to describe the coordinate transformation that brings the cameras from a parallel axes configuration to a convergent one.

The translation for the left and the right view volume can be obtained by applying the following translation matrix:

$$\mathbf{T}^{L/R} = \begin{bmatrix} 1 & 0 & 0 & \pm\frac{b}{2} \\ 0 & 1 & 0 & 0 \\ 0 & 0 & 1 & 0 \\ 0 & 0 & 0 & 1 \end{bmatrix} \tag{2}$$

Then the azimuthal rotation (α^L and α^R) and the elevation (β^L and β^R) are obtained with the following rotation matrices:

$$\mathbf{R}_\alpha^{L/R} = \begin{bmatrix} \cos\alpha^{L/R} & 0 & \sin\alpha^{L/R} & 0 \\ 0 & 1 & 0 & 0 \\ -\sin\alpha^{L/R} & 0 & \cos\alpha^{L/R} & 0 \\ 0 & 0 & 0 & 1 \end{bmatrix} \tag{3}$$

$$\mathbf{R}_\beta^{L/R} = \begin{bmatrix} 1 & 0 & 0 & 0 \\ 0 & \cos\beta^{L/R} & -\sin\beta^{L/R} & 0 \\ 0 & \sin\beta^{L/R} & \cos\beta^{L/R} & 0 \\ 0 & 0 & 0 & 1 \end{bmatrix} \tag{4}$$

The complete roto-translation of the view-volumes is:

$$\begin{bmatrix} \mathbf{O}^{L/R} \\ 1 \end{bmatrix} = \mathbf{R}_\beta^{L/R}\mathbf{R}_\alpha^{L/R}\mathbf{T}^{L/R}\begin{bmatrix} \mathbf{O} \\ 1 \end{bmatrix} \tag{5}$$

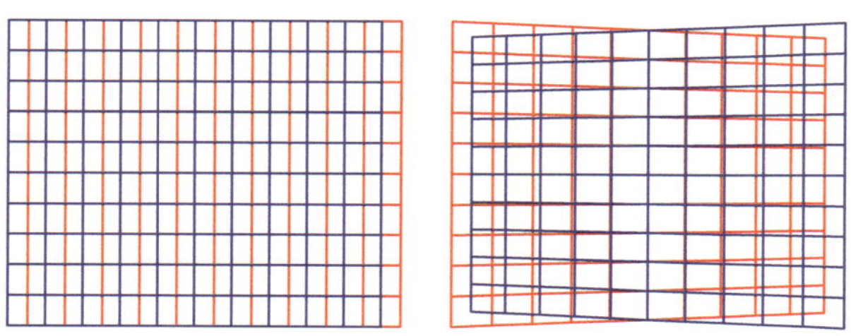

(a) (b)

Fig. 5. The projections of a fronto-parallel square onto the image planes, drawn in red for the left image and blue for the right. The texture applied to the square is a regular grid. (a) The projection obtained with the off-axis technique: only horizontal disparity is introduced. (b) The projection obtained with the toe-in technique: both vertical and horizontal disparities are introduced.

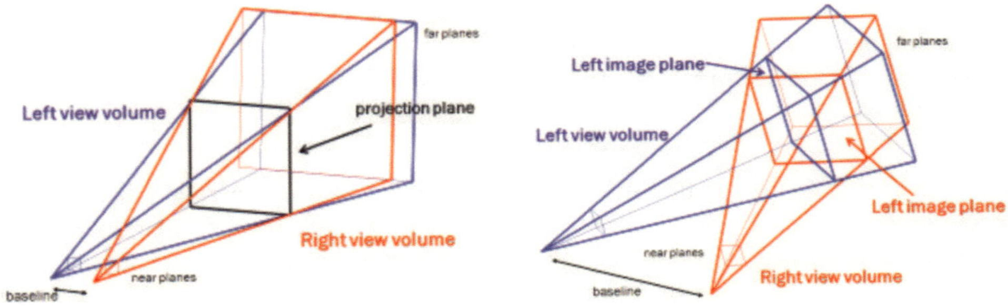

(a) (b)

Fig. 6. (a) The two skewed frustums for the off-axis technique. (b) The two view volumes of the stereo cameras for the toe-in technique.

Thus, the projection direction is set to the target point **F**, then the left and the right views project onto two different planes, as it can be seen in Figure 4b.
In this way, it is possible to insert a camera in the scene (e.g. a perspective camera), to obtain a stereoscopic representation with convergent axes and to decide the location of the fixation point. This emulates the behavior of a couple of verging pan-tilt cameras.

3.3.1 Camera rotations

In general, the frame transformation can be described by consecutive rotations (and translations), the specific rotation described by Eq. 5 is the Helmholtz sequence (neglecting the torsion of the camera, i.e. the rotation around the visual axis). This rotation sequence is related to the gimbal system of the actual camera (we are simulating). In particular, the horizontal axis is fixed to the robotic head, and the vertical axis rotates gimbal fashion around the horizontal axis (Haslwanter, 1995). That is, first we rotate through $\beta^{L/R}$ around the horizontal axis, then we rotate through $\alpha^{L/R}$ around the new updated vertical axis.
We can simulate a different gimbal system by using the Fick sequence (i.e., the vertical axis is fixed to the robotic head), described by:

$$\begin{bmatrix} \mathbf{O}^{L/R} \\ 1 \end{bmatrix} = \mathbf{R}_{\alpha}^{L/R}\mathbf{R}_{\beta}^{L/R}\mathbf{T}^{L/R}\begin{bmatrix} \mathbf{O} \\ 1 \end{bmatrix} \quad (6)$$

It is worth noting that the fixation point is described by different values of the angles.
For non conventional cameras, e.g. (Cannata & Maggiali, 2008), it is also possible to describe the camera rotation movements from the initial position to the final one through a single rotation by a given angle γ around a fixed axis $\mathbf{a}_{\gamma}$:

$$\begin{bmatrix} \mathbf{O}^{L/R} \\ 1 \end{bmatrix} = \mathbf{R}^{L/R}(\gamma, \mathbf{a}_{\gamma})\mathbf{T}^{L/R}\begin{bmatrix} \mathbf{O} \\ 1 \end{bmatrix} \quad (7)$$

In this way, we can study how the additive degrees of freedom of non conventional (e.g. bio-inspired) systems may have effects on the computational processing of visual features.

3.3.2 General camera model

A simple and widely used model for the cameras is characterized by the following assumptions: the vertical and horizontal axes of rotation are orthogonal, through the nodal points, and aligned with the image planes. However, the commercial cameras without a careful engineering can violate the previous assumptions, and also the cameras equipped with a zoom, since the position of the nodal point changes with respect to the position of the image plane as a function of focal length. A general camera model (Davis & Chen, 2003; Jain et al., 2006; Horaud et al., 2006) takes into account that the pan and tilt can have arbitrary axes, and the image plane are rigid objects that rotate around such axes. The actual camera geometry is described by:

$$\begin{bmatrix} \mathbf{O}^{L/R} \\ 1 \end{bmatrix} = \mathbf{T}_{pan}\mathbf{R}_{pan}\mathbf{T}_{pan}^{-1}\mathbf{T}_{tilt}\mathbf{R}_{tilt}\mathbf{T}_{tilt}^{-1}\begin{bmatrix} \mathbf{O} \\ 1 \end{bmatrix} \tag{8}$$

where **R** denotes a rotation around the tilt/pan axis, and **T** denotes a translation from the origin to each axis. In particular, the following steps are performed: first a translation **T** to the center of rotation, then a rotation **R** around the respective axis, and eventually a back translation for allowing the projection.

Figure 7 and 8 show the horizontal and vertical disparity maps for the different gimbal systems and for the general camera model. The stereo virtual cameras are fixating nine targets on a fronto-parallel plane, the central target is straight ahead and the other eight targets are symmetrically displaced at $\pm 14°$. The baseline of the cameras is 6.5 cm with a field of view of $21°$, and the plane is at 65 cm from the cameras. For the general camera model, we simulated a displacement of the nodal points of 0.6 cm, and a misalignment of the tilt and pan axes with respect to the image plane of $3°$.

4. Geometry of the motion flow

In many robotic applications it is important to know how the coordinates of a point and its velocity change as the camera moves. The camera frame is the reference frame and we describe both the camera motion and the objects in the environment relative to it. The coordinates of a point $\mathbf{X}_0$ (at time $t = 0$) are described as a function of time t by the following relationship (Ma et al., 2004):

$$\mathbf{X}(t) = \mathcal{R}(t)\mathbf{X}_0 + \mathcal{T}(t) \tag{9}$$

where $\mathcal{R}(t)$ and $\mathcal{T}(t)$ denote a trajectory that describes a continuous rotational and translational motion.

From the transformation of coordinates described by Eq. 9, the velocity of the point of coordinates $\mathbf{X}(t)$ relative to the camera frame (see Fig. 9) can be derived (Longuet-Higgins & Prazdny, 1980):

$$\dot{\mathbf{X}}(t) = \boldsymbol{\omega}(t) \times \mathbf{X}(t) + \mathbf{v}(t) \tag{10}$$

where $\times$ denotes the cross product, $\boldsymbol{\omega}(t)$ and $\mathbf{v}(t)$ denote the angular velocity and the translational velocity of the camera, respectively.

Figure 10 shows the motion fields for different kinds of camera movements. For the sake of simplicity, the visual axes are kept parallel and only the left frame is shown. The virtual set-up is the same of Fig. 7 and 8.

5. Software implementation

The virtual reality tool we propose is based on a C++ / OpenGL architecture and on the Coin3D graphic toolkit (`www.coin3D.org`). Coin3D is a high level 3D graphic toolkit for developing cross-platform real time 3D visualization and visual simulation software. It is portable over a wide range of platforms, it is built on OpenGL and uses scene graph data

structures to render 3D graphics in real time. Coin3D is fully compatible with SGI Open Inventor 2.1, the de-facto standard for 3D visualization in the scientific and engineering communities. Both OpenGL and Coin3D code co-exist in our application.
In order to obtain a stereoscopic visualization of the scene useful to mimic an active stereo system, rather than to make a human perceive stereoscopy (see Section 3 for further details), we have not used the stereo rendering of the `SoCamera` node in the library, since it adopts the off-axis geometry. We have created our own `Cameras` class, that contains a pointer to a `SoPerspectiveCamera`, which can be moved in the left, right and cyclopic position. The class stores the status of the head:

- 3D position of the neck;
- projection direction of the cyclopic view;

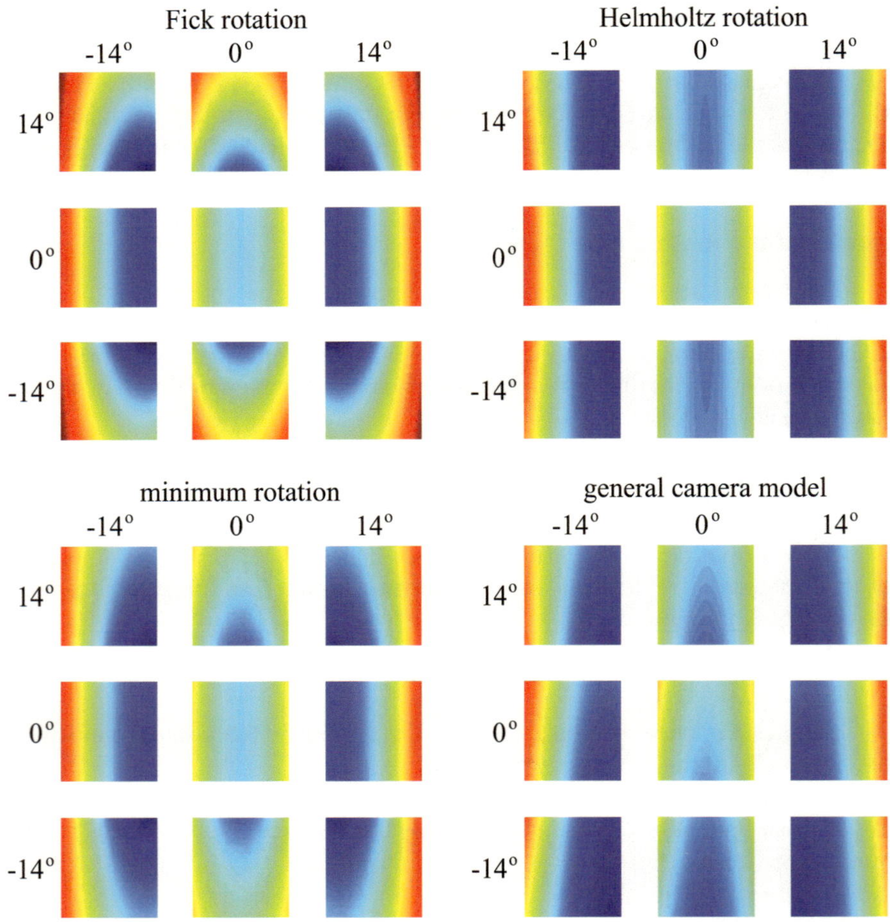

Fig. 7. Horizontal disparity patterns for different kinds of rotations and camera models. For each panel nine different gaze directions are shown. The disparity values are coded from red (uncrossed disparity) to blue (crossed disparity).

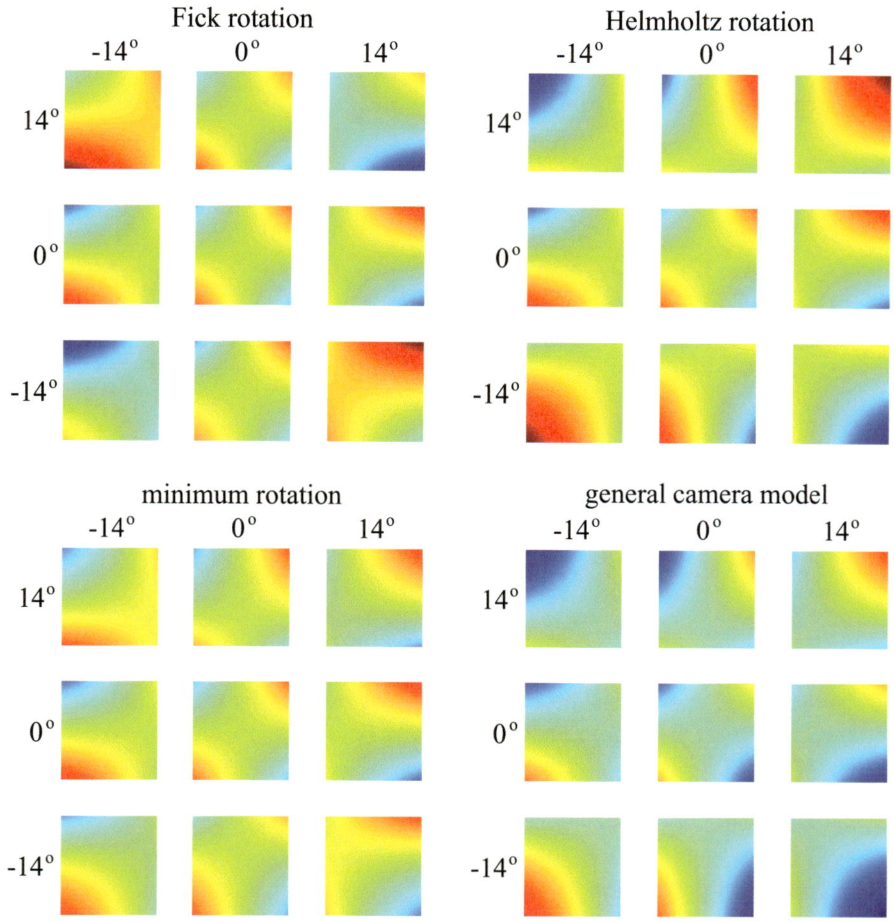

Fig. 8. Vertical disparity patterns for different kind of rotations and camera model. Same notation of Fig.'7

- direction of the baseline, computed as the cross product between the projection direction and the up vector;

and the status of each view:

- 3D position and rotation (R^R and R^L) computed with respect to the $(0,0,-1)$ axis;
- values of the depth buffer with respect to the actual position of the camera.

The left and the right views are continuously updated after having computed the rotation R^R and R^L necessary to fixate the target. Also the position of the neck, the projection direction, and the direction of the baseline can be updated if the neck is moving.

The scene from the point of view of the two stereo cameras is then rendered both in the on-screen OpenGL context and in the off-screen buffer. At the same time the depth buffer is read and stored. It is worth noting that, since Coin3D library does not easily allow the users to access and store the depth buffer, the `SoOffscreenRender` class has been modified in order to add this feature. After such a modification it is possible to access both the color buffer and the depth buffer.

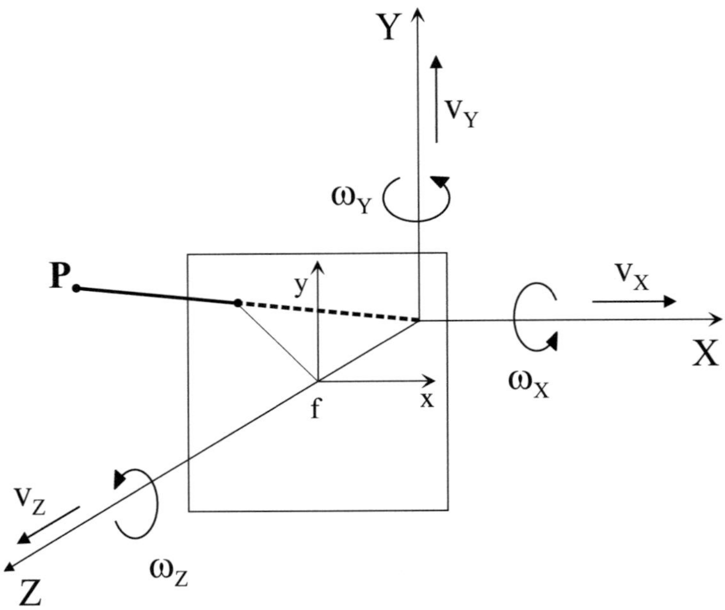

Fig. 9. Viewer-centered coordinate frame. The relative motion between an observer and the scene can be described at each instant t as a rigid-body motion, by means of two vectors (i.e., kinetic characteristics): the translational velocity $\mathbf{v} = (v_X, v_Y, v_Z)^T$, and the angular velocity $\boldsymbol{\omega} = (\omega_X, \omega_Y, \omega_Z)^T$.

The ground truth maps can be then generated and stored.

5.1 Ground truth data generation

To compute the ground truth data it is necessary to exploit the resources available from the graphics engine by combining them through the computer vision relationships that describe a 3D moving scene and the geometry of two views, typically used to obtain a 3D reconstruction.

5.1.1 Stereo cameras

Formally, by considering two static views, the two camera reference frames are related by a rigid body transformation described by the rotation matrix $\mathcal{R}$ and the translation $\mathcal{T}$ (see Eq. 1), thus the two projections (left and right) are related in the following way (Ma et al., 2004):

$$\lambda^R \mathbf{x}^R = \mathcal{R} \lambda^L \mathbf{x}^L + \mathcal{T} \tag{11}$$

where $\mathbf{x}^L$ and $\mathbf{x}^R$ are the homogeneous coordinates in the two image planes, and λ^L and λ^R are the depth values.

In order to define the disparity, we explicitly write the projection equations for Eq. 5 (Helmholtz sequence). The relation between the 3D world coordinates $\mathbf{X} = (X, Y, Z)$ and the homogeneous image coordinates $\mathbf{x}^L = (x^L, y^L, 1)$ and $\mathbf{x}^R = (x^R, y^R, 1)$ for the toe-in technique is described by a general perspective projection model. A generic point $\mathbf{X}$ in the world coordinates is mapped onto image plane points $\mathbf{x}^L$ and $\mathbf{x}^R$ on the left and right cameras, respectively. It is worth noting that the fixation point $\mathbf{F}$ in Figure 4b is projected onto the origins of the left and right image planes, since the vergence movement makes the optical

(a) (b) (c) (d) (e)

Fig. 10. Motion fields for different camera movements: (a) the v_Z camera velocity produces an expansion pattern with the focus of expansion in the center; the superposition of a v_X velocity moves the focus of expansion on the left (b) or on the right (c) as a function of its sign; (d) the cameras move with v_Z and a rotational velocity ω_Y. (e) The color-coding scheme used for the representation: the hue represents the velocity direction, while its magnitude is represented by the saturation.

axes of the two cameras to intersect in **F**. For identical left and right focal lengths f_0, the left image coordinates are (Volpel & Theimer, 1995):

$$x^L = f_0 \frac{X_+ \cos\alpha^L + Z \sin\alpha^L}{X_+ \sin\alpha^L \cos\beta^L - Y \sin\beta^L - Z \cos\alpha^L \cos\beta^L}$$
$$y^L = f_0 \frac{X_+ \sin\alpha^L \sin\beta^L + Y \cos\beta^L - Z \cos\alpha^L \sin\beta^L}{X_+ \sin\alpha^L \cos\beta^L - Y \sin\beta^L - Z \cos\alpha^L \cos\beta^L} \quad (12)$$

where $X_+ = X + b/2$. Similarly, the right image coordinates are obtained by replacing α^L, β^L and X_+ in the previous equations with α^R, β^R and $X_- = X - b/2$, respectively. We can define the horizontal disparity $d_x = x^R - x^L$ and the vertical disparity $d_y = y^R - y^L$, that establish the relationship between a world point **X** and its associated disparity vector **d**.

5.1.2 A moving camera

Considering the similarities between the stereo and motion problems, as they both look for correspondences between different frames or between left and right views, the generalizations of the two static views approach to a moving camera is in principle straightforward. Though, the description of the stereoscopically displaced cameras and of the moving camera are equivalent only if the spatial and temporal differences between frame are small enough, since the motion field is a differential concept, but not the stereo disparity. In particular, the following conditions must be satisfied: small rotations, small field of view, and v_Z small with respect to the distance of the objects from the camera. These assumptions are related to the analysis of video streams, where the camera motion is slow with respect to the frame rate (sampling frequency) of the acquisition device. Thus, we can treat the motion of the camera as continuous (Ma et al., 2004; Trucco & Verri, 1998; Adiv, 1985).

The relationship that relates the image velocity (motion field) $\dot{\mathbf{x}}$ of the image point $\mathbf{x}$ to the angular ($\boldsymbol{\omega}$) and the linear ($\mathbf{v}$) velocities of the camera and to the depth values is described by the following equation (see also Eq. 10):

$$\dot{\mathbf{x}} = \boldsymbol{\omega} \times \mathbf{x} + \frac{1}{\lambda}\mathbf{v} - \frac{\dot{\lambda}}{\lambda}\mathbf{x} \quad (13)$$

where λ and $\dot{\lambda}$ are the depth and its temporal derivative, respectively.

For planar perspective projection, i.e. $\lambda = Z$, we have that the image motion field $\dot{\mathbf{x}}$ is expressible as a function of image position $\mathbf{x} = (x, y)$ and surface depth $Z = Z(x, y)$ (i.e., the depth of the object projecting in (x, y) at current time):

$$\begin{bmatrix} \dot{x} \\ \dot{y} \end{bmatrix} = \frac{1}{Z} \begin{bmatrix} f_0 & 0 & -x \\ 0 & f_0 & -y \end{bmatrix} \mathbf{v} + \begin{bmatrix} -xy/f_0 & (f_0 + x^2/f_0) & -y \\ -(f_0 + y^2/f_0) & xy/f_0 & x \end{bmatrix} \boldsymbol{\omega} \quad (14)$$

To apply the relationship described by Eqs. 11 and 13 we first read the z-buffer (w) of the camera through the method added in the `SoOffScreenRenderer` class, then we obtain the depth values with respect to the reference frame of the camera in the following way:

$$\lambda = \frac{f\,n}{w(f-n) - f} \quad (15)$$

where f and n represent the values of the far and the near planes of the virtual camera, respectively.
Finally, from Eq. 11 it is possible to compute the ground truth disparity maps $\mathbf{d}$, and from Eq. 13 it is possible to obtain the ground truth motion field $\dot{\mathbf{x}}$.

6. Results for different visual tasks

The proposed VR tool can be used to simulate any interaction between the observer and the scene. In particular, in the following two different situations will be considered and analyzed:

1. Scene exploration, where both the head and the scene are fixed, and only ocular movements are considered.
2. Robotic navigation, by considering monocular vision, only.

6.1 Active vision - scene exploration

By keeping fixed the position and the orientation of the head, the described tool is active in the sense that the fixation point $\mathbf{F}$ of the stereo cameras varies to explore the scene. We can distinguish two possible scenarios: (1) to use the system to obtain sequences where the fixation points are chosen on the surfaces of the objects in the scene; (2) to use the system in cooperation with an algorithm that implements a vergence/version strategy. In the first case, it is not possible to fixate beyond or in front of the objects. In the second case, the vergence/version algorithm gives us an estimate of the fixation point, the system adapts itself looking at this point and the snapshots of the scene are then used as a new visual input for selecting a new target point.
To compute the fixation point in 3D coordinates, starting from its 2D projection, the `SoRayPickAction` class has been used. It contains the methods for setting up a ray from the near plane to the far plane, from the 2D point in the projection plane. Then the first hit, the one that corresponds to the first visible surface, is taken as the 3D coordinates, the system should fixate.
Figure 11 shows the active exploration of an indoor scene, representing a desktop and different objects at various distances, acquired by using a laser scanner. The simulator aims to mimic the behavior of a human-like robotic system acting in the peripersonal space. Accordingly, the interocular distance between the two cameras is set to 6 cm and the distance between the cameras and the center of the scene is about 80 cm. The fixation points have been chosen arbitrary, thus simulating an active exploration of the scene, and in their proximity the disparity between the left and the right projections is zero, while getting far from the

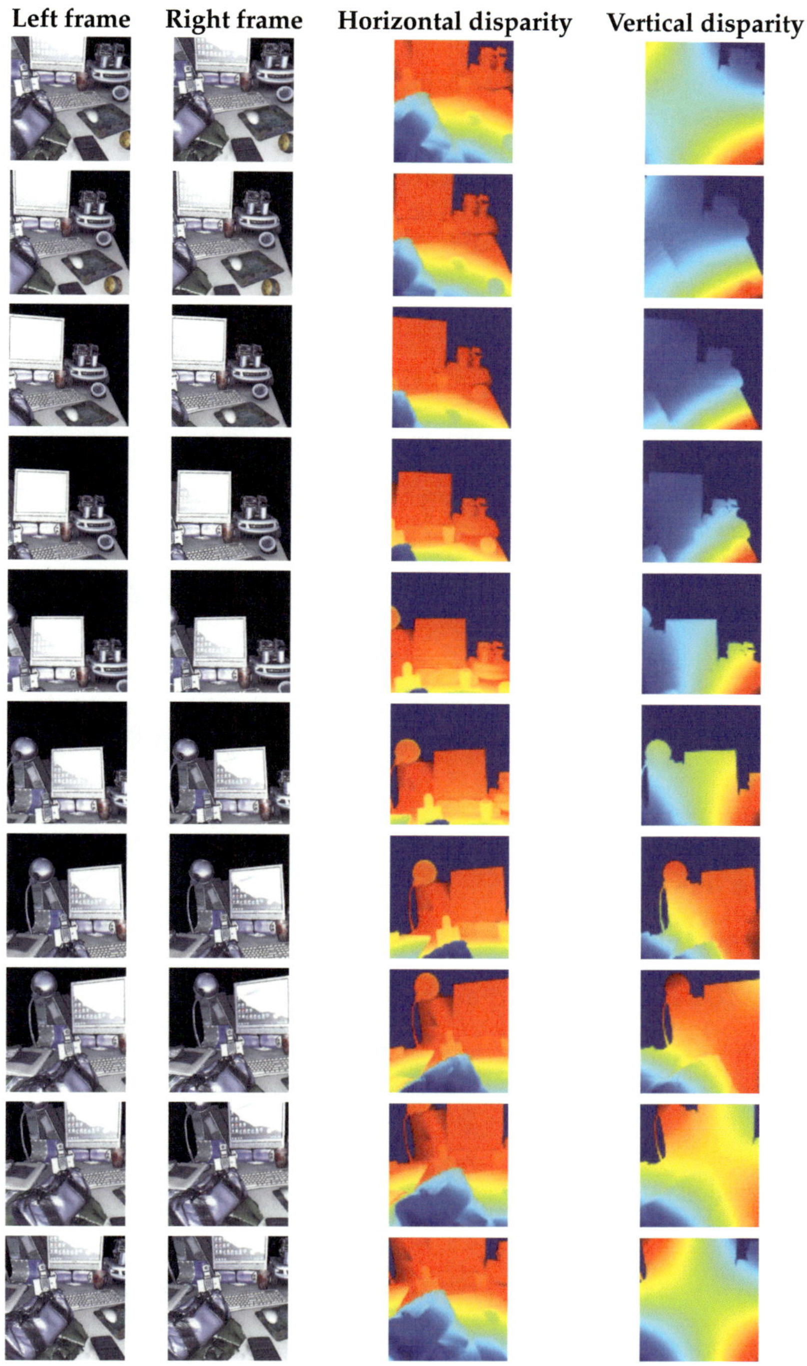

Fig. 11. Active exploration of a scene. The position and the orientation of the head is fixed, whereas the eyes are moving in order to explore the scene. The scenario mimics a typical indoor scene. The disparity values are coded from red (uncrossed disparity) to blue (crossed disparity).

fixation point both horizontal and vertical disparities emerge, as it can be seen in the ground truth data.
Instead of directly computing the 3D coordinates of the fixation points, it is possible to analyze the sequence of images and the corresponding disparity maps, while performing vergence movements. In Figure 12 (left) it is possible to see the red-cyan anaglyph of the stereo pairs, before having reached the fixation point (upper part of the figure) and when fixation is achieved onto a target (bottom). The plots on the right show the variation of the disparity in the center of the image at each time step (upper part) and the variation of the actual depth of the fixation point with respect to the desired value (bottom).

6.2 Robotic navigation

In this Section, the simulator is used to obtain sequences acquired by a moving observer. The position and the orientation of the head can be changed, in order to mimic the navigation in the virtual environment. For the sake of simplicity, the ocular movements are not considered and the visual axes are kept parallel. It is worth noting that the eye movements necessary to actively explore the scene, considered in the previous Section, could be embedded if necessary. Figure 13 shows the sequence of images and the related ground truth optic flow fields for the different movements of the observer.

7. Conclusion

In conclusion, a tool that uses the VR to simulate the actual projections impinging the cameras of an active visual system rather than to render the 3D visual information for a stereoscopic display, has been developed. The simulator works on the 3D data that can

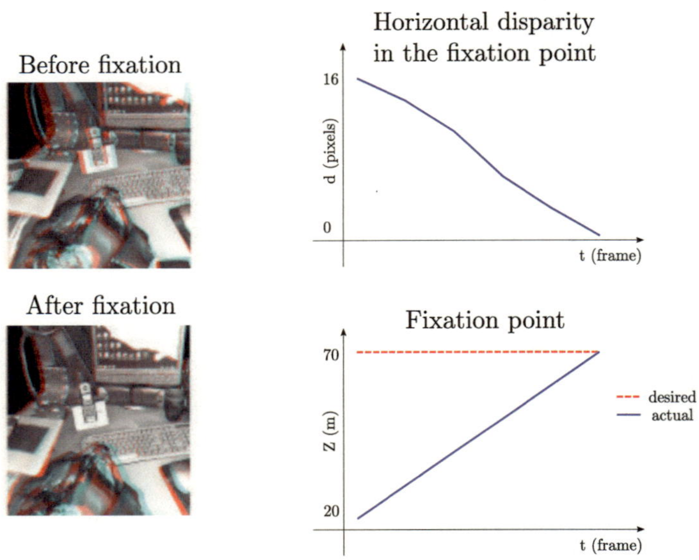

Fig. 12. (left) The anaglyph images before and after a vergent movement of the cameras in order to correctly fuse the left and right images of the target object. (right) The plots show the variation of the disparity in the center of the stereo images and the related depth of actual and desired fixation point. It is worth noting that the vergence movements are synthetically generated (i.e., not driven by the visual information).

be synthetically generated or acquired by a laser scanner and performs both cameras and robot movements following the strategies adopted by different active stereo vision systems, including bio-mimetic ones.

The virtual reality tool is capable of generating pairs of stereo images like the ones that can be obtained by a verging pan-tilt robotic head and the related ground truth data, disparity maps and motion field. To obtain such a behavior the toe-in stereoscopic technique is preferred to the off-axis technique. By proper roto-translations of the view volumes, we can create benchmark stereo sequences for testing vision algorithms under convergent-camera conditions. In more general terms, by exploiting the full knowledge of the 3D structure of the scene the proposed VR tool can be used to model active vision systems interacting with the scene. A data set of stereo image pairs and the related ground truth disparities and motion fields are available for the Robotics and Computer Vision community at the web site `www.pspc.dibe.unige.it/Research/vr.html`.

Although the main purpose of this work is to obtain sufficiently complex scenarios for benchmarking an active vision system, complex photo-realistic scenes can be easily obtained by using the 3D data and textures acquired by laser scanners, which capture detailed, highly accurate, and full color objects to build 3D virtual models at an affordable computational cost. In this way improving the photo-realistic quality of the 3D scene does not endanger the

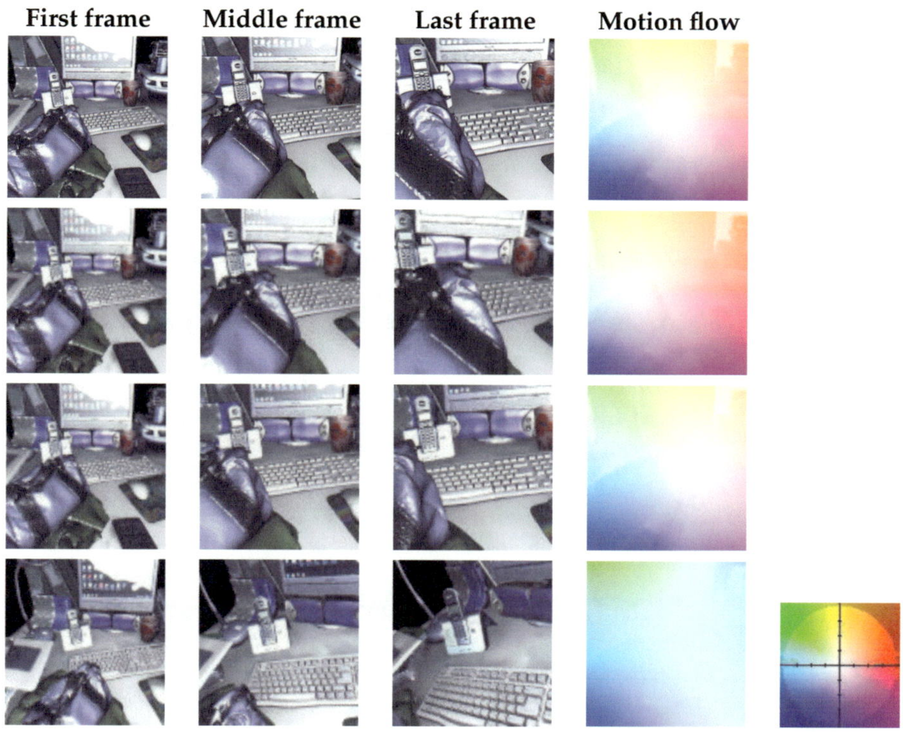

Fig. 13. Robotic navigation in an indoor scenario. Different situation are taken into account. First row: the robot has v_Z velocity, only. Thus the focus of expansion is in the center. Second and third row: positive and negative v_X are introduced, thus the focus of expansion move to the left and to the right, respectively. Fourth row: a rotation around the Y axis is combined with a translation aking v_Z. Same color-coding scheme of Fig.10.

definition of a realistic model of the interactions between the vision system and the observed scene. As part of a future work, we plan to modify the standard pan-tilt behaviour by including more biologically plausible constraints on the camera movements (Schreiber et al., 2001; Van Rijn & Van den Berg, 1993) and to integrate vergence/version strategies in the system in order to have a fully active tool that interacts with the virtual environments.

8. Acknowledgements

We wish to thank Luca Spallarossa for the helpful comments, and Andrea Canessa and Agostino Gibaldi for the acquisition, registration and post-processing of the 3D data.
This work has been partially supported by EU Projects FP7-ICT 217077 "EYESHOTS" and FP7-ICT 215866 "SEARISE".

9. References

Adelson, E. & Bergen, J. (1991). The plenoptic and the elements of early vision, *in* M. Landy & J. Movshon (eds), *Computational Models of Visual Processing*, MIT Press, pp. 3–20.

Adiv, G. (1985). Determining three-dimensional motion and structure from optical flow generated by several moving objects, *IEEE Transactions on Pattern Analysis and Machine Intelligence* 7: 384–401.

Awaad, I., Hartanto, R., León, B. & Plöger, P. (2008). A software system for robotic learning by experimentation, *Workshop on robot simulators (IROS08)*.

Baker, S., Scharstein, D., Lewis, J., Michael, S., Black, J. & Szeliski, R. (2007). A database and evaluation methodology for optical flow, *ICCV*, pp. 1–8.

Bernardino, A., Santos-Victor, J., Ferre, M. & Sanchez-Urn, M. (2007). Stereoscopic image visualization for telerobotics. experiments with active binocular cameras, *Advances in Telerobotics*, pp. 77–90.

Bourke, P. & Morse, P. (2007). Stereoscopy: Theory and practice, *Workshop at 13th International Conference on Virtual Systems and Multimedia* .

Cannata, G. & Maggiali, M. (2008). Models for the design of bioinspired robot eyes, *IEEE Transactions on Robotics* 24: 27–44.

Chessa, M., Sabatini, S. & Solari, F. (2009). A fast joint bioinspired algorithm for optic flow and two-dimensional disparity estimation, *in* M. Fritz, B. Schiele & J. Piater (eds), *Computer Vision Systems*, Vol. 5815 of *Lecture Notes in Computer Science*, Springer Berlin / Heidelberg, pp. 184–193.

Davis, J. & Chen, X. (2003). Calibrating pan-tilt cameras in wide-area surveillance networks, *Proc. of IEEE International Conference on Computer Vision*, IEEE Computer Society, pp. 144–150.

EYESHOTS (2008). *FP7-ICT 217077 "EYESHOTS"*, `http://www.eyeshots.it/`.

Ferre, P., Aracil, R. & Sanchez-Uran, M. (2008). Stereoscopic human interfaces, *IEEE Robotics & Automation Magazine* 15(4): 50–57.

Fleet, D. & Jepson, A. (1990). Computation of component image velocity from local phase information, *International Journal of Computer Vision* 5(1): 77–104.

Forsyth, D. & Ponce, J. (2002). *Computer Vision: A Modern Approach*, Prentice Hall.

Gibaldi, A., Chessa, M., Canessa, A., Sabatini, S. & Solari, F. (2010). A cortical model for binocular vergence control without explicit calculation of disparity, *Neurocomputing* 73(7-9): 1065 – 1073.

Grinberg, V., Podnar, G. & Siegel, M. (1994). Geometry of binocular imaging, *Proc. of the*

IS&T/SPIE Symp. on Electronic Imaging, Stereoscopic Displays and applications, Vol. 2177, pp. 56–65.

Haslwanter, T. (1995). Mathematics of three-dimensional eye rotations, *Vision Research* 35(12): 1727 – 1739.

Heeger, D. (1987). Model for the extraction of image flow, *Journal of the Optical Society of America A* 4(1): 1445–1471.

Horaud, R., Knossow, D. & Michaelis, M. (2006). Camera cooperation for achieving visual attention, *Machine Vision and Applications* 16: 331–342.

Hung, G., Semmlow, J. & Ciufferda, K. (1986). A dual-mode dynamic model of the vergence eye movement system, *Biomedical Engineering, IEEE Transactions on* BME-33(11): 1021–1028.

Jain, A., Kopell, D., Kakligian, K. & Wang, Y. (2006). Using stationarydynamic camera assemblies for wide-area video surveillance and selective attention, *In IEEE Conference on Computer Vision and Pattern Recognition*, Vol. 1, pp. 537–544.

Jørgensen, J. & Petersen, H. (2008). Usage of simulations to plan stable grasping of unknown objects with a 3-fingered schunk hand, *Workshop on robot simulators (IROS08)*.

Kooi, F. & Toet, A. (2004). Visual comfort of binocular and 3d displays, *Displays* 25(2-3): 99–108.

Liu, Y., Bovik, A. & Cormack, L. (2008). Disparity statistics in natural scenes, *Journal of Vision* 8(11): 1–14.

Longuet-Higgins, H. & Prazdny, K. (1980). The interpretation of a moving retinal image, *Phil. Trans. R. Soc. Lond. B* 208: 385–397.

Ma, Y., Soatto, S., Kosecka, J. & Sastry, S. (2004). *An Invitation to 3D Vision. From Images to Geometric Models*, Springer-Verlag.

McCane, B., Novins, K., Crannitch, D. & Galvin, B. (2001). On benchmarking optical flow, *Computer Vision and Image Understanding* 84(1): 126–143.

Michel, O. (2004). Webots: Professional mobile robot simulation, *International Journal of Advanced Robotic Systems* 1(1): 39–42.

Nakamura, Y., Matsuura, T., Satoh, K. & Ohta, Y. (1996). Occlusion detectable stereo-occlusion patterns in camera matrix, *Computer Vision and Pattern Recognition, 1996. Proceedings CVPR '96, 1996 IEEE Computer Society Conference on*, pp. 371 –378.

Okada, K., Kino, Y. & Kanehiro, F. (2002). Rapid development system for humanoid vision-based behaviors with real-virtual common interface, *IEEE/RSJ IROS*.

Otte, M. & Nagel, H. (1995). Estimation of optical flow based on higher-order spatiotemporal derivatives in interlaced and non-interlaced image sequences, *Artif. Intell.* 78(1-2): 5–43.

Scharstein, D. & Szeliski, R. (2002). A taxonomy and evaluation of dense two-frame stereo correspondence algorithms, *International Journal of Computer Vision* 47(1/2/3): 7–42.

Scharstein, D. & Szeliski, R. (2003). High-accuracy stereo depth maps using structured light, *Proceedings of the IEEE Conference on Computer Vision and Pattern Recognition*, Vol. 1, pp. 195–202.

Schreiber, K. M., Crawford, J. D., Fetter, M. & Tweed, D. B. (2001). The motor side of depth vision, *Nature* 410: 819–822.

Southard, D. (1992). Transformations for stereoscopic visual simulation, *Computers & Graphics* 16(4): 401–410.

Tikhanoff, V., Cangelosi, A., Fitzpatrick, P., Metta, G., Natale, L. & Nori, F. (2008). An open-source simulator for cognitive robotics research: The prototype of the iCub humanoid robot simulator, *Workshop on Performance Metrics for Intelligent Systems*

Workshop.

Trucco, E. & Verri, A. (1998). *Introductory Techniques for 3-D Computer Vision*, Prentice Hall.

Ulusoy, I., Halici, U. & Leblebicioglu, K. (2004). 3D cognitive map construction by active stereo vision in a virtual world, *Lecture notes in Computer Science* 3280: 400–409.

Van Rijn, L. & Van den Berg, A. (1993). Binocular eye orientation during fixations: Listing's law extended to include eye vergence, *Vision Research* 33: 691–708.

Volpel, B. & Theimer, W. (1995). Localization uncertainty in area-based stereo algorithms, *IEEE Transactions on Systems, Man and Cybernetics* 25(12): 1628–1634.

Wann, J. P., Rushton, S. & Mon-Williams, M. (1995). Natural problems for stereoscopic depth perception in virtual environments., *Vision research* 35(19): 2731–2736.

Yamanoue, H. (2006). The differences between toed-in camera configurations and parallel camera configurations in shooting stereoscopic images, *Multimedia and Expo, IEEE International Conference on* pp. 1701–1704.

Yang, Z. & Purves, D. (2003). Image/source statistics of surfaces in natural scenes, *Network: Comput. Neural Syst.* 14: 371–390.

5

Development of a Finger Pad Force Display for a Hand Haptic Interface

Haruhisa Kawasaki, Shinya Koide, Tetuya Mouri and Takahiro Endo
Gifu University,
Japan

1. Introduction

Most human interfaces in virtual environments use information of visual sensation and auditory sensation. By adding tactile sensation to these human interfaces, the human operator can handle objects with a realistic tactile sense and can perform complex tasks in the virtual reality environment. Haptic interfaces that present force and tactile feeling to the fingertips of a human operator have been investigated extensively over the last two decades [1]-[12]. Although some of these interfaces [9]-[12] provide three-dimensional force feeling to the human fingertip, few haptic interfaces cover the workspace of the human arm. These interfaces are classified into two types: wearable type interfaces [9], which are mounted firmly to the human hand, and opposed type interfaces [12], which are mounted in a position opposed to the human hand. These interfaces apply three-dimensional (3D) forces only to the human fingertips.

Medical doctors must use palpation in examining patients, and the force and tactile sensation on both the fingertips and the finger pads are important in such palpation. However, training doctors to perform palpation is difficult, because this requires the cooperation of the patient. Thus a breast palpation training system in a virtual reality environment [13] would be useful as a training tool for palpation. However, due to the limitation of human finger length, developing a haptic interface that displays 3D force feeling to both the fingertips and the finger pads is not easy.

The density of tactile sense organs in the human finger [14] is high in the fingertip and low in the finger pad. Hence, the human finger has a high sensitivity to 3D force at the fingertip but a low sensitivity at the finger pad. This suggests that a haptic interface that consists of 1D finger pad force display devices and a 3D fingertip force device would be effective for use in a virtual environment such as a virtual breast palpation training system.

The present paper describes a hand haptic interface for use in a virtual training system in which not only fingertip force display but also finger pad force display is required. The hand haptic interface consists of novel finger pad force display devices and a 3D fingertip haptic interface, known as HIRO II [12], which was developed by our group. The developed finger pad force display device is driven by a flat-type brushless DC motor and is easy attachable to the finger pad. The applied force is controlled by a time interval control, which is an open-loop control. Here we present the design concept of the hand haptic interface, the control method and specifications of the finger pad force display device, and the results of an experimental evaluation of manipulating a virtual object. We also provide a comparative evaluation between a case of using one force finger pad force display device and a case of using two force finger pad force display devices on an index finger when touching a rotating polyhedron.

2. Hand haptic interface

Humans manipulate objects using force and tactile feeling at the fingertip and the finger pad. For example, medical doctors search for tumors during breast palpation and manipulate internal organs during surgery using the fingertips and finger pads. To practice such medical procedures in a virtual environment, a hand haptic interface is required to apply forces to both the fingertips and finger pads.

The density of tactile sensory organs in the human finger is high in the fingertip and relatively low in the finger pad [14]. Hence, the human hand has a high sensitivity to 3D force at the fingertip [15] but a relatively low sensitivity at the finger pad. This suggests that a hand haptic interface that applies 3D force feeling to the finger tip and 1D force feeling to the finger pad would be effective for palpation training in a virtual reality environment, as shown in Fig. 1. In this figure, the human fingertip shows 3D force from the 3D fingertip force display device and the human finger pad shows 1D force, the direction of which is normal with respect to the surface of finger pad, from the 1D finger pad display device. The finger pad force display devices are attached to the proximal phalanges of the thumb and fingers and to the middle phalanges of the fingers. The total number of displayed points of the finger pads is nine.

The multi-fingered haptic interface robot HIRO II [12] shown in Fig. 2 is used to apply 3D fingertip forces. The haptic interface is described in detail in a previous report [8]. The mechanism of the haptic interface is outlined briefly herein to clarify the proposed hand haptic interface.

HIRO II can present force and tactile feeling at the five fingertips of the human hand. HIRO II is designed to be completely safe and is similar to the human upper limb both in shape and mobility. The mechanism of HIRO II consists of a six-degrees-of freedom (DOF) arm and a 15-DOF hand with a thumb and four fingers. Each finger has three joints, allowing three DOF. The first joint, relative to the base of the hand, allows abduction/adduction. The second joint and the third joint allow flexion/extension. The thumb is similar to the fingers except for the reduction gear ratio and the movable ranges of joint 1 and joint 2. To read the finger loading, a six-axis force sensor is installed in the second link of each finger. The user must wear finger holders over his/her fingertips to manipulate the haptic interface. Each finger holder has a ball attached to a permanent magnet at the force sensor tip and forms a passive spherical joint. This passive spherical joint has two roles. First, it adjusts for differences between the human finger orientation and the haptic finger orientation. Second, the operator is able to remove his/her fingers from the haptic interface in case of a malfunction. The suction force generated by the permanent magnet is 5 N.

3. Finger pad haptic display device

A. Mechanical design

A haptic device for the finger pad should be small and lightweight, so that it can be attached to the finger pad. The magnitude of the applied force must be sufficiently large, so that it can present realistic sensations during virtual object manipulation. The device should be easy to wear and should not obstruct the movement of the hand. Previously developed haptic devices for the finger tips or finger pads [16]-[19] have been problematic in that forces could not be applied to two finger pads of a finger simultaneously because of the size of the device or because the applied forces were insufficient. Therefore, we developed a novel finger pad force display device, as shown in Fig. 3(1), which can be attached to a finger at two points. This finger pad force display device consists of a body and a hook-and-loop fastener, which is wrapped around the finger pad. The mechanical structure of the device is shown in Fig. 3(2). The finger pad force display device is driven by a flat-type brushless DC motor (EC10, Maxon Motor) with a maximum torque of 0.176 mNm, a maximum rotational velocity of 22,000 rpm, a mass of 0. 81 g, and a diameter of 10 mm. Reduction gears with a reduction ratio of 3.67 are attached to the rotor of the motor, and a screw mechanism with a pitch of 0.5 mm is attached to the output gear axis of the reduction gears. The nut of the screw mechanism moves up and down with the rotation of the motor with a range of movement of 4 mm and contacts the finger pad. The mass and output force are 4.8 g and 2.6 N, respectively. Note that, in order to realize compactness and light weight, the finger pad force display device does not contain a force sensor. Hence, the contact force is open-loop controlled.

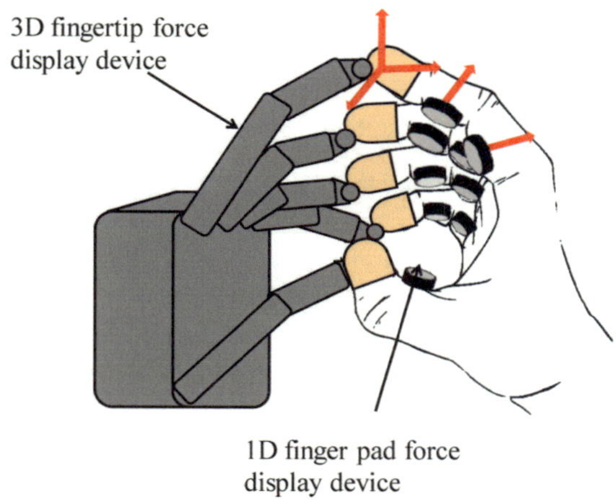

Fig. 1. Concept of proposed hand haptic interface

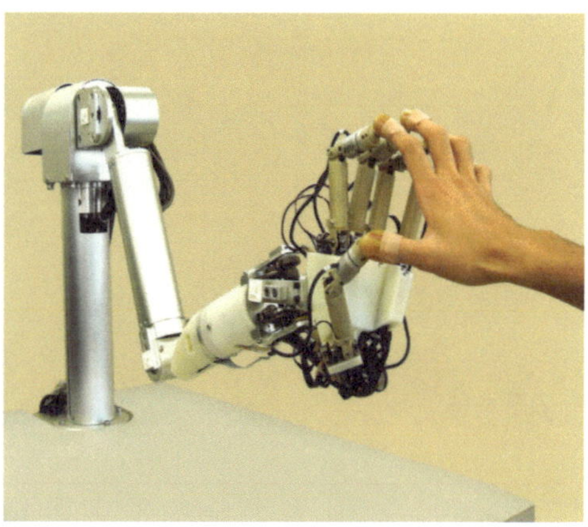

Fig. 2. Multi-fingered haptic interface robot HIRO II

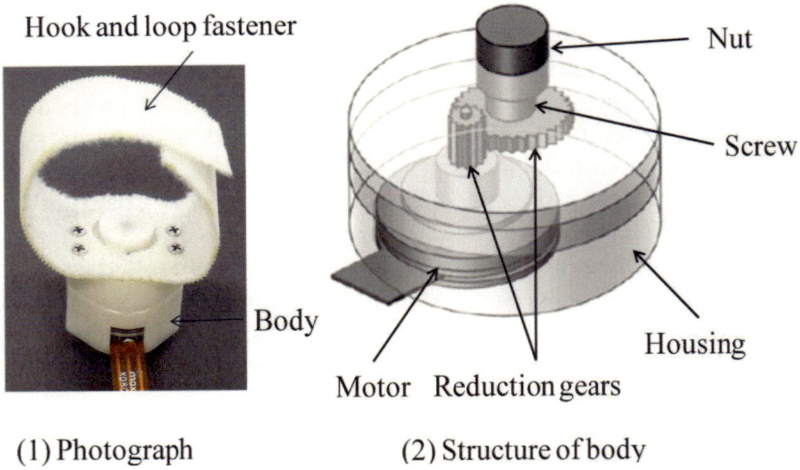

Fig. 3. Developed finger pad force display

B. Measurements of the displayed force

To determine force on the finger pad of the human hand, we measure the force responses on a rigid plate and a gel plate [20] (Exseal Co.). The measurement system for the case of the gel plate is shown in Fig. 4. The force is measured by means of a six-axis force sensor (NANO sensor, Nitta Co.). The gel plate, which has a thickness of 5 mm and a hardness of 5, as measured using an ASKER durometer (Type C) [20], is wedged between the sensor and the force display device. We selected this plate because it has a hardness that is similar to that of human skin. Fig. 4(1) shows the initial state, and Fig. 4(2) shows the end state after applying a force.

The step responses of the measured force are shown in Fig. 5. The displayed forces are 2.26 N for the rigid plate and 0.71 N for the gel plate, which is approximately 31% of the rigid plate case. This reduction is caused by the deformation of the gel plate, as shown in Fig. 4(2). A similar phenomenon will likely occur in the case of the finger pad of the human hand.

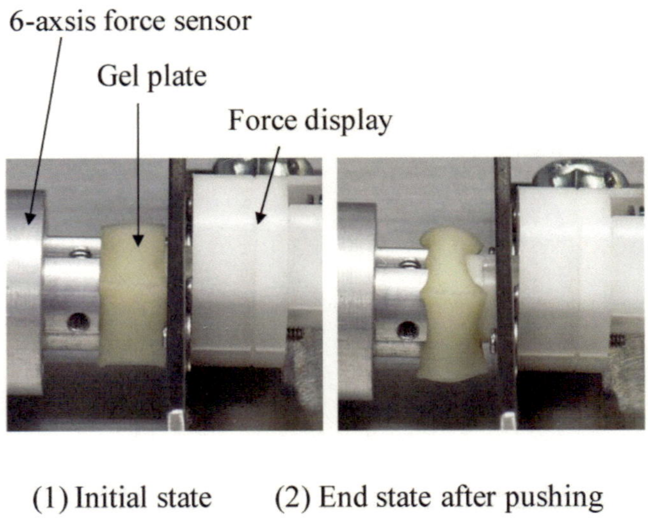

Fig. 4. Force measurement system

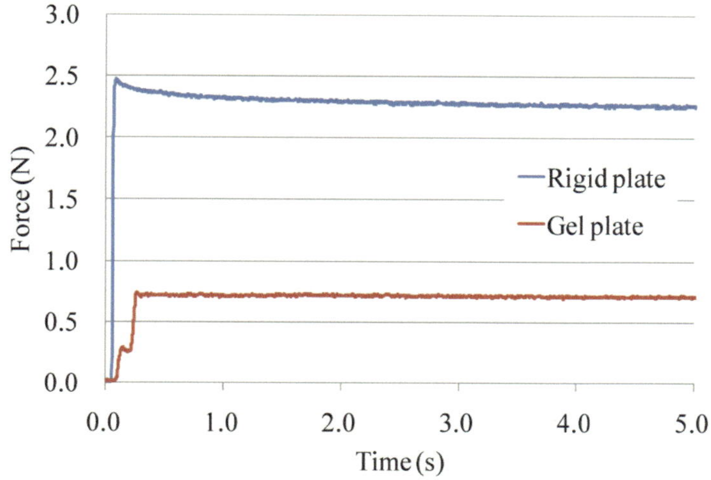

Fig. 5. Force responses by step input in case of rigid and gel plates

C. Time interval control

We adopt a time interval control in which the time interval of the input is controlled to adjust the applied force, because the finger pad force display device is not equipped with a force sensor. To confirm the effectiveness of the time interval control, we set the time interval of the input from 0.1 s to 0.5 s with intervals of 0.1 s, which yields five levels of applied force. The experimental results are shown in Fig. 6. The root-mean-square of the measured forces at each time interval control are 0.13, 0.26, 0.39, 0.56, and 0.71 N with standard deviations of 0.013, 0.01, 0.011, 0.013, and 0.011 N, respectively. Input of a longer time interval results in a higher level of force. These results reveal that the developed fingertip force display device can present a stepwise force to the finger pad of the human hand.

D. Experiment testing force sensation at the finger pad

We examined whether the human hand can distinguish the five levels of force applied by the finger pad force display device after nominal force (level 3) was applied. Ten subjects in their twenties, including eight male subjects and two female subjects, all right handed, tested the device. Each subject wore the finger pad force display device on the middle phalanx of the index finger and was asked to indicate whether the applied force was 'strong', 'the same as', 'weak', or 'unknown' compared to the nominal stimulus of level 3. The nominal stimulus and the comparison stimulus were presented alternately. The level of the comparison stimulus, i.e., from level 1 to level 5, was randomized, and the number of times each level of the comparison stimulus was presented was set to be 10 times. The results of the experiment are shown in Table I. When the difference between the nominal stimulus and the comparison stimulus was two levels, the correct answer rate was 98%. However, the correct answer rate was reduced to 62~78% when the difference between the nominal stimulus and the comparison stimulus was at the zero or one level. Note that there are significant differences between individuals. One of the subjects answered weak for 90% of the comparison stimuli, whereas another subject answered weak for only 10% of the comparison stimuli.

Next, we examined whether the human hand could distinguish the force level when the nominal force level had not been applied. The subjects were the same as those of the previous experiment. First, subjects were presented with five forces, from level 1 to level 5. The subjects were then presented with a comparison stimulus of a random level and asked to answer two questions. First, the subjects were asked to state the force level (levels 1 through 5, or unknown) of the presented stimulus. Second, the subjects were asked to state whether the force level of the stimulus was small, the same as, large, or unknown as compared to the previously applied stimulus. The results are shown in Table II. The average correct answer rate for the first question was 49.6%, with a standard deviation of 17.6%, and that for the second question was 84.4%, with a standard deviation of 13.4%. Although there were individual differences in the correct answer rate, we can say that the correct answer rate of the exact force level was not high and that the correct answer rate for the differences between the comparative stimuli was relatively high.

The results indicate that the stepwise force display device with the five-level time interval control can produce a recognizable force sensation.

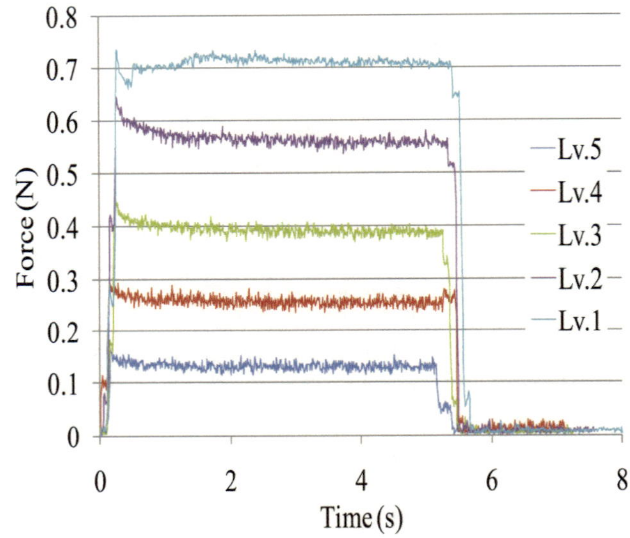

Fig. 6. Force responses by the time interval control in case of the gel plate

Displayed force level	Weak	Same	Strong	Unclear	Correct answer rate [%]
1	98	2	0	0	98
2	62	35	3	0	62
3	2	74	22	2	74
4	2	16	78	4	78
5	0	2	98	0	98

Note: Each subject wore the finger pad force display device on the middle phalanx of the index finger and was asked to indicate whether the applied force was 'strong', 'the same as', 'weak', or 'unknown' compared to the nominal stimulus of level 3.

Table 1. Correct Answer rates for Comparisons with Nominal Stimulus

Subject No.	1	2	3	4	5	6	7	8	9	10
First question	32	20	40	68	60	40	68	72	56	40
Second question	60	76	68	84	100	92	92	92	100	80

Note: Subjects were presented with five forces, from level 1 to level 5. Then, they were presented with a comparison stimulus of a random level and asked to answer two questions. First, the subjects were asked to state the force level (levels 1 through 5, or unknown) of the presented stimulus. Second, the subjects were asked to state whether the force level of the stimulus was small, the same as, large, or unknown as compared to the previously applied stimulus.

Table 2. Results Of Correct Answer rates

4. Virtual reality system

We have developed a hand haptic interface that incorporates a 3D fingertip force display device (HIRO II) and 1D finger pad force display devices, as shown in Fig. 7. The hand orientation of the operator is measured by a 3D orientation-tracking sensor (InertiaCube made by InterSense, Inc.), which is mounted on the back of the operator's hand. The hand position is measured by a 3D position-tracking sensor (Optorack Certus, Northern Digital Inc.). The operator wears five finger holders over the fingertips, for the connection with HIRO II, and nine finger pad force display devices on the middle phalanges of the fingers and the proximal phalanges of the thumb and fingers, as shown in Fig. 8.

The finger joint angles of the operator's hand are calculated using the inverse kinematics of the finger based on the positions of fingertips, measured by HIRO II, and the wrist point, measured by the 3D position tracking sensor. The solution of the inverse kinematics is not unique, because the human finger has three joints (distal interphalangeal joint, proximal interphalangeal joint, and metacarpophalangeal joint), each of which has four DOF. However, the fourth (distal interphalangeal) joint angle, q_4^i, depends on the third (proximal interphalangeal) joint angle, q_3^i, and can be approximated as $q_3^i = q_4^i$ [21], where the index i indicates the order of the fingers. Using this relation, the inverse kinematics has a unique solution. The results of the calculations are shown in Fig. 9, in which the large balls indicate the fingertips and the small balls indicate the locations of the finger pad force display devices.

The control system of the hand haptic interface consists of a haptic interface control PC (HPC) and a virtual environment modeling PC (VPC). The constrained forces at the contact points between the hand and the virtual object are computed in the VPC and are sent to the HPC with a sampling cycle of 1 ms through a local LAN. HIRO II is controlled by a hybrid control comprising a finger force control and an arm position control, in which the haptic hand attitude is controlled such that the hand manipulability is optimized in real time [12]. The finger pad force display device is controlled by the time interval control with five levels.

5. Experimental evaluation

We examined the effectiveness of the haptic interface through two psychological tests. One involved grasping a cylindrical virtual object and the other involved touching a rotating polyhedron. Ten subjects in their twenties, including nine male subjects and one female subject, all right handed, participated in the evaluation.

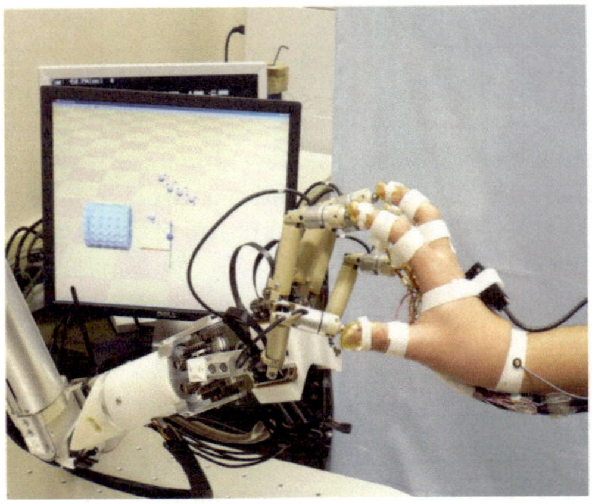

Fig. 7. Developed hand haptic interface

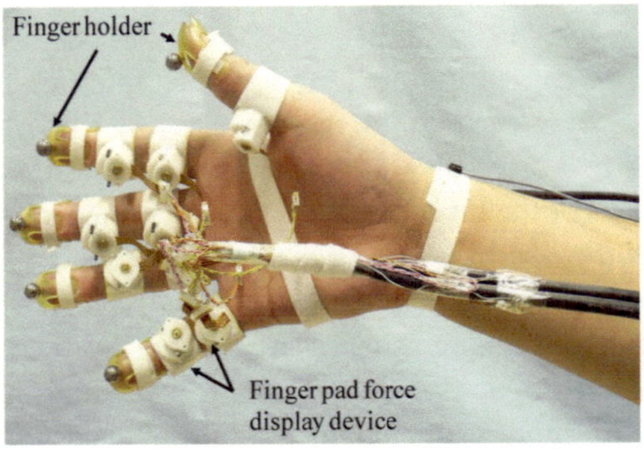

Fig. 8. Layout of the finger holders and the finger pad force display devices

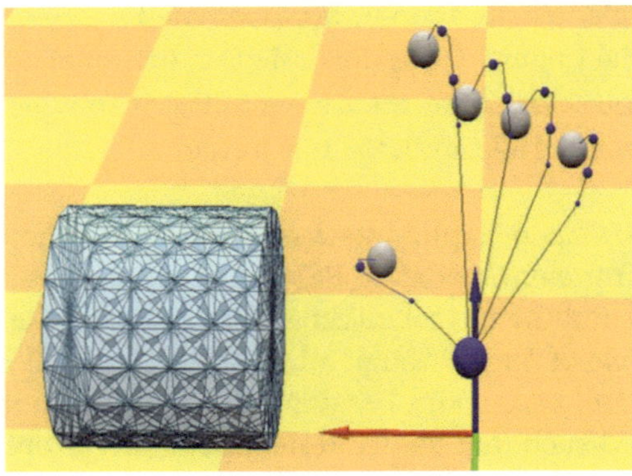

Fig. 9. Human hand model in computer graphics

A. Grasping of a cylindrical object.

In the experiment, the subjects were asked to grasp a virtual cylindrical object with an enveloping grasp and to move the object laterally for a distance of 300 mm. Trials were conducted using the newly developed hand haptic interface and using the fingertip force display device only. The diameter and mass of the cylindrical object were 100 mm and 50 g, respectively. After manipulation of the virtual object, the subjects were asked to rate the following criteria on a five-point scale, in which 1 was the lowest rating and 5 was the highest rating:

(a) Comfort while wearing the device
(b) Heaviness of the device
(c) Annoyance associated with wearing the device
(d) Existence of force feeling at the finger pad
(e) Operability
(f) Applied force consistency with virtual reality (VR)

The results of the questionnaire are shown in Fig. 10. The subjects rated the developed haptic interface as being less comfortable to wear, heavier, and more annoying to wear than the fingertip force display device only. However, the subjects rated the developed haptic interface higher in regard to the existence of force feeling at the finger pad, operability, and applied force consistency with VR as compared to the finger tip force display device only. This evaluation was the result of experiencing force display at the finger pads of the hand. We analyzed the statistical significance of evaluation items (e) and (f). A t-test with a 10% significance level indicated no significant difference between the trials conducted using the newly developed hand haptic interface and those conducted using the fingertip force display device only for evaluation item (e), and a t-test with a 5% significance level indicated a significant difference between the trials conducted using the newly developed hand haptic interface and those conducted using the fingertip force display device only for evaluation item (f).

Subjects indicated that grasping the virtual object with an enveloping grasp when using the newly developed hand haptic interface, was easy and that the shape of the object could be sensed based on the contact force applied to the hand. Subjects pointed out that it was not easy to put on the hand haptic interface by oneself.

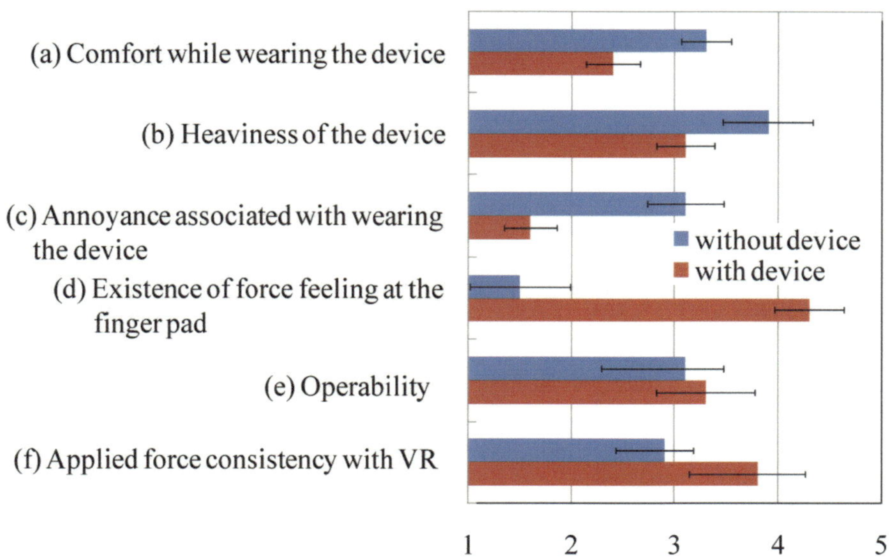

Fig. 10. Questionnaire results of cylindrical object handling in cases of with and without finger pad force display devices

B. Touching of rotating polyhedron

We made comparative evaluations of subjects' experiences when touching a rotating polyhedron by using the index finger only for the following three cases:in case A, subjects used a HIRO II with finger pad force display on the distal and proximal interphalangeal finger pads as shown in Fig.11 (a); in case B, subjects used a HIRO II with finger pad force display on the proximal interphalangeal finger pad, as shown in Fig.11 (b); and in case C, subjects used a HIRO II without finger pad force display. The object in a virtual environment was a polyhedron with 50 plates consisting of isosceles triangles and trapezoids, as shown in Fig. 12. The polyhedron was rotating at a rate of about 3 rad/s around an axis that was orthogonal with respect to the flexion/extension axis of the index finger. After contacting the virtual object, the subjects were asked to rate the following criteria on a five-point scale, in which 1 was the lowest rating and 5 was the highest rating:

- *(a)* Comfort while wearing the device
- *(b)* Heaviness of the device
- *(c)* Annoyance associated with wearing the device
- *(d)* Existence of force feeling at the distal interphalangeal
- *(e)* Existence of force feeling at the proximal interphalangeal
- *(f)* Operability
- *(g)* Consistency between force and computer graphics (CG)

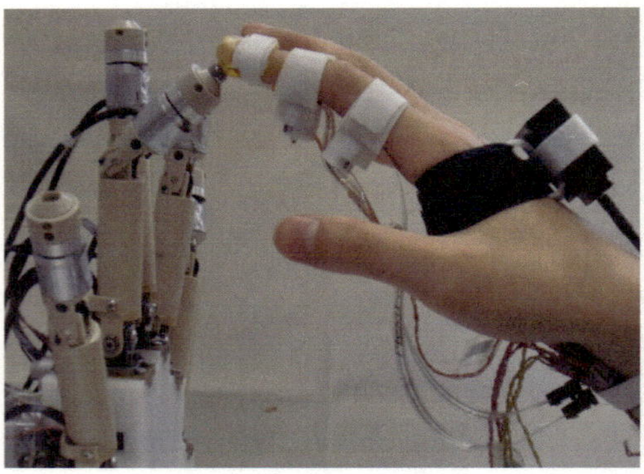

(a) Devices on distal and proximal interphalangeal finger pads

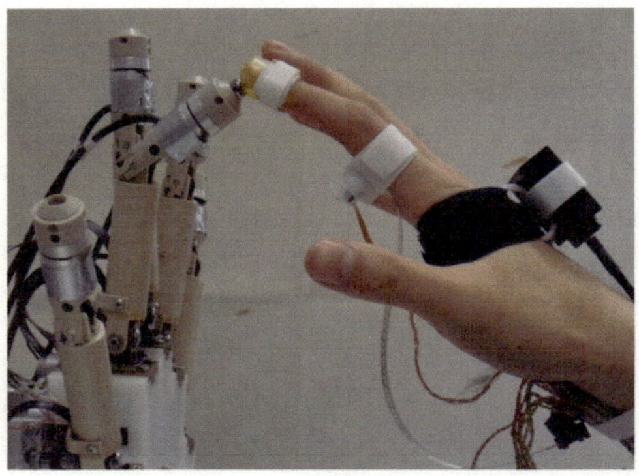

(b) Devices on proximal interphalangeal finger pad

Fig. 11. Two cases of experiment condition

The results of the questionnaire are shown in Fig. 13. Case A received the highest score in regard to the consistency between force and CG, but the lowest score in regard to the comfort, heaviness, annoyance, and operability. Case C received the highest score in regard to the comfort, heaviness, annoyance, and operability, but the lowest score in regard to the consistency. Case B received an intermediate score in all criteria. We analyzed the statistical significance of evaluation items a) to g). A Tukey test with a 5% significance level indicated no significant difference between case A and case B for evaluation items (a) and (e) and between case B and case C for evaluation item (d), and indicated a significant difference for the other times.

Most of the subjects mentioned that case B was better than case A for touching the rotating object, because this task was simple, it was easier to move the index finger, and the time needed to set up the finger pad display was smaller. These observations indicate that the finger pad force display contributes to enhancing the sense of reality in a virtual environment, but it generates a feeling of irritability in the subjects. This is a trade-off problem.

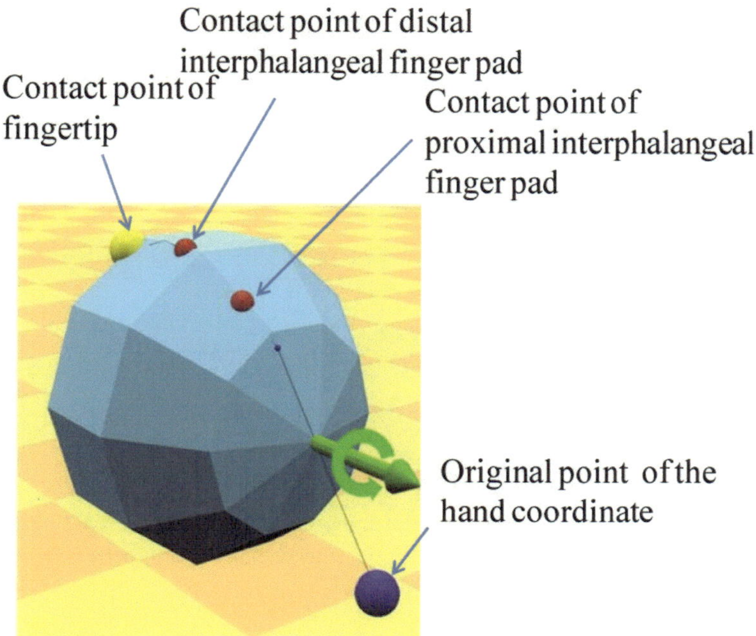

Fig. 12. Rotating polyhedron with 50 plates

6. Conclusions

We have presented a hand haptic interface for use in a virtual reality environment such as virtual palpation training. The hand haptic interface consists of novel finger pad force display devices and a 3D fingertip haptic interface (HIRO II). The developed finger pad force display device is driven by a flat-type brushless DC motor and can be attached at two points on the finger pads. The design concept of the hand haptic interface, the control method of the finger pad force display device, and results of an experimental evaluation have been presented. Questionnaire results revealed that the developed hand haptic interface is useful in virtual object manipulation. For a simple task such as touching a rotating polyhedron with an index finger, our evaluation showed that the use of HIRO II with one finger pad force display is better than that with two finger pad force displays to achieve both enhancement of reality in a virtual environment and reduction of discomfort when handling the haptic interface.

7. Acknowledgments

The present study was supported in part by the Strategic Information and Communications R&D Promotion Program (SCOPE) of the Ministry of Internal Affairs and Communications and by a Grant-in-Aid for Scientific Research from JSPS, Japan ((B) No. 19360190).

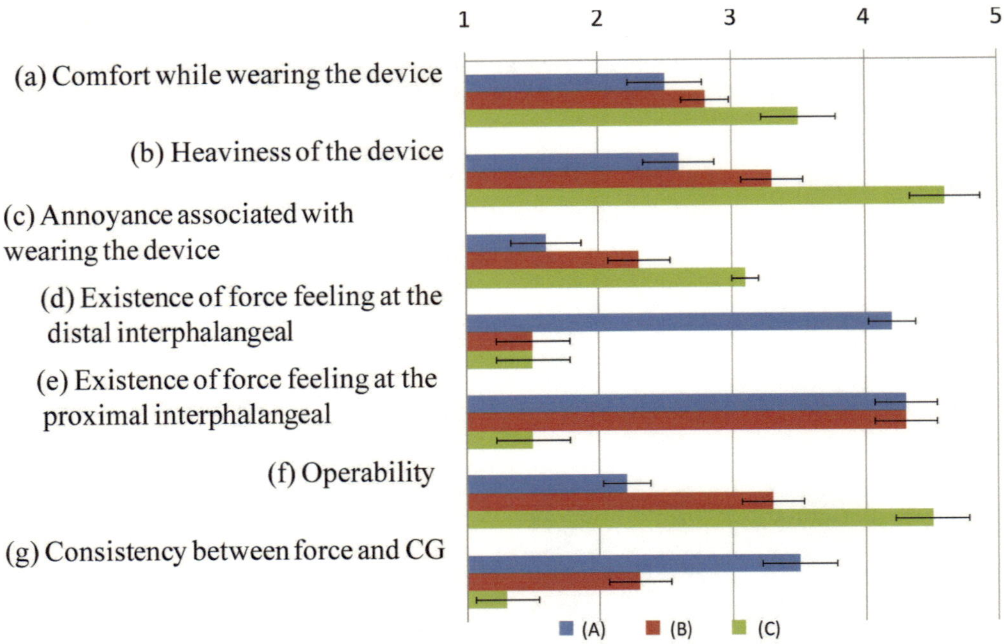

(A) Case A: with wearing device on distal and proximal interphalangeal finger pads

(B) Case B: with wearing device on proximal interphalangeal finger pad

(C) Case C: without wearing device

Fig. 13. Questionnaire results of rotating polyhedron object handling in three cases; Case A is HIRO II with finger pad force display devices on distal and proximal interphalangeal finger pads, Case B is HIRO II with finger pad force display devices on proximal interphalangeal finger pad, and Case C is only HIRO II.

8. References

[1] H. Kawasaki and T. Hayashi, Force Feedback Glove For Manipulation of Virtual Objects, Jour. of Robotics and Mechatronics, Vol. 5, No. 1, pp. 79-84, 1993.

[2] M. Bouzit, G. Burdea, G. Popescu, and R. Boian, The Rutgers Master II - New Design Force-Feedback Glove, IEEE/ASME Trans. on Mechatronics, Vol. 7, No. 2, pp. 256-263, 2002.

[3] T. Koyama, K. Takemura, and T. Maeno, Development of Ultrasonic Clutch for Multi-Fingered Exoskeleton Haptic Device using Passive Force feedback for Dexterous Teleoperation, Proc. of IROS 2003, pp. 2229-2234, 2003.

[4] M. Fontana, D. Dettori, F. Salsedo, and M. Bergamasco, Mechanical Design of a Novel Hand Exoskeleton for Accurate Force Displaying, Proc. of ICRA2009, pp. 1074-1709, 2008.

[5] ImmersionCorporation:CyberForce, http://www.immersion.com/3d/products/cyber_force.php.

[6] G. Inaba and K. Fujita, A Pseudo-Force-Feedback Device by Fingertip Tightening for Multi-Finger Object Manipulation, Proc. of EuroHaptics 2006.
[7] Y. Ueda and T. Maeno, Development of a Mouse-Shaped Haptic Device with Multiple Finger Inputs, Proc. of IROS2004, pp. 2886-2891(2004).
[8] T. Yoshikawa and A. Nagara, Development and Control of Touch and Force Display Devices for Haptic Interface, Proc. of SYROCO'00, pp. 427-432, 2000.
[9] Y. Adachi, et al., Development of a Haptic Device for Multi Fingers by Macro-Micro Structure, Journal of the Robotics Society of Japan, Vol. 20, No. 7, pp. 725-733, 2002.
[10] S. Walairacht, M. Ishii, Y. Koike, and M. Sato, Two-Handed Multi-Fingers String-Based Haptic Interface Device, IEICE Trans. on Information and Systems, Vol. E84D, No. 3, pp. 365-373, 2001.
[11] M. Montoy, M. Oyarzabal, M. Ferre, A. Campos, and J. Barrio, MasterFinger: Multi-finger Haptic Interface for Collaborative Environment, Proc. of EuroHaptics 2008, pp. 411-419, 2008.
[12] H. Kawasaki and T. Mouri, Design and Control of Five-Fingered Haptic Interface Opposite to Human Hand, IEEE Transaction on Robotics, Vol. 23, No. 5, October, pp. 909-918, 2007.
[13] M. O. Alharabi, V. Daniulaitis, H. Kawasaki, and T. Hori, Medical Training Simulation for Palpation of Subsurface Tumor Using HIRO, Proc. WorldHaptics2005, Pisa, pp. 623-624, 2005.
[14] S. J. Lederman, Skin and Touch, Encyclopedia of Human Biology, Vol. 7, pp. 51-63, 1991.
[15] T. Endo, H. Kawasaki, T. Kanno and T. Mouri, Perception of the Force Direction and Skill Transfer by using Five-Fingered Haptic Interface, Proceedings of the 13th International Conference on Virtual Systems and Multimedia (VSMM'07), Brisbane, 2007
[16] T. Grieve, Y. Sun, J. M. Hollerbach, and S. A. Mascaro, 3-D Force Control on the Human Fingerpad Using a Magnetic Levitation Device for Fingernail Imaging Calibration, Proc. of 3rd Joint Eurohaptics Conference and Symposium on Haptic interfaces for Virtual Environment and Teleoperator System, pp. 411-416, 2009.
[17] K. Minamizawa, S. Fukamachi, H. Kajimoto, N. Kawakami, and S. Tachi, Wearable Haptic Display to Present Mass and internal Dynamics of Virtual Objects, TVRSJ, Vol. 13, No. 1, 2008.
[18] T. Aoki, H. Mitake, S. Hasegawa, and M. Sato, Wearable Haptic Device to Present Contact Sensation, Based on Cutaneous Sensation using Thin Wires, TVRSJ Vol. 14, No. 3, pp. 421-428, 2009.
[19] I. M. Koo, K. Jung, J. C. Koo, J. Nam, and Y. K. Lee, Development of Soft-Actuator Based Wearable Tactile Display, IEEE Trans. on Robotics, Vol. 24, No. 3, pp. 548-558, 2008.
[20] WEB of Exseal Corporation:
http://www.exseal.net/.

[21] H. Kawasaki and T. Komatsu, Mechanism Design of Anthropomorphic Robot: Gifu Hand I, Journal of Robotics and Mechatronics, Vol. 11, No. 4, pp. 269-273, 1999.

6

Face-Touch: An Emotional Facial Expression Technique of Avatar Based on Tactile Vibration in Virtual Reality Game

Ahmad Hoirul Basori, Abdullah Bade,
Mohd. Shahrizal Sunar and Daut Daman
Universiti Teknologi Malaysia, Universiti Malaysia Sabah
Malaysia

1. Introduction

Nowadays we can see that avatar expresses their emotional expressions only by using facial animation, gesture and voice. In this research, we present an avatar in a creative way that can attract user attention while they play game and use computer. Human representations like virtual Assistants or virtual humans in the virtual environment are considered as an interface that can make harmonious relationships between human and computer (Wang et al., 2005). A virtual representation of human is expected to become a guideline in the virtual environment. Therefore, studies of artificial psychology have been conducted to create an interface that is able to comply with human satisfaction while they interact with computer. Considering this situation, we can see numerous applications such as Second Life or games like the SIMS manipulates a lot of avatars in their systems. If we look at this matter carefully, the substance of presence, which is the ultimate features for virtual environment application, requires further improvement. The root of the problem is caused by several factors such as: the complexity of virtual human model itself, emotional expression (Wang et al., 2005), or incoherent animation reaction(Rojas et al., 2008). Usually emotion is expressed by facial expression, voice intonation or even using hand gesture.
Researchers in image processing and computer graphics fields tried to combine facial expression with voice expression and hand gesture. Recently Haptics or 'sense of touch' attracted attention to be explored - especially Haptics that is related to emotional expression (Bailenson et al., 2007, Hashimoto and Kajimoto, 2008). In this study, our major concern is to grasp the ways to utilise haptic tactile vibration as an emotional expression of virtual human or avatar that can give the user more sensation during the interactions process. The procedure starts by mapping the human emotion colour diagram into several vibration frequencies. Considering this scenario, a group of frequencies are initiated as a magnetize stimulation to express particular emotional expression such as anger or happiness.

2. Literature review

Virtual environments are becoming more interesting and complex. Previous research like (Fabri et al., 1999) stated that non verbal communication in Collaborative Virtual

Environments (CVEs) can be conducted via face, gaze, gesture or even body posture. Now, researchers are making several improvising to human representation by means to increase the interaction and communication level between computer and human. (Wang et al., 2005) has created a virtual assistant that acts according to human emotion rules. He also mentions that there are two main problems with creating a virtual human: Construction of emotion and Generation of affection model. The avatar does not only represent human as physical representation, it also needs some believability context. According to (Rojas et al., 2006) the current avatars need to be improved due to believability setback. He proposed an individualisation method by putting personality, emotion and gender into the avatar. Other research such as (Zagalo and Torres, 2008) created additional features that can turn the avatar into unique character which improves the avatar capability to express their emotions through the involvement of touching process among two characters (Zagalo and Torres, 2008). Meanwhile ((Melo and Paiva, 2007) made some innovations in expressing the emotion of virtual character by putting aside body parts. They used element like light, shadow, composition and filter as tools for conveying the Character's emotion. The basic human emotions have been recognised and formatted into standard form. For example, the emotional facial expression can be detected from the eyes and lips of a human face (Ekman, 1982). Researchers like the following tried to recognise emotions from several ways such as: Colour(Farbenlehre, 1808-1810, Melo and Gratch, 2009, Nijdam, 2006, Sucontphunt et al., 2008), Haptic device(Bailenson et al., 2007, Salminen et al., 2008, Hashimoto and Kajimoto, 2008), Acoustic (Dai et al., 2009), Music (Shan et al., 2009), dance movement(Camurri et al., 2003).

2.1 Motivation and main contribution

The motivation of our study is inspired by haptic ability that can give different sensation compared to visual stimulation and acoustic stimulation. Haptic is widely used in games such as: to give impact sensation on racing game or fighting game. As we mentioned before, most users are much not affected by facial expression of avatar because they can only see the changes of avatar facial expression and various tone of voice intonation. These situations motivate us to make a bridge between avatar and user (human) when they communicating each other. See our illustration on Fig.1. Fig.1 explains that user able to see the car crashes with street barrier however, they cannot immerse with strong feeling about the situation. Therefore researcher tends to add vibration to the haptic device to give strong impression of impact. We simulate the same concept by conducting surveys to our students. As we expect, most of them did not impressed with the avatar expression through visual and acoustic. So, we proposed a unique avatar equipped with various range of haptic vibrations to creates better emotional expression than the previous avatar. The avatar has the following features:

Visual and brain sense: Provide user a sensation of facial expression based on Facial action coding system, data glove and brain activity.

Touch Sense: Stimulating user by creating particular tactile vibration frequency which is connected and synchronized with facial expression of avatar.

The problem on expressing emotion for avatar using vibration is less explored because previous researcher almost concentrates producing facial expression. To our concern, we then mapped the vibration values into emotion appearance followed by synchronizing the avatar facial expression as well as synchronizing the external control system like hand glove and mind controller. In other words we tried to create link between facial appearance and tactile vibration. What we proposed here is straightforward and can be reproduced by using cheap and commercial joystick.

Fig. 1. Tactile and visual representation on demonstrating car crash (collision) with barrier

3. Face-Touch construction method

Face-Touch is an integration of three human senses: visual, acoustic and haptic. Haptic is requiring preprocessing to classify the magnitude force into suitable range for emotion expression. The classification is based on colour theory which is mapping the human emotion characteristic into RGB mode, and then RGB property will be converted into magnitude force of vibration. The complete diagram of Face-Touch system can be viewed as Fig.2.

3.1 Calculating constant factor (f)

In term of color, emotion has been divided into certain color since long time ago. According to (Nijdam, 2006, Farbenlehre, 1808-1810) human emotion can be divided into areas of color like shown in Fig.3.

Shirley Willett (Nijdam, 2006), creates a circle that represent emotion classification into certain color. The outside circle gives positive impression, the inner circle represents six basic emotions and the centre of circle reassembles all negative impression. See Fig.4 for the detail.

Sucontphunt et.al(2008) propose 3D solid cube technique to convertemotion into color representation (Sucontphunt et al., 2008). It's said that Red equivalent to Anger, green symbolize Happiness and Blue is sadness. Other researcher like Melo also support that certain color, saturation and brightness are carry some emotion information like joy or sadness feeling (Melo & Gratch, 2009). In this pre-processing stage, several parameters

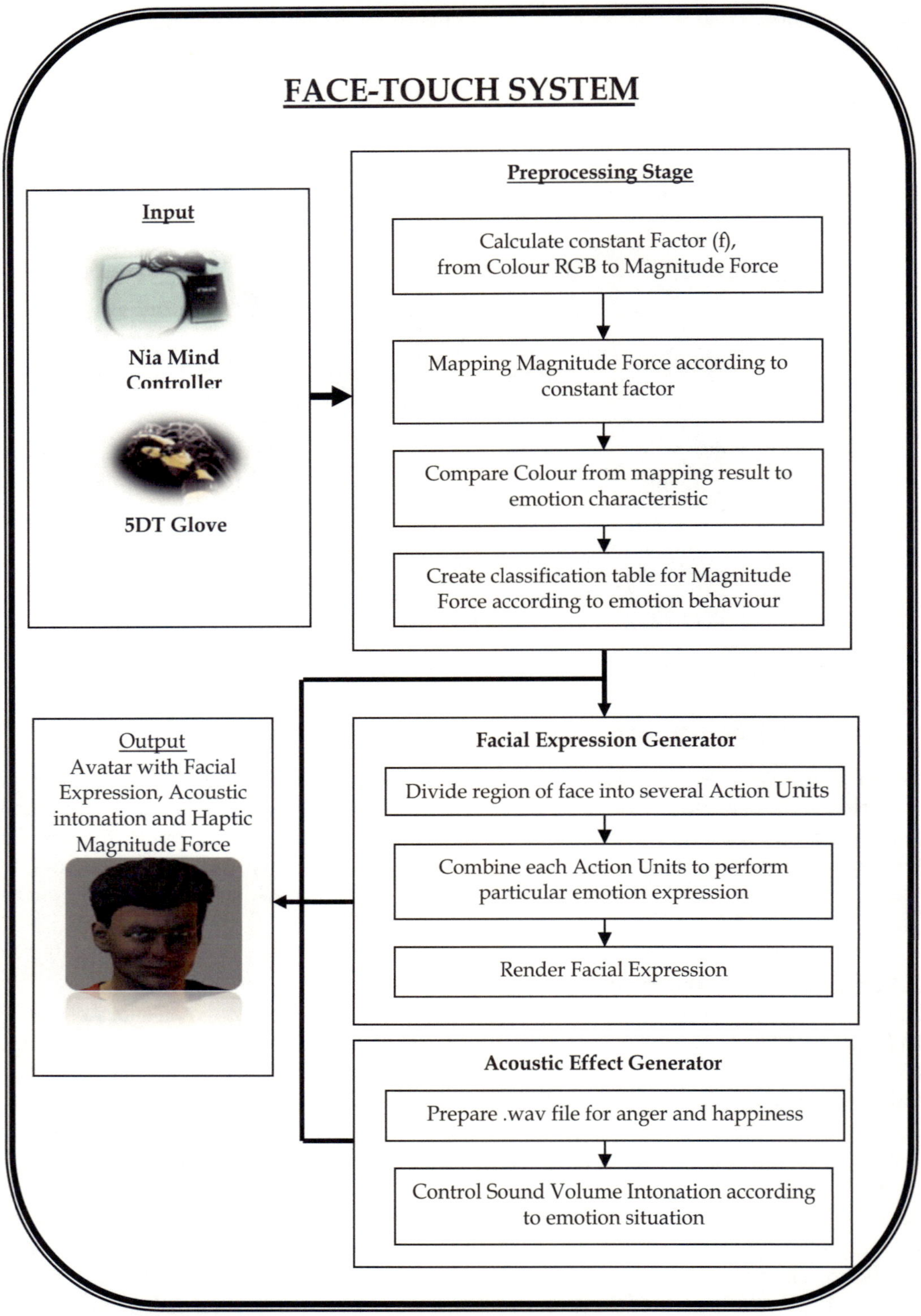

Fig. 2. Face-Touch System Architecture

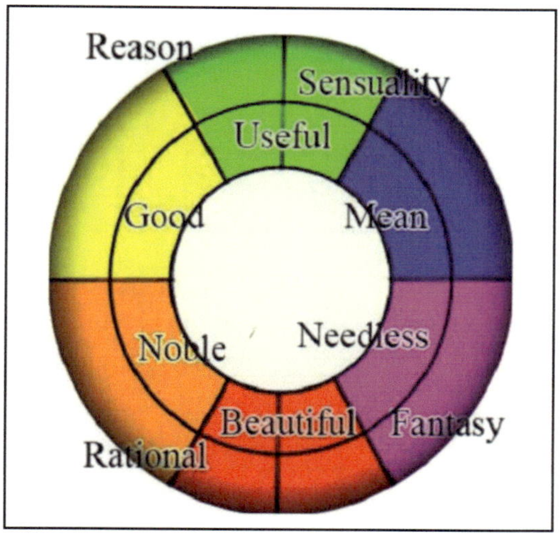

Fig. 3. Emotion-Color Classification(Farbenlehre, 1808-1810)

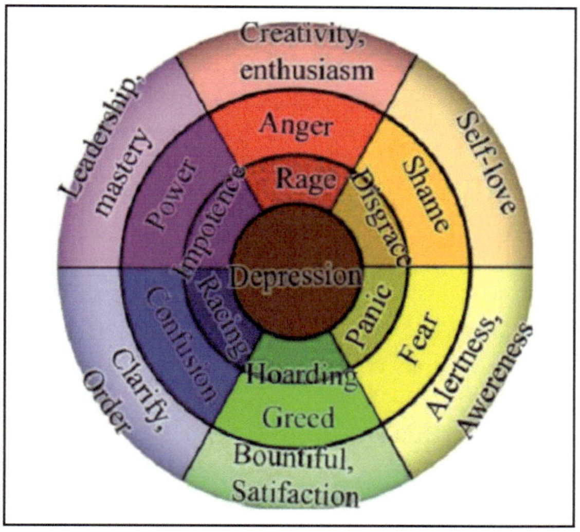

Fig. 4. Shirley Willett -Color mapping (Nijdam, 2006)

according to the previous researches are being considered when we convert the emotional expressions into vibration. Anger has the characteristics of negative and high, red and raise. This parameter is interpreted into high and long vibration. Happiness in the Circumplex model is represented as positive value but not high. In colour theory, happiness is being suggested as pink color, and also increases the heart rate. To justify our mapping process, the happiness mode is converted into low to medium vibration with short and long duration. High vibration in long duration usually will cause people uncomfortable feeling, anger, frustration and other negative feelings, while low vibration can cause relaxation, joy and even enthusiasm emotion (Griffin, 1990, Hashimoto & Kajimoto, 2008). The detail of emotion characteristic is described in Fig.5.

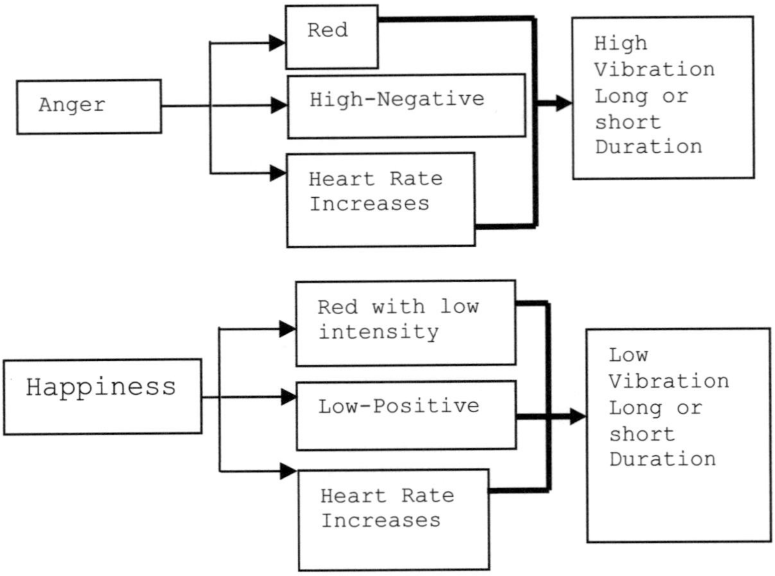

Fig. 5. Flow for mapping color to vibration

In this paper, the emotion value is transferred through red colour. Why red colour?, this is due to red colour has strong and close relationship with anger and happiness (Farbenlehre, 1808-1810, Melo & Gratch, 2009, Nijdam, 2006, Sucontphunt et al., 2008). In this case, each vibration from 0-1000 Hz will be segmented into red colour intensity from 0-255. In implementation, Hue of the colour is set to 0 and R (red) value hold in 255. The G (green) and B(blue) will run from 0-255 and colour will change from full red then degrade until close to white. From conducted experiment, we found out that the RGB values (1-255) can easily be mapped into given magnitude force (1-1000 Hz) as suggested by vibration frequency classification(Griffin, 1990, Hashimoto & Kajimoto, 2008). To plot the given vibration frequency into emotion we used the following equation where the constant factor (f) denoted for colour and vibration. When intensity of red colour need to be changed, this mean RGB value of red hold in 255, hue=0, saturation move from 100% to 0%, and RGB value green and blue move from 0-255.

$$f = \frac{V_{\max}}{RGB_{\max}} \tag{1}$$

$$Vcolour_i = f\ x \left| RGBblue - 255 \right|)_i \tag{2}$$

Note:
f = variable for constant
Vmax = maximum value for vibration (10000)
RGBmax = maximum RGB value for Red, Green or Blue Colour (255)

$$f = \frac{10000}{255} = 39.21$$

This conversion process can be illustrated like in Fig.6, where vibration magnitude power increase or decrease linearly according to colour intensity.

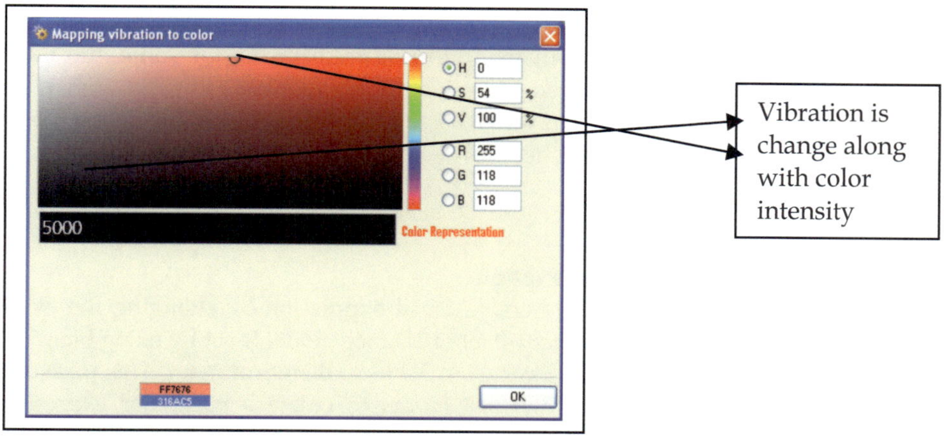

Fig. 6. Flow for mapping colour to vibration

3.2 Mapping magnitude force and create classification table

Based on mathematics formula in (1) and (2), the classification of emotion according to magnitude force can be described like in Table 1.

RGB Colour Value						Magnitude Force Based on Colour intensity ($Vcolour_i = f \times R_i$)	Colour	Emotion value
H	S	V	R	G	B			
0	8	100	255	234	234	823.536	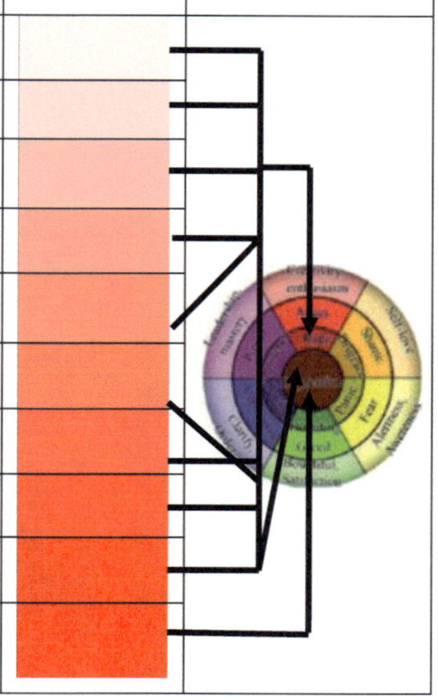	
0	16	100	255	215	215	1568.64		
0	26	100	255	190	190	2549.04		
0	37	100	255	162	162	3647.088		
0	46	100	255	137	137	4672.488		
0	57	100	255	110	110	5686.32		
0	66	100	255	85	85	6666.72		
0	77	100	255	60	60	7647.12		
0	86	100	255	35	35	8627.52		
0	100	100	255	0	0	10000.08		

Table 1. Conversion from emotion into vibration power based on colour theory

Data on Table 1 have proved that emotion can be mapped into magnitude force value by transferring the emotion in colour perception into magnitude force. High magnitude force more than 5000 is potential for carrying the 'anger' emotion and magnitude force lower than 5000 similar to emotion 'happiness' characteristic. This finding is very useful for foundation of synchronizing vibration tactile with facial expression and acoustic. By applying the formula, we successfully create the conversion procedure from colour value into vibration power. We found as well that the speed of motor rumble increases linearly with vibration frequency. For example, anger emotion will trigger high speed which is proving the initial experiment conducted by (Bailenson et al., 2007).

4. Facial expression generator

4.1 Facial region partition and combination

In this paper, FACS is also adopted to create facial expression by changing the eyebrow, eyes and the lips. The position of the face offset in 3D face model is set by using blender. The face offset of 3D face is created in x, y, z vertex in 3D virtual environment. This pose offset is implanted to FACS elements in our 3D face model to create a particular expression of emotion. The detailed illustration FACS in this research system can be described in detail in Fig.7. AU1 and AU2 are responsible to manage the eye brow area and generate wrinkle in forehead in order to show particular emotions. By creating an emotional expression, this means combining each action units (AU). This combination also shows the strength of certain emotion expressions. For example, in this study, an anger emotion is created by AU1+AU2. However, when the level of anger gets higher it also involves AU4. Furthermore, emotional expression is also expressed by the changing of the lips shape as well.

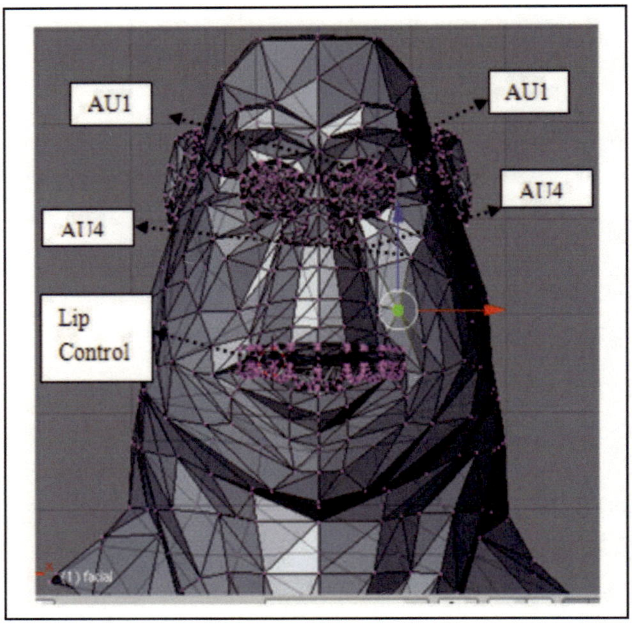

Fig. 7. 3D humanoid model

According to FACS, certain facial avatar expressions such as anger and happiness were created. In this study, we focus only on two emotions which are anger and happiness. According to the previous emotion theories, anger is usually related to something that makes people feel uncomfortable. This kind of feeling is represented in many ways such as: high speed of movements, high temperature, red colour, high heart rate, high blood pressure and high vibration frequency (Hashimoto & Kajimoto, 2008, Russell, 1980, Rollin McCraty, 1993, Rollin McCraty, 1995, Nijdam, 2006, Nasoz et al., 2003, Bailenson et al., 2007, Basori et al., 2008). The facial expression computation is based on calculation of each Auction point as shown in Fig.7. Every action units is responsible to the strength and type of the emotion that has been expressed. In this study, the expression of anger is more complex than happiness. The complexity will increase accordingly when the level of anger rises up.

$$AngryE= AU1+AU2+(Level*AU4)$$

AU1 and AU2 are used to control the expres-sion near to the eyebrow, while AU4 and Level generates the wrinkle and rise up the area near the nose. On the other hand, expression of happiness has different characteristics. It involves 4 controls to express the emotional condition.

$$HappyE= AU1+AU2+(Level*AU4)+(Level*lip\ Control)$$

AU1 and AU1 hold the role to manage the eyebrow muscle and together with AU4 to perform expression of happiness. Lip control manages lip movement while emotion is being generated. All elements work together to perform a happy appearance while Level is used as power control that determines how strong the expression of happiness needs to be made. Fig.8 shows happiness in facial expression of avatar in various level of happiness.

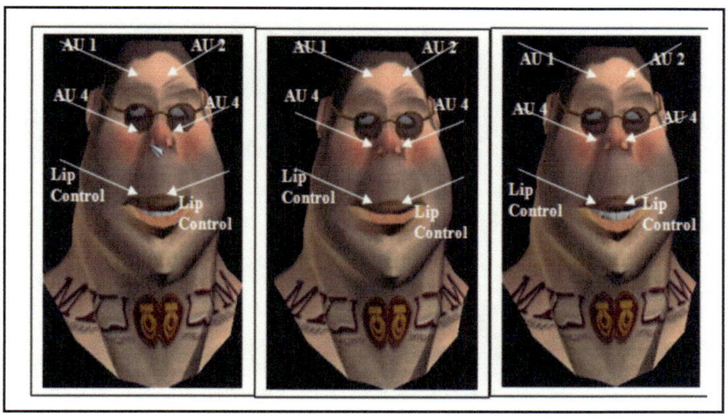

Fig. 8. Happiness mode of 3D humanoid model based on combination of Action Units(AUs)

4.2 Avatar rendering and controller synchronization

This study is run on PC Pentium 4 with RAM 2 GB and VGA card 512 MB. Three haptic devices that are commonly used by people such as XBOX windows controller and Wii mote were connected. In order to obtain the optimum functionality of haptic devices, the grip of haptic device is designed according to (Griffin, 1990). Fig.9 and Fig.10 illustrates the user interaction with avatar. Avatar model that we used is modified model of dr.headBunsen from OgreGameEngine (OGRE, 2010). Fig.9 and Fig.10 shows the interaction between user and avatar through haptic glove and mind controller to interact with 3D facial expression of humanoid model and Xbox joystick to feel touch sensation. 3D humanoid model will create emotional expression based on user current behaviour. Like in Fig. 9, user tried to show their anger by creating fist in his hand and it change facial expression of 3D humanoid model. The face of avatar will be changed to anger and the strength of anger is depending on glove and mind controller intensity. The magnitude force of this Xbox joystick is controlled by level of avatar emotion.

Fig. 9. User Interaction with avatar through XBOX windows controller and 5DT Data Glove-1

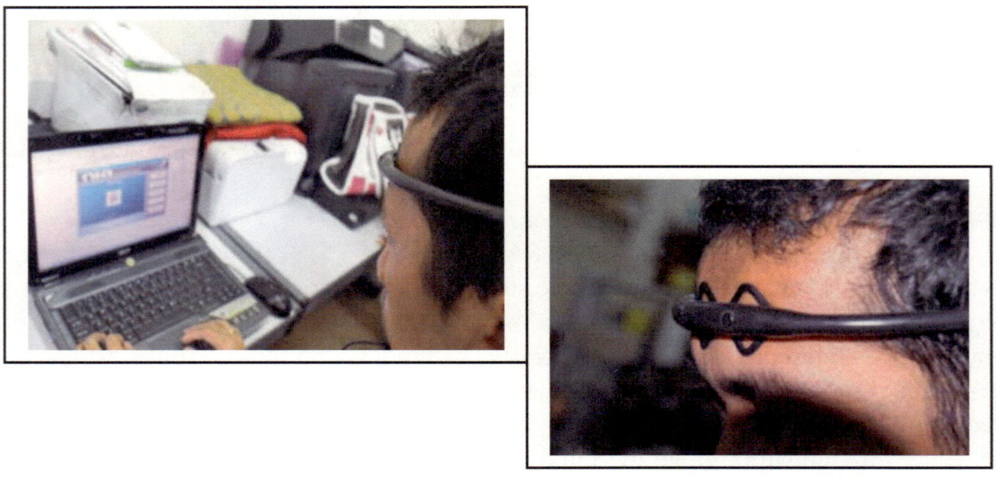

Fig. 10. User Interaction using NIA Mindcontroller

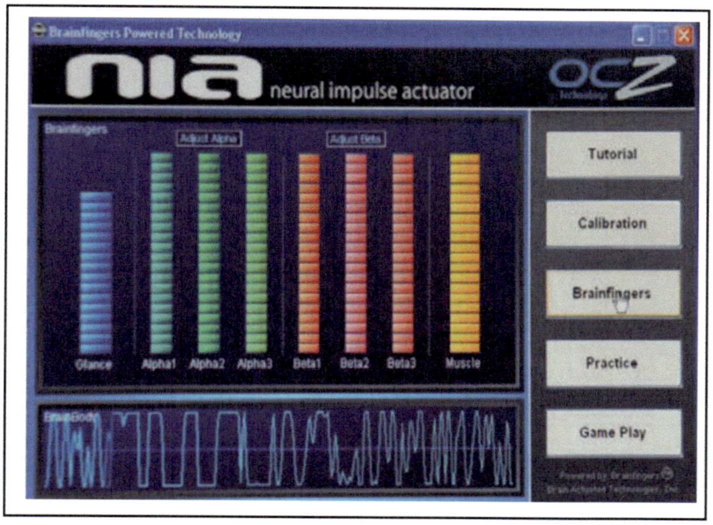

Fig. 11. Brain activity of users during interaction

Activity of user brain is illustrated in Fig.11.Glance sensor record eye muscle movement, Muscle responsible for forehead muscle activity, Alpha 1,2,3 and Beta 1,2,3 tell us what's going on brain activity. This neural impulse actuator is used to record the user activity during their interaction with the avatar. The result of this recording is utilized as benchmark parameter to user testing. The constructed avatar is produced based on facial expressions and mapping vibration parameters. Facial expressions of the avatar are used as the supporting visual element to the vibration frequency. Therefore, when the avatar is smiling, user will able to see their facial expressions and feel their emotions through haptic vibration. Nia mind controller will control the facial expression of avatar or it can be said as that nia mind controller is synchronized with facial expression of avatar. The anger emotion will increase brain activity and it will change the facial appearance as well.

The joystick that used in this experiment has two motor rumbles which are able to produce certain magnitude force and frequency. This subsection will proved empirically the effect of magnitude vibration power of joystick. Joystick has magnitude force, this force able to produce certain rotational speed or velocity (V) and acceleration (A). Based on (Griffin, 1990) there are several physic formulas that very important to this experiment .

$$\text{Velocity (V)} = 2\pi f = \frac{2\pi}{T} \tag{3}$$

$$\begin{aligned}\text{Acceleration (A)} &= (V)2\,X \\ &= (2\pi f)2\,X\end{aligned} \tag{4}$$

$$\text{r.m.s Magnitude } (\grave{A}) = \frac{A}{\sqrt{2}} \tag{5}$$

Note:
f = frequency of joystick
T = duration or period
X=displacement, the distance from rotational source

V in SI unit is symbolized with metre per second (ms-1)
A in SI unit is symbolized with metre per second (ms-2)
À is r.m.s Magnitude in symbolized with root mean square metre per second (ms-2r.m.s)
In the conducted experiment the velocity, acceleration and frequency of joystick in several magnitudes can be seen in Table 2, 3, 4.

Magnitude Force	Velocity (ms-1)									
	0.1s	0.2s	0.3s	0.4s	0.5s	0.6s	0.7s	0.8s	0.9s	1s
10000	63.333	73.333	63.333	62.292	60.833	60.972	60.833	59.792	58.889	58.750
9000	61.667	57.917	63.333	61.042	58.500	58.889	58.214	58.021	57.222	56.583
8000	53.333	56.667	58.056	57.500	55.833	56.250	55.119	56.875	53.241	53.167
7000	40.000	47.917	52.500	52.917	52.667	53.611	52.619	53.125	51.204	49.583
6000	32.500	39.167	40.833	39.792	40.333	40.417	39.643	40.417	39.907	38.750
5000	21.667	25.417	28.333	32.708	36.500	36.528	36.310	37.396	36.667	36.833
4000	0.000	13.333	20.278	21.250	24.667	25.139	27.381	30.521	31.574	30.333
3000	0.000	0.000	0.000	0.000	0.000	6.667	8.333	9.063	10.278	9.667
2000	0.000	0.000	0.000	0.000	0.000	0.000	0.000	0.000	0.000	0.000
1000	0.000	0.000	0.000	0.000	0.000	0.000	0.000	0.000	0.000	0.000

Table 2. Velocity of joystick based on conducted experiment

The graph representation of this velocity of motor rumble joystick vibration can be viewed as Fig.12.

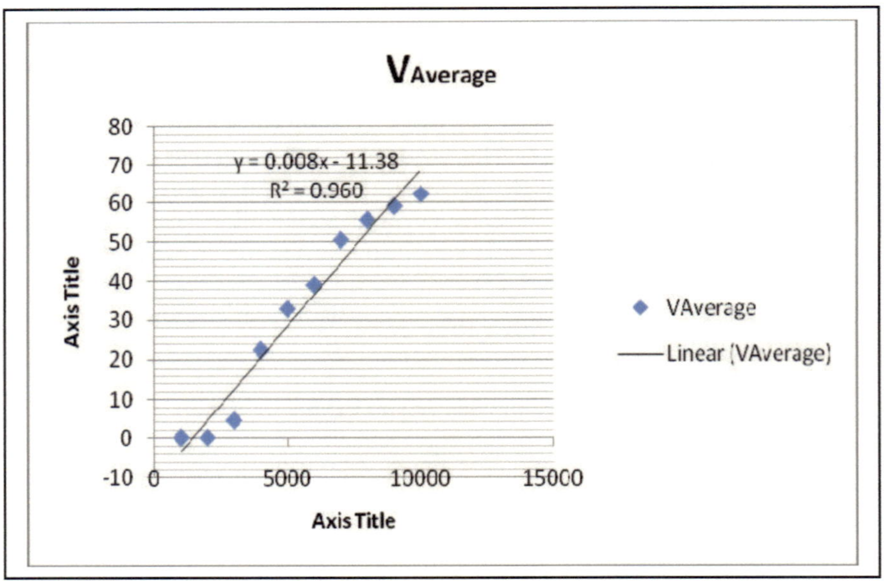

Fig. 12. Velocity of motor rumble joystick

Fig 12 shows that highest magnitude force will cause peak velocity that increase rapidly along with the magnitude force power level.

Magnitude Force\ Duration	Frequency(f) in Hz										
	f0.1	f0.2	f0.3	f0.4	f0.5	f0.6	f0.7	f0.8	f0.9	f0.10	f average
10000	31.67	36.67	31.67	31.15	30.42	30.49	30.42	29.90	29.44	29.38	28.18
9000	30.83	28.96	31.67	30.52	29.25	29.44	29.11	29.01	28.61	28.29	26.74
8000	26.67	28.33	29.03	28.75	27.92	28.13	27.56	28.44	26.62	26.58	25.14
7000	20.00	23.96	26.25	26.46	26.33	26.81	26.31	26.56	25.60	24.79	22.83
6000	16.25	19.58	20.42	19.90	20.17	20.21	19.82	20.21	19.95	19.38	17.65
5000	10.83	12.71	14.17	16.35	18.25	18.26	18.15	18.70	18.33	18.42	14.58
4000	0.00	6.67	10.14	10.63	12.33	12.57	13.69	15.26	15.79	15.17	9.71
3000	0.00	0.00	0.00	0.00	0.00	3.33	4.17	4.53	5.14	4.83	1.72
2000	0.00	0.00	0.00	0.00	0.00	0.00	0.00	0.00	0.00	0.00	0.00
1000	0.00	0.00	0.00	0.00	0.00	0.00	0.00	0.00	0.00	0.00	0.00

Table 3. Frequency of joystick based on conducted experiment

The frequency of joystick also has been measured as seen in Table 3, with graph representation like show in Fig.13 faverage ca be viewed as linear function with f(x)=0.003x-5.358.

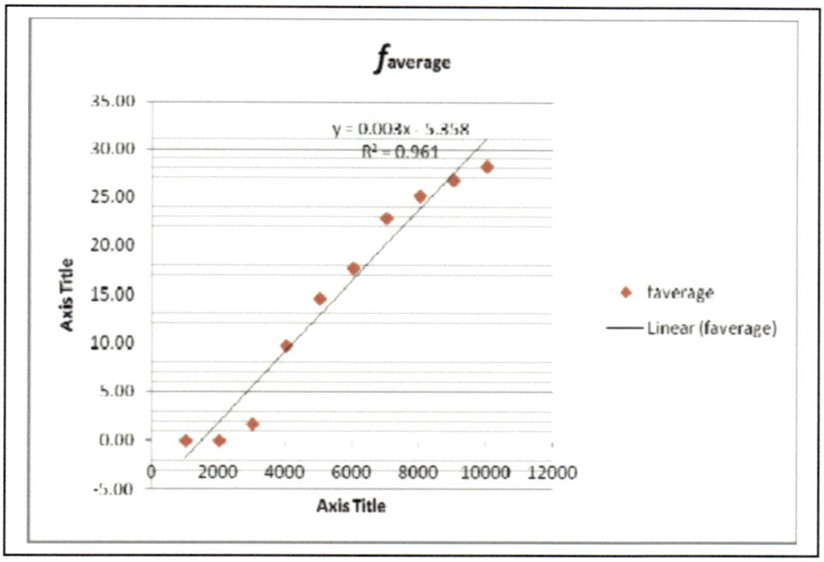

Fig. 13. Average frequency of joystick motor rumble

The acceleration of joystick has shown promising result like the further discussion. This acceleration is able to show particular emotion information. In Fig.14 Aaverage has function y=0.01x-3.217 while r.m.sA has function y=0.01x-2.275. Table 4 has listed all acceleration result for various magnitude force and duration.

These results have been compared with previous result to prove the similarity behaviour of vibration effect and emotion classification. Derived from Griffin (1990) there are numerous previous researchers have described the implication of vibration to human. (Oborne & Clarke, 1974) have classified the vibration based on mean magnitude and semantic scales:

Magnitude Force	Acceleration (ms-2)											
	$A_{0.1}$	$A_{0.2}$	$A_{0.3}$	$A_{0.4}$	$A_{0.5}$	$A_{0.6}$	$A_{0.7}$	$A_{0.8}$	$A_{0.9}$	$A_{1.0}$	Aaverage	r.m.s A
10000	12.03	16.13	12.03	11.64	11.10	11.15	11.10	10.73	10.40	10.35	11.67	8.25
9000	11.41	10.06	12.03	11.18	10.27	10.40	10.17	10.10	9.82	9.61	10.50	7.43
8000	8.53	9.63	10.11	9.92	9.35	9.49	9.11	9.70	8.50	8.48	9.28	6.57
7000	4.80	6.89	8.27	8.40	8.32	8.62	8.31	8.47	7.87	7.38	7.73	5.47
6000	3.17	4.60	5.00	4.75	4.88	4.90	4.71	4.90	4.78	4.50	4.62	3.27
5000	1.41	1.94	2.41	3.21	4.00	4.00	3.96	4.20	4.03	4.07	3.32	2.35
4000	0.00	0.53	1.23	1.35	1.83	1.90	2.25	2.79	2.99	2.76	1.76	1.25
3000	0.00	0.00	0.00	0.00	0.00	0.13	0.21	0.25	0.32	0.28	0.12	0.08
2000	0.00	0.00	0.00	0.00	0.00	0.00	0.00	0.00	0.00	0.00	0.00	0.00
1000	0.00	0.00	0.00	0.00	0.00	0.00	0.00	0.00	0.00	0.00	0.00	0.00

Table 4. Acceleration of joystick based on conducted experiment

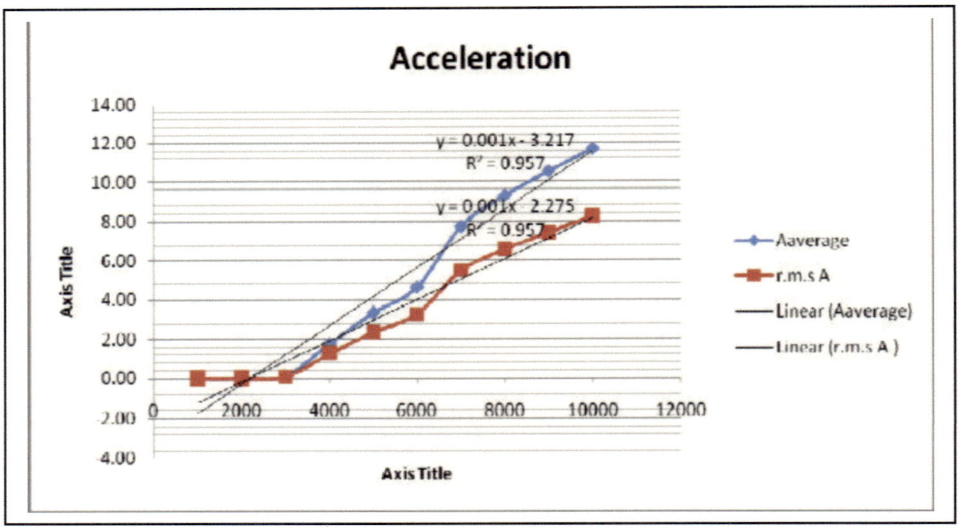

Fig. 14. Joystick acceleration

- Mean magnitude (ms-2r.m.s): >2.3 →very uncomfortable
- Mean magnitude (ms-2r.m.s): 1.2-2.3→Uncomfortable
- Mean magnitude (ms-2r.m.s): 0.5-1.2 } Fairly Uncomfortable / Fairly Comfortable
- Mean magnitude (ms-2r.m.s): 0.23-0.5 →Comfortable
- Mean magnitude (ms-2r.m.s):<0.23 →Very Comfortable

According to result on Table 2 until 4, we have found an interesting finding that magnitude force above 5000 potential to represent anger emotion and below 5000 has characteristic for happy emotion due to magnitude force more than 5000.

4.4 Acoustic effect generator

Acoustic is an element of human sense that affect human through ear. The sound effect will stimulate user from two aspects: "Emotional word" and intonation volume level that heard from sound. In term of sound environment the angle of sound position also determine user reaction for example surround system has better effect to user rather than normal stereo sound. The intonation of acoustic is consist of some parameters that related to emotion condition such as pitch, loudness and length (Banziger & Scherer, 2005).

In the paper, acoustic will focus on loudness level to increase the realism and synchronization process with facial expression through windows API by changing the master volume according to emotion that occur Face-Touch. The sound effect is based on emotion word that has been chosen before sound file is created. For example anger.wav that consists of word "Annoy" or for happy "Nice" or "Good".

5. Result analysis and discussion

Two analyses on measuring the systems were conducted. These three steps are designed to investigate the emotional characteristics and how strong is the impression that has been given to user through facial expression of avatar and haptic-tactile. Besides, this research also aims to make a comparison with the previous existing avatar like Alfred and Xface.

5.1 Analysis on emotion based on vibration characteristic

Earliest, we have evaluated our technique by measuring the speed and wave length based on joystick motor rumble characteristic. According to Microsoft MSDN one cycle is equivalent into full one wavelength. During our experiment, we have found that speed of motor rumble increase while vibration is rising up. Angry emotion will trigger high speed is similar with the result of previous research that conducted by (Bailenson et al., 2007). We are able to produce certain data to measure the characteristic of joystick from their period and speed. The vibration will follows the color intensity transformation as well like shown in Table 5 and Fig.15. The Fig.15 also shows that speed will rise linearly with the growth of vibration.

Magnitude Force based on color intensity	VAverage	faverage	Aaverage	r.m.s A
10000.08	62.23611	28.18	11.67	8.25
8627.52	59.13879	26.74	10.50	7.43
7647.12	55.60403	25.14	9.28	6.57
6666.72	50.61422	22.83	7.73	5.47
5686.32	39.17586	17.65	4.62	3.27
4672.488	32.83581	14.58	3.32	2.35
3647.088	22.44759	9.71	1.76	1.25
2549.04	4.400694	1.72	0.12	0.08
1568.64	0	0.00	0.00	0.00
823.536	0	0.00	0.00	0.00

Table 5. Data relationship between Velocity,Acceleration,r.m.s Acceleration, frequency and Magnitude force

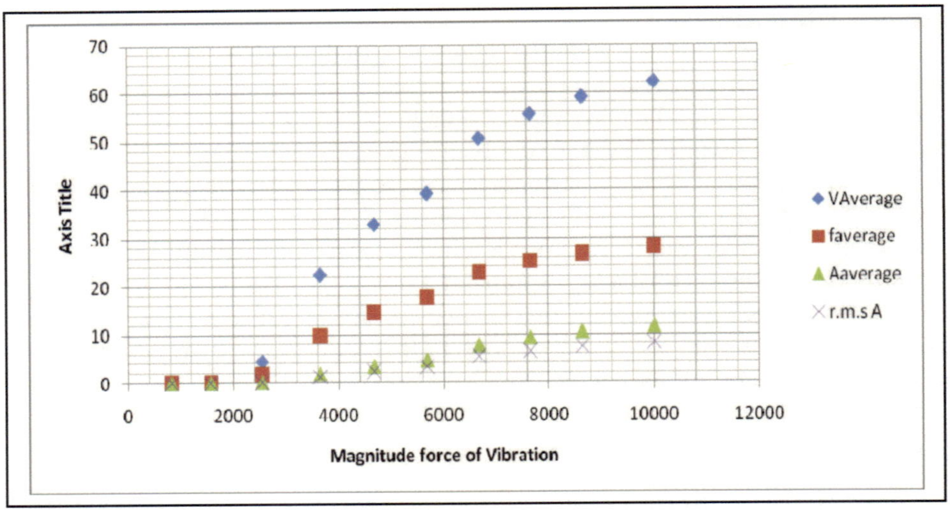

Fig. 15. Vaverage, faverage, average and vibration to colour relationship

5.2 Statistical analysis on usability testing

This study has recruited: 8 male and 13 female that comes from undergraduate, Post graduate student (Master and PhD). Each student is required to make interactive interaction with system and after interaction student will be asked to answer some questions in questionnaire. Question will base on data profile, emotion background, experience emotion, interaction, and benchmarking. This study conducts two user interactions. First, user will interact with Face-Touch system, and secondly, user will interact with Alfred and Xface (Balcı et al., 2007, Bee et al., 2009) system as our benchmarking system. Alfred initiated by Nikolaus, Bee in (Nikolaus et al., 2009) from university of Augsburg. While Xface was initiated by Balci from University of Trento (Balcı et al., 2007).

All participants are trained to interact with this study's application and Alfred for a certain period of time. During the interaction, user activity and expression through figure were gathered. Participants need to conduct interaction with this study's system and Alfred system for a certain period of time. The interactions with Alfred system and Xface system is to investigate whether users satisfied or not with current emotion expression (facial expression). See Fig.16A and Fig.16B for the task completion. This comparison has a goal to measure how realistic is the created avatar expression compares to Alfred system itself. In this section, statistic analyses have been computed to compare whether Alfred system or this study's system is more exciting for user.

In Fig.17, study's system obtains significant result. XFace able show emotion by facial expression and voice intonation while Alfred only capable by showing facial expression. This result is very interesting when user get more excited when they stimulated by combination of facial expression, voice intonation and magnitude fore vibration. Most of users are feel something different when they were triggered by numerous vibration frequencies. Some of Participants feel relax in particular low vibration and feel inconvenient when shocked by high vibration. Fig.17 and Table 6 show user rating on recognizing and ranking emotion.

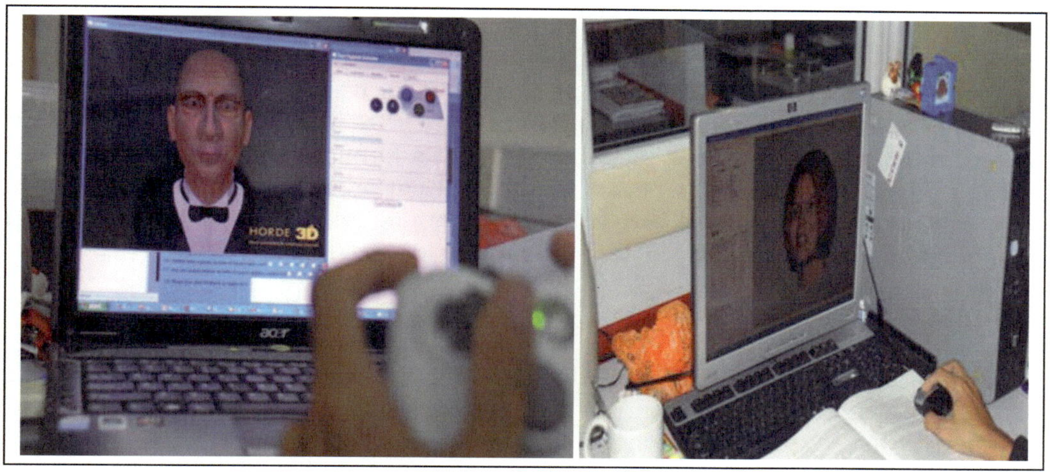

(a) (b)

Fig. 16. Task Completion by interacting with Alfred Sytems(A) and Xface(B)(Balcı et al., 2007, Bee et al., 2009)

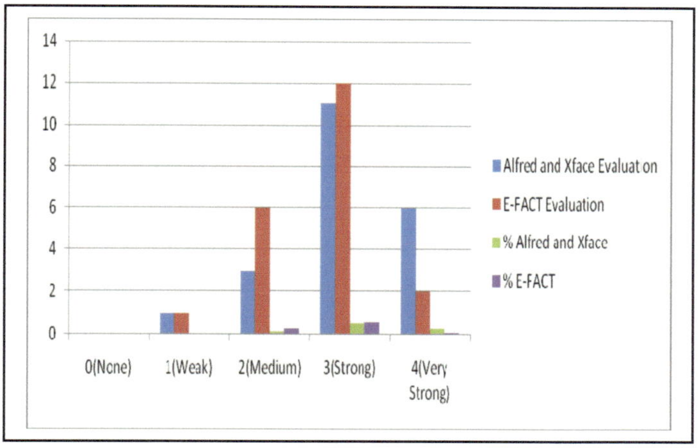

Fig. 17. Questioner Summary on usability user testing

Level of Emotion	Alfred and Xface Evaluation	Face-Touch Evaluation	% Alfred and Xface	% Face-Touch
0(None)	0	0	0%	0%
1(Weak)	1	1	5%	5%
2(Medium)	3	6	14%	29%
3(Strong)	11	12	52%	57%
4(Very Strong)	6	2	29%	10%
Mean	4.2	4.2		
Variance	15.76	19.36		
STDev	4.438468204	4.91934955		

Table 6. User rating on recognizing and ranking emotion representation strength

From the graph that shown in Fig.17, the experiment give significant positive result which is able to drive avatar to give more realistic expression. All users have strong confidence rate on differentiate and recognizing emotion of users. From the user testing, we obtain 67% user give strong and very strong impression that our system gives stronger emotional expression than Alfred systems. 29 % user give medium values to our system compare to Alfred system. Finally, around 5% users said that our system provide a little impression than Alfred system. Furthermore, we have found an interesting finding that all users agree that high vibration of joystick equivalent to anger emotion

6. Conclusion

The aim of this research is to integrate three element of human sense (visual,acoustic and haptic) to increase the realism of virtual reality game. Our conducted experiments proved that user manages to have strong feeling and impression while they interact and communicate with Face-Touch. The study has proved that high magnitude force of haptic device like joystick capable to create emotional sensation which is classified by intensity of RGB colour. Furthermore, it is able to be synchronized with facial expression of 3D humanoid model as well. From user study, the feedback from user is very exciting while 67% user give strong and positive response to Face-Touch system. In addition, 15 users from 21 participant (71%) agree with classification of magnitude force into emotion representation, they said high magnitude force create similar sensation when they feel anger. While low magnitude force is more relaxing to them. This integration between facial expression, acoustic and magnitude force is believed to bring strong impression and believability to user in real world and even strengthen the interactivity and immersiveness of virtual reality or serious game it self.

7. References

BAILENSON, J. N., YEE, N., BRAVE, S., MERGET, D. & KOSLOW, D. (2007) Virtual interpersonal touch: expressing and recognizing emotions through haptic devices. Hum.-Comput. Interact., 22, 325-353.

BALCı, K., NOT, E., ZANCANARO, M. & PIANESI, F. (2007) Xface Open Source Project and SMIL-Agent Scripting Language for Creating and Animating Embodied Conversational Agents. MM'07, September 23–28, 2007. Augsburg, Bavaria, Germany, ACM.

BANZIGER, T. & SCHERER, K. R. (2005) The role of intonation in emotional expressions. International Journal of Speech Communication, 46 252–267, Elsevier.

BASORI, A. H., DAMAN, D., BADE, A., SUNAR, M. S. & SAARI, N. (2008) The feasibility of human haptic emotion as a feature to enhance interactivity and immersiveness on virtual reality game. Proceedings of The 7th ACM SIGGRAPH International Conference on Virtual-Reality Continuum and Its Applications in Industry. Singapore, ACM.

BEE, N., FALK, B. & ANDR, E. (2009) Simplified facial animation control utilizing novel input devices: a comparative study. Proceedings of the 13th international conference on Intelligent user interfaces. Sanibel Island, Florida, USA, ACM.

CAMURRI, A., LAGERL, I. & VOLPE, G. (2003) Recognizing emotion from dance movement: comparison of spectator recognition and automated techniques. Int. J. Hum.-Comput. Stud., 59, 213-225.

DAI, K., FELL, H. & MACAUSLAN, J. (2009) Comparing emotions using acoustics and human perceptual dimensions. Proceedings of the 27th international conference extended abstracts on Human factors in computing systems. Boston, MA, USA, ACM.

EKMAN, P. (1982) Emotion in the Human Face, Cambridge University Press.

FABRI, M., MOORE, D. J. & HOBBS, D. J. (1999) The Emotional Avatar: Non-verbal Communication Between Inhabitants of Collaborative Virtual Environments. Proceedings of the International Gesture Workshop on Gesture-Based Communication in Human-Computer Interaction. Springer-Verlag.

FARBENLEHRE, J. W. V. G. Z. (1808-1810) Sechste Abteilung: Sinnlich-sittliche Wirkung der Farbe.

GRIFFIN, M. J. (1990) Handbook of Human Vibration, Academic Press.

HASHIMOTO, Y. & KAJIMOTO, H. (2008) Emotional touch: a novel interface to display "emotional" tactile information to a palm. ACM SIGGRAPH 2008 new tech demos. Los Angeles, California, ACM.

MELO, C. & PAIVA, A. (2007) Expression of Emotions in Virtual Humans Using Lights, Shadows, Composition and Filters. Proceedings of the 2nd international conference on Affective Computing and Intelligent Interaction. Lisbon, Portugal, Springer-Verlag.

MELO, C. M. D. & GRATCH, J. (2009) The Effect of Color on Expression of Joy and Sadness in Virtual Humans. The International Conference on Affective Computing and Intelligent Interaction Amsterdam, Netherlands, IEEE.

NASOZ, F., ALVAREZ, K., LISETTI, C. L. & FINKELSTEIN, N. (2003) Emotion Recognition from Physiological Signals for Presence Technologies. International Journal of Cognition, Technology, and Work - Special Issue on Presence,Springer London, 6(1), 1-32.

NIJDAM, N. A. (2006) Mapping emotion to color. http://hmi.ewi.utwente.nl/verslagen/capita-selecta/CS-Nijdam-Niels.pdf, Human Media Interaction (HMI) , Department of Electrical Engineering, Mathematics and Computer Science, (EEMCS) at the University of Twente, Last Accessed date :09 September 2009.

NIKOLAUS, B., BERNHARD, F. & ELISABETH, A. (2009) Simplified facial animation control utilizing novel input devices: a comparative study. Proceedings of the 13th international conference on Intelligent user interfaces. Sanibel Island, Florida, USA, ACM.

OBORNE, D. J. & CLARKE, M. J. (1974) The determination of equal comfort zones for whole-body vibration. Ergonomics, 17, 769-782.

OGRE (2010) Open Source 3D Ggraphics Engine.

ROJAS, A. G., GUTIRREZ, M. & THALMANN, D. (2008) Simulation of individual spontaneous reactive behavior. Proceedings of the 7th international joint conference on Autonomous agents and multiagent systems - Volume 1. Estoril, Portugal, International Foundation for Autonomous Agents and Multiagent Systems.

ROJAS, A. G., VEXO, R. & THALMANN, D. (2006) Individualized reaction movements for virtual humans. Proceedings of the 4th international conference on Computer graphics and interactive techniques in Australasia and Southeast Asia. Kuala Lumpur, Malaysia, ACM.

ROLLIN MCCRATY, M. A., WILLIAM TILLER,GLEN REIN, AND ALAN D.WATKINS (1995) The Effects of Emotions on Short-Term Power Spectrum Analysis of Heart Rate Variability. The American Journal of Cardiology, 76, 1089-1093.

ROLLIN MCCRATY, M. A. G. R. (1993) ECG SPECTRA:The Measurement of Coherent and Incoherent Frequencies and their relationship to mental and emotional states. The International Society for Study of Subtle Energy and Energy Medicine. Monterey, California.

RUSSELL, J. A. (1980) A circumplex model of affect. Journal of Personality and Social Psychology. Journal of Personality and Social Psychology, 39, 1161-1178.

SHAN, M.-K., KUO, F.-F., CHIANG, M.-F. & LEE, S.-Y. (2009) Emotion-based music recommendation by affinity discovery from film music. Expert Syst. Appl., 36, 7666-7674.

SUCONTPHUNT, T., YUAN, X., LI, Q. & DENG, Z. (2008) A Novel Visualization System for Expressive Facial Motion Data

Exploration. IEEE Pacific Visualisation Symposium 2008. 4 - 7 March, Kyoto, Japan, IEEE.

WANG, Z., CHENG, N., FAN, Y., LIU, J. & ZHU, C. (2005) Construction of Virtual Assistant Based on Basic Emotions Theory Construction of Virtual Assistant Based on Basic Emotions Theory Springer Berlin / Heidelberg.

ZAGALO, N. & TORRES, A. (2008) Character emotion experience in virtual environments. Vis. Comput.Springer-Verlag, 24, 981-986.

7

VR Development with InTml

Pablo Figueroa
Universidad de los Andes
Colombia

1. Introduction

Controlling complexity is the essence of computer programming. Brian Kernighan

VR applications are very interesting pieces of technology, not only from the point of view of final users who are immersed in a compelling experience, but also to developers. VR applications are a real challenge in terms of development constraints: they gather information from users through several and possibly redundant input devices, they have to compute a simulation in the order of miliseconds, and they have to deliver output through several devices and modalities at interactive rates. In terms of APIs, VR applications are built on top of a wide variety of software technologies in order to accomplish their goals: from low level drivers that communicate with devices to specialized 3D render APIs, from sockets to real time geometrical algorithms, from XML readers to streaming technologies. Developers should also know about several fields related to computing such as networking, data mangling, simulation, computer graphics, haptics, and human factors. There are several toolkits, libraries, and frameworks that developers could use in this endeavor, so applications can benefit from previous solutions.

However, to this date, VR development is still a challenge. On top of the steepy learning curve of most VR development toolkits, final applications may be unstable, prone to errors, hard to customize to particular user needs and features, difficult to deploy, and technology dependent, among other concerns. Part of these issues are related to the inherent complexity of the technologies involved in development, where the lack of standards and the wide variety of providers make work harder. Part is also related to the inherent focus of a particular VR application, which usually concentrates resources in certain goals (i.e. a particular user study), while treating others as not as important (i.e. code reusability).

Common solutions in VR development are VR toolkits and APIs, which may offer standard solutions to certain problems. Although there are examples of mature tools in the field, some of these may be either too difficult, too limiting, or too low level for novices. Some researchers such as Trenholme & Smith (2008) have tried to use tools and techniques from the game industry, which by far exceeds the size and economic force of its VR ancestor. Most of the success of the game industry is due to the vast amount of resources dedicated to improve gamer's experience, but it is also important to notice the availability of powerful game engines which help developers to handle complexity. A game engine allows developers to create compelling results in a short time, by hiding complex parts of a solution under specialized APIs. However, some solutions, shortcuts, and workarounds in games are not adequate for VR, where simulation fidelity and device support are very important.

Our long term goal is to facilitate VR and Mixed Reality (MR) development, by dividing its complexity among several people with different roles. For this reason we created the Interaction Techniques Markup Language (InTml) and a set of tools around this concept. InTml allows us to divide concerns in two main categories, one directed to architectural design, and the other related to code; one high level abstraction, and the other low level implementation. InTml offers an abstraction for the description of VR applications, independent from a particular set of device drivers, VR toolkits, libraries, and programming languages; an abstraction powerful enough to describe a wide variety of applications in the VR domain. This could make VR applications more portable in the future, since their abstract description in InTml may be ported to several technologies. Finally, InTml makes easier to identify particular devices and interaction techniques in an application, so they can be replaced if it is important to port an application to a new hardware environment. We call this process *application retargeting*, and we hope that in the future it will be an important element of VR application maintenance and evolution.

This chapter is organized as follows: First, we present some introductory examples and several relevant aspects in InTml development. Next, our development process and variability factors are presented. Later we present more examples of use and relevant related work. Finally, we describe future work.

2. An introduction to InTml

An InTml application is basically a set of components connected between them. Such components are called filters, which may represent devices, content, or behavior in an application. There is a library of available filter classes, and it is possible to add new classes to the system. This system can be executed in several runtime implementations, based on generic programming languages. We show first an abstract example of an InTml application and later we describe the concept of a filter class. Then, we show how such applications are created and executed in our IDE. Finally, we present the InTml's abstract execution model and an example of an execution, which can be implemented in both a parallel or sequential fashion. In general, InTml hides from designers certain elements of complexity, which will be described in Section 3.1, so developers can use or improve technologies behind the scene.

2.1 An InTml application

Our first example is shown in Figure 1, an application that allows a user to move a virtual hand with a tracker and touch virtual objects. In this example, a device (*handTracker*) gives position and orientation information to an object (*handRepr*). The behavior filter *SelectByTouching* receives the actual *handRepr* and *scene* objects, and any changes in position or orientation from *handRepr*. Once a collision is detected the selected objects are passed to *Feedback*, which activates a white bounding box around such objects. At the end of each execution step, *console* will render all objects in the scene (both *handRepr* and objects inside *scene*).

An InTml application is composed of instances of filter classes, constants, and object holders. Constants can give initial values to selected input ports in the system, and object holders are used as an indirection mechanism. Filters can also be sent as events through the dataflow, which is shown as an output port with a special decoration (two examples are *handRepr* and *scene* in Figure 1). We also use a special decoration for an output device (i.e. *console*), in order to avoid line cluttering of connections from all objects to the output device.

As we have mentioned, object holders are an indirection mechanism inside InTml. They are placeholders that can hold any piece of content in an application, i.e. any filter that represents

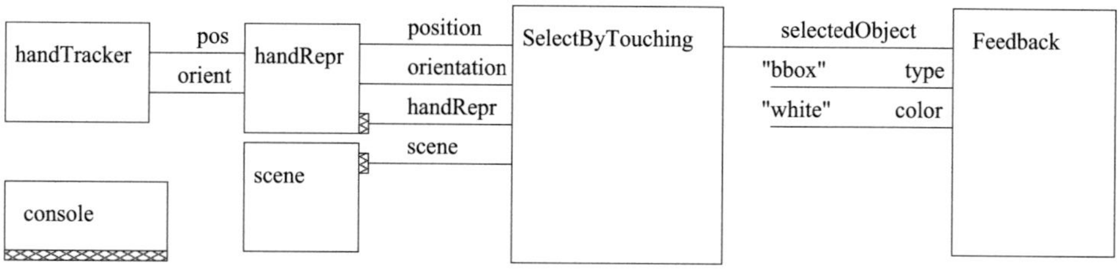

Fig. 1. Simple Application. Touching Objects with a Virtual Hand

content. They have an special input port that is used to change the contained object, and an output port that informs interested filters about changes in the contained object. Other filters can connect to and from an object holder, and those connections will be attached to the contained object during execution. Figure 2 shows examples of object holders inside a composite filter. *GoGoIT*, a composite filter that models the Go Go selection technique by Poupyrev et al. (1996), consists of three object holders (*cube, current, previous*) and three behaviors (*gogo, SelectByTouching, FeedbackOne*). *gogo* takes two configuration parameters (*K,D*) plus position and orientation of the user's head and hand in order to compute a virtual hand's position and orientation plus the visibility of a cube, that represents a user's real hand. *SelectByTouching* takes a computed virtual hand position, a virtual hand geometry, and a set of selectable objects in the scene in order to compute a selected object. Finally, *FeedbackOne* uses two object holders in order to modify color and bounding box of the current and previous selected objects. These two last object holders are a good example of the indirection mechanism: no matter which object is selected at any time, *FeedbackOne* can refer to it and send it events.

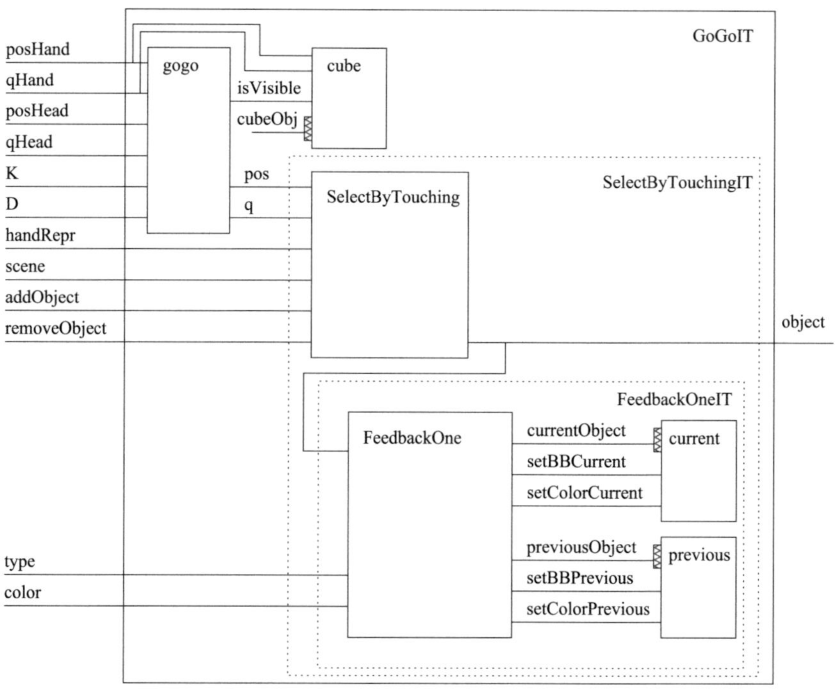

Fig. 2. GoGoIT, a Composite Filter

2.2 Filter classes

Each filter class defines a type of component that can be instantiated in an InTml application. A filter class' instance is a particular element in an application that receives the required information for its computation and produces certain information. Both required and produced information are modeled as a set of ports, which define the set of chunks of information the filter can receive or produce. Each port is defined in terms of a unique name and the type of information it may receive or produce. At any particular time, a filter can receive zero or more events in each one of its input ports, and produce zero or more events in its output ports.

Simple filter classes should encapsulate just one of the following elements: a piece of content, a behavior, or a device. A piece of content could be an interactive object in the 3D scene, a widget in the interface, a sound effect, or a haptic effect, with ports that allow developers to configure its initial state of modify such content during execution, i.e. activating an effect or changing an object's color. A behavior could be either the core algorithm for an interaction technique or an animation effect, with input ports for receiving the required information for its computation and output ports that carry the result of its computation. A device represents a physical device that users can see and manipulate, i.e. a joystick or a tracking system, with input ports for device configuration and output ports that capture and discriminate the information produced.

Instances of simple filters can be used to create applications or composite filters. A composite filter is a special type of filter class that can be used to hide complexity, and it can contain a set interconnected instances of simple or composite filters.

2.3 Abstract execution model

The abstract execution of an InTml application follows a pipeline model, with the following stages per execution frame:

- Data gathering. All data from input devices are gathered during a certain period of time. All events gathered during that period are considered simultaneous.
- Data propagation. Gathered information is propagated through the dataflow. All filters compute their output data from events in their input ports. Filters that represent content accumulate changes without affecting the object's state. This is to assure that any read operation over content will read a consistent state during an execution frame.
- Object holder's execution. If required, object holders change their contained objects first. After, they propagate received events to their contained filters.
- Changes in content. All content filters collect input events, compute their new state, and propagate changes through their output ports. Those changes will be received by interested filters in the coming frame of execution.

The computation of a filter, which occurs inside the data propagation stage or inside the changes in content stage, is divided in three main stages:

- Data gathering. All information generated in a certain time interval is collected. This stage is considered a preprocessing stage, in which filters select and manipulate the information they have received, in order to prepare for the next stage.
- Processing. In this stage a filter executes, given the collected input information and its internal state. Output information is generated, but not propagated
- Output propagation. Output information is propagated to all interested filters.

This model allows the parallel execution of filters, if the required computational resources are available, as we will show in Section 2.6.

2.4 Design and execution of InTml applications

By means of our IDE, an application is created by instantiating the appropriate filter classes. Filters may come from the predefined libraries of classes, organized by the three main categories: objects, devices, and behaviors. Developers can also add their own libraries of filter classes, if necessary, by creating the abstract description of each filter class (name, input and output ports). Figure 3 shows the application view the InTml IDE, that allows designers to load new libraries, create new filter instances, constants, filter holders[1], or links between filters. Figure 4 shows the library editor that allows the definition of new filter classes, by means of the specification of its input and output ports. This editor also allows code generation for each filter class in each one of the runtime environments[2].

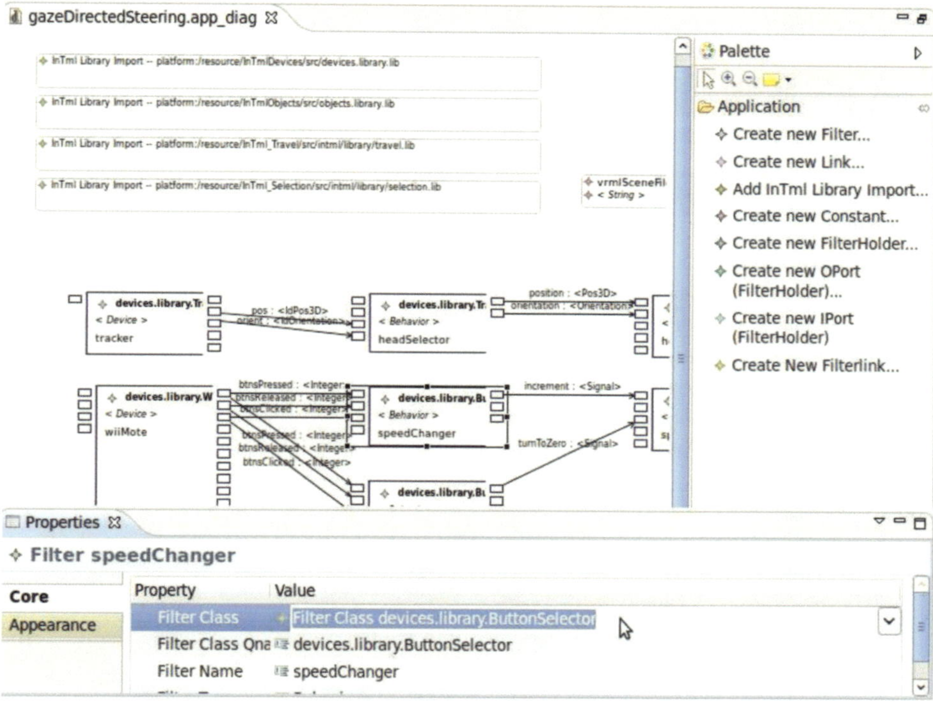

Fig. 3. Application View in the InTml IDE.

Applications can be run inside the IDE with the common method in eclipse, by the `Run As...` wizard.

The library of filter classes has been designed with reusability in mind, from a subset of interaction techniques presented in Bowman et al. (2004). However, this requires to rethink applications to an order that maximizes reuse. For example, Figure 5 shows a version of the application in Figure 1, with maximum reuse and extra functionality in mind. The *tracker*

[1]Object holders are called Filter holders in this interface, although they can only hold filters that represent objects. The creation of a filter holder involves the definition of its input and output ports. The IDE does not support yet composite filters.

[2]Currently, there are independent runtimes in C++, Java, and Actionscript.

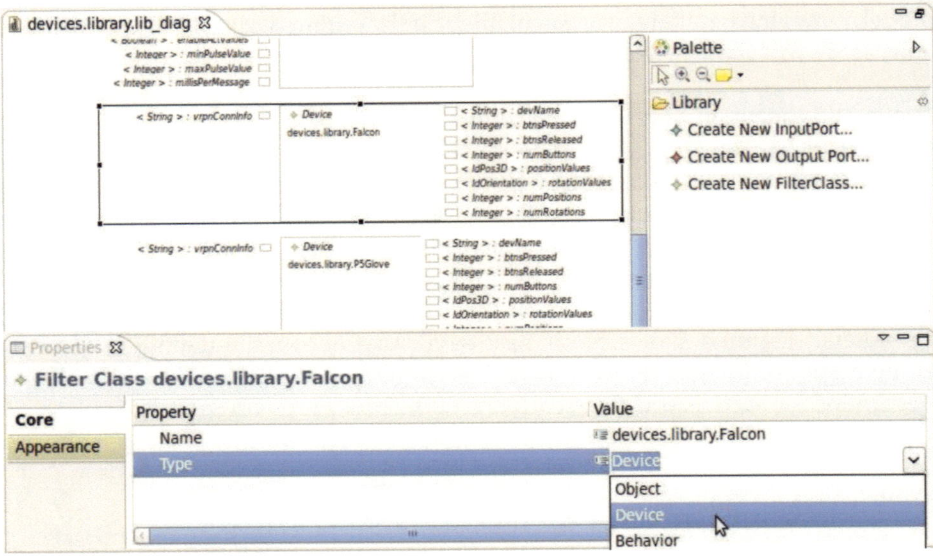

Fig. 4. Library View in the InTml IDE.

device receives a configuration string and outputs streams of positions and orientations, from all tracker elements it may have. The *handSelector* and *headSelector* filters separate from these streams the trackers with ids 0 and 1, and values from those devices can be transformed (i.e. moved, rotated, or scales) at *handOffset* and *headOffset*. The output of these two filters transform a *virtualHand* object and the system's *camera*. The *scene* filter loads and separates objects from an input file, and some of them are identified for selection at *objectsForSelection*. Finally, *collision* receives the *virtualHand* and the objects for selection and outputs objects that are collided by the virtual hand, which are visually enhanced by *feedback*. This diagram may be reduced to the one in Figure 1, by encapsulating *tracker*, *handSelector*, and *handOffset* into a composite filter, by eliminating the filters involved in camera movement, and by making explicit the *console* filter.

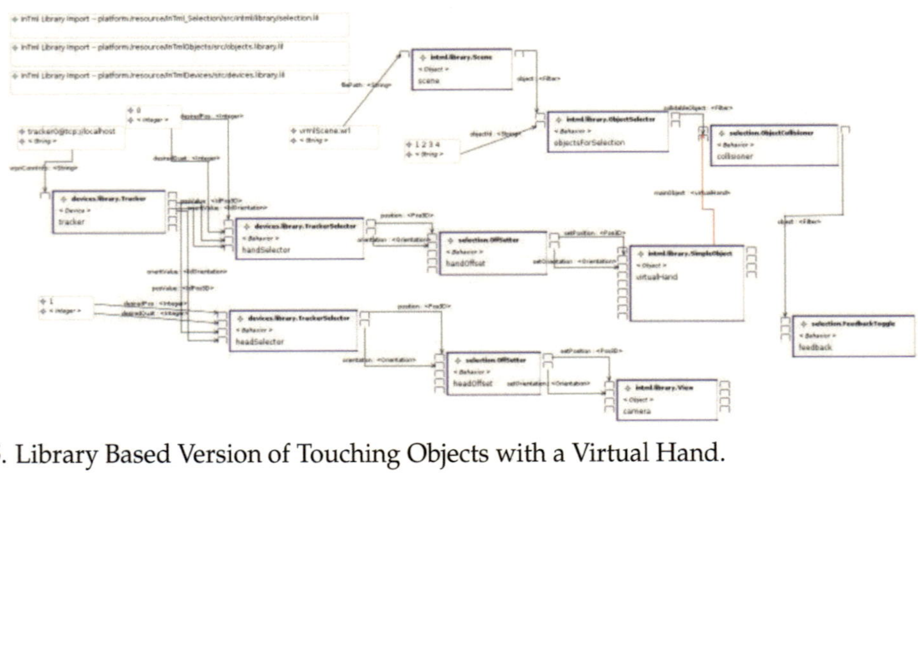

Fig. 5. Library Based Version of Touching Objects with a Virtual Hand.

2.5 IDE development

Our current IDE is based in the concepts of Model Driven Architecture by Stahl & Veolter (2006) and Software Product Lines by Clements & Northrop (2002); and it uses technologies such as The Eclipse Foundation (2007)'s IDE for the basic but extendable environment, EMF and GMF as frameworks inside eclipse for the visual programming environment and the openArchitectureWare.org (2008)'s oAW for code generation in Java, ActionScript, and C++.
This IDE has been developed as follows: first, an eCore[3] model of InTml is developed. Such model includes model constraints that help designers to identify errors during development. Then, graphic elements, graphic tools, and interface code are defined for the core model, as it is required by GMF. Based on this output, oAW's templates and constraints are defined in order to generate code for the targeted platforms. It is interesting to notice that both GMF and oAW provide mechanisms for constraint description, which provide a better interface and error feedback to designers. A side effect of this last development is a change in the final XML format for an InTml application: Initially we had defined our own format and DTD. With this final development, we have to use the XML format generated by GMF. This is a minor issue, since the visual programming environment provides a much better experience to designers than our previous XML editor.
During development we have performed two usability tests, the first one with VR developers and the second with non-programmers. In the first test we showed our IDE to 4 students with previous experience in VR development. Subjects received a short introduction to the IDE, see how a small example was developed, and were asked to answer some questions regarding the interface. Those comments were used in order to produce and improved version. In the second experiment 26 graduate students in an extension course of our Arts Department received training in InTml, and produced two designs in which they could optionally use our IDE. Finally, they were asked to fill a questionnaire about InTml's ease of learning, IDE's feedback, restrictions, consistency, and functionality. After 9 hours of exposure, they found InTml easy to learn, although some problems in understanding the execution model were detected. We believe this is due to the lack of experience they had with the actual application in execution, since they were required to design an application, not to execute it. In terms of the IDE they found issues with feedback, which are part of further changes to the environment.

2.6 An example of InTml's operational semantics

We have developed in the Z formal notation by Spivey (1992) a language and platform independent description of the InTml model. We describe in such a notation the concept of a filter, how filters can be composed of filters that hide complexity, how filters process information at any time step, how information gets propagated thoughout a dataflow of filters, and controlled ways to change the dataflow at runtime. The details of the formal description are mentioned in Figueroa et al. (2004). Although this description requires a good understanding of Z as a formal language and in consequence it may not be suited for general communication of the InTml capabilities, it is very precise and programming–language neutral. In particular, it has been used as blueprints for both C++ and Java implementations. Here we show with an example the main features that such a model gives to our VR applications. In Figueroa (2008) it is possible to find this description plus some motivations for this model.

[3]An eCore model is a UML class model with limited syntax.

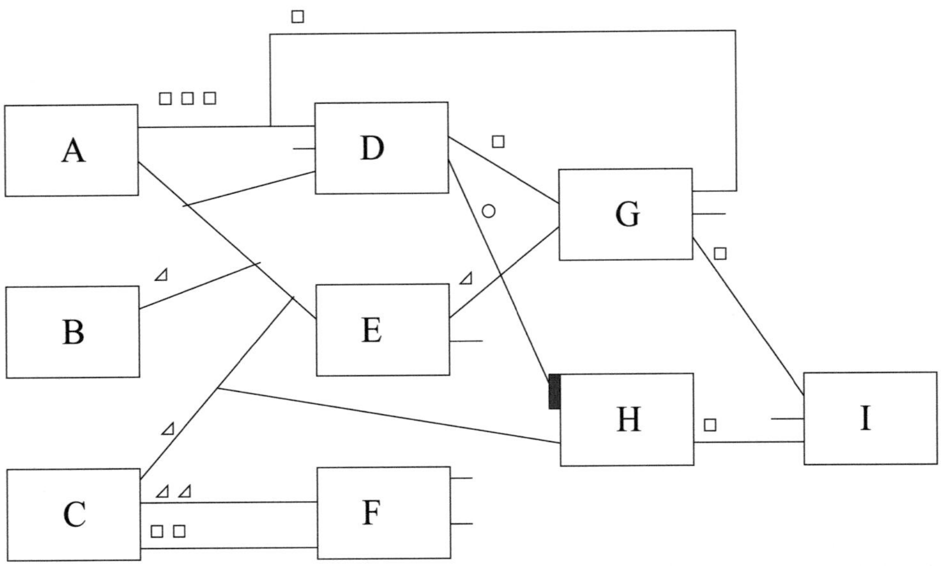

Fig. 6. A Time Step in an InTml Application. By convention, events are propagated from left to right.

Figure 6 shows an example of a the state of an InTml application in a particular time step, in which we consider **H** an object holder, **E** and **F** two content objects. This example shows the following features of an InTml application during execution:

- A filter can have several input and output ports, which may or may not be connected to other filters. In this way, filters can be reused in different scenarios without common restrictions imposed by standard function calls, which parameters are always mandatory.
- Different filter types such as devices, interactive content, and behavior are first class citizens of this description. Appart from the details already described in the execution of object holders and content objects, all filters seem equal from the design point of view.
- A time step defines a lapse of time in which all events from input devices are considered simultaneous. If **A**, **B**, and **C** are devices, all events they generate during such a small lapse of time will be processed together, no matter the particular generation rates from each device. In this example, **A** has generated three events in one of its output ports, **B** just one, and **C** outputs five events in total.
- Cycles are allowed in the description of an application, but they are broken for the execution of a time step. In the case of this example, the cycle **DGD** is broken and treated in a special way, i.e. delaying events from **G** to **D** to the next time step.
- Filters execute at most once in a time step, and the information they produce is considered simultaneous. A topological sort can be used in order to find a sequential execution order, i.e. **ADBCEGHFI** in the example. Such an order could be paralelized in the subsets [{**A,B,C**},{**D,E,F**},{**G,H**},{**I**}], without any effect on the inputs and outputs of each filter. In this regard, InTml guarantees a consistent execution no matter the number of execution threads.
- An object holder has a special input port that allows to replace the contained object (i.e. the connection from **D** to **H** will provide objects to be contained in **H**). Events received in other

ports are propagated to the contained object (i.e. events from **C** to **H**), and events generated from the contained object are propagated to registered filters (i.e. events from **H** to **I**).

- Since content objects can be related in structures that are not evident from the InTml dataflow (i.e. in a scene graph), which may require rule checking and change validation, and since content objects can be queried by several filters in the dataflow, all changes in objects are queued until the end of a time step. For example, **E**, **F**, and the object inside **H** could be parts of the same animated avatar, which have to fulfill certain rules and restrictions in its movements. Again in our example, this means that although all filters will execute at most once in a time step, output events from **E** and **H** will be delayed one step[4]. and the entire dataflow will require two frames of execution in order to execute each filter at least once.

3. Development process

Our development process is depicted in Figure 7. We divide tasks between two roles: a designer and a developer. A designer is a novice or non programmer that is interested in developing novel applications based on a set of predefined filters. A developer is a programmer that knows how to create novel filters and novel applications, or it could also be a support asset for a designer that requires to implement novel filter classes. We show here how we used this process from a designer's point of view for a family of applications described at Figueroa et al. (2005), a matching test that shows three objects and three copies of such objects, to be executed in four VR hardware setups.

Identify application goals We identify the set of use cases that the application has to fulfill: In this example it could be to select an object, move an object to the position and orientation of its copy, remove matched objects, define an initial state for objects, and save chronology of interesting events.

Describe application requirements in InTml documents For this stage we define a dataflow that fulfills all goals. We have found that it is more readable for designers to make one dataflow per goal, with cross references between them. Each dataflow is a subset of the entire application, and it is called a Task View. We do not show here the task views for this application, but examples of Task Views can be seen in Section 4.1.

Are current libraries enough? Members of this family of applications were consecutively developed. The first application of this family was developed from scratch, so there was no library at that time and all filters were application dependant. From this version on, each new application adapted existing filters in order to make them more reusable, or created new ones when necessary. In this case, the entire set of tasks for developers were performed as part of this step.

Check correctness in InTml documents Basic checking of InTml documents can be automatically done by tools: types and names of ports in instanced filters, type correspondence in port connections, or validity of filter classes, among other things. We have developed some tools in order to identify initial problems.

Execute/Test InTml application Once filter classes are implemented by developers, designers can run their design and test its usability. In our case we tested our prototypes with users from our staff, in order to identify improvements in their user interfaces.

[4] This example is not interested in the output of F, which is also delayed

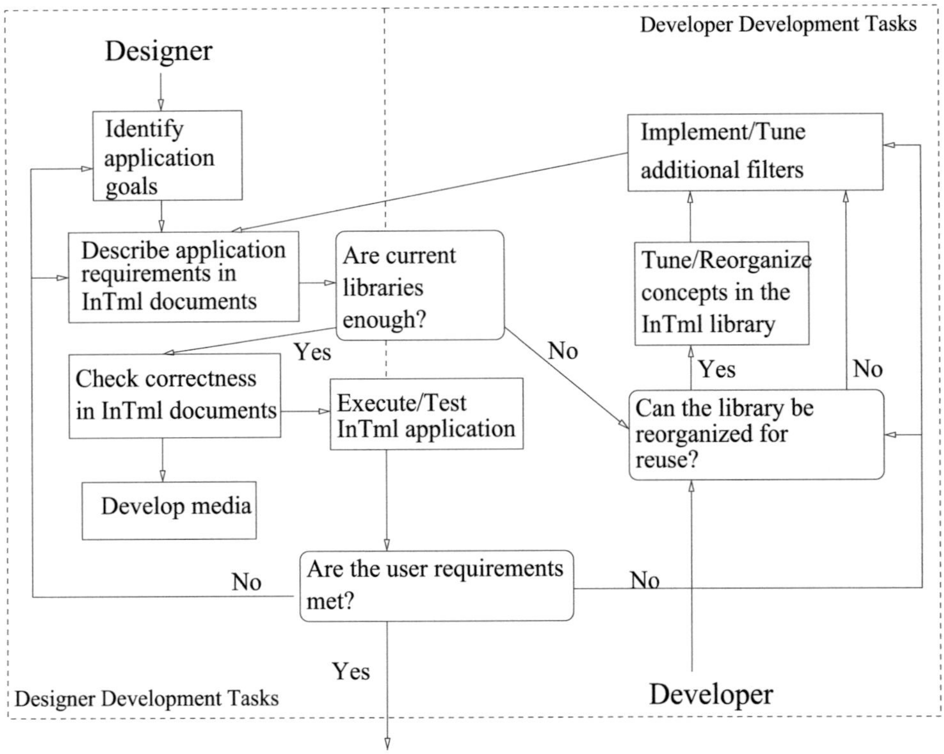

Fig. 7. InTml–Based Development Process

Develop media If required, specific application media should be developed in this step. Since it is possible to use basic models as surrogates in initial stages of development, it is possible to delay this task until the end, or even make this task in parallel. In the case of our example, 3D objects were obtained from public repositories.

Are the user requirements met? Once usability tests are performed, it is possible to identify improvements. Here such improvements are defined in terms of new goals, which are input for the new cycle in the development process.

3.1 Variability in application families

Variability is what makes different a set of applications with the same functionality but in different hardware setups. Variability's description in novel applications is very complex, due to the big variety of user types, devices, interaction techniques, visualization aids, frameworks, and libraries that may be used. We decided to ease development of non–programmers by dividing the variability spectrum in issues at the level of InTml language and issues at the level of the InTml implementation. An InTml family of applications consists of the following elements:

- A common set of basic types. Basic types in InTml are the equivalent of basic types in common programming languages, such as int or float. They have to be instantiated to available types in a particular InTml implementation.
- A library of filter types. Filter classes are reuse units. Such classes can use qualifiers in order to group them, in a similar way as packages can group Java classes.

- Applications. As we have seen, an InTml application is a set of interconnected instances of filter classes, constants and object holders. An application is divided in tasks, a subset of the application's dataflow. Each application can copy and redefine tasks from other applications in the family.

These elements allow us to address the following types of variability among applications in the same family:

- Devices. Each input and output device is represented by a filter in InTml, which may be instantiated or replaced in an application as desired.
- User types. Support for several user types is represented as different applications in the family, which may share common tasks.
- Interaction techniques. Developers can (and should) change the interaction techniques of a particular application depending on the type of user and devices in use. Such a change consists in the replacement of devices, behavior, or content related to a particular technique from one application to another. This replacement is feasible because filters clearly separate interaction techniques from the rest of the application.

Although also important, the following variation points in a MR application family are hidden from the InTml designer, and should be implemented one level below by an experienced programmer:

- Levels of detail and performance. A particular content could be shown at different levels of detail, depending on the capabilities of the available hardware. In the same way, a particular behavior could be adapted to the particular computational power of the underlying hardware.
- Context awareness. Devices could adapt their behavior to environmental factors, such as light conditions.
- Runtime adaptation. Several InTml applications can be combined in just one executable, which may switch between implementations depending on external factors such as user types.
- Particular APIs and frameworks. InTml can be implemented on top of a wide variety of APIs and frameworks, depending on the desired functionality at the high level and how convenient is to reuse a particular piece of software. A programmer should take into consideration reuse tradeoffs and integrate new elements when feasible.

This separation of variation points allows non–programmers to define by themselves their own prototypes, without special considerations about the InTml implementation. It is up to programmers at the InTml's implementation level to exercise low level variations.

4. Examples

We show now examples of how application families can be designed by highlighting three main concepts: The design of an application in terms of Task Views, the variability of a task among several applications in a family, and the basic software support for a prototype of a MR platform. The examples below show only the most important elements, which should be complemented as shown in Section 2.4[5].

[5]The InTml IDE does not support yet Task Views, so examples are shown in the abstract style.

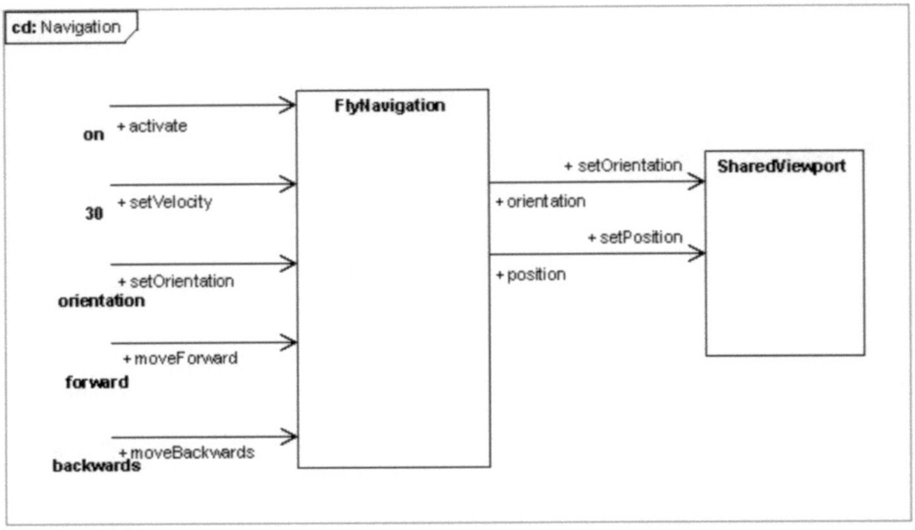

Fig. 8. CAVE Navigation in VWT

4.1 A client for a virtual steering application

We are collaborating in the development of heterogeneous and distributed clients for a virtual wind tunnel (VWT), that uses massive paralelism and fast algorithms for computational fluid dynamics by Boulanger et al. (2006). Figures 8, 9, and 10 show InTml diagrams for the following tasks: navigation in a CAVE environment, sharing viewpoints between clients, and control from a bluetooth–enable device. This application is going to be implemented in the following environments: a personal environment with a HMD and a Phantom, a Geowall–like environment, and a CAVE–like environment. Figures 9, and 10 apply to all implementations, while Figure 8 defines the navigation technique in a CAVE.
Navigation in a CAVE environment (Figure 8) uses a simple flying metaphor, in which a head tracker defines move direction, and wand buttons move backwards and forwards.

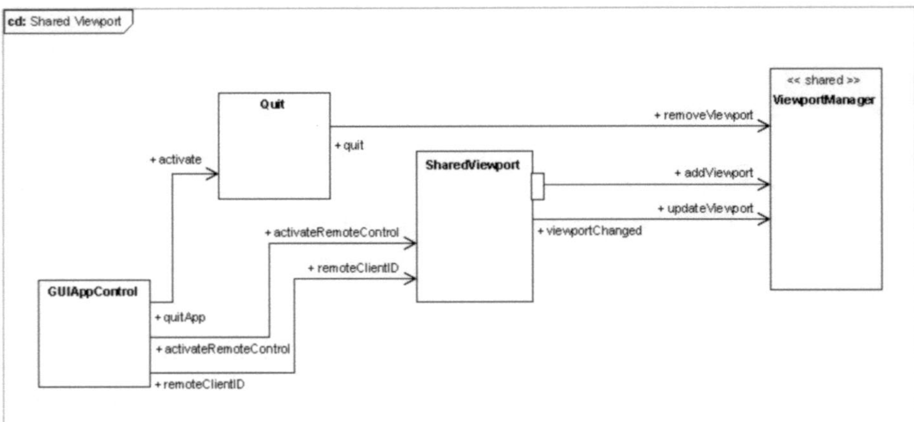

Fig. 9. Sharing a Viewport in VWT

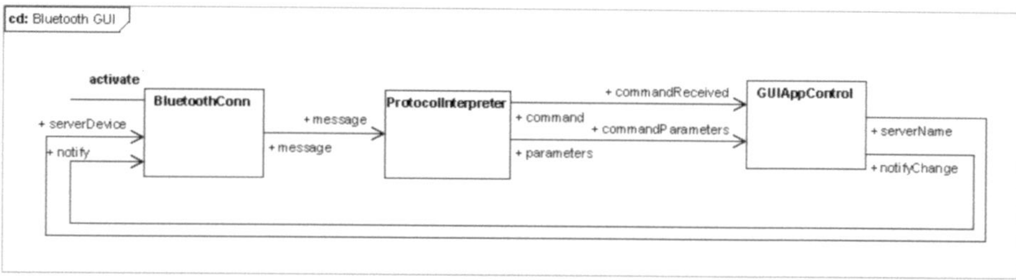

Fig. 10. VWT Control from a Bluetooth device

Shared Viewpoint in Figure 9 describes the task of sharing a representation of a user's viewpoint to all clients in a simulation. It shows the local viewpoint (*SharedViewport*) and how it is added to a pull of viewports, managed by *ViewportManager*. The implementation of this last filter handles the required networking, and the avatars' representation.
Finally, we have a PDA with a bluetooth connection, that allows us to send commands to the control of the application, represented by *GUIAppControl* in Figure 10.

4.2 Navigation tasks in a family

Let's assume we are interested in navigating and showing information about objects in a small but complex VR office, in three hardware platforms: a CAVE, a PC with a joystick, and a cell phone with graphics acceleration. If we concentrate on the navigation task, it is possible to think on interesting and different implementations for such a task in each platform, as follows:

- In a CAVE, a user can navigate to an interesting object by pointing to such an object and selecting it. The system should compute a path from the current viewpoint position to a position in front of such an object. This technique is similar to Fixed–Object Manipulation in (Bowman et al., 2004, p.215), with extra behavior for path planning.
- In a PC with a joystick, a navigation technique that resembles the WALK mode in VRML could be used (*P2D2NavInPlane*). This mode features collision detection between the avatar and objects in the environment.
- In a cell phone, due to computation restrictions and limitations on the input device, it is more convenient to select pre–recorded viewpoints and paths than using the previous navigation techniques. It could be also important to reduce the complexity of the scene as possible.

Figures 11 and 12 show the InTml diagrams of such navigation techniques.

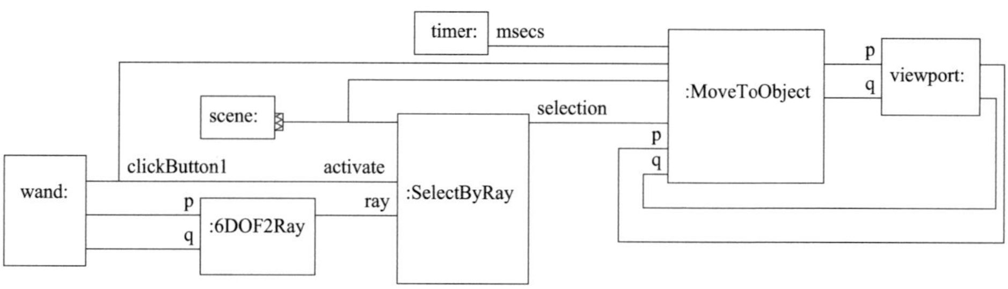

Fig. 11. Navigation in a Cave

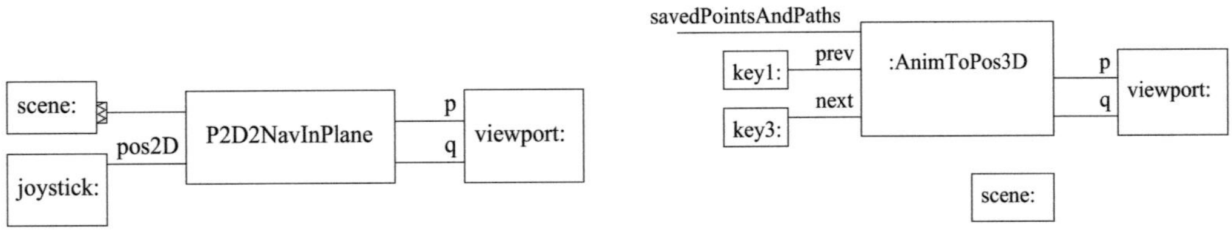

Fig. 12. Navigation in a PC and a Cell Phone

4.3 Software support for a new MR platform

We are developing an integrated MR platform based on the ARToolkit and VRPN, and we are designing a set of reusable filter classes as an API for developers. Such an API will facilitate development to a family of applications in that particular domain, and corresponds to the concept of core assets in the Software Product Line literature such as Clements & Northrop (2002). Figures 13 and 14 show some of the current set of platform-independent filter types, which correspond the following functionality:

- *MappedVRPNTracker*, which gives 6DOF data from an identified pattern and a definition of its local coordinate system.
- *Switch*, which sends as output one of the predefined inputs once a signal is received.
- *Scene*, which allows to select and copy an object by giving an id.
- *Map2DtoTerrain*, which outputs a 3D position over a terrain from a 2D one.
- *Collision*, which identify a collision between two objects.

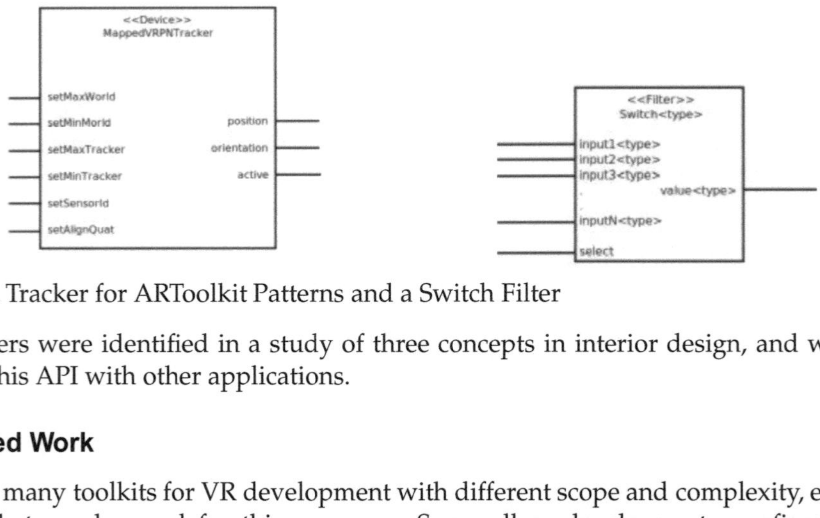

Fig. 13. A Tracker for ARToolkit Patterns and a Switch Filter

These filters were identified in a study of three concepts in interior design, and we plan to validate this API with other applications.

5. Related Work

There are many toolkits for VR development with different scope and complexity, even game engines that can be used for this purpose. Some allow developers to configure a wide

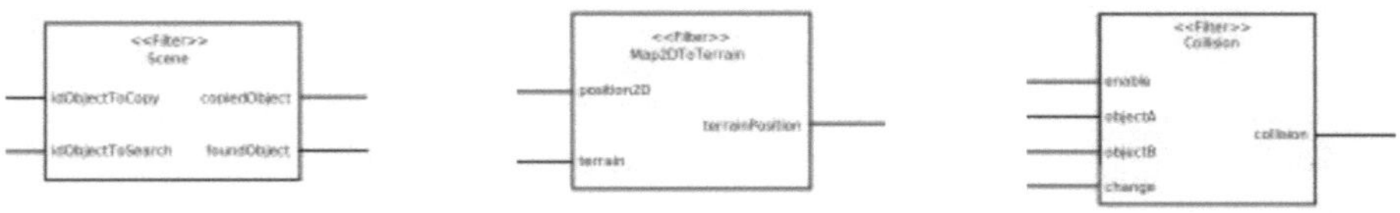

Fig. 14. A Scene and Terrain objects, plus A Colision Detection Filters

spectrum of aspects, while others hide some decisions in order to reduce complexity. Some environments are tailored to a particular hardware platform, and others allow developers to use a wide range of input and output devices. By reviewing the way VR programs are developed in several toolkits such as Shaw et al. (1992); VRCO (2003); SGI (2003); Blach et al. (1998); Sense8 (2000); CMU (1999); Bierbaum et al. (2001); Web3D Consortium (2003); Taylor et al. (2001); Sastry et al. (2001); Allard et al. (2004), it can be seen that most environments with wide coverage of hardware platforms require developers to take decisions on many detailed aspects at the same time, and to learn rather complex APIs in a general purpose programming language. Environments with easier to learn environments tend to limit support for devices and novel behavior, precluding the evolution of VR applications. However, there are some environments that offer a high level programming paradigm with a library of high level constructs and at the same time allow developers to create new high level constructs by writing code in a generic programming language. Such environments are at the same time easy to learn for novices and powerful enough for expert developers. Our solution follows this approach, and incorporates novel solutions related to application code structure, device management, and a scalable execution model.

One of the main problems of current environments, APIs and toolkits for VR development is the proposed structure for application-specific code. Developers should be able to easily incorporate novel devices, interaction techniques, or content to VR applications. However, this is not the case. Some environments such as the ones in Shaw et al. (1992); CMU (1999); Taylor et al. (2001) organize application-specific code around isolated callbacks, which process one event at a time. Each callback should include code related to parts of interaction techniques, event correlation, and modifications to output data structures. This scheme is difficult to scale to complex applications, since isolated callbacks are not enough as an organization scheme for an entire application and developers have to struggle in order to incorporate more advanced architectural styles. Other environments such as Bierbaum et al. (2001); SGI (2003) add new behavior around the main rendering loop. In this case, code with the new functionality can be written in specific callbacks, which are called at specific stages, usually before or after rendering. Again, this structure intertwines code related to interaction techniques, application behavior, or gathering input devices data. Finally, other environments allow developers to read as many devices as they want in a particular point of code, which is very convenient for event correlation, but can lead to coincidental coupling between devices. There are also limitations related to the core APIs in use and the way they handle novel input devices. Current environments usually define a fixed set of input types, for example, keyboard events and mouse events, with extra information from special keys on the keyboard (i.e. shift, alt, and ctrl). Events from other devices are usually translated to available ones. For example, joystick events can be translated to mouse events. This limits the number of devices that can be simultaneously used and the type of input events that an application can receive. Some toolkits provide extension mechanisms for new devices or new events, but these capabilities target senior developers, and are rarely used.

Despite their success with standard interfaces, traditional architectures have the following limitations for VR applications:

- There are no provisions for more complex structures between callbacks, and their interactions are difficult to model. Generally, all callbacks are just at one level from the dispatcher, without relations between them. Java3D by Sun Microsystems (1997) allows passing control from one callback to another, but the scheme is limited to relationships between two callbacks, and the code inside each callback has the same reusability problems mentioned here.

- Since all events are queued and serialized, there is no provision for treatment of simultaneous events from different devices with different generation rates.
- Addition of new events from novel input devices is a difficult task, so it is usually avoided by reusing events from standard devices that are not presently in use. This creates problems due to usability differences between devices, and conflicts if new and old devices are used at the same time.
- There are limited possibilities for composition and reuse of third-party components due to the lack of an interface standard, and a notion of composition. It is difficult to compose callbacks that were previously developed for other purposes.

Our proposal uses data flow as the high level model for passing control and data between components, similar to the one in Allard et al. (2004). With such a structure it is possible to model complex dependencies between tasks and interaction techniques. In contrast, the callback model does not scale well to more complex structures, where dependencies among callbacks are required. A model based on dataflow can better define relationships between different behavior components in the system, and it clearly exposes component dependencies. Some systems such as Carey & Bell (1997); Web3D Consortium (2005); Ava (2000); Blach et al. (1998); Virtools (2007) have used a similar structure, but they usually take the very simple execution model of propagating one event at a time. Our approach differs from the one in Allard et al. (2004) in the way we have adapted the traditional execution models from pipeline processing, such as Synchronous Data Flow architectures presented by Battacharyya et al. (1996), to the following characteristics of VR applications:

- Not all information from input devices needs to be processed in any given period of time. Depending on the computation speed and the refresh rate of output devices, some information from input devices could be irrelevant or outdated. We allow components to define an interval of time where all received information is considered simultaneous, so redundant information inside the interval can be eliminated. Such information does not affect successive intervals, so discarded information do not affect future executions. The model in Allard et al. (2004) uses extra control connections in order to handle computation distribution, and only allows one output per interval of time in each module.
- New input and output devices are common in new applications. It should be simple to add new devices to an application. Moreover, simultaneous events from different devices should be easy to detect. Filters with several input and output ports are our solution to this problem. They can model any type of device in an uniform way, and it is easy to create new types of filters for new types of devices. On the other hand, a filter interested in simultaneous events from different devices just needs to include them as input and read all events received in a time interval from all its inputs.

Some intrinsic characteristics of VR applications are still not directly addressed by the present proposal, such as the desirable fixed refresh rate for output devices. However, it is possible to integrate the work by Shaw et al. (1992) that decouple device reading from simulation execution and even distributed solutions such as Allard et al. (2004), with some limitations.
A dataflow architecture also allows us to consider dynamic and static scheduling algorithms for machines with several CPUs. This approach cannot be implemented in current dataflow-based solutions such as VRML and X3D, due to intrinsic limitations on the order

of execution of their components in a program. Kwok & Ahmad (1999) discuss several algorithms for static scheduling, and solutions for arbitrary graph structures with arbitrary computational costs per node, such as CP/MISF and DF/IHS, are promising for high performance solutions in VR.
Our work in InTml differs from previous approaches in several ways:

- InTml provides a way to both hide implementation details and allow changes in any behavior that the application may provide. There are some development environments with high level, user-friendly languages (e.g. Web3D Consortium (2003); CMU (1999)), but they assume some interaction techniques that are either impossible or very difficult to override.
- InTml provides a formally described language and a component-based development environment suitable for reuse on different hardware platforms. Some component-based solutions are available in Blach et al. (1998); Web3D Consortium (2003); Dachselt et al. (2002), but without a formal description of their semantics.
- InTml can be implemented on top of a wide variety of existing libraries and toolkits, so it can provide a unified and executable description for VR applications.
- InTml takes a novel approach to the treatment of simultaneous, multimodal events from several devices. We define a dataflow model with a periodic execution that handles several events as simultaneous. Such a model is an evolution of the traditional single-threaded, one event at a time model, inherited from traditional WIMP interfaces.
- InTml is a domain specific language for defining the architecture of VR applications. Some languages in the field such as Web3D Consortium (2003); Autodesk (2006) concentrate mostly on geometry and on the PC-based interaction environment. Others, such as Wingrave & Bowman (2005) use state machines as a design abstraction, which we believe is very powerful although more complex for non-programmers. The same is true of hybrid languages such as the one in Smith & Duke (1999), which proposes a way to combine notations for discrete and continuous signals, using extensions to Petri Nets and state machines. InTml allows unsophisticated developers to model devices, behavior and content, all of them as first-class concepts that are easy to understand and present in any VR hardware platform.
- Some authors such as Massó et al. (2005); Dachselt et al. (2002) have proposed portable ways for describing VR applications, but they have been used on a subset of VR applications, usually Desktop VR.

From the point of view of VR development methodologies, there are some options such as the one by Tanriverdi & Jacob (2001), the user-centered approach in Neale et al. (2002), a UML-based approach in Kim (2005), and a methodology in Sastry et al. (2001) based on a hybrid language. While such alternatives have similarities with, and are extensions to the one presented here, our approach introduces and depends on the key concepts of retargeting and separation of roles.
There have been some attempts to define a concept similar to VR retargeting but restricted to computer graphics. Scalable graphics is a field that studies methods for parallel rendering of scenes. Several authors such as Humphreys et al. (2001); Eldridge et al. (2000); Nishimura & Kunii (1996); Molnar et al. (1992) have proposed algorithms for load balancing of the rendering task over several computers. Application retargeting in VR requires this type of rendering solution, in order to use the capabilities of clusters and parallel machines.

However, retargeting also involves changes in other important elements of a VR application, as we have shown. IBM presented similar ideas in its interpretation of Scalable Graphics by Boier-Martin (2003), but too few details are presented. In summary, our proposal describes how to retarget devices and interaction techniques in VR applications, as opposed to changes in graphic content only.
More details about InTml and its implementation can be found at Figueroa et al. (2008) and Figueroa (2010).

6. Future work

Supporting VR and MR development is a complex task, that requires an important effort in several directions. We believe InTml might be an interesting solution, that allows both developers and designers to construct new applications that can survive despite changes in particular technologies. We need to offer a more friendly environment for both developers and designers, and more functionality in order to make their work easier. In particular, we are improving the support for rapid prototyping from the point of view of a designer, by means of more functionality at the IDE and a more complete library of filter classes. The work of a developer is by no means easier, so we need to find out ways to facilitate the creation of code attached to filter classes, and ways to make the overall architecture clearer for debugging and understanding purposes.
InTml code is published under several open source licenses at Figueroa (2007)

7. References

Allard, J., Gouranton, V., Lecointre, L., Limet, S., Melin, E., Raffin, B. & Robert, S. (2004). Flowvr: A middleware for large scale virtual reality applications, *Euro–Par 2004 Parallel Processing*, Vol. 3149/2004, Springer Berlin / Heidelberg, pp. 497–505.

Autodesk (2006). Autodesk FBX, http://usa.autodesk.com/adsk/servlet/index?id=6837478&siteID=123112.

Ava (2000). Avango: A distributed virtual reality framework, http://imk.gmd.de/docs/ww/ve/projects/proj1_2.mhtml.

Battacharyya, S. S., Murthy, P. K. & Lee, E. A. (1996). *Software Synthesis from Dataflow Graphs*, Kluwer Academic Publishers.

Bierbaum, A., Just, C., Hartling, P., Meinert, K., Baker, A. & Cruz-Neira, C. (2001). VR Juggler: A Virtual Platform for Virtual Reality Application Development, *Proceedings of IEEE Virtual Reality*, IEEE, pp. 89–96.

Blach, R., Landauer, J., Rosh, A. & Simon, A. (1998). A flexible prototyping tool for 3d real-time user interaction, *User-Interaction, Proc. of Virtual Environments*, Springer Wien, pp. 54–1–54–10.

Boier-Martin, I. M. (2003). Adaptive graphics, *Computer Graphics and Applications* 23(1): 6–10.

Boulanger, P., Garcia, M. J., Badke, C. & Ryan, J. (2006). An advanced collaborative infrastructure for the real-time computational steering of large CFD simulations, *European Conference on Computational Fluid Dynamics (ECCOMAS CFD 2006)*, TU Delft. http://www.eccomascfd2006.nl/.

Bowman, D., Kruijff, E., Joseph J. LaViola, J. & Poupyrev, I. (2004). *3D User Interfaces: Theory and Practice*, Addison Wesley.

Carey, R. & Bell, G. (1997). *The Annotated VRML 97 Reference*, chapter 2.10.

Clements, P. & Northrop, L. (2002). *Software Product Lines*, Addison Wesley.

CMU (1999). Alice: Easy interactive 3D graphics, http://www.alice.org. Carnegie Mellon University.

Dachselt, R., Hinz, M. & Meiner, K. (2002). Contigra: an XML–based architecture for component-oriented 3d applications, *Proceeding of the seventh international conference on 3D Web technology*, ACM, ACM Press, pp. 155–163.

Eldridge, M., Igehy, H. & Hanrahan, P. (2000). Pomegranate: a fully scalable graphics architecture, *Proceedings of the 27th annual conference on Computer graphics and interactive techniques*, ACM Press/Addison-Wesley Publishing Co., pp. 443–454.

Figueroa, P. (2007). Intml development tools, http://sourceforge.net/projects/intml.

Figueroa, P. (2008). Intml: Main concepts, examples, and initial lessons, *Proceedings of the IEEE Virtual Reality 2008 Workshop on Software Engineering and Architecture for Realtime Interactive Systems (SEARIS)*, Shaker-Verlag, pp. 3–6.

Figueroa, P. (2010). Insights on the design of intml, *Presence: Teleoperators and Virtual Environments* 19(2): 118–130.
URL:*http://www.mitpressjournals.org/doi/abs/10.1162/pres.19.2.118*

Figueroa, P., Bischof, W. F., Boulanger, P. & Hoover, H. J. (2005). Efficient comparison of platform alternatives in interactive virtual reality applications, *International Journal of Human-Computer Studies* 62(1): 73–103.

Figueroa, P., Bischof, W. F., Boulanger, P., Hoover, H. J. & Taylor, R. (2008). Intml: A dataflow oriented development system for virtual reality applications, *Presence: Teleoper. Virtual Environ.* 17(5): 492–511.

Figueroa, P., Hoover, J. & Boulanger, P. (2004). Intml concepts, *Technical report*, University of Alberta. Computing Science Department.

Humphreys, G., Eldridge, M., Buck, I., Stoll, G., Everett, M. & Hanrahan, P. (2001). Wiregl: a scalable graphics system for clusters, *Proceedings of the 28th annual conference on Computer graphics and interactive techniques*, ACM Press, pp. 129–140.

Kim, G. J. (2005). *Designing Virtual Reality Systems. The Structured Approach*, Springer.

Kwok, Y.-K. & Ahmad, I. (1999). Static scheduling algorithms for allocating directed task graphs to multiprocessors, *ACM Computing Surveys (CSUR)* 31(4): 406–471.

Massó, J. P. M., Vanderdonckt, J., Simarro, F. M. & López, P. G. (2005). Towards virtualization of user interfaces based on usixml, *Web3D '05: Proceedings of the tenth international conference on 3D Web technology*, ACM Press, New York, NY, USA, pp. 169–178.

Molnar, S., Eyles, J. & Poulton, J. (1992). Pixelflow: high-speed rendering using image composition, *Proceedings of the 19th annual conference on Computer graphics and interactive techniques*, ACM Press, pp. 231–240.

Neale, H., Cobb, S. & Wilson, J. (2002). A front ended approach to the user-centred design of ves, *Proceedings of IEEE Virtual Reality*, IEEE, pp. 191–198.

Nishimura, S. & Kunii, T. L. (1996). Vc-1: a scalable graphics computer with virtual local frame buffers, *Proceedings of the 23rd annual conference on Computer graphics and interactive techniques*, ACM Press, pp. 365–372.

openArchitectureWare.org (2008). openarchitectureware, http://www.openarchitectureware.org/.

Poupyrev, I., Billinghurst, M., Weghorst, S. & Ichikawa, T. (1996). The go-go interaction technique: non-linear mapping for direct manipulation in vr, *Proceedings of the 9th annual ACM symposium on User interface software and technology*, ACM, ACM Press, pp. 79–80.

Sastry, L., Boyd, D. & Wilson, M. (2001). Design review and visualization steering using the inquisitive interaction toolkit, *IPT/EGVE 2001: Joint 5th Immersive Projection Technology Workshop / 7th Eurographics Workshop on Virtual Environments.*

Sense8 (2000). Virtual reality development tools. The sense8 product line, http://www.sense8.com/products/index.html.

SGI (2003). Iris performer home page, http://www.sgi.com/software/performer.

Shaw, C., Liang, J., Green, M. & Sun, Y. (1992). The decoupled simulation model for virtual reality systems, *Proceedings of the SIGCHI conference on Human factors in computing systems*, ACM Press, pp. 321–328.

Smith, S. & Duke, D. (1999). The hybrid world of virtual environments, *Eurographics Proceedings*, Vol. 18, Blackwell Publishers, pp. 298–307.

Spivey, M. (1992). *The Z Notation: A Reference Manual*, 2nd edition edn, Prentice-Hall.

Stahl, T. & Veolter, M. (2006). *Model-Driven Software Development : Technology, Engineering, Management*, Wiley.

Sun Microsystems (1997). Java 3D Home Page, http://java.sun.com/products/java-media/3D/index.html.

Tanriverdi, V. & Jacob, R. J. (2001). VRID: A design model and methodology for developing virtual reality interfaces, *in* ACM (ed.), *Proceedings of the ACM Symposium of Virtual Reality Software and Technology*, ACM, ACM Press, pp. 175–182.

Taylor, R. M., Hudson, T. C., Seeger, A., Weber, H., Juliano, J. & Helser, A. T. (2001). VRPN: A device-independent, network-transparent VR peripheral system, *Proceedings of the ACM symposium on Virtual reality software and technology*, ACM Press, pp. 55–61.

The Eclipse Foundation (2007). Eclipse, http://www.eclipse.org/.

Trenholme, D. & Smith, S. P. (2008). Computer game engines for developing first-person virtual environments, *Virtual Reality* 12(3): 181–187.

Virtools (2007). Virtools, http://www.virtools.com/index.asp.

VRCO (2003). Cavelib library, http://www.vrco.com/products/cavelib/ cavelib.html.

Web3D Consortium (2003). Extensible 3D ($X3D^{TM}$) Graphics. Home Page, http://www.web3d.org/x3d.html.

Web3D Consortium (2005). ISO/IEC FDIS 19777-1:2005. extensible 3D (X3D) language bindings part 1: ECMAScript, http://www.web3d.org/x3d/specifications/ISO-IEC-19777-1-X3DLanguageBindings-ECMAScript/.

Wingrave, C. A. & Bowman, D. A. (2005). Chasm: Bringing description and implementation of 3d interfaces, *Proceedings of the IEEE Workshop on New Directions in 3D User Interfaces*, Shaker Verlag, pp. 85–88.

Part 3

Evaluation of Cognition and Behavior

8

Compelling Self-Motion Through Virtual Environments without Actual Self-Motion – Using Self-Motion Illusions ("Vection") to Improve User Experience in VR

Bernhard E. Riecke
Simon Fraser University
Canada

1. Introduction

While modern computer graphics and virtual reality (VR) simulations can have stunning photorealism, they are often unable to provide a life-like and compelling sensation of moving through the simulated world. This is in stark contrast to our real-world experience, where locomotion through the environment is naturally accompanied by the embodied sensation of self-motion, even when we are not actively walking but using other transportation devices like bicycles, cars, or buses. This fundamental difference in which we perceive simulated versus actual motions might negatively impact the perceived realism, behavioural effectiveness, user acceptance, and commercial success of virtual reality technology and applications. In this chapter, I propose and discuss how investigating, utilizing, and optimizing self-motion illusions ("vection") might be a lean and elegant way to overcome such shortcomings and provide a truly *"moving experience"* in computer-mediated environments without the need to physically move, thus reducing overall cost and effort.

The aim of this chapter is to provide an overview of the state of the art in research on visually-induced self-motion illusions in real and virtual environments. Specific focus will be on a topic that is of particular interest in the context of VR but has not been thoroughly reviewed before: Namely how self-motion illusions are not only affected by physical stimulus parameters themselves via bottom-up perceptual processes (as discussed in section 3), but also by the way we look at, perceive, and interpret the stimulus, how it is integrated into the overall display setup, and whether or not actual motion might be possible (see section 4). Knowledge of these factors can not only deepen our understanding of the complex processes underlying self-motion perception, but might also be of particular interest for VR simulations and other immersive/multi-media applications like gaming or movies, as these factors can often be manipulated with relatively little effort. Section 5 will provide a brief overview on recent studies on multi-modal contributions and interactions for vection. These indicate significant cross-modal benefits, which could, together with the results presented in earlier sections, be employed to design more effective-yet-affordable VR interfaces, as will be discussed in the final section and throughout this chapter. Possible side-effects of vection in VR are discussed in section 6.

2. Self-motion illusions ("vection")

Self-motion illusions induced by moving visual stimuli that cover a large part of the visual field have been first described more than a century ago (Mach, 1875; Wood, 1895), and were termed circular and linear vection for rotational and translational self-motion illusions, respectively (Fischer & Kornmüller, 1930; Tschermak, 1931). Many readers might have experienced the compellingness of visually-induced self-motion illusions themselves, as they can easily occur under natural conditions - for example, when sitting in a train waiting to depart from the station and looking out of the window where a train on the adjacent track starts moving, many people experience a rather convincing illusion that there own train started moving ("train illusion"). Similarly, when waiting in a car in front of a red light and a large truck slowly pulls up on the side, many of us instinctively hit the break as for a moment we believed that our own car was moving. One of the earliest occurrences of vection might have been when our ancestors were gazing at fast-moving clouds or looking down on a river and fixating onto a stationary object (like a rock) in the river and experienced a tilting sensation in the direction opposite of the visual (river) motion. More recently, large-screen theme park rides and cinemax or I-Max theatres utilize self-motion illusions to provide more compelling experiences to their audience, as was already done more than a century ago with the "haunted swing" illusion described by Wood (1895).

Why might we want to care about self-motion illusions in the context of VR and other immersive media? As mentioned above, most VR and immersive media setups and applications do not provide a compelling and believable sensation of moving through the simulated environments; despite often impressive visual realism, perceptual and behavioural realism is often lacking. That is, seeing a simulated self-motion does not necessarily imply experiencing and believing it, thus reducing overall believability and simulation quality. So what conditions are conducive to experiencing believable self-motion illusions?

There is more than a century of vection research investigating under what precise conditions moving visual and non-visual stimuli can induce embodied sensations of self-motion. I propose that revisiting, utilizing, and extending this body of knowledge can provide both inspiration and guidance for improving VR and other immersive media from the human/user perspective. In a nutshell, if we could provide users with a compelling illusion of moving through simulated worlds, we would not have to go through the effort of allowing for large-scale physical locomotion or could at least relax the requirement of those.

One of the biggest challenges in self-motion simulation is that some modalities simply cannot (yet) be simulated easily or switched off noninvasively: In particular, vestibular and most somatosensory cues cannot be simply "turned off" like visual cues (closing ones' eyes) or auditory cues (wearing earplugs and/or listening to masking noise). Hence, whenever self-motions are only simulated and not physically performed, there is a conflict between those cues suggesting self-motion (e.g., the visual simulation) and other cues indicating stationarity (e.g., vestibular cues indicating that there was no acceleration and we should thus still be stationary, or somatosensory cues from our feet touching solid ground). So how is this conflict and ambiguity resolved by the human system to form a coherent percept of one's current state of motion?

Indeed, self-motion perception is a complex phenomenon that includes multiple sensory and motor systems as well as both bottom-up processes and higher-level, cognitive influences, as will be discussed in the subsequent sections. There are several mathematical frameworks modelling how the different sensory and motor inputs might be integrated to form a coherent percept of self-motion despite conflicting or ambiguous information (e.g., Mergner & Becker, 1990; Mergner et al., 2000; Wertheim, 1994; Zacharias & Young, 1981). While vestibular motion cues immediately yield a sensation of self-motion, large-field visual motion can be interpreted as either object motion (where the observer is stationary) or self-motion (where the visual stimulus is stationary) or a combination thereof. When presented with coherent large-field visual motion, the observer typically perceives object motion during the first few seconds after motion onset (1-30s, depending on various stimulus parameters), followed by a sometimes very brief period of mixed object and self-motion, and finally exclusive self-motion and saturated vection (Dichgans & Brandt, 1978). During saturated vection, the moving stimulus is typically (but not always) perceived as earth-stationary, and vection occurs in the direction opposite of the visual motion (just as if we would be physically moving).

There is a long history of investigating how different stimulus parameters affect the onset, strength, and velocity of vection. General reviews on self-motion illusions can be found in (Andersen, 1986; Dichgans & Brandt, 1978; Howard, 1982, 1986; Mergner & Becker, 1990; Warren & Wertheim, 1990). Auditory vection has recently been reviewed by (Riecke et al., 2009; Väljamäe, 2009). Neurophysiological correlates of vection have been described in, e.g., (Hettinger, 2002; Kovacs et al., 2008) and references therein. Vection with a specific focus on motion simulation, virtual environments, and undesirable side-effects has been reviewed in (Hettinger, 2002).

The goal of the following section is to provide a current review on different stimulus parameters affecting visually-induced vection, and how these factors might be utilized in the design of VR and other immersive applications. Section 4 will focus on recent findings indicating that vection is not only affected by physical stimulus parameters themselves, but also by how we look at, perceive, and interpret the stimulus, by what is beyond the display itself, and by our sensation/knowledge whether actual motion might or might not be possible. The presented research findings lead to a number of possible applications and implications for VR and other immersive applications. Instead of summarizing them in a separate section, I decided to integrate them with the respective research findings to provide a stronger link and an improved understanding of their origin and underlying processes.

3. Stimulus parameters affecting visually-induced vection

Vection induced by moving visual stimuli has clearly received the most research attention so far and will thus be discussed in more detail below. Self-motion illusions can, however, also be induced by other modalities including auditory (see reviews by Riecke et al., 2009; Väljamäe, 2009), tactile (Dichgans & Brandt, 1978), or biomechanical cues (Bles, 1981; Brandt et al., 1977) or from direct galvanic stimulation of the vestibular system (Cress et al., 1997; Lepecq et al., 2006). In the following, I will review different factors that have been shown to facilitate vection, and how they might be utilized in VR and other immersive situations. Note that this information can, of course, equally be used to inhibit self-motion illusions were desired to avoid possible undesired side-effects, as discussed in section 6.

3.1 Up to an optimal velocity, higher stimulus velocities yield stronger vection

Higher stimulus velocities in general enhance vection, indicated by earlier vection onset, higher perceived self-motion velocity, and increased intensity and convincingness of the self-motion illusion (Allison et al., 1999; Brandt et al., 1973; Dichgans & Brandt, 1978; Schulte-Pelkum et al., 2003; Howard, 1986). For example, Brandt et al. (1973) showed that circular vection velocity increased linearly with increasing stimulus movement up to 120°/s and roughly matched the stimulus velocity. Further increasing stimulus velocity did not increase perceived self-rotation velocity further, such that the moving stimulus was no longer perceived to be earth-stationary. In terms of VR applications, this suggests that there might be maximum movement and/or optic flow velocities beyond which simulation effectiveness could deteriorate and the simulated world might no longer be perceived as stable.

3.2 Larger stimulus sizes increase vection

One major factor determining the onset and strength of vection is the solid angle (field of view, FOV) subtended by the moving visual stimulus. Although stimulus sizes as small as 7.5° have been shown to induce linear vection under carefully designed lab conditions (Andersen & Braunstein, 1985), larger stimulus sizes generally enhance vection in all measures, and full-field stimulation results in the strongest vection to a point where it cannot be suppressed any more and can be indistinguishable from actual self-motion (Berthoz et al., 1975; Brandt et al., 1973; Dichgans & Brandt, 1978; Held et al., 1975).

3.3 Central and peripheral vision is equally effective in inducing vection

While earlier studies reported that peripheral visual motion is more effective in inducing vection than central motion (Brandt et al., 1973; Dichgans & Brandt, 1978; Johansson, 1977), later studies demonstrated that peripheral and central motion have similar influences on vection when their display areas are equated (Andersen & Braunstein, 1985; Howard & Heckmann, 1989; Nakamura, 2008; Post, 1988; Wolpert, 1990). In fact, the peripheral dominance effect observed earlier was likely caused by peripheral stimuli being perceived as farther away than central stimuli. When perceived depth is held constant, vection strength linearly increases with increasing stimulus size, independent of stimulus eccentricity (Nakamura, 2008).

3.4 Optimal spatial frequency for vection depends on stimulus eccentricity

There is, however, an interaction between optimal frequency for central versus peripheral stimulation: Palmisano & Gillam (1998) showed that the most compelling circular vection is achieved when lower spatial frequency patterns are presented peripherally (where the eye's spatial resolution is also lower) and higher-spatial frequency stimuli are presented to central vision (where acuity is higher). From an applied perspective of improving self-motion simulations, the decreased peripheral sensitivity to high-frequency stimuli relaxes the need for high-resolution displays or imagery in the periphery unless the user needs to focus there (see also discussion in Wolpert, 1990). Even without a central display, vection can be reliably induced by peripheral stimulation: Brandt el al. (1973) demonstrated that circular vection was hardly reduced when the central 120° of the human visual field was blocked and participants saw motion only in the far periphery. Similar amounts of vection were achieved when visual motion was restricted to a horizontal streak of 60° height and full-field width. These results suggest that adding affordable low-resolution displays in the periphery of VR or other immersive setups might have surprisingly strong effects on perceived self-motion (and likely also presence and immersion).

3.5 Density of moving contrasts enhances vection

While single moving dots or objects can hardly induce vection, increasing their number and density can eventually induce vection, and vection strength seems to generally increase with the density of moving contrasts (Brandt et al., 1975; Dichgans & Brandt, 1978). Thus, care needs to be taken for simulations where there are only few objects (e.g., for flight, space, or diving simulations), especially if they are also far away (and thus have low image velocity for translations). If compelling vection is desired, it might thus be necessary to carefully add nearby objects to increase overall optic flow and relative motion with respect to stationary foreground objects. Ideally, this should be done in the context of the simulation scenario to ensure ecological validity. For flight simulations, this could, e.g., be achieved by adding clouds or haze.

3.6 Linear vs. circular vs. curvilinear vection

Trutoiu et al. (2009) demonstrated that linear vection in a panoramic projection setup was less convincing than circular vection, whereas curvilinear vection was perceived to be as convincing as circular vection. This has interesting implications for motion simulations, suggesting that even slight curvatures in the path might be able to increase the convincingness of the motion percept. Linear vection could be enhanced by adding a floor projection, though, possibly due to the special role that a perceivable moving ground plane seems to play in vection (Sato et al., 2007).

Overall, however, up-down (aka "elevator") vection tends to be more compelling and occur earlier than left-right or forward-backward vection, likely because up-down movements do not change the direction of the gravito-inertial vector, such that accelerational and gravitational forces are parallel (Giannopulu & Lepecq, 1998; Trutoiu et al., 2009). Similarly, continuous circular vection around the earth-vertical axis can be induced more easily than vection around earth-horizontal axes (roll or pitch). The latter can lead to paradoxical sensations of limited body tilt despite continuous sensations of tilting (Allison et al., 1999; Held et al., 1975; Young et al., 1975). This has been attributed to the conflict between the visually-suggested tilt in the gravitoinertial vector and the actual gravitoinertial vector (sensed by the otoliths in the vestibular system and the somatosensory system) which does not tilt. Without full-field stimulation and a naturalistic visual stimulus, it seems difficult to obtain pitch or roll vection that includes head-over-heels orientations. As most real-world situations do not include those extreme orientations, this might not be a major limitation for most VR and immersive media applications, though.

3.7 Simulated viewpoint jitter facilitates vection despite visuo-vestibular conflict

Traditionally, it was often believed that vection should be facilitated if the sensory conflict between visual cues (simulating motion) and vestibular cues (indicating stationarity) was reduced. This view is supported by findings that bilaterally labyrinthine defective participants perceive visual vection much earlier and more intense (Johnson et al., 1999), and can perceive unambiguous roll or pitch vection through head-over-heels orientations (Cheung et al., 1989). In a series of studies, Palmisano and colleagues challenged this notions by showing that forward linear vection occurred earlier, lasted longer, and was more compelling when coherent viewpoint jitter was added to the expanding optic flow display (Palmisano et al., 2000), whereas incoherent jitter impaired vection (Palmisano et al., 2003). Moreover, viewpoint jitter alone induced weak vection sensations, without any overall radial or lamellar optic flow (Palmisano et al., 2003).

3.8 Perceived rigidity of optic flow field enhances vection

Nakamura (2010) extended these findings in showing that coherent visual jitter can facilitate linear vection even when the stimulus does not contain any depth cues and appears flat, whereas incoherent jitter impaired vection. Nakamura proposed that coherent jitter increasing the perceived rigidity of the random dot display, which in turn facilitated vection. Increasing the perceived rigidity of a vection-inducing stimulus seems, however, not to be the only mechanism underlying the vection-facilitating effect of stimulus jitter, as the effect can also be observed for naturalistic stimuli, which are arguably readily perceived as inherently rigid: Using videos of translations along a hallway, Bubka & Bonato (2010) showed that adding image oscillations induced by walking motions considerably enhanced linear forward vection strength while reducing vection onset latencies. Similar facilitation of forward linear vection when including slow viewpoint oscillations has been reported for more abstract optic flow displays (Palmisano et al., 2007). Surprisingly, it did not matter whether the viewpoint oscillations were caused by active head oscillations or just passively viewed without any head motions (Kim & Palmisano, 2008).

While it is tempting to suggest to add coherent image jitter or oscillations to VR simulations in order to enhance self-motion perception and perceptual realism, this should be carefully evaluated on a case-by-case basis, as adding image jitter/oscillations has also been shown to increases motion sickness (Palmisano et al., 2007), likely due to the increased sensory conflict between visual and non-visual cues.

4. Beyond physical stimulus parameters: How we look at, perceive, and interpret the stimulus can also affect vection

As described above, previous vection research mostly focussed on how various physical parameters of the moving stimulus like the stimulus contrast or field of view affect vection via lower-level, bottom-up perceptual processes. As I will argue in this section, there is, however, increasing evidence that vection can also be affected by what is outside of the moving stimulus itself, by the way we move and look at a moving stimulus, our pre-conceptions, intentions, and how we perceive and interpret the stimuli. Vection might even be directly or indirectly affected by higher-level and cognitive/top-down processes (Andersen & Braunstein, 1985; Lepecq et al., 1995; Mergner & Becker, 1990; Riecke et al., 2005). While many of these findings are exploratory in nature and await further careful experimentation, they provide a fascinating glimpse into the complex processes and interactions underlying the phenomenon of perceived self-motion without actual self-motion. Apart from its theoretical relevance, potential higher-level/cognitive/intentional contributions to vection might be of considerable interest for many applications, as these factors can often be manipulated with relatively small effort and cost.

4.1 Eye movements and relative motion perception

Intent and eye movements: Fixation and staring facilitate vection, as compared to smooth pursuit

In the following, I will review research demonstrating that vection is not only determined by the physical parameters of the moving stimulus (i.e., strictly bottom-up perceptual processes), but also strongly influenced by our intent and specifically the way we look at a moving stimulus. When viewing a moving visual stimulus without explicit viewing instruction, our eyes smoothly follow the stimulus (optokinetic nystagmus). Likely one of the first observations on vection-facilitating factors was that fixating on a stationary foreground object (like our outstretched hand) facilitated vection (Fischer & Kornmüller, 1930; Mach, 1875; Wallach, 1940; Warren, 1895). However, fixation is not necessarily required, and inattentively staring at a moving pattern can also facilitate vection (Fischer & Kornmüller, 1930). Careful experimentation by Becker et al. (2002) showed that suppressing the optokinetic reflex by fixating a stationary fixation point yields higher perceived vection velocities and lower vection onset latencies, as compared to trying to suppress the optokinetic reflex without a fixation point or merely staring at the stimulus. Attentively following the moving pattern yielded the lowest vection velocity and highest onset latencies, although eye movements were similar to the staring condition. This suggests that not only retinal slip and the pattern of eye movements, but also one's intent (e.g., to follow vs. stare) can affect self-motion illusions, as has been shown and mathematically modeled in a series of studies (Becker et al., 2002; Mergner et al., & Becker, 2000; Mergner et al., 2000).

In terms of applications like motion simulations, differences in the user task, instructions, and intentions could thus have a considerable effect on the perceived self-motion and consequently on the overall believability and effectiveness of a simulation. For instance, instructions that require users to fixate on foreground objects moving with the observer instead of the simulated outside scene (e.g., checking the speedometer or operating the radio in a car or aircraft cockpit instead of looking at the surrounding outside environment) might somewhat surprisingly enhance self-motion perception and thus potentially overall simulation realism and effectiveness.

Note, however, that the combination of fast-moving stimuli and a limited update rate (typically 60Hz) of VR displays can induce undesirable perceptual artifacts like flicker and ghost images, especially when observers fixate or stare at the display and thus do not follow the visual motion with their eyes. Moreover, color-sequential displays like 1-chip dlp projectors or the commonly-used LCoS head-mounted displays (HMDs) can induce color separation for fast-moving sharp contrast edges, even without fixation or staring. Thus, applications where fast object or observer motion is required should be carefully tested and tuned to limit display artifacts.

Increasing retinal slip, local image velocities, and relative motion between moving stimulus and observer-fixed reference frame facilitates vection

Apart from fixation and staring, peripheral looking and gaze shifts between central and peripheral regions can also improve forward linear vection (Palmisano & Kim, 2009). Potential factors underlying this effect include faster local image velocities and increased retinal slip (local image velocity is higher in the periphery for radially expanding flow fields) as well as screen boundary effects as described in the following. Several studies demonstrated that vection depends not only on characteristics of the moving visual stimulus itself, but also on the relative motion between the moving visual stimulus and stationary reference objects. For example, circular vection was facilitated when the moving visual stimulus was surrounded by a stationary rectangular foreground viewing window (Howard & Heckmann, 1989). Merely adding two vertical thin bars as stationary foreground objects also enhanced vection, in particular for slowly (5°/s) moving stimuli where vection is otherwise hard to achieve (Howard & Howard, 1994). Howard and colleagues argued that the effect originated from the relative motion signal between the stationary foreground objects and the moving stimulus, although it seems that perceived object-background separation might also have contributed (Seno et al., 2009, see also subsection below). Even without physical depth separation, stationary objects can facilitate vection, as was shown by Lowther & Ware (1996) when adding a rectangular 5×5 grid to a projection screen displaying the moving stimulus or by Riecke et al. (2005, exp. 2) when adding hardly noticeable marks (scratches) to the projection screen.

This opens up interesting avenues and future research areas for facilitating vection in non-obtrusive ways, without the need for fixation or other restrictions of eye movements. Especially for slow image motions, adding a stationary (foreground) reference frame can provide relative motion cues that facilitate motion detection and vection. This can be achieved, e.g., though the frames of multi-monitor setups, through real or simulated window frames (like the windscreen pillar in driving or flight simulators), or through other means that should ideally be inspired by and match the motion metaphor and application scenario. Ironically, although large-FOV spherical or cylindrical projection setups have many advantages, they typically provide only limited relative motion cues due to the lack of visible screen boundaries or other foreground objects, which can reduce their vection-inducing potential.

4.2 Perceived background motion, not just physical depth determine vection

Already in 1975, Wist et al. (1975) demonstrated that the perceived self-rotation velocity (which is often used as a measure of the strength of circular vection) increases not only with the angular velocity of the visual stimulus as one might expect, but also linearly increases with the perceived distance of the moving stimulus. However, later research demonstrated that not only the absolute perceived distance, but in particular the relative depth structure and figure-ground (or object-background) separation seems critical, in that the stimulus that is *perceived* to be further away typically determines the occurrence, direction, and strength of vection (Brandt et al., 1975; Howard & Heckmann, 1989; Ito & Shibata, 2005; Nakamura, 2008; Nakamura & Shimojo, 1999; Ohmi & Howard, 1988; Ohmi et al., 1987). Several of these studies used perceptually bistable displays and demonstrated that not only physical stimulus parameters themselves, but in particular how the stimulus is perceived and interpreted at any moment in time can modulate or even determine self-motion perception. For example, monocular viewing of two optic flow displays in Ohmi et al. (1987) caused spontaneous reversals in their perceived depth order, without any physical stimulus changes. Results showed that the display that was currently perceived to be the further away dominated the self-motion percept, irrespective of the physical depth order and irrespective of which of the two displays was fixated or pursued.

Importance of perceived object-background relation for vection

As our visual system readily organizes visual stimuli into figure versus ground (i.e., perceptual objects versus background), the findings by Ohmi et al. (1987) could be interpreted as the perceived background dominating vection, whereas "figures" (e.g., objects in the foreground) having less, if any, effect on vection (Kitazaki & Sato, 2003; Ohmi et al., 1987). This hypothesis was confirmed and extended in a clever series of experiments by Seno et al. (2009), who used two independently moving luminance-defined gratings organized to form perceptually bistable displays like a Rubin's vase that show spontaneous reversals of the figure-ground (i.e., the object-background) relationship. When a moving stimulus was currently perceived as an "object", it's vection-inducing potential decreased to a point where it could no longer induce vection. Conversely, the part of the stimulus that was currently perceived as the "ground" or background determined vection responses, even if it was stereoscopically defined to be closer than the "object". Moreover, Experiment 5 of Seno et al. (2009) showed that upright shapes (face, apple, or human figure) produced stronger vection than inverted (upside-down) shapes, arguable because the inverted shapes were less likely to be perceived as an object.

Object-background and rest frame hypothesis provide a unifying framework

Seno et al. (2009) proposed that the object versus background hypothesis could provide a unifying framework for investigating and better understanding vection and vection-inducing stimuli. In particular, many factors that have been shown to facilitate vection are also typical properties of the perceived background, like occupying a large field of view, peripheral stimulation, lower spatial frequencies, rigidity and coherent visual motion, being a ground plane, being unattended, or being further away than other parts of the display. For example, paying particular attention to one of the two motion components in Kitazaki & Sato (2003) might have emphasized it's "object" or "foreground" status, such that other aspects of the stimulus were more likely to be perceived as a background and thus dominated vection. Similarly, fixating a stationary part of the display might have perceptually enhanced its object-likelihood, such that the other (now "background") stimulus dominated vection.

Note that the object-background hypothesis bears similarity with the *rest frame hypothesis* proposed earlier by Prothero (1998) and Prothero & Parker (2003). This hypothesis states that "a particular reference frame, the 'rest frame,' is selected as the comparator for spatial judgments" (Prothero & Parker, 2003, p. 47). In this sense, spatial presence as well as vection are proposed to be (in part) determined by the extent to which a presented stimulus is accepted and selected as a primary reference or rest frame, which in turn is related to the likelihood of it being perceived a as background (see also theoretical framework by von der Heyde & Riecke, 2002; Riecke, 2003, chap. IV).

The findings by Riecke et al. (2006) could also be interpreted in the context of the object-background hypothesis and rest frame hypothesis: They observed that vection was reduced when the naturalism of the visual stimulus was decreased by inverting the presented scene or making it globally inconsistent via scene scrambling (see section 4.6 for details). Both stimulus inversion and scrambling decreased spatial presence and arguably might also have reduced the likelihood that the moving stimulus was perceived as a background and accepted as a stable reference frame with respect to which visual motion is more likely to be interpreted as self-motion rather than object-motion. In particular, I propose that spatial presence and immersion in a real or simulated environment are tightly linked to the likelihood of the stimulus being perceived and accepted as a "background" or scene. That is, in order for strong spatial presence and immersion to emerge, the visual stimulus should not be perceived as an object, but instead as a scene or background that can act as a stable reference or rest frame (von der Heyde & Riecke, 2002; Prothero, 1998; Prothero & Parker, 2003; Riecke, 2003, chap. IV). Although further research is needed to explore the concept of perceptual object-background separation and rest/reference frames for vection, the simplicity and unifying nature of these concepts if promising and might ultimately enable a deeper understanding of the underlying processes and allow us to better predict how vection and other phenomena like spatial presence depend on various stimulus parameters.

Stationary foreground vs. background

In agreement with the object-background hypothesis and the rest frame hypothesis, adding stationary background stimuli has been found to reduce or even inhibit circular vection, especially when presented peripherally, whereas stationary foreground stimuli can facilitate circular vection, especially if centrally presented (Brandt et al., 1975; Howard & Howard, 1994; Nakamura, 2006). Moreover, stationary foreground stimuli in front of a moving background are typically perceived to be moving with the observer, suggesting they are localized in body coordinates (Brandt et al., 1975; Fischer & Kornmüller, 1930), whereas during saturated vection the moving background stimulus is perceived as stationary in external coordinates and thus might act like an allocentric reference frame or rest frame. This situation is similar to riding a vehicle, where close-by objects (being part of the vehicle) move with the observer and are thus likely represented in an egocentric (body-centered) reference frame, whereas the more distant (outside) stimuli are likely to be part of the stationary environment. This can easily be utilized in motion simulator design and other applications (Nakamura, 2006). If the goal is to enhance perceived self-motion and overall realism, providing centrally located physical foreground objects like a cockpit, instruments, or other objects that match the overall simulation/application metaphor would be instrumental. This way, the simulated scene (outside of the cockpit) will be more easily perceived as the background, thus facilitating vection and enhancing overall simulation effectiveness. Conversely, if desired, vection (and potentially also motion sickness) can be reduced or even suppressed by providing peripheral static backgrounds (Prothero & Parker, 2003). Incidentally, this mimics typical desktop VR/gaming situations, where the static visible background of the room typically suppresses self-motions that might otherwise occur from the visual motions presented on the centrally located monitor in the foreground.

4.3 Consistent stereoscopic depth cues facilitate vection

Displaying the vection-inducing stimulus stereoscopically has been shown to facilitate both circular and linear vection (Lowther & Ware, 1996; Palmisano, 1996). Furthermore, consistent stereoscopic cues can increase the speed and travelled distance for optic flow-induced linear forward vection, which might have mediated the vection-enhancing effect of stereoscopic cues (Palmisano, 2002). Palmisano argued that the vection-enhancing effect of stereoscopic presentation goes beyond merely increasing the perceived distance of the visual stimulus. With stereoscopic presentation becoming increasingly available and affordable, this opens up new opportunities for increasing vection and the overall simulation experience by not only providing stereoscopic information of the simulated scene, but also purposefully enhancing object-background separation, providing unobtrusive stationary foreground object that increase the relative perceived motion between the stationary (observer-fixed) foreground and background movement through the simulated scene, or by providing a more realistic and believable scene that can more easily be accepted as a primary reference or rest frame.

4.4 Head-tracking can facilitate vection for moving observers

Lowther & Ware (1996) demonstrated that vection occurs later when observers moved in front of the stationary display used to present the vection-inducing motion, possibly because of the increased cue conflict between visual and vestibular/somatosensory cues. Using head tracking to couple the simulated perspective to the observers' motion mitigated most of the motion-induced vection deterioration.

This highlights the importance of including head tracking whenever observer head position is not fixed, such as to provide a simulated scene that "behaves" like the real world and can be perceived as stable in 3D space despite head movements. Head tracking might have facilitated vection by stabilizing the simulated scene, thus making it more believable and increasing the likelihood that it is selected and accepted as a primary reference frame or rest frame with respect to which scene relative motions are more easily perceived as self-motion instead of object-motions (von der Heyde & Riecke, 2002; Prothero & Parker, 2003; Riecke, 2003, chap. IV).

4.5 Attention and cognitive demand can modulate vection

To investigate potential attentional biases in visual vection, Kitazaki & Sato (2003) presented participants with vertically moving patterns of red and green dots moving in opposite (up vs. down) direction, and asked participants to attend to either the red or the green dots. The perceived direction of vection was largely determined by the non-attended stimulus, both when the red and green dots were spatially separated (exp. 1) or superimposed (exp. 2). When the upward and downward moving patterns were presented in different depth planes, however, the far stimulus dominated the attentional modulation, although there was still some attentional contribution. Apart from a direct effect of attention on vection, it is also conceivable that the attended stimulus was perceived to be closer, such that perceived depth ordering and not attention per se determined vection (see discussion in Seno et al. 2009). Furthermore, the attended stimulus might have become the perceptual "object" or "figure", such that attention might have modulated the perceptual object-background relationship, which in turn might have determined vection. Recently, Trutoiu et al. (2008) showed that forward linear visual vection occurs earlier if participants were performing an attention-demanding working-memory task (counting specific targets moving by in the visual stimulus). This suggests that vection can be enhanced if one does not pay particular attention to the vection-inducing stimulus.

In summary, although it seems likely that attention can modulate vection, it remains to be determined if attention can directly affect vection or whether the effect is mediated by other factors like eye movement patterns or changes in the perceived depth structure or object-background relationships. No matter what the underlying processes, it is clear that we can modify the vection experience intentionally to some degree, which is relevant for both fundamental research, where task instructions should be carefully phrased, and for applications, where task requirements and expectations can likely affect the effectiveness of a motion simulation and the overall user experience.

4.6 Reference frames, naturalism, and ecological validity of vection-inducing stimuli

Already in 1954, Gibson put forth that "Perceived motion occurs in a perceptually stable space or environment. Another way of saying this is to assert that the perception of stability is part and parcel of the perception of motion; you cannot have the latter without the former" (Gibson, 1954, p. 310). Thus, when we see environmental motion, (illusory) self-motion might be inferred due to our conscious or unconscious assumption of a stable environment (Dichgans & Brandt, 1978; Prothero & Parker, 2003). If this were the case, one might posit that moving visual or auditory stimuli that depict objects that normally do not move (e.g., houses or the sound of church bells) should enhance vection, compared to moving objects where our experience does not suggest stationarity (e.g., the sight or sound of a moving car). In the following, I will review studies that explicitly tested this hypothesis for visual vection. Note that auditory vection can also be facilitated when the moving sound sources represent objects that normally do not move (so-called "acoustic landmarks" like

church bells) as compared to objects that move (e.g., the sound of a driving car) or are ambiguous (e.g., pink noise) (Larssonet al., 2004; Riecke et al., 2005; Väljamäe et al., 2009).
While most of the classic visual vection studies used abstract stimuli like polka-dotted or striped patterns, several researchers stressed that complex, naturalistic, and ecologically relevant stimuli should instead be used for studying self-motion perception (Gibson, 1954; Wann & Rushton, 1994). Indeed, when using naturalistic stimuli projected on a wide (142° × 110°) FOV dome projection of a flight simulator, van der Steen & Brockhoff (2000) observed surprisingly rapid vection buildup with saturated linear (forward) and circular (yaw) vection after only 2.7s and 3s, respectively. This is considerably faster than for abstract, non-naturalistic stimuli, where vection takes between 10s (Brandt et al., 1973) to 20-30s (Howard & Howard, 1994) until reaching saturation. This led van der Steen & Brockhoff (2000) to propose that the natural scene might have contributed to the unusually fast vection buildup. Unfortunately, this hypothesis was not directly tested, and a multitude of differences in the experimental setup, procedure, and response measures compared to classic vection studies makes direct comparisons problematic.

Naturalistic, globally consistent stimuli facilitate vection

To provide a more conclusive answer and assess if naturalistic stimuli do indeed enhance vection, we performed a series of experiments that directly manipulated the degree of naturalism and global scene consistency (i.e., higher-level factors) within one experimental paradigm (Schulte-Pelkum et al., 2003; Riecke et al., 2006). In a first study, circular yaw vection was induced by seating participants behind a curved projection screen (84°×63° FOV) displaying a rotating virtual environment created from either a naturalistic roundshot photograph (see Figure 1b) or a mosaic-like scrambled version of the same photograph (see Figure 1c)(Schulte-Pelkum et al. 2003, see also Schulte-Pelkum 2007, exp. 1). While the globally consistent scene was rendered perspectively correct and contained ample pictorial depth cues and might thus facilitate vection by providing a reference frame of a naturalistic environment on could feel spatially present in, the scrambled stimulus contained the same local image information and statistics, but could not be interpreted as a naturalistic scene one could feel present in. In addition, the scene scrambling procedure introduced additional high-contrast edges, which are known to increase perceived motion and facilitate vection (Dichgans & Brandt, 1978; Diener et al., 1976; Palmisano & Gillam, 1998). These lower-level factors thus worked against our higher-level hypothesis that naturalistic stimuli might enhance vection. Nevertheless, the naturalistic stimulus resulted in earlier vection onset and higher perceived vection intensity and convincingness than the scrambled stimulus.

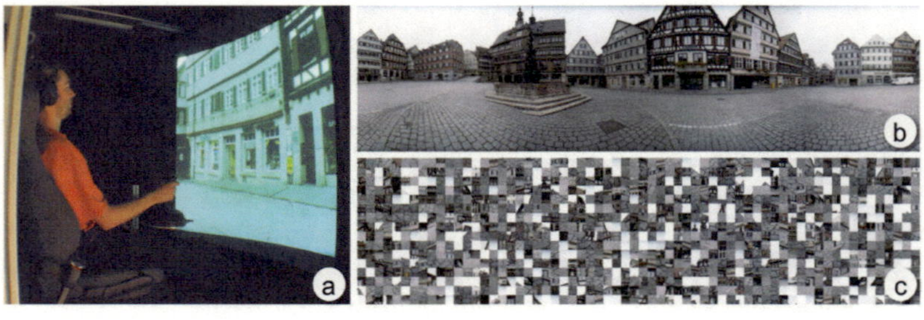

Fig. 1. (a): Participant seated behind curved projection screen showing the naturalistic circular vection stimulus based on a panoramic image (b). A globally inconsistent scene was created by mosaic-like scrabbling of the panoramic image (c).

Riecke et al. (2006) replicated and extended these results by systematically varying the degree of stimulus degradation and global inconsistency (see Figure 2, a-f). Results showed enhanced vection and presence for the naturalistic stimulus as compared to any of the sliced or scrambled stimuli, and hardly any influence of the type or degree of stimulus degradation. Figure 2, g-i contrasts the vection measures for the intact versus the least degraded stimulus. Together, these results suggest that higher-level factors related to scene consistency dominated over lower-level factors (more high-contrast edges for the scrambled stimulus) that would have predicted the opposite result.

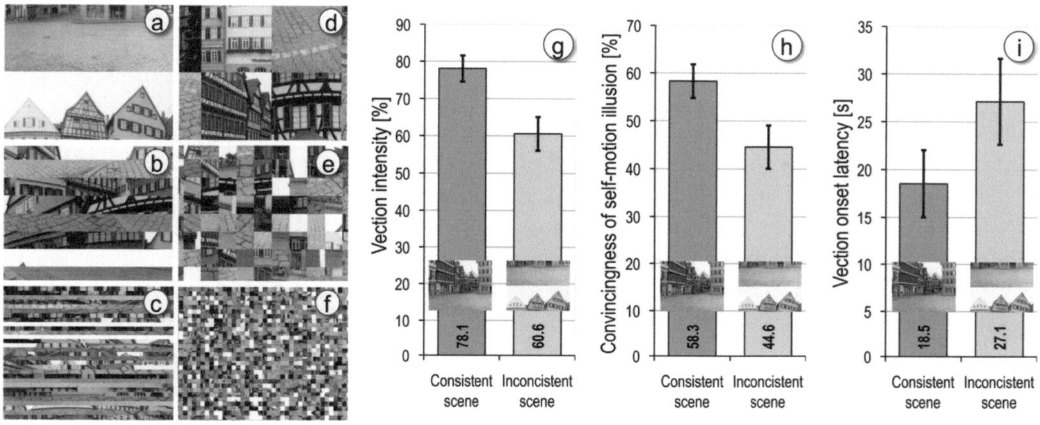

Fig. 2. 54°×45° view of the different horizontally sliced (a-c) and mosaic-like scrambled (d-f) vection-inducing stimuli as seen by participants in (Riecke et al., 2006) in addition to the globally consistent stimulus (cf. Figure 1, a & b). (g) – (i): Circular vection measures for the comparison of the globally consistent stimulus (left bar) and one of the globally inconsistent stimuli (the sliced version depicted in (a)). Note the vection impairment for the globally inconsistent (less naturalistic) stimulus, suggesting higher-level/cognitive influences. Depicted are mean ± one standard error of the mean, re-plotted from a subset of the original data of Riecke et al. (2006) for 40°/s stimulus velocity without data normalization.

There are at least three underlying mechanism that might explain the observed vection-facilitating effect of globally consistent, naturalistic stimuli:

1. The globally consistent stimulus contained ample pictorial depth cues arranged in a consistent, naturalistic environment. This might have increased the perceived distance of the stimulus, which is known to increase perceived vection velocity (Wist et al., 1975), which in turn is associated with enhanced vection. In fact, increasing stimulus velocities in (Schulte-Pelkum et al., 2003) from 20°/s to 40°/s to 60°/s reduced vection onset latencies and increased vection intensity and convincingness.
2. Previous studies showed that perceived foreground-background separation can affect vection: When vection-inducing stimuli are comprised of multiple parts (e.g., superimposed or spatially separated), vection is dominated by the motion of the perceived background (Howard & Heckmann, 1989; Nakamura & Shimojo, 1999; Ohmi et al., 1987; Seno et al., 2009). In our study, the naturalistic scene stimulus and pictorial depth contained therein might have resulted in a perceived foreground-background separation between the physical screen and setup acting as the foreground and the

projected scene being perceived as further away and thus acting as a moving background, thus indirectly facilitating vection.

3. Presence ratings were significantly higher for the naturalistic stimulus than any of the sliced or scrambled stimuli, and were consistently correlated with vection measures. Thus, the naturalistic scene might have provided a more believable and convincing, stable reference frame and primary rest frame than the globally inconsistent stimuli, such that stimulus motion might be more easily perceived or interpreted as self-motion than image or object motion (Dichgans & Brandt, 1978; Gibson, 1954; Prothero, 1998).

In sum, the data suggest that not only lower-level factors, but also higher-level factors like the interpretation of the stimulus as a believable and ecologically valid scene can affect self-motion perception.

Natural stimulus orientation enhances vection and presence

In a second experiment, Riecke et al. (2006) showed that inverting the naturalistic scene such that it appears upside-down reduced both the convincingness of vection and rated presence in the scene. Note that lower-level factors (e.g., image statistics) and scene consistency were identical between the upright and upside-down stimulus. This corroborates the relevance of higher-level/cognitive factors like the ecological validity and naturalism of the stimulus and the existence of optic flow from a believable ground surface, which has been shown to facilitate vection (Sato et al., 2007).

Naturalistic stimuli induce stronger vection than abstract geometric patterns

Further indication of potential higher-level influences stem from Richards et al. (2004), who investigated how postural stability during linear treadmill walking is affected by different moving visual stimuli presented on a projection screen (FOV: 65°×48°). Body sway in roll and pitch direction was more pronounced for a simple textured room display that contained intrinsic upright orientation cues (i.e., visual polarity defined by room geometry and clearly distinguishable ceiling, walls, and floor) as compared to a black and white polka-dotted cylindrical room that had no intrinsic upright cues. Furthermore, the room environment were rated as perceptually more compelling and resulted anecdotally in more frequent and intense vection experiences and reduced vection drop-outs. This supports findings by Riecke et al. (2006) and Schulte-Pelkum et al. (2003) that consistent, naturalistic visual cues enhance vection. Similarly, Wann & Rushton (1994) observed stronger circular vection for a naturalistic 3D environment presented via HMD as compared to the 2D texture stripes of a simulated optokinetic drum. Note, however, that the room versus polka-dotted stimuli in Richards et al. (2004) and the 3D environment versus texture stripes in Wann & Rushton (1994) differed not only in terms of naturalism and inherent upright-direction, but also with regards to other factors that are known to affect vection and could thus have contributed to the observed effects, including their spatial frequency content and the number of moving contrasts (Diener et al., 1976; Palmisano & Gillam, 1998; Hu et al., 1997) or perceived depth and foreground-background separation (Howard & Heckmann, 1989; Seno et al., 2009).

Tumbling sensation (roll vection) is facilitated by cue-rich, naturalistic environment

Additional support for the importance of naturalistic 3D environments comes from tumbling room studies, where stationary observers are surrounded by an (empty or fully furnished) room that can be rotated around the observers' roll axis. The perception of body tilt and roll vection was facilitated by a number of factors including the availability of a visual frame of reference, objects with clear visual polarity (i.e., intrinsic "up" direction), rotation velocity of the tumbling room, and field of view (Allison et al., 1999; Howard & Childerson, 1994). With 30°/s rotation of a fully furnished room with ample visual polarity cues and unrestricted FOV, up to 80% of observers experienced strong tumbling sensations including head-over-heels (cartwheel) roll vection. Tumbling (roll vection) occurred less frequently for smaller rotational velocities (15°/s instead of 30/s) and reduced field of views. These results highlight the vection-inducing power of naturalistic full-field visual motion. Further, carefully conducted research is, however, needed to more deeply understand what parameters of the visual stimulus make it more effective, and to disambiguate lower-level, bottom-up factors (like number of moving contrasts and edges) from higher-level perceptual and cognitive factors (like the "known" visual polarity of objects or the familiarity of "rooms"). Using wide-FOV VR simulators would give us the flexibility to more easily investigate these issues without the need to equip physical tumbling rooms with different objects and having to secure them for roll rotations.

4.7 Does the possibility of actual motion affect the illusion of self-motion?

Whenever self-motions are only simulated (e.g., through visual cues or a motion platform) and not actually performed, there is a conflict between some cues suggesting self-motion and others indicating stationarity. Apart from sensory cues directly indicating motion or no-motion, there are typically also other factors that might affect perceived self-motion. In particular, we are typically aware whether actual motion is, in fact, possible (e.g., when sitting on a moveable platform or vehicle) or not (e.g., when we stand/sit on solid ground). Thus, in order to provide compelling sensations of (illusory) self-motion, we might not only need to overcome the sensory conflict between sensory information suggesting self-motion versus stationarity, but potentially also "convince" us that actual motion is indeed possible.

Theme parks have long recognized the importance of providing a cognitive-perceptual framework of movability, e.g., by guiding users of a star wars fun ride (at Disney's Hollywood Studio theme park) through a (fake) space-craft airport before entering the "space-craft", which is a motion platform carefully disguised as a space ship such that users are unaware of the actual motion limitations of the system. Apart from being entertaining and avoiding that visitors get bored while waiting for the next ride, providing such a scenario and suggesting movability of the space craft might help to prime visitors to expect actual motion and more easily accept and believe the motion simulation. Although such suspension of disbelief is frequently used in consumer-market applications like theme parks and video arcades, there is surprisingly little published research investigating whether providing a cognitive-perceptual framework of movability can not only increase user enjoyment and fun but also enhance the effectiveness and believability of self-motion simulations.

As providing a cognitive-perceptual framework of movability can often be created at much lower cost and effort than increasing the actual motion range of VR simulations, pursuing this question could be of considerable interest for many applications. In addition, it can extend our understanding of higher-level influences on vection, and in particular on the integration of multi-modal sensory cues with higher-level cognitive/perceptual information. In the following, I will review and discuss research that explicitly investigated whether the perceived possibility of actual self-motion can enhance vection, for example by designing for situational awareness of movability by providing a cognitive-perceptual framework suggesting the possibility of actual self-motion.

Participants are often seated on movable devices to facilitate vection

In order to suggest movability and facilitate vection, a number of vection researchers have seated participants on rotating chairs when investigating circular vection (Lackner, 1977; Väljamäe, 2009) or on moveable carts when studying linear vection (Berthoz et al., 1975; Lackner, 1977; Pavard & Berthoz, 1977; Andersen & Braunstein, 1985) and demonstrated the possibility of motion prior to the actual vection experiments. Andersen & Braunstein (1985, p. 124) stated, for example, that "several subjects in pilot studies and other observers had previously reported that the experience of self-motion was inhibited by the observation that they were in an environment in which they could not be physically moved". Surprisingly, however, none of the above-mentioned studies provided actual data that vection was indeed facilitated when participants were seated on a moveable chair or cart.

Children experience vection earlier when sitting on moveable platform

To the best of our knowledge, the first study that explicitly addressed this issue was conducted by Lepecq et al. (1995) with children of seven and eleven years. Half of the participants were seated on a chair with rollers ("movement possible" condition) and were demonstrated prior to the actual experiment how the chair could move. The other half of the participants were seated on a stationary chair ("movement impossible" condition) and shown that the chair could not be moved. Although participants were always stationary during the subsequent backward linear visual vection experiment, knowledge about the possibility of motion reduced vection onset latencies. The frequency of vection occurrences remained unaffected by this cognitive manipulation, though. Nevertheless, Lepecq et al. (1995) provided first evidence that the knowledge and prior experience that actual motion is possible could facilitate vection, suggesting higher-level, cognitive contributions.

Is there a similar effect of perceived movability on vection in adults, or are they less easily "fooled to believe"? There are only a few studies that investigated this issue in adults, and the results provide somewhat mixed evidence.

Self-motion-bias versus object-motion-bias instructions affect vection reporting

Palmisano & Chan (2004) used adult participants and a similar overall procedure as Lepecq et al. (1995) to investigate if linear forward linear vection induced by an optic flow display is modulated by creating situations were physical movements are possible vs. impossible. While the "movement possible" (or self-motion-bias) group was instructed to report the onset and offset of *self-motion* as in Lepecq et al. (1995), the "movement impossible" (or object-motion-bias) group in Palmisano & Chan (2004) was instructed to report the onset and offset of *object motion*, and vection was inferred when no object motion was reported. This object-motion-bias reduced the occurrence of vection reports as compared to the self-motion-bias, although vection onset latencies were unaffected by the cognitive manipulation. Note that these results differ from Lepecq et al.'s findings, where the cognitive manipulation affected the onset latency, but not the occurrence of vection. It is conceivable that the object-motion-bias introduced a criterion shift and response bias in favor of reporting object-motion. Moreover, trials with only partial vection, where object- and self-motion co-exist, would have been identified as vection trials for the self-motion-bias group but as no-vection trials for the object-motion-bias group. Hence, it remains unclear whether the cognitive manipulation in Palmisano & Chan (2004) did indeed affect perceived self-motion.

Elevator vection occurs earlier if actual motion is possible

In a vertical oscillatory ("elevator") vection study with adults, Wright et al. (2006) showed that participants who were seated in a vertical oscillator and shown prior to the actual experiment how they could be moved reported more compelling vection than participants who saw the same vection stimulus, but were sitting on a stationary chair in a different room. Vection amplitudes and onset latencies remained unaffected by the cognitive manipulation, though. To explain their data, Wright et al. (2006) proposed two dissociable factors underlying vection: One process determining the compellingness of vection that is susceptible to cognitive manipulations, and a second process primarily driven by visual (bottom-up) cues that mainly affects vection onset latencies and the extend of the self-motion illusion. Note that this distinction does not fit the data by Lepecq et al. (1995), where the cognitive manipulation affected the onset latency, but not the occurrence of vection.

Visual circular vection not facilitated if actual motion is possible

While by Lepecq et al. (1995) and Wright et al. (2006) found a significant facilitation of linear visual vection when participants were previously demonstrated that actual motion is possible, circular visual vection might be less affected by such cognitive manipulations (Schulte-Pelkum, 2007; Schulte-Pelkum et al., 2004): When participants were seated on a 6 degree of freedom Stewart motion platform and previously shown how the platform can move, 2/3 of them did indeed believe that they were physically moving in at least some of the trials where the platform was switched on (see Figure 3, middle), and many of them were fairly certain that actual motion occurred (see Figure 3, right). Nevertheless, vection reports were unaffected by this cognitive manipulation, and vection onset times, intensity, and convincingness were identical between movement-possible and movement-impossible trials. As discussed in detail in Riecke (2009) and Schulte-Pelkum (2007), the lack of a clear vection-facilitating effect of the cognitive manipulation might be due to a number of differences in experimental procedures, as compared to Lepecq et al. (1995) and Wright et al.

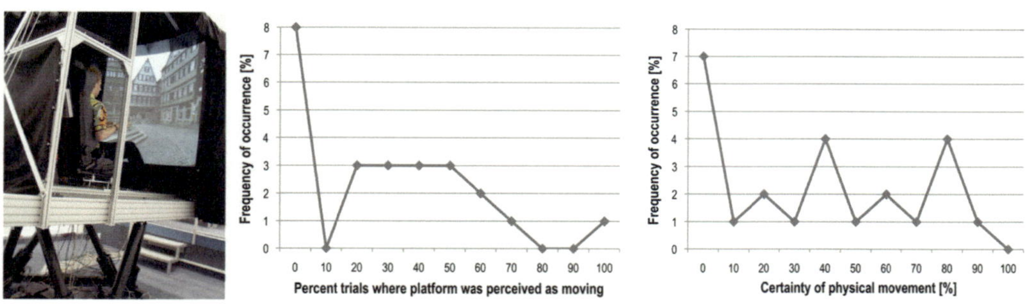

Fig. 3. **Left:** Participant seated on a motion platform that was either switched on ("motion possible" condition) or not ("motion impossible"). **Middle:** Histogram of participants' responses. Participants were asked to rate in what percentage of trials they perceived the platform to be physically moving. 8/24 participants (33.3%) stated that it never moved, whereas the remaining 66.7% stated that the platform moved in at least 10% of the trials. One participant stated that it always moved. **Right**: Participants were asked to rate how certain they were (on a 0-100% scale) that the platform did move in at least some trials. Only seven participants were certain that it never moved, and five participants were at least 80% certain that it moved. Data re-plotted from (Schulte-Pelkum et al., 2004; Schulte-Pelkum, 2007).

(2006), and we are currently planning experiments to assess if visual circular vection can indeed be affected by providing a cognitive-perceptual framework of movability.

Auditory vection can be facilitated by cognitive-perceptual framework of movability

While it remains to be demonstrated if a cognitive-perceptual framework of movability can affect visually-induced circular vection, there is recent evidence that it can affect auditorily-induced circular vection (Riecke, Feuereissen, & Rieser, 2009). In order to provide high-quality recordings of rotating sound fields for the auditory vection experiments, the lab was equipped with two easily distinguishable and localizable sound sources positioned 90° apart, and participants were seated on a hammock chair mounted above a circular treadmill (see Figure 4a) and passively rotated. Small in-ear microphones were used to generate individualized binaural recordings of what participants hear when actually rotating in the lab. During the subsequent vection experiment, participants sat on the hammock chair with the circular treadmill switched off while wearing blindfolds and noise-cancelling headphones displaying the previously recorded rotating sound fields. Participants' feet were either suspended by a chair-attached footrest (see Figure 4b, "movement possible" condition) or positioned on solid ground ("movement impossible" condition). Providing a cognitive-perceptual framework of movability in the "motion possible" condition yielded higher vection intensity ratings (see Figure 4d), and there was a marginally significant trend ($p<.1$) towards more frequent occurrence of vection (84% vs. 68%, see Figure 4c), reduced vection onset latencies (41s vs. 31s, see Figure 4e), and higher perceived realism of actually rotating in the lab. Hence, the common practice of seating participants on moveable chairs or platforms (Lackner, 1977; Väljamäe, 2007, 2009) does indeed seem to benefit auditory vection.

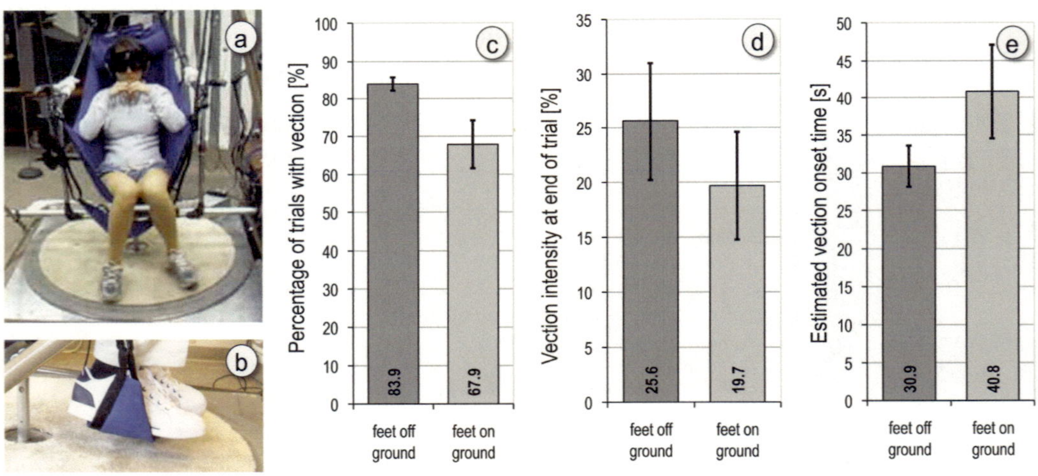

Fig. 4. (a): Participant wearing blindfold and noise-cancelling headphone, seated on a hammock chair mounted stationary above a circular treadmill. (b) In a "feet off ground" condition, participants' feet were suspended by a footrest, whereas in a "feet on ground" condition (a) participants' feet were on solid ground, thus acting as a "motion impossible" condition. (c) – (e): Auditory circular vection measures show slightly enhanced vection when participants' feet did not touch solid ground. Depicted are mean ± 1SEM, re-plotted from a subset of the original data of (Riecke et al., 2009) with no jitter.

The exact mechanisms underlying this effect await further experimentation, though: In the current experiment, both cognitive and perceptual factors might have contributed. On the one hand, resting one's feet on solid ground provides somatosensory and thus lower-level, perceptual cues indicating stationarity. On the other hand, it provides higher-level, cognitive "knowledge" that could have primed participants to believe that physical motion was impossible. From the current data, it is not possible to disambiguate between cognitive and perceptual factors, and they likely contributed both and might even support or depend on each other.

Touching the floor attenuates visual roll vection in weightlessness

The influence of touching the stationary floor on vection was also investigated by Young et al. (1983) and Young & Shelhamer (1990): While in weightlessness, visually induced roll vection was compared between a "free floating" condition, where only a bite bar fixated participants' orientation and position in space, and a "tactile" condition, where an additional shoulder harness pressed participants to the floor using elastic bands. Thus touching the floor resulted in more vection drop-outs and reduced the strength of roll vection. Some participants also reported prolonged vection onset latencies. Similar to the auditory vection study discussed above (Riecke et al., 2009) touching and being restrained to the floor in Young et al. (1983) and Young & Shelhamer (1990) might have attenuated visual roll vection via both lower-level perceptual processes, namely somatosensory cues indicating being tied to a stationary floor, and higher-level, cognitive factors like the knowledge that actual motion was impossible due to the restraints.

Conclusions

In summary, although it is often difficult to disentangle the possible influence of cognitive versus perceptual processes, there is converging evidence that providing a cognitive-perceptual framework of movability can under certain conditions facilitate self-motion perception. This is consistent with informal reports and common practice of seating participants on moveable platforms in situations where vection is difficult to achieve, as is the case for auditory vection (e.g., Lackner 1977; Väljamäe 2007) or visual vection with small field of views (Andersen & Braunstein, 1985). Although the above-mentioned results are promising, further research is necessary to enable us to more deeply understand why, how, and under which conditions perceptual and/or cognitive information suggesting movability versus stationarity can affect self-motion perception. While of clear theoretical interest, there is also a clear applied benefit, as cognitive-perceptual frameworks of movability can often be implement with relatively little effort, especially compared to the costs involved in allowing for large-scale physical locomotion or full-fledged motion simulators.

5. Cross-modal facilitation of vection

While an in-depth review of multi-modal aspect of vection would go beyond the scope of this chapter, it is important to realize that there are a number of cross-modal effects and facilitations of vection that could help to optimize VR simulations and other immersive applications. For example, galvanic vestibular stimulation can both directly induce self-tilt and affect visually simulated self-motions (Cress et al., 1997; Lepecq et al., 2006). Adding subtle vibrations to the observers' seat and footrest has been shown to enhance visual vection (Riecke et al., 2005; Schulte-Pelkum, 2007). Similarly, vibrations can enhance auditory vection (Riecke et al., 2009), especially if accompanied by a matching simulated engine sound (Väljamäe et al., 2006; Väljamäe et al., 2009). Although moving sound fields by themselves can only induce vection in about 20-75% of blindfolded listeners, they have been shown to enhance vection induced by other modalities, including visual circular vection (Riecke et al., 2009) and biomechanical circular vection induced by stepping along a circular treadmill (Riecke et al., 2010). Adding small physical motions (simple jerks) to the onset of visually simulated self-motion has been shown to significant enhance visually induced vection, both for passive movement (Berger et al., 2010; Riecke et al., 2006; Schulte-Pelkum, 2007; Wong & Frost, 1981) and for simple self-initiated motion cueing (Riecke, 2006). Note that these jerks facilitated vection despite being only qualitatively correct (i.e., they matched the direction and precise temporal onset of the visual motion, but not the extent or acceleration). This suggests that there might be a surprisingly large coherence zone within which visuo-vestibular conflicts go unnoticed or at least have little detrimental effect (Steen, 1998). Finally, applying vibrations and small physical movements (jerks) together enhanced visual vection more then either of them alone (Schulte-Pelkum, 2007, exp. 6). Together, these results suggest considerable cross-modal benefits for self-motion perception, even when cross-modal stimuli are only qualitatively matched. While proper motion cueing using 6DOF motion platforms is clearly desirable in many applications including flight or driving simulations, budgets and space are often limited. In such situations, vibrations and spatialized auditory cues can often be included at moderate cost and effort. Even simple commercially available motion seats or gaming seats might provide considerable benefits to self-motion perception and overall simulation effectiveness.

6. Potential undesirable side-effects of vection in VR

For all applications, the potential benefits of providing compelling self-motion illusions need to be carefully evaluated against potential undesirable side-effects (for a detailed discussion, see Hettinger 2002; Kennedy et al. 2003 and references therein). The occurrence of vection can, for example, correlate with undesirable side-effects like motion sickness or motion after-effects. It is, however, still unclear whether or how vection might be causally related to motion sickness, as vection generally seems to occur when visuo-vestibular cue conflicts are small, whereas motion sickness tends to occur for larger cue conflicts (Kennedy et al., 2003; Palmisano et al., 2007). Moreover, visually-induced motion sickness can occur without either vection or optokinetic nystagmus (Ji, So, & Cheung, 2009). Vection is also known to co-occur with body sway in standing observers (Howard, 1982). While small infants can indeed tip over due to large-field visual stimulation (Lee & Aronson, 1974), children older than five years and adults seem less affected and sway less. While vection and visually induced body sway likely share similar pathways and vection strength can be indicative of body sway, body sway occurs well before the onset of vection and does not necessarily match the direction of perceived self-motion, again questioning a direct causal relation between vection and body sway (Guerraz & Bronstein, 2008; Wang et al., 2010). In sum, further research is needed to carefully assess factors promoting undesirable side-effects like motion/simulator sickness, postural responses, after-effects, and (re)adaptation effects, and to what degree there might or might not be any causal relationships to vection.

7. Conclusions and outlook

Self-motion illusions are embodied illusions that can be quite compelling and thus critically affect the overall experience and effectiveness of VR and other immersive media. Hence, it is important to better understand the nature of the phenomenon of vection and the different contributing factors and their interactions, such that the illusion can be purposefully elicited or suppressed, depending on the specific goals and requirements of a given application. While this chapter provides a review on different factors that can enhance vection, this information can, of course, also be used to purposefully inhibit the illusion where desired. Depending on the goals and user task of an application, different degrees of vection and overall presence/immersion might be desirable, and it should be carefully evaluated on a case-by-case basis to what degree vection can or cannot contribute to the overall goal.

Given the increased availability and affordability of large, multi-screen displays setups, care should be taken that self-motion is only perceived where intended. For example, when manipulating 3D objects or CAD models on a screen, this should be perceived as object motion and not self-motion. Especially when users have to quickly switch between different tasks, screens, or simulated environments, vection as well as spatial presence and immersion should be avoided. Conversely, for architecture walkthroughs, vehicle simulation, telepresence, and other applications where perceptual/behavioral realism is of the essence, simulated observer motions should be perceived as self-motion and not object motion; else, the 3D model might be perceived as a small toy mockup instead of a full-sized, naturalistic environment. For disambiguating between perceived object versus self motion, manipulating the perceived object-background separation might be the most effective means, as discussed above.

Interestingly, many sought-after attributes in the design of VR systems and other immersive media seem to also be factors that are known to enhance vection, such as large FOVs, naturalistic and ecologically valid stimuli, stereoscopic presentation, perceived background motion, or multi-modal stimulation and consistency. In particular, presence in the simulated environment frequently correlates with vection, seems to benefit from similar factors as vection, and might even be mediated by vection (Riecke et al., 2006; Väljamäe, 2009), as predicted by the rest frame hypothesis (Prothero & Parker, 2003). I propose that utilizing and further developing promising comprehensive frameworks like the rest frame hypothesis (Prothero, 1998; Prothero & Parker, 2003), the object-background hypothesis (Seno et al., 2009), or the reference frame model (von der Heyde & Riecke, 2002; Riecke, 2003, chap. 4) can foster a deeper understanding of the mechanisms underlying phenomena like vection, presence, or spatial orientation and enable us to devise operation definitions and novel measurement methods (Prothero & Parker, 2003; Riecke, 2003, chapter IV). Ultimately, being able to integrate seemingly disparate findings into a conceptual framework will allow us to derive testable hypothesis and predictions that can guide future research and applications.

In conclusion, a growing body of evidence suggests that vection and overall simulation effectiveness is not only determined by physical stimulus parameters themselves, but also by other factors including how we look at, perceive, and interpret the stimulus, the perceived foreground-background separation, and a variety of higher-level phenomena like cognitive-perceptual frameworks of movability, naturalism and ecological validity, spatial presence, and reference/rest frames. Clearly, these factors deserve more attention both in basic research and applications. These factors might also turn out to be crucial especially in the context of VR applications and self-motion simulations, as they have the potential of offering an elegant and affordable way to optimize simulations in terms of perceptual and behavioral effectiveness. Compared to other means of increasing the convincingness and effectiveness of self-motion simulations like increasing the visual field of view or using a motion platform, higher-level factors can often be manipulated rather easily and without much cost, such that they might be an important step towards a lean and elegant approach to effective self-motion simulation. This is nicely demonstrated by many theme park rides, where setting up the proper cognitive framework and expectation (both highly cognitive factors) helps to draw users more easily and effectively into the simulation and into "believing". Thus, I posit that an approach that is centered around the perceptual and behavioral effectiveness and not only the physical stimulus realism is important both for gaining a deeper understanding in basic research and offering a lean and elegant way to improve a number of applications, especially in the advancing field of virtual reality simulations. This might ultimately allow us to come closer to fulfilling the promise of VR as a believable "window onto the simulated world", such that the virtual reality can be perceived and accepted as an alternate reality that enables natural and unencumbered human behavior.

8. References

Allison, R. S., Howard, I. P., & Zacher, J. E. (1999). Effect of field size, head motion, and rotational velocity on roll vection and illusory self-tilt in a tumbling room. *Perception, 28*(3), 299-306.

Andersen, G. J. (1986). Perception of Self-Motion - Psychophysical and Computational Approaches. *Psychological Bulletin, 99*(1), 52-65.

Andersen, G. J., & Braunstein, M. L. (1985). Induced Self-Motion in Central Vision. *Journal of Experimental Psychology – Human Perception and Performance, 11*(2), 122-132.

Becker, W., Raab, S., & Jürgens, R. (2002). Circular vection during voluntary suppression of optokinetic reflex. *Experimental Brain Research, 144*(4), 554-557.

Berger, D. R., Schulte-Pelkum, J., & Bülthoff, H. H. (2010). Simulating believable forward accelerations on a stewart motion platform. *ACM Trans. Appl. Percept., 7*(1), 1-27. doi:10.1145/1658349.1658354

Berthoz, A., Pavard, B., & Young, L. R. (1975). Perception of linear horizontal self-motion induced by peripheral vision (linearvection) - basic characteristics and visual-vestibular interactions. *Experimental Brain Research, 23*(5), 471-489.

Bles, W. (1981). Stepping around: circular vection and Coriolis effects. In J. Long & A. Baddeley (Eds.), *Attention and performance IX* (pp. 47–61). Erlbaum, Hillsdale, NJ.

Brandt, T., Büchele, W., & Arnold, F. (1977). Arthrokinetic nystagmus and ego-motion sensation. *Experimental Brain Research, 30*(2), 331-338. doi:10.1007/BF00237260

Brandt, T., Dichgans, J., & Koenig, E. (1973). Differential effects of central versus peripheral vision on egocentric and exocentric motion perception. *Experimental Brain Research, 16*, 476-491.

Brandt, T., Wist, E. R., & Dichgans, J. (1975). Foreground and Background in Dynamic Spatial Orientation. *Perception & Psychophysics, 17*(5), 497-503.

Bubka, A., & Bonato, F. (2010). Natural visual-field features enhance vection. *Perception, 39*(5), 627 – 635. doi:10.1068/p6315

Cheung, B. S. K., Howard, I. P., Nedzelski, J. M., & Landolt, J. P. (1989). Circularvection About Earth-horizontal Axes in Bilateral Labyrinthine-defective Subjects. *Acta Oto-Laryngologica, 108*(5), 336. doi:10.3109/00016488909125537

Cress, J., Hettinger, L. J., Cunningham, J., Riccio, G., Haas, M. W., & McMillan, G. (1997). Integrating vestibular displays for VE and airborne applications. *IEEE Computer Graphics and Applications, 17*(6), 46-52. doi:10.1109/38.626969

Dichgans, J., & Brandt, T. (1978). Visual-Vestibular Interaction: Effects on Self-Motion Perception and Postural Control. In *Perception*, Handbook of Sensory Physiology (pp. 756 - 804). Springer.

Diener, H. C., Wist, E. R., Dichgans, J., & Brandt, T. (1976). Spatial Frequency Effect on Perceived Velocity. *Vision Research, 16*(2), 169-176.

Fischer, M. H., & Kornmüller, A. E. (1930). Optokinetisch ausgelöste Bewegungswahrnehmung und optokinetischer Nystagmus [Optokinetically induced motion perception and optokinetic nystagmus]. *Journal für Psychologie und Neurologie*, 273-308.

Giannopulu, I., & Lepecq, J. C. (1998). Linear-vection chronometry along spinal and sagittal axes in erect man. *Perception, 27*(3), 363-372.

Gibson, J. J. (1954). The visual perception of objective motion and subjective movement. *Psychological Review, 61*(5), 304-314. doi:10.1037/h0061885

Guerraz, M., & Bronstein, A. M. (2008). Mechanisms underlying visually induced body sway. *Neuroscience Letters, 443*(1), 12-16. doi:10.1016/j.neulet.2008.07.053

Held, R., Dichgans, J., & Bauer, J. (1975). Characteristics of moving visual scenes influencing spatial orientation. *Vision Research, 15*(3), 357-365, IN1. doi:10.1016/0042-6989(75)90083-8

Hettinger, L. J. (2002). Illusory Self-motion in Virtual Environments. In K. M. Stanney (Ed.), *Handbook of Virtual Environments* (pp. 471-492). Lawrence Erlbaum.

von der Heyde, M., & Riecke, B. E. (2002). Embedding presence-related terminology in a logical and functional model. In F. Gouveia (Ed.), *Presence* (pp. 37-52).

Howard, I. P. (1982). *Human visual orientation*. Chichester, New York, Engl.: J. Wiley.

Howard, I. P. (1986). The perception of posture, self motion, and the visual vertical. In K. R. Boff, L. Kaufman, & J. P. Thomas (Eds.), *Sensory processes and perception*, Handbook of human perception and performance (Vol. 1, pp. 18.1-18.62). New York: Wiley.

Howard, I. P., & Childerson, L. (1994). The contribution of motion, the visual frame, and visual polarity to sensations of body tilt. *Perception, 23*(7), 753-762.

Howard, I. P., & Heckmann, T. (1989). Circular vection as a function of the relative sizes, distances, and positions of 2 competing visual-displays. *Perception, 18*(5), 657-665.

Howard, I. P., & Howard, A. (1994). Vection - the contributions of absolute and relative visual motion. *Perception, 23*(7), 745-751.

Howard, I. P., & Heckmann, T. (1989). Circular vection as a function of the relative sizes, distances, and positions of two competing visual displays. *Perception, 18*(5), 657 – 665. doi:10.1068/p180657

Hu, S. Q., Davis, M. S., Klose, A. H., Zabinsky, E. M., Meux, S. P., Jacobsen, H. A., Westfall, J. M., et al. (1997). Effects of spatial frequency of a vertically striped rotating drum on vection-induced motion sickness. *Aviation Space and Environmental Medicine, 68*(4), 306-311.

Ito, H., & Shibata, I. (2005). Self-motion perception from expanding and contracting optical flows overlapped with binocular disparity. *Vision Research, 45*(4), 397-402. doi:10.1016/j.visres.2004.11.009

Ji, J. T. T., So, R. H. Y., & Cheung, R. T. F. (2009). Isolating the Effects of Vection and Optokinetic Nystagmus on Optokinetic Rotation-Induced Motion Sickness. *Human Factors, 51*(5), 739-751. doi:10.1177/0018720809349708

Johansson, G. (1977). Studies on visual-perception of locomotion. *Perception, 6*(4), 365-376.

Johnson, W. H., Sunahara, F. A., & Landolt, J. P. (1999). Importance of the vestibular system in visually induced nausea and self-vection. *Journal of Vestibular Research - Equilibrium & Orientation, 9*(2), 83-87.

Kennedy, R. S., Drexler, J. M., Compton, D. E., Stanney, K. M., Lanham, D. S., & Harm, D. L. (2003). Configural scoring of simulator sickness, cybersickness, and space adaptation syndrome: Similarities and differences. In *Virtual and Adaptive Environments: Applications, Implications, and Human Performance Issues* (pp. 247–278).

Kim, J., & Palmisano, S. (2008). Effects of active and passive viewpoint jitter on vection in depth. *Brain Research Bulletin, 77*(6), 335-342. doi:10.1016/j.brainresbull.2008.09.011

Kitazaki, M., & Sato, T. (2003). Attentional modulation of self-motion perception. *Perception, 32*(4), 475-484. doi:10.1068/p5037

Kovacs, G., Raabe, M., & Greenlee, M. W. (2008). Neural correlates of visually induced self-motion illusion in depth. *Cerebral Cortex, 18*(8), 1779-1787. doi:10.1093/cercor/bhm203

Lackner, J. R. (1977). Induction of Illusory Self-Rotation and Nystagmus by a Rotating Sound-Field. *Aviation Space and Environmental Medicine, 48*(2), 129-131.

Larsson, P., Västfjäll, D., & Kleiner, M. (2004). Perception of Self-motion and Presence in Auditory Virtual Environments. In *Proceedings of 7th Annual Workshop of Presence* (pp. 252-258).

Lee, D. N., & Aronson, E. (1974). Visual proprioceptive control of standing in human infants. *Perception and Psychophysics, 15*(3), 529–532.

Lepecq, J. C., De Waele, C., Mertz-Josse, S., Teyssedre, C., Huy, P. T. B., Baudonniere, P. M., & Vidal, P. P. (2006). Galvanic vestibular stimulation modifies vection paths in healthy subjects. *Journal of Neurophysiology, 95*(5), 3199-3207. doi:10.1152/jn.00478.2005

Lepecq, J. C., Giannopulu, I., & Baudonniere, P. M. (1995). Cognitive effects on visually induced body motion in children. *Perception, 24*(4), 435-449.

Lowther, K., & Ware, C. (1996). Vection With Large Screen 3D Imagery. In *ACM CHI '96* (pp. 233-234).

Mach, E. (1875). *Grundlinien der Lehre von der Bewegungsempfindung*. Leipzig, Germany: Engelmann.

Mergner, T., & Becker, W. (1990). Perception of horizontal self-rotation: Multisensory and cognitive aspects. In R. Warren & A. H. Wertheim (Eds.), *Perception & Control of Self-Motion* (pp. 219-263). New Jersey, London: Erlbaum.

Mergner, T., Schweigart, G., Müller, M., Hlavacka, F., & Becker, W. (2000). Visual contributions to human self-motion perception during horizontal body rotation. *Archives Italiennes De Biologie, 138*(2), 139-166.

Mergner, T., Wertheim, A. H., & Rumberger, A. (2000). Which retinal and extra-retinal information is crucial for circular vection? *Archives Italiennes de Biologie, 138*(2), 123-138.

Nakamura, S. (2006). Effects of depth, eccentricity and size of additional static stimulus on visually induced self-motion perception. *Vision Research, 46*(15), 2344-2353. doi:10.1016/j.visres.2006.01.016

Nakamura, S. (2008). Effects of stimulus eccentricity on vection reevaluated with a binocularly defined depth. *Japanese Psychological Research, 50*(2), 77-86. doi:10.1111/j.1468-5884.2008.00363.x

Nakamura, S. (2010). Additional oscillation can facilitate visually induced self-motion perception: The effects of its coherence and amplitude gradient. *Perception, 39*(3), 320-329. doi:10.1068/p6534

Nakamura, S., & Shimojo, S. (1999). Critical role of foreground stimuli in perceiving visually induced self-motion (vection). *Perception, 28*(7), 893-902.

Ohmi, M., & Howard, I. P. (1988). Effect of Stationary Objects on Illusory Forward Self-Motion Induced by a Looming Display. *Perception, 17*(1), 5-11.

Ohmi, M., Howard, I. P., & Landolt, J. P. (1987). Circular Vection as a Function of Foreground-Background Relationships. *Perception, 16*(1), 17-22.

Palmisano, S. (1996). Perceiving self-motion in depth: The role of stereoscopic motion and changing-size cues. *Perception & Psychophysics, 58*(8), 1168-1176.

Palmisano, S. (2002). Consistent stereoscopic information increases the perceived speed of vection in depth. *Perception, 31*(4), 463-480. doi:10.1068/p3321

Palmisano, S., Bonato, F., Bubka, A., & Folder, J. (2007). Vertical display oscillation effects on forward vection and simulator sickness. *Aviation, Space, and Environmental Medicine, 78*(10), 951–956.

Palmisano, S., Burke, D., & Allison, R. S. (2003). Coherent perspective jitter induces visual illusions of self- motion. *Perception, 32*(1), 97-110.

Palmisano, S., & Chan, A. Y. C. (2004). Jitter and size effects on vection are immune to experimental instructions and demands. *Perception, 33*(8), 987-1000.

Palmisano, S., & Gillam, B. (1998). Stimulus eccentricity and spatial frequency interact to determine circular vection. *Perception, 27*(9), 1067-1077.

Palmisano, S., Gillam, B. J., & Blackburn, S. G. (2000). Global-perspective jitter improves vection in central vision. *Perception, 29*(1), 57-67.

Palmisano, S., & Kim, J. (2009). Effects of gaze on vection from jittering, oscillating, and purely radial optic flow. *Attention, Perception & Psychophysics, 71*(8), 1842-1853. doi:10.3758/APP.71.8.1842

Pavard, B., & Berthoz, A. (1977). Linear acceleration modifies perceived velocity of a moving visual scene. *Perception, 6*(5), 529-540.

Post, R. B. (1988). Circular vection is independent of stimulus eccentricity. *Perception, 17*(6), 737 – 744. doi:10.1068/p170737

Prothero, J. D. (1998). *The Role of Rest Frames in Vection, Presence and Motion Sickness* (PhD thesis). University of Washington. Retrieved from ftp://ftp.hitl.washington.edu/pub/publications/r-98-11/temp/r-98-11.pdf

Prothero, J. D., & Parker, D. E. (2003). A Unified Approach to Presence and Motion Sickness. In L. J. Hettinger & M. W. Haas (Eds.), *Virtual and Adaptive Environments: Applications, Implications, and Human Performance Issues* (pp. 47 - 66). Lawrence Erlbaum.

Richards, J. T., Mulavara, A. P., & Bloomberg, J. J. (2004). Postural stability during treadmill locomotion as a function of the visual polarity and rotation of a three-dimensional virtual environment. *Presence - Teleoperators and Virtual Environments, 13*(3), 371-384.

Riecke, B. E. (2003). *How far can we get with just visual information? Path integration and spatial updating studies in Virtual Reality* (PhD thesis). Eberhard-Karls-Universität Tübingen. Retrieved from www.kyb.mpg.de/publication.html?publ=2088

Riecke, B. E. (2006). Simple User-Generated Motion Cueing can Enhance Self-Motion Perception (Vection) in Virtual Reality. In *Proceedings of the ACM Symposium on Virtual Reality Software and Technology (VRST)* (pp. 104-107). Limassol, Cyprus: ACM. doi:http://dx.doi.org/10.1145/1180495.1180517

Riecke, B. E. (2009). Cognitive and higher-level contributions to illusory self-motion perception ("vection"): does the possibility of actual motion affect vection? *Japanese Journal of Psychonomic Science, 28*(1), 135-139.

Riecke, B. E., Feuereissen, D., & Rieser, J. J. (2009). Auditory self-motion simulation is facilitated by haptic and vibrational cues suggesting the possibility of actual motion. *ACM Trans. Appl. Percept., 6*(3), 1-22.

Riecke, B. E., Feuereissen, D., & Rieser, J. J. (2010). Spatialized Sound Influences Biomechanical Self-Motion Illusion ("Vection"). In *ACM Symposium on Applied Perception in Graphics and Visualization (APGV)* (p. 158). doi:http://doi.acm.org/10.1145/1394281.1394309

Riecke, B. E., Schulte-Pelkum, J., Avraamides, M. N., Heyde, M. V. D., & Bülthoff, H. H. (2006). Cognitive Factors can Influence Self-Motion Perception (Vection) in Virtual Reality. *ACM Transactions on Applied Perception, 3*(3), 194-216. doi:http://doi.acm.org/10.1145/1166087.1166091

Riecke, B. E., Schulte-Pelkum, J., & Caniard, F. (2006). Visually induced linear vection is enhanced by small physical accelerations. In *7th International Multisensory Research Forum (IMRF)*. Dublin, Ireland. Retrieved from http://www.kyb.mpg.de/publication.html?publ=3901

Riecke, B. E., Schulte-Pelkum, J., Caniard, F., & Bülthoff, H. H. (2005). Towards Lean and Elegant Self-Motion Simulation in Virtual Reality. In *Proceedings of IEEE Virtual Reality 2005* (pp. 131-138). Bonn, Germany. doi:http://doi.ieeecomputersociety.org/10.1109/VR.2005.83

Riecke, B. E., Väljamäe, A., & Schulte-Pelkum, J. (2009). Moving sounds enhance the visually-induced self-motion illusion (circular vection) in virtual reality. *ACM Trans. Appl. Percept., 6*(2), 1-27.

Riecke, B. E., Västfjäll, D., Larsson, P., & Schulte-Pelkum, J. (2005). Top-Down and Multi-Modal Influences on Self-Motion Perception in Virtual Reality. In *Proceedings of HCI international 2005* (pp. 1-10). Las Vegas, NV, USA. Retrieved from http://www.kyb.mpg.de/publication.html?publ=2765

Sato, T., Seno, T., Kanaya, H., & Fukazawa, H. (2007). Dominance of ground stimuli in vection induction. *Perception, 36*(ECVP Abstract Supplement), 180-181.

Schulte-Pelkum, J. (2007). *Perception of self-motion: Vection experiments in multi-sensory Virtual Environments* (PhD thesis). Ruhr-Universität Bochum.

Schulte-Pelkum, J., Riecke, B. E., & Bülthoff, H. H. (2004). Vibrational cues enhance believability of ego-motion simulation. In *International Multisensory Research Forum (IMRF)*. Retrieved from http://www.kyb.mpg.de/publication.html?publ=2766

Schulte-Pelkum, J., Riecke, B. E., von der Heyde, M., & Bülthoff, H. H. (2003). Circular vection is facilitated by a consistent photorealistic scene. *Proceedings of Presence 2003.*

Seno, T., Ito, H., & Sunaga, S. (2009). The object and background hypothesis for vection. *Vision Research, 49*(24), 2973-2982. doi:10.1016/j.visres.2009.09.017

Steen, F. A. M. V. D. (1998). *Self-Motion Perception* (PhD thesis). Technical University Delft, Netherlands.

Steen, F. A. M. V. D., & Brockhoff, P. T. M. (2000). Induction and impairment of saturated yaw and surge vection. *Perception & Psychophysics, 62*(1), 89-99.

Trutoiu, L. C., Mohler, B. J., Schulte-Pelkum, J., & Bülthoff, H. H. (2009). Circular, linear, and curvilinear vection in a large-screen virtual environment with floor projection. *Computers & Graphics, 33*(1), 47-58. doi:10.1016/j.cag.2008.11.008

Trutoiu, L. C., Streuber, S., Mohler, B. J., Schulte-Pelkum, J., & Bülthoff, H. H. (2008). Tricking people into feeling like they are moving when they are not paying attention. In *Applied Perception in Graphics and Visualization (APGV)* (p. 190). doi:http://doi.acm.org/10.1145/1394281.1394319

Tschermak, A. (1931). Optischer Raumsinn. In A. Bethe, G. Bergmann, G. Embden, & A. Ellinger (Eds.), *Handbuch der Normalen und Pathologischen Physiologie* (pp. 834-1000). Springer.

Väljamäe, A. (2007). *Sound for Multisensory Motion Simulators* (PhD thesis). Chalmers University of Technology.

Väljamäe, A. (2009). Auditorily-induced illusory self-motion: A review. *Brain Research Reviews, 61*(2), 240-255. doi:10.1016/j.brainresrev.2009.07.001

Väljamäe, A., Alliprandini, P. M. Z., Alais, D., & Kleiner, M. (2009). Auditory Landmarks Enhance Circular Vection in Multimodal Virtual Reality. *Journal of the Audio Engineering Society, 57*(3), 111-120.

Väljamäe, A., Larsson, P., Västfjäll, D., & Kleiner, M. (2006). Vibrotactile enhancement of auditory induced self-motion and spatial presence. *Journal of the Acoustic Engineering Society, 54*(10), 954-963.

Wallach, H. (1940). The role of head movements and vestibular and visual cues in sound localization. *Journal of Experimental Psychology, 27*(4), 339–368.

Wang, Y., Kenyon, R. V., & Keshner, E. A. (2010). Identifying the control of physically and perceptually evoked sway responses with coincident visual scene velocities and tilt of the base of support. *Experimental Brain Research, 201*(4), 663-672. doi:10.1007/s00221-009-2082-0

Wann, J., & Rushton, S. (1994). The illusion of self-motion in virtual-reality environments. *Behavioral and Brain Sciences, 17*(2), 338-340.

Warren, H. C. (1895). Sensations of rotation. *Psychological Review, 2*(3), 273-276. doi:10.1037/h0074437

Warren, R., & Wertheim, A. H. (Eds.). (1990). *Perception & Control of Self-Motion.* New Jersey, London: Erlbaum.

Wertheim, A. H. (1994). Motion perception during self-motion - the direct versus inferential controversy revisited. *Behavioral and Brain Sciences, 17*(2), 293-311.

Wist, E. R., Diener, H. C., Dichgans, J., & Brandt, T. (1975). Perceived distance and perceived speed of self-motion - linear vs angular velocity. *Perception & Psychophysics, 17*(6), 549-554.

Wolpert, L. (1990). Field-of-view information for self-motion perception. In R. Warren & A. H. Wertheim (Eds.), *Perception & Control of Self-Motion* (pp. 101-126). Erlbaum.

Wong, S. C. P., & Frost, B. J. (1981). The effect of visual-vestibular conflict on the latency of steady-state visually induced subjective rotation. *Perception & Psychophysics, 30*(3), 228-236.

Wood, R. (1895). The 'Haunted Swing' illusion. *Psychological Review,* 2(3), 277-278. doi:10.1037/h0073333

Wright, W. G., DiZio, P., & Lackner, J. R. (2006). Perceived self-motion in two visual contexts: dissociable mechanisms underlie perception. *Journal of Vestibular Research, 16*(1-2), 23–28.

Young, L. R., Oman, C. M., & Dichgans, J. M. (1975). Influence of head orientation on visually induced pitch and roll sensation. *Aviation, Space, and Environmental Medicine, 46*(3), 264-268.

Young, L. R., Crites, T. A., & Oman, C. M. (1983). Brief weightlessness and tactile cues influence visually induced roll. *Advances in Oto-Rhino-Laryngology, 30,* 230-234.

Young, L. R., & Shelhamer, M. (1990). Weightlessness Enhances the Relative Contribution of Visually-Induced Self-Motion. In R. Warren & A. H. Wertheim (Eds.), *Perception & Control of Self-Motion: Resources for Ecological Psychology*. Erlbaum, Hillsdale, NJ.

Zacharias, G. L., & Young, L. R. (1981). Influence of combined Visual and Vestibular Cues on Human Perception and Control of Horizontal Rotation. *Experimental Brain Research, 41,* 159-171.

9

Neck Motion Analysis Using a Virtual Environment

Dr. Sarig Bahat Hilla, BPT, M Phys, PhD
University of Haifa,
Israel

1. Introduction

Neck pain is common and constitutes a major cause of disability in the western world with significant ramifications to the injured individuals and to society at large (Hogg-Johnson, S. et al. 2008). A need exists for an objective evaluation of the impairments and disabilities associated with this disorder for both diagnostic and prognostic purposes. An objective assessment is needed in the subgroup of whiplash associated disorders, where secondary gains (e.g., monetary compensation) may have a significant effect on performance.
The overall purpose of our research project was to develop an objective and functional assessment of cervical motion. Using this assessment, it was aimed to investigate the effect of neck pain on cervical motion by kinematic analysis. The future goal is to use the developed system for treatment purposes.
This chapter will review the literature related to neck pain as a significant health problem, existing methods for neck assessment and the use of virtual reality (VR) in rehabilitation. This will be followed by description of the developed VR assessment, outcome measures, testing procedures, and statistical analyses. This chapter will present reliability, range of motion (ROM) and kinematic results. It will review the significance of findings in light of existing research, and will indicate contributions of current results to the understanding of the effect of neck pain on motion. Clinical applications, limitations and future goals will conclude this chapter.

1.1 Neck pain- definition, pathomechanisms and epidemiology

Neck pain as described by the Neck Task Force (Bone and Joint Decade 2000-2010) is pain located anywhere inferior to the superior nuchal line and superior to the line connecting the roots of both scapulae, with or without radiation to the head, and upper limb (Guzman, J. et al. 2008). The aetiology of neck pain may be traumatic, such as in cases of whiplash associated disorders (WAD) (Holm, L.W.D. et al. 2008) or may be non-traumatic i.e., of insidious onset (Hogg-Johnson, S. et al. 2008).
The pathological mechanism causing the symptoms associated with neck pain is mainly unknown (Childs, J.D. et al. 2008). Imaging is frequently used for primary screening of traumatic damage in the cervical spine, however the majority of cases of neck pain complaints are non-traumatic, with no structural damage identified in imaging as the cause of pain (Stiell, I.G. et al. 2003). Similarly to low back pain research, cervical imaging studies have been unable to provide answers as to which tissue is responsible for neck pain (Childs,

J.D. et al. 2008). The main limitation of imaging research is that it cannot correlate structural changes such as degenerative changes with symptoms associated with neck pain (Stiell, I.G. et al. 2003). Therefore, the patho-anatomical cause of neck pain is not identifiable and clinical assessment of disability and impairment of body function has remained the accepted approach for evaluation of patients complaining of neck pain (Childs, J.D. et al. 2008).

The incidence rate of neck pain ranges widely between studies with estimates that 22%- 70% of the western world population will experience neck pain sometime during their lives (Childs, J.D. et al. 2008; Cote, P. et al. 2001; Hogg-Johnson, S. et al. 2008). The incidence of neck pain has been constantly growing, and is now second after low back pain in annual worker's compensation (Cote, P.D.C.P. et al. 2008). Epidemiologic evidence showed that incidence of neck pain increases with age, however it peaks in middle age (45-54 years of age) and declines afterwards (Cote, P.D.C.P. et al. 2008; Hogg-Johnson, S. et al. 2008).

An important subgroup of neck pain complaints consist of WAD resulting from motor vehicle collisions (Holm, L.W.D. et al. 2008; Spitzer, W.O. et al. 1995). In spite of this relatively small proportion of WAD out of general cases of neck pain, it is the subject of much study due to the economic ramifications involved with WAD claims (Holm, L.W.D. et al. 2008). Moreover, a 10-fold increase in the number of patients complaining of neck pain attending an emergency department due to whiplash injuries was reported over the past 20 years (Holm, L.W.D. et al. 2008). A recent epidemiologic study by European insurance associations emphasised the need for an objective assessment of the cervical spine (Chappuis, G. and Soltermann, B. 2008). Similar conclusion as to the severity of the problem were reported based on collected data from the U.S.A, Australia, New Zealand and Switzerland (Barnsley, L. et al. 1994; Brison, R.J. et al. 2000).

The economic ramifications of these injuries are severe with the total costs related to whiplash injuries in the U.S.A being $29 billion per year (Spitzer, W.O. et al. 1995). The average cost for a whiplash injury in Europe was €35,000 (Chappuis, G. and Soltermann, B. 2008).

In spite of the difference in aetiology between traumatic WAD and non-traumatic cases with neck pain, both groups share similar impairments that are of similar severity (Woodhouse, A. and Vasseljen, O. 2008).

1.2 Impairments due to neck pain

Recognised impairments due to neck pain include range of motion (Childs, J.D. et al. 2008; Hogg-Johnson, S. et al. 2008), repositioning ability (Heikkila, H.V. and Wenngren, B.I. 1998; Treleaven, J. et al. 2003), isometric strength (Dvir, Z. and Prushansky, T. 2008), and endurance of the cervical flexor muscles (Jull, G.A. et al. 2008). The following section will critically review existing studies in the field of ROM and repositioning impairments due to neck pain, most relevant to our research topic.

1.2.1 Cervical range of motion

Limitation in cervical ROM is the one impairment most frequently studied and clinically observed (Chiu, T.T.W. and Lo, S.K. 2002; Dall'Alba, P.T. et al. 2001; Dvir, Z. et al. 2006; Heikkila, H.V. and Wenngren, B.I. 1998; Youdas, J.W. et al. 1991). In spite of cervical ROM being such a frequently studied impairment, the accuracy of this measure as a diagnostic tool has been controversial due to conflicting evidence concerning its specificity and sensitivity (Dall'Alba, P.T. et al. 2001; De Hertogh, W.J. et al. 2007). ROM assessment methods include eye-balling, (Chen, J. et al. 1999) radiographs, (Lind, B. et al. 1989; Penning, L. and Wilmink, J.T. 1987) goniometers and inclinometers, (Rix, G.D. and Bagust, J. 2001; Youdas, J.W. et al. 1991) potentiometer-based tools, (Feipel, V. et al. 1999) as well as more advanced technologies such as ultrasonic (Dvir, Z. et al. 2006; Dvir, Z. and Prushansky, T. 2000), optic (Marcotte, J. et al. 2002), and electromagnetic (Day, J.S. et al. 2000; Koerhuis, C.L. et al. 2003) three dimensional (3D) motion tracking devices. While goniometers and inclinometers are used extensively for clinical purposes, these devices only measure two dimensional (2D), static ROM (Rix, G.D. and Bagust, J. 2001; Youdas, J.W. et al. 1991). In contrast, motion tracking devices (Day, J.S. et al. 2000; Dvir, Z. et al. 2006; Dvir, Z. and Prushansky, T. 2000; Koerhuis, C.L. et al. 2003) measure 3D dynamic ROM, but their use is limited primarily to research due to cost and technical complexity.

Among the advanced 3D motion tracking devices, the FASTRAK electromagnetic tracking system (FASTRAK, Polhemus, http://www.polhemus.com/FASTRAK) was selected for this study. It was investigated for its reliability in evaluating 3D cervical motion (Amiri, M. et al. 2003; Jordan, K. et al. 2000) in asymptomatic individuals. Inter-tester reliability was shown to be greater than intra-tester reliability for most measures, suggesting variability of ROM in asymptomatic individuals over a period of a few days was greater than variability between repeated measures on the same day by two testers. These findings may indicate that there are normal physiological or biological changes in the human body which lead to changes in cervical ROM, representing the normal variability in population. Jordan et al. (Jordan, K. et al. 2000) additionally found that full-cycle measurements (i.e., flexion (F)+extension (E), right rotation (RR)+left rotation (LR)) were more reliable than half-cycle ones (i.e., F, E, RR, LR), recommending the use of full-cycle measures.

1.2.2 Cervical repositioning ability

Cervical repositioning ability, also known as kinaesthetic ability, is commonly measured by the difference in displacement between an original position and a reproduced position (Treleaven, J. 2008). Revel et al. (Revel, M. et al. 1991; Revel, M. et al. 1994) in the early 1990's led this field with 2D distance measurements between points on a cardboard. Participants wore helmets with a laser pointer attached to it, by which they pointed at a designated sign on a board in front of them (Revel, M. et al. 1991; Revel, M. et al. 1994). Using this simple set up, Revel et al.(Revel, M. et al. 1991; Revel, M. et al. 1994) showed that patients with neck pain presented with increased repositioning error as compared to control individuals without symptoms.

Three dimensional tracking, which emerged later, enabled measuring angular displacement of the cervical spine rather than the linear distance between visual targets, and therefore became more commonly used for cervical motion analysis (Heikkila, H.V. and Wenngren, B.-I. 1998; Treleaven, J. et al. 2003). Reported increased repositioning error (Heikkila, H.V. and Wenngren, B.-I. 1998; Revel, M. et al. 1991; Treleaven, J. et al. 2003) may indicated a deficit in kinaesthetic and/or vestibular sensibility, possibly affected by neck pain. However, this evidence is controversial for several reasons. First, the reported repositioning error is small (2°-5°) (Heikkila, H.V. and Wenngren, B.-I. 1998; Revel, M. et al. 1991; Treleaven, J. et al. 2003). Second, a group difference in repositioning error was found significant only for one subgroup (moderately-severely disabled patients with neck pain) (Sterling, M. et al. 2003). Third, repositioning ability was insufficient for differentiating patients with neck pain from non-symptomatic individuals due to its low sensitivity and specificity (Treleaven, J. et al. 2006). Forth, contrasting findings by four other studies (Edmondston, S.J. et al. 2007; Grip, H. et al. 2007; Rix, G.D. and Bagust, J. 2001; Woodhouse, A. and Vasseljen, O. 2008) showed no significant group difference in repositioning error between patients with non-traumatic chronic neck pain and non-symptomatic individuals. Therefore, the value of repositioning error measurement for evaluation of impairment due to neck pain remains uncertain. Lastly, repositioning assessments, as well as ROM measurement, are static measurements.

A more dynamic approach to kinaesthesia assessment was attempted in "the fly" (Kristjansson, E. et al. 2001; Kristjansson, E. et al. 2004) project, where the main task was to follow a displayed movement pattern with head motion, controlled by a tracking system. Three movement patterns, represented by closed curved line patterns, were projected on a computer screen, to be followed by head motion using tracking data (Kristjansson, E. et al. 2001; Kristjansson, E. et al. 2004). The error between the performed trajectory of head motion and the displayed movement pattern was increased in patients with WAD as compared to non-symptomatic individuals (Kristjansson, E. et al. 2001; Kristjansson, E. et al. 2004). The main advantage of the "Fly" is in measuring dynamic cervical motion. However, a limitation of this study should be noted. The use of a flat screen in front of the participant restricted the ROM stimulated in this method, and therefore could not assess maximal cervical ROM.

1.3 Cervical kinematics analysis

Patients presenting with neck pain often report difficulty in performing neck movements, especially fast movements, in their daily life. As the above literature review demonstrated, most existing methodologies analyse measures of a static position. Although part of our daily function is static, we much more frequently move our neck dynamically in response to multiple stimuli. Very few studies have analysed the dynamic kinematics of neck motion, (Gregori, B. et al. 2008; LoPresti, E.F. et al. 2003) and specifically in relation to neck pain (Dvir, Zeevi and Prushansky, Tamara 2000), (Sjolander, P. et al. 2008). The methods and results of studies that investigated cervical kinematics are presented in Table 1.

Dvir and Prushansky, (Dvir, Zeevi and Prushansky, Tamara 2000) in their reproducibility study, reported that mean velocity of voluntary neck motion ranged from 200/s to 300/s in 25 individuals without symptoms. A recent pilot study (Sjolander, P. et al. 2008) evaluated kinematic features of fast cervical motion. Electromagnetic tracking was used for assessment of 16 individuals with chronic neck pain and 16 control individuals (Sjolander, P. et al. 2008). The results did not demonstrate a significant difference in ROM or in velocity between the groups, but did show a significant group difference in smoothness of motion (Sjolander, P. et al. 2008). The lack of group difference in cervical ROM found by Sjolander et al. (Sjolander, P. et al. 2008) contrasts strong existing evidence for ROM restriction in patients suffering with neck pain as described above (Chiu, T.T.W. and Lo, S.K. 2002; Dall'Alba, P.T. et al. 2001; Dvir, Z. et al. 2006; Heikkila, H.V. and Wenngren, B.I. 1998; Youdas, J.W. et al. 1991).

LoPresti et al. (LoPresti, E.F. et al. 2003) used a head mounted display (HMD) to characterize how individuals with severe neurological disorders such as multiple sclerosis (without neck pain) control a computer mouse via cervical motion; the requested task was to select computer icons. The performance of this task and its kinematic characteristics were analysed and compared between the group of individuals with severe disabilities and a control

Study	Sjolander et al. (2008)	Gregori et al. (2008)	Lopresti et al. (2003)	Dvir & Prushansky (2000)	Present study
Population	16 patients with chronic neck pain; 16 control individuals	15 patients with cervical dystonia; 13 control individuals	10 subjects with severe neurological disorders; 15 control individuals	25 individuals without symptoms	25 patients with chronic neck pain; 42 control individuals
Motion analysed	Rotation	Rotation; Flexion-Extension	Rotation; Flexion-Extension	Rotation; Flexion-Extension; Lateral Flexion	Rotation; Flexion-Extension
Outcome measures	ROM, Vpeak, smoothness (jerk index)	ROM, MT, Vpeak	ROM, MT, RT, Vpeak, accuracy, smoothness (NVP)	ROM, Vmean	ROM, MT, RT, Vmean, Vpeak, TTP%, smoothness (NVP)
Movement initiation cut off	5% of Vpeak	10% of Vpeak	50% of Vpeak, or 3.68 cm/s	Not described	2.5% of Vpeak
Type of instruction	Verbal request for cervical motion	Verbal request for cervical motion	Computer icons selection task	Verbal request for cervical motion	Obtaining a virtual target, interactive task.
Requested motion	Fast	Fast	Naturally-paced	Naturally-paced	Fast
Tracking system	Electro-magnetic	Optic	Ultrasonic	Ultrasonic	Electro-magnetic
Mean Velocity (deg/s)	120-130	Not reported	Not reported	Flexion-extension ~ 19 Rotation ~ 30 Lateral flexion ~ 20	Flexion-extension ~ 30 Rotation ~50
Peak Velocity (deg/s)	Not reported	Flexion-extension ~ 300 Rotation~600	529.2 pixels/s*	Not reported	Flexion-extension ~ 120-130 Rotation~160
Significant group differences	Smoothness	ROM, MT, Vpeak	ROM, MT, Vpeak, accuracy, smoothness	No group comparison was performed	ROM, Vmean, Vpeak, MT, smoothness

Table 1. Characteristics of studies of cervical motion kinematic analysis. ROM- range of motion, MT- movement time, RT- response time, Vpeak- peak velocity, Vmean- mean velocity, TTP%- time to peak percentage out of movement time, NVP- number of velocity peaks. * Velocity units were non comparable to deg/s, and were not presented by direction.

group. Significant differences were shown in all kinematic features, indicating that the patient group presented with severe kinematic impairments, as expected in such severe disorders (LoPresti, E.F. et al. 2003). Gregori et al. (Gregori, B. et al. 2008) investigated cervical motion kinematics for the purpose of studying the effect of therapy with botulinum toxin type-A (BTX-A) in patients with dystonia. The values of cervical velocity reported in non-symptomatic individuals were very high compared to the other reports; no explanation for this was given. Unlike LoPresti et al. (LoPresti, E.F. et al. 2003), Gregori et al. (Gregori, B. et al. 2008) did not stimulate task-oriented motion, but simply requested participants to move their heads as fast as they could.

As indicated in Table 1, cervical motion was most commonly elicited using verbal instructions for neck motion, (Dvir, Zeevi and Prushansky, Tamara 2000; Gregori, B. et al. 2008; Sjolander, P. et al. 2008) with the exception of LoPresti et al. (LoPresti, E.F. et al. 2003) who used computer icon selection. Fast cervical motion was requested in two studies, (Gregori, B. et al. 2008; Sjolander, P. et al. 2008) and naturally-paced motion was recorded in two others (Dvir, Zeevi and Prushansky, Tamara 2000; LoPresti, E.F. et al. 2003).

The cervical velocity values reported in these studies were inconsistent, possibly due to the differences in types of populations and methodologies.

The above evidence leaves the issue of neck pain's effect on cervical velocity and smoothness of motion unresolved and consequently led to the investigation of this subject in present work, utilizing virtual reality (VR) for this purpose.

1.4 Virtual reality

Virtual reality entails the use of computers and multimedia peripherals, to produce a simulated environment comparable with real world scenario. VR users interact with images and sounds that stimulate responses while providing feedback concerning their performance (Rizzo, A. and Kim, G.J. 2005). Over the past decade, VR technologies have emerged as valuable tools for clinical assessment and intervention (Riva, G. et al. 1999; Rizzo, A.A. et al. 2006; Weiss, P.L. et al. 2003). Some of these applications include VR use for pain distraction, (Hoffman, H.G. et al. 2001) evaluation of cognitive function, (Grealy, M.A. et al. 1999; Wilson, P.N. et al. 1996) investigation of postural control, (Keshner, E.A. and Kenyon, R.V. 2000; Keshner, E.A. and Kenyon, R.V. 2004; Keshner, E.A. et al. 2004) and assessment of attention deficits (Rizzo, A.A. et al. 2006). The latter VR application for attention deficits assessment is the "virtual classroom" by Rizzo et al. (Rizzo, A.A. et al. 2006). This VR application monitored cervical motion in children with attention deficit hyperactive disorder, simulating a classroom scenario (Rizzo, A.A. et al. 2006). Auditory and visual distractive stimuli were programmed to appear unexpectedly, and the response of the child to the distraction, and his return to focus on the blackboard was monitored via head motion tracking (Rizzo, A.A. et al. 2006). Results showed significant differences in several parameters of performance and attention ability in children with ADHD, compared to children without ADHD (Rizzo, A.A. et al. 2006). The "virtual classroom" (Rizzo, A.A. et al. 2006) is the closest identified VR application to the present work in its set up as it involved head motion analysis, however the objectives, developed environment and population are completely different.

The important assets of using virtual reality for clinical application include interaction, motivation, and pain distraction. Active interaction within a VR environment has been previously demonstrated to enhance the effectiveness of exercise interventions in various applications (Holden, M.K. 2005; Mirelman, A. et al. 2009). Bryanton et al. (Bryanton, C. et al. 2006) compared compliance to lower limb VR exercises with compliance to conventional exercises in children with cerebral palsy, and found increased dorsiflexion ROM and higher motivation during the VR session. High motivation to participation in VR was also reported by Harris and Reid (Harris, K. and Reid, D. 2005) who used VR for exercise purposes, although they did not compare the VR methodology to other methods. Lee et al (Lee, J.H. et al. 2003) showed that VR was more effective than conventional methods for cognitive training purpose, with longer a duration of participation, increased motivation and prolonged attention as compared with the conventional method.

Clinical applications of virtual reality appear to be effective in reducing pain and anxiety (Hoffman, H.G. et al. 2001; Sharar, S.R. et al. 2008). A VR application for pain control was used during burn wound debridement in a hydrotherapy tank for 11 burn unit patients (Hoffman, H.G. et al. 2008). The use of VR for this purpose was found to be effective in reducing the reported pain level, and therefore offered a non-pharmacological pain reduction technique during wound care (Hoffman, H.G. et al. 2008). Recent evidence from functional magnetic resonance study showed VR distraction to have significant analgesic efficacy as represented by reductions in pain-related brain activity in the insula, thalamus, and secondary somatosensory cortex (Hoffman, H.G. et al. 2007).

1.5 Rationale

Most existing methodologies (Chen, J. et al. 1999; Nordin, M. et al. 2008; Sjolander, P. et al. 2008) for cervical assessment evaluated voluntary motion, elicited by instruction. This common methodology will be referred to as "conventional" throughout this dissertation. However, in day-to-day life, head movement is generally an involuntary response to multiple visual, auditory, tactile and/or olfactory stimuli. Therefore, measures obtained via conventional assessment may not truly represent functional ability. To achieve a more functional approach to objective cervical motion assessment, the current study aimed to develop a specialized VR system.

The rationale was that participants would be involved in a simple, yet engaging VR game, in which head motion is monitored via electromagnetic tracking. Such cervical assessment that is programmed to enhance performance, would potentially distract the participant from sensations of pain, and provide dynamic kinematic data. In doing so, such developed cervical assessment may help in improving screening processes, in evaluating effectiveness of interventions, in differentiating patients from healthy individuals, and consequently in improving health care of patients with neck pain, and in reducing financial burden due to neck pain.

Neck pain has become the focus of increased global attention by various health, research, and insurance bodies (Chappuis, G. and Soltermann, B. 2008; Childs, J.D. et al. 2008). These have emphasized the need for objective, reliable and valid method (Lidgren, L. 2008). This chapter presents an advanced and functional solution to neck assessment.

The overall objective of this research project was to develop an innovative assessment method for neck disorders, and to utilize it for the investigation of cervical kinematics in patients with chronic neck pain compared to individuals without symptoms. The new method took advantage of the unique characteristics of virtual reality to quantify, measure, and analyse cervical spine mobility. Furthermore, the virtual environment elicits neck motion in a fashion that is closer to real neck function than existing assessments, and is gradable and motivating.

2. Materials and methods

Upon completion of development of the VR system for cervical motion assessment, the reliability study commenced. Inter- and intra-tester reliability of range of motion (ROM) measures taken with the newly developed VR system and by the conventional assessment method were evaluated. Once the reliability of the new VR assessment was supported, the VR system was used for assessment of cervical motion in patients with chronic neck pain and in individuals without neck symptoms.

The first part of the comparative study investigated cervical ROM in the two groups of participants, by the VR and conventional methods of cervical ROM assessment, and will be referred to henceforth as the comparative ROM study. In addition to investigation of group differences, the comparative ROM study explored the differences between the VR and conventional methods of assessment, and between horizontal and sagittal cervical motion. The diagnostic ability of ROM measures was evaluated by logistic regression analysis for both VR and conventional methods of assessment.

The second part of the comparative study investigated kinematic measures representing the dynamic characteristics of cervical motion, and will be referred to as the comparative kinematics study. Kinematic outcome measures were assessed only by the developed VR method. In addition to the investigation of group differences, the comparative kinematic study explored differences between the four motion directions, as well as differences between horizontal and sagittal cervical motion.

This study was approved by the University of Haifa Institutional Review Board, and by the Helsinki Ethical Committee of the Rambam Medical Centre, Haifa. Each participant signed an informed consent form prior to testing.

2.1 Participants

The research sample included 30 participants without symptoms in the reliability study (22 females and 8 males, mean age ± SD =28.6 ± 7.5), and 67 participants in the comparative study. The comparative study population included two groups, 42 individuals without symptoms in the control group (31 females, 11 males, mean age ± SD =35.3±12.4 years), and 25 patients with chronic neck pain in the patient group (16 females, 9 males, mean age ± SD =39.0±12.7 years).

Inclusion criteria of participants with neck pain:

1. Complaint of neck pain for 6 weeks or more, with or without referral to the upper limb.
2. Etiology of either WAD or insidious onset of symptoms without trauma.

Exclusion criteria of participants with neck pain:

1. Neck pain caused by other pathological entities such as diffuse connective tissue diseases, rheumatic syndromes, metabolic and endocrine diseases, neoplasm, fractures or dislocations.
2. Regular intake of medication which may affect pain or motor performance, such as analgesics, relaxants, steroids, and non-steroidal anti inflammatory drugs.

Exclusion criteria for asymptomatic participants:

1. Current or past history of neck pain or WAD within the past 10 years.
2. Current history of vertigo, dizziness, or other vestibular disorder.
3. Visual impairment (uncorrected by optical devices).
4. Complaints of altered sensation (e.g., pins and needles), or weakness of the upper limbs, which can be caused by disorders such as multiple sclerosis, spinal stenosis, spinal cord injuries, neuropathies.

5. Cognitive impairment that could affect ability to follow instructions.

Participants were recruited from a local physiotherapy clinic and from the University of Haifa, respectively. Exclusion criteria for the control group were identical those presented above.

2.2 The developed VR cervical assessment system

A customized video game-like virtual environment was developed in order to encourage and motivate participants to achieve maximal cervical ROM (ROM analysis), and to stimulate fast cervical mobility (kinematics analysis). The VR system was constructed from off-the-shelf hardware and was operated using customized software.

Hardware consisted of two main components: an electromagnetic tracker (Fastrak, Polhemus, http://www.polhemus.com/FASTRAK) and a Head Mounted Display (HMD) (I-glasses HRV Pro, Virtual Realities, http://www.vrealities.com). The tracker sampled motion via two sensors at 60 Hz each. Sensors were placed at the back of the HMD, adjacent to the occipital protuberance, and on the sternal notch in order to differentiate trunk motion from that of the neck and remove it from the data.

A virtual environment was developed using Game Maker software (http://www.gamemaker.nl), and tracking data were analysed using Matlab software (version 12b, http://www.mathworks.com). We have used this system to study cervical motion charecteristics and compared conventional and VR methods (Sarig-Bahat, H. et al. 2009; Sarig-Bahat, H. et al. 2010). In the conventional method participants were orally instructed to move their head into flexion, extension, rotation, and lateral flexion. In the VR method, cervical motion was elicited by interaction with images in a video game that were displayed on the two monitors embedded in the HMD (Sarig-Bahat, H. et al. 2009; Sarig-Bahat, H. et al. 2010). The HMD and sensors are shown in Figure 1.

The VR gaming environment developed for this study enabled us to elicit cervical motion by the participants and to assess its dynamic characteristics. During the game, fly targets were displayed on the HMD monitors and the participant's task was to "spray" the flies. This was achieved by aligning each fly with a virtual target sign attached to a virtual spray canister. The position of the spray canister was controlled by the participant's head motion. The participant was instructed to spray the flies as fast as possible. In the ROM game the participant moved from one target to the other, and in the velocity game he had to return to mid-position after hitting each target. Directions of the targets were randomly ordered, eliciting fast cervical flexion (F), extension (E), right rotation (RR), and left rotation (LR). Two targets were placed at 100% of ROM and an additional two targets at 80% of ROM, as measured conventionally at the beginning of the experiment. An example of a fly target appearing on the left side of the screen to stimulate LR is shown in Figure 2.

The ROM game challenged participants with constantly increasing ROM required to hit target flies. Flies continued to appear at increasing distances from the central resting position until the participant failed to point the spray can nozzle at the fly in a given direction during three consecutive trials. However, in the velocity game there was a set number of trials at 80% and 100% conventional ROM.

2.3 Procedure

The experimental session commenced with an interview regarding possible exclusion criteria, and the completion of VAS, NDI, and TSK questionnaires by the participants with neck pain. A short warm up followed with two repeated cervical movements in all directions.

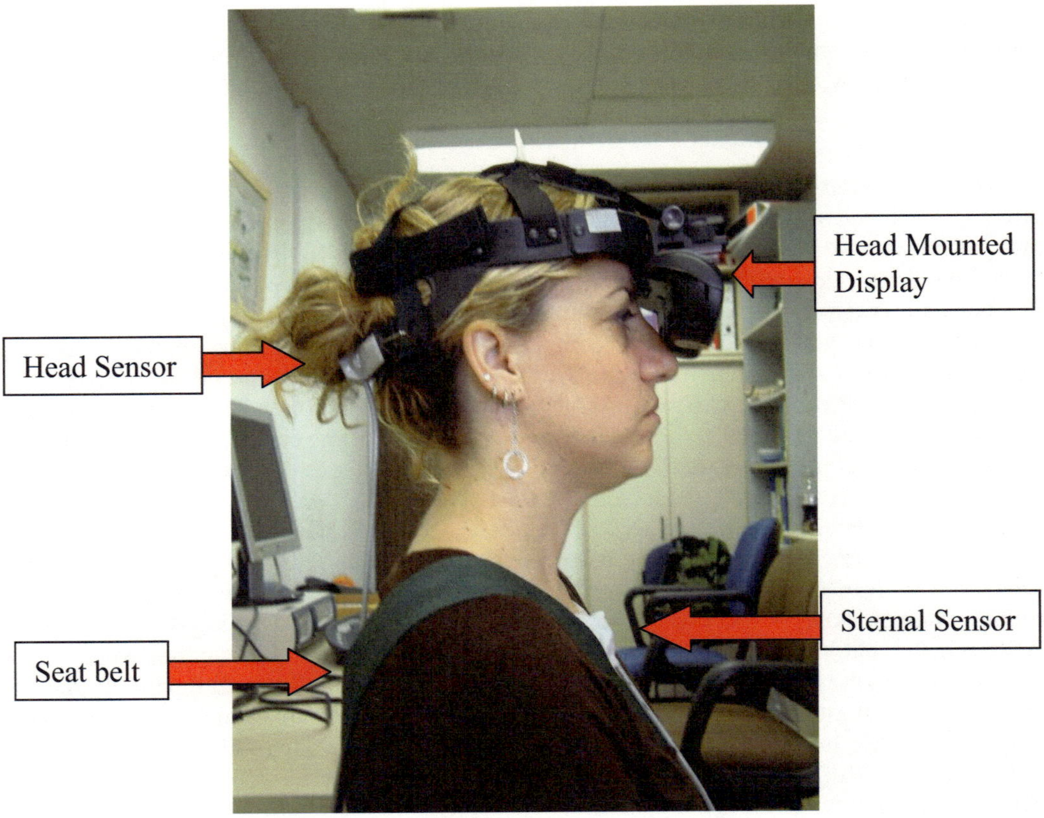

Fig. 1. Head Mounted Display with tracking sensors attached.

Fig. 2. A screen capture as viewed via the HMD, during the VR game. The Fly is the target; the task is to point the target sign (in the top of the spray canister) at the fly via movements of the head.

At the beginning of each assessment, participants were requested to place their head in what they perceived as mid-position, and this location was recorded and used for data analysis. Each assessment included the following stages: a conventional ROM assessment (Conv1), a VR assessment, including the ROM game and the velocity game, and a repeated conventional ROM assessment (Conv2).

During the reliability study each participant was assessed twice during the first session by two different testers, randomly ordered. The assessment was repeated by one of the testers 3-7 days later.

In the following comparative kinematic study, each participant was assessed once, and all by the same tester. Assessments were performed by a musculoskeletal physiotherapist.

2.4 Subjective outcome measures

Participants with neck pain completed three questionnaires, reflecting different aspects of their disorder:

Visual Analogue Scale (VAS) (Breivik, E.K. et al. 2000; Langley, G.B. and Sheppeard, H. 1985; Ogon, M. et al. 1996; Wainner, R.S. et al. 2003) is a 10 cm line representing pain intensity. Patients were requested to indicate on the line the point that best represented their level of neck pain at the beginning of the assessment. The VAS has been recognized as a valid and sensitive pain intensity instrument (Breivik, E.K. et al. 2000; Wainner, R.S. et al. 2003) and is reported to be the most cited pain intensity measure in studies of neck pain (Nordin, M. et al. 2008).

Neck Disability Index (NDI) is a self-rated instrument assessing disability due to neck pain (Vernon, H. 2008; Vernon, H. and Mior, S. 1991). It consists of 10 items related to daily living activities, such as working, reading, and sleeping, with each item rated on a six-point scale (0-5). The NDI has been widely used and has been shown to have good validity and reliability (Pietrobon, R. et al. 2002; Vernon, H. 2008).

Tampa Scale of Kinesiophobia (TSK) (Sullivan, M.J. et al. 2002) is a 17-item questionnaire used to assess fear of movement or re-injury, in which patients are asked to rate their level of agreement with each item on a four-point scale (1-4). The TSK has been shown to have adequate internal consistency and reliability (Cleland, J.A. et al. 2008) and to be associated with measures of behavioral avoidance and disability (Sullivan, M.J. et al. 2002).

2.5 Objective outcome measures

Objective measures included two main categories, ROM measures and kinematic measures. ROM measures were analysed in the reliability study and in the comparative ROM analysis. Kinematic measures were analysed in the comparative kinematic analysis.

Conventional ROM measures included half-cycle (F, E, RR, LR, RLF, LLF) and full-cycle (F+E, RR+LR, RLF+LLF) cervical ROM. Three repeated measurements were performed for each direction in the reliability study, and two, in the comparative ROM study. This change in number of repetitions was due to software adaptation following four cases of side effects in the reliability study, due to high total number of repetitions in high rate.

VR ROM measures collected included only full cycle measures as there was continuous motion between targets during the game with no return to a stationary central resting position between successive trials. The VR game elicited movements in F, E, RR, and LR, but not lateral flexion. The three greatest scores were collected from the VR assessment for statistic analysis.

Kinematic measures were analyzed from the data collected by the tracker for each of the 16 assessment trials throughout the virtual game. Each trial period was defined as the time from target appearance to target hit. Data were low pass filtered (Butterworth, 10 Hz, order = 10), and an angular velocity profile was computed for each trial from angular rotations (i.e., roll, pitch, and yaw). Mean values of the kinematic outcome measures were calculated for each of the four directions (flexion, extension, right rotation, and left rotation). The following variables were analyzed:

Response time extends from target appearance to motion initiation. Motion initiation towards the target was defined as the point where velocity passes a threshold value set at 2.5% of peak velocity. Compared to reported thresholds of 10% and more, (LoPresti, E.F. et al. 2003; Michaelsen, S.M. et al. 2001) 2.5% was preferred in order to prevent significant data loss during the analysis.

Peak velocity (Vpeak) refers to the maximal velocity value recorded throughout a trial.

Mean velocity (Vmean) refers to the mean value of velocity from motion initiation to target hit.

Time to peak percentage (TTP%) refers to the time from motion initiation to the peak velocity moment, as a percent of total movement time.

Number of velocity peaks (NVP) refers to the number of velocity peaks from motion initiation to target hit, indicating motion smoothness. NVP was defined by counting the number of times that the acceleration curve changed sign, i.e., crossed the zero line.

Impairment percentages were calculated for each kinematic measure in each direction by the following formula, where "value" refers to each kinematic measure:

(Mean value for patients - Mean value for controls) / Mean value for controls

2.6 Statistical analysis

The following section will discourse statistics methods performed in each part of the study. Significance was determined at $p \leq 0.05$. JMP® statistics software was used (S.A.S Institute, www.jmp.com), as well as SAS® software (Statistical Analysis Software, www.sas.com).

2.6.1 Reliability study

The mean value of three largest ROM results to each direction was used for statistical analysis. Repeatability was assessed based on methods developed by Bland and Altman (Bland, J.M. and Altman, D.G. 1986; Bland, J.M. and Altman, D.G. 2007). Repeatability coefficient r95% was calculated as 1.96 times the standard deviations of the differences between the two measurements (tester1 and tester2, or day1 and day2) (Bland, J.M. and Altman, D.G. 1986; Bland, J.M. and Altman, D.G. 2007). The r95% measure, with units of degrees in our study, represents the value below which the absolute difference between two repeated test results may be expected to lie with a probability of 95%.

In addition, Bland & Altman's analysis (Bland, J.M. and Altman, D.G. 1986; Bland, J.M. and Altman, D.G. 2007) was used to evaluate differences between assessment methods, comparing results from Conv1 and VR. In order to compare between the VR and the conventional methods, differences between the results of both assessment methods during each of the three experimental stages (Conv1, VR, and Conv2) were assessed by a mixed-model ANOVA, with stage as the fixed factor and participant as the random factor. When the ANOVA indicated significant overall differences between stages, pairwise differences were assessed by the Tukey-Kramer test.

2.6.2 ROM analysis

The mean value of the three largest ROM results in each direction was used for statistical analysis. Full cycle and half cycle measures were analysed by the conventional method, and full cycle measures alone were analysed by the VR method. Differences between the results of the two groups (patients vs. control), the two planes of motion (sagittal vs. horizontal), and the three experimental stages (Conv1, VR, and Conv2) were assessed by a mixed-model ANOVA, with group, plane of motion, and experimental stage as the fixed factors and participant as the random factor. When the ANOVA indicated significant overall differences between stages, pairwise differences were assessed by the Tukey-Kramer test.

Univariate and multivariate logistic regression analyses and receiver operating characteristic (ROC) curves were used to examine the predictive relationship between test parameters and status (patients vs. control groups). In addition to tests of model significance and ROC area under the curve, these analyses included determination of odds ratios and their confidence intervals, and sensitivity and specificity of different model cut-off thresholds.

2.6.3 Kinematic analysis

The mean value of four trials for each kinematic measure to each motion direction (F, E, RR, and LR) was calculated. Failure-to-hit trials were less than 1% of trials in both groups and were excluded. Differences between the two groups (patient vs. control), and between the four motion directions (F, E, RR, and LR) were assessed by a two-way repeated measures ANOVA (group x direction of motion). When the ANOVA indicated significant interactions (group x direction of motion), pairwise differences were assessed by the Tukey-Kramer test, and contrasts were analysed to evaluate differences between the sagittal (combination of F with E results) and horizontal (combination of RR with RR results) planes of motion.

3. Results

This part will cover results in four main categories: (a) reliability; (b) group differences; (c) VR vs. conventional methods of ROM assessment differences, and (d) dynamic kinematics differences.

3.1 Reliability

The inter- and intra-tester repeatability analysis using Bland and Altman's method4 resulted in no bias ($p>0.1$) in all full cycle measures for both conventional and VR assessments. r95% of full cycle results ranged from 19.90 to 29.20 by conventional method and from 15.00 to 22.60 by VR method. These results showed an advantage for the VR method compared to the conventional method, with smaller repeatability coefficient (r95%) values. Inter tester reliability was found to be higher as compared with intra tester reliability, with smaller repeatability coefficient (r95%) values.

Half-cycle reliability results (conventional method) were found to be non-biased, with the exception of RLL and LLF in the inter-tester analysis which demonstrated a trend ($0.05<P<0.1$). The r95% of half cycle conventional results ranged between 9.90 and 27.30. In summary, full-cycle measures were found more reliable than half-cycle measures, and VR measures were found more reliable than conventional ones, although both methods resulted no bias. Additional analysis in the reliability study compared between the conventional and VR methods of assessment with advantage found to the VR method for full-cycle measures (Sarig-Bahat, H. et al. 2009).

3.2 Comparative ROM study results

Following the reliability evaluation, the VR assessment was utilised for assessment of cervical ROM in patients with neck pain and in control participants without neck symptoms.

Cervical assessments were performed on all 67 participants. Comparable demographic baseline values for control and patient groups were found with no significant differences in age or in gender ($p=0.12$). Demographic characteristics of both groups are listed in Table 2. In addition, Table 2 presents the symptoms, function and fear of motion associated with neck pain as reported by the patients using the VAS, NDI and TSK.

Characteristic	Patient group (n=25)	Control group (n=42)
Age in years (Mean (SD), Range)	39.0 (12.7), 22 - 65	35.3 (12.4), 23 - 64
No. of females / males	16 / 9	31 / 11
Duration in months (Mean, SD, Range)	43.40 (53), 1.5 - 240	N/A
No. of cases with right / left / bilateral symptoms	12 / 6 / 7	N/A
No. of cases with / without whiplash injury	7 / 18	N/A
Neck Disability Index (Mean (SD), Range)	11.60 (4.88), 3 - 23	N/A
Tampa Scale of Kinesiophobia (Mean (SD), Range)	35.74 (5.71), 25 - 53	N/A
Visual Analogue Scale (Mean (SD), Range)	3.30 (2.05), 0 - 9	N/A

N/A- not applicable, SD- standard deviation.

Table 2. Characteristics of experimental groups.

Results of mixed-model three-way ANOVA indicated significant overall differences (a) between groups ($F(1,65.3)=15.2$, $p=0.0002$), (b) between experimental stages ($F(2,296)=121$, $p<0.0001$), and (c) between sagittal and horizontal planes of motion ($F(1,294)= 487.6$, $p<0.0001$). All interactions were non-significant ($p>0.1$) with one trend found in the interaction between plane and group ($p=0.06$).

The complementary Tukey-Kramer test for full cycle ROM measures showed significant differences ($p<0.05$) for every possible between-experimental stages pairwise comparison. Figure 3 shows the group difference in ROM, with patient group demonstrating reduced values. In addition, Figure 3 shows that Conv2 ROMs were significantly greater than Conv1 ROMs and VR-ROMs were significantly greater than both pre- and post VR assessments. In other words, a single VR session showed a significant motion enhancement effect in both groups, as demonstrated by greater ROM during the VR game, as compared with conventional ROM collected before and after the VR game (see Figure 3).

Horizontal plane measures of motion (right and left rotation) presented with greater ROM, compared to sagittal plane measures of cervical motion (flexion and extension).

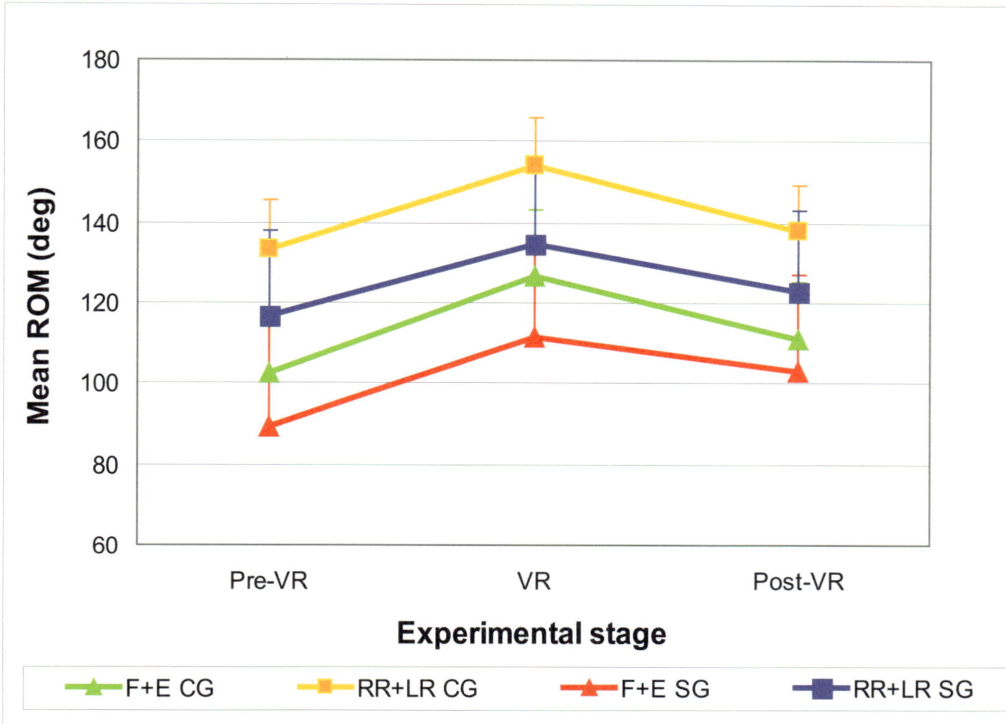

Fig. 3. Mean ± SD of cervical range of motion, as maintained in the three experimental stages.

Conv1- first conventional assessment; VR- virtual reality assessment; Conv2- second conventional assessment; F+E- flexion and extension, RR+LR- right rotation and left rotation; CG- control group; PG- patient group; ROM- range of motion.
ROM impairment percentage by the conventional method was 13.15% in FE, and 12.32% in rotation, and by the VR method, 12.15% and 12.60%, respectively.

3.3 Logistic regression results

Results of the logistic regression analysis performed for full cycle measures were found to be statistically significant diagnostic factors. The diagnostic values in Table 3 are sorted by sensitivity, from highest to lowest. For each outcome measure the actual predictor value is given, i.e., the optimal cut-off value based on the best overall accuracy (a trade-off between sensitivity and specificity). For example, for F+E ROM during VR (first row in Table 7), every 10 increase above 133.3 reduces the odds of being a true patient by a factor of 0.96. Thus, the larger the ROM, the more likely it is that the participant is well.
Two very important values reported in Table 3 are sensitivity and specificity. The sensitivity of VR F+E was found to be 88%, such that 22 out of the 25 patients were identified as true positive cases (i.e., they were diagnosed correctly). Specificity of VR F+E, however, was low, 43%; that is, only 18 out of the 42 control participants were identified as true negative cases

by this single measure. The results of high sensitivity and low specificity of VR F+E are consistent with the common trade-off between sensitivity and specificity. Good sensitivity (72%) was found for VR RR+LR, which also showed good specificity of 79%. Henceforth, VR RR+LR was found to be the most accurate measure. In contrast to the VR measures, conventional ROM measures demonstrated low sensitivity (<60%) however their specificity values were higher than those of the VR measures, 88% for conventional R+LR and F+E; i.e., 37 out of 42 control participants were identified correctly using conventional measures.

Outcome measures	F+E VR	RR+LR VR	RR+LR Conv.	F+E Conv.
Model significance	0.002	<0.0001	0.0002	0.009
Predictor significance	0.006	0.001	0.001	0.015
Optimal predictor value	133.3	146	119.3	81.8
Unit Odds Ratio	0.96	0.92	0.94	0.97
Odds Ratio 95% CL	0.93 - 0.99	0.88 - 0.97	0.90 - 0.98	0.94 - 0.99
Sensitivity	0.88	0.72	0.56	0.4
Specificity	0.43	0.79	0.88	0.88
Accuracy	0.31	0.51	0.44	0.28
Area Under Curve	0.7	0.79	0.74	0.66

Sig.- significance; CL-confidence limits, lower limit- higher limit; F- flexion; E- extension; VR- virtual reality; RR- right rotation; LR- left rotation; Conv- conventional.

Table 3. Diagnostic value of significant outcome measures

3.4 Comparative kinematic study results

VR assessments and kinematic analysis were performed on all 67 participants (25 patients and 42 controls) in the comparative part of the study.

Results of the mixed model ANOVA indicated significant group differences for (a) movement time ($F(1,65)=16.23$, $p=0.0001$); (b) Vpeak ($F(1,65)=22.3$, $p<0.0001$); (c) Vmean ($F(1,65)=23.91$, $p<0.0001$); and (d) NVP ($F(1,65)=9.11$, $p=0.0036$). Results showed that participants with neck pain performed with lower peak and mean velocities when they moved towards the virtual fly target, compared to control participants. The velocity curves of patients with neck pain also showed a greater number of peaks (maxima), indicating impaired motion smoothness. No significant group differences were found for response time and for TTP%. There was no significant interaction found between group and motion direction for most of the measures, except for Vmean and Vpeak where a significant interaction was found. Tukey-Kramer test and contrast analysis were performed only for the measures with significant interactions, i.e., Vmean and Vpeak. Group and direction differences are illustrated for peak velocity, and mean velocity in Figure 4 and Figure 5, respectively. Contrast results indicated significantly higher mean and peak velocities in the horizontal plane versus the sagittal plane (Figures 4 and 5).

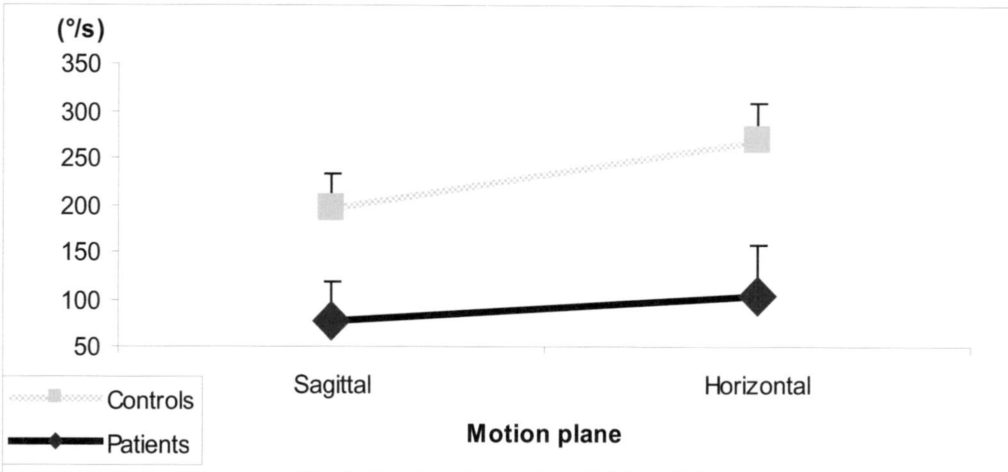

Fig. 4. Mean ± SD of peak velocity for control and patient groups, in sagittal and horizontal plane of motion. Higher peak velocity is demonstrated in horizontal motion as compared with sagittal motion, for both patient and control group. The difference between motion planes was greater in the patient group, as indicated by the interaction effect found.

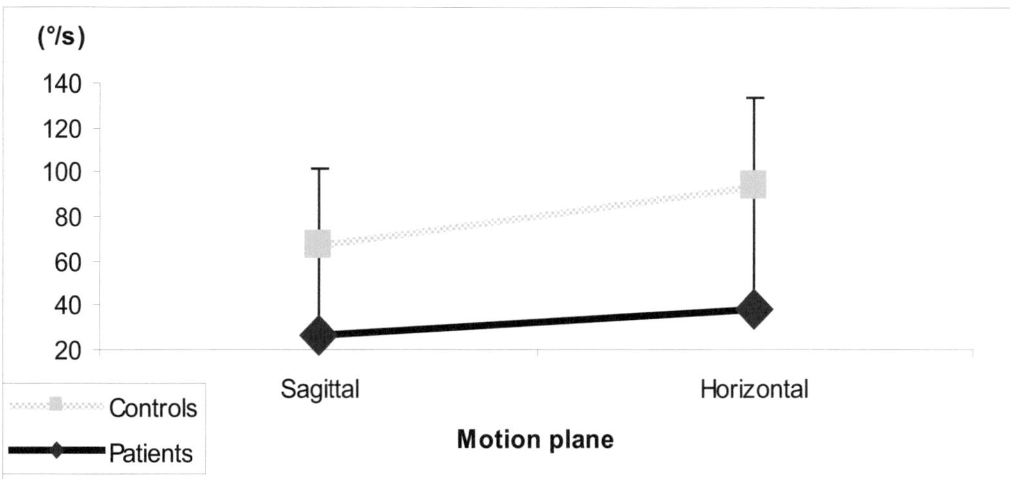

Fig. 5. Mean ± SD of mean velocity for control and patient groups, in sagittal and horizontal plane of motion. Higher mean velocity is demonstrated in horizontal motion as compared with sagittal motion, for both patient and control group. The difference between motion planes was greater in the patient group, as indicated by the interaction effect found.

The presented results showed that the developed VR system for cervical motion assessment is reliable, is capable of demonstrating ROM and kinematic differences between participants with neck pain and control participants, with good sensitivity and specificity. Furthermore, the VR system demonstrated a motion enhancement effect within a single session in both patient and control groups.

4. Discussion

Neck pain is a common and growing health problem in the western world, causing a heavy burden on society (Hogg-Johnson, S. et al. 2008). The scope of the problem, the high expenditure associated with it, as well as the limitations of existing methods for its assessment emphasise the need for an objective and reliable assessment of impairments due to neck pain (Chappuis, G. and Soltermann, B. 2008; Nordin, M. et al. 2008).

This chapter introduced a novel method developed to analyze cervical motion, which provides a more functional, task-oriented method, compared to existing conventional methodologies. It presented the development of the VR system for cervical assessment, evaluation of its reliability, and results of cervical motion analysis in patients with neck pain and in healthy individuals.

Reliability findings demonstrated non biased inter- and intra-tester reliability of the VR- and the conventional ROM assessments; inter-tester reliability was greater than intra-tester reliability, and horizontal motion measures were more stable than sagittal motion measures. The VR assessment was used to investigate cervical motion impairment in patients with neck pain compared to healthy control individuals. The findings demonstrated significantly reduced cervical ROM, motion velocity, and movement smoothness in patients with chronic neck pain. The findings of impaired velocity and smoothness of cervical motion, in particular, contribute new knowledge to the understanding of the impairments associated with neck pain, and establish a reference for future kinematic research in the cervical spine. The diagnostic ability of the VR system was evaluated by logistic regression analysis with findings of good sensitivity and specificity for many of the studied outcome measures. This demonstrated their ability to identify correctly patients suffering from neck pain and individuals without neck pain. In addition to its ecologic validity, reliability and diagnostic ability, the VR cervical motion assessment was found advantageous as compared to conventional assessment in its ability to enhance cervical mobility, in both groups of the study. This enhancement suggests its therapeutic potential.

4.1 Reliability

The non-biased inter- and intra-tester results determined here support the reliability of both the VR-based and conventional assessment methods tested in this study. Values of repeatability coefficients (r95%) ranged from 150 to 29.20, which may be considered fairly large. However, these values are similar to those reported by Assink et al., (Assink, N. et al. 2005) who also used electromagnetic tracking system, evaluated active ROM reliability using similar statistical method. Assink et al.(Assink, N. et al. 2005) reported repeatability coefficients ranged from 14.5° to 27°. From a clinical point of view, both previous and current findings show that substantial differences should be expected when measuring cervical ROM, despite accurate measuring equipment and a rigid measurement protocol.

In agreement with previous studies, (Chen, J. et al. 1999; Jordan, K. et al. 2000; Lantz, C.A. et al. 1999) the current analysis within the conventional assessment demonstrated that half cycle measures are less stable than full cycle measures.

The results of the reliability analysis indicate that maximal ROM results obtained via VR were more stable than those obtained via conventional assessments. VR appears to act as an engaging and motivating modality (Rizzo, A. and Kim, G.J. 2005), directing attention to an external stimulus rather than to the body motion itself (Wulf, G. et al. 1998; Wulf, G. et al. 2007), resulting in better performance. These unique features of the VR-based assessment may be responsible for the smaller repeatability coefficients obtained with this methodology.

4.2 ROM findings

Various measuring instruments and protocols have been used to characterize cervical ROM (Chen, J. et al. 1999; Nordin, M. et al. 2008). All reviewed studies reported using conventional protocols similar to the one used in the current study (Chen, J. et al. 1999). A very wide variability of ROM results in healthy subjects was documented with largest differences in between technologies up to 55° in full cycle rotation, 78° in full cycle lateral flexion, and 64° in full cycle flexion-extension (Chen, J. et al. 1999). Nevertheless, we note that the results of the present study fell within the ranges reported in the literature using electromagnetic tracking technology.

4.3 Motion enhancement effect by VR

Results of the comparison between the three experimental stages (Conv1, VR, and Conv2) demonstrated a significant motion enhancement effect by the developed VR assessment. ROM of both rotation and flexion-extension movements attained while the participants were engaged in a task in the virtual environment were significantly higher than those recorded conventionally, prior to, and post- the VR-based assessment. The phenomenon of motion enhancement by VR was demonstrated first in the reliability study in participants without symptoms, and second, in the comparative ROM study, in both patient and control groups. Future investigation of changes in ROM across trials could help explain the large intra-rater reliability.

Motion enhancement may be partially explained by the increased motivation obtained while the participants were involved in an engaging and challenging game. Motivation benefits of VR have been reported in numerous studies involving subjects with various disabilities (Bryanton, C. et al. 2006; Harris, K. and Reid, D. 2005; Holden, M.K. 2005; Mirelman, A. et al. 2009). It is likely that the participants with neck pain in the present study also benefited from pain-distraction induced by involvement in VR (Hoffman, H.G. et al. 2001; Hoffman, H.G. et al. 2008; Hoffman, H.G. et al. 2007). VR distraction has been shown to have a significant analgesic effect (Hoffman, H.G. et al. 2001; Hoffman, H.G. et al. 2008) as demonstrated by significant reductions in pain-related brain activity in the insula, thalamus, and secondary somatosensory cortex(Hoffman, H.G. et al. 2007).

The difference between VR and conventional results may be further explained by the difference in focus of attention between the two methods of cervical motion assessment. Multiple studies have shown the advantage of an external focus of attention over an internal focus of attention on motor performance and motor learning (McNevin, N.H. et al. 2003; Wulf, G. 2008; Wulf, G. et al. 1998; Wulf, G. et al. 1999; Wulf, G. and McNevin, N.H. 2001; Wulf, G. and Su, J. 2007; Zachry, T. et al. 2005). The fact that motion enhancement by VR was shown in both groups with no interaction effect strengthens the suggestion that the noted improvements may be due to a changed focus of attention and not to pain distraction. The shift in focus of attention may have contributed to the enhanced motion during VR game. The VR game seems to have therapeutic potential in improving motor performance and movement economy of the cervical region.

4.4 Kinematics analysis and neck pain

In the comparative kinematic study, the dynamic characteristics of neck motion, in patients with neck pain and in control subjects were examined. A dynamic assessment of cervical motion was needed due to (a) its functional value; (b) lack of existing evidence regarding kinematics of cervical motion, and (c) clinical experience with patients suffering from neck pain who often report difficulty in performance of fast neck movements.

In day to day living we normally move our heads in response to multiple sensory stimuli, such as turning our head when hearing a loud sound or smelling an attractive scent. The location and timing of these environmental stimuli is unknown and changing, often requiring head motion that is both fast and accurate. Most existing assessments of impairment due to neck pain collect measures of a static nature, such as ROM measurements, (Chen, J. et al. 1999) repositioning ability, (Treleaven, J. 2008) and isometric muscle strength (Dvir, Z. and Prushansky, T. 2008) evaluation. The VR based methodology developed in the present study elicited fast cervical motion in response to visual stimuli.

The effect of neck pain on cervical motion control via kinematic analysis has been seldom studied. Identified studies (Gregori, B. et al. 2008; LoPresti, E.F. et al. 2003) that have investigated cervical kinematics (described in Table 1, page 11) studied populations with neurological disorders and severe disabilities very different to neck pain.

Sjolander et al. (Sjolander, P. et al. 2008) was the sole study to have investigated kinematics of cervical motion in relation to neck pain. Sjolander et al. (Sjolander, P. et al. 2008) reported higher velocity values than ones reported here (see Table 1). They found that cervical motion smoothness was impaired in patients suffering from neck pain, whereas ROM and cervical motion velocity were not. In contrast, current results demonstrated that individuals suffering from neck pain moved more slowly and less smoothly towards virtual targets. The lack of ROM restriction in their patient group, no description of severity or disability, and investigation of rotation alone, are all methodological weaknesses that should be considered when referring to the study by Sjolander et al. (2008).

The present results play an important role in providing a reference for future research in cervical kinematics.

The overall impairment percentage in velocity and smoothness of cervical motion in patients with neck pain ranged from an impairment of 22% to 44%, compared to control participants. The overall ROM impairment percentage found in the comparative ROM analysis for the same population with the same VR technology, ranged from an impairment of 12.15% to 13.5%, compared to control participants. Therefore it seems that in the examined mildly disabled chronic population, velocity and smoothness of cervical motion were restricted by a relatively greater proportion to cervical ROM. This may be explained by the greater degree of difficulty in performance of fast motion compared to naturally-paced motion. Velocity and smoothness, unlike ROM measurement, reflect dynamic cervical motion, and therefore may reveal more of the impairment than ROM assessment.

Since the ability to move quickly in response to external stimuli is a necessary function, this deficit in cervical motion velocity and smoothness is probably meaningful and needs to be addressed. Further research should investigate if this finding of greater impairment in cervical velocity and smoothness as compared to ROM exists in more severely affected individuals.

4.5 Limitations and further research

Several limitations were identified in this study, and reflect on future research requirements. The VR game facilitated motion in F, E, RR, and LR directions; however it was not programmed to elicit lateral flexion, unless when coupled with rotation. In order to elicit isolated LF, a separate task or game is needed. From a clinical and functional point of view, it seemed that isolated LF is of least value compared to other directions of motion.

Reliability was evaluated only in non-symptomatic individuals, and should be evaluated on patients with neck pain in the future. The patient group assessed in this study was characterized by mild chronic disability, and a moderate level of kinesiophobia. Therefore furthere research should investigate a more heterogenic population.

Subjective and objective measures were not correlated in present study. Future research should assess the correlations between subjective and objective measures. The effect of subjective measures such as pain intensity and fear of motion on objective kinematic measures should be evaluated. This would help identify which subjective characteristics restrict performance. This finding may guide treatment. In addition, prognostic analyses should be evaluated using a prospective methodology, exploring risk factors for prolonged disability and poor treatment outcome, and positive predictive factors, for successful treatment outcomes.

The current findings of impaired motion velocity and smoothness in individuals suffering from chronic neck pain have clinical implications for both the assessment and management of neck pain.

Investigation of a patient's ability to perform fast and sudden neck movements should be included in any clinical examination. Subjective examination should include questioning relating to the ability to perform fast cervical motion.

Present ROM analysis showed a significant cervical motion enhancement effect by a single VR session. Future study should evaluate the therapeutic effectiveness of VR-training for cervical rehabilitation, using a randomized controlled trial methodology. Future development of VR-based management strategies may include training regime that challenge fast, task-oriented exercising, using visual/auditory stimuli, directed at external focus of attention. Further development is needed for treatment purposes to create a variety of games and tasks that will maintain motivation and interest in the VR game during several sessions.

The use of VR may play an additional role in overcoming fear of motion via pain distraction, and therefore VR training should be further studied for its effectiveness in reducing kinesiophobia and preventing chronicity.

5. Summary

Neck pain has recently drawn international attention as a growing health problem in western society (Lidgren, L. 2008; Rydevik, B. 2008). Consequently, a need for a reliable, objective and functional assessment was stressed in existing literature (Chappuis, G. and Soltermann, B. 2008; Nordin, M. et al. 2008). Qualities of VR technology were utilised in order to provide a solution for this need.

Our research included development of a novel VR assessment of cervical motion, reliability evaluation of the developed VR, and comparison of cervical motion kinematics between patients with chronic neck pain and control individuals without symptoms.

The described advantages of the VR assessment over existing conventional assessments include the interactive use of external visual stimuli; the VR motion enhancement effect demonstrated in ROM analysis; and the greater sensitivity found for VR ROM and kinematic measures compared to existing outcome measures.

The validation of the VR assessment was supported by two analyses, first by demonstrating group differences in range, velocity and smoothness of cervical motion, and second by showing good diagnostic value for outcome measures used.
As part of the investigation, and in agreement with previous literature, advantageous findings and better performance were shown for horizontal motion as compared with sagittal motion. This included differences in reliability, range and velocity of cervical motion.
The developed VR system may serve a platform for future therapeutic modalities, for training in rehabilitation of patients suffering from neck pain.

6. Acknowledgement

This chapter is based on the PhD dissertation completed on 2010 by the author under the dedicated supervision of Prof. Yocheved Laufer (School of Physical Therapy) and Prof. Tamar Weiss (School of occupational therapy), at the University of Haifa, Israel.

7. References

Amiri, M., et al. (2003). Measuring range of active cervical rotation in a position of full head flexion using the 3D Fastrak measurement system: an intra-tester reliability study. Man Ther, 8, (3), 176-179,

Assink, N., et al. (2005). Interobserver Reliability of Neck-Mobility Measurement by Means of the Flock-of-Birds Electromagnetic Tracking System. Journal of Manipulative and Physiological Therapeutics, 28, (6), 408-413,

Barnsley, L., et al. (1994). Whiplash injury. Pain, 58, (3), 283-307.,

Bland, J.M. and D.G. Altman (1986). Statistical methods for assessing agreement between two methods of clinical measurement. Lancet, 1, (8476), 307-310,

Bland, J.M. and D.G. Altman (2007). Agreement between methods of measurement with multiple observations per individual. J Biopharm Stat, 17, (4), 571-582,

Breivik, E.K., et al. (2000). A comparison of pain rating scales by sampling from clinical trial data. Clinical Journal of Pain, 16, (1), 22-28, 0749-8047

Brison, R.J., et al. (2000). A prospective study of acceleration-extension injuries following rear-end motor vehicle collisions. World Congress on Whiplash-Associated Disorders in Vancouver, British Columbia, Canada in February of 1999. Journal of Musculoskeletal Pain, 8, 97,

Bryanton, C., et al. (2006). Feasibility, motivation, and selective motor control: virtual reality compared to conventional home exercise in children with cerebral palsy. Cyberpsychol Behav, 9, (2), 123-128,

Chappuis, G. and B. Soltermann (2008). Number and cost of claims linked to minor cervical trauma in Europe: results from the comparative study by CEA, AREDOC and CEREDOC. Eur Spine J, 17, (10), 1350-1357,

Chen, J., et al. (1999). Meta-analysis of normative cervical motion. Spine, 24, (15), 1571-1578,

Childs, J.D., et al. (2008). Neck pain: Clinical practice guidelines linked to the International Classification of Functioning, Disability, and Health from the Orthopedic Section of the American Physical Therapy Association. J Orthop Sports Phys Ther, 38, (9), A1-A34,

Chiu, T.T.W. and S.K. Lo (2002). Evaluation of cervical range of motion and isometric neck muscle strength: reliability and validity, 16(8):851-858(8). Clin Rehab, 16, (8), 851-858,

Cleland, J. A., et al. (2008). Psychometric properties of the Fear-Avoidance Beliefs Questionnaire and Tampa Scale of Kinesiophobia in patients with neck pain. Am J Phys Med Rehabil, 87, (2), 109-117, 0894-9115

Cote, P., et al. (2001). The treatment of neck and low back pain: who seeks care? who goes where? Med Care, 39, (9), 956-967.,

Cote, P.D.C.P., et al. (2008). The Burden and Determinants of Neck Pain in Workers: Results of the Bone and Joint Decade 2000-2010 Task Force on Neck Pain and Its Associated Disorders. S60-S74,

Dall'Alba, P.T., et al. (2001). Cervical range of motion discriminates between asymptomatic persons and those with whiplash. Spine, 26, (19), 2090-2094.,

Day, J.S., et al. (2000). Calibration of position and angular data from a magnetic tracking device. J Biomech, 33, (8), 1039-1045,

De Hertogh, W.J., et al. (2007). The clinical examination of neck pain patients: The validity of a group of tests. Manual Therapy, 12, (1), 50,

Dvir, Z., et al. (2006). Cervical motion in patients with chronic disorders of the cervical spine: a reproducibility study. Spine, 31,(13), E394,

Dvir, Z. and T. Prushansky (2000). Reproducibility and instrument validity of a new ultrasonography-based system for measuring cervical spine kinematics. Clin Biomech (Bristol, Avon), 15, (9), 658-664,

Dvir, Z. and T. Prushansky (2008). Cervical muscles strength testing: methods and clinical implications. J Manipulative Physiol Ther, 31, (7), 518-524,

Edmondston, S.J., et al. (2007). Postural neck pain: An investigation of habitual sitting posture, perception of 'good' posture and cervicothoracic kinaesthesia. Manual Therapy, 12, (4), 363-371, 1356-689X

Feipel, V., et al. (1999). Normal global motion of the cervical spine: an electrogoniometric study. Clin Biomech (Bristol, Avon), 14, (7), 462-470,

Grealy, M.A., et al. (1999). Improving cognitive function after brain injury: the use of exercise and virtual reality. Arch Phys Med Rehabil, 80, (6), 661-667,

Gregori, B., et al. (2008). Fast voluntary neck movements in patients with cervical dystonia: A kinematic study before and after therapy with botulinum toxin type A. Clinical Neurophysiology, 119, (2), 273,

Grip, H., et al. (2007). Variations in the axis of motion during head repositioning-a comparison of subjects with whiplash-associated disorders or non-specific neck pain and healthy controls. Clin Biomech (Bristol, Avon), 22, (8), 865-873,

Guzman, J., et al. (2008). A new conceptual model of neck pain: linking onset, course, and care: the Bone and Joint Decade 2000-2010 Task Force on Neck Pain and Its Associated Disorders. Spine, 33, (4 Suppl), 14-23,

Harris, K. and D. Reid (2005). The influence of virtual reality play on children's motivation. Can J Occup Ther, 72, (1), 21-29,

Heikkila, H.V. and B.I. Wenngren (1998). Cervicocephalic kinesthetic sensibility, active range of cervical motion, and oculomotor function in patients with whiplash injury. Arch Phys Med Rehabil, 79, (9), 1089-1094.,

Hoffman, H.G., et al. (2001). Effectiveness of virtual reality-based pain control with multiple treatments. Clin J Pain, 17, (3), 229-235.,

Hoffman, H.G., et al. (2008). Virtual reality pain control during burn wound debridement in the hydrotank. Clin J Pain, 24, (4), 299-304,

Hoffman, H.G., et al. (2007). The analgesic effects of opioids and immersive virtual reality distraction: evidence from subjective and functional brain imaging assessments. Anesth Analg, 105, (6), 1776-1783, table of contents,

Hogg-Johnson, S., et al. (2008). The burden and determinants of neck pain in the general population: results of the Bone and Joint Decade 2000-2010 Task Force on Neck Pain and Its Associated Disorders. Spine, 33,(4 Suppl), S39-51,

Holden, M.K. (2005). Virtual environments for motor rehabilitation: review. Cyberpsychol Behav, 8, (3), 187-211; discussion 212-189, 1094-9313 (Print)

Holm, L.W.D., et al. (2008). The Burden and Determinants of Neck Pain in Whiplash-Associated Disorders After Traffic Collisions: Results of the Bone and Joint Decade 2000-2010 Task Force on Neck Pain and Its Associated Disorders. Spine, 33, (4S), S52-S59,

Jordan, K., et al. (2000). The reliability of the three-dimensional FASTRAK measurement system in measuring cervical spine and shoulder range of motion in healthy subjects. Rheumatology (Oxford), 39, (4), 382-388,

Jull, G.A., et al. (2008). Clinical assessment of the deep cervical flexor muscles: the craniocervical flexion test. J Manipulative Physiol Ther, 31, (7), 525-533,

Keshner, E.A. and R.V. Kenyon (2000). The influence of an immersive virtual environment on the segmental organization of postural stabilizing responses. J Vestib Res, 10, (4-5), 207-219,

Keshner, E.A. and R.V. Kenyon (2004). Using immersive technology for postural research and rehabilitation. Assist Technol, 16, (1), 54-62,

Keshner, E.A., et al. (2004). Postural responses exhibit multisensory dependencies with discordant visual and support surface motion. J Vestib Res, 14, (4), 307-319,

Koerhuis, C.L., et al. (2003). Neck mobility measurement by means of the 'Flock of Birds' electromagnetic tracking system. Clinical Biomechanics, 18, (1), 14-18,

Kristjansson, E., et al. (2001). Cervicocephalic kinaesthesia: reliability of a new test approach. Physiother Res Int, 6, (4), 224-235,

Kristjansson, E., et al. (2004). A new clinical test for cervicocephalic kinesthetic sensibility: "The fly". Archives of Physical Medicine and Rehabilitation, 85,(3), 490-495,

Langley, G.B. and H. Sheppeard (1985). The visual analogue scale: its use in pain measurement. Rheumatol Int, 5, (4), 145-148,

Lantz, C.A., et al. (1999). Clinical validity and stability of active and passive cervical range of motion with regard to total and unilateral uniplanar motion. Spine, 24, (11), 1082-1089, 0362-2436 (Print)

Lee, J.H., et al. (2003). A virtual reality system for the assessment and rehabilitation of the activities of daily living. Cyberpsychol Behav, 6, (4), 383-388,

Lidgren, L. (2008). Preface: Neck Pain and the Decade of the Bone and Joint 2000-2010. Spine, 33,(4S), S1-S2,

Lind, B., et al. (1989). Normal range of motion of the cervical spine. Arch Phys Med Rehabil, 70, (9), 692-695,

LoPresti, E.F., et al. (2003). Neck range of motion and use of computer head controls. J Rehabil Res Dev, 40, (3), 199-211,

Marcotte, J., et al. (2002). The kinematics of motion palpation and its effect on the reliability for cervical spine rotation. Journal of Manipulative and Physiological Therapeutics, 25, (7), E1,

McNevin, N.H., et al. (2003). Increasing the distance of an external focus of attention enhances learning. Psychological Research-Psychologische Forschung, 67,(1), 22-29,

Michaelsen, S.M., et al. (2001). Effect of trunk restraint on the recovery of reaching movements in hemiparetic patients. Stroke, 32, (8), 1875-1883,

Mirelman, A., et al. (2009). Effects of training with a robot-virtual reality system compared with a robot alone on the gait of individuals after stroke. Stroke, 40, (1), 169-174, 1524-4628 (Electronic)

Nordin, M., et al. (2008). Assessment of Neck Pain and Its Associated Disorders. Results of the Bone and Joint Decade 2000–2010 Task Force on Neck Pain and Its Associated Disorders. Spine, 33,(4S), S101-S122,

Ogon, M., et al. (1996). Chronic low back pain measurement with visual analogue scales in different settings. Pain, 64,(3), 425,

Penning, L. and J.T. Wilmink (1987). Rotation of the cervical spine. A CT study in normal subjects. Spine, 12, (8), 732-738,

Pietrobon, R., et al. (2002). Standard scales for measurement of functional outcome for cervical pain or dysfunction: a systematic review. Spine (Phila Pa 1976), 27,(5), 515-522,

Revel, M., et al. (1991). Cervicocephalic kinesthetic sensibility in patients with cervical pain. Arch Phys Med Rehabil, 72,(5), 288-291.,

Revel, M., et al. (1994). Changes in cervicocephalic kinesthesia after a proprioceptive rehabilitation program in patients with neck pain: a randomized controlled study cervicocephalic kinesthetic sensibility in patients with cervical pain. Arch Phys Med Rehabil, 75,(8), 895-899.,

Riva, G., et al. (1999). Virtual Environments in the Diagnosis, Prevention, and Intervention of Age-Related Diseases: A Review of VR Scenarios Proposed in the EC VETERAN Project. Cyberpsychol Behav, 2, (6), 577-591,

Rix, G.D. and J. Bagust (2001). Cervicocephalic kinesthetic sensibility in patients with chronic, nontraumatic cervical spine pain. Arch Phys Med Rehabil, 82, (7), 911-919.,

Rizzo, A. and G.J. Kim (2005). A SWOT analysis of the field of virtual reality rehabilitation and therapy. Presence-Teleoperators and Virtual Environments, 14, (2), 119-146, 1054-7460

Rizzo, A.A., et al. (2006). A virtual reality scenario for all seasons: the virtual classroom. CNS Spectr, 11, (1), 35-44,

Rydevik, B. (2008). Editorial preface: The bone and joint decade 2000-2010 task force on neck pain and its associated disorders. European Spine Journal, 17, S3-S3, 0940-6719

Sarig-Bahat, H., et al. (2009). Cervical motion assessment using virtual reality. Spine, 34, (10), 1018–1024,

Sarig-Bahat, H., et al. (2010). Neck Pain Assessment in a Virtual Environment. Spine, 35, (4), E105–E112,

Sharar, S.R., et al. (2008). Applications of virtual reality for pain management in burn-injured patients. Expert Rev Neurother, 8, (11), 1667-1674,

Sjolander, P., et al. (2008). Sensorimotor disturbances in chronic neck pain--Range of motion, peak velocity, smoothness of movement, and repositioning acuity. Manual Therapy, 13, (2), 122,

Spitzer, W.O., et al. (1995). Scientific monograph of the Quebec Task Force on Whiplash-Associated Disorders: redefining "whiplash" and its management. Spine, 20, (8 Suppl), 1S-73S.,

Sterling, M., et al. (2003). Development of motor system dysfunction following whiplash injury. Pain, 103, (1-2), 65-73,

Stiell, I.G., et al. (2003). The Canadian C-spine rule versus the NEXUS low-risk criteria in patients with trauma. N Engl J Med, 349,(26), 2510-2518,

Sullivan, M.J., et al. (2002). Differential predictors of pain and disability in patients with whiplash injuries. Pain Res Manag, 7, (2), 68-74,

Treleaven, J. (2008). Sensorimotor disturbances in neck disorders affecting postural stability, head and eye movement control. Manual Therapy, 13, (1), 2,

Treleaven, J., et al. (2006). The relationship of cervical joint position error to balance and eye movement disturbances in persistent whiplash. Man Ther, 11, (2), 99-106,

Treleaven, J., et al. (2003). Dizziness and unsteadiness following whiplash injury: characteristic features and relationship with cervical joint position error. J Rehabil Med, 35, (1), 36-43.,

Vernon, H. (2008). The Neck Disability Index: state-of-the-art, 1991-2008. J Manipulative Physiol Ther, 31, (7), 491-502,

Vernon, H. and S. Mior (1991). The Neck Disability Index: a study of reliability and validity. J Manipulative Physiol Ther, 14, (7), 409-415, 0161-4754 (Print)

Wainner, R.S., et al. (2003). Reliability and diagnostic accuracy of the clinical examination and patient self-report measures for cervical radiculopathy. Spine, 28, 52-62,

Weiss, P.L., et al. (2003). Design and testing of a virtual environment to train stroke patients with unilateral spatial neglect to cross a street safely. Occup Ther Int, 10,(1), 39-55,

Wilson, P.N., et al. (1996). Transfer of spatial information from a virtual to a real environment in physically disabled children. Disabil Rehabil, 18, (12), 633-637,

Woodhouse, A. and O. Vasseljen (2008). Altered motor control patterns in whiplash and chronic neck pain. BMC Musculoskelet Disord, 9, 90,

Wulf, G. (2008). Attentional focus effects in balance acrobats. Research Quarterly for Exercise and Sport, 79, (3), 319-325, 0270-1367

Wulf, G., et al. (1998). Instructions for motor learning: Differential effects of internal versus external focus of attention. Journal of Motor Behavior, 30, (2), 169-179, 0022-2895

Wulf, G., et al. (1999). The learning advantages of an external focus of attention in golf. Research Quarterly for Exercise and Sport, 70, (2), 120-126, 0270-1367

Wulf, G. and N.H. McNevin (2001). Further evidence for the benefits of an external attentional focus - Or: Preventing an internal focus is not enough. Journal of Sport & Exercise Psychology, 23, S60-S60, 0895-2779

Wulf, G. and J. Su (2007). An external focus of attention enhances golf shot accuracy in beginners and experts. Research Quarterly for Exercise and Sport, 78, (4), 384-389, 0270-1367

Wulf, G., et al. (2007). Attentional focus effects as a function of task difficulty. Research Quarterly for Exercise and Sport, 78, (3), 257-264, 0270-1367

Youdas, J.W., et al. (1991). Reliability of measurements of cervical spine range of motion--comparison of three methods. Phys Ther, 71,(2), 98-104; discussion 105-106.,

Zachry, T., et al. (2005). Increased movement accuracy and reduced EMG activity as the result of adopting an external focus of attention. Brain Research Bulletin, 67, (4), 304-309,

10

Handedness and Dexterity Evaluation System Using Haptic Virtual Reality Technology

Masanao Koeda, Mako Matsuyama,
Munetaka Sugihashi and Tsuneo Yoshikawa
Ritsumeikan University
Japan

1. Introduction

It is considered that the ratio of right-handed to left-handed persons is 9 to 1 approximately, and most products are created for right-handed persons. Right-handed persons are mostly unaware of the inconvenience, however, it is a deep problem for left-handed persons.

Quantitative evaluation of handedness of people will be useful in various situations. For example, handedness is an important factor in designing tools and devices that are to be handled by people using their hands. It will also be useful for knowing the degree of recovery of a person in rehabilitation stage suffering from injury or disease.

A well-known method for evaluating handedness of a person is LQ (laterality quotient)-method (Oldfield,R.C.1971) which is based on the answers to ten questions such as which hand 1 uses for writing letters. (Matsuda et al.,2003) propose to evaluate handedness based on the results of tests of tapping, peg-board, and picking up beans using discriminant function analysis.

There are many researches trying to find functional differences between dominant and non dominant hands. (Fujiwara et al.,2003) use a digital trace method for studying the difference of upper limb coordination between dominant and non-dominant hands. (Wu et al.,1996) examine the difference between the behaviors during the operation of touch panel by the dominant and non-dominant hands. (Bagesteiro et al.,2002) investigate interlimb differences in coordination through analysis of inverse dynamics and electromyography recorded during the performance of reaching movements. These studies assume that subjects in their experiments can be divided into 2 groups: right-handed persons and left-handed persons. However, there are many persons who are neither 100% right-handed nor 100% left-handed persons. In order to properly take these persons into consideration in various studies related to handedness of people, we need to consider the quantitative degree of handedness of each subject. One possible direction of future research will be to consider the quantitative degree of handedness of each subject.

We have also proposed a method for evaluating quantitatively the handedness and dexterity (Yoshikawa et al.,2007). The evaluation method is based on a performance of some test tasks in the virtual world that are constructed using haptic virtual reality technology. Haptic virtual reality is a technology which makes it possible for us to see and touch a virtual environment composed by a computer through a haptic display device. Various researches have been done so far in this field (Burdea,G.C.,1996). We have proposed a methodology for displaying the dynamics of virtual objects (Yoshikawa et al.,1995), and developed a system for observing human skill by using a virtual task space (Yoshikawa et al.,2000). The merits of virtual test tasks over real tasks in evaluating the handedness are that it is easier to provide a large variety of tasks, to change the values of parameters of these tasks, and to obtain detailed position and force data for evaluation. In this method, 3 test tasks were prepared: accurate positioning task, accurate force control task, and skillful manipulation task. Performance data for these test tasks taken from a group of subjects are analyzed using the factor analysis. Since the obtained factor scores for the right and left hands of each subject can be regarded as the skillfulness of the right and left hand, it was proposed to define the degree of handedness and dexterity of the subject based on the difference and average of these factor scores respectively. The results of the judgment of handedness from this method for the ten subjects were consistent with that from the conventional LQ method. However, these tests had some problems:

- The desired position was not indicated clearly in the position control test.
- The indication method of desired force was not easily viewable in the force control test.
- The grasping position was no specified clearly in the manipulation test, therefore some subjects were confused.

In this study, the problems of the tests of the previous method were modified, and we describe the following points:

1. A new test task was added to measure combined dexterity of position and force control of fingertips.
2. The learning effect of each test was investigated.
3. Three test tasks in the real space were conducted.

By using this system, experiments to measure handedness and dexterity were conducted to 12 subjects, and the performance of the new system is discussed.

2. Outline of handedness and dexterity evaluation system

An experimental system shown in Fig. 1 has been developed for measuring the dexterity of a finger from the following 4 viewpoints:

1. Position control
2. Force control
3. Manipulation of objects
4. Position-force combined control

The system consists of 2 force display devices (PHANToM OMNI), a display, and a computer for constructing a virtual task world. The specifications of the computer and the force display device are shown in Table 1, 2. The test task applications which is described in detail in the next section are all needed to be controlled using one's finger. Therefore, the original attachment which is shown in Fig. 2 was installed instead of the standard stylus.

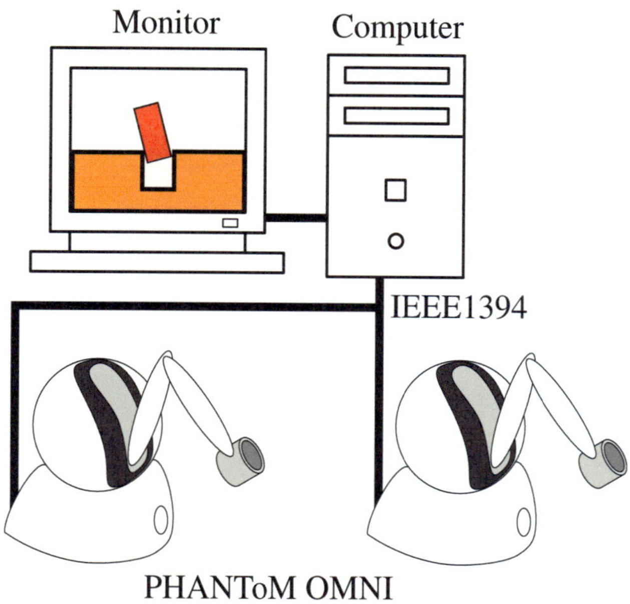

Fig. 1. System configuration

Fig. 2. Original attachment for our test tasks

3. Test tasks in virtual space

3.1 Position control test

This test is intended to measure the dexterity in positioning a fingertip accurately. The subject is asked to follow the desired point on the screen which moves along a circle with the constant velocity by using his/her index finger. The desired point turns around the circle 5 times taking 6 seconds for each turn. Fig.3-(a) shows the image on the monitor screen, and Fig.3-(b) shows the handling style of the attachment. In a right hand test, the desired point rotates in clockwise direction along the circle and in a left hand test, the desired point rotates in counterclockwise direction along the circle.

OS	Microsoft Windows XP Professional
CPU	Intel Xeon 5140 2.33 [GHz]
Memory	2 [GB]
GPU	NVIDIA Quadro FX 550
Bus Type	PCI Express × 16

Table 1. Specifications of computer

Force Feedback Workspace	160W x 120H x 70D[mm]
Position Resolution	0.055[mm]
Maximum Exertable Force	3.3[N]
Continuous Exertable Force	0.88[N]
Stiffness	X axis 1.26[N/mm] Y axis 2.31[N/mm] Z axis 1.02[N/mm]
Force Feedback	x, y, z
Interface	IEEE-1394 FireWire

Table 2. Specifications of PHANToM OMNI

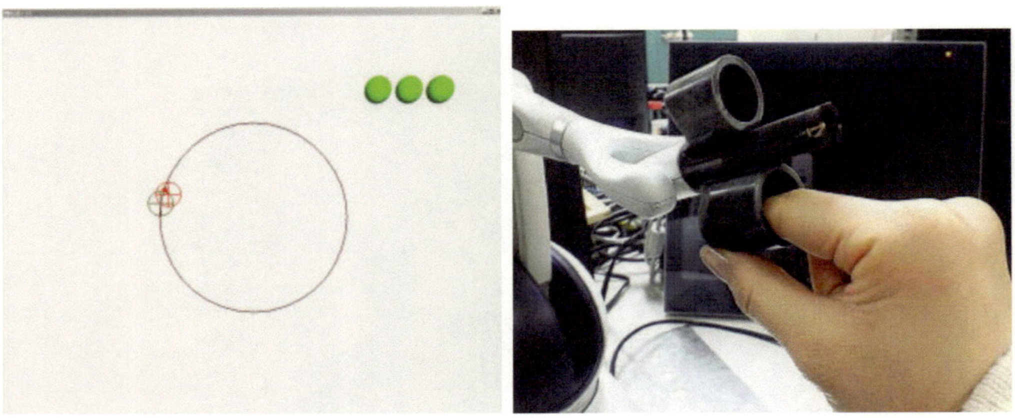

(a) Image on the monitor (b) Handling

Fig. 3. Position control test

The average of the tracking error during the 5 turns from the 2nd to the 4th turn is taken as the measure of performance of this task. As is shown in Fig.4, the tracking error $e_p(t)$ at time t is given by

$$\boldsymbol{P}(t) = [x(t) \;\; y(t)]^T \tag{1}$$

$$\boldsymbol{P}_d(t) = [x_d(t) \;\; y_d(t)]^T = [r\cos(\omega_p t) \;\; r\sin(\omega_p t)]^T \tag{2}$$

$$e_p(t) = \sqrt{||\boldsymbol{P}(t) - \boldsymbol{P}_d(t)||} \tag{3}$$

where $\boldsymbol{P}(t)$ is the position vector of the fingertip on the virtual plane shown by a red circle $\boldsymbol{P}_d(t)$ is the desired position vector of the fingertip shown by a green circle, and ω_p is the

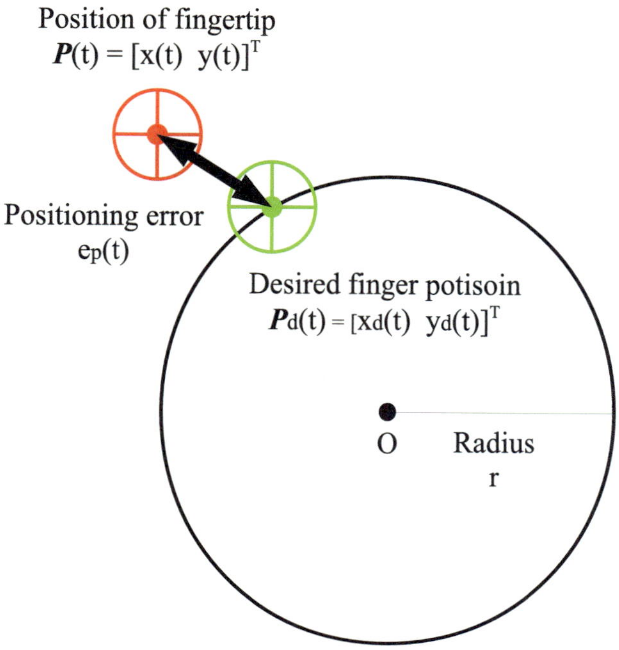

Fig. 4. Positioning error

rotational velocity of $\boldsymbol{P}_d(t)$ (= $-2\pi/6[\mathrm{s}^{-1}]$ in a right hand test, = $2\pi/6[\mathrm{s}^{-1}]$ in a left hand test). The measure of performance E_p is given by the average magnitude of tracking error, that is,

$$E_p^n = \frac{\int_0^T e_p(t)dt}{T} \tag{4}$$

$$E_p = \frac{\Sigma_{n=1}^N E_p^n}{N} \tag{5}$$

where E_p^n is the performance of the nth trial, N is the number of trial(=3), T is the total time (=30 [s]). The smaller the value E_p is, the more dexterous the subject is regarded in position control.

3.2 Force control test

This test is intended to measure the dexterity in exerting desired force on a virtual object by fingertips accurately. The subject is asked to pinch a green virtual object in the screen by using index and thumb finger. The both sides of the object are concaved to be pinched easily. Fig.5-(a) shows the image on the monitor screen and Fig.5-(b) shows the handling style of the attachment in this test. When the subject pinches the box, he/she can feel the reaction force through the force display device. The reaction force is calculated by using a spring-damper model of the surface of box. The subject can also watch the relative magnitude of the exerted force $\boldsymbol{F}(t)$ and the desired force $F_d(t)$ by the gauge which is placed in right side of the monitor. The task continues 30 seconds and the data is obtained during 6 through 24 seconds skipping the first and last 6 second.

The average of the force control error during the 18 seconds is taken as the measure of performance of this task. As is shown in Fig. 6, exerted force and desired force are displayed

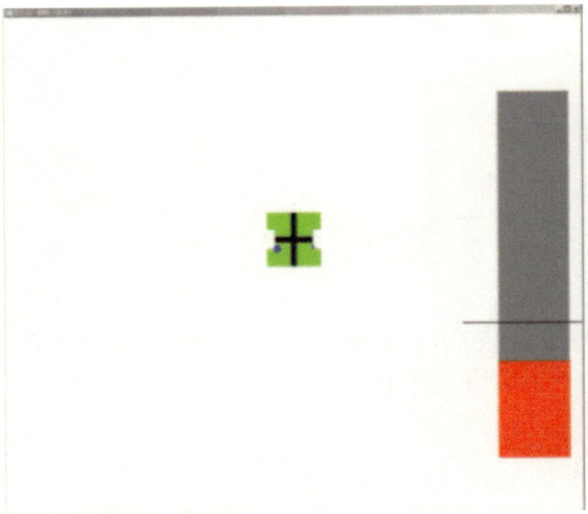

(a) Image on the monitor

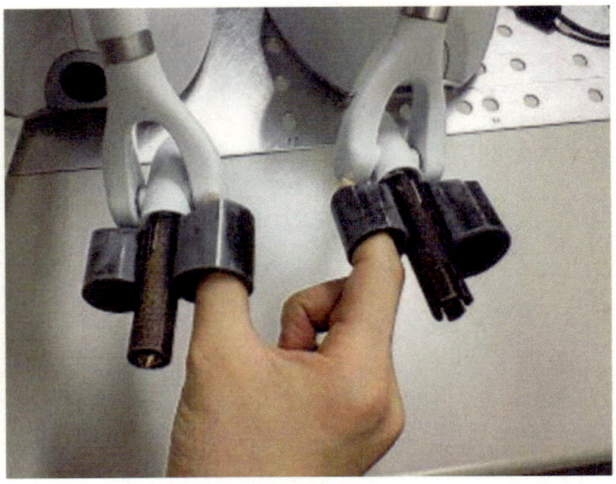

(b) Handling

Fig. 5. Force control test

and the force error is shown clearly to the subject than the previous force test. The force control error $e_f(t)$ at time t is given by

$$F(t) = \frac{||\boldsymbol{F}_l(t)|| + ||\boldsymbol{F}_r(t)||}{2} \quad (6)$$

$$F_d(t) = 1.5 + \sin(\omega_f t) \quad (7)$$

$$e_f(t) = |F(t) - F_d(t)| \quad (8)$$

where $\boldsymbol{F}_l(t)$ and $\boldsymbol{F}_r(t)$ is the force vector of left and right finger, $F_d(t)$ is the desired force, ω_f is the frequency of the desired force(=$2\pi/3[s^{-1}]$). The measure of performance E_f is given by

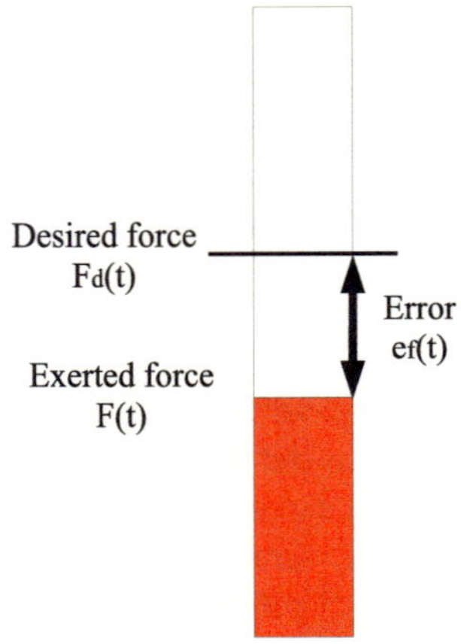

Fig. 6. Force error

$$E_f^n = \frac{\int_0^T e_f(t)dt}{T} \quad (9)$$

$$E_f = \frac{\Sigma_{n=1}^N E_f^n}{N} \quad (10)$$

where E_f^n is the performance of the nth trial, N is the number of trial(=3), T is the total time (=18 [s]). The smaller the value E_f is, the more dexterous the subject is regarded in force control.

Here, we describe the method for generating the contact force between a finger and a virtual object in this test. To generate virtual space and force to the force display device (PHANToM OMNI), we used Haptic Library API (HLAPI). HLAPI is distributed from SensAble Technologies, Inc. (SensAble Technologies,Inc.) and it provides a lot of useful functions to develop applications for PHANToM OMNI. By using this library, it is easy to measure the position and orientation of the device and control the force in virtual space in real time. The control period of the force display device using this library is 1[ms].

Now, let us suppose the situation that is illustrated in Fig. 7, where $\boldsymbol{P}_m(t)$ and $\boldsymbol{P}_c(t)$ indicate the measured and current position of a finger in a virtual space respectively.

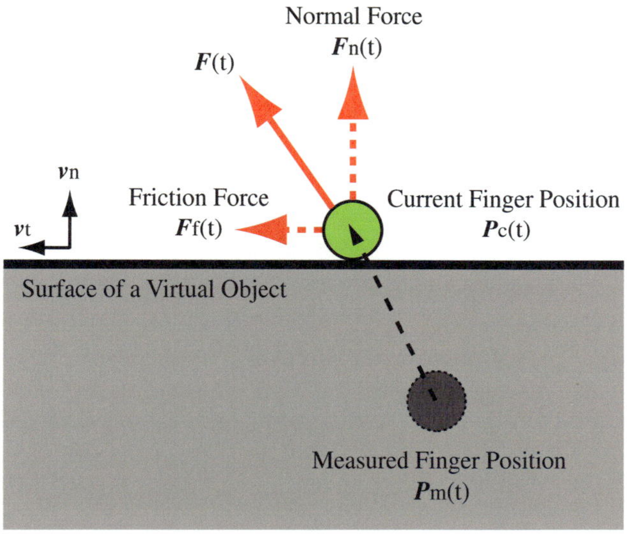

Fig. 7. Virtual object, finger position, and exerted force

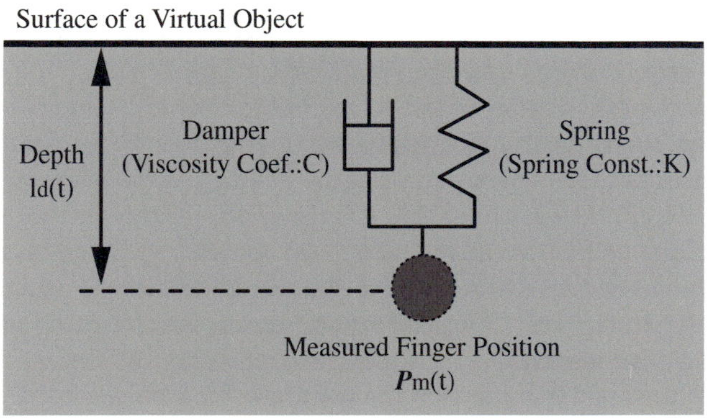

Fig. 8. Spring-damper model

(a) Image on the monitor

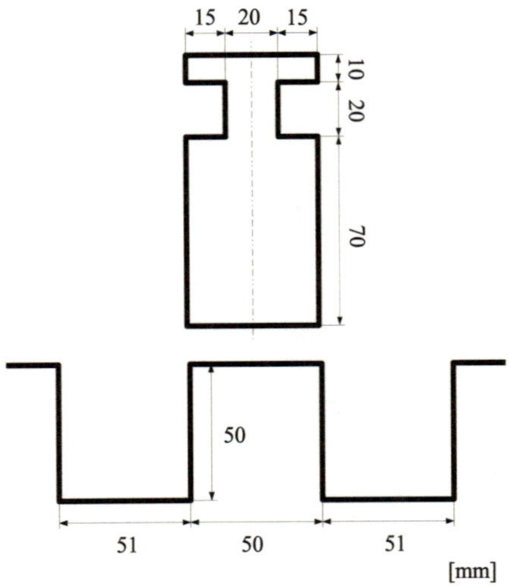

(b) Size of peg and holes

Fig. 9. Manipulation test

To display the force from the virtual object, spring-damper model is estimated shown in Fig. 8, and normal force vector $\boldsymbol{F}_n(t)$ and friction force vector $\boldsymbol{F}_f(t)$ is defined as following equations:

$$\boldsymbol{F}_n(t) = \left\{ K l_d(t) + C \dot{l_d}(t) \right\} \boldsymbol{v}_n \quad (11)$$

$$\boldsymbol{F}_f(t) = \mu \left\| \boldsymbol{F}_n(t) \right\| \boldsymbol{v}_t \quad (12)$$

where $l_d(t)$ is the depth of measured finger position, $\dot{l_d}(t)$ is the velocity of finger motion, $\boldsymbol{v}_n$ is the unit normal vector of the surface, $\boldsymbol{v}_t$ is the unit tangent vector of the surface, K is the spring constant, C is the viscosity coefficient, and μ is the friction coefficient.

3.3 Manipulation test

This test is intended to measure the dexterity of a subject in manipulating objects by his/her hand. The subject is asked to insert a peg into a hole in virtual world, which is constructed by using a dynamics simulator: Open Dynamics Engine (Smith,R.,2000). The interaction forces among the fingertips, peg, and hole are calculated based on the intrusion distance among them following the approach described in (Yoshikawa et al.,2000).
The gravitational acceleration is assumed to be 9800 [mm/s^2]. The task is specified in the 2-dimensional space by constraining the motion of peg in a plane parallel to the monitor screen. The subject is asked to pick up a peg of 50[mm] wide, 20[mm] wide at handling position, 100[mm] long, and weighing 75[g], by his/her thumb and index finger. The size of hole is 50[mm] deep and 51[mm] wide. Fig.9-(a) shows the image on the monitor screen and Fig.9-(b) illustrates the detail of the size of the peg and holes. The handling style is same as the force test shown in Fig.5-(b). To specify the grasping position and manipulate easily, the both sides of the peg are concaved.
The subject is asked to insert the peg into the next hole by 4 times. (see Fig.10). The time E_m^n needed to perform this insertion task is taken as the measure of performance.

$$E_m = \frac{\Sigma_{n=1}^{N} E_m^n}{N} \quad (13)$$

where N is the number of trial(=3). The smaller the value E_m is, the more dexterous the subject is regarded in manipulation control.

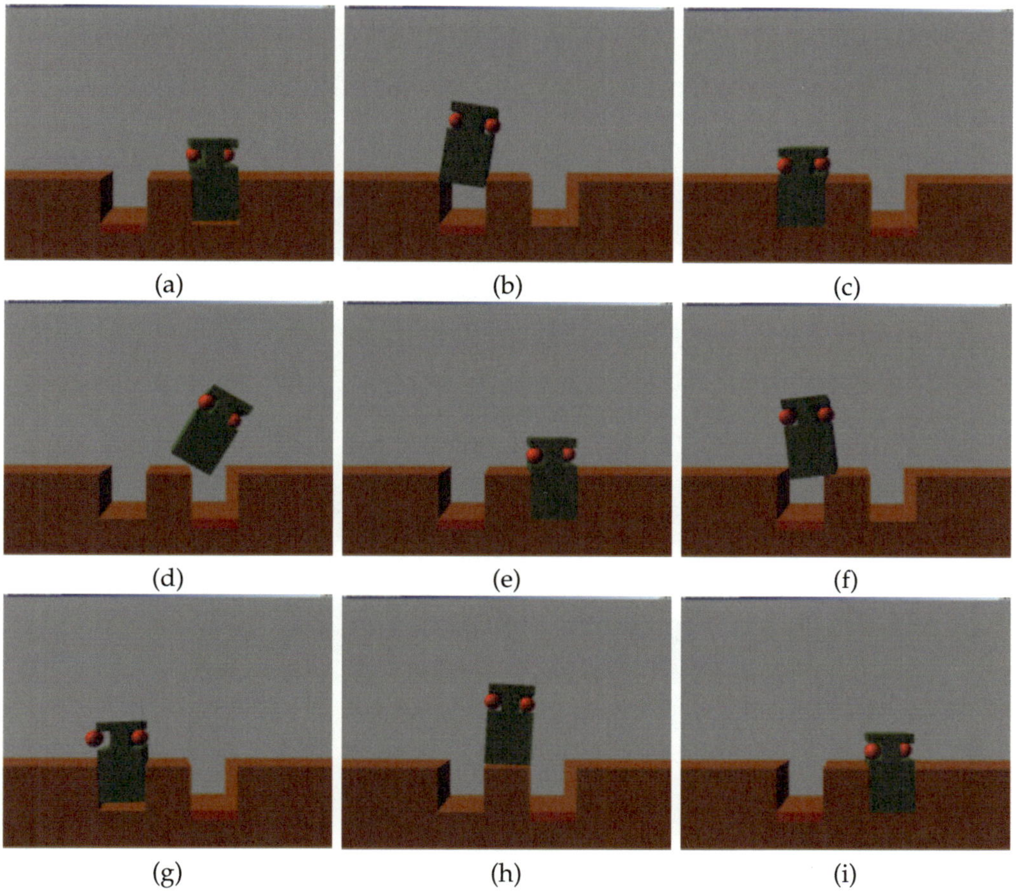

Fig. 10. Snapshots in manipulation test task

3.4 Position-Force combined test

This test is intended to measure the dexterity of a subject in simultaneous control of position and force by his/her fingertips. Fig.11 shows the image on the monitor screen of this test, and the handling style is same as the force test shown in Fig.5-(b). This test was constructed by combining the 2 tests previously described: position control test and force control test. The subject is asked to pinch a green virtual object in the screen with the constant force by using index and thumb finger, and the subject is also asked to follow the marker which indicates desired finger point. The marker moves along a circle with the constant velocity. The desired point turns around the circle 5 times taking 6 seconds for each turn. The average of the tracking error during the 5 turns from the 2nd to the 4th turn is taken as the measure of performance of this task. The gauge which is placed in center of the monitor indicates the exerted force and the desired force. The handling style is same as the force test shown in Fig.5-(b).
The measure of performance E^n_{cp} and E^n_{cf} are given by the same method of the position control test and force control test as previously described. Note that desired force $F_d(t)$ is constant

value(=0.93[N]) in this test.

$$E_{cp} = \frac{\Sigma_{n=1}^{N} E_{cp}^{n}}{N} \tag{14}$$

$$E_{cf} = \frac{\Sigma_{n=1}^{N} E_{cf}^{n}}{N} \tag{15}$$

where E_{cp}^{n} and E_{cf}^{n} are the performance of the nth trial, N is the number of trial(=3).

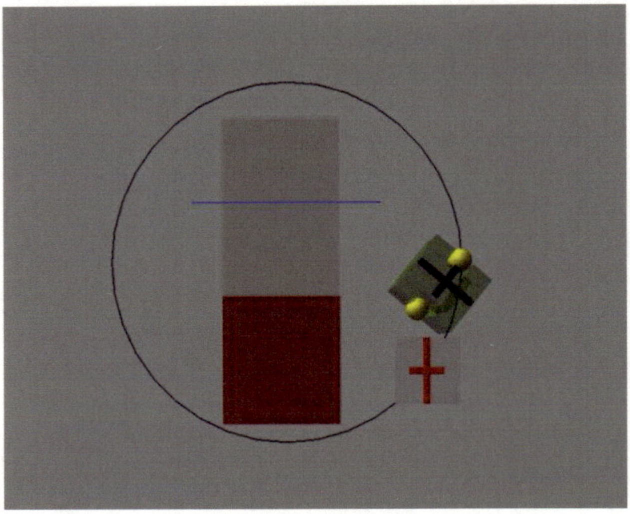

Fig. 11. Image on the monitor of Position-force combined test

4. Experimental results

4.1 LQ test

10 male and 2 female subjects of age 21–24 have taken the LQ tests. The questionnaire form of the test is shown in Table. 3. According to the conventional LQ test, 9 subjects (Subject A–J) were right-handed, 1 subject (Subject L) was left-handed, and subject K was ambidexterity (see Table 4).

4.2 Test tasks in virtual space

First of all, we investigated learning effect of the proposed test tasks. This investigation was conducted to subject M. Fig.12 shows learning curves of each test. It seems that all tests except manipulation test are not affected by learning so much. However, manipulation test is needed a little training for stable data acquisition.

Then, 1 minute training was imposed before all tests, and tests were repeated 3 times for the right and left hands of each subject.

Their averages were regarded as the measured performance data denoted as

$$\{E_{ihp}, E_{ihf}, E_{ihm}, E_{ihcp}, E_{ihcf}\}$$

where subscript i means subject $i = A, B, \cdots, L$, subscript h means left hand ($h = l$) or right hand ($h = r$), and subscripts p, f, m, cp, and cf mean the position control, the force control, the manipulation, position control in the combined test, and force control in the combined test respectively. Table 5,6 and Fig.13 show the measured data.

No.	Question	Left Hand	Right Hand	Both
1	Which hand do you use when writing?			
2	Which hand do you use when using chopsticks?			
3	Which hand do you use when drawing a picture?			
4	Which hand do you use when throwing a ball?			
5	Which hand do you use when using scissors?			
6	Which hand do you use when brushing teeth?			
7	Which hand do you use when using a spoon?			
8	Which hand do you use when sweeping by a short broom?			
9	Which hand do you use when lighting a match?			
10	Which hand do you use when unscrewing a bottle cap?			

Table 3. LQ questionnaire form

	Question No.										
Subject	**1**	**2**	**3**	**4**	**5**	**6**	**7**	**8**	**9**	**10**	**LQ Value**
A	R	R	R	R	R	R	R	R	R	R	**100**
B	R	R	R	R	R	R	R	R	R	R	**100**
C	R	R	R	R	R	R	R	R	R	R	**100**
D	R	R	R	R	R	R	R	R	R	R	**100**
E	R	R	R	R	R	R	R	R	R	R	**100**
F	R	R	R	R	R	R	R	R	R	R	**100**
G	R	R	R	R	R	R	R	R	R	R	**100**
H	R	R	R	R	R	R	R	R	R	R	**100**
I	R	R	R	R	R	R	R	R	R	R	**100**
J	R	R	R	R	R	R	R	R	R	L	**80**
K	R	R	R	L	L	R	R	B	R	B	**40**
L	L	L	L	L	L	L	L	L	L	L	**-100**

Table 4. Results of LQ value (R: Right Hand, L: Left Hand, B:Both)

5. Test tasks in real space

To investigate the relativity between virtual space and real space, we conducted 3 tests in real space: Picking up beans, moving pegs, and hitting counter test. Since this research is under investigation, overview of the experiments and experimental results are just shown in this paper.

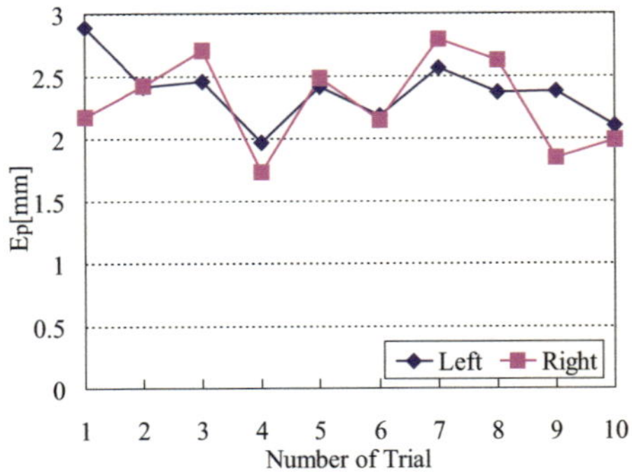

(a) Position control test

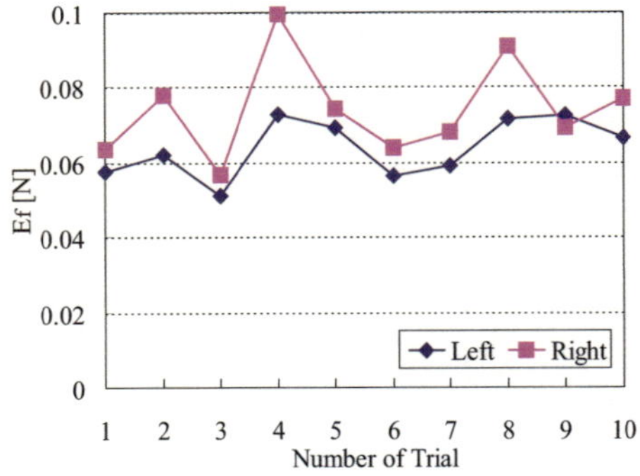

(b) Force control test

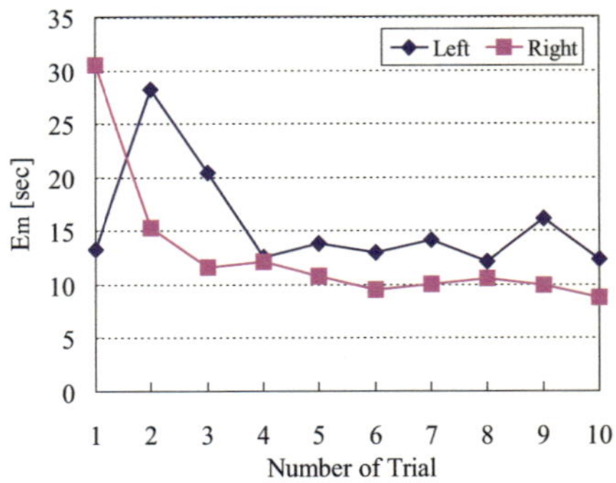

(c) Manipulation test

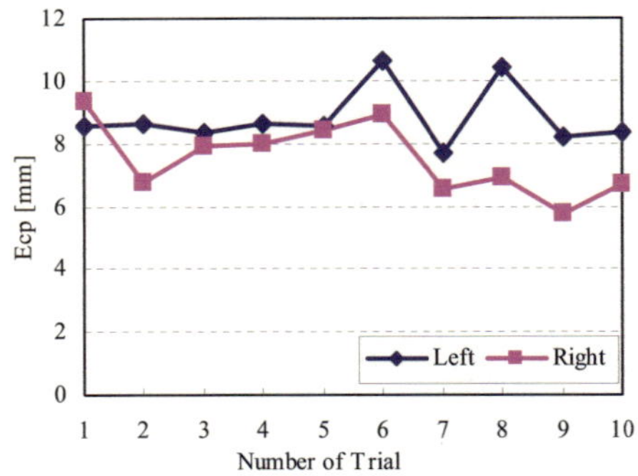

(d) Combined test (Position)

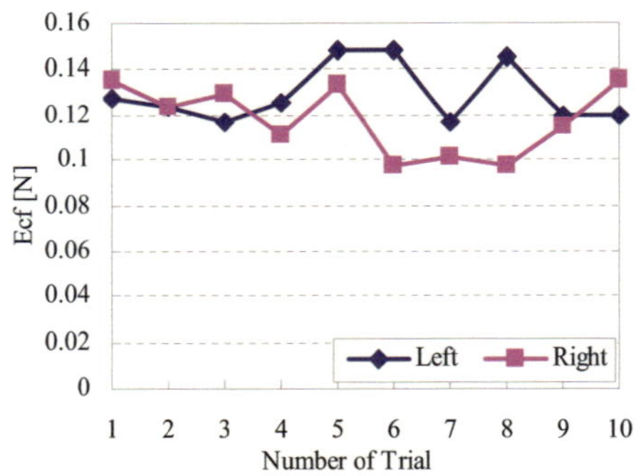

(e) Combined test (Force)

Fig. 12. Learning curves of subject M for the virtual space tests

5.1 Picking up beans test

The subject is asked to pick up a bean (soy bean, about 10[mm] in diameter) and move it to the next dish by using chopsticks, repeating 5 times for each hand. The size of dish is 100[mm] in diameter, and the distance between two dishes is 50[mm]. The dishes are fixed to the table by the double-stick tape. The experimental setup of this test and the experimental result are shown is shown in Fig.14-(a), Table 7, and Fig. 15-(a).

Subject	Position test [mm]		Force test [N]		Manipulation test [s]	
	L.H. E_{ilp}	R.H. E_{irp}	L.H. E_{ilf}	R.H. E_{irf}	L.H. E_{ilm}	R.H. E_{irm}
A	2.805	2.210	0.1463	0.0918	7.686	5.626
B	2.503	1.673	0.1060	0.0702	5.848	5.757
C	2.810	1.801	0.0747	0.0783	10.013	9.035
D	2.137	1.710	0.0848	0.0709	9.880	8.314
E	2.774	2.170	0.0763	0.0931	7.803	6.881
F	2.717	2.571	0.1209	0.0910	8.330	9.358
G	2.946	2.854	0.1122	0.1263	13.523	11.190
H	1.614	1.551	0.0638	0.0770	8.852	8.630
I	2.619	2.462	0.1039	0.0813	8.508	9.613
J	2.301	2.137	0.1014	0.0907	6.747	5.248
K	1.696	1.850	0.0765	0.0789	7.880	8.730
L	2.141	2.177	0.1066	0.0965	7.092	7.930

Table 5. Experimental results of position, force and manipulation test in virtual space (L.H.: Left Hand, R.H.:Right Hand)

Subject	Position [mm]		Force [N]	
	L.H. E_{ilcp}	R.H. E_{ircp}	L.H. E_{ilcf}	R.H. E_{ircf}
A	8.519	8.108	0.130	0.125
B	11.208	6.833	0.286	0.095
C	6.194	6.193	0.219	0.134
D	8.056	7.175	0.236	0.200
E	5.521	4.798	0.255	0.149
F	8.072	8.125	0.191	0.144
G	13.398	12.293	0.156	0.115
H	5.424	4.811	0.271	0.148
I	8.953	8.530	0.322	0.222
J	6.346	5.517	0.134	0.104
K	7.576	5.586	0.271	0.153
L	6.020	6.334	0.175	0.152

Table 6. Experimental results of the combined test in virtual space (L.H.: Left Hand, R.H.:Right Hand)

5.2 Moving pegs test

The subject is asked to pick up a small peg and move it to the hole below, repeating 20 times for each hand. The size of peg is about 6[mm] in diameter, 10[mm] deep, and the distance between holes is 12[mm] approximately. The board with holes is fixed to the table by the double-stick tape. The experimental setup of this test and the experimental result are shown in Fig.14-(b), Table 7, and Fig. 15-(b).

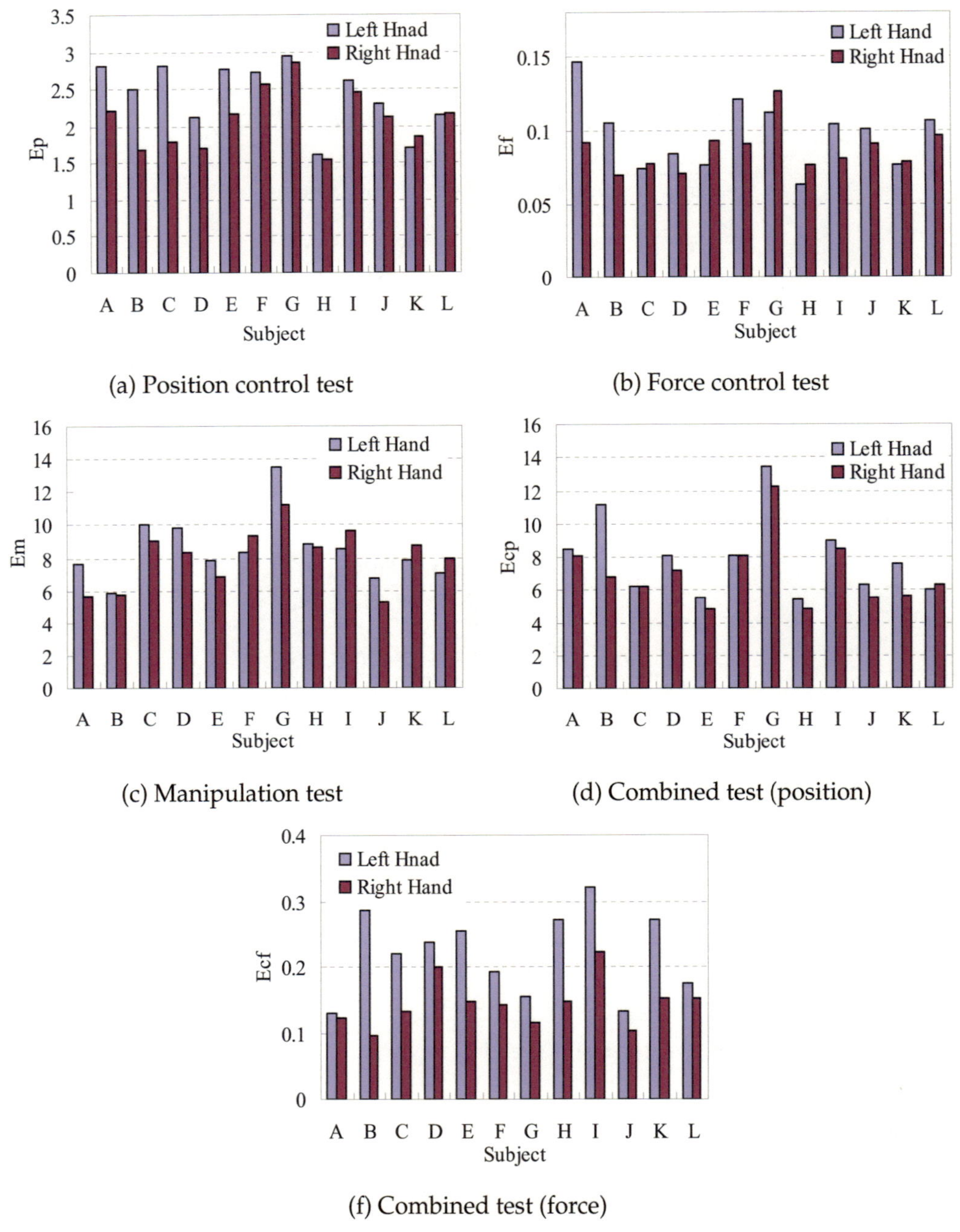

Fig. 13. Results of the virtual space tests

5.3 Hitting counter test

The subject is asked to hit counters alternately, repeating 100 times for each hand. The counter is fixed to the table by the double-stick tape. The experimental setup of this test and the experimental result are shown in Fig.14-(c), Table 7, and Fig. 15-(c).

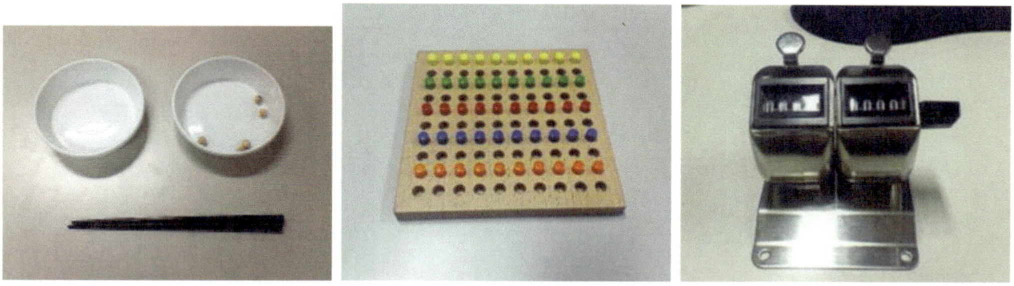

(a) Picking up beans (b) Moving pegs (c) Hitting counter

Fig. 14. Experimental setups of real space test

Subject	Picking up beans [s]		Moving pegs [s]		Hitting counter [s]	
	L.H.	R.H.	L.H.	R.H.	L.H.	R.H.
A	32.15	12.08	16.62	15.19	26.81	20.75
B	85.40	14.96	18.93	13.00	25.20	19.41
C	100.79	17.97	16.74	16.30	23.02	20.50
D	37.81	14.65	16.17	13.33	21.49	14.97
E	23.92	22.48	16.71	15.63	32.28	22.72
F	71.42	27.54	15.82	13.27	27.28	15.96
G	28.06	16.59	17.10	14.68	24.65	21.85
H	39.12	17.85	20.96	21.72	21.29	20.04
I	51.49	26.14	29.81	19.16	28.86	23.77
J	24.96	12.28	17.28	15.37	29.55	21.78
K	59.14	48.25	22.36	21.96	19.08	18.18
L	17.21	26.68	16.45	22.24	21.69	22.33

Table 7. Experimental results of real space tests (L.H.: Left Hand, R.H.:Right Hand)

6. Definition and evaluation of handedness and dexterity

We have proposed a quantitative definition of the handedness and dexterity based on the factor analysis in (Yoshikawa et al.,2007). Based on this method, we adapt and apply it for the new test tasks.

To analyze the obtained data by the factor analysis, we first standardize the measured performances for each test as follows. The standardized value z of datum E is given by

$$z_{iht} = \frac{E_{iht} - \overline{E}_t}{v_t}, \quad t = p, f, m, cp, cf \tag{16}$$

where $\overline{E}_t$ and v_t are, respectively, the average and the standard variation of the data $\{E_{iht}\}$ of each test t.

Let the standardized performance data for hand h of subject i for the test t be z_{iht}. Then from the basic formula of the factor analysis we adopt the one-factor model given by

$$z_{iht} = a_t d_{ih} + e_{iht} \tag{17}$$

where d_{ih} is the factor score, a_t are the factor loading coefficients for the 4 tests, and e_{iht} are the independent errors.

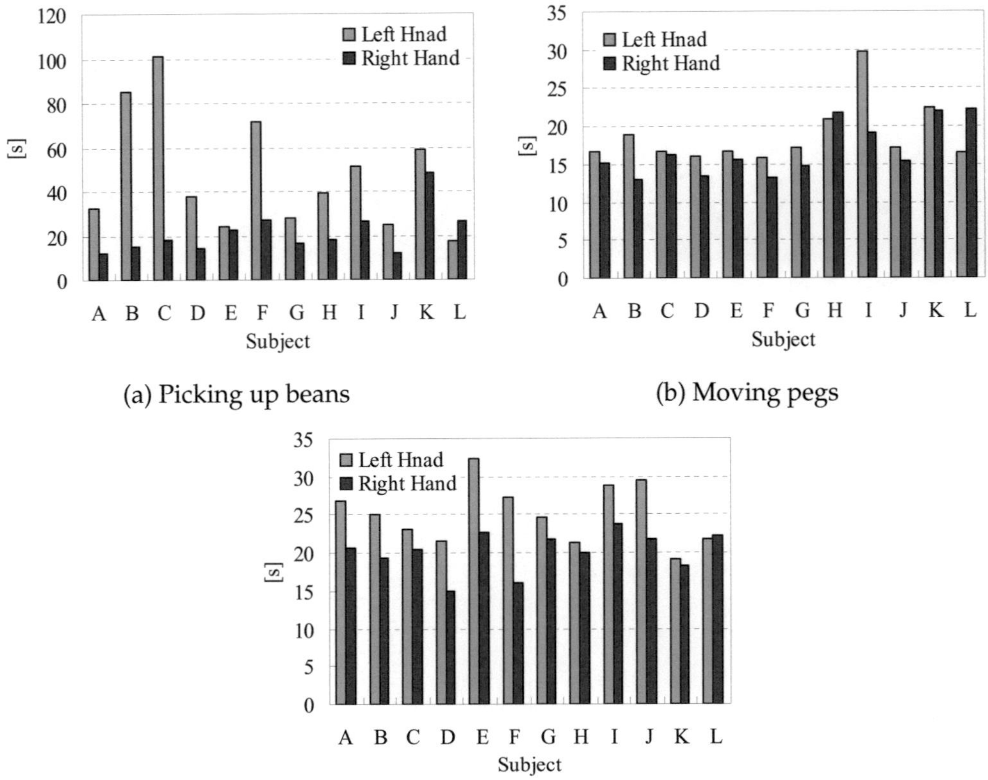

(a) Picking up beans

(b) Moving pegs

(c) Hitting counter

Fig. 15. Experimental results in real space test

In order to calculate the factor score, we first obtain the values of factor loadings. Let the factor loading matrix $\boldsymbol{A}$ be

$$\boldsymbol{A} = [a_p \ a_f \ a_m \ a_{cp} \ a_{cf}]^T \tag{18}$$

then the relation between $\boldsymbol{A}$ and the correlation matrix $\boldsymbol{R}$ is given by

$$\boldsymbol{R} = \boldsymbol{A}\boldsymbol{A}^T + \boldsymbol{R}_e \tag{19}$$

where $\boldsymbol{R}_e$ is the diagonal covariance matrix of the independent errors. The correlation matrix $\boldsymbol{R}$ is also calculated from the performance data Table 5, 6,

$$\boldsymbol{R} = \begin{bmatrix} 1 & 0.670 & 0.360 & 0.590 & 0.078 \\ 0.670 & 1 & 0.100 & 0.565 & -0.212 \\ 0.360 & 0.100 & 1 & 0.485 & 0.114 \\ 0.590 & 0.565 & 0.485 & 1 & 0.097 \\ 0.078 & -0.212 & 0.114 & 0.097 & 1 \end{bmatrix} \tag{20}$$

Using the Principal Factor Method, factor loading matrix $\boldsymbol{A}$ satisfying (19) is given by

$$\boldsymbol{A} = [-0.839 \ -0.690 \ -0.418 \ -0.804 \ -0.022]^T \tag{21}$$

Now we can obtain the factor score d_{ih} based on the relation

$$d_{ih} = [z_{ihp} \ z_{ihf} \ z_{ihm} \ z_{ihcp} \ z_{ihcf}]\boldsymbol{R}^{-1}\boldsymbol{A} \tag{22}$$

Note that, although matrix $-\boldsymbol{A}$ can also be a solution of (19), the above solution with negative components was intentionally chosen. This way, we can obtain the factor score such that the larger the factor score is, the more dexterous the subject is.
Based on the above considerations, we define the dexterity d_i and handedness h_i of a subject using the factor score of his/her right hand d_{ir} and left hand d_{il} :

$$d_i = \frac{d_{ir} + d_{il}}{2} \tag{23}$$

$$h_i = \frac{d_{ir} - d_{il}}{2} \tag{24}$$

7. Discussion

The factor scores of the right and left hands of each subject are given in Table 8 and in Fig.16.

Subject	Factor score		Handedness	Dexterity	LQ
	d_{il}	d_{ir}	h_i	d_i	
A	-1.104	-0.104	0.500	-0.604	100
B	-1.024	0.862	0.943	-0.081	100
C	-0.308	0.829	0.568	0.261	100
D	0.093	0.815	0.361	0.454	100
E	-0.095	0.640	0.367	0.273	100
F	-0.769	-0.537	0.116	-0.653	100
G	-2.162	-1.898	0.132	-2.030	100
H	1.373	1.433	0.030	1.403	100
I	-0.670	-0.394	0.138	-0.532	100
J	0.121	0.510	0.195	0.316	80
K	0.786	0.910	0.062	0.848	40
L	0.393	0.300	-0.047	0.347	-100

Table 8. Evaluation results of dexterity and handedness

The dexterity is shown in Fig.17. The handedness and the LQ value of each subject are shown in Fig.18. From the LQ value, subject L was only regarded left-handedness, and our method conducted the same result. Though, the LQ values of subject A–L were in the same value 100, and the results of the handedness h_i were different widely. It can be said that our method can indicate the handedness in detail than the LQ method. The values of the handedness h_i of Subject F, G and H make a little difference. However, the values of the dexterity d_i are much different because of the difference of the factor scores d_{il}, d_{ir}. Thus, it requires attention when they have similar handedness value.
Fig.19 shows the result of the factor score, handedness and dexterity, which are analyzed by using the three test method in the previous paper: position, force, and manipulation test, excepting the combined test results (this will be call Three-Test Method hereafter). Subject K was determined as left-handedness based on the Three-Test Method. By contrast, from the LQ value, he uses right hand mainly in daily life, so he can be regarded as right-handedness in this time. From an interview after the experiment, he talked that he had been used the left

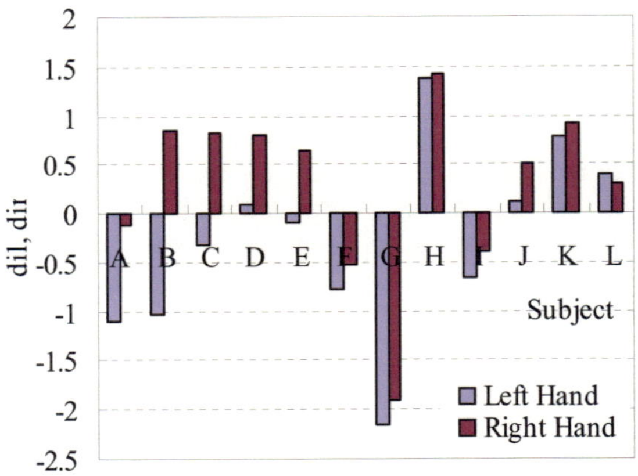

Fig. 16. Factor scores

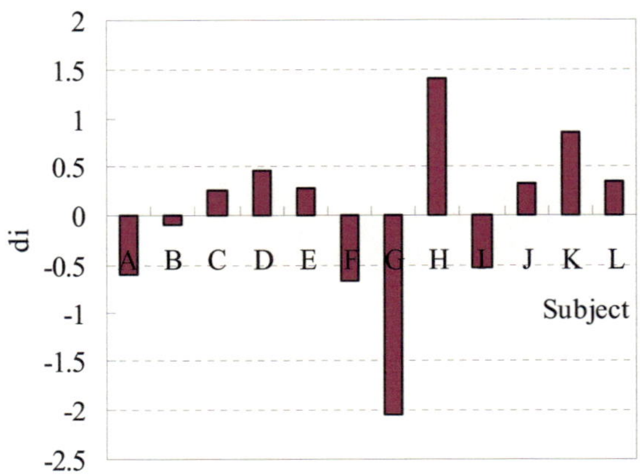

Fig. 17. Dexterity

hand mainly in childhood. The new method indicates weak right-handedness to subject K. It may be that the new method can analyze the handedness more precisely.

8. Conclusion

In this paper, a new handedness and dexterity evaluation system was presented. In this system, for accuracy evaluation of handedness and dexterity, 4 test tasks in virtual space are constructed: position control, force control, manipulation and position-force combined control. By using the evaluation method based on the factor analysis which was applied from the previous work (Yoshikawa et al.,2007), experiments to evaluate the handedness and dexterity were conducted to 12 subjects. As a result, the judgment of handedness from our method was consistent with the LQ method, and the new method may analyze the handedness more precisely. Additionally, for the future investigation, 3 tests in real space were conducted and shown the experimental results.

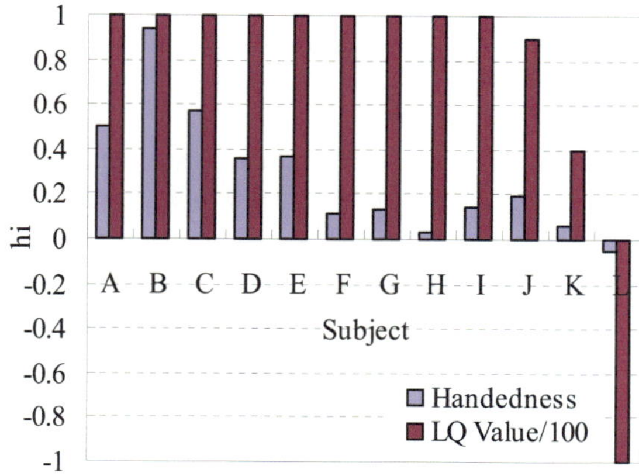

Fig. 18. Handedness

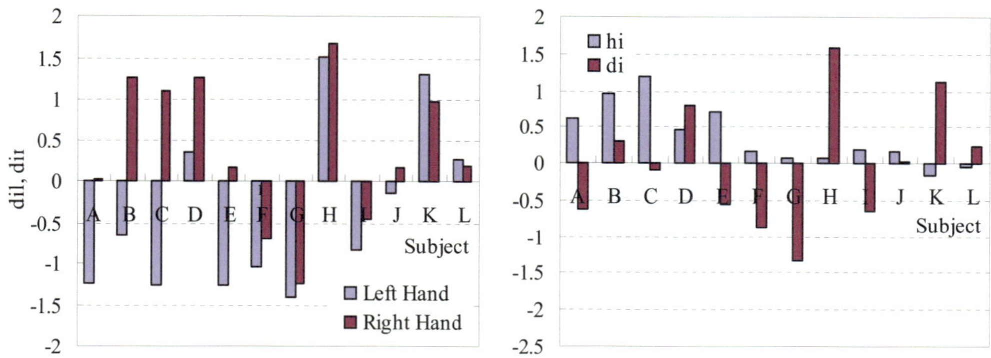

(a) Factor scores (b) Handedness and Dexterity

Fig. 19. Evaluation by Three-Test Method

For future works, much more subjects should be investigated by our evaluation system, especially, left-handedness and ambidexterity persons. The investigation between virtual and real space is also needed.

9. References

[Bagesteiro et al.,2002] Bagesteiro, L.B. and Sainburg, R.L., Handedness: Dominant Arm Advantages in Control of Limb Dynamics, *Journal of Neurophysiology*, Vol. 88, No. 5, p. 2408–2421, (2002)

[Burdea,G.C.,1996] Burdea, G.C.,A Wiley-Interscience Publication, John Wiley & Sons, Inc., Force and Touch Feedback for Virtual Reality, (1996)

[Fujiwara et al.,2003] Fujiwara, N. and Kushida, N. and Murakami, T. and Fujimoto, S.,Upper Limb Coordination Differs Among Ages and Between Dominant and Non-dominant Hands Utilizing Digital Trace Test, *Journal of health sciences, Hiroshima University*,Vol. 2,No. 2, p. 22–28, (2003)

[Matsuda et al.,2003] Matsuda, I. and Yamaguchi, M. and Yoshida, K.,Quantitative Discrimination of Handedness – Preliminary Study Using Discriminant Analysis Approach –, *Sagyouryouhou (Journal published by Japanese Association of Occupational Therapists*,Vol. 5, p. 40–41 (in Japanese), (2003)

[Oldfield,R.C.1971] Oldfield, R.C., The Assessment and Analysis of Handedness: The Edinburgh Inventory, *Neuropsychologia*,Vol. 9, No. 1,p. 97–113, (1971)

[Wu et al.,1996] Wu, J. and Morimoto, K. and Kurokawa, T., A Comparison between Effect of Handedness and Non-handedness on Touch Screen Operation, *Transactions of Human Interface Society*, Vol. 11, No. 4, p. 441–446 (in Japanese), (1996)

[Yoshikawa et al.,1995] Yoshikawa, T. and Yokokohji, Y. and Matsumoto, T. and Zheng, X-Z., Display of Feel for the Manipulation of Dynamic Virtual Objects, *Journal of Dynamic Systems, Measurement, and Control*, Vol. 117, No. 4, p. 554–558, (1995)

[Yoshikawa et al.,2000] Yoshikawa, T. and Yoshimoto, K., Haptic Simulation of Assembly Operation in Virtual Environment, *Proceedings of the ASME, Dynamic Systems and Control Division–2000*, p. 1191–1198, (2000)

[Smith,R.,2000] Smith, R., Open Dynamics Engine, `http://www.ode.org/`, (2000)

[SensAble Technologies,Inc.] SensAble Technologies, Inc., `http://www.sensable.com/`, (1993)

[Yoshikawa et al.,2007] Yoshikawa, T. and Koeda, M. and Sugihashi, M.A Quantitative Evaluation Method of Handedness Using Haptic Virtual Reality Technology, *Proceedings of the 16th IEEE International Symposium on Robot & Human Interactive Communication*, p. 298–303, (2007)

11

An Exploratory Study on the Relationship between Orientation Map Reading and Way-finding in Unfamiliar Environments

Chieh-Hsin Tang[1], Chin-Wei Chang[2], Ying-Ji Chuang[2] and Ching-Yuan Lin[2]
[1]*Tungnan University,*
[2]*National Taiwan University of Science and Technology,*
Taiwan

1. Introduction

There are many ways to familiarize oneself with an unfamiliar environment, but most people use orientation maps to help them. In more complicated buildings, orientation maps may be posted everywhere, since they serve as important references for spatial cognition and way-finding for users. A study on way-finding by Best (1970) identified a positive relationship between the number of choice points (hallway intersections) within a building and way-finding difficulty. Weisman (1981) defined a number of environmental variables that people use to help orient themselves during way-finding, and categorized these variables into four classes: (1) *signs*, which provide directional information within a setting; (2) *perceptual access*, which provides a view to landmarks within or exterior to a building; (3) *architectural differentiation*, which is the ease with which different regions or landmarks within a building can be recognized; and (4) *plan configuration*, which is the configuration of a building's floor plan. Beaumont *et al.* (1984) interviewed building occupants and found that the layout of floor plans is equal in importance to other architectural features, such as the availability of signs, with respect to reported ease of way-finding. O'Neill (1991a) found that incremental increases in floor plan complexity reduce both the accuracy of one's cognitive map and one's way-finding performance. O'Neill (1991b) also found that floor plan complexity reduces way-finding performance, despite the presence of directional signage. Nichols *et al.* (1992) reported that the primary cause of way-finding difficulties in transportation centers is the complexity of possible paths. The accuracy of the information in one's cognitive map can influence one's way-finding performance (O'Neill, 1991a, 1991b). The cognitive map can store *route* and *survey* representations (Tolman, 1948), where *route representations* contain knowledge about individual places and the way in which they are connected through experience; in other words, the 'travel-ability' that exists between places (Kuipers, 1983). Montello (1991) proposed that the asymmetric structural design of streets is likely to mislead users: subjects tend to make more mistakes pointing out the position of an object and direction (east, west, south, and north) when on asymmetric streets than on intersecting ones. Passini (1999) argued that the acquisition of knowledge about places plays an important role in way-finding and determines one's chance of finding one's way successfully. If pedestrians acquire incorrect information about a place during way-finding, the chances are that they will get lost.

As for how environmental design contributes to effective way-finding, Lynch (1960) pinpointed many concepts from which subsequent researchers can learn. According to Lynch (1960), an environment should have, among other things, the following elements - paths, edges, districts, nodes, and landmarks - because they offer environmental clues during way-finding. Darken (1995) also believed that environments without proper structures are not preferred, because men normally feel terribly uncomfortable in an environment in which there are no clues for reference; they rely heavily on any environmental structures or objects to determine what direction they are pointing and which direction to take.

One's cognitive map reflects one's mental image of a place. A distinction must be made between two concepts - *cognitive map* and *cognitive mapping*. The difference between them is that *cognitive mapping* is a dynamic process, during which information about individual's spatial environments are processed, whereas a *cognitive map* is a network concept that represents the relative locations between different objects (Johns, 2003). Garling *et al.* (1984) used a vivid example to illustrate this difference: "a cognitive map is like an end product, whereas cognitive mapping is similar to the process of acquisition." A cognitive map cannot reproduce the original environment completely: on the contrary, it is a product constructed by each human's cognitive system (Tversky, 2000). According to Tversky & Lee (1998), a cognitive map demonstrates spatial information complementarily, in both illustrative and descriptive fashions. Elvins (1997) identified three important facets of a cognitive map – it must be identifiable; it must be structural; and it must be meaningful; in other words, the objects in an environment must be identifiable and comprehensible to be preserved within a person's cognitive map. Other empirical studies also have shown that individuals will attempt to seek out whatever reference points they can identify, when trying to find their way, so as to reorganize information about an unfamiliar environment. The subsequent storage of these points in the cognitive map indicates that landmarks are visual, cognitive, and structural, as proposed by Sorrows and Hirtle (1999). Furthermore, Golledge & Stimson (1997) reported that cognitive mapping is a process that builds understanding about different environments, and interprets and deals with a series of complex information. This so-called 'information' is not only spatial; it also refers to the value and meaning of a place's existence. The cognitive map, on the other hand, is concerned with the retrieval and use of an object from spatial knowledge as an anchor, after the acquisition of spatial knowledge, and is the linking of all the anchors in an environment to establish an interdependent network, which is the so-called cognitive map. It can be referred to as a map previously saved in the human brain, so that one has a clearer picture of the complete layout of a place (Golledge, 1999). As a result, an accurate and complete cognitive map is a key determinant of successful way-finding performance. Kitchin (1994) gave direct support to the idea that it is imperative to formulate a cognitive map. He believed that the main function of a cognitive map is to tackle spatial problems, which primarily are way-finding and navigating processes.

From the viewpoint of Evans (1980), people are more likely to feel well oriented in buildings consisting of regular structures (such as a crisscross or a right angle) than in those with irregular structures and/or angles. The concept of the cognitive map can be dated back to 1913, when Trowbridge conducted a study and concluded that behavioral responses to environments confirm the existence of image schemas in human cognitive systems. In the study of Liben (1981), in terms of spatial ability and spatial representation, a cognitive map contains four types of composition difference which are *spatial product*, *spatial thought*, *spatial storage*, and *memory storage*. Montello (1999) defined *spatial ability* as the ability to use maps, explore new environments, and describe a surrounding, using words, in a very large space in the real world. Collins and Quillian (1969) proposed that the knowledge system of human beings is a hierarchical network. The issue of how human internal cognitive systems interact with the external environment during way-finding, thereby influencing way-finding performance, should be addressed (Garling *et al.*, 1984). The information about the environments in which human beings exist can be subdivided into three categories: *information about location*; *information about properties*; and *information about time*. The three categories of information determine the behaviors and activities of men moving between locations (Krieg-Bruckner *et al.*, 1998). Siegel and White (1975) outlined three learning steps that occur while one acquires spatial knowledge: *landmark recognition*; *path/route development*; and the *coordination of clusters*. For Thorndyke and Hayes-Roth (1982), spatial knowledge comes from paths and from a bird's eye view. Passni (1939) stressed that the understanding of spatial orientation plays a fairly important role as people develop a concept of space, and it is the generic term for direction and location. Judgment on orientation is closely interrelated with that for direction, because both represent the ability to continuously move forward. One can identify his own position based on his location relative to things around him.

Zeitzer (1994) stated that virtual reality is an advanced user interface which generates real-time simulations and interactions through many sensory modalities. Wilson (1999) pointed out that virtual reality enables users to observe simulated worlds from any perspective, and to further interact with any objects in those worlds. Weyrich (1999) noted that virtual reality, which is generated by computer models with the integration and application of computers and peripherals, creates three dimensional (3D) scenes through which users can navigate. When in virtual reality, users activate their perceptual and cognitive systems, as they do in the real world, to interact with simulated objects, and the experience is very close to those of the real world (Stanney, 2003). Considerable research on spatial cognition, like studies on human beings' way-finding performance, has employed virtual reality as a medium through which to understand navigational behaviors (Darken & Silbert, 1996). Virtual reality is an appropriate research medium for studying spatial cognition, because the investigators have total control over operating the variables; and they are able to simulate and represent any environments, real or hypothetical (Jansen-Osmann, 2002). Since virtual reality is a computer-simulated environment, computers can conduct real-time calculations, based on user behaviors, and respond with suitable simulated scenes that users are supposed to see (Grammenos *et al.*, 2002). Among the benefits brought about by virtual reality is that researchers can add different environmental variables, on their own terms, to control the variable that might affect way-finding performance, something which is less likely to be orchestrated in the real world (Booth, Fisher, Page, Ware, and Widen, 2000). The evidence provided by Witmer, Bailey, Knerre and Parsons (1996) indicate that the route knowledge gained by participants in highly-simulated worlds is transferred to and applied in real life successfully.

In addition, Tang *et al.* (2008) once conducted an experiment on reading cognition and way-finding, using building evacuation plan diagrams without virtual reality, and the result revealed that different backgrounds do affect diagram-reading and way-finding. As a result, this study aims to investigate the relationship between the orientation of maps and the reading cognition of users. Our specific objectives are as follows:

1. To probe the time required to read and comprehend orientation maps, in order to examine the level of descriptiveness of existing maps;
2. To analyze factors that lead to differences in map cognition, so as to reduce the gap in reading cognition; and
3. To examine the correlation between map-reading and way-finding, in order to measure the efficacy of maps in way-finding.

2. Methods

2.1 Simulated space

The simulated buildings used in this experiment represented two hospitals, and the simulated areas included the ground and first floors. On each floor were four emergency staircases that led to other floors. The building at the front was 15 m tall and 36 m wide; the other building, at the back, was 20 m tall and 56 m wide, with a ceiling height of 3.2 m. The area of one floor was roughly 1660 m^2. The front building housed the reception and registration desks; the rear building housed the emergency room and several consultation rooms. In addition to the four emergency escapes, an additional seven public elevators and two elevators for sickbeds were arranged in a crisscross pattern. The only corridor, which was 2.5 m wide, connected the front and rear buildings.

2.2 Experimental facilities

The computer employed to conduct the experiments was an ASUS V6 laptop. A DLP projector, serving as the user interface for the experiment, was connected to the laptop. The simulated scenes were presented on an 80" color screen with a screen resolution of 1024×768. The ambient illuminance for the experimental environment was measured by SEKONIC L-508. The design of the simulation workstation is shown in Figure 1. The monitor was placed above the desk, which was 75 cm tall, and the centre of the screen was 40 cm above the desk, with a screen inclination of 90 degrees. The above-mentioned figures were fixed and not subject to change. Prior to the experiments, subjects could adjust the height of their chair accordingly; the visual range was set at 250 cm.

2.3 Design of the experiment

Prior to their participation, subjects were informed that they were to be in a simulated way-finding experiment. The path of the simulated journey was set to start in the lobby on the ground floor (starting point), and then proceeded through a corridor and up staircases, to the final destination (the blood draw room on the first floor). The maps provided are shown in Figure 2. Since floor plans are posted at elevator lobbies at the scene, the computer also simulated the floor plans for this experiment (see Figures 3~4). Figures 5~10 demonstrate the simulated nodes. During the experiment, subjects moved a mouse to simulate the way they would travel through the buildings. By left clicking and dragging the mouse button, subjects moved ahead (at a speed of 1 m/sec); conversely, right clicking and dragging the mouse caused them to step backwards. Subjects could turn left or right simply by moving the mouse in the desired direction.

2.4 Participants

A total of 45 subjects completed the study. They were comprised of both students and members of the general public who agreed to participate in the experiment. To be eligible, an individual had to have a basic working knowledge of computers. Twenty-three of the 45 subjects were male (51.1%) and 22 were female (48.9%); 21 (46.7%) of all participants were architecture- or design-related professionals. The vast majority of subjects (91.1%) were between the ages of 20 and 39 years. No subject was color blind or had any eye disease, with all corrected eyesight between 20/25 and 24/20. All were tested once only. No subject was permitted to observe other subjects being tested.

Description: the term 'front building' refers to the map posted in the elevator lobby in the front building; and 'rear building' refers to the map posted in the elevator lobby in the building behind it. Each map shows the floor plan of the building in which it is located. Since maps were posted in different locations, the floor plan for the ground floor of the rear building is rotated 90 degrees.

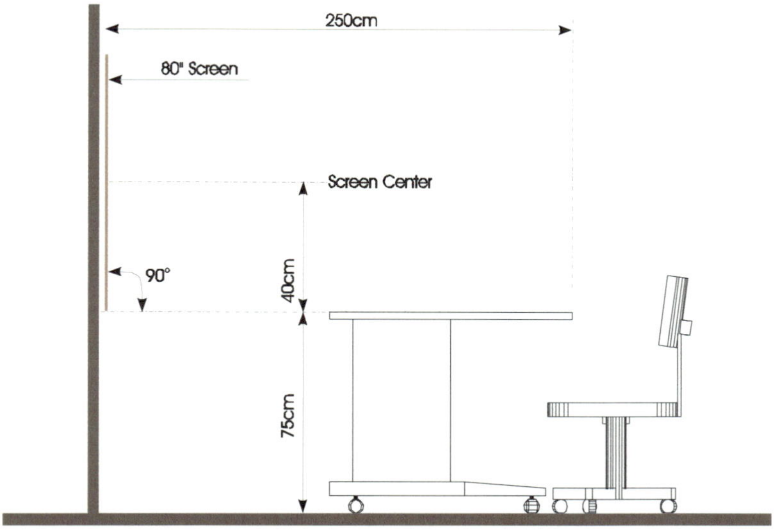

Fig. 1. Simulation workstation

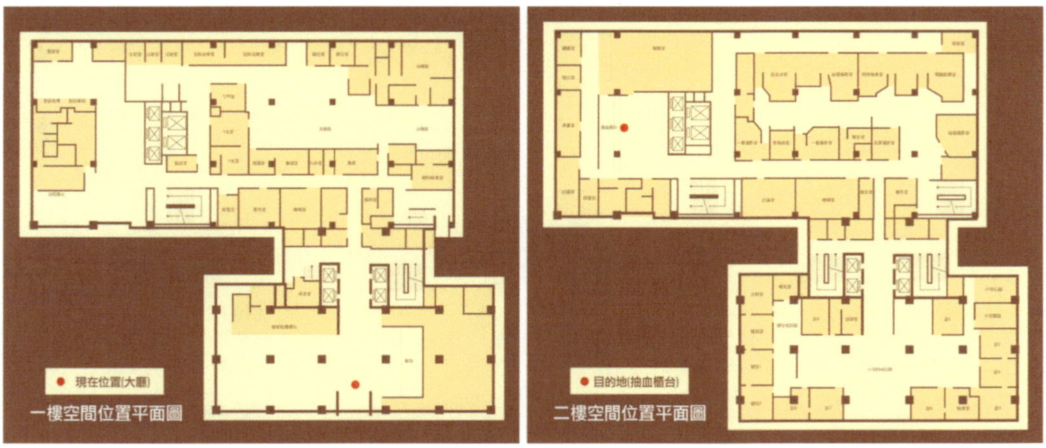

(a) 1 Floor (b) 2 Floor

Fig. 2. Map adopted in experiments

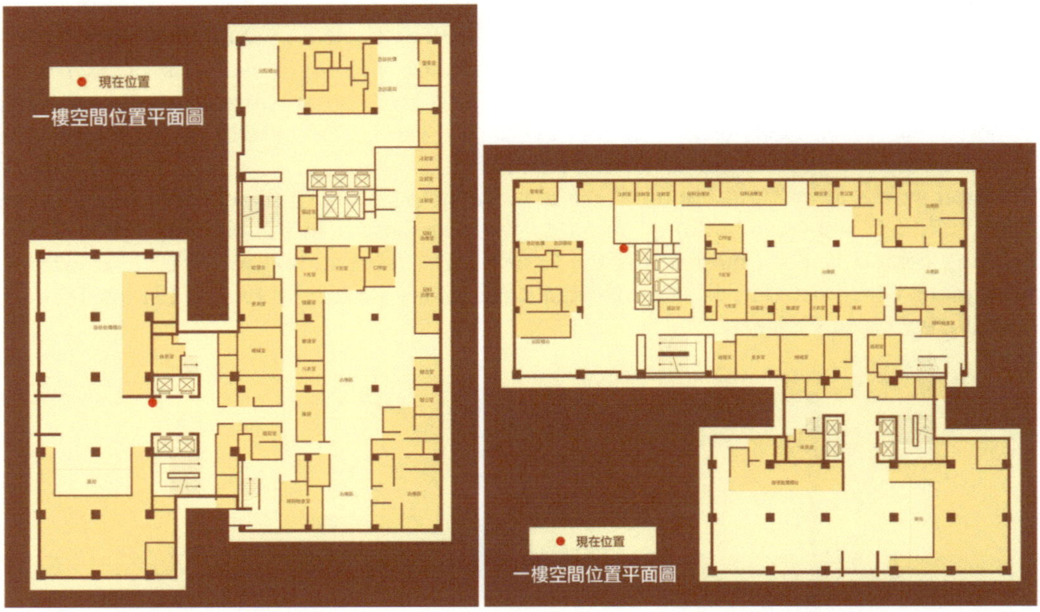

(a) Front Building (b) Rear Building

Fig. 3. Map posted in the elevator lobby on the ground floor

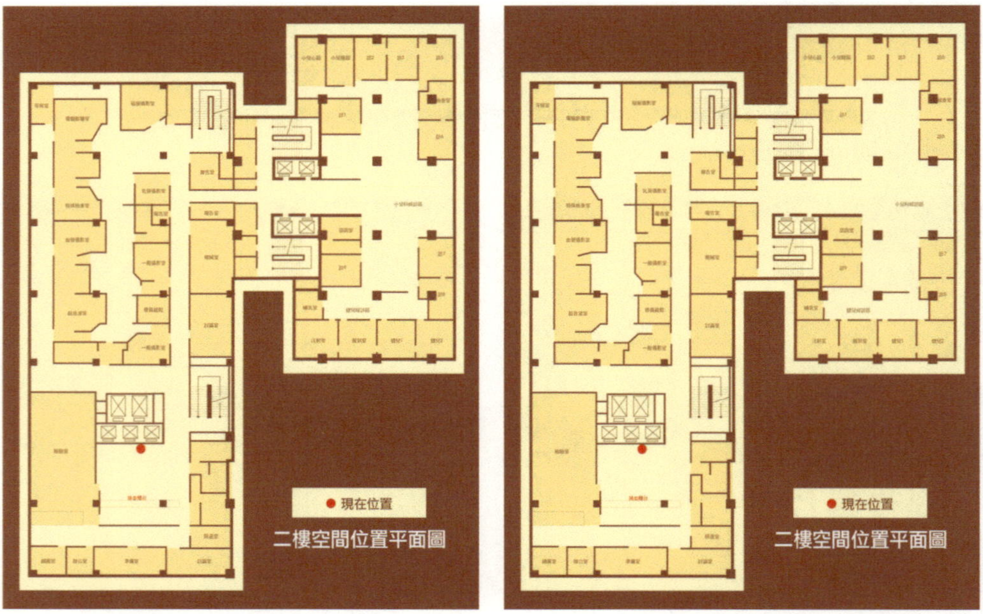

(a) Front Building (b) Rear Building

Fig. 4. Map posted in the first floor elevator lobby

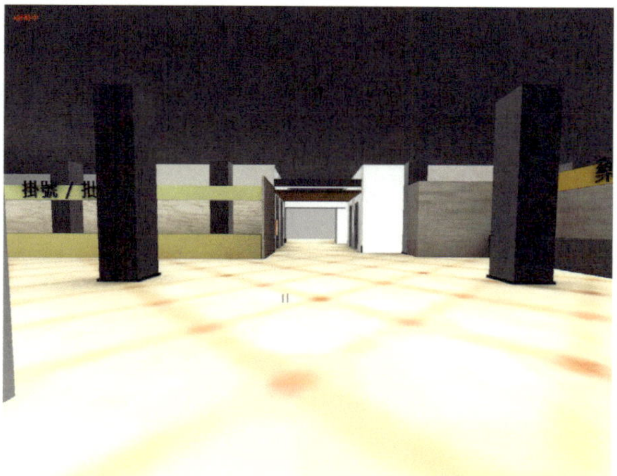

Fig. 5. Simulated node (starting point)

Fig. 6. Simulated node (ground floor elevators)

Fig. 7. Simulated node (#2 staircase on the ground floor)

Fig. 8. Simulated node (1st floor elevators)

Fig. 9. Simulated node (1st floor corridor)

Fig. 10. Simulated node (destination)

2.5 Limitations

The core experiment conducted in this study took place in a virtual-simulated hospital, in which we sought to measure the relationship between orientation maps and reading cognition. The maps used in the experiment were the same as those in the hospital. As we focused on the correlation between orientation maps and reading cognition, several limitations arose in this study.

1. Prior to this study, a pilot study simulated by computer was carried out, based upon which we concluded that this work was of an exploratory nature. Also, since participants needed to be familiar with computers, the vast majority of subjects were between 20 and 39 years old. Most people outside of this age range were excluded.
2. In order to avoid any possible influence of the existence of other objects on spatial perception, there were no other objects in the simulated areas.
3. Since the simulation was done with a computer, it was hypothesized that the level of computer literacy would not affect the results of the experiment, and obtained data outliers were excluded from analysis.
4. It is difficult to control the actual psychological reaction of people in a hospital; consequently, in the VR experiment, the simulation was predetermined to take place under normal conditions, instead of under physical duress.
5. Map-reading time and way-finding time were measured and their means calculated separately. Measurement of map-reading time started off as soon as floor plans appeared, indicated by a red dot to signify the subject's current position; and stopped as soon as subjects reported understanding the maps. The measurement of way-finding time did not start until after subjects understood the maps, determined their current position, entered the virtual reality world, and started to move their mouse; that first mouse movement initiated measurement, which ceased as soon as the subjects arrived at their final intended destination.

3. Reading of orientation maps and analysis

3.1 Reading of orientation maps

When showing the orientation maps, two maps depicting the starting point (ground floor) and the destination (first floor) were displayed simultaneously on the same screen. Time measurement began as soon as the maps appeared on the screen and stopped when subjects realized where the starting point and destination were and completed their route planning. The mean time required to read the map was 49 seconds (Table 1, Fig. 11~13), but this was not the median time, as 60% of the subjects finished reading the maps in less than 49 seconds, 42% within 20 to 39 seconds.

Background	Map-reading time (s)	SD	Maximum time (s)	Minimum time (s)	Map-rereading time (s)
Entire group	49	26	150	16	14
Male	41	18	79	16	6
Female	57	32	150	18	8
Professional	32	13	63	16	6
Non-professional	63	27	150	29	8

Table 1. Map-reading time

The shortest distance between the starting and ending point, with a staircase in between, was 50 m, in accordance with the actual scale of the physical building. Under this circumstance, the time required for reading cognition was considerably less for men than for women (m:f = 1:1.39), and the map-reading time for women was 1.4 times that of men. The standard deviation for reading time was considerably narrower among men than among women, also indicating less variability in males. Comparing architecture-related professionals versus those without such a background, professionals exhibited superior reading map performance, as well as less variability; professionals used half the time required by non-professionals for map-reading (professionals:non-professionals = 1:1.97), indicating that architecture-related education enhanced their map reading skills. This suggests that there were certain technical symbols in the maps that delayed comprehension among those not already familiar with the field. If and how different subject backgrounds influenced reading cognition will be analyzed and reported later.

Subjects were informed prior to the experiment that they could reread floor plans (posted at certain locations, based on locations in the actual buildings) at the elevator lobbies if they became lost. Fourteen of 45 subjects (31%) chose to reread the floor plans during way-finding. One reread the maps twice, while others reread them once. Six of 23 males (26%) and 8 of 22 females (36%) reread the maps; 6 of 21 professionals (29%) and 8 of 24 non-professionals (33%) chose to reread the maps. In general, then, irrespective of gender or background, approximately 30% of the subjects decided to reread floor plans when they were lost during way-finding.

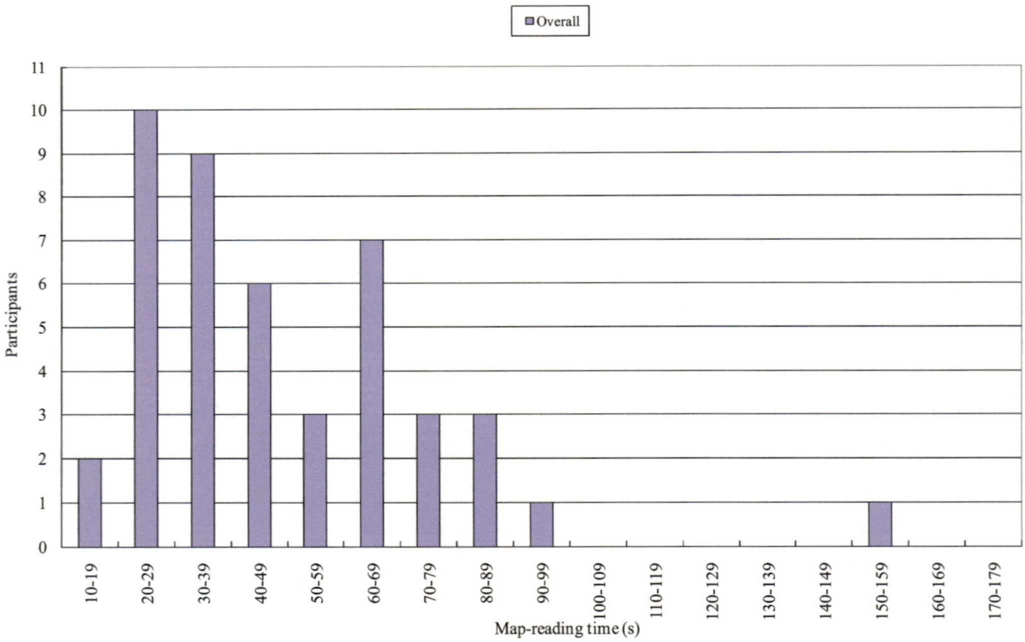

Fig. 11. Distribution of map-reading time of all subjects

In addition to the earlier report on differences in map-reading by gender and professional background, it is clear from Figures 12 and 13 that most men spent 20 to 49 seconds reading maps, whereas there was a greater range of time requirements for map-reading among women. Architecture professionals generally spent 20-39 seconds map-reading, while there was a much greater range among non-professionals and the average in the latter group was more than 20 seconds longer.

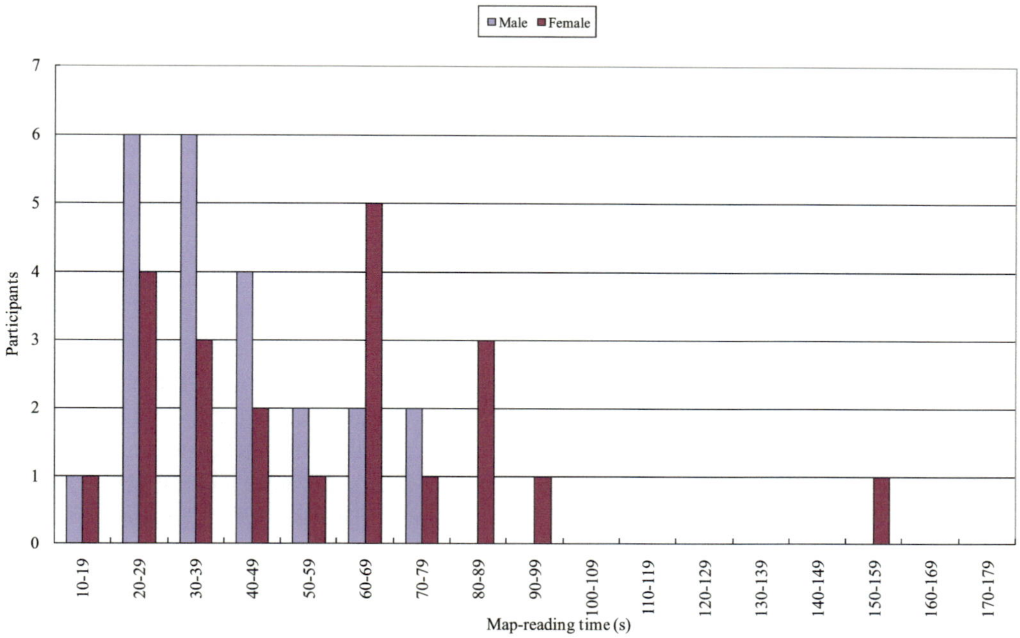

Fig. 12. Distribution of map-reading time of males and females

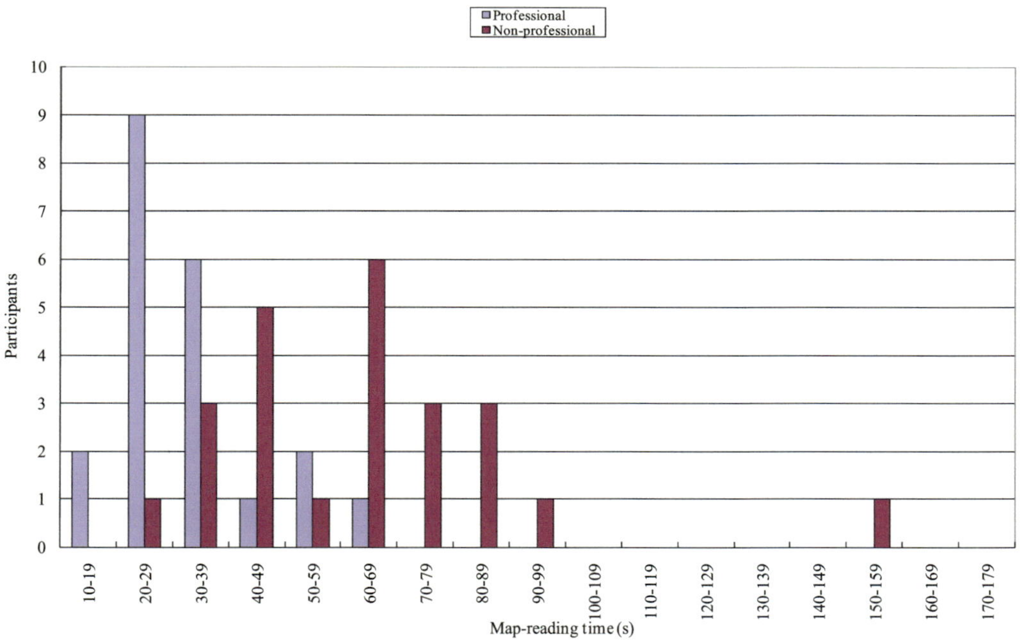

Fig. 13. Distribution of map-reading time of professionals and non-professionals

3.2 Factors leading to differences in reading cognition

Preliminary analysis of the experimental data suggest that different backgrounds did influence outcomes; but whether or not these outcomes are statistically different between groups is yet to be verified. As a result, an attempt was made to determine which factors might contribute to significant differences in reading cognition in the public. The two demographic variables - gender and professional status - were processed and analyzed by means of t-tests for independent samples.

In the case of reading cognition, significant differences were apparent both for gender (p=0.030) and professional status (p=0.014), indicating that there were differences in reading cognition between men and women; and between those with versus those without architecture-related professional backgrounds. In other words, men and women, and professionals and non-professionals require different amounts of time to understand maps. Assessing the issue of professional status, it already has been shown that there are technical signs in maps that the public cannot comprehend easily; consequently, removing such symbols, at least to an appropriate extent, might be advantageous. Furthermore, 52% of male subjects had been in architecture-related professions, and 48% not; so it is obvious that having a professional background did not contribute to the difference between men and women, in terms of reading cognition. What truly makes a difference is the better reading cognition ability that is inherent in men. We concluded, therefore, that professionals and males have better map reading comprehension skills than non-professionals and females.

4. Simulation and analysis of way-finding

4.1 Time required for way-finding

In this instance, way-finding time was the time needed for the subject to proceed from the starting point on the ground floor to the end point on the first floor. The average time required across all subjects was 90 seconds, with a maximum of 174 seconds (a female non-professional) and a minimum of 53 seconds (a male professional). The maximum was almost three times the minimum (see Table 2). Moreover, the way-finding time for men was less than for women (m:f = 1:1.28) and the standard deviation for men was slightly less, as well. The times required by professionals and non-professionals, on the other hand, were pretty close (professionals: non-professionals = 1:1.08), as were the standard deviations. In the experimental design, the walking speed per second was set at 1 m, and the shortest walking distance was 50 m, so the shortest time path could not possibly be less than 50 seconds. Generally speaking, the way-finding time needed was between 50 and 89 seconds (62% of all subjects), with a steady decline in the numbers of individuals requiring times greater than 90 seconds (see Figure 14). Based upon the 50-second minimum time requirement, the following observations can be made: (1) the way-finding time required by men was 1.6 times the reference time; women 2.0 times; professionals 1.7 times; and non-professionals 1.9 times. Standard deviations were the least for men, suggesting an overall consistency in way-finding skills in males, relative to females.

The overall distributions of times for professionals and non-professionals were quite similar, mostly falling between 60 and 69 seconds. After the 70th second, the numbers dropped steadily. Preliminary analysis showed that professionals were not as efficient and effective in way-finding as expected (see Figures 15 and 16).

Background	Way-finding time (s)	SD	Maximum time (s)	Minimum time (s)
Entire group	90	33	174	53
Male	79	30	150	53
Female	101	32	174	58
Professional	86	31	155	53
Non-professional	93	34	174	58

Table 2. Way-finding time

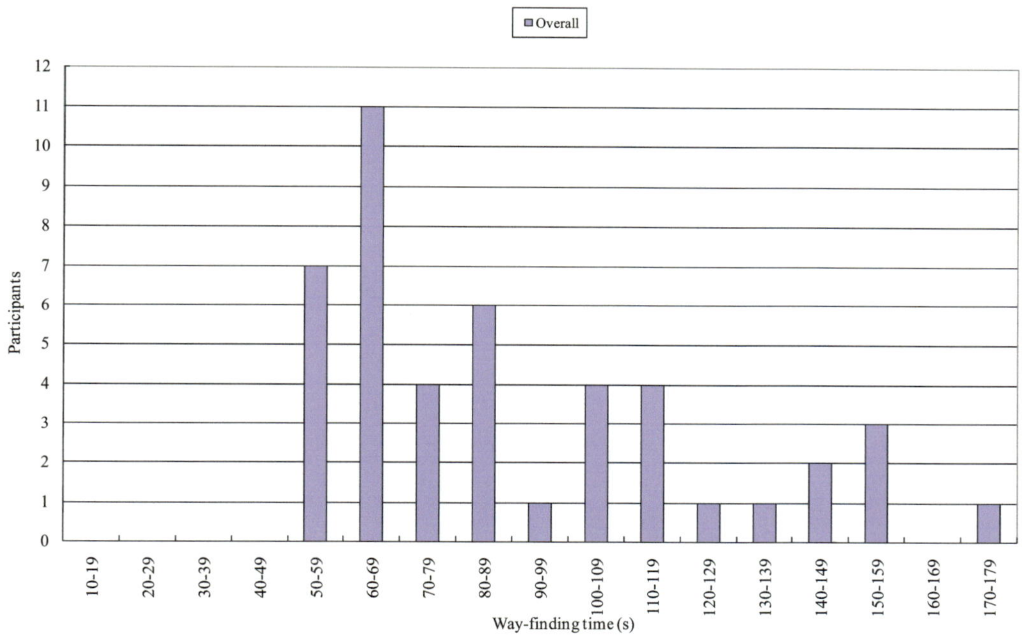

Fig. 14. Distribution of way-finding time of all subjects

4.2 Analysis of way-finding time

The results of way-finding time were analyzed using t-tests for independent samples, as was done for map-reading time. This analysis failed to identify any statistically significant differences by either gender (p=0.514) or professional status (p=0.542); in other words, gender and professional differences did not appear to influence way-finding time. What is noteworthy here is that professionals in the architecture field normally would be expected to be equipped with better spatial cognition and comprehension abilities, both of which should be conducive to way-finding, than those without such a background; but our findings argue against this. Architectural expertise did not facilitate the way-finding process, which suggests that difficulties exist in the transfer of knowledge from map-reading comprehension to the cognition of physical space. Whether or not other factors, like one's seniority or field of expertise (e.g., design versus engineering), cause these difficulties should be evaluated in future studies.

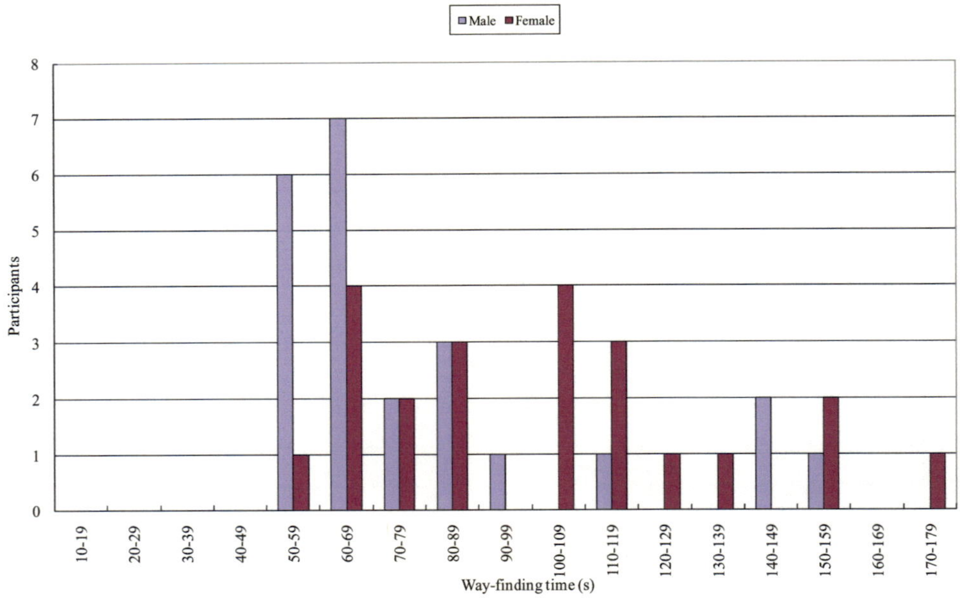

Fig. 15. Distribution of way-finding time of males and females

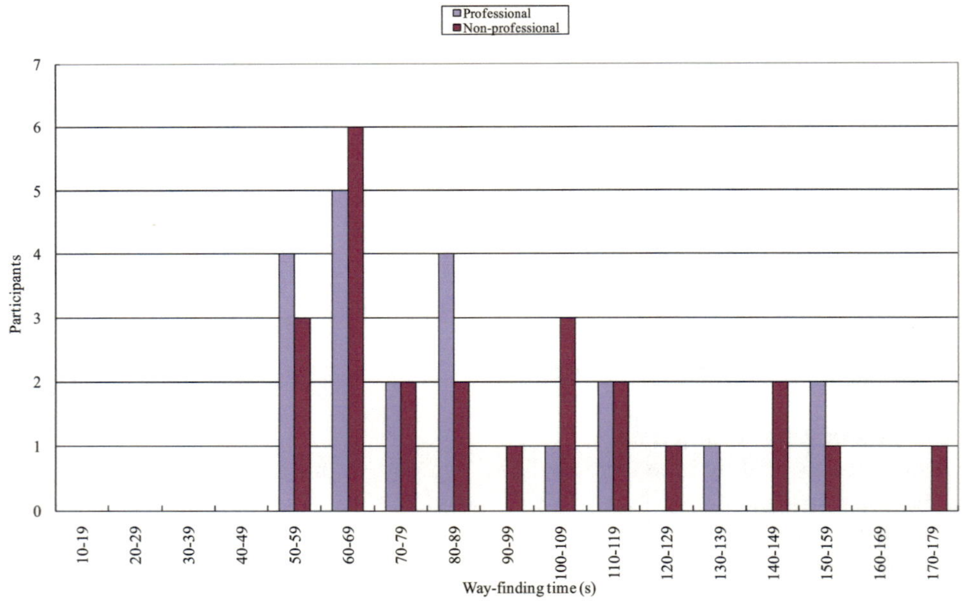

Fig. 16. Distribution of way-finding time of professionals and non-professionals

5. Correlation between cognition and behavior

5.1 Correlation between map-reading and way-finding

This section will discuss map-reading and way-finding, and issues related to the transfer of reading cognition to spatial perception, in particular. When discussing the correlation between map-reading and way-finding, demographic data should be analyzed first. In this study, there are two binomial variables - gender, composed of males and females; and professional status, composed of those with versus those without expertise in the architectural field (see Table 3 for details). The purpose of conducting t-tests was to determine whether different demographic backgrounds result in correlation between or differences in map-reading and way-finding. Results indicate that among males (p=0.010) and non-professionals (p=0.008), map-reading time and way-finding time were correlated; conversely, among females (p=0.263) and professionals (p=0.395), map-reading time and way-finding time were not correlated. A correlation coefficient (r) of 0.529, which we considered to be moderate degree of correlation, was identified for map-reading time and way-finding time among males; and much the same was observed in non-professionals. Furthermore, looking at the trend line for the entire group, it is apparent that the slope is positive, meaning that, as map-reading time increases, way-finding time does, as well (Fig. 17). For details related to the relationships between each variable and map-reading time and way-finding time, please refer to Figures 18 and 19.

Variables	Map-reading time (s)	Way-finding time(s)	Coefficient of correlation	Significance
Male (Map-reading vs. way-finding)	41	79	0.523	0.010*
Female (Map-reading vs. way-finding)	57	101	0.249	0.263
Professional (Map-reading vs. way-finding)	32	86	0.196	0.395
Non-professional (Map-reading vs. way-finding)	63	93	0.529	0.008*

Table 3. Correlation coefficient of map-reading and way-finding

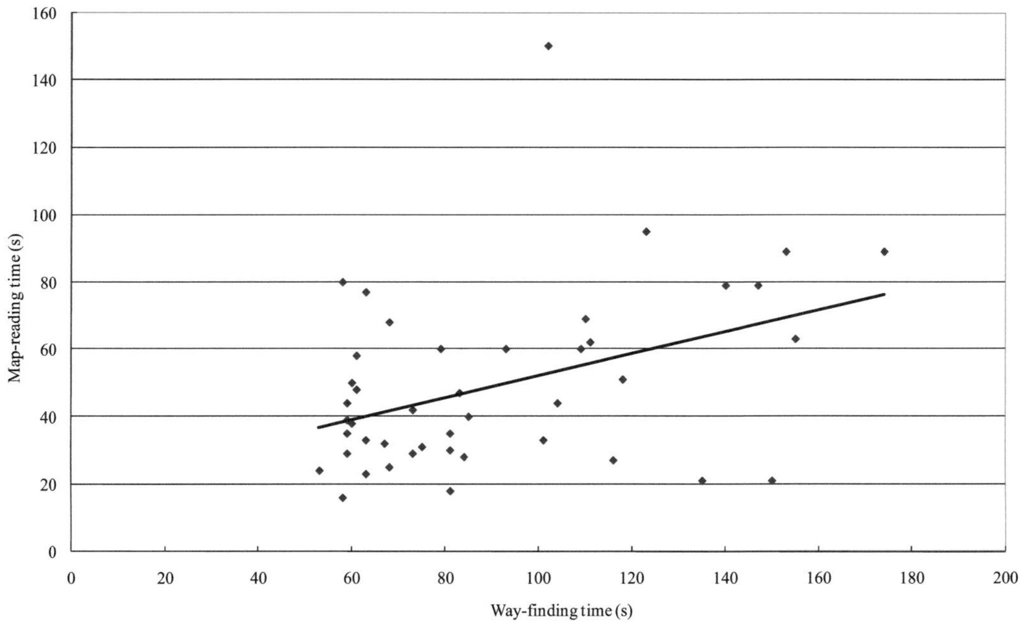

Fig. 17. Correlation between map-reading by all subjects and way-finding

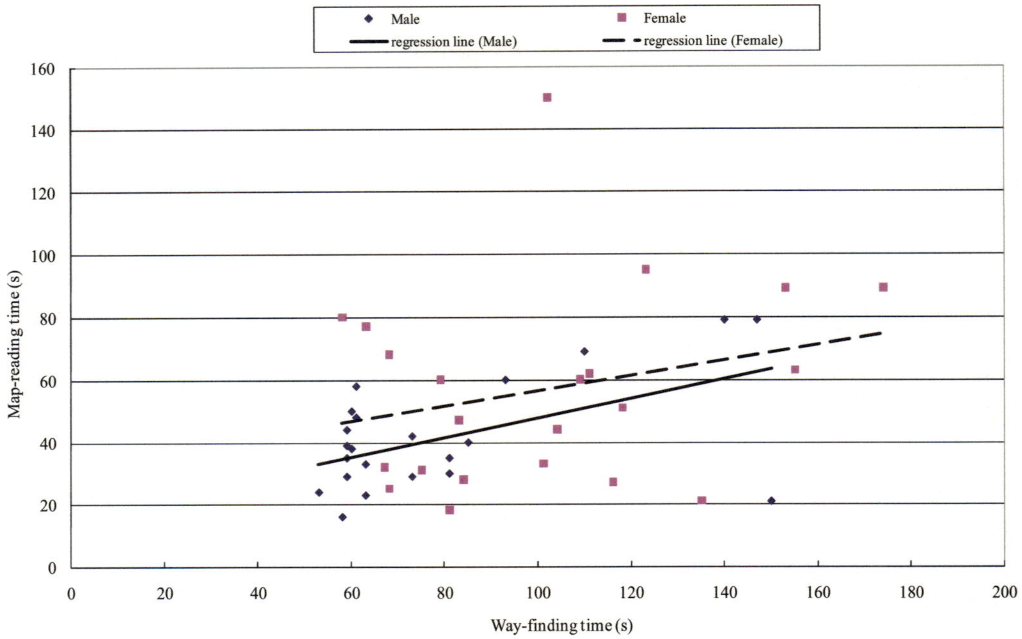

Fig. 18. Correlation between map-reading by different genders and way-finding

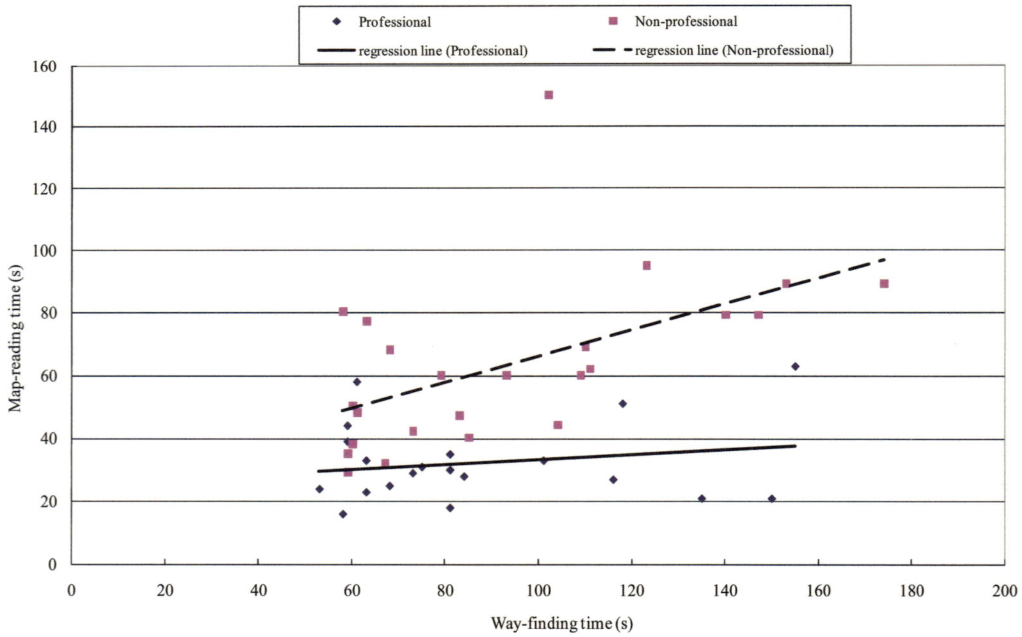

Fig. 19. Correlation between map-reading by non-/professionals and way-finding

A moderate correlation between map-reading time and way-finding time was observed for men. That is, when map-reading time increased, so did way-finding time. This phenomenon also was found for non-professionals. Among women and professionals, no such correlation was identified, and this is worth investigating. During the experimental process, possibly because professionals were equipped with prior architectural knowledge, they finished reading their maps more quickly. One assumption is that, in their hurry to complete the map-reading task, the professional respondents overlooked relevant information on the maps, because they thought they understood the maps thoroughly. Once they entered the 3D virtual reality world, however, they became unable to apply their spatial knowledge from the maps to the physical space. Therefore, this author infers that education for architecture design professionals-to-be should be designed to enhance the students' 3D spatial perceptual abilities, so that consistency between their knowledge of maps and their physical space can be achieved.

To determine the relative influence of each variable on the total time needed by the entire subject group, multiple regression analysis was conducted. Here, *total time* refers to map-reading time plus way-finding time. The results are shown in Table 4. The p-values for both map-reading time and way-finding time were less than 0.05, indicating a statistically significance impact of each on the total time; however, beta coefficients reveal a greater influence of way-finding time (beta=0.659) than map-reading time (beta=0.532). Both are positively correlated with total time. All other variables were eliminated during the regression analysis procedure, indicating that whatever influence they exerted on total time was overshadowed by the influence of these two previously noted variables.

Variables	Standardized coefficient (Beta)	Significance
Gender	------	------
Professional background	------	------
Staircase choice	------	------
Map-rereading	------	------
Subjective sense of direction	------	------
Map-reading time	0.532	0.000*
Way-finding time	0.659	0.000*

Table 4. Correlation between variables and total time required

5.2 Analysis of subjective sense of direction, maps, and path time

Prior to the virtual reality experiment utilized in this study, subjects were asked to give their opinion about their sense of direction, using a five-point Likert scale (1 very good, 2 good, 3 fair, 4 bad, 5 very bad) to indicate their response. Among the 45 subjects, 4.4% chose very good, 40.0% good, 24.4% fair, 22.2% bad, and 8.9% very bad. In other words, roughly half of the subjects believed that they had at least a good sense of direction, and roughly one quarter felt their sense of direction was fair. Moreover, self perception of sense of direction was inversely correlated with way-finding time, such that those with a more positive subjective sense of direction spent less time on way-finding. What is more, the trend line shown in Figure 20 demonstrates a strong correlation in men, but a weak correlation in women.

Further, correlation analysis (Table 5) found that subjective sense of direction was correlated with map-reading time (p=0.006), but not way-finding time (p=0.234). In other words, participants with a positive perception of their sense of direction tended to perform better understanding maps after reading them, but they failed to exhibit the same degree of way-finding skill, suggesting that they had over-estimated their way-finding ability.

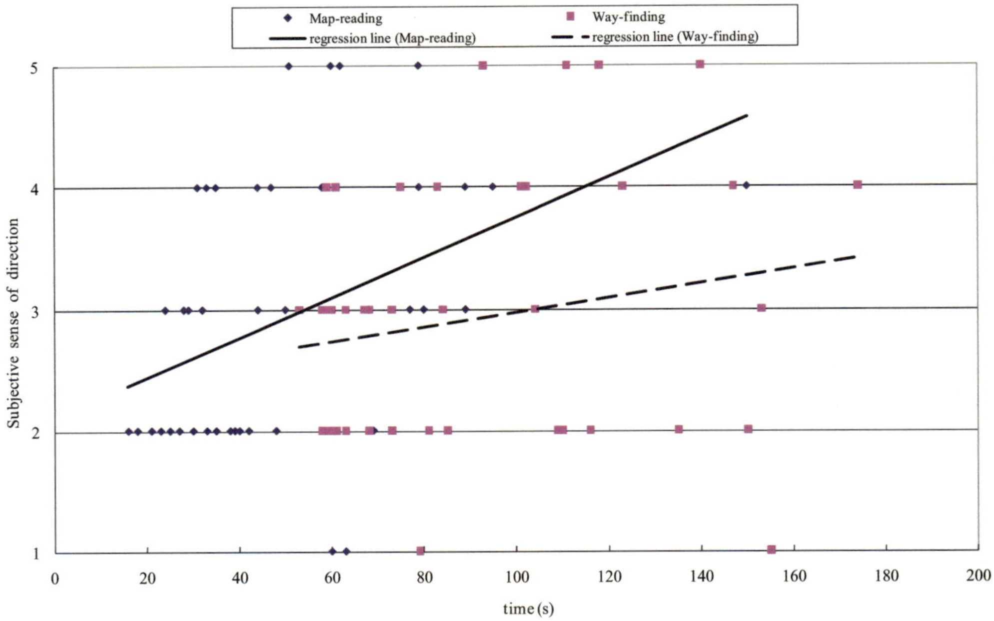

Fig. 20. Correlation among subjective sense of direction, maps, and path time

Variables	Coefficient of correlation	Significance
Subjective sense of direction vs. Map-reading	0.401	0.006*
Subjective sense of direction vs. Way-finding	0.181	0.234

Table 5. Correlation of subjective sense of direction

5.3 Analysis of choice of staircase during way-finding

In the virtual model floor plans employed in this study, there were four staircases, two (#1、#2) in the front building, and the other two (#3、#4) in the rear building. Their relative positions are shown in Figure 21. During the experiment, no clues as to which staircase leads to the first floor were provided. Subjects needed to make their own decisions based upon their understanding of the maps. As such, 13.3% of the subjects selected staircase #1, 57.8% #2, 22.2% #3, and 6.7% #4 (Table 6). Analyzing the data from the perspective of which staircases were nearest to the starting and finishing points of the intended path, #1 and #2 were closest to the starting point, and #3 closest to the final destination. Nevertheless, because of regulations related to map drawing, only half of staircase #1 was drawn, so it was not easily detected by subjects. Most subjects, therefore, selected staircases #2 and #3. This proves that clear and conspicuous representation of staircases exerts an influence on the reading and understanding of maps. It also shows that there is room for discussion as to whether the drawing of staircases in orientation maps should comply with the regulations set out by CNS 11567. For instance, if the depiction of staircase #1 was the same as for #2, our results might have been different. Additionally, approximately 40% of the subjects reported being unable to locate any staircases or having no idea where they were, suggesting that the representation of staircases in maps often is incomprehensible to the public. As a result, it may be necessary to appropriately adjust representations of staircases to reinforce staircase identification, or provide the lay public with training to establish a staircase schema.

Fig. 21 Relative position of staircases on floor plan

	#1 staircase (%)	#2 staircase (%)	#3 staircase (%)	#4 staircase (%)
Male	8.7	65.2	21.7	4.3
Female	18.2	50.0	22.7	9.1
Professional	14.3	61.9	14.3	9.5
Non-professional	12.5	54.2	29.2	4.2
Average	13.3	57.8	22.2	6.7

Table 6. Preference of staircase choice

Variables	Coefficient of correlation	Significance
Staircase choice vs. Map-reading	-0.044	0.772
Staircase choice vs. Way-finding	-0.029	0.849

Table 7. Correlation of staircase choices

We were not able to identify any significant correlations between staircase choice and either map-reading or way-finding. The choice of staircase did not affect way-finding performance (p=0.849); nor did it affect map-reading comprehension (p=0.772) (Table 7). Using t-tests to determine if gender and/or professional background influences stair choice, no significant influences were uncovered (gender: p=0.225; professional background: p=0.961). In other words, subjects generally selected the same staircases, irrespective of their gender or profession.

6. Conclusions

Tables and figures have to be made in high quality, which is suitable for reproduction and print, taking into account necessary size reduction. Photos have to be in high resolution. Tables and figures should be embedded in the text. A short descriptive title should appear under each table / figure / photo with a clear legend. (Table 1. Title, left justified / Fig. 1. Title, left justified). All units must be included.
This study employed a virtual reality (VR) approach to measure the time required both to read and comprehend a map, and to find one's way to a predetermined destination within a hospital, in an attempt to examine for differences in reading cognition and comprehension skills. Using VR platforms, simulations involving a variety of environments and signs/cues can be conducted effectively. In fact, virtual reality simulations have many incomparable advantages over on-site experiments, and play an important role in the spatial cognition of unfamiliar environments. Our findings were as follows.

6.1 Time required for reading cognition

The average map-reading time, across all subjects, was 49 seconds. Females were 39% slower at map-reading than their male counterparts; and those without a professional background in an architecture-related field were 97% slower (i.e., half as fast) than those with. This suggests that maps must have certain technical symbols that cannot be understood by those without some background in architecture, and that appropriate changes should be made to the representation in maps. Additionally, approximately 30% of subjects, irrespective of their professional backgrounds, decided to reread floor maps when they felt lost during way-finding.

6.2 Factors contributing to differences in reading cognition

It can be concluded from the t-test results that professionals and males have better map reading comprehension than non-professionals and females, the former finding again supporting the hypothesis that maps generally contain technical symbols that cannot be understood by most people and that should be considered for removal.

6.3 Results of way-finding

Overall, subjects averaged 90 seconds in finding their way through the VR simulation, but the range was broad, from a high of 174 seconds in a female non-professional, to a low of 53 seconds in a male professional. However, contrary to the results with map-reading, neither gender nor professional background appears to significantly influence way-finding time. This is surprising, given that those with professional backgrounds in an architecture-related field would be expected to have better spatial cognition and comprehension. One potential explanation for the lack of superiority of this group of individuals in way-finding is that they experienced difficulties in the transfer of knowledge derived from map reading comprehension to spatial cognition in the real world.

7. Acknowledgements

The authors would like to thank the National Science Council of the Republic of China for financially supporting this research under Contract No. NSC 99-2221-E-236-010.

8. References

Best, G. A. (1970). Direction-finding in large buildings. In D. Canter, Ed., Architectural Psychology. London: RIBA Publications, pp. 72-91.

Beaumont, P. B., Gray, J., Moore, G. T. and Robinson, B. (1984). Orientation and wayfinding in the Tauranga departmental building: A focused post-occupancy evaluation. Environmental Design Research Association Proceedings, 15, pp. 77-91.

Booth, K.S., Fisher, B.R. Page, S., Ware, C., and Widen, S. (2000). Wayfinding in a virtual environment. Poster presentation in supplement to Proceedings of Graphics Interace 2000. May 15-17, Montreal, QC.

Collins, A. M., & Quillian, M. R. (1969). Retrieval time from semantic memory, Journal of Verbal Learning and Verbal Behavior, 8, pp. 240-247.

Darken, R.P. (1995). Wayfinding in Large-Scale Virtual Worlds. Conference Companion ACM SIGCHI `95, pp. 45-46.

Darken, R.P., & Sibert, J.L. (1996). Wayfinding Strategies and Behaviors in Large Virtual Worlds. Proceedings of ACM SIGCHI `96, pp. 142-149.

Elvins, T. T. (1997). Virtually lost in virtual worlds - way-finding without a cognitive map. Computer Graphics, 31(3), pp. 15-17.

Evans, G. W. (1980). Environmental cognition. Psychological Bulletin, 88(2), pp. 259-287.

Garling, T., Book, A., & Lindberg, E. (1984). Cognitive Mapping of Large-scale Environments. Environment and Behavior, 16(1), pp. 3-34.

Golledge, R. G. (1999). Human way finding and cognitive maps. In R. Golledge (Ed.), Way finding behavior: Cognitive mapping and other spatial processes, pp. 5-45. Baltimore: John Hopkins Press.

Golledge, R. G., and R. J. Stimson. (1997). Spatial behavior: A geographic perspective. New York: Guilford Press.

Grammenos, D., Filou, M., Papadakos, P., & Stephanidis, C. (2002). Virtual Prints: Leaving trails in Virtual Environments. In Proceedings of the Eighth Eurographics Workshop on Virtual Environments, pp. 131-139, Barcelona, Spain, 30-31 May.

Jansen-Osmann, P. (2002). Using desktop virtual environments to investigate the role of landmarks Computers in Human Behavior, 18(4), pp. 427-436.

Johns,C. (2003). Spatial learning: cognitive mapping in abstract virtual environments. Paper presented at the Proceedings of the 2nd international conference on Computer graphics, virtual Reality, pp.7-16, visualisation and interaction in Africa.

Kitchin, R.M. (1994). Cognitive maps: What are they any why study them? Journal of Environmental Phychology, 14(1), pp. 1-19.

Krieg-Bruckner, B., Rofer, T., Carmesin, H.-O. and Muller, R. (1998). A Taxonomy of Spatial Knowledge for Navigation and its Application to the Bremen Autonomous Wheelchair. In C. Freksa, C. Habel, K. F. Wender (Eds.), Spatial Cognition, No. 1404, pp. 373–397, Lecture Notes in Artificial Intelligence.

Kuipers, B.J. (1983). The cognitive map: could it have been any other way? In: acredolo, L. and Pick, H. (Eds), Spatial Orientation: Research, Application, and Theory, pp. 345-359, New York: Plenum.

Liben L. S. (1981). Spatial representation and behavior: Multiple perspectives, In L. S. Liben, A. H. Patterson , & N. Newcombe (Eds.), Spatial representation and behavior across the life-span, pp. 3-36, New York: Academic Press.

Lynch, K. (1960). The Image of the City, Cambridge (Mass.): MIT Press.

Montello, D. R. (1991). Spatial Orientation And The Angularity Of Urban Routes A Field Study. Environment and Behavior, 23(1), pp. 47-69.

Montello, Daniel R., Kristin L. Lovelace, Reginald G. Golledge, and Carol M. Self. 1999. Sex-related differences and similarities in geographic and environmental spatial abilities. Annals of the Association of American Geographers, 89(3), 515-534.

Nichols, F., Canete, I. & Tuladhar, S. (1992). Designing for Pedestrians: A CAD Network Analysis Approach. In: Y.E. Kalay, Editor, Evaluating and Predicting Design Performance, Wiley & Sons, New York.

O'Neill, M. J. (1991b). Effects of signage and floor plan configuration on way-finding accuracy. Environment and Behavior, 23(5), pp. 553-574.

O'Neill, M. J. (1991a). Evaluation of a conceptual model of architectural legibility. Environment and Behavior, 23(3), pp. 259-284.

Passini, R. (1999). Way-finding: backbone of graphic support systems. Visual Information for Everyday Use, London: Taylor & Francis, pp. 241–256.

Passini, R. (1992). Wayfinding in architecture,Van Nostrand Reinhold Company Inc.

Siegel, A. and White, S. (1975). The development of spatial representations of large-scale envi-ronments, Academic Press, New York.

Sorrows, M. E., & Hirtle, S. C. (1999). The Natural of Landmarks for Real and Electronic Spaces. In C. Freksa & D. Mark (Eds.), Spatial Information Theory. Lecture Notes in Computer Science , pp. 37-50.

Stanney, K. M. (2003). Virtual Environment. In J. A. Jacko & A. Sears (Eds.), The Human-Computer Interaction Handbook: Fundamentals, Evolving Technologies and Emerging Applications., pp. 621-634: Lawrence.

Tang, C.-H., Lin, C.-Y., Hsu, Y.-M. (2008). Exploratory research on reading cognition and escape-route planning using building evacuation plan diagrams. Applied Ergonomics, 39(2), pp. 209-217.

Thorndyke, P. and Hayes-Roth, B. (1982). Differences in spatial knowledge acquired from maps and navigation, Cognitive Psychology, 14(4), pp. 560-589.

Tolman, Edward C. (1948). Cognitive maps in rats and men. Psychological Review 55(4), pp. 189-208.

Trowbridge, L. W., & Bybee, R. W. (1996). Teaching secondary school science: Strategies for developing scientific literacy (6th ed.). Englewood Cliffs, N.J.: Merrill.

Tversky, B. Remembering Space.In E. Tulving & C.F.I.M. (2000).(Eds.),Oxford Handbook of Memory, pp. 363-379. Oxford: Oxford University Press.

Tversky, P. Lee, (1999). Pictorial and verbal tools for conveying routes, Spatial Information Theory: Cognitive and Computational Foundations of Geographic Information Science, Springer Verlag, pp. 51-64.

Weisman, G D. (1981). Evaluating architectural legibility: way-finding in the built environment. Environment and Behavior, 13(2), pp. 189-204.

Weyrich, M., & Drews, P. (1999). An Interactive Environment for Virtual Manufacturing: the Virtual Workbench, Computers in Industry, 38(1), pp. 5-15.

Wilson, J. R. (1999). Virtual Environments Applications and Applied Ergonomics, Ergonomics, 30(1), pp. 3-9.

Witmer, B. G., Bailey, J. H., & Knerr, B. W. (1996). Virtual space and real world places: transfer of route knowledge. International Journal of Human-Computer Studies, 45(4), pp. 413-428.

Zeltzer D., Johnson M. (1994). Virtual Actors and Virtual Environments, Interacting with Virtual Environments, MacDonald L., Vince J. (Ed), pp. 229-256.

Part 4

VR as a Therapeutic Tool

12

Virtuality Supports Reality for e-Health Applications

Giovanni Saggio and Carlo Alberto Pinto
University of Rome "Tor Vergata"
Italy

1. Introduction

The "virtualization" process of the reality is unavoidable and cannot be arrested since it goes deeply towards the process of dematerialization initiate with the post-industrialization era. Formerly, in fact, the power and the richness were in the hands of people with large amounts of goods or lands, but nowadays are in the hands of people who sell intangible applications (software and firmware) or goods with poor material but highly rich contents (notebooks, mobile phones, ipods,..) or even only no matter services (telecom, web, educational,.. companies).
Hence the "virtualization" is more and more becoming a so powerful tool that can have the capability to reproduce, augment and even overcome "reality".
In this view the "virtuality", joined to the know-how, is the successful key for new fundamental achievement in really many fields, but some in particular deserve special attention, i.e. the health-focused disciplines, so important because there are highly concentrated the monetary, political and social interests. In this context our aim is to furnish an overview on how nowadays the virtuality supports reality for e-health applications.

2. Virtuality reproduces, augments and overcomes reality

Even if the term "virtual" was born for unreal things, over the time it tends to be more and more used in reference to things that mimic their "real" equivalents, especially via pc applications. So we know of virtual library, virtual earth, virtual work, virtual museum, virtual tour, and so on.
We can refer the "real" mimed by the "virtual" as a "virtualization" process, which has now also the aim to enrich, enhance and, in some way, boost the possibilities offered by the "restricted" real world.
Limiting, for the moment, out attention to the mere aspect of reproduction of the reality, the "virtuality" expresses a virtual vision of the real world. Nowadays this process can be produced by interesting 3D techniques such as stereoscopy and holography.
Actually the stereoscopy was invented in the remote 1832 by Charles Wheathstone, but did not present any practical application till now. This technique exploits the human binocular vision to place virtual objects in a 3D space. An example is reproduced in Fig. 1 where users with special glasses have the impression of seeing "floating" planets in the room. The application in Fig. 1 has been developed by our collaborators of the PFM Multimedia Company (www.pfmmultimedia.it).

Fig. 1. Users donning special glasses see "floating" planets in the room (Courtesy by PFM Multimedia Company)

The holography was theorized for the first time in 1947 by Dennis Gabor and the first practical applications were possible only few years later by the adoption of the laser technology. One of the latest holography technique has been applied and can be appreciated in the site of Pompei (Naples, Italy) where in the ancient house of Polibio an hologram illustrates to the visitors the characteristics of the *domus* (see Fig. 2). This is a new technique indeed, being based on ultrasonic transducers which diffuse micro-particles of air mixed with nebulized water, as a support to the projection of the images. Again, this application has been developed by our collaborators of the PFM Multimedia Company.

Fig. 2. A 3D holographic virtualization of Polibio in his *domus* in Pompei (Courtesy by PFM Multimedia Company)

The reported examples deal not only with the possibility to reproduce reality in a virtual world, but also demonstrate how virtuality "augments" reality, giving visibility to ancient no more existing world.

Among all the virtual pc applications, which "copy" the reality, one of the most interesting is more and more becoming the avatar reproduction of measured real human postures, possible thanks to the current availability of suitable sensors and electronic stuff.
In this view, we can refer to mere shoots of postures by cameras or webcams which can "see" the reality from a multi-point-of-view, but one at time. An example of this is represented by the known *gait analysis system*, which consists in the systematic study of human/animal locomotion, augmented by instrumentation for measuring body movements, but mainly by means of multiple cameras view.

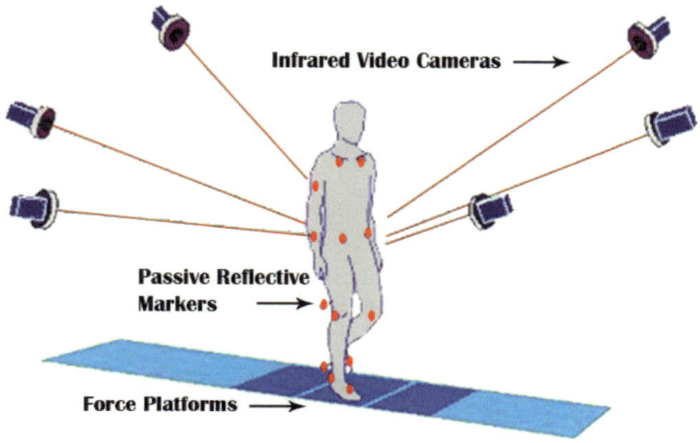

Fig. 3. A schematization of the camera based gait analysis system

But actually here we want to consider the new, more interesting and innovative, wearable sensorized systems which can accurately measure all the angles of human joints, pointing out finger, wrist, pelvis, neck, knee,.. movements, and spatial positions of arms, trunk, head, legs,.. The "wearability" of these new systems allow the advantage of unnecessity of a prepared scenario and have the capability to quantitatively measure the movements in every time and every space without limitations. The wearable systems make it possible to measure every single pose and movement of a person, so allowing the real time reproduction in Virtual Reality (VR), by means of complex avatars which can be incredibly similar to the original. We are here treating of new frontier systems capable to measure all human postures (or single parts of them) and to reproduce such postures in VR.
These systems have a potential huge number of applications, covering several different areas: working, sporting, gaming,.. with implications on social, military, medical, musical, edutainment, .. fields.
In the social area the measure and the subsequent "virtualization" of human postures can lead to a process capable to translate the sign language into single words and phrases, in home automation a real movement can be virtually recognized and an action can be associated to it, the virtualization of real acts can be very useful for improving the ergonomics of some stuff, etc.
In the work area the "virtualization" of real human actions can be useful for simulating dangerous activities, for verifying "off-line" the effect of some actions, for simulating the manipulation of hazardous stuff, for designing assistance, etc.
In the computer science area the "virtualized" reality can be useful for realizing new input interfaces or for implementing new automatic programming tools. In particular, within such frame, we realized a computer interaction system with no necessity of mouse and keyboard

inputs, being the commands obtained by the "translation" of finger movements of the user (see Fig. 4).

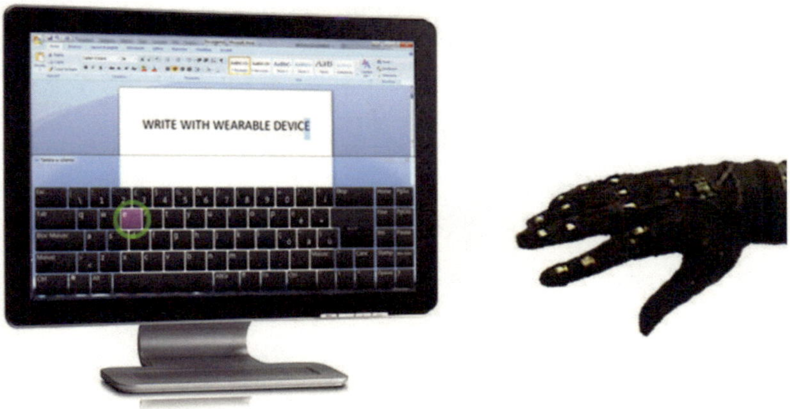

Fig. 4. Mouse and keyboard are unnecessary if computer interactions are made by a sensorized glove capable to accept commands obtained by finger motions.

In the music area the "virtualization" can reproduce real music instruments with good accuracy avoiding the expenses and spaces paid in reality, and the virtual instruments can be played simulating the action of the player or associating a single note/chord to a real human body posture (Costantini et al., 2010).

Perhaps the army, the navy and the air forces are the more potentially interested in the "virtualization" process of human movements, since the necessity of simulating war scenarios, and the necessity of predicting the consequences of soldier acts in several potential environments.

So going ahead for all the other previous mentioned fields, "virtuality" can reproduce "reality" for the aims of training, educating, assisting, experiencing people.

But it is in the health-focused areas that the measure of real human postures, and the subsequent reproduction by means of pc avatars, can lead to the most fascinating and useful applications. In fact the virtualization process of patient's postures can be very useful in motor therapy, so that doctors can better identify pathologies, in rehabilitation, so to rightly evaluate pre-post effect of surgery, in functional analysis, so to create a database to classify the residual movements of the patient, and so on. On the other end not only the measure of patient's postures can be so useful, but even the doctor's ones! In fact, measuring the doctor's hand movements can be fundamental for surgical training or skills evaluation for virtual implementations of new procedures, for realizing minimal invasive surgery techniques, even for implementing tele-surgery in a way that the doctor's movements are faithfully remotely replayed by robot's arms.

In such a frame is the so called *augmented reality* which plays a winning role (Geisen, 2005). The concept of Augmented Reality, short AR (sometimes referred as Mixed Reality), comes from a fusion of digital data together with the human perception of the environment, so that the virtual objects overlay the reality on a pc screen (see Fig. 5). To the aim of upgrading performances and accuracies of the overall system and increasing the comfort for the user, we think here to the digital data obtained by means of the previously mentioned wearable systems. Augmented and Mixed Reality technology offer seamless visualization of text-based physiological data and various graphical 3D data onto the patient's body. Thanks to the wearable sensors together with the AR the user can see himself into the real world, with the virtual objects superimposed upon or composited with it. So AR supplements reality and, ideally, "it would appear to the user that the virtual and real objects coexisted in the same space." (Azuma, 1997)

Fig. 5. An example of AR imagine. Information about bones are superimposed over the real picture

Potentials and limits of current AR in surgery have been reported elsewhere (Shuhaiber, 2004) , so here our aim is not to discuss about that, but the introduction of novel possibilities which comes from different interfaces thanks to the wearable systems, not applied till now, which can even overcome the, for some aspect, still futuristic AR.

As already mentioned, the AR technology is both for real and for simulate surgery. An example of the latter comes from the ImmersiveTouch™-SENSIMMER® system (www.immersivetouch.com), which integrates a haptic device with a head and hand tracking system and a high resolution high pixel-density stereoscopic display. The haptic device is in some way "merged" with the high resolution 3D graphics, giving the user a more realistic and natural means to manipulate and modify 3D data in real time.

Since the key element in AR for surgery is becoming more and more the exact measure of doctor's hand postures, our argumentation will be especially focused on that in the following paragraphs.

The virtualization can be even enhanced and extended thanks to 3D visualisation-related knowledge. Examples come from the 3DVisA (3dvisa.cch.kcl.ac.uk), Altair4 Multimedia (www.altair4.it), PFM Multimedia (www.pfmmultimedia.it). So virtuality results a key element even for hidden, inaccessible or alternative reality.

The VR can boost the possibilities of the real world since it can even represents the hidden reality. Let's think, for instance, to the wearable sensorized system donned by soldiers: even if no camera pictures are possible, we can have in any case their postures real-time reproduces in a remote location, so to guarantee information otherwise impossible to obtain (see Fig. 6)

Fig. 6. The wearable sensorized system makes it possible to obtain fundamental posture data of soldiers even if no camera shootings are possible. On the left the real situation, on the right the visualization of the obtained information from the sensorized garments.

2.1 From reality to virtuality

To reproduce reality in a virtual environment, let's start analyzing the so called Virtual World and all its components. To transpose reality into a 3D scenario three key topics should be considered: *Models*, *Textures* and *Lights*.

Modelling is the art and science of creating a surface that mimics the shape of a real object. Each object of the virtual world has a shape and a size and this entity is called *Mesh*. In meshes everything is built from three basic structures: *Vertices*, *Edges* and *Faces* (see Fig. 7).

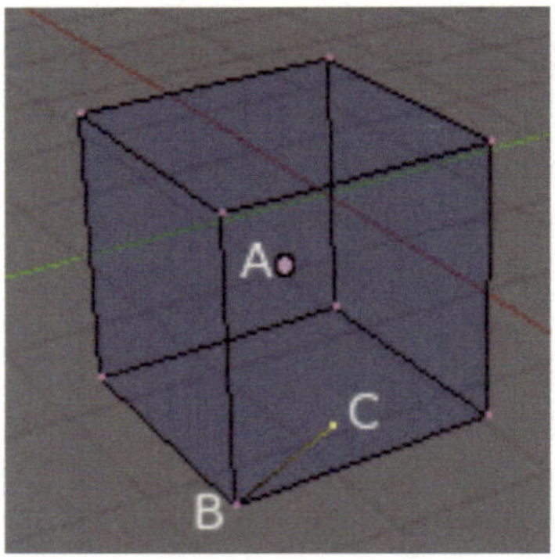

Fig. 7. Vertices, Edges and Faces: C is a vertex, between B and C there is an edge and A is the mesh center point

A vertex is primarily a single point or a position in a 3D space. A straight line connecting two vertices is an edge; this is the wire that is seen when a mesh is looked at in wireframe view. Vertices and edges are usually invisible on the rendered image.

Edges are used to construct faces which are the highest level structure in a mesh and are used to build the surface of the object. A face locates the area between either three or four vertices (respectively triangles and quadrangles), with an edge on every side. The mentioned mesh can be defined as a set of connected vertices and sometimes thousands of vertices are necessary to built complex objects.

It is possible to assemble the vertices in groups forming the so called *Vertex Groups*, so to reusing parts of a mesh for making copies and, eventually, hiding "everything else" while

details are worked and so on. Vertex Groups identify sub-components of an object, like the joints of a hand or the hinges of a door. With vertex groups we can easily select and work on them in isolation without the necessity to create apart objects.
The "virtual world", how described till now, produces smooth, uniform objects that can be animated, but such objects are not yet particularly similar to the real counterpart, because uniformity tends to be uncommon and out of place. In order to approach a more realistic scenario, a 3D model Textures can be applied so to modify the reflectivity, specularity, roughness and other surface qualities of a material (see Fig. 8).

Fig. 8. This image is an example of results obtained from texture application

The third issue, Lighting, is a very important topic in rendering, standing equal to models and textures. A simple model can become very realistic if a light source is skillfully adopted, while without a proper lighting scheme the most accurately modeled and textured scene will yield poor results. We have to apply the same "lighting-rules" as in the real world, which is never lit by a single light source, indeed even if a single light is present, its rays can bounce off objects being re-irradiated all over the scene. In this way every single part of the image or 3D space is softly shadowed, partially lit and not pitch black.
If it is required to animate a mesh and make it move, we have to define an armature which is made of a series of invisible bones connected to each other via parenting or constraints, that allow we to pose and deform the geometry that surrounds it. The armature is used for building skeletal systems to animate the poses of characters and everything else which needs to be posed. By adding an armature system to an object, it can be deformed accurately so that geometry doesn't have to be animated "manually". The armature modifier allows objects to be deformed simply by specifying the name of the virtual bone. As a bone moves, it deforms or moves the vertices, but not necessarily all of them, only the ones assigned to it. The mesh surface is analogous to the skin of the human body. The armature is also referred as *Skeleton*. In some complex 3D programs there are more complex skeleton systems defined bipeds. These elements are pre-designed and are customizable in order to fit with the mesh. An example of biped is in Fig. 9.

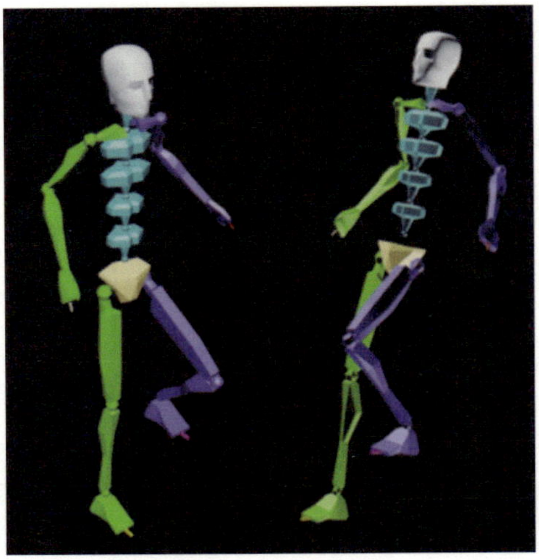

Fig. 9. Biped: a complex customizable skeleton system

By the 3D software an user can define how many fingers each hand has and how many phalanxes each finger has or how many sections for the torso and so on. Then the virtual representation of a real element (an object, a person or whatever) can be defined as a virtual alter-ego immersed in the virtual space.

In order to represent a human character we need to create a 3D body model, more often called *Avatar* (see Fig. 10). In a real-time virtual environment an avatar is a textured mesh obviously rigged, with a skeleton inside as reported.

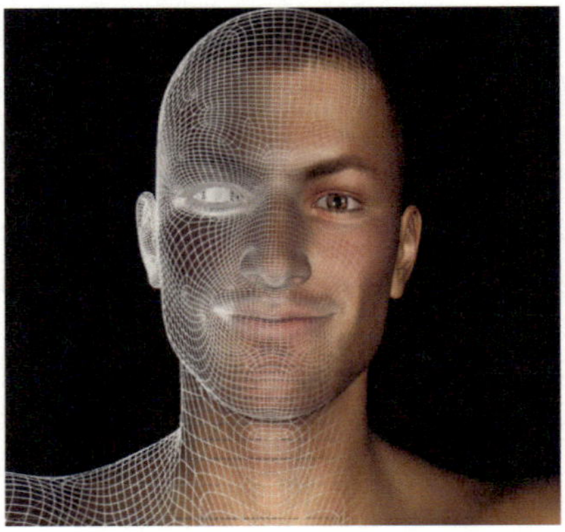

Fig. 10. 3D male avatar

There are many ways of creating a 3D model: starting from zero with a software for graphical applications by modeling a solid, as a sculptor would, or by editing an existing base model, or by creating a new one with external tools like 3D scanners for surface or volume acquisition. In any case we have to use a 3D graphic software to edit one or more meshes in a virtual complete environment, called *Scene*. There are several interesting software, freeware or under license, for such a purpose, and the best choice cannot necessarily correspond to the highest price. Usually the most expensive software is also too complicate to be utilized by beginner users. Among 3D design packages with commercial license, the most common and popular are *3DS Studio Max*, *Maya* and *Lightwave 3D*. Two of the best freeware solutions are *DAZ 3D* and *Blender*. The latter is not only free of charge but even open source and with a wide available toolset, defining a complete pipeline (from modeling to sequence editing) controlled by a flexible and consistent user interface. With Blender it is possible to create a scene that is a way to organize the 3D environment with objects, textures and lights. Each scene can contain multiple objects, which can contain multiple materials, which can contain many textures, and so on.

A 3D scene is like a real space with its own coordinate system. In a 3D cartesian coordinate system, a generic point is referred to by three real numbers (the coordinates), indicating the positions of the perpendicular projections from the point to three fixed, perpendicular, graduated lines, called the axes, which intersect at the origin. Stands the several possible choices among softwares, unfortunately it has not be defined a unique coordinate reference set yet. 3D graphics applications use two types of Cartesian coordinate systems: right-handed (Fig. 11B), and left-handed (Fig. 11A).

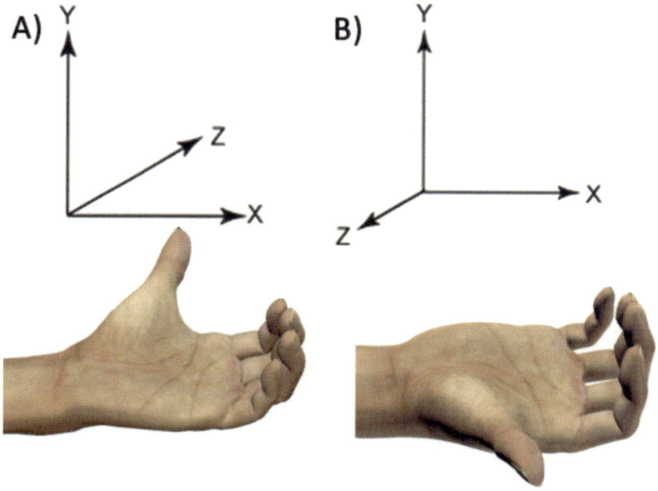

Fig. 11. A) left handed and B) right handed coordinate systems.

In both coordinate systems, the positive x-axis points to the right, and the positive y-axis points up. It is possible to remember which direction the positive z-axis points by pointing the fingers of either left or right hand in the positive x-direction and curling them into the positive y-direction. The thumb points in the positive z-axis direction for that coordinate system.

The basic operations performed on objects, defined in a 3D coordinate system, are *rotation, translation* and *scaling*. It is possible to combine these basic transformations to create a transform matrix, as it will be detailed explained in the next section. Likewise our eyes see the reality, in the virtual reality the scene is observed by virtual cameras. Just like the corresponding real cameras, the virtual ones may be located in a three-dimensional space, capturing the scene from their point of view. Everything located inside the virtual camera field of view is called *viewport*.

2.2 Reality-virtuality interactions

The previous section deals with the elements existing in a virtual artificial world in order to reproduce reality. This section is dedicated to specify how to import a real action or movement in a 3D virtual scene and consequently how reality and virtuality can interact and the tools devoted to this aim.

As a starting point we need to define the medium of interaction between the real and the virtual world. In this sense we can utilize several interfaces such as mouse, touchpad, keyboard, joystick and so on, but the most interesting ones are the devices that allow users to move naturally within the environment, giving them an "immersive" experience. These systems can be based on webcams, capable to track human movements, or can be based on motion sensors directly sewn on garments (as is the so called data glove detailed afterwards).

Referring the sensors as the key elements capable to reveal the states of the (active or passive) sources, the commercial human movement tracking systems fit basically into three different classifications depending on where the sensors and the sources are respectively placed (Wang, 2005):

Inside-Out Systems: the sensors are positioned on the body while the sources are somewhere else in the world. The problem with these systems is that they tend to be bulky.

Outside-In Systems: the sources are attached to the body while the sensors are somewhere else in the world. These systems are less intrusive to the subject but are particularly sensitive to occlusion problems.

Inside-In Systems: the sensors and sources are on the user's body. These systems can be used to study relative movements between specific parts of the body.

Obviously each system exhibits both advantages and disadvantages: to increase accuracy and to reduce latency the best choice is an Inside-In System (like wearable devices can be). On the other hand, a good choice to obtain an intrusion decrease, is an Outside-In System.

As an example, let's consider the acquisition of the human hand movement: the first issue is to find all degrees of freedom, taking into account that for each finger's joint not all movements are possible. The distal interphalangeal joint and the proximal interphalangeal joint have only the possibility to move in the flexion/extension plane (Fig. 12c), so 1 Degree of Freedom (1 DoF). The metacarpo phalangeal joint has 2 DoF: one on the flexion/extension plane and the other one on abduction/adduction plane (Fig. 12d). The first thumb joint and the wrist have 3 DoFs and 2 DoFs respectively.

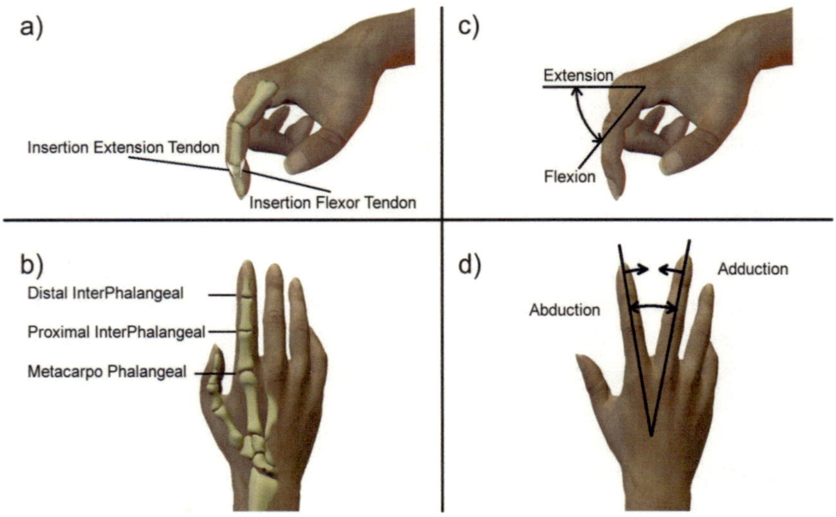

Fig. 12. a) and b) details of finger joints. c) and d) possible movements.

After DoFs have been identified, we can measure all of them or restrict the interest to the ones which are strictly necessary to our aims and, consequently, focus on the subset of sensors, necessary to measure the requested DoFs.
After the most suitable acquisition system has been chosen and an appropriate 3D reproduction software has been selected, then it is possible to reproduce every recorded movements in a 3D virtual space with a high and realistic immersion degree.
A data glove, as for instance our Hiteg-Glove (http://hiteg.uniroma2.it), is an example of Inside-In System. Thanks to this wearable device it is possible to track real hand's movements (1 sensor for each DoF), and converting them into electric signals. Once data are acquired and converted into digital form, all values are sent to PC with a specific protocol useful to disambiguate and recognize the exact sensor under investigation and its value. The data can be tidily stored in a specific database, in such a way each information can be simply re-called and utilized in a simple numerical format or, more effectively, converted into a graphical representation useful for replicating the real hand movement by a virtual avatar on a PC screen. The software converts the digital values into bending values, expressed in degrees or radians, applying such bending to the corresponding virtual model.

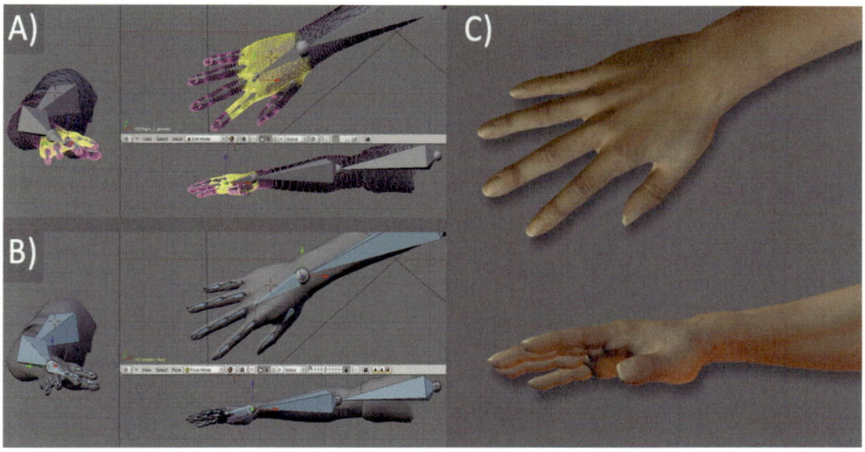

Fig. 13. A 3D human hand model: A) Mesh with vertex group (yellow selection). B) Armature: hidden hand bones. C) Final rendering of the rigged model with textures and lights

In a vectorial virtual space every bone is described by two matrixes: a local one (local transform) and a combined one (combined transform). The local matrix describes translations and rotations with respect to its pivot. Obviously the bones are connected in a way that translation and rotation of one bone influences the others in a cascading way. This means that for every junction movement the combined matrix of all the junctions is recomputed in a recursive way:

$$C_i = L_i \, C_{i-1} \quad (1)$$

The combined matrix of the *i-th* junction (C_i) is computed multiplying its local matrix (L_i) by the combined matrix of the "father junction" (C_{i-1}).
By a constant application of these transformations, the virtual model is consistent with the movements and the postures of the user.

Once it has been established the way to move the mesh in the virtual world, it is necessary to make it interact with the objects or other animated meshes (other avatars) and in general there are two ways to do it. The first way is to recognize the posture or the action the user is making and to start a pre-set animation, if the action is known and allowed in that context. For example, the user indicates or touches an object in the virtual world and the software moves the object of a default measure, not related to real strength, speed or angle of the user. The second, more complex, way is to introduce a "physical engine" in the virtual world. A physical engine is a computer program that simulates Newtonian physic models using variables such as mass, velocity, friction, etc.. So it is possible to obtain simulated occurrences of collisions, rebounds, trajectories. With this engine, each object interacts with the surroundings according to its own characteristics.

We developed an interesting application just taking advantages of the virtual interaction possibilities in the virtual world. Actually one of the project carried on by our group named Hiteg (Health Involved Technical Engineering Group) is oriented to virtual architecture: the aim is to reconstruct entire monuments starting from pieces of ruins acquired by 3D scanner (see Fig. 14 and Fig. 15).

In such a way the real reconstruction can be made only after it is well known the exact location for every single pieces, so saving even a huge amount of money and time.

So far we have seen how you can act in the virtual world, but actually in reality the interaction is bidirectional: the world also affects the person. In this case it is necessary to use an haptic device.

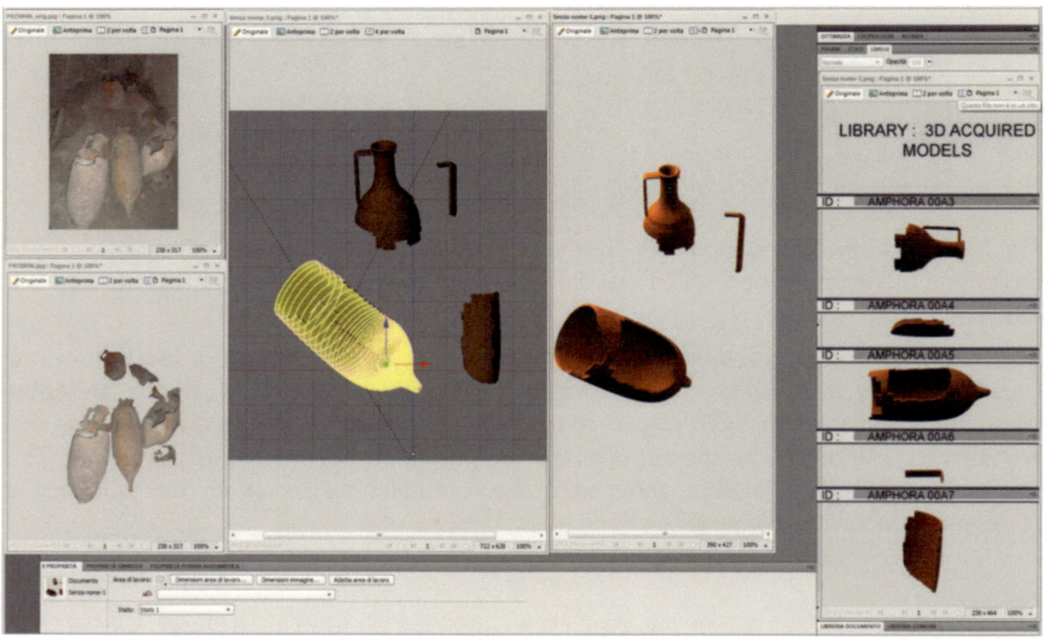

Fig. 14. The 3D scanned parts of an ancient pillar are virtually reproduced in a VR environment.

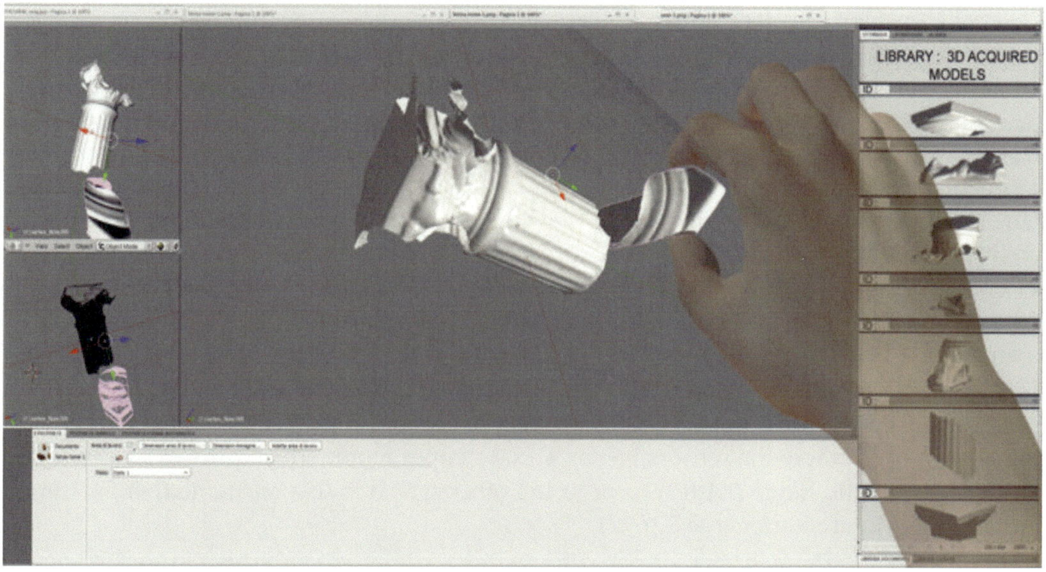

Fig. 15. 3D scanned parts of an ancient pillar are virtually recombined into the original form utilizing our Hiteg-glove as an interaction tool

Fig. 16. When an object is virtually touched, the haptic device can give the sensation of the real touch.

The word haptic comes from the Greek verb άπτικός, haptes, with the meaning of "contact" or "touch". Haptic technology, or haptics, is a tactile feedback technology that applies forces, vibrations, and/or motions to the user. This mechanical stimulation may be used to assist the user in the remote control of machines and devices (tele-operations).

Now we have a world as close as possible to reality, which enjoys some of the fundamental laws of physics, we have an avatar, that represents the user, and a set of objects that enrich the environment.

2.3 Hiteg glove

Generally speaking, a data glove is intended as the ensemble of mechanical to electrical transducers, a support (usually Lycra based), a powered conditioning electronic, a (wired or wireless) transmission system, all useful to measure all the DoFs of wrist and finger joints.
In our laboratory we developed a version of data glove, referred as HITEG glove (stands our name "Health Involved Technical Engineering Group"), which is mostly based on bend sensors capable of measuring bending angles thanks to the piezoresistive effect by means of which, in correspondence of each angle to which the sensors are subjected, it is measured a distinct resistance value.
In order to obtain high level performances of our data glove, in the sense of reliability, reproducibility and sensibility, we measured and characterized several piezoelectric sensors, manufactured by Flexpoint Sensor System Inc. (www.flexpoint.com) and Image S.I. (www.imagesco.com), different in length and encapsulation materials.
Sensors resistance variation vs. bending angle was measured thanks to a home-made setup based on hinges where the sensors lay on, and a stepper motor which provides the rotation of one wing of the hinge (with respect to the other which is fix constrained) simulating a human finger joint rotation (see Fig. 17).

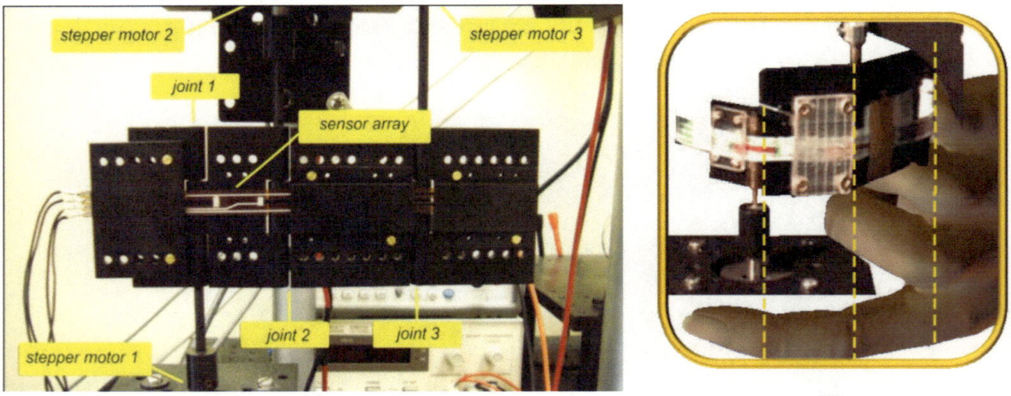

A) B)

Fig. 17. A) A three motor system to measure a sensor array, simulating movements of B) a real human finger

The motor which rotates the hinge's wing is a Trinamic PD-109 two phase hybrid stepper, microstepping optimized. It is provided with a Trinamic Motion Control Language (TMCL) which consists of an instruction set of motion control commands. On the basis of a host computer PC software development environment, the TMCL-IDE, motion control commands are provided to the motors. A rigid frame provides the necessary stability to the system. The motor is fixed on an optical bench by angular Newport EQ80-E shores. The motor motion is transmitted to the hinge's axis thanks to an universal rigid joint in order to obtain an excellent stability.
With the described measurement set-up, each sensor can be characterized in a -90° to 180° (from inward to outward) range with programmable step value of bending angle, number of measurement repetitions and mechanical actuator speed. At known angles, the resistance values of the sensors are measured by an Agilent 34405A multimeter.

The investigated piezoelectric sensors or array of sensors, for the specific application of the data glove, have a large measurement range for chosen outward angles from 0° to 120°, and correspondingly the resistance normally changes from 10 to 170 kΩ. The hysteresis of the sensors is really negligible and measurement repeatability is exceptional. Among all the performed measurements, some relevant results are showed in Fig. 18. It reports measurement results, resistance mean values (including standard deviations), on 6 different 2 inches length polyimmide encapsulated Flexpoint sample sensors: each sensor is characterized repeating measurements 10 times, varying bending angle from 0° to 120° and vice versa.

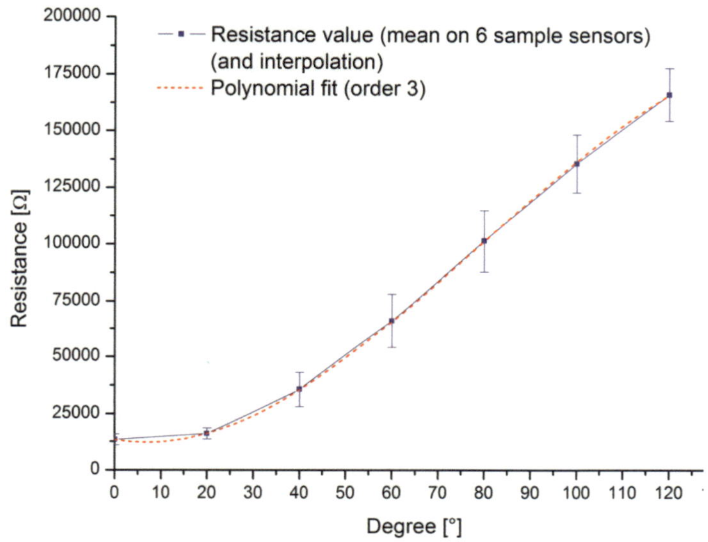

Fig. 18. Resistance variation vs. bending angle: mean on 6 sample sensors and standard deviation

After the characterization, the sensors are sewn on a Lycra based glove, each corresponding to a single finger joint so to measure flex-extension movements and between fingers to evaluate abdu-adduction movements. The Fig. 19 shows our Hiteg glove.
The resistance variation vs. bending angle characteristic of each sensors is utilized to correctly convert the electric resistance value into the corresponding finger joint flexed angle.

3. E-health applications

Healthcare is one of the areas potentially dramatically reshaped by the introduction of the new virtual tools. In fact, over the past few years there has been a rapid increase in the application of VR technology for e-health purposes in particular in diagnosis, healing, motor and neurological rehabilitation, motor therapy, instruction and surgery simulation, study, even in explanation to patients. With the aim of VR in motor therapy doctors have a multi-view vision so to better catch pathologies (Saggio et al., 2009), in rehabilitation to quantitatively, not qualitatively, evaluate pre-post effect of surgery (Castagnaro et al., 2010), in functional analysis so to create a database to classify the residual movement of the

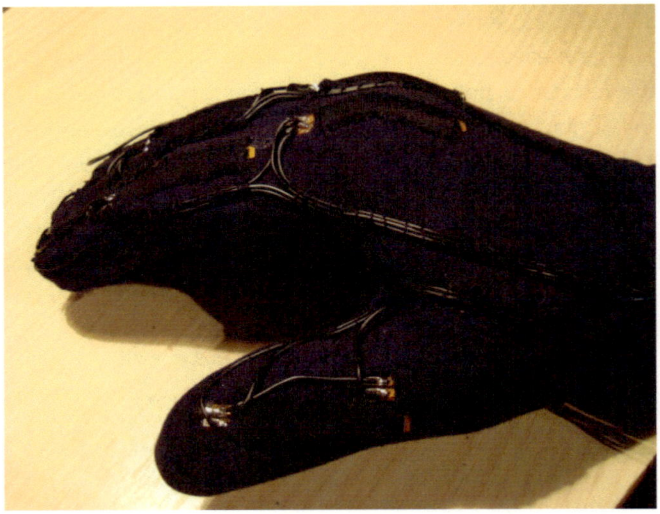

Fig. 19. The Hiteg glove

patient, in doctor training so to evaluate their surgical skills, in understanding the genesis and treatment of special symptoms (Zányi et al., 2009), in biomechanical evaluation during work and daily-life activities (Draicchio et al., 2010), in pain reduction treatments (Shahrbanian et al., 2009), even in developing an additional therapy tool for eating and impulse control disorders (Jiménez-Murcia et al., 2009), etc.

In the following paragraphs, we will focus our attention on some e-health applications of VR. In particular we will detail of surgery simulations, neurological and motor rehabilitations, brain computer interface facilities for severe neuromuscular impaired people.

3.1 Surgery simulator

Surgery simulator is an excellent example of application of virtuality and reality-virtuality interaction. Differing from classic computer graphics, with the surgery simulator the user can touch and interact with objects such as organs or human tissue.

The first historical simulator was invented by Edwin Albert Link in 1929. It was a flight simulator called the "Blue Box" or "Link Trainer" by which it was possible to evaluated the pilot performances "off-line". Many years passed since that date before the idea could be applied in medicine, but in the latest years it is having an increasing implementation. Just to refer the importance of the surgery simulator for the market, looking at the U.S. market for instance, the surgical training systems sold had a value of approximately 9.9M$ in 2004, over 11M$ in 2005, till more than 26M$ in 2009. It is believed that worldwide sales more than double U.S. sales. But there is not only a market for the surgery simulator itself: the system providers can generate percentage on the revenue by providing updates to software, training, and system support.

The surgery simulator is more and more becoming an important, or somewhat fundamental, tool useful to train novice surgeons to practice complex operative tasks before entering the operating room. To practice a procedure or a given gesture repeatedly can dramatically increase surgical training, so surgery simulator can even become useful for those who are already practice but want to gain greater proficiency outside the operating room. It is somewhat ascertained how simulators are helping to accelerate that learning curve, so improving the fundamental Patient Safety (www.oregonsimulation.com, www.surgical-science.com). Using VR concepts (navigation, interaction, immersion), surgical planning, training, and teaching even for complex surgical procedure may be possible. A hypothesis regards even visionary leaders examining the VR as an educational technique integrated into traditional curricula of novice surgeons (Dawson, 2006).

At the end, the simulator can record errors and provide an operative efficiency measure, so functioning both as an educational tool and a skills validation instrument.

Nowadays VR is exploited in some specific surgery simulator applications: hepatic surgery (Marescaux et al., 1998), arthroscopy trainer (www.insightarthrovr.com), laparoscopic surgery (Ho, 2006; Schijven & Jakimowicz, 2003), endoscopic procedures (Soler et al., 2009), virtual cholecystectomy (www.surgical-science.com), thoracic surgery, orthopedics, urology, and gynecology (Haluck et al., 2002), arterial/duct clipping (Chaudhry et al., 1999), endovascular procedures (Van Herzeele & Aggarwal, 2008) and so on, but with time it is reasonable to think that the real most part of surgery will be computer simulated.

Since the peculiar application, for which virtual environments are interactive and reactive, the interactions which can occur are of unpredictable nature, so it is not possible to pre-compute images for each of the ~20 frames/s that are needed to provide an immersive VR experience. As if not enough, the physical correct behaviour of objects have to be modelled in real-time too. So, in practice, at present there is a limit to the desired realism of the physical models, and it must be balanced against the need for speed. In any case there are interesting studies and applications which demonstrate surgery simulations with an acceptable real-time occurrences. Since now modelling deformation in virtual anatomy has been realized by using surface models (Cover et al., 1993), but more recently the volumetric mass-spring models (Kuhn, et al., 1996), the Finite Element models (Bro-Nielsen & Cotin, 1996), and the Fast Finite Element models (Bro-Nielsen, 1996), demonstrate a 3D volumetric deformable patient organs in a more than acceptable real-time modelling.

The other key element is the possibility for a doctor to have a force feedback to his/her movements/action. In fact to correctly act, it can be fundamental to have in his/her hands a force feedback that mimics, for instance, how tissue and blood vessels feel and behave or heart beats in real life. A dissertation on methods and fundamental considerations for adding force feedback to a surgery simulator has been reported elsewhere, where an example of the virtual endoscopic surgery trainer "VS-One", developed at the Forschungszentrum Karlsruhe, is treated (Maass et al., 2003).

3.2 Virtual Reality in rehabilitation

Virtual Reality in rehabilitation treatments is becoming more and more applied. The new VR technologies can potentiality improve the dynamic posturography for a better understanding of standing balance in clinical settings, may improve gait for people with amputations, can visualize how ultrasound and laser treatments may benefit wound healing, and so on. Within all the possibilities, we will focus our discussion on some of the most important rehabilitation treatments, especially respect the cognitive/neurological and postural training/motor rehabilitation.

Cognitive and Neurological Rehabilitation

Only in the U.S., traumatic brain injuries (TBI) resulting from car crashes, falls, gunshot wounds, and sports injuries is 500,000 to 1.9M persons (Rizzo et al., 1998), and accounts around 200,000 hospitalized cases per year. Over 1.7M persons suffer a mild TBI that results in a temporary disability (Torner et al., 1999), while 100,000 people suffer varying degrees of permanent disability from TBI. So, it becomes obvious the importance of the following rehabilitation which can greatly contribute to reduce impairment, disability and handicap (Rose, 1996). Since it has been shown that the activity of mental stimulation induced by virtual reality can change the brain metabolic activity, it follows that exercising in a virtual environment offers the potential for significant gains in cognitive function (Grealy et al., 1999) greatly improve the rehabilitation process.

In order to achieve restoration of cognitive functions, a subject must repetitively perform appropriate retraining exercises. In this view, VR can help people with brain injuries to regain the ability to do simple activities by retraining damaged brain areas or enabling patients to learn to use new areas. VR can also prepare people who have lost some sensory functions for navigation in an unfamiliar place by letting them first experience a virtual (e.g. audio and haptic) layout of that setting. The fully advantages of VR technology for rehabilitation of the activities of daily living has been reported (Lee et al., 2003). Among the advantages of adopting the VR technique, is the fact that it allows to easily vary training parameters and to explore especially effective scenes that may be difficult or unsafe to construct in the real world.

The VR can be not necessary intended as a substitute of standard techniques useful for rehabilitation abilities after brain damage, but novel and standard methods often strictly coexist together being applied in a parallel or series way (Koenig, 2009). In addiction to VR, also mixed reality demonstrates its efficacy for the assessment of post-traumatic stress disorder with (or without) TBI (Fidopiastis et al., 2009).

Postural training and motor rehabilitation

Visual, vestibular, and proprioceptive sensory information play a key role in postural and motor effectiveness, and the integration of multisensory information from the environment is the basis for the control of body spatial orientation and movement (Cinelli & Patla, 2008). On the other end, the adoption of postural measurements and VR can allow new paradigms aimed at altering the multisensory information contribution thus opening up many new research possibilities. These arguments imply that the tools offered by VR can be dangerous or can produce benefits in postural training and motor rehabilitation (Menegoni, 2009), so particular attention must be paid and *ad-hoc* protocols must be carefully developed (Boechler et al., 2009; Trotti et al., 2009).

Several requirements and long time repetitive practices are necessary for effective postural training and motor rehabilitation intervention. But the average situation for hospitalized stroke patients is that they receive half an hour session daily by a therapist, so the healing time is often too long. The use of the VR technology can drastically reduce this problem by allowing patients to perform long time and high frequency rehabilitation exercises using a computer, even simply at home. Last frontier in this field is the Haptic Motor Rehabilitation since it offers force and tactile feedback which can be crucial for many upper and lower extremity rehabilitation (Kayyali et al., 2007).

A recent study demonstrates how virtual environments and VR can offer, if correctly adopted, a valid tool in motor rehabilitation with respect those achieved in real-world applications (Sveistrup, 2004).

So, many efforts have been paid to develop valid systems based on VR. As an example, the *NeuroVR 1.5* is a cost-free virtual reality platform based on open-source components, allowing professionals to easily modify a virtual world, to best suit the needs of the clinical setting (Algeri et al., 2009).

By our side, we developed a complete VR system specific for the upper limb motor rehabilitation, which is now being tested on hand injured patients at the Hospital structure of the ASL Viterbo (Italy), Hand Surgery Dept., thanks to Dr. Antonio Castagnaro and Dr. Anna De Leo (Castagnaro et al., 2010). The overall system consists of a wearable sensorized device (the data glove), an electronic circuitry for conditioning and A/D converting electrical signals, a wireless data transmission board based on ZigBee protocol, a database on SQL platform useful for data storage for further data utilization, a virtualization software capable to in-line and off-line reproduce the recorded movements by avatars (see a schematic representation in Figs. 20 and 21).

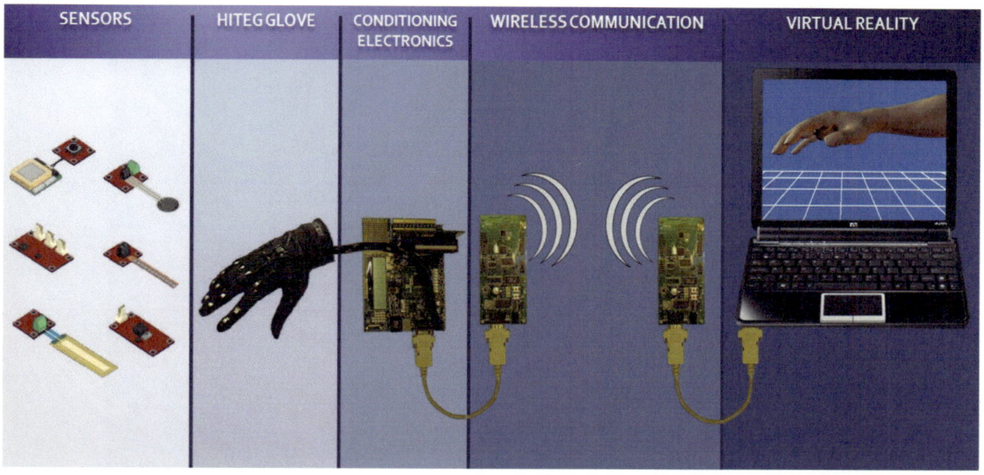

Fig. 20. A schematization of the overall system made of sensors, Hiteg glove, electronic for conditioning the signals, wireless communication board based on ZigBee protocol, and Virtual Reality reproduction

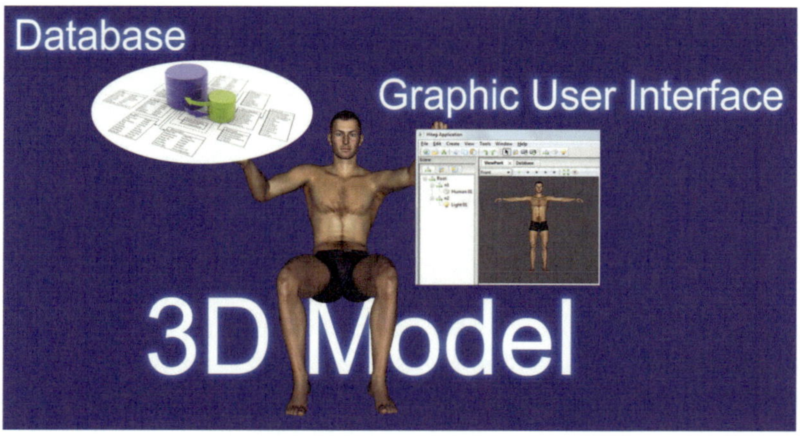

Fig. 21. A schematization of the VR system we adopted for motor rehabilitation. It is made of a 3D model, a database where recorded user movements are stored and a Graphic User Interface (GUI).

During the post-processing data phase, thanks to the model, it is possible to replay all the fingers and hand movements in slow / rapid / frame-by-frame motion (see Fig. 22) and to isolate even just one finger at a time, removing the others from the view, in order to focus the operator's attention only on some important details.
The overall VR system is believed to become, in a near future, fully integrated to the surgery follow-up.

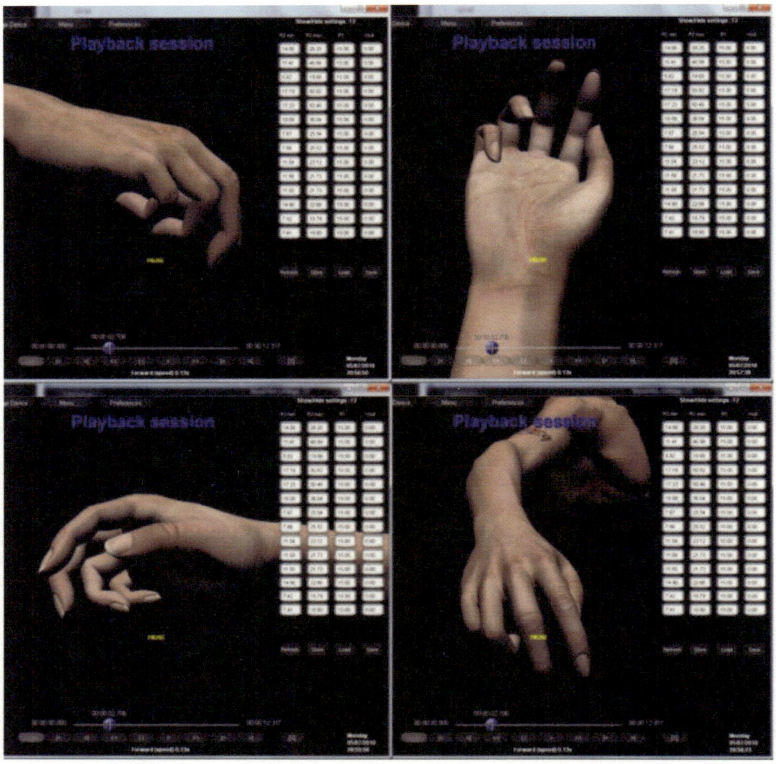

Fig. 22. A reproduction session: software allows user to see an acquisition session off-line, and by rotating 3D model in any direction, it is possible to analyze reproduction from different viewpoints.

3.3 Brain Computer Interface

Many people in the world are affected by severe neuromuscular impairments, which make them lose the control on their muscular voluntary activities thus isolating them from the environment. Brain Computer Interface (BCI) systems try to facilitate for these people the communication of their intents by translating some electrophysiological signals into commands towards external peripherals without making use of the classical pathways of nerves and muscles (Wolpaw et al. 2002). Basically BCI is adopted to assist and support impaired people. BCIs bypass the user's peripheral nervous system (nerves) and his/her muscles, establishing a direct connection between the central nervous system (brain) and the environment the user operates in. In this interaction paradigms, it is not needed that the user contracts even a single muscle (e.g. to press a button, to vocalize his/her intent, or to direct his/her gaze), because the interface is able to recognize specific commands by recognising his/her "brain states" (Cincotti et al., 2009).

There are different adopted methods to interface brain with computer, and these methods can be invasive (electrodes implanted directly into the gray matter of the brain, subdural Electro Cortico Graphy "ECoG", Stereotactic Electro Encephalo Graphy "SEEG",..) or non invasive (Electro Encephalo Graphy "EEG", Magnetic Resonance Image "MRI", Magneto Encephalo Graphy "MEG", functional Magnetic Resonance Imaging "fMRI" systems, ..).
One of the most fruitful areas of BCI research is the development of devices that can be controlled by thoughts, so giving to the severely disabled people the possibility to act independently.
Obviously the research look forward in adopting the less possible invasive interfacing technique, so particular attention is being paid to BCI systems essentially based on EEG recording (Costantini et al., 2009). But since the performance of BCI strictly depends on the ability of users to control and modulate their own EEG signals, it is of fundamental importance to develop a system capable to increase such a control. In this view studies emphasize how it is possible to improve the EEG control via feedback presentation (Bianchi et al., 2008). To get this objective, VR technology is becoming a powerful tool by its graphical possibilities to improve BCI-feedback presentation, with the capability of creating immersive and motivating environments (Angevin, 2009).
Let's consider an user with upper limb immobility, or affected by a stroke with consequently motor decreasing. In this case, it can be useful to reproduce the hands of the user in a virtual environment and to stimulate his/her motor imagery with a visual stimulus (like a spotlight on a specific arm). The user, connected to a BCI system, holds his/her hands on a real desk; his/her arms are hidden by a towel or a panel, on which a projector displays virtual hands reproduced as avatars. It is important that the 3D model is much similar as possible to the user real counterpart, in order to increase the realism and the positive response. For the same reason, it is very important that the perspective of the virtual model corresponds to the user's point of view. During a trial, the software creates some visual stimuli and records the EEG activity of the user. If the BCI system recognises the user's brain state, by means of classifiers (Saggio et al., 2010), then the avatars are animated so to reproduce the thought movement. A schematization of this feedback path is in Fig. 23, where the system provides as an output the movements of a robotic arm. At present, the overall system works thanks to a team we collaborate with, at the *Santa Lucia IRCSS* foundation in Rome, Italy.

4. Conclusion

Nowadays the knowledge and understanding of the reality pass through the virtual world. This is practically true for all the human disciplines, but it is particularly true in e-health applications, for healing treatment, therapy, rehabilitation, surgery and support for impaired people. Since health is a widespread top priority, and will remain so in the context of an ageing society, it appears evident how every possible contribute to the increase of medical solutions and the decrease of time and cost of healing, are welcome. From this point of view VR is a really great opportunity within this challenge.
This chapter dealed with the techniques usefully adopted to convert the real into virtual and the advantages this passage offers having, in some way, assisted and/or enriched the real world. We treated also of our and our collaborators efforts and results in designing, developing and applying 3D visualization techniques (stereoscopy and holography), human

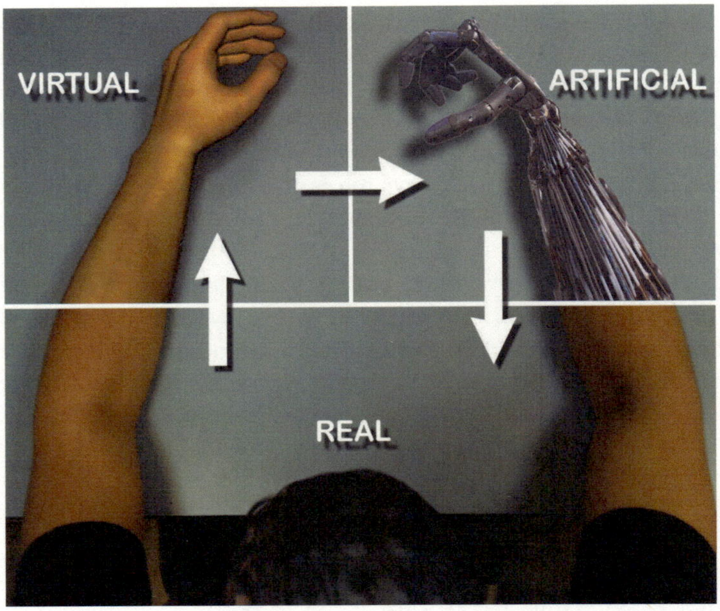

Fig. 23. The user wear a 61 electrodes cap by which his/her mental status is recorded. When the BCI system recognizes a "closing hand" gesture, the virtual hand reproduces the gesture. The artificial limb can be driven as well.

postures measurements (Hiteg glove), avatar representation, human machine interaction (virtual mouse and keyboard), virtual interactions (reconstructions of ancient monuments), motor rehabilitation (for hand injured patients), communication for neuromuscular impaired people (BCI systems).

Special attention was paid to the basic processes necessary for reproducing reality in a virtual environment and the methodology for the reality-virtuality interactions. Some e-health applications have been detailed, especially for surgery simulations and assisted rehabilitation processes.

We explained how the VR markets can be considered on the application areas of: rehabilitation and therapy (cognitive/neurological, postural/motor, pain distraction,..), surgery (simulations, pre-operative planning, assisted surgery), education and training (for novice surgeons, to practice procedures, to certify experienced surgeons,..), diagnostic tool also by means of visualization of medical data (2D, 3D modelling).

In conclusion we can state that, if correctly utilized, Virtual Reality can be a really valid support for e-health applications, especially because it can reduce time and cost for effective therapy/treatment for health-focused disciplines, and provide doctors an opportunity to perform tasks in a risk-free environment. In addiction patient acceptance can be quite high since the VR implementation can have a low invasive impact.

5. References

Algeri D., Carelli L., Gaggioli A., Riva G. (2009). A Free Tool for Motor Rehabilitation: NeuroVR 1.5 with CamSpace. *Annual Review of CyberTeraphy and Telemedicine*, Brenda K. Wiederhold, Giuseppe Riva (Ed.), vol. 7, 2009, ISSN: 15548716, 99-101

Angevin, R. R. (2009). *Annual Review of CyberTeraphy and Telemedicine,* Brenda K. Wiederhold, Giuseppe Riva (Ed.), vol. 7, 2009, ISSN: 15548716, 184-188

Azuma, Ronald T. (1997). A Survey of Augmented Reality, *Teleoperators and Virtual Environments 6,* 1997, 355-385, Malibu

Bianchi L., Pronestì D., Abbafati M., Quitadamo L. R., Marciani M. G., Saggio G. (2008). A New Visual Feed-Back Modality for the Reduction of Artifacts in Mu-Rhythm Based Brain-Computer Interfaces. *30th Annual International Conference of the IEEE Engineering in Medicine and Biology Society, EMBC,* August 20-24, 2008, Vancouver, Canada

Boechler P., Krol A., Raso J. Blois T. (2009). Virtual Reality Interventions for Rehabilitation: Considerations for Developing Protocols. *Annual Review of CyberTeraphy and Telemedicine,* Brenda K. Wiederhold, Giuseppe Riva (Ed.), vol. 7, 2009, ISSN: 15548716, 102-104

Bro-Nielsen M. (1996). Surgery Simulation Using fast Finite Elements. *Proceedings of the 4th International Conference on Visualization in Biomedical Computing,* 1996, 529 - 534

Bro-Nielsen M., Cotin S. (1996). Real-time volumetric deformable models for surgery simulation using finite elements and condensation. *Computer Graphics Forum* (Eurographics'96), vol. 15, no. 3, 1996, 57-66

Castagnaro A., De Leo A., Inciocchi S., Saggio G., Tarantino U. (2010). Nuova biotecnologia: il guanto sensorizzato per misurare la cinesi della mano. *48° Congresso Nazionale Società Italiana Chirurgia della Mano SICM 2010, "Stato dell'arte nella chirurgia articolare del gomito, polso e mano: protesi e tecniche alternative",* 29 Sept - 2 Oct, Savona, Italy, 2010

Chaudhry A., Suttont C., Wood J., Stonet R., McCloy R. (1999). Learning rate for laparoscopic surgical skills on MIST VR, a virtual reality simulator: quality of human-computer interface. *Ann R Coll Surg Engl.,* vol.81, 1999, 281-286

Cincotti F., Quitadamo L. R., Aloise F., Bianchi L., Babiloni F., Mattia D. (2009). Interacting with the Environment through Non-invasive Brain-Computer Interfaces. In *Universal Access in Human-Computer Interaction. Intelligent and Ubiquitous Interaction Environments,* Springer Berlin / Heidelberg (Ed.), Vol. 5615, 2009, 483-492

Cinelli M. E., Patla A. E. (2008). Task-specific modulations of locomotor action parameters based on on-line visual information during collision avoidance with moving objects. *Human Movement Science,* vol. 27, 2008, 513-31.

Costantini G., Casali D., Carota M., Saggio G., Bianchi L., Abbafati M., Quitadamo L. R. (2009). SVM Classification of EEG Signals for Brain Computer Interface. *WIRN'09; 19th Italian Workshop on Neural Networks;* May 28-30, 2009, Salerno, Italy

Costantini G., Todisco M., Saggio G. (2010). A Data Glove to Control a Real Time Granular Sound Synthesis Process. *The International Multi-Conference on Complexity, Informatics and Cybernetics: IMCIC 2010,* April 6th - 9th, 2010, Orlando, Florida USA

Cover S. A., Ezquerra N. F., O'Brien J. F., Rowe R., Gadacz T., Palm E. (1993). Interactively deformable models for surgery simulation. *IEEE Computer Graphics & Applications,* Nov. 1993, 68-75

Dawson S. (2006). Procedural Simulation: A Primer, *Radiology,* Vol. 241, Number 1 October 2006, 17-25

Draicchio F., Silvetti A., Amici F., Iavicoli S., Ranavolo A., Muscillo R., Schmid M., D'Alessio T., Sandrini G., Bartolo M., Orengo G., Saggio G., Conte C. (2010). Global Biomechanical Evaluation during Work and Daily-Life Activities. *BIODEVICES - International Conference on Biomedical Electronics and Devices: part of BIOSTEC The 3rd International Joint Conference on Biomedical Engineering Systems and Technologies,* Valencia, Spain, 20-23 January 2010, 108-112

Fidopiastis C., Hughes C. E., Smith E.. (2009). *Annual Review of CyberTeraphy and Telemedicine,* Brenda K. Wiederhold, Giuseppe Riva (Ed.), vol. 7, 2009, ISSN: 15548716, 216-220

Geisen, S. (2005). Term paper - Augmented Reality in surgery, *Seminar Medical Images,* Universität Paderborn, Fakultät für Elektrotechnik/ Informatik / Mathematik

Grealy M., Johnson D., Rushton S. (1999). Improving cognitive function after brain injury: The use of exercise and virtual reality. *Archives of Physical Medicine and Rehabilitation,* Vol. 80, Issue 6, 1999, 661-667

Haluck R. S., Gallagher A. G., Satava R. M., Webster R., Bass T. L., Miller C. A. (2002). Reliability and validity of Endotower, a virtual reality trainer for angled endoscope navigation, *Stud Health Technol Inform.,* vol.85, 2002, 179-84

Ho I. K. (2006). Laparoscopic Surgery. *The American College of Gastroenterology,* January 2006

Jiménez-Murcia S., Fernández-Aranda F., Kalapanidas E., Konstantas D., Ganchev T., Kocsis O., Lam T., Santamaría J. J., Raguin T., Breiteneder C., Kaufmann H., Davarakis C. (2009). *Annual Review of CyberTeraphy and Telemedicine,* Brenda K. Wiederhold, Giuseppe Riva (Ed.), vol. 7, 2009, ISSN: 15548716, 163-166

Kayyali R., Shirmohammadi S., El Saddik A., Lemaire E. (2007). Daily-Life Exercises for Haptic Motor Rehabilitation. *HAVE 2007 - IEEE International Workshop on Haptic Audio Visual Environments and their Applications,* Ottawa - Canada, 12-14 October 2007, 118-123

Koenig S. T., Crucian G. P., Dalrymple-Alford J. C., Dünser A. (2009). *Annual Review of CyberTeraphy and Telemedicine,* Brenda K. Wiederhold, Giuseppe Riva (Ed.), vol. 7, 2009, ISSN: 15548716, 105-107

Kuhn Ch., Kuhnapfel U., Krumm H-G., Neisius B. (1996). A virtual reality based training system for minimally invasive surgery. *Proceedings of Computer Assisted Radiology (CAR'96),* 1996, 764-769

Lee J. H., Ku J., Cho W., Hahn W. Y., Kim In Y., Lee S.-M., Kang Y., Kim D. Y., Yu T., Wiederhold B. K., Wiederhold M. D., Kim Sun I. (2003). Virtual Reality System for the Assessment and Rehabilitation of the Activities of Daily Living. *Cyberpsychology & Behavior,* Vol. 6, No. 4, 2003, 383-388

Maass H., Chantier B. B. A. , Çakmak H. K, Kühnapfel U. G. (2003). How to Add Force Feedback to a Surgery Simulator. *Surgery Simulation and Soft Tissue Modeling.* Vol. 2673, 2003, ISBN 978-3-540-40439-2

Marescaux J., Clement J-M., Tassetti V., Koehl C., Cotin S., Russier Y., Mutter D., Delingette H., Ayache N. (1998). Virtual Reality Applied to Hepatic Surgery Simulation: The Next Revolution. *Annals of Surgery,* Vol. 228, No. 5, 1998, 627-634

Menegoni F., Albania G., Bigonia M., Priano L., Trotti C, Galli M., Mauro A. (2009). Walking in an Immersive Virtual Reality. *Annual Review of CyberTeraphy and Telemedicine*, Brenda K. Wiederhold, Giuseppe Riva (Ed.), vol. 7, 2009, ISSN: 15548716, 72-76

Rizzo, A., Buckwalter, J. G., Neumann, U. (1998). Basic issues in the application of virtual reality for the assessment and rehabilitation of cognitive impairments and functional disability. *CyberPsychology & Behavior*, vol. 1, 1998, 59–78

Rose F. D.. (1996). Virtual reality in rehabilitation following traumatic brain injury. *Proc. 1st Euro. Conf. Disability, Virtual Reality & Assoc. Tech.*, Maidenhead, UK, 1996, 5-12

Saggio G., Latessa G., De Santis F., Bianchi L., Quitadamo L. R., Marciani M. G., Giannini F. (2009). Virtual reality implementation as a useful software tool for e-health applications, *1th IEEE International WoWMoM Workshop on Interdisciplinary Research on E-Health Services and Systems*, IREHSS 2009, Kos, Greece

Saggio G., Cavallo P., Quitadamo L. R., Marciani M. G., Bianchi L., Costantini G., Susi G. (2010). Comparison of Different Classifiers on a reduced set of features for Mental Tasks-Based Brain-Computer Interface. *BIOSIGNALS - International Conference on Bio-inspired Systems and Signal: part of BIOSTEC The 3rd International Joint Conference on Biomedical Engineering Systems and Technologies*, Valencia, Spain, 20-23 January 2010, 174-179

Schijven M., Jakimowicz J. (2003). Virtual reality surgical laparoscopic simulators. *Surgical Endoscopy* (2003) 17: 1943–1950

Shahrbanian S., Ma X., Korner-Bitensky N., Simmonds M. J. (2009). Scientific Evidence for the Effectiveness of Virtual Reality for Pain Reduction in Adults with Acute or Chronic Pain. *Annual Review of CyberTeraphy and Telemedicine*, Brenda K. Wiederhold, Giuseppe Riva (Ed.), vol. 7, 2009, ISSN: 15548716, 40-43

Shuhaiber, Jeffrey H. (2004). Review article - Augmented Reality in Surgery. *Archives of Surgery*, Vol. 139, Feb 2004, pp. 170-174

Soler L., Nicolau S., Hostettler A., Fasquel J-B., Agnus V., Charnoz A., Moreau J., Dallemagne B., Mutter D., Marescaux J. (2010). Virtual Reality and Augmented Reality applied to Endoscopic and notes procedures. *World Congress on Medical Physics and Biomedical Engineering*, 362-365, 2010, Springer Berlin Heidelberg, 978-3-642-03905-8, Munich, Germany

Sveistrup H. (2004). Motor rehabilitation using virtual reality. *Journal of NeuroEngineering and Rehabilitation*, 2004, 1-10

Torner J. C., Choi S., Barnes T. Y. (1999). Epidemiology of Head Injuries. *Traumatic brain injury*, Donald W. Marion (Ed.), 990-991, E. Thieme, 3-13-783402-3, New York

Trotti C., Menegoni F., Baudo S., Bigoni M., Galli M., Mauro A., (2009). Virtual Reality for the Upper Limb Motor Training in Stroke: A Case Report. *Annual Review of CyberTeraphy and Telemedicine*, Brenda K. Wiederhold, Giuseppe Riva (Ed.), vol. 7, 2009, ISSN: 15548716, 257-260

Van Herzeele I., Aggarwal R. (2008). Virtual Reality Simulation in the Endovascular Field. *Interventional Cardiology*, Touch Briefings 2008, pp. 41-45

Wang, Yifei. Human movement tracking using a wearable wireless sensor network. Master Thesis. Iowa State University, 2005. Ames, Iowa

Wolpaw J. R., Birbaumer N., McFarland D. J., Pfurtscheller G., Vaughan T. M. (2002). Brain–computer interfaces for communication and control. *Clinical Neurophysiology*, 113(6), 2002, 767–791

Zányi E., Selmanovic E., Broome M., Czanner S., Birchwood M., Chalmers A., Singh S. (2009). *Annual Review of CyberTeraphy and Telemedicine*, Brenda K. Wiederhold, Giuseppe Riva (Ed.), vol. 7, 2009, ISSN: 15548716, 138-140

13

Simulation of Subject Specific Bone Remodeling and Virtual Reality Visualization

Ajay Sonar, Laurel Kuxhaus and James Carroll
Clarkson University
U.S.A.

1. Introduction

Bone is a dynamic tissue. The dynamic nature is the result of the remodeling process, in which the skeleton is renewed continuously. The external mechanical loading affects the remodeling process which in turn affects the internal structure. German anatomist Julius Wolff first noticed this phenomenon in 1892 (Wolff, 1986). The purpose of remodeling is to prevent the accumulation of damage, adapt the internal architecture to the external loads and maintain homeostasis (Van Der Linden et al., 2001; Pivonka et al., 2008; Lemaire et al., 2004).
Compressive fractures caused by osteoporosis are common in the lower vertebrae is a frequent region for compressive fracture due to osteoporosis (Melton et al.,1989; Melton et al.,1999; Scane,1994). Figure 1 shows the overall structure of a lumbar vertebrae. The outer dense bone is called cortical bone and the inner porous bone is called cancellous bone. To understand the remodeling process it is important to understand the role of the cells involved in the process. Osteoblasts are the cells responsible for the bone formation. They have a single eccentric nucleus. Osteoclasts are multi-nucleated cells responsible for bone resorption. Together they are called the Basic Multicellular Unit (BMU). During bone formation some of the osteoblasts get trapped in the matrix that they secrete and become Osteocytes. Another type of cells are lining cells which cover the entire bone surface. These are quiescent osteoblasts. The osteocytes are connected to each other (Figure 2) and to the lining cells through narrow channels called the Canaliculi (Parfitt, 1984).
Remodeling involves the coordinated actions of osteoclasts, osteoblasts, osteocytes and bone lining cells. The remodeling process involves removal of packets of bone from the surface followed by formation of new bone within the cavity created. This is a cyclic process involving five stages - quiescence, activation, resorption, reversal, formation and back to quiescence. Remodeling happens in adult animals. In younger animals in which the bone is still growing the process is called modeling. The fundamental difference between the two processes is that the remodeling is a cyclic process of erosion and formation on the bone surface, whereas in modeling, either bone resorption or formation occur continuously for a long period of time without interruption (Parfitt, 1984). In adults, bone is continuously remodeled at discrete locations. The balance between bone resorption and formation determines the bone mineral content.
Osteoclast activity determines the extent of the depth of resorption and the osteoblast activity controls the amount of bone formation. The osteocytes, with their interconnected cellular network, play an important role in communication and transportation between cells within the bone matrix. When there is a balance between the bone formation and bone resorption

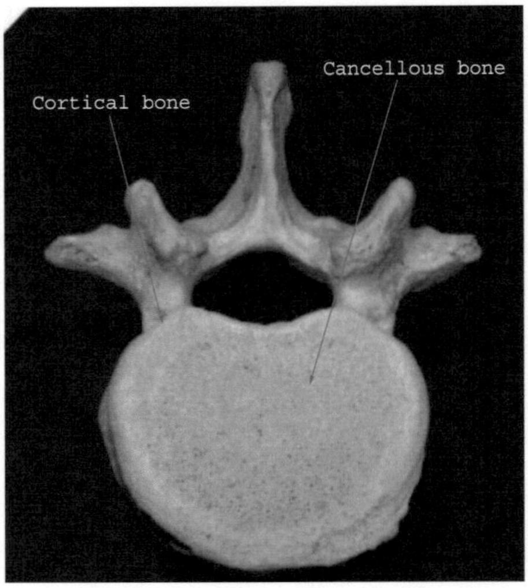

Fig. 1. Transverse view of a lumbar vertebrae (http://biology.clc.uc.edu/Fankhauser/)

there is no bone loss. In younger animals the rate of bone formation is more than bone resorption, hence the bone mass keeps increasing. In adults this process reaches a steady state therefore there is no significant change in the bone mass but the geometry keeps changing. In older animals the rate of bone resorption is more than bone formation which results in bone loss. The process of remodeling is illustrated in Figure 3 (Parfitt, 1984).
The osetocytes and the canalicular network play an important role in the modeling and remodeling process. Osteocytes act as load sensors. Frost proposed that a minimum effective strain (MES) is required to trigger remodeling (Frost, 1983). According to the supporting experiments the range of MES was determined to be 0.0008-0.002 unit bone surface strain. Strains below MES do not evoke modeling and strains above do. Since the maximum deformations in bone tissue are relatively small, another theory suggest that bone cells respond to stress generated flow of interstitial fluid through the canalicular network, which transmit this information to other osteocytes and to the lining cells (Weinbaum et

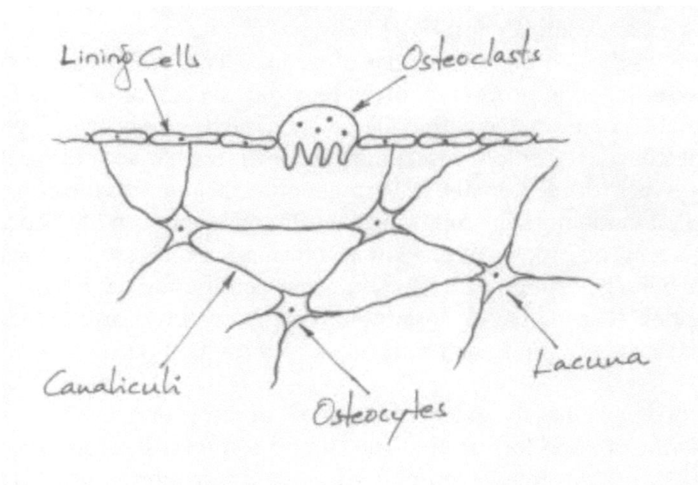

Fig. 2. Bone cells

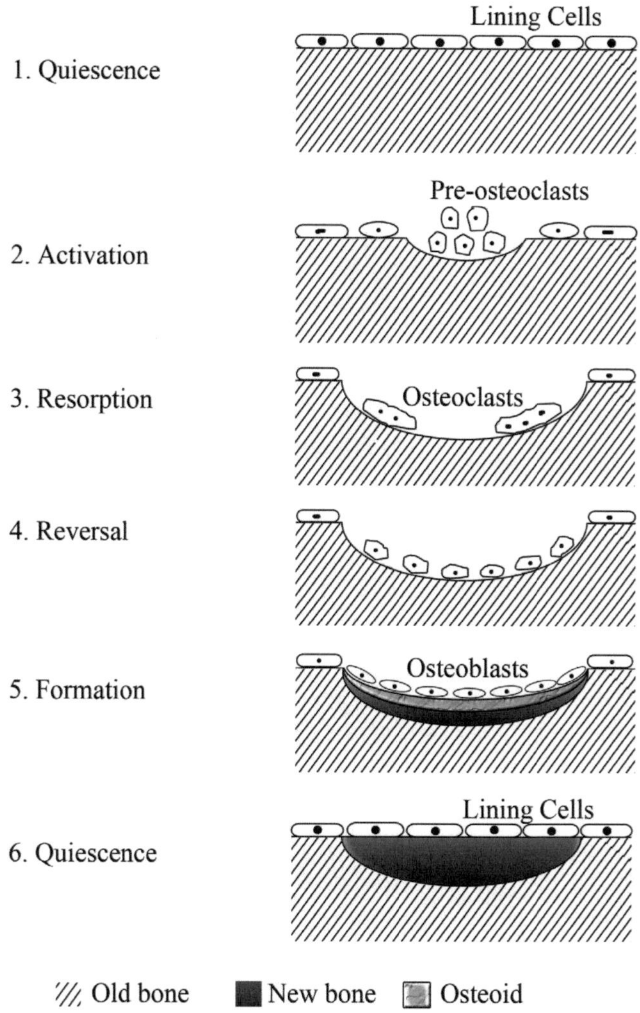

Fig. 3. Remodeling cycle in adult bone (Parfitt, 1984)

al.,1994; Turner et al.,1995). The response to overuse or disuse is formation or resorption respectively. When the osteocytes sense a mechanical stimulation which is more than the normal physiological use, they send signals to the lining cells and more osteoblasts cells are recruited. These osteoblast form new bone on the surface in that area which restores the normal level of use. Disuse reduces the stress and also transportation of nutrients. This will cause the death of osteocyte, which is a signal to recruit new osteoclasts (Bronckers et al., 1996). This process is illustrated in Figure 4(a) (Burger & Klein-Nulend, 1999).
Remodeling also occurs due to fatigue damage. Fatigue damage occur due to repetitive loading in the normal physiological range. When accumulated over time they result in microcracks. These micro cracks run through the mineralized matrix, which may disrupt the canalicular network and the osteocytes. This creates a situation similar to disuse in which the communication between the osteocytes and the bone lining cells is severed, resulting

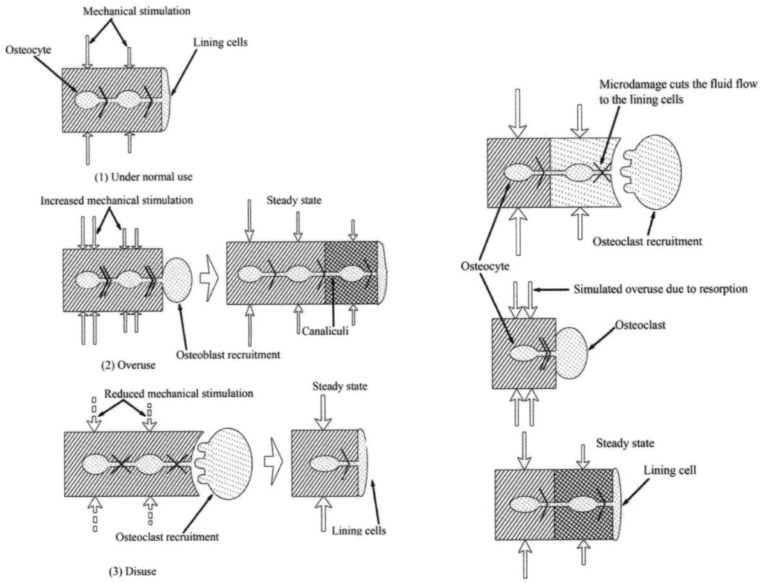

(a) (b)

Fig. 4. (a)Schematic representation of bone modeling and (b) Schematic representation of bone remodeling due to microdamage (Burger & Klein-Nulend, 1999)

in osteocyte recruitment. Osteoclast resorb the damaged bone until the undamaged bone is reached. The local loss of bone results in local overuse of the remaining bone. The resulting increased fluid flow through the canalicular network triggers the recruitment of osteoblasts. The osteoblasts build the bone matrix until a steady state is reached. This is illustrated in Figure 4(b).

The trajectorial hypothesis put forward by Wolff (Wolff, 1986) suggests that the architecture of the bone is transformed to align the trabeculae with the principal stress orientation. Remodeling, also called as maintenance, is an adaptive process which is regulated by the bone cells influenced by the local state of stress. The proposed hypothesis in this study is as follows: by appropriately simulating the external loading conditions on the bone a more realistic change in the geometry of trabecular structure can be estimated.

2. Literature review and present work

The bone is continuously being remodeled. This occurs at multiple spatially and temporally discrete sites. It happens in both the trabecular bone and the cortical bone. This prevents the accumulation of damage (Burr, 1993), helps in adapting the architecture to external load and provides a way for the body to alter the balance of the essential minerals by accessing the stores of calcium and phosphate (Burr, 2002). Bone goes through a continuous process of modeling in younger animals. It reaches a peak mass at approximately 30 years of age and decreases gradually after that (Van Der Linden et al., 2001). This decrease in mass is caused by the formation deficit, the osteoblast formation is less relative to osteoclast resorption. The remodeling process as described by Parfitt (Parfitt, 1984) is illustrated in Figure 3. Normally 80% of the bone surface is quiescent with respect to remodeling. Activation requires recruitment of osteoclasts, a means for them to gain access to the bone and a mechanism to attach to the bone surface. Activation is a function of age, sex and metabolic state. It occurs partly at random and partly in response to the biomechanical requirement. After coming in contact with the bone, the osteoclasts begin to resorb the bone. It is referred to as Howship's lacuna in trabecular bone and as cutting cone in cortial bone. The resorption cavity has a charecteristic shape and dimension. The resorption cavity grows at a rate of 5-10μm/day perpendicular to the surface and 20-40μm/day parallel to the surface. After the resorption ends, it enters a reversal phase. The rough surface of the resorption cavity is smoothed and thin layer of highly mineralized matrix is laid down, preparing the surface for bone formation. Once the surface is ready, osteoblast cells are recruited. This phase has two parts, matrix synthesis and mineralization. Mineralization follows matrix synthesis. The newly laid unmineralized bone matrix is called osteoid. This seperates the osteoblasts and the newly mineralized bone. Synthesis terminates after the cavity is filled. Mineralization continues slowly until the osteoid seam disappears. The osteoblasts that remain on the surface transform in to lining cells.

Bone adapts its structure much more readily during growth than after skeletal maturation because it is intrinsically responsive to strain (Frost, 1982). During modeling there is no need for activation of the surface since it is continuously active from earliest embryonic stage until growth ceases. Whereas in the adult bone, for the adaptive change to occur, the quiescent surface needs activation.

Unlike cortical bone which is dense, trabecular bone is porous and extremely anisotropic. It consists of numerous interconnected struts mostly with thick vertical struts and thinner horizontal struts. There are two distinct types of struts present in the structure, plates and rods. As the name suggest the rods are more cylindrical and long whereas the plates are more flat. In a study on the age related change by Mosekilde (Mosekilde, 1988; 1989), on individuals between the age of 15 to 87, a significant thinning and disappearance of the horizontal supporting struts and total removal of some of the vertical struts were observed. A significant increase in both the horizontal and vertical trabecular distance was also shown. A pronounced loss of bone strength was shown in females around the age of 40-50 (Mosekilde, 1989).

Many theoretical and computational models have been proposed to investigate and simulate the dynamic behavior of the bone (Van Der Linden et al.,2001; Lemaire et al.,2004; Thomsen et al.,1994; Langton et al.,1998). With high resolution imaging methodologies such as μCT becoming more accessible, the study of trabecular remodeling began to take in to account the influence of cellular activity in 2 and 3 dimensions (Liu et al., 2008; Van Der Linden et al., 2001; Müller & Hayes, 1997). Simulation involving effect of metabolic bone formation deficit and the micro structural bone formation deficit are also developed (Van Der Linden et al., 2001; Linden et al., 2003). Effect of trabecular plate thickness and the trabecular plate density on the age related changes showed that the plate density is more significant predictor of bone loss than a decrease in the plate thickness (Parfitt et al., 1983).

Different mathematical control models of mechanical bone mass regulation have been proposed (Cowin & Hegedus,1976; Mullender & Huiskes,1995; Huiskes et al.,1987). These models assumed a continuous feedback loop between the maintenance of bone mass and local strain values in the tissue. This enabled mathematical predictions of local bone regulation based on external loads. These models differ in the kind of mechanical signal used to control the feedback loop. Finite element methods are used to link the external loads to local mechanical signal. These models were validated to produce accurate prediction of long term formation and resorption (Van Rietbergen et al., 1993; Weinbaum et al., 1994). The results of these models showed that the orientation of the trabeculae is directly related to the external principal stress orientation, and when the orientation of the principal stress is rotated the trabecular architecture transformed to realign to the new orientation.

Apart from the visual assessment of the structural changes, different structural parameters are used to characterize these changes (Parfitt et al., 1987; Müller & Rüegsegger, 1996; Müller & Hayes, 1997; Liu et al., 2008). In the past, these parameters were studied by the examination of the two dimensional crossections of cancellous bone biopsies. The three dimensional morphometric parameters are then derived from two dimensional images using stereological methods (Parfitt et al., 1987). The bone volume fraction,which is a ratio of bone volume to the total volume of the structure (BV/TV), and the surface density, which is the ratio of the bone surface area to the bone volume (BS/BV), can be obtained directly from the two dimensional images, whereas trabecular thickness (Tb.Th), trabecular separation (Tb.Sp) and the trabecular number (Tb.N) are derived indirectly assuming a fixed structural model. Typically an ideal plate or rod model is assumed. The problem with this method is that, it will lead to errors in the indirectly derived parameters if the structure deviates from the assumed model. It has been shown that the error due to deviation could be up to 52% depending on the method used (Simmons & Hipp, 1997). Cancellous bone structure continuously changes is structural type. Since the stereological method assumes a certain structural model, the initial parameters calculated on a trabecular bone undergoing remodeling cannot be compared with the subsequent calculated parameters because the remodeling changes the type of the structure from plate-like to rod-like (Hildebrand & Ruegsegger, 1997). Recent advances in μCT have made it possible to acquire these parameters directly from 3D μCT image (Hildebrand et al., 1999) without any underlying model assumptions. The values obtained by this method were shown to correspond well with the stereological method (Thomsen et al., 2005). The trabecular thickness is determined by filling maximal spheres into the structure, then the average thickness of all points in the bone is calculated to give Tb.Th (Hildebrand & Ruegsegger, 1997). The Tb.Sp is calculated in the same way but the points representing the non bone region or the marrow region are used to fill the maximal spheres (Hildebrand et al., 1999). The Tb.N is taken as the inverse of the mean distance between the midaxis of the trabecular structure. The calculated midaxes of the cancellous structure can also be used to decompose the bone in to rods and plates (Stauber & Müller, 2006; Ju et al., 2007). Further, the orientation of the rods can also be calculated. By decomposing the cancellous bone in to rods and plates, the trabecular thickness can be calculated for the rods and plates seperately. A comparison between the indirect calculated values assuming fixed model structure and the model independent direct calculation is made in (Hildebrand et al., 1999).

The idea proposed in this research is the use of the realistic mechanical loading data to run a remodelling algorithm to predict the structure of trabecular bone after real-world loading conditions are applied. This can be achieved by gathering the motion capture data of an individual performing different activities (eg., walking, running, lifting weights etc.). These activities can be grouped into different categories like easy, medium or hard based on their intensity. This data can be collected with any motion capture system. This data can be used in virtual human modeling and musculoskeletal simulation software to calculate forces and displacements at various joint locations or at specified marker locations. This force data is then used in the remodeling algorithm to accurately predict the modified trabecular structure. This data could be useful to predict and change the lifestyle/physical habits to avoid severe chronic damage/injury. The schematic of the proposed method is shown in the Figure 5.

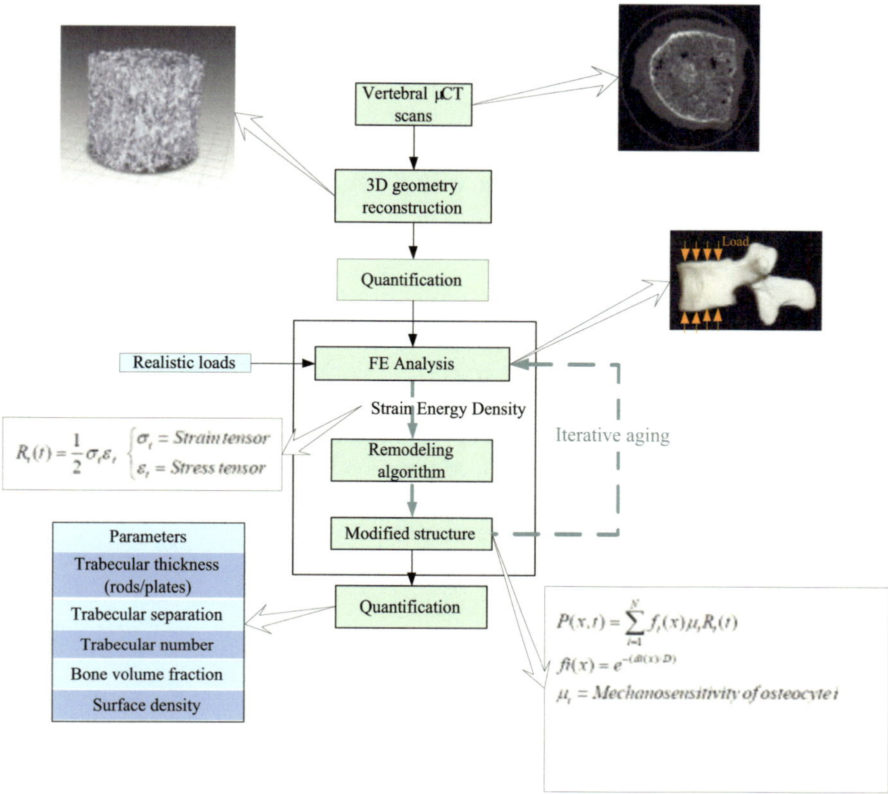

Fig. 5. Schematic of the proposed method

3. Materials and methods

For this study μCT images of fourth lumbar vertebrae (L4) were used. The original μCT images have a resolution of 18μ x 18μ x 36μm. The steps involved in the simulation process are outlined below.

3.1 Image processing

This step involves reading the images, thresholding, segmentation and 3D geometry reconstruction. In the initial phase of the project, a core of the vertebra was used instead of the entire vertebra. The region of interest (ROI) was chosen to be at the center of the vertebra to avoid artifacts present at the edges during scanning. Because of the physical limitation on the size of the specimen that can be physically manufactured and tested for another part of the project, the ROI was chosen to be 480 pixels in diameter. The aspect ratio (diameter/height) of a single vertebral body is 1.33. To maintain this aspect ratio in the cored sample, a total of 384 images were chosen from the entire set. These cored images were then thresholded to separate the bone matrix form the surrounding marrow. Each image is thresholded individually with a value of 22.4% of its maximal gray value (Rüegsegger et al., 1996).
Once all the images are segmented and thresholded, the next step is to construct the 3D geometry from them. 3D geometry can be represented in many ways. One way is to store a list of vertices on the surface and a list of indices that form connected triangular facets from

those vertices. An isosurface algorithm is used to extract this information. The images are stored in a three dimensional array. The isosurface algorithm connects the points that have a value equal to the one specified by the user, which is called the isovalue. In this experiment, the pixels in each image have two values, 0 for marrow or the pixels in the background space and 1 for the region that represents the bone. Hence an isovalue of 1 would generate a list of points on the surface of the bone along with a list of combination of indices that form triangular facets.

3.2 Quantification

The parameters selected to quantify the bone structure are, bone volume fraction which is a ratio of bone volume to the total volume (BV/TV), surface density which is the ratio of bone surface area to the bone volume (BS/BV), trabecular thickness (Tb.Th), trabecular separation (Tb.Sp) and the trabecular number (Tb.N) (Hildebrand et al., 1999). The bone volume (BV) is the volume enclosed by the bone surface. Total volume (TV) is the volume of the bone including the marrow space. The bone surface area is calculated by adding the area of all the triangles, generated by the isosurface function, forming the surface. The area of a triangle formed by its vertices a, b, and c is give by equation 1.

$$\begin{aligned} A &= a - b \\ B &= c - a \\ Area &= (A \times B)/2 \end{aligned} \tag{1}$$

Since the bone geometry is irregular it is difficult to calculate the volume of it and there are different ways this can be accomplished. One way to overcome this problem is to chop the whole geometry in to smaller known geometry and add the volume of each element. The 3D geometry representing the bone volume is split in to tetrahedral mesh elements using a tetrahedral mesh generation algorithm (*http://iso2mesh.sourceforge.net/cgi-bin/index.cgi*, Nov 2010). The volume of the bone is the sum of the volume of all the tetrahedral elements (Sommerville, 1959). Another reason to split the geometry in to tetrahedral elements is that this information can be used in the later stage of the project in the stress analysis using finite elements techniques. The volume of an irregular tetrahedron is calculated using the following equation 2

$$\begin{aligned} D &= \begin{bmatrix} 0 & u^2 & v^2 & w^2 & 1 \\ u^2 & 0 & W^2 & V^2 & 1 \\ v^2 & W^2 & 0 & U^2 & 1 \\ w^2 & V^2 & U^2 & 0 & 1 \\ 1 & 1 & 1 & 1 & 0 \end{bmatrix} \\ Volume &= \sqrt{\det(D)/288} \end{aligned} \tag{2}$$

where (U,u), (V,v) and (W,w) are opposite edge length pair, illustrated in the Figure 6.
Before calculating the other three parameters, an additional step of calculating the medial axis of the structure is introduced. A medial axis is a plane for a plate like structure and a line for a rod like structure (Figure 7). A voxel model of the bone structure is constructed. A voxel is a three dimensional pixel element, i.e. a cube of user specified dimensions. The voxel reconstruction is performed by first building a voxel space that is approximately the same

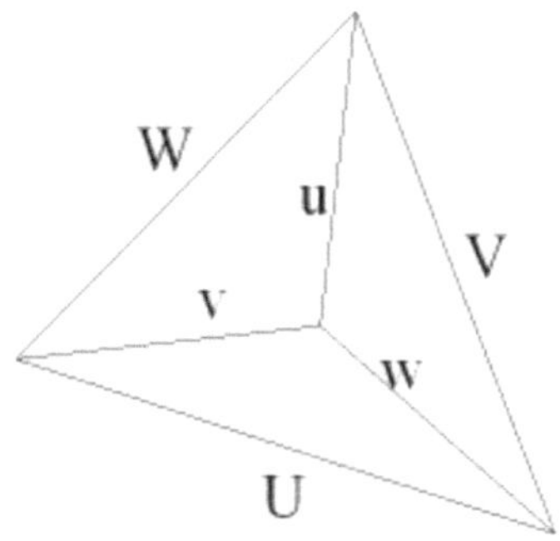

Fig. 6. Edge lengths for calculation of volume

size as the specimen. The size of the voxel element defines the resolution of the final model, i.e., smaller the voxel, higher the resolution. Each layer of the voxel form the voxel space is projected on to the binary μCT scan. The voxels that intersect the cancellous bone region, i.e., the white region in the binary images, are retained and the rest are discarded. After this process is repeated on all the images, the remaining voxels represent the volume of the specimen. The calculation of the medial axis is an iterative algorithm where in each iteration the boundary voxels of the structure is calculated. Each of these voxels are tested to see if it is a critical point. If the removal of a particular boundary voxel changes the topology of the structure then it is tagged as critical. The other non-critical voxels are removed. This process is repeated until there are no more voxels to be removed. The result of this algorithm is a set of voxels representing the skeleton of the structure. This can be further broken down in to set of points representing the skeleton of the rods, called curves, and a set of points representing the skeleton of the plates, called surfaces. The advantage of this addition step is that, the medial axis can be used to separate each individual trabecule and to calculate the orientation of these trabeculae. This information is useful in the simulation because studies have shown that the orientation of the trabeculae affects the age related thinning process (Mosekilde, 1988; 1989). The direct 3D method is used to calculate the trabecular thickness (Tb.Th). Maximal spheres are fitted to every point in the structure and take the mean to calculate the mean thickness. For efficient implementation of the algorithm distance map for every point in the structure is calculated by the distance transformation, which assigns euclidean distance from that point to the nearest background point. The mean of these values give the mean trabecular distance. The trabecular thickness of the rods and plates can be calculated separately to study the effects

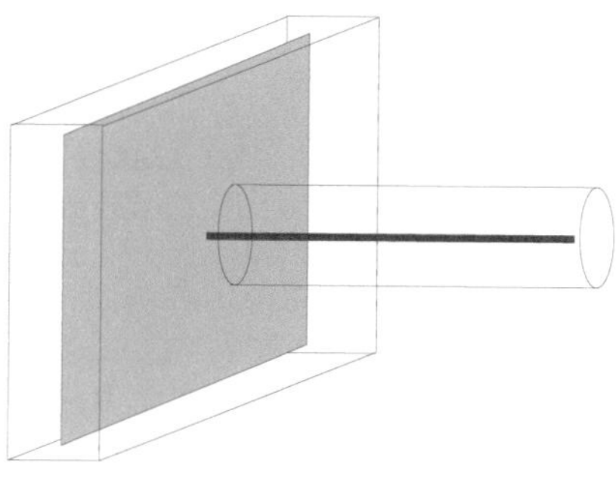

Fig. 7. Medial axis: Shaded gray area represent the mid plane of the plate and the red line represents the mid axis of the rod like structure

of the age related thinning on them. The trabecular separation is calculated in the same way, but on the background voxels. The background voxels are calculated by finding the background pixels on each slice of the image. For this, the convex hull of each image slice is calculated. The pixels representing the bone area are removed from this convex hull. The remaining pixels represent the background pixels. Once this process is repeated on all the image slices the voxel model representing the background is constructed. The same process of calculating the trabecular thickness is repeated on these background voxels which give the trabecular separation (Tb.Sp). A slight modification of the process of the trabecular separation give trabecular number. Maximal spheres are fitted to the background voxels, but this time the boundary of the sphere is not to the surface of the bone, but all the way till the mid-axis of the trabecular structure. The inverse of this value give trabecular number and is defined as the number of plates per unit length (Hildebrand et al., 1999).

3.3 Simulation using finite element methods

Osteocytes located within the bone matrix measure the mechanical signal, the strain energy density rate, which is the result of recent loading history. They stimulate the actor cells (osteoblasts and osteocytes) within their vicinity to adapt the bone mass depending on the difference between the measured signal and the reference signal. The influence of the ostecytes on its environment is decreases exponentially with increase in distance from the actor cells. This relation is given by the following equation (Mullender & Huiskes, 1995)

$$f_i(x) = e^{-(d_i(x)/D)} \tag{3}$$

where $d_i(x)$ is the distance between osteocyte i and location x. The parameter D is the distance from osteocyte i to the location where its effect has reduced to e^{-1} or 36.8%.
The relative density of the bone at location x is controlled by the stimulus value P(x,t), to which all the osteocytes within the vicinity contribute, based on the distance relationship. This is given by the following equation (Mullender & Huiskes, 1995; Huiskes et al., 2000)

$$P(x,t) = \sum_{i=1}^{N} f_i(x)\mu_i R_i(t) \tag{4}$$

where μ_i is the mechanosensitivity of the osteocyte i, and $R_i(t)$ is the strain energy density rate at osteocyte location i. The local change in the relative density of the bone m is expressed as (Huiskes et al., 2000),

$$\frac{dm}{dt} = \begin{cases} \tau\{P(x,t) - k_{th}\} - r_{oc} & \text{for } P(x,t) > k_{th} \\ -r_{oc} & \text{for } P(x,t) \le k_{th} \end{cases} \tag{5}$$

where k_{th} is the threshold of bone formation, r_{oc} is the relative amount of bone resorbed by osteoblasts and τ is the time constant regulating the rate of the process. The relative density of the bone varies between 0 (for no bone) and 1 (for fully mineralized bone). It is assumed that the osteocytes disappear at location where the mineral density goes to 0 and new osteocytes are formed at locations where the density reaches 1. The resorption is regulated by the presence of micro cracks or by disuse (Huiskes et al., 2000; Ruimerman et al., 2001). In this work, resorption due to the presence of micro cracks is assumed to be constant.

$$p(x,t) = d \quad (spatially\ random) \tag{6}$$

Resorption due to disuse is dependent on the strain and is given by the following equation,

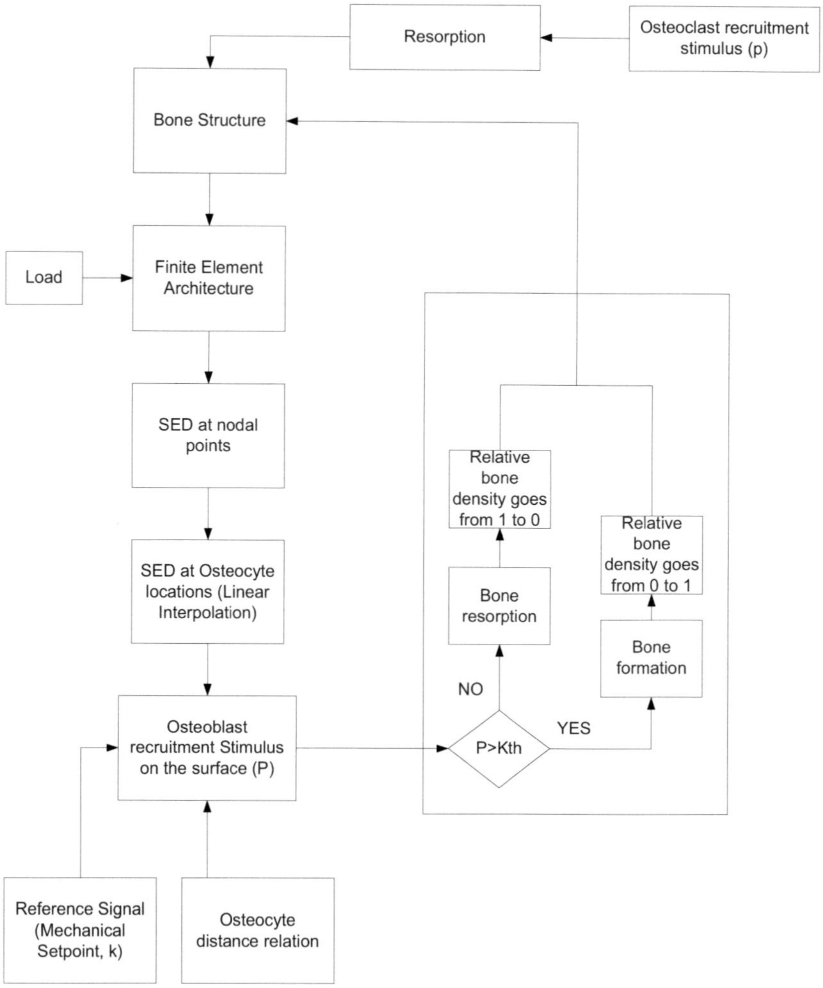

Fig. 8. Regulatory mechanism for Wolff's Law

$$p(x,t) = \begin{cases} c[a - P(x,t)] & \text{if } P < a, \\ 0 & \text{if } P \geq a \end{cases} \tag{7}$$

where $c = 12.5$ and $a = 1.6$.
This entire process of regulation of the bone mass and architecture is illustrated in the block diagram in Figure 8.
The objective is to supply the load information to the algorithm which is representative of realistic everyday activity by a person. Due to the size of the data and the time consumed to process it, it is intended to use the parallel computing functionality of the Matlab software on a cluster of machines.

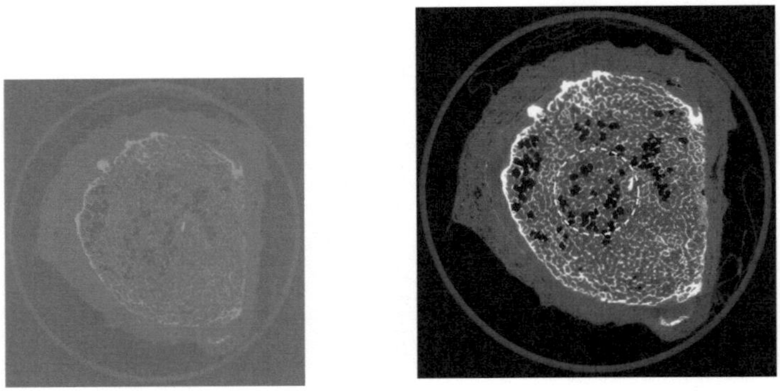

(a) (b)

Fig. 9. (a)Original μCT scan (b)Enhanced CT scan showing the ROI

4. Results

4.1 Image processing

The original μCT scan is shown if Figure 9(a). The region of interest (ROI) is shown in Figure 9(b) by the yellow circle.

Figure 10(a) shows the cored images and Figure 10(b) shows the thresholded core image. The thresholded core images are stored in a 3D image matrix. An isosurface algorithm is used to generate the surface geometry of the bone with an isovalue of 1. The result of this is a 3D surface geometry which is shown in Figure 11.

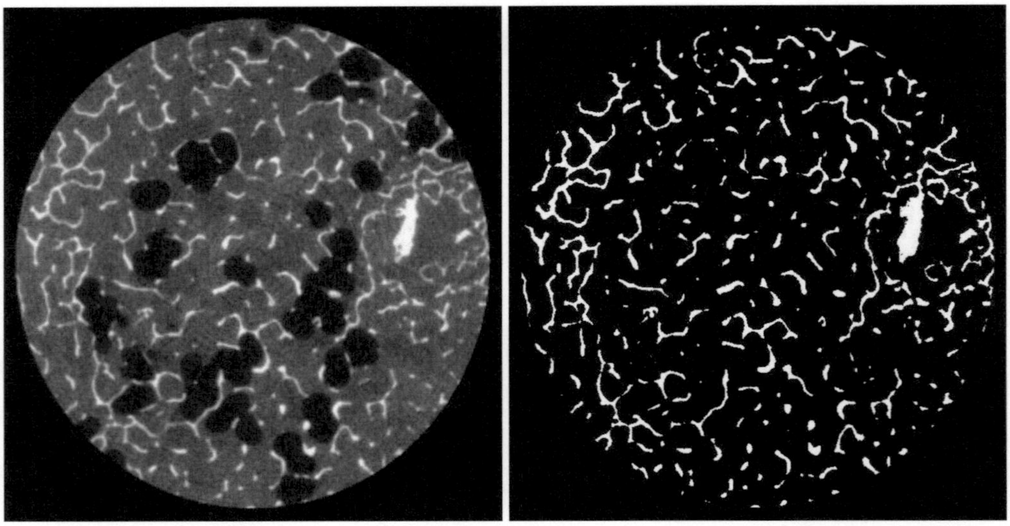

(a) (b)

Fig. 10. (a)Extracted Core image (b)Binary image after thresholding

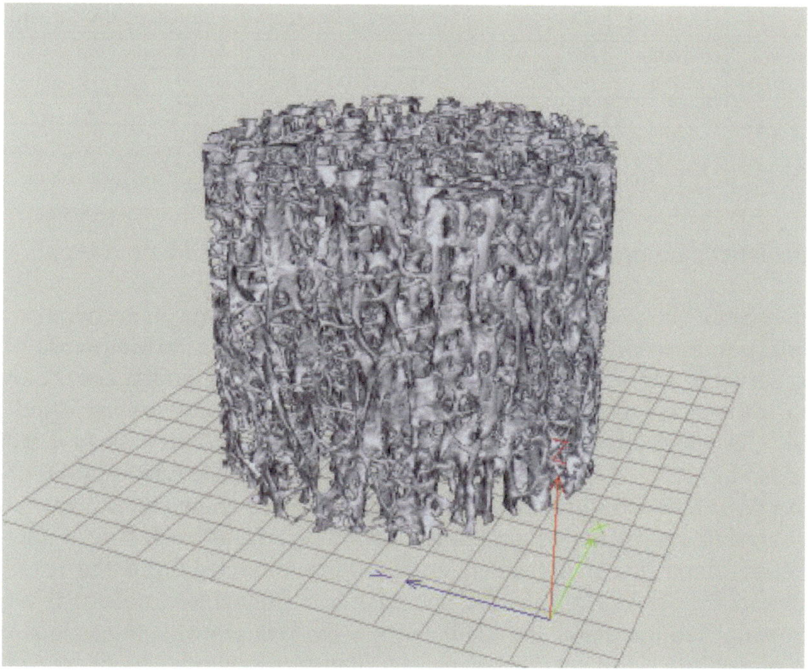

Fig. 11. Surface model of the segmented core

5. Quantification

The calculated midaxis is shown overlapped on to the original section of cancellous bone in Figure 12(a). The blue voxels represent the rods and the red voxels represent the plates. The midaxis of the rods are segmented in to individual struts and their orientation is calculated. These are then classified as horizontal strut (if the orientation is less than 45 degrees with respect to the horizontal plane) or vertical struts (if the orientation is $\geq$45 degrees). This is shown in Figure 12(b).

Several small sections of bone were extracted from the 4th Lumbar vertebra core. The parameters to quantify the bone were calculated on these sections. These sections were

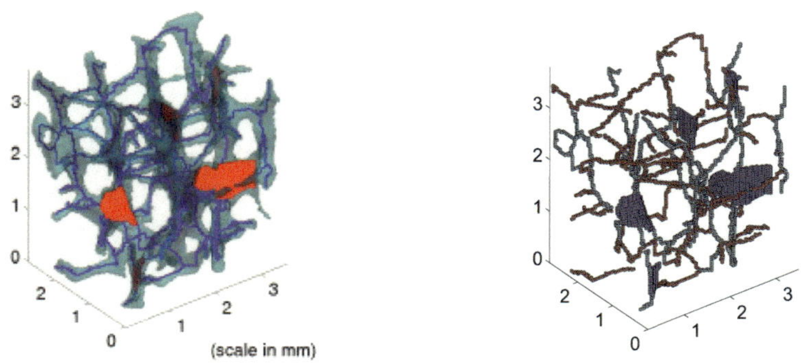

(a) (b)

Fig. 12. (a) Cancellous bone overlapped on the medial axis. (b) Orientation of the rods. Cyan voxels represent the vertical struts.

	Dataset1	Dataset2	Dataset3	Dataset4	Clinical Study (Mean)	SD
rTb.Th (mm)	0.1202	0.1121	0.1186	0.0919	0.139	0.028
pTb.Th (mm)	0.1498	0.1262	0.1381	0.1034	0.139	0.028
Tb.Sp (mm)	0.13	0.1126	0.0694	0.0973	0.854	0.143
Tb.N (mm^{-1})	2.788	3.3931	4.9932	2.8502	1.161	0.181
BV/TV (%)	12.1537	33.5976	17.2474	12.3187	8.7	0.033
BS/BV (mm^{-1})	22.0369	9.7129	30.2927	28.1630	21.17	3.59

Table 1. Calculated parameters compared to Hildebrand et al. (Hildebrand et al., 1999)

approximately $3mm^3$ in size. Calculations were done on these smaller sections because of the computational power needed to do it on the whole core. Tools like the Mathwork's Distributed Computing Server/Parallel Computing toolbox (*http://www.mathworks.com/*, Nov 2010) can be used to do the calculations on the whole core. These parameters are listed in Table 1. The column, Clinical Study, shows the data collected form 52 donars in a clinical study (Hildebrand et al., 1999). It shows the mean and the standard deviation (SD) of the values calculated on the whole 4th Lumbar vertebra. The Figure 13 shows the comparison between the clinical data and the calculated parameters on the sections extracted form the core.
The remodeling algorithm was applied on a section extracted from the core. The load signal generated by LifeMOD (LifeModeler Inc. San Clemente, California) was used for this experiment. This illustrates the ability to use the real world motion data to drive the remodeling algorithm. The results of this simulation are shown in Figure 14. The top row is the principal stress, middle row is the strain energy density and the bottom row is the geometry of the trabecular bone. Column (a) is the initial geometry, column (b) is the configuration after 7 iterations and column (c) is configuration after 14 iterations.

6. Virtual reality visualization

An initial effort has been made to facilitate interactive navigation through the complex 3D geometry of the cancellous bone structure using human computer interfaces, e.g., gyro mouse and stereoscopic head mounted display with Intersense-based head tracking. The resulting visualization facilitates more efficient study of the complex biological structures. For example, the original and the aged bone can be interactively viewed/navigated, the results of the FEA can be texture-mapped onto the 3D geometry of the bone to augment the researcher's ability to identify the stress localization in bone structure. Virtools, a virtual reality simulation and modeling software, was used for interactive visualization and navigation. A screen shot of the cancellous bone in the virtual environment is shown Figure 15.

7. Conclusion

The proposed method can be used to produce a subject-specific structure. The generated structure can be used to predict the effect on the overall trabecular bone structure (e.g., strength of the bone). Based on these results the loading conditions on the bone can be changed to produce more desirable results, i.e., stronger or at least not a weak structure. This can have applications in physiotherapy, help avoid injuries in various sports and study the effects of different types of bone implants over a period of time.

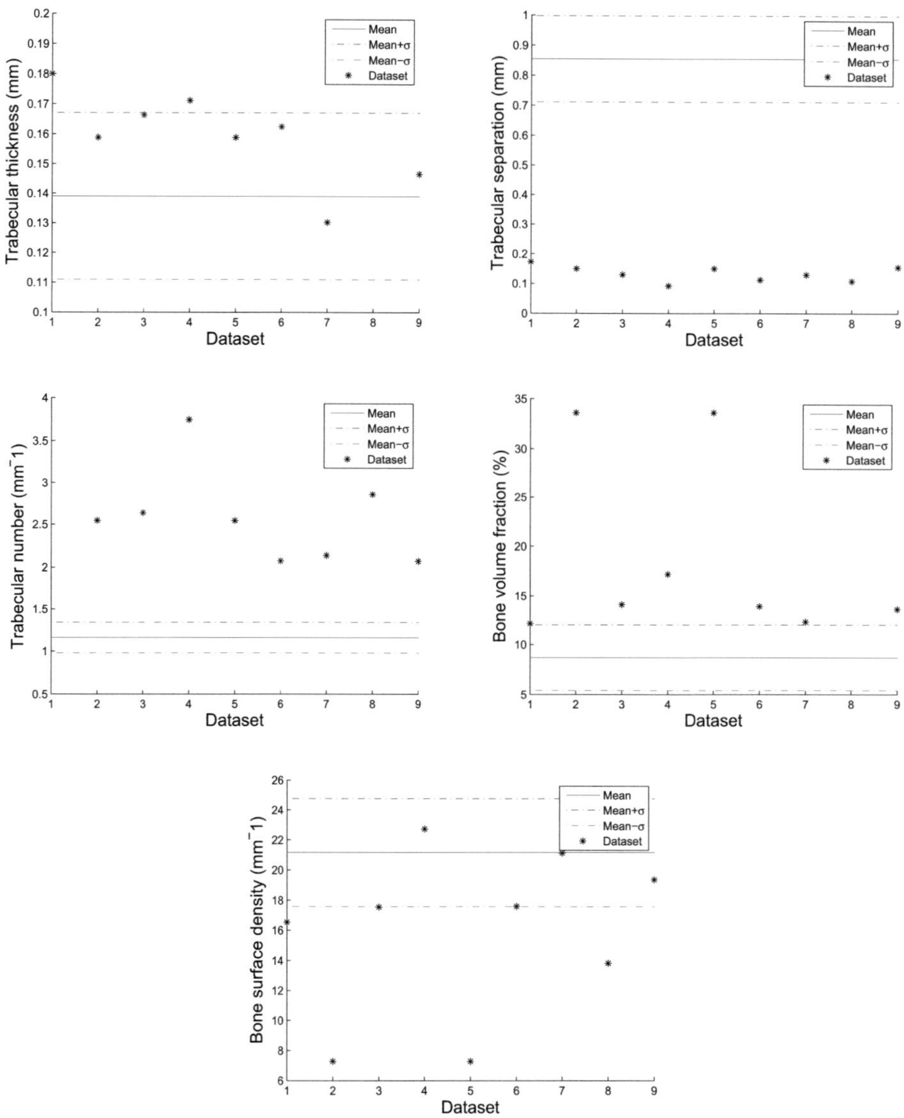

Fig. 13. Comparison of the calculated parameters (∗) in comparison with the clinical data (blue, red, magenta lines)

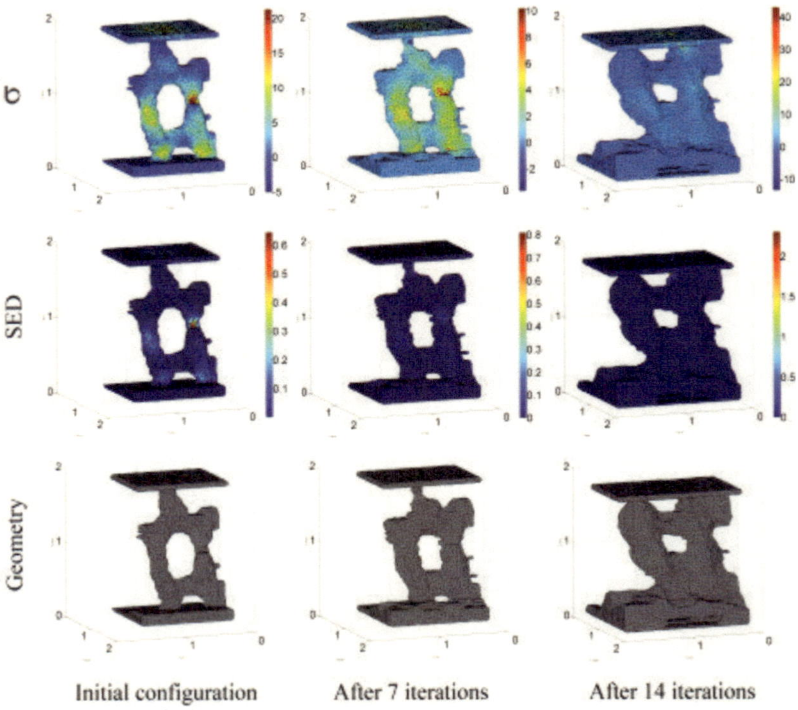

Fig. 14. Results of remodeling algorithm simulation (a) initial geometry (b) after 7 iterations (c) after 14 iterations

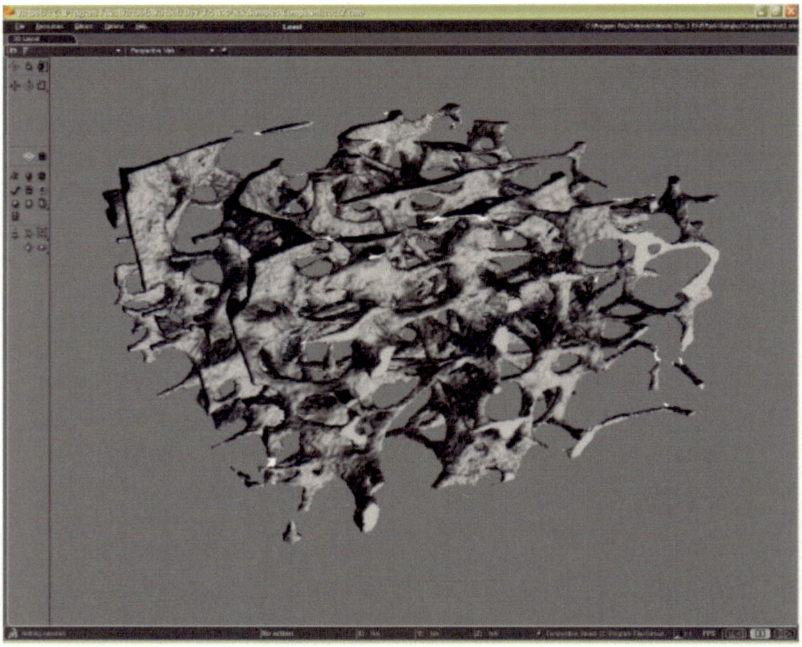

Fig. 15. Virtual reality visualization of the cancellous bone

8. References

Bronckers, A., Goei, W., Luo, G., Karsenty, G., D'Souza, R., Lyaruu, D. & Burger, E. (1996). DNA fragmentation during bone formation in neonatal rodents assessed by transferase-mediated end labeling., *Journal of bone and mineral research: the official journal of the American Society for Bone and Mineral Research* 11(9): 1281.

Burger, E. & Klein-Nulend, J. (1999). Mechanotransduction in bone-role of the lacuno-canalicular network, *The FASEB Journal* 13(9001): 101.

Burr, D. (1993). Remodeling and the repair of fatigue damage, *Calcified tissue international* 53: 75–81.

Burr, D. (2002). Targeted and nontargeted remodeling, *Bone* 30(1): 2–4.

Frost, H. (1982). Mechanical determinants of bone modeling., *Metabolic bone disease & related research* 4(4): 217.

Frost, H. (1983). A determinant of bone architecture: the minimum effective strain, *Clinical Orthopaedics and Related Research* 175: 286.

Hildebrand, T., Laib, A., Müller, R., Dequeker, J. & Rüegsegger, P. (1999). Direct three-dimensional morphometric analysis of human cancellous bone: microstructural data from spine, femur, iliac crest, and calcaneus, *Journal of Bone and Mineral Research* 14: 1167–1174.

Hildebrand, T. & Ruegsegger, P. (1997). A new method for the model-independent assessment of thickness in three-dimensional images, *Journal of Microscopy* 185(1): 67–75.

http://iso2mesh.sourceforge.net/cgi-bin/index.cgi (n.d.).

http://www.mathworks.com/ (Nov 2010).

Huiskes, R., Ruimerman, R., van Lenthe, G. & Janssen, J. (2000). Effects of mechanical forces on maintenance and adaptation of form in trabecular bone, *Nature* 405(6787): 704–706.

Ju, T., Baker, M. & Chiu, W. (2007). Computing a family of skeletons of volumetric models for shape description, *Computer-Aided Design* 39(5): 352–360.

Lemaire, V., Tobin, F., Greller, L., Cho, C. & Suva, L. (2004). Modeling the interactions between osteoblast and osteoclast activities in bone remodeling, *Journal of theoretical biology* 229(3): 293–309.

Linden, J., Verhaar, J., Pols, H. & Weinans, H. (2003). A simulation model at trabecular level to predict effects of antiresorptive treatment after menopause, *Calcified tissue international* 73(6): 537–544.

Liu, X., Huang, A., Zhang, X., Sajda, P., Ji, B. & Guo, X. (2008). Dynamic simulation of three dimensional architectural and mechanical alterations in human trabecular bone during menopause, *Bone* 43(2): 292–301.

Mosekilde, L. (1988). Age-related changes in vertebral trabecular bone architecture–assessed by a new method., *Bone* 9(4): 247–50.

Mosekilde, L. (1989). Sex differences in age-related loss of vertebral trabecular bone mass and structure–biomechanical consequences., *Bone* 10(6): 425.

Mullender, M. & Huiskes, R. (1995). Proposal for the regulatory mechanism of Wolff's law, *Journal of orthopaedic research* 13(4): 503–512.

Müller, R. & Hayes, W. (1997). Biomechanical competence of microstructural bone in the progress of adaptive bone remodeling, *Proceedings of SPIE*, Vol. 3149, SPIE, p. 69.

Müller, R. & Rüegsegger, P. (1996). Analysis of mechanical properties of cancellous bone under conditions of simulated bone atrophy, *Journal of Biomechanics* 29(8): 1053–1060.

Parfitt, A. (1984). The cellular basis of bone remodeling: The quantum concept reexamined in light of recent advances in the cell biology of bone, *Calcified Tissue International*

36: 37–45.
Parfitt, A., Drezner, M., Glorieux, F., Kanis, J., Malluche, H., Meunier, P., Ott, S. & Recker, R. (1987). Bone histomorphometry: Standardization of nomenclature, symbols, and units, *J Bone Miner Res* 2(6): 595–610.
Parfitt, A., Mathews, C., Villanueva, A., Kleerekoper, M., Frame, B. & Rao, D. (1983). Relationships between surface, volume, and thickness of iliac trabecular bone in aging and in osteoporosis. Implications for the microanatomic and cellular mechanisms of bone loss., *Journal of Clinical Investigation* 72(4): 1396.
Pivonka, P., Zimak, J., Smith, D., Gardiner, B., Dunstan, C., Sims, N., John Martin, T. & Mundy, G. (2008). Model structure and control of bone remodeling: A theoretical study, *Bone* 43(2): 249–263.
Rüegsegger, P., Koller, B. & Müller, R. (1996). A microtomographic system for the nondestructive evaluation of bone architecture, *Calcified tissue international* 58(1): 24–29.
Ruimerman, R., Huiskes, R., Van Lenthe, G. & Janssen, J. (2001). A computer-simulation model relating bone-cell metabolism to mechanical adaptation of trabecular architecture, *Computer Methods in Biomechanics and Biomedical Engineering* 4(5): 433–448.
Simmons, C. & Hipp, J. (1997). Method-Based Differences in the Automated Analysis of the Three-Dimensional Morphology of Trabecular Bone, *Journal of Bone and Mineral Research* 12(6): 942–947.
Sommerville, D. (1959). *Analytical geometry of three dimensions*, The University Press.
Stauber, M. & Müller, R. (2006). Volumetric spatial decomposition of trabecular bone into rods and plates - A new method for local bone morphometry, *Bone* 38(4): 475–484.
Thomsen, J., Laib, A., Koller, B., Prohaska, S., Mosekilde, L. & Gowin, W. (2005). Stereological measures of trabecular bone structure: comparison of 3D micro computed tomography with 2D histological sections in human proximal tibial bone biopsies, *Journal of Microscopy* 218(2): 171–179.
Van Der Linden, J., Verhaar, J. & Weinans, H. (2001). A Three-Dimensional Simulation of Age-Related Remodeling in Trabecular Bone, *J Bone Miner Res* 16(4): 688–696.
Van Rietbergen, B., Huiskes, R., Weinans, H., Sumner, D., Turner, T. & Galante, J. (1993). The mechanism of bone remodeling and resorption around press-fitted THA stems, *Journal of biomechanics* 26(4-5): 369–382.
Weinbaum, S., Cowin, S. & Zeng, Y. (1994). A model for the excitation of osteocytes by mechanical loading-induced bone fluid shear stresses, *Journal of biomechanics* 27(3): 339–360.
Wolff, J. (1986). The Law of Bone Remodeling.(Das Gesetz der Transformation der Knochen, Kirschwald, 1892). Translated by Maquet, P., Furlong, R.

14

Application of Advanced Virtual Reality and 3D Computer Assisted Technologies in Computer Assisted Surgery and Tele-3D-computer Assisted Surgery in Rhinology

Ivica Klapan[1,2], Pero Raos[3], Tomislav Galeta[3], Ljubimko Šimičić[4], Juraj Lukinović[5], Željko Vranješ[2,6], Josip Maleš[6], Stanko Belina[7] and Višeslav Ćuk[7]

[1]*Klapan Medical Group Polyclinic, Zagreb,*
[2]*Faculty of Medicine at University of Osijek,*
[3]*Mechanical Engineering Faculty in Slavonski Brod at University of Osijek,*
[4]*Department of Physics at University of Zagreb,*
[5]*ENT Department, Faculty of Medicine at University of Zagreb,*
[6]*ENT Department, Faculty of Medicine at at University of Osijek,*
[7]*Division of Radiology and Otorhinolaryngology, General Hospital Zabok,*
Croatia

1. Introduction

Every physician using computer for diagnostic and therapeutic purposes should know that images are processed by use of graphic and computer systems, as well as by specialized program systems, in order to better present the anatomy of a particular part of the body with identified diseased areas (Ecke et al., 1998; Urban et al., 1998).The possibility of exact preoperative, non-invasive visualization of the spatial relationships of anatomic and pathologic structures, including extremely fragile ones, size and extent of pathologic process, and of precisely predicting the course of surgical procedure, allows the surgeon to achieve considerable advantage in the preoperative examination of the patient and to reduce the risk of intraoperative complications (Knezović et al., 2007), all this by use different virtual reality (VR) methods (Fig.1.).

Beside otorhinolaryngology, this has also been used in other fields (Klimek et al., 1998; Hassfeld et al., 1998). The more so, in addition to educational applications, virtual endoscopy (VE), virtual surgery (VS), application of 3D models, etc., has offered us the possibility of preoperative planning in rhinology (sinus surgery), and has become a very important segment in surgical training and planning of each individual surgical intervention. These analyses are becoming routine procedures in other otorhinolaryngology, oral, maxillofacial and plastic surgery, etc.

Classical endoscopic procedures performed with rigid endoscopes are invasive and often uncomfortable for patients, and some of them may have serious side effects such as perforation, infection and hemorrhage (Belina et al., 2008). VE is a new method of diagnosis

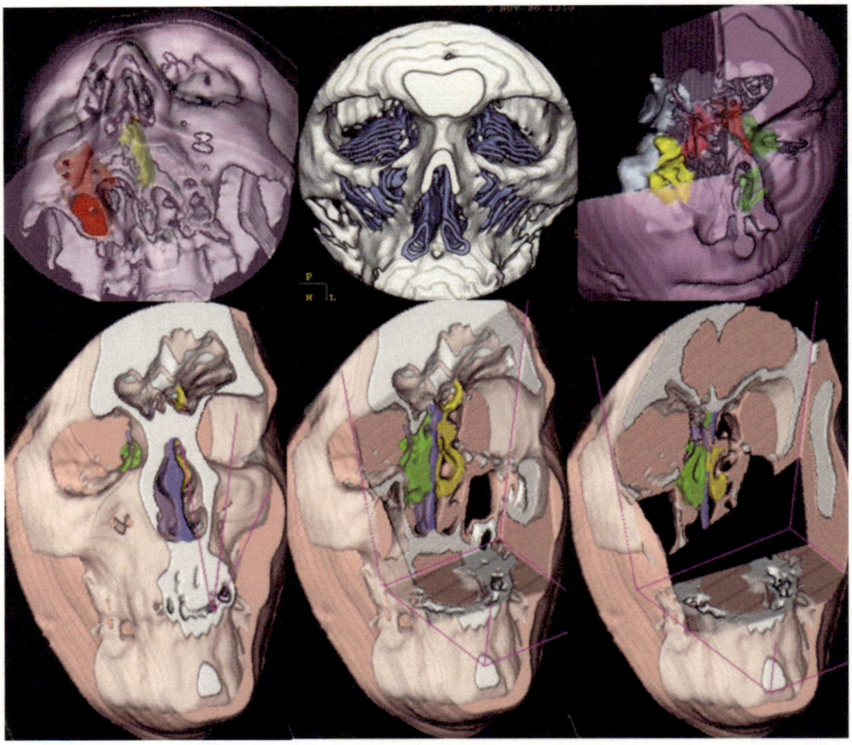

Fig. 1. 3D models of the human head in different projections. Visualization of the paranasal sinuses and surrounding regions from different 3D aspects (taken with permission from Klapan et al., Otolaryngology Head Neck Surg, 2002 and Klapan Medical Group Polyclinic, Zagreb, Croatia).

using computer processing of 3D image datasets (such as 2D multi slice computed thomography - MSCT and/or MRI scans) to provide simulated visualizations of patient specific organs similar or equivalent to those produced by standard endoscopic procedures (Rob, 2000; Wickham et al., 1994). Development of new computer techniques and fly through algorithms offer valuable non-invasive additional tools in diagnostics and preoperative planning in otorhinolaryngology (Fig.2.). Virtual endoscopy visualization avoids the risks associated with real endoscopy, and when used prior to performing an actual endoscopic exam can minimize procedural difficulties and decrease the rate of morbidity, especially for endoscopists in training (Robb, 2000), which was proved in our first Croatian 3D computer assisted- functional endoscopic sinus surgery (3D-CA-FESS) in June 3, 1994 (Klapan et al., 1997).

Definitely, the basic goal of 3D-computer assisted (3D-CA) support in diagnostic and surgical activities is to achieve safer surgical procedure using new computer and medical technologies in surgical (Anon et al., 1998) and /or telesurgical procedures (Fig.3.), and provide visualization of the anatomy as well the pathology in the 2D as well as in the form of 3D-models. Using our own approach in computer assisted-endoscopic surgery, we were able to "look inside" the patient during the real surgical procedure. According to our original idea, the computer network, essential for computer collaboration between surgical sites for telesurgical purposes, has to be built in parallel to the video network. Every

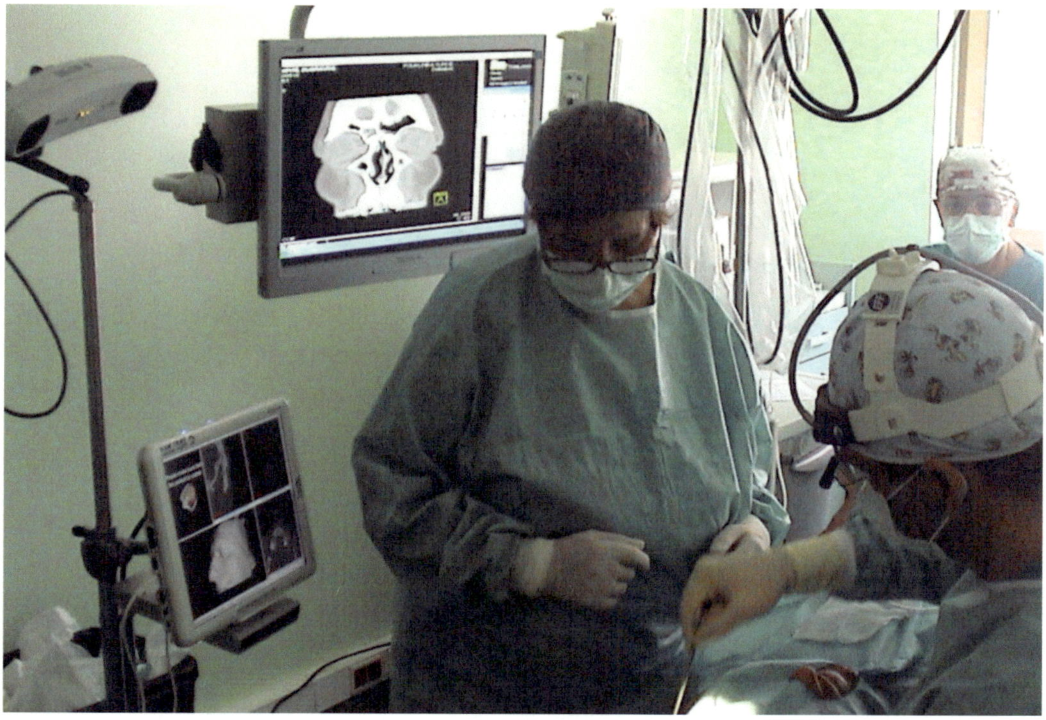

Fig. 2. An example of 3D-computer assisted navigation surgery of the nose and paranasal sinuses with simulation and planning of the course of subsequent endoscopic operation *per viam* VE which overcomes some difficulties of conventional endoscopy, such as "standard" FESS or tele-FESS (taken with permission of Klapan Medical Group Polyclinic, Zagreb, Croatia)

telesurgical site must have compliant collaboration software. On computer workstations, all sites have computed thomography (CT) images and 3D models with appropriate movies, and then the consultant, an experienced surgeon, assists the less experienced surgeon to reach the pathology in the operating field.

This kind of our Tele-3D-computer assisted surgery (Tele-3D-CAS) has to enable less experienced surgeons to perform critical surgeries using guidance and assistance from a remote, experienced surgeon. In telesurgery, more than two locations can be involved; thus less experienced surgeon can be assisted by one, two or more experienced surgeons, depending on the complexity of the surgical procedure. Our Tele-3D-CAS provides also the transfer of computer data (images, 3D-models) in real time during the surgery and, in parallel, of the encoded live video signals. Through this network, the two encoded live video signals from the endocamera and operation room camera have to be transferred to the remote locations involved in the telesurgery/consultation procedure (Klapan et al., J Telemed Telecare, 2002).

The first kind of our Tele-3D-C-FESS took place between two locations in the city of Zagreb, 10 km apart, with interactive collaboration from a third location. A surgical team carrying out an operative procedure at the Šalata ENT Department, Zagreb University School of Medicine and Zagreb Clinical Hospital Center, received instructions, suggestions and guidance through the procedure by an expert surgeon from an expert center. The third

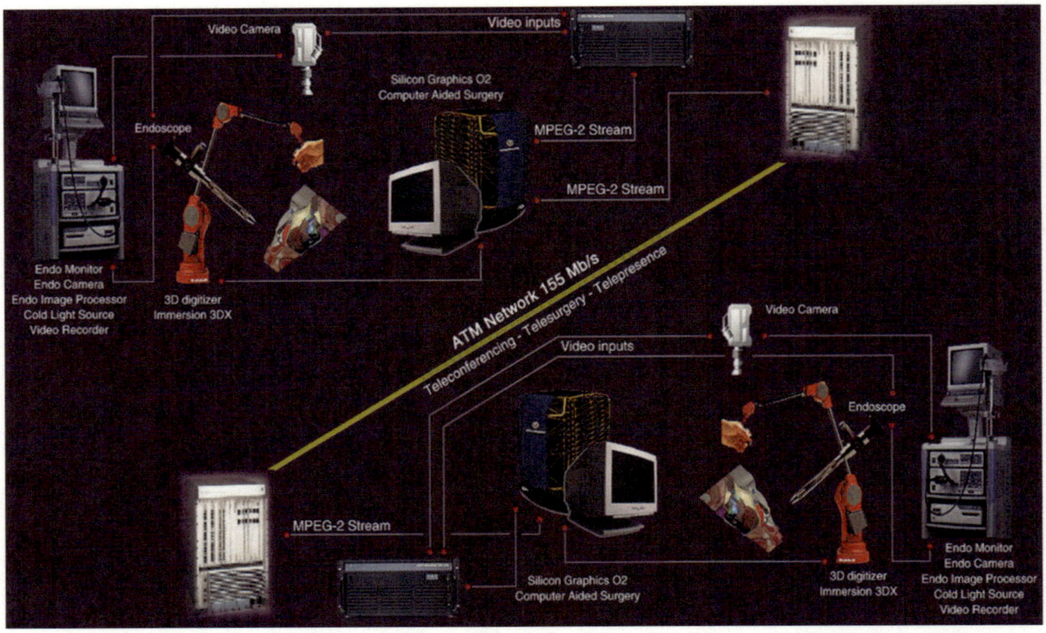

Fig. 3. Our tele-3D-computer assisted surgery of the nose and paranasal sinuses realized during our 3D computer assisted-FESS in June 3, 1994., proved the main advantage of VE and/or tele-VE that there are no restrictions on the movement of virtual endoscope prior the real procedure, and requires no hospitalization (taken with permission from Klapan et al., Otolaryngology Head Neck Surg, 2002 and Klapan Medical Group Polyclinic, Zagreb, Croatia)

active point was the Faculty of Electrical Engineering and Computing. The 2nd Tele-3D-C-FESS took place between two locations, two cities in Croatia (Osijek and Zagreb, 300 km apart). The surgical team carrying out an operative procedure at the ENT Department, Osijek Clinical Hospital, received instructions, suggestions and guidance through the procedure by an expert surgeon and radiologist from the Expert Center in Zagreb. This Tele-3D-C-FESS surgery, performed as described above, was successfully completed in 25-30 minutes.

Taking into account the opinion of the leading world authorities in endoscopic surgery, we believe that each endoscopic operation is a demanding procedure, including those described in the first two Tele-3D-C-FESS surgeries presented. Nevertheless, we would like to underline herewith that ordinary, and occasionally even expert surgeons may need some additional intraoperative consultation (or VE/3D support), for example, when anatomical markers are lacking in the operative field due to trauma (war injuries) or massive polypous lesions/normal mucosa consumption, bleeding, etc. Now, imagine that we can substitute artificially generated sensations for the real standard daily information received by our senses. In this case, the perception system in humans could be deceived, creating an impression of another 'external' world around the man (e.g., 3D navigation surgery). In this way, we could replace the true reality with the simulated reality that enables precise, safer and faster diagnosis as well as surgery. All systems of simulated reality share the ability to offer the user to move and act within the apparent worlds instead of the real world.

What do experts think about additional support *per viam* computer assisted reconstruction of the anatomy and pathology of the head and neck; what is the truth and level of reliability of the computer reconstruction of CT images in telesurgery transmission; the question of availability and very expensive equipment; 3D image reality; control parameters; what is the use of computer 3D image of the surgical field and isn't a real live video image much better for telesurgery? Computer simulation by use of the simulated reality system allows for the medical diagnostic procedure to repeat over and over again on the virtual body, many functions can be simulated for realistic simulation as it is usually done, the surgeon is warned if the procedure does not proceed correctly, etc.

Sinus CT scan in coronal projection is a term familiar to every radiologist dealing with CT in the world. Layer thickness, shift, gantry, and window are internationally standardized and accepted values, thus being reproducible all over the world. The method is standardized, reproducible and distinctly defined (Stewart et al., 1999, Kenny et al., 1999), and it is by no means contradictory. But on the other side, the basic CT diagnostics has also limited possibilities, first of all because it presents summation images in a single plane (layer) but cannot present the continuity of structures. This has been solved by 3D reconstruction which is now available on PCs equipped with Pentium IV processors/2,0 GHz, or better. By presenting the continuity of structures (0.5-1 mm sections), this reconstruction allows visualization of the region as a whole, avoiding the loss of images by use of the standard approach in sinus CT imaging (3-5 mm sections).

During the 3D-CA-telesurgery, the computer with its operative field image allows the surgeon, by means of up-to-date technologies, to connect the operative instrumentarium to spatial digitalizers connected to the computer. Upon the completion of the tele-operation, the surgeon compares the preoperative and postoperative images and models of the operative field, and studies video records of the procedure itself. Using intraoperative records, animated images of the real tele-procedure performed can be designed. By means of computer records labelled coordinate shifts of 3D digitalizer during the surgery, an animated image of the course of operation in the form of journey, i.e. operative field fly-through in the real patient, can be designed. Beside otorhinolaryngology (Klimek et al., 1998; Ecke et al., 1998; Mann et al., 1998), this has also been used in other fields. The more so, in addition to educational applications, VS offers the possibility of preoperative planning in sinus surgery, and has become a very important segment in surgical training and planning of each individual surgical or telesurgical intervention, not only in the region of paranasal sinuses (Keeve et al., 1998; Hassfeld et al., 1998).

The complex software systems allow tele-visualization of CT or MRI section in its natural course (the course of examination performed), or in an imaginary, arbitrary course. Particular images can be transferred, processed and deleted, or can be presented in animated images, as it was done during our first telesurgery (Fig. 6). Multiple series of images can be simultaneously observed in different color tables and at various magnifications, with various grades of transparency, observing them as a unique 3D model system. The work with such models allows different views, shifts, cuts, separations, labelling, and animation. The series of images can be changed, or images can be generated in different projections through the volume recorded, as we have showed in our OR (Klapan et al., 2001).

Before the development of 3D spatial model, each individual image or the whole series of images have to be segmented, in order to single out the image parts of interest, because the basic requirement, in human medicine, resulting from the above mentioned needs refers to the use of a computer system for visualization of anatomic 3D-structures and integral operative field to be operated on. Thus, separate models of bones, healthy tissue, affected tissue, and all significant anatomic entities of the operative field can be developed (Klapan et al., Am J ORL, 2002). The complete tele-3D-CA-procedure planned can be developed on computer models and a series of animations describing the procedure can be produced.

Comparative analysis of 3D anatomic models with intraoperative finding, in any kind of telesurgery, shows the 3D volume rendering image to be very good, actually a visualization standard that allows imaging likewise the real intraoperative anatomy (Burtscher et al., 1998; Holtel et al., 1999; Thral., 1999) · Mentioned technologies represent a basis for realistic simulations that are useful in many areas of human activity (including medicine), and can create an impression of immersion of a physician in a non-existing, virtual environment (John et al., 2004).

Using routable shared and switched Ethernet connections (Fig. 4), 25 frames were transferred *per* second in full PAL (phase alternating line or phase alternation by line) resolution but with 20% of dropped frames. After some tests, it was found that the routing protocol between two or more sites could not offer a constant frame rate. Packages sent from the source travel to the destination using different network paths, thus some packages may be lost during communication or some may reach the destination with unacceptable delays.

Another problem we faced with video signals was how to transfer multiple video signals to remote locations. The native, uncompressed video required a bandwidth of about 34Mb/s, thus the video signals had to be compressed for the transfer of multiple video streams to remote locations using 155Mb/s.

The video image is critical in tele-endoscopic surgery and must be of the highest quality. Using software and hardware M-JPEG compression, it was found that one video stream from the endocamera in full PAL resolution and with audio required a bandwidth of about 20-30Mb/s. Our M-JPEG encoders were upgraded with MPEG1 and later with MPEG2 encoders, because we had a bandwidth of only 155Mb/s for data, video, audio and control communication. MPEG1 seems very good for conferencing; however, the endoscope video signal of the operating field required better image quality. The encoded MPEG1 video stream with audio was transferred to the remote location in full frame resolution using a bandwidth of about 6Mb/s (multiple T1 lines). When our encoder was upgraded to the MPEG2 standard, the quality of the video image was adequate for the operating field endocamera. A bandwidth of 8Mb/s produced a high quality video stream at the remote site. Using MPEG streams, the video signal could be transferred from the endocamera to the remote location for consultancy or education.

As known in the circles of telemedicine/telesurgery, the basic cost of the presented system is known. It includes standard telemedicine equipment which should be mounted at any institution for the institution to be connected to the telemedicine network. This equipment allows for transfer of live video image of the operative field, CT images, commentaries, surgery guidance, etc. In addition, a computer with appropriate volume rendering software support should be introduced in the operating theater. All these devices are now standard equipment available on the market at quite reasonable prices. For comparison, the overall price of these devices is by far lower than the price of a system for image guided surgery, currently mounted in many hospitals all over the world. Once installed and tested, the whole system can be used without any special assistance of technical personnel (computer experts and/or network specialties). Clinical institutions (e.g., Klapan Medical Group Polyclinic, Zagreb, Croatia), which have expert clinical work places, employ properly educated and trained technical personnel who can be readily included in the preparation and performance of tele-3D-C-FESS surgery as well as in the storage of the procedure itself

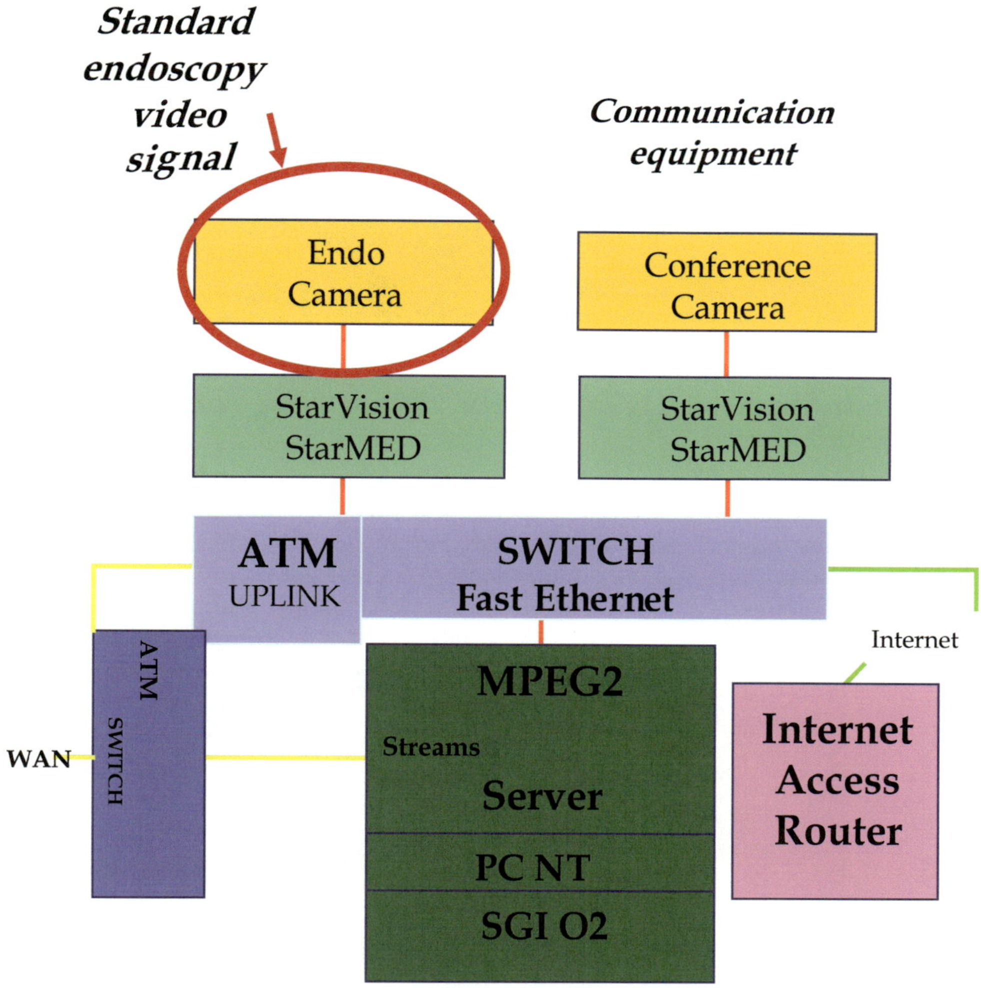

Fig. 4. Using routable shared and switched Ethernet connections, 25 frames/sec were transferred in full PAL resolution (taken with permission from Klapan et al., Otolaryngology Head Neck Surg, 2002)

and of intraoperatively generated computer 3D animations. It is of the higher importance, because if we would like to understand the idea of virtual reality (VR), it is necessary to recognize that the perception of surrounding world created in our brain is based on information coming from the human senses and with the help of a knowledge that is stored in our brain. The usual definition says that the impression of being present in a virtual environment, such as virtual endoscopy (VE) of the patient's head, that does not exist in reality is called virtual reality. The physician, e.g., any member of our surgical team, has impression of presence in the virtual world and can navigate through it and manipulate virtual objects. A VR system may be designed in such a way that the physician is completely immersed in the VE.

It should be made clear that the main message of the tele-3D-CA-endoscopic surgery, as differentiated from the standard telesurgeries worldwide, is the use of the 3D-model operative field, and thus of VE and VS (Fig. 5).

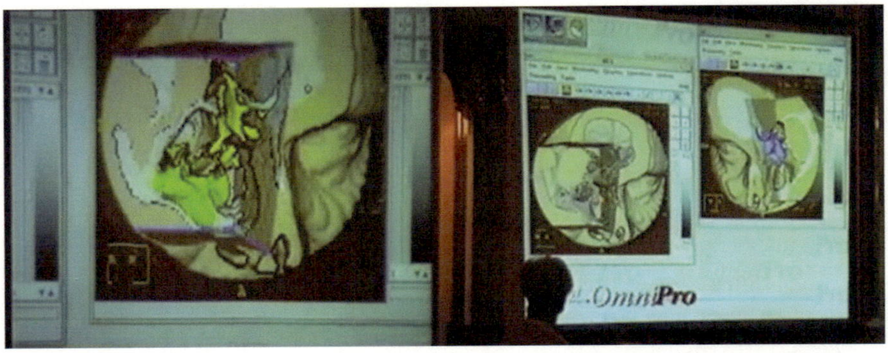

Fig. 5. Virtual endoscopy, realized during our tele-3D-C-FESS in 1999 (taken with permission from Klapan et al., J Telemed Telecare, 2002 and Klapan Medical Group Polyclinic, Zagreb, Croatia)

Research in the area of 3D image analysis, visualization, tissue modelling, and human-machine interfaces provides scientific expertise necessary for developing successful 3D visualization of the human head during 3D-CAS (Fig. 6), Tele-3D-CAS (Fig. 7), and other VR applications. Such an impression of immersion can be realized in any medical institution using advanced computers and computer networks that are required for interaction between a person and a remote environment, with the goal of realizing tele-presence.

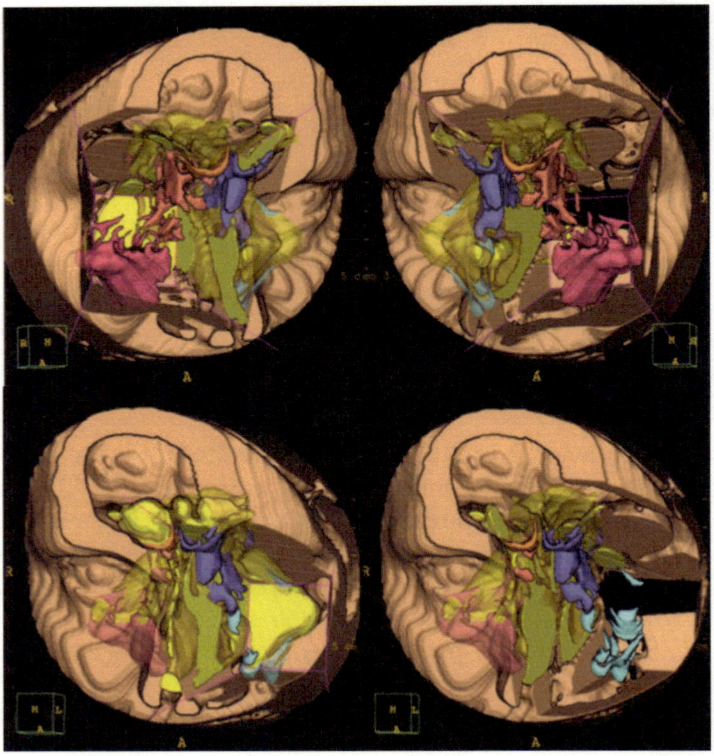

Fig. 6. Transmission of 3D models as virtual endoscopy (VE) of the human head, realized during one of the first Croatian 3D-CA-navigation endoscopic surgeries in October 1994 (taken with permission from Klapan et al., J Telemed Telecare, 2002)

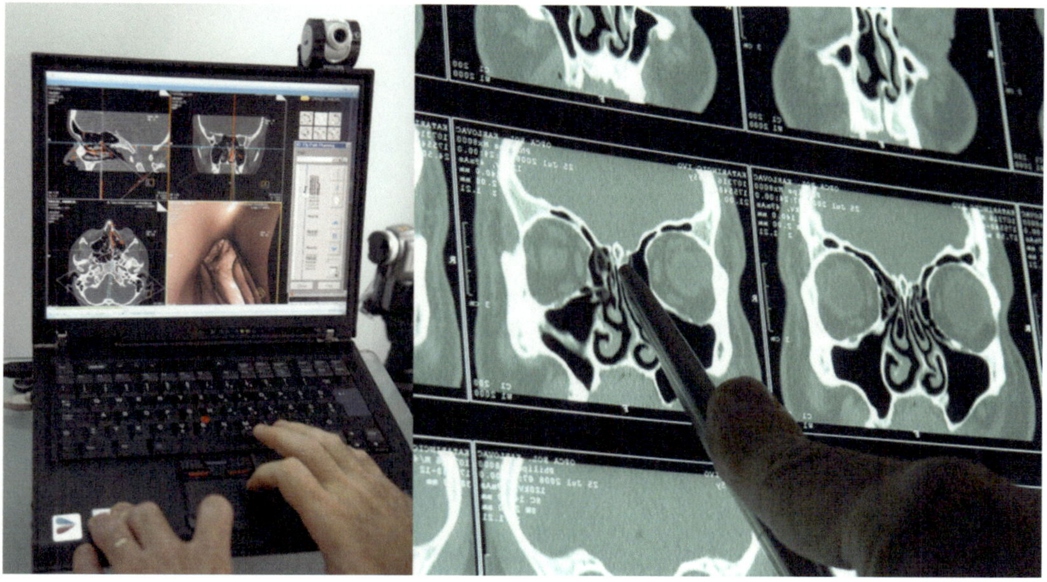

Fig. 7. 3D-VE-navigation of the human head during tele-3D-computer assisted-FESS (taken with permission of Klapan Medical Group Polyclinic, Zagreb, Croatia)

In human medicine, extremely valuable information on anatomic relationships in particular regions while planning and performing endoscopic surgery is provided by high quality CT or MRI diagnosis (Mladina et al., 1995), thus contributing greatly to the safety of this kind of surgery (Rišavi et al., 1998). Once created from 2D cross-section images with 3D modeling software, virtual 3D surface models or volume rendered models can be further used in virtual reality for measuring, operation planning, simulations, finite element analysis. However, virtual 3D models also can be used in actual reality for tangible models obtained from rapid prototyping applications. Rapid Prototyping (RP) techniques look most promising to satisfy medical need for tangible models. While prototyping is a usually slow and expensive process of building pre-production models of a product to test various aspects of its design, rapid prototyping techniques are methods that allow quick production of physical prototypes (Fig. 8.). Nowadays even more often, rapid prototyping techniques provide to medicine actual products e.g. prosthesis and implants with the important benefit in significant shortening of the Time to Market (Raos & Galeta, 2004).The mode of computer visualization of anatomic structures (Elolf et al., 1998) of the human body used to date could only provide diagnostic information and possibly assist in the preoperative preparation. Intraoperative use of computer generated operative field 3D-model has not been widely adopted to date. The intraoperative use of computer in real time requires development of appropriate hardware and software to connect medical instrumentarium with the computer, and to operate the computer by thus connected instrumentarium and sophisticated multimedia interfaces.In rhinology, such an revolutionary approach is of paramount importance for the surgeon because of the proximity of intracranial structures and limited operative field layout hampering spatial orientation during the "standard" operative procedure.

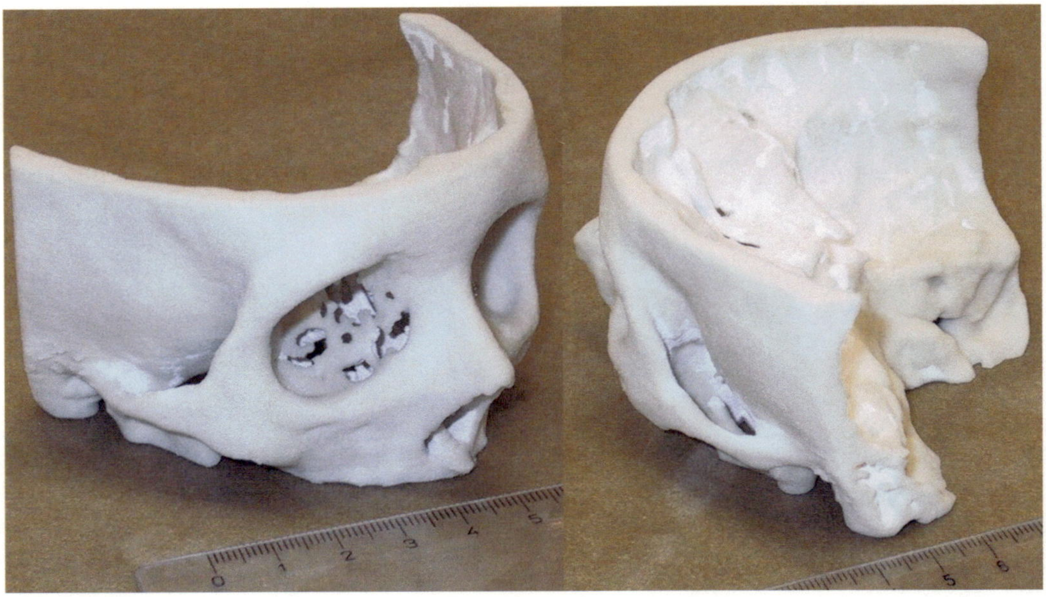

Fig. 8. Real 3D model produced with Rapid Prototyping technique

2. Methods

2.1 High quality diagnosis (DICOM standard)

High quality diagnostic image is the main prerequisite for appropriate utilization of computer systems during the preparation, performance and analysis of an operative procedure (Fig. 9.). Development of a system for data exchange between multiple medical diagnostic devices as well as between diagnostic devices and computer networks has led to the establishment of DICOM (digital imaging and communication in medicine) standards describing the forms and modes of data exchange.

Before the introduction of DICOM standards, image recordings were stored on films, where the information obtained from the diagnostic device was in part lost (Knezović et al., 2007). In ideal conditions, sixteen different image levels could be distinguished on films at the most. When film images were to be stored in computer systems, films had to be scanned, thus inevitably losing a part of significant data and probably introducing some unwanted artefacts. The level setting and window width to be observed on the images could not be subsequently changed. Visualization of the image on the diagnostic device monitor was of a considerably higher quality, thus it was quite naturally used for record receipt and storage in computer media. Video image allows for the receipt of 256 different levels at the most. Neither it is possible to subsequently modify the level setting and window width to be observed on the images that have already been stored in the computer system. When stored in computer systems by use of DICOM protocol, images are stored in the form generated by the diagnostic device detector. These image recordings can then be properly explored by use of powerful computer systems. This is of special relevance when data in the form of images are to be used for complex examinations and testing, or in preoperative preparation where rapid and precise demarcation between the disease involved and intact tissue is required (Knezović et al., 2007). It is also very important for the images to be visualized in various

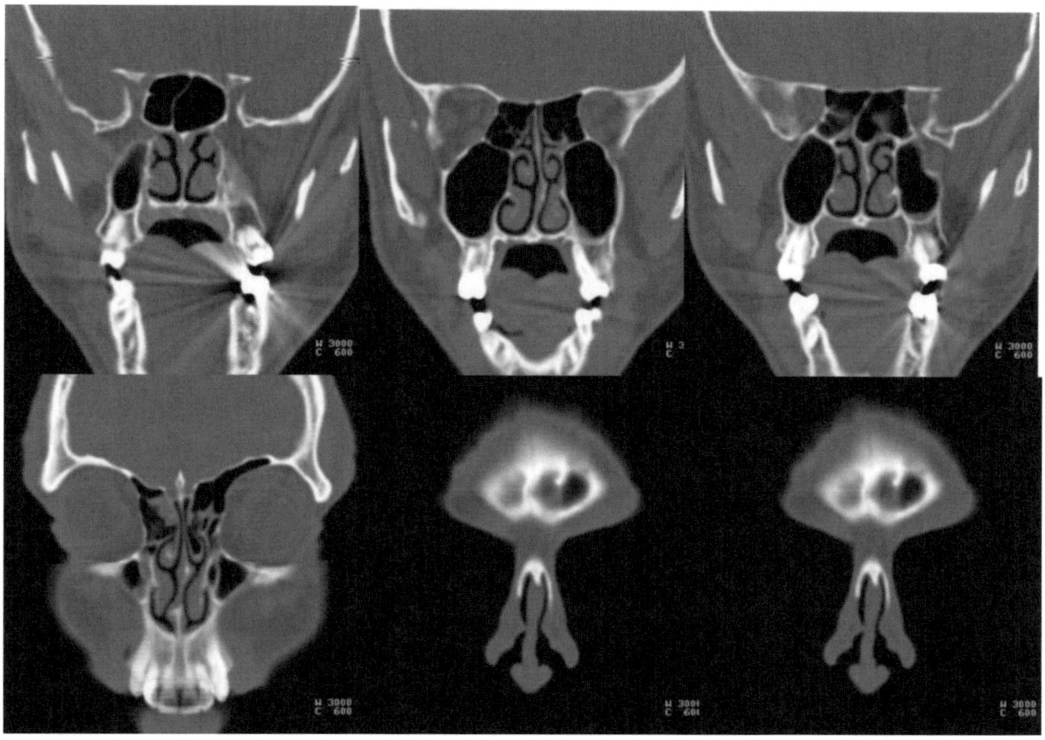

Fig. 9. MSCT slices of the nose and paranasal sinuses (taken with permission of Klapan Medical Group Polyclinic, Zagreb, Croatia)

forms and from different aspects and then - which is most demanding indeed - to develop spatial models to aid the surgeon in preparing and performing the procedure as well as in postoperative analysis of the course of the procedure.

The entire operative procedure can be simulated and critical areas avoided during the real procedure by employing real patient images in the operation preparatory phase using complex spatial models and simulated operative field entry (VE,VS) (Klapan et al., 2001).

2.2 Preoperative preparation

The real-time requirement means that the simulation must be able to follow the actions of the user that may be moving in the virtual environment. The computer system must also store in its memory a 3D model of the virtual environment (3D-CAS models). In that case a real-time virtual reality system will update the 3D graphical visualization as the user moves, so that up-to-date visualization is always shown on the computer screen. For realistic simulations it is necessary for the computer to generate at least 30 such images per second, which imposes strong requirements to computer processing power.

Use of the latest program systems enables development of 3D spatial models, exploration in various projections, simultaneous presentation of multiple model sections and, most important, model development according to open computer standards (Open Inventor) (Knezović et al., 2007). Such a preoperative preparation can be applied in a variety of program systems that can be transmitted to distant collaborating radiologic and surgical work sites for preoperative consultation as well as during the operative procedure in real time (telesurgery) (Klapan et al., J Telemed Telecare, 2002) (Fig. 10.).

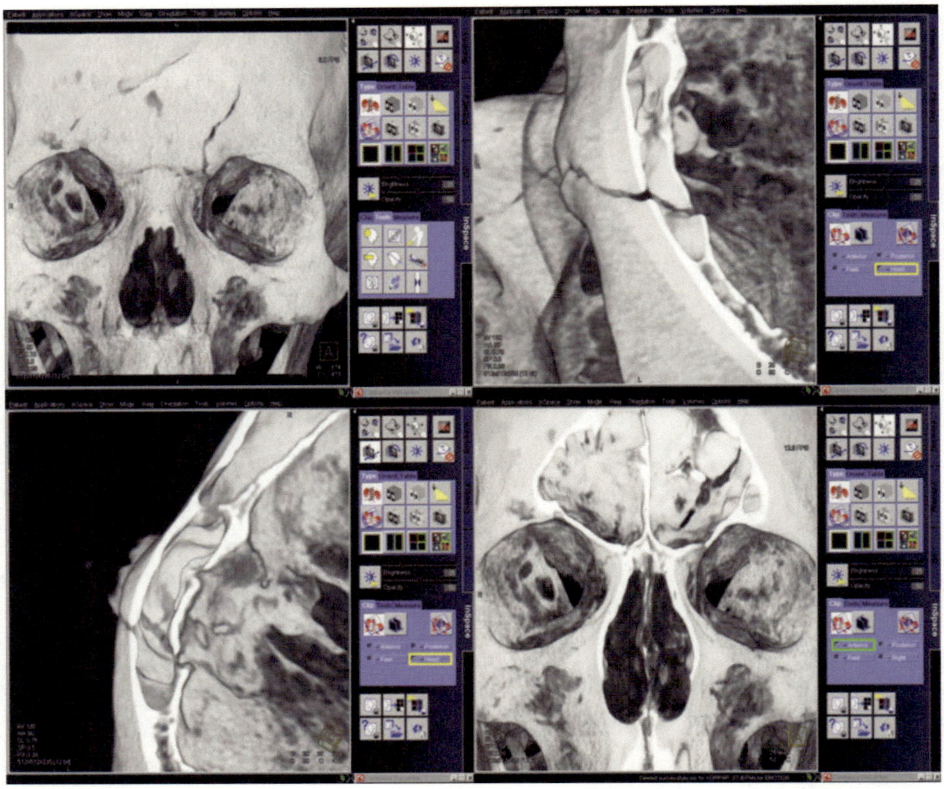

Fig. 10. Our 3D models of the human head in different projections. Virtual reality systems may be used for visualization of anatomical structures, virtual endoscopy, 3D-image-guided surgery as well as of pathology and/or anatomy during the planning of therapy (taken with permission from Belina et al., 2009)

Such a model in medical applications will enable simulation of changes that the tissue undergoes when compressed, stretched, cut, or palpated. The computer must then generate, in real-time, an appropriate visualization of the tissue as it is deformed by the user. Biological tissue modeling represents an important research area with applications in many medical areas. In this context, physics-based deformable models represent a powerful simulation tool. In the context of VR applications, 3D visualization techniques in real-time are particularly important. The goal here is to develop methods for fast and realistic visualization of 3D objects that are in the VE.Advanced technologies of exploring 3D spatial models allow for simulation of endoscopic surgery and planning the course of the future procedure (VE) or telesurgery (Tele-VE). By entering the models and navigating through the operable regions the surgeon becomes aware of the problems he will encounter during the real operation. In this way, preparation for the operation could be done including identification of the shortest and safest mode for the real operation to perform (Klapan, J Telemed Telecare, 2002; Klapan, Am J ORL, 2002) (Fig. 11).

The two main approaches to visualization are surface rendering and volume rendering (Burtscher et al., 1998; Vannier, 1996). Surface rendering is a classical visualization method where object surfaces are approximated using a set of polygonal shapes such as triangles. Most general-purposed computers use this approach and such wide availability represents

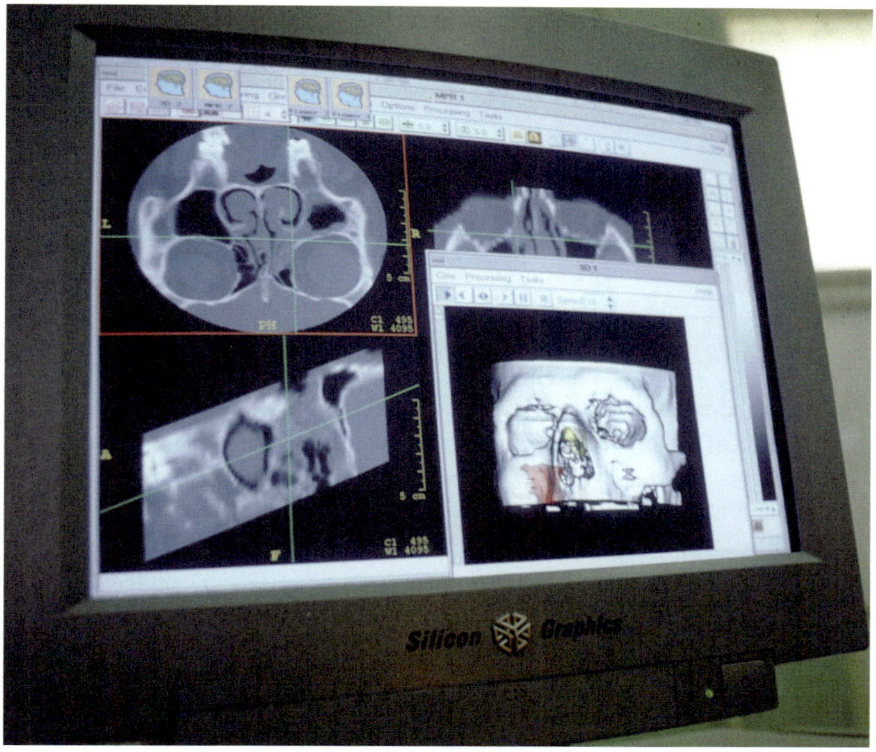

Fig. 11. An example of 3D-CA-FESS of the nose and paranasal sinuses with simulation and planning of the course of subsequent endoscopic operation (VE) (November 1994) (taken with permission from Klapan et al., Orbit 2001)

an important advantage of surface rendering. A disadvantage is that surface rendering cannot represent volume interior. Volume rendering can create very nice visualizations of volume interiors, but a disadvantage is that a special hardware is required for acceleration because of computational complexity.

2.3 Virtual endoscopy

Siemens Somatom Emotion 16 MSCT (from 2004) and 64 MSCT (from 2006) scanners were used for image acquisition from the very beginning of our VE acitivities (2004). CT images were stored in DICOM format and transferred to Xeon-based workstation running standard postprocessing software 3D Syngo CT 2006G from Siemens Medical Systems. Initial postprocessing was performed by radiologist and ENT specialist working together on In-space and Fly-through software. Working area during fly-through was divided in four windows showing CT image reconstruction in three major planes and resulting 3D rendered VE view for current position of virtual endocamera. Fly-through path planning was performed by moving mouse pointing device. Recordings of VE images together with appropriate CT images in three major planes during fly-through was performed with Camtasia recorder in real-time. 3D Syngo CT 2006G is the overall platform for the imaging workstation of Siemens Medical Systems. VE on the Syngo platform is performed using ray casting method with space leaping as major acceleration technique, and provides an automatic navigation mode (Fig. 12.).

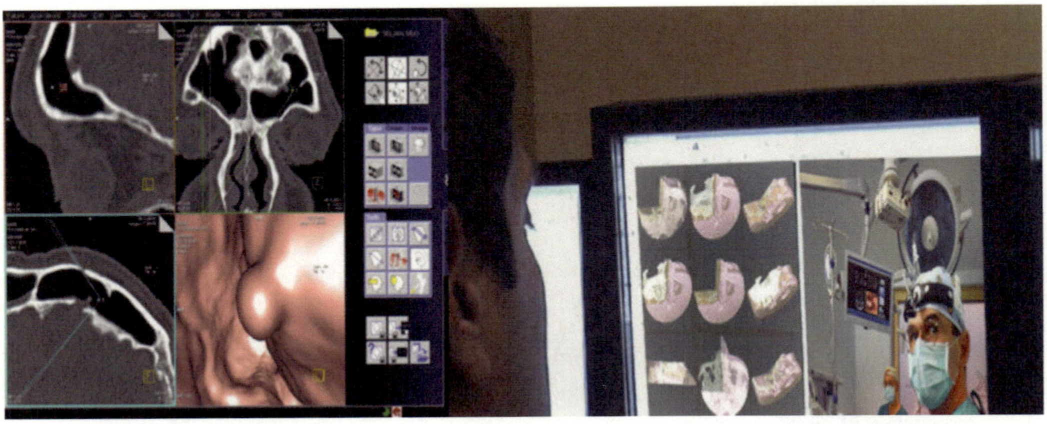

Fig. 12. An example of VE of the nose and paranasal sinuses with CT image reconstruction in three major planes and resulting 3D rendered VE view for current position of virtual endocamera (taken with permission from Belina et al. 2009, and Klapan Medical Group Polyclinic, Zagreb, Croatia)

We performed 644 VEs of the nasal cavity, scull base, and paranasal sinuses of patients with different pathology of paranasal sinuses as a part of diagnostic or preoperative management, such as: chronic sinus diseases, maxillary sinus cancer, different head traumas which involved paranasal sinuses, with multifragment fractures of maxillary sinus walls, ethmoids and lamina papiracea as well as the fracture of the sphenoid sinus wall.

2.4 Rapid prototyping models

In a rapid prototyping process, the product is firstly designed on a computer and then created based on the computer data. Therefore an essential prerequisite is the digital computer representation, usually made in a 3D geometrical modelling computer system like a CAD system, a 3D scanner, computer tomography, etc. Precision of a computer representation is a key parameter for controlling the tolerances of the future model. An important difference between rapid prototyping and traditional techniques is the fact that most of these new techniques build parts by adding material (e.g. layer by layer) instead of removing it (Raos & Galeta, 2004).

The first commercial rapid prototyping process - Stereo Lithography was brought on the market in 1987. Today, there are many different rapid prototyping techniques with high accuracy and large choices of materials available on the market. However, some of specially developed rapid prototyping techniques are still not commercialized. The most successfully developed techniques are: Stereo Lithography, Selective Laser Sintering, Laminated Object Manufacturing, Fused Deposition Modelling, Solid Ground Curing and nowadays the most popular 3D Printing.

During last two decades rapid prototyping techniques have been tested and used in many different areas in medicine (Petzold et al., 1999). Such areas include:

- The physical models of human organs that are extremely effective in realizing the anatomy and enhancing discussion and collaboration among teachers, students, researchers and physicians;
- Virtual planning and simulation of operation for orthopaedic surgery, vascular surgery and maxilla surgery with complex spatial relationships;

- Prosthesis like titanium dental cast crowns, free of porosity, with excellent functional contour and a smooth surface finish, could be obtained from the first casting trial;
- Implants are also very interesting for possible rapid production, therefore many researches' have been;
- Biomedical devices like a rapid produced polymeric implant consisted of a drug embedded in a polymeric matrix that was surgically implanted into the body.

Some of common advantages of rapid prototyping techniques when used in medicine are: speed; manufacturing flexibility; high degree of control over part microstructure; wide variety of engineering and medical materials.

Existing rapid prototyping techniques also have some common shortcomings like: lack of required mechanical properties depending on material combination; low accuracy; high computational demands and poor bio-compatibility. Yet, most of listed shortcomings can be successfully avoided in particular case with proper selection of techniques and materials (Galeta et al., 2008).

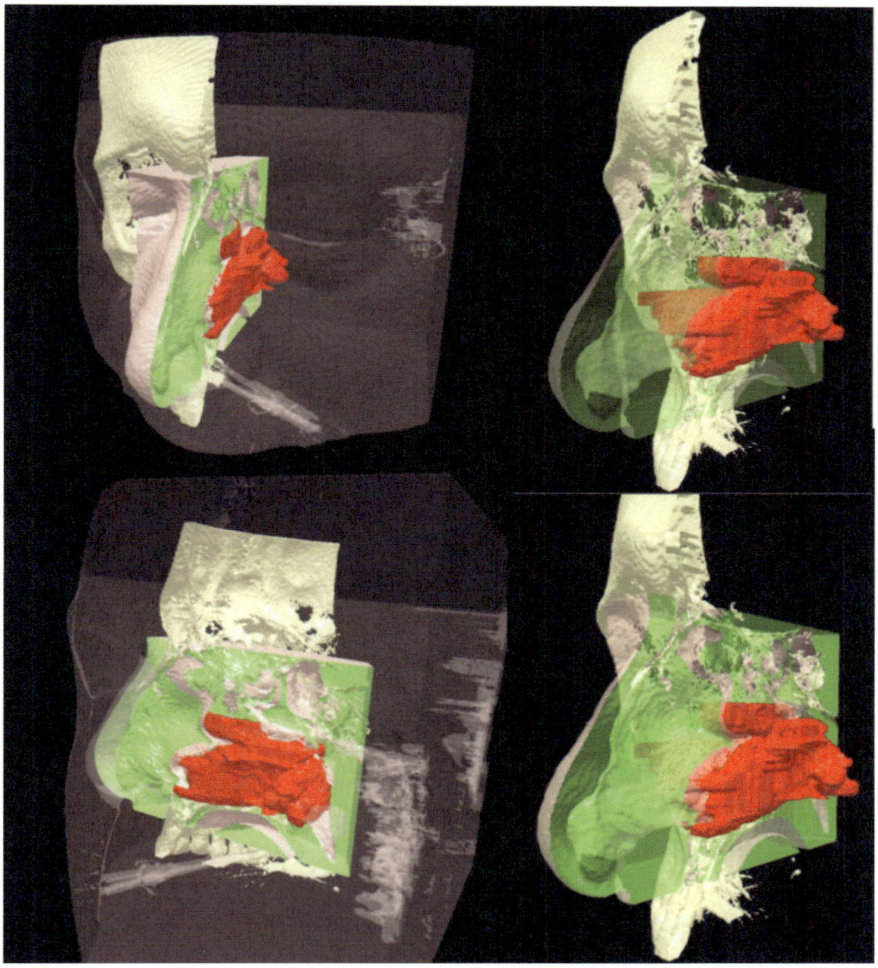

Fig. 13. Rapid prototyping models (taken with permission of Klapan Medical Group Polyclinic, Zagreb, Croatia)

2.5 Computer assisted navigation surgery

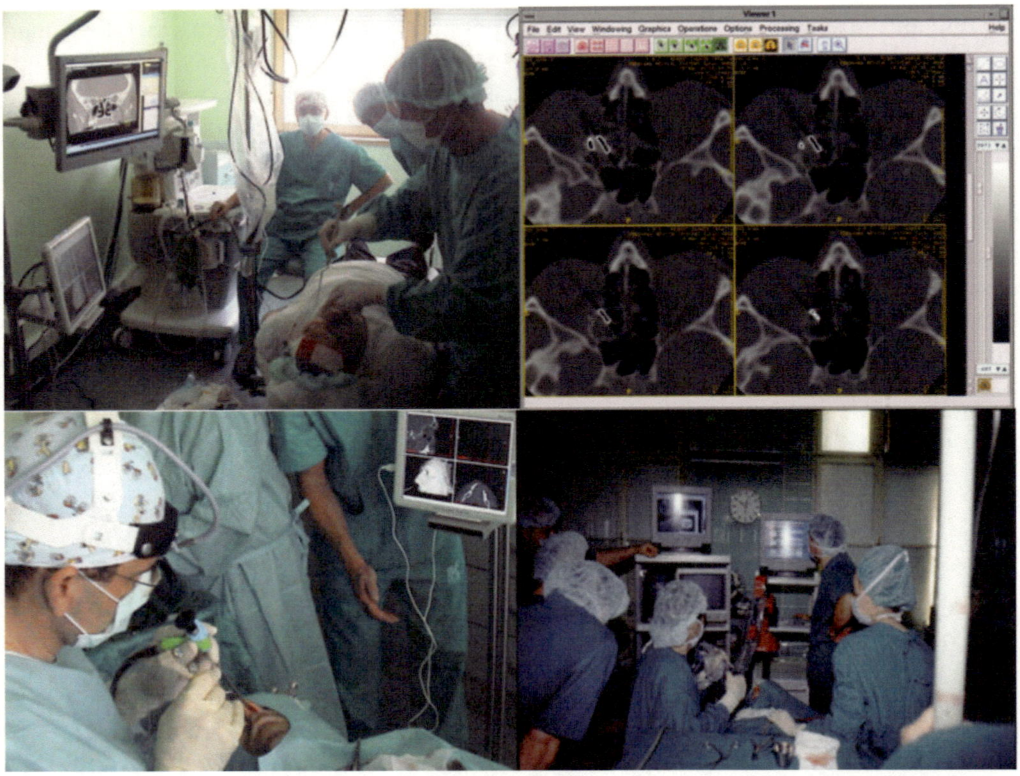

Fig. 14. Computer assisted navigation operations (taken with permission of Klapan et al., Orbit, 2001., and Klapan Medical Group Polyclinic, Zagreb, Croatia)

2.6 Computer assisted telesurgery

Computer technologies allow for computer assisted surgery to be performed at distance. The basic form of telesurgery can be realized by using audio and video consultations during the procedure. Sophisticated endoscopic cameras show the operative field on the monitor mounted in the operating theater, however, the image can also be transmitted to a remote location by use of video transmission. The latest computer technology enables receipt of CT images from a remote location, examination of these images, development of 3D spatial models, and transfer of thus created models back to the remote location (Klapan et al., 2006). All these can be done nearly within real time. These procedures also imply preoperative consultation. During the surgery, those in the operating theater and remote consultants follow on the patient computer model the procedure images, the 'live' video image generated by the endoscopic camera, and instrument movements made by the remote surgeon (Klapan et al., 1999). Simultaneous movement of the 3D spatial model on the computers connected to the system providing consultation is enabled (Klapan et al., J Telemed Telecare 2002; Klapan et al., ORL H&N Surg, 2002). It should be noted that in most cases, intraoperative consultation can be realized from two or more locations, thus utmost care should be exercised to establish proper network among them.

The extreme usage of computer networks and telesurgery implies the use of robot technologies operated by remote control. In such a way, complicated operative procedures could be carried out from distant locations. The main idea considering the use of computer networks in medicine is: *it is preferable to move the data rather than patients* (Fig. 15). In the future, we can expect more applications of VR in medicine. Advances in computer science will make possible more realistic simulations. VR, 3D-CAS, and Tele-3D-CAS systems of the future will find many applications in both medical diagnostics and computer-aided intervention.

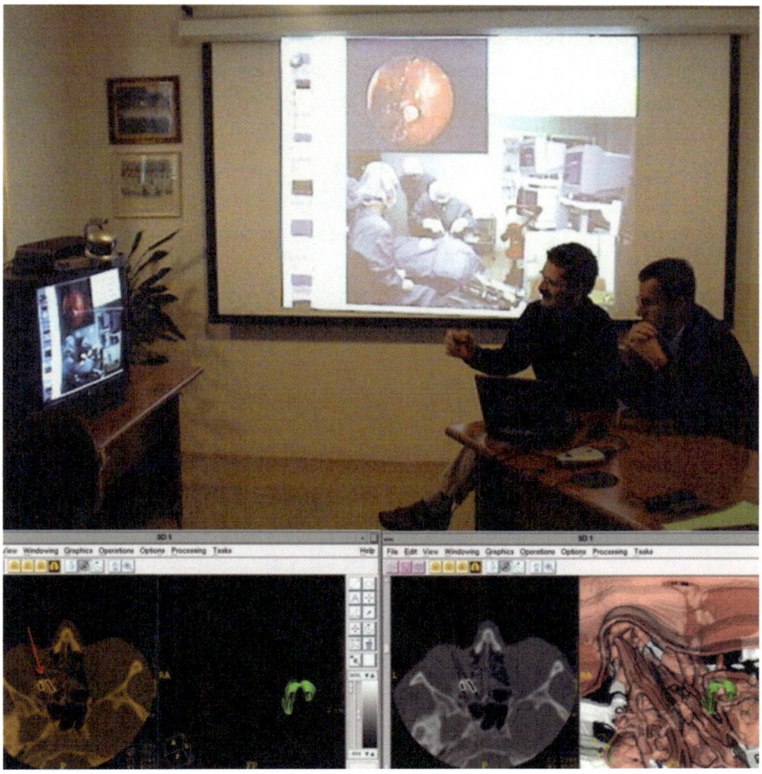

Fig. 15. An example of our tele-3D-CA-surgeries of the nose and paranasal sinuses in 1998/2000., representing the use of 3D imaging of the organ of interest (e.g using CT, or MRI) (taken with permission from Klapan et al., Otolaryngology Head Neck Surg 2002., and Klapan Medical Group Polyclinic, Zagreb, Croatia)

2.7 Computer networks

Very important factor for realization of 3D-CAS, and Tele-3D-CAS applications which represent a typical VR philosophy in routine daily diagnostic and surgical practice, and VR systems is a fast computer network. The network is the basis for any tele-activity. Fast computer networks are also the basis for telemedical applications, which may also be viewed as a kind of teleoperation systems.

Following the application of computers in surgery and connecting diagnostic devices with computer networks by use of DICOM protocol, the next step is directed toward connecting these local computer networks with broad range networks, i.e. within a clinical center, city,

country, or countries. The establishment of complex computer networks of diagnostic systems across the country offers another significant application of computer networks in medicine, i.e. telemedicine. Current computer networks using ATM technology allow for very fast and simultaneous communication among a number of physicians for joint diagnostic or therapeutic consultation. Textual, image, audio and video communication as well as exchange of operative field spatial models are thus enabled. Patient images and 3D spatial models can be simultaneously examined by a number of phyisicans, who then can outline and describe image segments by use of textual messages, indicator devices, sound or live image. The course and conclusions of such a consultation can be stored in computer systems and subsequently explored, used or forwarded to other users of the computer assisted diagnostic system.
The use of computer networks in medicine allows for high quality emergency interventions and consultations requested from remote and less equipped medical centers in order to achieve the best possible diagnosis and treatment (e.g., surgery). In addition to this, through consultation with a surgeon, a physician in a remote diagnostic center can perform appropriate imaging of a given anatomic region, which is of utmost importance for subsequent operation to be carried out by the consultant surgeon from the remote hospital center.

2.8 Video technologies

During telesurgical transmission, two video signals have to be transferred from the OR site and one video signal from every remote site involved in the telesurgery procedure. As about 24 Mb/s of bandwidth are needed for the native video signal, and there are only 155 Mb/s or multiple 2Mb/s lines of bandwidth, the video signals must be compressed using standard video compression systems (Satava, 1996; Klapan et al., 1999). At each of the four locations involved in the telesurgical procedure there was a remotely controlled video switch with 8 video inputs and 8 video outputs. At the expert location, remote from the OR, there was a video processor for the acquisition of all video signals from all sites involved in the telesurgery procedure and software for the remote control of all video inputs/outputs and pan/tilt/zoom cameras of all locations. Thus, from this point in the telesurgery network, a consultant or conference moderator (Schlag et al, 1998) can view all the video signals or just the primary display. For all these possibilities, a bandwidth of at least 155Mb/s asynchronous transfer mode (ATM OC-3) is needed.

2.9 Network technologies

ATM switches and adaptation layer type 5 (AAL-5) were used for video transmission and native or LANE for TCP/IP (transmission control protocol/internet protocol) computer communications in our tele-3D-CAS.

2.10 Collaboration

InPerson teleconferencing software and the native TCP/IP network was used for communication between all sites in our tele-3D-CAS. Consultations using computer images and 3D-models were performed using the video network; outputs from the computer were encoded into video stream and transmitted to the remote locations through video communication protocols. The advantage is that only standard video equipment, without any type of computer, needs to be installed at the remote location; the disadvantage is the image or 3D-model from the local computer can only be viewed at the remote location and cannot be manipulated with computer software.

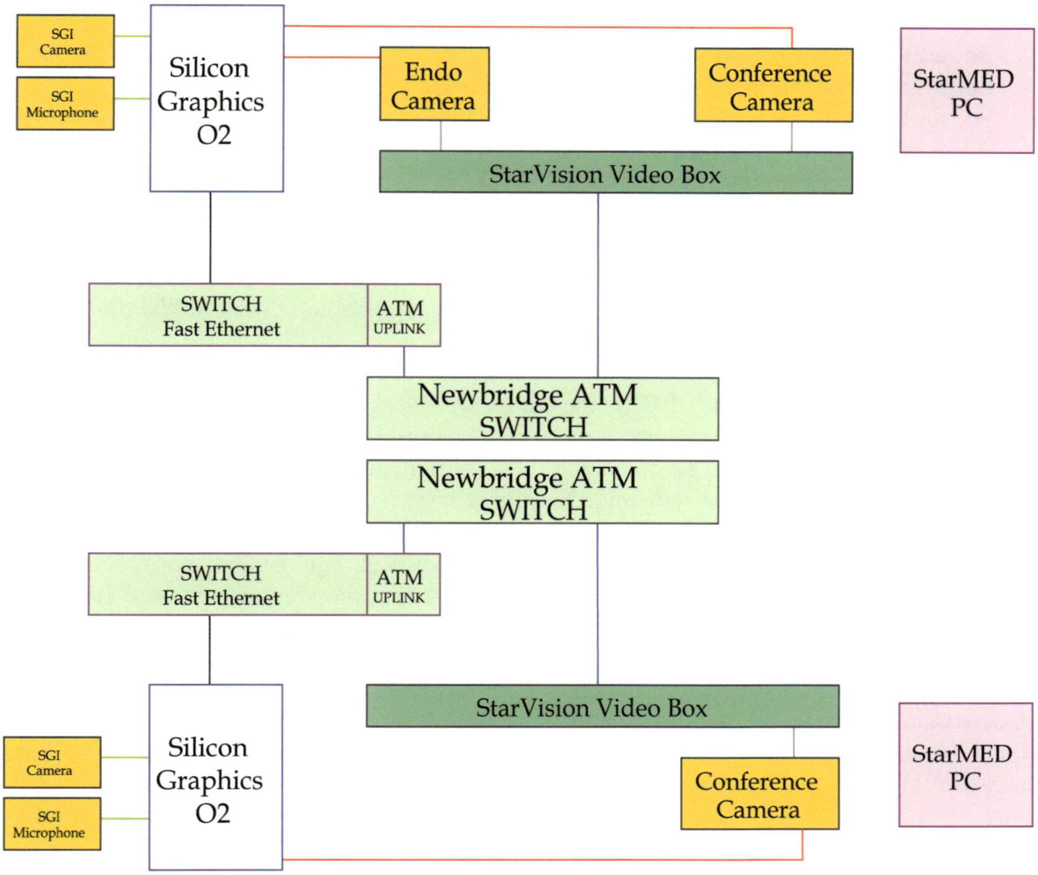

Fig. 16. Our Telesurgical equipment in ATM Network (OC-3, 155Mb/s) (taken with permission from Klapan et al., J Telemed Telecare 2002)

Video records of the procedure, MPEG streams of the procedure in combination with CT images and 3D models are essential for the creation of a computer database system for education and the preparation of future surgical procedures (Broadcasting, Tele-education, DVD-ROM, CD-ROM, www). In the real procedure, 3D computer models (Open Inventor) can be texture-mapped using the live video signal from the endocamera. The live video signal can be positioned using a 3D digitizer or any other spatial localizer. The texture mapped 3D model, with live video signal during the surgery, provides the surgeons with a more realistic computer presentation of the real surgical field. In our the 1st tele-3D-CAS, we used the following (Klapan et al., J Telemed Telecare 2002) (Fig. 16):

- SGI O2 workstation,
- Newbridge ATM Switch,
- ATM switched networks,
- Video streams over AAL-5,
- Computer communications over LANE (TCP/IP),
- 3Com Inverse Multiplexing (4xT1),
- Optivision MPEG1/MPEG2 encoders,
- Newbridge M-JPEG/MPEG1/MPEG2 encoders.

Network topologies:

- point to point T1 lines,
- nonroutable/routable shared FastEthernet/Ethernet,
- nonroutable/routable switched FastEthernet/Ethernet,
- ATM switched networks with AAL-5 and LANE,
- multiple T1 lines (today).

Usage of collaboration tools (H.120, H.323):

- SGI InPerson (Video, Audio, WhiteBoard),
- SGI Meeting (Whiteboard, Application Share/Collaboration),
- Microsoft NetMeeting(Video, Audio, Whiteboard, Application Share/Collaboration),
- StarVison StarMED, StarED.

From the very beginning of our 3D-CAS (Klapan et al., 2006; Klapan et al., 2008), and tele-3D-CA-surgeries (Klapan et al., 1997), the modeling was done by use of the VolVis, Volpack/Vprender, GL Ware programs on a DEC Station 3100 computer .With the advent of 3D Viewnix V1.0 software, we started using this program, and then 3D Viewnix V1.1 system, AnalyzeAVW system, T-Vox system and OmniPro 2 system on Silicon Graphics O2, Origin200 and Origin2000 computers. Our team used several standards to encode live video signals in telesurgery, such as M-JPEG, MPEG1, MPEG2 and MPEG4. For conferencing/consultation cameras used between two or more connected sites during the surgery, we used JPEG and MPEG1 stream with audio. Operation rooms (OR) were connected using several computer network technologies with different bandwidths, from T1, E1 and multiple E1 to ATM-OC3 (from 1Mb/s to 155Mb/s). For computer communications using X-protocol for image/3D-models manipulations, we needed an additional 4Mb/s of bandwidth, instead of the 1Mb/s when we used our own communication tools for the transfer of surgical instrument movements (Table 1.).

	First tele-3D-CAS	Second tele-3D-CAS
Video technology	M-JPEG, H.323	MPEG1/2, H.323
Network technology	ATM OC-3 155Mb/s	Inverse multiplexing 4xT1 8Mb/s
Collaborative computing	N.A.	SGImeeting, NetMeeting, T.120
Consultancy	Through video	Collaborative tools T.120 Through video
Preoperative consultancy	Through video InPerson, H.323	Collaborative computing T.120, H.323
Number of involved locations	3	2
Video acquisition/processing	Multiple In/Out (8/8) Quad split	N.A. Manually controlled switch
Number of video signals	2 from O.R. 1 from other sites	1 from O.R. 1 from other sites
Hardware	SGI O2, PC	SGI O2
Software	SGI IRIX, MS Windows, StarMED, OmniPro, InPerson	SGI IRIX, MS Windows, OmniPro, SGImeeting, NetMeeting, InPerson

Table 1. Comparison between our first and second Tele-3D-CAS (FESS) (taken with permission from Klapan et al., J Telemed Telecare, 2002)

3. Discussion

In 1992, when we tried to establish the first system implementation for our CA-surgery, a scientific research rhinosurgical team was organized at the University Department of ENT-Head & Neck Surgery, Zagreb University School of Medicine and Zagreb University Hospital Center in Zagreb, who have developed the idea of a novel approach in head surgery. This computer aided FESS with 3D-support has been named 3D-CA-FESS. The first 3D-CA-FESS operation in Croatia was carried out at the Šalata University Department of ENT, Head & Neck Surgery in June 3, 1994., when a 12-year-old child, was inflicted a gunshot wound in the region of the left eye. Status: gunshot wound of the left orbit, injury to the lower eyelid and conjunctiva of the left eye bulb. Massive subretinal, retinal and preretinal hemorrhage was visible. The vitreous diffusely blurred with blood. The child was blinded on the injured eye (today, sixteen years after the operation, 29 year old patient shown in the Fig. 17) (Klapan et al., 1996, 1997, 2002).

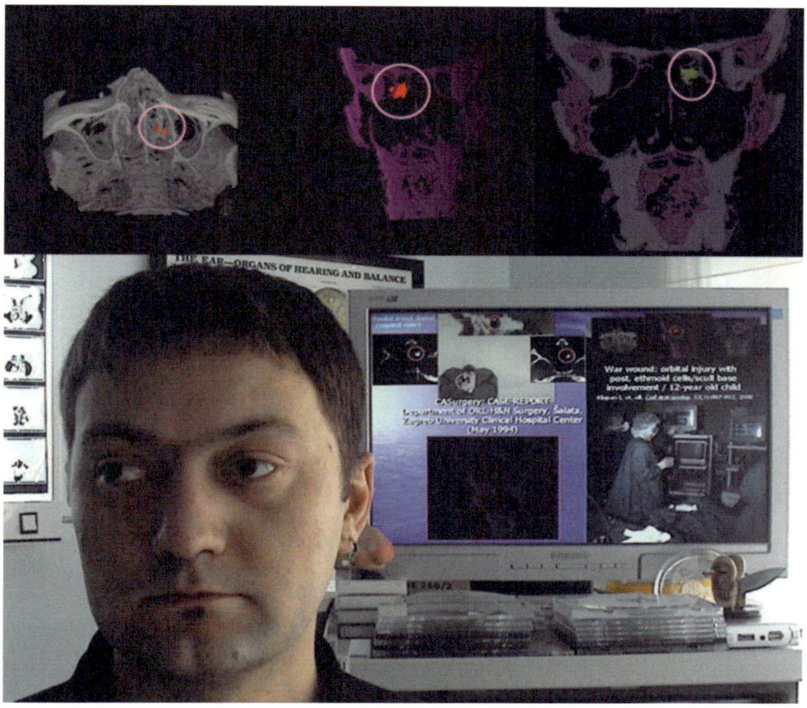

Fig. 17. Different 3D models with evidence of the metallic foreign body. Using the *static 3D model* elaborated from 2D CT sinus section, we obtained relative relationships of the borderline areas that are important for the diagnosis of pathologic conditions in the region, which proved to be a significant improvement in comparison with 2D visualization in the form of stratified images (taken with permission from Klapan et al., Am J Otolaryngol, 2002. and Klapan Medical Group Polyclinic, Zagreb, Croatia)

Additionaly, with due understanding and support from the University Department of ENT, Head & Neck Surgery, Zagreb University Hospital Center; Merkur University Hospital; T-Com Company; InfoNET; and SiliconMaster, in May 1996 the scientific research rhinosurgical team from the Šalata University Department of ENT-Head & Neck Surgery organized and successfully conducted the first distant radiologic-surgical consultation (teleradiology) within the frame of the 3D-C-FESS project. The consultation was performed before the operative procedure between two distant clinical work posts in Zagreb (Šalata University Department of ENT, Head & Neck Surgery and Merkur University Hospital) (outline/network topology).In October 1998, and on several occasions thereafter, the team conducted a number of first tele-3D-computer assisted operations as unique procedures of the type not only in Croatia but worldwide (www.mef.hr/MODERNRHINOLOGY and www.poliklinika-klapan.com) (Klapan et al., 1997; Klapan et al., 1999). During the first telesurgry of this kind, a surgical team carrying out an operative procedure at the Šalata ENT Department, Zagreb University School of Medicine and Zagreb Clinical Hospital Center, received instructions, suggestions and guidance through the procedure by an expert surgeon from an expert center. The third active point was the Faculty of Electrical Engineering and Computing, where ENT specialists, students and residents took an active part in the entire surgical procedure. This tele-3D-CA-FESS surgery, performed as described above, was successfully completed in 15 minutes (Fig. 18).

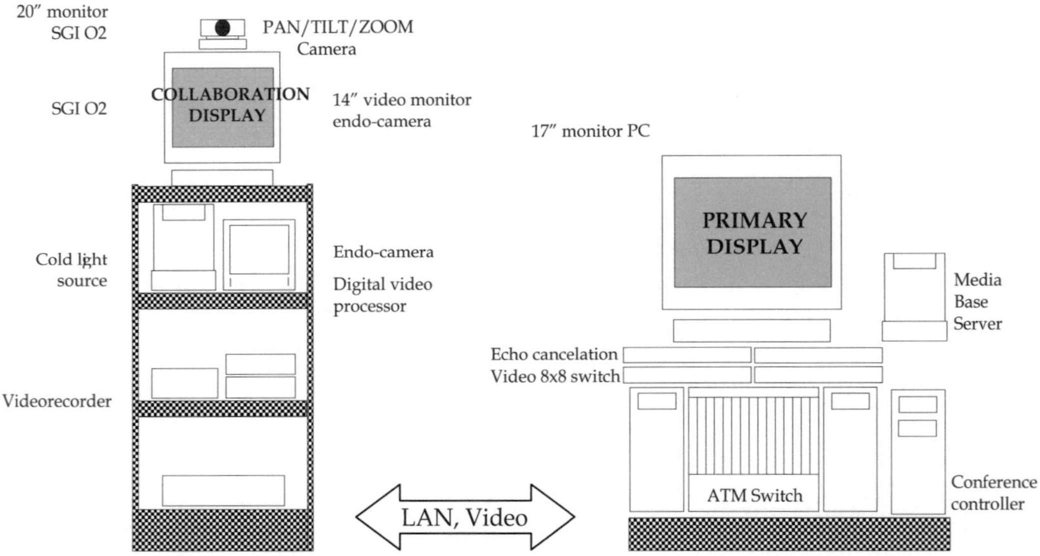

Fig. 18. An example of our Tele-3D-C-FESS surgery initially performed in 1998 (taken with permission from Klapan et al., Otolaryngology Head Neck Surg, 2002)

The complex software systems allow visualization of a 2D CT or MRI section in its natural course (the course of examination performed), or in an imaginary, arbitrary course. Particular images can be transferred, processed and deleted, or can be presented in animated images. The series of images can be changed, or images can be generated in different projections through the volume recorded.

Before the development of 3D spatial model, each individual image or a series of images have to be segmented, in order to single out the image parts of interest. 3D-model completely presents the relative relations of borderline areas that are of utmost diagnostic importance, which is a considerable advancement compared with standard 2D stratified imaging. Comparative analysis of 3D anatomic models with intraoperative finding shows the 3D volume rendering image to be very good, actually a visualization standard that allows imaging likewise the real intraoperative anatomy (Mann & Klimek, 1998; Hamadeh et al., 1998).

The technique of examination intended to realize in the proposed study provides, according to many authors, optimal visualization of the paranasal sinus anatomy. Moreover, by use of this approach, some substantial advancements are achieved in the diagnosis of the pathologic state of paranasal sinuses, based on CT analysis, e.g. (a) basic CT diagnostics has become an important aid in the diagnosis of chronic sinusitis, in terms of the follow-up and prognosis of the course and treatment outcome; (b) additional axial or coronal sections are avoided by the development and use of 3D model (so-called volume-rendering technique) for diagnostic purposes; (c) as indicated in (b), the dose of irradiation to which the patient is exposed is considerably reduced by the use of volume rendering technique; etc.

Therefore, we made endeavors to implement all these concepts and advantages of the new mode of 3D visualization not only in daily 3D-CAS performed in our operating theaters but also as a specific form of telesurgery with 3D computer assisted support, currently a completely new and original type of telesurgery in the world, with the use of most sophisticated computer technology in any OR. The surgeon and consultants view four split video signals (quad split video processing) on the primary video display: one from the endocamera, one from the OR camera, one from the first remote site and one from the second remote site. However, during real surgery, all locations involved in such telesurgery usually view only the video signal from the endocamera procedure on their primary displays. In real surgery, there is one patient at one location included in the "telesurgical procedure", with one or more consultants at one or more remote locations (the local location is where the surgery is performed, and remote locations are the other locations included in the telesurgery procedure) (Sezeur, 1998). As we already discussed, two video streams (the endocamera and the conference camera) have to be transferred from the local location (patient location), and one video stream (the conference camera) has to be transferred from each remote location (consultants). At each location, video monitors are needed for video streams from any other location included in the telesurgery procedure (up to four video streams on one large video monitor, quad-split, can be used). An LCD/TFT video projector can be put in the OR. Using such tele-CA-system, the possibility of exact preoperative, non-invasive visualization of the spatial relationships of anatomic and pathologic structures, including extremely fragile ones (Hauser et al., 1997, Vinas et al., 1997), size and extent of pathologic process (Elolf et al., 1998; Burtcher et al., 1998), and to precisely predict the course of surgical procedure (Man & Klimek, 1998), definitely allows the surgeon in any 3D-CAS or Tele-CAS procedure to achieve considerable advantage in the preoperative examination of the patient, and to reduce the risk of intraoperative complications, all this by use of VS or diagnosis. With the use of 3D model, the surgeon's orientation in the operative field is considerably facilitated (Burtcher et al., 1998) ("patient location" as well as the "location of the tele-expert consultant"), and all procedures and manipulations are performed with higher certainty and safety (Olson & Citardi, 1999).

As it can be seen, one of their main applications of Tele-3D-C-FESS is 3D-navigation (VE) in the study of anatomy and surgery ("computed journey through the nose and paranasal sinuses"). From this point of view this approach can be compared with similar simulator systems for the training of endoscopic sinus surgery presently available on the market, but definitely we have to be aware that it is not the study of or training in anatomy or surgery, but pure implementation of live surgical procedure with computer support in real time, the prime and foremost aim being the achievement of faster and safer procedure. So, it should be made clear that the main message of our Tele-3D-C-FESS surgery, as differentiated from the standard tele-surgeries worldwide, is the use of the 3D-model operative field, and thus of "VS", which in addition to higher safety allows for successful course of operation, especially in small, detached medical institutions where advanced endoscopic techniques are not available. This is of paramount importance for emergency surgical interventions which have to be performed in distant medical institutions where the service of "well known surgical experts" (e.g., skull base surgery) is not available.

3.1 Postoperative analysis

Surgical workstation includes 3D vision, dexterous precision surgical instrument manipulation, and input of force feedback sensory information. The surgeon and/or telesurgeon operates in a virtual world (Klapan et al., 2006). The use of computer technology during preoperative preparation and surgery performance allows for all relevant patient data to store during the treatment. CT images, results of other tests and examinations, computer images, 3D spatial models, and both computer and video records of the course of operation and teleoperation are stored in the computer and in CD-R devices for subsequent analysis (www.mef.hr/MODERNRHINOLOGY). Also, these are highly useful in education on and practice of different approaches in surgery for surgery residents as well as for specialists in various surgical subspecialties.

VR has many applications in CA-surgery. Statistical studies show that physicians are more likely to make errors during their first several to few dozen surgical procedures. Surgical training may be done on cadavers, but the problem is a chronical shortage of cadavers for medical research. It would be helpful if medical training could be performed using a realistic imitation of a human body inside the computer. Such computer-based training can be used for minimally invasive surgery, and for open surgery. Training on cadavers has several drawbacks: a) if trainee cuts a nerve or a blood vessel in a cadaver nothing will happen, b) no action can be reversed on cadavers (what is cut is cut), c) dead tissue is harder, color is changed, and arteries do not pulsate. Advantages of computer simulations are that the procedures can be repeated many times with no damage to virtual body, virtual body does not have to be dead - many functions of living body can be simulated for realistic visualizations, and organs can be made transparent and modeled. The trainee may be warned of any mistakes in the surgical procedure using a multimedia-based context-sensitive help.

In this way, the real surgery and/or telesurgery procedures can be subsequently analyzed and possible shortcomings defined in order to further improve operative treatment. The use of latest computer technologies enables connection between the computer 3D spatial model of the surgical field and video recording of the course of surgery to observe all critical points during the procedure, with the ultimate goal to improve future procedures and to develop such an expert system that will enable computer assisted surgery and telesurgery with due account of all the experience acquired on previous procedures (Klapan et al., ORL H&N Surg, 2002) . Also, using the computer recorded co-ordinate shifts of 3D digitalizer during the telesurgery procedure, an animated image of the course of surgery can be created in the form of navigation, i.e. the real patient operative field fly-through, as it was done from the very beginning (from 1998) in our telesurgeries.

The real-time requirement means that the simulation must be able to follow the actions of the user that may be moving in the virtual environment (Belina et al., 2008). The computer system must also store in its memory a 3D model of the virtual environment, as we did in our first activities in 1994 (3D-CAS models; Fig. 19). In that case a real-time virtual reality (VR) system will update the 3D graphical visualization as the user moves, so that up-to-date visualization is always shown on the computer screen (Belina et al., 2009) (Fig. 20).

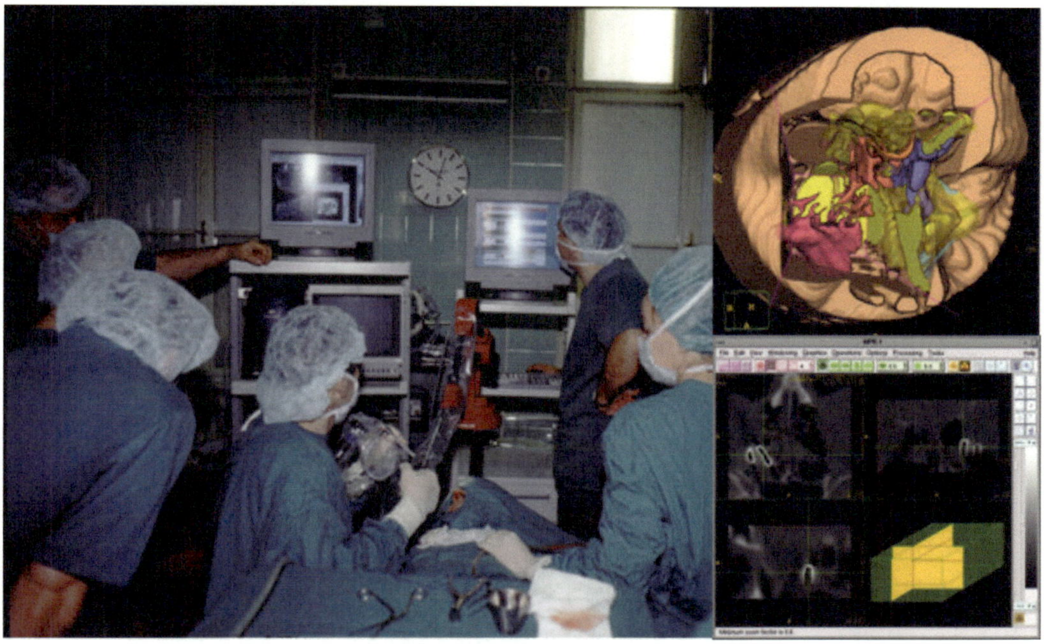

Fig. 19. Transmission of 3D-models as VE of the human head, realized during our tele-3D-CA-endoscopic sinus surgeries in 1998., when we used 3D image analysis to create the model of the desired anatomical structures (segmentation) (taken with permission from Klapan et al., Ear Nose Throat J, 2006. and Klapan Medical Group Polyclinic, Zagreb, Croatia)

Upon the completion of the CAS and/or tele-CAS-operation, the surgeon compares the preoperative and postoperative images and models of the operative field, and studies video records of the procedure itself. In otorhinolaryngology, especially in rhinology, research in the area of 2D and 3D image analysis, visualization, tissue modelling, and human-machine interfaces provides scientific expertise necessary for developing successful VR applications (Johnson, 2007). The basic requirement in rhinology, resulting from the above mentioned needs refers to the use of a computer system for visualization of anatomic 3D-structures and integral operative field to be operated on (Fig. 21). To understand the idea of 3D-CAS/VR it is necessary to recognize that the perception of surrounding world created in our brain is based on information coming from the human senses and with the help of a knowledge that is stored in our brain. The usual definition says that the impression of being present in a virtual environment, such as virtual endoscopy (VE) of the patient's head, that does not exist in reality, is called VR.

The physician has impression of presence in the virtual world and can navigate through it and manipulate virtual objects. A 3D-CAS/VR system may be designed in such a way that the physician is completely impersed in the virtual environment.

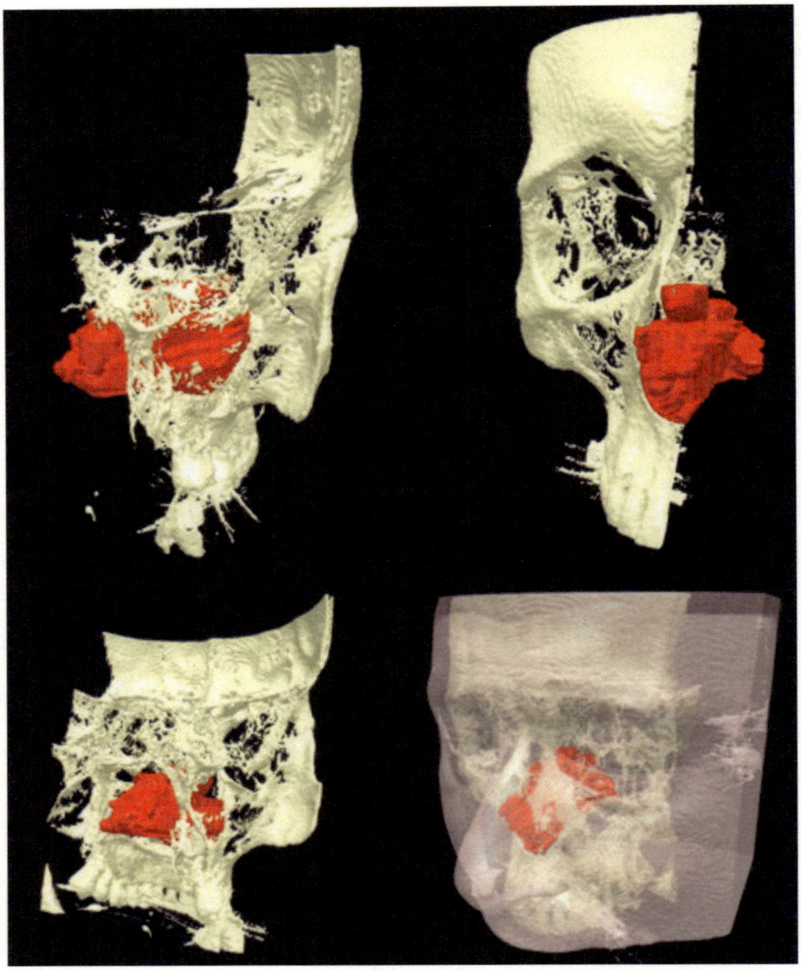

Fig. 20. 3D volume rendering technique can show the surface of the air-tissue interfaces, using a separate segmentation of air, soft tissue, bone, and pathologic tissue (taken with permission of Klapan Medical Group Polyclinic, Zagreb, Croatia)

4. Conclusions

Different VR applications become a routine preoperative procedure in human medicine, as we already shown in our surgical activities in the last two decades (from June 03, 1994), providing a highly useful and informative visualization of the regions of interest, thus bringing advancement in defining the geometric information on anatomical contours of 3D-human head-models by the transfer of so-called "image pixels" to "contour pixels" (Rubino et al., 2002).

Telemedicine attempts to break the distance barrier between the provider and the patient in health-care delivery. VR is able to simulate remote environments and can therefore be applied to telemedicine. Physicians can have VR produced copy of a remote environment including the patient at their physical location. One of the simplest telemedical applications is medical teleconsultation, where physicians exchange medical information, over computer

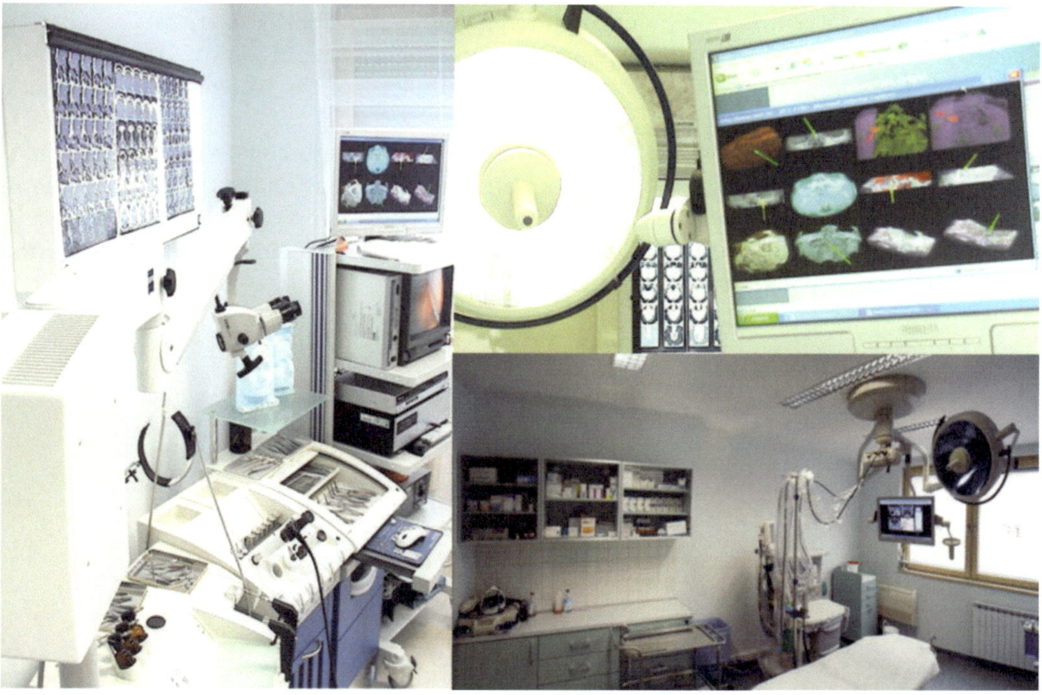

Fig. 21. Postoperative analysis, done after one our tele-3D-CA-sugreries in rhinology, where we defined the precise relationships of the borderline areas that are important for the diagnosis of pathologic conditions in the patient's head (taken with permission of Klapan Medical Group Polyclinic, Zagreb, Croatia)

networks, with other physicians in the form of image, video, audio, and text. Teleconsultations can be used in radiology, pathology, surgery, and other medical areas. One of the most interesting telemedical applications is tele-surgery. Telesurgery is a telepresence application in medicine where the surgeon and the patient are at different locations, but such systems are still in an early research phase. Patients, who are too ill or injured to be transported to a hospital, may be operated remotely. In all these cases, there is a need for a surgeon specialist who is located at some distance. Generaly speaking, the purpose of a tele-presence system is to create a sense of physical presence at a remote location. Tele-presence is achieved by generating sensory stimulus so that the operator has an illusion of being present at a location distant from the location of physical presence. A tele-presence system extends operator's sensory-motor facilities and problem solving abilities to a remote environment. A tele-operation system enables operation at a distant remote site by providing the local operator with necessary sensory information to simulate operator's presence at the remote location. Tele-operation is a special case of tele-presence where in addition to illusion of presence at a remote location operator also has the ability to perform certain actions or manipulations at the remote site. In this way it is possible to perform various actions in distance locations, where it is not possible to go due to a danger, prohibitive price, or a large distance. Realization of VR systems require software (design of VE) for running VR applications in real-time. Simulations in real-time require powerful computers that can perform real-time computations required for generation of visual displays.

Different goals can be achieved by using different VR applications. These goals range from teaching, diagnosis, intervention planning, providing insight into the potentially complicated and non-standard anatomy, as well pathology of the patients, intra-operative navigation, etc.

VE or fly-through methods which combine the features of endoscopic viewing and cross-sectional volumetric imaging provided more effective and safer endoscopic procedures in diagnostics and management of our patients, especially preoperatively, as we already discussed (Fig.22). This approach can also be applied for training and familiarize the surgeon with endoscopic anatomic appearance.

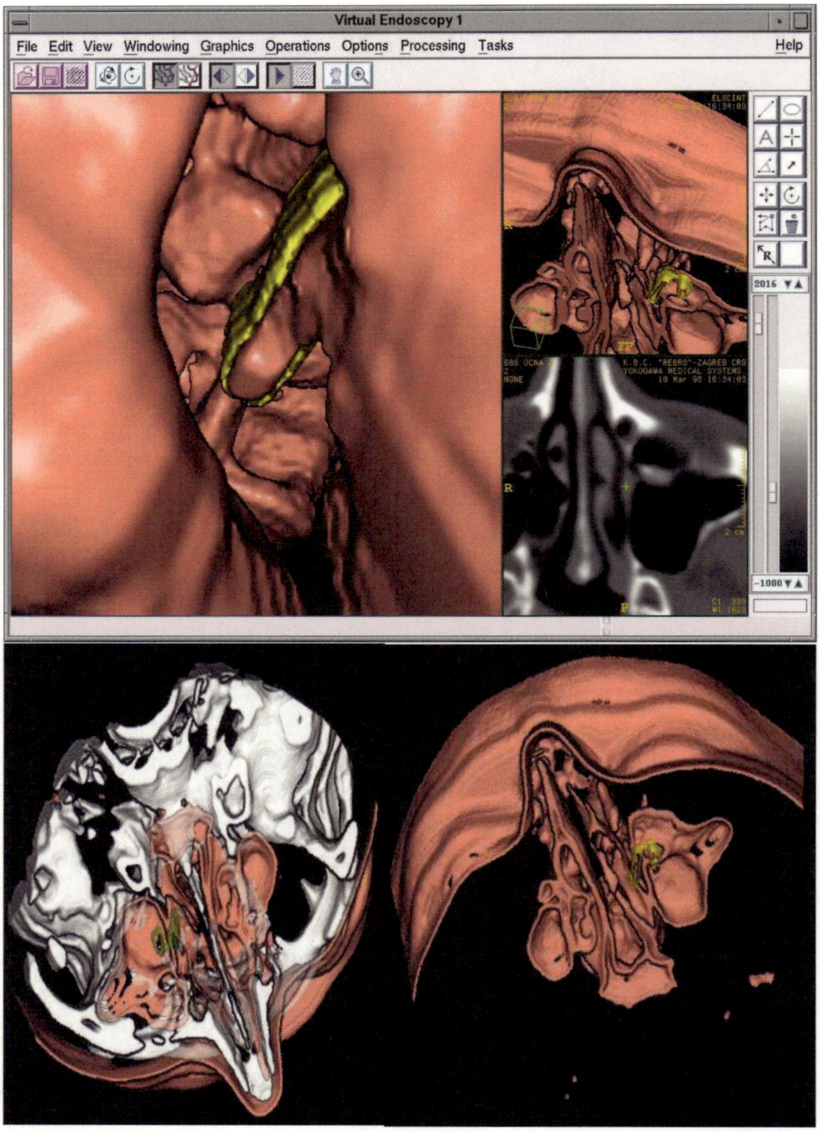

Fig. 22. Virtual endoscopy during our 3D-CA-endoscopic surgery (taken with permission of Klapan Medical Group Polyclinic, Zagreb, Croatia)

Definitely, the presentation of image data in such a way enables the operator not only to explore the inner wall surfaces but also to navigate inside the virtual organs extracted from MSCT and/or MR images of nasal cavity, paranasal sinuses and scull base, and in combination with in-space skull bone rendering, offers plastic and accurate additional 3D information for head and neck surgeon in combination with classical 2D black and white CT images (Belina et al., 2008). Interactive display of correlated 2D and 3D data in a four-window format may assist the endoscopist in performing various image guided procedures. In comparison with real endoscopy, the VE is completely non-invasive. It is possible to repeat the same procedure several times, therefore it may be a valuable tool for training, as well as the interactive control of all virtual camera parameters, including the field-of-view, and the viewing as opposed to the extend of lesions within and beyond the wall which gives the potential to stage tumors by determining the location and the extent of transmural extension (Belina et al., 2008). In the nasal or sinus cavity, VE can clearly display the anatomic structure of the paranasal sinuses (Di Rienzo et al., 2003), nasopharyngeal cavity and upper respiratory tract, revealing damage to the sinus wall caused by a bone tumor or fracture (Tao et al., 2003; Belina et al., 2009), and use the corresponding cross-sectional image or multiplanar reconstructions to evaluate structures outside the sinus cavity. A major disadvantage of VE is its inability to make an impact on operating room performance, as well as the considerable time consumption (Caversaccio et al., 2003), to evaluate the mucosal surface (Belina et al., 2008), or to provide a realistic illustration of the various pathologic findings in cases with highly obstructive sinonasal disease (Bisdas et al., 2004).

Even more, our vision of 3D-CA-navigation surgery and/or tele-3D-CA-navigation surgery allows surgeons not only to see and transfer video signals but also to transfer 3D computer models and surgical instrument movements with image/3D-model manipulations in real time during the surgery (Šimičić et al., 1998) (Fig. 23). Considering the specificities and basic features of 3D-CA-navigation surgery and tele-3D-CAS, we believe that this type of surgery would be acceptable to many surgeons all over the world for the following reasons: a) the technology is readily available in collaboration with any telecom worldwide, b) the improved safety and reduced cost will allow the inclusion of a greater number of patients from distant hospital institutions in such a telesurgical expert system, c) the "presence" of leading international surgical experts as tele-consultants in any OR in the world will thus be possible in the near future, which will additionally stimulate the development of surgery in all settings; and d) the results obtained in the tele-3D-CAS project in Croatia are encouraging and favor the further development of the method.

The possibility of data analysis and storage in the 3D form and development of 3D centers at clinical institutions, as well as the development of the surgery using a remote-controlled robots (Vilbert et al., 2003) should provide a new quality in proper training of future surgeons in 3D-CAS as well as tele-3D-CAS activities (www.mef.hr/MODERNRHINOLOGY and www.poliklinika-klapan.com).

Finally, modelling of the biological material and tissue properties is an important field of research. In the future, we can expect a new generation of diagnostic imaging techniques that use simulated reality techniques for effective visualization of organ anatomy and function. Such systems will enable not only better medical diagnosis but also more appropriate intervention.

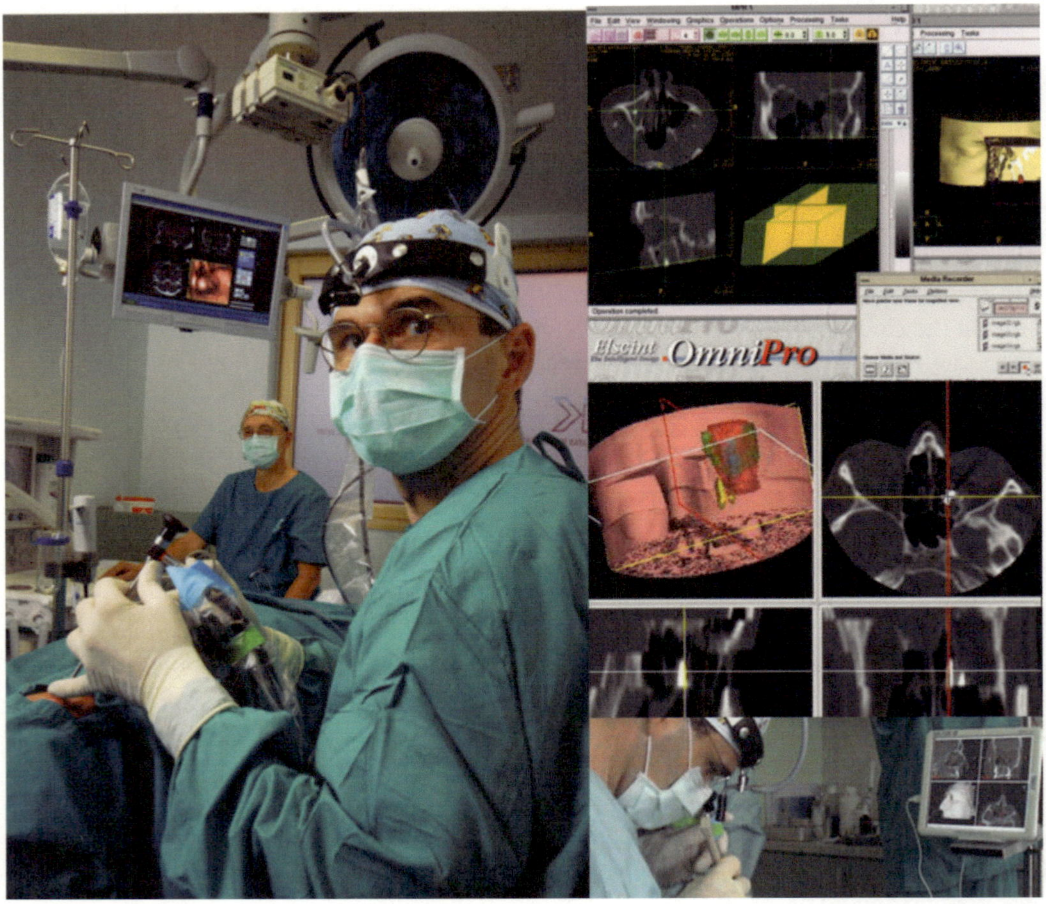

Fig. 23. Different VR applications can be applied for preoperative analysis, intraoperative surgery (as well as postoperative training and education), and completely familiarize the surgeon with endoscopic anatomy and pathology in the real operation (taken with permission from Klapan et al. Coll Anthrop 2008., and Klapan Medical Group Polyclinic, Zagreb, Croatia)

5. References

Aleid, W.; Watson, J.; Sidebottom, AJ.; Hollows, P. (2009). Development of in-house rapid manufacturing of three-dimensional models in maxillofacial surgery. *British Journal of Oral and Maxillofacial Surgery*, Article in press, 2010.

Anon, J. (1998). Computer-aided endoscopic sinus surgery. *Laryngoscope*, 108 (1998):949-961.

Bisdas, S.; Verink, M.; Burmeister, HP.; Stieve, M. & Becker, H. (2004). Three-dimensional visualization of the nasal cavity and paranasal sinuses. Clinical results of a standardized approach using multislice helical computed tomography. *J Comput Assist Tomogr*, 28(5) (2004):661-9.

Belina, S.; Ćuk, V.; Klapan, I.; Vranješ, Ž. & Lukinović, J. (2008). Our experience with virtual endoscopy of paranasal sinuses. *Coll Antropol*, 32(3) (2008) :887-892.

Belina, S.; Ćuk, V. & Klapan, I. (2009). Virtual endoscopy and 3D volume rendering in the management of frontal sinus fractures. *Coll Antropol*, 33(2) (2009) :115-119.

Burtscher, J.; Kremser.; C, Seiwald.; M, Obwegeser, A.; Wagner, M.; Aichner, F.; Twerdy, K. & Felber, S. (1998). 3D-computer assisted MRI for neurosurgical planning in parasagittal and parafalcine central region tumors. *Comput Aided Surg*, 3 (1998):27-32.

Caversaccio, M.; Eichenberger, A. & Hausler, R. (2003). Virtual simulator as a training tool for endonasal surgery. *Am J Rhinol*, 5 (2003) :283-90.

Di Rienzo, L.; Coen Tirelli, G.; Turchio, P.; Garaci, F. & Guazzaroni, M. (2003). Comparison of virtual and conventional endoscopy of nose and paranasal sinuses. *Ann Otol Rhinol Laryngol*, 112(2) (2003) :139-42.

Ecke, U.; Klimek, L.; Muller, W.; Ziegler, R. & Mann, W. (1998) Virtual reality: preparation and execution of sinus surgery. *Comput Aided Surg*, 3 (1998):45-50.

Elolf, E.; Tatagiba, M. & Samii, M. (1998). 3D-computer tomographic reconstruction: planning tool for surgery of skull base pathologies. *Comput Aided Surg* ,3 (1998):89-94.

Galeta, T.; Kljajin, M. & Karakašić, M. Geometric Accuracy by 2-D Printing Model. *Strojniški vestnik - Journal of Mechanical Engineering*, Vol. 10, No. 54, April 2008, 725-733, 0039-2480.

Hamadeh, A.; Lavallee, S. & Cinquin, P. (1998). Automated 3D CT and fluoroscopic image registration. *Comput Aided Surg*, 3 (1998):11-19.

Hassfeld, S. & Muhling, J. (1998). Navigation in maxillofacial and craniofacial surgery. *Comput Aided Surg*, 3 (1998):183-187.

Hauser, R.; Westermann, B. & Probst, R. (1997). Non.invasive 3D patient registration for image guided intranasal surgery. *Medical Robotics Comput Assisted Surg*, New York, Springer, str. 1997; 327-336.

Holtel, MR.; Burgess, LP. & Jones, SB. (1999). Virtual realiry and technologic solutions in Otolaryngology. *Otolaryngol Head Neck Surg*, 121(2) (1999):181.

Johnson, E. (2007). Surgical simulators and simulated surgeons: reconstituting medical practice and practitioners in simulations. *Social Studies of Science*, 37: 585-608

Keeve, E.; Girod, S.; Kikins, R. & Girod, B. 1998). Deformable modeling of facial tissue for craniofacial surgery simulation. *Comput Aided Surg*, 3 (1998):228-238.

Kenny, T.; Yildirim, A.; Duncavage, JA.; Bracikowski, J.; Murray, JJ. & Tanner, SB. (1999).Prospective analysis of sinus symptoms and correlation with CT scan. *Otolaryngol Head Neck Surg,* 121(2) (1999):111.

Klapan, I.; Šimičić, Lj.; Kubat, M. & Rišavi, R. (1996). Fracture of the ethmoid and medial orbital wall. Removal of the bullet per viam 3D C-FESS technique, In: *3rd EUFOS* (ed. Ribari O, Hirschberg A), Monduzzi Editore, Bologna, 2 (1996):83-87.

Klapan, I.; Šimiči,ć, Lj. & Kubat, M. (1997).. Our three-dimensional Computer Assisted Functional Endoscopic Sinus Surgery (3D C-FESS). In*: McCafferty GJ, Coman WB, eds. XVI World Congress of Otorhinolaryngology, Head and Neck Surgery, Sydney, Australia.* Bologna: Monduzzi Editore, (1997):1543-1547.

Klapan, I.; Šimiči,ć Lj. & Rišavi, R. (1999). Tele-3D-Computer Assisted Functional Endoscopic Sinus Surgery (Tele-3D-C-FESS). In: *Proceedings of the 13th CARS'99,* Lemke HU, Vannier MW, Inamura K, Farman AG (Eds.), Elsevier, Amsterdam, NewYork, Oxford, Shannon, Singapore, Tokyo, (1999):784-789.

Klapan, I.; Šimičić, Lj.; Rišavi, R.; Bešenski, N.; Bumber, Ž.; Stiglmajer, N. & Janjanin, S. (2001). Dynamic 3D computer-assisted reconstruction of metallic retrobulbar foreign body for diagnostic and surgical purposes. Case report: orbital injury with ethmoid bone involvement. *Orbit,* 20 (2001):35-49.

(a) Klapan, I.; Šimičić, Lj.; Bešenski, N.; Bumber, Ž.; Janjanin, S.; Rišavi, R. & Mladina, R. (2002). Application of 3D-computer assisted techniques to sinonasal pathology. Case report: war wounds of paranasal sinuses with metallic foreign bodies. *Am J Otolaryngol,* 23 (2002):27-34.

(b) Klapan, I.; Šimičić, Lj.;, Rišavi, R.; Bešenski, N.; Pasarić, K.; Gortan, D.; Janjanin, S.; Pavić, D. & Vranješ, Ž. (2002). Tele-3D-computer assisted functional endoscopic sinus surgery: new dimension in the surgery of the nose and paranasal sinuses. *Otolaryngology Head Neck Surg,* 127 (2002):549-557.

(c) Klapan, I.; Šimičić, Lj.; Rišavi, R.; Pasarić, K.; Sruk, V.; Schwarz, D. & Barišić, J. (2002). Real time transfer of live video images in parallel with three-dimensional modeling of the surgical field in computer-assisted telesurgery. *J Telemed Telecare,* 8 (2002):125-130.

Klapan, I.; Vranješ, Ž.; Rišavi, R.; Šimičić, Lj.; Prgomet, D. & Glušac, B. (2006). Computer assisted surgery and computer-assisted telesurgery in otorhinolaryngology. *Ear Nose Throat* J, 85(5) (2006):318-321.

Klapan, I.; Vranješ, Ž.; Prgomet, D. & Lukinović, J. (2008). Application of advanced virtual reality and 3D computer assisted technologies in tele-3D-computer assisted surgery in rhinology. *Coll Antropol,* 32(1) (2008):217-219.

Klimek, L.; Mosges, M.; Schlondorff, G. & Mann, W. (1998). Development of computer-aided surgery for otorhinolaryngology. *Comput Aided Surg,* 3 (1998):194-201.

Knezović, J.; Kovač, M.; Klapan, I.; Mlinarić, H.; Vranješ, Ž.;, Lukinović, J. & Rakić M. (2007). Application of novel lossless compression of medical images using prediction and contextual error modeling. *Coll Antropol,* 31 (4) (2007):315-319.

Mann, W. & Klimek, L. (1998). Indications for computer-assisted surgery in otorhinolaryngology. *Comput Aided Surg,* 3 (1998):202-204.

Mladina, R.; Hat, J.; Klapan, I. & Heinzel, B. (1995). An endoscopic approach to metallic foreign bodies of the nose and paranasal sinuses. *Am J Otolaryngol,* 16(4) (1995):276-279.

Olson, G. & Citardi, M. (1999). Image-guided functional endoscopic sinus surgery. *Otolaryngol Head Neck Surg,* 121 (1999):187.

Petzold, R ; Zeilhofer, H.-F. & Kalender, W. A. Rapid prototyping technology in medicine - basics and applications. *Computerized Medical Imaging and Graphics,* 23 (1999) 277-284.

Raos, P. & Galeta, T. (2004). Rapid Prototyping. In : *Proceedings of 2nd Croatian Congress on Telemedicine with International Participation (TeleMED),* pp. 74-75, Fakultet elektrotehnike i računarstva, May 2004,.Zagreb, Croatia

Rišavi, R.; Klapan, I.; Handžić-Ćuk, J. & Barčan, T. (1998). Our experience with FESS in children. *Int J Pediatric Otolaryngol,* 43 (1998):271-275.

Robb, RA. (2000). Virtual endoscopy: Development and evaluation using the Visible Human Datasets. *Computerized Medical Imaging and Graphics,* 24 (2000):133-151.

Rubino, F.; Soler, L.; Marescaux, J. & Maisonneuve, H. (2002). Advances in virtual reality are wide ranging. *BMJ,* 324 (2002): 612-612

Satava, RM. (1996). Telesurgery - acceptability of compressed video for remote surgical proctoring - invited commentary. *Arch Surg,* 131 (1996): 401.

Schlag, PM.; Engelmurke, F. & Zurheyde, MM. (1998).*Teleconference and telesurgery. Chirurg,* 69 (1998):1134-1140.

Sezeur, A. (1998). Surgical applications of telemedicine. *Ann Chir,* 52 (1998):403-411.

Stewart, MG.; Donovan, D.; Parke, RB. & Bautista, M. (1999). Does the sinus CT scan severity predict outcome in chronic sinusitis? *Otolaryngol Head Neck Surg,* 121(2) (1999):110.

Šimičić, Lj.; Klapan, I.; Simović, S.; Brzović, Z.; Vukoja, M.; Rišavi, R. & Gortan, D. (1998). Computer assisted functional endoscopic sinus surgery. Video texture mapping of 3D models. *Proceedings of ERS&ISIAN Meeting,* pp. 281-285.,Vienna, Austria, 1998 (ed. H. Stammberger, G. Wolf), Monduzzi Editore, Bologna.

Tao, X.; Zhu, F.; Chen, W. & Zhu, S. (2003). The application of virtual endoscopy with computed tomography in maxillofacial surgery. *Chin Med J,,* 116(5) (2003):679-81

Thrall, JH. (1999).Cross-sectional era yields to 3D and 4D imaging. *Diagn Imaging Eur,* 15(4) (1999):30-31.

Urban, V.; Wapler, M.; Neugenbauer, J.; Hiller, A.; Stallkamp, J. & Weisener, T. (1998). Robot-assisted surgery system with kinesthetic feedback. *Comp Aided Surg,* 3 (1998):205-209.

Vannier, MW. & Marsh, JL. (1996). 3D imaging, surgical planning and image guided therapy. *Radiol Clin North Am,* 34 (1996):545-563.

Vibert, E.; Denet, C. & Gayet, B. (2003). Major digestive surgery using a remote-controlled robot: the next revolution. *Arch Surg,* 138 (2003): 1002-1006.

Vinas, FC.; Zamorano, L.; Buciuc, R. &, Shamsa, F. (1997). Application accuracy study of a semipermanentm fiducial system for frameless stereotaxis. *Comput Aided Surg,* 2 (1997):257-263.

Wickham, J.E.A. (1994). Minimally invasive surgery: future developments. *BMJ*,3 08(1994):193-6.

Winder, J. & Bibb, R. (2005). Medical Rapid Prototyping Technologies: State of the Art and Current Limitations for Application in Oral and Maxillofacial Surgery. *Journal of Oral and Maxillofacial Surgery*, 63 (2005):1006-1015, 02782391

15

Development of a Medical Training System with Integration of Users' Skills Assessment

Ronei M. Moraes and Liliane S. Machado
Federal University of Paraíba
Brazil

1. Introduction

Virtual Reality (VR) joins several areas to produce environments that contain elements with realistic behaviour. The real-time processing of users interactions is a mandatory requirement and one or more user senses can be explored in VR systems. Machado & Moraes (2010) presented the multidisciplinary aspect of the VR systems and pointed out their importance for training.

Particularly, the training of medical procedures can be improved by VR systems. It occurs due to the fact that traditional training in medicine is frequently performed with cadavers or guinea pigs, which do not present the same characteristics of live bodies. Practice supervised by a tutor, with real patients, is another usual situation used for training. Both cases present problems: dead bodies, besides the degradation along the time, cannot be reused if cuts or punctures were done and need to be discarded after some manipulation; and supervised training can be risky or even uncomfortable for patients. Additionally, supervised training depends directly on the cases attended, what could not represent the variability and diversity of cases that students must learn. These observations make VR powerful to improve training, since it can rebuild digitally the same components of real procedures and can present virtual bodies with similar features of live bodies. Moreover, it can allow realistic and interactive simulation, in safe conditions, for users and patients; can provide variability of cases and offers reusability of the structures.

A very important aspect related to VR for medical simulation is the possibility of monitoring users' actions. Since VR systems are computational applications, all input and output data can be stored and used to assess users. This feature allows users to know their skills and to identify the points that must be improved in the execution of the procedure. This is particularly important in blind procedures in which a videotape of the execution cannot give possibilities of assessment by an expert. However, only recently this resource has been explored (Machado et al., 2000; Machado & Moraes, 2010).

This chapter will present the development process of a medical training system for bone marrow harvest procedure, a minimally invasive procedure. The problem approached will be described in order to identify the senses involved in the real procedure. Then, difficulties to assess trainees' skills and problems present in a real procedure, such as risks for donors, will be discussed allowing the identification of key points in the conception of a simulator based on VR. Those key points, the project budget and technological limitations will help to define the main features to be included in the computational architecture of the simulator.

The use of a framework that integrates several tools and methods will be introduced to demonstrate how this kind of software can decrease implementation time and standardize the development of this kind of application.

2. Development difficulties

There are four aspects related to the development of simulations for medical training: know the procedure, presence of a multidisciplinary team, presence of methods to assess the quality of training performed in the simulator and knowledge of computational tools and technologies for programming the application. It makes challenging the activities of the researchers to produce advances that could benefit all areas involved, without duplicity of efforts.

Know the procedure refers to obtain a detailed description about all elements involved in it: objects, structures, tools, anatomical parts, ways to perform the procedure and its variations, senses included (sight, touch, hearing, smell), range of expected time necessary to perform the procedure, and other aspects necessary to have a complete description. That information should be analysed according to the project budget and the technology available and can demand changes in the approach to be adopted. However, any decision must be discussed among the team: computer scientists and engineers will point out the technological possibilities and physicians will evaluate the approaches proposed, as example. The method to be used to assess users in the simulator must also be discussed according to the simulator subject. The detailed description will provide information that will allow identifying the type of variables included in the procedure. It must be discussed with a statistician or mathematician to define an adequate and good assessment method capable to deal with input and output data of simulator. During the implementation and after it, the development team will continuously refine and correct the approach adopted. Finally, the physicians must do the validation of the simulator.

A simulator based on VR must contain the same steps present in a real procedure and can use volumetric models, stereoscopic visualization, haptic systems, deformation methods and interactive cut. The use of all those features requires a lot of processing and can compromise the real-time performance. Thus, a VR simulator for medicine is defined and developed to deal with specific parts of the human body and present some limitations: according to the procedure requirements, some VR techniques are more explored than others. The architecture components could present educational aspects beyond training. Educational contents include explanations of the procedure, models with transparent view, attach, detach and other 3D manipulation tools, that only can be present by a VR application, to help users to solve some doubts about the procedure. Additionally, data collected during interaction in a VR-based simulation can be used to assess users' performance in training and to allow them to identify mistakes and improve their skills. An online assessment tool coupled to the simulator can do it.

A difficulty related to the development of simulators, which explore more than one human sense, is the integration of the tasks related to each sense and their synchronization. Most of the simulators found in literature were developed through the implementation and integration of all routines necessary. Because there are several devices and specific APIs (Application Programming Interface) dedicated to their programming, a programmer with experience to deal with each device or API is necessary to develop the VR simulators. Methods for collision detection, deformation, and stereoscopic visualization also need to be completely implemented each time an application is developed. Besides, the several methods need to deal with the same models and interaction devices. Then, all this information and all application tasks must be synchronized to avoid delays or inconsistencies that can compromise the realism. Figure 1 presents a diagram with some tasks that can be present in a simulator for medical training: the tasks can depend on process from other tasks. Finally, there isn't any guarantee of compatibility among simulators and codes are not usually shared among groups, fact that causes constant duplicity of efforts and recoding of the same tasks.

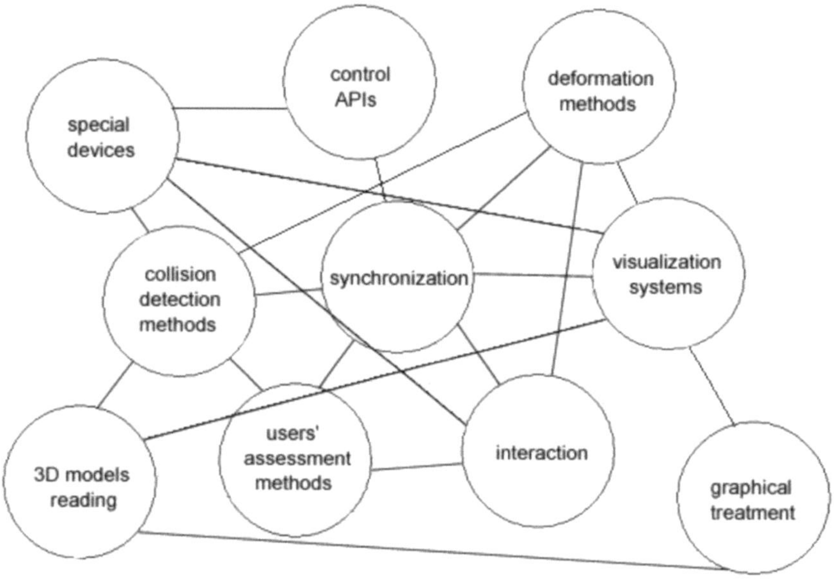

Fig. 1. Tasks that could compose medical simulators based on VR and their relation.

2.1 The framework CyberMed

To programming a simulator it is necessary to know a set of methods and tools: the method for generation of stereoscopic images and their adequacy to the visualization device chosen must be considered; the haptic device has specific API for programming; there are different methods for collision detection between objects in virtual environments; deformation methods depends on collision detection and can be more or less complex, depending on the one chosen; assessment is related to the type of input data (interaction) and demand the knowledge of mathematical or statistical concepts; the models must be readable; and, finally, all processes must be synchronized.

The use of frameworks was recently adopted to minimize duplicity of efforts, to make interoperable the simulators and to allow fast development. It means that the stage of implementation can be accelerated if programmers do not need to learn and develop all methods and tools related to each task. Examples of frameworks for the development of medical simulators are the GiPSi, Spring, SOFA, SSVE, Chai3D, ViMeT, and CyberMed (Machado et al., 2009; Correa et al., 2009). In Table 1 is possible to observe that most of them are open source, feature that augments the possibilities of discussion and code exchange among programmers. Support to haptics is also an important component since it allows including routines that provide sense of touch and force feedback for users. However, only the CyberMed presents support to assessment and can be pointed as a framework for the development of training simulator capable to provide feedback about users' skills.

Framework	Open Source	Free License	Support to haptics	Support to assessment
GiPSi	X	X	X	
SSVE				
Spring	X		X	
SOFA	X	X		
CHAI3D	X	X	X	
ViMeT	X	X	X	
CyberMed	X	X	X	X

Table 1. Comparison among frameworks for medical development based on VR.

CyberMed is a framework to the development of VR simulators based on VR for commodity computers (Souza et al., 2007). It is composed by a set of open and free libraries that allows integrating new methods or supporting new devices. It also supports low cost devices as much as high-end devices, depending on the budget of the project. This flexibility permits to attend a large group of applications and programmers can select the resources available according to the goal and public of the final system. It allows programming in high-level but permit expanding its functionalities in a low-level programming. It is available for download at http://cybermed.sourceforge.net/. Figure 2 presents CyberMed layers and their disposition inside the system.

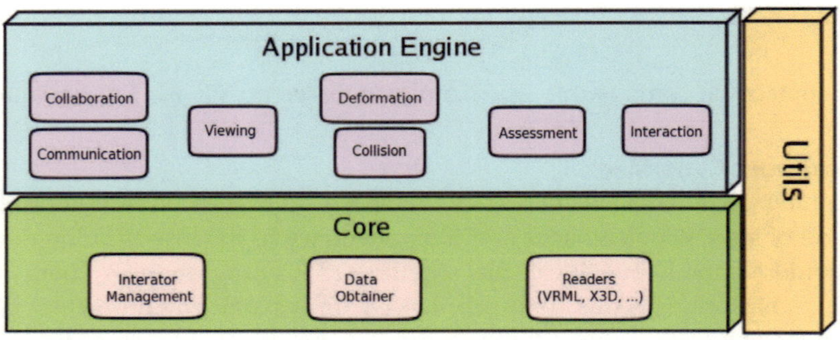

Fig. 2. CyberMed architecture.

The architecture of CyberMed is based on the object-oriented paradigm and follows some pattern designs to guarantee software reuse and agile development. Then, *singleton* and *Abstract Factory* were patterns applied in CyberMed development: *singleton* offers a single instance of a class to allow singleness of information; and *Abstract Factory* allows the creation of interfaces to make new objects with common operations.

The framework is composed by a set of layers that provide services for its users. Each layer abstracts several concepts to facilitate the development of VR applications. Nowadays, CyberMed offers support to: three different modes of stereoscopy, mass-spring deformation, two collision detection modes, import 3D meshes, optical and magnetic tracking, haptics, network collaboration, synchronization, and three different assessment methods.

3. Design of the simulator

The design of the simulator starts with the complete description of the procedure. The bone marrow transplant is a minimally invasive medical procedure to treat recently considered incurable diseases, as some specific occurrences of cancer. It is used to replace the cells of the immune system, mainly after chemotherapy or radiotherapy sessions. To obtain bone marrow it is necessary to extract it through many material aspirations from the iliac crest bone marrow (sometimes it includes the sternum bone also) of a donator under general anaesthesia. The harvest is executed blindly without any visual feedback except the external view of the donor's body. So, the physician needs to touch patient's body and identify the position of the iliac crest. After, he will insert a needle from this position to reach the bone marrow. In order to do that, he must apply adequate force and feel the tissue layers pierced by the needle.

The knowledge of the anatomic structures of the pelvic region, as well as the physician ability to find the iliac crest under the skin and the perception of the tissues pierced by the needle are essential to perform the bone marrow harvest procedure. Thus, it is possible to observe that the sense of touch is essential to perform the procedure and will be from it that the physician will decide the correct position to insert the needle and when to stop doing it. The dexterity of the physician will determine his skills.

The process of learning the bone marrow harvest procedure can be divided in three stages: understand the anatomy of the pelvis, learn how to identify the iliac crest and acquire dexterity to insert the needle, with correct force and precision, to reach the bone marrow. The elements necessary to compose these stages are: anatomical models of structures of the iliac region; needle for harvest; hand or fingers for palpation; hardness and elasticity properties of tissues from each structure; colour of structures.

Factors that determine a correct execution are related to the time of harvest, correctness of place in needle insertion, and adequate application of forces during the piercing. This information can be used for decision making about users dexterity and their skill level.

3.1 Assessment methodologies

The research area on training assessment for simulators based on VR is recent (Burdea & Coiffet, 2003). The early works in that area probably were proposed by Dinsmore et al. (1996; 1997) (Langrana et al., 1997) that used a quiz to assess users of a VR environment to identify subcutaneous tumors. The quiz contained questions related to the diagnosis and hardness of tumor. Similarly, Wilson et al. (1997) created a minimally invasive system (MIST) in which each task could be programmed for different difficulty levels. Performance data of each user could be saved to post analysis (offline) by an expert or statistical methods.

In parallel, methods to assess surgical skills have been developed by several research groups. Some of them use statistical models to do that offline (Derossis et al., 1998) and others use statistical methods to show that through VR based systems is possible to discriminate between expert and novice physicians (Taffinfer et al., 1998; Gallagher et al., 2001). It was showed also that surgeons trained in VR systems could obtain better results (Gallagher et al., 1999) when compared to others trained by traditional methods. Additionally, the assessment of psychomotor skills in VR systems that include haptic devices can quantify surgical dexterity with objective metrics (Darzi et al., 1999). Thus, VR systems for training can be used to provide metrics to a proficiency criterion of learning (Darzi et al., 1999; Gallagher et al., 2005). Due to those reasons, McCloy & Stone (2001) pointed out the assessment of psychomotor skills as the future of medical teaching and training.

The first proposal for online training assessment in VR systems was presented by (Burdea et al., 1998) and was based on a boolean logic that compared diagnoses provided by users with correct ones stored in the simulator. However, ordinary computers of that generation were not able to run simultaneously virtual reality environments/simulators and online assessment systems if several interaction variables were monitored. After that, more sophisticated assessment methods were proposed for several training systems (McBeth et al., 2002; Huang et al., 2005; Mackel et al., 2006; Kumagai et al., 2007; Farber et al., 2008).

Apart from methods for evaluating a user, have also been proposed methodologies for evaluation of multiple users interacting in the same VR environment (Moraes & Machado, 2007). It is important to note that there are evaluations systems for training systems based on Web (Moraes & Machado, 2005b; 2006; Machado & Moraes, 2006). Some methodologies, which cannot be able to run in real time in commodity computers, can be implemented using embedded systems, coupled to them (Moraes & Machado, 2008).

The choice of an assessment methodology is strongly related to the procedure itself. For example, in a procedure in which information can be obtained from procedures performed in simulators based on VR are fully quantitative, numerical methods based on probability distributions can be most appropriate (Machado & Moraes, 2006). However, one should take into consideration what types of such information specialists are able to interpret. In cases where such information coming from specialists are imprecise or vague, modelling from fuzzy sets (Moraes & Machado, 2009a) or hybrid modelling can be good choices (Moraes & Machado, 2010). Can still be used in knowledge-based modelling, such as rule-based expert systems (classical or fuzzy) (Machado et al., 2000). Approaches based on models for discrete variables or statistical models based on binomial or multinomial distributions are not indicated, since the need for changes on the original variables that can cause loss of information (Moraes & Machado, 2009b). In cases where information is qualitative, the use of expert systems can be a good solution (Machado et al., 2008). Other approaches based on multinomial probability models (Moraes & Machado, 2009a; 2009b) can also be used for these cases. There are still cases in which information is obtained from both qualitative and quantitative variables. In these cases, evaluation method to be used should take into consideration these aspects and be able to analyse the two types variables simultaneously (Machado & Moraes, 2009).

Because users can have forgotten some decisions and actions done during the training, the main problem in this kind of evaluation is the interval between training and evaluation. Additionally, some performances cannot be classified as good or bad due to procedure complexity. Thus, the existence of an evaluation system coupled to a simulation allows fast feedback that can be used improve user performance. However, it demands low computational complexity in order to not compromise the simulation performance and high accuracy to do not compromise the quality of evaluation. Figure 3 shows the independence between simulator and evaluation systems in spite of their simultaneous action.

Theoretically, the system can collect any information related to position, forces, torque, resistance, velocity, acceleration, temperature, angle of visualization, sound, smells, temperature, velocity and shape. Spatial position can be captured by tracking devices attached to some part of users' body or to an object manipulated by them. Those devices can collect movements in three or more degrees of freedom in constant intervals of time. Such information allows VR system to calculate object position in the virtual scene, the velocity of the movement and its acceleration. In a similar way, haptic devices (Burdea & Coiffet, 2003) also can do the same, but in a limited physical space. In both examples, sampling rates vary according to the device chosen. The positioning of objects manipulated by users can allow the identification of collision with other objects of the virtual scene, besides the direction of contact and its intensity. In order to achieve this, position vectors with last and present position are used to determine the collision velocity and intensity.

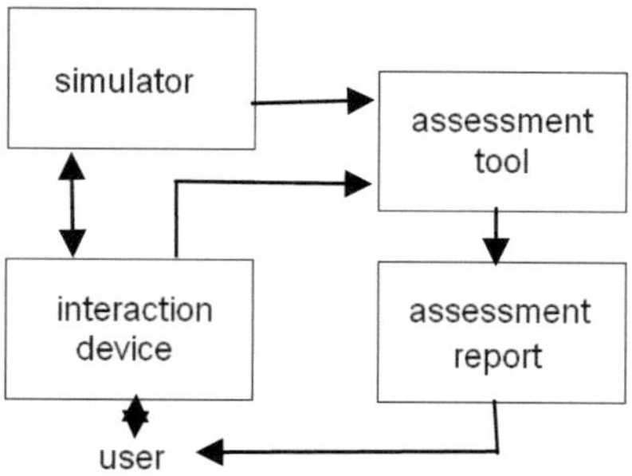

Fig. 3. Assessment and its relation with VR simulator.

Reactions from data processing collected from interaction can be send to users as force feedback, a new point of view of the scene, deformation of objects, sound, increase or decrease of temperature, change of objects (as cuts or divisions) and smells. The intensity of feedback will depend on device capabilities. However, the continuity of reaction is an important factor in the levels of immersion.

a. Maximum Likelihood

Maximum Likelihood decision rule is the most common statistical technique used in data classification. Its application for training evaluation based on VR was presented by Moraes & Machado (2005a). Formally, the classes of performance for an user are done by: w_i , $i=1,...,M$, where M is the total number of classes of performance. It is possible to determine the most probable class of a vector of training data X, by conditional probabilities (Johnson & Wichern, 2001):

$$P(w_i \mid X), \text{ where } i=1,...,M. \qquad (1)$$

The probability done by (1) gives the likelihood that for a data vector X, the correct class is w_i. Classification rule is performed according to

$$X \in w_i \textit{ if } P(w_i \mid X) > P(w_j \mid X) \text{ for all } i \neq j. \qquad (2)$$

However, all the probabilities done by (1) are unknown. So, probabilities denoted by $P(X \mid w_i)$ can be estimated if there is sufficient information available for each class of performance. Using the Bayes Theorem:

$$P(w_i \mid X) = [P(X \mid w_i)\, P(w_i)] / P(X), \qquad (3)$$

where $P(X) = \sum^{M}_{i=1} P(X \mid w_i)\, P(w_i)]$.
As $P(X)$ is the same for all classes w_i, then it is not relevant for data classification. In Bayesian theory, $P(w_i)$ is called *a priori* probability for w_i and $P(w_i \mid X)$ is *a posteriori* probability for w_i where X is known. Then, the classification rule done by (2) is modified:

$$X \in w_i \text{ if } P(w_i \mid X)\, P(w_i) > P(w_j \mid X)\, P(w_j) \text{ for all } i \neq j. \qquad (4)$$

Equation (4) is known as the maximum likelihood decision rule or maximum likelihood classification. However, it can be convenient to use (Johnson & Wichern, 2001):

$$g(X) = ln\ [P(X \mid w_i)\ P(w_i)] = ln\ [P(X \mid w_i)] + ln\ [P(w_i)] \quad (5)$$

where $g(X)$ is known as the log-likelihood function and it is known as discriminant function. Equation (5) can be used to modify the formulation done by (4):

$$X \in w_i \text{ if } g_i\ (X) > g_j\ (X) \text{ for all } i \neq j. \quad (6)$$

It is important to note that if statistical distribution of training data can assume multivariate Gaussian distribution, the use of (6) has interesting computational properties (Johnson & Wichern, 2001). If training data cannot assume that distribution, (6) can provide a significant reduction of computational cost of implementation. Thus, the user's interactions with the system are monitored and the information is sent to the evaluation system, where Maximim Likelihood is in its kernel. This method can produce good results even with small bases calibration. However it is necessary that these data are able to translate the scope of the problem addressed.

For the calibration of the evaluation system, an expert executes several times the procedure, labelling each one into a class of performance among M classes available. For each one, the vectors of each variable are storage. At the end of calibration, the information of variability about each one procedure class is acquired by calculate the mean vector and covariance matrix. These parameters are sufficient to characterize the multivariate Gaussian distribution for each class of performance. When it is done, the evaluation system is ready to run.

The users perform their training in the VR simulator and the Evaluation Tool based on Maximum Likelihood collects the data from that manipulation. All probabilities of data for each class of performance are calculated by evaluation tool and a w_j class of performance is assigned to the user at the end of simulation, according (4) or (6), which is reported to the trainee.

b. General Bayesian Network (GBN)

A Bayesian network is a probabilistic model that can represent a set of probabilities distributions from all variables in a complex process and also establish their relationships (Neapolitan, 2003). Formally, a Bayesian network is defined as directed acyclic graphs, denoted by *G* and a probabilistic distribution denoted by *P*. The graph *G* is a set of nodes and oriented arcs, where nodes represent variables in process and oriented arcs encode conditional dependencies between variables (Neapolitan, 2003). The dependencies are modeled by specific conditional probabilistic distributions (Krause, 1998).

Cheng & Greiner (2001) proposed a classification for Bayesian networks, according to their graph structure, in five classes: Naive-Bayes, Tree Augmented Naive-Bayes, Augmented Naive-Bayes, Bayesian Multi-net nets e General Bayesian Networks (GBNs). The choice of a specific structure to knowledge representation depends on dependencies relationship between variables, which describe that process. That choice is critical, because it changes the final results. The GBN is a generalized form of Bayesian networks, which allows nodes to form an arbitrary graph, rather than just a tree. Another important characteristic is that each child node cannot be connected to the final classes of evaluation.

The General Bayesian Network is convenient to serve as base for a training evaluation due to its generality. In that network, the dependencies between nodes can adjust itself to real

dependencies. Thus, it is possible to verify dependencies between variables during network modelling and put them in structure nodes of GBN, which did not occur in other structures.
Formally, let the classes of performance be in space of decision Ω with M classes of performance. Let be w_j, $j \in \Omega$ the class of performance for a user and X_i, $1 \leq i \leq n$, represents a node in GBN with n as the number of nodes in a graph. The joint probability distribution in GBN for an event is done by:

$$P(X_1, X_2, \ldots, X_n) = \prod^{n}_{i=1} P(X_n \mid X_{n-1}, X_{n-2}, \ldots, X_1) \quad (7)$$

where $P(X_1, X_2, \ldots, X_n)$ is the joint probability distribution and $P(X_n \mid X_{n-1}, X_{n-2}, \ldots, X_1)$ is the conditional probability of X_n conditioned by its predecessor nodes $X_{n-1}, X_{n-2}, \ldots, X_1$.
If the conditional independence between variables is verified, this permits simplifications in (7). Then,

$$P(X_1, X_2, \ldots, X_n) = P(X_1 \mid w_j)\, P(X_2 \mid w_j)\, P(X_3 \mid w_j) \quad (8)$$

The node probabilities are associated to probability distribution. For example, a node A can have a Gaussian distribution and a node B, which depends on A, can have a bivariate Gaussian distribution, with a mean vector and a covariance matrix (Johnson & Wichern, 2001).
The structure of GBN is learned from data, as well as the parameters of conditional probabilities. By the use of probabilities calculus is possible to find dependencies among nodes in a Bayesian network. If those dependencies are founding and, if is possible to assume Gaussian distribution for nodes, dependencies can be estimated using multivariate linear regression (Neapolitan, 2003). Scores are used to help the estimation of the final structure of GBN for each class of assessment. In a first moment, a network is created with all independent nodes and an initial score is calculated. Following, all combinations are searched and an arc is designed between two nodes to obtain an increment of initial score. Then, the parameters for that nodes set are re-estimated using linear regression. This cycle is repeated until the total network score could be less than a predetermined value or a fixed number of cycles. This methodology has the ability to obtain better results for larger calibration databases.
Previously, an expert calibrates the system, according M classes of performance. The information of variability about these procedures is acquired using GBN based method (Moraes et al., 2009). The users perform their training in the VR simulator and the Assessment Tool based on GBN collects the data from that manipulation. All probabilities of data for each class of performance are calculated by GBN and a w_j class of performance is assigned to the user at the end of simulation, according to (7) or (8), depending on the particular case. At the end of the training, the assessment system reports the classification to the trainee.
For the calibration of the evaluation system, an expert executes several times the procedure, labeling each one into a class of performance among M classes available. For each one, the vectors of each variable are storage. At the end of calibration, the structure of GBN is learned from data, as well as the parameters of conditional probabilities for each class of performance. Using probabilities calculus is possible to find dependencies among nodes in a Bayesian network. If those dependencies are founding and, if is possible to assume Gaussian distribution for nodes, dependencies can be estimated using multivariate linear regression (Neapolitan, 2003). Scores are used to help estimate the final structure of GBN for each class

of assessment. In a first moment a network is created with all independent nodes and an initial score is calculated. Next, all combinations are searched and an arc is designed between two nodes for which an increment of initial score is obtained. Then, the parameters for that nodes set are re-estimated using linear regression. This cycle is repeated until total network score is less than a predetermined value or a fixed number of cycles.
The users perform their training in the VR simulator and the Evaluation Tool based on GBN collects the data from that manipulation. All probabilities of data for each class of performance are calculated by evaluation tool and a w_j class of performance is assigned to the user at the end of simulation, according (7) or (8), which is reported to the trainee.

c. Expert system based on Fuzzy Rules

As it is possible that some variables in the training system do not present an exactly correspondence to the real world, some measures cannot be exact. Then we must use fuzzy sets to measure those variables (Dubois & Prade, 1980).
In classical set theory a set A of a universe X can be expressed by means of a membership function $\mu_A(x)$, with $\mu_A: X \rightarrow \{0,1\}$, where for a given $a \in A$, $\mu_A(a)=1$ and $\mu_A(a)=0$ respectively express the presence and absence of a in A. Mathematically:

$$\mu_A(x) = \begin{cases} 1, & \text{if } x \in A \\ 0, & \text{if } x \notin A \end{cases} \tag{9}$$

Zadeh (1965) introduced the fuzzy set theory in 1965. A fuzzy set or fuzzy subset is used to model an ill-known quantity. A fuzzy set A on X is characterized by its membership function $\mu_A: X \rightarrow [0,1]$. We say that a fuzzy set A of X is "precise" when $\exists\, c^* \in X$ such that $\mu_A(c^*)=1$ and $\forall c \neq c^*$, $\mu_A(c)=0$. A fuzzy set A will be said to be "crisp", when $\forall\, c \in X$, $\mu_A(c) \in \{0,1\}$.
The intersection and union of two fuzzy sets are performed trough the use of *t-norm* and *t-conorm* operators respectively, which are commutative, associative and monotonic mappings from $[0,1] \rightarrow [0,1]$. Moreover, a t-norm Γ (respec. t-conorm $\perp$) has 1 (respec. 0) as neutral element (e. g.: Γ=*min*, $\perp$=*max*) (Dubois & Prade, 1988). Thus, we can define intersection and union of two fuzzy sets as:
The intersection of two fuzzy sets A and B, with membership functions $\mu_A(x)$ e $\mu_B(x)$ is a fuzzy set C with membership function given by:

$$C=A \cap B \Leftrightarrow \mu_C(x)= \Gamma\{\mu_A(x),\mu_B(x)\},\ \forall\ x \in X. \tag{10}$$

The union of two fuzzy sets A and B, with membership functions $\mu_A(x)$ e $\mu_B(x)$ is a fuzzy set C with membership function given by:

$$C=A \cup B \Leftrightarrow \mu_C(x)= \perp\{\mu_A(x),\mu_B(x)\},\ \forall x \in X. \tag{11}$$

The complement of a fuzzy set A in X, denoted by $\neg A$ is defined by:

$$\mu_{\neg A}(x) = n(\mu_A(x)),\ \forall x \in X. \tag{12}$$

where: $n: [0,1] \rightarrow [0,1]$ is a negation operator which satisfies the following properties:

- $n(0)=1$ and $n(1)=0$
- $n(a) \leq n(b)$ if $a>b$
- $n(n(a))=a$, $\forall\ x \in [0,1]$

and a negation is a strict negation if it is continuous and satisfies

- $n(a)<n(b)$ if $a>b$.

The main negation operator which satisfies these four conditions is $n(a) = 1-a$.
The implication function between two fuzzy sets A and B, with membership functions $\mu_A(x)$ e $\mu_B(x)$, is a fuzzy set C with membership function given by:

$$C=A \Rightarrow B \Leftrightarrow \mu_C(x,y)= \nabla\{\mu_A(x),\mu_B(y)\},\ \forall x \in X,\ \forall y \in Y \quad (13)$$

where ∇: $[0,1]^2 \rightarrow [0,1]$ is an implication operator which obeys the following properties: $\forall a, a', b, b' \in [0,1]$:

- If $b \le b'$ then $\nabla(a,b) \le \nabla(a,b')$;
- $\nabla(0,b)=1$;
- $\nabla(1,b)=b$.

The pure implications obeys too:

- If $a \le a'$ then $\nabla(a,b) \ge \nabla(a',b)$;
- $\nabla(a, \nabla(b,c))= \nabla(b, \nabla(a,c))$.

Expert systems (Rich & Knight, 1993) use the knowledge of an expert in a given specific domain to answer non-trivial questions about that domain. For example, an expert system for image classification would use knowledge about the characteristics of the classes present in a given region of the image to classify a pixel of that region. This knowledge also includes the "how to do" methods used by the human expert. Usually, the knowledge in an expert system is represented by rules in the form:

IF <condition> THEN <conclusion>.

Most rule-based expert systems allow the use of connectives AND or OR in the premise of a rule and of connective AND in the conclusion. From rules and facts, new facts will be obtained through an inference process.
In several cases, we do not have precise information about conditions or conclusions, then the knowledge in the rules cannot be expressed in a precise manner. Thus, it can be interesting to use a fuzzy rule-based expert system (Zadeh, 1988). However, it is important to emphasize that obtaining rules from an expert can be a long process and eventually must be done in several stages. This is the major limitation of this methodology.
For example, using a fuzzy expert system coupled to a surgical simulator based on virtual reality, experts can define, in an imprecise way, regions of tissue and bones in where is possible to find bone marrow harvest. To evaluate a user, values of variables are collected by a haptic device and sent to expert system for evaluation. The system must analyse each step performed by users and classify users, at the end of training, according to predefined performance classes. Machado et al. (2000) used five performance classes, described by the following fuzzy sets: *you need much more training, you need more training, you need training, your training is good* or *your training is excellent*, to identify if more training of bone marrow harvest procedure is or not necessary. The fuzzy rules of expert system are modelled by membership functions according to specifications of experts. Several types of membership functions can be used as trapezoidal, triangular and pi-functions and the fuzzy inference system used is Mamdani-type (Mamdani & Assilian, 1975). An example of rule for this expert system is:

IF Position_x is left_center AND Position_y is up_center

AND Position_needle is acceptable AND Marrow_harvest is yes

THEN Trainee_class is you_need_training

where: Position_x, Position_y are coordinates which the needle touch the patient body; Position_needle is the angle of needle input to body of patient; Marrow_harvest shows the success or failure of trainee to harvest bone marrow and Trainee_class is the classification of trainee.

In a different way from previous methods, the calibration of an expert system based on fuzzy rules is made by extraction of knowledge from one or several experts. In general, the experts explain the procedure and which variables must be taking in account in evaluation process. From those variables is necessary to know their parameters (which translate by fuzzy numbers) and as they are related with evaluation process to create rules to express each one of the M classes of performance. The number of rules depends on the complexity of procedure. When users perform their training, the Evaluation Tool based on Expert System collects the data from that manipulation. All rules are applied over data and, according to the expert system, one class of performance w_j is assigned to the user at the end of simulation, which is reported to the user.

4. Implementation

A simulator based on VR must contain the same steps present in a real procedure and can use volumetric models, stereoscopic visualization, haptic systems, deformation methods and interactive cut. The use of all those features requires a lot of processing and can compromise the real-time performance. Thus, a VR simulator for medicine is defined and developed to deal with specific parts of the human body and present some limitations: according to the procedure requirements, some VR techniques are more explored than others. The architecture components could present educational aspects beyond training. Educational contents include explanations of the procedure, models with transparent view, attach, detach and other 3D manipulation tools, that only can be present by a VR application, to help users to solve some doubts about the procedure. Additionally, data collected during interaction in a VR-based simulation can be used to assess users' performance in training and to allow them to identify mistakes and improve their skills. An online assessment tool coupled to the simulator can do it.

In order to deal with the main points of the learning of bone marrow harvest (BMH), the three stages described in the design were considered. It was also decided that learning and practice should be treated in different moments, and the simulator was conceived to present these two possibilities. When is learning the anatomy and understanding the procedure, the user should be able to view internally the virtual body and become familiarized with the tools and tissues properties. However, the practice should reproduce exactly the reality of the procedure and the user must be assessed in this process. Figure 4 presents how the different moments were approached in the simulator and the tasks related to each one.

Sight and touch are the two senses identified as fundamental in the procedure. The touch is necessary for the palpation of the virtual body and for the puncture with the needle. In this case, the use of a haptic device is mandatory to simulate the tissues properties and provide touch feedback for users. Haptic devices are special devices that incorporate sensors and

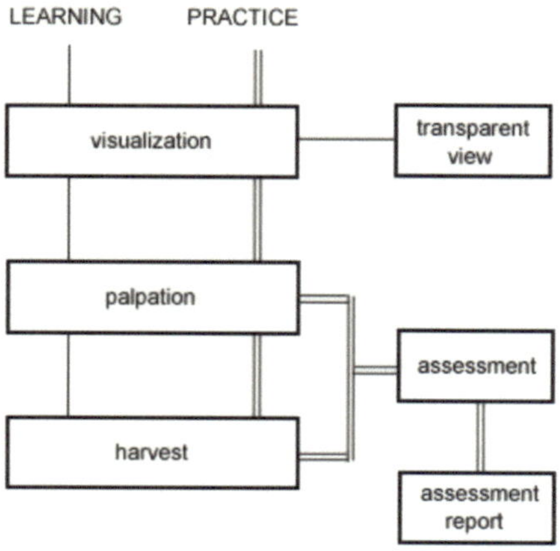

Fig. 4. Learning (I) and practice (II) tasks defined for the bone marrow harvest simulator.

actuators to capture user actions and provide touch and force feedback. The perception of touch allows identifying texture of objects and force feedback allows feeling sense of position and movement associated to the interaction with objects. Haptic devices with 6DOF[1] permit spatial movements and are the type of device necessary to the simulator for BMH. If the manipulation will occur in three dimensions, the visualization must follow the same principle and stereoscopic visualization will also be necessary. Figure 5 presents the haptic and visualization devices selected for BMH simulator.

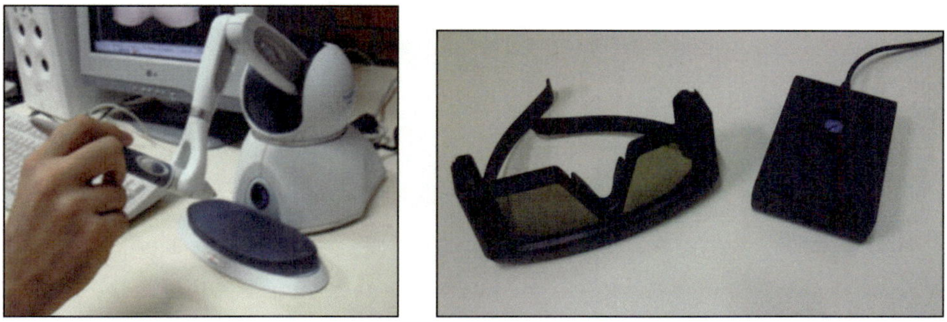

Fig. 5. 6DOF haptic device (left) and shutter glasses for stereoscopic visualization (right).

Five models compose the application: three for the human body structures and two for the interaction object. The interaction objects, finger and needle, were modelled with the Blender package and saved in VRML 2.0 format. The models of human body structure were obtained from a previous work (Machado, 2003) and represent the skin of the pelvic region, the iliac bone and the bone marrow (Figure 6).
The tissues properties are important information for the simulator. They are used to give to models the same properties of the real tissues. In this case, textures can be acquired or designed, and colours must be defined. Touch properties, as hardness, elasticity and roughness must also be acquired. Because several tissues do not have a numerical value to describe their properties, it is common to acquire them from physicians' impressions. A haptic calibrator was used to do that (Figure 7). Then, some virtual spheres were presented to

[1] DOF = degrees of freedom

physicians and they could select and refine their properties according to what they feel when manipulate the real tissues: first they do for it for skin, after for bone and, finally, for bone marrow. The properties they could calibrate were: hardness, roughness, friction and viscosity.

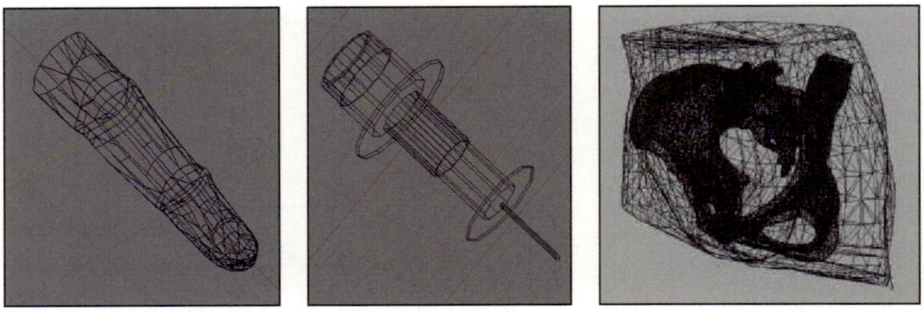

Fig. 6. Models conceived to represent the interaction device and pelvic structures (skin, iliac bone and bone marrow).

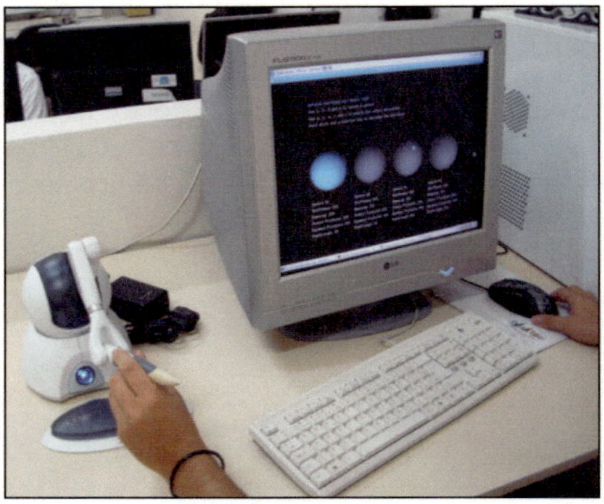

Fig. 7. Tool for calibration of material properties from physicians' impressions.

There is a last information necessary to make the simulator and it refers to the correct and wrong ways to perform the bone marrow harvest. However, describe it in natural language with details is not an easy tasks, even for physicians. Thus, the best way to do that will be making the physicians use the simulator and perform the procedure in several ways labelling what is correct and what is not correct. In this case, their interactions can be saved and used to construct models for users' assessment.

4.1 Coding with CyberMed

The application was implemented using the follow CyberMed classes: CybView, CybMouse, CybParameters, OF, CybInterator, CybHaptics and CybAssess. These classes offer the functionalities, respectively: visualization, mouse interaction, storage and management of 3D models, interaction control, haptic control and online user's assessment.
The five tasks defined in the design process were implemented. The CybView class allowed choosing the visualization mode of the application. In spite of CyberMed support four different view modes, the simulator was defined to provide only the monoscopic and temporal multiplexing visualization modes (using shutter glasses). With this class two light

sources were defined and an illumination model was enable to the visual scene and its objects. The menu entries were also made in the CybView. The objects used in the visualization are obtained from the OF and CybParameters classes which store the models topology, the model used to represent the interaction device and the transformation matrixes of the scene. The CybInterator class was used to choose the interaction object. The CybAssess will access in real-time the transformation matrixes and CybInterator to the user's assessment. In order to reach that, it was used the CybAssess with an assessment method based on Maximum Likelihood. The CybHaptics class allowed setting the material properties of the models and enabling the haptic device. This class provided an abstract layer for several API used to programming haptic devices and did not demand knowledge about the device API.

Figure 8 shows parts of the implementation with the CyberMed used to read the models and set the material properties for the haptic interaction. In that figure, it is possible to observe the reading of five VRML models in lines 1 to 8. The lines 10 to 16 define the properties of the first layer, the skin, as being touchable and pierceable. Observe that there isn't any mention of the haptic device in use. It is done in a single way with the class CybInterator and is independent of device manufacturer.

The visualization mode chosen does not need any special programming and the only thing necessary is instance the view mode and start it:

```
/*instance view mode for shutter glasses */
   CybViewShutter view;
/*Initialize visualization*/
   view.init();
```

```
1  int numLayer = 5;
2
3  // read the models
4  char *arqname[30] = {"1.wrl","2.wrl","3.wrl","4.wrl", "5.wrl"};
5  ofMesh<cybTraits> malha[numLayer];
6  CybDataObtainer<cybTraits> data(numLayer);
7  ofWrlReader<cybTraits> entrada;
8  CybParameters cybCore;
9
10 // set haptic material properties for the skin
11 interator.hapticDevice.createHapticLayers(0,true);
12 interator.hapticDevice.createMaterialPropertyContext(numLayer, true);
13 interator.hapticDevice.setMaterialPropertyValue(0, POPTHROUGH, 1.0f);
14 interator.hapticDevice.setMaterialFace(0, POPTHROUGH, FRONT);
15 interator.hapticDevice.setMaterialPropertyValue(0, DYNAMIC_FRICTION, 0.6f);
16 interator.hapticDevice.setMaterialFace(0, DYNAMIC_FRICTION, FRONT);
17
18 // set haptic material properties for the bone
19 interator.hapticDevice.createHapticLayers(1,true);
20
21 // association of the contact point to a model point
22 interator.setObjectType(0, -0.020913, 0.078050, -10.034132);
23
24 // enable material property for haptics
25 interator.hapticDevice.enableHapticMaterialProperty();
```

Fig. 8. Code of the BMH simulator using CyberMed 1.2.

The menu was implemented to be dynamically modified, according to user choices. A visual exploration is enable in the Study module and the user can choose which structures he wants to see and set their transparency. Figure 9 shows the Study module and the menu options available. The user can also modify the position and orientation of the structures through mouse interaction. If shutter glasses were available, it is possible to start the stereoscopy visualization.

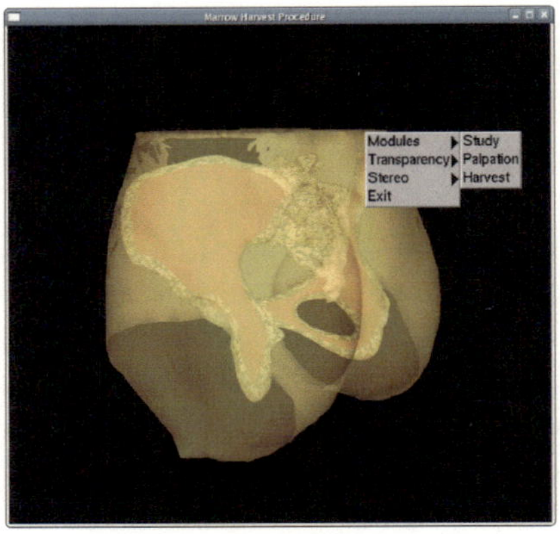

Fig. 9. Screenshot of the transparent view task and menu options available.

The second module available is the Palpation module. For this step of the training, all interaction with the objects was disabled and the position of the objects was fixed. In fact, the only visualization possible is from the backside of the skin model. Because the visualization of the bone and bone marrow models is not allowed, these models were disable and will not be rendered. However, they can be identified by touch since the user starts the haptic interaction (Figure 10). With the haptic device the user will be able to feel the different material properties throughout the skin and identify a hardest area, located under the iliac crest (not visible). In this module, the finger model was related to the haptic device and the point of contact is located on its tip.

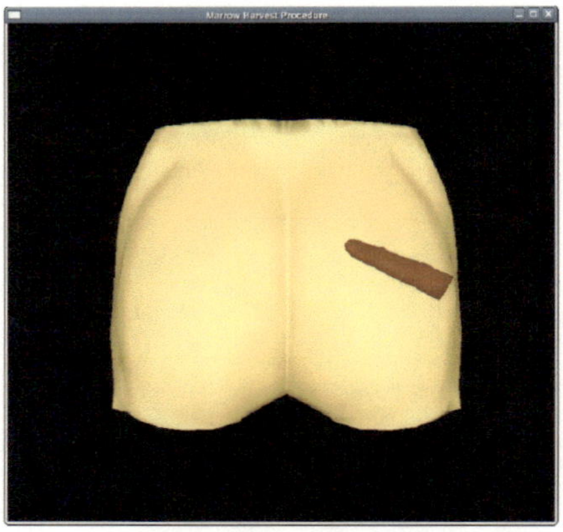

Fig. 10. Palpation tasks and the representation of the haptic device by a finger.

In the last module, the Harvest, the user can practice how to harvest the bone marrow. As in the Palpation module, movements with the body models are not allowed and a needle represents the haptic device. In this module is possible to penetrate into the models with the haptic device and all body structures - skin, bone and bone marrow - are haptically displayed. It allows reaching the bone marrow under the skin and inside the bone.
To the online user's assessment the simulation had to be executed several times to calibrate the assessment tool. This stage allows acquiring the assessment parameters to be used in the on-line assessment. In order to reach that, an expert executes several times the training and at the end of that, he/she labels each one into M classes of performance (M=5 in the Figure

8: "Well Qualified", "Qualified", "Need Some Training", "Need More Training" and "Novice"). This procedure is necessary to measure the statistical variability for each class of performance and improve the accuracy of the assessment method. It was used the Maximum Likelihood based method (Moraes & Machado, 2005a). Figure 11 shows the calibration stage of the simulator in the harvest module. The only difference between the calibration procedure for training assessment and the final training application is the presence of calibration options in the menu. In the calibration procedure, these options will be selected by an expert to label the class of performance for each calibration procedure. In the final application this menu option is replaced by an assessment option which can be selected by the user to receive his assessment report at the end of the simulation.

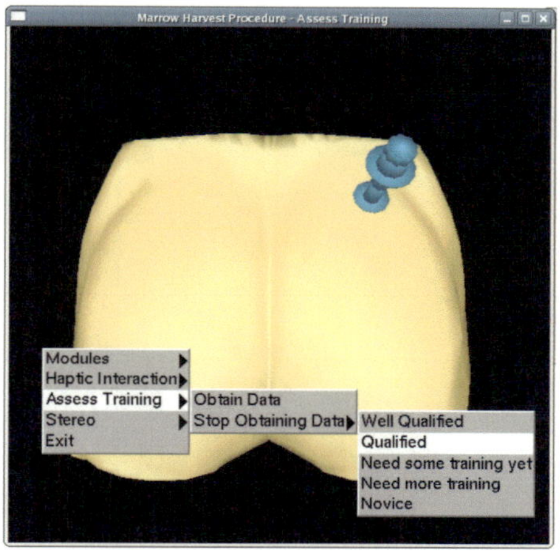

Fig. 11. Assess of training: acquisition of the assessment parameters.

5. Results

The bone marrow harvest simulator was designed and developed by Machado (2003). The present work used the same models and material property parameters of the previous work to develop a new application, with the same training goal but using a framework in its development. To compare the applications, the previous simulator will be called BMHSimulator and the new application CybBMH. Table 2 shows the main differences between BMHSimulator and CybBMH.
The CybBMH was developed only using free tools: GNU C++ language and the CyberMed system. The modeling package used to model the needle and the finger was the Blender, also free. Because the CyberMed integrates and synchronizes visual and haptic routines, it was not necessary the use of other tools for the development of the CybBMH. In opposite, the BMHSimulator required the use of several tools that must to be integrated, besides the necessity of synchronization of the visual and haptic tasks. The use of a single class to store the models topology allows utilizing the same three objects for visual and haptic scenes in the CybBMH. Additionally, two models were used to represent the haptic device in the visual scene. The illumination treatment offered by the CyberMed also allows providing a better visual quality. The visual quality of the simulators can be observed in the Figure 12. The BMHSimulator used three models for the visual scene and other three models for the haptic scene. Due to performance reasons, the haptic models were simplified and the

number of vertexes was reduced. Then, visual and haptic scenes did not share the same object and was necessary to use six different models in the past simulator. The representation of the haptic device was done through textures applied on crossed plans. In spite of optimizing the rendering process, this approach presented graphic imperfections.

	BMHSimulator	CybBMH
Operational system	Windows™	Linux
programming tools	- Visual C++ - OpenGL - Ghost API - Microsoft Foundation Classes	- GNU C++ - CyberMed
Haptic device	Phantom Desktop	any Phantom family device
Stereoscopy method	temporal multiplexing	temporal multiplexing
Number of models	6	5
Time for application development	~1 year	~2 months

Table 2. Main differences between the simulator previously developed and the new simulator.

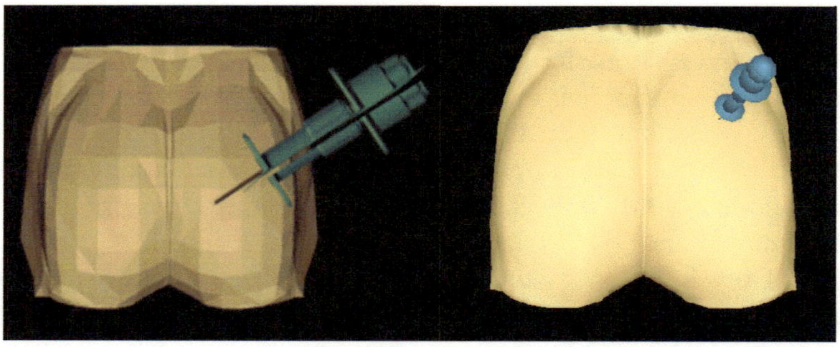

Fig. 12. Visual results of a previous application (left) and of the simulator developed with the CyberMed (right).

Both simulators support the use of shutter glasses and haptic devices. However, in the BMHSimulator the use of this hardware required a previous study of OpenGL functions to implement the routines for stereoscopic images generation. The same effort was necessary to integrate the haptic device and its routines to the application through the device API. In that simulator, the application window and menus were defined using the Visual C++ IDE (Integrated Development Environment) and the Microsoft Foundation Classes. The efforts needed to learn how to use all the tools mentioned above and to the implement the application demanded approximately one year for the complete development of the simulator. The CybBMH also demanded efforts to its development. However, it was focused in the use of the CyberMed classes. By the definition of objects and by the access to their of methods, it was possible to use methods, already integrated, ready to deal with stereoscopy, haptic devices and menus. It allowed reducing the time of development of the simulator to approximately two months. Additionally, the CyberMed classes provided an on-line assessment method to assess user's performance. This functionality offers a performance feedback to the user and can be used to know his ability level.

The sequence of the steps of the simulation is the same in both applications. The dissection and the transparency settings available in the Study module can be equally performed through menus. However the illumination model provided by the CyberMed classes allowed to offer better graphic results in the CybBMH, especially in the Study module, due to the presence of three models composed by thousands of points (skin, bone and bone marrow).

Two haptic devices of the Phantom family (Sensable, 2010) were tested and used with the CybBMH: the Omni and the Phantom Desktop. The exchange of the haptic devices did not require any change in the final code of the application. The main differences between the two devices are the size of the workspace, the precision and the amount of force which can be exerted.

The time consumed in the development of the BMHSimulator and the CybBMH did not include the acquisition of the simulation parameters or the design of models used in the application.

5.1 Assessment of users

The framework CyberMed presents a higher level of abstraction, is dedicated to the development of medical applications and presents methods for on-line assess users' performance. In the version 2.0 of CyberMed, three evaluation methods are available: Maximum Likelihood, General Bayesian Network and Expert system based on Fuzzy Rules, which were described early. All of them can be applied to bone marrow harvest simulator.

When a training system based on VR is implemented, always need to involve experts in the area object of the system, not only in the design and calibration properties, but also to assess the final version of the system. The ideal way to evaluate is to perform procedures under various specific conditions in which the system is able to allow. So, the experts through questionnaires record their impressions about the system. Another option is doing usability tests with the experts. At this stage, some problems still can be detected and should be fixed, after which another round of evaluation is performed. Once the experts qualify the system, it really becomes useful for the medical community that will use it.

In the case of development of the bone marrow harvest system, experts followed its conception from the Children Hospital of the University of São Paulo (Brazil). They calibrated the system properties and tested them. At the end of development, system qualification tests were performed (Machado, 2003). When redesigning the system using CyberMed framework, these experiences have been incorporated and the configuration parameters were reused from the previous system (Souza et al., 2007).

For the problem of bone marrow harvest, it is possible to choose any one of three methods of assessment in CyberMed. However, in this case was chosen the method of maximum likelihood, due to limitation of other methods on the size of the database and the expert knowledge.

To verify performance of the method of maximum likelihood and for reasons of general performance of the VR simulator, the following variables were chosen to be monitored: spatial position, velocities, forces and time on each layer. Previously, an expert, according to M classes of performance defined by him, calibrated the system. The calibration process consists in to execute several times the procedure and to classify each one according to classes of performance. The number of classes of performance was defined as M=3: 1) correct procedures, 2) acceptable procedures, 3) badly executed procedures. So, the classes of performance for a trainee could be: "you are well qualified", "you need some training yet", "you need more training". Sixty samples of training (twenty of each class of performance) were used for calibration of evaluation system. After that, users performed 150 procedures. The information of variability about these procedures was acquired using the maximum likelihood method. In our case, we assume that the source of information for w_j classes is the vector of the sample data D. The user makes his/her training in the virtual reality simulator and the evaluation tool collects data from his/her manipulation. All probabilities of data for each class of performance are calculated and at the end the user is assigned to a w_j class of performance. So, when a trainee uses the system, their performance is compared with each expert's class of performance and the assessment tool assigns the most appropriated class, according to the trainee's performance. At the end of the training, the assessment system reports the classification to the trainee.

The Cohen's Kappa Coefficient was used to perform the comparison of the classification agreement, as recommended in the literature (Duda et al., 2000) because it is known to be over conservative. The classification matrix obtained for the method is presented in the Table 3. The Kappa coefficient was K=81.0% with variance 1.6×10^{-3} %. In 19 cases, the evaluation tool made mistakes and at least one classification was made incorrectly in all classes. That performance is good and shows that maximum likelihood method is a competitive approach in the solution of assessment problems.

Class of performance according to experts	Class of performance according to Evaluation Tool		
	1	2	3
1	46	0	4
2	1	49	0
3	8	6	36

Table 3. Classification Matrix for the Evaluation Tool based on Maximum Likelihood.

In statistical terms, the performance of maximum likelihood method is acceptable. About computational performance the average of CPU time consumed was 0.0160 seconds, showing the method is qualified as online.

6. Conclusion

The development of applications based on VR for medical training involves knowledge of several areas and demands a multidisciplinary team. The union of ideas is important in all stages of the development as: definition of scope, design, modelling, definition of assessment method, implementation, tests and validation.

A simulator based on VR must contain the same steps present in a real procedure and can use volumetric models, stereoscopic visualization, haptic systems, deformation methods and interactive cut. The use of all those features requires a lot of processing and can compromise the real-time performance. Usually, the development team defines the most important features to integrate the simulator. It will also depend on the budget available.
Several systems were developed to the design and implementation of VR applications. Some of them are not free and demands specific non-free platforms. There are also, free systems to allow the development, integration and synchronization of tasks and tools in VR systems. In particular, the framework CyberMed presents a higher level of abstraction, is dedicated to the development of medical applications and presents methods for on-line assess users' performance.
A bone marrow harvest simulator was developed with CyberMed, explaining their facilities when compared to the full implementation of techniques and devices support routines. Thus, this Chapter showed the challenges and possible solutions related to the development of VR-based simulators for training. Particularly, was presented the importance of a user assessment included in the system to allow identifying mistakes and points for improvement. In this context, CyberMed is the only framework that provides assessment methods ready for use.
In particular, an assessment tool can, in real-time, to modify simulation aspects, as variables and functions responsible for feedback. Besides, this information can also be utilized to verify the degree of accuracy of users when performing the simulation. In the bone marrow harvest simulator implementation was used an assessment tool based on maximum likelihood, which achieved good results in a performance test.
Nowadays, there are other simulators been developed with CyberMed. The inclusion of new classes and methods already allow the development of tutoring applications over Internet. However, the framework has been expanded with new functionalities for synchronous collaboration (Sales et al., 2010).
As future works, is intended to make tests and statistical comparisons among the others assessment methodologies presented in this Chapter, as well as, to make a statistical comparison between trainees that use the VR system in their training and other trainees that do not use.

7. References

Burdea, G.; Patounakis, G.; Popescu, V.; Weiss, R.E. (1998) Virtual Reality Training for the Diagnosis of Prostate Cancer. Proc. IEEE Virtual Reality Annual Int. Symposium (VRAIS'98), pp. 190-197.

Burdea, G & Coiffet, P. (2003) Virtual Reality Technology. Wiley Interscience.

Cheng, J. & Greiner, R. (2001) Learning Bayesian Belief Network Classifiers: Algorithms and System, Proc. 40th Canadian Conference on Artificial Intelligence.

Correa, C.G.; Nunes, F.L.S.; Bezerra, A. (2009) Evaluation of VR Medical Training Applications under the Focus of Professionals of the Health Area. Proc. ACM-SAC Symposium on Applied Computer, pp. 821, Hawaii, ACM, Honolulu.

Darzi, A.; Smith, S.; Taffinder, N. (1999) Assessing operative skills. British Medical Journal, v.318, n.7188, pp.887-888.

Derossis, A.M. et al. (1998) Development of a model for training and evaluation of laparoscopic skills. American Journal of Surgery, v. 175, n.6, pp. 482-487.

Dinsmore, M. (1996) Virtual reality simulation: training for palpation of subsurface tumors. Master's Thesis, Department of Mechanical and Aerospace Engineering, Rutgers University, October.

Dinsmore, M.; Langrana, N.; Burdea, G.; Ladeji, J. (1997) Virtual Reality Training Simulation for Palpation of Subsurface Tumors. Proc. IEEE VRAIS 1997, pp. 54-60.

Dubois, D. & Prade, H. (1980) Fuzzy sets and systems - theory and applications. New York: Academic Press.

Dubois, D. & Prade, H. (1988) Possibility theory: An approach to computerized processing of uncertainty. Plenum Press.

Duda, R.O.; Hart, P.E.; Stork, D.G. (2000) Pattern Classification. 2nd ed. Wiley.

Färber, M. et al. (2008) Heinz Handels Training and evaluation of lumbar punctures in a VR-environment using a 6DOF haptic device, Studies in Health Technology and Informatics v.132, p.112-114.

Gallagher, A. G. et al. (1999) Virtual Reality training in laparoscopic surgery: A preliminary assessment of minimally invasive Surgical trainer Virtual Reality (MIST VR). Endoscopy, v.31, n.4, pp. 310-313.

Gallagher, A. G. et al. (2001) Objective psychomotor skills assessment of experienced, junior, and novice laparoscopists with virtual reality. World Journal of Surgery, v.25, n.11, pp. 1478-1483.

Gallagher, A. G. et al. (2005) Virtual Reality Simulation for the Operating Room: Proficiency-Based Training as a Paradigm Shift in Surgical Skills Training. Annals of Surgery, v.241, n.2, pp. 364-372.

Huang, J.; Payandeh, S.; Doris, P.; Hajshirmohammadi, I. (2005) Fuzzy Classification: Towards Evaluating Performance on a Surgical Simulator. Studies in Health Technology and Informatics v.111, pp. 194-200.

Johnson, R.A. & Wichern, D.W. (2001) Applied Multivariate Statistical Analysis, Prentice Hall, 5 edition.

Kumagai, K.; Yamashita, J.; Morikawa, O.; Yokoyama, K. (2007) A New Force-Based Objective Assessment of Technical Skills in Endoscopic Sinus Surgery. Studies in Health Technology and Informatics v.125, pp. 235-237.

Krause, P. J. (1998) Learning Probabilistic Networks, Knowledge Engineering Review, vol. 13, pp. 321-351.

Langrana, N.; Burdea, G.; Ladeji, J.; Dinsmore, M. (1997) Human Performance Using Virtual Reality Tumor Palpation Simulation. Computer & Graphics, v.21, n.4, pp.451-458.

Machado, L.S. (2003) Virtual Reality to Modeling and Simulation of Invasive Procedures for Pediatrics Oncology: A Case Study in Bone Marrow Transplant. PhD Thesis. Dept. of Electrical Engineering, University of Sao Paulo. (In Portuguese)

Machado, L.S. & Moraes, R.M. (2006). Evaluation of Training Executed by Web Using Multilayer Perceptron Based Systems. Proceedings of World Congress on Computer Science, Engineering and Technology Education (WCCSETE'2006). March, Santos, Brasil, p. 228-232.

Machado, L.S. & Moraes, R.M. (2009). Qualitative and Quantitative Assessment for a VR-Based Simulator. Studies in Health Technology and Informatics, v. 142, p. 168-173.

Machado, L.S. & Moraes, R.M. (2010) Intelligent Decision Making in Training Based on Virtual Reality. In: Da Ruan. (Org.) Computational Intelligence in Complex Decision Systems, Chapter 4. Atlantis Press, 9789078677277 , Paris.

Machado, L. S.; Moraes, R. M.; Zuffo, M. K. (2000)A Fuzzy Rule-Based Evaluation for a Haptic and Stereo Simulator for Boné Marrow Harvest for Transplant. In: Annals of Phantom Users Group. Aspen.

Machado, L. S.; Valdek, M. C. O.; Moraes, R. M. (2008) On-Line Assessment System for a Training System with Multiple Stages Based on Virtual Reality. Journal of Multiple-Valued Logic and Soft Computing, v.14, n.3-5, p.511-524.

Machado, L.S.; Moraes, R.M.; Souza, D.F.L; Souza, L.C.; Cunha, I.L.L. (2009) A Framework for Development of Virtual Reality-Based Training Simulators. Studies in Health Technology and Informatics, v. 142, pp. 174-176. IOSPress.

Mackel, T.; Rosen, J.; Pugh, C. (2006) Data Mining of the E-Pelvis Simulator Database: A Quest for a Generalized Algorithm for Objectively Assessing Medical Skill, Studies in Health Technology and Informatics 119, 355-360.

Mamdani, E.H. & Assilan, S. (1975) An experiment in linguistic synthesis with a fuzzy logic controller. International Journal of Man-Machine Studies, v. 7, no. 1, pp.1–13, 1975.

McBeth, P.B. et al. (2002) Quantitative Methodology of Evaluating Surgeon Performance in Laparoscopic Surgery. Studies in Health Technology and Informatics v. 85. 2002, pp. 280-286.

McCloy, R. & Stone, R. (2001) Science, medicine, and the future: Virtual reality in surgery. British Medical Journal, v.323, n.7318, p. 912–915.

Moraes, R.M. & Machado, L.S. (2005a) Maximum Likelihood for On-line Evaluation of Training Based on Virtual Reality. Proc. Global Congress on Engineering and Technology Education (GCETE'2005). March, Santos, Brasil, p.299-302.

Moraes, R.M. & Machado, L.S. (2005b) Evaluation of Training Executed by Web Using Fuzzy Rule Based Expert Systems. Proc. Global Congress on Engineering and Technology Education (GCETE'2005). March, Santos, Brasil, p.857-860.

Moraes, R.M. & Machado, L.S. (2006) Continuous Evaluation in Training Systems Based on Web. Proceedings of World Congress on Computer Science, Engineering and Technology Education (WCCSETE'2006). Março, Santos, Brasil, p. 223-227.

Moraes, R.M. & Machado, L.S. (2007) Multiple Assessment for Multiple Users in Virtual Reality Training Environments. Lecture Notes in Computer Science. Berlim. v. 4756, p. 950-956. Springer.

Moraes, R.M. & Machado, L.S. (2008) Using Embedded Systems to Improve Performance of Assessment in Virtual Reality Training Environments. Proc. Int. Conference on Engineering and Technology Education 2008 (Intertech'2008). March, Santos, Brasil, p. 140-144.

Moraes, R.M. & Machado, L.S. (2009a) Online Training Evaluation in Virtual Reality Simulators Using Possibilistic Networks. Proc. Safety Health and Environmental World Congress 2009 (SHEWC'2009). July, Mongaguá, Brasil, p. 67-71.

Moraes, R.M. & Machado, L.S. (2009b) Another Approach for Fuzzy Naive Bayes Applied on Online Training Assessment in Virtual Reality Simulators. Proc. Safety Health and Environmental World Congress 2009 (SHEWC'2009). July, Mongaguá, Brazil, p. 62-66.

Moraes, R.M. & Machado, L.S. (2010). Fuzzy Gaussian Naive Bayes Applied to Online Assessment in Virtual Reality Simulators. Proc. 9th Int. FLINS Conf. Foundations and Applications of Computational Intelligence (FLINS'2010). August, Chengdu, China, p. 243-248.

Moraes, R.M.; Machado, L.S.; Souza, L.C. (2009) Online Assessment of Training in Virtual Reality Simulators Based on General Bayesian Networks. In: Proc. VI International Conference on Engineering and Computer Education (ICECE 2009). Mongaguá, Brazil. CDROM.

Neapolitan, R.E. (2003) Learning Bayesian Networks, Prentice Hall. Series in Artificial Intelligence.

Rich, E. & Knight, K. (1993) Artificial Intelligence. McGraw Hill.

Sales, B.R.A.; Machado, L.S.; Moraes, R.M. (2010) Interactive Collaboration for Virtual Reality Systems related to Medical Education and Training. In: Proc. 6th Int. Conference on Technology and Medical Sciences (TMSi), Porto, Portugal. CDROM.

Sensable Technologies - Haptic Devices. Online: http://www.sensable.com/products-haptic-devices.htm. Access in July, 2010.

Souza, D.F.L.; Cunha, I.L.L.; Souza, L.C.; Moraes, R.M.; Machado, L.S. (2007) Development of a VR Simulator for Medical Training Using Free Tools: A Case Study. In: Proc. of Symp. Virtual and Augmented Reality (SVR2007), p. 100-105, Brazil, SBC.

Taffinder, N. et al. (1998) Validation of virtual reality to teach and assess psychomotor skills in laparoscopic surgery: results from randomised controlled studies using the MIST VR laparoscopic simulator. Medicine Meets Virtual Reality. Amsterdam: IOS Press, p. 124-130.

Wilson, M.S.; et al. (1997) MIST VR: a virtual reality trainer for surgery assesses performance. Annals of the Royal College of Surgeons of England, v.79, p. 403-404.

Zadeh, L.A. (1965) Fuzzy Sets. Information Control. n 8., pp. 338-353.

Zadeh, L.A. (1988) Fuzzy Logic. Computer, v. 1. pp.83-93.

16

Virtual Reality Simulators for Objective Evaluation on Laparoscopic Surgery: Current Trends and Benefits.

Ignacio Oropesa[1,2], Pablo Lamata[1], Patricia Sánchez-González[1,2], José B. Pagador[3], María E. García[1], Francisco M. Sánchez-Margallo[3] and Enrique J. Gómez[1,2]
[1] Bioengineering and Telemedicine Group, (ETSIT, Technical University of Madrid),
[2]Networking Research Center on Bioengineering, Biomaterials and Nanomedicine,
[3]Minimally Invasive Surgery Centre Jesús Usón,
Spain

1. Introduction

1.1 Laparoscopic surgery

Minimally Invasive Surgery (MIS) has changed the way surgery is performed in Operating Rooms (OR). MIS techniques are increasing their relevance in almost all surgical specialities, and have become the recommended standard in many procedures, displacing open surgery. Laparoscopy, one of the most common MIS approaches, has been adopted by several surgical sub-specialties including gastrointestinal, gynaecological and urological surgery (Fig. 1). It has become the standard technique for certain pathologies, like those associated with anti-reflux diseases, and procedures such as cholecystectomy (Cuschieri, 2005).

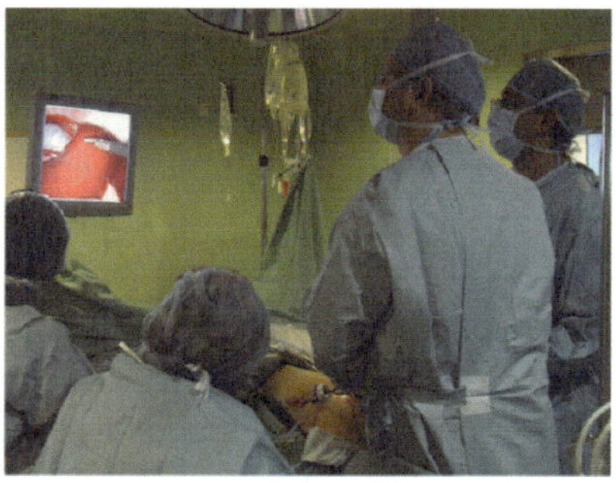

Fig. 1. Operating theatre view during a laparoscopic surgical intervention

MIS techniques bring important advantages to patients, such as less postoperative complications, faster recoveries or shorter hospitalization periods. However, they also bring forth considerable limitations and changes for physicians. Specifically, need of high degree of manual dexterity, complexity of instrument control, difficult hand-eye co-ordination, and lack of tactile perception, are the major obstacles. These difficulties involve a challenge for surgeons in getting used to a reduced workspace and to a limited sensory interaction, caused by indirect manipulation and visualization of the patient. They have to acquire new cognitive and motor skills, and they have to accommodate to the reduced workspace and to visualizing the intervention through a 2D monitor.

Due to these limitations, acquisition of MIS skills requires a long learning curve. Moreover, there is also a crescent pressure for safer, transparent and reproducible training programs. They should also allow for practice anywhere at any time, and make use of structured and objective training curricula to determine accurately the trainee´s preparation.

1.2 A historical framework on surgical evaluation

Effective training and assessment of surgeons have become one of the major concerns of hospitals and clinics in recent decades, fuelled mostly by patients' and society's demand for safer surgeries and prepared professionals. Much focus is thus set on the goal of developing structured curricula for surgical qualification and excellence.

1.2.1 Theoretical background

In order to understand the implications of designing training and assessment curricula, it is necessary to bear in mind some of the different pedagogical models and theories for adult learning. More specifically, we will consider the Bloom taxonomy (Bloom et al., 1956) and the Miller pyramid (Miller, 1990).

According to the learning objectives of a training program, Bloom's taxonomy defines three categories of learning objectives: knowledge, skills and attitudes. *Knowledge* refers to cognitive aspects, the assimilation and transformation of information; *skills* to psychomotor competences; and *attitudes* to the growth in feelings or emotional areas.

Most important in clinical education, however, is Miller's pyramid, which establishes four training levels: (1) *Knows* (knowledge), (2) *Knows How* (competence), (3) *Shows How* (performance) and (4) *Does* (action). The first two levels deal with declarative knowledge (knowing *what* to do), and thus can be established by means of examinations or essays. The two top levels are related to procedural knowledge (knowing *how* to do it), where establishment of proficiency levels is not so obvious due to the complex mixture of cognitive, motor, judgment and emotional skills involved.

In a broad sense, these models and theories convey the existence of a double plane of skills to be acquired: cognitive and motor skills. A third level could be arguably considered, involving the trainee's own judgement and applied knowledge to the problem at hand. Whilst in surgery cognitive skills' evaluation can easily be determined by validated methods such as examinations, motor and judgement skills are not so easily established. Thus they have been the focus of attention on recent years, implying the need for standardised and objective training programs (Tavakol et al., 2008).

1.2.2 Towards objectively structured curricula

Traditionally, training of surgeons has been based on the mentor-trainee relationship known as Halsted's model (Halsted, 1904). Motor skills' evaluation is performed with periodic In-Training Evaluation Reports (ITERs), along with aspects such as patient care, communication skills or professionalism (Sidhu et al., 2004). However, these reports are subjective, expensive, and prone to two undesirable side effects: The first is the halo effect, which refers to the influence that the relationship with a trainee can have on the mentor's report, for good or bad. Secondly, as these reports are periodically written, they are subject to the evaluators' long term memory, and provide little or none constructive feedback to the trainee (Fried & Feldman, 2008).

A need for structured, objective curricula was thus detected, and one of the first efforts to remedy the situation were the Objective Structured Clinical Examinations (OSCE), introduced on 1975 by Harden et al., and developed together between the University of Dundee and the Western Infirmary of Glasgow (Scotland). OSCE established a report based on trainee's performance on different clinical stations by means of checklists and assessment reports, with the process and end-product analysis of the task clearly distinguished (Harden et al., 1975).

As successful as OSCEs were, technical skill evaluation is buried between its much more ambitious examination goals, focused on other aspects such as procedural knowledge or attitude towards the patient. As a result of this, and in the wake of their popularity, the Objective Structured Assessment of Technical Skills (OSATS) were developed (Martin et al., 1997). Like OSCE, they employ assessment techniques such as operation checklists and end product-analysis, but always centred on the technical and motor skills of the surgeon. They are usually employed in laboratory settings, using box trainers or human cadavers, and ultimately, live animals in the OR (Sidhu et al., 2004). A counterpart of OSATS for Minimally Invasive Surgery was developed by Vassiliou et al., the Global Operative Assessment of Laparoscopic Skills (GOALS) (Vassiliou et al., 2005).

OSATS validity has been fully established, for skill training ranging from simple tasks to advanced chores (Moorthy et al., 2003). However, the resources needed are high, ranging from the number of experts required at each station to evaluate the trainees, to the marginal costs of each exam per candidate. Laparoscopic video offline-evaluation has been proposed to reduce some of these costs (Datta et al., 2002) with good reliability results; but still the presence of a reviewer is required, and immediate feedback is lost for the trainee.

On the last few years, there has been a been a growing interest on researching automatic methods for measuring the surgeon's motor skills; to provide him precise and immediate feedback on his performance, without requiring the constant presence of a supervisor. Training methods are being gradually changed, leaving the traditional ways behind on behalf of criterion-based curricula (Satava, 2008). This tendency has been boosted thanks to the development and advances on tracking and computing technologies, which have lead, for example, to the appearance of Virtual Reality simulators for surgical training. A new vast research field has opened, were efforts focus not only on the development of training and assessment systems such as said simulators; but on determining what these systems should measure and how should that information be handled (Lamata, 2006a). The present chapter will present an in-depth view on how Virtual Reality simulators have steadily become a part of motor skill formation programs on Minimally Invasive Surgery.

2. Metrics definition: How is surgical skill defined?

2.1 Difficulties on metrics definition

Since the need for structured and objective assessment programs became apparent, there has been much research to identify which parameters characterise surgical skills. This research has been boosted with the availability of automated tracking and registering systems such as simulators. Number, precision and accuracy of the potential metrics have grown due to the processing capabilities these systems provide (Satava et al., 2003).

Determination of valid metrics is a complex process where great difficulties arise when defining quantitatively a surgical motor skill, considering how relative that definition can be. Different validation studies for a given metric may vary on the conclusions obtained; often, due to the nature and difficulty of the task associated to it. Definition must thus be carefully considered, as some metrics also require *ad hoc* characterization for a given task. Error-related metrics, for example, will be closely associated to that task's goal.

Metrics must be taken into account in relationship with each other rather than on their own. For example, time taken on a task is not a valid parameter if the trainee commits many errors during the exercise. When considering several metrics, it has to be regarded that their nature may vary, and thus also the means for registering them. One may consider, for example, a movement tracking device to capture the tool's motion for analysis of the path length; but to combine that information with input on the errors performed, it will be necessary a supervisor or a post-exercise video-review. In this sense, Virtual Reality simulators excel themselves, due to their ability to determine qualitative parameters such as errors committed and perform final-product analysis.

2.2 Metrics taxonomy

Much research has been devoted to the definition of new valid metrics for performance assessment (Cotin et al., 2002; Lamata, 2006a), as well as on determining the ideal skills, tasks and parameters to measure (Satava et al., 2003). Metrics can generally be classified into two main categories: Efficiency and Quality metrics (Fried & Feldman, 2008). Some of the most important metrics identified in the literature are shown on Table 1.

Metrics for objective skills' assessment			
Efficiency	*Force Analysis*	Tool - tissue forces Torsion	(Rosen et al., 2002)
		Force sensitivity	(Lamata, 2006a)
	Motion Analysis	Time Path Length Motion Smoothness Depth Perception Tool Rotation	(Cotin et al., 2002)
		Speed & Acceleration Optimal Path Deviation IAV (Energy Expenditure)	(Cavallo et al., 2005)
		Angular Area Volume	(Chmarra et al., 2010)
Quality		Task Outcome Errors Manoeuvres' Repetitions Manoeuvres' Order Idle States	(Fried & Feldman, 2008)

Table 1. Metrics for objective skills' assessment

For meaningful skill assessment, both efficiency and qualitative metrics should always be considered on any training curricula. Efficiency metrics are related with measurable physical parameters, and thus their definition is usually precise and has a strong theoretical background behind them. These metrics always require the use of some sensor-based device in order to be acquired, either on physical or virtual simulators; and thus are objective, reproducible and little prone to misinterpretation. A distinction can be made between motion- and force- derived metrics. The first ones include all those related with movements of hands and tools performed during a task: total path length, economy of movements, speed, motion smoothness, etc. Force related metrics, such as tool-tissue interactions, have also been studied by Rosen et al. (Rosen et al., 2002), and, more recently, by Horeman et al. (Horeman et al., 2010).

Quality metrics, on the other hand, relate to the task's definition and execution. Most prominent among these metrics are the errors committed, the final product analysis, the sequence of steps performed in an exercise or procedure, etc. Objective and automatic measurements of these parameters can be difficult, and usually they call for the presence of a trained supervisor and the definition of clear structured checklists, such as those provided by OSATS (Fried & Feldman, 2008).

2.3 Validation of metrics for skills' assessment

As shown above, there are many potential metrics to be considered for surgical assessment; however, not all of them prove to be as decisive for the task. A process of validation must be carried out in order to determine their relevance and suitability for the evaluation process.

2.3.1 Concepts on validation

In order for a test, or measurement within it, to be considered useful for the determination of surgical skills, proof of its reliability and validity must be given (Fried & Feldman, 2008).

Reliability is a measure of the consistency of the test; the extent to which the assessment tool delivers the same results when used repeatedly under similar conditions. It is measured by a reliability coefficient, quantitative expression of the consistency of the tests ranging between 0 and 1. A good reliability coefficient has been approximated at values >0.8. Other useful measures of reliability are α, coefficient α, Cronbach's α, or internal consistency (Gallagher et al., 2003). Three different aspects are involved:

- **Inter-rater Reliability:** Extent to which two different evaluators give the same score in a test made by a user. This feature has little interest in Virtual Reality simulators, where metrics are already automatically acquired.
- **Intra-rater Reliability:** Internal consistency of an evaluator when grading on a given test on different occasions.
- **Test-retest Reliability:** Extent to which two different tests made by the same person in two different time frames give the same result.

Validity relates to the property of "being true, correct, and in conformity with reality". In testing, the fundamental property of any measuring instrument, device, or test is that it "measures what it purports to measure". Within the testing literature, a number of benchmarks have been developed to assess the validity of a test or testing instrument. They are the following (Gallagher et al., 2003):

- **Face validity:** defined as "a type of validity that is assessed by having experts review the contents of a test to see if it seems appropriate". It is a very subjective type of validation and is usually used only during the initial phases of test construction. For example a simulator has face validity when the chosen tasks resemble those that are performed during a surgical task.

- **Content validity:** defined as "an estimate of the validity of a testing instrument based on a detailed examination of the contents of the test items". Experts perform a thorough examination of the contents of the tests to determine if they are appropriate and situation specific. Establishing content validity is also a largely subjective operation and relies on the judgments of experts about the relevance of the materials used. For example a simulator has content validity when the tasks for measuring psychomotor skills are actually measuring those skills and not anatomic knowledge.
- **Construct validity:** degree to which the test captures the hypothetical quality it was designed to measure. A common example is the ability of an assessment tool to differentiate between experts and novices performing a given task (Schijven & Jakimowicz, 2003).
- **Concurrent validity:** defined as "the extent to which the test scores and the scores on another instrument purposing to measure the same construct are related". When the other instrument is considered a standard or criterion, the validity test is called "criterion validity" Discriminate validity is defined as "an evaluation that reflects the extent to which the scores generated by the assessment tool actually correlate with factors with which they should correlate".
- **Predictive validity:** defined as "the extent to which the scores on a test are predictive of actual performance". An assessment tool used to measure surgical skills will have predictive validity if it can ascertain who will perform surgical tasks well and who will not.

2.3.2 State of the art

Despite all of the metrics stated previously, many of them still require proper validation in order to be considered representative of surgical skill level. Time, total path length and economy of movements are considered in general as valid metrics, on the basis that an expert surgeon will perform a task more swiftly and denoting a more clear perception of the surgical space and the strategic approach to the task at hand (Thijssen & Schijven, 2010). Path deviation is also a very popular metric, usually considering the optimal path as the straight line between two points (although this has been accurately questioned by Chmarra et al. (Chmarra et al., 2008), pointing out the existence of a retraction movement in the correct *modus operandi*). Quality metrics such as end-product analysis and error count, although much more variable in their definition, are also considered basic for a correct determination of surgical level (Satava et al., 2003).

New metrics are proposed continuously as the means to acquire and process them become available. Their validation and study pose as key research aspects in the development of new objective assessment programs. Analysis of speed profile was studied by (Sokollik et al., 2004), with inconclusive results. Sinigaglia et al. identified acceleration of movements as a key factor for determining surgical expertise, studying their power spectra (Sinigaglia et al., 2005). A related parameter, motion smoothness, has been proposed and used by authors such as Stylopoulos et al. (Stylopoulos et al., 2004). Chmarra et al. proposed measuring the angular area and volume of the movements performed (Chmarra et al., 2010) and employed them for automatic detection of surgical skills. Overall, the clinical significance of these metrics has yet to be further determined, and thus thorough validation is required before being clinically adapted to training curricula.

3. Virtual Reality simulators for objective skills' assessment

Ethical concern on patient safety has led to a tendency to bring the training and assessment processes out of the OR as much as possible. Live animals and human cadavers are used as bench models, which generates a moral debate. Box trainers have also become popular training means, offering simple but key tasks to develop the necessary basic and advanced surgical skills. Examples on different box trainers can be found in (Rosser et al., 1997; Scott et al., 2000; Fichera et al., 2005). However, the real breakthrough came with the first Virtual Reality simulators, which allowed for controlled training and objective skills' assessment, on exercises ranging from simple tasks to complex laparoscopic procedures.

3.1 Advantages and limitations

Virtual Reality simulators offer some advantages that can add certain value to the training and assessment of surgical skills. They allow for training on controlled environments, and are always available for the trainee, without the need of a supervisor (thus reducing associated costs). They are ideal for monitoring a surgeon's learning curve, and offer a wide range of metrics which can be used for objective assessment, both efficiency and quality driven. More importantly, they deliver immediate constructive feedback of results and errors to the trainee, which some authors identify as basic in any effective training program (Issenberg et al., 2005).

However, some limitations have slowed down their clinical implantation (Lamata, 2006a). First, there are resource-derived constraints, such as trainees' loaded schedules, which leave them little time for practice; or the costs resulting from the expensive technologies behind the simulators. There are cases in which these advanced and sophisticated systems are available in the hospital but residents do not find the time or motivation to train their skills with them. Secondly, Virtual Reality environments show limitations in realism and interaction, which might not be critical for their didactic value, but are nevertheless of key importance to gain the acceptance of physicians. Thirdly, there are mentality-driven constraints, such as thinking of a surgical simulator as a videogame with no didactic value. Prior experience with videogames can also be a handicap when facing virtual simulators. It can even happen that such systems will lull oneself to a false sense of security, built on the development of incorrect habits while getting used to a virtual environment.

3.2 State of the art

Over the past fifteen years, virtual simulation has become a reference on the field of surgical training, with many attempts, some more successful than others, to develop, and most importantly, validate diverse models.

Surgical simulators can be classified according to the interventional procedures they are aimed for. Thus, we may find examples of arthroscopic simulators for knee and shoulders, as the InsightArthroVR (GMV Healthcare, Spain); cystoscopy and colonoscopy oriented, such as UroMentor and GIMentor respectively (Simbionix, Israel); intravascular simulators as CathSim (Immersion Medical, USA) and VIST-VR (Mentice, Sweden); and even focused on ophthalmological procedures, as the EYESi simulator (VRMagic, Germany).

In the field of laparoscopic surgery, we can find several well-positioned simulators on the market. As of this day, the principal laparoscopic simulators currently on the market can be found in Table 2. To further characterise each of them we can establish (1) whether tasks offered are basic, advanced (motor skill training) or complex (motor and cognitive training); (2) whether they offer realistic anatomic scenarios for procedures' simulation, and (3) whether they offer force feedback to the trainee.

LapMentor (Simbionix, Lod, Israel - Cleveland, USA) • Simple and advanced tasks, surgical procedures • Realistic scenarios • Force feedback	
LapSim (Surgical Science Ltd, Göteborg, Sweden) • Simple and advanced tasks, surgical procedures • Realistic scenarios • Optional force feedback	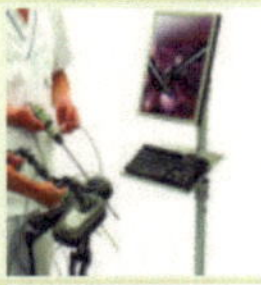
MIST-VR (Mentice AB, Göteborg, Sweden) • Simple tasks • Non-realistic scenarios • Optional force feedback	
Promis (Haptica, Dublin, Ireland - Boston, USA) • Simple tasks, surgical procedures • Real scenarios (Hybrid Simulator) • Optional force feedback	
SIMENDO (DeltaTech, Delft, Netherlands) • Simple tasks • Non-realistic scenarios • No force feedback	

Table 2. Main simulators currently on the market

A final mention must be done to the many prototypes, which, without reaching commercial status, contribute to the validation and recognition of simulators as useful educational tools. Among the research prototypes we may mention some as Vesta (Tendick et al., 2000), Kalsruhe (Kühnapfel et al., 2000), GeRTiSS (Monserrat et al., 2004), and SINERGIA (Lamata et al., 2007), which will be thoroughly presented in Section 4.

3.3 Taxonomy of didactic resources for Virtual Reality simulation

Virtual Reality simulators can be conceived as training and evaluation means built using different didactic resources. These resources are classified into three main categories (Lamata et al., 2006b) based upon the extent to which simulators (1) emulate reality (*fidelity resources*); (2) exploit computer capabilities such as new ways of interaction and guidance (*teaching resources*); (3) measure performance and deliver feedback (*assessment resources*).

Regarding this taxonomy, there are three main directions in the design of a simulator, which can be taken independently or in a combined fashion (see Fig. 2): (1) the improvement of Virtual Reality technologies for providing a better fidelity, (2) the enhancement of simulation by augmenting the surgical scene for providing guidance, and (3) the development of evaluation metrics for giving a constructive feedback to the trainee. This framework will now be used to evaluate and compare existing simulators, and to address the development of an optimal solution by assessing the value of these didactic resources.

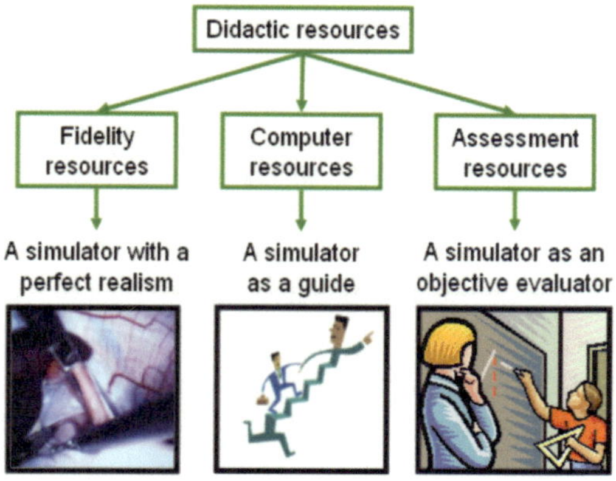

Fig. 2. The three conceptions of a Virtual Reality surgical simulator driven by the use of different didactic resources.

3.3.1 Evaluation and comparison of Virtual Reality simulators

Laparoscopic simulators, from simple box trainers with standardized tasks to advanced Virtual Reality simulators, are designed to train laparoscopic skills; but they make use of different didactic resources. A comparative analysis between some of the commercially available products is provided in Fig. 3.

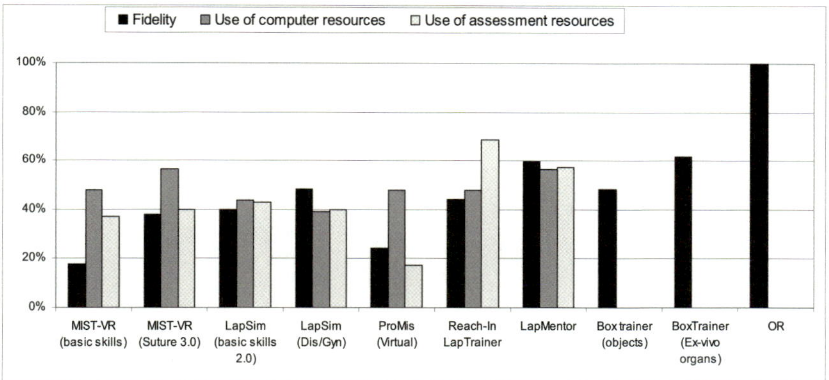

Fig. 3. Fidelity and use of computer and assessment resources by laparoscopic simulators.

Approaches to simulator design can be identified after studying how laparoscopic simulators make use of different didactic resources. The simplest one is an abstract conception of the surgical workspace focusing attention on the basic psychomotor skills that have to be developed by the trainee. MIST-VR "basic skills" was designed in this way, with an extremely simple interaction, almost no deformation and useful interaction indicators. The second approach aims at simulating a virtual patient with perfect realism, which is normally requested by surgeons. Force feedback is incorporated, organs are more realistic and interaction is enhanced. This is the trend usually followed by research institutions and companies, a trend lead by LapMentor as the simulator with the highest fidelity in almost every field (see Fig. 3).

But there is one last approach that might have a great potential: to enhance a simulator with a "virtual instructor" to guide the trainee through the procedure and deliver constructive feedback. Simulators make use of computer and assessment resources that build this "virtual instructor" capability. MIST-VR "Suture 3.0", which has the highest use of computer resources together with LapMentor (57%), offers an interesting guided interaction to teach trainees stitching and knotting skills. Reach-In Lap Trainer (nowadays integrated with MIST-VR), which had the highest use of assessment resources (69%), gave feedback about surgical performance not with low significant measurements like time or movements, whereas with what could be the advice of a surgical expert, with messages like "too much tissue bitten". The value of these types of resources has not yet been properly studied.

3.3.2 Towards an optimal design of a surgical simulator

Designing an optimum Virtual Reality surgical simulator for surgical training and assessment requires a suitable combination of Virtual Reality didactic resources. The value and importance of each of these didactic resources should therefore be assessed.

An important research question to be answered is to find the relationship between fidelity and training effectiveness. It would be really useful to assess how an increment in the realism of a simulation enhances or not the didactic capability. Fig. 4 shows a hypothetical line that relates these two variables for a given training objective, for example the acquisition of hand-eye coordination. The shape of this line is driven by three hypotheses. (1) *"A low degree of fidelity is enough to provide a good training effectiveness. It could even be the most efficient alternative"*, based in the fact that skills acquired with a simple surgical simulator, MIST-VR, are transferred to the operating room (Seymour, 2002); (2) *"Incorporation of force feedback in simulation delivers an increase of training effectiveness in training"*; and (3) *"Stress present in real operating theatres decreases training effectiveness"*. Several experiments are needed to figure out the real shape of this relationship between fidelity and training outcome.

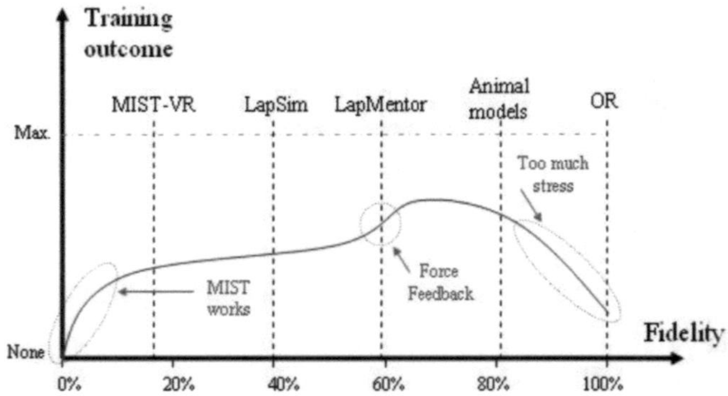

Fig. 4. Hypothetical relationship between simulation fidelity and training outcome. Fidelity values of commercial simulators are taken from (Lamata et al., 2006b).

On the other hand it is important to assess the value of computer and assessment resources offered. It could be contrasted if (1) *"Computer and assessment resources can overcome some lack of fidelity and result in an even more didactic simulator"*, based on the fact that many times some interaction limitation is solved with a virtual interaction paradigm, for example when some colour code substitutes force feedback (Kitawaga et al., 2005). Other hypotheses are (2) *"Growing semitransparent spheres are a good forces substitute in suture training"*; (3) *"Suture training in Virtual Reality is enhanced with a guided training strategy focusing the fidelity resources on pre-defined ways of interaction compared to a non-guided one"*; (4) *"A guided training strategy with constructive feedback in Virtual Reality can enhance suture training outcome beyond that of physical trainers despite some fidelity limitations"*; or even (5) *"Computer and assessment resources can substitute an expert teacher behind the surgical trainee"*.

3.4 Technical development of a Virtual Reality simulator

There are basically three main components in a Virtual Reality simulator: (1) a haptic interface to emulate the laparoscopic tools; (2) a monitor that simulates the abdominal cavity; and (3) a computer that manages both interfaces and runs the simulator's software, which in turn comprises four main modules (Fig. 5) (Lamata et al., 2007):

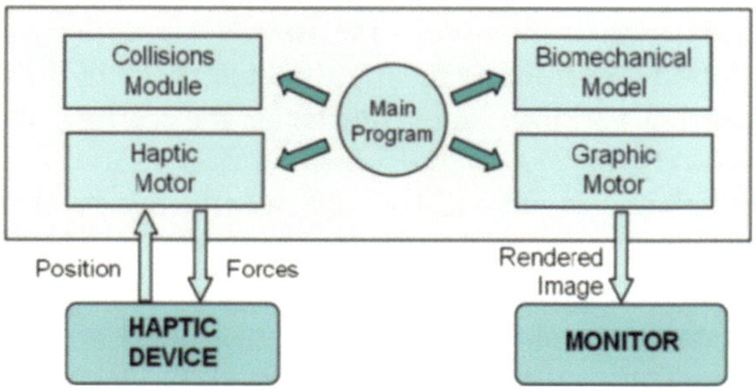

Fig. 5. Main Components in a Virtual Reality simulator

- **Biomechanical model:** Due to their very restrictive conditions, which imply update rates of at least 25Hz, robustness, satisfaction with visual result and precision, a trade-off must be achieved between complexity and speed when designing biomechanical models. There are two main approaches to be adopted (Meier et al, 2005): (1) heuristic models, (e.g. mass-spring models), or (2) models based on continuum mechanics, (e.g. finite elements models). There are several difficulties in this modelling process: biomechanical properties must be correctly acquired and tissue characteristics such as anisotropy, incompressibility and non-linearity considered (Picinbono et al., 2002). The models must represent surgical alterations that occur on real interventions, like cuts, dissections and other topological changes. Simplifications are made to address these problems, mainly assuming linear elasticity (valid for small deformations) and reducing the models' requirements. These have the drawback of being less realistic and prone to anomalous deformations (Picinbono et al., 2002).
- **Collisions' detection module:** Responsible of detecting overlapping objects and handling these detected collisions. There are three main types of collisions to manage: (1) tool-tool, (2) tool-tissue and (3) tissue-tissue. Implementation must consider the time constraints derived by fast-moving instruments. It is usually addressed with a coarse remodelling of the objects present in the scene to reduce their complexity. One simple alternative consists on defining boundary boxes on objects, and detecting any overlapping between them (Teschner et al, 2005). A recent advance introduces a fuzzy logic approach for handling tool-tissue collisions (García-Pérez et al., 2009).
- **Haptic rendering:** Delivering force feedback is still an unripe technology compared to visual rendering. This sensorial information requires a minimum update rate of 300Hz, which is technologically much more demanding compared to the 30Hz of visual display. There are several approaches for implementing it, like using the biomechanical

model (Delingette, 1998) or with a simplified geometric constraint force calculation proportional to the penetration depth of the tool (Balaniuk & Laugier, 2000).

- **Visual rendering:** Thanks to the many advances on computer graphics and the great deal of open source libraries available, visual rendering is a mature technology. Advances are focused now on photorealistic rendering and simulation of fumes and bleeding (Aggarwal et al., 2003).

3.5 Validation and acceptance of Virtual Reality simulators as assessment tools

As explained before, to be considered a suitable assessment tool, a measuring test or device and its related metrics must comply with a series of validation milestones. Virtual Reality simulators are not an exception to this, and so we can find in the literature many examples on the efforts to validate the different models available.

In the beginning, validation as a training means attracted much of the attention, focusing on concepts such as concurrent validity, skills transfer or the learning curve associated to the simulator (Lamata, 2006a). It is safe today to assume that Virtual Reality simulators are a valid supplementary method for surgical training, as effective as that provided by video-based box trainers. For further information, the reader is referred to (Gurusamy et al., 2009) for a complete meta-analysis of surgical simulators' validation for surgical training.

When it comes to validation as assessment tools however, there are more doubts about their reliability and fidelity (Thijssen & Schijven, 2010). For one, the limitations exposed previously still continue to hold sway among many clinicians. Indeed, validation studies up to today are sometimes inconclusive, and many surgeons are still mistrustful about their assessment capabilities.

3.5.1 Validation strategies

Different strategies are employed to carry out the validation studies necessary for a simulator (Fried & Feldman, 2008). Face and content validation, being for the most part subjective studies, are usually done by means of structured questionnaires and reviews. Face validity questionnaires usually call for personal opinions on the simulator's usefulness "at face value"; whilst content validation requires a more thorough and complete review of the tasks, skills assessed and metrics employed by the expert reviewer, before passing judgment.

Construct validation is usually granted if the simulator is able to determine differences between groups of surgeons with known different skill levels (as for example, residents and expert surgeons). The strategy employed is to divide the test population according to these levels, and measure their performance and the differences observed on the simulator. Some factors may however dampen the results of a study if not properly considered. Test subjects should not have prior experience with the simulator, as their learning curve may be enhanced because of this. Also, some studies have shown the influence of video-gaming experience as an influential concern (McDougall et al., 2006). Well designed studies, as well as increasing the test population, may help to mitigate these issues.

Concurrent and predictive validations require an alternative and valid assessment method to be deployed (a *gold standard*), in order to compare the results obtained on both scenarios. Test subjects are usually grouped by levels, and similar tasks performed and measured in both settings. Finding a gold standard for this comparison is not always easy; usually, comparison is done via OSATS, motion tracking systems, or employing another virtual simulator. If the comparison is done in a similar time period, it is considered concurrent validation; if on the contrary the time lapse between them is considerable, it is predictive validation which is being measured.

3.5.2 Validation studies on commercial simulators

There are many reports considering assessment validation of surgical simulators in the literature, especially where construct and concurrent validity are concerned. This is reasonable if we consider that these two parameters are essential for the automatic and immediate assessment they intend to carry out. Table 3 briefly summarizes the conclusions arrived at on the main studies performed on commercial simulators for the last few years.

Simulator as a skill assessment tool		
Face validity		
Simulator	*Reference*	*Valid?*
MIST-VR	(Maithel et al., 2006)	Yes
LapSim	(Schreuder et al, 2009)	Yes
SIMENDO	(Verdasdoonk et al., 2006)	Yes
LapMentor	(McDougall et al., 2006)	Yes
	(Ayodeji et al., 2007)	Yes
ProMis	(Botden et al., 2008)	Yes
Content validity		
Simulator	*Reference*	*Valid?*
SIMENDO	(Verdasdoonk et al., 2006)	Yes
LapMentor	(McDougall et al., 2006)	Yes
Construct validity		
Simulator	*Reference*	*Valid?*
MIST-VR	(Gallagher et al., 2004)	Yes
LapSim	(Sherman et al., 2005)	Yes
	(Ro et al., 2005)	No at the first exposure to simulator
	(Langelotz et al., 2005)	Yes, but time and path metrics only
	(Hassan et al., 2005)	Yes, more patent in second
	(Eriksen & Grantcharov, 2005)	Yes
	(Woodrum et al., 2006)	Yes, but only some parameters
	(Larsen et al., 2006)	Yes
	(Schreuder et al., 2009)	Yes
SIMENDO	(Verdasdoonk et al., 2007)	Yes
LapMentor	(McDougall et al., 2006)	Yes
	(Zhang et al., 2008)	Yes
	(Aggarwal et al., 2009)	Yes
ProMIS	(Broe et al., 2006)	Yes
	(Neary et al., 2007)	Yes
	(Pellen et al., 2009)	Yes
Concurrent validity		
Simulator	*Reference*	*Valid?/ Concurrent with...?*
MIST-VR	(Gallagher et al., 2004)	A little, with OR metrics
LapSim	(Youngblood et al., 2005)	Yes, with box trainer
	(Newmark et al., 2007)	Yes, with box trainer
SIMENDO	(Verdasdoonk et al., 2006)	Yes
LapMentor	(Okrainec et al., 2008)	Yes, with GOALS metrics in the OR
ProMis	(Ritter et al., 2007)	Yes, with OR metrics
	(Botden et al., 2007)	Yes, with LapSim
Predictive validity		
Simulator	*Reference*	*Valid?*
LapSim	(Hassan et al., 2008)	Yes
LapMentor	(Greco et al., 2008)	Yes
ProMis	(McCluney et al., 2006)	Yes

Table 3. Validation studies on commercial Virtual Reality simulators for skills' assessment

As promising as these results are, they are only but the first milestone on the slow road to integrating simulators on the design of structured assessment curricula.

4. Designing a Virtual Reality simulator for surgical training and assessment: The SINERGIA experience

There is little specific literature about how to develop an efficient didactic design for a simulator. It can be found that an ergonomic task analysis (Stone & McCloy, 2004) was used for the design of the MIST-VR, but without any further detail. The construction of the SINERGIA laparoscopic Virtual Reality simulator is one of the best documented examples of the development process (Lamata, 2006a), and this section highlights its main aspects. For a more detailed and thorough description of the design and development process of surgical systems the reader is referred to (Freudenthal et al., 2010).

4.1 Didactic design of simulator tasks

Design of the didactic contents of a simulator is based on a thorough analysis of the training needs, driven by a surgical training curriculum. Existing solutions and validation studies are also an important reference for the definition of specifications, which are described with a suitable use of simulation technologies. The third main pillar in the designing process is understanding the capabilities and reach of Virtual Reality technologies.

Human beings have perceptual limitations of the sensory, motor and cognitive system. Laparoscopy is characterised by a loss of sensory stimuli of the surgeon, which leads to the need of developing new skills. Knowing and understanding how surgeons interact in the surgical theatre and develop their skills is an important issue in order to address the design of a surgical simulator. This contributes to the definition of the required degree of simulation fidelity, a very controversial issue. For example, it is unclear the role of force feedback in surgical training (Kneebone, 2003). Comprehension of the laparoscopic interaction leads also to the definition of objective metrics of surgical skill. For example, an analysis of tissue consistency perception (Lamata et al, 2006c) led to the definition of "Force sensitivity" training tasks in the SINERGIA simulator (Lamata et al., 2007).

Training objectives and needs of the SINERGIA laparoscopic simulator were grounded on the vast training experience of the Minimally Invasive Surgery Centre Jesús Usón (MISCJU, Cáceres, Spain). This Centre has a thoroughly validated methodology of training based on four levels: (1) basic and advanced skills with box trainers, (2) anatomical protocols and advanced skills with animal models, (3) advanced procedural skills with tele-surgical applications and (4) practice in the OR (Fig. 6).

The SINERGIA laparoscopic simulator was conceived as a means for training and assessment on the first level in the pyramidal model. An analysis of the laparoscopic skills acquired at this stage led to the definition of seven didactic units: hand–eye coordination, camera navigation, grasping, pulling, cutting, dissection and suture.

4.2 Technical development

SINERGIA was developed in C++ language, with WTK libraries (WorldToolKit, Engineering Animation Inc., Mill Valley, CA-USA) and in a Windows environment. The chosen haptic interface was the Laparoscopic Surgical Workstation (Immersion Medical, Gaithersburg, USA) (Lamata et al., 2007).

Fig. 6. MISCJU Formation Pyramid

Biomechanical modelling was solved employing T2-Mesh mass spring models for hollow objects. A T2-Mesh model is a surface model that seeks for simplicity and speediness of calculi, in detriment of a realistic behaviour. Nodes in the model have a mass assigned to them. They are linked with linear springs which act as energy storage and react against deformations. The equations' system is relatively small and, therefore, fast in its resolution. Nevertheless it is an iterative model and consequently mined by the risk of instabilities and oscillations (Meier et al., 2005). Solid object handling was improved by the use of ParSys, which are fast and stable models composed by a set of interconnected volumetric elements, also called particles. Volumetric behaviour is given and guaranteed by its structure and volume conservation by the constant number of particles in an object (Pithioux et al., 2005).
Collision detection was performed by an *ad hoc* library built for SINERGIA, which tests geometrically the interaction between tools (rigid objects) and deformable objects, and manages topological changes. Assuming that the objects are modelled by means of a triangular mesh, **collision handling** is posed as finding the new positions of the vertices of the triangles involved in the collision. The problem is based on the tool kinematics (the tool velocity vector) and the normal vectors to the triangles involved in the collision. Therefore, each of its vertexes are displaced out of the tool bearing in mind the fuzzy nature of the tool motion, which is modelled as penetration or sliding (García-Pérez, 2009).
Graphical design of the scenarios was done with Blender (Blender Foundation, Amsterdam, Netherlands), an open source and multi-platform tool for 3D design and modelling, with a python-command interface. It provided the advantages of the ability to share 3D scenes from different platforms, and the feasibility to share models generated from real medical images. It was employed to design scenes (including exercises) and add the effects of texture and realism. Fig. 7 shows an example of a pig's abdominal cavity built using these models.

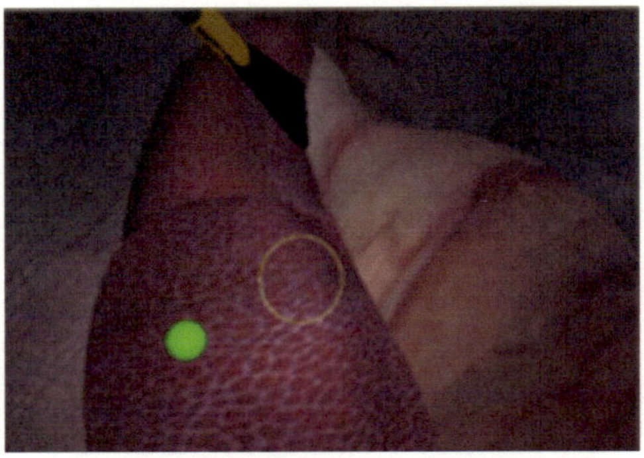

Fig. 7. Example of a surgical scene

4.3 SINERGIA objective assessment module

Addressing the needs described for surgical assessment, the SINERGIA Virtual Reality simulator includes an objective evaluation system, in order to monitor trainees' learning curves (Fig. 8). Objective metrics' definition allows trainees to learn from their mistakes by means of indications when errors are performed (*formative feedback*) or by visualization of the global practice score (*summative feedback*).

This evaluation component can be used by three different groups: (1) trainees, who perform the tasks and whose metrics are stored and managed by the system; (2) teachers, who monitor and follow-up the trainees' progress by means of the evaluation interface; and (3) administrators, tasked with system and user management. Security is an important issue in the evaluation system. Thus, a teacher is only able to follow his pupils' results, and a trainee tracks only his own data, but can compare these results with an average mark of the global users' community.

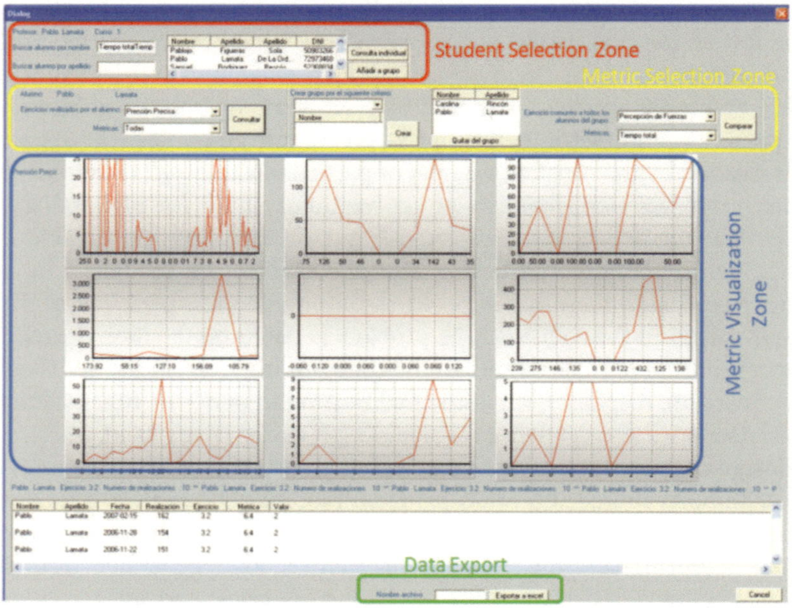

Fig. 8. SINERGIA Assessment Module

In order to manage all evaluation data, different graphics modalities are implemented for easy monitoring and understanding of the surgical skills' evolution of the trainee. Comparisons between different individuals or groups of pupils and data exchange for statistical analysis are possible in the user interface.
Moreover, the system offers an easy to use interface which allows efficient metric management, while dealing with huge amounts of information. Its design has been validated by expert surgeons of the Minimally Invasive Surgery Centre Jesús Usón.

4.4 SINERGIA face and construct validation

First validation of SINERGIA consisted on two tests to determine face and construct validity (Sánchez-Peralta et al., 2010). Among all tasks provided, five were selected for the study (hand-eye coordination, camera navigation, navigation and touch, accurate grasping and coordinated pulling, as shown in Fig. 9).

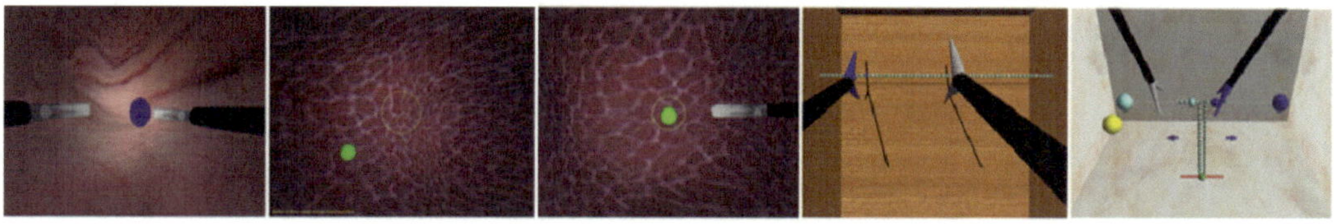

Fig. 9. Tasks performed in the validation process: From left to right: hand-eye coordination, camera navigation, navigation and touch, accurate grasping and coordinated pulling.

10 novices and 6 expert surgeons took part in the validation experiment. Each subject performed each task in the SINERGIA Virtual Reality simulator once and filled in demographic and face validity questionnaires after performance. No external help was given during the exercises; only a brief explanation of the task prior performance. Results are shown in Table 4.
Significance was calculated using the Mann-Whitney U test for $P<0.05$. Statistical analysis highlighted significant differences between the experienced and non-experienced groups in 60% of the evaluated metrics, which implies a partial construct validity being reached. Face validity is confirmed in the questionnaires, where there are no significant differences in any of the evaluated aspects. Results also showed that both groups considered the most remarkable characteristic in SINERGIA its usefulness as a learning tool for basic laparoscopic skills, rating it with the highest possible score.

5. Alternative technologies for objective surgical evaluation

In order to give a complete picture of the current state of the art on surgical assessment technologies, and to understand where Virtual Reality simulators stand in the bigger picture, we will briefly present other ways for acquiring efficiency measurements for objective evaluation.
On the last few years several systems have been developed for force and movement analysis (Moorthy et al, 2003). All these have in common the need for some means to capture the value of objective metrics. This is usually achieved by active or passive tracking devices. Active tracking relies on optical, electromagnetic or mechanical sensors mounted on the surgical tools. Passive tracking relies on the external detection of markers placed on the instruments, using ultrasound or electromagnetic technologies. The reader is referred to (Chmarra et al., 2007) for more information behind the technologies behind tracking systems.

SINERGIA construct validity				
Tasks	**Metrics**	**Novices (n = 14)**	**Experts (n = 6)**	**P value**
Coordination	Total time (s)	75.16 ± 9.72	61.97 ± 11.11	0.033
	Partial time (s)	2.98 ± 0.49	2.48 ± 0.45	0.062
	Fulfilment (%)	75.14 ± 8.18	85.33 ± 8.26	0.051
	L-I efficiency (%)	36.80 ± 11.48	46.97 ± 10.67	0.062
	R-I efficiency (%)	37.06 ± 8.48	47.27 ± 10.78	0.033
	Harms to background (#)	11.43 ± 5.45	4.67 ± 2.88	0.006
Navigation	Total time (s)	104.71 ± 10.95	97.50 ± 12.93	0.353
	Partial time (s)	7.86 ± 0.73	7.36 ± 0.57	0.207
	Fulfilment (%)	76.36 ± 14.48	88.00 ± 8.39	0.076
	L-I efficiency (%)	40.93 ± 8.19	47.52 ± 3.89	0.033
	Harms to background (#)	0.29 ± 0.61	0.67 ± 0.82	0.353
Navigation and touch	Total time (s)	106.79 ± 19.92	85.33 ± 11.36	0.005
	Partial time (s)	7.48 ± 1.27	5.97 ± 0.92	0.007
	Fulfilment (%)	71.64 ± 15.83	95.50 ± 4.93	0.007
	L-I efficiency (%)	40.93 ± 10.03	55.45 ± 3.84	0.014
	Harms to background (#)	95.36 ± 94.01	11.33 ± 4.46	0.002
Precise grasping	Total time (s)	50.14 ± 12.66	32.50 ± 5.58	0.002
	Partial time (s)	5.01 ± 1.30	3.27 ± 0.52	0.002
	Fulfilment (%)	100.00 ± 0.00	100 ± 0.00	1
	Deviation from central point (cm)	0.06 ± 0.01	0.04 ± 0.01	0.003
	L-I efficiency (%)	6.43 ± 2.62	8.33 ± 2.16	0.091
	R-I efficiency (%)	8.21 ± 2.75	10.17 ± 3.54	0.207
	Grasps out of the area (#)	4.71 ± 6.39	1.00 ± 1.26	0.02
	Grasps with excessive pressure (#)	3.00 ± 2.08	0.00 ± 0.00	0.002
Coordinate Traction	Total time (s)	123.71 ± 45.41	87.00 ± 24.58	0.051
	Partial time (s)	41.33 ± 15.24	29.11 ± 8.32	0.062
	Fulfilment (%)	69.05 ± 20.52	94.44 ± 13.61	0.026
	L-I distance from ideal line (cm)	836.93 ± 352.73	501.33 ± 201.78	0.02
	R-I distance from ideal line (cm)	748 ± 285.64	504.67 ± 184.19	0.041
	L-I efficiency (%)	4.31 ± 1.03	6.61 ± 1.42	0.002
	R-I efficiency (%)	5.10 ± 1.66	7.11 ± 2.22	0.062
	Non-coordination moments (#)	31.64 ± 36.56	1.33 ± 3.27	0.001

Table 4. Metrics results for novices and experts

The technology behind these devices is all but the same than that employed by the haptic systems of Virtual Reality simulators (indeed, they can be exchangeable), so the main difference resides in the tracking system's application: instead of software-based virtual tasks, they are used as training and assessment means on box trainers and even the OR.

Force sensing has been mainly approached by Rosen et al. (Rosen et al., 2002). They demonstrated that experienced surgeons apply higher force/torque magnitudes during tissue dissection than novices, and vice versa for tissue manipulation. Sensing was performed by a specially built system, the BlueDragon, a bulky device with built-in mechanical sensors. More recently, Horeman et al. have approached tool/tissue forces detection by means of a pressure platform placed under the box trainer task (Horeman et al., 2010).

However, movement sensing has been one of the most common approaches followed. Motion tracking systems register both the position (x,y,z coordinates) and orientation (yaw, pitch and roll) of the surgical tools. Systems have been developed that place position sensors on tools or on hands and fingertips, such as ADEPT (Hanna et al., 1998), ICSAD (Datta et al., 2001), CELTS (Stylopoulos et al., 2004), or TrEndo (Chmarra et al., 2006). Among other things, measuring trajectories has been used for speed and acceleration calculi, optimal path and economy of movement determination, depth perception and movement sequences analysis, and repetitions or idle states detection. Active sensing has the disadvantages of introducing new elements on the surgical theatre, thus altering it, and also of modifying the tools' ergonomics. Passive sensing systems have thus been also developed for motion tracking, such as the Zebris (Sokollik et al., 2004).

An interesting approach for passive sensing can be the analysis of the laparoscopic videos, which allow tracking of movements employing computer vision techniques. This way, information about position and trajectories can be acquired, which can then be used to obtain speeds and accelerations, and for metrics calculation such as economy of movements, efficiency, optimal path, etc. The challenge of this approach is to exploit the 2D information of the surgical scenario captured by the endoscope in order to assess the laparoscopic tool's 3D position. This approach solves the problem of calculating the 3D position and orientation of a tool with only the 2D information extracted from each frame of a video sequence. Combining segmentation and edge detection techniques, position of the surgical tools' borders is determined. Knowing the tool's cylindrical geometrical dimensions and its 2D projection as denoted by the detected borders, real 3D tool's pose is calculated (Fig. 10). The mathematical equation for this calculus is a description of the geometrical relations between the tools, trocars and the optical centre of the camera; its complete description and explanation can be found in (Cano et al., 2008). Current tracking performance of these methods, with an accuracy of 9.28mm, is good enough for gesture analysis and objective evaluation of surgical manoeuvres.

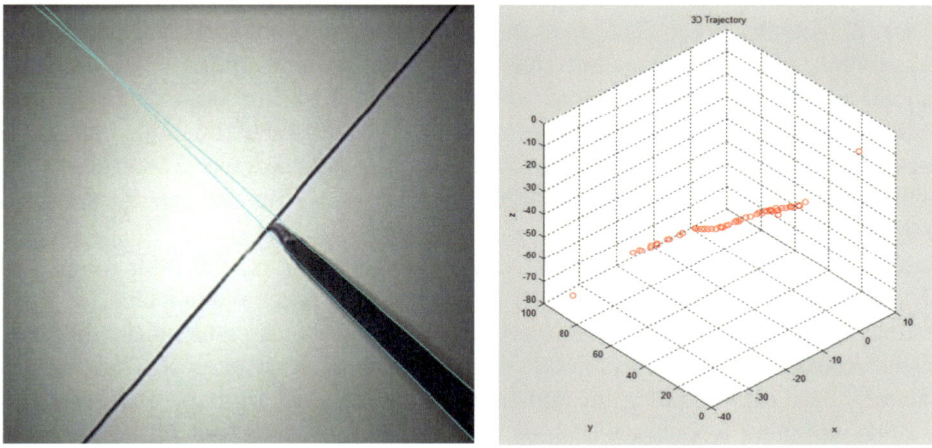

Fig. 10. Video tool tracking: Left, 2D detection of the instrument's borders; right, 3D trajectory determination

6. Discussion

Developing structured training curricula for laparoscopic surgery has become a priority in the past few decades. There are several reasons behind this: primarily, there is an ever-growing social concern on patient safety, whether on medical errors or on the ethics behind training on real patients. It has become also necessary to optimize resident's timetables, and evolve efficient training programs around them. Finally, there is a need to maximize the efficiency/cost ratios of these programs.

Within these new curricula, Virtual Reality simulators, along with the aforementioned tracking systems, present themselves as useful methods for training and assessing skills in laboratory settings. In these conditions, the trainee is able to practice his skills in a stress-free environment and receive objective feedback of his technical performance. A good example on trying to integrate Virtual Reality simulators on surgical curricula can be found in (Aggarwal et al., 2009).

However, controversy has surrounded their use since the very first models. Their lack of realism has been one of the strongest arguments employed against them. Much work is still required in this field; some authors have even pointed out that surgeons and trainees seem to prefer training on physical simulators due to the more realistic visual and tactile sensations involved (Chmarra et al., 2008; Gurusamy et al., 2009). Validation studies have, however, proved over the last few years that these limitations do not diminish the training effectiveness; indeed, where the ultimate goal is the acquisition of motor skills such as hand-eye coordination or depth perception, a realistic scenario does not necessarily add much value to the training process.

But whilst training effectiveness seems to be generally accepted, the same cannot still be said of their assessment capabilities (Thijssen & Schijven, 2010). This, however, can be partly blamed on the difficulties of defining a standardized training curriculum, and its associated metrics. Although this problem could be extended to other areas of surgical training besides Virtual Reality simulators, in their case it becomes magnified if considered along their limitations and their slow acceptance (Liselotte & Dewan, 2009).

The truth is that, no matter what, the possibilities of Virtual Reality simulators as evaluation tools are potentially great. The fact that they are ever available for training, their reproducibility and the immediate feedback they provide mean that training and assessment of skills can be easily accommodated to the trainee's schedule. Also, their unrivalled ability to capture and acquire not only efficiency metrics but also quality based ones gives them an important advantage over other acquisition devices. The variety of tasks available, from simple exercises to complex interventions, allows also extending their range to the field of cognitive knowledge.

No doubt in the future Virtual Reality simulation will focus on the improvement of the visual and tactic experience for the user; as technologies become available. But it will be interesting to see their clinical evolution concerning their assessment capabilities. One promising research area is the automatic determination of surgical level. These techniques have already been explored by some authors (Rosen et al., 2002, Chmarra et al., 2009; Megali et al., 2006), applying techniques such as Hidden Markov Models or Linear Discriminant Analysis. Their inclusion on future generations of Virtual Reality simulators could help improve their value as objective assessment tools.

To conclude, it is necessary to stress the complimentary role that Virtual Reality simulators and other tracking devices play in the much larger scope of the surgical structured curricula. Despite the need for objectivity, the fact remains that final expertise accreditation should come by the hand of an expert mentor. There will always be a subjective component to the determination of a surgeon's readiness, which will imply judging abilities such as reaction time, mentality, patient care, handling of stress or group working capability. These are all important factors that add a human dimension to the qualification process, and thus should always be considered.

7. Conclusion

Studies on Virtual Reality simulators over the last few years have focused especially on their training capabilities, determining whether motor skills acquisition on them is really effective and if they really translate to the OR afterwards. The present chapter has presented them from a different, although related, perspective: their usefulness as skills' assessment tools. While acceptance of Virtual Reality simulators is growing by the day as validation studies prove their usefulness, the development of training curricula to determine surgical expertise is not being so easy. It has been the authors' goals in this chapter to convey to the reader the actual state of the art of Virtual Reality simulators in the field of skills assessment, in relation to other devices such as sensor-based tracking systems; to point out to him their limitations and advantages; and further still, to give him insight on the development and validation process of a surgical simulator (SINERGIA) in order to prove that, despite their limitations and the complications surrounding them, we believe that in the near future, Virtual Reality will play an important role on structured and objective skills assessment.

8. References

Aggarwal, R.; Bhasin, Y.; Raghupathi, L. & Devarajan, V. (2003). Special visual effects for surgical simulation: Cauterization, irrigation and suction. *Medicine Meets Virtual Reality 11*, Nextmed: Health Horizon, 94, pp. 1-3.

Aggarwal, R. ; Crochet, P.; Dias, A.; Misra, A.; Ziprin, P. & Darzi, A. (2009). Development of a virtual reality training curriculum for laparoscopic cholecystectomy. *British Journal of Surgery*, 96 pp. 1086–1093

Ayodeji, I.D.; Schijven, M.; Jakimowicz, J. & Greve, J.W. (2007). Face validation of the Simbionix LAP Mentor virtual reality training module and its applicability in the surgical curriculum. *Surgical endoscopy*, 21, 9, pp. 1641-1649.

Balaniuk, R. Y. & Laugier, C. (2000). Haptic interfaces in generic virtual reality systems, Proc. *IEEE/RSJ International Conference on Intelligent Robots and Systems, 2000, (IROS 2000)*, Takamatsu Japan, 2, pp. 1310-1315.

Bloom, B.; Englehart, M.; Furst, M.; Hill, W. & Krathwohl, D. Taxonomy of educational objectives: The classification of educational goals. New York: David McKay Company, Inc.; 1956.

Botden, S.M.B.I.; Buzink, S.N.; Schijven, M.P. & Jakimowicz, J.J. (2007). Augmented versus Virtual Reality Laparoscopic Simulation: What is the difference? *World journal of surgery*, 31, 4, pp. 764-772.

Botden, S.M.; Berlage, J.T.; Schijven, M.P. & Jakimowicz, J.J. (2008). Face Validity Study of the ProMIS Augmented Reality Laparoscopic Suturing Simulator. *Surgical technology international*, 17, pp. 26-32.

Broe, D.; Ridgway, P.F.; Johnson, S.; Tierney, S. & Conlon, K.C. (2006). Construct validation of a novel hybrid surgical simulator. *Surgical endoscopy*, 20, 6, pp. 900-904.

Cano, A.M.; Gayá, F.; Lamata, P.; Sánchez-González, P & Gómez, E.J. (2008). Laparoscopic tool tracking method for augmented reality surgical applications. Lecture Notes in Computer Science, vol. 5104, pp. 191-196, 978-3-540-70521-5_21.

Cavallo, F.; Megali, G.; Sinigaglia, S.; Tonet, O. & Dario, P. (2005). A Biomechanical Analysis of Surgeon's Gesture in a Laparoscopic Virtual Scenario. *Studies in health technology and informatics*, 119, pp. 79.

Chmarra, M.K.; Bakker, N.H.; Grimbergen, C.A. & Dankelman, J. (2006). TrEndo, a device for tracking minimally invasive surgical instruments in training set-ups. *Sensors and Actuators*, 126, pp. 328-334

Chmarra, M.K.; Grimbergen, C.A. & Dankelman, J. (2007). Systems for tracking minimally invasive surgical instruments. *Minimally Invasive Therapy & Allied Technologies*, 16, 6, pp. 328-340

Chmarra, M.K.; Dankelman, J.; Van Del Dobbensten, J.J. & Jansen, F.W. (2008). Force feedback and basic laparoscopic skills, *Surgical Endoscopy*, 22, pp. 2140–2148.

Chmarra, M.K.; Klein, S.; de Winter, J.C.F.; Jansen, F.W. & Dankelman, J. (2010). Objective classification of residents based on their psychomotor laparoscopic skills. *Surgical Endoscopy*, 24, 5, pp. 1031-1039.

Cotin, S.; Stylopoulos, N.; Ottensmeyer, M.; Neumann, P.; Rattner, D. & Dawson, S. (2002). Metrics for Laparoscopic Skills Trainers: The Weakest Link! *Proceedings of Medical Image Computing and Computer-Assisted Intervention – MICCAI 2002*, Tokyo, Japan, September 2002.

Cuschieri, A., (2005). Laparoscopic surgery: current status, issues and future developments. *Surgeon*, 3, 3, 125-138.

Datta; V., Mackay, S., Mandalia, M. & Darzi, A. (2001). The use of electromagnetic motion tracking analysis to objectively measure open surgical skill in the laboratory-based model. *Journal of the American College of Surgeons*, 193, 5, pp. 479-485.

Datta, V.; Mandalia, M.; Mackay, S.; Chang, A.; Cheshire, N. & Darzi, A. (2002). Relationship between skill and outcome in the laboratory-based model, *Surgery*, 131, 3, pp. 318-323.

Delingette, H. (1998). Toward realistic soft-tissue modeling in medical simulation, *Proceedings of the IEEE*, 86, 3, pp. 512-523.

Eriksen, J.R. & Grantcharov T. (2005) Objective assessment of laparoscopic skills using a virtual reality stimulator, *Surg. Endosc.*, 19, 9, pp. 1216-1219.

Fichera, A.; Prachand, V.; Kives, S.; Levine, R. & Hasson, H. (2005). Physical reality simulation for training of laparoscopists in the 21st century. A multispecialty, multi-institutional study. *Journal of the Society of Laparoendscopic Surgeons*, 9, 2, pp. 125-129.

Freudenthal, A.; Stüdeli, T.; Lamata, P. & Samset ,E (2010). Collaborative co-design of emerging multi-technologies for surgery. *Journal of Biomedical Informatics* (in press)

Fried, G.M. & Feldman, L.S. (2008). Objective Assessment of Technical Performance. *World journal of surgery*, 32, 2, pp. 156-160.

Gallagher A.G.; Ritter E.M. & Satava R.M.. (2003). Fundamental principles of validation, and reliability: rigorous science for the assessment of surgical education and training. *Surgical Endoscopy*, 17, pp. 1525-1529.

Gallagher, A.; Lederman, A.; Mcglade, K.; Satava, R. & Smith, C. (2004). Discriminative validity of the Minimally Invasive Surgical Trainer in Virtual Reality (MIST-VR) using criteria levels based on expert performance. *Surgical endoscopy*, 18, 4, pp. 660-665.

García-Pérez, V.; Muñoz-Moreno, E.; Aja-Fernández, S. & Alberola-López, C. (2009). A 3-D Collision Handling Algorithm for Surgery Simulation Based on Feedback Fuzzy Logic. *IEEE Transactions on Information Technology in Biomedicine,* 13, 4, pp. 451-457.

Greco, E. M.D.; Escallon, J. M.D.; Grantcharov, T. M.D.; Okrainec, A. M.D. (2008). Do Performance Measures on the LapMentor VR Simulator Predict FLS Performance? *In Canadian Association of General Surgeons Annual Meeting,* September 2008, Halifax, Nova Scotia, Canada.

Gurusamy, K. S.; Aggarwal, R.; Palanivelu, L. & Davidson, B. R. (2009). Virtual reality training for surgical trainees in laparoscopic surgery. *Cochrane Database of Systematic Reviews.,* Jan 21, 1, CD006575.

Halsted, W.S. (1904). The training of the surgeon. *Bulletin of the Johns Hopkins Hospital* 15, pp. 267-275.

Hanna, G.; Drew, T.;Clinch, P.; Hunter, B. & Cuschieri, A. (1998). Computer-controlled endoscopic performance assessment system. *Surgical endoscopy,* 12, 7, pp. 997-1000.

Harden, R.M.; Stevenson, M.; Downie, W.W. & Wilson, G.M. (1975). Assessment of clinical competence using objective structured examination. *British Medical Journal,* British Medical Association, 1, 5955, pp. 447-451.

Hassan, I.; Sitter, H.; Schlosser, K.; Zielke, A.; Rothmund, M. & Gerdes B. (2005). A virtual reality simulator for objective assessment of surgeons' laparoscopic skill. *Chirurg,* 76, 2, pp. 151-156.

Hassan, I.; Osei-Agymang, T.; Radu, D.; Gerdes, B.; Rothmund, M. & Fernandez, E.D. (2008). Simulation of laparoscopic surgery--four years' experience at the Department of Surgery of the University Hospital Marburg. *Wiener klinische Wochenschrift,* 120, 3-4, pp. 70-76.

Horeman, T.; Rodrigues, S.P.; Jansen, F.W.; Dankelman, J. & van den Dobbelsteen, J.J. (2010). Force measurement platform for training and assessment of laparoscopic skills. *Surgical Endoscopy.* Published online.

Issenberg, S.B.; McGaghie, W.C.; Petrusa, E.R.; Lee, G.D. & Scalese, R.J. (2005). Features and uses of high-fidelity medical simulations that lead to effective learning: a BEME systematic review. *Medical Teacher,* 27, 1, pp. 10-28.

Kitagawa, M.; Dokko, D.; Okamura, A.M. & Yuh D.D. (2005). Effect of sensory substitution on suture-manipulation forces for robotic surgical systems. *The Journal of Thoracic and Cardiovascular Surgery,* 129, 1, pp. 151-158.

Kneebone R. (2003). Simulation in surgical training: educational issues and practical implications. *Medical Education,* 37, 3, pp. 267-277.

Kühnapfel, U.; C. Akmak, H. K. & Maass, H. (2000). Endoscopic surgery training using virtual reality and deformable tissue simulation. *Computers & Graphics,* 24, pp. 671-682.

Lamata, P., (2006). *Methodologies for the Analysis, design and evaluation of laparoscopic surgical simulators.* Similar Network of Excellence, UCL Presses, Universitaires de Louvain. Available at www.i6doc.com.

Lamata, P.; Gómez, E. J.; Bello, F.; Kneebone, R. L.; Aggarwal, R. & Lamata, F. (2006). Conceptual framework for laparoscopic VR simulators. *IEEE Computer Graphics and Applications.,* Nov-Dec, 26, 6, pp. 69-79.

Lamata, P.; Gómez. E.J.; Sánchez-Margallo, F.M.; Lamata, F.; del Pozo; F. & Usón, J. (2006). Tissue consistency perception in laparoscopy to define the level of fidelity in virtual reality simulation. *Surgical Endoscopy*, 20, 9, pp. 1368-75.

Lamata, P.; Gómez, E. J.; Sánchez-Margallo, F. M.; López, O.; Monserrat, C.; García, V.; Alberola, C.; Florido, M. A.; Ruiz, J. & Usón, J. (2007). SINERGIA laparoscopic virtual reality simulator: didactic design and technical development. *Computer Methods and Programs in Biomedicine*, 85, 3, pp. 273-83.

Langelotz, C.; Kilian, M.; Paul, C.; & Schwenk W. (2005). LapSim virtual reality laparoscopic simulator reflects clinical experience in German surgeons. *Langenbecks Arch. Surg*, 390, 6, pp. 534-537.

Larsen, C.R.; Grantcharov, T.; Aggarwal, R.; Tully, A.; Sørensen, J.L.; Dalsgaard, T. & Ottesen, B. (2006). Objective assessment of gynecologic laparoscopic skills using the LapSimGyn virtual reality simulator. *Surgical endoscopy*, 20, 9, pp. 1460-1466.

Liselotte, L.M. & Dewan, P. (2009). Virtual Reality simulators in gynecological surgery: A surging new wave. *Journal of the Society of Laparoendscopic Surgeons,* 13 pp. 279–286.

Maithel, S.; Sierra, R.; Korndorffer, J.; Neumann, P.; Dawson, S.; Callery, M.; Jones, D. and Scott D. (2006). Construct and face validity of MIST-VR, Endotower, and CELTS: are we ready for skills assessment using simulators? Surgical Endoscopy, 20,1, pp. 104-112.

Martin, J.; Regehr, G.; Reznick, R.; Macrae, H.; Murnaghan, J.; Hutchison, C. & Brown, M. (1997). Objective structured assessment of technical skill (OSATS) for surgical residents. *British Journal of Surgery*, 84,2, pp.273-278.

McCluney, A.; Feldman, L. & Fried, G. (2006). Validation of the ProMIS Hybrid Simulator using a standard set of laparoscopic tasks. *Proc.Sages*.

McDougall, E.M.; Corica, F.A.; Boker, J.R.; Sala, L.G.; Stoliar, G.; Borin, J.F.; Chu, F.T. & Clayman, R.V. (2006). Construct Validity Testing of a Laparoscopic Surgical Simulator. *Journal of the American College of Surgeons*, 202, 5, pp. 779-787.

Meier, U.; Lopez, O.; Monserrat, C.; Juan, M. C. & Alcaniz, M. (2005). Real-time deformable models for surgery simulation: a survey. *Computer Methods and Programs in Biomedicine*, 77, 3, pp. 183-197.

Miller, G.E. (1990). The assessment of clinical skills/competence/performance. Academic Medicine, 65, 9, pp. S63-S67.

Monserrat, C.; López, O.; Meier, U.; Alcañiz, M.; Juan, C. & Grau, V. (2003). GeRTiSS: A Generic Multi-model Surgery Simulation, *Proc. IS4TM*, Juan-Les-Pinnes (Fr), LNCS, 2673, 59-66.

Moorthy, K.; Munz, Y.; Sarker, S.K. & Darzi, A. (2003). Objective assessment of technical skills in surgery. *British Medical Journal*, 327, 7422, pp. 1032.

Neary, P.C.; Boyle, E.; Delaney, C.P.; Senagore, A.J.; Keane, F.B.V. & Gallagher, A.G. (2008). Construct validation of a novel hybrid virtual-reality simulator for training and assessing laparoscopic colectomy; results from the first course for experienced senior laparoscopic surgeons. *Surgical endoscopy*, 22, 10, pp. 2301-2309.

Newmark, J.; Dandolu, V.; Milner, R.; Grewal, H.; Harbison, S. & Hernandez, E. (2007). Correlating virtual reality and box trainer tasks in the assessment of laparoscopic surgical skills. *American Journal of Obstetrics and Gynecology*, 197, 5, pp. 546-546.

Okrainec, A.; Greco, E.; Arts, M.A. & Grantcharov, T. (2008), Does assessment during virtual surgery predict actual intraoperative performance? *Association for Surgical Education Annual Meeting*, Toronto, Canada.

Pellen, M.G.C.; Horgan, L.F.; Barton, J.R. & Attwood, S.E. (2009). Construct validity of the ProMIS laparoscopic simulator. *Surgical endoscopy*, 23, 1, pp. 130-139.

Picinbono, G.; Delingette, H. & Ayache, N. (2002). Non-linear elastic deformable models for real-time surgery simulation. *Comptes rendus biologies*, 325, 4, pp. 335-344.

Pithioux, M.; Lopez, O.; Meier, U.; Monserrat, C.; Juan, M.C. & Alcaniz, M. (2005). ParSys: a new particle system for the introduction of on-line physical behaviour to three-dimensional synthetic objects. *Comput. Graphics – UK* 29 pp. 135–144.

Ritter, E.M.; Kindelan, T.W.; Michael, C.; Pimentel, E.A. & Bowyer, M.W. (2007). Concurrent validity of augmented reality metrics applied to the fundamentals of laparoscopic surgery (FLS). *Surgical endoscopy*, 21, 8, pp. 1441-1445.

Ro, C.Y.; Toumpoulis, I.K.; Ashton, R.C.Jr.; Jebara, T.; Schulman, C.; Todd, G.J.; Derose, J.J. Jr. and McGinty J.J. (2005). The LapSim: a learning environment for both experts and novices. *Stud. Health Technol. Inform.*, 111, pp. 414-417.

Rosen, J.; Solazzo, M.; Hannaford, B. & Sinanan, M. (2002). Biomedical Paper Task Decomposition of Laparoscopic Surgery for Objective Evaluation of Surgical Residents' Learning Curve Using Hidden Markov Model. *Computer Aided Surgery*, 7, pp. 49-61.

Rosser, J.C.; Rosser, L.E. & Savalgi, R.S. (1997). Skill acquisition and assessment for laparoscopic surgery. *Archives of Surgery*, 132, 2, pp. 200.

Sánchez-Peralta, L.F.; Sánchez-Margallo, F.M.; Moyano-Cuevas, J.L.; Pagador, J.B.; Enciso-Sanz, S.; Sánchez-González, P.; Gómez-Aguilera, E.J. & Usón-Gargallo, J. (2010). Construct and face validity of SINERGIA laparoscopic virtual reality simulator. *Int J Comput Assist Radiol Surg*; 5, 4, pp. 307-15.

Satava, R.M.; Cuschieri, A.; Hamdorf, J. (2003). Metrics for objective assessment: Preliminary summary of the Surgical Skills Workshop. *Surgical endoscopy*, 17, 2, pp. 220-226.

Satava, R.M. (2008). Historical Review of Surgical Simulation—A Personal Perspective. *World journal of surgery*, 32, 2, pp. 141-148.

Schijven M & Jakimowicz J. (2003). Construct validity - Experts and novices performing on the Xitact LS500 laparoscopy simulator. *Surgical Endoscopy and Other Interventional Techniques*, 17, 1, pp. 803-810.

Schreuder, H.W.; van Dongen, K.W.; Roeleveld, S.J.; Schijven, M.P. & Broeders, I.A. (2009). Face and construct validity of virtual reality simulation of laparoscopic gynecologic surgery. *Am J Obstet Gynecol*. May,200,5, pp. 540.e1-8.

Scott, D.J.; Bergen, P.C.; Rege, R.V.; Laycock, R.; Tesfay, S.T.; Valentine, R.J.; Euhus, D.M.; Jeyarajah, D.R.; Thompson, W.M. & Jones, D.B. (2000). Laparoscopic training on bench models: better and more cost effective than operating room experience? *Journal of the American College of Surgeons*, 191, 3, pp. 272-283.

Seymour, N. E.; Gallagher, A. G.; Roman, S. A.; O'Brien, M. K.; Bansal, V. K.; Andersen, D. K. & Satava, R. M. (2002). Virtual reality training improves operating room performance: results of a randomized, double-blinded study. Annals of Surgery, 236, 4, pp. 458-463.

Sherman, V.; Feldman, L.S.; Stanbridge, D.; Kazmi, R. & Fried G.M. (2005). Assessing the learning curve for the acquisition of laparoscopic skills on a virtual reality simulator. *Surgical Endoscopy,* 19, 5, pp. 678-682.

Sidhu, R.; Grober, E.; Musselman, L. & Reznick, R. (2004). Assessing competency in surgery: where to begin? *Surgery,* 135, 1, pp. 6-20.

Sinigaglia, S.; Megali, G.; Tonet, O.; Pietrabissa, A. & Dario, P. (2005). Defining metrics for objective evaluation of surgical performances in laparoscopic training. *International Congress Series 2005,* Elsevier, pp. 509-514.

Sokollik, C.; Gross, J. & Buess, G. (2004). New model for skills assessment and training progress in minimally invasive surgery. *Surgical endoscopy,* 18, 3, pp. 495-500.

Stone, R. & McCloy, R. (2004). Ergonomics in medicine and surgery, *BMJ,* 328, 7448, pp. 1115-1118.

Stylopoulos, N.; Cotin, S.; Maithel, S.; Ottensmeyer, M.; Jackson, P.; Bardsley, R.; Neumann, P.; Rattner, D. & Dawson, S. (2004). Computer-enhanced laparoscopic training system (CELTS): bridging the gap. *Surgical endoscopy,* 18, 5, pp. 782-789.

Tavakol, M.; Mohagheghi, M.A. & Dennick, R. (2008). Assessing the skills of surgical residents using simulation. *Journal of surgical educatio*n, 65, 2, pp. 77-83, 1931-7204, United States.

Tendick, F.; Downes, M.; Goktekin, T.; Cavusoglu, M. C.; Feygin, D.; Wu, X.; Eyal, R.; Hegarty, M. & Way, L. W. (2000). A Virtual Environment Testbed for Training Laparoscopic Surgical Skills. *Presence,* 9, 3, pp. 236-255.

Teschner, M.; Kimmerle, S.; Heidelberger, B.; Zachmann, G.; Raghupathi, L.; Fuhrmann, A.; Cani, M. P.; Faure, F.; Magnenat-Thalmann, N.; Strasser, W. & Volino, P. (2005). Collision detection for deformable objects. *Computer Graphics Forum,* 24, 1, pp.61-81.

Thijssen, A.S. & Schijven, M.P. (2010). Contemporary virtual reality laparoscopy simulators: quicksand or solid grounds for assessing surgical trainees?, The American Journal of Surgery, 199, 4, pp. 529-541.

Vassiliou, M.C.; Feldman, L.S.; Andrew, C.G.; Bergman, S.; Leffondré, K.; Stanbridge, D. & Fried, G.M. (2005). A global assessment tool for evaluation of intraoperative laparoscopic skills. *The American Journal of Surgery,* 190, 1,, pp. 107-113.

Verdaasdonk, E.G.G.; Stassen, L.P.S.; Monteny, L.J. & Dankelman, J. (2006). Validation of a new basic virtual reality simulator for training of basic endoscopic skills. *Surgical endoscopy,* 20, 3, pp. 511-518.

Verdaasdonk, E.G.G.; Stassen, L.P.S.; Schijven, M.P. & Dankelman, J. (2007). Construct validity and assessment of the learning curve for the SIMENDO endoscopic simulator. Surgical endoscopy, 21, 8, pp. 1406-1412.

Woodrum, D.T.; Andreatta, P.B.; Yellamanchilli, R.K.; Feryus, L.; Gauger, P.G. & Minter R.M. (2006). Construct validity of the LapSim laparoscopic surgical simulator. *Am. J. Surg.,* 191, 1, pp. 28-32.

Youngblood, P.L.; Srivastava, S.; Curet, M.; Heinrichs, W.L.R.; Dev, P. & Wren, S.M. (2005). Comparison of training on two laparoscopic simulators and assessment of skills transfer to surgical performance. *Journal of the American College of Surgeons,* 200, 4, pp. 546-551.

Zhang, A.; Hünerbein, M.; Dai, Y.; Schlag, P.M. & Beller, S. (2008). Construct validity testing of a laparoscopic surgery simulator (Lap Mentor): evaluation of surgical skill with a virtual laparoscopic training simulator. *Surgical endoscopy,* 22, 6, pp. 1440-1444.

Part 5

Neuroscience and Neuro-rehabilitation

17

Research in Neuroscience and Virtual Reality

Beatriz Rey and Mariano Alcañiz
Instituto Interuniversitario de Investigación en Bioingeniería y Tecnología Orientada al Ser Humano, Universidad Politécnica de Valencia
Spain

1. Introduction

Virtual reality is one of the most challenging applications of computer graphics and is currently being used in many fields. Participants of immersive virtual environments have unique experiences which were never before possible. Although they know from a cognitive point of view that the virtual environment is not a real place, they act and think as if the virtual environment were real. Virtual environments take advantage of the imaginative ability of people to psychologically transport them to other places.
In this chapter, we are going to analyze the two-way relationship between virtual reality and neuroscience.
First, it will be described how virtual reality can be a useful tool in neuroscience research, as long as it can be used to create controlled environments where participants can perform tasks while their responses are monitored in order to achieve a more detailed understanding of the associated brain processes. Previous work and research in this field will be detailed and discussed.
Secondly, the applications of neuroscience in the virtual reality field will be analyzed. There are aspects of the virtual reality experience such as presence that can be an object of study for neuroscientists (Sanchez-Vives & Slater, 2005). Results from neuroscience studies can help virtual reality researchers to improve their knowledge about the processes that occur in the brain during the exposure to virtual environments and generate more compelling and effective versions of the virtual environments that they develop.
At the end of the chapter, some general conclusions and implications that the research in virtual reality and neuroscience may have for future work will be described.
The different kinds of studies that will be described in this chapter are listed in Table 1.

2. Virtual reality for neuroscience

Virtual reality can be a perfect tool to generate controlled environments that can be used to observe human behaviour. Different aspects can be analyzed from a neuroscience perspective, including perception, control of movement, learning, memory, and emotional aspects.
Usually, in order to analyze human responses to different kinds of events or tasks, the participant behaviour has to be monitored in a real situation or during the execution of experimental tasks designed to analyze the influence of specific variables on human behaviour.

Virtual reality for neuroscience	Study of human navigation with highly immersive virtual environments	(Warren et al., 2001; Tarr & Warren, 2002; Kearns et al., 2002; Foo et al., 2004; Foo et al., 2005; Waller et al., 2007; Richardson & Waller, 2007)
	Virtual versions of classical neuroscience tests to study navigation and spatial memory	(Astur et al., 1998; Jacobs et al., 1997; Jacobs et al., 1998 ; Driscoll et al., 2003; Astur et al., 2004; Astur et al., 2005; Duncko et al., 2007; Cornwell et al., 2008)
	Animal navigation	(Astur et al., 2003; Hölscher et al., 2005; Harvey et al., 2009)
	Human social interaction	(Bailenson et al., 2001; Schilbach et al., 2006; Slater et al., 2006)
Neuroscience for virtual reality	Presence research – Electroencephalogram	(Schlögl et al., 2002; Baumgartner et al., 2006; Kober, 2010)
	Presence research – functional magnetic resonance	(Hoffman et al., 2003; Baumgartner et al., 2008; Jäncke et al., 2009)
	Presence research – Transcranial Doppler	(Alcañiz et al., 2009; Rey et al., 2010)
	Virtual representation of the body	(Slater et al., 2008)

Table 1. Classification of previous studies combining virtual reality and neuroscience

Those previous approaches have both positive and negative points that have to be taken into account when applying them to study human behaviour.

Laboratory experimental tasks allow the controlled study of any of the variables that may be having an influence on the participant's responses. However, the situation presented to the user is not realistic, and usually the participant has to execute the task in a laboratory setting and isolated from other contextual factors that are also associated with the situations or tasks that are being analyzed.

On the other hand, the analysis of human responses in real situations is complicated because the stimuli that are intervening in the experience cannot be controlled (or, at least, not completely controlled) by the experimenter.

However, with virtual reality, it is possible to design a virtual environment and situation with key elements analogous to those of a similar situation in the real world, but, in this case, the presentation of stimuli to the participant can be controlled in a precise way. Furthermore, virtual reality can also be used to create virtual versions of classical neuroscience tests that had only been applied to animals because of their characteristics. Virtual reality allows that the virtual version of the test can be conveniently applied to human participants.

In the following subsections, different kinds of studies about human behaviour that have been conducted up to now with the help of virtual reality settings will be described:

1. Study of human navigation with highly immersive virtual environments. Behavioural neuroscientists have been interested in analyzing how humans learn routes to get from one place to another. Highly immersive virtual environments provide a virtual laboratory where this kind of studies can be conducted and easily controlled.

2. Virtual versions of classical neuroscience tests to study navigation and spatial memory.
3. Animal navigation. In these cases, neural circuits underlying navigation have been studied in animals such as mice using specifically designed virtual environments.
4. Human social interaction. There are other aspects, apart from navigation and spatial memory, that have been analyzed with virtual reality settings. Studies that have analyzed the neural correlates of social interaction will be described.

2.1 Study of human navigation with highly immersive virtual environments

Human navigation is one of the issues that have been analyzed using virtual environments. Users can navigate in a virtual reality system with specific goals, while their behaviour is analyzed to obtain conclusions about how humans learn routes to get from one place to another.

Tarr & Warren (2002) considered that three sources of information were available for this learning process: visual information in the form of optic flow (the pattern of visual motion at the moving), visual information about objects distributed in the environment (which can be used as landmarks) and body senses including vestibular and proprioceptive information. In order to analyze the influence of each of those factors, it is necessary that the subject moves through an environment where the experimenter can manipulate aspects such as the optic flow and the objects that appear in the environment. Virtual reality can be used to generate this controlled environment where the participant can navigate freely.

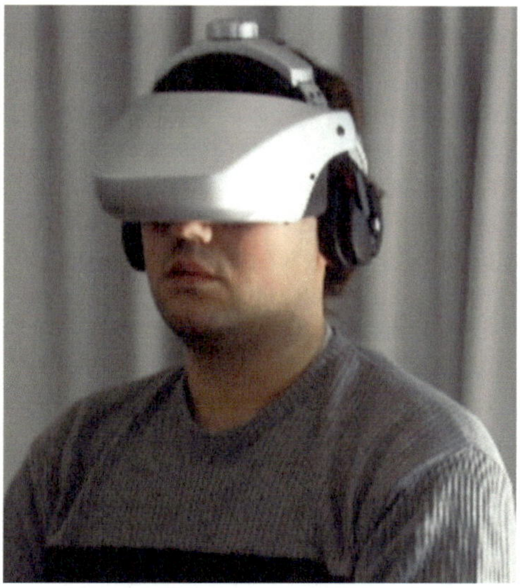

Fig. 1. Subject of a virtual reality experiment wearing a head mounted display

Tarr & Warren (2002) created a highly immersive virtual reality system, which they called VENLab, in which users visualized the environment using a stereo head mounted display. A photograph of a subject wearing a head mounted display is shown in Figure 1. Participants navigated in the VENLab using real walking (a wide-area head tracker was attached to the head tracker)

In different studies conducted with the VENLab, they analyzed the role of each of these sources of information while participants navigated in a virtual world where optic flow and landmarks could be controlled by the experimenter.

In one of the studies, Warren et al. (2001) analyzed if optic flow information is actually used when users have to walk towards a goal. Two different hypotheses had been proposed in the literature. The optic flow hypothesis indicated that the observer would walk to cancel the error between the heading perceived from optic flow and the goal navigation. On the other hand, the egocentric direction hypothesis considered that the observer just walks in the perceived visual direction of the goal with respect to the body. As the two hypotheses usually predict the same behaviour, it was fundamental the use of a virtual environment to be able to dissociate them. The virtual environment that was designed made it possible to displace the heading direction specified by the optic flow by an angle from the actual direction of walking. Different experimental conditions with growing levels of optic flow were analyzed, including an initial condition where no surrounding flow was available. It was found that subjects walked in the visual direction of a target, but increasingly relied on optic flow as it was added to the display.

In another study, Kearns et al. (2002) analyzed the role of visual information and body senses during a homing task. In this kind of tasks, the participant must be able to return to a home location after following a trajectory in the environment. Path integration is defined in this context as a navigation strategy in which information about one's velocity or acceleration is integrated on-line to estimate the distance travelled and the angles turned from an initial point (Loomis et al., 1999). Both optic flow information and body senses information (such as vestibular information and proprioception from receptors in muscles, tendons and joints) can provide information about distances and rotations. In order to analyze the role of the different variables, three experiments were proposed in the study. The task was a triangle completion task, in which participants walk two specified legs of a triangle and then they have to return to the starting position. In the first two experiments, only optic flow was analyzed, by making users navigate in a virtual environment using a joystick during the homing task. In the third experiment, the combined influence of visual and body senses was analyzed, by making the user navigate in the virtual environment with real walking. Results from the first two experiments showed that optic flow can be used for path integration in a homing task. Results from the third experiment showed a different pattern of results. Participants were more consistent, exhibited a pattern of overturning instead of underturning, and had similar responses independently of the presence of optic flow. These results seemed to indicate that, even if participants can perform path integration from optic flow if it is required, they usually rely more on body senses if this information is available.

Later, Foo et al. (2004) analyzed the influence of landmarks in navigation when compared with path integration. The task was also a triangle completion one. Four repetitions of the task with different triangles were conducted. In the first and last repetition, no landmarks were available. In the intermediate ones, a red post was placed near the starting position, but slightly displaced, with viewing angles from the final point ranging from 0 to 28 degrees. The participants did not notice the displacement, and followed the direction of the landmark. In a second experience, they were told that the landmark was unreliable, and in this case, they used path integration instead. It seems that, even if both systems provide information for homing tasks, landmarks are the factor that usually dominates navigation.

In a more recent study, Foo et al. (2005) continued the comparison of landmarks with path integration. In this case, they analyzed if the participant was able to find shortcuts in different environments during a triangle completion task. The subjects were trained on the two legs of the triangle and the angle between them in the context of a specific environment. After training, they had to find a shortcut between the endpoints of the two legs of a triangle. The first virtual environment that was used was a virtual desert world, which contained minimal optical aids. Optic flow and body senses information provided information for path integration, but no other sources of information were present. It was compared with a forest environment that contained multicoloured posts, to provide the user with a landmark strategy that could be used for navigation. Participants could not find successful shortcuts in the desert environment, but they could find them in the forest with multicoloured posts. These results seem to support that subjects rely on the potential landmarks when they are available and use them as a reference to guide navigation.

Apart from the VENLab, other special virtual reality systems have been developed to study spatial cognition. One of them is the HIVE - Huge Immersive Virtual Environment (Waller et al., 2007). This system consists of a large tracking area that lets users move through virtual worlds as they would in the real world, thus allowing the analysis of mental processes that require extensive movements through an environment. The system makes it possible to include in the experiments body-based sources of sensory information (such as vestibular and proprioceptive data), as happened also with the VENLab. Technically, the HIVE is based on an eight-camera optical tracking system that monitors user's position data, which are sent wirelessly to a rendering computer worn by the user. The environment is shown to the participant using a head-mounted display. The system is completed with an orientation tracking device. The HIVE has been used, for example, to analyze the influence of a user's physical environment on distance underestimation in immersive virtual environments. Previous research has found that egocentric distances are underestimated in immersive virtual environments (i.e., Lampton et al., 1995; Witmer & Kline, 1998). Using systems like the HIVE, it is possible to analyze if this underestimation occurs also when navigation is controlled by real physical walking. Richardson & Waller (2007) conducted an experiment which showed that the execution of an interaction task in the immersive virtual environment significantly corrected the underestimation that has been observed in previous studies.

All the studies described in this section have in common two main factors:

- The user can navigate using real walking in a wide area. Tracking systems designed to monitor the user position in large areas are used.
- The appearance and responses (such as optical flow) of the virtual environment can be controlled and changed between the different experimental conditions.

These are issues that should be taken into account when designing a virtual environment for the study of human navigation.

2.2 Virtual versions of classical neuroscience tests to study navigation and spatial memory

Virtual reality has also been used by other researchers to create virtual versions of classical neuroscience tests to study navigation.

In previous non-human research, the gold standard for analyzing place learning ability in rodents is the Morris water task (Morris, 1981). In this task, the rat has to swim to a fixed hidden platform (that cannot be seen, heard or smelt) in a circular pool, making use of distal spatial cues outside the pool. The apparatus used when this task was first applied was a circular pool with dimensions of 1.30 m diameter by 0.60 m high (Morris, 1981). The platform used in the experiment was put at a specific location in the pool, either visible or invisible (under water). Research has found that the ability to learn to navigate in this task is highly influenced by the integrity and plasticity in the hippocampus (Sutherland et al., 1982).

In order to apply the Morris water task in human research about navigation and spatial learning, practical difficulties appear. One requisite would be that humans and non-human animals should be tested in comparable spatial domains. A big pool would be required, and the manipulation of the platforms and monitoring of the experiment in this real pool would be more difficult than in the small circular container used in the experiments with rats. Furthermore, participants would probably find the task uncomfortable.

However, with virtual reality, virtual versions of the Morris water task can be prepared and applied in experiments about the analysis of place learning and spatial memory in humans. The advantages that virtual reality can provide are the following:

- A virtual pool environment with adequate dimensions for human participants can be generated and applied in the experiments.
- Subjects can navigate using virtual reality hardware for navigation. There is no necessity to physically swim.
- As the navigation occurs in a controlled computer system, it is possible to program it to easily control experimental variables such as the initial position of the participant, the position of the platforms inside the pool and the position of any visual cues in the environment.
- Furthermore, as the instantaneous position of the subject at each moment is known by the system, it is possible to store the exact trajectories that the participant has followed until arriving to the platform, allowing posterior analyses about different aspects such as the required time to find the platform or the length of the followed trajectory.

Astur et al. (1998) developed a computerized version of the test to analyze if the observed results in experiments with rats would generalize into the human domain. In their experiment, the virtual environment consisted of a circular pool in a room where several distal cues were present. No local cues were used. Participants had to swim in the pool navigating with a joystick. They had to find a platform hidden under the surface of the water from different initial locations. The fact of starting from different locations requires that a cognitive map is formed using the distal cues on the surrounding walls. Performance can be established using objective values that can be calculated, such as the path length or the required time to reach the platform. Different studies with a virtual version of the Morris water task have been developed and have shown the feasibility of applying it in human research (Astur et al., 1998; Jacobs et al., 1997; Jacobs et al., 1998; Driscoll et al., 2003; Duncko et al., 2007). These studies have shown that it is possible to apply a computerized Morris water task in human research. Each of them has focused on a different aspect of the experience. Differences in the performance of the Morris water task have been found associated to different factors such as sex, age or stress.

Posterior studies have combined the virtual Morris water maze with a virtual analogue of another task that has been used classically to analyze spatial memory in animals: an eight-arm radial maze. Radial arm mazes are composed of a central area with a number of identical arms radiating outwards (Olton & Samuelson, 1974). A schema of the eight arm radial maze has been represented in Figure 2.

In the eight-arm radial maze, four of the arms have food at the end, but the other four arms do not have anything. In the first experimental trial, the rat should be able to find the food that is placed in four of the arms. Afterwards, the animal is removed from the maze. In the

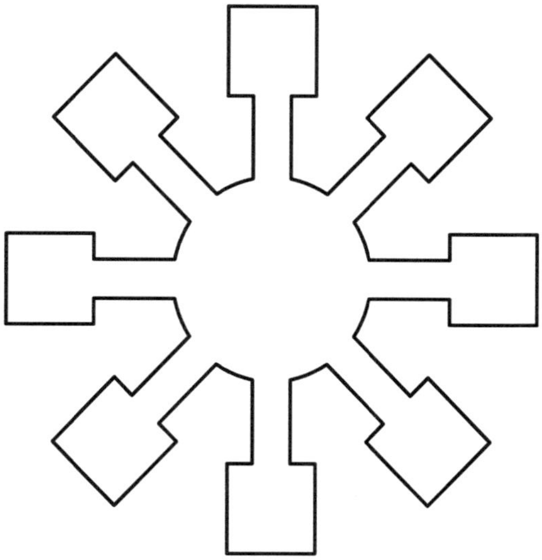

Fig. 2. Distribution of the eight arm radial maze

following experimental trials, the location of the food is maintained. With training, the rodents learn to find the food without entering in the empty arms.

Astur et al. (2004) combined the virtual Morris water maze with an eight-arm radial maze. The virtual eight-arm radial maze consisted of a virtual room that had eight runways extending out of a round middle area. Participants knew that in four of the runways there was an award at the end, and that in the other four runways there was not. They had to retrieve all the awards as soon as possible. Results of the study showed that men performed significantly better than women when trying to find the hidden platform in the virtual Morris water task. However, there are no sex differences in working memory errors, reference memory errors or distance to find the rewards in the virtual radial maze. These results seemed to indicate that the virtual Morris water task and the virtual eight-arm radial maze assess spatial memory in different ways.

Other studies with the virtual Morris water task and the radial mazes have monitored brain activation associated with these tests, specially analyzing the activity in the hippocampus.

Cornwell et al. (2008) recorded neuromagnetic activity using magnetoencephalography (MEG), which is a technique that records magnetic fields produced by electrical activity in the brain and that can be used for mapping brain activity. Participants had to navigate to the hidden platform in a virtual Morris water task. The objective was to determine if hippocampal / parahippocampal theta activity was related to behavioural performance on the virtual Morris task. Source analysis of the MEG data captured during the study showed an increase in the power in the theta band of the spectrum (4-8 Hz) in hippocampus and parahippocampal structures during goal-directed navigation. It was also found a linear relationship between these theta responses and navigation performance on the virtual Morris task.

Astur et al. (2005) conducted an experiment with a radial arm maze to assess the function of the hippocampus and to see if the results from non-human research could be extrapolated to humans. Participants of the study had to perform a virtual radial arm task during functional magnetic resonance imaging (fMRI). An image of an fMRI machine can be visualized in Figure 3.

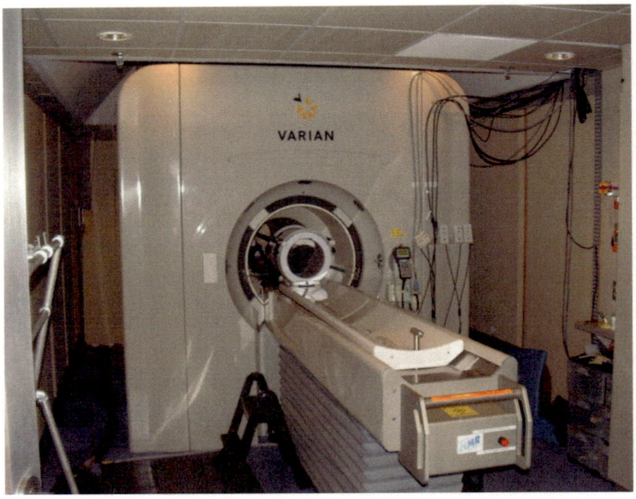

Fig. 3. 4T fMRI, part of the Brain Imaging Center, in: Helen Wills Neuroscience Institute at the University of California, Berkeley

fMRI is used for the study of metabolic and vascular changes that accompany changes in neural activity. The technique is based on the Blood Oxygen Level Dependent method (BOLD), which measures the ratio of oxygenated to deoxygenated haemoglobin in the blood across regions of the brain. As oxygen is extracted from the blood, increases in deoxyhaemoglobin can lead to an initial decrease in BOLD signal. However, this is followed by an increase, due to overcompensation in blood flow that tips the balance towards oxygenated haemoglobin. It is this that leads to a higher BOLD signal during neural activity.
fMRI is not a tool that can be easily combined with virtual reality environments. First of all, a test platform has to be developed to allow the exposition to the virtual environment while capturing the fMRI images without altering in a significant way any of both technologies. Moreover, the user has to be inside the magnetic resonance machine in supine position and with minimum head movement, and devices used to navigate and interact in the virtual environment have to work inside high magnetic fields with minimum electromagnetic interference.
Astur et al. (2005) used an fMRI-adapted joystick to allow participants to navigate in the virtual environment. As happened with other previous studies, significant changes were found in the activity of the hippocampus during the performance of the task. However, a decrease in activity occurred during the spatial memory component of the task. On the other hand, frontal cortex activity was also found, which could indicate activity associated to working memory circuits.

2.3 Animal navigation

Virtual reality has also been used in neuroscience experiments with non-human animals. There have been some studies that have shown that primates, similarly to humans, can also interpret interactive two-dimensional projections as a virtual environment in which they can move (Leighty & Fragaszy, 2003; Nishijo et al., 2003; Towers et al., 2003). Astur et al. (2003), for example, examined if rhesus monkeys could learn to explore virtual mazes. In their experiment, four male macaques were trained to locate a target in a virtual environment. The monkeys controlled the navigation by moving a joystick. They completed successfully the task, and were able to locate the target. The search pattern that the animals followed within the maze was similar to the navigation pattern observed on more traditional two-dimensional computerized mazes and was in accordance with predictions made from actual patterns in physical space.

But not only primates have been immersed in virtual reality experiences to analyze navigation patterns and spatial memory. Recently, it has been proven that rats are also able to navigate in virtual environments. Hölscher et al. (2005) built a virtual reality set-up and tested it with rats. It was shown that rodents could learn spatial tasks in this virtual reality system. One important point that had to be taken into account in the design of the virtual reality setting was to consider the wide-angle visual system of rats into account. That is why, while immersed in the virtual environment, the rat was surrounded by a toroidal screen of 140 cm diameter and 80 cm height. This screen covers a large part of the rat's visual field (360° azimuth, -20° to +60° of elevation).

Recently, Harvey et al. (2009) used this kind of virtual reality system to study the neural circuits underlying navigation in mice. The purpose was to measure the intracellular dynamics of place cells during the navigation in a virtual environment. However, intracellular recording methods require a mechanical stability which cannot be obtained when the animals can move freely in the real world. In this study, the mouse was allowed to run on top a spherical treadmill while its head was maintained stable using a head plate. Regarding the projection of the virtual environment, similarly to the previous study, the environment was projected on a toroidal screen that surrounded the rodent and that was designed to cover a wide area according to the large field of view of the animal. The movements of the mouse were measured as rotations of the spherical treadmill using an optical computer mouse. The mice were trained to run along a virtual linear track (180 cm long) with local and distal cues in the walls. Small water rewards were given to the animal when it has run between opposite ends of the track. The intracellular dynamics of hippocampal place cells were measured during the navigation with precision, because the mouse's head was stationary. The observed dynamics in the hippocampal place-cells had similar properties to those recorded in real environments.

2.4 Human social interaction

Virtual reality can also be a technology that can help to analyze other aspects of human behaviour. In this subsection, some studies that have been made in the social cognitive neuroscience field will be summarized.

There are several factors that contribute to make virtual reality a useful technology to address questions related to human behaviour in social situations. Participants of virtual reality experiences can feel that they are present in the virtual environment. This means that they have the sense of being in the virtual environment instead of being in their physical location, for example, the experimental room (Held & Durlach, 1992; Schumie et al., 2001). Presence is a multi-dimensional concept, and one of the dimensions that are analyzed when studying this complex experience is social presence, which occurs when part or all of a person's perception fails to accurately acknowledge the role of the technology that makes it appear that s/he is communicating with other people or entities. Virtual characters convey social information to human participants of virtual reality experiences. Furthermore, they are perceived by the participants as social agents, who exert social influence on human subjects that participate in the virtual reality experience (Bailenson et al., 2003).

Consequently, virtual reality has started to be applied in social psychological research (de Kort et al., 2003). In the following paragraphs, different studies that have analyzed several aspects of human interaction using virtual reality will be described.

Bailenson et al. (2001) analyzed the equilibrium theory specification (Argyle & Dean, 1965), which specified an inverse relationship between mutual gaze and interpersonal distance. In order to analyze this theory, participants were exposed to a virtual environment in which a male virtual character stood. The users were told to remember certain features about the agent's shirt. The participants' positions were tracked by the system, so the distance between participants and the virtual agent were continuously monitored. The results showed that the space between the participant and the virtual character was higher than the distance between the participants and objects with similar size and shape, but without human appearance. On the other hand, the interpersonal distance was higher in the case of women interacting with agents who did engage them in eye contact than with agents who did not. This effect was not observed in men. Results seem to indicate that factors such as non-verbal expressions of intimacy are in the origin of changes in the personal space.

Schilbach et al. (2006) studied the differences between being personally involved in a social interaction or being just a passive observer of a social interaction between other people, using virtual characters to generate the social situations. The virtual characters that were used in the study would gaze directly to the human observer, or look away towards a third person situated at an angle of approximately 30º (and not visible by the human participant). The virtual characters would show changing facial expressions similar to the ones that they would have in real-life social interaction situations or they would show arbitrary and socially irrelevant movements. fMRI was used to monitor brain activity while the participants of the study observed the virtual characters. The sequences were projected onto a screen inside the fMRI scanner. After each repetition of the task, the participant had to answer two questions about how s/he has interpreted the behaviour of the virtual character. In order to allow this interaction inside an fMRI scanner, compatible keypads were used. Eye movements during conditions were also monitored using an infrared video-based eye-tracking system. The results showed that higher neural activity was found in the anterior medial cortex when the virtual character was looking at the participant. Furthermore, if facial expressions were perceived as socially relevant, increased neural activity was observed in the ventral medial prefrontal cortex. Finally, the perception of arbitrary facial movements activated the middle temporal gyrus. Globally, the results showed that different regions of the medial prefrontal cortex contributed differentially to social cognition.

The interaction with a virtual character in an extreme social situation such as the conflict created within Milgram's paradigm (Milgram, 1963) has also been studied. This paradigm creates a social dilemma in which participants try to follow the experimenter's commands to administer pain to another person, but at the same time they feel that they have to avoid causing any harm to that person. This paradigm has been partially replicated within an immersive virtual environment (Slater et al., 2006). The participants of the virtual reality experience showed discomfort and increased arousal over the course of the conflict, and some of them stopped administering pain to the avatar, or expressed that they did not want to continue with the experience.

3. Neuroscience for virtual reality

In the previous section, a review of studies in which virtual reality has been applied as a tool for neuroscience has been presented. However, as has already been stated, neuroscience tools can also be used in virtual reality studies and can provide useful information for researchers in this field.

Some of the studies in which neuroscience has been a tool for virtual reality research are going to be described. They have been grouped in two different fields of application:

1. Presence studies. Neuroscience research can provide useful information to better understand the concept of presence in virtual environments. Different techniques and their combinations have been proposed and used to measure presence in virtual environments (Insko, 2003). These techniques have been classified in two main groups: subjective tools and objective tools. Subjective techniques have been mainly based on the application of psychological measurement instruments like rating scales and subjective reports. On the other hand, objective techniques include behavioural measures and physiological measures. These measures are usually obtained during the virtual reality experience rather than following it, so they can be used for real-time monitoring during the exposure. However, although they are called objective, they do not generate a direct measure of presence. Instead, presence is assumed to be related in some way with the degree of change in parameters that can be obtained from physiological measures or from behavioural observation. It has been only in recent years that it has been studied applying neuroscience tools. Different neurological measures have been applied to analyze brain activity during the exposure to virtual environments in order to look for brain correlates of the presence experience. Three main neurological measures have been applied:
   a. Electroencephalogram (EEG).
   b. Functional magnetic resonance imaging (fMRI).
   c. Transcranial Doppler (TCD).

   In the following subsections, the advances in the presence research field that have been obtained in recent years using these three different techniques will be described.
2. Virtual representation of the body. Other works have applied neuroscience tools to analyze the interpretation of participants of virtual reality experiences about the virtual representation of their own body. For virtual reality researchers, it is necessary to know the interpretation that the participants of the experience attribute to the virtual representation of their bodies. The studies in this area will also be summarized in the following points.

3.1 Presence research: Electroencephalogram

Electroencephalogram (EEG) reflects the brain's electrical activity, and in particular postsynaptic potentials in the cerebral cortex. Scalp-recorded EEG signals are thought to be generated by the addition of excitatory and inhibitory post-synaptic potentials in the cortical pyramidal neurons (Speckman et al., 1993). EEG signals always represent the potential difference between two electrodes, an active electrode and the reference electrode. This technique has a high temporal resolution, which makes it possible to analyze both fluctuations of EEG dependant of task demand, and differentiate between functional inhibitory and excitatory tasks.

EEG was proposed as a possible tool for obtaining objective indicators of presence, to detect brain states and transitions in the user, who can feel present in the virtual world and then change to feel present in the real world (Schlögl et al., 2002).

Baumgartner et al. (2006) were the first to use EEG to analyze neural correlates of spatial presence in arousing virtual environments without interaction. The virtual environment used was a virtual roller coaster scenario. Twelve children and eleven adolescents participated in the study. There was a control session, with a horizontal roundabout track, and several realistic rides (with ups, downs and loops). EEG and skin conductance were captured during the experience. It was found in both groups that spatial presence was higher in the realistic rides (when compared with the control condition). Furthermore, this was accompanied by increased electrodermal reactions and activations in parietal brain areas known to be involved in spatial navigation. Parietal processing centres in turn stimulated the insula as the core region for generating body sensations and the posterior cingulated which is strongly involved in emotion processing. On the other hand, children showed higher spatial presence, but less activity in some prefrontal areas than adolescents. These prefrontal areas are involved in the control of executive functions. The higher increase in spatial presence observed in children can have its origin on the fact that their frontal cortex function is not fully developed.

Recently, preliminary results from a study to analyze the parietal activity in interactive virtual reality were presented (Kober, 2010). The goal of the study was to analyze if the parietal activity that was found in the study from Baumgartner et al. (2006) would also appear during a free navigation in a virtual environment. The environment was a virtual maze in which the participant performed a wayfinding task while EEG activity was monitored. Results showed that parietal activation also occurred in this interactive virtual reality.

3.2 Presence research: functional magnetic resonance imaging

In the first fMRI study related to virtual reality and presence (Hoffman et al, 2003), subjects reported experiencing an illusion of presence in virtual reality via a magnet-friendly image delivery system despite the constraint of lying down with their head immobilized in an enclosed environment. fMRI results were not reported in the study.

Recent works (Baumgartner et al., 2008; Jäncke et al., 2009) have complemented the previously described study that used the roller coaster scenario as stimulus and EEG to monitor brain activity. These recent works have analyzed fMRI data captured during the exposure to the same virtual environment. Each ride lasted 102 s in total, whereas the different phases where divided into the following time scheme: anticipation phase 30 s, dynamic phase 60 s and end phase 12 s. In total, eight different roller coaster rides were presented, four High Presence and four Low Presence roller coaster rides. Results from the fMRI analysis show that the presence experience evoked by the virtual roller coaster scenario is associated with an increase in activation in a distributed network, which comprises extrastriate areas, the dorsal visual stream, the superior parietal cortex (SPL) and inferior parietal cortex (IPL), parts of the ventral visual stream, the premotor cortex (PMC), and the brain structures located in the basal and mesiotemporal parts of the brain. The network is modulated by the dorso lateral prefrontal cortex (DLPFC). The DLPFC activation strongly correlates with the subjective presence experience (the right DLPFC controlled the sense of presence by down-regulating the activation in the egocentric dorsal visual processing stream, the left DLPFC up-regulated widespread areas of the medial prefrontal cortex known to be involved in self-reflective and stimulus-independent thoughts). In contrast, there was no evidence of these two strategies in children. This difference is most likely attributable to the prefrontal cortex that is not fully matured in children.

3.3 Presence research: Transcranial Doppler

Transcranial Doppler monitoring (TCD) has also been applied recently to analyze cognitive states related with presence during the exposure to virtual environments in different immersion and navigation conditions. TCD is a secure and non-invasive ultrasound diagnosis technique with high temporal resolution which is used to analyze hemodynamic variations in the brain. It monitors blood flow velocity in the main vessels of the brain: the left and right Middle Cerebral Arteries (MCA-L and MCA-R), the left and right Anterior Cerebral Arteries (ACA-L and ACA-R) and the left and right Posterior Cerebral Arteries (PCA-L and PCA-R). These velocity variations constitute a reliable source of information about brain activity. When the neurovascular coupling is adequate (Iadecola, 1993), the velocity variations that are detected by TCD reflect changes in regional cerebral blood flow due to brain activation in the brain areas supplied by the monitored vessel (Daffertshofer, 2001). Consequently, the spatial resolution of the technique is delimited by the size of the cortical areas supplied by the vessels selected for a particular study. In order to apply the measurement, two probes (transducers) are required, one for each cerebral hemisphere. In functional studies, each probe is placed in its correct location by attaching it to a headpiece that the user has to wear during the whole experiment.

Alcañiz et al. (2009) used the TCD technique to compare two different navigation conditions (user-controlled vs. system-controlled navigation) potentially associated with different levels of presence in the participants of the study. The study was carried out in a CAVE-like environment with four sides (three walls and the floor), using a wireless joystick and an optical tracking system to navigate in the environment. The virtual environment that was used in the study was a maze composed of several rooms and corridors. The virtual maze was designed specifically for this task. An image of one of the rooms of the virtual environment can be visualized in Figure 4.

Results from the study showed that it was possible to use TCD to monitor brain activity during virtual reality studies. The percentage variations between mean blood flow velocity in the user-controlled navigation and its preceding baseline (repose period), and between the mean blood flow velocity in the system-controlled navigation and its preceding baseline, were positive in all the arteries under study (MCA-L, MCA-R, ACA-L and ACA-R). Significant differences between the percentage variations in the two navigation conditions were observed in the case of the left arteries: MCA-L and ACA-L. Motor tasks to control the joystick with the right hand might be the origin of the observed variations in MCA-L blood flow velocity. However, the variations in ACA-L are not directly related to this issue, and can only be explained by other factors related to the virtual reality experience, such as decision making and emotional aspects. In fact, it is expected that the user may be more emotionally involved in the free navigation condition. Furthermore, during this experimental condition, more decisions have to be made, specially associated to navigation factors. All these issues are related with the level of presence that the user is experiencing during exposure to the different navigation conditions. Presence questionnaires confirmed that the level of presence was significantly higher during the free navigation condition.

Rey et al. (2010) compared the same navigation conditions (user-controlled vs. system-controlled), but in two different immersion configurations (corresponding to two different virtual reality settings: the CAVE-like system and a single projection screen). In this case, only MCA-L and MCA-R were considered. The navigation factor had a significant influence on the observed blood flow velocity variations in both monitored vessels. Higher percentage

Fig. 4. Image of one of the rooms of the virtual maze that was used in the studies that analyzed presence in virtual environments using TCD

variations were observed in the free navigation condition than in the automatic navigation condition. As in the previous study, the observed differences in MCA-L can have their origin in the motor tasks differences between navigation conditions. On the other hand, a possible explanation of the differences in MCA-R percentage variations between navigation conditions could be found in the higher degree of involvement of the user in the creation of a motor plan in the free navigation condition. Results from questionnaires also found higher values of presence during the free navigation condition.

3.4 2 Virtual representation of the body

Other works have applied neuroscience tools to analyze the interpretation of participants of virtual reality experiences about the virtual representation of their own body. Virtual reality can be used to replace a person's real body by a virtual representation. For example, a virtual limb can be made to feel part of the participant's body if appropriate multisensory information is provided. Slater et al. (2008) created this illusion on participants of a virtual reality experience using a tactile stimulation on a person's hidden real right hand while, simultaneously, a 3D virtual arm was projected out of their shoulder. Questionnaire responses and behavioural analyses showed that participants were experiencing the virtual arm as part of themselves. These results open up the possibility that the whole virtual body could be interpreted by participants as part of themselves in the future.

4. Conclusion

This chapter has summarized the contributions and implications that advances on the virtual reality field may have for behavioural neuroscience studies. Virtual reality can provide a virtual laboratory where experiments can be conducted in a controlled way and with the desired conditions. Applications in neuroscience studies related to spatial navigation and social interaction have been described. Based on the results of these studies, it can be foreseen that virtual reality may be the basis to develop further studies about human behaviour in the following years.

On the other hand, neuroscience tools have provided the virtual reality research field with new techniques that may contribute to the understanding of human factors and human responses during the virtual reality experience. Although neurological correlates of virtual reality experiences have still to be further analyzed, advances in this area may help virtual reality researchers to design more compelling and effective versions of the virtual environments that they develop.

The two-way cooperation between virtual reality and neuroscience can be the basis of many advances in these research areas in the following years. Both fields of research can take advantage of the results from the studies that combine the use of virtual environments with neuroscience techniques that study aspects of human behaviour inside these environments.

5. References

Alcañiz, M.; Rey, B.; Tembl, J. & Parkhutik, V. (2009). A Neuroscience Approach to Virtual Reality Experience Using Transcranial Doppler Monitoring. *Presence: Teleoperators & Virtual Environments*, 18(2), 97-111.

Argyle, M. & Dean, J. (1965). Eye-Contact, Distance and Affiliation. *Sociometry*, 28:289-304.

Astur, R.S.; Ortiz, M.L. & Sutherland, R.J. (1998). A characterization of performance by men and women in a virtual Morris water task: A large and reliable sex difference. *Behavioral Brain Research*, 93, 185-190.

Astur, R.S.; Tropp, J; Sava, S; Constable, R.T. & Markus, E.J. (2004). Sex differences and correlations in a virtual Morris water task, a virtual radial arm maze and mental rotation. *Behavioral Brain Research*, 151, 103-115.

Astur, R.S.; St. Germain, S.A.; Baker, E.K.; Calhoun, V.; Pearlson, G.D. & Constable R.T. (2005). fMRI hippocampal activity during a virtual radial arm maze. *Applied Psychophysiology and Biofeedback*, 30: 307-317.

Bailenson, J.N.; Blascovich, J.; Beall, A.C. & Loomis, J.M. (2003). Interpersonal distance in immersive virtual environments. *Personality and Social Psychology Bulletin*, 29: 819-833.

Baumgartner, T.; Valko, L.; Esslen, M. & Jäncke, L. (2006). Neural correlate of spatial presence in an arousing and noninteractive virtual reality: an EEG and psychophysiology study. *CyberPsychology & Behavior*, 9(1), 30-45.

Baumgartner, T.; Speck, D.; Wettstein, D.; Masnari, O.; Beeli, G. & Jäncke, L. (2008). Feeling present in arousing virtual reality worlds: prefrontal brain regions differentially orchestrate presence experience in adults and children. *Frontiers in Human Neuroscience*, 2: 8.

Cornwell, B.R.; Johson, L.L.; Holroyd, T.; Carver, F.W. & Grillon, C. (2008). Human hippocampal and parahippocampal theta during goal-directed spatial navigation predicts performance on a virtual Morris water maze. *The Journal of Neuroscience*, 28(23): 5983-5990.

Daffertshofer, M. (2001). Functional Doppler testing, In: *Cerebrovascular ultrasound: Theory, practice and future development*, S. Meairs & M.G. Hennerici (Eds.), 341-359, Cambridge University Press, ISBN 0 521 63223 4, Cambridge.

de Kort, Y.A.W.; IJsselsteijn, W.A.; Kooijman, J. & Schuurmans, Y. (2003). Virtual laboratories: Comparability of real and virtual environments for environmental psychology. *Presence: Teleoperators & Virtual Environments*, 12(4): 360-373.

Driscoll, I.; Hamilton, D.A.; Petropoulos, H.; Yeo, R.A.; Brooks, W.M.; Baumgartner, R.N. & Sutherland, R.J. (2003). The aging hippocampus: cognitive, biochemical and structural findings. *Cerebral Cortex*, 13: 1344-1351.

Duncko, R.; Cornwell, B.; Cui, L.; Merikangas, K.R. & Grillon, C. (2007). Acute exposure to stress improves performance in trace eyeblink conditioning and spatial learning tasks in healthy men. *Learning & Memory*, 14: 329-335.

Foo, P.; Harrison, M.; Duchon, A.; Harren, W.H. & Tarr, M.J. (2004). Humans follow landmarks over path integration. *Journal of Vision*, 4(8), article 892.

Foo, P.; Harren, W.H.; Duchon, A. & Tarr, M.J. (2005). Do humans integrate routes into a cognitive map? Map- versus Landmark-based navigation of novel shortcuts. *Journal of Experimental Psychology: Learning, Memory, and Cognition*, 31(2), 195-215.

Harvey, C.D.; Collman, F.; Dombeck, D.A. & Tank, D.W. (2009). Intracellular dynamics of hippocampal place cells during virtual navigation. *Nature* 461, 941-949.

Held, R. & Durlach, N. (1992). Telepresence. *Presence: Teleoperators & Virtual Environments*, 1(1): 109-112.

Hoffman, H.G.; Richards, T.; Coda, B.; Richards, A. & Sharar, S.R. (2003). The illusion of presence in immersive virtual reality during an fMRI brain scan. *CyberPsychology & Behavior*, 6(2):127-131.

Hölscher, C.; Schnee, A.; Dahmen, H.; Setia, L. & Mallot, H.A. (2005). Rats are able to navigate in virtual environments. *Journal of Experimental Biology*, 208: 561-569.

Iadecola, C. (1993). Regulation of the cerebral microcirculation during neural activity: Is nitric oxide the missing link? *Trends in neuroscience*, 16(6): 206-214.

Insko, B.E. (2003). Measuring presence: Subjective, behavioural, and physiological methods, In: *Being there: Concepts, effects and measurement of user presence in synthetic environments*, G. Riva, F. Davide & W. IJsselsteijn (Ed.), 109-120, IOS Press, ISBN 978-1586033019, Amsterdam.

Jacobs, W.J.; Laurance, H.E. & Thomas, K.G.F. (1997). Place learning in virtual space. I. Acquisition, overshadowing, and transfer. *Learning and Motivation*, 28: 521-541.

Jacobs, W.J.; Thomas, K.G.F.; Laurance, H.E. & Nadel, L. (1998). Place learning in virtual space. II. Topographical relations as one dimension of stimulus control. *Learning and Motivation*, 29:288-308.

Jäncke, L.; Cheetam, M. & Baumgartner, T. (2009). Virtual reality and the role of the prefrontal cortex in adults and children. *Frontiers in Neuroscience* 3(1): 52-59.

Kearns, M.J.; Warren, W.H.; Duchon, A.P. & Tarr, M.J. (2002). Path integration from optic flow and body senses in a homing task. *Perception* 31, 349-347.

Kober, S. (2010). Cortical correlate of spatial presence in 2-D and 3-D interactive virtual reality: An EEG study. *Proceedings of the 3rd RAVE (Real Actions, Virtual Environments) Workshop,* Barcelona, March 2010.

Lampton, D.R. ; McDonald, D.P.; Singer, M. & Bliss, J.P. (1996). Distance Estimation in Virtual Environments, *Proceedings of the Human Factors and Ergonomics Society Annual Meeting,* pp. 1268-1272(5), ISSN 1071-1813, San Diego, California, October 1995, Human Factors and Ergonomics Society, Santa Monica, CA, USA.

Leighty, K.A. & Fragszy, D.M. (2003). Primates in cyberspace: using interactive computer tasks to study perception and action in nonhuman animals. *Animal cognition*, 6: 137-139.

Loomis, J.M.; Klatzky, R.L., Golledge, R.G., Cicinelli, J.G., Pellegrino, J.W., Fry, P.A. (1993). Nonvisual navigation by blind and sighted: assessment of path integration ability. *Journal of Experimental Psychology: General* 122: 73-91.

Milgram, S. (1963). Behavioral study of obedience. *Journal of Abnormal Psychology* 67, 371-378.

Morris, R.G.M. (1981). Spatial localization does not require the presence of local cues. *Learning and motivation* 12: 239-260.

Nishijo, H.; Kazui, K.; Hori, E.; Tabuchi, E.; Umeno, K.; Sasaki, K. & Ono, T. (2003). Spatial correlates of monkey hippocampal neurons during navigation in a virtual space. *Society of Neuroscience Abstracts*, 32: 717.14.

Olton, D.S. & Samuelson, R.J. (1976). Remembrance of places passed: spatial memory in rats. *Journal of Experimental Psychology: Animal Behavior Processes*, 2(2): 97-116.

Rey, B.; Alcañiz, M.; Tembl, J. & Parkhutik, V. (2010). Brain Activity and Presence: a Preliminary Study in Different Immersive Conditions Using Transcranial Doppler Monitoring. *Virtual Reality* 14, 55-65.

Richardson, A.R. & Waller, D. (2007). Interaction with an immersive virtual environment corrects users' distance estimates. *Human Factors* 49, 507-517.

Schilbach, L.; Wohlschlaeger, A.M.; Kraemer, N.C.; Newen, A.; Shah, N.J.; Fink, G.R. & Vogeley, K. (2006). Being with virtual others: Neural correlates of social interaction. *Neuropsychologia* 44(5): 718- 730.

Schuemie, M.; van der Straaten, P.; Krijn, M. & van der Mast, C. (2001). Research on presence in virtual reality: A survey. *CyberPsychology & Behavior*, 4(2): 183-201.

Slater, M.; Antlye, A.; Davison, A.; Swapp, D.; Guger, C.; Barker, C.; Pistrang, N. & Sanchez-Vives, M.V. (2006). A virtual reprise of the Stanley Milgram obedience experiments. *PLoS ONE* 1, e39.

Slater, M.; Perez-Marcos, D.; Ehrsson, H.H. & Sanchez-Vives, M.V. (2008). Towards a digital body: the virtual arm illusion. *Frontiers in Human Neuroscience*, 2: 6.

Schlögl, A.; Slater, M. & Pfurtscheller, G. (2002). Presence research and EEG, *Proceedings of Presence 2002, 5th Annual International Workshop on Presence*, pp. 9-11, Porto, October 2002.

Speckman, E.J.; Elger, C.E. & Altrup, U. (1993). Neurophysiologic basis of the EEG, In: *The treatment of epilepsy: Principles and practices*, E. Wyllie (Ed.), 149-164, Lippincott Williams & Wilkins, ISBN 978-0781723749, Philadelphia.

Sutherland, R.J.; Kolb, B. & Whishaw, I.Q. (1982). Spatial mapping: definitive disruption by hippocampal and frontal cortex damage in the rat. *Neuroscience Letters*, 31: 271-276.

Tarr, M.J. and Warren, W.H. (2002). Virtual reality in behavioral neuroscience and beyond. *Nature neuroscience* 5, 1089-1092

Towers, D.; Ellmore, T. & McNaughton, B. (2003). Spatial navigation by Rhesus monkeys in a virtual environment by exclusively visual cues. *Society of Neuroscience Abstracts*, 32:518.6.

Warren, W.H.; Kay, B.A.; Zosh, W.D.; Duchon, A.P. & Sahuc, S. (2001). Optic flow is used to control human walking. *Nature Neuroscience* 4, 213-216.

Waller, D.; Bachman, E.; Hodgson, E. & Beall, A.C. (2007). The HIVE: A huge immersive virtual environment for research in spatial cognition. *Behavior Research Methods* 39(4), 835-843.

Witmer, B.G. & Kline, P. (1998). Judging perceived and traversed distance in virtual environments. *Presence: Teleoperators & Virtual Environments* 7, 144-167.

18

Exploring the Potential of Virtual Reality for the Elderly and People with Disabilities

Felix Kamieth[1], Patrick Dähne[1], Reiner Wichert[1], Juan Luis Villalar[2], Viveca Jimenez-Mixco[2], Antonella Arca[2] and Maria Teresa Arredondo[2]
[1]*Fraunhofer Institute for Computer Graphics Research IGD (Fh-IGD),Darmstadt*
[2]*Life Supporting Technologies, Technical University of Madrid (LST-UPM)*
[1]*Germany*
[2]*Spain*

1. Introduction

Nowadays society is facing a process where life expectancy is gradually but constantly increasing. As a result, the group of elderly people is growing to become one of the most significant in the entire population (Giannakouris, 2008). This also means that the prevalence of physical and cognitive impairments is increasing in proportion. Elderly people usually suffer from vision deficiencies (yellowish and blurred image), hearing limitations (especially at high frequencies) motor impairments (for selection, execution and feedback) and slight deterioration of their cognitive skills (Lillo & Moreira, 2004). In this context, providing the elderly and people with disabilities (E&D) with accessible systems and services that could improve their level of independence and thus enhance their quality of life has become a must for ICT –Information and Communication Technologies– developers such as usability engineers and interaction designers.

Ambient Assisted Living (AAL) is one of the solutions that are beginning to address this technological challenge. The AAL concept represents a specific, user-oriented type of Ambient Intelligence (AmI). It comprises technological and organisational-institutional solutions that can help people to live longer at the place they like most, ensuring a high quality of life, autonomy and security (Steg et al., 2006). AAL solutions are sensitive and responsive to the presence of people and provide assistive propositions for maintaining an independent lifestyle (De Ruyter & Pelgrim, 2007).

Within this complex and continuously evolving framework, it is very challenging to technologically meet all users' needs and requirements regarding accessibility and usability along the development process. Accessibility is a prerequisite for basic use of products by as many users as possible, in particular elderly persons and persons with sensory, physical or cognitive disabilities. Usability denotes the ease with which these products or services can be used to achieve specified goals with effectiveness, efficiency and satisfaction in a specified context of use (Wegge & Zimmermann, 2007). These aspects should be taken into account during the product design ideally from early stages, following a more interactive and iterative design-development-testing procedure. The major problem lies in the global cost of the design and development process, which can be critically increased, since AmI solutions involve complex features such as ubiquity, context awareness, smartness, adaptiveness and computing embedded in daily life goods.

The continuous advance of ICT is gradually increasing the ability of the E&D to perform daily activities independently, decreasing the amount of effort required for completing sensitive tasks. In this sense, Virtual Reality (VR) –at a broader scope, Virtual & Mixed Reality (VMR)– is growing to become a very useful tool for the empowerment of a large number of people. The potential usefulness of VR for these persons were already summarised in four main points almost two decades ago (Lanier, 1992; Middleton, 1992):

- It offers them the possibility to perform tasks and experience situations that they might not otherwise because of any physical or cognitive limitation, since VR can transform the sensory information that they cannot perceive into other modalities.
- VR can present a world where people may learn in a simplified way, applying afterwards the skills acquired to more complex real environments.
- VR technologies can be adapted to a wide range of individual senses and capabilities of the user. E.g. blind users can receive more audio information; visual information can be reinforced for deaf users, etc. Also, individual abilities of the users can be assessed so that the adaptation is optimal for them.
- VR allows people with special needs to interact with other users in the same conditions.

At present, costs of emerging VR technologies are being constantly reduced while becoming adaptable to a wider range of environments and individual requirements. Therefore they may offer significant opportunities to support user interaction in technological environments, while helping to reduce the existing usability gaps. As a consequence, VR has become the central research issue for a new generation of technologies that may be used to help E&D.

Since many years, the two research groups responsible of this book chapter - Fh-IGD and LST-UPM- have been advancing in the potential of ICT to overcome access limitations to environments and services, particularly addressing the convergence of VR, domotics and accessibility. As a natural step in this collaborative process, both groups are exploring the convenient application of VR technologies in the process of designing and developing accessible solutions for the E&D. An overview of this complementary work is depicted below.

2. State of the art

Probably the main advantage of VR is the possibility to create realistic environments. The experience of feeling immersed in a virtual scenario helps the user to overlook that s/he is actually in an artificial testing environment, allowing the assessment of the user experience under more natural circumstances. Another important benefit is the capability for controlling the type, number, speed and order of stimulus that are to be presented to the user of the virtual scenario, which enables the specialists to improve their interventions by personalising the environments, adapting them to the special conditions of each user. In the same way, trial and error methods can be easily applied into virtual environments; VR may then be used to analyse the user's behaviour in potential dangerous situations without any risk. Finally, by selecting different sets of stimulus to be presented to the user, the level of complexity of test exercises can be gradually increased, so the specialist is able to individualise the treatment or training scenario.

At the moment, the most significant domains for using VR applied to E&D are training, learning, rehabilitation, leisure or even tele-operation. Most of these systems are designed to establish a flexible and efficient *interface* between user and specialist, allowing the latter to define activities, measurements and protocols to quantitatively evaluate the user's progress. In contrast, a major weakness of VR is that nowadays there are still few applications that cover all the expectations created. Anyway, there are remarkable products coming out from laboratories that seem rather close to predictions. Some of them are analysed next.

2.1 VR applied to people with physical, sensorial and cognitive disabilities

VR technologies can be a great help for people with dysfunction or complete loss of specific interaction functions such as motion or speech. Techniques are progressing, and today certain applications and devices, which were used at first only to interact with VR, are now useful in the real world as assistive technologies (e.g. VR gadgets for transforming sign language into speech).

Furthermore, VR can be applied to rehabilitate specific disorders of people with motor limitations by training exactly those functions that can be improved. In this field of motion rehabilitation, force feedback devices like haptic interfaces and exoskeletons are commonly used (Ghedini et al., 2008). These devices are mainly robots able to apply controlled forces upon the user, to enable perception of the virtual environment by means of touch. The therapy may be adapted by calibrating the forces, hindering or facilitating the patient's motion for a specific exercise. There are several types of robots for this purpose, depending on the functionality required or the interaction mode. Some of them allow either 2D or 3D movements, some are wearable, others are in contact only with the part of the body that is going to be rehabilitated, etc.

People with physical disabilities can also use VR to perform the same complex tasks as non-handicapped people. VR may provide an adaptable mechanism for taking advantage of a convenient physical ability of one person to operate an input device for a computer program and, therefore, go around his limitation. E.g. there are systems based on data gloves that allow users to record custom-tailored gestures and map these gestures into actions (Micelli et al., 2009). In this way, people with vocal impairments could even enhance their communication skills by mapping specific hand gestures to speech phrases.

Another area of use is creating simulations for people with sensory impairments like blind or deaf people. In these applications the focus is helping them to learn the use of new tools like a walking stick or sign language. VR systems are also used for testing the usefulness and accessibility of products and environments before they are actually built. Virtual buildings can be designed in advance and displayed through a head mounted display to a wheelchair user who will move around and check for potential obstructions or non-accessible places (Pithon et al., 2009).

Educational inclusion for children with sensorial disabilities is also an important research goal for VR developers. The overall objective of virtual learning environments is to allow students to interact physically and intellectually with a new generation of instructional materials, and the focus of a significant number of researchers is to offer the same opportunities to users with disabilities to access and take advantage of all these resources. For example, there are virtual environments for visual impaired or blind children, which focus on the creation of mental structures of navigable objects using only spatial audible information and no visual information; there are also virtual environments for the education and training of children with spatial problems caused by movement limitations; hearing impaired children can also benefit from virtual environments by helping them to improve in structural inductive processes and flexible-thinking ability (Sik Lányi et al., 2006).

One type of application is the improvement of training results for people with cognitive impairments. Here, VR environments provide a safe and completely controlled surrounding that removes many stresses caused by natural human interactions and thus allows a gradual development of social abilities that are impossible to attain through real-life interactions. Work in this area includes the development of special VR scenarios for children with autism to promote creative activity (Parés et al., 2005). An interactive environment with stimuli of different modalities like visual, aural and vibrotactile was created for autistic children without verbal communication abilities, looking forward to providing these children with a reproducible and ordered environment in which they can expand their underdeveloped sense of agency, an essential factor of the autistic condition. It means that autistic children are unconscious of their ability to influence their environment. A virtual environment with clear input-reaction mappings can isolate this problem and provide a space where sense of agency can be developed.

Finally, therapeutic leisure is one of the most extended applications of VR for all kind of users, still offering long-distance research paths. Its ease of use and adaptability makes it a feasible option for E&D. This way, impaired participants have the experience to control over their environment and success in activities that are usually inaccessible to them (Yalon-Chamovitz & Weiss, 2008).

2.2 VR applied to the elderly

VR appears to provide varied and motivating opportunities for the rehabilitation of elderly people with chronic diseases, like stroke patients. In stroke rehabilitation, animal studies have suggested that, through the use of intensive therapy -which implies the repetition of individual movements hundreds of times per day-, a significant amount of the motor control lost by the stroke can be recovered. Human therapy approaches supplement this approach with keeping patients informed about their progress. Since sessions with therapists usually only cover a small set of motions and significant recovery requires more effort, patients are required to stick to an extensive home exercise regimen. However, only a fraction of the patients actually perform these exercises as recommended. Here, VR games are investigated for improving rehabilitation involvement by increasing patient motivation and quantifying recovery progress, with a focus on supporting the re-development of proprioception (Alankus et al., 2010; Cho et al., 2010). In the case of brain damage, VR approaches not only include direct rehabilitation work but also give the opportunity for tele-rehabilitation (Flores et al., 2008). A further use of VR in healthcare is the involvement of so-called *virtual humans* in elderly assistance scenarios. In this framework, simulated doctors or healthcare workers are being used to let a system communicate with patients. Similarly, VR representations of patients are being used by healthcare personnel for bed-side soft-skills training (Cabrera-Umpierrez et al., 2006).

A further area of use of VMR solutions is in the development of products and services tailored to elderly people with cognitive issues, in order to support them in their daily lives. An example for this is an augmented reality approach for helping elder drivers with spatial recognition problems though a GPS navigation system suited for the needs of elderly people (Kim & Dey, 2009). Existing navigation systems, while helping with orientation and navigation, tend to increase the in-vehicle information load, creating problems with divided attention between the information display on the navigation system and the road itself. The solution realised is the projection of navigation information directly onto the windshield, thus requiring no switching between looking at the road and the navigation system since they are both integrated. As in-vehicle augmented reality displays are being seriously considered by car manufacturers as a display option, this system has potential to be used in field once the underlying technological issues of creating reliable high-quality images on the windshield have been solved. Evaluations show that augmented reality displays are preferred by elderly and younger drivers alike, supporting them to understand context-sensitive information and reduce cognitive load.

Further usage of VR solutions in product development takes place in the development of mobile services for the elderly, for instance through avatar-based VR simulation systems (Asghar et al., 2009). Real world sensors help to map user movement and interactions to the virtual scene, running simulating services in parallel, so as to support the adaptation of the final products to the elderly requirements.

Another area of research for elderly people is the improvement of their access to real environments through the use of VR interfaces (Pittarello & De Favieri, 2006) by adding a semantic description of different zones and objects in the environment. This description is then mapped onto a 3D simulated environment used for navigation and object descriptions, providing a different level of assistance based on user skills and/or cognitive deficiencies.

A main area to consider is the wide range of solutions developed in the AAL field, such as the creation of VMR development and simulation environments for debugging AAL solutions. Some of these initiatives (Arca et al, 2009; Maly et al, 2009; Schäfer et al., 2009; Schätzlein et al., 2009) are developed in the framework of the VAALID project, so they will be described in more detail in a later section.

3. Experimenting with VR & accessible domotics

The Life Supporting Technologies group (LST-UPM) has a long experience in research on the application of ICT solutions towards the *accessible digital home*. The emergence of accessible and adapted spaces -and particularly the development of domotics and environment control systems- holds a key role in supporting the independent living of the E&D. Since almost two decades, concepts such as Universal Design (Connell et al., 1997) or Design for All, Assistive Technologies (Tiresias, 2010) or Web Accessibility (WAI, 2010) have been exploited in this group to advance in the development of accessible approaches to domotic installations, taking advantage of a fruitful, direct and continuous cooperation with the E&D. As a result of this research line, a dedicated smart home infrastructure was arranged as the Laboratory for Domotic Usability Evaluations at the University premises, providing a preliminary testbed to assess user experience of E&D and their carers in a controlled home environment. In this framework, emerging VR technologies appears as a potential next step to offer significant opportunities to support user interaction, helping to reduce the existing usability gaps in such technological environments (Stanney et al, 1998). The idea of integrating VR into domotic spaces as a new environment control modality has implied for a long time the exploration of a very testable research area with promising perspectives for supporting independent living (Meisel et al, 1993). Following these arguments, this section describes an innovative VR-based interaction strategy which was fully integrated within an accessible domotic platform (Jimenez-Mixco et al., 2009), providing an evaluation framework to analyse and extract those applications with better acceptance for the users by making use of a multimodal approach to adapt the interaction mechanisms to their needs, skills and preferences.

3.1 Configuration of the smart home demonstrator

The core of the smart home demonstrator is an accessible domotic installation, which is composed of several home appliances (lights, window blind, door, water tap and heating) and environment sensors (presence, smoke, gas, flood and temperature) connected through an EIB[1] gateway. An open architecture platform derived from an OSGi[2] middleware allows software-based environment control, while a set of accessible web-based interfaces enable both local and remote, secure, personalised access to domotic services (Conde-Alvarez et al., 2006).

A new virtual environment has been aggregated to the demonstrator trying to replicate the real appearance of the laboratory, using Multigen Creator[3] for 3D design and EON Studio[4] for interactivity. Users may interact with the system through a combination of different displays and devices: 6 m^2 Stewart retro-projection screen for stereoscopic glasses[5]; Trivisio AR-vision-3D stereoscopic binocular display[6]; 5DT HMD 800 head mounted display[7]; 5DT Data Glove 5 for detecting finger motion[5]; Intersense InterTrax 2 tracking system with 3-DOF[8]; stereo sound system and different models of tactile screens, mice and keyboards.

The design and implementation of the VR-based solution followed the Design for All philosophy by taking into account concepts such as usability, adaptability, multimodality or standards-compliance, going through the following phases: (1) graphical design of the virtual elements for a realistic 3D representation; (2) compilation of individual components into the simulated lab; (3) integration and configuration of multimodal –visual, tactile, acoustic and haptic– interaction devices; (4) incorporation of animation and interactivity to the virtual scene; (5) development of a bi-directional communication interface between the virtual and real environments based on web services; and (6) deployment of the VR solution over most web browsers, by taking advantage of EON Reality's web plug-in. The resulting architecture of the system is represented in Fig. 1.

3.2 Virtual design considerations

One of the key factors that support accessibility is the provision of multimodal user interfaces. Multimodality –as the possibility of using in parallel more than one interaction modalities for communication between user and system– has been implemented in four modes: whereas *visual* and *acoustic* modalities are used for system outputs, inputs are achieved through *tactile* and *haptic* methods. Acoustic input (i.e. voice recognition) was left out for future platform versions. A more detailed description of each modality is included below:

---

[1] http://www.knx.org
[2] http://www.osgi.org
[3] http://www.presagis.com
[4] http://www.eonreality.com
[5] http://www.stewartfilmscreen.com
[6] http://www.trivisio.com
[7] http://www.5dt.com
[8] http://www.isense.com

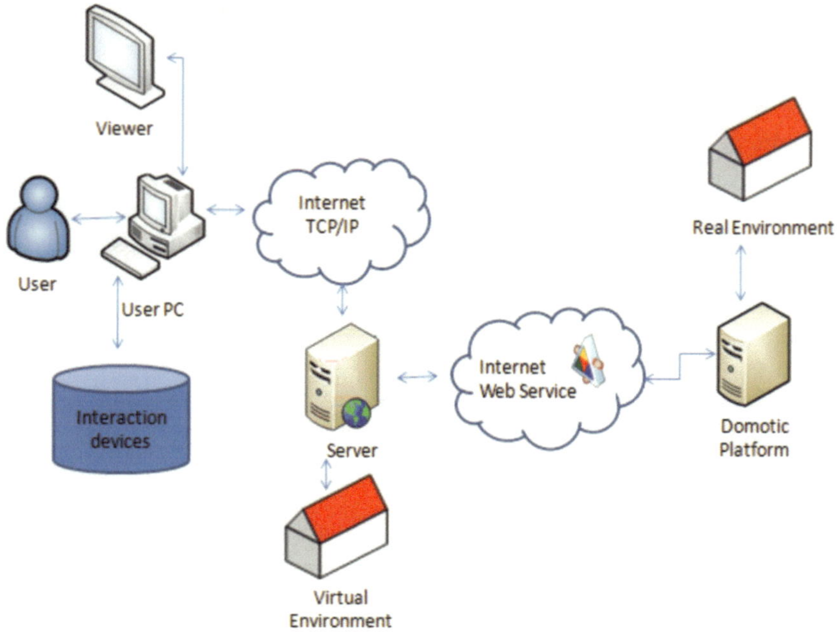

Fig. 1. System architecture of the VR demonstrator

- *Visual:* The 3D representation of the virtual lab and its components gives the main feedback to the user: virtual doors have been provided with open/close motion; lights change their colour to differentiate between on/off status, conveniently updating the overall light condition of the virtual environment; water pours from the tap when open; etc. Interaction options are highlighted through a helping tool, both textual and graphical, to facilitate user's navigation along the scene. Moreover, the user has also the possibility to visualise the real living lab at any time through an integrated web camera. The different screens and VR displays allow the customisation of the 2D or 3D visualisation scenario.
- *Acoustic:* In addition to the visual helping tools, acoustic messages guide the user in the navigation and interaction with the scene. For instance, when the user faces an interactive device–e.g. the door–, a voice message informs about the different interaction possibilities –i.e. open/close–. Virtual elements are also complemented with acoustic signs to increase the user's immersion feeling, like the sounds of the window blinds that are raising or some water pouring from the tap. This modality is implemented through a stereo sound system, either integrated in the virtual scenario or through personal headphones.
- *Tactile and haptic:* These two modalities allow the user to navigate in the virtual scene and control its elements. Navigation provides the user with a feeling of presence into the virtual environment, as s/he can move all over the scene (forward, backward and around), collide with the virtual objects, observe in any direction, make zoom and even change the point of view. The different interactive devices of the scene (e.g. lights, doors, webcam) can be controlled too, changing their status through a combination of these modalities. Complete tactile interaction is possible by pressing keyboard buttons, moving and clicking the mouse or touching the tactile screen. Haptic communication is

implemented by detecting commands from hand-based gesture recognition (using the VR glove) as well as by aligning user perspective along with head or arm real-time orientation (through the 3-DOF motion tracker).

Furthermore, the integrated system has been designed according to various guidelines and recommendations in order to make it accessible and user-adapted (Tiresias, 2010; ETSI, 2008):

- Users are able to select any of the input and output devices available as any input device -such as mouse, keyboard, tactile screen or data glove- can perform the same tasks effectively.
- The virtual environment provides object descriptions that are meaningful to users (when interactivity is enabled). Visual objects that are primarily decorative and contain little or no information need not be described.
- Users can easily activate a graphical menu to personalise different interaction features (e.g. acoustic signals).
- Users are provided with both acoustic and visual feedback when they interact with the elements in the scene (including alerts).
- Users are allowed to change the point of view and make zoom in the scene so as to find the most comfortable perspective.
- Every interaction has been implemented with at least two modalities: e.g. users can turn on/off the light either by touch (tactile screen, keyboard, mouse) or haptically (data glove), whereas feedback is obtained both graphically (screen, VR display) and acoustically (stereo system, headphones).
- Immersiveness can be adapted according to user preferences, from selecting specific visualisation devices (e.g. head mounted display instead of 2D screen) to simulating the own user's hand in the virtual scene. The inclusion of a virtual avatar is under consideration for further research.
- Users can combine the different interaction devices and modalities as they wish, to achieve the most usable solution for them. At present, most VR interfacing devices are wired, presenting tough usability concerns. Emerging wireless gadgets are to provide a relevant step forward in this sense.

3.3 Outcome of the experiment

The proposed solution has resulted in a running living lab for testing VR applications in the smart home domain, especially devoted for the E&D. It can be accessed locally or remotely through the Internet, and enables both real and simulated control of the domotic platform. Furthermore, it supports multimodal interaction, by means of specific VR devices, such as head mounted display, position tracker or data glove, and commonly used interaction gadgets (e.g. mouse, keyboard, tactile screen). This approach permits that users move around and interact with home appliances in a virtual environment, allowing them to check and change online the status of real devices directly through the 3D virtual elements (Fig. 2). To keep consistency between both real and virtual environments, status and orders for each device are shared by means of continuous feedback through an Internet connection and a typical web browser. Because of the collection of displays and interactive devices included, users may play around with different interaction modalities and degrees of immersion. Also some visual and acoustic guidance and help tools have been provided, to facilitate navigation within the interface and make it more intuitive.

Fig. 2. Views of the LST-UPM living lab: real picture (left) vs. virtual representation (right)

In addition, by adjusting a number of configuration elements on the user interface, the same interactive application may be validated for different settings and user profiles. In case the virtual environment is disconnected from the real lab, the application can be used by elderly or cognitive disabled to learn how to manage domotic installations in a non-threatening environment, while those with physical impairments may exploit the system to find the most convenient combination of modalities and interaction devices. By keeping both labs interconnected, confident users can go one step further and take the application directly as a ubiquitous remote control of the smart home, enabling them to check, both indoors and outdoors, the status of any home alarm or change in advance the temperature of the heating system. Moreover, carers, relatives or informal assistants are able to monitor in a non-intrusive way the real environment of any person requiring external supervision.

A preliminary evaluation phase has been carried out to validate the system in terms of performance, reliability and usability. 25 volunteers were able to assess combinations of the different displays and interaction mechanisms, both in simulated and real running modes. The results have been satisfying in terms of system usability, supporting the interest in VR technologies applied to smart home interaction. Although a complete validation plan was arranged to assess the whole system considering several user profiles from the E&D, professional assistants and informal carers, unfortunately some last-minute logistic problems made it postponed until the new living lab -which is actually under construction-becomes available, expected by the last quarter of 2010.

4. VR & AAL environments: the VAALID project

Nowadays, an innovative area of research and development is usability testing to make sure that special needs of the E&D are taken into account in the design and deployment of AAL environments. Conducting such tests in a VR environment can save time and money whereas improving the quality of products and services. In this sense, the above-described living labs resulted in a useful tool for interaction designers and usability engineers to immerse users in a virtual environment and assess, through the application, their experience in terms of interaction devices, modalities and reactions within smart home environments. Based on this assessment, designers would be able to develop new interaction concepts with users, improve existing solutions, and explore the potential of innovative AAL products and services. The preliminary encouraging results allowed envisioning multiple possibilities of VR on the process of providing the E&D with more adapted access to domotic-related applications.

However, current solutions have important limitations, especially as they require a significant amount of implementation effort to finally address the assessment of user experience in just one single environment integrating a pre-defined set of products and services. This section presents an approach proposed in the context of the European-funded VAALID project (VAALID, 2010) that extends the key concepts applied in these living labs, providing an easier method to create virtual environments and implement interactivity, enabling dynamic changes of environment conditions and characteristics, and allowing a thorough evaluation of user performance with real time interaction techniques. A dedicated toolkit has been developed in order to enable real rapid prototyping and validation of accessible and usable AmI solutions, by integrating VR tools and appropriate user interfaces. This approach will bridge the gap between planning AAL scenarios and their refinement and assessment in reality from the very beginning in the development process, reducing the global design and development effort.

4.1 The VAALID concept

VAALID is a European research project that aims to develop advanced computer aid engineering tools that will allow ICT developers, especially those ones that design AAL products and services, to optimise and make more efficient the whole process of user interaction design, and to validate usability and accessibility at all development stages, following a User Centred Design (UCD) process. The VAALID platform makes use of VR technologies to provide an immersive environment with 3D virtual ambients, specifically created for each possible use scenario, where AAL users can experience new interaction concepts and techno-elements, interactively. The usage of VAALID tools will make feasible, both economically and technically, the Universal Design of AAL solutions which have the potential of being acceptable by most persons since their needs are taken into account proactively during the development phases.

The methodology proposed to address AAL solutions (Naranjo et al., 2009) is based on a UCD approach, drawing together the practical, emotional and social aspects of people's experience and bringing on the needed innovation that delivers real user benefit. For that reason, UCD is particularly useful when a new product or service is to be introduced, as it is the case of AAL solutions. The methodology consists of four iterative phases (concept, design, development & validation), where both usability engineers and interaction designers must participate, while involving AAL users –i.e. the E&D– all along the process:

- *Concept.* First, AAL solution requirements must be extracted, including the functions that the proposed solution provides and how it reacts and behaves, as well as the constraints that should be considered in the design process.
- *Design.* Once the requirements are well-identified, developers define the specifications of the AAL solution, taking into account all significant facets that may have influence on the development process. Low-fidelity virtual prototypes of the AAL solution, including 3D virtual AAL-enabled spaces, are built to reflect all aspects of the conceptual design, and further evaluated by users. Design iterations are driven by users' feedback in terms of acceptance and accessibility issues until requirements are met.

- *Implementation.* This phase involves the creation of real and fully-functional high-fidelity AAL prototypes, with the aim of transforming the validated conceptual design into a concrete and detailed solution. The components developed at this stage must be tested against its accessibility features, and improvements or corrective actions must be addressed accordingly.
- *Validation.* Finally, the implementation of AAL solution prototypes are evaluated and assessed, detecting usability issues both automatically and with real end-users.

This methodology allows virtually simulating each aspect of an AAL product/service and validating it before the real implementation. The whole process involves both virtual and mixed reality elements. The simulation in the design phase requires mainly 3D virtual environments to reproduce the conceptual design of the solution; the implementation phase goes a step further and adds the possibility to use mixed reality elements, so that both real functional prototypes can be tested within virtual environments and product/service virtual mock-ups may be integrated in a real living lab scenario for final assessment.

In order to permit developers to apply this methodology across all the stages of the design cycle -and thus allow rapid development of AAL solutions and further assessment with users-, the VAALID platform is structured in two complementary frameworks: Authoring and Simulation. The *Authoring Framework* provides the ICT designer with the appropriate components to deal with the three main pillars of an AAL solution: users, environment and services. In particular it involves the creation of user profiles, the modification of AAL-enabled 3D spaces (including sensors, networks and interaction devices and functions), the creation of virtual user-interaction devices (which may be embedded in daily life objects) and new service concepts. The designer may then interconnect these individual components to create different evaluation scenarios so as they can be validated afterwards as integrated simulations. The *Simulation Framework* is based on the *instant**reality***[9] framework (from the Fh-IGD group in Darmstadt, Germany) to run the 3D environment in the available VR infrastructure and activate the different virtual devices and services, providing the ICT designer with a number of tools to assess how the user interacts within the virtual scenario.

From the VAALID usage perspective, target users can be divided into three main groups:

- *Primary users*: designers of AAL solutions that will use VAALID as a professional instrument. This group includes interaction engineers -who design the structure of the simulation, building the seniors' profile and defining the interaction modes with the environment- and usability engineers -who plan the interface between AAL services and senior citizens, through the study of their interactions with the VAALID system-.
- *Beneficiaries (or users, by default)*: the main target group of users who will benefit from the results of using VAALID tools:
  - Elderly people over 60 years old that may have light hearing/sight problems, mobility impairments or the typical declined cognitive and physical abilities related to age
  - Young people with hearing/sight/mobility problems
  - Any other group of users that may profit from accessible AAL solutions
- *Secondary users*: all those users that may benefit indirectly from VAALID, using it as a consultancy service:

[9] http://www.instantreality.org/

- Architects, construction planners, care centres, suppliers of interaction devices, public administration, interior designers and other stakeholders who work for companies that buy and develop AAL services.
- System designers, who implement AAL solutions validating usability and accessibility of their products, like sensors, actuators or control software.

4.2 The VAALID Authoring Framework

The main purpose of the VAALID Authoring Framework (Villalar et al., 2009) is to support interaction designers and usability engineers in building the core elements that compose an AAL simulation context. It follows the Rapid Application Development (RAD) methodology (Mackay et al., 2000), enabling a quick iteration between the design, execution and refinement phases for each individual element that will be integrated and afterwards executed within the Simulation Framework. One AAL simulation is created from a conjunction of several models (or *Templates*) which are stored together in a so-called *Project* – i.e. the basic component of the VAALID data repository–. Every simulation scenario is saved as a single Project that, according to the VAALID modelling framework, is basically composed of three main models: User Model, Environment Model and AAL Service Model. Each of these elements is created by editing pre-existing characteristics described as properties and behaviours. Properties are defined through *ontologies* (Mocholí et al., 2010) that represent static features of a single model; behaviours are described as *workflows* (Fernández-Llatas et al., 2010) that define how the element relates with others by means of interaction. Through this kind of information the designer can build models in a rapid way trying to cope with the user requirements.

The Authoring Framework workspace is then divided into three tools, one for each type of model (Fig. 3):

- *User Model Builder:* The User Editor defines the user (i.e. E&D) profile in terms of interaction capabilities -physical, sensory, cognitive- according to pre-defined ontological templates. This information is collected during the design phase and may be refined while testing the AAL solution. With this tool, the designer may create a new User Model, import or export an existing one from/to the VAALID library and remove the User Model associated to the current Project.
- *Environment Model Builder:* The Environment Model holds a virtual representation of one specific place, similarly to the living lab experiences described above. This tool allows importing VRML files from any CAD or 3D animation software as the start-up for the 3D simulation environment where users will be finally immersed. Pre-existing 3D objects can be added –defining their relative position and dimensions– and deleted from the Project to complete the desired environment. These objects are the interactive devices of the scene (i.e. sensors, actuators and a combination of both), which are the basis for defining the interaction between users and AAL services. The tool enables the characterisation of these objects by means of defining their properties and behaviours through the appropriate ontology and workflow editors using a graphical language.
  Environments, devices and workflows can be imported and exported from/to the VAALID library for being reused in other Projects.
- *AAL Service Compositor:* This editor creates an AAL Service Model, which describes the potential interactions between users and objects in the scene. It is essentially composed of a workflow that defines how to process information coming from environment

sensors (i.e. active or passive user inputs) to consequently activate the relevant actuators (e.g. security systems, lighting, automatic phone calls), including those devoted to give feedback to the user. Services can be also imported and exported from/to the VAALID library.

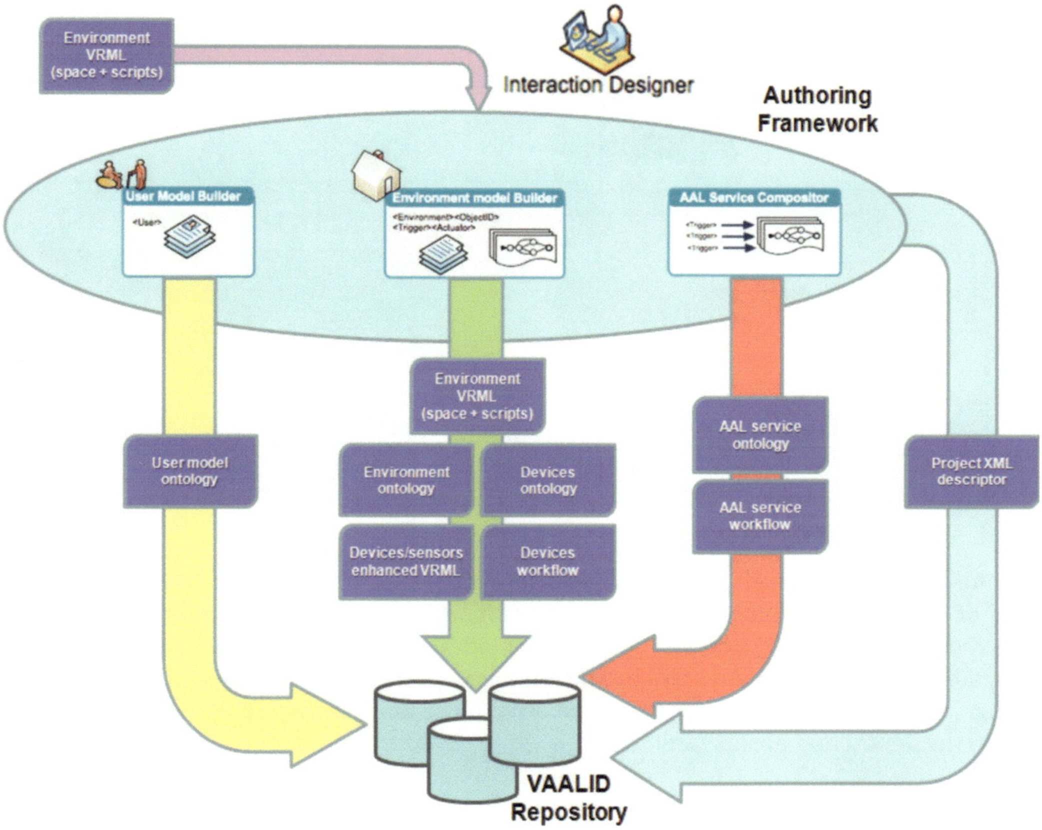

Fig. 3. Structure of the VAALID Authoring Framework

Finally, there is a *Project Editor* that integrates these three tools in a common framework in order to manage all the files involved in each simulation scenario as one single Project. Projects can be saved and opened in the traditional way and is the input element for the Simulation Framework.

Regarding implementation facts, the Authoring Framework (Fig. 4) is based on the architecture and look-and-feel of Eclipse[10] so that a highly-familiar user interface could help developers in rapidly getting managed with the tools. The development framework can then be personalised, configured to fit the needs of each designer, providing help hints whenever required along the development process. The following technologies have been integrated to create the Authoring Framework: Eclipse RCP as main IDE; GForge for cooperative software development; SWT for user interface components; Java3D/VRML97 for 3D management; Protégé, Jena & Jastor for ontologies; jBPM for workflows.

[10] http://www.eclipse.org

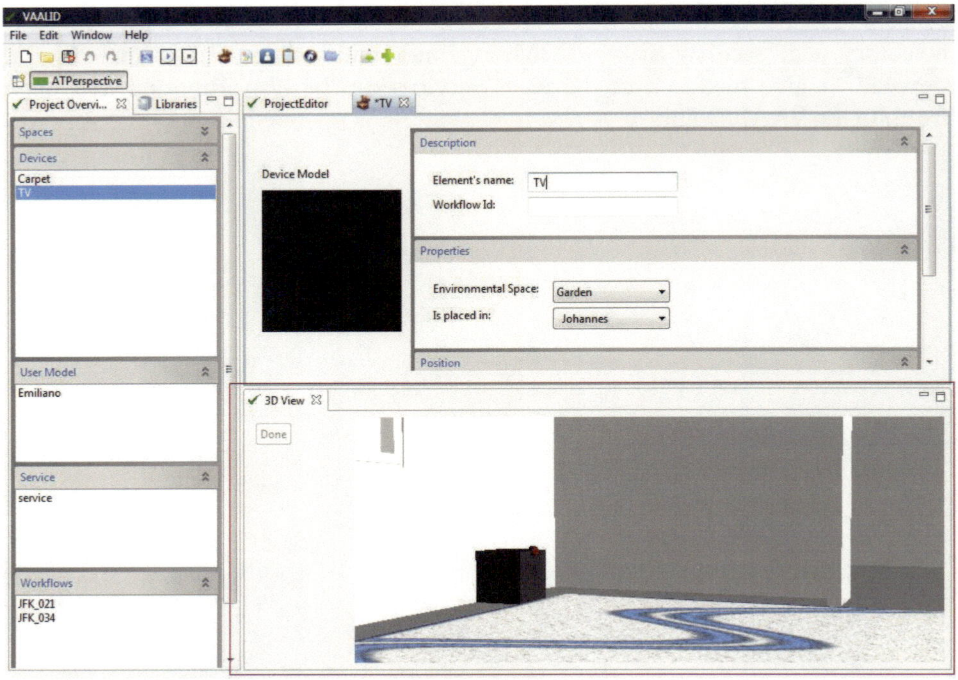

Fig. 4. Screenshot of the Authoring Framework prototype

The Authoring Framework will be deployed as open source software so, in case of success, a kind of development community may grow around it in the near future. This community may be oriented to: (a) the development of additional tool functionalities, by simply integrating new Eclipse-based plugins; (b) the creation and exchange of individual elements though the VAALID library; (c) the cooperative reuse and refinement of VAALID Projects due to the import and export facilities.

4.3 The VAALID Simulation Framework

The purpose of the VAALID Simulation Framework is to provide the possibility to perform AAL system evaluations and validations at earlier stages of development in a fast and cost-effective fashion, thus saving development time and cost while incorporating end-users into earlier stages of development. The Simulation Framework takes care of displaying the virtual AAL solution to end-users for validation and evaluation purposes. It consists of several components which simulate different aspects of the virtual solution (Fig. 5).

From an AAL system designer perspective, the core component is the *Simulation Control Panel* (SCP) as it lets the designer setup, configure, run, manipulate and analyse a simulation session. This module is integrated with the Authoring Framework and distributes the different output files (3D environment, workflows and ontologies) among the other components of the Simulation Framework architecture. It has the control for executing and stopping all these components, each of which simulates an aspect of the developed solution. Besides, the SCP includes an *Accessibility Verifier* which allows performing preliminary checks for the early detection of accessibility constraints depending on the user profile (e.g. using acoustic outputs for hearing impaired users will automatically raise an alarm for the AAL designer before the simulation starts).

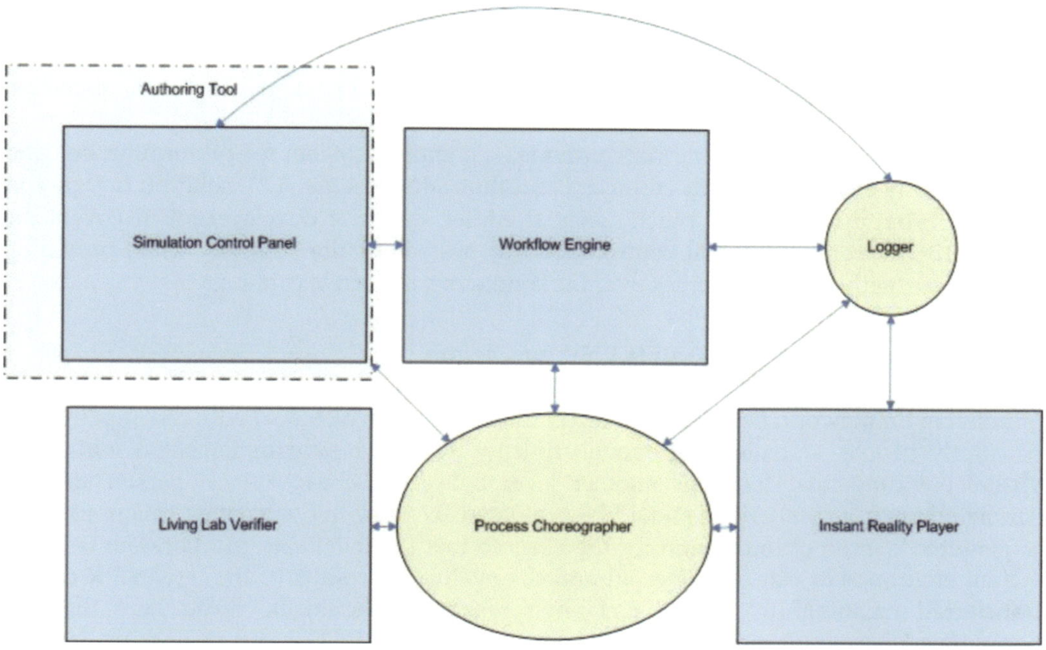

Fig. 5. Architecture of the VAALID Simulation Framework

The *instant**reality*** player is a complete VMR system, which is used for rendering the 3D-model of the simulated AAL environment, coming as a VRML file from the Authoring Framework. At the same time it provides the connection framework for the interaction devices used to navigate through and interact with the scene. The *instant**reality*** player allows the use of common 2D-displays and modern 3D-displays as well as CAVE or other multi-projector display systems.

In parallel, the *Workflow Engine* (WE) executes the different workflows created with the Authoring Toolkit to simulate the functionalities of all functional components within the scene, like TV screens, stereo systems, ambient displays, doors or windows. The other main feature of the WE is the simulation of AAL services such as health monitoring, personal security services or daily life support services which make use of the simulated devices' functionalities. Once the simulation is running, the SCP can be used to intervene in the execution of these workflows and change some system functions in real time.

The WE is connected to the *instant**reality*** player through the *Process Choreographer* component. This module facilitates the communication between the Simulation Framework components by coordinating the exchange of the XML-structured messages previously defined.

The *Living Lab Verifier* module enables the AAL designer to replace simulated devices and sensors with their real counterparts, thus including real-world components into the simulation environment. Following this process iteratively with every simulated device, in the latter stage of the development cycle for the AAL solution the simulation environment is fully replaced by a real laboratory for final solution testing.

Finally, the *Logger* is connected to the Process Choreographer, WE and *instant**reality*** player, capturing all the communication messages between the components as well as all user inputs to the simulated scene through the *instant**reality*** player. The aggregation of these collected data is available in the SCP after the simulation run has been ended and lets the AAL designer analyse key indicators of the simulation (e.g. task completion, time between events, number of events of a kind) and perform semi-automatic analyses of the extracted information.

This way, the Simulation Framework provides a complete system for performing fast and effective early evaluations with end-users and thus supports the AAL solution designer in moving through UCD cycles much faster at earlier stages of development. It covers the entire process from simulation configuration to post-simulation analysis while providing the designer with complete control over the simulation while it is running.

4.4 Further research on accessible VMR interaction

The interaction with VMR for testing AAL environments poses an extra challenge to the Simulation Framework. Developing interaction modalities which deal with the impairments of elderly people, a challenging enough task by itself, is now complemented with a 3D virtual environment. This adds another layer between the elderly test person and the simulated environment which should be evaluated. The key to overcoming this problem is to generate a sense of immersion for the user, so that the inevitable gap between real and virtual environment can be neglected and the evaluation results of the test in VR can be transferred meaningfully to the real environment. It should be noted here that the Simulation Framework is meant for quick feedback in early UCD cycles, so as more detailed feedback still requires real-world implementation. However, these first results regarding the feasibility of an AAL service for elderly people can meaningfully complement the early stages of AAL solution design and lead to a stronger involvement of end users in the development process.

For the interaction in the VAALID system, the end user can navigate through the scene and manipulate the environment using different simulation control devices, which range from standard input devices like a space mouse or a gamepad to specialised devices more suited for elderly people like wheelchairs, which serve the needs of the elderly in the VR setting. This wheelchair allows elderly people to sit down in front of the environment, thus eliminating the strain of standing or the fear of falling down. The interaction with the wheelchair is quick and intuitive, since there already exists a clear mental model for its function even among technology-averse people. An aversive response to the wheelchair as stigmatising was not confirmed in tests. On the contrary, the fact that one could sit down in front of the wall and have an easy-to-learn interface was regarded as beneficial.

While there are clear limits to the use of VR technology among the cognitive disease spectrum -patients with epilepsy, for example, should not be confronted with a virtual reality environment-, the VAALID system aimed at an extensible interaction system which allowed the incorporation of a variety of different input modalities for simulation control, both in terms of navigation and interaction.

For interaction, an abstraction was used which lets the elderly user interact with the system in an intuitive fashion (Kamieth et al., 2010). A virtual hand (Fig. 6) can be moved through the scene and be used to touch, grab and interact with objects and devices within the scene. Opening doors, windows, controlling televisions and touch screens for example, can be implemented with the virtual hand abstraction. For first evaluations of AAL scenarios, this metaphor allows a clear and intuitive way for interaction that facilitates end-user immersion within the scene and thus helps in closing the gap between VR and reality, supporting the transferability of results from VR testing to real world test outcomes.

Fig. 6. Virtual hand used for interacting with the simulated environment

For transferability of results -an important issue in the development of AAL solutions-, the question of end-user immersion is crucial. Some authors argue that, in the development of a feeling of presence, scene realism is of secondary importance (Nunez, 2004). Instead, the support of user expectations needs a high degree of consideration. Thus, the analysis of end-user expectations -in this case, the expectations of elderly people in VR environments- requires extended research for the realisation of better scenario simulations. Especially the manipulation of cognitive load leads to an improvement of a feeling of presence. Based on these findings, further research would include the testing of this concept with elderly people. However, the question of presence is also being approached in the sense of earlier research focusing on realism and the coverage of different sensory channels.

The literature suggests that immersion is made up of two main components which can be called *Depth of information* and *Breadth of Information* (Steuer, 1995). The term *Depth of information* refers to the quality of the signals presented to the user (for example, the sound quality or the resolution and colour depth of the displays used for the simulation). The term *Breadth of information* refers to the variety of sensory data sent to the user during the simulation. This means that the more senses are stimulated during a simulation, the higher is its breadth of information. In this area the main focus in the research community has usually been on visual and auditory stimuli with an even stronger focus on visual display. This focus has shifted in recent years toward incorporating haptic systems too, which provide the user furthermore with data in the form of touch.

The VAALID approach takes these requirements for immersion into account. At the pilot site in Fh-IGD, either the HEyeWall (a high-resolution 3D-projection wall) or the CAVE (a small room in which five walls are 3D-projector displays) is being used, providing state-of-the-art solutions in the area of immersive visual displays. Furthermore, the VRML-standard used for the description of the simulation environment allows a complex modelling of directional sound sources, which provide the illusion of moving past sound sources through a change in sound volume and direction. To increase the sense of immersion in the dimension of *breadth of information*, the VAALID system incorporates haptic interaction devices like the Novint Falcon[11], which enables the user to interact with the scene through a natural mapping of hand movements to VR interactions. Apart from the abovementioned wheelchair device, a pressure board is also used for travelling through the scene, which allows a natural mapping of stepping on a board to travelling through a scene.

Along the VAALID lifetime, the project is exploring the feasibility and accessibility of integrating other simulation controls to the platform (Fig.7), either based on the Nintendo Wii remote controller[12], head/hand trackers, infrared data gloves, visual hand controls or smart phone accelerometers. The most suitable simulation controls will be extensively assessed during the final pilot tests, with the aim of finding the most adapted solutions for each user.

Fig. 7. Testing VR using a wheelchair and Falcon (left), smart phone (centre) and infrared data gloves (right)

5. Discussion & conclusion

Accessibility and usability concepts are currently considered within a limited range of ICT applications and services, mostly constraining its usage to research and development activities and presenting significant reserves when dealing with production and deployment phases. Although the seven principles of the Universal Design or Design for All are well-known and applicable to a wide variety of domains, business stakeholders are still highly reticent to apply them in practice. This lack of commitment with the elderly and disabled community, in particular when designing AAL solutions, is mainly due to the high costs involved in the iterative design-development-testing procedure and the considerable effort in time and resources needed to meet user's needs.

On the other hand, the adoption of VR technologies seems to confront with the purpose of designing services for the E&D, as rather few initiatives have been carried out in this field regarding accessibility requirements. Most of them deal with people with cognitive disabilities (dementia, autism, schizophrenia, Down's syndrome, etc.), proposing simple virtual worlds where users get immersed in order to learn some tasks, acquire some habits or recover some capabilities under a controlled scenario. Nevertheless, VR has been proven to offer significant advantages for persons with all kinds of disabilities. It can present virtual worlds where users can be trained or learn in a controlled environment, and then apply the skills acquired to a real context. VR technologies can be adapted to a wide range of individual requirements and, at the same time, user's abilities and experience can be assessed in order to reach an optimal adaptation. Particularly, the multimodal approach

[11] http://www.novint.com/

[12] http://www.nintendo.com/wii/

inherent to VR and the low-effort interaction techniques followed can make VR-based interfaces especially valuable for users with disabilities or special needs. The conjunction of these facts may enhance the variety of accessible solutions for addressing the specific impairments and preferences of each person, especially in terms of interaction limitations. This involves not only physical, but also cognitive disabilities.

The work described in this chapter brings together all these issues into a technological approach that will have a beneficial impact for all the involved parts: the ICT designers will be able to evaluate the suitability of the proposed solutions with a significant reduction of the global design and development effort; business stakeholders will have a cost-effective solution and therefore new market opportunities; and finally, the E&D will be provided with new services to improve their quality of life, and even better, they will be able to active and critically participate in the creation process of these services.

This chapter has explored the most promising technologies and applications in the field of VR applied to the E&D. It presents the outcomes of assessing user experience through innovative approaches, bringing together VR and other technologies such as environment control systems. The objective is to develop a convenient framework to evaluate the accessibility and usability of AAL solutions, focusing on their adequacy to increase quality of life and improve autonomy of different target users. The possibility of performing assessment phases during the design process of AAL solutions -before building up real living labs- has key benefits such as saving of time and costs. In addition, users can participate in a controlled environment, since VR technologies assure safe and secure interaction. This does not mean that evaluation in a real living lab has to be avoided, but that any further interaction experiment will be enriched by the results obtained in the preliminary design process.

The suitability of different multimodal interaction mechanisms integrated with VR has been studied, including visual, acoustic, tactile and haptic modalities. Besides, several potential functionalities of the solutions are explored, such as training, cognitive therapy or domotic control. Considering the collected data, preliminary results show that users feel comfortable in using the VR devices and defined the experience as realistic, although there are valuable suggestions to improve the user interaction (e.g. allow sensitiveness calibration). From a technical point of view, this can be taken as a good starting point for future work with VR-based applications, although further research is required concerning its suitability for elderly users.

The current research work aims at giving answer to a number of open issues such as: (a) the adequacy of VR for enhancing user experience for the E&D; (b) the chances of VR as widespread usable human-computer interaction method; (c) the convenience of VR for a daily handling of smart home environments. In this sense, the addition of other modalities, like natural language voice recognition or augmented reality, or new interfacing devices coming from the emerging generation of intuitive wireless gadgets for entertainment or telecommunication, might be the starting point for definitely spreading VR technologies while fostering their key role in improving accessibility for people with special needs.

The next evaluation phase of the VAALID project (which will involve dozens of designers and beneficiaries in three European pilot sites until April 2011) as well as the imminent finalisation of the new LST-UPM living lab will certainly help to clarify some of the above open topics. Conclusions will feed -and will be afterwards expanded by- the VERITAS project (VERITAS, 2010), the next collaboration initiative where both research groups are engaged. VERITAS aims at developing an extensive list of VMR tools for supporting accessibility testing at all stages of development of five application domains (automotive, smart living spaces, workplace design, infotainment, personal healthcare and wellbeing), moving ahead in the convergence between VMR and accessibility of environments, services and devices.

6. Acknowledgements

Part of this work has been accomplished under the VAALID and TRAIN-ON projects. VAALID is a cooperative research project partially funded by the European Union (ICT-2007-224309). TRAIN-ON is a research initiative partly funded by the Office of Universities and Research of the Community of Madrid and the Technical University of Madrid.

7. References

Alankus, G.; Lazar, A.; May, M. & Kelleher, C. (2010). Towards customizable games for stroke rehabilitation, *Proceedings of the 28th ACM Conference on Human Factors in Computing Systems (CHI 2010)*, pp. 2113-2122, ISBN 978-1-60558-929-9, Atlanta, Georgia, USA, April 2010, ACM, New York, NY

Arca, A.; Villalar, J.L.; Diaz-Nicolas, J.A. & Arredondo, M.T. (2009). Haptic Interaction in Virtual Reality Environments through Android-based Handheld Terminals. *Adjunct Proceedings of 3rd European Conference on Ambient Intelligence (AmI09)*, pp. 259-263, ISBN 978-3-902737-00-7, Salzburg, Austria, November 2009, M. Tscheligi et al. (Eds.), ICT&S Center, University of Salzburg

Asghar, Z.; Hickey, S. & Kazmi, S. (2009). Developing mobile services for specific user groups using virtual environments, *Proceedings of the 8th International Conference on Mobile and Ubiquitous Multimedia (MUM '09)*, article no. 17, ISBN 978-1-60558-846-9, Cambridge, UK, November 2009, ACM, New York, NY

Cabrera-Umpierrez, M.F.; Ramirez, C.M.; Sevillano, A.; Arredondo, M.T. & De Smedt, A. (2006). Medical Educational e-Platform through Virtual Reality technologies, *Proceedings of IEEE Mediterranean Electrotechnical Conference (MELECON 2006)*, pp. 453-456, ISBN 1-4244-0087-2, Benalmadena, Malaga, Spain, May 2006, F. Sandoval et al. (Eds.), IEEE

Cho, S.W.; Ku, J.H.; Kang, Y.J.; Lee, K.H.; Song, J.Y.; Kim, H.J.; Kim, I.Y. & Kim, S.I. (2010). A Pilot Study for Development of Shoulder Proprioception Training System Using Virtual Reality for Patients with Stroke: The Effect of Manipulated Visual Feedback, In: *IFMBE Proceedings, XII Mediterranean Conference on Medical and Biological Engineering and Computing (MEDICON 2010)*, 29, 4, R. Magjarevic et al. (Eds.), pp. 722-724, ISBN 978-3-642-13039-7, Springer Berlin Heidelberg, Germany

Conde-Alvarez, E.; Rodriguez-Ascaso, A.; Montalva, J.B. & Arredondo M.T. (2006). Laboratory for domotic usability evaluations, *Proceedings of the I Workshop on Technologies for Healthcare and Healthy Lifestyle (WTHS'06)*, ISBN 978-84-611-1311-8, Valencia, Spain, April 2006

Connell, B.R.; Jones, M.; Mace, R.; Mueller, J.; Mullick, A.; Ostroff, E.; Sanford, J.; Steinfeld, E.; Story, M. & Vanderheiden, G. (1997). *The Principles of Universal Design*, Version

2.0, January 1997, Raleigh, NC: North Carolina State University, The Center for Universal Design, USA

De Ruyter, B. & Pelgrim, E. (2007). Ambient Assisted-Living Research in CareLab. *Interactions*, 14, 4, (July + August 2007) pp. 30-33, ISSN 1072-5520, New York, NY, USA

ETSI EG 202 487 (2008): *Human Factors (HF); User experience guidelines; Telecare services (eHealth)*. Version 1.1.2 (February 2008)

Fernández-Llatas, C.; Mocholí, J.B.; Sánchez, C.; Sala, P. & Naranjo, J.C. (2010). Process choreography for Interaction simulation in Ambient Assisted Living environments, In: *IFMBE Proceedings, XII Mediterranean Conference on Medical and Biological Engineering and Computing (MEDICON 2010)*, 29, 4, R. Magjarevic et al. (Eds.), pp. 757-760, ISBN 978-3-642-13039-7, Springer Berlin Heidelberg, Germany

Flores, E.; Tobon, G.; Cavallaro, E.; Cavallaro, F.I.; Perry, J.C. & Keller, T. (2008). Improving patient motivation in game development for motor deficit rehabilitation, *Proceedings of the 2008 International Conference on Advances in Computer Entertainment Technology (ACE '08)*, 352, pp. 381-384, ISBN 978-1-60558-393-8, Yokohama, Japan, December 2008, ACM, New York, NY, USA

Ghedini, F.; Faste, H.; Carrozzino, M. & Bergamasco, M. (2008). Passages: a 3D artistic interface for children rehabilitation and special needs, *Proceedings of 7th ICDVRAT with ArtAbilitation*, pp. 185-189, ISBN 07-049-15-00-6, Maia, Portugal, September 2008, University of Reading, UK

Giannakouris, K. (2008). Ageing characterises the demographic perspectives of the European societies. *Population and Social Conditions*. Eurostat, Statistics in focus, 72/2008, ISSN 1977-0316

Jimenez-Mixco, V.; de las Heras, R.; Villalar, J.L. & Arredondo, M.T. (2009). A New Approach for Accessible Interaction within Smart Homes through Virtual Reality. In: *Universal Access in Human-Computer Interaction. Intelligent and Ubiquitous Interaction Environments*, C. Stephanidis (Ed.), LNCS 5615/2009, pp. 75–81, ISBN 978-3-642-02709-3, Springer Berlin Heidelberg, Germany

Kamieth, F.; Hellenschmidt, M. & Dähne, P. (2010). Interaction Framework for Evaluation of Barrier-free environments, In: *Ambient Assisted Living 2010*, A. Hartmann et al. (Eds.), article nº 76, VDE VERLAG GMBH, ISBN 978-3-8007-3209-8, Berlin, Offenbach, Germany

Kim, S. & Dey, A.K. (2009). Simulated Augmented Reality Windshield Display as a Cognitive Mapping Aid for Elder Driver Navigation, *Proceedings of the 27th ACM Conference on Human Factors in Computing Systems (CHI 2009)*, pp. 133-142, ISBN 978-1-60558-246-7, Boston, MA, USA, April 2009, ACM, New York, NY

Lanier, J. (1992). Virtual reality and persons with disabilities, *Proceedings of Virtual Reality and Persons with Disabilities Conference*, Los Angeles, March 1992, Office of Disabled Student Services, California State University, USA

Lillo, J. & Moreira, H. (2004). Envejecimiento y diseño universal. *Anuario de Psicología*, 35, 4, (December 2004) pp. 493-506, ISSN 0066-5126 (in Spanish)

Mackay, H.; Carne, C.; Beynon-Davies, P. & Tudhope, D. (2000). Reconfiguring the User: Using Rapid Application Development. *Social Studies of Science*, 30, 5, (October 2000) pp. 737-757, ISSN 0306-3127

Maly, J.; Savall, A.; Schäfer, J. & Machate, J. (2009). The VAALID authoring tool: User Interface Concept. *Adjunct Proceedings of 3rd European Conference on Ambient Intelligence (AmI09)*, pp. 243-246, ISBN 978-3-902737-00-7, Salzburg, Austria, November 2009, M. Tscheligi et al. (Eds.), ICT&S Center, University of Salzburg

Meisel, A.H.; Meisel, H. & Marsh, C.H. (1993). Virtual Reality, Human Evolution, and the World of Disability. *Proceedings of the 1st Annual International Conference: Virtual Reality and Persons with Disabilities*, San Francisco, June 1993, Center On Disabilities, California State University-Northridge, USA

Micelli, V.; Rosiello, F.; Aleotti, J. & Caselli, S. (2009). Design of Gestural Interfaces for Simulated Smart Environments, *Adjunct Proceedings of 3rd European Conference on Ambient Intelligence (AmI09)*, pp. 231-234, ISBN 978-3-902737-00-7, Salzburg, Austria, November 2009, M. Tscheligi et al. (Eds.), ICT&S Center, University of Salzburg

Middleton, T. (1992). Matching virtual reality solutions to special needs. *Proceedings of Virtual Reality and Persons with Disabilities Conference*, Los Angeles, March 1992, Office of Disabled Student Services, California State University, USA

Mocholí, J.B.; Sala, P.; Fernández-Llatas, C. & Naranjo, J.C. (2010). Ontology for Modeling Interaction in Ambient Assisted Living Environments, In: *IFMBE Proceedings, XII Mediterranean Conference on Medical and Biological Engineering and Computing (MEDICON 2010)*, 29, 4, R. Magjarevic et al. (Eds.), pp. 655-658, ISBN 978-3-642-13039-7, Springer Berlin Heidelberg, Germany

Naranjo, J.C; Fernandez, C.; Sala, P.; Hellenschmidt, M. & Mercalli, F. (2009). A modelling framework for Ambient Assisted Living validation. In: *Universal Access in Human-Computer Interaction. Intelligent and Ubiquitous Interaction Environments*, C. Stephanidis (Ed.), LNCS 5615/2009, pp. 228–237, ISBN 978-3-642-02709-3, Springer Berlin Heidelberg, Germany

Nunez, D. (2004). How is presence in non-immersive, non-realistic virtual environments possible? *Proceedings of the 3rd International Conference on Computer Graphics, Virtual Reality, Visualisation and interaction in Africa (AFRIGRAPH'04)*, pp. 83-86, ISBN 1-58113-863-6, Stellenbosch, South Africa, November 2004, ACM, New York, NY, USA

Parés, N.; Carreras, A.; Durany, J.; Ferrer, J.; Freixa, P.; Gómez, D.; Kruglanski, O.; Parés, R.; Ribas, J.I., Soler, M. & Sanjurjo, À. (2005). Promotion of creative activity in children with severe autism through visuals in an interactive multisensory environment, *Proceedings of the 2005 Conference on Interaction Design and Children (IDC'05)*, pp. 110-116, ISBN 1-59593-096-5, Boulder, Colorado, USA, June 2005, ACM, New York, NY

Pithon, T.; Weiss, T.; Richir, S. & Klinger, E. (2009). Wheelchair simulators: A review. *Technology and Disability*, 21, 1-2, (July 2009) pp. 1-10, ISSN 1055-4181

Pittarello, F. & De Faveri, A. (2006). Improving access of elderly people to real environments: a semantic based approach, *Proceedings of the Working Conference on*

Advanced Visual Interfaces (AVI'06), pp. 364-368, ISBN 1-59593-353-0, Venetia, Italy, May 2006, ACM, New York, NY, USA

Schäfer, J.; Schätzlein, F.; Maly, J.; Unger, A.; Sala, P. & Mercalli, F. (2009). Evaluation of the VAALID authoring user interface. *Adjunct Proceedings of 3rd European Conference on Ambient Intelligence (AmI09)*, pp. 239-242, ISBN 978-3-902737-00-7, Salzburg, Austria, November 2009, M. Tscheligi et al. (Eds.), ICT&S Center, University of Salzburg

Schätzlein, F.; Kamieth, F.; Röder, P.; Schäfer, J. & Burmester, M. (2009). Evaluation of interaction techniques for AAL in virtual reality with senior citizens. *Adjunct Proceedings of 3rd European Conference on Ambient Intelligence (AmI09)*, pp. 235-238, ISBN 978-3-902737-00-7, Salzburg, Austria, November 2009, M. Tscheligi et al. (Eds.), ICT&S Center, University of Salzburg

Sik Lányi, C.; Geiszt, Z.; Károlyi, P.; Tilinger A. & Magyar, V. (2006). Virtual Reality in Special Needs Early Education. *The International Journal of Virtual Reality*, 5, 4, (December 2006) pp. 55-68, ISSN 1081-1451

Stanney, K.M.; Mourant, R.R. & Kennedy R.S. (1998). Human Factors Issues in Virtual Environments: A Review of the Literature. *Presence: Teleoperators and Virtual Environments*, 7, 4, (August 1998) pp. 327-351, ISSN 1054-7460

Steg, H.; Strese, H.; Loroff, C.; Hull, J. & Schmidt, S. (2006). *Europe Is Facing a Demographic Challenge. Ambient Assisted Living Offers Solutions*. Ambient Assisted Living - European Overview Report, (March 2006) Berlin, Germany

Steuer, J. (1995). Defining virtual reality: dimensions determining telepresence, In: *Communication in the Age of Virtual Reality*, F. Biocca et al. (Eds.), Lea'S Communication Series, pp. 33-56, ISBN 0-8058-1550-3, L. Erlbaum Associates Inc., Hillsdale, NJ, USA

Tiresias web site. *Guidelines for the design of accessible information and communication technology systems*. Available online: http://www.tiresias.org/research/guidelines/index.htm (last access: August 2010)

VAALID web site. *Accessibility and Usability Validation Framework for AAL Interaction Design Process*. Research Project. 7th EC Framework Programme. Contract n° ICT-2007-224309. Available online: http://www.vaalid-project.org/ (last access: August 2010)

VERITAS web site. *Virtual and Augmented Environments and Realistic User Interactions to Achieve Embedded Accessibility Designs*. 7th EC Framework Programme. Contract n° 247765. Available online: http://veritas-project.eu/ (last access: August 2010)

Villalar, J.L. et al. (2009). *D3.1: Authoring Environment Functional Specification*. VAALID project deliverable. Version 1.0 (June 2009)

WAI web site. *W3C Web Accessibility Initiative*. Available online: http://www.w3.org/WAI/ (last access: August 2010)

Wegge, K.P. & Zimmermann, D. (2007). Accessibility, Usability, Safety, Ergonomics: Concepts, Models, and Differences, In: *Universal Access in Human Computer Interaction. Coping with Diversity*, C. Stephanidis (Ed.), LNCS 4554/2007, pp. 294-301, ISBN 978-3-540-73278-5, Springer Berlin Heidelberg, Germany

Yalon-Chamovitz, S. & Weiss, P.L.T. (2008). Virtual reality as a leisure activity for young adults with physical and intellectual disabilities. *Research in Developmental Disabilities*, 29, 3, (May-June 2008) pp. 273–287, ISSN 0891-4222

19

Common Issues of Virtual Reality in Neuro-Rehabilitation

Man, D.W.K.
Department of Rehabilitation Sciences, The Hong Kong Polytechnic University
Hong Kong, PRC

1. Introduction

Use of virtual reality (VR) has been developing rapidly in the rehabilitation field. The efficacy and efficiency of VR application in either an immersive or a non-immersive type, has been demonstrated for different client groups during the last few decades. This book chapter provides a review of "what, how and why" of virtual reality application for neuro-rehabilitation, with a focus on cognitive rehabilitation. Examples of technology transfer to VR-assessment (such as retrospective and prospective memory assessment) and -intervention for persons with special needs (for examples, everyday memory, community living skills and vocational training skills) will be highlighted. The client groups include persons with stroke, traumatic brain injury, schizophrenia, older adults with mild cognitive impairment and dementia. Ecological validity of VR-test will be discussed in terms of transfer ratio from training to real-life task. Hints in better designing, structuring the content in virtual environment (VE) for navigation, interaction, presence and immersion functions will be outlined. New development including tele-VR rehabilitation, artificial intelligence (AI) application in cognitive rehabilitation in neurological patients and vocational rehabilitation for schizophrenic trainees will be introduced.

2. What is the problem?

Virtual reality has been considered as a cutting-edge technology. Its development is sporadic and can possibly be used in rehabilitation for persons with neurological conditions and those with long-hauled cognitive problems. It is clear the VR has its strengths and "room for expansion", its limitations should not be under-estimated. We need to be cognizant of VR's development in terms of technology advancement, as well as its working mechanism in order to develop evidence-based practice. To a certain extent, the above question has been partially answered, but a lot more to be explored. This chapter may serve as a bridge between what we knew, we know and we will know.

3. What is virtual reality (VR)?

It is a cutting-edge computer technology which has its origins in visually coupled system (Kalawksy, 1993) and formed the basis of the first flight simulator. VR is a computer generated environment. It was based on computer simulation and real-time visual, auditory and touch feedback (Katz et al., 2005). Schultheis and Rizzo (2001) defined it as a way for humans to visualize, manipulate, and interact with computers and extremely complex data. VR could also be viewed as an advanced form of human-computer interface that allowed users to "interact" with and become "immersed" in a computer-generated environment in a naturalistic fashion (Riva, 2002). Characteristics of virtual reality systems include navigation (exploring, orientating), interaction (opportunities to engage in virtual environment or VE), presence (subjective feeling of being present in a simulated environment) and immersion (objective measure –VR platform, technology-based) (Aguinis et al., 2001; Vince, 1998). VR is now being widely applied in many fields including engineering, architecture, design, medicine, education and training. The potential of virtual environments (VEs) in the field of neurological rehabilitation has been noted (Rose et al., 1998).

4. "How VR works?"

Virtual reality can be of two types, immersive and non-immersive. In its immersive form the visual and auditory aspects of the computer generated environment are delivered to the user via visual display units and speakers situated in a head mounted display while tactile sensations can be delivered via data gloves or a body suit. In the non-immersive form of VR the visual aspects of the environment are presented to the user on a PC monitor (or projected onto a large screen) and the auditory array is presented through speaker. Through VR's capacity to control dynamic 3-dimensional, ecologically valid stimulus environments within which behavioral responding can be recorded and measured, it offers clinical assessment and rehabilitation options that are not available with traditional methods (Schultheis, 2001). VR has several advantages including cost- effectiveness and a good match between the current capabilities of VR technology and generalization issues (Rizzo et al., 1997; 1998). In studying the relative advantages of immersive and non-immersive type of VR, it was commented that immersive VR (IVR) applications might cause some side-effects such as motion sickness. It is believed to occur when there is a conflict between perceptions in different sense modalities, e.g., auditory, visual, vestibular, or proprioceptive (Rizzo et al., 1997; Galimberti et al., 2001). Morganti and associates (2006) also suggested the benefits and challenges in VR neurological rehabilitation (See Figure 1).

VR can only work well according to good guidelines in development (Castelnuovo et al., 2003; Munro et al., 2002; Tarr & Warren, 2002). Fidelity, target client characteristics and purpose of assessment or treatment are closely considered. Observers must be able to move freely, and the VR system can respond to his/her actions on close to real time. They will be provided with significant portion of visual view for a sense of "embeddedness", viewing multiple 3D objects with realistically shaded and textured surfaces. Thus accurate representation of the real world (physical fidelity) should be provided. Factors contributing to the users' sense of presence has also been proposed (Weiss et al., 2005). Apart from users' characteristics (age, gender, immersive tendencies, prior experience, and disability), the VR system characteristics (e.g. dimensionality, representation, multimodality, and encumbrance) and VR task characteristics (meaningfulness, realism, and interaction) also contribute to presence (also see Figure 2).

5. Why VR works?

May be it is more important to provide answers to the key question on "Why VR works?" In recent years, several papers on VR efficacy have been published in which the effects of exposure to VR on the activity of the nervous system have been discussed (Pugnetti et al,

VR Application	Benefits	Challenges
Neuro-muscular	• Improve compliance • Fine time resolution • Rehabilitation at home • On-line data gathering	• Equipment cost • Technical expertise • Safety at home • Network bandwidth
Post-stroke	• Engaging/motivation • Repetitive intensive • Adaptable to patient education • Usable in chronic phase • Activities of daily living	• Clinical acceptance • Technical expertise • Abnormal limb configuration • Upper functional population applicability • Cognitive load
Cognitive functions	• More realistic assessment • Reduced therapy cost • Increased safety • Learning transfer	• Equipment cost • Safety at home • Psychological factor

Fig. 1. Benefit/challenges in VR neurological rehabilitation (Adapted from Morganti, 2006)

Key questions	Possible answers
1. Are virtual environments (VEs) useful, effective and efficient in clinical applications?	Evaluations of possible advantages and limits , cost-benefit analysis
2. Do VEs reproduce the physical and perceptual characteristics of real environments?	Attentions to graphics and technical characteristics. Focus on realism and technical issues
3. Do VEs allow users to function in an ecologically valid way?	Attention on cultural and social aspects. Focus on interaction, importance of relationships and context

(Adapted from Castelnuovo et al., 2003)

Fig. 2. Possible issues to consider in designing virtual environments (VEs) (Adapted from Castelnuovo et al., 2003)

1998). Positive effects in functional outcome, transfer of skills and *f*MRI studies have been shown (Bertella et al., 2001; Mcgeorge et al., 2001; Rose et al., 1998; Zhang et al., 2003). One possible explanation would be brain plasticity resulted from environmental stimuli and essential for therapeutic strategies development and for many cerebral disorders. For examples, virtual-reality training environment was suggested to induce cortical organization and associated locomotor recovery in chronic stroke (Sung et al., 2005). VR-based program was used to conduct motor training of affected upper limb in people with hemiparetic stroke. Functional improvements in affected limb were showed in VR group, but not in control group. Cortical reorganization was found in the primary sensorimotor cortex under *f*MRI examination. These findings supported that the effect of VR exposure was not limited to functional gains, but also in the activities in nervous system.

The high training effectiveness of VR in neurological (e.g. Burke et al., 2009; Grealy & Heffernan, 2001) and cognitive rehabilitation (e.g. Dou et al., 2006; Pascoe, 2010; Yip & Man, 2009) had been explained by "environmental enrichment" (EE; Kolb, 1999) that environmental effect was very important to patients' recovery from brain injury. From animal studies, enriched VR environments might stimulate neuroplastic change in the cerebral cortex, enhance learning and problem-solving, and reduce cognitive impairment caused by brain-damage (Rose et al., 1998).This was further evidenced by neuro-imaging studies and psychophysiological studies (McComas & Jayne, 1998). Relatively complex and stimulating environment had better training effect than impoverished environment (Johansson, 2004; Kolb, 1999). Virtual environment thus could offer rich and vivid visual and auditory stimulations. Better training effects were expected as compared to other training strategies on which the application of visual and auditory stimulation was not focused. In addition, the "naturalistic" training environment created by VR matched the principle of learning such as contextual learning (Gordon et al., 2006). The focus on training in real life situation and day-to-day problem had been found to be more effective than training isolated cognitive skills. While real life training may impose potential hazard to both patients and therapists, virtual environment was a good substitution. This is supported by studies that training in virtual environment yielded equivalent training effect as training in real environment (Brooks et al., 1999). Moreover, modern functional imaging technology indicated the activation of hippocampus under functional imaging during virtual navigation (Astur et al., 2005). It means that virtual environment or tasks may produce a similar stimulation to corresponding neural structure just like the real environment does. On the same "learning theory" vein, constructivist therapy for theory of VR learning also suggested that people could learn through first-person, non-symbolic experience. VR allows them to construct knowledge from direct experience by the "perceptual illusion of non mediation" between themselves and the computer. People assimilate knowledge more effectively when they have the freedom to move and engage in self-directed activities within their learning context. VR facilitates the active process of making sense of new information, by creating their own version of reality instead of simply receiving others' view (Mantovani, 2001).

Another possible explanation would be the "transfer of skills to real world". It was suggested that training established association between physical aspects of the task and cognitive organization learnt during task performance resulting in a learnt cognitive response to the task. Thus visual picture may result in more autonomic real world performance, due to possible freeing up cognitive capacity to deal with interfering tasks (Rose et al., 2000). In addition, training skill transfer should be best when training mimics performance as closely as possible virtual reality fulfills the principles for generalization (Lathan et al., 2002). During the design phase, generalization is already a key issue of programming: identification of naturalistic reinforcement, selection of appropriate transfer measurement, use of sufficient examples and repetitions, stimuli common to both the training environment and the example of repetition (Rizzo & Buckwalter, 1997).

When applying VR to cognitive rehabilitation, VR was proposed to be able to reduce the required attentional resource and prevent overload by simplifying the tasks (Grealy et al., 1999). In the learning process, the virtual environment can reduce brain's work load by easier recognition of objects, spatial ordering, large-size environment (Seidel & Chatelier, 1997). Using VR in training may reduce cognitive load by eliminating the need for a trainee to convert two-dimensional training materials into three-dimensional representation, thus enable them to utilize more cognitive resources on learning the task (Johnson & Hyde, 1997).

Last but not the least, use of VR may serve as a motivational factor. Usability and motivational factors seem to be an important reason for the success of computer-based rehabilitation. VR is considered as the more advanced evolution of the relationship between man and computers. VR designers typically aim to create a convincing, engaging, environment in which sense of presence has to be recreated (Priore et al., 2003)

6. VR for assessment and treatment

Presence of an "e-supervisor" through VR may provide a more valid, reliable and less-threatening assessment situation, and may better reinforce/ structure the disabled individual's residual self-management skills in a somewhat familiar, simulated environment. For instance, executive function deficits are revealed only when the individual is alone, or fails to maintain awareness when left unsupervised, but being observed by the VR program. In VR training, responsibility for the activities will be transferred to the patient, including the generalization to the environment of daily life and sustain training efforts and bringing about behavioral changes (Trepagnier, 1999). In the context of cognitive rehabilitation, virtual environment may be valuable when assessment and training in "real-life" situations is made difficult. For instance, brain injured patients' sensory, motor and cognitive disabilities may not allow them to threatening real-life situation, or cause danger by "pre-mature" exposure. It is also suggested that VR-based tests overcome several limitations of traditional paper-and pencil tests, and are at least as sensitive to target cognitive impairments, while providing a richer range of opportunities for measuring behavior (Pugnetti et al., 1998). VR can thus be a useful tool for assessment and treatment in neurological and cognitive rehabilitation. Moreover, different cognitive rehabilitation approaches rest upon the assumption that what is learnt in training transfers to the equivalent real world task. There have been preliminary findings that a clear positive transfer effect from virtual and real training suggests that the cognitive strategy elements and cognitive loads of the training is broadly equivalent (Rose et al., 2000). Moreover, VR has been used in conjunction with traditional therapeutic techniques to promote cognitive and visual perceptual functioning (Cunningham & Krishack, 1999). Virtual reality has proven useful in enhancing human perceptions and thus resulting behaviors, psychological health and well being (Thomas et al., 1996).

6.1 More examples to illustrate

The potential for VR applicable in neuro-rehabilitation and cognitive rehabilitation has been found to be great. For instances, VR has been used in unilateral neglect and hemineglect in stroke (Myers & Bierig, 2000; Tsirlin, et al., 2009), brain injury assessment and rehabilitation (Pugnetti et al., 1998; Rizzo et al., 2000; Rose et al., 2005), physical rehabilitation in stroke (Saposnik, et al., 2010) and spinal cord injury (Kizony et al., 2003), functional evaluation and training (Lee et al., 2003), as well as tele-rehabilitation (Tam et al., 2003; Rizzo, et al., 2004).

There are also precedents for use of VR in memory rehabilitation (Brooks & Rose, 2003), executive dysfunction (Mendozzi et al., 1998), perceptual disorders and learning difficulties (Wann et al., 1997). VR has also been proposed for the relearning of community living skills (Christiansen et al., 1998; Gourlay et al., 2000), as VR environments are precisely controlled, entirely safe environments within which patients' learning outcome and behaviours can be minutely monitored.

More specific examples include the assessment of children with attentional deficits through a virtual classroom (Rizzo, et al, 2002), spatial and episodic memory of brain damaged patients through a virtual town (Spier et al, 2001), prospective memory assessment of stroke through a virtual four-room bungalow (Brooks, et al, 2004), and acquired brain injury through a virtual shopping mall (Man et al., 2010a, under review), evaluating brain injured patients' daily living skills through a simulated kitchen (Zhang et al., 2003).
Recently, there has been memory training in older adults with mild cognitive impairment (MCI) using a virtual model home and a convenience shop (Man et al., 2010b, under review), community living skill training (room crossing, bus-taking, shopping, use of bank services and meeting friends) through a virtual city and a supermarket (da Costa et al., 2000; Tam et al., 2005; Yip & Man, 2009), motivation of stroke survivors through VR leisure program (Reid & Hirji, 2003), virtual play in children with cerebral palsy (Reid, 2004), driving skills training for persons with brain injury (Schultheis & Peterson, 2000). Application to persons with schizophrenia for vocational training using a virtual boutique has also been noted (Tsang & Man, in preparation).

6.2 Artificial intelligence-based virtual reality program

The innovative use of artificial intelligence (AI) techniques such as Case-Based Reasoning has been proposed (Yip & Man, 2010, under review) to develop the VR system allows some flexibility to facilitate individual learning. The main advantage in integrating VR systems with embedded AI software can be the ability of providing instant analysis of the user's behavior. Therefore, immediate feedbacks and assistance can be given to the users in the forms of additional clues and objects in the virtual world. This will allow for individual styles of learning and their relative stages of recovery. A recent development would be an AI based VR system for prospective memory training for shopping skills (Yip & Man, 2010, under review). By altering three parameters, namely number of items in a shopping list (S), number of prospective memory task (P) and level of assistance (A). After gathering the training performance of each trial/session, AI system can plan the level of difficulty in the next session.

7. Conclusion

It is optimistic that application of VR is wide-spreading and feasible for neurological and cognitive rehabilitation. VR can be especially valuable when training in real life situations will be impractical, dangerous, logistically difficult, unduly expensive, and too difficult to control (Rose et al., 2000). VR has the capacity, and greater flexibility, to simulate a greater range of situations and environments as compared to other simulation-based techniques (Aguinis et al., 2001). VR holds people's attention for a longer period of time than other methods because it is immersive, interactive, imaginable and interesting (Albani et al., 2002). Limitations of VR might result in a decreased sense of presence due to heavy and cumbersome headsets, low spatial resolution, narrow field of view that may presently be available in the headsets, primitive methods of force and tactile feedback, inappropriate time lags in tracking performance, induction of stimulator/motion sickness/cyber sickness (Gaggioli, 2001; Priore et al., 2003). Further development depends how we resolve these problematic issues and reduce the technological and financial demand. The initial demonstration of VR using commercial games such as Wii game technology in stroke rehabilitation (Sapnosnik et al., 2010) might be an alternative way to provide VR rehabilitation in motor recovery and possibly more in rehabilitation arena.

8. References

Aguinis, H., Henle, C.A. & Beaty, J.C. (2001). Virtual Reality Technology: A New Tool for Personnel Selection, *International Journal of Selection and Assessment* 9(1/2): 70-83.

Albani, G., Pignatti, R., Bertella, L., Priano, L., Semenza, C. & Molinari, E. (2000). Common daily activities in the virtual environment: a preliminary study in parkinsonian patients, *Neurological Sciences* 23: S49-S50.

Astur, R.S.,Germain, S.A., Baker, E.K., Calhoun,V., Pearlson G.D. & Constable, R.T. (2005). fMRI hippocampal activity during a virtualradial arm maze. *Applied Psychophysiology and Biofeedback*: 30(3), 307-316.

Bertella, L., Marchi, S. & Riva, G. (2001). Virtual environment for topographical orientation (VETO): Clinical rationale and technical characteristics, *Presence, 10*: 440 - 449.

Brooks, B. M., McNeil, J. E., Rose, F. D., Greenwood, R. J., Attree, E. A. & Leadbetter, A. G. (1999). Route learning in a case of amnesia: A preliminary investigation into the efficacy of training in a virtual environment, *Neuropsychological Rehabilitation* 9(1): 63-76.

Brooks, B.M. & Rose, F.D. (2003). The use of virtual reality in memory rehabilitation: current findings and future direction, *Neurorehabilitation* 18: 147-157.

Brooks, B.M., Ross, F,D,Potter, J. Jayawardena, S. & Morling, A. (2004). Assessing stroke patients's prospective memory using virtual reality, *Brain Injury*: 18(4), 391-401.

Burke, J.W., McNeill, M.D.J., Charles, D.K., Morrow, P.J., Crosbie, J.H. & McDonough, S.M. (2009). Optimising engagement for stroke rehabilitation using serious games, *Visual Computer* 25: 1085-1099.

Castelnuovo, G., Priore, Liccione C. L. & Cioffi, G. (2003). Virtual reality based tools for the rehabilitation of cognitive and executive functions: the V-store, *PsychNology Journal* 1(3): 310-325.

Christiansen, C., Abreu, B., Ottenbacher, K., Huffman, K., Masel, B. & Culpepper, R. (1998). Task performance in virtual environments used for cognitive rehabilitation after traumatic brain injury, *Archives of Physical and Medical Rehabilitation* 79: 888-892.

Cunningham, D. & Krishack, M. (1999). Virtual reality promotes visual and cognitive function in rehabilitation, *CyberPsychology and Behavior* 2(1): 19-23.

da Costa, R., de Carvalho, L. & de Aragon, D.F. (2000). Virtual reality in cognitive training, Proceedings of 3rd International Conference on Disability, Virtual Reality & Associated Technology, Alghero, Italy, pp. 221-224.

Dou, Z.L., Ou, N.H., Zheng, J.L., Man, D.W.K. & Tam, S.F. (2006). Computerized errorless learning-based memory rehabilitation for Chinese patients with brain injury: a preliminary quasi-experimental clinical design, *Brain Injury* 20(3): 219-225.

Gaggioli, A. (2001). Using virtual reality in experimental psychology. *In* Riva, R. & Galimberti, C. (ed.), *Towards cyberpsychology: mind, cognition and society in an internet age*, IOS Press, The Netherlands, pp.157-174.

Galimberti, C., Ignazi, S., Vercesi, P. & Riva, G. (2001). Characteristics of interaction and cooperation in immersive and non-immersive virtual environments. *In* Giuseppe, R. & Galimberti, C. (ed.), *Towards cyberpsychology: Mind, cognition and society in the internet age*, IOS Press, The Netherlands, pp. 129-155.

Gordon,W.A., Cantor, J., Ashman, T. & Brown, M. (2006). Treatment of post-TBI executive dysfunction: application of theory to clinical practice, *Journal of Head Trauma Rehabilitation* 21(2): 156-167.

Gourlay. D, Lun, K.C., Lee, Y.N. & Tay, J. (2000). Virtual reality for relearning daily living skills, *International Journal of Medical Informatics* 60(3): 255-261.

Grealy, M. A., & Heffernan, D. (2001). The rehabilitation of brain injured children: the case for including physical exercise and virtual reality, *Pediatric Rehabilitation* 4(2): 41-49.

Grealy, M. A., Johnson, D. A. & Rushton, S. K. (1999). Improving cognitive function after brain injury: the use of exercise and virtual reality, *Archives of physical medicine and rehabilitation* 80: 661-666.

Johnson, S. & Hyde, B.G. (1997). *Training for a rapidly changing workplace: applications of psychological research*, American Psychological Association, Washington.

Kalawksy, R.S. (1993). *The science of virtual reality and virtual environments*. AddisonWesley Publishing Co,UK.

Katz, N., Ring, H., Naveh, Y., Kizony, R., Feintych, U. & Weiss, P. L. (2005). Interactive virtual environment training for safe street crossing of right hemisphere stroke patients with Unilateral Spatial Neglect, *Disability and Rehabilitation 27:* 1235-1243.

Kizony, R., Katz, N., Weiss, P.L. (2003). Adapting an immersive virtual reality system for rehabilitation,*The Journal of Visualization and Computer Animation* 14: 261-268.

Kolb, A. & Kolb D. A. (2001). *Experiential Learning Theory Bibliography 1971-2001*, McBer and Co, Boston.

Lathan, C.E., Tracey, M. R., Sebrechts, M. M., Clawson, D. M. & Higgins, G. A. (2002). Using virtual environments as training simulators: Measuring transfer. *In* Stanney, K. M. (ed.), *Handbook of virtual environments: Design, implementation, and applications,* Erlbaum, Mahwah, NJ, pp. 403-414.

Lee, J.H., Ku, J., Cho, W., Hahn, W.Y., Kim, I.Y., Lee, S.M., Kang, Y., Kim. D, Y., Y. T., Wiederhold, B.K., Wierderhold, M.D. & Kim S.I. (2003). A virtual reality system for the assessment and rehabilitation of the activities of daily living, *CyberPsychology & Behavior* 6(4): 383-388.

Man, D.W.K., Shum, D. & Fleming, J. (2010a, under review). Development and validation of a prospective memory test - a shopping mall.

Man, D.W.K., Chung, J.C.C. & Lee. G.Y.Y. (2010b, under review). Evaluation of a virtual reality-based memory training programme for Hong Kong Chinese older adults with Mild Cognitive Impairment (MCI).

Mantovani, F. (2001). VR learning: potential and challenges for the use of 3D environments in education and training. *In* Riva, R. & Galimberti, C. (ed.), *Towards cyberpsychology: mind, cognition and society in an internet age*, IOS Press, The Netherlands, pp: 207-223.

McComas, J.P. & Jayne, L.M. (1998). Children's transfer of spatial learning from virtual reality to real environments, *CyberPsychology and Behavior* 1(2): 121-128.

McGeorge, P., Phillips, L.H., Crawford, J.R., Garden, S.E., Sala, S.D. & Mine, A.B. et al. (2001). Using virtual environment in the assessment of executive dysfunction, *Presence* 10: 375 - 383.

Mendozzi, L., Motta, A., Barbieri,E., Alpini, D. & Pugnetti, L. (1998). The application of virtual reality to document coping deficits after a stroke: report of a case study, *Cyberpsychology and Behavior* 1:79-91.

Meyer, R.L. & Teresa, A.B. (2000). Virtual reality and left hemineglect: a technology for assessment and therapy, *CyberPsychology & Behavior* 3(3): 465-468.

Morganti, F., Goulene, Gaggioli, A., StrambaBadiale, M. & Giuseppe, R. (2006). Grasping virtual objects: a feasibility study for an enactive interface application in stroke, PsychNology 4(2):181-197.

Munro, A., Breaux, R. & Patrey, J. (2002). Cognitive aspects of virtual environments design. *In* Stanney, K. M. (ed.), *Handbook of virtual environments: design, implementation, and applications*, Erlbaum, Mahwah, NJ, pp. 415-434.

Pascoe, J. (2010). The effect of an enriched environmental language-accessing programme on the reacquisition of language in a person with traumatic brain, *Social Care and Neurodisability* 1(2): 4-15.

Priore, C.L., Castelnuovo, G., Liccione, D. & Liccione, D. (2003). Experience with V-STORE: considerations on presence in virtual environments for effective neuropsychological rehabilitation of executive functions, *CyberPsychology & Behavior* 6(3): 281-287.

Pugnetti, L., Mendozzi, L., Attree, E., Barbieri, E., Brooks, B. BM., Cazzullo, C.L., Motta, A. & Rose, F. D. (1998). Probing memory and executive functions with virtual reality: Past and present studies, *CyberPsychology and Behavior* 1(2):151-161.

Reid, D. (2004). The influence of virtual reality play in children with cerebral palsy, *Occupational Therapy International* 11: 131-144.

Reid, D. & Hirji, T. (2003). The influence of a virtual reality leisure intervention program on the motivation of older adult stroke survivors: a pilot study, *Physical and Occupational Therapy in Geriatrics* 21(4): 1-19.

Riva, G. (2002). Virtual reality for health care: the status of research, *CyberPsychology & Behavior* 5(3): 219-225.

Rizzo, A. A. Buckwalter, J. G. & Neumann, U. (1997). Virtual reality and cognitive rehabilitation: a brief review of the future, *Journal of Head Trauma Rehabilitation* 12(6): 1-15.

Rizzo, A. A., Buckwalter, J.G., Neumann, U., Kesselman, C. & Thiebaux, M. (1998). Basic issues in the application of virtual reality for the assessment and rehabilitation of cognitive impairment and functional disabilities, *CyberPsychology and Behavio*r 1(1): 59-78.

Rizzo, A.A., Buckwalter, J.G., Bowerly, T., van Der Zaag, C., Humphrey, L., Neumann U., Chua, C., Kyriakakis, C., Van Rooyen, A. & Sisemore, D. (2000), The virtual classroom: a virtual reality environment for the assessment and rehabilitation of attention deficits, *CyberPsychology & Behavior* 3(3): 483-499.

Rizzo, A.A., Strickland, D.M. & Bouchard, S. (2004). The challenge of using virtual reality in telerehabilitation, *Telemedicine Journal and e-Health* 10(2): 184-195.

Rose, F. D., Attree, E. A., Brooks, B. M. & Johnson, D. A. (1998). Virtual environments in brain damage rehabilitation: A rationale from basic neuroscience. In Riva, G., Wiederhold, B. K. (eds.), Virtual environments in clinical psychology and neuroscience: Methods and techniques in advanced patient-therapist interaction. *Studies in health technology and informatics, Vol. 58,* IOS Press, Amsterdam, Netherlands Antilles, pp. 233-242.

Rose, F. D., Attree, E. A., Brooks, B. M., Parslow, D. M., Penn, P. R. & Ambihipahan, N. (2000).Training in virtual environments: transfer to real world tasks and equivalence to real task training, *Ergonomics* 43 (4): 494-511.

Rose, F.D., Brooks, B.M, Rizzo, A. (2005). Virtual reality in brain damage rehabilitation: review, *CyberPsychology & Behavior* 8(3): 241-262.

Saposnik, G., Mamdani, M., Baytley, M., Thorpe, K.E., Hall, J., Cohen, L.G. & Teasell, R. (2010). Effectiveness of virtual reality exercises in stroke rehabilitation (EVREST): rationale, design, and protocol of a pilot randomized clinical trial assessing the Wii gaming system. *International Journal of Stroke* 5: 47-51.

Schultheis, M. T. & Rizzo, A.A. (2001). The application of virtual reality technology in rehabilitation, *Rehabilitation Psychology* 46(3): 296-311.

Schultheis, M. & Peterson, W. (2000). *The use of virtual reality technology for assessment of driving skills following acquired brain injury,* RehabWire, 2(8) (http://www.naric.com/RehabWire/000901.html)

Seidel, R. J. & Chatelier, P. R. (1997). Virtual reality, training's future. Plenum Press, New York.

Spier, H.J., Burgess, N., Maguire, E.A., Baxendale, S.A., Harley, T., Thompson, P.J. & O'Keefe, J. (2001). Unilateral temporal lobectomy patients show lateralized topographic and episodic memory deficits in a virtual town, *Brain* 124 (12):2476-2489.

Sung, H. Y., Jang, S.H., Kum, Y.H., Hallet, M., Ahn, S.H., Kwon, Y.H., Kim, J.H. & Lee, M.Y. (2005). Virtual-reality training environment was suggested to induce cortical organization and associated locomotor recovery in chronic stroke, Stroke 36:1166-1171.

Tam, S.F., Man, D.W.K., Chan, Y. P., Sze, P.C. & Wong, C.M. (2005). Evaluation of a computer-assisted, 2-D virtual reality system for training people with intellectual disabilities on how to shop, *Rehabilitation Psychology* 50(3): 285-291.

Tam, S.F., Man, W.K., Hui-Chan, C. W.Y., Lau, A., Yip, B. & Cheung,W. (2003). Evaluating efficacy of tele-cognitive rehabilitation for functional performance, *Occupational Therapy International* 10(1): 20-38.

Tarr, M. J. & Warren, W. H. (2002). Virtual reality in behavioral neuroscience and beyond, *Nature Neuroscience* 5: S1089-S1092.

Thomas, G. P., Fraizer, S., Tittle, A., Babula, M., Ferlic E. & Riggs, E. (1996). Does virtual reality enhance the psychological benefits of exercise? *Proceeding of 1st European Conference on Disability, Virtual Reality & Associated Techology,* Maidenhead, UK, p.5.

Trepagnier, C.G. (1999). Virtual environments for the investigation and rehabilitation of cognitive and perceptual impairments, *Neurorehabilitation* 12(1): 63-72.

Tsang, M., Man, D.W.K. (in preparation). A virtual reality-based vocational training system (VRVTS) for people with schizophrenia in vocational rehabilitation.

Tsirlin, Dupierrix, E., Chokron, S., Coquillart, S. & Ohlmann, T. (2009). Uses of virtual reality for diagnosis, rehabilitation and study of unilateral spatial neglect: review and analysis, *CyberPsychology & Behavior* 12(2): 175-181.

Vince, J. (1998). Essential Virtual Reality Fast: How to Understand the Techniques and Potential of Virtual Reality, Springer-Verlag, New York.

Wann, J.P., Rushton, S.K., Smyth, M. & Jones, D. (1997). Rehabilitative environments for attention and movement disorders. *Communcations of the ACM,* 40, 49-52.

Weiss, P.L., Kizony, R., Feintuch, U. & Kazt, N. (2005). Virtual reality in neurorehabilitation, *Selzer* 2-13: 182-197.

Yip, B. C.B. & Man, D. W.K. (2009). Virtual reality (VR)-based community living skills training for people with acquired brain injury: a pilot study, *Brain Injury 23(13-14: 10107-1026.*

Yip, B. C.B, Man, D. W.K. (2010, under review). Intelligent virtual reality (IVR) cognitive rehabilitation programme for everyday prospective memory training.

Zhang, L., Abreu, B., Seale, G., Masel, B., Christiansen, C. & Ottenbacher, K. (2003). A virtual environment for evaluation of a daily living skill in brain injury rehabilitation: reliability and validity, *Archives of Physical Medicine and Rehabilitation* 84: 1118-1124.

20

Application of Virtual Reality in Neuro-Rehabilitation: an Overview

Lucia F Lucca[1], Antonio Candelieri[1,2] and Loris Pignolo[1]
[1]*S. Anna Institute and RAN - Research in Advanced Neuro-rehabilitation, Crotone,*
[2]*Laboratory of Decision Engineering for Health Care Delivery, University of Cosenza,*
Italy

1. Introduction

Virtual reality (VR) collectively refers to the realistic, albeit artificial environments that are simulated by computer and are experienced by end-users via human-machine interfaces involving multiple sensory channels. In this respect, comparable technical solutions are applicable across different domains such as *cyberspace, virtual environments, teleoperation, telerobotics, augmented reality,* and *synthetic environments.* This makes application possible in a variety of conditions such as (1) design, engineering, manufacturing, and marketing; (2) medicine and healthcare; (3) online monitoring of children and the elderly at home and accident prevention; (4) hazardous operations in extreme or hostile surroundings; and (5) training in military and industrial machine operation, medical teaching and surgery planning/training. An implement of VR with live direct or indirect view of a physical real-world environment whose elements are purportedly enhanced (*augmented*) by virtual computer-generated imagery to meet the viewer needs, Augmented Reality is extensively used in open surgery, virtual endoscopy, radiosurgery, neuropsychological assessment and medical rehabilitation. Application in psychotherapy ranked 3rd among 38 psychotherapy interventions predicted to increase in use in the next future (Gorini & Riva, 2008a; Gorini & Riva, 2008b).
Application in rehabilitation is increasing and expanding; innovative technical solutions in motor and sensory-cognitive rehabilitation result in substantial developments from the available procedures and in prototypes for clinical testing. The clinical results appear promising.

2. Rationale for VR-mediated neuro-rehabilitation

The rationale for application mainly rests on the available evidence that a functional re-arrangement of the injured motor cortex can be induced with the mediation of the mirror neurons system (Eng et al, 2007; Holden, 2005; Rose et al, 2005) or through the subject's motor imagery and learning (Gaggioli et al, 2006). Intensive training (*repetition*) facilitating re-arrangement of cortical function and *motivation* reinforced by *feedback information* about the ongoing improvement are necessary for motor learning to be possible after brain damage. These conditions are easily made available in VR-mediated neuro-rehabilitation paradigms. Motor impairment and recovery can be measured in real time (*e.g.* at the end of each trial or a series of trials) to give the user the knowledge-of-performance (about his/her movement patterns) and knowledge-of-results (about the outcome predictable at each time point during rehabilitation) that reinforce motivation and the training procedure itself. VR allows online or offline feedback, that has been extensively investigated with a general agreement that it improves learning (Bilodeau & Bilodeau, 1962; Gentile, 1972; Khan & Franks, 2000; Newell & Carlton, 1987; Winstein, 1991; Young & Schmidt, 1992; Woldag & Hummelsheim, 2002). The expectation is, that VR-mediated rehabilitation should improve the approach efficacy and the outcome by making tasks easier, less demanding and less tedious/distractive, and more informative for the subject. Interactive VR environments are flexible and customizable for different therapeutic purposes; individual treatments can be personalized in order to facilitate movement retraining, to force the user to focus on the task key elements, and to facilitate transfer of motor patters learned in VR environments to the real world.

3. Studies

3.1 VR in the upper limb motor rehabilitation

VR was first applied in the rehabilitation of the paretic upper-limb after stroke in a setting designed to promote motor (re)learning for different movements (hand, elbow and shoulder) and functional tasks or goals (Holden et al, 1999). The approach implemented a learning-by-imitation paradigm through three components: a motion tracking device to record the trajectories to be performed in the VR environment, a desktop computer display and a VR editing software specifically developed to create suitable 3D-simulated tasks at varying level of complexity. Once the scenario had been defined, the programmed motor learning tasks to be performed within the virtual environment were stored into the motion tracking device. Patients were then requested to reproduce the trajectories set by the *virtual teacher* or to devise appropriate trajectories in the absence of it, while the upper limb movements were monitored by the *virtual teacher*, displayed in real time and recorded. The approach also assessed the degree of matching between the *virtual teacher* and the patient's trajectories and provided trainer and trainee with a measure of each trial efficency. In a pilot study (Holden et al, 1999), two chronic patients with massive stroke were trained on a reach-and-grasp task involving shoulder flexion, elbow extension and forearm supination at six increasing levels of complexity. Efficacy was assessed through a 3D kinematic reach test performed in the real world before and after VR-supported rehabilitation; the Fugl-Meyer Test of Motor Recovery for Stroke test (Fugl-Meyer et al, 1975) and the motor task section of the Structured Assessment of Independent Living Skills (SAILS) test of UE function (Mahurin et al, 1991) were used for clinical evaluation. The patients were able to export the abilities learned in VR to the real world and to similar but untrained activities, but hand orientation proved difficult to learn. In successive studies (Holden et al, 2001; Holden et al, 2002), information about the specific (as measured in real tasks designed to evaluate generalization in space, gravitoinertial force, combined spatial/gravitoinertial force, and in tasks requiring novel recombination of trained movement elements, and control tasks with untrained elements) and non-specific (as measured by variations in motor recovery tests after VR-supported training activity) motor generalization was used to measure in detail the ability to transfer to the real world what learned in VR. Patients improved in three standard clinical tests of function, even if practicing in two movements only during VR training. It was suggested that VR-mediated rehabilitation is an effective and efficient approach to (re)train a set of basic tasks with upgrading to a wide variety of skilled movements (Holden, 2005).

Piron et al. (2005) replicated these results in a study on 50 patients with impaired upper limb motion after stroke. The VR-supported rehabilitation system included a virtual environment (a

PC workstation with a wall screen), a motion tracking device and the dedicated software for editing 3D-scenarios in a learning-by-imitation rehabilitation process with a *virtual teacher*. Therapists set the virtual scenarios characteristics and the motor training complexity to match each patient's motor impairment and rehabilitation protocol, set the starting position, target location and orientation, designed simple/complex tasks, added or removed non-pertinent virtual objects (distractive elements) to increase/reduce the task level of difficulty, recorded trajectory of the desired movement to be (re)learned by the subject, with *the virtual teacher* visible or hidden as advisable. The degree of motor impairment or recovery and the attained levels of autonomy in daily living activities were measured by the Fugel-Meyer (FM) UE score and the Functional Independence Measure scale (FIM) before and after the therapy, and by means of kinematic measures such as the movement morphology and mean duration and speed. Improvement was observed in the FM UE and FIM mean scores (with 15% and 6% increases, respectively) and in the movement mean duration (18%) and speed (23%), with better regularity of trajectories. Improvements do not appear to have been influenced by age, time since stroke or site of brain damage, as already noted in previous studies (Jeffery & Good, 1995; Johnston et al, 1992; Bagg et al, 2002; Tangeman et al, 1990; Dam et al, 1993). Instead, the severity of impairment was crucial for the outcome and a severe initial impairment was more difficult to rehabilitate. Comparison between the degrees of recovery attained after standard or VR-reinforced learning in two randomly assigned post-stroke patient groups (Turolla et al, 2007) showed significantly increased FM UE scores in all 30 patients, but improvement was greater after VR-supported therapy. The different outcome was ascribed, at least in part, to the feedback information about knowledge-of-results and knowledge-of-performance provided by the system (Todorov et al, 1997; Schmidt & Young, 1991; Winstein et al, 1996) and to the reinforced learning provided by the VR-based rehabilitation approach (Barto, 1994; Doya, 2000; Fagg & Arbib, 1992; Rummelhart et al, 1986).

3.2 VR in the lower limb motor rehabilitation

Several VR applications were designed to recover efficient walking in patients with lower limb motor impairment after stroke (Deutsch et al, 2002 and Deutsch et al, 2004). Fung, et al. (Fung, et al 2004, 2006), performed studies on gait training by using a treadmill mounted on a 6-degree-of-freedom motion platform with a motion-coupled VR environment. The system provided the unique feature of simulated turning within the environment; also provided auditory and visual cues as positive/negative feedback. Subjects were required to wear 3D stereo glasses to visualize the virtual environment. Test results from this project demonstrated improved gait speed with training. More recently, Mirelman et al. studied the effects on impaired gait kinetics of robot-assisted rehabilitation with or without VR support (Mirelman et al, 2007). Subjects in the two subgroups were trained with the same exercises; requested movements were inversion and eversion, dorsiflexion and plantar flexion, or combinations of these. A motion capture system was used to measure movements in association with a force-feedback system permitting navigation within a virtual environment displayed on a computer screen. Gait was estimated at baseline, one week after the training session, and three months after end of the therapy. Feedback information was provided directly by the system to the patients treated in the VR setting and by the therapist to those undergoing rehabilitation withouth VR support. Both groups improved, but patients treated with VR support did better, with increased ankle strenght at the end of treatment and at follow-up. Patients undergoing robotic- assisted rehabilitation without VR support reported fatigue earlier.

Park and colleagues (Park et al, 2007) developed a VR system for motor rehabilitation with a PC camera and two markers of movement in a very simple virtual scenario with a crossing-stepping stone task. The success rate in 9 hemiplegic patients with stiff-knee gait after stroke was computed as the ratio of successful trials to the total gait cycles, with a ~30% improvement after treatment.

3.3 VR and telemedicine: the upper limb tele-rehabilitation

VR settings are usable in the transfer of available occupational treatments to a platform for rehabilitation at home, with remote control by therapist. Broeren and coworkers have emphasized the reduced labor, logistics and costs of the state-of art web-based video/audio systems for telemedicine and tested their protocol in a case study, with VR associated to the haptic force feedback necessary for VR object manipulation. The hand fine dexterity and grip improved after treatment (Broeren et al, 2002). More recently, Trotti and colleagues proposed VR-supported training as an integration of the conventional rehabilitation protocols (Trotti et al, 2009). They used kinematics indexes (such as movement execution time and precision) and validated clinical scales, such as Nine-Hole Peg Test (NHPT) (Mathiowetz, 1985), Frenchay Arm Test (FAT) (Heller, 1987), Medical Research Council (MRC) (Florence, 1992), Motricity Index (MI) (Bohannon, 1999), and the Motor Evaluation Scale for Upper extremity in Stroke Patients (MESUPES) (Van de Winckel, 2006) to measure the upper limb impairment in a patient with stroke before and after therapy with VR-supported upper limb rehabilitation. Kinematic analysis and most clinical scales (MRC of fingers, MESUPES and NHPT time, but not MI and FAT) showed a decrease in movement execution time and increase in precision, with improved muscle strenght and movement control (Trotti et al, 2009).
VR-mediated telerehabilitation was further investigated (Piron et al, 2009) by comparing two groups (18 subjects each) of patients with stroke treated for four weeks by a VR-assisted rehabilitation program operated through Internet or by conventional therapy. Motor impairment was assessed one month before, at the beginning and end of therapy, and one month later by means of the Fugl-Meyer Upper Extremity (FM EU), Abilhand (Penta et al, 2001) and Ashworth (Bohannon & Smith, 1987) scales. The setting included a *virtual teacher* showing the correct trajectories as set by the therapist in association with the patient's actual movement. The knowledge-of-performance was provided via videoconference. No differences were observed when comparing the assessments one month before and at beginning of therapy, but both groups improved after therapy and the improvement was evident also one month after the end of therapy. The FM UE showed better recovery for patients treated through VR-based telerehabilitation.

4. Systems and applications

4.1 Systems and applications for VR-supported upper limb rehabilitation

A VR system purported to measure the impairment in speed, strength, fractionation and range of fingers movements was designed to be distributed over three sites connected via Internet (for rehabilitation, data storage and data access, respectively) (Boian et al, 2002). At the rehabilitation site, the system featured a workstation and two sensing (cyber and haptic) gloves; the data storage site organized the information acquired during the VR-supported rehabilitation; open access to data was through Internet. An algorithm was implemented to increase or decrease according to the achieved performance the difficulty of the target task. The system was tested in a pilot study on 4 patients with stroke. A screen provided the patients with knowledge-of-results and performance (feedback) through a transparent hand

representing the target and numerical scores about the trial execution. Trained patients achieved various degrees of improvement, with a good retention in gains and a positive evaluation of the system both by patients and therapists. A virtual tabletop environment for the upper limb rehabilitation after traumatic brain injury was developed (Wilson et al, 2007) to measure the residual function and kinematic markers like speed, precision, distance, accuracy of targeting. The system was innovative because flexible, automated, and relatively inexpensive, with components specifically designed to be user-friendly: LCD panels easy to carry and reducing the set-up time were favored; the virtual environment was displayed on the LCD panel placed horizontally on a tabletop surface, and users could interact with the system by moving sensing-objects over it; knowledge of results was provided to the patient via another LCD panel. Distractive elements appeared on the LCD to increase or decrease the task difficulty. Low-cost implements, such as commercial game controllers and marker tracking were used. Wilson and coworkers suggested that psychometric measures should be preferred in the future and predicted broad application in assessing movement impairment after stroke and ischemic or traumatic brain damage or in movement disorders (e.g. Parkinson or Huntington's diseases).
Therapy WREX (T-WREX) was designed by Reinkensmeyer and Housman (2007) for the hand and arm rehabilitation after stroke to make rehabilitation possible also in the absence of the therapist, with exercises mimiking the daily living activities in VR environment and a feedback information procedure. The system featured a passive gravity-balancing orthosis based on the Wilmington Robotic Esoskeleton (WREX) (Rahman et al, 2007), a hand grip sensor and the software needed for VR and performance evaluation, but was not a robotics/VR integration because WREX assisted patients only against gravity and by elastic bands. It focused on the re-training of function on a plane, therefore displaying the movement on the plane of interest. The system bypassed the problems of 3D complexity, but limitated the movements to be re-learned. Most patients nevertheless found T-WREX less boring than conventional therapy and their progress during rehabilitation easier to track. Reiteration of motor training by T-WREX reduced motor impairment (as measured by the Fugl-Meyer scale) in a preliminary randomized controlled study (Reinkensmaeyer & Housman, 2007).

4.2 Low-cost and open source systems for VR-supported tele-rehabilitation

Interest on tele-rehabilitation as a possible alternative to the traditional treatment of inpatients in hospital increased in recent years with the increment of costs and commitment by the private and public healthcare. Sugarman and colleagues assumed it is impossible for the therapist to monitor patients performing rehabilitation at home, emphasized the therapist's role in motivating the patient and the need of efficient communication between the therapist and patients at any time and place, including home (Sugarman et al, 2006). Approaches combining VR and mechanical devices for rehabilitation (Fasoli et al, 2004; Coote & Sokes, 2005; Broeren et al, 2004; Reinkensmeyer et al, 2002; Jadhav & Krovi, 2004) appear encouraging, but the systems specifically developed for these purposes have high costs. In alternative, Sugarman and colleagues adopted a commercial feedback joystick in association with a specifically designed armrest and a PC with Internet connection. Their proposed VR solution could be operated in two different modes: stand-alone or cooperative. In the former, patients exercised at home without Internet connection; in the latter, the patient and therapist were online and the therapist could monitor and tutor the patient performing.

Open-source tools stand as inexpensive alternatives to promote the development of user-friendly, customized VR systems for rehabilitation and are being tested. Riva and colleagues proposed NeuroVR, a cost-free software platform based on open-source available solutions (Riva et al, 2009). The platform allows users with no technical background to easily interface with the virtual environment and modify the scenario according to the specific needs; 2D and 3D objects may be selected from a database and incorporated into the virtual environment by a user-friendly graphical interface; therapists can supplement the database with pictures of persons or objects belonging to the patient's real life and suitable as stimuli or stressors. A further improvement of NeuroVR (Algeri et al, 2009) was the integration with the open-source software CamSpace aimed at developing a cost-free system overcoming some operational limits related to the joypad, mouse or keyboard use. A further extention was CamSpace 7, through which patients can interact with the virtual environment simply by hand or body movements and allowing design both motor and balance rehabilitation exercises (Weiss Tamar et al, 2004). NeuroVR is also in use in the treatment of a variety of conditions, including obesity (Riva et al, 2006), alcohol abuse (Gatti et al, 2008), anxiety disorders (Gorini & Riva, 2008a,b), and in the rehabilitation of cognitive impairment (Morganti et al, 2007).

4.3 VR-based systems for sensory, cognitive and behavioural rehabilitation

The traditional protocols for cognitive-behavioural rehabilitation are mostly based on imaginary or *in-vivo* exposure; the Virtual Reality Exposure Therapy (VRET) is an altered form of behavioral therapy and may be a possible alternative to standard in vivo exposure, for example in the therapy of anxiety disorders (Krijn, 2004). VR allows immersive or semi-immersive interaction with virtual environments incorporating suitable stimuli, therefore reducing the limits of representing real tools to brain damaged subjects unable to chategorize (Rizzo et al, 2005). VR systems are today in use in the management of patient with stroke, to support cognitive rehabilitation by providing logopaedic help and reducing the somatic effects of paresis though a multi-sensorial brain stimulation approach (Probosz et al, 2009). Marusan and colleagues (Marusan et al, 2006) and other groups (Rose et al, 1998; Tomasino & Rumiati, 2004) suggested the use of mental rotation paradigms (Shepard & Metzler, 1971) in VR neuro-rehabilitation setting, with extention to the brain injured of the use of mental images that is critical in cognitive tasks involving memory, reasoning and problem solving in everyday life (Zacks et al, 1999; Podzebenko et al, 2005). Marusan and coworkers main goal was to develop a VR-based technical solution for neurorehabilitation of traumatic brain injury (TBI) patients; their secondary goal was ease of use for the patient at home via common technical supports such as PC, mouse and keyboard devices to be available anywhere and anytime without special equipment (3D glasses, gloves, suits, etc) requiring expert help.

Koenig and colleagues (Koenig et al, 2009) proposed a VR approach to assess the patient's performance in tasks of way-finding and in the training of spatial orientation skills in brain injured patients. Several standardized outcome measures were used: Money Road-Map Test (Money et al, 1965), Zoo Test (Wilson et al, 1996), Object Perspective Taking Test (Kozhevnikoy & Hegarty, 2001), Virtual Reality Navigation Task, Real-World Navigation Task, Santa Barbara Sense of Direction Scale (Hegarty et al, 2002), Mental Rotation Task, Card Rotation Task, and Surface Development Task (Ekstrom et al, 1976). Complexity was increased with the protocol and subject's progressing in order to promote generalization of regained abilities, with the addition of naturalistic features or constraints (*e.g.* locked doors or detours) and varying conditions of illumination. Performance was evaluated as navigation errors, timing and orientation behaviour.

Interactive multimodal rehabilitation may enhance the efficacy of cognitive rehabilitation after cerebrovascular brain injury. Salva and co-workers (Salva et al, 2009) have developed a novel Mixed Reality (MR) approach reportedly promoting neural plasticity. An evolution of classical VR merging and overlapping virtual and real environments, MR creates an augmented reality without losing contact with the real setting and preserving sensory feedback and interaction without any requirement for adaptation. The Mixed Reality Rehabilitation System (MRRS) was meant to avoid crucial problems in the traditional therapy such as the limitations in resources and decreasing levels of participation and interest. Pilot studies seem to indicate remarkable potentialities in neurorehabilitation though MR, mostly by allowing patients to interact with and experience both the virtual scenario and the real world (Standen and Brown, 2005). Also based on Augmented Reality tools is GenVirtual (Correa et al, 2007), a musical game helping patients in colors and sounds memorization tasks. The approach proved acceptable to the patient with cognitive deficits and useful in rehabilitation, inexpensive and applicable to integrate standard rehabilitation in hospital as well as at home.

5. Comment

VR stands as a potentially useful tool for diagnosis, therapy, education and training. Application in neuro-rehabilitation is still unsystematic and limited, yet there is evidence supporting its applicability in a variety of paradigms that can allow the patients avoid the real world challenges in a secure environment and to freely explore, experiment, feel, live and experience feelings and thoughts. Motor rehabilitation has been applied in patients with acquired brain injury with some success, but application in the rehabilitation of these subjects' cognitive deficits remains unsystematic and its potentialities appear high but still undocumented.

The differences among studies in the design, procedures for data acquisition and analyses, and criteria of admission do not allow a direct comparison of the efficacy of different VR setups. VR is a new tool for upper limb stroke rehabilitation, but evidence about its efficacy is still regarded as weak to moderate (Henderson, 2007). Application of VR procedures in the rehabilitation of the upper limb emphasizes the lack of agreed criteria to assess the kinetics and kinetic impairment in neurology and these limitations are only in part compensated for by the motor scales in use in neuro-rehabilitation (Lucca, 2009). The training conditions to be favored in the clinical practice and/or in research on large populations therefore remain unidentified. Systematic neuroimaging research is today mandatory for the cortical functional re-arrangement to be correlated in full detail with the neurorehabilitation clinical effects irrespective of the applied rehabilitative procedures. It would allow document the cortical functional damage as well as the efficacy of training. In this prospective, today's limits in the long-term efficacy of VR rehabilitation procedures may challenge physicians, physiatrists, psychologists and bio-engineers without questioning the potentialities of the approach.

Rehabilitation needs to be intensive over long periods of time and requires dedicated staff, resources and logistics. The duration of the rehabilitation effects after discontinuing VR training is crucial and should be determined in controlled follow-up studies, which remain unsystematic to date. This discrepancy contrasts with the increased availability of advanced and limited-cost technologies and the need for reliable criteria to help define cost/benefit ratios and priorities in private and public health facilities. VR would also mediate between the therapist's and the real world and is forseen as possibly promoting the patients' earlier

AUTHOR,YEAR	PATIENT	INTERVENTION
UPPER LIMB REHABILITATION		
Holden et al, 1999	Stroke	Learning-by-imitation paradigm.
Holden et al, 2002	Stroke	Motor generalization: ability to transfer to the real world what learned in VR.
Boian et al, 2002	Stroke	VR system and two sensing cyber and haptic gloves) measures the impairment in speed, strength, fractionation and range of fingers movements. Difficulty of the target task increases or decreases according to the achieved performance.
Piron et al, 2005	Stroke	Different level of difficulty: the motor training complexity to match each patient's motor impairment and rehabilitation protocol.
Wilson et al, 2007	Traumatic brain inj.	A virtual tabletop environment to measure the residual function and kinematic markers.
Reinkensmeyer and Housman, 2007	Stroke	Hand and arm rehabilitation in absence of the therapist, with exercises mimiking the daily living activities in VR environment. The system featured a passive gravity-balancing orthosis.
LOWER LIMB REHABILITATION		
Fung et al, 2004, 2006	Stroke	Gait training by using a treadmill mounted on a 6-degree-of-freedom motion platform with a motion-coupled VR environment. Auditory and visual cues as positive/negative feedback.
Mirelman et al, 2007	Stroke	Robot-assisted rehabilitation with or without VR support Force-feedback system permits navigation within a virtual environment displayed on a computer screen.
Park et al, 2007	Stroke	VR system for motor rehabilitation in a very simple virtual scenario with a crossing-stepping stone task.
COGNITIVE REHABILITATION		
Rizzo et al, 2005	Brain injury	VR immersive or semi-immersive with suitable stimuli, reduces the limits of representing real tools to subjects unable to chategorize.
Marusan et al, 2006	Traumati cbrain inj.	Use of mental rotation paradigms in VR neuro-rehabilitation setting.
Correa et al, 2007	Brain injury	Augmented Reality: a musical game helping patients in colors and sounds memorization tasks.
Probosz et al, 2009	Stroke	VR systems support cognitive rehabilitation by providing logopaedic help and reducing the somatic effects of paresis though a multi-sensorial brain stimulation approach.
Koenig et al.,2009	Brain injury	VR approach to assess the patient's performance in tasks of way-finding and in the training of spatial orientation skills.

Table 1. Summary of studies

discharge from hospital and transfer to programs for rehabilitation at home, with improved quality of life and clinical outcome.
In general, the scenario would motivate research to achieve widespread application, possibly by making home rehabilitation under remote control a realistic option and by extending VR use to the computer or technology illiterate.

6. References

Algeri, D., Carelli, L., Gaggioli, A. and Riva, G. (2009). A free tool for motor rehabilitation: NeuroVR 1.5 with CamSpace. In *Annual Review of Cybertherapy and Telemedicine*, 7. 1554-8716

Bagg, S., Paris Pombo, A. and Hopman, W. (2002). Effect of age on functional outcomes after stroke rehabilitation. *Stroke*, 33, 179-185. 0039-2499

Barto, A. G. (1994). Reinforcement learning control. *Curr Opin Neurobiol*, 4, 888-893. 0959-4388

Bilodeau, E. A. & Bilodeau, I. M. (1962). Motor skills learning. *Annual Reviews of Psychology*, 13, 243–280. 0066-4308

Boian, R., Sharma, A., Han, C., Merians, A., Burdea, G., Adamovich, S., Recce, M., Tremaine, M. and Poizner, H. (2002). Virtual-reality-based post-stroke hand rehabilitation. *In Proceedings of Medicine Meets Virtual Reality 2002 Conference*, IOS Press, Newport Beach CA, January 23-26 2020, 64-70.

Bohannon, R. W., Smith, M. B. (1987). Interrater reliability of a modified Ashworth scale of muscle spasticity. *Phys Ther*, 67, 2, 206-7. 1538-6724

Bohannon, R. W. (1999). Motricity Index Scores are Valid Indicators of Paretic Upper Extremity Strength Following Stroke. *Journal of Physical Therapy Science*, 11, 59-61. 09155287

Broeren, J., Georgsson, M., Rydmark, M. and Stibrant Sunnerhagen, K. (2002). Virtual reality in stroke rehabilitation with the assistance of haptics and telemedicine. *In Proc. 4th Intl Conf. Disability, Virtual Reality & Assoc. Tech., Veszprém, Hungary. ICDVRAT/University of Reading*, UK; ISBN 07 049 11 43 4

Broeren, J., Rydmark, M. and Sunnerhagen, K. S. (2004). Virtual reality and haptics as a training device for movement rehabilitation after stroke: a single case-study. *Archives of Physical Medicine and Rehabilitation*, 85, 1247-1250. 0003-9993

Coote, S. and Stokes, E. K. (2005). Effect of robot-mediated therapy on upper extremity dysfunction post stroke – a single case study. *Physiotheraphy*, 91, 250-256. 0031-9406

Correa, A. G. D., De Assis, G. A., do Nascimento, M., Ficheman, I., and de Deus Lopes, R. (2007). GenVirtual: An augmented reality musical game for cognitive and motor rehabilitation. *In Proceedings of Virtual Rehabilitation Conference, IEEE*, 27-29 Sept. 2007; 1–6.

Dam, M., Tonin, P. Casson, S., Ermani, M., Pizzolato, G., Iaia, V. and Battistin, L. (1993). The effects of long-term rehabilitation therapy on poststroke hemiplegic patients. *Stroke*, 24, 1186-1191. 0039-2499

Deutsch, J. E., Merians, A. S., Adamovich, S., Poizner, H. and Burdea, G. C. (2002). Development and application of virtual reality technology to improve hand use and gait of individuals post-stroke. *Restorative Neurology and Neuroscience*, 20, 1-16. 0922-6028

Deutsch, J. E., Paserchia, C., Vecchione, C., Mirelman, A., Lewis, J. E., Boian, R. and Burdea, G. (2004). Improved Gait and Elevation Speed of Individuals Post-Stroke After Lower Extremity Training In Virtual Environments. *JNPT*, 28, 4, 185-186. 1557-0576

Doya, K. (2000). Complementary roles of basal ganglia and cerebellum in learning and motor control. *Curr Opinion Neurolbiol*, 10, 732-739. 0959-4388

Ekstrom, R. B., French, J. W., Harman, H. H. and Dermen, D. (1976). Kit of factor-referenced cognitive tests. Educational Testing Service, Princeton, NJ.

Eng K., Siekierka E., Pyk P., Chevrier E., Hauser Y., Cameirao M., Holper L., Hägni K., Zimmerli L., Duff A., Schuster C., Bassetti C., Verschure P. & Kiper D. Interactive visuo-moto therapy system for stroke rehabilitation. *Medical & Biological Engineering & Computing 2007*, September, 45, 9, 901-907

Fagg, A. H. and Arbib M. A. (1992). A model of primate visual-motor conditional learning. *Adaptive Behavior*, 1, 3-37. 1059-7123

Fasoli, S. E., Krebs, H. I. and Hogan, N. (2004). Robotic technology and stroke rehabilitation: translating research into practice. *Topics in stroke Rehabilitation*, 11, 11-19. 1074-9357

Florence, J. M. (1992). Intrarater reliability of manual muscle test (Medical Research Council scale) grades in Duchenne's muscular dystrophy. *Phys Ther*, 72, 115-122. 1538-6724

Fugl-Meyer, A.R., Jaasko, L., Leyman, I., Olsson S & Steglind S. (1975). The post-stroke hemiplegic patient: a method for evaluation of physical performance. *Scandanavian Journal of Rehabilitation*, 7, 13–31. 1650-1977

Fung, J., Malouin, F., McFadyen, B. J., Comeau, F., Lamontagne, A., Chapdelaine, S., Beaudoin, C., Laurendeau, D., Hughey, L. and Richards, C. L. (2004). Locomotor rehabilitation in a complex virtual environment. *EMBC 2004 Conference Proceedings 26th Annual International Conference*. 4859-4861

Fung, J., Richards, C. L., Malouin, F., McFadyen, B. J. and Lamontagne, A. (2006). A Treadmill and Motion Coupled Virtual Reality System for Gait Training Post Stroke. *CyberPsychology Behavior*. 9, 2, 157-162. 2152-2715

Gaggioli, A., Meneghini, A., Morganti, F., Alcaniz, M. & Riva, G. (2006). A strategy for computer-assisted mental practice in stroke rehabilitation. *Neurorehabilitation and Neural Repair*. 20, 4, 503-507. 1545-9683

Gatti, E., Massari, R., Saccelli, C., Lops, T., Gatti, R. and Riva, G. (2008). Why do you drink? Virtual reality a san experimental medium for the assessment of alcohol-dependent individuals. *Stud Health Technol Inform*, 132, 232-137. 0926-9630

Gentile, A. M. (1972). A working model of skill acquisition with application to teaching. *Quest*, 17, 3-23. 1011-226X

Gorini, A. and Riva, G. (2008a). Virtual reality in anxiety disorders: the past and the future. *Expert Review of Neurotherapeutics*, 8, 2, 215-233. 1473-7175

Gorini, A. and Riva, G. (2008b). The potential of Virtual Reality as anxiety management tool: a randomized controlled study in a sample of patients affected by Generalized Anxiety Disorder. *Trials*, 9, 25. 1745-6215

Hegarty, M., Richardson, A. E., Montello, D. R., Lovelace, K. and Subbiah, I. (2002). Development of a selfreport measure of environmental spatial ability. *Intelligence*, 30, 425-447. 0160-2896

Heller, A. (1987). Arm function after stroke: measurement and recovery over the first three months. *Journal of Neuroloy, Neurosurgery, and Psychiatry*, 50, 714-719. 0022-3050

Henderson, A., Korner-Bitensky, N., Levin M. (2007). Review Virtual reality in stroke rehabilitation: a systematic review of its effectiveness for upper limb motor recovery. *Top Stroke Rehabil*, 14, 2. 52-61. 17517575

Holden, M.K., Todorov, E., Callahan, J. & Bizzi E. (1999). Virtual environment training improves motor performance in two patients with stroke: case report. *Neurology Report*. 23, 57–67. ISSN 1085-049X

Holden, M.K., Dyar, T., Callahan, J., et al. (2001). Quantitative assessment of motor generalization in the real world following training in a virtual environment in patients with stroke. *Neurology Report*, 25,129–130.

Holden, M.K., Dyar, T. (2002). Virtual environment training: a new tool for rehabilitation. *Neurology Report*. 26, 62–71.

Holden, M., Dyar, T.A., Schwamm, L., et al. (2005). Virtual-environment based telerehabilitation in patients with stroke. *Presence: Teleoperat Virtual Environ*. 14(2), 214-233.

Holden, M. (2005). Virtual enviroments for motor rehabilitation: review. *Cyberpsychol Behav* 8, 3, 187-211, 10949313

Jadhav, C. G. and Krovi, V. (2004). A Low-cost framework for individualized interactive telerehabilitation. In *26th Annual International Conference in IEEE Engineering in Medicine and Biology Society (EMBS)*, San Francisco.

Jeffery, D. R. and Good, D. C. (1995). Rehabilitation of the stroke patient. *Curr. Opin. Neurol.*, 8, 62-68, 1473-6551

Johnston, M. V., Kirshblum, S. Zorowitz, R. and Shiflett, S. C. (1992). Prediction of outcomes following rehabilitation of stroke patients. *Neuro. Rehabil.*, 2, 4, 72-97. 1053-8135

Khan, M. A. & Franks, I. M. (2000). The effect of practice on component submovements is dependent on the availability of visual feedback. *J. Motor Behav.*, 32, 227-240. 0022-2895

Koenig, S.T., Crucian, G.P., Dalrymple-Alford, J.C., Dünser, A. (2009). Virtual reality rehabilitation of spatial abilities after brain damage. *Stud Health Technol Inform.*, 144, 105-107. 1959-2742

Kozhevnikoy, M. and Hegarty, M. (2001). A dissociation between object-manipulation spatial ability and spatial orientation ability. *Memory and Cognition*, 29, 745–756. 0090-502X

Krijn, M., Emmelkamp, P. M. G., Olafsson, R. P., and Biemond, R. (2004). Virtual reality exposure therapy of anxiety disorders: A review. *Clinical Psychology Review*, 24, (3), 259-281. 1524-5832

Lucca, L.F. (2009). Virtual Reality and motor rehabilitation of the upper limb stroke patients: a generation of progress? *J Rehabil Med*, 41, 1003-1006. 1650-1977

Mahurin, R. K., Debettignies, B. J. & Pirozzolo, F. J. (1991). Structured assessment of independent living skills: preliminary report of a performance measure of functional abilities in dementia. *Journal of Gerontology*. 46, 58–66, 0022-1422

Marusan, M., Kulistak, J. and Zara, J. (2006). Virtual Reality in neurorehabilitation: mental rotation. In *Proceedings of the Third Central European Multimedia and Virtual Reality Conference*. Veszprèm: Pannonian University Press. 77-83. 963 9495 89 1

Mathiowetz, V. (1985). Adult norms for nine hole peg test of manual dexterity. *Occup Ther J Res*. 5, 24-37. 0276-1599

Mirelman, A., Patritti, B. L., Bonato, P. and Deutsch J. E. (2007). Effects of Robot-Virtual Reality Compared with Robot Alone Training on Gait Kinetics of Individuals Post Stroke. *Virtual Rehabilitation*, 65-69, 978-1-4244-1204-4

Money, J., Alexander, D. and Walker, H. T. (1965). A standardized road-map test of direction sense. *Johns Hopkins Press*, Baltimore.

Morganti, F., Gaggioli, A., Strambi, L., Rusconi, M. L. and Riva, G. (2007). A virtual reality extended neuropsychological assessment for topographical disorientation: a feasibility study. *Journal of Neuroengineering and Rehabilitation*, 4, 26. 1743-0003

Newell, K. M. & Carlton, M. J. (1987). Augmented information and acquisitionof isometric tasks. *J. Motor Behav.*, 19, 4-12. 0022-2895

Park, J., Ku, J., Cho, S., Kim, D., Kim, J., Kim, I. Y. and Kim, S. I. Development and Clinical Test of Virtual Reality Rehabilitation Training System for stiff-knee gait of stroke patients. *Virtual Rehabilitation*, 81-81, 978-1-4244-1204-4

Penta, M., Tesio, L., Arnould, C., Zancan, A., Thonnard, J.L. (2001). The ABILHAND Questionnaire as a Measure of Manual Ability in Chronic Stroke Patients Rasch-Based Validation and Relationship to Upper Limb Impairment. *Stroke*. 32, 1627-1634, 0039-2499

Piron, L., Tonin, P., Piccione, F., Iaia, V. and Trivello, E. (2005). Virtual environment training therapy for arm motor rehabilitation. *Presence*, 14, 6, 732–740

Piron, L., Turolla, A., Agostini, M., Zucconi, Cortese, F., Zampolini, M., Zannini, M., Dam, M. and Tonin, P. (2009). Excercises for paretc upper limb after stroke: a combined virtual-reality and telemedicineapproach. *Journal of Rehabilitation Medicine*, 41, 12, 1016-1020, 1650-1977

Podzebenko, K., Egan, G. F. and Watson, J. D. G. (2005). Real and imaginary rotary motion processing: functional parcellation of the human parietal lobe revealed by fMRI. *Journal of Cognitive Neuroscience*, 17, 1, 24-36. 0898-929X

Probosz, K., Wcislo, R., Otfinoski, J. Slota, R., Kitowski, J., Pisula, M. and Sobczyk, A. (2009). A multimedia holistic rehabilitation method for patients after stroke. In *Annual Review of Cybertherapy and Telemedicine*, 7, 261-263. 1554-8716

Rahman, T., Sample, W., Seliktar, R., Scavina, M.T., Clark, A.L., Moran, K., Alexander, M.A. (2007). Design and testing of a functional arm orthosis in patients with neuromuscular diseases. *Neural Systems and Rehabilitation Engineering, IEEE*. 15, (2), 44 - 251. 1534-4320

Reinkensmeyer, D. J., Pang, C. T., Nessler, J. A. and Painter, C. C. (2002). Web based telerehabilitation for the upper extremity after stroke. *IEEE Transactions on Neural Systems and Rehabilitation Engineering*, 10, 102-108. 1534-4320

Reinkensmeyer, D. J., Housman, S. J. (2007). "If I can't do it once, why do it a hundred times?": Connecting volition to movement success in a virtual environment motivates people to exercise the arm after stroke. *Virtual Rehabilitation*, 44-48. 978-1-4244-1204-4

Riva, G., Bacchetta, M., Cesa, G., Conti, S., Castelnuovo, G., Mantovani, F. and Molinari, M. (2006). Is severe obesity a form of addiction? Rationale, clinical approach, and controller clinical trial. *CyberPsychology and Behaviour*, 9, 4, 457-479. 10949313

Riva, G., Carelli, L., Gaggioli, A., Gorini, A., Vigna, C., Algeri, D., Repetto, C., Raspelli, S., Corsi, R., Faletti, G., Vezzadini; L. (2009). NeuroVR 1.5 in Practice: Actual Clinical

Applications of the Open Source VR System. *Annual Review of Cybertherapy and Telemedecine Volume 7, 57-60. ISSN: 1554-8716*

Rizzo, A., Pair, J., McNerney, P. J., Eastlund, E., Manson, B., Gratch, J., Hill, R. and Swartout, B. Development of a VR therapy application for Iraq war military personnel with PTSD. (2005). *Stud Health Technol Inform*, 111, 407-413. 0926-9630

Rose, F. F., Atree, E. A., Brooks, B. M., Johnson, D. A. (1998). Virtual environments in brain damage rehabilitation: a rationale from basic neuroscience. *Virtual environments in clinical Psychology and Neuroscience.* In Giuseppe Riva, Brenda K. Wiederhold, Enrico Molinari (Eds.), Ios Press: Amsterdam, Netherlands.

Rose F. D., Broocks B. M. & Rizzo A. A. (2005). Virtual reality in brain damage rehabilitation: review. *Cyberpsychol Behav.* 8, 3, 241-262, 10949313

Rummelhart, D. E., Hinton, G. E. and Williams, R. J. (1986). Learning internal representations by error propagation. In Parallel distributed processing: explorations in the microstructure of cognition. In Rummelhart D. E. and McClelland J. L. (Eds) Bradford Books/MIT Press, 1, 318-362. Cambridge, Massachusetts.

Salva, A. M., Wiederhold, B. K., Alban, A. J., Huges, C., Smith, E., Fidopiastis, C., and Wiederhold, M. D. (2009). In *Annual Review of Cybertherapy and Telemedicine*, 7, 1554-8716. 1554-8716

Schmidt, R. A. and Young, D. E. (1991). Methodology for motor learning: a paradigm for kinematic feedback. *J Motor Behav*, 23, 13-24. 0022-2895

Shepard, R. N. and Metzler, J. (1971). Mental rotation of three-dimensional objects. *Science*, 171, 701-703. 0036-8075

Standen, P. J. and Brown, D. J. (2005). Virtual Reality in the rehabilitation of people with intellectual disabilities: Review. *CyberPsychology & Behaviour Journal*, 8, 3, 155-159. 10949313

Sugarman, H., Tiran, J., Weisel-Eichler, A. and Dayan, E. (2006). Low-cost Telerehabilitation using force feedback joysticks. In Annual Review of Cybertherapy and Telemedicine, 4, 137-143. 1554-8716

Tangerman, P. T., Banaits, D. A. and Williams, A. K. (1990). Rehabilitation of chronic stroke patients: Changes in functional performance. *Arch. Phys. Med. Rehabil.*, 71, 876-880.

Todorov, E., Shadmehr, R. and Bizzi, E. (1997). Augmented feedback presented in a virtual environment accelerates learning of a difficult motor task. *J Motor Behav*, 29, 147-158. 0022-2895

Tomasino, B. and Rumiati, R. I. (2004). Effects of strategies on mental rotation and hemispheric lateralization: neurophysiological evidence. *Journal of Cognitive Neuroscience*, 16, 5, 878-887. 0898-929X

Trotti, C., Menegoni, F., Baudo, S., Bigoni, M., Galli, M. and Mauro, A. (2009). Virtual Reality for the Upper Limb Motor Training in Stroke: A Case Report. In *Annual Review of Cybertherapy and Telemedicine, 2009.* 7, 257-260. 1554-8716

Turolla, A., Tonin, P., Zucconi, C., Agostini, M., Piccione, F., Dam, M. and Piron, L. (2007). Reinforcement Feedback in Virtual Environment vs Conventional Physical Therapy for arm motor deficit after Stroke. Virtual Rehbilitation, 49-52. 978-1-4244-1204-4

Van de Winckel, A. (2006). Can quality of movement be measured? Rasch analysis and inter-rater reliability of the Motor Evaluation Scale for Upper Extremity in Stroke Patients (MESUPES). *Clin Rehabil*, 20, 871-884. 0269-2155

Weiss Tamar, P., Rand, D., Katz, N., Kizony, R. (2004). Video capture virtul reality as a fleaxible and effective rehabilitation tool. *Journal of Neuroengineering and Rehabilitation*, 1, 12. 1743-0003

Wilson, B. A., Alderman, N., Burgess, P. W., Emslie, H. and Evans, J. J. (1996). Behavioural Assessment of the Dysexecutive Syndrome (BADS). *Thames Valley Test Company*, Bury St. Edmunds.

Wilson, P.H., Thomas, P.R., Shum, D., Duckworth, J., Gugliemetti, M., Rudolph, H., Mumford, N., and Eldridge, R. (2007). A virtual tabletop workspace for the assessment of upper limb function in Traumatic Brain Injury (TBI). *Proceedings of the Annual Conference on Virtual Rehabilitation.* Venice, Italy, September 27-29, 2007

Winstein, C. J. (1991). Knowledge of results and motor learning implication for physical therapy. *Phys Ther.*, 71, 140-149. 0190-6011

Winstein, C. J., Pohl, P. S., Cardinale, C., Green, A., Scholtz, L. and Waters, C. S. (1996). Learning a partial-weight-bearing skill: effectiveness of two forms of feedback. *Phys Ther*, 76, 985-993. 1538-6724

Woldag, H. & Hummelsheim, H. (2002). Evidence-based physiotherapeutic concepts for improving arm and hand function in stroke patients. *J. Neurol.*, 249, 518-528, 0340-5354

Young, D. E. & Schmidt, R. A. (1992). Augmented kinematic feedback for motor learning. *J. Motor Behav.*, 24, 261-273, 0022-2895

Zacks, J., Rypma, B., Gabrieli, J. D. E., Tversky, B. and Glover, G. H. (1999). Imagined transformations of bodies: an fRMI investigation. *Neuropsychologia*, 37, 9, 1029-1040. 0028-3932

Part 6

Psychiatric Evaluation and Therapy

21

Virtual Reality in Evidence - Based Psychotherapy

Aurora Szentágotai[1], David Opriş[1] and Daniel David[1,2]
[1]*Babeş-Bolyai University,*
[2]*Mount Sinai School of Medicine,*
[1]*Romania*
[2]*USA*

1. Introduction

In his 1957 *Annual Review of Psychology* article, Winder defines psychotherapy as an interpersonal relationship characterized by the following attributes (p. 309): (1) at least one of the participants (i.e., therapist) is an expert in human relationships; (2) at least one of the participants (i.e., client) displays intrapersonal or interpersonal adjustment problems; (3) the objective of the relationship is to change these maladaptive intrapersonal and interpersonal patterns. Psychotherapy thus circumscribes a group of psychological procedures that are applicable and delivered to individuals with emotional, behavioral and somatic pathology severe enough to be included in clinical diagnostic categories (e.g., the Diagnostic and Statistical Manual of Mental Disorders), and more generic strategies targeted at promoting growth and personal development (David, 2006; Huppert et al., 2006).

Based on their underlying theory of mental health and illness, and on theoretically derived treatment strategies, there are three major paradigms in psychotherapy: the cognitive-behavioral approach, the psychodynamic approach and the humanistic-existential approach; each of these paradigms, in its turn, encompasses a number of theoretically and procedurally individualized schools. Regardless of paradigm, the therapeutic process involves several distinct components, generally described as (David, 2006): (1) assessment; (2) conceptualization; (3) treatment (intervention); (4) therapeutic alliance (relationship).

Over the last years, there has been a dramatic interest in and expansion of psychotherapy research. A large number of studies have focused on the process and outcomes of psychotherapy, approaching them either from the point of view of theoretical and practical elements specific to a particular type of psychotherapy (e.g., cognitive-behavioral psychotherapy) (see Butler et al., 2005) or from a "common factors" view, looking at the non-specific ingredients which make psychotherapy, in general, work (Lambert, 1992; Lambert & Ogles, 2004).

This focus on research and its results have led to the justification of psychotherapy as a legitimate practice. Indeed, hundreds of studies show that psychotherapy works better than no intervention (Kopta et al., 1999), with some forms (e.g., cognitive-behavioral therapy) faring somewhat better than others (see, for example, the National Institute for Health and Clinical Excellence - NICE - guidelines for evidence-based treatments).

Despite the notable progress, research also systematically points to a segment of patients who are non-responsive, prompting professionals to advocate for improving the efficacy of treatments and for exploring and developing new efficient and cost-effective intervention strategies (David et al., 2008). One such direction has been the integration of new technological developments (e.g., computer technology) into the therapeutic process.

The current chapter discusses some of the main applications and advantages of virtual reality (VR) technologies in psychotherapy assessment, intervention and rehabilitation, using cognitive-behavioral therapy (CBT) as a case example. We have chosen to focus on CBT for at least two reasons: it is the best researched form of psychotherapy and it is (both in which research and intervention are concerned) the most likely and frequent "host" for VR intervention strategies.

2. Evidence-based psychotherapy

The number of available psychological treatments has grown exponentially during the last decades; in the field of psychotherapy only, there are over 200 distinct schools and hundreds of individual techniques (Bergin & Garfield, 1994). In a review of the scientific foundations of clinical work, published in 1966, Edward Bordin concluded that *"The present state of our knowledge is such that strong doubts can be expressed about virtually all psychological practices . . . none of them rest upon a firmly verified foundation of knowledge"* (p. 119).

Increasing criticism eventually led to a more firm commitment to research in psychotherapy. In this context, one of the significant changes in the field has been the development, validation and dissemination of evidence-based treatments for various clinical conditions. This movement is consistent with the past 20 years of work in evidence-based medicine, advocating for improved outcomes by informing clinical practice with research data (Woolf & Atkins, 2001). Among the factors that have converged in recent years resulting in the evidence-based movement are an increased understanding of the mechanisms of various disorders, leading to the need of developing interventions specifically targeted at these mechanisms, the improvement of clinical research methodologies, resulting in higher quality data, and the rising costs and inadequacies of health care, prompting governments to advocate for quality and evidence-based services (Huppert et al., 2006).

During the mid 1990s, the Task Force on the Promotion and Dissemination of Psychological Procedures (Society of Clinical Psychology, Division 12, American Psychological Association; APA) published specific guidelines to determine if a treatment was empirically validated (Anthony & Rowa, 2005). A decade later, the APA Presidential Task Force on Evidence-Based Practice defined Evidence-Based Practice in Psychology (EBPP) as *"the integration of the best available research with clinical expertise in the context of patient characteristics, culture and preferences"* and stated that *"the purpose of EBPP is to promote effective psychological practice and enhance public health by applying empirically supported principles of psychological assessment, case formulation, therapeutic relationship, and intervention."* (APA Presidential Task Force on Evidence-Based Practice, 2006). The definition of evidence-based practice argues for the importance of the harmonious integration of the three components (i.e., research, clinical expertise, patient characteristics). Many medical and psychological scientists, however, consider research to be the most important element of this partnership (Goodheart, 2006).

Although the need for data supporting the accountability, efficacy, effectiveness and cost-effectiveness of various assessment and intervention strategies is widely recognized, there are differences in the extent to which professionals emphasize the importance of "evidence" in psychotherapy (Goodheart, 2006). One approach toward the movement (see Wampold and Bahti, 2004) cautions against an excessive focus on treatments, draws attention to the importance of not omitting the therapist and the subjective experience of the client from the equation, and recommends conceptualizations that focus on common factors in psychotherapy and broader research perspectives (Goodheart, 2006).

A different approach is illustrated by Barlow (2004) who, based on the recent advancements and the current status of the field, suggests that a terminological distinction should be made between "psychological treatments" (i.e., supported, manualized treatments, addressed to specific disorders) and "psychotherapy" (i.e., a more generic term that could be eventually dropped, or kept to refer to interventions directed at self-development, adjustment and living problems). David & his colleagues (David, 2004; David, 2006; David & Montgomery, in press) take this approach a step further, suggesting that for a psychotherapy to be considered "evidence-based" it would require a validation not only of its therapeutic package (by efficacy and effectiveness studies), but also of its underlying theory (i.e., the mechanisms of change it proposes).

3. Cognitive-behavioral psychotherapy as a model of evidence-based psychotherapy

Based on the APA established criteria, psychological treatments have been classified into "well-established treatments", "probably efficacious treatments" and "experimental treatments". Cognitive-behavioral psychotherapy is well-represented as a standard treatment for many disorders in the APA list of empirically validated treatments. Although there are several different schools of CBT, they all share the same basic assumptions (Hollon, 1998).

Cognitive-behavioral therapies are based on Albert Ellis' ABCDE model (Ellis, 1962). According to this model, people experience undesirable activating events (A) about which they have rational (i.e., adaptive, healthy or functional) and irrational (i.e., maladaptive, unhealthy or dysfunctional) beliefs (B). These beliefs lead to emotional, behavioral and cognitive consequences (C). Rational beliefs lead to functional consequences, while irrational beliefs lead to dysfunctional consequences. Clients who engage in therapy are encouraged to actively dispute (D) their irrational beliefs and to assimilate more efficient (E) rational beliefs, with a positive impact on their emotional, cognitive, and behavioral responses (Ellis, 1994; David & Szentagotai, 2006).

CBT is an approach to mental health promotion and the treatment of psychological disorders based on the idea that the way an individual thinks about an event determines, to a large extent, the way he or she responds to that event, both in terms of emotions and behavior. According to cognitive theory, dysfunctional beliefs and maladaptive information processing styles are at the heart of emotional disorders, and the therapeutic process is focused on helping the patient learn to identify and correct them in order to reduce unhealthy emotions and behaviors (Hollon, 1998).

The cognitive approach is linked to research in cognitive science, which suggests that information processes are dominated by strategies and heuristics that are conservative in nature and structured to maintain existing beliefs, even in the absence of motivation; the patient therefore suffers as a consequence of these misperceptions, with no underlying motivation of maintaining them (Hollon, 1998). CBT also assumes that most complex human responses (e.g., emotional, cognitive, behavioral) are cognitively penetrable. Cognitive penetrability refers to two things: that a response (e.g., behavior) is an outcome of cognitive processing, be it conscious or unconscious, and that a change in cognition, by various procedures, will induce a change in the expressed response. It is important to note that the limits of cognitive penetrability are the limitations of CBT. In other words, because some basic human responses are not cognitively penetrable (some basic behaviors are genetically determined), they are not typically considered within the realm of CBT (David & Szentagotai, 2006).

CBT is an active, directive, collaborative, structured, problem-oriented, solution-focused and psychoeducational model of treatment (Freeman et al., 2004). Since its development, (Beck, 1972; Ellis, 1962) hundreds of papers examining the theory and practice have been published. Some of these studies have confirmed the main aspects of the original theory, while others have made critical contributions to its evolution. Furthermore, meta-analytic studies substantiate the conclusion that CBT is an empirically supported form of psychotherapy (Butler et al., 2005). Thus, CBT appears to be a gold standard for psychological treatments, as it has a well-defined theory and a well-supported effectiveness (David & Szentagotai, 2006).

Similar to most psychotherapy interventions, CBT involves an assessment (diagnostic) component, a conceptualization component, and an intervention component, all unfolding on the background of the therapeutic alliance (David, 2006).

3.1 Assesment and conceptualization

Psychological formulations view medical and psychological diagnostic reasoning as a process of hypothesis testing; solutions to diagnostic problems are found by generating a successive number of hypotheses and using them to guide subsequent data collection within a complex problem-solving process (Elstein & Scwartz, 2002).

The therapeutic process in CBT begins by an assessment phase that provides a diagnosis and an initial conceptualization, used for treatment planning and clinical decision making. Data is collected from multiple sources, including the clinical interview, structured clinical interviews (e.g., Structured Clinical Interview for DSM Disorders; SCID) self-report scales, self-monitoring forms, reports from family members and other mental health professionals (Pearson, 2008). Diagnosis is important for various reasons, including establishing a common language among scientists and practitioners and the fact that most evidence-based treatments are linked to a diagnosis.

Once a diagnosis has been established, however, the assessment shifts form nomothetic to ideographic, exploring the way a certain diagnosis is manifested in the case of a particular client. The role of the therapist is to translate a nomothetic model (e.g., Beck's cognitive theory of depression) into an individualized one. This process includes the development of a problems list, the evaluation of the patient's environment and characteristics, an individualized analysis of specific problems (e.g., functional analysis of behaviors), of their origins and of the individual's coping strategies. The information is used to develop the case conceptualization, a hypothesis about the psychological mechanisms and other factors that are causing and maintaining the patient's problems. A complete case formulation ties the following elements into a coherent whole (David, 2006; Pearson, 2008):

- clinical diagnosis and specific symptoms and problems
- hypothesized mechanisms causing the symptoms and problems

- recent precipitants of current challenges
- the origins of these mechanisms
- intervention strategies to overcome the disorder.

3.2 Treatment / intervention

One of the main functions of the first phase of therapy is to guide effective treatment by establishing the targets of intervention, which are generally the mechanisms that the conceptualization proposes as causing the symptoms (Pearson, 2008). In the case of CBT, these mechanisms are usually cognitive (e.g., maladaptive schemas, irrational beliefs) or behavioral (e.g., conditioning processes) in nature.

Cognitive techniques are intended at modifying maladaptive thinking patterns that cause dysfunctional emotions and behaviors. They address several dimensions of this process: (1) identification of maladaptive thinking patterns; (2) interrupting automatic information processing which contains the dysfunctional, habitual and uncritically accepted negative thoughts; (3) challenging and replacing dysfunctional/irrational cognitions (e.g., self-downing); (4) altering maladaptive information processing (e.g., overgeneralization).

Behavioral techniques have always been an important part of CBT - change can not be considered complete unless the person's behavioral patterns are modified (Freeman & Oster, 1998). These techniques include: exposure (in vivo and imaginary), relaxation training, behavioral rehearsal, contingency management, graded task assignment, assertiveness training and so on. Although behavioral in nature, the cognitive aspects of these techniques (e.g., attributions, expectancies) are highlighted and exploited by the cognitive-behavioral therapist (Freeman & Oster, 1998). For example, in vivo exposure for phobias is regarded not only as a way of altering conditioning processes that might have led to the problem, but also as an opportunity of testing, challenging and restructuring the patient's catastrophic interpretations of the feared situation (David, 2006).

Another cluster of strategies employed in CBT - rehabilitation strategies - is particularly worth mentioning in the context of this discussion of virtual reality and psychotherapy. Over the last few decades, this field has undergone substantial growth and development (Sohlberg & Mateer, 2001), with cognitive-behavioral interventions being among the most widely used and accepted treatments in rehabilitation psychology (Elliot & Jackson, 2004). There is significant evidence supporting the fact that people who have social and cognitive adaptive skills experience better adjustment following disability (Frank & Elliot, 2000), justifying the need for intervention in the case of patients and their families. The range of beneficiaries of such interventions is very broad (Elliot & Jackson, 2004), including individuals with central neurological conditions (e.g., stroke), peripheral neurological conditions (e.g., spinal cord injury), orthopedic conditions (e.g., fractures), medical conditions (e.g., major surgery) and psychiatric illnesses (e.g., schizophrenia, dementia, mental retardation).

Cognitive rehabilitation approaches can be broadly classified into two categories (Rizzo et al., 2001): *restorative* approaches, which focus on the retraining of individual cognitive processes (e. g., attention, memory) and *functional* approaches, which emphasize the stepwise training of skills and behaviors. Developments in this field rely significantly on research in cognitive science, which helps understand cognitive processes at a computational level and has shown that the brain is a far more plastic organ than it was thought to be, capable of considerable reorganization following damage and injury

(Sohlberg & Mateer, 2001). On the other hand, rehabilitation psychology has been profoundly influenced by the technological advancements of the last years, with increasingly complex technologies available for individuals with cognitive and physical limitations.

3.3 Therapeutic alliance

The idea that the relationship between the therapist and the client has an important effect on the therapeutic process can be traced back to Sigmund Freud's writings. Although his understanding of the therapeutic alliance has been dramatically challenged and modified over the years by other developments in psychotherapy (e.g., CBT), the interest in it remains and a variety of ideas have been advanced regarding the essential components of this relationship and about the mechanisms through which it actually works (Horvath, 2006).

The empirical testing of these ideas has shown that alliance is indeed a predictor of treatment outcome (Horvath & Luborsky, 1993; Shrik & Carver, 2003). In fact, alliance has been found to be one of the most robust predictors of positive psychotherapy outcome, regardless of the type of therapy used or whether assessed by therapist, client or independent observers (Horvath, 2001). Early alliance is particularly predictive of the results, and attrition from therapy can also be predicted by the quality of therapist-client interaction as early as the end of the first session (Robins et al, 2003). These associations are also consistent across therapies (e.g., cognitive-behavioral, psychodynamic) (Creed & Kendall, 2005). A recent analysis by Hilsenroth and Cromer (2007) of "evidence-based" clinician behaviors useful in the initial phase of alliance building, lists several elements traditionally considered key aspects of the CBT approach: adopting a collaborative stance toward the client, speaking with emotional and cognitive content, actively exploring problem issues, maintaining active focus on topic, offering psychoeducation on symptoms and treatment process, collaboratively developing treatment goals and tasks.

4. Virtual reality and psychotherapy

Despite the obvious strengths and the notable progresses made by psychotherapy during the last decades, research also systematically points to a segment of patients who are non-responsive to interventions, prompting professionals to advocate for improving the efficacy of treatments and for exploring and developing new efficient and cost-effective intervention strategies (David et al., 2008). Virtual reality (VR) has lately emerged as a promising tool in several areas of psychological intervention (Rizzo & Kim, 2005).

The first computer programs for CBT were developed in the 1980s in the United Kingdom and the United States. They relied on written text, checklists, and multiple-choice questions for communication with the patient (Wright & Small, 2004). Among the benefits of using computer programs in psychotherapy and the factors motivating the continued development of computer-assisted cognitive-behavioral therapy (CCBT) are the possibility of providing unique learning experiences to clients, leading to a faster attainment of treatment goals, the reduction of therapy costs and increased access to psychological treatments for people who are unable or unwilling to attend traditional treatment (Wright & Small, 2004).

Based on the assessment of available data, the National Institute for Health and Clinical Excellence (NICE) has included computer-based anxiety (i.e., panic, phobia,) and depression interventions among its recommended treatments (NICE, 2006; 2009).

More recently developed computer tools for CBT have incorporated virtual reality, and continuing advances in the field have led to the development of VR systems that are uniquely suited for targeting a variety of psychological conditions. Their main advantage resides in the potential of creating cost-effective, systematic assessment, training and treatment environments that allow for the precise control of complex, immersive and dynamic 3D stimulus presentations and for sophisticated interaction, behavior tracking and performance recording (Rizzo & Kim, 2005).

VR uses complex computer graphics and a variety of input and output devices to construct a virtual environment where the observer feels immersed (Peck, 2007). Thus, the person is no longer mere external observer of the images on the computer screen, but an active participant in the computer-generated three-dimensional world (Rothbaum, 2000). This three-dimensional interaction is what generates presence. Presence refers to the interpretation of the virtual environment as if it were real (Lee, 2004; Price & Anderson, 2006). Although the individual is conscious of his or her experience being produced by the technology, perception to a certain extent overlooks this aspect and interprets the environment as if technology were not involved (Krijn et al., 2004).

The main strategies used to immerse subjects into virtual environments and generate presence are head mounted displays (HMD) and computer automatic virtual environments (CAVE). HMD systems are for individual use; they are image display systems worn on the head that remain optically coupled to the user's eyes as he or she turns or moves (Schultheis & Rizzo, 2001). They are often used in combination with tracking systems, earphones, gesture-sensing gloves and haptic-feedback devices (Schultheis & Rizzo, 2001). The HMD is typically connected to a computer operated by the therapist, who guides the process. The CAVE is a multiuser, projection-based VR system. The patient and therapist are surrounded by computer generated images projected on more sides. Glasses are worn and a tracking system is attached to them, to generate a correct perspective (Krijn et al., 2004).

VR basically brings "the outside world" into the clinician's office, and allows for a higher level of control and the appropriate tailoring of the therapeutic process to the individual needs of the client, making a valuable addition to all components of the therapeutic process.

4.1 Virtual reality contributions to assessment

An accurate and comprehensive assessment is essential to a coherent conceptualization and treatment planning. A variety of combined strategies (e.g., clinical interviews, scales, observation) are typically used by clinicians to get a clear picture of the client's circumstances and problems before starting intervention. For example, in order to get an accurate image of the client's specific emotional and behavioral reactions in a given situation, the therapist can rely on psychological tests/interviews or try to gather the information by exposing the client to the situation, either imaginary or in vivo. While all these strategies can lead to valuable information, they also have their downsides.

Clinical tests are employed to measure various constructs (e.g., irrational beliefs, maladaptive schemas), and their results used to make predictions about the individual's behaviors and emotions in certain situations (e.g., speaking in front of an audience). Thus, a particular measure - the predictor - is used to make predictions of a specific outcome - the criterion. The limitations of this method are related to two factors (Sechrest et al., 1998): (1) the reliability of the test for the particular population to which the individual belongs and (2) the fact that predictions are based on a relationship between predictor and criterion, and are limited by the validity of the predictor to the context in question (Sechrest et al., 1998). Another problem with clinical tests is their lack of ecological validity, for some situations. Interviews, on the other hand, are post-factum and often biased by memory processes.

Imaginary and in vivo exposure offer direct access to the client's thoughts, emotions and behaviors in a given context. However, they are not without limitations: while imaginary exposure may be affected by the inability of the client to recall and relive relevant aspects of the situation, in vivo exposure may often prove difficult, expensive or impractical to conduct.

A discussion of these assessment-related challenges gives us a picture of where virtual reality fits in into the puzzle. VR offers the therapist the opportunity of observing and recording cognitive, behavioral, subjective and physiological patterns in environments that are very much like the real world or where the person acts as in the real world, while retaining control and eliminating potential confounded variables (Rizzo et al., 2004). This provides an understanding of human behavior and human cognition that is challenging to achieve in any other fashion (David, 2010). While the possibility of conducting assessment as the patient interacts with a relevant environment is important in all cases, it becomes all the more valuable in situations where exposure to real-life contexts is impossible or impractical (e.g., due to high costs). For example, VR fear of flying programs are not only useful for intervention, but also for the assessment of the cognitive, emotional, behavioral, and physiological responses of patients in a context very similar to the one they fear, and that is significantly more difficult to access.

One such VR assessment tool, called Virtual Classroom, has been developed by a group of researchers at the University of Southern California in collaboration with Digital MediaWorks Inc., Canada (Rizzo et al., 2000). The system is specifically aimed at the assessment of attentional processes. The scenario consists of a classroom environment, containing objects (desks, blackboard) and persons (teacher, children) that are normally found in this context. A window on a side wall looks out onto a playground, and at each end of opposite walls there is a door through which activity occurs (Schultheis & Rizzo, 2001). The child sits at a desk in the virtual classroom and is given a task to complete. Attention can be assessed while a series of typical classroom distracters (e.g., noise, people moving, activity on the playground and at the doors) are controlled and manipulated by the therapist (Schultheis & Rizzo, 2001).

Virtual environments have also been used to evaluate cognitive functioning in individuals with various limitations. In a recent study, Josman and colleagues (Josman et al., 2009) employed VR to evaluate executive functioning in patients diagnosed with schizophrenia. The VR environment simulated shopping activity, and the authors found it highly suitable for the assessment of executive function deficits in schizophrenia. Although these deficits are well documented in the literature, they are generally assessed by neuropsychological tests, which provide important information, but consist of isolated, artificial tasks, with a fairly limited ability to predict the daily functioning of the patient (Chaytor et al., 2006; Josman et al., 2009). VR environments, on the other hand, have high ecological validity and cue habitual responses, thus giving the clinician more insight into the day-to-day behavior of the patient.

With VR technologies becoming more accessible as their price decreases, they can definitely develop into a valuable addition to the assessment process, providing the therapist information and an understanding of the client's emotions and behavior that would be otherwise difficult to access.

4.2 VR contributions to intervention and to the understanding of underlying mechanisms of psychological disorders

It is interesting to note that the technical (r)evolution in psychotherapy was anticipated by the results of a poll conducted by Norcross and colleagues in 2002, published in an article entitled *"The face of 2010: A Delphi poll on the future of psychotherapy"*. A panel of 62 psychotherapy experts involved in the poll predicted trends in the field for the following decade. Among the future scenarios that they considered most likely was the expansion of evidence-based interventions, of practice guidelines and of technology in psychotherapy (Norcross et al., 2002). These predictions have turned out to be accurate, both in which the evidence-based movement and computer-based interventions are concerned.

The nature of VR-based interventions makes them highly suitable for integration into CBT treatment programs. Over the last decade, applications have expanded as costs have dropped and hardware has improved. VR interventions have been developed for a variety of clinical conditions ranging from anxiety to eating disorders. In addition to generating presence, there are other features of VR that make it so appealing to psychotherapy (Glantz et al., 2003, p. 56): the possibility to precisely control what is presented to the client, the ability to tailor the treatment to the needs of the patient and the ability to expose the client to a wide range of conditions that would otherwise be unsafe or unpractical.

In addition, and just as important, recent research points to the potential of VR-based studies to clarify the mechanisms underlying various psychological disorders, which will eventually pay off in the development of increasingly efficient treatment packages. To give just one example, recent studies of acrophobia have pointed out that motion combined with simulated height, rather that height per se, lead to the phobic response (Coelho et al., 2006; Coelho et al., 2008), suggesting the need to also explore visuo-vestibular and motion mechanisms as possible diathesis factors in this disorder (Coelho et al., 2009). Similar progresses are being anticipated in the case of substance abuse (e.g., the association of environmental and personal factors leading to drug abuse; Culbertson et al., 2010) and psychotic disorders (e.g., mechanisms leading to symptom generation; Fornells-Ambrojo et al., 2008).

Most of the data that is currently available on VR interventions and their efficacy comes from studies of anxiety. Anxiety disorders are among the most common and frequently occurring mental disorders and they have been shown to be responsive to both medication and psychological interventions, CBT being widely employed in their management (Bush, 2008). While for the vast majority of other disorders data regarding VR interventions are based on case studies and uncontrolled studies, several randomized controlled trials have already been published for anxiety. This is not surprising considering the importance of exposure in the treatment of anxiety and the fact that VR environments provide a safe and controllable way of confronting the patient with the feared stimuli and situations. The first VR applications for psychotherapy were in fact designed to treat specific phobias (North & North, 1994; Rothbaum et al., 1995). To date, virtual reality exposure therapy (VRET) applications have been developed and used for a variety of anxiety disorders including panic disorder with agoraphobia, acrophobia, spider phobia (arachnophobia), fear of flying, claustrophobia, fear of driving, social phobia and post traumatic stress disorder (PTSD).

Two recent quantitative meta-analyses (both published in 2008) summarize the results of these studies. One was conducted by Parsons and Rizzo and included 21 studies, based on the following criteria (Parsons & Rizzo, 2008, p. 252): (1) report of interval or ratio data; (2) anxiety symptom data presented before and after VRET; (3) use of at least one affect assessment instrument; (4) sufficient report of study results to allow effect size computation. Effect sizes were calculated for 6 affective domains: PTSD, social phobia, spider phobia, acrophobia, panic disorder with agoraphobia, fear of flying. An overall effect size across affective domains was also computed. Results indicated statistically significant large effects (Cohen's ds ranging between 0.87-1.79,) on all affective domains, with the largest effect sizes for fear of flying (1.59) and panic with agoraphobia (1.79). The overall effect size was also large (0.95). These are important findings in support of the potential benefits of VR exposure despite the somewhat limited number of subjects (particularly for certain affective domains) and the inclusion of uncontrolled studies in the analysis (Parsons & Rizzo, 2008).

Similar results were reported in the meta-analysis of Powers and Emmelkamp, which included 13 studies, meeting the following criteria (Powers & Emmelkamp, 2008, p. 563): (1) at least one virtual reality exposure therapy condition; (2) random assignment or matched condition; (3) either an active or inactive control group. Patients in these studies met the criteria for various types of specific phobia, social phobia, panic disorder and PTSD. Results indicated a large overall effect for VRET (assessed by domain specific measures) compared to control conditions, and medium to large effects for VRET on several other outcome categories (i.e., general subjective distress, cognitive, behavioral, psychophysiological). An interesting finding of this study was that, while both VR and in vivo exposure were more effective than no treatment, VR slightly outperformed in vivo exposure (small effect). The authors interpret these results as reflecting the higher credibility and expectancy for VRET and by the patients progressing more rapidly through the hierarchy due to a higher perception of control and safety (Powers & Emmelkamp, 2008).

The few studies combining VR treatments with cognitive techniques were excluded from this meta-analysis, due to procedural aspects that precluded the accurate evaluation of the independent effects of cognitive restructuring. One recent study, not included in this meta-analysis (Krijn et al., 2007), compared VRET alone to VRET combined with cognitive self-statements, and found no difference between the two conditions in patients with acrophobia. It is interesting to mention, however, that the meta-analysis indicated a very large effect size of VRET for cognitive outcome measures (g=1.30; Powers & Emmelkamp, 2008). This result supports the idea that behavioral techniques, such as exposure, also lead to cognitive change, affecting the patients' attributions and expectancies (David, 2006; Freeman & Oster, 1998). We believe that studies evaluating the added value of integrating VR techniques into already established CBT treatment protocols are quite important in order to clarify the most effective ways of delivering interventions to patients.

The majority of studies addressing VR applications for psychotherapy have focused on anxiety disorders. However, VR interventions for other psychological conditions have also been proposed. It is not the scope of this chapter to offer a comprehensive review of these applications, but we mention some of them as follows (but see Glantz et al., 2003 and Krijn et al., 2004 for reviews).

Experiential Cognitive Therapy was developed by Giuseppe Riva and his colleagues (Riva, 1998; Riva et al., 1999; Riva et al., 2002) to address obesity and eating disorders, particularly body image disturbance and the negative emotions associated with it. The VR component is integrated into a CBT approach and it consists of exposing patients to critical contexts and stimuli (e.g., kitchen, restaurant, commercials) and helping them deal with their emotional reactions and develop adaptive coping strategies. Patients' false assumptions about their own body are also confronted in the virtual environment. The authors report positive results of this strategy, particularly in which body dissatisfaction and self-efficacy are concerned (Riva et al., 2002).

More recently, it has been suggested that VR application could be developed not only for the assessment (see above), but also for the treatment of patients diagnosed with psychotic disorders. In a study published in 2008, Fornells-Ambrojo and colleagues used a socially relevant environment to evaluate the acceptability and safety of using VR with individuals with persecutory delusions. Their results indicate that brief experiences in VR are both safe and acceptable to people with psychosis, and that they are also relevant from the point of view of presence and of eliciting delusional thoughts (Fornells-Ambrojo, 2008). Acceptability and lack of side effects of VR exposure were also reported by Stinson and colleagues (Stinson et al., 2010). Future studies are needed, but these data suggest the potential of VR strategies to be integrated into cognitive behavioral interventions for psychosis (Fornells-Ambrojo, 2008).

VR technologies have also been explored as potential skills training instruments for individuals with autistic spectrum disorders (ASD). A series of studies have discussed the viability and utility of VR in developing the social skills of people diagnosed with ASD (Cobb et al., 2002; Parsons & Mitchell, 2003; Parsons et al., 2004; Parsons et al., 2006). Virtual environments are considered to be fit for this task, as they can depict complex social contexts, but they are at the same time controllable and predictable, eliminating the anxiety that social interactions often elicit in people with ASD (Parsons et al., 2006). As in the case of psychotic disorders, research on this topic is still at the beginning, but the results so far are encouraging.

Another promising line of research is related to addictions. Several studies have already looked at the potential of VR environments to elicit craving and at the possibility of using these environments as assessment (e.g., Saladin et al., 2006; Culbertson et al., 2010) and intervention tools (Lee at al., 2007). Saladin and colleagues (2006) evaluated the ability of a VR environment to generate craving and emotional reactivity in cocaine dependent individuals. Their results showed that scenes related to cocaine use, compared to neutral scenes, elicited craving, physiological reactivity (e.g., increased heart rate) and emotional responses (e.g., anticipatory anxiety and a reduction in positive affect). Similar results were reported by Culbertson and colleagues (2010) in a group of methamphetamine users. VR drug cueing systems have also been developed for tobacco, cannabis and heroin (Baumann & Sayette, 2006; Bordnick et al., 2009; Kuntze et al., 2001). These systems allow an accurate and individual assessment of factors that induce craving and drug-use behavior and provide the opportunity of designing and testing treatments for drug addiction (Culbertson et al., 2010). In which intervention is concerned, exposure to cues eliciting craving (cue-exposure therapy) has already been assessed and proposed as a strategy of extinguishing the association between the substance and substance-related cues and contexts (e.g., Lee et al., 2007).

4.3 VR contributions to rehabilitation

Recent research also points to the broad usability of VR in targeting a range of physical, cognitive and behavioral rehabilitation issues. Beginning with the early 1990, there has been an increased interest in the study and promotion of these strategies. According to Rizzo and Kim (2005) ecological validity, stimulus control and repetitive delivery, real-time feedback, self-guided exploration, the safe environment and the opportunity to tailor the interface to the individual's impairment are just some of the factors that make VR a feasible intervention tool in rehabilitation.

Several research teams have already integrated VR in the assessment and rehabilitation protocols of cognitive processes in patients suffering from developmental disorders, neurological conditions (e.g., traumatic brain injury) and psychiatric conditions (e.g., schizophrenia). VR applications have been developed and tested for attention processes (e.g., Rizzo et al., 2000; Rizzo et al., 2001), spatial abilities (e.g., Rizzo et al., 1998), memory (e.g., Brooks, 1999) and executive functions (e.g., Costa & Carvalho, 2004; Pugnetti et al., 1998). VR scenarios have also been designed to teach patients daily activities such as meal preparation (e.g., Christiansen et al., 1998), use of public transportation (e.g., Lam et al., 2005), street crossing (Josman et al., 2008) and shopping (Tam et al., 2005)

The focus of CBT on promoting adjustment, well being and personal health among individuals with disabling conditions has led to it becoming one of the most widely accepted treatments in rehabilitation psychology (Elliot & Jackson, 2004). Although clinical data on VR rehabilitation strategies is still insufficient (particularly in which controlled studies are concerned), their integration into CBT packages holds significant promise, considering the documented adequate match between the two (Wright & Small, 2004). Moreover, CBT rehabilitation protocols are usually complex interventions that, depending on the patient's condition, not only address issues of cognitive and behavioral skills (re)training and development, but also aspects of coping with the disorder, treatment adherence, vocational reintegration, lifestyle change, patient and family education (Elliot & Jackson, 2004).

4.4 VR and the therapeutic alliance

While there are some studies that have looked at the limits (e.g., side effects, costs) and acceptability of VR strategies by various categories of patients, little attention has been given to their effects on the therapeutic alliance. A typical VR-related concern regarding alliance has to do with the reduction of face to face interaction between therapist and client (Chu et al., 2004). Future research must address this issue in a systematic manner and reconcile the apparently conflicting data on the importance of the therapeutic alliance on the one hand, and the effectiveness of treatments that involve limited therapist input on the other hand (Peck, 2007). According to Chu et al. (2004), technological developments and their inclusion in therapy challenge the traditional conceptualization of the clinician's role, and the study of alliance must be extended to take into account a variety of new therapeutic relationship forms.

However, a difference must be made here between entirely computer-based psychotherapy interventions, where the process takes place without a therapist being involved, and the integration of VR strategies into traditional CBT protocols. In this latter situation, the four basic components of the therapeutic process (i.e., assessment, conceptualization, intervention, alliance) are not altered. In other words, VR strategies are a valuable addition to the therapy process, which retains and strengthens all its other active ingredients. This assumption seems to be confirmed by studies that have found high levels of acceptability, involvement and preference of patients for VR technologies.

5. A virtual reality cognitive-behavioral environment and treatment protocol for attention-deficit and hyperactivity disorder (ADHD) (Based on Anton et al., 2009a)

Attention-deficit and hyperactivity disorder (ADHD) is among the most prevalent psychiatric childhood disorders, affecting 8% to 10% of children (Baren, 2002). Although it persists into adolescence in up to 80% of cases (Schubiner et al., 2002), it is considered a childhood disorder, and largely diagnosed during childhood. The accurate diagnosis and treatment of ADHD is of significant importance, considering that, when left untreated, it can lead to school underachievement, affect professional prospects and cause relational problems (Baren, 2002). Adolescents with ADHD are more likely to display risk-taking behaviors such as reckless driving, risky sexual activities, substance abuse and criminal behavior (Barkley et al., 1990).
Over the past few years, clinical research and consensus guidelines have established the most effective treatment approaches for ADHD. A recent review of evidence-based psychosocial treatments for children and adolescents with ADHD identifies behavioral parent training and behavioral school interventions as empirically validated interventions (Chronis et al., 2006). Both approaches involve teaching parents and educators to use behavior modification strategies such as praise, positive attention and rewards to increase positive behavior, and ignoring, time-out and response-cost to decrease unwanted behavior. Overall, medication and behavioral approaches have been shown to be effective in the clinical management of ADHD, but they do have limitations that advocate for the need of developing additional intervention strategies (Anton et al., 2009a). To some extent, the limitations of behavioral approaches overlap with those of medication as: (1) effects appear to be short-term; (2) not all children respond to treatment; and (3) data do not support the long-term benefits of these interventions (Waschbusch & Hill, 2003). Multimodal programs, such as the one proposed by Dopfner and colleagues (Dopfner et al., 2006) are considered to be the best alternative (Anton et al., 2009a). Multilevel programs involve work on the cognitions and behaviors of the child, using a combination of parent training and child-focused cognitive behavioral intervention. The CBT component of multimodal programs includes: (1) reinforcement techniques (e.g., positive reinforcement, guidance, shaping) (2) techniques for eliminating maladaptive behavior (e.g., extinction, response-cost) and (3) cognitive restructuring techniques (e.g., disputation, hypothesis testing)

5.1 From assessment to treatment - Development of a VR treatment tool for ADHD

The goal of the research project we describe bellow was to develop a VR intervention tool that could be integrated into a traditional CBT approach for ADHD (Anton et al., 2009a). Our intention was to create a high ecological validity instrument that would allow us to conduct intervention in a context simulating the everyday environment of the child. This instrument is being developed, in collaboration, by the members of the Department of Clinical Psychology and Psychotherapy, Babeş-Bolyai University, Cluj-Napoca Romania, Dr. Albert "Skip" Rizzo from the Institute for Creative Technologies, University of Southern California, San Diego and Digital Media Works (DMW) Canada. The team at Babeş-Bolyai University is led by Dr. Daniel David and its members are Raluca Anton (MA), Anca Dobrean (PhD), David Opris (MA), and Aurora Szentagotai (PhD).
Our starting point was the Virtual Classroom program, developed by Rizzo and colleagues (Rizzo et al., 2000). The Virtual Classroom was intended and tested as a study and

assessment tool, but its creators had envisioned the possibility of the system being used for treatment (Rizzo et al., 2000). It is a head mounted display (HMD) system, and the scenario consists of a classroom environment, containing objects (desks, blackboard) and persons (teacher, children) that are normally found in this context. A window on a side wall looks out onto a playground, and at each end of opposite walls there is a door through which activity occurs (Schultheis & Rizzo, 2001). The child sits at a desk in the virtual classroom and is given a task to complete. Attention can be assessed through tasks of various difficulties, while a series of typical classroom distracters are controlled and manipulated by the therapist (for detailed descriptions see Rizzo et al., 2000; Rizzo et al., 2006).

This objective and reliable evaluation strategy addresses and eliminates some of the problems of traditional assessment techniques in ADHD (e.g., issues related to low ecological validity) (Rizzo et al., 2006). An initial clinical trial comparing 6-12 years old children diagnosed with ADHD (n=8) and non-diagnosed children (n=10) has shown significant differences between the two groups on a number of variables such as reaction times under distracting conditions, number of omission and commission errors and levels of motor activity. No negative side-effects were reported by the participants (Rizzo et al., 2006).

Our aim was to transfer the advantages of using VR with children diagnosed with ADHD from the assessment to the intervention level. Based on the literature showing that multimodal interventions are the most efficient in the clinical management of the disorder, we decided to build on this approach (Dopfner et al., 2006) by implementing some of its components into a virtual environment. In other words, the program relies on established behavioral and cognitive techniques, but they are used in a virtual school context.

Focus on school behavior is an important aspect of the program, as it allows clinical work to be conducted in an environment that normally raises multiple challenges to children with ADHD. Given the ecological nature of the intervention, our expectation was that skills acquired during therapy would be easier transferred into the real classroom, improving the child's functioning in this important area of everyday life. While most parents support the implementation of newly learned skills at home, this is often not the case at school. Our intervention was designed to address this problem and give children the opportunity of practicing new behaviors in the (virtual) classroom as well.

It is important to mention that we do not propose a new therapeutic paradigm. We instead "relocate" the intervention from the clinician's office into the virtual classroom. As far as we know, this is the first VR program that allows the clinician to use relevant CBT techniques in the treatment of ADHD. A number of features were introduced in the program to support the CBT intervention:

- Graphic display of child performance
- Pause button
- Self-talk event recording
- Distracters/environment control
- Reward/punishment system
- Feedback component
- Tasks difficulty grading component
- Head movement tracking.

These features are designed to serve several purposes, such as: (1) give the therapist control of the virtual environment (pause button; distracters control); (2) offer the therapist information regarding the child's performance and behavior (graphic display of child performance; head movement tracking); (3) support the application of cognitive (self-talk event recording; feedback component) and behavioral (reward/punishment system; task difficulty grading) techniques.

From a technical point of view, the system consists of two computers connected through a wired or wireless network. One computer (the patient's computer) is running the ClinicaVRtm Classroom, while the other one (the therapist's computer) is running the School Master. An eMagin Z800 head mounted display is used for presenting the virtual environment to the patient. Using a graphical control interface, the therapist controls the ClinicaVRtm Classroom and gets real-time feedback on the patient's performance.

Fig. 1. ClinicaVRtm Classroom adapted for intervention. Patient interface copyright © 2010 Digital MediaWorks Inc.

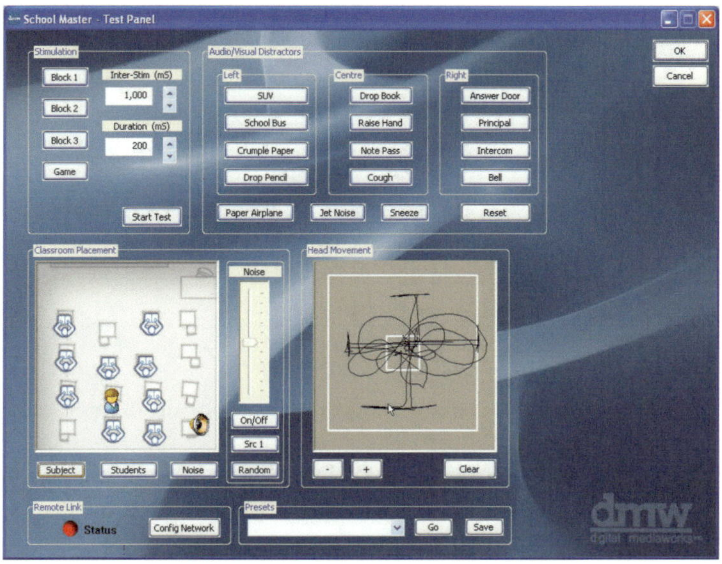

Fig. 2. ClinicaVRtm Classroom adapted for intervention. Therapist interface copyright © 2010 Digital MediaWorks Inc.

5.2 Intervention protocol

The protocol designed to include this modified version of the ClinicaVR[tm] Classroom is based on the program proposed by Dopfner, Shurmann and Frolich (2006). This is a flexible, family-based program and the strategy varies from family to family and from child to child. Flexibility does not refer, however, to modifying cognitive or behavioral techniques but, for example, to skipping certain phases if they are not considered useful for the client.

A number of studies have shown that family-based interventions are quite efficient for managing children with defiant behavior (McMahon & Forehand, 1984) and that combining family intervention with self-education techniques significantly improves the child's behavior. However, one problem during therapy is related to the difficulties of exposing children and their families to real environments where they can practice newly acquired skills. We expect the learning and practice process to be much easier in a virtual environment that simulates real-life situations.

The intervention involves 16 weekly sessions (see Table 1; this protocol is based on Anton et al. 2009a, republished in Anton et al., 2009b). Each session focuses on teaching the child and the family cognitive and behavioral techniques that they are required to practice daily. One part of the intervention is addressed to the parent, and one part to the child. Each session a story of a boy with ADHD, named Peter, is red and discussed with the child. VR strategies are not used in all meetings, but only in sessions where they are considerer useful for the implementation of cognitive and behavioral strategies.

Session number and objective	Session Content
Initial Assessment	Focused on: behavioral assessment cognitive abilities evaluation family diagnostic
Session 1: Defining behavioral problems	Individualized description of child and family problems Objectives in terms of behavioral change Work on problems list VR assessment I
Session 2: Case conceptualization I	Integration of material from child and parent into common conceptualization
Session 3: Case conceptualization II	Conceptualization at case (general) level and at the problems (specific) level (continued from Session 2)
Session 4: Intervention objectives	Specific objectives detailed VR assessment II
Session 5: Focusing on positive interactions with the child	Discussion on positive and negative child-parent interactions Parents helped to focus on positive interactions with their children VR game to model positive interactions
Session 6: Building positive interactions through games	Games introduced as opportunities for positive interactions
Session 7: Family rules	Discussion and assessment of family rules Formulation of efficient family rules

Session 8: Efficient requirements	Parents taught to formulate efficient requirements
Session 9: Social reinforcements when requests are followed	Parents taught how to use social reinforcements Graded difficulty VR task (opportunity to model social reinforcements)
Session 10: Social reinforcements when child does not interrupt	Parents taught to give the child the attention he or she needs Parents taught to involve the child in independent activities Parents taught to reinforce the child when he or she does not interrupt
Session 11: Efficient monitoring (only if needed)	Assessment of problem behaviors when the child is on his or her own Establishing rules Reinforcing compliance with rules and managing non-compliance
Session 12: "Natural" negative consequences	Analysis of individual situations (if any) where established rules and principles do not work Establishing negative consequences for individual situations Graded difficulty VR task (opportunity to illustrate negative consequences)
Session 13: The "POINTS System"	Implementation of token economy principles for situations where social reinforcements do not work: points earned are exchanged for rewards Graded difficulty VR task - points earned for each correct answer
Session 14: Awarding points	Establishing rules for awarding points Graded difficulty VR task - feedback component is introduced to teach the child to cope with negative feedback – points earned for correct answers and points lost for incorrect answers
Session 15: Reinforcement withdrawal	Parents taught to withdraw benefits Contest between parent and child started: child gains a point when he or she follows a rule and parent gains a point when the child does not follow an established rule Graded difficulty VR task - points earned for correct answers and points lost in favor of opponent for incorrect answers
Session 16: Time-out	Time-out principles are discussed and introduced for managing highly resistant behavior
Session 17: Stabilizing gains	Overview of the sessions Overview of gains Rehearsal for future situations

Table 1. ADHD intervention protocol illustrating the integration of VR strategies into a CBT treatment program

6. Conclusions

The goal of this chapter was to discuss the applications and advantages of VR technologies in psychotherapy assessment, intervention and rehabilitation, using CBT as a general example, and the development of a VR intervention technology for ADHD as a specific example. We feel it is important to end our endeavor by stressing that VR psychotherapy (interventions) do not constitute a (new) form of psychotherapy in and of themselves. Even when playing a key role in therapy, they are basically tools that extend and complement the skills of well-trained clinicians and lead to the improvement of all components of the therapy process (David, 2010). Their contribution to the advancement of the evidence-based movement, through the stimulation of high quality research, the increasing of clinical expertise, and the tailoring of interventions to patient characteristics and preferences, makes them highly valuable instruments in the mental health field. Nevertheless, in order to make the most of their advantages, thoroughly planned studies and careful consideration of research evidence are needed before recommending them as viable treatment options (Bush, 2008).

7. References

Anderson, P.; Jacobs, C. & Rothbaum, B. O. (2004). Computer supported cognitive behavioral treatment of anxiety disorders. *Journal of Clinical Psychology,* 60., 3., (March 2004) 253–267, ISSN: 0021-9762

Anton, R.; Opris, D.; Dobrean, A.; David, D. & Rizzo, A. S. (2009a). Virtual reality in rehabilitation of attention deficit/hyperactivity disorder. The instrument construction principles. *Proceedings of Virtual Rehabilitation International Conference,* 2009, pp. 59-64, ISBN: 978-1424441884, Haifa, June-July 2009, IEEE, Haifa

Anton, R.; Opris, D.; Dobrean, A.; David, D. & Rizzo, A. S. (2009b). Virtual reality in rehabilitation of attention deficit/hyperactivity disorder. The instrument construction principles. *Journal of Cognitive and Behavioral Psychotherapies,* 9., 2., (September 2009) 935-946, ISSN: 1582-6694

Antony, M. A. & Rowa, K. (2005). Evidence-Based Assessment of Anxiety Disorders in Adults. *Psychological Assessment,* 17., 3., (September 2005) 256–266, ISSN: 1040-3590

APA Presidential Task Force on Evidence-Based Practice (2006). Evidence-Based Practice in Psychology. *American Psychologist,* 61., 4., (May-June 2006) 271–285, ISSN: 0003-066X

Baren, M. (2002). ADHD in adolescents: will you know it when you see it? *Contemporary Pediatrics,* 19., 4., (April 2002) 124–143, ISSN: 8750-0507

Barlow, D. H. (2004). Psychological treatments. *American Psychologist,* 59., 9., (December 2009) 869–878, ISSN: 0003-066X

Baumann, S. B. & Sayette, M. A. (2006). Smoking cues in a virtual world provoke craving in cigarette smokers. *Psychology of Addictive Behavior*, 20., 4., (December 2006) 484–489, ISSN: 0893-164X

Beck, A.T. (1972). *Depression: Causes and Treatment.* University of Pennsylvania Press, ISBN: 978-0812276527, Philadelphia

Brooks, B. M. (1999). Route learning in a case of amnesia: A preliminary investigation into the efficacy of training in a virtual environment. *Neuropsychological Rehabilitation*, 9., 1., (February 1999) 63-76, ISSN: 0960-2011

Bordin, E. S. (1966). Curiosity, compassion, and doubt: The dilemma of the psychologist. *American Psychologist,* 21., 2., (February 1966) 116–121, ISSN: 0003-066X

Bordnick, P. S.; Copp, H. L.; Traylor, A.; Graap, K. M.; Carter, B. L.; Walton, A., et al. (2009). Reactivity to cannabis cues in virtual reality environments. *Journal of Psychoactive Drugs,* 41., 2., (June 2009) 105-121, ISSN: 0279-1072

Bush, J. (2008). Viability of virtual reality exposure therapy as a treatment alternative. *Computers in Human Behavior,* 24., 3., (May 2008) 1032-1040, ISSN: 0747-5632

Butler, A. C.; Chapmann, J. A.; Forman, E. M. & Beck, A. T. (2006). The empirical status of cognitive-behavioral therapy: A review of meta-analyses. *Clinical Psychology Review,* 26., 1., (January 2006) 17-31, ISSN: 0272-7358

Chaytor, N.; Schmitter-Edgecombe, M. & Burr, R. (2006). Improving the ecological validity of executive functioning assessment. *Archives of Clinical Neuropsychology,* 21., 3., (April 2006) 217–227, ISSN: 0887-6177

Chronis, A. M.; Jones, H. A. & Raggi, V. L. (2006). Evidence-based psychosocial treatments for children and adolescents with attention-deficit/hyperactivity disorder. *Clinical Psychology Review,* 26., 4., (August 2006) 486–502, ISSN: 0272-7358

Christiansen, C.; Abreu, B.; Ottenbacher, K.; Huffman, K.; Masel, B. & Culpepper, R. (1998). Task performance in virtual environments used for cognitive rehabilitation after traumatic brain injury. *Archives of Physical Medicine and Rehabilitation,* 79., 8., (August 1998) 888-892, ISSN: 0003-9993

Chu, B. C.; Choudhury, M. S.; Shoru, A. I.; Pincus, D. B.; Creed, T. A. & Kendall, P. C. (2004). Alliance, technology and outcome in the treatment of anxious youth. *Cognitive Behavioral Practice*, 11., 1., (December 2004) 44-55, ISSN: 1077-7229

Coelho, C. M.; Santos, J. A.; Silverio, J. & Silva, C. F. (2006). Virtual reality and acrophobia: one-year follow-up and case study. *CyberPsychology and Behavior,* 9., 3., (June 2006) 336–341, ISSN: 1094-9313

Coelho, C. M.; Silva, C. F.; Santos, J. A.; Tichon, J. & Wallis, G. (2008). Contrasting the effectiveness and efficiency of virtual reality and real environments in the treatment of acrophobia. *PsychNology Journal,* 6., 2., 203–216, ISSN: 1720-7525

Coelho, C. M.; Waters, A. M.; Hine, T. J. & Wallis, G. (2009). The use of virtual reality in acrophobia research and treatment. *Journal of Anxiety Disorders,* 23., 5., (June 2009) 563-574, ISSN: 0887-6185

Cobb, S.; Beardon, L.; Eastgate, R.; Glover, T.; Kerr, S.; Neale, H., et al. (2002). Applied Virtual Environments to support learning of Social Interaction Skills in users with Asperger's Syndrome. *Digital Creativity,* 13., 1., (March 2002) 11–22, ISSN: 1462-6268

Costa, R. M. & Carvalho, L. A. (2004). The acceptance of virtual reality devices for cognitive rehabilitation: a report of positive results with schizophrenia. *Computer Methods and Programs in Biomedicine,* 73., 3., (March 2004) 173-182, ISSN: 0169-2607

Creed, T. A. & Kendall, P. C. (2005). Therapist alliance-building behavior within a cognitive behavioral treatment for anxiety in youth. *Journal of Consulting and Clinical Psychology,* 73., 3., (June 2005) 498-505, ISSN: 0022-006X

Culbertson, C.; Nicolas, S.; Zaharovits, I.; London, E. D.; De La Garza, R.; Brody, A. L., et al. (2010). Methamphetamine craving induced in an online virtual reality environment. Pharmacology, *Biochemistry and Behavior,* doi:10.1016/j.pbb.2010.07.005, ISSN: 0091-3057

David, D. (2004). Special Issue on the cognitive revolution in clinical psychology: Beyond the behavioral approach - conclusions: Toward an evidence-based psychology and psychotherapy. *Journal of Clinical Psychology* 60., 4., (April 2004) 447-451, ISSN: 0021-9762

David, D. (2006). *Handbook of cognitive-behavioral psychotherapies (*Romanian title: *Tratat de psihoterapii cognitive şi comportamentale),* Polirom, ISBN: 978-9734604913, Iaşi

David, D. (2010). Cutting edge developments in psychology: virtual reality applications. Interview with two leading experts. *Journal of Cognitive and Behavioral Psychotherapies,* 10., 1., (March 2010) 115–125, ISSN: 1582-6694

David, D. & Szentagotai, A. (2006). Cognitions in cognitive-behavioral psychotherapies; toward an integrative model. *Clinical Psychology Review,* 26., 3., (May 2006) 284-298, ISSN: 0272-7358

David, D.; Szentagotai, A.; Lupu, V. & Cosman, D. (2008). Rational Emotive Therapy, Cognitive Therapy and medication in the treatment of major depressive disorder: A randomized clinical trial. *Journal of Clinical Psychology,* 64., 6., (June 2008) 728–746, ISSN: 0021-9762

David, D. & Montgomery, G. H. (in press). The scientific status of psychotherapies: A new evaluative framework for evidence-based psychosocial interventions. *Clinical Psychology: Science and Practice,* ISSN: 0969-5893

Dopfner, M.; Shurmann, S. & Frolich J. (2006). *Therapeutic program for children with hyperkinetic and oppositional behavioral problems (Romanian title: Program terapeutic pentru copiii cu probleme comportamentale de tip hiperchinetic şi opozant),* RTS, ISBN: 973-8633729, Cluj-Napoca

Dreier, O. (2008). *Psychotherapy in everyday life,* Cambridge University Press, ISBN: 978-0511369995, Cambridge

Ellis, A. (1962). *Reason and emotion in psychotherapy,* Lyle Stuart, ASIN: B000NI34HA, New York

Ellis, A. (1994). *Reason and emotion in psychotherapy: A comprehensive method of treating human disturbances: Revised and updated,* Citadel, ISBN: 978-1559722483, Secaucus NJ

Elstein, A. S. & Schwarz, A. (2002). Clinical problem solving and diagnostic decision making: selective review of the cognitive literature. *British Medical Journal,* 324., 23., (March 2002) 728-723, ISSN: 0959-8138

Elliot, T. R. & Jackson, W. T. (2004). Rehabilitation psychology, In: *Encyclopedia of Cognitive Behavior Therapy,* A. Freeman; S. H. Felgoise; A. M. Nezu; C. M. Nezu & M. A. Reinecke (Eds.), 324-327, Springer, ISBN: 978-306485810, New York

Fornells-Ambrojo, M.; Barker, C.; Swapp, D.; Slater, M.; Antley, A. & Freeman, D. (2008). Virtual reality and persecutory delusions: Safety and feasibility. *Schizophrenia Research,* 104., 1., (September 2008) 228-236, ISSN: 0920-9964

Freeman, A. & Oster, C. L. (1998). Cognitive therapy and depression, In: *International handbook of cognitive behavioral treatments for psychological disorders,* V. E. Caballo (Ed.), 489-520, Elsevier Science Ltd., ISBN: 0-08-043433-9 Oxford

Goodheart, C. D. (2006). Evidence, endeavor and expertise in psychology practice, In: *Evidence-based psychotherapy. Where practice and research meet,* C. D. Goodheart; A. E. Kazdin & R. J. Sternberg (Eds.), 37–61, American Psychological Association, ISBN: 978-1591474036, Washington DC

Hilsenroth, M. J. & Cromer, T. D. (2007). Clinician interventions related to alliance during the initial interview and psychological assessment. *Psychotherapy: Theory, Research, Practice, Training,* 44., 2., (June 2007) 205-218, ISSN: 0033-3204

Hollon, S. D. (1998). What is cognitive-behavioral psychotherapy and does it work? Commentary. *Current Opinion in Neurobiology,* 8., 2., (April 1998) 289-292, ISSN: 0959-4388

Horvath, A. O. (2001). The Alliance. *Psychotherapy: Theory, Research, Practice, Training,* 38., 4., (Winter 2001) 365–372, ISSN: 0033-3204

Horvath, A. O. (2006). The alliance in context: accomplishments, challenges, and future directions. *Psychotherapy: Theory, Research, Practice, Training,* 43., 3., (October 2006) 258-263, ISSN: 0033-3204

Horvath, A. O. & Luborsky, L. (1993). The role of the therapeutic alliance in psychotherapy. *Journal of Consulting and Clinical Psychology,* 61., 4., (August 1993) 561–573, ISSN: 0022-006X

Huppert, J. D.; Fabbro, A. & Barlow, D. (2006). Evidence-Based Practice and Psychological Treatments. In: *Evidence-based psychotherapy. Where practice and research meet,* C. D. Goodheart; A. E. Kazdin & R. J. Sternberg (Eds.), 131–152, American Psychological Association, ISBN: 978-1591474036, Washington DC

Josman, N.; Milika Ben-Chaim, H.; Friedrich, S. & Weiss, P. L. (2008). Effectiveness of Virtual Reality for Teaching Street-Crossing Skills to Children and Adolescents with Autism. *International Journal on Disability and Human Development,* 7., 1., 49-56, ISSN: 1565-012X

Josman, N.; Schneiderman, A. E.; Klinger, E. & Shevil, E. (2009). Using virtual reality to evaluate executive functioning among persons with schizophrenia: A validity study. *Schizophrenia Research,* 115., 2-3., (December 2009) 270-277, ISSN: 0920-9964

Kopta, M. S.; Lueger, R. J. & Saunders, S. M. (1999). Individual psychotherapy outcome and process research: Challenges leading to greater turmoil or a positive transition? *Annual Review of Psychology,* 50., (February 1999) 441-469, ISSN: 0066-4308

Krijn, M.; Emmelkamp, P. M. G.; Olafsson, R. P. & Biemond, R. (2004). Virtual reality exposure therapy of anxiety disorders: A review. *Clinical Psychology Review,* 24., 3., (July 2004) 259-281, ISSN: 0272-7358

Krijn, M.; Emmelkamp, P. M. G.; Olafsson, R. P.; Schuemie, M. J. & van der Mast, C. A. (2007). Do self statements enhance the effectiveness of virtual reality exposure therapy? A comparative evaluation in acrophobia. *CyberPsychology and Behavior,* 10., 3., (June 2007) 362-370, ISSN:1094-9313

Kuntze, M. F.; Stoermer, R.; Mager, R.; Roessler, A.; Mueller-Spahn, F. & Bullinger A. H. (2001). Immersive virtual environments in cue exposure. *CyberPsychology and Behavior,* 4., 4., (August 2001) 497–501, ISSN: 1094-9313

Lam, Y. S.; Man, D. W. K; Tam, S. F. & Weiss, P. L. (2005). Virtual reality training for stroke rehabilitation. *NeuroRehabilitation,* 21., 3., (December 2006) 245-253, ISSN: 1878-6448

Lambert, M. J. (1992). Psychotherapy Outcome Research: Implications for Integrative and Eclectic Therapists, In: *Handbook of Psychotherapy Integration,* J. C. Norcross & M. R. Goldfried (Eds.), 94-129, Basic Books, ISBN: 978-0195165791, New York

Lambert, M. J. & Ogles, B. M. (2004). The efficacy and effectiveness of psychotherapy, In: *Bergin and Garfield's handbook of psychotherapy and behavior change,* J. Lambert, (Ed.), 139-193, John Wiley & Sons, ISBN: 978-0471377559, New York

Lee, K. M. (2004). Presence explicated. *Communication Theory*, 14., 1., (February 2004) 27–50, ISSN: 1050-3293.

Lee, J. H.; Kwon, H.; Choi, J. & Yang, B. H. (2007). Cue-exposure therapy to decrease alcohol craving in virtual environment. *CyberPsychology and Behavior*, 10., 5., (October 2007) 617-623, ISSN: 1094-9313

National Institute for Health and Clinical Excellence (NICE). Depression and anxiety – computerized cognitive behaviour therapy (CCBT). (Review of Technology Appraisal 51). http://www.nice.org.uk/guidance/TA097 (accessed 3 August 2010)

Norcross, J.; Hedges, M. & Prochaska, J. (2002). The face of 2010: A Delphi poll on the future of psychotherapy. *Professional Psychology, Research and Practice*, 33., 3., (June 2002) 316-322, ISSN: 0735-7028

North, M. & North, S. (1994). Relative effectiveness of virtual environment desensitization and imaginal desensitization in the treatment of aerophobia. *Electronic Journal of Virtual Culture*, 2., 4., (September 1994) 37–42, ISSN: 1068-5327

Parsons, S. & Mitchell, P. (2002). The potential of virtual reality in social skills training for people with autistic spectrum disorders. *Journal of Intellectual Disability Research*, 46., 5., (June 2002) 430–443, ISSN: 0964-2633

Parsons, S.; Mitchell, P. & Leonard, A. (2004). The use and understanding of virtual environments by adolescents with autistic spectrum disorders. *Journal of Autism and Developmental Disorders*, 34., 4., (August 2004) 449–466, ISSN: 1573-3432

Parsons, T. A. & Rizzo, A. A. (2008). Affective outcomes of virtual reality exposure therapy for anxiety and specific phobias: A meta-analysis. *Journal of Behavior Therapy and Experimental Psychiatry*, 39., 3., (September 2008) 250-261, ISSN: 0005-7916

Pearson, J. (2008). *The case formulation approach to cognitive-behavior therapy*, Guilford Press, ISBN: 978-1593858759, New York

Peck, D. (2007). Computer-guided cognitive-behavioral therapy for anxiety states. *Psychiatry*, 6., 4., (April 2007) 166-168, ISSN: 0033-2747

Price, M. & Anderson, P. (2007). The role of presence in virtual reality exposure therapy. *Journal of Anxiety Disorders*, 21., 5., (June 2007) 742-751, ISSN: 0887-6185

Pugnetti, L.; Mendozzi, L. & Attree, E. (1998). Probing memory and executive functions with virtual reality: Past and present studies. *CyberPsychology and Behavior*, 1., 2., (January 1998) 151-162, ISSN: 1094-9313

Rizzo, A. A.; Buckwalter, J. G.; Neumann, U.; Kesselman, C.; Thiebaux, M.; Larson, P. et al. (1998). The virtual reality mental rotation/ spatial skills project: Preliminary findings. *CyberPsychology and Behavior*, 1., 2., (January 1998) 107-113, ISSN: 1094-9313

Rizzo, A. A.; Buckwalter, J. G.; Humphrey, L.; van der Zaag, C.; Bowerly, T.; Chua C. et al. (2000). The virtual classroom: A virtual environment for the assessment and rehabilitation of attention deficits. *CyberPsychology and Behavior*, 3., 3., (June 2000), 483-500, ISSN: 1094-9313

Rizzo, A. A.; Buckwalter, J. G.; Bowerly, T.; Humphrey, L. A.; Neumann, U.; Rooyen, A. et al. (2001). The virtual classroom: a virtual reality environment for the assessment and rehabilitation of attention deficits. *Revista Espanola de Neuropsicologia*, 3., 3., 11-37, ISSN: 1139-9872

Rizzo, A. A.; Schultheis, M. T.; Kerns, K. A. & Mateer, C. (2004). Analysis of assets for virtual reality applications in neuropsychology. *Neuropsychological Rehabilitation,* 14., 1-2., (March 2004) 207–239, ISSN: 0960-2011

Rizzo, A. & Kim, G. J. (2005). A SWOT Analysis of the Field of Virtual Reality Rehabilitation and Therapy. *Presence,* 14., 2., (April 2005) 119–146, ISSN: 1054-7460

Robbins, M. S.; Turner, C. W. & Alexander, J. F. (2003). Alliance and dropout in family therapy for adolescents with behavior problems: Individual and systemic effects. *Journal of Family Psychology,* 17., 4., (December 2003) 534–544, ISSN: 0893-3200

Rizzo, A. A.; Bowerly, T.; Buckwalter, G.; Klimchuk, D.; Mitura, R. & Parsons T. D. (2006). A virtual reality scenario for all seasons: the virtual classroom. *CNS Spectrums,* 11., 1., (January 2006) 35-41, ISSN: 1092-8529

Riva, G. (1998). Virtual environment for body image modification: virtual reality system for the treatment of body image disturbance. *Computers in Human Behavior,* 14., 3., (September 1998) 477-490, ISSN: 0747-5632

Riva, G.; Bachetta, M; Baruffi, M.; Rinaldi, S. & Molinari, E. (1999). Virtual reality based experiential cognitive treatment of anorexia nervosa. *Journal of Behavior Therapy and Experimental Psychiatry,* 30., 3., (September 1999) 221–230, ISSN: 0005-7916

Riva, G.; Bachetta, M; Baruffi, M. & Molinari, E. (2002). Virtual-reality-based multidimensional therapy for the treatment of body image disturbances in binge eating disorders: a preliminary controlled study. *IEEE Transactions on Information Technology in Biomedicine,* 6., 3., (September, 2002) 224-234, ISSN: 1089-7771

Rothbaum, B. O.; Hodges, L. F.; Kooper, R.; Opdyke, D.; Williford, J. & North, M. (1995). Effectiveness of computer-generated (virtual reality) graded exposure in the treatment of acrophobia. *American Journal of Psychiatry,* 152., 4., (April 1995) 626-628, ISSN: 0002-953X

Rothbaum, B. O.; Hodges, L. F; Smith, S.; Lee, J. H. & Price, L. (2000). A controlled study of virtual reality exposure therapy for the fear of flying. *Journal of Consulting and Clinical Psychology,* 68., 6., (December 2000) 1020-1026, ISSN: 0022-006X

Saladin, M. E.; Brady, K. T.; Graap, K. & Rothbaum, B. O. (2006). A preliminary report on the use of virtual reality technology to elicit craving and cue reactivity in cocaine dependent individuals. *Addictive Behaviors,* 31., 10., (October 2006) 1881-1894, ISSN: 0306-4603

Schubiner, H.; Robin, A. L. & Neustern, L. S. (2002). School problems. In: *Adolescent health care: a practical guide,* L. S. Neinstein (Ed.), 1124-1142, Lippincott Williams & Wilkins, ISBN: 978-0781728973, Baltimore

Schultheis, M. T. & Rizzo, A. A. (2001). The application of virtual reality technology in rehabilitation. *Rehabilitation Psychology,* 46., 3., (August 2001) 296-311, ISSN: 1939-1544

Sechrest, L.; Stickle, T. R. & Stewart, M. (1998). The role of assessment in clinical psychology, In: *Comprehensive Clinical Psychology,* A. S. Bellack & M. Hersen (Eds.), 1-29, Pergamon, ISBN: 978-0080427072, New York

Shirk, S. R. & Karver, M. (2003). Prediction of treatment outcome from relationship variables in child and adolescent therapy: A meta-analytic review. *Journal of Consulting and Clinical Psychology,* 71., 3., (June 2003) 452–464, ISSN: 0022-006X

Sohlberg, M. M. & Mateer, C. A. (2001). *Cognitive rehabilitation. An integrative neuropsychological approach.* The Guilford Press, ISBN: 1-57230-613-0, New York

Stinson, K.; Valmaggia, L. R.; Antley, A.; Slater, M. & Freeman, D. (2010). Cognitive triggers of auditory hallucinations: An experimental investigation. *Journal of Behavior Therapy and Experimental Psychiatry,* 41., 3., (September 2010) 179-184, ISSN: 0005-7916

Tam, S. F.; Man, D. W. K; Chan, Y. P; Sze, P. C. & Wong, C. M. (2005). Evaluation of a Computer-Assisted, 2-D Virtual Reality System for Training People With Intellectual Disabilities on How to Shop. *Rehabilitation Psychology,* 50., 3., (August 2005) 285-291, ISSN: 0090-5550

Wampold, B. E. & Bhati, K. S. (2004). Attending to the omissions: A historical examination of evidence based practice movements. *Professional Psychology: Research and Practice,* 35., 6., (December 2004) 563–570, ISSN: 0735-7028

Waschbusch, D. A. & Hill, G. P. (2003). Empirically supported, promising, and unsupported treatments for children with Attention-Deficit/Hyperactivity Disorder. In: *Science and Pseudoscience in Clinical Psychology,* S. O. Lilienfield; S. J. Lynn & J. M. Lohr (Eds.), 333-362, The Guilford Press, ISBN: 978-1572308282, New York

Winder, C. L. (1957). Psychotherapy. *Annual Review of Psychology,* 8., (February 1957) 309–330, ISSN: 0066-4308

Woolf S. H.; & Atkins, D. A. (2001). The evolving role of prevention in health care: contributions of the US Preventive Service Task Force. *American Journal of Preventive medicine,* 20., 3., Suppl. 1., (April 2001) 13–20, ISSN: 0749-3797

Wright, J. H. & Small, D. K. (2004). Computer programs for cognitive-behavior therapy, In: *Encyclopedia of Cognitive Behavior Therapy,* A. Freeman; S. H. Felgoise; A. M. Nezu; C. M. Nezu & M. A. Reinecke (Eds.), 324-327, Springer, ISBN: 978-306485810, New York

22

Application of “Virtual Realities” in Psychotherapy: Possibilities, Limitations and Effectiveness

Dr. Christiane Eichenberg
University of Cologne (Institute of Clinical Psychology and Psychological Diagnosis)
Germany

1. Introduction

In numerous projects, the Internet has proven to be a useful enhancement and a helpful support to psychosocial and psychotherapeutic methods. Key words such as online-therapy, e-therapy, and e-mental health are frequently used in this context (for an overview, see Bauer & Kordy, 2008; Eichenberg, 2008; Eichenberg & Ott, in press; Ott & Eichenberg, 2003; Bauer & Kordy, 2008). Another tool considered useful is mobile media, which can effectively be applied to the entire spectrum of clinical-psychological interventions (Döring & Eichenberg, 2007). Virtual Reality (VR) technologies go one step further by enabling the creation of computer-based models of the real world that can be interacted via man-machine interfaces. VR applications can also be accessed via the Internet, but only singular and stationary programs exist so far. The observation that virtual stimuli trigger real anxiety, often accompanied by physiological symptoms (elevated blood pressure, sweating and nausea), has led to the integration of these modern applications into the spectrum of therapeutic intervention techniques.

Two conditions are necessary in order for people to experience virtual environments as "real" and thus render the environments therapeutically useful. These two conditions are referred to as "immersion" and "presence".

An individual's involvement with the virtual environment due to objective, stimulating conditions is referred to as immersion. On the one hand, the virtual environment's visual, auditory, and tactile designs create the three-dimensional perception that the VR model is the real world. On the other hand, the perception of the virtual environment is facilitated by specific output devices (e.g. data-goggles, monitor) and special input devices (e.g. data gloves, voice recognition software, geolocation systems, and line-of-sight trackers). These special devices and systems enable synchronous activity and communication with the computer generated model using gestures, mimicry, language, body position, etc.

The subjective experience of physically being in a virtual environment and that this environment is real is referred to as presence. Characteristics of presence are the perception of the environment being real, blanking out real-world stimuli as well as involuntary and objectively meaningless body movements. For example, a person might crouch to feel his feet firmly planted on the real floor while crossing a virtual bridge over a virtual abyss.

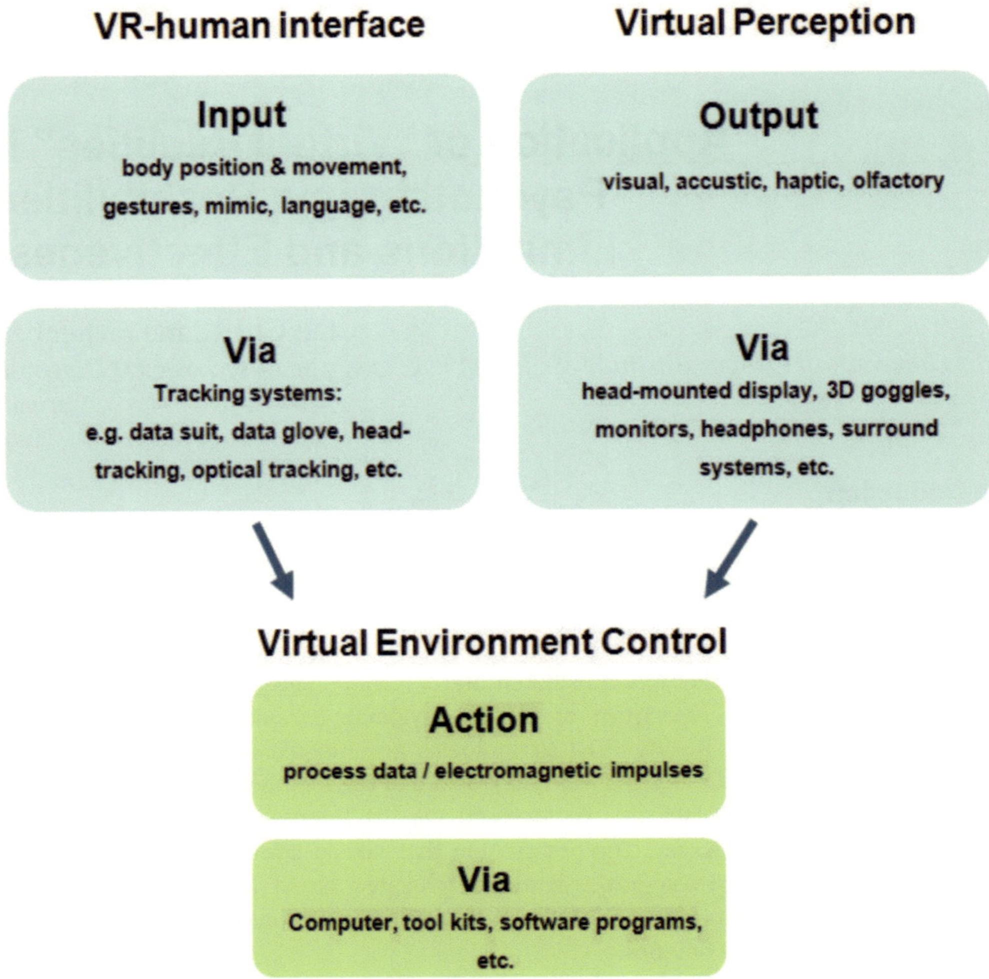

Fig. 1. Technical requirements of VR applications (source: proprietary graphic)

2. Use in psychotherapy

Initially, VR technologies were applied in various areas of medicine (comp. Kaltenborn, 1994). The development of a three-dimensional visualization system facilitated laparoscopic surgery. In the field of rehabilitation of physically disabled patients, carrying out everyday tasks was simplified with the aid of VR devices. Mute patients, for example, could carry on verbal conversations using a data glove that captures gestures, which are interpreted by the computer and forwarded to a language system. The language system then translates the gestures into a synthetic language.

Since 2000, VR applications have been systematically tested in the field of psychotherapy, particularly in behavior therapy and proven to be effective in the treatment of various specific phobias, as first studies show. According to the theories of behavior therapy, in order to treat phobias the anxiety provoking situation must be sought, avoidance amplifies the notion that the stimulus is dangerous and thus prevents corrective experiences. Being able to experience and tolerate anxiety is an essential part of the therapy. The aim of the treatment is to revise maladjusted concepts and to learn new behavior. There are two different forms of exposure therapy. Immediate exposure to the feared situation or object in reality is referred to as "in vivo" exposure. Exposure to the situation or object in imagination only is referred to as "imaginal" exposure. Both methods involve incremental, i.e. graduated exposure. Starting with stimuli that trigger only low levels of fear, the exposure is incrementally or massively increased. In the latter case, patients are exposed to their most extreme fear ("flooding" or, in imaginal exposure, "implosion").

Consequently, exposure treatments that employ VR applications go one step further than imaginal confrontation because they present a three-dimensional and interactively explorable environment. As a medium between imaginal and in-vivo exposure to anxiety-provoking stimuli, the effectiveness of these methods is outlined in the following article.

3. Empirical evidence of the effectiveness of exposures using VR

Most studies of the effectiveness of VR applications have examined their use in treating specific phobias such as fear of heights, fear of flying, fear of animals, and social phobias. A few studies have been made using VR to treat other disorders, though some of these applications are questionable not only ethically but also by current psychotherapeutic standards.

Firstly, two current meta analyses regarding the effectiveness of VR environments in treating anxiety disorders are summarily presented. Subsequently, exemplary studies of the treatment of anxiety disorders, including posttraumatic stress disorder, and the therapeutic VR components used in the treatments are introduced.

3.1 Meta analyses

There are currently two meta analyses that analyze and document the present state of research on the effectiveness of VR-based exposure treatments for anxiety disorders.

N=21 evaluation studies (N=300 subjects) substantiating the effectiveness of VR-based exposure therapy were evaluated by Parsons and Rizzo (2008). All studies with pre-post measurements were included in this study; using a controlled study design was not a prerequisite for admission to the analysis. Regarding the reduction of symptoms by using VR therapies, the authors found an average effect size of d=.95 (SD=.02). Aside from fear of flying (d=1.5; SD=.05), the effect size was largest for the treatment of panic disorder with agoraphobia (d=1.79; SD=.02). The effect size was nearly identical for the treatment of social phobia (d=.96; SD=.10), acrophobia (d=.93; SD=.06) as well as arachnophobia (d=.92; SD=.12), with that of PTSD being the smallest (d=.87, SD=.01). The authors assumed a series of determining factors (e.g. degree of immersion and presence, duration of the disorder, socio-demographic aspects), but were unable to make empirically funded statements based on the data at hand, because too few studies provided information about these aspects.

Powers and Emmelkamp (2008) chose a more rigid design and used only 13 controlled studies (with N=397 subjects) as a basis. They surmised that VR treatment for anxiety disorder is highly effective (in comparison to the waiting control group: median d=1.11) and at least as effective as in-vivo therapy (median d=.34).

Overall, the findings at hand show that VR treatment for anxiety disorders is highly effective, although it seemed more effective in treating diffuse phobias (e.g. fear of flying) than more complex anxiety disorders (e.g. social phobia, PTSD). However, the weaknesses common to meta analyses (e.g. publication bias, as studies with insignificant results are less frequently published, with the consequence that effects tend to be overestimated) need to be considered. Conversely, the limitations of the studies involved need to be taken into account in particular (e.g. sample sizes that are too small, partially missing data about the time of the follow-up ratings and the conjunctive lastingness of a successful treatment). Introducing varied levels of immersion (e.g. head-mounted display or VR-cave) as independent variables and generally ensuring that no measurement instruments are used that might favor one treatment environment over the other (e.g. imaginal vs. VR) is an important consideration for future studies.

3.2 Exemplary studies of various syndromes

The meta studies on hand reveal that the effectiveness of VR has been studied mainly in behavior therapy for patients with anxiety disorders. Anxiety disorders are among the most frequently diagnosed psychological disorders. In the federal health survey of 1998/99, a 12-month prevalence was established among 14.5% of the adult German population (Jacobi et al., 2004). Consequently, comprehensive research efforts to optimize existing treatment methods come as no surprise. Anxiety disorders lie within the traditional treatment range of behavioral procedures and lend themselves well to the VR setting due to their concept of exposure (as opposed to psychodynamic therapy procedures, which center on the relationship aspect). Thus, anxiety disorders present the first syndrome category for which the use of modern media such as the Internet or VR technology as a setting for interventions was scientifically evaluated (Eichenberg & Portz, 2005).

The two major diagnostic classification systems differ in their definition of anxiety disorders. While the DSM-IV (the American Psychiatric Association's Diagnostic and Statistical Manual of Mental Disorders; Saß et al., 1998) contains an individual chapter named „Anxiety Disorders", they are included in the chapter „Neurotic, Stress and Somatoform Disorders" in the ICD-10 (the World Health Organizations' International Classification of Diseases, 1991). The ICD-10 distinguishes between the subgroups of *phobic* disorders (agoraphobia, social anxiety disorder, as well as specific phobias) and other *anxiety disorders* (panic disorder, generalized anxiety disorders). *Posttraumatic stress disorder* is consequently dealt with in the same chapter as anxiety disorders.

Fear of heights

The fear of situations involving heights (acrophobia) is frequently reported among the public. In a survey of over 8000 adults, 20% admitted to having experienced an exaggerated fear of heights at least once in their lifetime, but not to the extent that would meet the clinical criteria of acrophobia (Curtis et al., 1998). In the cited study, acrophobia ranks immediately behind the fear of animals, which was reported most often (22%). 5.3% of those surveyed met the criteria for diagnosis of acrophobia. Contrary to the common observation that women develop a specific phobia more frequently than men, this is not distinctively the case with acrophobia. While 55-70% of acrophobia sufferers are female, 75-90% of adults suffering from fear of animals are women (comp. DSM-IV, Saß et al., 1998).

Empirical research of VR-based exposure therapy began with individual case studies of patients suffering from acrophobia. Rothbaum et al. (1995) described an acrophobic student who had five therapy sessions after being shown anxiety reducing relaxation techniques. During these sessions, he was exposed to several virtual environments within which he

could gradually move up to increasingly higher planes. On each plane, the student used relaxation techniques to habituate himself to the height. Standardized instruments (e.g. Avoidance Scale, Attitude Towards Heights) measured an improvement of his symptoms in a pre-post comparison. Even if these first studies show methodical deficits (effects of relaxation techniques were not distinguished from effects of exposure techniques), they do illustrate the fundamental advantages of imaginal confrontation. On the one hand, actual locations, in this case high bridges, can often only be reached with great effort and pedestrians can disturb the intervention. On the other hand, the stimulus can be applied in measured doses and the anxiety-provoking situation can be accessed in a safe and individually remodelable environment.
The therapeutic potential of VR exposure as part of behavior therapy to treat acrophobic patients was confirmed in a study series by Emmelkamp et al. (2001). In the first study, a within-subjects design was used. Ten acrophobic patients were gradually exposed to heights in VR during sessions and then went in-vivo to heights in the company of the therapist. The extent of their acrophobia was measured before treatment, after VR exposure, and after in-vivo exposure. Various scales indicated significant improvement after VR exposure, while only one variable (Fear of Heights, Cohen) registered additional improvement after in-vivo exposure. The authors assumed that a blanket effect had happened in the sense that VR treatment was so effective that no further significant improvement could be achieved after repeated in-vivo exposures. In a second study (Emmelkamp et al., 2002), VR and in-vivo exposure were compared in a between-subject design. N=33 acrophobic patients with an average age of 44 (SD=9.3) and having suffered from the disorder for an average of 31.5 years (SD=11.3) were randomly exposed to both VR and real settings. Each exposure was

Fig. 2. VR-environment used to treat fear of flying (source: A. Mühlberger)

graduated over the course of three sessions. In order to increase the comparability of the two scenarios, the real environment used for in-vivo exposures was replicated in the virtual environment. Thus, three environments - virtual or real - had to be visited: A shopping mall in Amsterdam with four floors, escalators, and bridge railings, a 50 meter high fire escape, and the roof garden on a university's grounds (65 feet high). The patients rated their anxiety levels on the SUDS-scale (Subjective Units of Disturbance) at specified points in time. Each time patients had habituated themselves to a particular situation, they were encouraged to switch to a more challenging exercise. The evaluation results demonstrated that both forms of treatment were equally effective. VR as well as the in-vivo variant lead to equally significant improvements that continued to last after six months. Krijn et al. (2004) found no differences in effectiveness regarding the dependence upon different levels of presence, i.e. operationalized with VR via Cave (high degree of presence) or head-mounted-display (low degree of presence).

Fear of flying

According to references, phobic *fear of flying* affects approximately 10% of the population (e.g. Nordlund, 1983). Another 20% fly with considerable unease (Institute of Demoscopy Allensbach, 2003). There is a frequent comorbidity with other disorders: According to Kinnunen (1996), 43% of those suffering from fear of flying also suffer from claustrophobia, while another 53% suffer from acrophobia. The situations that trigger fear in individuals suffering from fear of flying differ greatly. In a study with 144 subjects suffering from fear of flying (Mühlberger & Hermann, 1997), 5% of subjects reported fear of an accident happening, 29% fear of heights, 26% fear of enclosed rooms, 25% fear of an anxiety attack, 14% fear they might not receive medical attention, 12% fear of being subjected to fear itself, and just as many were afraid of their fear being noticed by others.

Schubert and Regenbrecht (2002) refer to some of these anxiety-specific characteristics that, on a conceptual basis alone, support using VR in regard to treating fear of flying. In particular, they highlight the logistical and financial expenditure that is far lower in comparison to in-vivo exposure. They also emphasize the privacy and familiarity of the treatment setting compared to the public exposure during a regular commercial flight. Mühlberger et al. (2008) add the ease of repeating VR exposure. Rothbaum et al. (2000) introduced a controlled study comparing VR supported therapy to in-vivo exposure. Forty-five subjects with fear of flying were randomly assigned to either VR or in-vivo therapy. Both treatment environments resembled each other in the first four sessions (cognitive intervention, breathing exercises, and thought stopping training). In the next four sessions of VR treatment, patients were seated in a virtual airplane that they visualized using data goggles. The visualization was supplemented with realistic airplane ambiance noises or the simulation of turbulent weather. The patients were gradually exposed to increasingly anxiety-provoking situations (from simply sitting in a parked airplane to turbulence during takeoff, to actual flying or landing). In the in-vivo environment the subjects spent two double sessions at an airport. First they took part in flight preparation training, then they entered parked airplanes and visualized takeoff, flight and landing of the plane (combination of in-vivo and imaginal treatment). A pre-post comparison using several standardized measuring instruments showed significant improvement of symptoms in both treatment groups. No significant differences were apparent between the two treatment groups, even after the follow up rating after six months, and the improvements remained consistent. The subjects in the waiting condition showed no reduction in symptoms; however, it should be critically mentioned that the stimuli were not identical in the two

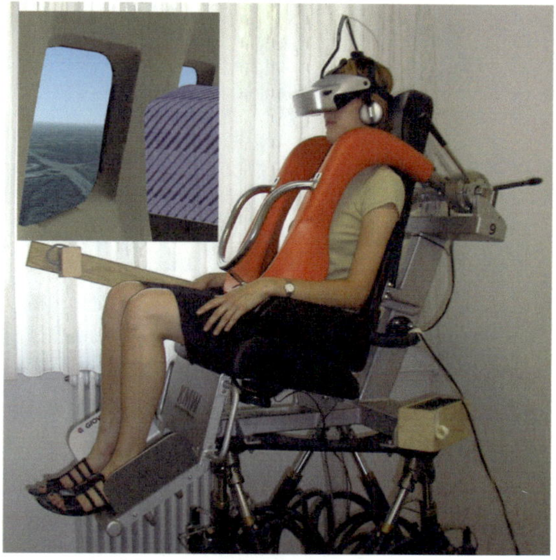

Fig. 3. Fear of flying: simulator (source: A. Mühlberger)

treatment environments, because an actual flight was not part of the therapy. A further study conducted by Wiederhold et al. (2003) revealed that graduated VR treatment combined with the feedback of physiological parameters (breathing, heart frequency, skin resistance) was most effective in comparison to pure VR therapy and imaginal exposure using the same graduated exposure to fear. In a randomized study, the authors found that 20% of the patients in the imaginal environment, 80% of the patients in the VR treatment and 100% of the patients who received VR exposure with additional feedback of biological parameters were able to fly again after eight weeks of therapy. Study series by German scientists from the University of Würzburg also substantiated the effectiveness of VR: Even short-term VR exposure therapy in only one session is useful for treating fear of flying in the long run. The authors demonstrated the participation in a completion flight is important for long-term therapy success, while the attendance of a therapist during this flight has little influence (Mühlberger et al., 2006). The following pictures show the simulator as well as a section of the VR (inside of the airplane) the way they were used in the Würzburg studies.

Fear of spiders

In the ICD-10, fear of spiders (arachnophobia) is assigned to the category of zoophobias, subgroup of specific phobias. Zoophobias are the most common specific phobias, the exaggerated fear of small, crawling, scuttling animals like spiders, snakes and rats being predominant. According to references, the prevalence of arachnophobia is 3.5-6.1% of the population, a large percentile of them women (Schmitt et al., 2009). A person suffering from arachnophobia will experience intense fear paired with physical reactions as well as avoidance and flight behavior when exposed to a spider. This can impede a person's daily life, such as being limited when choosing an apartment or needing help when confronted with a spider (comp. casuistic). Since spontaneous recovery is rare, behavior therapy is the preferred method in treating this disorder.

Single case studies (Carlin et al., 1997) as well as controlled studies have documented successful treatments of arachnophobia with VR.

Fig. 4. VR-environment used for exposure treatment of arachnophobia (source: www.hitl.washington.edu)

Case example (from Carlin et al., 1997)

Mrs. M. (37 years old) had suffered from arachnophobia that severely affected her daily life for 20 years. Before she drove to work in the mornings, she would search her car for spiders, spray pesticide, and leave a burning cigarette in the ashtray with the car windows closed, because she had heard that spiders do not like smoke. She routinely sealed the bedroom windows with tape and the door with towels before she went to bed to make sure no spiders could enter the room. After washing her clothes, she would put each piece of clothing into an individual plastic bags, sealing the bags to make sure the clothing stayed free of spiders.

Mrs. M. took part in 12 VR sessions of 60 minutes each over the course of three months. Before the first session, she was exposed to photos and later to plastic models of spiders over the course of several hours. Despite these preparative exposures, she remained extremely phobic. The therapist saw the advantage of using VR exposure because it enabled him to control the anxiety-provoking stimulus. Virtual spiders obey commands and can be touched without risk and brought to a desired position.

During the first VR sessions, Mrs. M. was exposed to two virtual spiders in a simulated kitchen - one large brown spider and one smaller black one. One month later (5th session), the visual simulation of one of the spiders was interfaced with a furry toy spider. This spider carried a sensor so that movement of the toy resulted in the movement of the virtual spider ("tactile augmentation"). The addition of a tactile stimulus was supposed to add to a maximum degree of presence and maximum transfer to the "real world".

The combination of tactile and visual stimuli triggered intense fear responses in Mrs. M. She experienced physical symptoms such as dry mouth, uncontrollable shaking of her hands and legs, and profuse sweating.

After completion of therapy, however, she showed a visible reduction in fear towards spiders.

While her self-rating of experienced fear during the visual-tactile exposure was 7.9 on a scale of 1-10, she rated her fear at a level of 3 by the end of therapy and showed no more physical symptoms. Off the 280 students who, like Mrs. M., completed a self-rating scale of arachnophobia, 29% were just as afraid or even more afraid of spiders than Mrs. M.
Mrs. M.'s improvement is so profound that she is now able to go camping.
The success of the treatment described above was also confirmed in follow-up studies (comp. Garcia-Palacios et al., 2002). At the same time, these studies revealed that VR treatments that combine the use of tactile and visual elements are more effective than purely visual VR exposures (Hoffmann et al., 2003).

Social Phobia

The fear of being critically observed by others, leading to avoidance of social situations, is referred to as social phobia. More extensive social phobias usually occur in combination with low self-esteem and fear of criticism. Social phobias symptomatically escalate in form of blushing, shortness of breath, cramping, speech impediment and frequent slips of the tongue, shaky hands, nausea, the urge to urinate, and even panic attacks. Typically, those affected fear that their nervousness or fear could be noticed, which only increases their anxiety. In an attempt to avoid all of this from happening, individuals with social phobias often avoid situations that could expose them to being observed by others to begin with. This can have a negative impact on a person's private and career life and lead to social isolation. About 11% of the male and 15% of female population suffer from social phobia at least once in their lifetime (Maggee et al., 1996).
Studies using clinical random samples also exist for the treatment of social phobia using VR settings. In a randomized design, Klinger et al. (2005) studied the effectiveness of VR supported therapy in comparison to cognitive behavior therapy with 36 patients who had, on average, been suffering from social phobia for 15 years. Various rating scales as well as therapist ratings were used to measure the effectiveness of the treatment after 12 sessions. Both VR and cognitive behavior therapies were found to be highly effective treatment forms for this specific phobia as well, successfully reducing fear and avoidance. Distinctions between the two forms of treatment were insignificant (comp. also Roy et al. 2003). Specific VR environments have also been developed to treat public speaking fear, a potential characteristic of social phobia (e.g. Anderson et al., 2003; Herbelin et al., 2002; Pertaub et al., 2001).
The use of VR in therapy to treat further anxiety disorders (e.g. claustrophobia: see single case study by Botella, 1998) and other psychological disorders (eating disorders: see Riva et al., 2001, alcoholism: see Lee et al., 2007) was examined as well. Studies on the effectiveness of VR in treating posttraumatic stress disorder are also available.

Posttraumatic stress disorder

Approximately 30% of individuals who experience a traumatic event suffer from a psychological disorder as a result. One of these disorders is the posttraumatic stress disorder (PTSD), which has been recognized as a formal diagnosis since 1980. According to the ICD-10, PTSD comprises the following symptoms: Those affected were exposed to a short or long-lasting event or situation of an exceptionally threatening or catastrophic nature, which is likely to cause pervasive distress in almost anyone. This leads to symptoms such as intrusions (flashbacks, repeating dreams), avoidance of activities and situations reminiscent of the trauma, the partial or complete inability to recall some important aspects of the event or situation, or symptoms of hyperarousal (e.g. increased startle reaction, sleeping disorders). Potentially traumatic events can be divided into two groups: manmade disasters (war, torture, and exile; sexual abuse, violent crimes, bullying) and natural disasters (e.g. earthquakes, accidents, life-threatening diseases) (Fischer, Weber & Eichenberg, in print).

There are a handful of studies that examine the utilization and effectiveness of VR in treating PTSD, in particular PTSD as a result of *terrorist attacks* and *wartime experiences*.

Difede and Hoffmann (2002) developed a VR environment for patients suffering from PTSD as reaction to the events of September 11, 2001 in New York. In their initial case study, the authors describe the treatment of a 26-year-old woman whose 9/11-related posttraumatic stress disorder had not responded to traditional imaginal exposure therapy. Having witnessed the attacks from across the street, she had survived without serious physical injury, but developed severe PTSD symptoms. She suffered from flashbacks, avoidance, hypervigilance, and difficulty falling and staying asleep.

The patient was treated with six VR sessions of 45-60 minutes. She was exposed to the following virtual scenarios:

1. A jet flies over the WTC towers, but doesn't crash, normal New York city street sounds.
2. Then a jet flies over, hits building, but no explosion
3. Then a jet flies over, crashes with explosion, but no sound effects
4. Then a jet flies over, crashes with explosion and explosion sound effects
5. Burning and smoking building (with hole where jet crashed), no screaming
6. Burning and smoking building (with hole where jet crashed) and screaming
7. Burning and smoking building (with hole where jet crashed), screaming, and people jumping
8. Second jet crashes into second tower with explosion and sound effects
9. Second tower collapses with dust cloud
10. First tower collapses with dust cloud
11. The full sequence

According to standardized clinical and self-report measures, the patient's symptoms were reduced immediately following the VR exposure treatments. This result was validated in a controlled study using a small random sample (Difede et al., 2006).

In Israel, Josman et al. (2008) developed the VR environment "BusWorld" with the aim of using VR therapy to help individuals who had experienced terrorist bombings. To test the functionality of the system, they ran a pilot test with 30 healthy subjects and gradually exposed them to four levels containing a re-enacted attack. The psychotherapeutic treatment comprised of ten VR sessions of 90-120 minutes each.

There are several studies about using VR to treat patients suffering from PTSD as a result of wartime experiences. Rothbaum et al. (2001) examined the effectiveness of VR in a controlled study with 10 Vietnam veterans. The veterans were exposed to authentically recreated war scenes (e.g. flight over Vietnam accompanied by auditory and visual effects of rockets and explosions) in eight VR sessions. While they experienced a reduction in PTSD symptoms after the sessions, the intrusion-score increased after the 6-month catamnesis.

Gerardi et al. (2008) tested the environment "Virtual Iraq" in a single case study of a 29-year-old soldier who had spent a year-long tour in Iraq. He was exposed to "Virtual Iraq" in four sessions of 90 minutes each; the exposure included olfactory elements (e.g. the smell of burnt rubber).

Fig. 5. „BusWorld" (source: research.haifa.ac.il)

Overall these study designs give rise to ethical concerns. Exposing Vietnam veterans suffering from severe PTSD symptoms to authentically recreated war scenarios or exposing witnesses of the 9/11 attacks to the same, dramatic virtual situation is a form of exposure that is contra-indicated as far as current research on trauma therapy is concerned. Several phases (i.a. stabilization, developing a therapeutic relationship, resolution of the traumatic memory, where the course of the traumatic situation is outlined and thus encapsulated) must precede re-experiencing and processing the traumatic experience (comp. Fischer, 2000; 2007). None of these phases were considered in the studies referred to here. Therefore, the risk of re-traumatization in VR exposure therapy is higher than the likelihood of successful processing of the traumatic experience. (For more critical issues, e.g. risk of renewed traumatization because the presented stimuli do not exactly depict the traumatic situation that the patient experienced, see Wagner & Maercker, 2009). At the same time, VR can be used to educate health professionals about recognizing symptoms by practicing adequate negotiation using a simulated case (see Kenny et al., 2008).

4. Conclusion

First studies show that virtual realities are an effective instrument within behavior therapy treatment of anxiety disorders. There are no indications that VR treatment of fear of heights and fear of flying, for example, are less effective than traditional in-vivo exposure therapy. Meanwhile several aspects that are immanent to a VR setting seem to accommodate some patients, for example in their willingness to be exposed to anxiety-provoking stimuli in the first place. There are also advantages to therapists that are summarized in Table 1.

At the same time, however, VR applications hold a number of restrictions and disadvantages for patients because of the risk of new or re-traumatization and ethical considerations and to therapists because VR technology requires technical equipment and the familiarization with this equipment.

Possibilities	Limitations / Risks
For the patient • Increased willingness to be confronted with the anxiety-provoking stimuli (increased subjective perception of safety and control over the presented stimuli) in the first place • A more private atmosphere, lower logistic and financial expenditure (fear of flying) • For patients with limited ability to visualize: VR aids the imagination of the anxiety-provoking situation	**For / To the patient** • „Simulator sickness" • Risk of new traumatization if the specific VR does not reflect the patient's traumatic situation accurately • Risk of re-traumatization if certain phases (i.a. stabilization) do not precede re-experiencing and processing the traumatic experience • Habituation to war and violence: Ethics?!
For the therapist • Exposure is possible in the practice • Possibility of subtler graduation in progression and intensity • In training: learning by simulated cases	**For / To the therapist** • Technology-based treatment: interference-prone • Acquisition is expensive • Training is necessary

Table 1. Advantages and disadvantages of using VR in psychotherapy

Overall, the results at hand are definitely in need of additional data if they are to be considered validated and differential evidence of the effectiveness of VR. The number of studies and random samples is too small to make general statements; moreover, they have pilot study character. In addition, long-term catamneses are missing. Examining personality variables (e.g. attitude towards technology, comprehension of reality and identity, ability to visualize) as possible moderators in order to develop criteria for the *intra- and inter-individual integration* of VR in psychotherapy is advised. With the integration of any kind of media application in therapy, the effects on therapist and patient variables as well as the effects on the therapeutic relationship should be examined.

VR exposure should be seen as a media reception, where the individual experiencing it plays an active and constructive role. The presented stimuli are processed on a cognitive level and assembled to a mental model that is linked to memories and conceptions. Hence, the research results of perception and media psychology are important fundaments in the further development of VR therapy settings. One prerequisite for the effectiveness of VR treatments is that the virtual world has to reflect the real world in a way that enables coherent cognitive and emotional processing. This means that the presentations of VR worlds are enhanced to provide ideal visual, auditory, and tactile stimuli. The VR applications so far have been prototypes. They have not been widespread enough, nor has the technical equipment involved been affordable enough so that VR could be used by behavioral therapists in regular practices to benefit their patients.

Although VR exposure therapy is the traditional domain of behavior therapy, *psychodynamic therapy* has been expanded with the conceptual integration of media-based interventions and training techniques. For an in depth report, refer to Eichenberg (2007). This reference states that media can also be integrated in psychodynamic therapies as long as the primacy "establishment of a relationship comes before technology" is ensured. (For an example see the integration of the self-help book "New ways out of trauma" [Fischer, 2005] in psychodynamic trauma therapies (refer to Angenendt, 2003).

5. References

Anderson P, Rothbaum BO, Hodges LF (2003) Virtual reality exposure in the treatment of social anxiety. *Cognitive and Behavioral Practice 10*: 240-247

Angenendt G (2003) *Entwicklung eines Beratungs- und Therapiemanuals zur Begleitung der Selbsthilfebroschüre "Neue Wege aus dem Trauma"*. Dissertation an der Philosophischen Fakultät der Universität zu Köln

Bauer S, Kordy, H. (Hrsg.) (2008) *E-Mental-Health. Neue Medien in der psychosozialen Versorgung*. Springer, Berlin

Bering R (2005) *Verlauf der Posttraumatischen Belastungsstörung. Grundlagenforschung, Prävention, Behandlung*. Shaker, Aachen

Botella C, Banos RM, Perpina C, Villa H, Alcaniz M, Rey, A (1998) Virtual reality treatment of Claustrophobia: a case repot. *Behaviour Research and Therapie 36*: 239-246

Botella C, Quero S, Baños RM, Perpiña C, Garcia-Palacios A, Riva G (2004) Virtual Reality and Psychotherapy. In: Riva G, Botella C, Légeron P, Optale G (Hrsg) *Cybertherapy, Internet and Virtual Reality as Assessment and Rehabilitation Tools for Clinical Psycology and Neuroscience.* IOS Press, Amsterdam

Carlin AS, Hoffmann HG, Weghorst S (1997) Virtual reality and tactile augmentation in the treatment of spider phobia: a case study. *Behaviour Research and Therapie 35*: 153-158

Curtis, GC, Magee, WJ, Eaton, WW, Wittchen, H-U & Kessler, RC (1998) *Specific fears and phobias. Epidemiology and classification. The British Journal of Psychiatry 173: 212-217*

Difede, J., Cukor, J., Patt, I, Giosan, C. & Hoffman, H. (2006) The Application of Virtual Reality to the Treatment of PTSD Following the WTC Attack. *Ann. N.Y. Acad. Sci. 1071:* 500-501

Difede, J & Hoffman, HG (2002). Virtual Reality Exposure Therapy for World Trade Center Post-traumatic Stress Disorder: A Case Report. *CyberPsychology & Behavior 5*(6): 529-535

Döring N, Eichenberg C (2007) Klinisch-psychologische Interventionen mit Mobilmedien: Ein neues Praxis- und Forschungsfeld. *Psychotherapeut 2*: 127-135

Eichenberg C (2008) Bedeutung der Medien für klinisch-psychologische Interventionen. In B. Batinic, & M. Appel (Hrsg.), *Medienpsychologie* (S. 503-530). Springer, Berlin

Eichenberg, C (2007). Der Einsatz von „Virtuelle Realitäten" in der Psychotherapie: Ein Überblick zum Stand der Forschung. *Psychotherapeut* 5: 362-367

Eichenberg, C & Ott R (in press) Klinisch-psychologische Intervention im Internet: Ein Review zu empirischen Befunden störungsspezifischer Angebote. *Psychotherapeut*

Eichenberg C, Portz K (2005) Angststörungen: Information und Intervention online. *Psychotherapie im Dialog 4:* 452-458

Emmelkamp P, Bruynzel M, Drost L, van der Mast C (2001) Virtual realitiy treatment in acrophobia: a comparison with exposure in vivo. *Cyberpsychologie and Behavior 3*: 335-341

Emmelkamp P, Krijn M, Hulsbosch L, de Vries S, Schuemie MJ, van der Mast C (2002) Virtual reality treatment versus exposure in vivo: a comparative evaluation in acrophobia. *Behavior Research and Therapie:* 509-516

Fischer G (2000) *Mehrdimensionale Psychodynamische Traumatherapie MPTT. Manual zur Behandlung psychotraumatischer Störungen.*Asanger, Heidelberg

Fischer, G (2005) *Neue Wege nach dem Trauma - Erste Hilfe bei schweren seelischen Belastungen.* Düsseldorf: Patmos.

Fischer G (2006) *Kausale Psychotherapie. Ätiologieorientierte Behandlung psychotraumatischer und neurotischer Störungen Manual zur Behandlung psychotraumatischer Störungen.* Asanger, Heidelberg

Fischer, G, Weber, T & Eichenberg, C (in press) Posttraumatische Belastungsstörung. In S. Letzel & D. Nowak (Hrsg.), *Handbuch Arbeitsmedizin.* Landsberg: ecomed MEDIZIN.

Garcia-Palacios A, Hoffman H, Carlin A, Furness TA III, Botella C (2002) Virtual reality in the treatment of spider phobia: A controlled study. *Behaviour Research and Therapy 40*: 983-993

Gerardi, M, Rothbaum, BO, Ressler, K & Heekin, M (2008) Virtual Reality Exposure Therapy Using a Virtual Iraq: Case Report. *Journal of Traumatic Stress 21*(2): 209-213

Herbelin B, Riquier F, Vexo F, Thalmann D (2002) *Virtual Reality in Cognitive Behavioral Therapy : a preliminary study on Social Anxiety Disorder,* 8th International Conference on Virtual Systems and Multimedia, VSMM2002. [Online Available]. http://vrlab.epfl.ch/Publications/pdf/Herbelin_and_al_VSMM_02.pdf

Hoffman HG, Garcia-Palacios A, Carlin C, Furness TA III, Botella-Arbona C (2003) Interfaces that heal: Coupling real and virtual objects to cure spider phobia. *International Journal of Human-Computer Interaction 16*: 283-300

Institut für Demoskopie Allensbach (2003) *Allensbacher Berichte Nr. 16: Wieder mehr Flugreisen*. Institut für Demoskopie Allensbach.

Jacobi F, Klose M, Wittchen H–U (2004) Psychische Störungen in der deutschen Allgemeinbevölkerung: Inanspruchnahme von Gesundheitsleistungen und Ausfalltage. *Bundesgesundheitsblatt -Gesundheitsforschung Gesundheitsschutz 8*: 736-744

Josman, N, Reisberg, A, Weiss, PL, Garcia-Palacios, A & Hoffman, HG (2008) BusWorld: an analog pilot test of a virtual environment designed to treat posttraumatic stress disorder originating from a terrorist suicide bomb attack. Cyberpsychol Behav. 11(6): 775-777

Kaltenborn K-F (1994) Virtuelle Realität - Anwendungen, Möglichkeiten und Grenzen einer neuen Computertechnologie. *Biomedical Journal 39*: 4-14

Kenny, P, Parsons, TD, Pataki, C, Pato, M, St-George, C, Sugar, J & Rizzo, A (2008) Virtual Justina: A PTSD Virtual Patient for Clinical Classroom Training. *Annual Review of CyberTherapy and Telemedicine 6*(1): 113-118

Klinger, E, Bouchard S, Légeron P, Roy S, Lauer F, Chemin I & Nugues P (2005) Virtual Reality Therapy Versus Cognitive Behavior Therapy for Social Phobia: A Preliminary Controlled Study. *Cyberpsychology and Behavior 1*: 76-88

Kinnunen, P (1996) *Flugangst bewältigen*. Weinheim: Psychologie Verlags-Union.

Krijn, M, Emmelkamp, PM, Biemond, R, de Wilde de Ligny, C, Schuemie, MJ & van der Mast, CA (2004). Treatment of acrophobia in virtual reality: the role of immersion and presence. *Behav Res Ther. 42* (2) 229-39

Lee, J-H, Kwon, H, Choi, J & Yang, B-H (2007) *Cue-exposure therapy to decrease alcohol craving in virtual environment*. CyberPsychology & Behavior 10 (5): 617-623

Maggee, WJ, Eaton, WW, Wittchen, H-U, McGonagle, KA & Kessler RC (1996) Agoraphobia, siple phobia and social phobia in the National Comorbidity Survey. *Archives of General Psychiatry, 53* (2): 159-168

Mühlberger, A & Hermann, MJ (1997) *Allgemeiner Flugangstfragebogen*. Unpublished Manuscript, Julias-Maximilians-Universität Würzburg.

Mühlberger, A, Krebs, H & Pauli, P (2008) Expositionsbehandlung von Flugphobie mithilfe virtueller Realität. In Bauer, S & Kordy, H (Hrsg.), *E-Mental-Health*. Neue Medien in der psychosozialen Versorgung (pp. 163-173). Berlin: Springer.

Mühlberger, A , Weik, A., Pauli, P. & Wiedemann, G (2006) One-session virtual reality exposure treatment for fear of flying: 1-Year follow-up and graduation flight accompaniment effects. *Psychotherapy Research 16*(1): 26-40

Nordlund, CL (1983) A Questionnaire Study of Swedes´s Fear of Flying. *Scandinavian Journal of Behaviour Therapy 12:* 150-168

Ott R, Eichenberg C (2003) (Hrsg.). *Klinische Psychologie und Internet. Potenziale für klinische Praxis, Intervention, Psychotherapie und Forschung*. Hogrefe, Göttingen

Pertaub DP, Slater M, Barker C (2001) An experiment on fear of public speaking in virtual reality. *Studies in Health Technology and Informatics* Bd. 81: 372-378

Powers MB, Emmelkamp PMG (2008) Virtual reality exposure therapy for anxiety disorders: A metaanalysis. *Journal of anxiety disorders 22* (3): 561-569

Riva G, Bacchetta M, Baruffi M, Molinari E (2001) Virtual Reality–Based Multidimensional Therapy for the Treatment of Body Image Disturbances in Obesity: A Controlled Study. *Cyberpsychology & Behavior 4*: 511-526

Rothbaum BO, Hodges LF, Kooper R, Opdyke D, Williford J, North M (1995) Virtual reality graded exposure in the treatment of acrophobie: a case report. *Behavior Therapie 26*: 547-554

Rothbaum, BO, Hodges, L, Ready, D et al. (2001) Virtual reality exposure therapy for Vietnam veterans with posttraumatic stress disorder. *J Clin Psychiatry 62*: 617-622

Roy S, Klinger E, Légeron P, Lauer F, Chemin I, Nugues P (2003) Definition of a VR-Based Protocol to Treat Social Phobia. CyberPsychology & Behavior 6: 411-420.

Saß, H, Wittchen, H-U & Zaudig, M (1998) *Diagnostisches und Statistisches Manual Psychischer Störungen (DSM-IV)*. Göttingen: Hogrefe.

Schmitt, WJ & Müri, RM (2009) Neurobiologie der Spinnenphobie. Schweizer *Archiv für Neurologie und Psychiatrie 160(8)* 352–355

Schubert T, Regenbrecht H (2002) Wer hat Angst vor virtueller Realität? Angst, Therapie und Präsenz in virtuellen Welten. In: Bente G, Krämer N, Petersen A (Hrsg.) *Virtuelle Realtitäten* (S. 255-274). Hogrefe, Göttingen

Thönes P (2006) *Der Einsatz bibliografischen Materials in der kardiologischen Rehabilitation – eine qualitative Studie*. Unveröffentlichte Diplomarbeit am Institut für Klinische Psychologie und Psychotherapie der Universität zu Köln

Wagner, B & Maercker, A (2009) Neue Medien für die Intervention bei Traumafolgestörungen. In BU Stetina & I Kryspin-Exner (Hrsg.), *Gesundheit und Neue Medien. Psychologische Aspekte der Interaktion mit Informations- und Kommunikationstechnologien* (S. 135-155). Wien: Springer.

Weltgesundheitsorganisation (1991) *Internationale Klassifikation psychischer Störungen. ICD-10 Kapitel V (F). Klinisch-diagnostische Leitlinien*. Bern: Huber. 978-3456841243

Wiederhold BK, Gevirtz RN, Spira JL (2003) Virtual Reality Exposure Therapy vs. Imagery Desensitization Therapy in the Treatment of Flying Phobia. In Riva G, Galimberti C (Eds), *Towards CyberPsychology: Mind, Cognitions and Society in the Internet Age* (Kap. 14). IOS Press, Amsterdam

23

Virtual Reality-Based Assessment of Social Skills and Its Application to Mental Illnesses

Jae-Jin Kim, MD, PhD[1], Joseph Kim, BA[2]
[1]*Department of Psychiatry, Yonsei University, Seoul,*
[2]*Department of Psychology, Vanderbilt University, Nashville, Tennessee,*
[1]*Korea*
[2]*USA*

1. Introduction

Appropriate usage of social skills by individual members ensures the survival of communities in the human society. Social skills include the cognitive abilities as well as verbal and nonverbal behaviors indispensable for interpersonal interactions. Abnormal social skills have been reported in patients with mental illnesses including schizophrenia and bipolar disorder. Various methods, including self-report, interviews, behavioral observation, and clinical rating scales, have been used for the assessment of social skills, but their usefulness has been undermined by subjective or observational biases. Given that a virtual reality system could provide viable environments for individuals to interact with social avatars, it may be one of the most promising tools for assessing social skills that can minimize concerns of assessment related biases.

2. Characteristic and significance of social skills in patients with mental illnesses

Social skills encompass a set of cognitive abilities and interactive behaviors that facilitate efficient social interaction among individuals in a shared environment. Even though social skills as a whole cannot be claimed as a feature exclusive to human behavior, they nevertheless constitute an irreplaceable part of human interaction by making social communication among one another more articulate and intelligible. This is made possible because social skills can help convey and decode extra information not carried by direct communication using verbal means. As such, social skills can be likened to adding multiple layers of communicative information to relevant social messages (Couture et al., 2006). For example, imagine introducing yourself to someone you have never seen before. In such occasion, it is certainly not considered unusual to smile at the person you are introducing yourself to while offering a handshake as a gesture of salutation. You may even add a cheerful intonation on top of the customary "Nice to meet you" that one might verbalize to a stranger. In this example, the ability to initiate an interaction, smile with your face and to offer your hand to an unfamiliar person can be regarded as non-verbal social skills whereas one's ability to use the idiomatic expression, "Nice to meet you", and aptly topping it with a cheerful intonation when vocalizing the phrase can be regarded as part of a verbal social skill set. These verbal as well as non-verbal usages of social skills in combination convey a cogent social message of geniality and hospitality.

As evident from the example above, social skills can take verbal as well as non-verbal forms, and may be additionally and simultaneously manifested through different sensory channels (e.g., visual, auditory, or tactile) of conveying the relevant information. By simultaneously utilizing multiple channels available, individuals involved in social interactions could use the information to more easily disambiguate other's intentions and may also strengthen the potency of their social communication. In the previous example of introducing oneself to an unfamiliar person, it would seem quite bizarre to merely offer one's hand for a handshake without displaying any affect through facial expressions (or worse, make an angry face). In a similar vein, it would probably seem rather odd to say "Nice to meet you" in a very monotonous tone, even with the smiling and the offering of your hand. In fact, such incongruence in manifestation of social cues may evoke a different interpretation from the observer and trigger suspicions of an ulterior message beneath the superficial friendliness This, however, extends the scope of our discussion to a whole another realm of issues relating to irony and deception in social communication, which will not cover in this chapter.

Social skills usage is not necessarily confined to one specific sensory modality, but can be embedded in multiple kinds. In fact, simultaneously using a wide array of social skills through various sensory modalities can be regarded as an indication of the integrative nature of social skills. "Verbal" social skills are often received through auditory channels. But "non-verbal" social skills such as facial expressions and social gestures are produced via motor output and received through visual input. Having multiple nodes of social skills available at one's disposal for interpersonal interactions allows exploiting individuals to exploit varigated combinations of different social cues and tack subtleties onto relevant communicable messages. What follows from human kinds' such an extraordinary ability to operate social skills using multiple channels is the complexity of the task to decode social messages.

Depending on the manifested symptoms and their severity, a mental illness can take its toll on the quality of very different types of social skills. Taking a detailed account regarding the effect of a mental illness on the affected individual's social skills and vice versa thus becomes all the more critical in order to fully appreciate a patient's mental health status. For example, patients experiencing depressive episodes from bipolar disorder or major depressive disorder often lack the interest to initiate and engage in social interaction, whereas patients with schizophrenia have difficulty in maintaining a meaningful social interaction due to their abnormal thought content and disorganization of speech (Brüne et al., 2010). In both cases, the quality of social interaction should be greatly reduced, however for disparate reasons. The former maybe more heavily influenced by the lack of motivation albeit having intact social skills, whereas the latter should be more affected by aberrant behaviors.

A specific social skills deficit in patients suffering from a mental illness may be an important indicator of how severely they are affected by the disorder. For example, lack of sustained eye contact during interpersonal interaction has long been regarded as a hallmark of social skills deficit in autistic disorders. The degree to which their eye contact is lacking has shown to correlate with their difficulty in social interaction (Pelphrey et al., 2005). Not surprisingly, measuring one's competency in social skills has been widely recognized as a critical step for a comprehensive assessment of a mental illness by scholars across the field of psychiatry and clinical psychology (Harvey et al., 2007). Moreover, assessment of social skills based on our knowledge of diverse elements of social interaction could help us trace mentally ill patients' ability to recognize and generate socially salient cues, ability to use linguistic means of producing and comprehending social messages, as well as the ability to recognize one another's intentions and emotions through non-verbal means such as gestures, facial expressions, eye-gaze, and so on.

3. Limitations of conventional methods of social skills assessment

Despite their acknowledgeable contribution to measuring and documenting of social skill competency in mentally ill patients, traditional measures of social skills have often come short of the expectation scholars have projected onto them (Bedell et al., 1998). The contexts in which social skills are used are inherently interactive, since social interaction by definition involves two or more parties. Naturally, such interactive nature of social skills has contributed to the difficulty assessing social skills that reflect multi-faceted features of a "real-life" social interaction. Even with such difficulty, there still have been different approaches developed to assess individual social skills. Two conventional measures of social skill competency come from clinician's assessment and self/peer-reports. Both of these reports are based on anecdotal and retrospective evidence retrieved from the rote memory of a patient or a patient's peer. Therefore, data acquired using this method may often not reflect an accurate assessment of the patient's social skills, but rather indicate a record of the memory of social skills being used. This is not to claim that the measure is entirely useless, however, they still seem at times incomplete and inexact given we would like as precise assessment of the patient's social skills as possible.

Moreover, even though these measures are useful in gauging rough levels of social functioning in patients, they are not entirely unadulterated measures of social skills as one might assume. Because these measures are subjectively rated by clinicians or told to them laden with the personal feelings of patients and patient peers, the assessment can be subject to at least a moderate degree of human interpretation, if not more. Unless a specific assessment of patients is based on direct observation of social skills being used in a naturalistic context, the assessment is only as good as "second-hand" information filtered through another individual's interpretation. Clinicians are not free from biases of their own when meeting with patients for an assessment. Their prior beliefs about specific mental illnesses or evaluation of the patient's previous assessment record can provide a context in which the assessment can be more thoroughly executed but at the same time unwittingly engender biases that go along with one's prior experiences. Such clinicians' subjective interpretations and biases can occur against the clinicians' best intention and judgment not to influence the measure with subjectivity.

Additionally, the conventional paper and pencil method of clinician-driven social skills assessment have limited range of quantifying the acquired data. Needless to say these measures neglect to reflect the multi-sensory and interactive nature of the context in which social skills are often used by individuals. But central to the problem is that proper record keeping of quantitative measurements acquired using human senses is not an easy feat. For example, one could mention in the clinical report of a child autism patient that she exhibits very little sustained eye contact. But what if she was to later show slight improvement on the duration of eye contact after a cognitive behavioral treatment, but then the clinician might not notice? If there was a way to track the patient's eye movement and the duration while engaging another person, it would provide a more accurate and reliable data that could be an informative indicator of a tangible improvement.

4. Virtual reality-based social skills assessments as complements to conventional methods

Recent development and technological advances have allowed the use of the virtual reality system to present socio-affective stimuli to human subjects, thus enabling scholars to measure behavioral characteristics of participants during social interaction with virtual avatars. Technological advancements in graphics and other human motion tracking hardware should be able to promote pushing "virtual reality" closer to "reality," and thus virtual reality can be used to assess social cognition and behavior in real life-like situations (Tarr and Warren, 2002). Subjects in a virtual environment tend to treat virtual persons as actual humans, and respond to them in a naturalistic way regarding personal space, social presence and affect (Blascovich et al., 2002; Bailenson et al., 2003). Virtual reality's faithful renditions of the real world provide a tremendous advantage in terms of offering human subject users a realistic experience.

In particular, virtual reality can provide a more realistic and convincing sensory environment in which mentally ill patients may be able to engage in social interaction that clinicians could later base their assessment on. The author's research team performed a pilot study to examine whether a virtual avatar could be applied to acquiring the patients' behavioral characteristics in a short conversation situation (Ku et al., 2006). Tasks to approach to a visually presented avatar on a screen using a joystick, initiate a talk, and answer to avatar's questions was assigned to patients with schizophrenia, and one of the behavioral parameters was the interpersonal distance. The results showed that the interpersonal distance was negatively correlated with the negative syndrome scale, which was consistent with a previous research reporting a similar relationship in the interpersonal distance using a real person's image (Nechamkin et al., 2003). We concluded, therefore, that the virtual avatar could be perceived as a real human by patients with schizophrenia and the avatar could draw the patients' behavior characteristics. This pilot study suggested that virtual reality would be useful in investigating the interpersonal behavior of mentally ill patients when a virtual environment populated by virtual avatars is properly used.

Based on the findings from this pilot study, our works were extended to various assessing tools evaluating social characteristics on the virtual environment. In another pilot study, using a morphing technique, we were able to evoke varied perception of emotional faces of virtual avatars by effectively manipulating affective information on the virtual avatar's faces and to validate the prototype for further use (Ku et al., 2005). In order to further test hypotheses about social cognition in mentally ill patients, we have developed these virtual reality based sociality-measuring systems for evaluating communication skills, eye gaze behavior, social cue perception, social problem solving, and emotional expression (Han et al., 2009). Using these systems which were set in specially fitted room (Fig 1), we have used virtual avatars for various applications which need to communicate with other person or to educate by showing humanlike behavior.

5. Measuring personal space using the virtual reality system

Our main work for social assessment was a system for measuring personal space. Personal space, an invisible boundary surrounding an individual that others cannot intrude upon, is an important nonverbal component of social skills (Hayduk, 1983; Bellack et al., 1997). It is a good, measurable parameter of social cognition in mentally ill patients, and virtual reality can be a favorable way to objectively study it. In order to investigate personal space, we

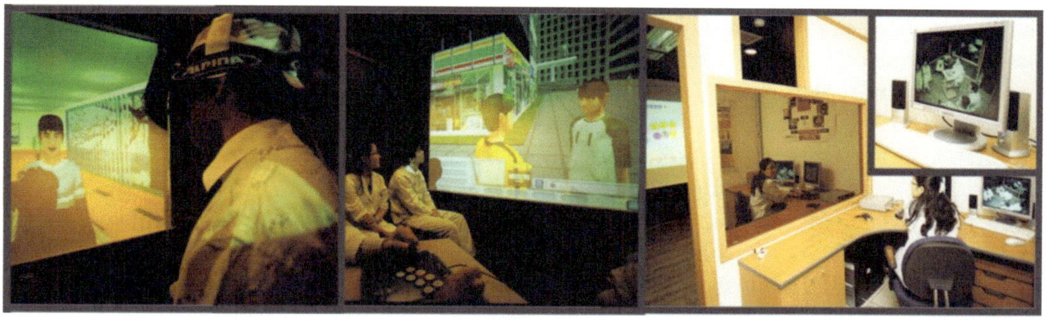

Fig. 1. Virtual reality presentation chamber. The chamber consists of the meeting room and the monitoring room. The meeting room is equipped with a head mounted display, a tracker, a beam projector, a screen, a camcorder, a speaker, and so on. In the monitoring room, a computer system controls all facilities in the meeting room and a situation in the meeting room can be observed through a one-way mirror.

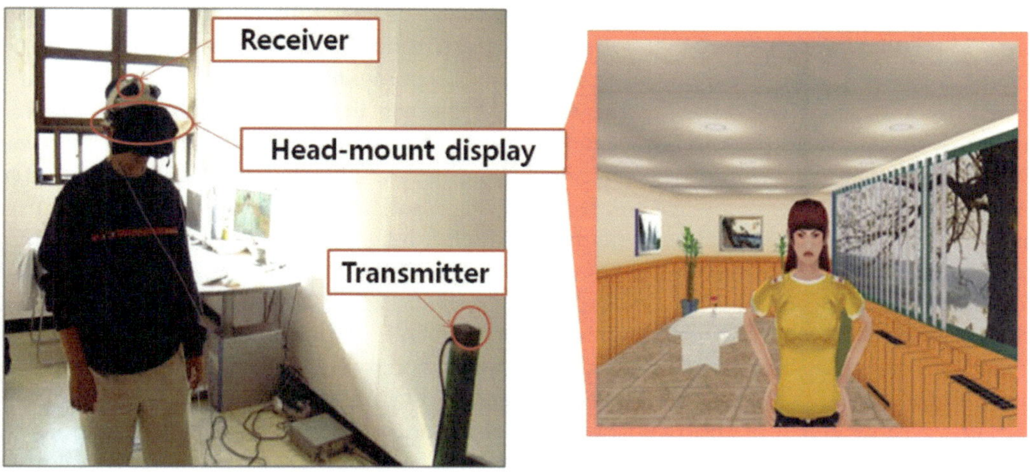

Fig. 2. Virtual reality social encounter task for measuring personal space. A participant is wearing a head-mounted display and enters into a virtual room. A receiver is placed on the vertex of the participant and represents the position and head orientation from a transmitter. A computer system calculates the distance and angle of head orientation from an avatar on the basis of the information from the receiver.

developed a virtual reality social encounter task (Kim et al., 2009; Park et al., 2009a; Park et al., 2009d). As shown in Fig. 1, the behavioral task assigned to the participant was to talk to an avatar in a virtual room. To present visual stimuli, participants put on a head-mounted display (HMD) that included a display monitor over each eye. The receiver that is needed to compute the position and head orientation in the virtual environment was placed on the vertex of the participant, and earphones were used for auditory stimuli.

To start the task, participants were instructed to walk in front of the avatar and to say "hello." The avatar was programmed to respond by saying "hello", introduce itself by talking about where it was born, where it lived, what it liked or detested, its hobbies and family members, and then ask participants to introduce themselves. There were three male and 3 female avatars displaying happy, neutral, and angry facial expressions, and thus the task consisted of 6 sessions for which six different scripts were prepared. To make the introduction more naturalistic, an experimenter controlled the timing that the avatars would start introducing themselves. In order to increase the degree of realism, the avatars were made to look at participants, blink their eyes seemingly spontaneously, open their mouths in accordance with the recorded voices, and make gestures that matched their facial expressions. All avatars displayed a manner of talk, prosodic expressions, facial expressions, and gestures that were matched in happy, neutral, or angry emotions.

Participants' verbal response onset time and duration were measured during each session. Participants' viewpoint in the virtual environment was rendered by tracking the head position and orientation by the receiver worn on the head. The distance and angle of head orientation were indexed as the average distance and the average angle during the conversation with the avatar in each of six task conditions. The angle of head orientation was used as an indirect measure of the eye gaze of the participant.

In an empirical research for patients with bipolar disorder experiencing manic episodes, the virtual reality social encounter task permitted us to demonstrate negativistic social cognition behavior indicated by increased interpersonal distance as measured by how far the patients were in relation to the avatar in the virtual reality environment, as well as through increased aversion of eye gaze compared to healthy normal control subjects (Kim et al., 2009). In a separate study using the same system, we could confirm that patients with schizophrenia also showed increased personal space, and further their disturbances in personal space had a close relationship with negative symptoms (Park et al., 2009d). The severity of negative symptoms had significant inverse correlations with the distance from the angry and neutral avatars and with the angle of head orientation toward the happy and angry avatars.

A novel finding that patients with bipolar disorders and patients with schizophrenia tended to show significantly increased personal space in relation to a virtual avatar could only be properly obtained using the virtual reality system. Even though anecdotal evidence existed, these studies were the first of its kind to parametrically demonstrate the existence of a meaningful tangible difference displayed in mentally ill patients' social interaction patterns. Larger personal space of the patients may reflect their discomfort in close situations or cognitive deficits. Showing these profiles to patients could help them realize the amount of personal space they need.

In addition, emotional responses including social anxiety are very important factors in a social situation. By using the virtual reality social encounter task, we tried to elucidate the relationship between emotional perception and response during social interactions in patients with schizophrenia (Park et al., 2009a). In this study, emotional valence and arousal of the avatars were rated after completing the task, and the patients significantly underestimated the valence and arousal of angry emotions (Fig. 3A). While valence and arousal ratings of happy avatars were comparable between the patient group and the normal group, the patients reported significantly higher state anxiety in response to happy avatars (Fig. 3B). State anxiety ratings significantly decreased from encounters with neutral to happy avatars in normal controls while no significant decrease was observed in the patient group. Negative symptoms including anhedonia, blunted affect, emotional withdrawal, and passive/apathetic social withdrawal items were significantly correlated with state anxiety ratings of the encounters with happy avatars. These results suggest that patients with schizophrenia may encounter interference with the experience of pleasure in virtual social interactions, and their interference may be associated with negative symptoms.

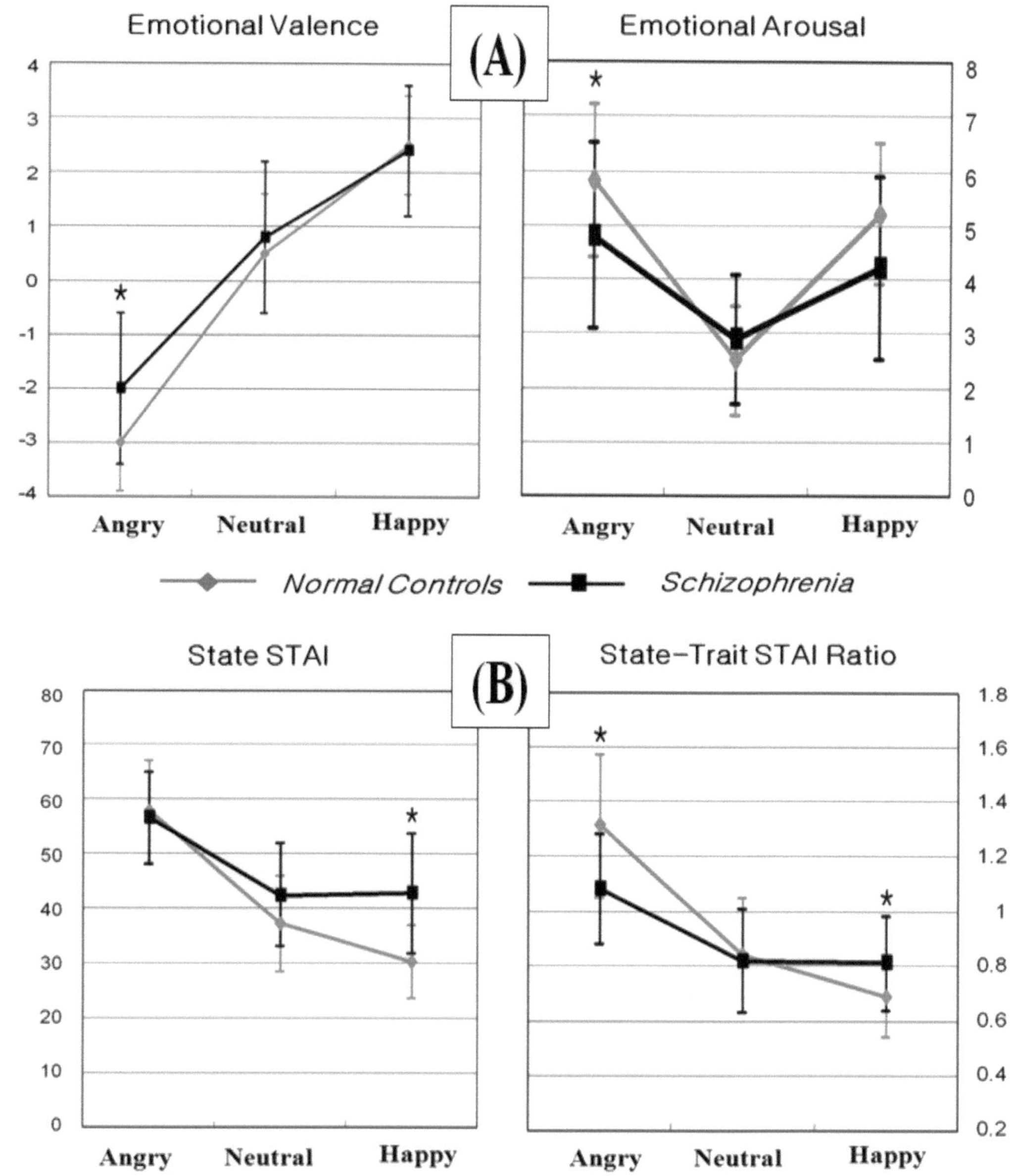

Fig. 3. Emotional perception and anxiety response during the virtual reality social encounter task with angry, happy and neutral emotion-expressing avatars. (A) Significant between-group difference (*) in both valance and arousal was observed at $p < 0.05$. (B) The State-Trait Anxiety Inventory (STAI) score representing the state anxiety experienced during the task. State-Trait STAI ratio represents the state anxiety experienced during the task divided by trait anxiety. Group x condition interaction was significant ($F=15.2$, $df=1.67$, $p<0.001$) without significant anxiety decrease from neutral to happy conditions only in the patient group (patients $t=0.32$, $df=26$, $p=0.75$; controls $t=3.81$, $df=26$, $p<0.01$).

Our next study taking advantage of the customizability of the virtual reality system examined eye gaze patterns of patients with schizophrenia towards agents involved in multi-person interpersonal interaction (Song et al., 2010). Presented with two avatars at the same time, one as the main avatar and the other as the assistant avatar, patients with schizophrenia or healthy normal controls performed a mock conversation (both listening to and speaking to) with avatars in both positive and negative affect-related scenarios (Fig. 4A). Eye gaze to both the main and the assistant avatar were measured and compared between the two groups. Interestingly, for conversation engagement during both scenarios, the patients showed aberrant distribution of eye gaze manifested by shorter eye gaze duration spent towards the main avatar and longer duration towards the assistant avatar compared to healthy controls (Fig. 4B). This pattern of result was more pronounced during the negative affect related scenario. This research not only once again demonstrated the possibility of using virtual reality to measure behavioral correlates of social cognition but additionally exhibited the potential that customizability of the virtual reality system such as utilizing multiple avatars in this case can be of great service to research methods.

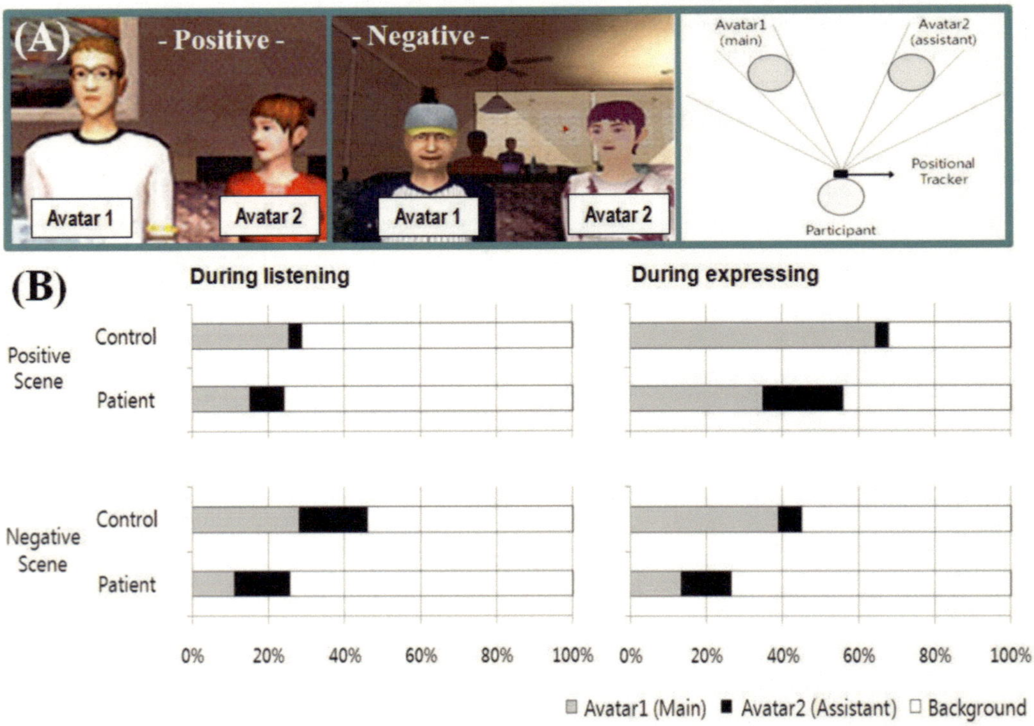

Fig. 4. A virtual reality task for measuring multi-person interpersonal interaction. (A) Positive emotion provoking scene was a conversation with family members who celebrate of father's promotion in the living room, whereas negative emotion provoking scene was a conversation with friends who make fun with participant's nickname at Café. A sectioned diagram on the right represents the experimental setting. (B) Proportion of watching time during listening and expressing showed decreases in staring at the main avatar and increases in staring at the assistant avatar in patients with schizophrenia when compared with normal controls.

6. Expanded uses of virtual reality-based social skills assessments for clinical trials

The utility of the virtual reality system as an assessment tool has also been demonstrated for measuring the effectiveness of therapy or clinical trials of new medications. Such utility has been particularly noticeable in research programs that test the efficacy of antipsychotics that supposedly help rehabilitate social competence in schizophrenia. Most clinical trials for social functioning in patients with schizophrenia have depended on reports from either patients or caregivers and direct observations of patients, but these measures are likely to be influenced not only by antipsychotic medication but also by environmental factors that encourage performance of the skills (McKibbin et al., 2004). On the other hand, performance-based measures of functional skills seem to occur more closely in time with changes in underlying cognitive performance, and thus these unbiased measures are considered to be suitable in clinical trials for schizophrenia to date (Buchanan et al., 2005; Harvey et al., 2007). Using such performance-based measures, one study indicated that treatment with both risperidone and quetiapine resulted in medium to large improvement in social competence (Harvey et al., 2006), whereas another study showed that medication with both clozapine and risperidone produced only very small improvement in social competence (Bellack et al., 1994). The contradictory findings on the effectiveness of atypical antipsychotics to social competence in schizophrenia may be at least in part attributable to the performance-based measure's limitations that rating distributions can vary by the raters' ability and the raters may be unable to discriminate subtle changes of functional skills (Bellack et al., 2006).

In order to avoid such shortcomings, automatic assessment of patients' performances is more likely to be advantageous. Not surprisingly, the author's research team devised the virtual reality system to provide an automatic assessment of patients' performance (Fig. 5), which was named the virtual reality functional skills assessment (VRFSA) (Park et al., 2009c). The VRFSA consisted of six virtual reality scenarios that were produced to represent common conversational situations. Two scenarios included a conversation concerned with a self-introduction with a stranger, two scenarios included a conversation related to making an appointment with a friend, and the final two included a conversation about the conduct of business with a co-worker. Each scenario consisted of two consecutive skills phases: the receptive skills phase during which the subjects listened to the avatar's narration, and the expressive skills phase during which they expressed their answers after the avatar asked questions. Four parameters representing a distinct functional skill were obtained; initiation (the response latency to the avatar's voice for the receptive skills phase and to the avatar's question for the expressive skills phase), duration (the percentage of time spent watching the avatar), proxemics (the average distance from the avatar), and eye contact (the average angle of head orientation from the avatar's eyes).

In a 6-week, randomized, open-label, and flexible dose study for 24 patients with paranoid schizophrenia and 15 healthy controls (Park et al., 2009c), there was a significant difference in the VRFSA between the patients and the healthy controls ($p < 0.05$). Significant treatment skills phase group interaction effect was found, and particularly, compared with risperidone, aripiprazole was more effective in improving social skills competency.

This study suggests that the virtual reality based measures are strongly sensitive to changes in social competence and thus especially well-suited for short-term clinical trials. Here, utilizing the virtual reality system has other several advantages over other conventional choices such as self-report and clinician's assessment. Importantly, virtual reality allows

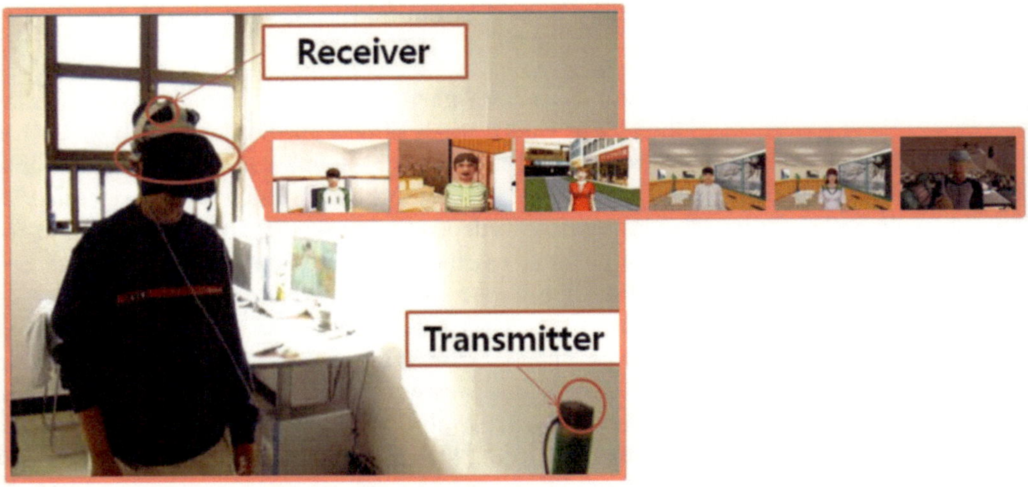

Fig. 5. Virtual Reality Functional Skills Assessment. The system consisted of a head-mount display with a receiver, a transmitter and connections to the computer system. Participants had a conversation with an avatar in the three-dimensional virtual environments with 6 scenarios, and a therapist monitored them using a video screen image captured by a video camera and input data of the times that they initiated and ended their response. The receiver measured the distance between the participants and the transmitter and the angle of the participants' head orientation from the transmitter. Next, the computer system calculated 4 parameters such as initiation, duration, proxemics, and eye contact, based on the information from the therapist's input and the receiver.

raters to present consistent social and affective stimuli, which on the other hand can be very difficult with human raters due to potential noise from various sources including raters' bias towards a specific experimental condition/group (not being blind to the subject assignment) or knowledge about the hypothesis (not being blind to the hypothesis). This is an especially weighty issue for clinical trials because subjectivity during social skills assessment when using conventional assessment methods can be a strong point of criticism in assessment involving human raters. Providing consistent social stimuli using virtual reality can adeptly address the subjectivity issue of effectiveness of a clinical treatment whether it be medications or behavioral therapy.

7. Assessment of problem-solving ability during a social situation

Our next work was to develop an easily applicable tool for an assessment of problem-solving function in various social situations using the virtual reality technique. Social problem-solving is a multidimensional psychosocial variable in the pathogenesis of mental health problems (Elliott et al., 2004) and a cognitive-behavioral process by which a person attempts to discover effective solutions for problems encountered during the course of everyday living (Nezu, 2004). We expected that virtual reality would also be useful for assessing social problem-solving, and made four virtual reality tasks including decision-making after the situational change, getting on an appropriate bus, making judgment against an inadequate request, and coping in the negatively emotional situation. Fig. 6A showed scenes from a task of getting on an appropriate bus. Using such realistic scenarios that are probable in real life, we could investigate the cognitive inflexibility that mentally ill patients might show during situations of social interaction.

Actually, a pilot study was performed to investigate characteristics of patients with schizophrenia for problem-solving in the social situations (Chun et al., 2006). In this study, 30 patients with schizophrenia and 30 healthy normal controls were to make choice judgments on each of 4 scenarios, and social problem-solving abilities of the patients were compared to those of the controls. In the results, the patients tended to consider mother's asking to be less important than meeting with a friend, and to select a deviated choice rather than a flexible solving. They made significantly less appropriate choices in the task of getting on the bus, and felt more intense negative emotion than the control group on the task of copying in the negatively emotional situation. Those results were interpreted to suggest that the patients with schizophrenia have a deficit of problem-solving function in the social situations.

Especially, as shown in Fig. 6B, the patients did show patterns of inflexibility subsequent to situational change. They had a tendency to obsess over the bus a virtual mother proposed in spite of the existence of more appropriate bus. Concreteness attributed to cognitive inflexibility is considered to be an important factor for the deficits in patients with schizophrenia. Providing realistic visual as well as auditory stimuli, this experiment capitalized on another example of the advantage that virtual reality has on its capacity to immerse human subjects to the virtual environment as if it were a real situation.

8. Uses of virtual reality for social skills training

Beyond considering virtual reality systems as a mere assessment tool, recent studies suggest the virtual reality system's potential utility as a therapeutic and social skills training tool. The author's group reported a novel method of implementing a role playing conversational skills training program using virtual avatars (Ku et al., 2007). In this study, computer generated virtual avatar's emotional stimuli could complement or even overcome the shortcomings of conventional role playing approach to social skills training. The strength of using virtual avatar for role playing training came from taking advantage of the fact that computer generated avatars can consistently present emotional stimuli at will of the clinician whereas the efficacy of conventional role playing methods are often limited to the expressive capacity of the clinician/trainer.

Another strength of using virtual reality and virtual avatars for social skills training of patients with mental illness is that they provide a safe, harmless, and well-controlled environment in which to practice social interaction without repercussions of emotional frustration and feeling of failure expected in the real world. Stigma associated with mental illness can be detrimental to rehabilitation training in mental health patients (Link et al., 2001; Rüsch et al., 2005). Especially for patients with severe symptoms, utilizing a virtual environment without the expectation of negative consequences of the real world may be a favorable method that readily allows behavioral activation which can jump start the social skills training among other rehabilitation processes that the patients are encouraged to engage in.

It is also very encouraging to note that the vast majority of patients who underwent social skills training using the virtual reality based conversation training program evaluated the program positively after it was finished (Ku et al., 2007). Providing an extra motivation to the patient is another factor that cannot be ignored when counting the efficacy of social skills

Order	Bus No.	Destination	No. of Stations to Site A
1	21	Site A	14
2	41	Site A	5
3	18	Site B	-
4	41	Site A	5
5	3	Site C	-
6	31	Site A	8

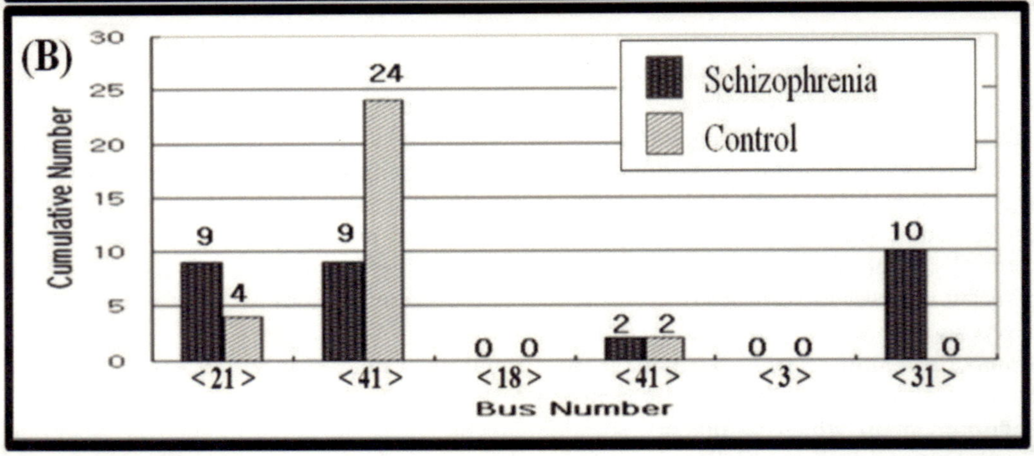

Fig. 6. An example of the virtual reality social problem-solving tasks and the experimental results. (A) In a task of getting on an appropriate bus, participants should get on a bus to site A. They had three options such as No. 21, 41 and 31. No. 21 bus was firstly arrived but had a lot of stations because it would use a detour. No. 41 bus was secondly and fourthly arrived and used the shortest way. No. 31 bus was finally arrived and had more stations to site A than No. 41 bus. However, participants could give priority to No. 31 bus because a virtual mother recommended them to get on No. 31 bus at the scene of home before the scene of getting on a bus. (B) Most normal controls tended to choose the first arrival of No. 41 bus, whereas most patients tended to choose the finally arrived No. 31 bus that a virtual mother proposed.

training. In addition, it is rather unrealistic to expect preparing a real world social interaction in order to help train social skills for a patient, so often time it is the responsibility of a clinician to help train social skills. Therefore, virtual reality based social skills training can also be a more cost-effective method in the long run compared to using clinician-based methods.

9. Integration of virtual reality and neuroimaging methods

One promising future direction in expanding the usage of virtual reality as a social skills assessment tool is to integrate the virtual reality system with neuroimaging methods such as functional magnetic resonance imaging (fMRI). Through the emergence of social neuroscience, there has been an explosion of neuroimaging research with much of its concentration on brain-mapping of various social cognition abilities. Based on an on-going accumulation of extensive neuroimaging research in social cognition and social skills, integration of neuroimaging methods and virtual reality promises to help form a synergistic relationship between the two fields whiling building on the past knowledge about the brain mechanisms involved in social skills.

Recent studies have shown promising trend of such integration. For example, an fMRI study investigated brain activity evoked by mutual and averted gaze in a compelling and commonly experienced social encounter (Pelphrey et al., 2004). In this study, subjects wearing virtual-reality goggles viewed a man who walked toward them and shifted their neutral gaze either toward (mutual gaze) or away (averted gaze), and the results showed that the superior temporal sulcus was involved in processing social information conveyed by shifts in gaze within an overtly social context. Another fMRI study using a virtual reality task during which subjects experienced themselves walking towards a complex scene composed of animate and/or inanimate objects also demonstrated strong activity in the superior temporal sulcus while the observer approached the social scene, but only when the virtual human was making gestures, suggesting the importance of biological motion in inferring the intentions of others (Morris et al., 2005).

Using our accumulated knowledge to assess individuals' condition relating to the neurocognitive basis of social skills germane to mental health problems provides new and exciting possibilities. For example, in order to evaluate attributional style which means how people typically infer the causes of emotional behaviors, a virtual reality attribution task was developed, and patients with schizophrenia and healthy controls underwent fMRI while performing three (happy, angry, and neutral) conditions of the task (Park et al., 2009b). The results showed that the patients may have functional deficits in mirror neuron system when attributing positive behaviors, which may be related to a lack of inner simulation and empathy and negative symptoms. In contrast, the patients may have increased activation in the precuneus/posterior cingulate cortex related to self-representations while attributing negative behaviors, which may be related to failures in self- and source-monitoring and positive symptoms.

Integration of neuroimaging methods and virtual reality systems offers benefits that are reciprocal in nature between the two methods. First of all, neuroimaging and human brain-mapping research can benefit from the improvement on the degree of realism depicted via presentation of social stimuli using virtual reality. On the other hand, behavioral research previously using the virtual reality system could now benefit from an extra layer of measure that may inform more in-depth neurocognitive mechanisms relevant to mental health assessment and the evaluation of social skills among other things. This of course is based on a caveat that the progress on the social neuroscience end of the research provides enough certainty in order to execute dependable social skills assessment. We cautiously but at the same time optimistically approach such assertion since advances in neuroimaging research methods and accumulation of social neuroscience research via in vivo human neuroimaging research allows for a realistic expectation that in the near future, we may begin using integrated assessment set up using both virtual reality and neuroimaging methods. Positron emissions tomography (PET), as well as certain optical imaging methods may also be considered for integration with virtual reality systems. Such integrative uses will not only allow collection of more in-depth data. But also provide more extensive data on what neurological region is involved in the patients' social skills deficit or improvement.

In addition to neuroimaging methods, other bio-feedback tools can be integrated with virtual reality system for assessment and training of social skills. For example, galvanic skin response measures can readily be used in conjunction with virtual reality methods to provide real time feedback to participants. Such real-time biofeedback may be especially beneficial in social skills training setting. With the help of visible feedback on one's own physiological responses, patients may be able to regulate their own emotion and cognition, both crucial factors in engaging in orderly social interaction.

10. Conclusion

In summary, virtual reality systems can provide an opportunity for people to experience interpersonal and social situation. A virtual avatar can be perceived as a real human by the participants in the virtual environment, and can influence on their behavior, emotion and memory. Since a virtual reality task using the avatar can draw the participants' behavioral and emotional characteristics and assess those objectively, it provides a potential to be used for assessing a social ability of mentally ill patients who have deficits in social function. Because impairment of social skills is often a cardinal feature in most mental illnesses, virtual reality may play an important role in objectively evaluating symptoms of mental illnesses and measuring effectiveness of treatments designed to rehabilitate social skills in patients with mental illnesses. In addition, it can be used to train patients by eliciting various emotions close to reality as well as to find out the clinical characteristics related to patients' symptoms. It may be expected that the neural basis of various social functions and their deficits will be able to be elucidated by combined uses of virtual reality and function neuroimaging techniques.

11. Acknowledgement

This material was based a grant from the Korea Health 21 R&D Project, Ministry of Health, Welfare and Family, Republic of Korea (A090537), and is based upon work supported by the National Science Foundation under Grant No. 1015659 awarded to Joseph Kim. Any opinions, findings, and conclusions or recommendations expressed in this material are those of the author(s) and do not necessarily reflect the views of the National Science Foundation.

12. References

Bailenson JN, Blascovich J, Beall AC, Loomis JM. Interpersonal distance in immersive virtual environments. *Pers. Soc. Psychol. Bull.* 2003; 29:819-833.

Bedell J, Lennox SS, Smith AD, Rabinowicz EF. Evaluation of problem solving and communication skills of persons with schizophrenia. *Psychiatry Res.* 1998; 78(3):197-206.

Bellack, A.S., Mueser, K.T., Gingerich, S., Agresta, J. Social Skills Training for Schizophrenia: A Step-by-Step Guide. The Guilford Press, New York. 1997.

Blascovich J, Loomis J, Beall AC, Swinth KR, Hoyt CL, Bailenson JN. Immersive virtual environment technology as a methodological tool for social psychology. *Psychological Inquiry* 2002; 13:103–124.

Brüne M, Schaub D, Juckel G, Langdon R. Social skills and behavioral problems in schizophrenia: The role of mental state attribution, neurocognition and clinical symptomatology. *Psychiatry Res.* 2010, Epub ahead of print

Buchanan RW, Davis M, Goff D, et al. A summary of the FDA-NIMH-MATRICS workshop on clinical trial design for neurocognitive drugs for schizophrenia. *Schizophr. Bull.* 2005; 31: 5-19.

Chun JY, Kim JJ, Jang HJ, Kim SY, Kim CH, Kim J, Kim K, Ku J, Kim IY, Kim SI. Characteristics of patients with schizophrenia for problem-solving function in social situations evaluated by a virtual reality program. *Korean J. Schizophr. Res.* 2007; 10:62-70.

Couture SM, Penn DL, Roberts DL. The functional significance of social cognition in schizophrenia: a review. *Schizophr. Bull.* 2006; 32:S44-63.

Elliott T, Grant J, Miller D. Social problem-solving abilities and behavioral health. In: Chang EC, D'Zurilla TJ, Sanna LJ, editors. Social Problem Solving: Theory, Research, and Training. Washington, DC: American Psychological Association; 2004.

Han K, Ku J, Kim K, Jang HJ, Park J, Kim JJ, Kim CH, Choi MH, Kim IY, Kim SI. Virtual reality prototype for measurement of expression characteristics in emotional situations. *Comput. Biol. Med.* 2009; 39:173-179.

Harvey PD, Patterson TL, Potter LS, Zhong K, Brecher M. Improvement in social competence with short-term atypical antipsychotic treatment: a randomized, double-blind comparison of quetiapine versus risperidone for social competence, social cognition, and neuropsychological functioning. *Am. J. Psychiatry* 2006; 163:1918-1925.

Harvey PD, Velligan DI, Bellack AS. Performance-based measures of functional skills: usefulness in clinical treatment studies. *Schizophr. Bull.* 2007; 33(5):1138-1148.

Hayduk LA. Personal space: where we now stand. *Psychol. Bull.* 1983; 94:293-335.

Kim E, Ku J, Kim JJ, Lee H, Han K, Kim SI, Cho HS. Nonverbal social behaviors of patients with bipolar mania during interactions with virtual humans. *J. Nerv. Ment. Dis.* 2009; 197:412-418.

Ku J, Han K, Lee HR, Jang HJ, Kim KU, Park SH, Kim JJ, Kim CH, Kim IY, Kim SI. VR-Based Conversation Training Program for Patients with Schizophrenia: A Preliminary Clinical Trial. *Cyberpsychol. Behav.* 2007; 10(4):567-574.

Ku J, Jang HJ, Kim KU, Kim JH, Park SH, Lee JH, Kim JJ, Kim IY, Kim SI. Experimental results of affective valence and arousal to avatar's facial expressions. *Cyberpsychol. Behav.* 2005; 8: 493-503.

Ku J, Jang HJ, Kim KU, Park SH, Kim JJ, Kim CH, Nam SW, Kim IY, Kim SI. Pilot study for assessing the behaviors of patients with schizophrenia towards a virtual avatar. *Cyberpsychol. Behav.* 2006; 9: 531-539.

Link BG, Struening EL, Neese-Todd S, Asmussen S, Phelan JC. Stigma as a barrier to recovery: The consequences of stigma for the self-esteem of people with mental illnesses. *Psychiatry Serv.* 2001; 52(12):1621-1626.

McKibbin CL, Brekke JS, Sires D, Jeste DV, Patterson TL. Direct assessment of functional abilities: relevance to persons with schizophrenia. *Schizophr. Res.* 2004; 72:53-67.

Morris JP, Pelphrey KA, McCarthy G. Regional brain activation evoked when approaching a virtual human on a virtual walk. *J. Cogn. Neurosci.* 2005;17(11):1744-1752.

Nechamkin Y, Salganik I, Modai I, Ponizovsky AM. Interpersonal distance in schizophrenic patients: relationship to negative syndrome. *Int. J. Soc. Psychiatry* 2003; 49(3):166-174.

Nezu AM. Problem solving and behavior therapy revisited. *Behav. Ther.* 2004; 35:1–33.

Park IH, Kim JJ, Ku J, Jang HJ, Park SH, Kim CH, Kim IY, Kim SI. Characteristics of social anxiety from virtual interpersonal interactions in patients with schizophrenia. *Psychiatry* 2009a; 72:79-93.

Park KM, Kim JJ, Ku J, Kim SY, Lee HR, Kim SI, Yoon KJ. Neural basis of attributional style in schizophrenia. *Neurosci. Lett.* 2009b; 459(1):35-40.

Park KM, Ku J, Park IH, Park JY, Kim SI, Kim JJ. Improvement in social competence in patients with schizophrenia: A pilot study using a performance-based measure using virtual reality. *Hum. Psychopharm. Clin. Exp.* 2009c; 24:619-627.

Park SH, Ku J, Kim JJ, Jang HJ, Kim SY, Kim SH, Kim CH, Lee H, Kim IY, Kim SI. Increased personal space of patients with schizophrenia in a virtual social environment. *Psychiatry Res.* 2009d; 169:197-202.

Pelphrey KA, Morris JP, McCarthy G. Neural basis of eye gaze processing deficits in autism. *Brain* 2005; 128: 1038-1048.

Pelphrey KA, Viola RJ, McCarthy G. When strangers pass: processing of mutual and averted social gaze in the superior temporal sulcus. *Psychol. Sci.* 2004; 15(9):598-603.

Rüsch N, Angermeyer MC, Corrigan PW. Mental illness stigma: concepts, consequences, and initiatives to reduce stigma. *Eur. Psychiatry* 2005; 20(8):529-539.

Song M, Ku J, Han k, Kim SI, Choi SH, Kim JJ. Characteristics of eye gaze distribution of patients with schizophrenia during the emotion-provoking conversation with several virtual persons. *J. Korean Neuropsychiatric Association* 2010; in press.

Tarr MJ, Warren WH. Virtual reality in behavioral neuroscience and beyond. *Nat. Neurosci.* 2002; 5 Suppl:1089-1092.

24

Emotions and the Emotional Valence Afforded by the Virtual Environment

Stéphane Bouchard, Ph.D,
Geneviève Labonté-Chartrand, Psy.D. Candidate
Université du Québec en Outaouais, Canada

1. Introduction

For decades, researchers have been concerned about the effectiveness of traditional tools used by clinicians to treat mental disorders and have been trying to develop more and more innovative techniques. The emergence of virtual reality presents new clinical and experimental opportunities in psychology. Virtual reality, as defined as "an application allowing a user to navigate and interact in real time with a computer-generated three-dimensional environment" (Pratt et al., 1995, p.17), can be distinguished from other media by the real-time interaction with synthetic stimuli. The potential of virtual reality has encouraged more scientific research exploring the mechanisms involved in the efficacy of using virtual environments.

Various applications to mental health problems have been the subject of virtual reality experiments. Virtual reality's usefulness in inducing anxiety for curative purposes has been reiterated many times (Robillard et al., 2003; Moore, Wierderhold et al., 2002), and the effectiveness of this tool for psychological treatment of certain anxiety disorders is documented by numerous studies (Bouchard et al., 2006; Côté & Bouchard, 2008; Gerardi et al., 2010; Weiderhold & Weiderhold, 2005).

It may seem astonishing that virtual reality would put an end to phobic avoidance even though virtual scenarios are not totally realistic. The feeling of presence gives users the subjective impression that the virtual environment in which they are immersed really exists. Seven dimensions may modulate presence: the realism of pictograms and images, social interactions in the environment, the ease of interactions, the user's power or perception of control, the duration of exposure, social factors such as relationships with others and, finally, characteristics related to the virtual reality system (Stanney & Sadowski, 2002). In addition, some variables such as the participant's propensity to be absorbed in an activity, the tendency to concentrate and to dispose of distractions (Witmer & Singer, 1998) and, certain data even suggests, the ability to be hypnotized could be involved in an increased feeling of presence (Wiederhold & Wiederhold, 2000). Ijsselsteijn and Riva (2003) asserted that the effectiveness of virtual immersion is partly attributable to the degree of presence felt by the immersed user. Similarly, Wiederhold and Wiederhold (1999) suggested that the degree of presence could be related to the success of the treatment.

The relationship between the feeling of presence and the intensity of the emotions felt in a virtual environment is especially relevant for clinicians using VR with people suffering from emotional disorders. Robillard et al. (2003) reported a significant correlation ($r = .74$, $< p$ .001) between anxiety and the feeling of presence. To assess the direction of the relationship between anxiety and presence, Bouchard, St-Jacques, Robillard and Renaud (2008) manipulated anxiety while participants suffering from a phobia of snakes were immersed in virtual reality, then evaluated the impact of anxiety on the feeling of presence. The results showed that the feeling of presence was significantly higher when the researchers induced anxiety. Changes in the level of anxiety felt and in the feeling of presence were also strongly and significantly correlated. Using multilevel hierarchical linear regression analyses, Riva et al. (2007) suggested the existence of a bidirectional relationship between emotions and presence. Based on these sophisticated analyses, their study suggests that anxiety is not only a predictor of presence, but the level of presence is also a significant predictor of the level of anxiety. Such a bidirectional relationship has been confirmed by an experimental study (Michaud et al., 2004) where presence was manipulated in a sample of 33 heights phobics. When the immersion in the virtual environment was conducted in a high-presence setting, the level of anxiety was significantly higher than when the immersion was conducted in a low-presence setting. These results all confirmed that emotions, at least anxiety, felt during an immersion have an impact on the feeling of presence.

Theoretically, one may wonder why the fact of feeling anxiety more intensely would make a person feel more present in the virtual environment. Can the causal relationship between emotions and presence be explained simply by a non specific emotional arousal, or does the emotion has to be consistent with the experience felt during the immersion? Feeling an emotion while immersed could validate the user's impression of the realism of the virtual stimuli. Post immersion, users of virtual reality systems sometimes say, "I fell from the balcony and was so surprised and nervous that it shows how much your virtual environment is realistic and how much I felt really there". Their feeling of being present appears to be strengthened by the emotional arousal. But what if that arousal was not confirming the realism of the virtual stimuli? Such as being anxious in a relaxing environment, or depressed in a joyful environment? Would a dissonance destroy the illusion and perceived realism of the immersion? There is a need to clarify whether people immersed in a virtual situation feel more present merely because they are feeling an emotion, or because the emotion feel is congruent with what is to be expected to felt in the virtual environment (i.e., which emotional valence is afforded by the virtual environment). In order to sort out the role of emotions and of the message they transmit to the user immersed in virtual reality, it would be necessary to induce emotions that do not match the virtual environment. If a user feels an emotion that is not supposed to be felt during the immersion, we can determine whether it is the emotional arousal itself that foster presence or if the meaning of the emotional arousal is important as well.

It is worth noting how emotions have been manipulated in previous studies on presence. In some cases, the virtual environments were carefully designed to induce emotions (Banos et al., 2004; Robillard & al., 2003). It is hard to see how an experimenter could create a mismatch between an emotion and the expected valence of a virtual environment by using procedures from Banos al (2004) or Riva et al. (2007) who used the virtual environment to induce the emotion. The alternative strategy is to induce the mood prior to the immersion, as Bouchard et al. (2008) did. However, their strategy was applied with phobics, who are people already sensitized to react very strongly to specific frightening stimuli. No study has attempted to induce positive and negative emotions in non-clinical participants without manipulating the virtual environment.

This chapter reports on two experiments examining the impact of inducing emotions on the feeling of presence among non-clinical samples. The objective of the studies consisted of verifying whether feeling an emotion that doesn't match with what the virtual environment is expected to induce leads to less presence than feeling an emotion that does match the emotional contents afforded by the environment. In the first experiment, a virtual environment judged *a priori* to be pleasant was used to evaluate the impact of positive and negative emotions on the presence felt by participants. Given the results, a second experiment was designed with a virtual environment that has a more saddening content.

2. Experiment 1

In order to examine the match between emotions felt by the user and those that should be induced by the virtual stimuli, the emotions have to be induced experimentally *in vivo*. The *in vivo* method means that the emotions will be induced in the user before the latter is immersed in virtual reality (*in virtuo*). Although the emotion of anxiety is quite easy to induce intensely among subjects suffering from anxiety disorders (e.g., Bouchard et al., 2008; Robillard et al., 2003), one may wonder whether it is possible to induce other types of emotions as intensely as anxiety. For this study, it was decided to induce positive and negative emotions among healthy subjects during immersion in an attractive virtual environment.

2.1 Sample and procedures

Twenty-eight adults participated in the study (18 women and 10 men). The non-clinical sample was made up of subjects varying in age from 19 to 53 (M = 28.54, sd = 10.36). The participants were recruited by ads posted on the university's campus. The inclusion criteria required that participants never had a virtual reality experience before and be 18 years of age or older. A telephone prescreening form was used to exclude participants suspected of epilepsy, having a physical condition that could exacerbate simulator sickness (diseases of the inner ear), cardiovascular problems, high blood pressure or diabetes.

The equipment used in the study included an IBM computer (Pentium IV™ with an ATI Radeon 128 MB graphics card) and a CY-Visor virtual headset (field of vision of 31 degrees, 800 x 600 resolution). An Intersense Intertrax² tracker (3 degrees of liberty, angular resolution of .02 degrees, latency of 4 ms) was attached to the virtual headset. The virtual environment was an adaptation of the level the Temple of Horus from the game "Unreal Tournament: Game of the year edition®", where the user walks in pyramids and into a mythical temple located in the Egyptian desert. The adaptation was limited and consisted in removing the violent content of the game, enabling the motion tracker to emulate the mouse of the player and using the headset to display the images to the user. The environment was chosen because of its availability and *a priori* positive features.

The participants who met the study selection criteria were invited to participate in the experiment and randomly assigned either one of the following conditions: (1) positive emotion (joy) induced or (2) negative emotion (sadness) induced. Each participant filled in the consent form, was advised of the nature of the research and the overall course of the experiment. Two pre-test questionnaires ("Immersive Tendencies Questionnaire" and "Simulator Sickness Questionnaire") were completed to assess and control for predisposition to feel present and to develop simulator sickness. This step was followed by a first 5-minute immersion in a neutral / irrelevant virtual environment in order to familiarize the participant with how to navigate in virtual reality and appraise the concept of "being there" in a virtual environment. After inducing emotions experimentally and taking measures with the Brief Mood Introspection Scale, the participant was immersed in the positive environment for seven minutes. This experimental immersion was followed by the completion of a battery of questionnaires. Finally, subjects had to wait fifteen minutes before leaving the lab to make sure that no significant simulator sickness was induced by the immersions.

The experimental manipulation of emotions consisted of inducing emotions *in vivo* prior to the experimental immersion. The effectiveness of various techniques for inducing emotions (music, films, facial expressions, autobiographical memories, etc.), including Velten's technique, varies between 50 and 75% (Gerrards-Hesse et al., 1994; Martin, 1990; Westermann, Spies, Stahl, & Hesse, 1996). Among these techniques, the procedure developed by Velten (1968) was used given its popularity and effectiveness (Gerrards-Hesse et al., 1994; Martin, 1990). The procedure consists of reading short statements that include emotional dimensions with positive, or negative, valence. Thus the participant had to read 25 short statements developed by Velten (1968) and expressing an emotional state of joy or depression/sadness. The person had to try to adopt the emotional state suggested by the statement. Each statement, written on a card, was read silently at the participant's own pace.

2.2 Measures

The Brief Mood Introspection Scale (Mayer & Gaschke, 1988) measures the intensity of various 16 emotions. The emotions are divided into two sub-scales and items are rated on a scale from 1 to 9 (1: does not correspond at all; 9: corresponds perfectly). The first sub-scale measures the strength of positive emotions (happy, calm, cheerful, etc.) and the second sub-scale measures the intensity of negative emotions (e.g., melancholy, depressed, sad, angry, etc.). This measure was used to check for the impact of the manipulation.

The Immersive Tendencies Questionnaire (Witmer & Singer, 1998) measures to what point the individual succeeds in cutting off outside distractions and concentrating on different tasks (i.e., watching a video) and thus provides an indication of a subject's capacity to feel immersed in a virtual environment. It consists of 18 items rated on a Likert scale (1 "never", 7: "often") assessing four domains: (1) focus: (degree of concentration, capacity to cut off distractions); (2) involvement: (feeling of being "absorbed" in a task); (3) emotions: (intensity of emotions, for example, during or after seeing a film); (4) play: (how often the person plays video games). The ITQ is used to control for potential pre-experimental differences among participants randomized in the two conditions.

The Simulator Sickness Questionnaire by Kennedy, Lane, Berbaum and Lilienthal (1993) is composed of 16 items. It measures on a 4-point scale (0 "not at all" to 3 "severely") the degree of discomfort felt by the individual (nausea, vertigo, eyestrain, etc.). The questionnaire includes three dimensions: (1) nausea; (2) oculomotor problems and (3) disorientation. It should be administered once before the immersion to enable excluding symptoms that are present before the experiment. This measure is used to document the potential side effects of the experiment and control for differences in side effects generally experienced during the study.

A Brief Measure of Presence was used to quantify the feeling of presence using one item and a rating scale of 0 to 100 by answering the question: "On a scale of 0 to 100, how much did you have the impression of really being *there* in the virtual environment?" The sensitivity of this brief measurement to changes and experimental manipulations was validated by Bouchard, Robillard, St-Jacques, Dumoulin, Patry and Renaud (2004). This measure represents one of the two dependent variables and is used to compare the scores in the neutral and the experimental immersions.

The Presence Questionnaire (Witmer & Singer, 1998) uses a 7-point Likert scale (1 "not at all" to 7 "completely") to measure the following dimensions: (1) realism (extent to which virtual environments appear natural or can be confused with reality); (2) possibility of action (active exploration and control of events); (3) quality of the interface (delay or awkwardness of the device); (4) possibility of examination (observation of objects from different angles); (5) self-evaluation of performance (feeling of competence and adaptation related to carrying out tasks); (6) auditory and (7) haptic (possibility of touching certain objects). This measure of presence relates more to the properties of the hardware and the software to induce presence than it related to the subjective experience of the user (Stanney & Sadowski, 2002). This is the second dependent variable and is used to compare the scores after the experimental immersion.

2.3 Results

The descriptive statistics show that scores on the Immersive Tendencies Questionnaire are comparable to the normative samples (M = 64.11, sd = 13.11), indicating that the participants seemed adequately predisposed to feel "absorbed" in the virtual environment (M = 66.43, sd =13.39). No differences were found between the two conditions. No difference was found on side effects of the immersion, although participants felt mild simulator sickness during the neutral immersion (M = 124.56, sd = 151.66) and intensity of the side effects increased at the second immersion (M = 256.97, sd = 224.47).

The manipulation check (see Figure 1) showed important findings on the Brief Mood Introspection Scale. As detailed in Table 1, repeated measures ANOVAs on the positive emotions revealed that a positive mood was induced with success in participants in the condition where joy was induced. Consistently, the negative mood in that group of participants was low and remained as such after the experimental immersion. However, among participants where sadness was induced, the level of positive mood was low post induction and increased significantly during the experimental immersion. The level of negative mood was moderate post induction but decreased significantly after the experimental virtual immersion. The induction procedure was therefore successful in inducing the expected emotions, but the immersion in the virtual environment was powerful enough to counter the negative mood.

As shown by the average scores on the dependent measures of presence (see Table 2) and results of the statistical analyses (see Table 1), the experimental manipulation of mood did not have a statistically significant effect on presence. The effect-sizes observed for the interaction on the Brief Measure of Presence (η^2 = .006) and between the conditions on the Presence Questionnaire (η^2 = .02) were minimal, suggesting that the lack of a significant difference is probably not explained merely by the size of the sample.

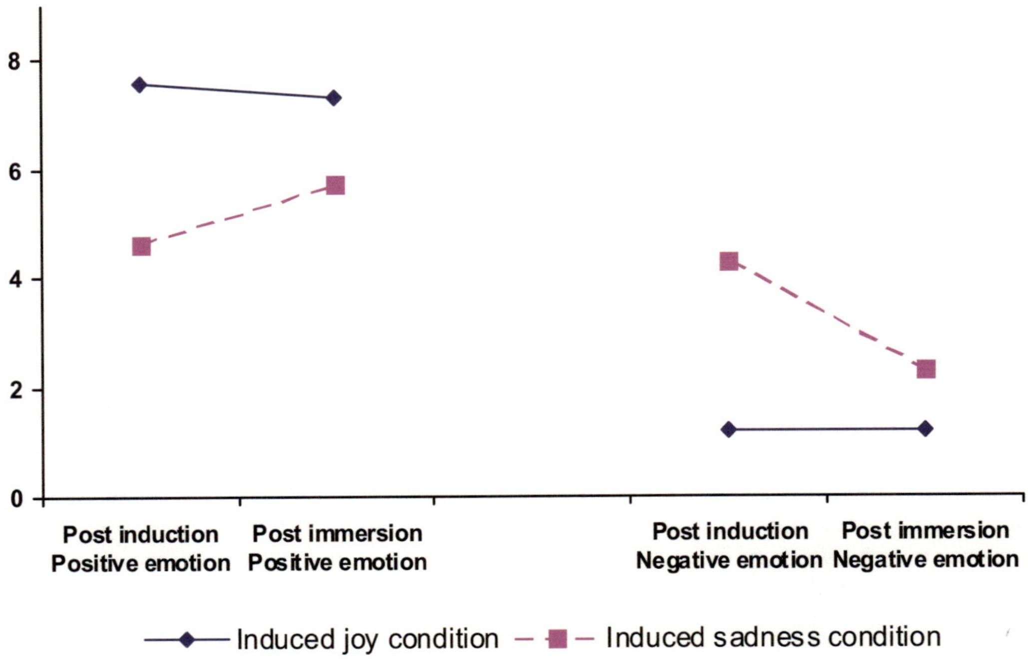

Fig. 1. Positive and negative mood after the induction and the immersion in a virtual environment with a positive valence.

	Condition main effect	Time main effect	Interaction main effect
Brief Mood Introspection Scale			
Positive emotions	32.36***	4.30*	8.20***
Negative emotions	26.28***	8.09**	8.09**
Brief Measure of Presence	.02	18.06***	.16
Presence Questionnaire	.52		

Note: Repeated measures ANOVAs were performed for the first two instruments and a two-way ANOVA was performed with the Presence Questionnaire. * $p < .05$, ** $p < .01$, *** $p < .001$

Table 1. Statistical analyses for mood and presence in a virtual environment with a positive valence.

	Conditions	
	Induced Joy	Induced sadness
Brief Measure of Presence - post immersion in the neutral / irrelevant environment	37.14 (26.01)	39.86 (33.22)
Brief Measure of Presence - post experimental immersion	50.71 (26.52)	51.07 (35.04)
Presence Questionnaire - post experimental immersion	100.79 (19.75)	94.36 (26.83)

Table 2. Mean (and standard error) for the measures of presence in Experiment 1.

2.4 Discussion for experiment 1

The objective was to verify whether feeling an emotion that matched the valence of a virtual environment induces a greater feeling of presence than feeling an emotion that does not match the emotional valance afforded by the same virtual environment. The hypothesis advanced was that inducing a negative emotion in a virtual environment that was expected *a priori* to be attractive would disturb and decrease the feeling of presence. The results first confirmed that the experimental manipulation was effective: the expected mood state of joy and sadness were induced. However, the valence of the virtual environment seemed positive enough to reduce the saddening effect of the mood induction. In addition, the manipulation did not produce the expected effect on the presence measures and the hypothesis cannot be confirmed. The effect-sizes suggest that the kind of emotions induced had no influence on the level of presence during virtual immersions. However, the induction of emotions in general, no matter whether the valence fits or not with the virtual environment, was associated with a significant increase in presence on the Brief Measure of Presence.

The weak level of negative mood reported after the experimental immersion among participants in the sadness condition may explain the results on the presence measures. The discrepancy between the emotional valence of the virtual environment and the induced negative mood was not that strong. Maybe a stronger discrepancy between mood and valence of the virtual environment would have had a significant impact. To reach that goal, the use of a negatively valence environment and the induction of positive emotion may be more fruitful than trying to induce more sadness in participants.

One possible explanation for the observed decrease in negative mood among participants where sadness was induced may be the inherent attractiveness of the virtual environment used for the immersion. Visiting a mythological Egyptian temple may represent a positive experience for most participants in the sample. It is important to point out however that virtual environments used by other researchers to induce positive mood (Banos et al., 2004; Riva et al., 2007) were especially designed to have a strong positive valence. No such efforts were invested in the current environment and, therefore, it was not expected to have such a soothing effect. Since the attractiveness of the environment chosen for the experiment may be blurring the results, and given the difficulty to induce a very negative mood that would be incongruent with the valence of the environment, a second experiment was designed with a virtual environment that has a negative valence, with the hope to verify whether a positive emotion which doesn't match the valence of a virtual environment would decrease the feeling of presence.

3. Experiment 2

This experiment used the same design and procedure for inducing emotions as Experiment 1, but a virtual environment depicting a grayish virtual city with dark building and broken-down cars was chosen. As well, some additional questions were added to complement the single-item measure of presence. The hypothesis was still that an emotion that does not match the virtual environment's affective valence would lead to a poorer feeling of presence than a matched emotion.

3.1 Sample and procedures

The sample was composed of 31 adults (19 women and 12 men) from a non-clinical population. Three participants were excluded because of excessive simulator sickness during the experiment. The 28 completers' age varied from 18 to 62 ($M = 30.55$, $sd = 11.79$). The recruitment procedures and selection criteria were identical to those described in the previous experiment.

The computer used was the same as in Study 1, except for the VR equipment. The use of a high-end headset (nVisor Sx from NVIS; visual field 60 degrees, resolution 1280 x 1024) and more precise tracker (Inertia cube^2 from InterSense; 3 degrees of liberty, angular resolution .05 degrees, latency of 8 ms, angular extent of 360 degrees) were expected to provide a better immersive experience. The virtual environment used for the experiment was a virtual city adapted from the 3D game Max Pain and used to treat height phobia (Bouchard et al., 2008). A pilot study was done to verify the valence of the virtual environment. In total, ten people who were not part of the experimental groups evaluated on a scale from 0 to 10 the valence of the Temple of Horus environment (see Experiment 1) and the virtual city. They confirmed that the virtual environment used in Experiment 2 did indeed had a more negative valence ($t_{(9)} = 4.54$, $p < .001$) than the Egyptian desert.

As in the previous experiment, emotions were induced using Velten's technique (1968). The experimenter explicitly reminded participants to try to hold their emotion during the experimental immersion. Also, participants were requested to complete the Brief Mood Introspection Scale not only after the emotions were induced but also before the mood induction, when they arrived at the lab. The addition of a baseline for their mood state was expected to allow confirming that the mood induction was indeed the cause of their mood state. The same measures were used in the experiment. Three items were added post-immersion to broaden the assessment of the subjective feeling of presence. One positively worded item assessed the perceived realism of the virtual environment and two items were negatively worded (reverse scoring) to document to what extent the user was aware that the virtual environment was created artificially and that he or she was in an office and not "there" in the virtual environment. An average score was calculated for this Gatineau Presence Questionnaire.

3.2 Results

The mood of participant was induced with success (see Figure 3 and Table 3). The scores on the negative emotion scale revealed a significant interaction effect. A more specific repeated-measures Condition X Time interaction contrast revealed a significant increase in negative mood from the baseline to after the sadness induction ($F_{(1,26)}$ = 16.09, p < .001). The mood state during the experimental immersion was consistent with the mood induction, with a significant repeated-measure Condition X Time interaction contrast ($F_{(1,26)}$ = 5.09, p < .05) on the negative mood scale. Therefore, a stronger negative mood was reported in participants where a sad mood was induced, and the virtual environment had a saddening effect on the mood of those where a joyful mood was induced. The effectiveness of the mood induction was also confirmed with similar repeated measures Condition X Time interaction contrast on the positive mood scale. A stronger positive mood was reported from baseline to post-induction in participants where joy was induced compared to those where sadness was induced ($F_{(1,26)}$ = 37.74, p < .001). The saddening effect of the virtual environment on the positive mood scale was not limited to participants where joy was induced, as revealed by the significant Time effect detected for that contrast ($F_{(1,26)}$ = 18.66, p < .001) and the lack of statistical significance of the repeated measures Condition X Time interaction contrasts between post-induction and post-immersion ($F_{(1,26)}$ = 4.90, ns).

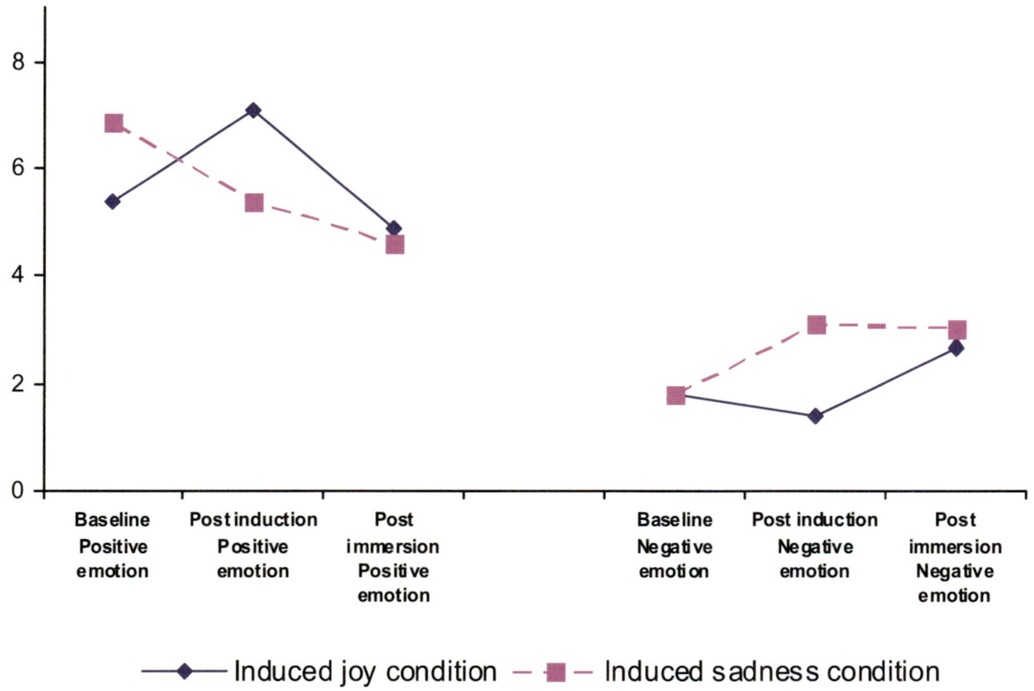

Fig. 2. Positive and negative mood at baseline, post induction and post immersion in a virtual environment with a negative valence.

Tables 3 and 4 show descriptive statistics and results of the analyses for the presence measures. The experimental manipulation had no significant impact on presence, even when measured only with one item, with all four items of the Gatineau Presence Questionnaire and with the Presence Questionnaire. The effect sizes were all small ($\eta^2 < .015$). Finally, let's mention that participants felt mild simulator sickness during the neutral virtual exposure (M = 30.29, sd = 23.55), that the intensity of the sickness increased during the second virtual immersion (M = 40.59, sd = 25.73) and that immersive tendency was good (M= 70.03, sd= 17.11) for both conditions.

	Condition main effect	Time main effect	Interaction main effect
Brief Mood Introspection Scale			
Positive emotions	.4	16.42**	8.39***
Negative emotions	2.45	6.77**	5.19*
Brief Measure of Presence	.00	.8	.00
Gatineau Presence Questionnaire	.34		
Presence Questionnaire	.19		

Note: A 2 X 3 repeated measures ANOVA was performed for measure of mood, a 2 X 2 repeated measures ANOVA was performed for the Brief Measure of Presence and two-way ANOVAs were performed for the remaining two instruments. * $p < .05$, ** $p < .01$, *** $p < .001$

Table 3. Statistical analyses for mood and presence in a virtual environment with a negative valence.

	Conditions	
	Induced Joy	Induced sadness
Brief Measure of Presence – post immersion in the neutral / irrelevant environment	63.82 (21.33)	63.18 (18.61)
Brief Measure of Presence – post experimental immersion	67.0 (22.03)	66.82 (23.23)
Gatineau Presence Questionnaire - post experimental immersion	51.74 (20.53)	46.52 (27.06)
Presence Questionnaire – post experimental immersion	86.94 (14.62)	84.36 (16.54)

Table 4. Mean (and standard error) for the measures of presence in Experiment 2.

3.3 Discussion for experiment 2.

The results of this second experiment suggest, as does the data from the first experiment, that effectively inducing emotions was possible but it did not has an impact on presence. The participants were able to use Velten's technique (1968) for inducing a positive or negative mood, but the immersion counteracted the effect of the positive mood induction. The mood states of the participants were not different at the end of the experiment. The hypothesis of the impact of a mismatch between the emotions and the valence of the virtual environment was not supported. This data replicate findings from Experiment 1, this time with an environment that has a negative valence. These converging findings raise important questions about emotions.

4. General discussion

Previous findings have shown a correlation between emotions and presence (Riva et al., 2007; Robillard et al., 2003) and a bidirectional relationship between these constructs (Bouchard et al., 2008; Michaud et al., 2004; Riva et al., 2007). Riva et al. (2007) showed that positive and negative mood could be efficiently induced by immersions in carefully designed virtual environments. The hopes behind the two experiments reported in this chapter were to document if the impact of emotions on presence was related to emotional arousal in general or to the realism of the experience. A mismatch between the emotions felt by the participant and what should be expected given the emotional valence of the virtual environment was expected to have a detrimental impact on presence. Both experiments used a classical method for inducing emotions (Velten, 1968). However, despite the use of two different virtual environments (one with a positive valence and another with a negative valence), it was impossible to confirm our hypothesis.

Although these are non significant findings, they deserve to be examined carefully as they can be interpreted differently whether they are considered from the angle of presence or emotions. From a presence standpoint, few conclusions could be reached since the manipulations could not create a mismatch. In Experiment 1, participants where sadness was induced were not in a negative mood throughout the immersion in the positive valence environment and in Experiment 2 participants where joy was induced were not in a positive mood throughout the immersion in the negative valence environment. Even if there was a slight mismatch in Experiment 1, the difference in mood was certainly too small to have an impact on presence. The only relevant observation is that immersion in the positive emotional valence environment lead to an increase in presence when compared to the training environment and this effect was not observed when comparing the training and the negative valence environments.

When the results are appraised from an emotion standpoint, one striking finding is that immersion in a virtual environment can counteract the effect of a mood induction performed with the classical and popular Velten's (1968) approach. This method has been extensively used and validated (Gilet, 2008). Immersions in moderately positive and negative valence virtual environments, as opposed to other environments designed following carefully planned strategies to impact on emotions (Banos et al., 2004; Bouchard et al., 2006; Riva et al., 2007), can improve moderately negative mood or reduce positive mood. This in itself is a significant, and replicated, finding. Experimental mood induction procedures do not always cause intense emotions (Gilet, 2008) and scores on the Brief Mood Introspection Scale are supporting this notion especially with the negative mood. The saddening induction did not lead to scores as high as the joyful induction. But the immersion in the positive emotional valence environment was able to counter very efficiently the negative induction. The negative emotional valence environment did not increase the negative mood of the participant but induced a negative mood in joyful people and reduced positive mood in all users.

Two conclusions can be reached from this chapter: (a) much stronger and long lasting mood induction techniques have to be found and used to induce *in vivo* emotions that would not match with the emotional valence of a virtual environment; (b) even simple virtual environments can counteract effectively the mood induced by traditional strategies. We cannot conclude, however, whether to increase presence an adequate fit is needed between relevance of emotions felt in virtual reality and emotions afforded by the content of the virtual environment. The question about the role of emotional arousal versus the relevance of the emotions remains.

Unpublished results on the relevance of olfactory cues on presence suggest that mismatch may not be that detrimental (Bouchard & Baus, in preparation). For example, in a study where participants were exposed to odors that match (i.e., smell of apple pie in a kitchen and of urine in a bathroom) or don't match (i.e., smell of apple pie in a bathroom and of urine in a kitchen) with the context of the virtual environment, the presentation or not of an odor had more impact on presence than the effect of a match or a mismatch. In case of mismatches, participants would fill-in for the irrelevance of odors by commenting, for example, that the pies must be really well cooked if they smell that strong in the bathroom, or that the garbage bag is due to be changed because of the awful smell in the kitchen.

Presence should be approached like an advanced perceptual illusion based on the integration of multisensory information. Emotions felt during an immersion can stem from the automatic appraisal of the stimuli and their meaning. But once emotional arousal is felt by the user, it could reinforce the illusion of being *there* in the virtual environment. Depending on the strength and meaning given to these emotions, we think they could foster presence or break the illusion.

5. References

Banos, R.M., Botella, C., Alcaniz, M. et al., (2004). Immersion and emotion : their impact on the sense of presence. *CyberPsychology and Behavior, 7*, 734-741.

Bouchard, S., Côté, S., & Richard, D. C. S. (2006). Virtual reality applications for exposure. In D. C. S. Richard (Éd.). *Handbook of exposure* (pp. 347-388).

Bouchard, S., Robillard, G., & Renaud, P. (2007). Revising the factor structure of the Simulator Sickness Questionnaire. *Annual Review of CyberTherapy and Telemedecine, 5*, 117-122.

Bouchard, S., Robillard, G., St-Jacques, J., Dumoulin, S., Patry, M.J., & Renaud, P. (2004). Reliability and validity of a single-item measure of presence in VR. *IEEE International workshop on haptic virtual environments and their applications, 3*, 59-61.

Bouchard, S., St-Jacques, J., Robillard, G., & Renaud, P. (2008). Anxiety increases the sense of presence in virtual reality. *Presence: Teleoperators and Virtual Environments.*

Côté, S., & Bouchard, S. (2008).Virtual reality exposure's efficacy in the treatment of specific phobia. *Journal of CyberTherapy and Rehabilitation*, 1(1), 75-92.

Gerardi, M., Cukor, J., Difede, J., Rizzo, A., & Rothbaum, B. A. (2010). Virtual reality exposure therapy for post-traumatic stress disorder and other anxiety disorders. *Current Psychiatry Reports, 12* (4), 298-305.
Gerrards-Hesse, A., Spies, K., Hesse, F. W. (1994). Experimental inductions emotional states and their effectiveness: A review. *British Journal of Psychology, 85,* 55-78.
Gilet, A. L., (2008). Mood induction procedures: A critical review. *Encephale 34* (3), 233-239.
Ijsselsteijn, W., & Riva, G. (2003). Being there: The experience of presence in mediated environments. In G. Riva, F. Davide, & W. A. Ijsselsteijn (Ed.), *Being There. Concepts, Effects and Measurements of User Presence in Synthetic Environments* (p. 3-17).Washington, DC: IOS Press.
Kennedy, R. S., Lane, N. E., Berbaum, K. S., & Lilienthal, M. G. (1993). Simulator Sickness Questionnaire: An enhanced method for quantifying simulator sickness. *International Journal of Aviation Psychology, 3,* 203-220.
Krijn, M., Emmelkamp, P. M. G., Olafsson, R. P., & Biemond, R. (2004). Virtual reality exposure therapy of anxiety disorders: A review. *Clinical Psychology Review, 24,* 259-281.
Martin, M. (1990). On the induction of mood. *Clinical Psychology Review, 10,* 669-697.
Mayer, J. D., & Gaschke, Y. N. (1988). The experience and meta-experience of mood. *Journal of Personality and Social Psychology, 55*(1), 102-111.
Michaud, M., Bouchard, S., Dumoulin, S., & Zhong, X.-W. (2004). *Manipulating presence and its impact on anxiety*. Presented at the Cybertherapy Conference 2004, San Diego, January 10-12 2004.
Moore, K., Wiederhold, B. K., Wiederhold, M. D., & Riva, G. (2002). Panic and agoraphobia in a virtual world. *Cyberpsychology and Behavior, 5,* 197-202.
Pratt, D. R., Zyda, M., & Kelleher, K. (1995). Virtual reality: In the mind of the beholder. *IEEE Computer, 28*(7), 17-19.
Riva, G., Mantovani, F., Capideville, C. M., Preziosa, A., Morganti, F., Villani, D., Gaggioli, A., Botella, C., & Alcaniz, M. (2007). Affective interactions using virtual reality: The link between presence and emotions. *CyberPsychology and Behavior, 10*(1), 45-56.
Robillard, G., Bouchard, S., Fournier, T., & Renaud, P. (2003). Anxiety and presence during VR immersion: A comparative study of the reaction of phobic and non-phobic participants in therapeutic virtual environment derived from computer games. *Cyberpsychology and Behavior, 6*(5), 467-476.
Stanney, K., & Sadowski, W. (2002). Presence in virtual environments. In K. M. Stanney (Ed.), *Handbook of virtual Environments. Design, Implementation, and applications* (p.791-806). Mahwah, New Jersey: Lawrence Erlbaum Associates, Publishers.
Velten, E. (1968). A laboratory task for induction of mood state. *Behaviour Research & Therapy, 6,* 473-482.
Westermann, R., Spies, K., Stahl, G., & Hesse, F. W. (1996). Relative effectiveness and validity of mood induction procedures: a meta-analysis. *European Journal of Social Psychology, 26,* 557-580.
Wiederhold, B. K., & Wiederhold, M. D. (1999). Clinical observations during virtual reality therapy for specific phobias. *Cyberpsychology and Behavior, 2*(2), 161-168.
Wiederhold, B. K., & Wiederhold, M. D. (2000). Lessons learned from 600 virtual reality sessions. *Cyberpsychology and Behavior*, 3, 393–400.

Wiederhold, B.K., & Wiederhold, M. D. (2005). *Virtual reality therapy for anxiety disorders. Advances in evaluation and treatment*. Washington (DC): American Psychological Association Press.

Witmer, B.G., & Singer, M. J. (1998). Measuring Presence in Virtual Environments: a Presence Questionnaire. *Presence, 7*(3), 225-240.

25

Serious Games for Serious Problems: from *Ludicus* to Therapeuticus

Pedro Gamito[1,2], PhD, Jorge Oliveira[1], PhD, Diogo Morais[1], Pedro Rosa[1,3] and Tomaz Saraiva[1]
[1]*Universidade Lusófona de Humanidades e Tecnologias,*
[2]*Clínica S. João deDeus,*
[3]*ISCTE-IUL/CIS,*
Portugal

1. Introduction

Within the primate family, the members of our species are the ones that present the longest period of immaturity. Originally thought as an adaptive evolutionary strategy, since natural selection would only opt for the characteristics that are more "cost-efficient", the longer period of dependency from progenitors is now perceived as a spin-off of another trait-intelligence. As a result of the relative narrow birth canal, humans' offspring need longer time, when compared to other primates, to puff up the cranial volume compatible to the volume and complexity of the brain from where our intelligence levels arise. This means that the cost of brightness leans on the necessity of further time to allow the brain to develop. More specifically, social intelligence seems to be the driving agent. According to Alexander (1987), as humans accomplished dominance over the other species, competition was shifted to their fellow members, which boosted the need to cope with the complex systems of relationships within the group.

The long period of brain development accounts for an increased ability towards the behavioral flexibility needed to deal with such multidimensional network which, according to Bjorklund (2007) is responsible for our species success. This flexibility, and the resulting social, competence are particularly acquired during the time young humans are playing. Since they are born, babies´s senses are stimulated, learn how to use their muscles, learn how to control their body, and, develop the strategies to interact and cope with other individuals by playing games (Papalia et al., 2005). In fact (Rakoczy, 2007) states that games because of the make-believe, in one hand, and of the associate inherent rules, in the other, are the doorway to the entrance on the structured institutional adulthood reality.

Children's interaction with the surrounding elements enables them to understand that the others are potential cooperators which allows them to accept their role as persons and, specially, the opportunity of sharing the same cultural background with others from which they acquire new ways of behavior and new ways of thinking (Rakoczy, 2007). Games enable children to engage more easily in this process.

Playing games is therefore a medium for learning the complexities of human systems. Huizinga (1971) states on his book *Homo ludens*, that playing is the basis of all human societies and civilizations. According to this author, civilizations appear and developed from and through gaming. At this light all human activities emerged from gaming. Philosophy derives from playing with concepts; the language formation relies on playing with sounds and meanings; war rests upon strategy and tactics, two pillars of gaming and art is a form of interacting, or playing, with a perceived reality.

Also, gaming replicate several aspects of a certain reality through a set of pre-established rules. When playing one obey and incorporate the inherent laws of the game. And because of its playful character rules are assimilate with minor effort. Even for games that have no previous standardized rules, the formal guidelines naturally appear along the way with participant consensus.

Even the production of knowledge process is, according to Huizinga (1971), a game. Like a children's game, knowledge production is full with doubts resulting from the uncertain outcome of ones and others players' actions, being, at the same time bound to rules. And it is this duality that provides the ability for knowledge to be produced. The rules made the superstructure, defining the pathway. The uncertainty enables the ability of the player to learn from their attempts and errors, which, is according to Popper the only way to comprehend and acknowledge a certain reality. So gaming seems to be a propeller of human intellectual and social activities.

The impact of gaming as a social activity is underlined by the entertainment industry where the gaming industry is leading the way. The revenues from video games release has relegate the film industry to a supporting role. Video games industry revenues in 2007 were $ 41.9 billion, whereas the movies industry accounted for $ 27 billion (PWC, 2008). Despite most of the innovative techniques came from the military and the academy (the internet, motion detection, artificial intelligence, animation physics and collision detection, among others), video games' companies have picked up from there and open up the Pandora's box to the general public.

Nowadays, many areas of activity use off-the-shelf video games graphic engines to produce simulations. Professionals from fields like urban planning (http://wwics.si.edu/foresight/index.htm), journalism (http://eciencia.urjc.es/dspace/bitstream/10115/.../texto_final_serious_games.pdf), the military (http://citeseerx.ist.psu.edu/viewdoc/download?doi=10.1.1.151.4796...), the police (www.dcs.shef.ac.uk/.../SeriousGames4thePolice_AhmedBinSubaih-1.pdf), education (Ritterfeld et al., 2009), or even, cultural heritage (Anderson et al., 2009) were converted to the thrilling visual and audio ascendancy of video games.

When the first goal of such games is other than entertainment they are coined as serious games (SG) (Micheal & Cohen, 2006). SG are upgrades of plain numerical simulations. One of the main goals of computing was, initially, to make possible, within a reasonable frame of time, the execution of long iterative calculi for simulation. The simulation of what-if scenarios was, and still is, a desirable path to follow every time an uncertain outcome arises. In the 60's of last century the USA Apollo program was an example. The Digital Simulation for the Verification of Apollo Flight Software was devised to emulate spaceship flight maneuver (Glick & Femino, 1970). Spaceship trajectory, gravity and sensor errors, among other features, were displayed as form of numbers and letters that were computed while the crew replied back by clicking on a 12 button keyboard (Dunbar et al, 1966). The result of simulations appeared as numerical or alphanumerical data. Nowadays, SG do the same thing. However, and on account of graphic boards and computer generated imagery (CGI) techniques, it is now possible to interact with the computer in a more fashionable way. 3D computer graphics' techniques, invented also in the 1960's, enabled that computer based simulations could be carry on more user-friendly environments.

SG are one of the most notorious off-springs of these developments. The concept behind SG rests on the ability of channeling videogames properties like graphic interfaces, animation, realism, interaction and simulation to a target other than pure entertainment. Zyda (2005, p.26) defined SG as "a mental contest, played with a computer in accordance with specific rules, that uses entertainment to further government or corporate training, education, health, public policy, and strategic communication objectives." But, perhaps what differentiates SG from their videogame ancestry is the ability in producing knowledge and skills that are focused within the application context (Susi et al, 2007). Under this light, Yusoff and colleagues (2009) produced a conceptual framework where learning, within a SG context, is a result of an iterative process that derives from the level of achievement of each player. According to player performance, the system should produce data or information that acknowledges every accomplishments and failures by providing feedback to the player. For each feedback, knowledge is produce enabling to move forward. It is also stressed that the SG must take into consideration its own game attributes that sustain learning and engagement, and the intended learning outcomes i.e. the major goals to attain.

As seen, nowadays simulation is, in most cases, made through the help of 3D models. The 3D perspective enables a better comprehension of the phenomenon under simulation, particularly if the phenomenon presents itself on a 3D fashion, such is the case, of most aspects of our daily lives. Visual perception on human brain relies on different brain areas in the cortex that are specialized in processing different aspects of visual information. For example, color, form and depth are processed on V1 and V2 occipital areas and motion on the medial temporal cortex. This means that the fully understanding, or cognition, of a real three dimensional phenomenon summons up different areas of the brain. Consequently, the cognitive load can be reduced if the object or situation presents itself as much as real as possible. And that is why one image worse thousand words. More effort is required for analyzing and comprehending a complex structure if it is described in the form of words. The same occurs if a 3D reality is displayed in 2D. The load on our brain is higher.

Along with simulation another a pattern arises. Interaction. The user ability to freely experience the digital world is, along with the meaning of the experience, a decisive contribution for a full engagement within the gaming context. Meaningfulness and interaction are therefore responsible for tricking ones brain perception making believe that the participant is actually in the synthetic set. This sense of being there, also defined as presence, is responsible for turning a 3D experience into a virtual reality (VR) adventure. And VR is the keystone of any modern SG.

The ability of the end user to freely and easily interact with the complex synthetic world, alone, or with others have ignited a modern "gold rush". As a consequence, millions are currently engaged on online 3D/VR games. This fact boosted a brave new world. Interacting with the PC is no longer a "thing" for software engineers. In future generations it will be probably hard to find anyone with no proficiency in computing interaction. And this is the casus belli for SG. Due to their inherent characteristics, SG are probably the best option when one needs to replicate a certain reality, real or oniric. Such is the case of the treatment of several mental health disorders or the case of motor and cognitive rehabilitation.

Concerning mental health disorders, more often than not chemical and pharmacological strategies do not work. One common way out is to empower patients through cognitive and behavioral therapies. In these therapies the patient is confronted with situations aimed at reeducating erroneous beliefs. For example, patients with arachnophobia face spider images or the spider itself as many times needed, until the disruptive fear ceases (Garcia-Palacios et al, 2002).

Regarding motor and cognitive rehabilitation, traditional exercises are more often than not, repetitive and boring, causing, after a few sessions, a break on the meaningfulness of the exercise. Setting games where patient's next action is unknown and where interaction is the keynote may engage more efficiently the patient on the rehabilitation process. Rand et al (2001), developed an augmented reality SG where paraplegic patients exercise torso posture by attempting to reach out for balls that randomly appear on a virtual screen.

2. Serious games for neuropsychological rehabilitation

2.1 Neuropsychological rehabilitation

The cognitive consequences of acquired brain injury can be very diverse and differ in their nature. Lesions can result from infectious or degenerative diseases in the central nervous system (e.g. Alzheimer, Parkinson disease), brain tumors, stroke (e.g. cerebrovascular accident) and traumatic brain injury. According to each condition, lesions can be focal or diffuse, resulting in deficits that range from cognitive impairment or attention/concentration deficits to motor disability. Cognitive impairment is defined by Cooper et al. (2008) as a limitation in the capacity for mental tasks and is often associated with deficit in executive functions. In fact, according to Wang and collaborators (2004) patients suffering from traumatic brain injuries need, in most cases, to relearn almost all daily life activities.

Brain injury can affect all human domains, such as cognitive, emotional, behavioral and social functioning, leading to selective effects in terms of motor or sensory losses, cognitive disability (e.g. memory deficits) and emotional problems, namely, anxiety and depression.

Neuropsychological rehabilitation is related with the improvement of cognitive and motor deficits caused by brain injury. In this way, the major goal of cognitive rehabilitation is to enable patients to overtake cognitive and emotional deficits and to achieve social adjustment and better quality of life (Wilson, 2003).

The scientific literature is in agreement regarding the development of new neuropsychological approaches that need to take on board the scientific knowledge from different areas of psychology. Cognitive rehabilitation can be considered as the use of cognitive theories in rehabilitation of patients with brain injury. The use of theoretical models from cognitive psychology has been quite influential on neuropsychological approaches (Sohlberg & Mateer, 2001). For example, theoretical models for working memory of Baddeley and Hitch (1974) have been critical for memory recover in cognitive rehabilitation programs, as well as the models of behavior and theories of learning (Baddeley, 1993) and cognitive behavior therapy models (Beck, 1976; 1996) for treatment of emotional consequences that are common in patients who suffer brain injury. The study of memory and attentional deficits is also important for many patients with acquired brain injury, even when they are not a primary problem. Once the patient is required to apply skills in real-world settings, demands on attention and working memory often exceed their processing and response capabilities. Patients with acquired brain injuries may find it difficult to train both a primary task and a simultaneous secondary task. Wilson and colleagues (2006) suggest that these procedures should be supported by visual and verbal cues that can signal attention to obstacles and forthcoming events. According to Wilson (2003) the self-regulation of frustration and loss feelings is another crucial factor in rehabilitation processes. In this way, the main goals of neuropsychological rehabilitation are to promote recovery of patients through the complete understanding of the impact of cognitive and behavioral impairments in their functional disabilities (Ylvisaker et al., 1998).

All validated approaches of cognitive rehabilitation start from a neuropsychological assessment. The complete neuropsychological assessment is important to determine and estimate the impact of each intervention. Cognitive rehabilitation has two different perspectives: internally and externally focused interventions. Regarding the internally focused protocols, interventions aim at training a specific function, whereas externally focused interventions are more related to the environmental adjustment of these patients.

Despite the nature of each intervention protocol, meaningful improvement in patient's everyday life activities is one critical aspect of neuropsychological rehabilitation. However, the focus on function has supported the development of more structured protocols and tools that may benefit the overall adjustment of these patients.

Sohlberg and Mateer (1989) claim that neuropsychological rehabilitation should be based on a theoretical background. For instance, cognitive retraining suggested by Sohlberg and colleagues (2001) is based in the assumption that stimulation of affected functions may help to recover from disability, which can be the case of using computer games to assist neuropsychological rehabilitation.

2.2 Serious games and IT in neuropsychological rehabilitation

Serious games (SG) can be defined, as seen, as games that do not have the entertainment as a primary goal and can contribute to a specific purpose.

Research with videogames has focused mainly in the negative effects of video games at an individual and social level, while other perspectives suggest that videogame play can help to develop cognitive abilities, such as visual and spatial skills.

Early in 1984, Greenfield has suggested that video games could enhance visuo-motor and cognition skills. Later, Green and Bavelier (2003) showed in a controlled study that playing videogames improves the overall capacity of the attentional system measured by the number of objects that can be attended in specific task.

Green and Bavelier (2006a) also studied spatial distribution of attention with video game play. These authors carried out a controlled study to test whether gamers have more attentional resources than non-gamers. The results showed that gamers attend more effectively to stimuli presented in the periphery and in central vision, revealing higher visuospatial attention.

The latest videogames are very challenging and can promote visuospatial attention resources by training task-related attention or vision skills (Green & Bavelier 2006b). For example, "heavy" gamers can train visual skills in an unusually challenging situation, since they are daily exposed to very demanding visual tasks that require visual processing of multiple items. Green and Bavelier (2007) also suggest that videogames could require, in a great extent, the efficient neglect of distracting items, which can enhance visual processing and, thus allocation of attentional resources.

One of the most common procedures in rehabilitation is the repeated and systematic training of the impaired functions, where patients need to practice and relearn lost cognitive and motor functions (Allred et al., 2005). In this way, the study of neural mechanisms involved in learning is a key component for the understanding of video-game practice in rehabilitation.

A study of Koepp and collaborators (1998) found that videogame play may change the release of neurotransmitters (e.g. dopamine) in the brain. Dopamine is a neurotransmitter involved in many functions with important roles in cognition and behavior through reward and learning modulation. The authors studied dopamine levels with positron emission tomography scans during an action video game play and actually observed an increase in dopamine levels during videogame play.

In agreement with these assumptions and according to Sohlberg and colleagues (2001) theory, cognitive retraining is one crucial aspect for neuropsychological rehabilitation. Virtual environments in terms virtual reality SG can provide training environments where repetition, visual and auditory feedback can be systematically manipulated according to each individual differences.

Levin and collaborators (2005) argued that using SG applications in rehabilitation may benefit training purposes, mainly through the 3D spatial correspondence between movements in the real world and movements in the virtual worlds, which may facilitate real-time performance feedback. As stated before, the repetitive practice is an important aspect in motor and cognitive training as it improves performance in disabled patients (Chen et al, 2004). For example, these authors used SG environments in children with cerebral palsy and observed that the repetitive practice of a particular motor aspect enables the coordination of a specific muscular system. While, repeating the exercises, patient's senses are provided with feedback on the accomplishments achieved during each task.

Another example of SG contribution in rehabilitation is the study of Viau and colleagues (2004). The authors studied movements performed by participants with hemiparesis with virtual objects in VR and real objects in real life and found no differences between conditions, suggesting that this VR can be effective as training technique for rehabilitation

Another important issue with neuropsychological rehabilitation is the patient's motivation to perform the predetermined exercises. Mainly because SG and VR are usually presented on a multimodal platform with several sorts of immersive cues, such as images and sounds, patients may be more willing to engage and pursue with the exercise when are performed within a SG or VR setups. In agreement with this notion, Bryanton and collaborators (2006) claim that children with cerebral palsy had more fun and tended to repeat more often at home the exercises in the virtual environments than the conventional exercises.

The wideband technology provides mobile and remote application of the SG virtual environments and brought about a new area of application, the telerehabilitation. Due to the disability characteristics or to the distance from the rehabilitation clinic, or both, an important part of the patients neglect training sessions (Sugarman et al., 2006). The neuropsychological telerehabilitation may take the cognitive and motor exercises to the patients. Lewis and colleagues (2006) developed a telerehabilitation application that enables therapist to communicate, control and monitoring patient's exercises remotely. This system comprises rehabilitation devices such as gloves and head-mounted display on the patient's side and a web camera and headphones on the remote therapist side. Although, it requires the effective participation of the therapist on rehabilitation procedure, this limitation may be overcome by the replacement of the therapist by an avatar. This synthetic person, armed with artificial intelligence, can coach the patient throughout the rehabilitation exercises dismissing therapist's involvement. However, there is lack of information regarding the effectiveness of this approach and the results are unclear at this point.

More recently, Gamito and collaborators (in press) have addressed this issue and studied an online portal to train memory and attention in patients with traumatic brain injury (Figure 1). The study was carried out on single 20 years old male patient with traumatic brain injury where the he had to complete a set of 10 online VR sessions. The patient was assessed before, during and after training with neuropsychological measures for working memory and attention. In this case study, the authors found an improvement in cognitive abilities suggesting that this online VR platform can be effective for cognitive rehabilitation of TBI patients.

Fig. 1. Online VR platform for cognitive telerehabilitation of TBI patients (Gamito et al. in press).

The same authors suggest that on a virtual environment, training can be perceived more as a game and less than a task, engaging the patients in the rehabilitation process more than the conventional methods.

In the future, the dissemination of these procedures may benefit with the development of game platforms, such as Wii, Xbox, Playstation that may also contribute to enhanced and more user-friendly training environments, where systematic training and real-time feedback can occur, as can be seen on the last section of chapter.

The principles of rehabilitation are grounded in different theories, however, it appears that the common procedure to all different approaches is that stimulation of impaired functions can promote faster recovery of the affected cognitive or motor skills and, as consequence, may contribute also to self-esteem, emotional well being and the overall social adjustment of these patients. Within the cognitive retraining perspective of (Sohlberg et al., 1989) and with virtual environments derived from SG and VR applications, training can be more effective since it provides a more ecologically valid technique which will ensure the transfer of learned skills to real-life situations.

3. Serious games for mental disorders

3.1 Mental diseases: facts, numbers and traditional treatments

One may think that mental disorders affect just a small part or specific layers of society; however, they are widespread in the population (Kessler, et al., 2005a), being the leading cause of disability in the U.S. and Canada (WHO, 2003). It has been shown that around 57.7

million people have diagnosable mental disorders (U.S. Census Bureau, 2004), according to a reliable established criteria (APA, 2000). Around 26 % of the Americans suffer from a mental disorder in any given year and 45 % of those meet the criteria for two or more disorders, usually related to co-morbidity (Kessler et al., 2005b).

Under the *mundus* of mental illness, a wide range of psychopathologies can be found. The most common type of mental disorders in psychiatric population are the anxiety disorders (AD) with a 18,1% of incidence and a lifetime prevalence of 28,8%, (Kessler et al., 2005b). AD is a supra category which include panic disorder, obsessive-compulsive disorder, post-traumatic stress disorder, generalized anxiety disorder, and phobias (social phobia, agoraphobia, and specific phobia) (APA, 2000). It is estimated that nearly 40 millions of American adults have an AD in a given year, representing 18 % of the American population (U.S. Census Bureau, 2004; Kessler et al., 2005b). Furthermore, AD commonly co-occur with others mental disorders and normally lead to relapses (Kessler et al., 2005b).

Another very common type of mental disorders are the mood disorders, which include the depression disorders and the bipolar disorders (APA, 2000). The unipolar depression and bipolar affective disorders are on the top ten of the leading causes of disability worldwide (Murray & Lopez, 1996). It is estimated that major depression affects approximately 14.8 million American adults (U.S. Census Bureau, 2004; Kessler et al., 2005b). Moreover, major depression is the leading cause of disability in the U.S. for ages 15-44 (WHO, 2004).

Although, not so common, schizophrenia is known to be a highly disabling disorder. In a 1999 a study conducted in 14 countries, schizophrenia was ranked as the third-most-disabling condition just after quadriplegia and dementia (Üstün et al., 1999). A meta-analyses study conducted by Bhugra (2005) revealed that the median prevalence of schizophrenia was 4.6/1,000 for point prevalence, 3.3/1,000 for period prevalence and 4.0/1000 for lifetime prevalence.

The typical treatments for mental disorders can be categorized in pharmacological or nonpharmacological (Gazzaniga & Heatherton, 2006). Pharmacological treatment includes several main groups. In mood disorders, Tricyclic antidepressants (TCAs), Selective Serotonin Reuptake Inhibitors (SSRIs) and Serotonin and Norepinephrine Reuptake Inhibitors (SNRIs) are the mostly employed (Hirschfeld & Vornik, 2004). Anxiolytics are used, generally shorter-term, for AD (APA, 2000). A sort of anxiolytics, like benzodiazepines prescribed for short-term relief, azapirones, barbiturates, meprobamate and non-cardioselective beta-receptor blocker are the mostly applied for AD (Goodman, 2004;). On other hand, antipsychotics are usually prescribed in schizophrenia (Davis & Adams, 2001). However, antipsychotics may provoke extrapyramidal reactions with a range of side effects like dystonias, akathisia, parkinsonism, tardive dyskinesia, tachycardia, hypotension or even impotence (Bellack, 2006).

Among nonpharmacological treatments, cognitive–behavioural therapy (CTB) is the most frequent in AD (Hofmann & Smits, 2008) , mood disorders (Gloaguen et al., 1998) and schizophrenia (Wykes et al., 2008). Interpersonal psychotherapy is also commonly applied, with positive outcomes in depression (Weissman et al., 2000).

Indeed, a larger body of literature suggests that CBT for AD are the non-pharmacological most effective approach (Craske, 1999), with an effectiveness relatively similar across AD and most efficacious that non-CBT treatments (e.g., Abramowitz, 1997; Fedoroff & Taylor, 2001;). These findings are not surprising, since that most treatments consist of therapeutic techniques of education, self-monitoring, cognitive restructuring and exposure therapy.

For treatment of AD, exposure therapy is the most common and effective psychotherapeutic technique (Foa et al., 2000). This efficacy in AD, may be explain by the common denominator for all AD, that is, a distinctly and abnormal increased fear response. When fear becomes more disproportionate than what is justified by the external threat and there is a clearly interference with the ability to function optimally, then the criteria for an anxiety spectrum disorder is met (APA, 2000).

This fear response has been related to an amygdalar dysfunction (Williams et al., 2006). The amygdala consists of 13 nuclei located in the anterior medial temporal lobe and has a key role in fear regulation (Hamm & Weike, 2005). Three of these nuclei, the basal amygdala, lateral amygdale, and central nuclei, are implicated in the pathways of fear response (Paré et al., 2004). Threatening cues are received by the sensory thalamus, sent to the lateral amygdale, and subsequently transmitted to the central nucleus. This circuit is known as "short loop" pathway. The long information processing circuit (long loop pathway) sends signals to the lateral amygdale from the sensory cortex, insula, and prefrontal cortex (LeDoux, 2000). From there, the information is projected to the effector spots in the brain stem and hypothalamus, which produce the autonomic and behavioral expressions of fear response.

Similarly, a number of studies reported an increase in amygdalar activity in specific phobias (Larson et al., 2006). According to Ledoux (2000), a threatening cue representing a potential danger, causes an automatic, quick protective response that occurs without the need for conscious thought. Despite the influence of neurobiological aspects, some models refer the weight of cognitive factors on AD development and maintenance.

Exposure therapy as a therapeutic technique involves the exposure to the feared stimulus or context without any danger while the psychotherapist relieves patient's anxiety (Rothbaum & Schwartz, 2002). Traditionally, exposure therapy adopts two different paths: imagination or *in vivo*. In imagination exposure, the patient will be exposed himself/herself to all the scary parts of ansiogenic situation - but just mentally. *In vivo* exposure consists on direct confrontation to feared objects, activities, or situations by a patient (Leahy, 2003). However, new forms of treatment (with preference low-priced, fast, creative and effective) are being been wished for not only for patients but for therapists as well. The advance of technology brought new approaches and new therapeutic techniques.

3.2 Serious gaming: a new iceberg peak is emerging

Exposure therapy, within in CBT context is the most reliable intervention type when it comes to treat AD. In some of these disorders, *in vivo* and in imagination exposure fails to deliver sound results (Parsons & Rizzo, 2008).

For example, imagination exposure is somewhat ineffective in PTSD and *in vivo* exposure is far from being cost efficient in fear of flying. It is difficult to

compel patients with PTSD that had suffered traumatic events to re-experience or relive those events through imagination (i.e. War PTSD, Motor Vehicle Accidents, sexual abuse). And regarding fear of flying, the amount of time spent and the associated costs of *in vivo* exposure narrows down the number of possible patients.

VR-based SG can replicate almost in perfection any of these ansiogenic situations, with less costs and in less time, given a better solution (ratio cost/efficacy) in AD treatment.

To bypass impediments such as these, SG were developed as a reliable and alternative therapeutic technological technique (TTT). The increasing accessibility to powerful personal computers and 3D visualization techniques made the development of SG and its use on psychotherapy, a tool for treating most AD. VR is actually one of the fields that, within the SG application content, yields a more promising future since it allows an even greater immersive experience and a more realistic approach.

VR holds a set of important features that, allied to the characteristics of SG, ensure a fruitful solution for many situations. One of these characteristics is the rich interactive simulation that VR encloses. The interactivity on a full sensory environment created to a specific end ensures that the objectives of exposure (in whatever field of application) are met in an easier and more controlled way than in traditional imagination exposure. In this way, VR-based SG might be an adequate technique due a better approximation to the real word (Vincelli & Molinari, 1998; Vincelli & Riva, 2002), inducing higher levels of immersion when compared to imagination exposure (Botella et al., 2000; Rothbaum et al., 1995; Vincelli & Riva, 2002).

Furthermore, VR allows the development of settings that ensure that ecological validity is taking in consideration. For instance, in cases of fear of subway, before getting in the railway carriage, patient should enter in the subway station; buy the traveling ticket, stamp it and then wait for the train to come (Figure 2).

Fig. 2. Screenshots of VR-based Serious Game for Agoraphobia Treatment developed by the Psychology Computional Laboratory of the Universidade Lusófona de Humanidade e Tecnologias, Lisbon, Portugal.

This element, in conjunction with the increased engagement that VR brings to any (serious or not) videogame, is an important feature for every multimedia application, and was taken into consideration since the beginning of the development of these tools. In some situations, namely psychotherapy, the novelty of the situation in which the participant is involved also ensures that the objective of SG is pursued in an easier way.

The impact VR-based SG has been felt in a far-reaching range of fields over the last years, being effective on treatment for anxiety, phobia, PTSD, stress inoculation training, pain and drug and alcohol addiction (Wiederhold & Wiederhold, 2008). More specifically, VR-based SG are being used to in clinical populations with acrophobia (Emmelkamp et al., 2001), arachnophobia (Garcia-Palacios et al., 2002), claustrophobia (Botella, 2000), fear of flying (Rothbaum et al., 2000), fear of driving (Saraiva et al., 2007) or PTSD (Gamito et al., 2008, 2009, 2010).

The hyper realistic threatening stimuli provided by SG lead to higher attention (Vincelli, 2000), and subsequent encapsulation, which means, once the fear system is activated it is difficult to control fear response by verbal instructions or stimulus consciousness (Hamm & Weike, 2005). According to Vincelli and Riva (2002) SG reduce then, the gap between reality and imagination, by diminishing potential distraction or cognitive avoidance to the threatening stimuli.

These and other studies revealed that this type of gaming enables patients to be immersed in the virtual world creating the so called "sense of being there". This sense, also coined as presence as mentioned in the introductory section of this chapter, allows patient to interact with virtual world like if he or she were truly in a real environment (Ditton et al. 1997). In addition, in SG, therapist may also have full control on the virtual world, being able to add, or withdraw, threatening cues according to patient and treatment requirements (Gamito et al., 2008).

SG can be thought in the prior terms as a masked exposure therapy technique with specific features embedded like novelty, playfulness, control and security that rely on the key process - the desensitization (Wolpe, 1973). Controlled studies have continuously shown that this combination of SG with traditional therapies results in more successful outcomes (Hoffman et al. 2000; Gamito et al., 2008, 2009, 2010).

The potentialities and benefits of SG have been demonstrated specially in PTSD studies (Rizzo and et al., 2006; Gamito et al., 2008; 2009). PTSD is a special case of AD, characterized by unique symptoms (e.g. dissociation, nightmares, flashbacks) which are not present in other AD, suggesting either different or deep emotion deregulation. (Ethin & Wager, 2007). PTSD patients typically re-experience the disturbing incident and engage the avoidance to stimuli linked to the traumatic scenario. These patients also present an impairing recall of events connected to traumatic scene and an autonomic hyper reactivity (APA, 2004). It has been also suggested that PTSD patients tend to have abnormal levels of key hormones implicated in fear response, namely lower cortisol levels and higher levels of epinephrine and norepinephrine when compared to non-patients (Yehuda, 1998).

Now is possible to reproduce in SG cues of events that are not replicable in a real life situation (Rizzo et al., 2006). SG appears to promote the visual, auditory and olfactory memory, activating other related memories and experiences such as cognition, affect, and physical sensation. Under SG, PTSD patients report physical (sweating, shaking knees) and emotional symptoms (feeling scared or uncomfortable) associated with the stored memories of the traumatic events. In general, SG provide a link between the patient's reality formed by his or her memories of the traumatic event and the objective world. The current studies with VR-based SG revealed that gaming aspect of the treatment also helps to reduce the stigma associated with getting therapy (Gamito et al., 2008, 2009, 2010).

In the field of specific phobias (e.g. snakes, spiders, dogs, pigeons, etc.), SG may become the first option for exposure therapy, in the way that is safer, less embarrassing, and less costly than reproducing the real world situations. The traditional exposure therapy can be, more often than not, a barrier to treatment. It is known, that only about 20% of phobic individuals seek treatment because they are too stressed by the thought of being exposed to the feared/avoiding stimuli (Bender, 2004).

In traditional exposure therapy, patient engagement in the therapeutically process is sometimes compromised. Phobic individuals tend to have difficulty in imagining, visualizing or describing the phobic situations, which, eventually, makes it hard to reproduce *in vivo* or to assess the level of avoidance in imagination exposure. This is the point that VR-based SG can be of distinctive help, by immersing phobic patients into a not-so-virtual world, in which they can live and relive as their own.

Regarding patients with fear of flying (Rothbaum et al., 2000), and acrophobia (Emmelkamp et al., 2001), SG can offer a superb visual and auditory cuing, allowing simultaneously therapists to generate and control the entire virtual world via computer. The virtual worlds allows then a simultaneous delivery of trigger stimuli including visual, auditory and tactile (bass shaker or vibration platform) originating an immersive and multimodal experience (Gorini & Riva, 2008).

SG has improved the chances of recovery in wide range of AD. Therapeutic benefits of SG not just take place in PTSD or specific phobias. The effectiveness of SG has been also tested with non-specific phobias.

A non-specific phobia is a more generalized fear, similar to specific phobias, but where the fear appears to be associated to something less discrete (APA, 2000), such as the fear of open spaces or agoraphobia.

Agoraphobics were exposed to VR-based SG, in which virtual open spaces were presented, revealing that the negative attitudes toward agoraphobic situations decreased significantly (North et al., 1996, Botella et al., 2004).

Also in claustrophobia, SG proved its efficacy. A VR-based SG was played throughout several sessions, in which patients were exposed to a customized hierarchy of feared situations. The results showed that anxiety was reduced and maintained at one month follow-up (Botella et al., 2004). It is also important to stress, that the previous claustrophobic related SG were enough real to produce a significant level of anxiety in patients. Another advantage found in SG derives from the possibility to return to lesser anxiogenic level every time the anxiety level becomes overwhelming. Similar to a remote control, a gameover order is at a click distance. The SG also gives an additional benefit to recreate physical sensations that agoraphobics or claustrophobics feel during their panic attacks, such as shortness of breath or blurred vision. (Botella et al., 2004). In a gastronomic analogy, SG allows therapists "to serve" à la carte anxiogenic scenarios, depending on the severity and specificity of each client.

SG benefits may also be spread to other range of psychopathology like schizophrenia. SG developed for social phobia, claustrophobia, and other AD are likely to be applicable to psychosis (Freeman, 2008). VR-based SG can be used with schizophrenic patients, where some complex deficits are able to be measured. It looks like that SG can be also a promising TTT for the understanding of schizophrenia and other brain disorders. SG in schizophrenia is not only a TTT, but a methodology that helps the understanding of functioning of schizophrenia and a new form of diagnostic as well (Josman et al, 2009). According to Freeman (2008), there are some SG applied on schizophrenia treatment, which can teach about the factors that make symptoms better or worse by indicating how emotional state affects hallucinations, or by helping the schizophrenics to learn about the effects focus of attention or style of reasoning.

Regarding mood disorders, SG has not been applied as a TTT itself, but rather, as a method to understand depression. VR-based SG are seen as new tools for assessing the link between depression and the hippocampus. According to Gould and colleagues (2007), when the spatial memory is challenged by a VR-based SG, patients with depression perform poorly on game compared with non-patients, suggesting that their hippocampi were not working appropriately.

The employment of SG in mental illness does not stop here. The VR-based SG are frequent applied on eating disorders (Perpiña et al., 2003) or in sexual disorders (Optale et al., 2004). A VR-based SG, including a cognitive behavioral therapy (in order to have an influence on the sensations of displeasure) and a visual-motor therapy (to mediate the body perception levels) showed effectiveness in the eating behaviors (Riva et al., 2003, 2004). Furthermore,

SG cannot be only a TTT, but also can be used as a method in the evaluation process, in order to assess the body image perception (Riva et al., 1998).
In relation to sexual disorders, SG were applied by Optale and colleagues (1998, 2004) in several studies. All of them revealed that SG increase the positive outcomes. The results suggest that SG when combined with psychotherapy may accelerate the therapeutic process, leading to a satisfactory sexual performance.
Not so related with mental illness, but still an important topic, is pain distraction. It is common during medical procedures patients feeling excessive pain (Melzack, 1990), especially during severe burn injuries care (Carrougher et al., 2003). Hoffman and colleagues (2001) found that VR-based SG can perform as a virtual nonpharmacological analgesic. The patients who played SG reported significant decreases in their pain ratings during the game as an important part of the patient's attentional focus was shifted away from the pain. These results are corroborated with large range of studies in pain, which point out SG as a reliable method for use as an adjunct to medication in pain control (e.g. Gerson, 2003; Stelle, 2003).

4. A shining and bright new future

The future of SG technology and its fields of applications is intimately related to the development of traditional videogames, medical science and military industry. SG have evolved at the same pace traditional videogame industry have, following however some other strategies to ensure that their specific demands are met.
This is the case, as discussed before, of virtual reality (VR), which has been one of the most used technologies in SG and constitutes an important leap towards the full implementation of these type of games as a valuable resource in many issues.
One of the most important technologies associated with VR, the Head Mounted Displays (HMD), which are supposed to promote an engagement experience through head tracking and stereoscopy, have been developing at a good pace. In the early days of VR in SG, most of the fields concerning VR applications were centered along the constraints, such as cybersickness, equipment ergonomy and image definition of these equipments, in a pursuit of a fully immersive experience, without compromising comfort and usability.
Recent developments in multimedia industry, such as high definition (HD) and 3D TV sets may contribute for bridging the gap between reality and the virtual reality exhibit on HMD. High definition and 3D displays improves the sense of realism and provide stereoscopic perception, reducing discomfort for the user.
If interactivity in SGs is an important feature, one can state that motion detection is a very interesting technology concerning SG, and more specifically, neurological/physical rehabilitation. This technology has suffered a dramatic evolution in the last 10 years, and its use is now widespread in the videogame industry. Nintendo was the first big company to tackle this issue, and most of the attention being drawn upon this technology can be attributed to the Japanese manufacturer. This success had to be met by their competitors, and both Playstation 3 (Sony) and Xbox 360° (Microsoft) now offer similar solutions on this engaging technology, that allows that real movements on the user to be recognized as virtual movements by the console and, therefore, a substantial increase in the level of interaction and meaningfulness can be achieved. This is an important resource for the professionals of both motor and neurorehabilitation, and even though some studies have proven the efficacy of SG as a method of rehabilitation (Rizzo, A. & Kim, G., 2005; Broeren,

et al. 2006), there are still some bumps to cross, concerning this technologies. The major issue is that Wii games (which are the ones currently in sale worldwide) were not created to this specific end. These games were created to deliver entertainment and in order for them to work as SG, investments in some of the available applications must be made, or a ground-up development of new ones, must be done, including, of course, the involvement of neurorehabilitation professionals. Even though Wii is a closed system, in the sense that all the development of new applications have to be approved by Nintendo, some game development tools, like Unity 3D, offer the possibility of developing new products for neurorehabilitation by third-party development teams. These projects, frequent in the Personal Computer (PC) scene, would clearly benefit with a parallel development in this particular system due to its almost unique features.

Another prospective feature that will increase the level of realism in this sort of applications will be the continuous development of graphic engines used in videogames. In the last five years, the increased power of both development and end-user equipments has brought up a surge of more realistic features in most videogames, which can, in the long run, allow for more sophisticated applications especially in the areas where SG are still unable to achieve the desired results, such as Post-traumatic Stress Disorder (Rizzo et al, *in press*), depression (Baños et al, 2006) or autism (Strickland, 1997). It is important however to affirm, that in some pathologies, the problem is not merely related to technological issues. In fact, and considering PTSD, the problem may reside much more in the inadequacy of therapeutic approaches than in the technological development. Nevertheless, the so called new generation videogames consoles and PC that use Direct X 10.0 and 11.0 still have an enormous margin for improvement, and the most pressing issue is to create synergies with the videogame industry, in order to get the most out of current and future videogames in a "more serious" perspective.

SG will also amplify its presence in the educational context, as more and more solutions are being found to increase the appeal and effectiveness of teaching. The main reason is that traditional formats of teaching find it hard to reach children that are getting more and more used to rich-media contents. Therefore, SG are a fun and integrated way to maximize the educational potential at school or at home, giving learning the same resources that entertainment has for competing for children's attention. An interesting experience being implemented using SG is the Magellan Initiative in Portugal, which is a similar project to the One Laptop per Child (OLPC) initially developed in the US. Both includes a series of applications that attempt to conjugate the potential of videogames with the learning process of early years. The initial results where a little off what was initially expected, especially because of some issues regarding the updates and configuration of the software. However, most teachers considered it a valuable resource for years to come, if the abovementioned issues can be resolved quickly. This is just an example of the role that SG can have in education, but in this case, the development of the application was specifically made to this purpose.

Furthermore, online collaborative 3D environments, especially taking into account the massive success of MMORPG (Massive Multiplayer Online Role-Playing Game), can also pose as an excellent tool for online and distance learning. In fact, many universities offer distance learning solution in some of their courses, and some online 3D communities have developed far beyond their initial role. One the most compelling examples is Second Life.

This online community has allowed, in the last few years, a sound display of the potential of Internet and online communities as places of knowledge and information exchange. Many universities and even some individuals scholars have used this platform to give some conferences and lectures, where hundreds and even thousands of people can gather, from all over the world, and watch is for free. This platform was conceived to work as similar videogames (like The Sims series, one of the most successful videogame in history), but allowing oneself to interact fully with others, living a virtual "second life".

Some other applications are now being tried. Governments of countries, like USA and the UK, are turning to SG in order to find a way to make people understand the consequences of social and political issues that are changing the geopolitical landscape after the financial crisis that started in 2008. Furthermore, and in a more holistic approach, some of these games (which are still in development in some of the world's most well known software houses) intend to ask players some out-of-the-box solutions for these "serious" problems. Therefore, SG are beginning to play an important role as a liaison between politicians and the people they represent. This can also be seen in the attempt that the British Government is doing to use Facebook as a tool for feedback and solution discussion for some of the most pressing issues concerning this financial and economic crisis.

Some other less conventional forms of SG have been developed in the last years. Some of these games can be employed as propaganda, using an apparent form of entertainment to get some message across. One of the clearest examples is Full Spectrum Warrior. This is a war simulation videogame that was used, by the United States Army, to display its military prowess and technological edge over other nations (Dgansetheman, 2005). This game, however, was not developed with this objective, but was then adapted to fit the US Army's agenda. This is just a new way to reach people with a specific political agenda, and it is no different than other forms used in the past (like comic books or cinema). But the most prolific example of the extraordinary reach of SGs and the investment being made in this format is America's Army (AAs) videogame (Becker D., 2004). As is a videogame developed by Virtual Heroes for the US Army as a traditional videogame. However, its scope goes far beyond entertainment since its major goal was to create an online platform for recruitment. The enormous success of the videogame (even though there are no clear numbers as far as the efficacy of this recruitment method) is very clear, since there are more than 5 million registered users and is one of the top five most played online videogames. Results like this are evidence enough to support similar endeavors in the future and probably other military forces will develop similar applications for the same end.

SG are also playing a role on a community with a diverse agenda. Advertisements on videogames is now a reality turning entertainment games into platforms that have other than the cheerful objective of playing (Susi et al. 2007). Nevertheless, like political propaganda or army recruitment, advergaming is a strategy being used by many companies to achieve a greater connection with its audience, but most of all, to ensure that a specific brand or product builds its base of consumers of the younger generations. The most troubling issue is that most of these products are very similar to traditional videogames which can be a bit of a problem to some consumers. Moreover, it is important that the "intrusion" of advertisement in videogames, that is becoming a more serious investment for major companies, does not "backfire", as there is still a high level of resistance to these sort of advertising strategies.

5. References

Abramowitz, J.S. (1997). Effectiveness of psychological and pharmacological treatments for obsessive-compulsive disorder: A quantitative review of the controlled treatment literature. Journal of Consulting and Clinical Psychology, 65, 44-52.

Alexander, R.D. (1987). *The Biology of Moral Systems (Evolutionary Foundations of Human Behavior)*. Aldine Transaction.

Allred, R.P., Maldonado, M.A., Hsu, J.E. & Jones, T.A. (2005). Training the "lessaffected" forelimb after unilateral cortical infarcts interferes with functional recovery of the impaired forelimb in rats. *Restorative Neurology and Neuroscience*, 23, 297-302.

Anderson, E., McLoughlin, L.; Liarokapis, F.; Peters, C; Petridis,P.; Freitas, S. (2009). Serious Games in Cultural Heritage. *The 10th International Symposium on Virtual Reality, Archaeology and Cultural Heritage VAST - State of the Art Reports*. M. Ashley and F. Liarokapis (Editors).

APA (2000). Diagnostic and Statistical Manual of Mental Disorders -TR (4th ed., test revision.). Washington, DC: American Psychiatric Association

Baddeley, A.D. & Hitch, G. (1974). Working memory. In G. H. Bower (Ed.), *The psychology of learning and motivation*, 8, 47-89. New York: Academic Press.

Baddeley, A.D. (1993). A theory of rehabilitation without a model of learning is a vehicle without an engine: a comment on Caramazza and Hillis. *Neuropsychological Rahabilitation*, 3, 235-244.

Baños R.M., Liaño V., Botella C., Alcañiz Raya M., Guerrero B. & Rey B. (2006). Changing Induced Moods Via Virtual Reality, *Proceedings of Persuasive 2006: 1st International Conference on Persuasive Technology*, Lecture Notes in Computer Science 3962, Springer 7-15

Beck, A.T. (1976). *Cognitive therapy and emotional disorders*. New York: Internation Universities Press.

Beck, A.T. (1996). Beyond belief: A theory of modes, personality and psychopathology. *In P.M. Salkovskis (Ed.) Frontiers of cognitive therapy*, 1-25, New York: The Guilford Press.

Becker D. (2004). US Army pushes video game Recruitment. *http://management.silicon.com/itpro/0,39024675,39120639,00.htm*

Bellack A. (2006). Scientific and consumer models of recovery in schizophrenia: concordance, contrasts, and implications. Schizophrenia Bulletin, 32 (3), 432–42.

Bender, E. (2004). Virtual Reality Treatment Combats Phobias, PTSD. *Psychiatric News*, 39 (13), 45.

Bjorklund, D (2007). *Why Youth is Not Wasted on the Young: Immaturity in Human Development*. Wiley-Blackwell.

Botella, C.; Banos, RM.; Villa, H.; Perpiñá, C. and Garcia - Palacios, A.. (2000). Virtual reality in the treatment of claustrophobic fear: a controlled, multiple-baseline design. *Behavior Therapy* 31:583-595.

Botella C., Villa, H., García-Palacios, A., Baños, R., Perpiñá, C., & Alcañiz. M. (2004). Clinically Significant Virtual Environments for the Treatment of Panic Disorder and Agoraphobia. *CyberPsychology & Behavior*, 7(5): 527-535.

Botella, C., Quero, S., Banos, R. M., Perpina, C., Garcia Palacios, A., & Riva, G. (2004). Virtual reality and psychotherapy. *Studies in Health Technology and Informatics, 99*, 37–54.

Broeren, J., Dixon M., Stibrant Sunnerhagen, K. & Rydmark, M. (2006). Rehabilitation after Stroke Using Virtual Reality, Haptics (Force Feedback) and Telemedicine. *Proceedings of MIE2006.*

Bryanton, C., Bossé, J., Brien, M., Mclean, J., McCormick, A. & Sveistrup, H. (2006). Feasibility, Motivation, and Selective Motor Control: Virtual Reality Compared to Conventional Home Exercise in Children with Cerebral Palsy. *CyberPsychology & Behavior*, 9, 123-128.

Carrougher, G., Ptacek, J., Sharar, S., Wiechman, S., Honari, S., patterson, D. & Heimbach, D. (2003) Comparison of patient Satisfaction and Self-Reports of Pain in Adult Burm-Injured Patients. J Burn Care Rehabilitation, 24, 1-8.

Cooper, R.A., Dicianno, B.E., Brewer, B., LoPresti, E., Ding, D., Simpson, R., Grindle, G. & Wang, H. (2008). A perspective on intelligent devices and environments in medical rehabilitation. *Medical Engineering & Physics*, 30, 1387–1398.

Craske, M. (1999). Anxiety Disorders: Psychological Approaches to theory and treatment. Boulder, CO: Westview.

Chen, Y., Kang, L.J., Chuang, T.Y., Doong, J.L., Lee, S.J. Tsai, M.W. et al. (2004). Use of Virtual Reality to Improve Upper-Extremity Control in Children With Cerebral Palsy: A Single-Subject Design. *Physical Therapy*, 87, 11, 1441-1457.

Danish. B. (2005). The Global Prevalence of Schizophrenia. PLoS Med., 2(5) e151. Published online 2005 May 31. doi: 10.1371/journal.pmed.0020151

David, A. & Adams, C. (2001). Depot antipsychotic medication in the treatment of patients with schizophrenia: (1) meta-review; (2) patient and nurse attitudes. Health Technology Assessment, 5, 1–61.

Dgansetheman, (2005). Military Steps Up Recruitment. *http://www.oppapers.com/essays/Military-Steps-Up-Recruitment/53006.*

Difede, J., Cukor, J., Patt, I., Giosan, C., & Hoffman, H. (2006). The application of virtual reality to the treatment of PTSD following the WTC attack. Annals of the New York Academy of Sciences,1071, 500-501.

Ditton, T. & Lombard, M. (1997). At the Heart of it all: The concept of presence, Journal of Computer-Mediated Communication, 3(2). Available online: http://www.ascusc.org/jcmc/vol3/issue2/lombard.html

Dunbar, J.C., Larson, R.A. & Augart, P.T. (1966). *An Automated Documentation Technique for Integrating Apollo Crew Procedures and Computer Logic.*

Emmelkamp, P. M., Krijn, M., Hulsbosch, A. M., de Vries, S., Schuemie, M. J., & van der Mast, C. A. (2002). Virtual reality treatment versus exposure in vivo: A comparative evaluation in acrophobia. Behavior Research and Therapy, 40 (5), 509-516.

Etkin, A. & Wager T. (2007). Functional neuroimaging of anxiety: a metaanalysis of emotional processing in PTSD, social anxiety disorder, and specific phobia. Am. J. Psychiatr., 164(10):1476–1488.

Fedoroff, I.C.& Taylor, S. (2001). Psychological and pharmacological treatments for social phobia: A meta-analysis. Journal of Clinical Psychopharmacology, 21(3), 311-324.

Foa, E., Keane, T, & Friedman M. (2000). Effective treatments for PTSD: practice guidelines from the International Society for Traumatic Stress Studies. Guilford Press, Guilford Press.

Freeman, D. (2008). Studying and treating schizophrenia using virtual reality (VR): a new paradigm. Schizophrenia Bulletin, 34, 605-610.

Gamito P, Oliveira J, Morais D, et al. (2009). Virtual reality therapy controlled study for war veterans with PTSD. Preliminary Results. Studies in Health Technology & Informatics, 144, 269–72.

Gamito, P., Oliveira, J., Pacheco, J., Morais, D., Saraiva, T., Lacerda, R., Baptista, A., Santos, N., Soares, F., Gamito, L & Rosa, P. (in press). Traumatic Brain Injury memory training: a Virtual Reality online solution. *Proceedings of the 8th International Conference on Disability, Virtual Reality & Associated Technologies.*

Gamito, P., Oliveira, J., Rosa, P., Morais, D., Duarte, N., Oliveira, S. & Saraiva, T., (2010). PTSD Elderly War Veterans: A Clinical Controlled Pilot Study.Cyberpsychology, Behavior, and Social Networking, 13(1), 43-48.

Gamito, P., Saraiva, T., Oliveira, J., Morais, D., Rosa, P., Pombal, M., Gamito, L, & LealA. (2008). Physiological assessment during VR PTSD treatment of a motorvehicle accident patient. Journal of CyberTherapy and Rehabilitation , 1(3),258-266.

Garcia-Palacios, A., Hoffman, H. G., Carlin, A., Furness, T. A., & Botella, C. (2002). Virtual reality in the treatment of spider phobia: A controlled study. Behaviour Research and Therapy, 40, 983-993

Gazzaniga, M.S. & Heatherton, T.F. (2006). The Psychological Science: Mind, Brain, and Behavior (2nd edition). New York: W.W. Norton & Company

Gershon J. (2003). Use of virtual reality as a distractor for painful procedures in a patient with pediatric cancer: a case study. Cyberpsychehav 2003; 6, 657–61.

Glick, F. K. & Femino, S. R. (1970). A Comprehensive Digital Simulation for the Verification of Apollo Flight Software. *MIT Charles Stark Draper Laboratory.*

Gloaguen, V., Cottraux, J., Cucherat, M., Blackburn, I. (1998): A meta-analysis of the effects of cognitive therapy in depressed patients. J. Affect Disord, 49, 59-72.

Goodman, W.(2004). Selecting pharmacotherapy for generalized anxiety disorder. J Clin Psychiatry, 65(13), 8-13.

Gorini, A. & Riva, G. (2008). Virtual reality in anxiety disorders: the past and the future. Expert Rev. Neurotherapeutics 8(2), 215–233.

Gould, N., Holmes, M., Fantie, B., Luckenbaugh, D., Pine, D., Gould T., Burgess, N., Manji, H. & Zarate, C. (2007). Performance on a Virtual Reality Spatial Memory Navigation Task in Depressed Patients. American Journal of Psychiatry, 164:516-519.

Green, C.S. & Bavelier, D. (2006). *The Cognitive Neuroscience of Video Games.* In Messaris, P. & Humphreys, L. (eds). Digital Media: Transformations in Human Communication. New York, Peter Lang.

Green, C.S., & Bavelier, D. (2003). Action video game modifies visual selective attention. *Nature*, 423, 534-537.

Green, C.S., & Bavelier, D. (2006). Effect of Action Video Games on the Spatial Distribution of Visuospatial Attention. *Journal of Experimental Psychology: Human Perception and Performance*, 32, 6, 1465–1478.

Green, C.S., & Bavelier, D. (2007). Action-Video-Game Experience Alters the Spatial Resolution of Vision. *Psychological Science*, 18, 1, 88-94.

Greenfield, P.M. (1984). *Mind and Media: The Effects of Television, Video Games, and Computers.* Cambridge: Harvard University Press.

Hamm, A. & Weike, A. (2005). The neuropsychology of fear-learning and fear regulation. International Journal of Psychophysiology, 57, 5-14.

Hirschfeld, R. & Vornik, L. (2004). Course and treatment of bipolar depression. Diagnosis and Management of Bipolar Disorder. Science Press Inc., London, 28–40.

Hoffman, H. G., Doctor, J. N., Patterson, D. R., Carrougher G. J., & Furness T. A., III. (2000). Use of virtual reality for adjunctive treatment of adolescent burn pain during wound care: A case report. Pain, 85(1–2), 305–309.

Hoffman, H.G., Patterson, D.R., Carrougher, G.J., & Sharar, S. (2001). The effectiveness of virtual reality based pain control with multiple treatments. Clinical Journal of Pain. 17, 229-235.

Hofmann, S. & Smits, J. (2008). Cognitive-behavioral therapy for adult anxiety disorders: a meta-analysis of randomized placebo-controlled trials. J Clin Psychiatry, 69(4), 621-32.

Huizinga, J. (1971) "*Homo Ludens*". Boston: Beacon Press.

Josman, N., Schenirderman, A., Kingler, E. & Shevil, E. (2009). Using virtual reality to evaluate executive functioning among persons with schizophrenia: A validity study. Schizophrenia Research, 115 (2), 270-277.

Kessler, R., Berglund, P., Demler, O., Jin, R., & Walters EE (2005b). Lifetime prevalence and age-of-onset distributions of DSM-IV disorders in the National Comorbidity Survey Replication (NCS-R). *Archives of General Psychiatry*. 62(6), 593-602.

Kessler, R., Chiu, W., Demler, O., & Walters E. (2005a). Prevalence, severity, and comorbidity of twelve-month DSM-IV disorders in the National Comorbidity Survey Replication (NCS-R). *Archives of General Psychiatry*, 62(6), 617-27.

Koepp, M.J., R.N. Gunn, A.D. Lawrence, V.J. Cunningham, A. Dagher, T. Jones, D.J. Brooks, C.J. Bench, & P.M. Grasby (1998). Evidence for striatal dopamine release during a video game. *Nature*, 393, 266-268.

Leahy, R. L. (2003). *Cognitive therapy techniques: A practitioner's guide.* New York: Guilford Press.

LeDoux, J. (2000): Emotion circuits in the brain. *Annual Review Neuroscience, 23*:155–184.

Levin, M. F., Musampa, N. K., Henderson, A. K. & Knaut, L. A. (2005). New approaches to enhance motor function of the upper limb in patients with hemiparesis. *Hong Kong Physiotherapy Journal*, 23, 2-5.

Lewis, J., Deutsch, J., & Burdea, G. (2006). Usability of the Remote Console for Virtual Reality TeleRehabilitation: Formative Evaluation. *Cyberpsychology & Behavior*, 9, 2, 142–147.

Mark, T., Levit, K., Coffey, R., McKusick, D., Harwood, H., King, E., Bouchery, E., Genuardi J., Vandivort-Warren, R., Buck, J., & Ryan, K. (2007). *National Expenditures for Mental Health Services and Substance Abuse Treatment, 1993–2003: SAMHSA Publication SMA 07-4227.* Rockville, Md, Substance Abuse and Mental Health Services Administration

Melzack, R. (1990). The tragedy of needless pain. *Scientific American, 262*, 27-33.

Michael, D. & Chen, S. (2006) *Serious games: Games that educate, train, and inform.* Boston: Thomson Course Technology.

Murray, C., & Lopez, A. (1996). Evidence-Based Health Policy: Lessons from the Global Burden of Disease Study. *Science*, *274* (5288), 740 - 43.

North, M., North, S., & Coble, L. (1996). Effectiveness of virtual environment desensitization in the treatment of agoraphobia. Presence-Teleoperators and Virtual Environments, 5, 346–352.

Optale, A., Munari, A., Nasta, A., Pianon, C., Baldaro Verde, J. & Viggiano G. (1998). A VR based therapy for the treatment of impotence and premature ejaculation. Stud Health Technol Inform , 58, 136-9.

Optale, G, Pastore, M, Marin, S., Bordin, D., Nasta A. & Pianon, C. (2004). Male sexual dysfunctions: immersive virtual reality and multimedia therapy. Stud Health Technol Inform., 99, 165-78.

Papalia, D.E., Olds, S.W., Feldman, R.D. (2005). *Child's World with LifeMAP CD-ROM and PowerWeb*. McGraw-Hill Higher Education.

Paré, D, Quirk, G., & LeDoux JE.(2004) New vistas on amygdala networks inconditioned fear. J Neurophysiol 92, 1–9.

Parsons, T.D., & Rizzo, A.A. (2008). Affective Outcomes of Virtual Reality Exposure Therapy for Anxiety and Specific Phobias: A Meta-Analysis. Journal of Behavior Therapy and Experimental Psychiatry, 39, 250-261.

Perpiña, C., Botella C. & Baños R. (2003).Virtual reality in eatingdisorders. Eat Disord Rev, 11, 261-78.

PWC (2008). *Global Entertainment and Media Outlook: 2008-2012*, Price Waterhouse Coopers.

Rakoczy, H. (2007). Play, games,and the development of collective intentionality. *Conventionality in cognitive development: How children acquire representations in language, thought and action. New Directions in Child and Adolescent Development.* 115, 53-67. San Francisco: Jossey-Bass.

Rand, D., Gottlieb, D. and Weiss, P.L (2001). Recovery of patients with a combined motor and proprioception deficit during the first six weeks of post stroke rehabilitation. *Physical and Occupational Therapy in Geriatrics*, 18, 69-87.

Ritterfeld, U., Shen, C., Wang, H., Nocera, L. & Wong, W. (2009). Multimodality and Interactivity: Connecting Properties of Serious Games with Educational Outcomes. *Cyberpsychology & Behavior*, 12, 6, 691-697.

Riva, G., Bacchetta, M., Cesa, G., Conti, S. & Molinari, E. (2003). Six-month follow-upof in-patient Experiential-Cognitive Therapy for binge eating disorders. CyberPsychol Behav, 6, 251-8.

Riva, G., Bacchetta, M., Cesa, G., Conti, S. & Molinari, E. (2004). The use of VR in the treatment of eating disorders. Stud Health Technol Inform, 99, 121-63.

Riva, G.; Bacchetta, M.,;Baruffi, M., Rinaldi, S. & Molinari, E. (1998). Experiential Cognitive Therapy: VR based Approach for the Assessment and Treatment of Eating Disorders. Virtual Environments in Clinical Psychology and and Neuroscience, Eds. G. Riva, B. Wiederhold, E. Molinari; IOS Pres, Netherland.

Rizzo, A., Pair J., Graap K., Manson, B., McNerney, P., Wiederhold, B., Wiederhold M., & Spira J. (2006). A Virtual Reality Exposure Therapy Application for Iraq War Military Personnel with Post Traumatic Stress Disorder: From Training to Toy to Treatment. In: Roy. M. (Ed.). NATO Advanced Research Workshop on Novel Approaches to the Diagnosis and Treatment of Posttraumatic Stress Disorder. IOS Press, Washington D.C., 235-250.

Rothbaum, B. & Schwartz, A. (2002). Exposure therapy for posttraumatic stress disorder. Am. J. Psychother, 56, 59-75, 2002.

Rothbaum, B. O., Hodges, L. F., Kooper, R., Opdyke, D., Williford, J. S., & North, M. (1995). Effectiveness of computer generated (virtual reality) graded exposure in the treatment of acrophobia. American Journal of Psychiatry, 152, 626 628.

Saraiva ,T., Gamito, P., Oliveira, J., Morais, D., Pombal, M. Gamito, L., Anastácio, M. 2007. The use of VR exposure in the treatment of motor vehicle PTSD: A case-report. Annual Review of Cybertherapy and Telemedicine, Vol. 5. Interactive Media Institute.

Sohlberg, M.M. & Mateer, C. A. (1989). *Introduction to cognitive rehabilitation: theory and practice.* New York: Gildford Press.

Sohlberg, M.M. & Mateer, C.A. (2001). *Cognitive rehabilitation: An integrative neuropsychological approach.* New York: Gildford Press.

Steele E. (2003). Virtual reality as a paediatric pain modulation technnique: a case study. Cyberpsych Behav, 6, 633–8.

Strickland, D. (1997). Virtual reality for the treatment of autism. *In G. Riva (Ed.), Virtual reality in neuropsycho- physiology*, 81-86. Amsterdam.

Sugarman, H., Dayan, E., Weisel-Eichler, A. & Tiran, J. (2006). The Jerusalem TeleRehabilitation System, a new Low-Cost, Haptic Rehabilitation Approach. *Cyberpsychology & Behavior*, 9, 2, 178–182.

Susi, T., Johanesson, M. & Backlund, P. (2007). *Serious Games - An Overview (Technical Report).* Skövde, Sweden: University of Skövde.

Sveistrup, H. (2004). Motor rehabilitation using virtual reality. *Journal of NeuroEngineering and Rehabilitation*, 1-10.U.S. Census Bureau (2004, May 9). Population Estimates by Demographic Characteristics. Available online: http://www.census.gov/popest/national/asrh/

Üstün, T., Rehm, J.; Chatterji S.; Saxena, S.; Trotter, R.; Room, R.; Bickenbach J. & WHO/NIH Joint Project CAR Study Group (1999). Multiple-informant ranking of the disabling effects of different health conditions in 14 countries. Lancet, 354(9173), 111-115.

Viau, A., Levin, M.F., McFadyen, B.J. & Feldman, A.G. (2004). Reaching in reality and in virtual reality: a comparison of movement kinematics. *In Proceedings of the 15th International Society of Electrophysiology and Kinesiology Congress*, 51.

Vincelli, F. & Riva, G. (2002). Virtual Reality: a new tool for panic disorder therapy». Expert Review of Neurotherapeutics 2(3): 89-95Weissman, M., Markowitz, J. & Klerman G. (2000). Comprehensive guideto interpersonal psychotherapy. New York: Basic Books.

Wang, P., Kreutzer, I.A., Bjärnemoa, R. & Davies, R.C (2004). A Web-based cost-effective training tool with possible application to brain injury rehabilitation. *Computer Methods and Programs in Biomedicine*, 74, 235—243.

WHO (2004). *The global burden of disease: 2004 update.* Table A2: Burden of disease in DALYs by cause, sex and income group in WHO regions, estimates for 2004. Available online: http://www.who.int/healthinfo/global_burden_disease/GBD_report_2004update_Annexa.pdf

Wiederhold, B.K., Wiederhold, M.D. (2008). Virtual Reality for Posttraumatic Stress Disorder and Stress Inoculation Training. Journal of CyberTherapy and Rehabilitation, 1(1), 23-35.

Wilson, B. (2003). *Neuropsychological rehabilitation: Theory and practice.* Swets & Zeitlinger B. V., Lisse, The Netherlands.

Wilson, P.H., Thomas, P., Sum, D., Duckworth, J., Gugliemetti, M., Rudolph, H., Mumford, N. & Eldridge, R. (2006). A multilevel model for movement rehabilitation in Traumatic Brain Injury (TBI) using Virtual Environments. *IEEE, 5th International Workshop of Virtual Rehabilitation (IWVR 2006).*

Wolpe, J. (1973). The practice of Behaviour Therapy. London: Pergamon Press.

Williams, L, Kemp, A, Felmingham, K., Barton, M., Olivieri, G., Peduto, A, Gordon, E., & Bryant R. (2006). Trauma modulates amygdalaand medial prefrontal responses to consciously attended fear. Neuroimage, 29, 347–357.

Wykes, T., Reeder, C., Landau, S. , Everitt, B., Knapp, M., Patel A. and Romeo, R. (2007). Cognitive remediation therapy in schizophrenia. Randomised controlled trial. British Journal of Psychiatry, 190, 421-427.

Yehuda, R. (1998). Psychoneuroendocrinology of post-traumatic stress disorder. Psychiatric Clinics of North America, 21, 359–379.

Ylvisaker, M., Szekeres, S.F., & Feeney, T. (1998). Cognitive rehabilitation: Executive functions. *Traumatic brain injury rehabilitation: children and adolescents. Boston: Butterworth-Heinemann*, 221-269.

Yusoff, A., Crowder, R., Gilbert, L. and Wills, G. (2009). A conceptual framework for serious games. *2009 Ninth IEEE International Conference on Advanced Learning Technologies*, 15 - 17 Juy 2009, Riga, Latvia.

Zyda, M. (2005). From visual simulation to virtual reality to games. *Computer*, 38, 9, 25-32.

Part 7

Educational and Industrial Applications

26

Integrating Low-Cost Virtual Reality into Engineering Design Curricula

Shana Smith
National Taiwan University
Taiwan, R.O.C.

1. Introduction

One way to enhance students' ability to visualize 3-D objects is to make their experience of the objects, while learning, as realistic as possible. However, in general, it is very difficult to clearly describe to students a 3-D object and the spatial relationship between the object components, without using a physical mockup. Physical mockups take a lot of time to construct, especially for more complex objects. As a result, graphics educators have started to use 3-D computer-aided design (CAD) tools to help students understand the spatial relationships between objects. However, CAD tools only allow students to examine 3-D models from outside flat computer monitors. In other words, the models and the viewers are in different realms. Using traditional CAD tools, students cannot view models with natural stereoscopic vision.

Virtual reality (VR) is a computer technology of simulating or replicating a physical environment to give users a sense of being there, taking control, and physically interacting with the environment (Ausburn & Ausburn, 2004). VR technology breaks down barriers between humans and computers by immersing viewers in a computer-generated stereoscopic environment. With advances in hardware and software, most PC computers now have the capability to support VR use. Thus, VR has now become an affordable visualization tool that can be used in classrooms.

As Ausburn and Ausburn (2004) indicated, there is a significant opportunity to expand and explore the use of VR in classrooms. Research suggests that VR is an effective tool that enhances learning in areas such as engineering (Sulbaran & Baker, 2000). In addition, VR engages the intellectual, social, and emotional processes of learners. The impact of VR is due to its ability to encourage interaction and ability to motivate learners (Winn et al., 1997). Salzman (1999) found that VR applications in education depends on VR features, class contents, students' characteristics, and students' prior experiences.

The emphasis of engineering graphics education has been placed on design, problem-solving, presentation, and communication skills. Three dimensional spatial visualization ability is the core requirement for successfully developing those skills. The use of VR may also represent an effective strategy that supports the development of spatial skills. It is important to combine exposure to VR models with activities such as sketching or drawing as a means for developing a capacity for visual imagery and creativity (Deno, 1995; Devon et al., 1994; Sorby, 1999). Sorby (1999) explained that in most cases, graphics curricula begin with multi-view sketching/drawing and then move to pictorial sketching. However, this sequence of topics is opposite of how most educational psychologists say that students learn.

Although there are many advantages in VR applications, it is important to consider challenges in integrating VR into classrooms. There is little guidance regarding the instructional design and classroom facilitation of VR technologies (Ausburn & Ausburn, 2004). These challenges include lack of necessary computing equipment for testing VR applications (Riva, 2003), lack of standardization of VR systems (Riva, 2003), and difficulty in establishing equivalent control groups (Crosier et al., 2000).

This paper examines the use of VR at three higher education institutions, including one four-year university and two two-year community colleges. This paper considers how the use of new technology in the classrooms affects faculty and students. Experiences and survey results are presented for interested practitioners to follow.

2. Project activities

A VR software tool, VRCADViewer, and instructional materials necessary for class use such as a variety of VR models were developed. The university developed a VR software tool (VRCADViewer) which utilized an open source from Open SceneGraph (www.openscenegraph.org). VRCADViewer can separate left-eye images and right-eye images of a model, so that the model can be viewed stereoscopically. Polarized VR projectors, Da-Lite silver matte tripod polarized screens, polarized 3-D glasses from 3-D ImageTek Corp, and Dell computers equipped with dual graphics output were purchased each of the participating institution.

2.1 Class activities

During the project years, this tool was used for engineering design courses for both first and second year students. Figure 1 shows a VR model projected on a screen in one of the design classes.

Fig. 1. A VR model was projected on a screen

Students were taught about orthographic projection as a part of their drafting studies. Traditionally, this unit of instruction requires the students to identify surfaces and classify them (normal, inclined, and oblique). They were also asked to examine a drawing of an object with a set of orthographic views and to identify and classify surfaces according to information from the drawing. With the advent of computer technology, VR becomes another avenue by which the instructors can attempt to reach these students.
During the classes, VR models were projected onto the Da-Lite screen. Students wore polarized 3-D glasses to view the models stereoscopically. Once students had shown an understanding of the differences between the surfaces, and their roles within the orthographic representational system, more complex models were presented for the students to practice. Through these exercises, students were allowed to develop an understanding of the process of relating surfaces and edges to their representation in orthographic views.

2.2 Summer camp

Ninety-five high school students and 8 teachers were invited to attend a 3-day VR4U! summer camp. During the summer camp, hands-on CAD courses, VR presentations, team work projects, design competitions, industry tours, and career talks were provided. Figure 2 shows high school students presented their VR models at the end of the summer camp. During the final presentation, parents were invited.

Fig. 2. High school students presented their VR models

After attending the summer camp, most participants demonstrated increased interest in pursuing careers in science and technology. Approximately 74% of the participants in the VR4U! summer camp indicated that availability of VR would be a factor in their college choice. More male students than female students indicated that the availability of VR would be a more important factor in their college choice. Most high school students also expressed that learning with VR is more engaging than by traditional teaching methods.

Before students attended the VR4U! summer camp, there was also a significant difference between male and female students in their responses concerning their interest in pursuing a career in science and technology. However, the differences in male and female students' attitudes faded away after they were exposed to VR in the summer camps. After they attended the summer camp, there was no statistically significant difference in their attitudes concerning STEM careers. In fact, the number of female students who indicated that they were interested in a science and technology career doubled after they were exposed to VR.

3. Evaluation

In this project, various tests and surveys were administrated to examine students' conceptual growth and changes in their spatial abilities and class engagement.

Reports from the focus groups conducted in the project years, and comments from the open-end questions from the student survey supported the quantitative evaluation activities. The results from the evaluation provided clear evidence on how the use of VR influenced students' understanding of spatial concepts and course contents.

3.1 Influences on spatial ability

Spatial ability has been shown to be positively correlated with retention and achievement in engineering disciplines (His et al., 1997). Spatial ability has identified several different spatial domains, including spatial visualization and spatial orientation. Spatial visualization refers to the ability to image the movements of objects and spatial forms, and involves tests of mental rotation. Spatial orientation refers to the ability to imagine the appearance of objects from different orientations of the observers. The improvements of students' spatial abilities were measured with specific measures, such as the Mental Rotation Test (MRT) and the Picture Test (PT) developed by Hegarty and Waller (2004).

Survey results showed that VR was an efficient instructional method to develop the spatial ability of students who performed poorly by the traditional instructional method. Students who performed poorly in the pre-PT were more likely to improve their posttest scores than those who did better in the pretest. In surveys, students also noted that, with the new VR tools and learning methods, they were able to better see and understand examples that related to course content. Students further explained that they were able to see inside models and to visualize objects. Other survey results concerning students' spatial ability are as follows.

- After exposure to VR, students' spatial visualization abilities were statistically significantly improved.
- After exposure to VR, students' spatial orientation abilities were improved, but the differences between the pre- and post-tests were not statistically significant.

- About 80% of the poor performers in the pre-MRT reported their posttest scores increased by 10% or more.
- More than 68% of the students reached the project's goal, improving their spatial visualization abilities and test scores by 10% or above in the post-MRT.
- About one-half (53%) of the students increased their scores in the post-PT.

3.2 Efficiency of VR

Efficiency in the evaluation is about efficiency in learning and teaching, including students' perceptions or experiences with VR as an easy, fun, and motivational instruction method as well as instructors' experiences with VR as an interactive and time-efficient tool for teaching.

VR was fun, non-threatening, and interesting

Survey results concering VR was fun, non-threatening, and interesting are as follows.

- About 92% of the high school students said that VR was fun.
- Students agreed that VR was easy to use and very user-friendly.
- More than 90% of the college students said that VR was not frustrating and they did not consider dropping out of the program.
- More than 90% of the students responded that the VR courses were not frustrating.

VR was efficient for students' acquisition of advanced concepts or skills in graphic design

Survey results showed that VR was an efficient instructional method to increase knowledge bases of graphic design among those students who performed poorly by the traditional instructional method. Due to fun, non-threatening, and the interesting nature of VR, students reported high achievements in mastering the advanced or difficult concepts or skills in graphic design. Other survey results are as follows.

- About 87% of the students indicated that the VR courses improved their abilities in engineering design, graphics communication, confidence in 3-D visualization, and so on.
- More than 90% of the students reported attainment of the advanced course objectives, such as 3-D solid modeling.
- About 83% of the students perceived VR and the instructional materials positively.
- Over 96% of the student did not perceive VR and the materials negatively.

Students' comments from focus groups also supported the results stated above.

- It was hard to draw and visualize from the textbook. When you see a bunch of lines and hidden lines, it is hard to understand what it is. It is easier when it is actually shown as an object. You can spin it and see what it is.
- It helps students recognize the views (front, top, right) of objects.

VR was efficient for both male and female students

Female students were more likely to report a lower mean than male students in the pretest; and were more likely to belong to the poor performer group in the pretest than male students. However, after female students were exposed to VR in their courses, they were more likely to have higher mean scores than male students on the posttest. Female students also responded to VR learning methods more positively and less negatively than male students.

- Both male and female students improved in their posttest of MRT and PT.
- Female students or students who performed poorly with the traditional instructional method showed greater improvement after they were exposed to VR.

Time efficiency and increasing interactions in the class

VR was a time-efficient instructional tool for students and instructors. Instead of spending time trying to understand how parts of a mechanism interact during normal operation, the presentation of a VR model allows them to move their attention to later phases of the problem-solving process. Students commented:

- Each faculty member used coaching strategies and group activities to encourage self-directed problem solving.
- VR was useful to explain complex concepts to students.
- VR allowed students to go inside, zoom in, or go through the part.

Also, it was time efficient for instructors. VR enhances the likelihood of interactions between teacher-students and among students because the instructors were able to quickly provide example models through VR. Thus, additional time was available. Rather than focusing on either the development of physical models or attempting to help students visualize specific components of an object, instructors are able to concentrate on the learning objective and to coach students in achieving this goal.

4. Discussions

Survey results showed that students were more confident when sketching projection views after visualizing VR models. Students gave VR instruction high ratings for stimulating their interest in learning. Project results also showed that VR instruction stimulates better interaction between instructors and students because students often have higher engagement and are more interested in discussing, with their instructors, what they see or discover during VR instruction.

In one class, students were asked to locate surfaces on objects, identify the type of surface (e.g., inclined, oblique, or normal), and to identify how edges were formed at the intersection of surfaces. This exercise requires students to visualize an object in order to successfully locate and identify characteristics. By using the VR technology, students were able to concentrate on basic concepts before focusing on the development of their visualization skills.

In addition, it was discovered that during the summer camp, one of the students was epileptic. This was unanticipated and was a valuable lesson learned. This realization informed future participating classes, summer camps, and project activities about VR regarding precautions needed and potential risk. From this experience, the physical comfort measures were developed and incorporated into the VR student survey. About 91% of the students expressed physical comfort in using VR; whereas, 8.6% did not. Female students were more sensitive and expressed less physical comfort in VR than male students, although the difference was not statistically significant. These results will provide valuable information for future VR-related projects.

5. Conclusions

VR is an emerging visualization tool in STEM education which can help viewers acquire better knowledge about data or images. Many major companies or research institutions now use VR to enhance their visualization activities. It is important to use VR in classrooms, not only for enhancing visualization, but also for helping students to become familiar with the important emerging technology before they enter into the workforce.

As demonstrated by this project, VR technology is now readily available, both technically and financially, for classroom use. This paper describes our experiences in integrating low-cost VR into design and technical graphics curricula. The project was a collaborative effort between a four-year university and two community colleges. A low-cost VR tool, consisting of hardware and software was developed to enhance instructional delivery and students' 3-D visualization skills. Using the innovative tools in teaching will also provide competitive advantages in recruiting and retaining students interested in design and graphics, and will promote student engagement in lifelong learning, by stimulating interest in leading-edge technology.

6. References

Ausburn, L. & Ausburn, F. (2004). Desktop virtual reality: A powerful new technology for teaching research in industrial teacher education, *Journal of Industrial Teacher Education,* Vol. 41, No. 4, pp. 33-58.

Sulbaran, T. & Baker, N. (2000, October). Enhancing engineering education through distributed virtual reality, The 30th ASSEE/IEEE Frontiers in Education Conference.

Winn, W.; Hoffmann, H.; Hollander, A.; Osberg, K.; Rose, H. & Char, P. (1997, March). *The effect of student construction of virtual environments on the performance of high and low-ability students.,* The meeting of the American Educational Research Association, Chicago, IL.

Salzman, M.; Dede, C.; Loftin, R. & Chen, J. (1999). *A Model for Understanding How Virtual Reality Aids Complex Conceptual Learning.* Retrieved from http://www.virtual.gmu.edu/pdf/presence.pdf.

Deno, J. (1995). The relationship of previous experiences to spatial visualization ability, *Engineering Design Graphics Journal,* Autumn, pp. 5-17.

Devon, R.; Engel, R.; Foster, R.; Sathianathan, D. & Turner, F. (1994). The effect of solid modeling on 3d visualization skills, *The Engineering Design Graphics Journal,* Vol. 58, No. 2, pp. 4-11.

Sorby, S. A. (1999). Developing 3-D spatial visualization skills, *Engineering Design Graphics Journal,* Vol. 63, No. 2, pp. 21-32.

Riva, G. (2003). Applications of virtual environments in medicine, *Methods of Information in Medicine,* Vol. 42, pp. 524-534.

Crosier, J.; Cobb, S. & Wilson, J. (2000). Experimental comparison of VR with traditional teaching methods for teaching radioactivity. *Education and Information Technologies,* 5 (4), 329-343.

Hsi, S.; Linn, M. & Bell, J. (1997, April). The role of spatial reasoning in engineering and the design of spatial instruction, *Journal of Engineering Education,* pp.151-159.

Hegarty, M & Waller, D. (2004). A dissociation between mental rotation and perspective thinking spatial abilities, *Intelligence,* Vol. 32, pp. 175-191.

27

Virtual Reality and Computational Design

Michael S. Bittermann and I. Sevil Sariyildiz
Delft University of Technology
The Netherlands

1. Introduction

Virtual reality (VR) has been used for diverse purposes, including medical surgery training, visualizing metabolic pathways, socio psychological experiments, flight and driving simulation, as well as industrial and architectural design [1-5]. In these applications the role of VR is to represent objects for visual experience by a human expert. In engineering and design applications the purpose is to verify the performance of a design object with respect to the criteria involved in the task during a search for superior solutions. In computational design, where this verification and search process are performed by means of computation, the instantiation of objects in virtual reality may become a necessary feature. The necessity occurs when the verification process requires the presence of 'physical' object attributes beyond the parameters that are subject to identification through search. For example, in an architectural design the goal may be to determine the most suitable position of an object, while the suitability is verified based on visual perception characteristics of the object. That is, the verification requires the presence of object features beyond the object's location in order to exercise the evaluation of the object's performance regarding the perception-based requirements. These features are provided when the object is instantiated in VR. This way a measurement process driving the evaluation, such as a virtual perception process in the form of a stochastic sampling process, can be executed to assess the perceptual properties of the object concerned.

This paper elucidates the role of VR in computational design by means of two applications, where VR is a necessary feature for the effectiveness of the applications. The applications concern a computational design system implemented in VR that identifies suitable solutions to design problems. The effectiveness of the system has been established in previous work [6], while the general significance of the role that VR plays in the system has not been addressed. This will be accomplished in this paper, which is organized as follows. In section two the computational system is described. In section three the role that VR is playing in the system is described and demonstrated with two applications from the domain of architectural design. This is followed by conclusions.

2. A computational design system implemented in Virtual Reality

In several instances during a design process VR enables decision makers to better comprehend the implications of design decisions. Two aspects can be distinguished in this process.

First, a design's implication in terms of the degree that it satisfies the objectives pursued is subject to assessment. This process may be termed as *verification,* as it entails the verification of the requirements' satisfaction during a search to maximize the satisfaction degree. It is noted that the concept of Pareto optimality plays an important role in the search for optimality. Namely in general it is problematic for a decision maker to commit himself for a specific relative importance among the major goals for the design at hand prior to knowing the implications of such a commitment. This is due to the generally abstract nature of the goals in design. For example the aims to have high functionality or low cost, clearly are difficult to put in perspective prior to knowing what solutions may be attained when maximizing the satisfaction of these goals in the present task. Pareto optimality addresses this issue by permitting to postpone the commitment on relative importance until a set of equivalent solutions is obtained that cannot be improved further. This is achieved by establishing those solutions where no others exist that outperform them in all goals at the same time.

A second process concerns *validation* of the objectives. That is, the question if the right objectives are pursued during verification is addressed. The latter process requires insights beyond knowing how to reach optimality for the given goals at hand. Namely contingent requirements that have not been put into the play during verification are to be pin-pointed. It is clear that the latter process requires verification to occur before it, since otherwise there is no rationale to modify the objectives. That is, based on the Pareto optimal solutions found, a designer is to compare these solutions against his/her preferences, yielding clues on the modification of criteria. The relation between the verification and validation process in design are shown in figure 1.

The reason why VR facilitates validation is that it allows considering the solution in the physical domain beyond an abstract description of the targeted performance features, so that a decision maker may become aware of directions for modifying the objectives. The validation process is especially soft, since it is highly contingent to circumstances so that potentially a vast amount of desirable objectives may be subject to inclusion in a design task, and it is generally problematic to have a hint about which ones to include as well as their relative importance [7]. Therefore it is a challenging issue to provide computational support for the validation process.

In order to investigate the role of VR in the search for optimality during verification, we take a closer look at verification and its associated search process. A computational system accomplishing this task is shown in figure 2. It aims to establish set of Pareto optimal solutions for a number of requirements, where the requirements are allowed to be *soft* in character, i.e. they may contain imprecision and uncertainty.

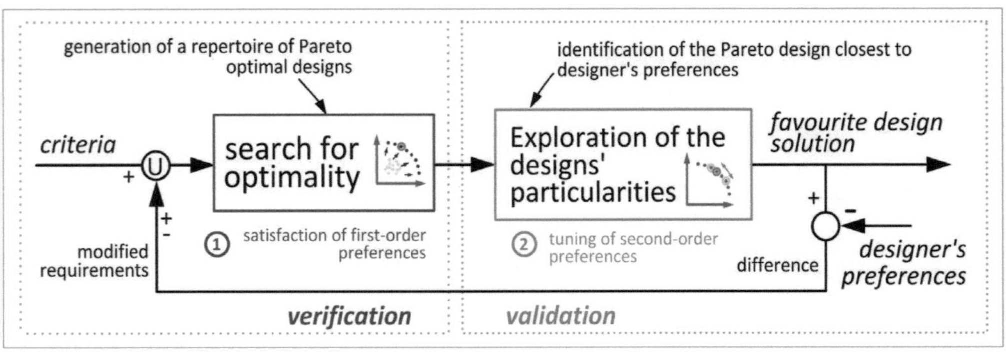

Fig. 1. Verification and validation in design

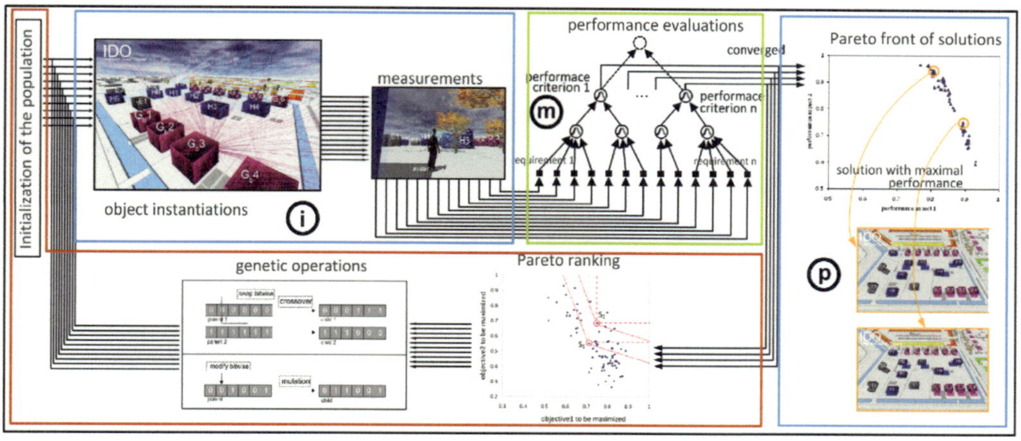

Fig. 2. Computational design system implemented in virtual reality

From the figure it is noted that the system consists of four components: a multi-objective genetic algorithm; a neuro-fuzzy model; object instantiation in VR; and instantiation of Pareto optimal solutions in VR. The genetic algorithm is marked by the red box, the fuzzy model is marked by the green box. The two components involving VR are shown in the blue boxes. In order to pin-point the role VR plays in the system, first it is necessary to explain the evolutionary and the fuzzy system components. The role of VR is described in section three.

2.1 Evolutionary search for multi-objective optimality

The task of the multi-objective search algorithm in the design system above is to gear the process towards desirable solutions. Multi-objective optimization deals with optimization where several objectives are involved. In design generally multiple objectives are subject to simultaneous satisfaction. Such objectives e.g. are high functionality and low cost. These objectives are conflicting or in competition among themselves. For a single objective case there are traditionally many algorithms in continuous search space, where gradient-based algorithms are most suitable in many instances. In discrete search spaces, in the last decade evolutionary algorithms are ubiquitously used for optimization, where genetic algorithms (GA) are predominantly applied. However, in many real engineering or design problems, more than two objectives need to be optimized simultaneously. To deal with multi-objectivity, evolutionary algorithms with genetic operators are effective in defining the search direction for rapid and effective convergence [8]. Basically, in a multi-objective case the search direction is not one but may be many, so that during the search a single preferred direction cannot be identified and even this is not desirable. To deal with multi-objectivity evolutionary algorithms are effective in defining the search direction, since they are based on a population of solutions. Basically, in a multi-objective case the search direction is not one but may be many, so that during the search a single preferred direction cannot be identified. In this case a population of candidate solutions can easily hint about the desired directions of the search and let the candidate solutions during the search process be more probable for the ultimate goal. Essential machinery of evolutionary algorithms is the principles of GA optimization, which are the genetic operations. Genetic operations entail the probabilistic combination among favourable solutions in order to provoke the emergence of more suitable solutions. Use of these principles is inspired from the phenomenon of biological evolution. It proves to be effective for multi-modal objective functions, i.e. problems involving many local optima. Therefore the evolutionary approach is robust and suitable for real-world problems.

Next to the evolutionary principles, in Multi-objective (MO) algorithms, in many cases the use of Pareto ranking is a fundamental selection method. Its effectiveness is clearly demonstrated for a moderate number of objectives, which are subject to optimization simultaneously. Pareto ranking refers to a solution surface in a multidimensional solution space formed by multiple criteria representing the objectives. On this surface, the solutions are diverse but they are assumed to be equivalently valid. The driving mechanism of the Pareto ranking based algorithms is the conflicting nature of criteria, i.e. increased satisfaction of one criterion implies loss with respect to satisfaction of another criterion. Therefore the formation of Pareto front is based on objective functions of the weighted N objectives $f_1, f_2, \ldots, f_N$ which are of the form

$$F_i(\boldsymbol{x}) = f_i(\boldsymbol{x}) + \sum_{j=1, j\neq i}^{j=N} a_{ji} f_j(\boldsymbol{x}), i = 1,2,\ldots,N \quad (1)$$

where $F_i(x)$ are the new objective functions; a_{ji} is the designated amount of gain in the j-th objective function for a loss of one unit in the i-th objective function. Therefore the sign of a_{ji} is always negative. The above set of equations requires fixing the matrix a. This matrix has all ones in its diagonal elements. To find the Pareto front of a maximization problem we assume that a solution parameter vector $\boldsymbol{x}_1$ dominates another solution $\boldsymbol{x}_2$ if $F(\boldsymbol{x}_1) \geq F(\boldsymbol{x}_2)$ for all objectives. At the same time a contingent equality is not valid for at least one objective.

In solving multi-objective optimization, the effectiveness of Pareto-ranking based evolutionary algorithms has been well established. For this purpose there are quite a few algorithms which are running quite well especially with low dimensionality of the multidimensional objective space [9]. However, with the increase of the number of objective functions, i.e. with high dimensionality, the effectiveness of the evolutionary algorithms is hampered. Namely with many objectives most solutions of the population will be considered non-dominated, although the search process is still at a premature stage. This means the search has little information to distinguish among solutions, so that the selection pressure pushing the population into the desirable region is too low. This means the algorithm prematurely eliminates potential solutions from the population, exhausting the exploratory potential inherent to the population. As a result the search arrives at an inferior Pareto front, and with aggregation of solutions along this front [10]. One measure of effectiveness is the expansion of Pareto front where the solution diversity is a desired property. For this purpose, the search space is exhaustively examined with some methods, e.g. *niched Pareto ranking*, e.g. [11]. However these algorithms are rather involved so that the search needs extensive computer time for a satisfactory solution in terms of a Pareto front. Because of this extensive time requirement, distributed computing of Pareto-optimal solutions is proposed [12], where multiple processors are needed.

The issue of solution diversity and effective solution for multi-objective optimization problem described above can be understood considering that the conventional Pareto ranking implies a kind of *greedy* algorithm which considers the solutions at the search area delimited by orthogonal axes of the multidimensional space, i.e. a_{ji} in Eq. 1 becomes zero. This is shown in figure 3 by means of the orthogonal lines delimiting the dominated region.

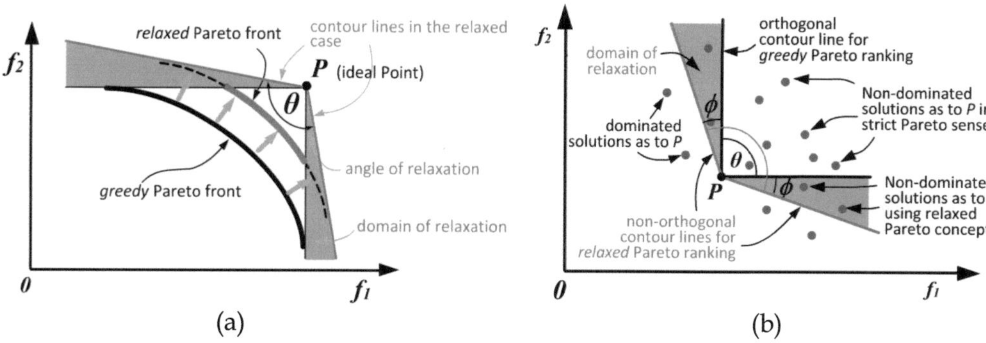

Fig. 3. Contour lines defining the dominated region in relaxed versus greedy case (a); implementation of the relaxation concept during the evolutionary search process (b)

The point *P* in figure 3a is ultimately subject to identification as an ideal solution. To increase the pressure pushing the Pareto surface towards to the maximally attainable solution point is the main problem, and relaxation of the orthogonality with a systematic approach is needed and applied in this work. From figure 3a it is noted that by increasing the angle at *P* from the conventional orthogonal angle to a larger angle implies that the conventional dominated region is expanded by domains of relaxation. This also entails that theoretically a Pareto front is to be reached that is located closer towards the ideal Point *P*.
Such an increase of the angle delimiting the search domain implies a deviation from the conventional concept of Pareto dominance, namely the strict Pareto dominance criterion is relaxed in the sense that next to non-dominated solutions also some dominated solutions are considered at each generation. This is seen from figure 3b, where the point ***P*** denotes one of the individuals among the population in the context of genetic algorithm (GA) based evolutionary search. In the greedy search many potential favourable solutions are prematurely excluded from the search process. This is because each solution in the population is represented by the point ***P*** and the dominance is measured in relation to the number of solutions falling into the *search domain* within the angle $\theta=\pi/2$. To avoid the premature elimination of the potential solutions, a relaxed dominance concept is implemented where the angle θ can be considered as the *angle for tolerance* provided $\theta>\pi/2$. The resulting Pareto front corresponds to a non-orthogonal *search domain* as shown in figure 3. The wider the angle beyond $\pi/2$ the more tolerant the search process and vice versa. For $\theta<\pi/2$, θ becomes the *angle for greediness*. Domains of relaxations are also indicated in Figure 3b. In the greedy case the solutions are expected to be more effective but to be aggregated. In the latter case, the solutions are expected to be more diversified but less effective. That is because such dominated solutions can be potentially favourable solutions in the present generation, so that they can give birth to non-dominated solutions in the following generation.
Although, some relaxation of the dominance is addressed in literature [13, 14], in a multidimensional space, to identify the size of relaxation corresponding to a volume is not explicitly determined. In such a volume next to non-dominated solutions, dominated but potentially favourable solutions, as described above, lie. To determine this volume optimally as to the circumstantial conditions of the search process is a major and a challenging task. The solution for this task is essentially due to the mathematical treatment of the problem where the volume in question is identified adaptively during the search that

it yields a measured pressure to the Pareto front toward to the desired direction, at each generation as follows.
The fitness of the solutions can be ranked by the fitness function

$$\boldsymbol{R}_{\boldsymbol{fit}} = \frac{1}{N(\theta)+n} \tag{2}$$

where n is the number of potential solutions falling into the *search domain* consisting of the conventional orthogonal quadrant, with the added areas of relaxation. To obtain n in Eq. 2, for each solution point, say P in Figure 3b, the point is temporarily considered to be a reference point as origin, and all the other solution points in the orthogonal coordinate system are converted to the non-orthogonal system coordinates. This is accomplished by means of the matrix operation given by Eq. 3 [15],

$$F = \begin{bmatrix} F_1 \\ F_2 \\ \cdots \\ F_n \end{bmatrix} = \begin{bmatrix} 1\ a_{21}\ .....\ a_{n1} \\ a_{12}\ 1\ .....\ a_{1n} \\ .... \\ a_{1n}\ a_{2n}\ .....\ 1 \end{bmatrix} \begin{bmatrix} f_1 \\ f_2 \\ ..... \\ f_n \end{bmatrix} = \begin{bmatrix} 1 & \tan(\phi_2)\ .....\ \tan(\phi_n) \\ \tan(\varphi_2) & 1\ .....\ \tan(\varphi_n) \\ .... & \\ \tan(\theta_2)\ \tan(\theta_n)\ ..... & 1 \end{bmatrix} \begin{bmatrix} f_1 \\ f_2 \\ ..... \\ f_n \end{bmatrix} \tag{3}$$

where the angles ϕ, φ, ... θ represent the respective relaxation angles between one axis of the coordinate system and the other axes. After coordinate transformation using Eq 3, all points which have positive coordinates in the non-orthogonal system correspond to potential solutions contributing to the next generation in the evolutionary computation. If any point possesses a negative component in the new coordinate system, the respective solution does not dominate P and therefore is not counted. This is because otherwise such a solution may lead the search in a direction away from P. The importance of this coordinate transformation becomes dramatic especially with greater amounts of objective dimensions. In such cases the spatial distribution of domains of relaxation becomes complex and is therefore difficult to implement. Namely, in multidimensional space the volume of a relaxation domain is difficult to imagine, and more importantly it is difficult to identify the population in such domains. Therefore many different methods for effective Pareto front formation in the literature [10, 16] are reported. However Eq. 3 provides a decisive and easy technique revealed in this work for the same goal. The approach through the coordinate transformation is a systematic and elegant approach, alleviating the bottleneck of conventional Pareto ranking dealing with many objectives to some extend, so that the evolutionary paradigm becomes more apt for applications in design usually containing a great many requirements.
In order to maximize the effectiveness of the relaxation, the determination of the suitable relaxation angle is a contingent issue, i.e. it depends on the particular conditions occurring during the stochastic search process. For instance, during a prematurely developed Pareto front, applying large relaxation angles may not permit effective distinction among the solutions regarding their suitability for the ultimate goal. Or during later stages of Pareto front development, a smaller angle will exhaust the diversity in the population and thus diminish the selection pressure towards the desirable regions. This means fixing the relaxation angle in advance may not be able to let the population arrive at a Pareto front as close to the ideal point compared to a strategy where the angle is adaptively changing during the search, taking the present conditionality of the Pareto front into account.

Adaptively changing the angle implies that the angle used to grade the individual solution's suitability is considered in perspective with the relaxation angles presently associated to the other solutions in the population. This is implemented by means of Eq. 4, where the ratio between the relaxation angle and average relaxation angle is used. $N(\theta)$ in Eq. 4 can be considered as expressing the amount of virtual solutions that are accrued to the counted number of dominant solutions given by n in Eq. 2, reflecting the fact that when we take the greedy dominance concept solutions that are dominated by s more solutions may turn out to be favourable in the search process although they normally would be eliminated due to greediness of the algorithm.

$$N(\theta) = \frac{s}{1 + \left(\theta / \bar{\theta}\right)} \tag{4}$$

Considering Eq. 2 and Eq. 4 together it is clear that the purpose is to reward a chromosome for affording a wide relaxation angle θ, relative to the average angle of the population $\bar{\theta}$, and still having a low dominance count, denoted by n. The wide angle provides more diversity in the population for the next generation. However, when the relaxation angle would be excessively big, the population for the next generation can be crowded with trivial solutions. To prevent that, in Eq. 2 the number of non-dominated solutions with respect to the particular solution considered denoted by n, is summed up with the function of the angle $N(\theta)$. This means that between two solutions with the same amount of non-dominated solutions, the one with the wider angle is preferred. This is done for every solution in the population. This implies that the average angle $\bar{\theta}$ is changing for every generation adaptively. It is noted that the number s appearing in Eq. 4 is a constant number, used to adjust the relative significance of relaxation angle versus count n. This means the value of s should be selected bearing in particular the population size in mind, so that for instance solutions using wide angles are adequately rewarded.

2.2 A fuzzy model for performance evaluation

The fuzzy model marked by the letter m in figure 2 enables the multi-objective search process to evaluate the solutions it generates and combines genetically, using some human-like reasoning capabilities. That is, the solutions are evaluated with respect to complex, vague objectives having a linguistic character. Design tasks, in particular in the domain of built environment, involve goals with such properties, e.g. functionality, or sustainability. During the search for optimality in design the suitability of a solution for the goals needs to be estimated. This means beyond observing the direct physical features of a solution, they need to be interpreted with respect to the goals pursued. For example, designing a space it may be desirable that the space is *large* or it is *nearby* another space. Clearly these requirements have to do with the size of the space, and the distance among spaces respectively, which are physical properties of the design. However, it is clearly noted that largeness is a concept, i.e. it does not correspond immediately to a physical measurement, but it is an abstract feature of an object. It is also noted that there is generally no sharp boundary from on which one may attribute such a linguistic feature to an object. For instance there is generally no specific size of a room from on which it is to be considered large, and below which it is not large. Many design requirements have this character, i.e. they do not pin-point a single acceptable parameter value for a solution, but a range of

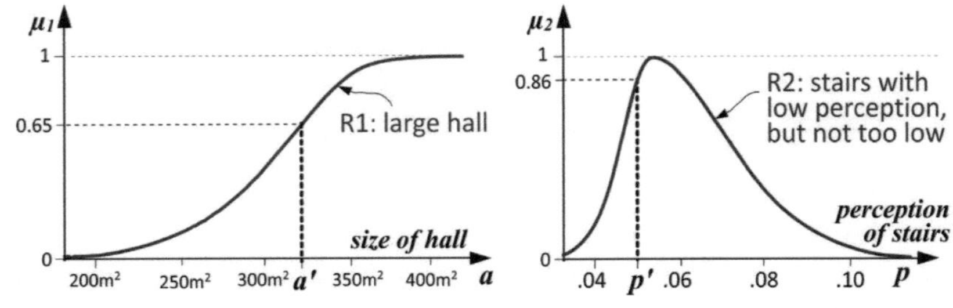

Fig. 4. Two fuzzy sets expressing two elemental design requirements

values that are more or less satisfactory. This is essentially because design involves conflicting requirements, such as spaciousness versus low cost. Therefore many requirements are bound to be merely partially fulfilled. Such requirements characterized as *soft*, and they can be modelled using fuzzy sets and fuzzy logic from the soft computing paradigm [17]. A fuzzy set is characterized via a function *termed fuzzy membership function* (mf), which is an expression of some domain knowledge. Through a fuzzy set an object is associated to the set by means of a membership degree μ. Two examples of fuzzy sets are shown in figure 4. By means of fuzzy membership functions a physical property of a design, such as size, can be interpreted as a degree of satisfaction of an elemental requirement. The degree of satisfaction is represented by the membership degree.

The requirements considered in figure 4 are relatively simple, whereas the ultimate requirement for a design - namely a high design performance - is complex and abstract. Namely the latter one is determined by the simultaneous satisfaction of a number of elemental requirements.

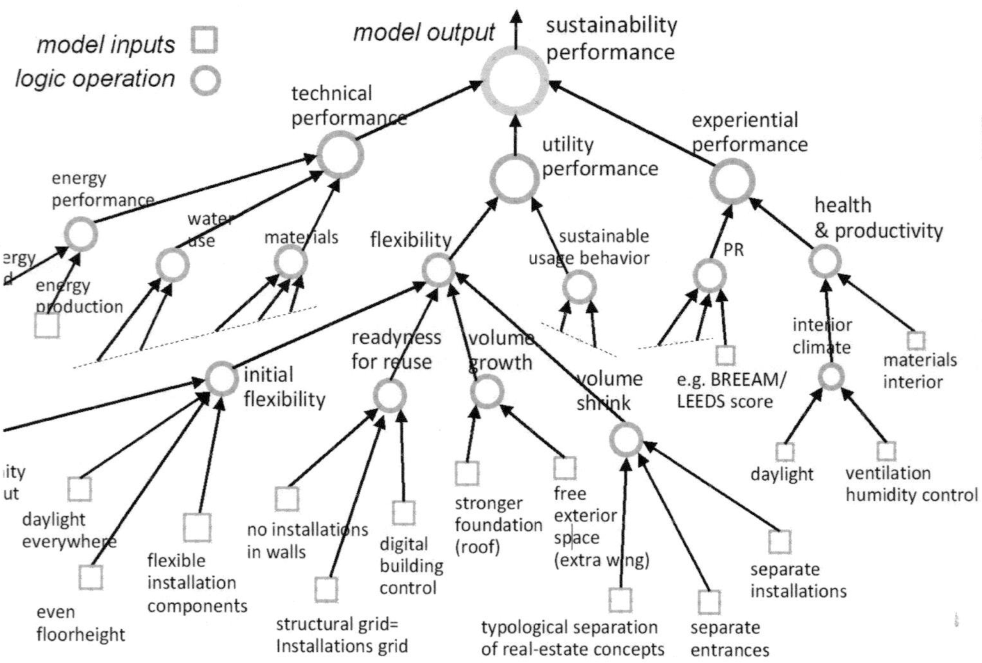

Fig. 5. The structure of a fuzzy neural tree model for performance evaluation

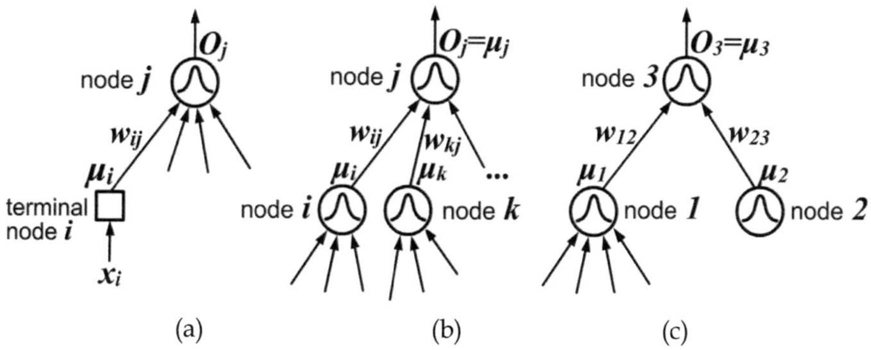

Fig. 6. Different type of node connections in the neuro-fuzzy model in figure 5

In this work the performance is computed using a fuzzy neural tree. It is particularly suitable to deal with the complex linguistic concepts like performance of a design. A neural tree is composed of one or several model output units, referred to as *root nodes* that are connected to input units termed *terminal nodes,* and the connections are via logic processors termed *internal nodes.* An example of a fuzzy neural tree for performance evaluation of a design is shown in Figure 5. The neural tree is used for the evaluation by structuring the relations among the aspects of performance. The root node takes the meaning of *high sustainability performance* and the inner nodes one level below are the aspects of the performance. The meaning of each of these aspects may vary from design project to project and it is determined by experts. The model inputs are shown by means of squares in Figures 5 and 6, and they are fuzzy sets, such as those given in Figure 4.

The detailed structure of the nodal connections with respect to the different connection types is shown in Figure 7, where the output of i-th node is denoted μ_i and it is introduced to another node j. The weights w_{ij} are given by domain experts, expressing the relative significance of the node i as a component of node j.

The centres of the basis functions are set to be the same as the weights of the connections arriving at that node. Therefore, for a *terminal node* connected to an *inner node,* the inner node output denoted by O_j, is obtained by [18].

$$O_j = \exp(-\frac{1}{2}\sum_{i}^{n}\left[\frac{(\mu_i - 1)}{\sigma_j / w_{ij}}\right]^2) \tag{5}$$

where j is the number of the node; i denotes consecutive numbers associated to each input of the inner node; n denotes the highest number of the inputs arriving at node j; w_i denotes the degree of membership being the output of the *i-th* terminal node; w_{ij} is the weight associated with the connection between the i-th terminal node and the inner node j; and σ_j denotes the width of the Gaussian of node j.

It is noted that the inputs to an inner node are *fuzzified* before the AND operation takes place. This is shown in Figure 7a. It is also noted that the model requires establishing the width parameter σ_j at every node. This is accomplished by means of imposing a consistency condition on the model [18]. This is illustrated in figure 7b where the left part of the Gaussian is approximated by a straight line. In figure 7b, optimizing the σ_j parameter, we obtain

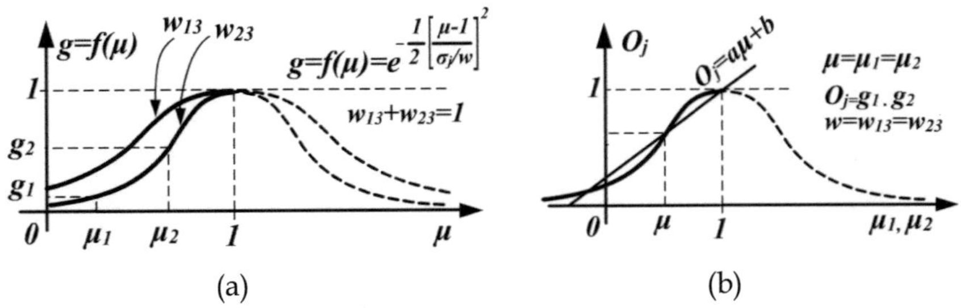

Fig. 7. Fuzzification of an input at an inner node (a); linear approximation to Gaussian function at AND operation (b)

$$O_j \cong \mu \quad (6)$$

for the values μ and O_j can take between zero and one. In any case, for a node in the neural tree, Eq. 6 is satisfied for $\mu=O_j=0$ (approximately) and for $\mu=O_j=1$ (exact) inherently, while g_1 and g_2 are increasing function of μ_1 and μ_2. Therefore a linear relationship between O_j and μ in the range between 0 and 1 is a first choice from the fuzzy logic viewpoint; namely, as to the AND operation at the respective node, if inputs are equal, that is $\mu=\mu_1=\mu_2$ then the output of the node of μ_1 AND μ_2 is determined by the respective *triangular membership functions* in the antecedent space. Triangular fuzzy membership functions are the most prominent type of membership functions in fuzzy logic applications. For five inputs to a neural tree node, these membership functions are represented by the data sets given by Table 1 and Table 2.

.1	.2	.3	.4	.5	.6	.7	.8	.9
.1	.2	.3	.4	.5	.6	.7	.8	.9
.1	.2	.3	.4	.5	.6	.7	.8	.9
.1	.2	.3	.4	.5	.6	.7	.8	.9
.1	.2	.3	.4	.5	.6	.7	.8	.9

Table 1. Dataset at neural tree node input

.1	.2	.3	.4	.5	.6	.7	.8	.9

Table 2. Dataset at neural tree node output

In general, the data sets given in Table 1 and Table 2 are named in this work as '*consistency conditions*'. They are used to calibrate the membership function parameter σ. This is accomplished through optimization. The consistency condition is to ensure that when all inputs take a certain value, then the model output yields this very same value, i.e. $\mu_1=\mu_2\approx O_j$ This is illustrated in Figure 7b by means of linear approximation to the Gaussian. The consistency is ensured by means of gradient adaptive optimization, identifying optimal σ_j values for each node. It is emphasized that the fuzzy logic operation performed at each node is an AND operation among the input components μ_i coming to the node. This entails for instance that in case all elemental requirements are highly fulfilled, then the design performance is high as well. In the same way, for any other pattern of satisfaction on the elemental level, the performance is computed and obtained at the root node output. The fuzzy neural tree can be seen as a means to aggregate elemental requirements yielding fewer requirement items at higher levels of generalization compared to the lower level requirements. This is seen from Figure 8.

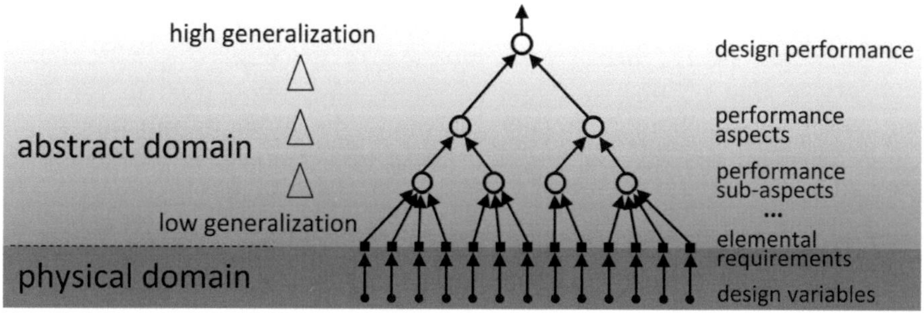

Fig. 8. Degrees of generalization in the neuro-fuzzy performance evaluation

At this point a few observations are due, as follows. If a weight w_{ij} is zero, this means the significance of the input is zero, consequently the associated input has no effect on the node output and thus also the system output. Conversely, if a w_{ij} is close to unity, this means the significance of the input is highest among the competitive weights directed to the same node. This means the value of the associated input is extremely important and a small change about this value has big impact on the node output O_j. If a weight w_{ij} is somewhere between zero and one, then the associated input value has some possible effect on the node output determined by the respective AND operation via Eq. 5. In this way, the domain knowledge is integrated into the logic operations. The general properties of the present neural tree structure are as follows: If an input of a node is small (i.e., close to zero) and the weight w_{ij} is high, then, the output of the node is also small complying with the AND operation; If a weight w_{ij} is low the associated input cannot have significant effect on the node output. This means, quite naturally, such inputs can be ignored; If all input values coming to a node are high (i.e., close to unity), the output of the node is also high complying with the AND operation; If a weight w_{ij} is high the associated input x_i can have significant effect on the node output. It might be of value to point out that, the AND operation in a neural-tree node is executed in fuzzy logic terms and the associated connection weights play an important role on the effectiveness of this operation.

3. The role of VR in the system

3.1 General considerations

From the descriptions of the two components in the previous section, it is clear that in order for the genetic algorithm to be effective, the suitability of the solutions it generates needs to evaluated using the fuzzy model. In conventional applications of Multi-objective GA, for instance maximizing the strength of a structural component and minimizing its weight at the same time, this evaluation is rather simple. The simplicity is in the sense that the fitness function is crisp and the parameters of the function, such as geometric parameters of the beam's cross-section, are directly those parameters that are subject to evolutionary identification. In these cases there is no necessity for instantiation of the beam object during the search for optimality. However, in other search tasks, as they occur for instance in architectural design, the problem requires more elaborate treatment, in particular object instantiation in virtual reality. This necessity arises when the parameters that are subject to identification through the genetic algorithm cannot be used as parameters in a fitness function because the evaluation of fitness requires the information from other object features. As an example let us consider a problem, where optimal positions for a number of design elements are pursued, while the determination of the suitability of the positioning requires information on the perceptual properties of the objects. A virtual perception process is needed that obtains the required input information used in the human-like reasoning during the evaluation process. Obtaining the input information requires the instantiation of object features beyond the parameters that are subject to identification through the search.

This is seen from figure 2, where the role of VR in the design system is to permit instantiation of the candidate solutions, as indicated by the letter *i*, so that measurements required for the fuzzy performance evaluation are executed for these solutions. The measurements deliver input information for the human-like reasoning about the suitability of a solution using the neuro-fuzzy model marked with the letter *m*. With this understanding the role of VR in the search process can be considered as the *interface* between the two components evolutionary algorithm and fuzzy performance evaluation. In particular, referring to figure 8, the instantiation of objects in VR permits the execution of measurement procedures that deliver input information from the parameter domain for the interpretations with respect to the abstract goals.

It is noted that for the effective multi-objective optimization in the application below the relaxation angle is computed adaptively for every chromosome, and at every generation. This is implemented by having the angle be a part of the chromosome of every solution. The fitness of a chromosome is obtained by considering two properties of the solution at the same time. One is the degree of dominance in terms of the amount of solutions dominating an individual, the second is the relaxation angle used to measure this amount. Based on Eqs. 2 and 4 the fitness in the applications is assessed with s=20, i.e. explicitly

$$R_{fit} = \frac{1}{\dfrac{20}{1+\left(\theta/\overline{\theta}\right)} + n} \qquad (7)$$

It is noted that the amount of chromosomes used in the tasks to be described in the following sections is 80.

Next to the need for object instantiation in VR during the search for optimal solutions there is a second instance during a design process when virtual reality plays a significant role. This is indicated by the letter *p* in figure 2, and concerns the investigation of the Pareto optimal solutions previously obtained. It is noted that generally multi-objective optimization involves no information on the relative importance among the objectives. This is in particular due to the abstract nature of the major goals making such a-priori commitment problematic. It is emphasized that in the present work this is the reason why the optimization takes place for the nodes at the penultimate neural level and not for the root node. Due to the lacking information on the relative importance among the criteria, generally Pareto optimal solutions cannot be distinguished without bringing into play higher-order criteria. That is, once a Pareto front is established, the difference among the solutions is subject to analysis, in order to determine a preference vector grading the objectives w.r.t. each other. In order for this process to be informative, it is required that the solutions found through evolutionary search be located at diverse positions on the Pareto front. This is to avoid that potentially interesting regions in objective space remain unexplored during the analysis of the Pareto front. It is emphasized that this diversity is obtained through the relaxation of the Pareto angle in this work.

With a diversely populated Pareto front it is possible to explore the front in a way that allows a decision-maker to intuitively grasp the relation between parameters of the solutions and corresponding performance characteristics, and in this way a decision maker is able to approach his most preferred solution among the Pareto optimal ones. Namely, the very nature of Pareto front implies that the trade-off that is afforded when moving along the Pareto surface is the inevitable trade-off inherent in the problem. This means, in case one is moving along the Pareto surface in a certain direction, for example towards better cost performance, the reduction of performance in the other dimensions, say the loss of functionality, is as small as possible through the definition of Pareto front. This means when a decision maker is observing a solution instantiated in virtual reality, i.e. in the parameter domain, he may decide to move in objective domain into the direction he wishes to 'improve' this solution, while minimal loss in the other objectives occurs. Clearly, the consideration whether the former or the latter solution is better matching the decision-makers preferences requires instantiation of the new solution in VR, too.

However, in complex problems the amount of solutions a decision maker needs to consider may be high in order to approach to his favourite solution, so that it becomes desirable to start the exploration from a solution among the Pareto solutions that is preferable in an unbiased sense. This is possible due to the involvement of fuzzy modelling in this work, as follows.

Although Pareto optimal solutions are equivalent in Pareto sense, it is noted that the solutions may still be distinguished. From figure 5, at the root node, the performance score is computed by the defuzzification process given by

$$w_1 f_1 + w_2 f_2 + w_3 f_3 = p \tag{8}$$

where f_1 is the output of the node *technical performance;* f_2 of node *utility performance;* f_3 of node *experiential performance.* That is, they denote the performance values for these aspects of the design, which are subject to maximization. The variable p denotes the design performance which is also requested to be maximized. In (32) w_1, w_2, and w_3 denote the weights associated to the connections from f_1, f_2 and f3 to the design performance. It is noted that $w_1+w_2+w_3=1$.

In many real-world optimization tasks the cognitive viewpoint plays an important role. This means it is initially uncertain what values $w_1,\dots w_3$ should have. Namely, the node outputs $f_1, \dots, f_3$ can be considered as the *design feature vector,* and the reflection of these features can be best performed if the weights w_1 ; ...; w_3 define the same direction as that of the feature vector. This implies that the performance p_{max} for each genetic solution is given by [19]

$$p_{\max} = \frac{f_1^2 + f_2^2 + f_3^2}{f_1 + f_2 + f_3} \tag{9}$$

Therefore, Eq. 9 is computed for all the design solutions on the Pareto front. Then the solution having maximal value of p_{max} is selected among the Pareto solutions. This way the particular design is identified as a solution candidate with the corresponding w_1, w_2, ..., w_n weights. These weights form a priority vector w^*. If for any reason this candidate solution is not appealing, the next candidate is searched among the available design solutions with a desired design feature vector and the relational attributes, i.e., $w_1, w_2, \ldots, w_n$. One should note that, although performance does not play role in the genetic optimization, Pareto front offers a number of design options with fair performance leaving the final choice dependent on other environmental preferences. Using Eq. 9, second-order preferences are identified that are most promising for the task at hand, where ultimately maximal design performance is pursued.

To this end, to make the analysis explicit we consider a two-dimensional objective space . In this case, Eq. 9 becomes [15]

$$p = \frac{f_1^{\,2} + f_2^{\,2}}{f_1 + f_2} \tag{10}$$

which can be put into the form

$$f_1^{\,2} + f_2^{\,2} - pf_1 + pf_2 = 0 \tag{11}$$

that defines a circle along which the performance is constant. To obtain the circle parameters in terms of performance, we write

$$f_1^{\,2} + f_2^{\,2} - pf_1 + pf_2 \equiv (x - x_1)^2 + (y - y_1)^2 - R^2 \tag{12}$$

From Eq. 12 we obtain the center coordinates x_1 , y_1 and the radius R of the circle in terms of performance as

$$\begin{aligned} x_1 &= p / 2 \\ y_1 &= p / 2 \\ R &= p / \sqrt{2} \end{aligned} \tag{13}$$

The performance circle with the presence of two different Pareto fronts are schematically shown in figure 9a. From this figure, it is seen that the maximum performance is at the locations where either of the objectives is maximal at the Pareto front. If both objectives are equal, the maximal performance takes its lowest value and the degree of departing from the equality means a better performance in Pareto sense. This result is significant since it reveals that, a design can have a better performance if some measured extremity in one way or other is exercised. It is meant that, if a better performance is obtained, then most presumably extremity will be observed in this design. It is noted that the location of an expected superior Pareto optimal solution in this unbiased sense depends on the shape of the Pareto front, in particular on the degree of symmetry the Pareto front has w.r.t. the line passing from the origin of the objective space through the ideal point. This is illustrated in figure 9b, where it is seen that for a Pareto front that is asymmetrical w.r.t. to this diagonal a unique location of a solution with a superior performance may exist.

3.2 Implementation nr. 1

This implementation of the system in VR concerns the design of an interior space. The space is based on the main hall of the World Trade Centre in Rotterdam in the Netherlands. The aim is to optimally position a number of design objects in this space. The objects are a

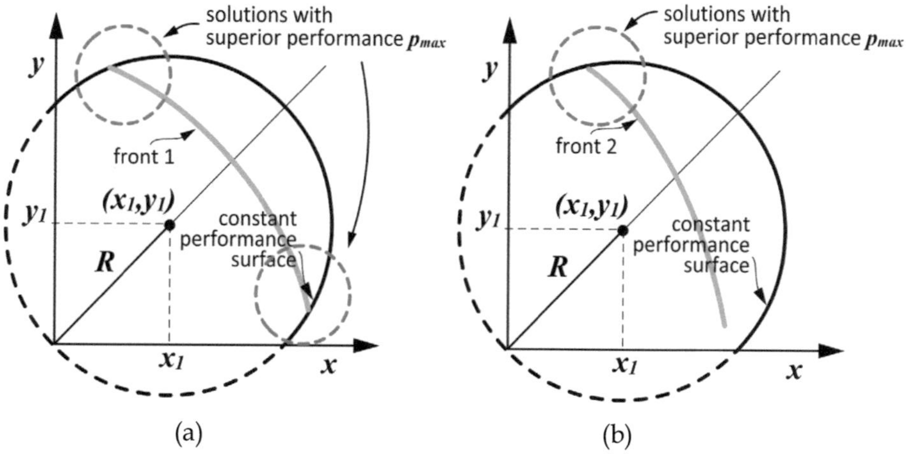

Fig. 9. Dependence of the location of desirable solutions on the shape of Pareto front

vertical building core hosting the elevators, a mezzanine, stairs, and two vertical ducts. The perception of a virtual observer plays a role in this task, because the objective involves a number of perception-based requirements. The function $f_x(x)$ shown in figure 10b is a probability density function (pdf) and given by Eq. 14 [20]. It models the visual attention of an *unbiased* virtual observer along a plane perpendicular to the observer's frontal direction. The unbiasedness refers that the observer has no a-priori preference for any particular direction within his visual scope over another one. Integral of the pdf over a certain length domain, i.e. of an object, yields perception expressed via a probability in this approach. The probability expresses the degree by which the observer is aware of the object.

The implementation of this model in virtual reality using a virtual observer termed *avatar* is illustrated in figure 11. From the figure it is noted that the avatar pays attention to the objects in the space equally in all directions in his visual scope. This is illustrated by means

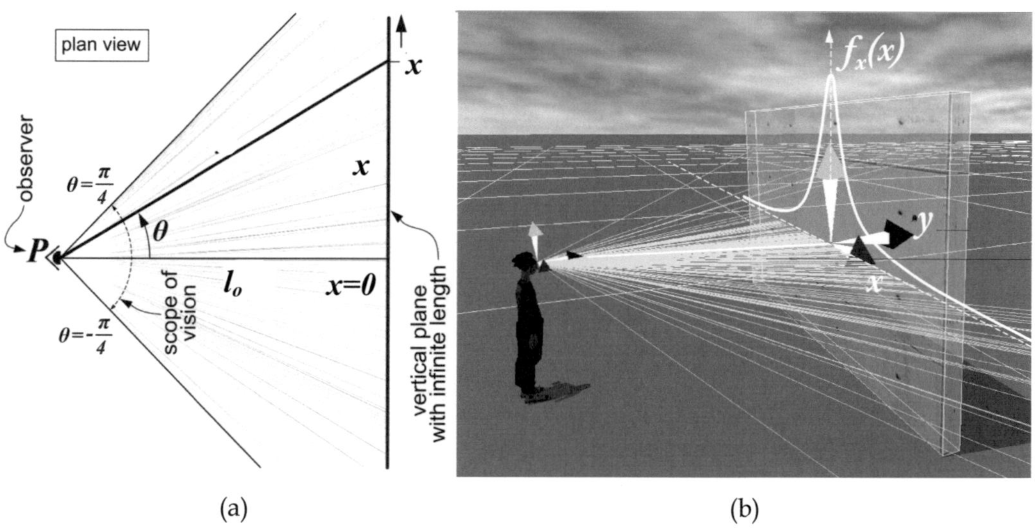

Fig. 10. Probabilistic perception model for a basic geometric situation, where the probability density $f_x(x)$ models visual attention along a plane object. Plan view (a); perspective view (b)

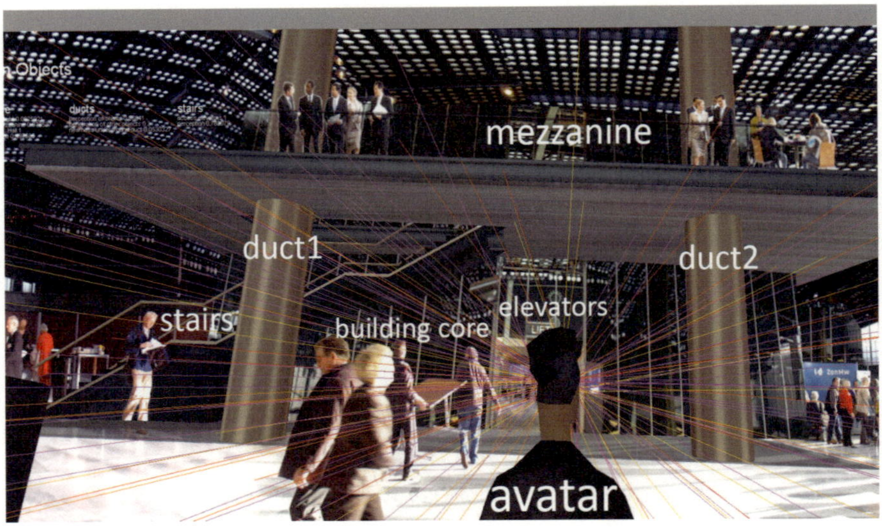

Fig. 11. Perception measurement by means of an avatar in virtual reality based on a probabilistic theory of perception

of the rays sent from the eyes of the avatar in random directions and intersecting the objects in the scene. The randomness has a uniform probability density w.r.t. the angle θ in figure 10a. In virtual reality implementation the amount of rays impinging on an object are counted and averaged in real time to approximate the perception expressed by a probability.

$$f_x(x) = \frac{2}{\pi} \frac{l_o}{\left(l_o^2 + x^2\right)}, \quad -l_o < x < l_o \tag{14}$$

The perception model requires instantiation of objects to obtain the probability quantifying perception. That is, the GA determines the position of the objects, however their geometric extent is responsible for the perception of the observer. So, once a candidate scene is instantiated in virtual reality, the perception computations involving the geometric features of the scene objects are executed.

The results from the perception measurement are probabilities associated with the objects of the scene, that indicate to what extend an object comes to the awareness of an observer paying unbiased visual attention to the scene. This crisp information needs to be further evaluated with regards to the satisfaction of the goals at hand. The present design task involves several perceptual requirements. Two of them are shown in figure 12 as examples. One example is that the stairs should not be very noticeable from the avatar's viewing position, in order to increase the privacy in terms of access to the mezzanine floor. At the same time the stairs should not be overlooked too easily for people who do need to access the mezzanine floor. This is seen from the mf in figure 12a, where x_{12} denotes the perception degree and w_o12 denotes the fuzzy membership degree. A second example is that the elevators should be positioned in such a way that they are easily noticed from the avatar's viewing position, so that people who wish to access the office floors above the entrance hall easily find the elevators. This requirement is expressed by means of the fuzzy membership function in figure 12b, where increasing perception denoted by x_3 yields increasing membership degree w_o3.

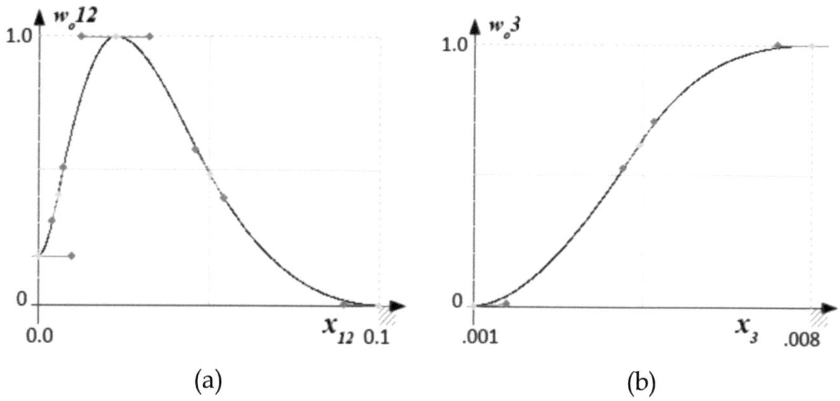

Fig. 12. Two requirements subject to satisfaction: perception of the stairs (a) and elevators (b)

It is noted that the perception computation using the probabilistic perception model yields x_{12} in figure 12b. The task is to optimally place the design objects satisfying a number of such perception requirements, and also some functionality requirements. The functionality requirements concern for instance the size of the space, which is influenced by the position of the building core object. The elemental requirements and their relation with the ultimate goal are seen from the fuzzy neural tree structure shown in figure 13. From the structure we note that the performance of the entrance hall depends on the performance of the design objects forming the scene. From this we note that the amount of objectives to be maximized is four, namely the outputs of nodes 4-7, whereas the elemental requirements total an amount of 12.

Figure 14 shows the results from the relaxed Pareto ranking approach. It is noted that the objective space has four dimensions, one for the performance of every design object. The representation is obtained by first categorizing the solutions as to which of the four

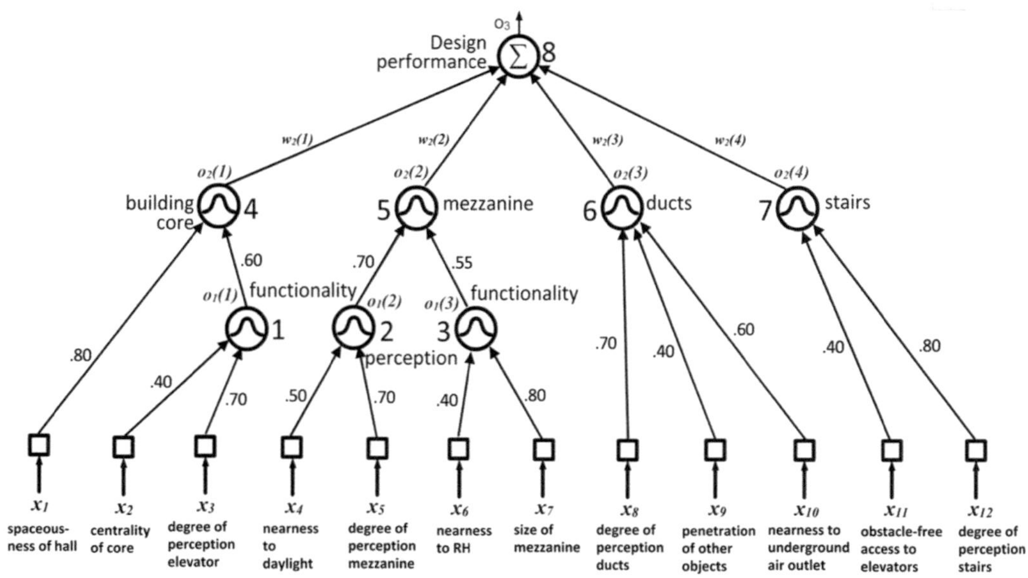

Fig. 13. Neural tree structure for the performance evaluation

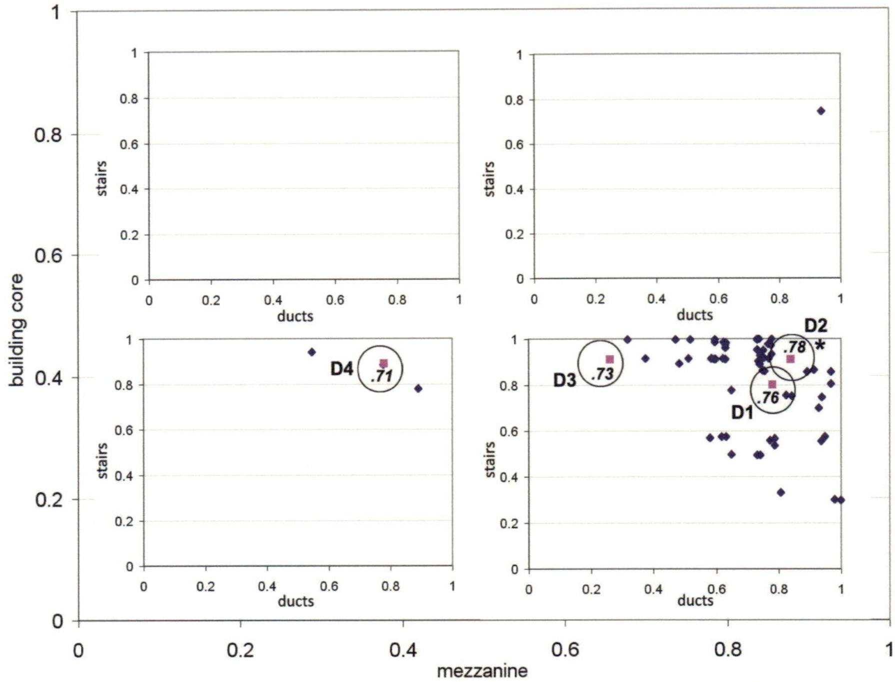

Fig. 14. Pareto optimal designs with respect to the four objective dimensions using relaxed Pareto ranking

quadrants in the two-dimensional objective space formed by the building core and mezzanine performance they belong, and then representing in each quadrant a coordinate system showing the stairs and ducts performance in this very quadrant. This way four dimensions are represented on the two-dimensional page.

Two Pareto optimal designs are shown in figures 15 and 16 for comparison. The maximal performance score as well as the performance feature vector for these solutions is shown in Table 1.

	core	mezzanine	ducts	stairs	p_{max}
D2	0.27	0.73	0.83	0.93	0.78
D4	0.48	0.49	0.78	0.89	0.71

Table 1. Performance of design D2 versus D4

From the table it is seen that design D2 outperforms design D4 with respect to the maximal performance p_{max} obtained using Eq. 9. It is also noted that the performance of D4 as to its features varies less compared to D2. The fact that D2 has a greater p_{max} confirms the theoretical expectation illustrated by figure 9 that solutions with more extreme features generally have a greater maximal performance compared to solutions with little extremity. The greatest absolute difference among D2 and D4 is the performance of the mezzanine. In D2 the mezzanine is located closer to associated functions, and this turns out to be more important compared to the fact that D4 yields more daylight on the mezzanine. Therefore D2 scores higher that D4 regarding the mezzanine. Additionally D2 slightly outperforms D4

Fig. 15. Pareto-optimal design *D2* in Figure 14

regarding the performance of the ducts. This is because the ducts do not penetrate the mezzanine in D2, whereas in D4 they do. The latter is undesirable, as given by the requirements. Regarding the building core D2 is inferior to D4, which is because the spaciousness in D4 is greater and also the elevators are located more centrally. Regarding the stairs' performance, the difference among D2 and D4 is negligible. The latter exemplifies the fact that an objective may be reached in different ways, i.e. solutions that are quite different regarding their physical parameters may yield similar scores as to a certain goal. In the present case the greater distance to the stairs in D2 compared to D4 is compensated by the fact that the stairs is oriented sideways in D2, so that the final perception degree is almost the same. It is noted that D2 is the solution with the greatest maximal performance p_{max}, so that from an unbiased viewpoint it is the most suitable solution among the Pareto optimal ones. This solution is most appealing to be selected for construction. This result is an act of machine cognition, as it reveals that pursuing maximal performance in the present

Fig. 16. Pareto-optimal design *D4* in Figure 14

task the stairs and ducts are more important compared to the building core from an unbiased viewpoint. This information was not known prior to the execution of the computational design process. It is interesting to note that the solution that was chosen by a human architect in a conventional design process without computational support was also similar to solution D2. The benefit of the computational approach is that it ensures identification of most suitable solutions, their unbiased comparison, and precise information on their respective trade-off as to the abstract objectives. This is difficult to obtain using conventional means. The diversity of solutions along the Pareto front, which is due to the relaxation of the Pareto concept is significant especially in order to facilitate the process of ensuing validation.

3.3 Implementation nr. 2

In the second implementation of the computational design system, object instantiation in VR is used for evaluation of solutions in a layout problem of a building complex for a performance measurement involving multiple objectives. In this task the spatial arrangement of a number of spatial units is to be accomplished in such a way that three main goals are satisfied simultaneously. These goals are maximizing the building's functionality and energy performance, as well as its performance regarding form related preferences. It is noted that the spheres shown in ensuing figures represent the performance of a number of alternative solutions for the three objectives of the design task.

The building subject to design consists of a number of spatial units, referred to as design objects, where every unit is designated to a particular purpose in the building. The task is to locate the objects optimally on the building site with respect to the three objectives forming suitable spatial arrangements. The objects are seen from figure 17 and their properties, which play role during the fitness evaluation of solutions generated by the algorithm, are given in table 3.

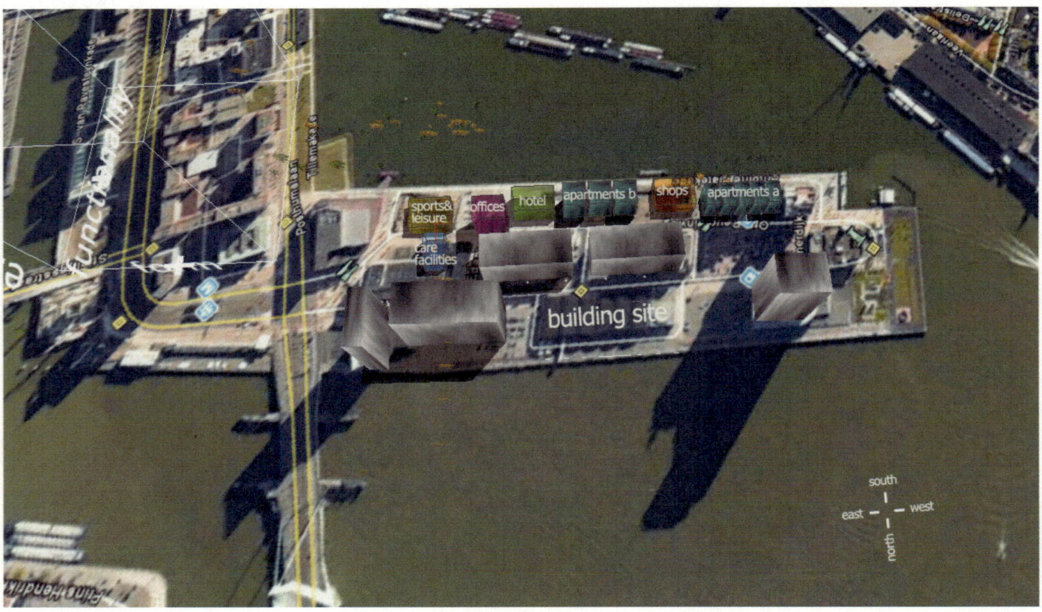

Fig. 17. Design objects subject to optimal positioning on the building site

	floorsurface (m²)	ceiling height (m)	Specific power q_I of inner heat sources (W/m²)	surface amount of glass in façades (%)
apt_a_1	22000	2.7	2.1	30
apt_a_2	22000	2.7	2.1	30
apt_a_3	18500	3.2	2.1	40
apt_a_4	22000	2.7	2.1	30
apt_a_5	22000	2.7	2.1	30
apt_b_1	45000	2.7	2.1	30
apt_b_2	37000	3.2	2.1	40
apt_b_3	45000	2.7	2.1	30
hotel	74000	3	2.1	40
care	32000	3	2.1	20
shops	34000	5	4	50
offices	115000	3.5	3.5	70
sport	28000	6	3.5	70

Table 3. Properties of the design objects

The attributes given in Table 1 play an important role in particular in the evaluation of the energy performance of the solutions, which is described in the Appendix A. It is noted that the site is located in Rotterdam in the Netherlands, so that climate data from this location is used in the energy computations. It is further noted that the energy computations require information of the insulation value of the facades expressed by the U-value of the walls, U-value of windows and glass façade, as well as the g-value of the glass. In this task the U-value of the walls is 0.15 W/m²K; U-value of windows is 1.00W/m²K; and g-value of the glass is 0.5.

In order to let the computer generate a building from the components shown in figure 17, i.e. for a solution to be feasible, it is necessary to ensure that all solutions have some basic properties. These are that spaces should not overlap, and objects should be adjacent to the other objects around and above; also the site boundaries should be observed, in particular on the ground floor to permit pedestrian traffic along the waterfront. This is realized in the present application by inserting the objects in a particular sequential manner into the site. This is illustrated in figure 18. Starting from the same location, one by one the objects are moved forward, i.e. in southern direction, until they reach an obstacle. An obstacle may be the site boundary or another object previously inserted. When they touch an object they change their movement direction from the southern to the eastern direction, moving east until they again reach the site boundary or another object. As a final movement step the object will move down until it touches the ground plane, which is in order to account for different heights the objects have. Packing objects in two dimensions in this way is known as *bottom-left two heuristic packing routine* in literature, e.g. [21]. After the final object has been placed in this way, due to the fact that the sum of the objects' groundplanes exceeds the available surface on the site, some objects will overlap the site boundary or be situated entirely outside the site boundary. This is illustrated in figure 18d, where in the present example two building units - *apartments a* and *sports & leisure* are located outside of the southern site boundary. The boundary is indicated by means of a white line in the figure.

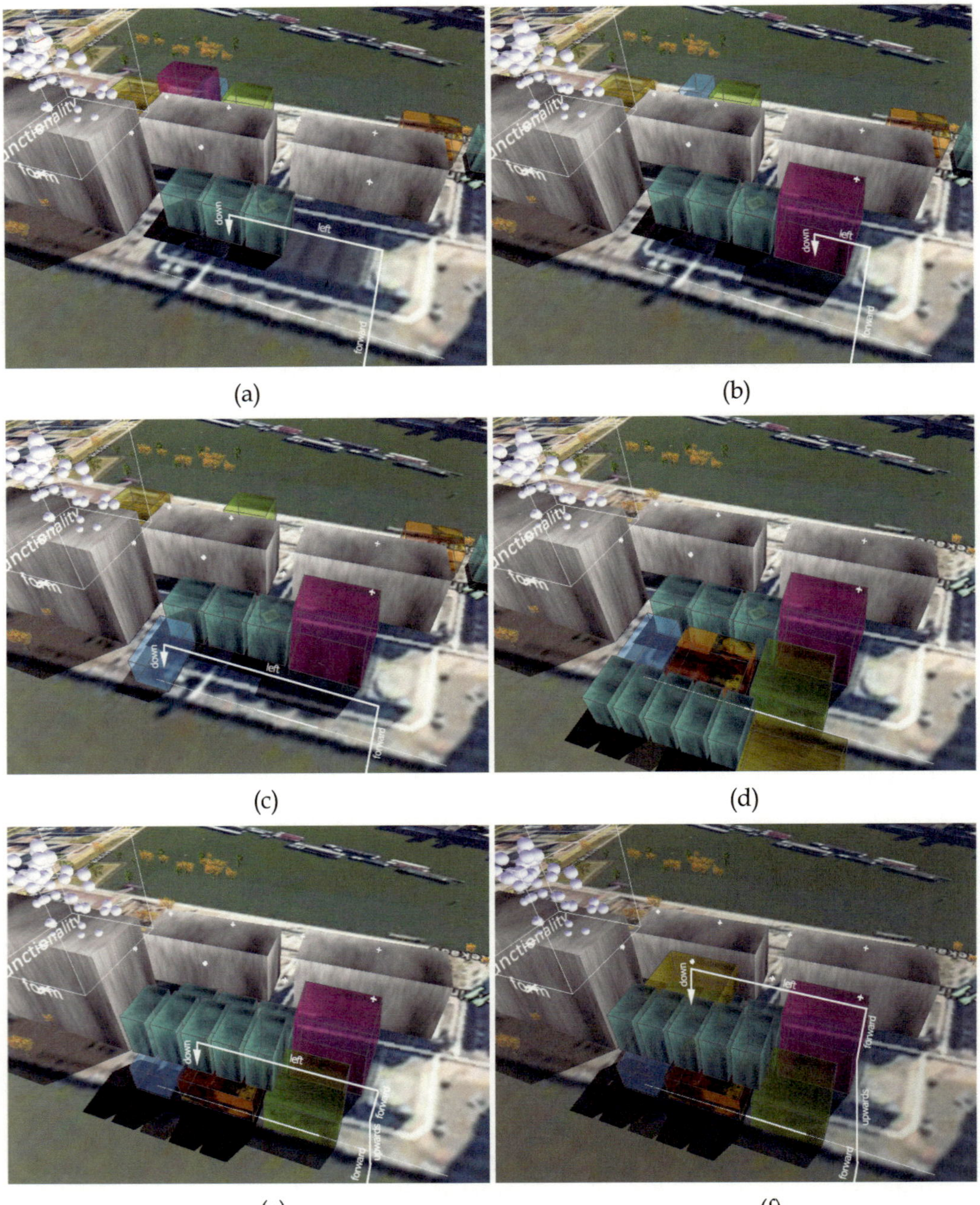

Fig. 18. Generation process of a solution through sequential insertion of the design objects in 3D

The objects exceeding the site will be inserted using a second movement procedure, where first the object is moved forward until it reaches an obstacle; then it is moved upwards until it reaches an upper boundary for the building, which is set to 140m and not visible in the figures. Then the object is moved forward again, until it touches an obstacle. Thereafter it is moved in eastern direction until touching an obstacle, and then down, so that it comes to rest on top the building below it.

It is noted that the decision from which side to insert the building components, and which location to use as the starting point for insertion is a matter of judgement, and it will strongly influence the solutions obtained. The insertion used in this application is due to the preference of the architect is to have the objects line up along the street, which is in northern boundary of the site.

In this task object instantiation is required for several reasons. One of the reasons can be already noted considering the above insertion process during the generation of feasible solutions. Namely, during the movement of an object into the site it is formidable to establish a formalism that can be used to predict the exact geometric condition of the configuration that is already found on the site when the object moves into it. The reason is that the amount of possible geometric configurations is excessive due to the amount of objects and also due to the fact that two of the objects, namely the offices and the hotel unit are permitted to have different amounts of floor levels, which is a parameter in the GA. As the floor surface amount is requested to remain constant, consequently both the object's height and floor plan is variable for these two objects.

Effectively, the spatial configuration an object will encounter during its insertion into the scene can only be known through execution of the insertion process, i.e. through instantiation of the objects on site as well as letting objects move into the site and testing for collisions during the movement. In this respect it is noted that the accuracy of placement is subject to determination, where the step length of the movement at every time frame during object insertion should be set to a small value, however not too small to avoid that the collision detection routine is called excessively. Next to the need for VR during this solution generation procedure, the instantiation is needed to execute the measurements indicated by the letter *m* in figure 2 as follows.

For the evaluation of the energy performance of the building it is necessary to compute the *transmission heat loss* denoted by Q_T [22]. Q_T quantifies how much energy will be lost through the facades of every building component over the period of one year due to temperature difference between inside and outside air temperature. In order to obtain this value it is necessary to verify for every façade of a building unit, whether it is adjacent to another building component, or adjacent to outside air. Also it is necessary to compute the solar gain Q_S, which quantifies the amount of solar energy that penetrates into the building unit through the glazing of the facades. For a certain façade surface, Q_S depends, among other factors, on the distance from another building unit located in front of the facade causing a shadow. Therefore, to accomplish computation of Q_T and Q_S it is necessary to measure if another object is adjacent to the façade in question, located in front of the facade at some distance close enough to cause a shadow, or if there is no object in front of the façade causing a shadow on it. For this purpose a test procedure is executed in the virtual reality, where for every façade the distance to objects in front of it is measured. It is clear that this test requires object instantiation due to the manifold possible geometric configurations in the search. The test is executed by means of rays that are emitted from the centre point of the building component in question and the intersection with other objects is detected. This is shown in figure 19a. The resulting information is then used in the computations of Q_T and Q_S in order to compute the heat energy Q_H required to heat the building over the period of one year per m^2 of floor surface area. The output Q_H is the result from energy computations using a steady state model given in the Appendix. From the neural tree in figure 20 it is seen that the energy performance evaluation involves a single fuzzy membership function, i.e. it does not involve inner nodes.

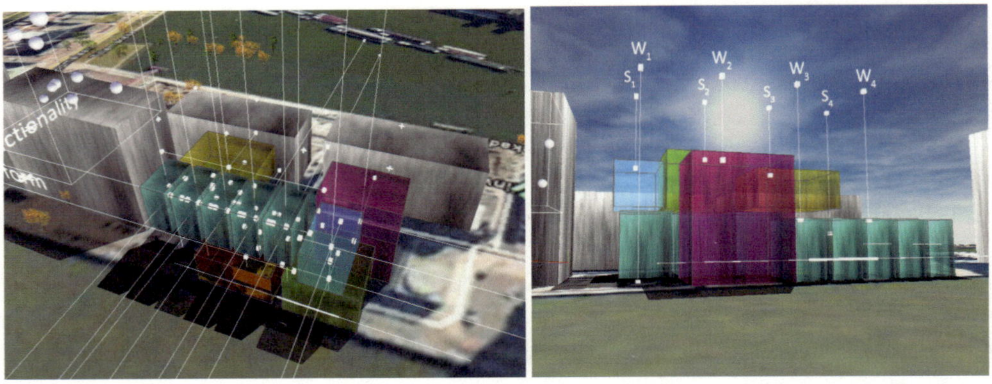

(a) (b)

Fig. 19. Verification of thermal environment by means of ray intersection tests for heat loss computation (a); measurement of heights of the building for estimating the satisfaction of form preferences

The membership function is shown in figure 21a, where it is seen that the input information for the energy evaluation is the heat energy Q_H expressed as energy per m^2 of floor surface area and per year. From figure 21a we note that the satisfaction of the energy requirement increases with decreasing energy, and that the satisfaction, expressed by the membership degree μ reaches its maximum for heat energy consumption below 2.2 kWh/m^{2}a, and satisfaction diminishes for energy amount beyond 4.4 kWh/m^{2}a. It is noted that this range concerns relatively low amount of energy compared to most contemporary building projects. This mainly due to the large size of the building units, where the amount of exterior surfaces with respect to the floor is relatively small.

For the evaluation of the performance regarding form preferences for the building, object instantiation in VR is required in order to execute other measurements. This is shown in figure 19b. From the figure it is seen that from 8 locations above the building test rays are sent downwards to measure the building's height at these locations. This information is used to compute to what extend the shape of the building satisfies some form preferences of the architect. The form preferences are seen from the fuzzy neural tree shown in figure 20.

The evaluation of the form preferences has two major aspects, the first one concerns the variations of heights in the building's skyline; the second one concerns the average height of the building. For both aspects two sub-aspects are distinguished in the model: the situation along the side facing the street (along the southern site boundary), and the side along the waterfront (along the northern boundary). For the height variation assessment, the difference in height measured between two adjacent measurement points S_n or W_n is obtained using the ray-tracing in VR seen from figure 19b. This difference is used as input in the membership function shown in figure 21b. From the membership function it is seen that the height variation is demanded to be rather large, i.e. the architect aims for a non-monolithic shape of the building, so that it is deemed to express what may be termed as a *playful* looking shape. This is seen from the maximum of the membership function being located at about 76m of height difference.

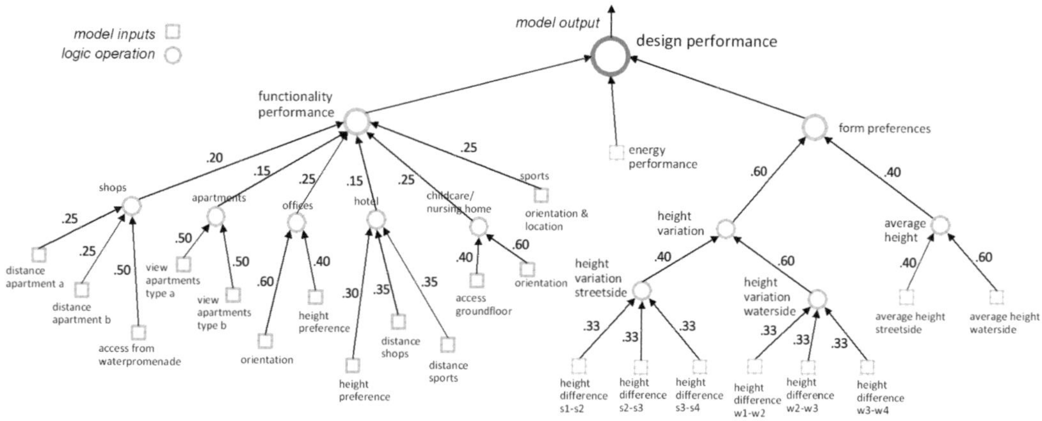

Fig. 20. Fuzzy neural tree for performance evaluation of the candidate solutions

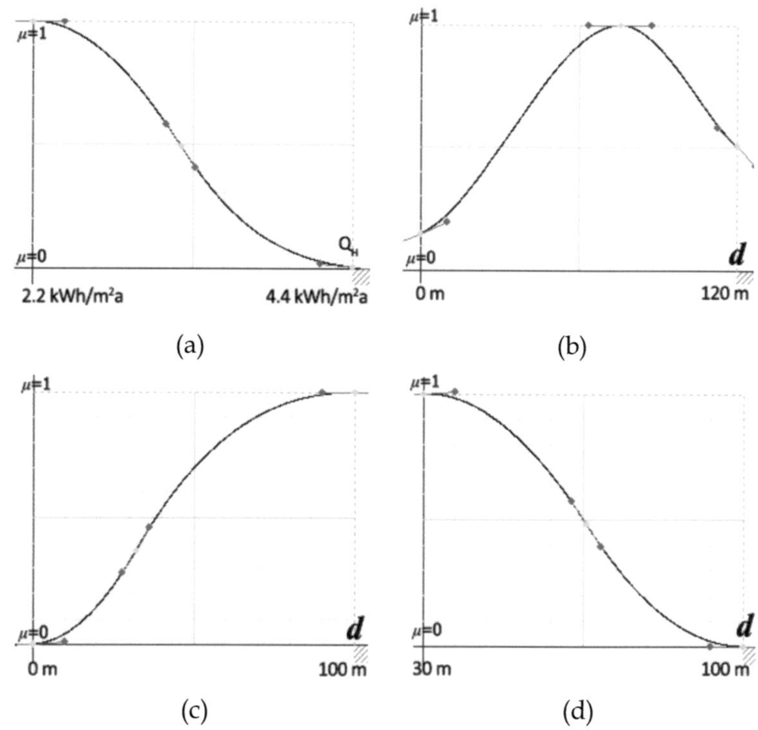

Fig. 21. Fuzzy membership functions used for energy performance evaluation (a); for evaluation of the height variation in the building's skyline (b); for evaluation of the average height along the street-side (c); along the waterfront (d)

Concerning the requirements on average height of the building the architect prefers to have a high average height along the street side, and a low average height at the waterfront. This is to emphasize the urban character of the street, whereas the lower height along the waterfront is to give the building a more accessible expression when perceived by people walking along the waterfront. The requirement for a high average height along the street-side is seen from the membership function in figure 21c, yielding maximum membership degree at 100m and diminishing as the height reduces. The requirement for a low average height along the water-front is seen from the membership function in figure 21d, where the membership degree diminishes with increasing height.

In the same way, during evaluation of a design alternative the tree is provided with input values obtained from the virtual building instantiated in VR, and the fuzzification processes are carried out at the terminal nodes. The fuzzification yields the degree of satisfaction for the elemental at the terminal nodes of the neural tree.

The root node of the neural tree shown in figure 20 describes the ultimate goal subject to maximization, namely the design performance and the tree branches form the objectives constituting this goal. The connections among the nodes have a weight associated with them, as seen from the figure. In the same way as the membership functions at the terminals, the weights are given by a designer as an expression of knowledge, and the latter specify the relative significance a node has for the node one level closer to the root node. In particular the weights connecting the nodes on the penultimate level of the model indicate how strongly the output of these nodes influences the output at the root node. It is noted that in the multi-objective optimization case the latter weights are not specified a-priori, but they are subject to determination after the optimization process is accomplished.

The fuzzified information is then processed by the inner nodes of the tree. These nodes perform the AND operations using Gaussian membership functions as described above, where the width-vector of the multi-dimensional Gaussian reflects the relative importance among the inputs to a node. Finally this sequence of logic operations starting from the model input yield the performance at the penultimate node outputs of the model. This means the more satisfied the elemental requirements at the terminal level are, the higher the outputs will be at the nodes above, finally increasing the design performance at the root node of the tree. Next to the evaluation of the design performance score, due to the fuzzy logic operations at the inner nodes of the tree, the performance of any sub-aspect is obtained as well. This is a desirable feature in design, which is referred to as *transparency*

The multi objective optimization is accomplished using a multi-objective genetic algorithm with adaptive Pareto ranking. It is used to determine the optimal sequence of insertion, so that the three objectives are maximally fulfilled. Every chromosome contains the information for every object, at which rank in the insertion sequence it is to be inserted, as well as the information for the relaxation angle to use during the Pareto ranking for the particular solution. It is noted that the information a chromosome contains in order to determine the sequence of insertion is in the form of float numbers, where one float number is assigned to every object. The objects are then sorted based on the size of the float numbers, so that an object with a higher number will be inserted before one with a lower number. Using float numbers in the chromosome, as opposed to e.g. an integer number denoting a unique sequence of insertion, allows a genetic algorithm with conventional crossover procedure to generate more suitable solutions from the genetic combination of two successful ones. This is because the float number sequence is unbiased with respect the objects to be inserted, whereas an integer coding of the sequences has an inherent bias making it necessary to reflect this bias in the crossover procedure.

The performance evaluation model is used during the evolutionary search process aiming to identify designs with maximal design performance. In the present case we are interested in a variety of alternative solutions that are equivalent in Pareto sense. The design is therefore treated as a multi-objective optimization as opposed to a single-objective optimization. In single-objective case exclusively the design performance, i.e. the output at the root node of the neural tree, would be subject to maximization. In the latter case, the solution would be the outcome of a mere convergence and any cognition aspect would not be exercised. In the multi-objective implementation the outputs of the nodes *functionality*, *energy*, and *form preferences*, which are the penultimate nodes, are subject to maximization. Their values are used in the fitness determination procedure of the genetic algorithm. Employing the fuzzy neural tree in this way the genetic search is equipped with some human-like reasoning capabilities during the search. The part of the tree beyond the penultimate nodes is for the de-fuzzification process, which models cognition, so that ultimately the design performance is obtained at the root node.

3.4 Application results

To exemplify the solutions on the Pareto front, three resulting Pareto-optimal designs D1-D3 are shown in figures 22-24 respectively. In the left part of the figures the location of the particular solution in the three-dimensional objective space is seen together with the locations of the other solutions.

The solutions in objective space are represented by spheres. The size of the sphere indicates the maximal performance value of the corresponding solution. That is, a large sphere indicates a high maximal design performance, and conversely a small sphere indicates a low performance.

Design *D1* is the design among the Pareto solutions having the highest maximal design performance, as obtained by Eq. 9, namely *p=.75*. It has a high *energy* and *form* performance, namely .76, and .88 respectively, while its *functionality* performance is moderate, being only .50. The high performance as to *form* is due to the strong variations of building-height along the building's skyline and the lower water-front versus higher street side, which match to the requirements. The low functionality performance is mainly due to low performance of office and childcare facilities, where the offices are expected to be a tall building-unit and offer a good view of the waterside.

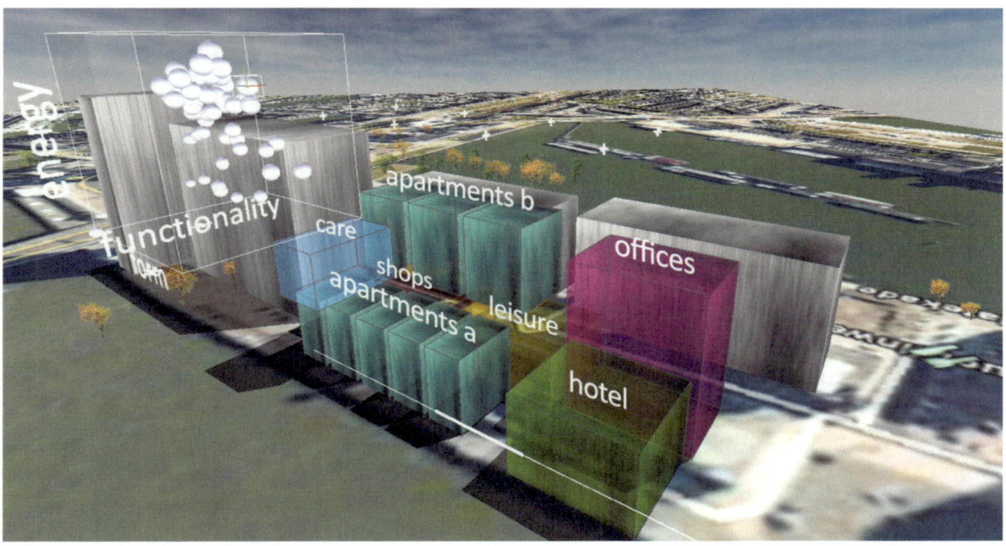

Fig. 22. Design D1 having a p_{max} of .75 being the highest among the Pareto solutions

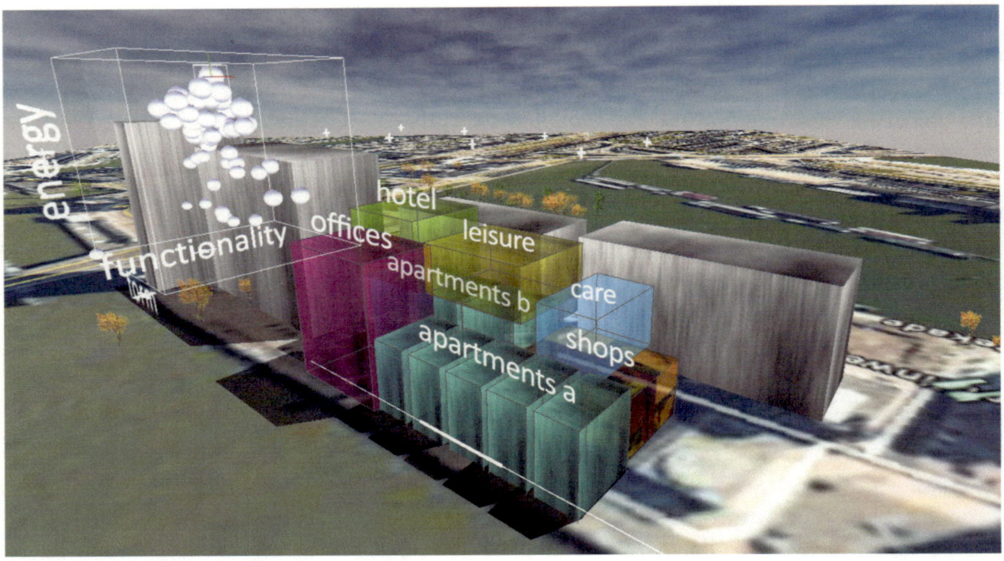

Fig. 23. Design D2 having a high energy performance

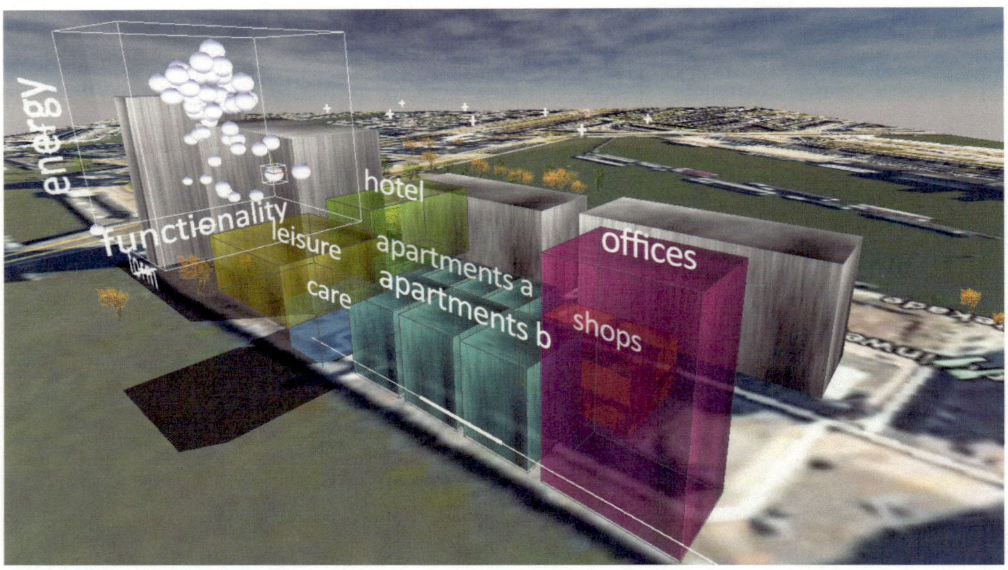

Fig. 24. Design D3 having a high functionality performance

Design *D2* has the highest *energy* performance among the Pareto solutions (.91) while *form* and *functionality* are moderate (.55 and .47). Its maximal design performance is *p=.70*. The high energy performance is due to the very compact overall shape, and also due to the fact that the office building, having a large amount of glazing percentage, has a compact shape implying few energy loss.

Design *D3* has a high functionality performance (.81), while energy performance is low (.23) and form performance is moderate (.41). Its maximal design performance is *p=.61*. The functionality performance is high, because the requirements for office, shops and care are highly satisfied. The energy performance is low, because the overall building is not compact

and most of the envelope of the office building component is exposed to outside air, which yields undesirably high heat energy consumption of the building.
From the results we note that design *D1* has a maximal performance that is higher than for the other Pareto optimal designs described by factor 1.07 and 1.23 respectively. That is, D1 clearly outperforms the other designs regarding their respective maximal performance. This means that when there is no a-priori bias for any of the three objectives, it is more proficient to be less concerned with functionality, but to aim for maximal energy performance and form qualities in the particular design task at hand. That is, in absence of second-order preferences, design D1 should be built, rather than the other designs.

4. Conclusions

The role of object instantiation in virtual reality during a computational design process is described by means of a computational intelligence approach implemented in virtual reality. The approach establishes Pareto front in a multi-objective optimization involving a stochastic search algorithm and a fuzzy model of the design requirements. The instantiation of solutions in VR plays a necessary role in the search process, as it permits evaluating solutions with respect to abstract object features that are not readily obtained from the parameters subject to identification through the search. Next to its role during the search for optimality, VR also facilitates the selection process among the Pareto optimal solutions, and the process of validating the criteria used in the search, which is also exemplified. The necessary role of VR during the search for optimality is demonstrated in two applications from the domain of architectural design, where the object instantiation is needed for the effectiveness of several procedures during the search process. In one application it is required for execution of a measurement procedure to quantify perceptual qualities of the design objects involving a virtual observer. In this task optimal positioning of a number of interior elements is obtained satisfying perceptual and functionality related requirements. In the second application instantiation in VR is required to facilitate the solution generation using a two heuristic packing strategy. Next to that it is needed in this application in order to permit measurement of functionality, energy, and form related performance of the solutions. A building consisting of several volumes is obtained, where these objectives are maximally satisfied. This is accomplished by identifying an optimal sequence of arranging the volumes, so that the three objectives pertaining are satisfied. In both applications the linguistic nature of the requirements is treated by using a fuzzy neural tree approach that is able to handle the imprecision and complexity inherent to the concepts, forming a model. This model plays the role of fitness function in the adaptive multi-objective evolutionary search algorithm, so that the search process is endowed with some human-like reasoning capabilities. The involvement of a fuzzy model requires the crisp input information for fuzzification and further processing via the fuzzy model. This is provided through the instantiation of objects and ensuing measurements in virtual reality. With this understanding VR can be considered to act as interface between the domain of quasi physical object features and the domain of abstract goals during the search for optimality.

Appendix - Energy Computations

The input of the fuzzy membership function expressing the energy performance shown in the neural tree in figure 21a requires as input the energy demand for heating over the period of one year and per floor surface area. This value is denoted by Q_H and given in the unit kWh/m²a. The size of the floor surface areas are given in Table 1. Q_H is computed as follows [22].

$$Q_H = Q_L - Q_G \tag{A1}$$

where Q_L denotes the sum of the energy losses and Q_G denotes the sum of energy gains of the building unit. Let us first consider the losses:

$$Q_L = Q_T + Q_V \tag{A2}$$

In Eq. A2 Q_T denotes losses through transmission via the building envelope, and Q_V denotes losses through ventilation. Q_T is computed by for every façade element n delimiting the unit as given by

$$Q_T = \sum_n A_n \cdot U_n \cdot f_t \cdot G_t \tag{A3}$$

where A_n denotes the surface amount of the n-th façade element in m²; U_n denotes the U-value of the façade element given in the unit W/m²K; f_t denotes a temperature factor to account for reduced losses when a façade is touching the earth (.65) versus the normal condition of outside air (1.0); G_t denotes the time-integral of the temperature difference between inside and outside air temperature given in the unit kKh/a. In this implementation G_t=79.8 kKh/a.
Q_V is computed for a building unit by

$$Q_V = V \cdot n_V \cdot c_{air} \cdot G_t \tag{A4}$$

where V denotes the air volume enclosed within the unit given in m³; n_V denotes the energetically effective air exchange rate of the ventilation system during the heating period given in the unit 1/h, which is n_V=0.09/h in this implementation; c_{air} denotes the heat capacity of air c_{air}=0.33 Wh/m³K.
Considering the energy gain: Q_G is obtained by

$$Q_G = \eta_G \cdot Q_F \tag{A5}$$

where η_G is a factor denoting the effectiveness of the heat gains, and Q_F denotes the free heat energy due to solar radiation and internal gains, given by

$$Q_F = Q_S + Q_I \tag{A6}$$

where Q_S denotes the gain due to solar radiation and Q_I denotes the internal gain:

$$Q_S = \sum_n f_r \cdot g_w \cdot A_{n,w} \cdot G_d \tag{A7}$$

In Eq. A7 for the n-th façade of a building unit f_r denotes a reduction factor that models the effect of a shadow on the façade. In the present implementation this factor is computed online using a measurement in VR. The factor g_w in Eq. A7 denotes the *g-value* of the window glazing used in the façade. This value expresses the total heat energy flux rate permitted through the glass. In the present case g_w=0.5. $A_{n,w}$ denotes the amount of window

surface in the façade in m²; G_d denotes the direction dependent solar radiation energy given in the unit kWh/m²a. In the present climatic situation G_{south}=321 kWh/m²a; G_{north}=145 kWh/m²a; G_{east}=270 kWh/m²a and G_{west}=187 kWh/m²a.
Q_I in Eq. A6 is given by

$$Q_I = 0.024 \cdot t \cdot q_I \cdot A_f \tag{A8}$$

where the number 0.024 is a conversion factor having the unit kh/d; t denotes the length of the heating period in days. In the present case t=205d. P_S denotes the specific power q_I of inner heat sources like people, lighting, computers, etc. given in the unit W/m². For the different building units subject to positioning in this task the different values for q_I are given in Table 3. The factor η_G in Eq. A5 is obtained by

$$\eta_G = \frac{1-(Q_F / Q_V)^5}{1-(Q_F / Q_V)^6} \tag{A9}$$

5. References

[1] L. J. Hettinger and M. W. Haas, Virtual and Adaptive Environments: Applications, Implications, and Human Performance Issues: Lawrence Erlbaum, 2003.

[2] S. K. Ong and A. Y. C. Nee, Virtual Reality and Augmented Reality Applications in Manufacturing. London: Springer, 2004.

[3] Y. Yang, L. Engin, E. S. Wurtele, C. Cruz-Neira, and J. A. Dickerson, "Integration of metabolic networks and gene expression in virtual reality," Bioinformatics, vol. 21, pp. 3645-3650, 2005.

[4] J. Blascovich, J. M. Loomis, A. C. Beall, K. R. Swinth, C. L. Hoyt, and J. N. Bailenson, "Immersive virtual environment technology as a methodological tool for social psychology," Psychological Inquiry, vol. 13, pp. 103-124, 2002.

[5] J. Whyte, Virtual Reality and the Built Environment. Oxford: Architectural press, 2002.

[6] M. S. Bittermann, "Intelligent Design Objects (IDO) - A cognitive approach for performance-based design," in Department of Building Technology. vol. PhD Delft, The Netherlands: Delft University of Technology, 2009, p. 235.

[7] J. A. Wise, V. D. Hopkin, and P. Stager, (eds.), "Verification and validation of complex systems: Human factors issues," in NATO Advanced Study Institute - ASI, Vimeiro, Portugal, 1992, p. 705.

[8] K. Deb, Multiobjective Optimization using Evolutionary Algorithms: John Wiley & Sons, 2001.

[9] C. A. C. Coello, D. A. Veldhuizen, and G. B. Lamont, Evolutionary Algorithms for Solving Multiobjective Problems. Boston: Kluwer Academic Publishers, 2003.

[10] E. J. Hughes, "Evolutionary many-objective optimisation: many once or one many?," in IEEE Congress on Evolutionary Computation CEC'2005, Edinburgh, Scotland, 2005, pp. 222-227.

[11] J. Horn, N. Nafploitis, and D. E. Goldberg, "A niched Pareto genetic algorithm for multiobjective optimization," in First IEEE Conf. on Evolutionary Computation, 1994, pp. 82-87.

[12] K. Deb, P. Zope, and A. Jain, "Distributed computing of pareto-optimal solutions with evolutionary algorithms," in 9th annual conference on Genetic and evolutionary computation London, England, 2003, pp. 532-549.
[13] J. Branke, T. Kaussler, and H. Schmeck, "Guiding multi-objective evolutionary algorithms towards interesting regions," AIFB University of Karlsruhe, Germany 2000.
[14] K. Deb, J. Sundar, U. Bhaskara, and S. Chaudhuri, "Reference point based multi-objective optimization using evolutionary algorithm," Int. J. Comp. Intelligence Research, vol. 2, pp. 273-286, 2006.
[15] Ö. Ciftcioglu and M. S. Bittermann, "Adaptive formation of Pareto front in evolutionary multi-objective optimization," in Evolutionary Computation, W. P. d. Santos, Ed. Vienna: In-Tech, 2009, pp. 417-444.
[16] A. Jaszkiewicz, "On the computational efficiency of multiple objective metaheuristics: The knapsack problem case study," European Journal of Operational Research, vol. 158, pp. 418-433, 2004.
[17] L. A. Zadeh, "Fuzzy logic, neural networks and soft computing," Communications of the ACM, vol. 37, pp. 77-84, 1994.
[18] O. Ciftcioglu, M. S. Bittermann, and I. S. Sariyildiz, "Building performance analysis supported by GA," in 2007 IEEE Congress on Evolutionary Computation, Singapore, 2007, pp. 489-495.
[19] M. S. Bittermann and O. Ciftcioglu, "A cognitive system based on fuzzy information processing and multi-objective evolutionary algorithm," in IEEE Conference on Evolutionary Computation - CEC 2009 Trondheim, Norway: IEEE, 2009.
[20] Ö. Ciftcioglu, M. S. Bittermann, and I. S. Sariyildiz, "Towards computer-based perception by modeling visual perception: a probabilistic theory," in 2006 IEEE Int. Conf. on Systems, Man, and Cybernetics, Taipei, Taiwan, 2006, pp. 5152-5159.
[11] E. Hopper and B. C. H. Turton, "An empirical investigation of metaheuristic and heuristic algorithms for a 2D packing problem," Eur. J. Oper. Res., vol. 128, pp. 34-57, 2001.
[22] W. Feist, E. Baffia, J. Schnieders, R. Pfluger, and O. Kah, Passivhaus Projektierungs Paket (PHPP) 2007. Darmstadt: Passiv Haus Institut, 2007.

28

Didactic Models in Civil Engineering Education: Virtual Simulation of Construction Works

Alcínia Z. Sampaio, Carlos O. Cruz and Octávio P. Martins
Technical University of Lisbon, Dep. Civil Engineering and Architecture, Lisbon Portugal

1. Introduction

Concerning educational tasks, the interaction allowed by three-dimensional (3D) geometric models could bring an end to passive learner attitudes which are often found in traditional academic teaching situations. In addition, Virtual Reality (VR) technology could be applied as a complement to 3D modelling, leading to better communication between the various stakeholders in the process, whether in training, in education or in professional practice. This role is particularly relevant to the presentation of processes which are defined through sequential stages as generally is the case in the learning of new curricular subjects. Besides this constant updating of training in the new graphic resources available to and in widespread and frequent use in professions in the fields of engineering or architecture, the school should also adapt its teaching activities to the new tools of visual communication. In fact, today, in practical subjects a variety of engineering software is used, but this requires skills and knowledge to develop economical and feasible solutions.

Educational institutions can use communication technology to access information, as a form of collaboration and communication with teachers, or as a tool for conveying educational contents, as well as a means of online teaching. A communication platform allows participants to exchange information about specific domains and interact and learn cooperatively, therefore, an aspect that must be improved is the preparation of didactic materials to support teaching (Gomes & Caldeira, 2004).

Today, 3D models and VR technology are used in engineering schools to aid both the lecturers and students. They offer students the opportunity to visualize the engineering concepts they learn in the classroom. Gibbon, in Electrical Engineering, uses laboratories containing operational amplifiers and a resonant circuit, based in 3D modelling tools in order to achieve a better understanding of circuit issues presented in formal lectures (Gibbon, 2008). Other examples of computer simulation and VR projects supporting the teaching of engineering students are remote physics experiments (Ozvoldova et al., 2006), simulation control testing (Su et al., 2006) and virtual laboratories (Safigianni & Pournaras, 2008).

Techniques of 3D modelling and VR were applied to the development of models related to the construction process. The 3D models created to support rehabilitation design emerge as an important tool for the monitoring of anomalies in structures and to assist decisions based on the visual analyses of alternative solutions. Didactic interactive models showing construction works were also developed. These applications allow the visual simulation of the physical progression of each type of work and also assist in the study of the necessary equipment needed and how it functions on site. The introduction of CAD and VR techniques in school is helpful to students in order to prepare them to consider these technologies as important supports, later in their professional practice.

The aim of the practical application of the didactic virtual models is to provide support in Civil Engineering education namely in those disciplines relating to drawing, bridges and construction process both in classroom-based education and in distance learning based on e-learning technology. Engineering construction work models were created, from which it was possible to obtain 3D models corresponding to different states of their shape, simulating distinct stages of the carrying out processes. In order to create models, which could visually simulate the progressive sequence of the process and allowing interact with it, techniques of virtual reality were used. Virtual instruments could complete or replace the experimental part in various cases. These applications allow users to conduct process and present briefly fundamental theory of the phenomena or provide full information concerning the experiments. So, the educational virtual experiments must be well framed in the lesson context.

In addition VR technology was applied on the development of a model concerning the management of lighting systems in buildings. It allows the visual and interactive transmission of information related to the physical behaviour of the elements, defined as a function of the time variable. The model was created by students involved in a research project. This kind of work gives the student capacities to develop, after in there professional activity, software that can help them to resolve engineering problems using the VR technology. That's a new tool that they know how to use.

2. VR models in AEC

The use of CAD and VR systems is helpful in areas such as Architecture, Engineering and Construction (AEC). However, the introduction of these new technologies into designers' actual practice has been anything but smooth (Duarte, 2007). At present, when carrying out a project, the use of graphic systems and, in particular, those relating to 3D modelling, makes a very positive contribution towards improving the transmission of rigorously correct technical information and, in general, to the understanding of spatial configurations in their environment. This means of expression surpasses a drawing, a picture or a diagram (Sampaio & Henriques, 2008).

Virtual Reality is a technology that allows users to explore and manipulate, in real time, computer-generated 3D interactive environment. This technology offers advantages such as: representational fidelity with a high degree of realism caused by the rendering capacity for objects; the ability to look at objects from different viewpoints, and the ability to pick up, examine and modify components within the virtual world; the feeling of presence or immersion, as a consequence of the realism of the images and a high degree of interaction. It makes the VR environment motivating and engaging by giving the users the possibility to be part of the world, and by allowing them to focus entirely on the task in hand.

VR is also seen today as an integrating technology, with great potential for communication between project participants, and most recently, as a tool for the support of decision-making, made possible by the integration of specific computer applications in the virtual model.

2.1 Construction

The results of the architectural design of a building are usually several drawings, which, lately, are often complemented by 3D models. Architects create 3D models of houses so that their clients can more clearly understand what the house will look like when built.
Models concerning construction need to be able to generate changes in the project geometry. The integration of geometric representations of a building together with scheduling data related to construction planning information is the basis of 4D (3D + time) models. Thus, in this field, 4D models combine 3D models with the project timeline, and VR technology has been used to render 4D models more realistic allowing interaction with the environment representing the construction site. 4D models are being used to improve the production, analysis, design management and construction information in many phases and areas of construction projects (Fischer & Kunz, 2004). VTT Building Technology has been developing and implementing applications based on this technique providing better communication between the partners in a construction project (Leinonen et al., 2003). Note the contribution of VR to support conception design (Petzold et al., 2007), to introduce the plan (Khanzode et al., 2007) and to follow the progress of constructions (Fischer, 2000).
The didactic VR models presented in the text shows the sequence of construction processes allowing step-by-step visualization. The models concern a wall, as a significant component of a building, two methods of bridge construction, each with different degrees of detail and technical information and a roof, namely the graphical process. The target users of these models are Civil Engineering students. Here, the VR technology was applied for educational purposes.

2.2 Maintenance of buildings

The main aim of a research project, which is now in progress at the Department of Civil Engineering of the Technical University of Lisbon, is to develop virtual models as tools to support decision-making in the planning of construction management and maintenance. The virtual models give the capacity to transmit, visually and interactively, information related to the physical behaviour of materials, components of given infrastructures, defined as a function of the time variable. In this context, the research project presents the development of a VR application, involving knowledge of the physical aspects of materials, particularly those which have a short-term function. This knowledge includes their use and environmental factors, and the application integrates these items into digital spatial representations. In this way, the indisputable advantage of the ease of interpretation and perception of space provided by the visualization of 3D models, and of the technical content underlying the real characteristics of the observed elements are brought together. The interactive application allows decisions to be made on conception options in the definition of plans for maintenance and management.
In farther work, several elements have been studied and implemented in the same virtual application. Until now, the model includes exterior closure of walls and façades, and, now in progress is the implementation of the floor element. The characteristics of different surfaces materials have been implemented as have some strategies of maintenance and rehabilitation for these construction elements of a building. The goal is to generate a model that can analyse, from a management perspective, the most important components of the building, a model which must be interactive.
A first prototype concerning the lighting system was developed (Sampaio et al., 2009). It integrates VR system and a computer application implemented in Visual Basic (VB)

language. The model allows the examination of the physical model, visualizing, for each element modelled in 3D and linked to a database, the corresponding technical information concerned with the wear and tear aspects of the material, defined for that period of time. In addition, the analysis of solutions for maintenance work or substitution and inherent cost are predicted, the results being obtained interactively and visibly in the virtual environment itself. In addition the model of lighting management can support analyses of preventive maintenance, the application in larger building and the study of the effects of lighting intensity.

3. Didactic models

The aim of the practical application of the virtual models is to provide support in Civil Engineering education namely in those disciplines relating to drawing, bridges and construction process both in classroom-based education and in distance learning based on e-learning technology. Engineering construction work models were created, from which it was possible to obtain 3D models corresponding to different states of their shape, simulating distinct stages of the carrying out processes. In order to create models, which could visually simulate the progressive sequence of the process and allowing interact with it, techniques of virtual reality were used. Virtual instruments could complete or replace the experimental part in various cases. These applications allow users to conduct process and present briefly fundamental theory of the phenomena or provide full information concerning the experiments. So, the educational virtual experiments must be well framed in the lesson context.

Specialist in construction processes and bridge design were consulted and implicated in the execution of the educational models in order to obtain efficient and accurate didactic applications:

a. In construction, the selected examples are three elementary situations of works, one concerns the execution of an external wall, a basic component of a building (Sampaio & Henriques, 2007), the second presents the cantilever method of bridge deck construction (Sampaio et al., 2006), a frequent construction technique and the last attends the incremental launching method of bridge deck construction (Martins & Sampaio, 2009). The developed applications make it possible to show the physical evolution of the works, the monitoring of the planned construction sequence, and the visualization of details of the form of every component of each construction. They also assist the study of the type and method of operation of the equipment necessary for these construction methodologies;
b. The roof model supports the explanation of subject matter pertaining to elevation projection representations applied to the design of roofs (Sampaio et al. 2009). This model presents the method of designing a roof using the usual graphic elements of plan drawing but displaying them in their 3D form. The model shows in animation the intersection between two simple roofs in order to explain how to define a more complex roof. In this way the model supports the learning of the methodology pertaining to the practical aspects in drawing roofs.

The pedagogic aspect and the technical knowledge are presented on the selection of the quantity and type of elements to show in each virtual model, on the sequence of exhibition to follow, on the relationship established between the components of both type of construction, on the degree of geometric details needed to present and on the technical information that must go with each constructive step. Further details complement, in a positive way, the educational applications bringing to them more utility and efficiency. Namely, the model of the wall shows the information concerning construction activity of interest for students corresponding to the geometric stage displayed in each moment and the cantilever deck construction model shows particularly the movement of the equipment in operation during the progressive activity. So when students go to visit real work places, since the essential details were previously presented and explained in class, they are able to better understand the construction operation they are seeing.

When modelling 3D environments a clear intention of what to show must be planned, because the objects to display and the details of each one must be appropriated to the goal the teacher or designer want to achieve with the model. For instance, if the objective is to explain the relationship between construction phases and the financial stages, the 4D model must represent the correspondent physical situation according to the established construction diagram and with the degree of detail appropriated. Developing didactic models for students concerns technical tasks, at a level that could be understood by undergraduate students, but also demands pedagogical attitudes.

In addition, the use of techniques of virtual reality on the development of these didactic applications is helpful to education improving the efficiency of the models in the way it allows the interactivity with the simulated environment of each activity. The virtual model can be manipulated interactively allowing the teacher or student to monitor the physical evolution of the work and the construction activities inherent in its progression. This type of model allows the participant to interact in an intuitive manner with the 3D space, to repeat the sequence or task until the desired level of proficiency or skill has been achieved and to perform in a safe environment. Therefore, this new concept of VR technology applied to didactic models brings new perspectives to the teaching of subjects in Civil Engineering education.

3.1 Model of the wall

The model of a masonry cavity wall corresponds to one of the basic components of a standard construction. To enable the visual simulation of the wall construction, the geometric model generated is composed of a set of elements, each representing one component of the construction. The definition of the 3D model of an exterior wall of a conventional building comprises (Fig. 1): the structural elements (foundations, columns and beams), the vertical filler panels (with the thermal isolation plate placed between the brick panels and the stone slabs placed on the exterior surface) and two cavity elements (door and window).

Fig. 1. Steel reinforcements 3D models of the structural elements, the vertical filler panels and the door and window openings.

The complete geometric model was transferred to the VR system *EON* (EON, 2009). In this system, the visual simulation of the wall building process was programmed, following a realistic plan of the construction progress. The order in which components are consecutively exhibited and incorporated into the virtual model, properly represent the real evolution of the wall under construction (Fig. 2): (a) During the animation, the student can control the length of time that any phase is exhibited and observe the model using the most suitable camera and zoom positions for a correct perception of the details of construction elements;

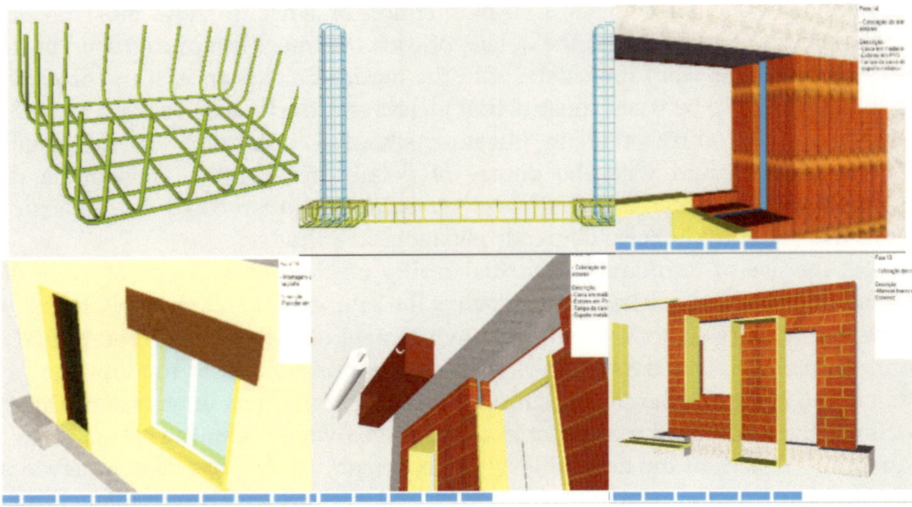

Fig. 2. Time length control, zoom positions and elements from the global model of the wall.

(b) It is possible to highlight the incorporated component at each new phase and to examine it in detail; (c) Included, under the window in which the virtual scene is exhibited, is a bar, which shows the progress of the construction. Throughout the animation, the bar is progressively filled, with small rectangles symbolizing the percentage of each phase, in relation to the completed wall construction. Through symbols it represents the diagrams normally used on construction plans; (d) Simultaneously, with the visualization of each phase, a text is shown (in the upper right corner of the window), giving data related to the shown stage, namely, its position within the construction sequence, the description of the activity and the material characteristics of the element incorporated.
The development of the model was supported by a specialised engineer working in construction which guarantees that the model shows a valid construction sequence and that the configuration of each component was defined accurately. The models support CAD and Construction subjects.

3.2 Model of the cantilever method of bridge construction

The second model created allows the visual simulation of the construction of a bridge using the cantilever method. Students are able to interact with the model dictating the rhythm of the process, which allows them to observe details of the advanced equipment and of the elements of the bridge (pillars, deck and abutments). The sequence is defined according to the norms of planning in this type of work.

The North Viaduct of the Bridge Farm, in Madeira, Portugal, was the case selected for representation in the virtual environment. In cross-section, the deck of the viaduct shows a box girder solution, its height varying in a parabolic way along its three spans. The most common construction technique for this typology is the cantilever method. A computer graphic system which enables the geometric modelling of a bridge deck of box girder typology was used to generate, 3D models of deck segments necessary for the visual simulation of the construction of the bridge (Fig. 3).

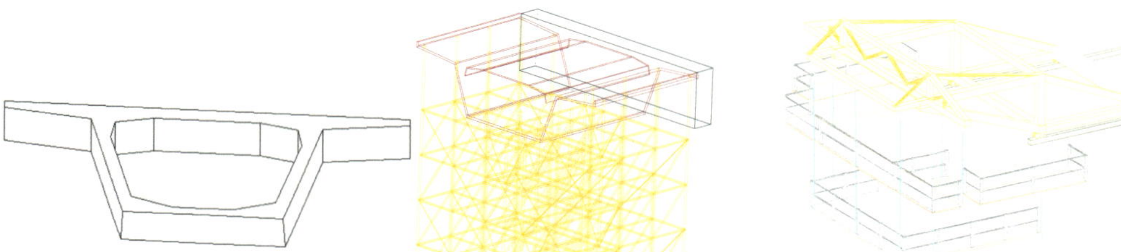

Fig. 3. 3D model of a deck segment, the scaffolding and the advanced equipment.

To complete the model of the bridge, the pillars and abutments were modelled. Then followed the modelling of the advanced equipment, which is composed not only of the form traveller, but also the formwork adaptable to the size of each segment, the work platforms for each formwork and the rails along which the carriages run (Fig. 3). As, along with the abutments, the deck is concreted with the false work on the ground, the scaffolding for placement at each end of the deck was also modelled (Fig. 3). The 3D model of the construction environment was then transposed to the virtual reality *EON system*.

The support of a bridge design specialist was essential in obtaining an accurate model, not only of the geometry definition of components of the bridge and devices, but also of the establishment of the progression sequence and of the way the equipment operates (Fig. 4): (a) This method starts by applying concrete to a first segment on each pillar, the segment being long enough to install the work equipment on it; (b) The construction of the deck proceeds with the symmetrical execution of the segments starting from each pillar, using the advanced equipment; (c) The continuation of the deck, joining the cantilever spans, is completed with the positioning of the closing segment; (d) Finally, the zone of the deck near the supports is constructed, using a false work resting on the ground.

Fig. 4. Sequence of the bridge deck construction.

Moving the camera closer to the bridge model and applying to it routes around the zone of interest, the student, interacting with the virtual model, can follow the sequence specifications and observe the details of the configurations of the elements involved (Fig. 5).

Fig. 5. Camera positioned closer to the model.

3.3 Model of the incremental launching method of bridge construction

Another interactive model concerning construction of deck bridges to support Civil Engineering education was created. The construction of bridge decks using the method on incremental launching has existed since the 60s. The incremental launching method consists of casting 15m to 30m long segments of the bridge deck in a stationary formwork which push a completed segment forward with hydraulic jacks along the bridge axis.

Every element needed in the virtual scenario was modelled and then the interaction was programmed using the some software based on the VR technology, the *EON Studio*. The 3D model of all elements was generated using *AutoCAD*: (a) The metal elements supporting the form and the formwork itself composed by beams and panels, made of wood, were created; (b) To represent the reinforcements a steel mesh was designed; (c) With the objective of allowing some immersive capacity to the model, the river was represented by a surface with mixed colours and the selected panorama simulated a typical environment of river banks.

During the animation, the position of the camera and its movement are synchronized to show the details of the elements or the assembly type and also an overview of the working place (Fig. 6): (a) In order to report an overview of the construction site the camera points initially to the casting yard. At this stage just the abutments, piers and beams of the foundation of the yard are visible. Next, is the building up the exterior form work composed of 26 identical elements, and only the assembly of one element being visualized in detail; (b)

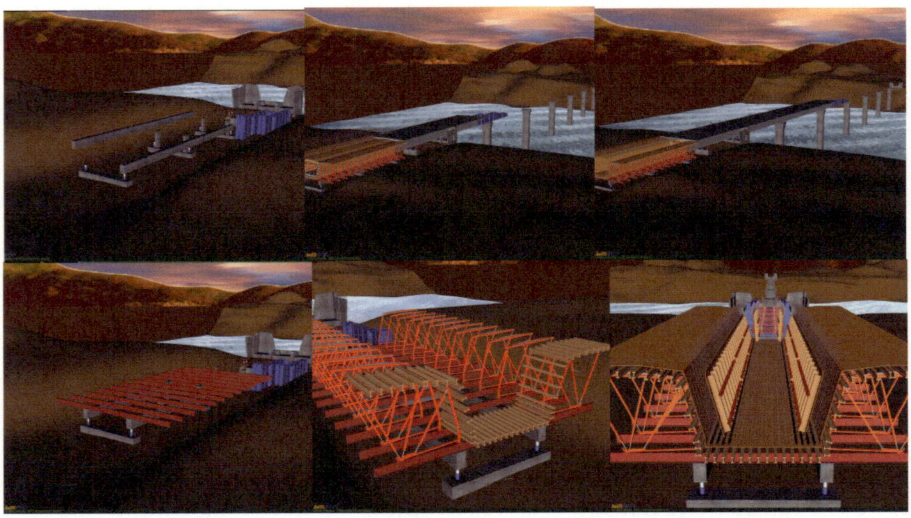

Fig. 6. The casting yard and a sequence of the incremental launches of the deck.

After placing the external panels of the shuttering and the reinforcement mesh, starts the visual simulation of the casting work. The elements that make up the interior false work are placed incrementally, starting with the metallic support, followed by the longitudinal beams and finishing with the implementation of shuttering panels; (c) Next, the assembly of the launching nose is installed. The camera is adjusted to allow the correct visualization of this work. After casting the first segment the displacement of this element takes place. For that the temporary support of the nose is removed and the segment is separated from the shuttering; (d) The arrival of the nose to the first pier is achieved during the advance of the second segment. In it the small brown parallelepipeds are the launch pads and are placed manually by workers between the nose and the temporary support placed over each pier (Fig. 7); (e) Already in the final phase of construction the casting equipment is removed and the area is covered with soil. Finally the guards along with other finishing elements are positioned.

The model was them made accessible to students and teachers of other institutions related to Civil Engineering using the platform developed by the Lisbon Technical University as part of their e-school activities. This model presents a great complexity of geometry and material concerning the different elements used in a real work process. It provides an immersive capacity inherent in the virtual world and it has a menu of events which allows the students and teachers to select a specific part (Fig. 7). The user is able to grasp the most important details of the construction method because of the camera movement which consistently shows the model throughout all the sequences of events: http://www.octaviomartins.com/lancamentoIncremental.

Fig. 7. The metallic launching nose, the guards and a menu of events.

3.4 Model of the roof

Following from those examples, a proposal was put forward to generate an educational model related to the graphic construction of a roof 3D model. Drawings using elevation projection is one of the topics in the subject of Technical Drawing included in the syllabus of the module on Computer Assisted Drawing. This representation uses only the view obtained by horizontal projection, the plan. However, the drawing is complemented by the relevant data, the elevations value and the graphics related to the three-dimensional space.

As far as the roof drawing is concerned the initial data needed are: the specification of the geometric outline of the roof and the slope of each of the roof planes of which it is made up. Based on this information the plan of the corresponding roof is drawn (Fig. 8). So, when defining drawings and 3D models some geometric elements must be used: the slopes represented by their corresponding right-angled triangles and the elevation lines. These are shown traced on a plan but they identify three-dimensional elements (Fig. 8).

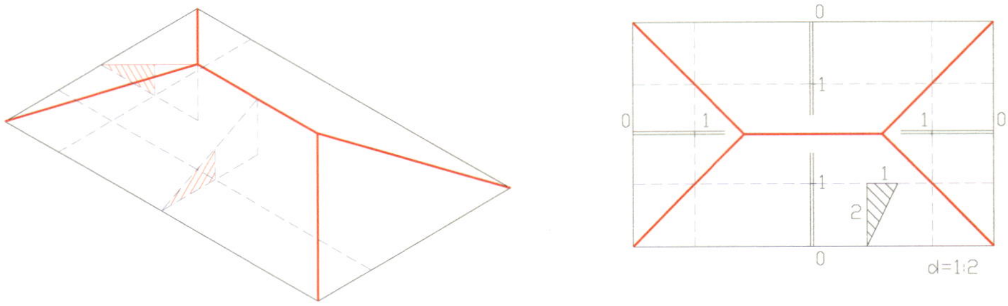

Fig. 8. Perspective and drawing of a roof.

In order to facilitate the ability to understand the spatial aspect inherent in the process, a didactic model was created in which all the methodology underlying its construction is presented in a virtual interactive environment. So, when defining drawings and 3D models of the roof some geometric elements must be used: the base, the slopes represented by their corresponding right-angled triangles and the elevation lines. These are shown traced on a plan but they identify three-dimensional elements. In order to facilitate the ability to understand the spatial aspect inherent in the process, the didactic model presents, in a virtual interactive environment all the methodology underlying the construction of a roof.
Two basic blocks of roof composes the selected example. Fig. 9 shows the outline of the roof under consideration and the slope value for each of the roof planes. When making plan drawings for roofs made up of more than four planes the initial form has to be subdivided into quadrangles. In order to define the virtual environment for the simulation a 3D representation of all its constituent elements was required. The modeling was carried out using *AutoCAD*. The components thus generated were rendered by the virtual reality system *EON Studio*, leading to the definition of the desired interactive animation.

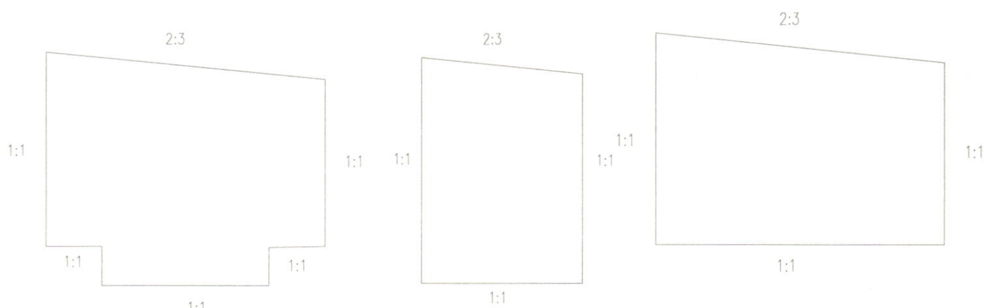

Fig. 9. Initial outline of the roof and gradient of roof planes and the breakdown into two quadrangles.

The model was programmed to show the detailed construction of the roof over one of the trapezoidal bases followed by the process of intersecting the two blocks. Thus solid models had to be used in order to achieve 3D representation (Fig. 10): (a) Two individualized wire-frame trapezoids (the base of two roofs composed of four planes); (b) Two right-angled triangles representing the established value for the slopes of each water-plane (1:1 and 2:3); (c) The unitary elevation roof lines with homogeneous elevation for each of the roof planes, referring to one of the roof block, forming a closed polygonal line; (d) The surfaces of 4 roof water planes for each of the block.

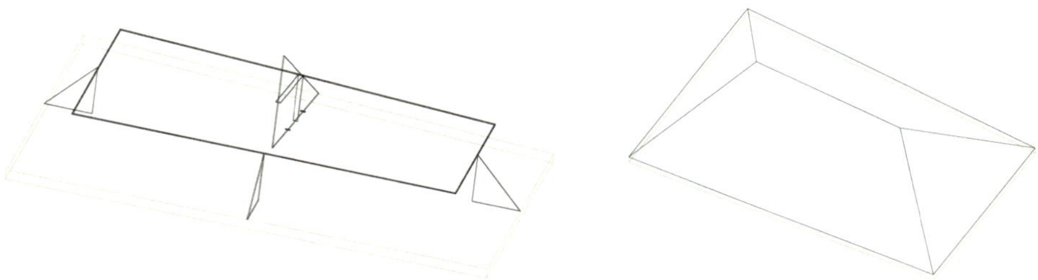

Fig. 10. 3D Models of the graphical elements of the roof.

The animation of the model follows the sequence of operations illustrated in Fig. 11: (a) Presentation of the initial base shape; (b) Subdivision of this shape into two polygons; (c) Placement of the triangle representing the slope value 2:3 next to one of the edges; (d) Insertion of the triangles with 1:1 pitch in normal positions for each of the edges; (e) Introduction of the polygon of the appropriate elevation; (f) Inclusion of the plane surfaces representing the 4 roof planes; (g) Representation of the second of the two blocks which make up the roof; (h) Intersection of the two roof blocks.

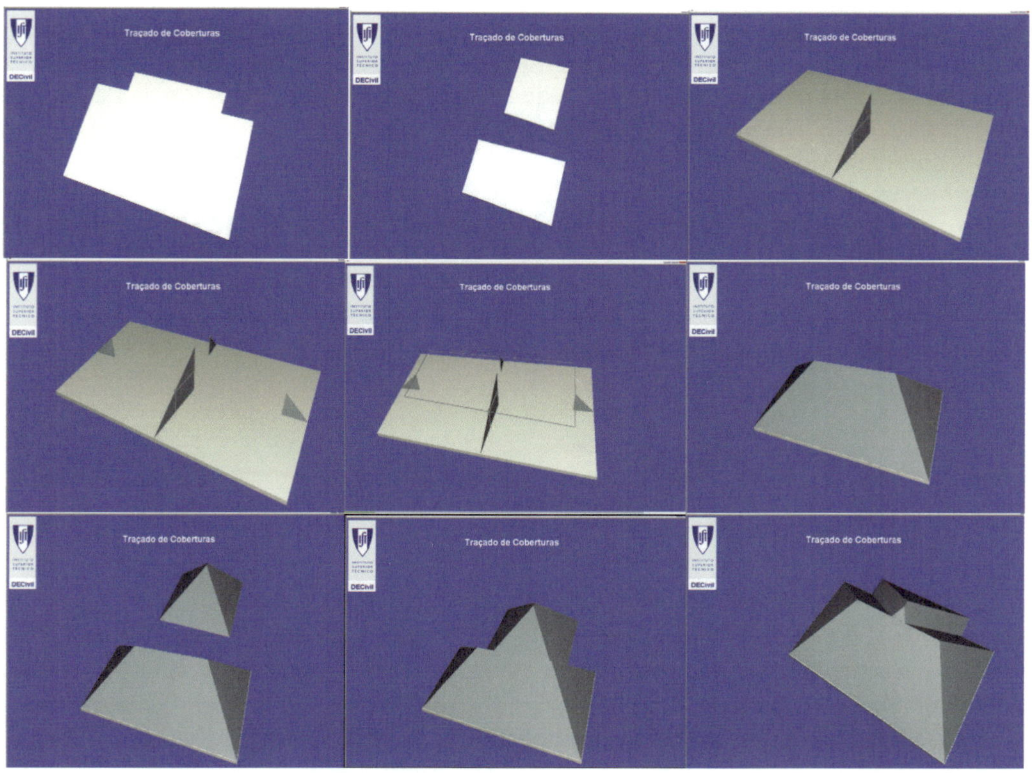

Fig. 11. A sequence of the construction progress.

The model allows interaction with the building process sequence enabling the user to backtrack and manipulate the camera position and distance in relation to the model. The final objective of this model is to show the complete roof constructed on a basis of the concepts of engineering drawing applied to the plan drawing of that structure. The intersection of the two blocks of the roof clearly illustrates how roofs with more than four planes must be executed (Fig. 12).

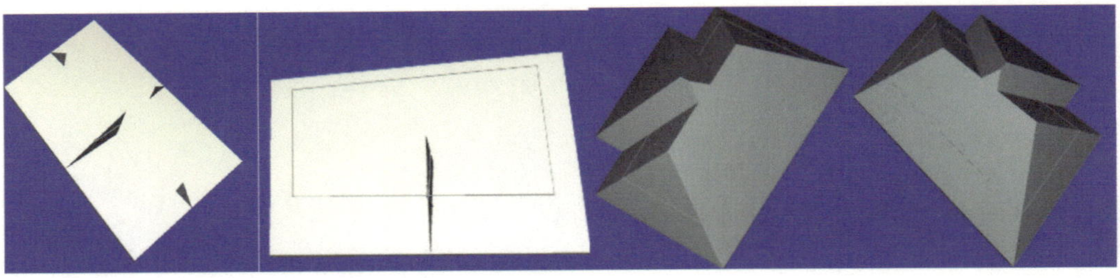

Fig. 12. Backtracking and different viewpoints.

3.5 Learning aspects

At present, didactic models are used in face-to-face classes of subjects of Civil Engineering curricula: Computer Aided Drawing (1st year) Construction Process (4th year) and Bridges (5th year). They are placed on the webpage for each subject thus being available for students to manipulate. The student should download the *EON Viewer* application available at, http://www.eonreality.com/. The traditional way to present the curricular subjects involved in those virtual models are 2D layouts or pictures. Now, the teacher interacts with the 3D models showing the construction sequence and the constitution of the modelled type of work. Essentially, the models are used to introduce new subjects.

As in **Computer Aided Drawing**, students have to define and draw structural plants over the architectural layouts, the virtual model of the wall helps to explain the connection between the architectural drawings and the structural solutions needed to support the building configuration (Fig. 13).

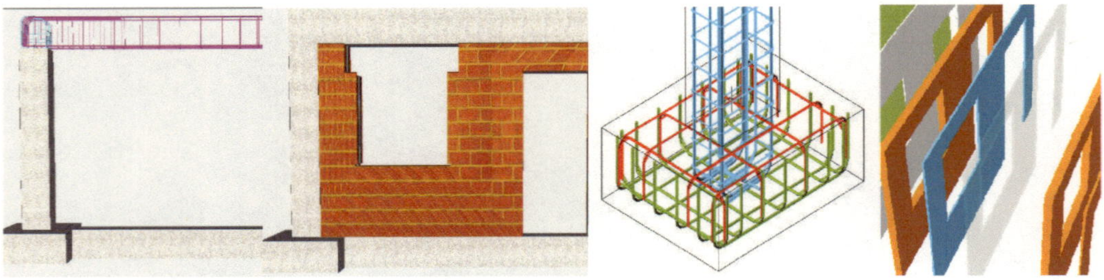

Fig. 13. Details of the virtual model of the wall.

In the discipline of **Construction Process**, in order to prepare students to visit real work sites, the teacher shows the construction animation and explains some items of the construction process of the wall, in particular, the way the iron grid work defined inside a beam or a column and specially the complexity of the relationship between the distinct types of ironwork near the zone where the structural elements connect to each other (Fig. 13). In order to explain this issue related to the structural elements, the iron networks were created as 3D models with distinct colours. They appear on the virtual scenario following a specific planned schedule. In addition, the type, sequence and thickness of each vertical panel that composes a cavity wall are well presented in the virtual model showing, step by step, the relationship between each other (Fig. 13).

The deck **bridge** models, in particular, show the complexity associated to the construction work of the deck and illustrate in detail the movement of the equipment. In class, the teacher must explain why the process must follow both sequence of steps and the way the equipment operates (Fig. 14).

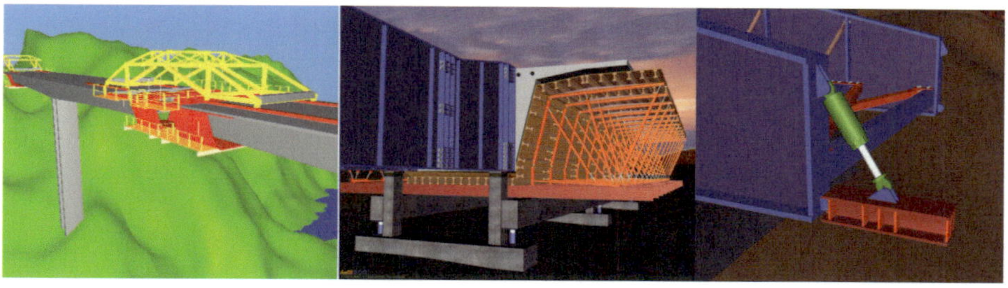

Fig. 14. The models show in detail the movement of the equipment.

When the student, of the 5th year, goes to a real work site he can observe the complexity of the work and better understand the progression of construction previously explained.
The roof model is an educational application to support the discipline **Computer Aided Drawing** (1st year). The issues involved require three-dimensional awareness which, in traditional methods of teaching, transmitted through plane view. This application supports the explanation of topics related to the construction of both simple roofs and more complex ones (that is, those that are more difficult for students to grasp). The model shows, in an animated way, the intersection between two simple blocks defining a more complex roof (Fig. 15).

Fig. 15. Definition of a more complex roof based in two simple blocks.

4. The virtual lighting prototype

The first component of the virtual prototype concerns the management of lamps in a lighting system. In addition, the analysis of solutions for substitution and inherent cost are predicted, the results being obtained interactively and shown in the virtual environment itself (Sampaio et al., 2009). Effective integration of advanced visualization capacities is incorporated into the interactive simulation system. The present project integrates a VR system and a computer application implemented in Visual Basic (VB) language. The scholarship holders involved, in this work, are 5th year students of Civil Engineering, who had, therefore, to learn advanced software of geometric modelling and visualization and to explore the capacities of a RV technology system, the *EON Studio*. They had to devise a

research bibliography regarding lamp devices usually applied in a building and they also had to develop their programming skills in order to be able to successfully integrate the elements needed in the creation of a virtual lighting system.
The characteristics of different types of bulbs were collated in order to create a database. An adequate database structure had to be implemented, integrating different types of information, needed to create an efficient and accurate virtual model. The VR model links the 3D objects of the model to this database. The database concerns the lighting system management within a collaborative virtual environment and the respective technical data associated with each component of the model is an integral part of the application, allowing the consultation of required data at any point in time.

4.1 The database

The visualization of information related to lamps requires an understanding of the essential characteristics of those elements and of the planning strategy of lighting system maintenance. The lighting VR model must support the following essential aspects: (a) The system must include a database containing the characteristics of bulb types, with wattage and the corresponding compatibility. These data are important parameters in the drawing up of management schemes. The data base must also include an image of each type of bulb (Fig. 16);

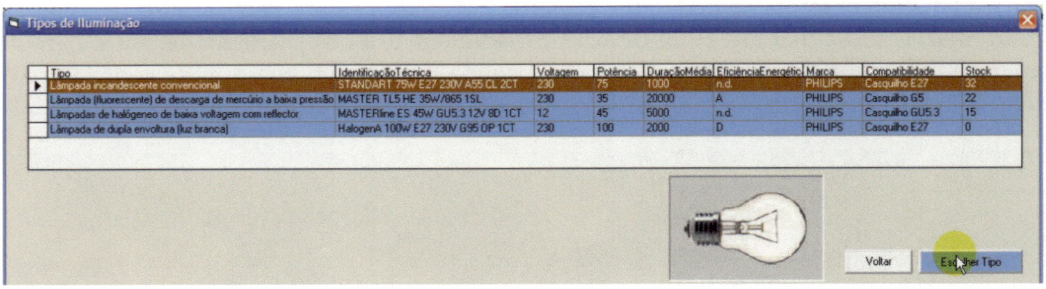

Tipo	IdentificaçãoTécnica	Voltagem	Potência	DuraçãoMédia	EficiênciaEnergética	Marca	Compatibilidade	Stock
Lâmpada incandescente convencional	STANDART 75W E27 230V A55 CL 2CT	230	75	1000	n.d.	PHILIPS	Casquilho E27	32
Lâmpada (fluorescente) de descarga de mercúrio a baixa pressão	MASTER TL5 HE 35W/865 1SL	230	35	20000	A	PHILIPS	Casquilho G5	22
Lâmpadas de halógeneo de baixa voltagem com reflector	MASTERline ES 45W GU5.3 12V 8D 1CT	12	45	5000	n.d.	PHILIPS	Casquilho GU5.3	15
Lâmpada de dupla envoltura (luz branca)	HalogenA 100W E27 230V G95 DP 1CT	230	100	2000	D	PHILIPS	Casquilho E27	0

Fig. 16. Details of the database of the model.

(b) A lamp is a replaceable component in a building. As the light source has a discrete lifestyle the VR system must incorporate the control of bulb stock (Fig. 17). The model must include alerts for periodic local inspections of the actual state of each bulb in the building. After inspection, there is an automatic process in which, the compatibility of the socket of each broken bulb can be checked on the database, the element replaced, the installation date and the lighting stock updated;

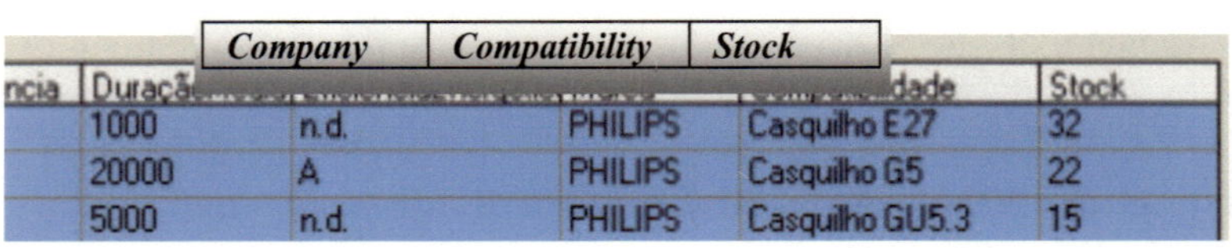

Duraçã...			...dade	Stock
1000	n.d.	PHILIPS	Casquilho E27	32
20000	A	PHILIPS	Casquilho G5	22
5000	n.d.	PHILIPS	Casquilho GU5.3	15

Fig. 17. Compatibility and stock of bulbs.

(c) The database has other characteristics relating to, light power, energy efficiency and lighting intensity of each bulb type. Based on these parameters the model can calculate the luminosity in a room or analyse the energy efficiency of the whole building (Fig. 18).

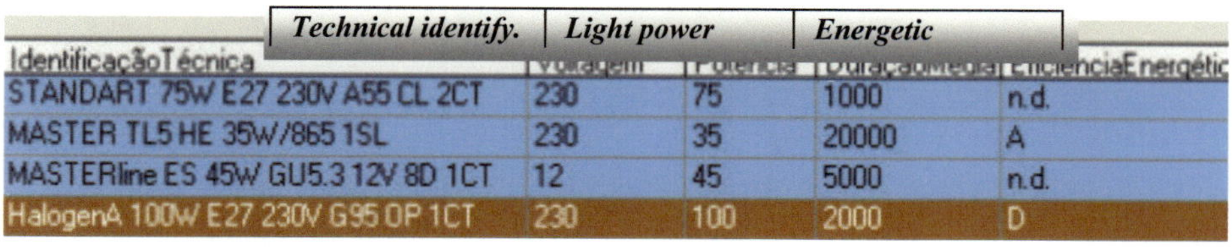

IdentificaçãoTécnica	Voltagem	Potência	DuraçãoMedia	EficiênciaEnergétic
STANDART 75W E27 230V A55 CL 2CT	230	75	1000	n.d.
MASTER TL5 HE 35W/865 1SL	230	35	20000	A
MASTERline ES 45W GU5.3 12V 8D 1CT	12	45	5000	n.d.
HalogenA 100W E27 230V G95 OP 1CT	230	100	2000	D

Fig. 18. Some characteristics of bulbs.

The system must calculate as a function of the time parameter the predicted functional life-time of lamps or the time remaining to the next planed inspection. The database therefore, must include for each bulb the installation date, the statistics for its average lifetime, the average number of hours of its predicted functionality and the next periodic inspection date (Fig. 19).

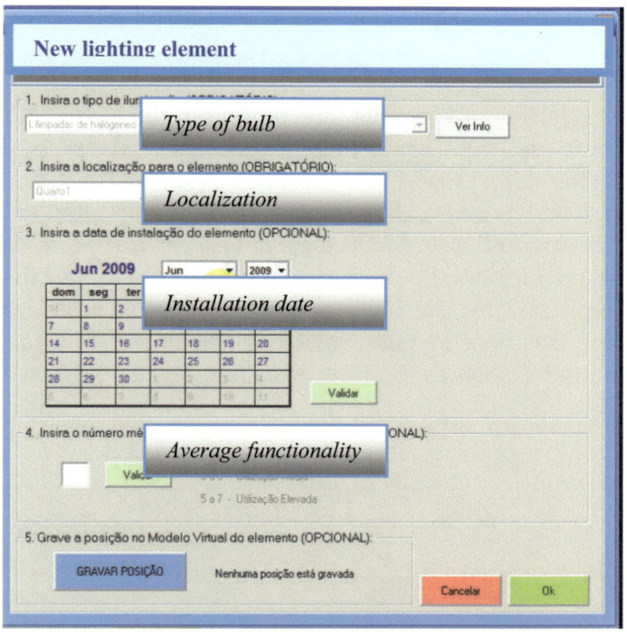

Fig. 19. Interface used to specify data values.

4.2 The 3D geometric model

A 3D geometric model of a building was created. The building consists of a ground-floor, a 1st floor and an attic allocated as living space. The model was generated based on architectural design drawings: plans, vertical views and vertical sections (Fig. 20). Some lighting equipment considered in the building was also modelled and incorporated into the 3D model (Fig. 20). The 3D model was created as 3ds file and exported to *EON Studio*.

4.3 The interface

The process of developing the prototype interface considers the purposes of defining an interactive environment. Human perceptual and cognitive capabilities were taken into account when designing this visualization tool. It uses an interactive 3D visualization

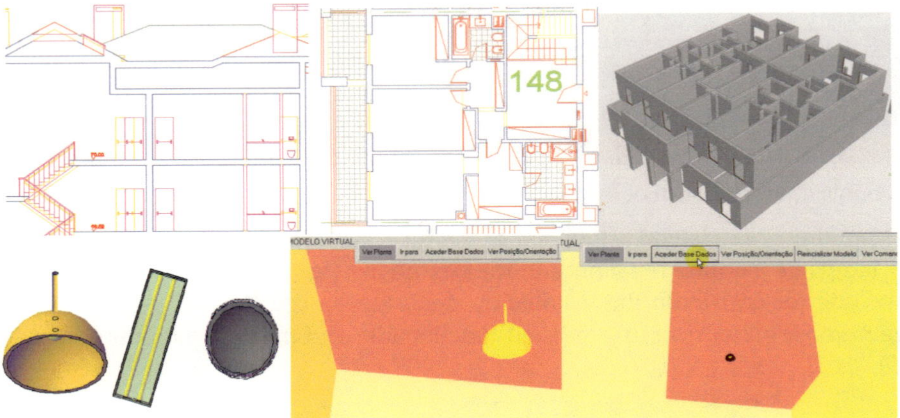

Fig. 20. 3D models of the building and of the lamp devices.

system based on the selection of elements directly within the virtual 3D world. The model enables users to pick up lighting elements, associate values to them and modify characteristics within the virtual world, which makes it easy to use.

First, the lamp is identified as a new element and a bulb is associated to it, together with all information on the chosen bulb included in the database. At this point, the lamp is properly identified as a monitored element. For each element the model allows the determination: (a) Of the predicted break-time for the bulb based on the installation data and the statistic period of lifetime for that type of bulb; (b) Of the temporal data for a specific date of interaction with the model, such as the time remaining to the predicted break-time or the percentage of use (Fig. 21).

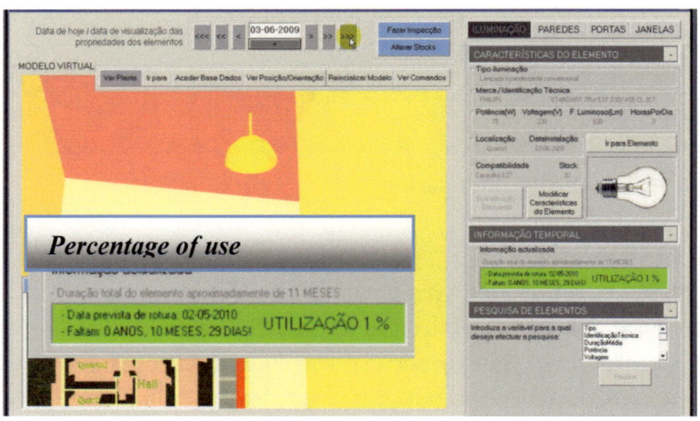

Fig. 21. Temporal data.

The percentage of use changes with the date when the model is used. The colour in the interface that shows this information changes accordingly, from green (less then 20%) to red (near 100%). Fig. 22 illustrates this capacity of the model. When 100% of use is reached an alert message (in red) is shown on the interface.

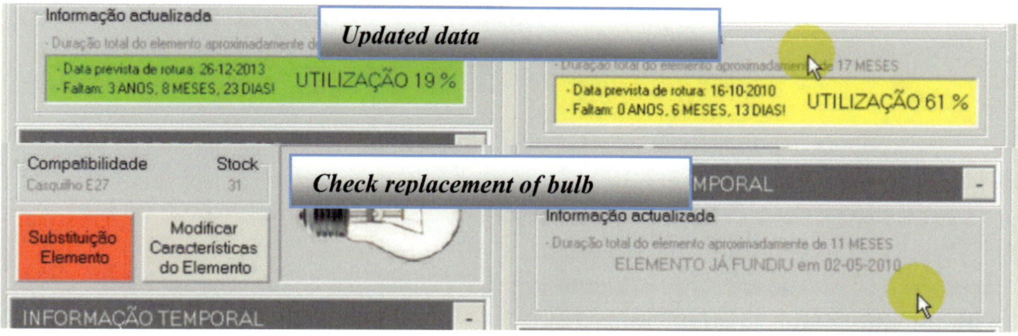

Fig. 22. Colours associated to percentage of use.

4.4 Expected benefits

The virtual model of lighting management can support analyses of preventive maintenance, the application in larger building and the study of the effects of lighting intensity.

Preventive maintenance: All elements of the model must be identified. After that, the model searches by specific characteristics: location within the building (room, kitchen), technical identification (incandescent, halogen), wattage or energetic efficiency. As a strategy of preventive maintenance the light bulbs could be replaced when the time of useful life is nearing its end. In this way, the non-functional period of the lamp left in place can be minimized. The model can list the elements of the building by predicted break-date order. Fig, 23 shows a search by predicted break-date.

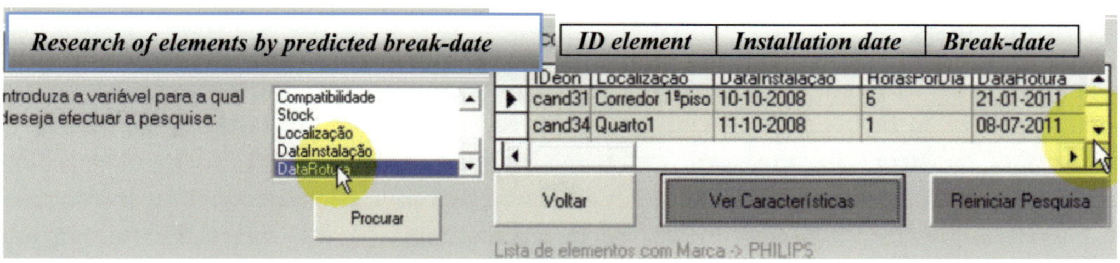

Fig. 23. List of elements ordered by break-date.

Variation of lighting intensity: The VR model allows the control of the lighting intensity of each bulb in a room environment. The *EON* system allows the redefinition of colour obtained by an algorithm of calculation defined as a function of the value of intensity associated with each type of light bulb. A colour is defined as a set of values: R (red), G (green) and B (blue). The algorithm determines a value for each primary colour, defining in this way the colour of the surfaces of the elements in a room. Fig. 24 illustrates different colours controlled by RGB values. This capacity allows the luminosity of a room to be analysed.

Management support on buildings of great dimensions: The application of the VR prototype in buildings of great dimensions, such as hospitals or schools brings benefits since it can support the control of stocks and the management of periodic inspections. Only the 3D geometric model needs to be defined and then this prototype can be automatically incorporated over it, resulting in a virtual model which allows the management of a great

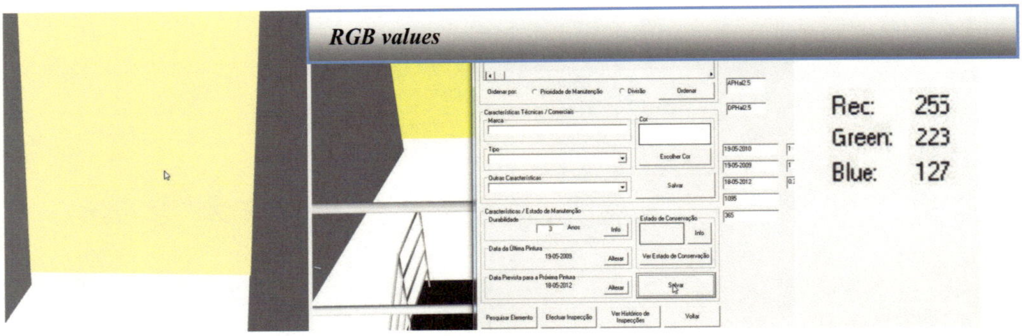

Fig. 24. Intensity of the light bulb related to the degree of luminosity.

amount of elements concerning the lighting system. The 3D geometric model is usually created by an architect. The link between the 3D model and the management prototype is defined in exactly the same way as the model presented in this paper was.

Bulbs monitored remotely: Because the model has a user-friendly interface it can be used by any manager, who can interact with the model in order to select elements from the building and update the associated information. The system supports the management of stocks for each type of bulb and alerts to the planning of local visits. Additionally, each lamp can be monitored remotely. For that a sensor must be fixed to each real lamp and connected to the virtual model. In this way any anomaly (deficient functionality or rupture) is transmitted to the virtual model, and the manager is alerted to the occurrence. In a building with large quantity of elements to be monitored the developed prototype is an important support in management.

5. Conclusions

It has been demonstrated, through the examples presented here, how the technology of virtual reality can be used in the elaboration of teaching material of educational interest in the area of construction processes and to give capacities to students to manage a new technology that can support later there engineering activity. The advantage of introducing new technologies into the creation of didactic material suitable for university students and technical instruction should be made known and applied. It was also focused the importance of teaching CAD systems at school, not only as a good executer of "drawings" but mostly as an helpful tool to be use to develop research work and, as a professional support in there activity as engineers, and also with the VR technology.

The three first applications represent standard situations of constructions. The student can interact with the virtual models in such a way that he can set in motion the construction sequence demanded by actual construction work, observe the methodology applied, analyze in detail every component of the work and the equipment needed to support the construction process and observe how the different pieces of a construction element mesh with each other and become incorporated into the model. The VR technology was also applied to a roof model in order to create an educational application of interest to the teaching of CAD. The issue involved requires three-dimensional location of drawing elements which, in traditional methods of teaching, are putted out using only the horizontal projection. This application supports the explanation of topics related to the construction of both simple roofs and more complex ones. These models are used in disciplines involving construction and drawing in courses in Civil Engineering and Architecture. The main objective of the practical application of the didactic models is to support class-based learning. In addition, it can be used in distance training based on e-learning platform technology. The involvement of virtual reality techniques in the development of educational applications brings new perspectives to Engineering education. There are many other possibilities for the creation of computational models mainly where the subject matter is suitable for description along its sequential stages of development. The applications with these characteristics make the advantage of using techniques of virtual reality more self-evident, especially when compared to the simple manipulation of complete models which cannot be broken down. The pedagogical aspects and the technical concepts must be attended on the elaboration of those models.

A virtual model concerning the management of the lighting system of a building was defined. The presented example concerns only one type of element, the illumination devices, but it was found to be efficient in the identification of elements, in the promotion of alerts of inspection and in the management of stock, all activities related to the maintenance and management of a building. The benefits of using the model are identified as: preventive maintenance, application in large buildings and control of the lighting intensity effect over the wall surface. This is an innovative tool that can be used with advantages later in the engineering activity.

6. Acknowledgments

The authors gratefully acknowledge the financial support of the Foundation for Science and Technology, a Governmental Organization for the research project PTDC/ ECM/67748/ 2006, now in progress.

7. References

Duarte, J. (2007). Inserting new technologies in undergraduate architectural curricula: A case study, *Proceedings of the 24th eCAADe Conference Education in Computer Aided Architectural Design in Europe*, pp.423-430, Frankfurt am Main, Germany, September 2007.

EON, (2009). Introduction to working in EON Studio, EON Reality, Inc. http://www.eonreality.com/

Fischer, M. & Kunz, J. (2004). The scope and role of information technology in construction, *CIFE Centre for Integrated Facility Engineering in Finland*, technical report #156, Stanford University.

Fischer, M. (2000). 4D CAD - 3D Models incorporated with time schedule, *CIFE Centre for Integrated Facility Engineering in Finland*, VTT-TEKES, Helsinki, Finland.

Gibbon, G. J. (2008). Combining theory and experimentation to develop inductive learning skills in an electric circuits course, *Proceedings of ICEE 2008* (cd rom 5pgs), Pécs and Budapest, Hungary, February 2008.

Gomes, C. & Caldeira, H. (2004). Virtual learning communities in teacher training, *Proceedings of International Conference on Education, Innovation, Technology and Research in Education. IADAT, International Association for the Development of Advances in Technology*, pp. 82-85, Bilbao, Spain, July 2004.

Khanzode, A., Fisher, M. & Reed, D. (2007). Challenges and benefits of implementing virtual design and construction technologies for coordination of mechanical, electrical, and plumbing systems on large healthcare project, *Proceedings of CIB 24th W78 Conference*, pp. 205-212, Maribor, Slovenia, June 2007.

Leinonen J., Kähkönen, K. & Retik A., (2003). New construction management practice based on the virtual reality technology. (eds.) Raja R.A., Flood I, William J & O'Brien, *4D CAD and Visualization in Construction: Developments and Applications*, pp. 75-100, A.A. Balkema Publishers, ISBN 9058093549.

Martins, O. & Sampaio, A.Z., (2009). The incremental launching method for educational virtual model, *Proceedings of CDVE2009, 6th International Conference on Cooperative Design, Visualization and Engineering*, pp. 329–332, Luxembourg City, Luxembourg, September 2009.

Ozvoldova, M., Cernansky, P. Schuer, F. & Lustig, F. (2006). Internet remote physics experiments in a student laboratory. (ed.) W. Aung, et al., *Innovations 2006* Chapt.. 25, pp. 297-304, iNEER, Arlington, VA 22205, USA, ISBN 1553-9911.

Petzold, F., Bimber O. & Tonn, O. (2007). CAVE without CAVE: on-site visualization and Design Support in and within existing building, *Proceedings of eCAADe 07, 25th Conf. of Education and Research in Computer Aided Architectural Design in Europe*, pp. 161-168, Frankfurt, Germany, September 2007.

Safigianni, A.S. & Pournaras, S.K. (2008). Virtual laboratory arrangement for measuring characteristic power system quantities. (eds.) W. Aung, et al., *Innovations 2008*, Chapt. 34, pp. 379-391, iNEER, Arlington, VA 22205, USA, ISBN 1553-9911.

Sampaio, A.Z. & Henriques, P.G. (2007). Building activities visualized in virtual environments, *Proceedings of eCAADe 07, 25th Conference of Education and Research in Computer Aided Architectural Design in Europe*, pp. 85-89, Frankfurt, Germany, September 2007.

Sampaio, A.Z. & Henriques, P.G. (2008). Visual simulation of Civil Engineering activities: Didactic virtual models, *Proceedings of WSCG 2008, 16th International Conference in Central Europe on Computer Graphics, Visualization and Computer Vision*, pp. 143-149, Plzen, Czech Republic, . February 2008.

Sampaio, A.Z. Henriques, P.G. & Cruz, C.O. (2009). Visual simulation of construction activity supported on VR models: e-Learning tools, *Proceedings of IADIS International Conference e-Society*, pp. 284-291, Barcelona, Spain, February 2009.

Sampaio, A.Z., Ferreira, M.M. & Rosário, D.P. (2009). Interactive virtual application on building maintenance: The lighting component, *Proceedings of IRF2009, 3rd International Conference on Integrity, Reliability and Failure: Challenges and opportunities, Symposium Visualization and human-Computer Interaction*, pp. 221-222, Porto, Portugal, July 2009.

Sampaio, A.Z., Henriques, P.G. & Ferreira, P.S. (2006). Virtual Reality technology applied in Civil Engineering education, *Proceedings of m-ICTE 2006, IV International Conference on Multimedia and ICT's in Education*, pp. 1351-1355, Seville, Spain, November 2006.

Su, J., Hu, J. & Ciou, Y. (2006). Low-cost simulated control experimentation conducted in Electrical Engineering Department of National Yulin University of Science and Technology. (eds.) W. Aung, et al., *Innovations 2006*, Chapt. 35, pp. 397-408, iNEER, Arlington, VA 22205, USA, ISBN 1553-9911.

Application of Augmented Reality to Evaluate Invisible Height for Landscape Preservation

Nobuyoshi Yabuki
Osaka University
Japan

1. Introduction

Landscape is the visible cognition of human environment, including natural objects such as mountains, rivers, the sea, forests and artificial objects such as buildings, bridges, and other structures. Landscape can be recognized and evaluated differently, depending on the viewer. However, people who share the same or similar local culture or aesthetics have the common recognition and evaluation of the landscape. A landscape can give a strong impact and make a socially, aesthetically, environmentally, or religiously desired outcome. On the other hand, if a mismatched object is laid out in the faborable landscape, people may feel that the good landscape is being destroyed. Recently, many good landscapes from viewpoint fields have been destroyed by constructing high rise buildings on the background area of the aesthetically pleasing structure. Figure 1 shows examples which singular landscapes of a Japanese historical Shinto shrine and a Buddhist temple are impaired by a modern tall glassy building and a tall broadcasting tower behind, respectively.

(a) (b)

Fig. 1. (a) A Japanese historical Shinto shrine and a new tall glassy building behind, (b) A Japanese historical Buddhist temple and a tall broadcasting tower behind

In order to prevent such landscape destruction, regulation of height of buildings and other structures must be enforced not only in the vicinity but also in considerably wide background area of the interested structure. To properly set the height regulation, it is necessary to compute the maximum height that does not disturb the landscape from the viewpoint fields for all the locations in the landscape preservation area. Such maximum height is called invisible height (Higuchi, 1988) and can be measured by drawing a vertical cross section as shown in Figure 2. However, it takes much cost and time to measure invisible height for all locations if we perform manually using a map or make a 3D computer graphics (CG) urban model, as described in the next section.

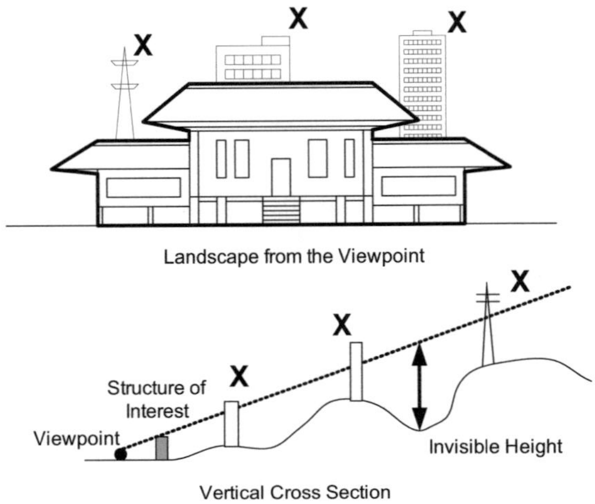

Fig. 2. Invisible height and regulation of height of structures for landscape preservation

Augmented Reality (AR) technology provides a facility to overlap real video images with virtual computer graphics images. The author perceived that invisible heights from multiple and moving points can be evaluated using AR technology without making an expensive and time-consuming 3D physical or numerical urban model. In this chapter, a new AR-based methodology for evaluating invisible height to support making regulations to preserve good landscapes is described.

2. Related work

2.1 Previous methods for measuring invisible height

In order to evaluate the invisible height for all the points behind the specific objects which make good landscape, the following four methods have been considered or employed in practice: (1) drawing sections from a map, (2) making a physical model of the area and buildings; (3) interpreting aerial photographs; and (4) making a numerical 3D terrain and building model. These methods require much time and cost.

As for the method (1), for each viewpoint, a large number of vertical cross sections must be drawn, and for each vertical cross section, invisible height must be measured at many points. Since there are a number of viewpoint fields for the interested structure, above mentioned work must be done iteratively. Furthermore, there may be other aesthetically pleasing structures nearby so that the above mentioned work must be done for all such structures and minimum invisible height must be selected for each location. Moreover, the height of the

interested structure is usually not uniform. The background terrain is usually not flat but uneven. As buildings and structures which already exist can make new hypothetical structure invisible, existing structures have to be drawn in the vertical cross section.
The method (2) is apparently expensive. The method (3) requires a special device called a stereophotogrammetry. The method (4) is also expensive and time-consuming.
Recently, Digital Terrain Model (DTM) (Lin et al., 2005), which represents elevations of terrain surface and Digital Surface Model (DSM), which represents elevations of surface of buildings, structures, trees, etc., may be available in some areas. If both of these data are obtained, the process of computing invisible height would be straightforward. However, such data are usually coarse and thus, not appropriate for this purpose. Even if the Laser imaging Detection and Ranging (LIDAR) method is used to make the 3D model, it takes much time and cost for processing the point cloud and making a surface model.

2.2 Virtual reality and augmented reality

VR technology is often used for observation and evaluation of landscape by city planners, designers, engineers, developers, and administrators (Yabuki et al., 2009). VR and 3D urban and natural models allow the user to explore various landscape scenes from multiple and moving viewpoints (Soubra, 2008; Dawood et al., 2009). However, if VR is employed in order to evaluate the invisible height for wide area behind the historical or valuable buildings or structures, one must develop a detailed and precise 3D city model with existing buildings, trees, and other objects. This could take a long time and high cost. If such a city model has already been built for other reasons, it can be used without additional cost. Unless otherwise, making a large 3D VR model may not be a suitable choice just for obtaining the invisible height alone in terms of cost-benefit performance.
On the other hand, AR has attracted attention as a technology similar to but different from VR (Wang & Wang, 2009). AR technology provides a facility to overlap real video images with virtual computer graphics images. According to Azuma (Azuma, 1997), AR has three characteristics, i.e., AR combines the real and virtual worlds, has real-time interaction with the user, and is registered in a 3D space. There are three types of displays for AR: Head Mounted Displays (HMDs), hand-held displays, and spatial displays (projection to the real world). The advantage of HMDs is that they provide the immersive effect to multiple moving users. There are two types of HMDs, i.e., video see-through type and optical see-through type. The HMD must be tracked with six degree of freedom (6DOF) sensors for registering the virtual images to the real world. The sensors can be either 1) position/posture sensors consisting Ground Positioning System (GPS) and gyroscope sensors (Feiner et al., 1997; Thomas et al., 1998) image sensors such as charge coupled device (CCD) cameras with markers (Kato & Billinghurst, 1999), or 3) feature point detection software (Jiang & Neumann, 2001; Golparvas-Fard et al., 2009). So far, the marker-based AR seems to be most popular because a free open source AR software package called ARToolKit (Kato & Billinghurst, 1999) is available. With ARToolKit, all you have to do is to make markers and purchase a web camera in order to start experiments of AR. Thus, ARToolKit has been used in this research. The marker in ARToolKit is a square with a black frame and some letter or shape inside the frame. ARToolKit can detect a marker from a video image and register the viewer's location by measuring the size and distorted shape of the marker on the video display image. The marker is linked with a virtual CG object and the system shows the object image on the video screen.

AR seems to be more often used indoors rather than outdoors because of the difficulty in registration of the user in the 3D world. A number of outdoor AR research projects have been reported (You et al., 1999; Kameda et al., 2004; Reitmayr & Drummond, 2006; Steinbis et al., 2008; Abawi et al., 2004; Ota et al., 2010). AR has been used for inspection of constructed objects such as steel columns (Shin & Dunston, 2009) and reinforcing bars (Yabuki & Li, 2007) in their research.

3. Proposed method for evaluation of invisible height

3.1 Overview of the proposed method

The main idea of the proposed method is when the user observes the landscape object under consideration from the viewpoint fields, wearing a HMD and a video camera connected to a PC, the AR system displays gridded virtual vertical scales (Figure 3(a)) that show elevations from the ground level and that are located behind the landscape object, on the HMD with overlapped real video images (Figure 3(b)). The user, then, captures the image and observes the maximum height that does not disturb the landscape for each virtual vertical scale. This process is iterated for various viewpoints, and appropriate maximum height for each location behind the landscape object is determined. Then, virtual vertical, maximum height scale models that should not disturb the landscape are generated and the user confirms whether the virtual objects are surely invisible, while walking around the viewpoint fields and wearing the AR system.

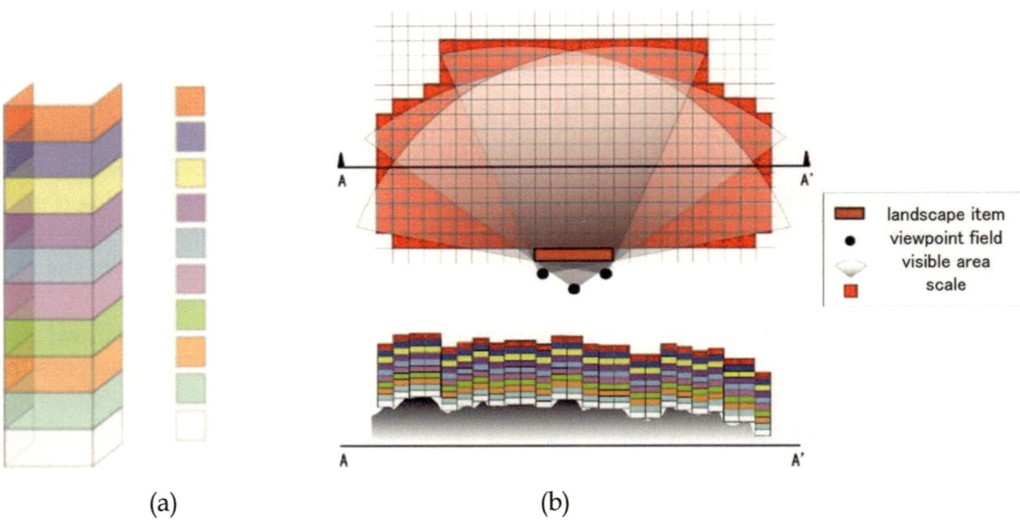

Fig. 3. (a) A color-coded CG scale and (b) Placement of scales

The first step of the proposed method of this research is to set multiple viewpoints of the interested structure. Viewpoints are usually determined by the advisory panel of academic experts in architecture, arts, landscapes, history, religions, etc., and representatives of the citizens. The panel members walk around the interested structure and decide multiple viewpoints making good landscapes.

Then, the area of the background region of the structure from the viewpoints is determined on the map. The area is then gridded with a certain interval such as 10m, 50m, 100m. For each grid point, the elevation of the terrain is measured. The terrain data can be borrowed from DTM provided by public agencies if available. Otherwise, the user can obtain it by scanning the contour map, converting it to vector data, interpolating the elevation data from the Triangulated Irregular Network (TIN) data. In the AR system, a translucent color-coded vertical computer graphics (CG) scale is placed on each grid point of the background area. Note that the terrain is usually uneven so that the scales are placed as shown in Figure 3(b). For each viewpoint, the location of the marker is determined.

Now, the user visits the site and sets the marker at the designated location using surveying equipment. Then, the user wears a HMD with a video camera and starts the AR system. On the screen of the HMD, the marker, real video image, and a number of CG scales are shown. The user can select one row of CG scales for displaying at a time because overlapping scales may not be readable. For each row, the user captures a screen image and this process is iterated at all viewpoints.

After returning to the laboratory, the user reads the invisible height for all scales from the captured images. Then, for each grid point, the minimum invisible height from the data of multiple viewpoints is determined. Then, upper portions of all the vertical CG scales are cut out so that the height of each scale is equal to the minimum invisible height. The user visits the site again and checks whether all the CG scales of invisible height are shorter than the visible structures at all the viewpoints. The confirmed data is the baseline for making the height regulation for preserving good landscape.

3.2 Implementation of the proposed method

A prototype system was developed for validating the methodology proposed in this research. As for the AR, ARToolKit was used because it is commonly and widely used for AR research in the world. The author used a standard spec laptop PC, SONY VGN-SZ94PS with RAM of 2.0 GB, VRAM of 256MB, a 1280x800 display, OS of Microsoft Windows XP. A HMD of eMagin, Z800, 3D Visor and a web camera of Logicool QCam Pro for Notebooks with 1600x1200 pixels were used. The web camera was attached with the HMD, as shown in Figure 4. Although the PC and the web camera have high resolutions, the screen size of 800x600 pixels were used for AR due to the limitation of ARToolKit.

(a) (b) (c)

Fig. 4. (a) Head Mounted Display, (b) Web camera, (c) Wearing HMD with Web camera

A marker of the AR system was made for identifying the location and viewing direction of the user. Markers are usually small, for example, 50x50 mm, for the use of tabletop or desktop AR. However, as the landscape objects are buildings in this research, the typical size of the virtual, vertical scale is about 300m, and the distance of the scale from the

viewpoint can be up to 5 km, small markers such as 50x50mm may not be visible from the viewpoints and the numerical errors due to the small size of the marker can be very large. Thus, a marker of which size is 900x900mm was made (Figure 5). The reason the edge size was 900mm is that the maximum width of wood plates typically available in Japan is 900mm. Although a larger marker such as 1.8m x 1.8m can be made by bonding four panels, handling would be very difficult and it could be extremely heavy in order to make it rigid.
Virtual vertical scale was developed as an OpenGL computer graphics (CG) object (Figure 3(a)). The shape of each scale is a rectangular solid which consists of multiple 5m-depth colored layers. Each layer has different color so that the user can read the height of the scale. In addition, the scale object must be see-through or very thin. Otherwise the scales would cover the target buildings and the user could not read the maximum invisible elevation for each scale.

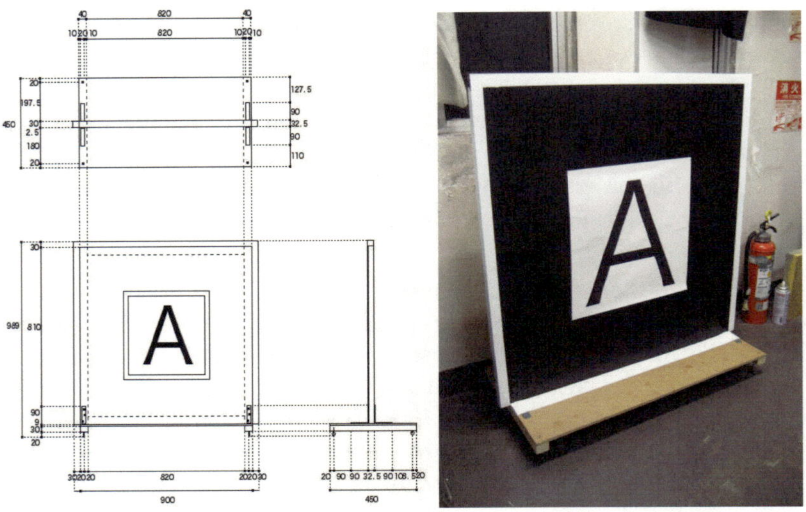

Fig. 5. Drawings and a photograph of the marker

4. Demonstration experiment and result

To demonstrate the proposed methodology and the developed prototype system, an experiment was executed. First, Convention Center and adjacent Gymnastic Hall of Osaka University (Figure 6) were selected as an experimental landscape preservation target because these buildings have highly evaluated property of aesthetic design and no permission was necessary to perform the experiment. Then, the horizontally flat and open square in front of the center and the hall was selected as a viewpoint field. The marker was installed at the square.
Then, 50m grid was drawn on the map of Suita Campus, Osaka University (Figure 7). The horizontal axis was named alphabetically, i.e., a, b, c, etc., and the vertical axis was named in number order, i.e., 1, 2, 3, etc. Each grid cell was named according to the horizontal and vertical number, e.g., d12, k16, m9, etc. The highest elevation in each grid cell was measured on the map and was assumed to represent the elevation of the cell. The virtual vertical scale of rectangular solid was placed so that its bottom elevation is the same as the ground elevation of the cell. This can be done by measuring the location, including the elevation, of

the marker, computing the elevation difference for each cell, and linking the marker and all the scale objects. Table 1 shows the elevation difference between the marker and all the cells. Figure 8 shows all the scales on the gridded area. If all the virtual scales are displayed on the screen, the scale would be invisible or illegible. Thus, for each time, one row is selected and shown on the screen, and then, the next row is selected and shown, and so forth.

Fig. 6. Convention Center (left) and Gymnastic Hall (right) of Osaka University

Fig. 7. Gridded map of Osaka University

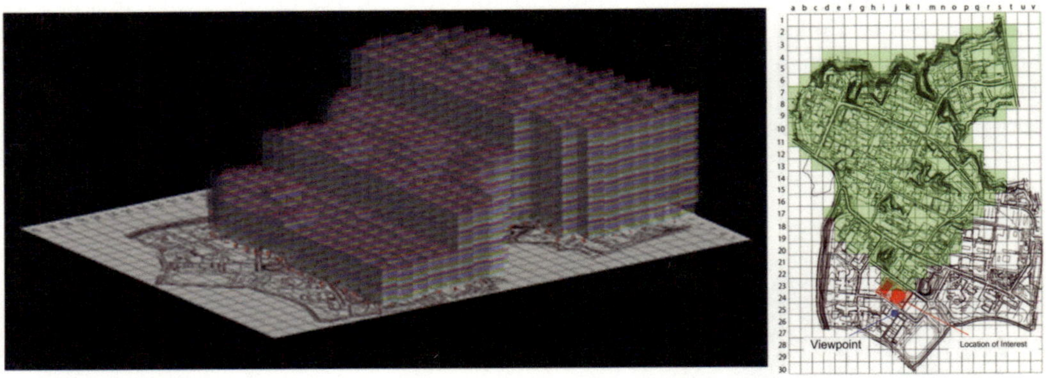

Fig. 8. All 3D CG scales placed on the gridded map of Osaka University

	a	b	c	d	e	f	g	h	i	j	k	l	m	n	o	p	q	r	s	t	u	v
1																			26.6			
2																32.6	29.6	37.1	32.7	13.3		
3														43.7	39.5	34.6	33.6	31.6	26.6	10.8		
4				36.6	31.7	42.6	45.6	45.6	36.6	41.6	44.6	43.6	44.9	44.9	39.5	24.1	21.1	10	12.5	9.6		
5			37.8	34.8	33.6	42.6	46.6	45.6	36.6	42.6	43.6	43.7	32.6	28.6	28.6	28.6	10.1	10.2	10	10.9		
6		34.6	36.6	19.7	15.7	32.6	32.6	42.6	40.6	36.6	20.7	34.1	29.6	23.6	16.7	19.9	12	11.2	11.1	11		
7	21.9	21.2	21.6	14.8	14.3	32.6	32.6	29.6	17.7	17	16.9	35.7	32.7	16.9	17.1	16.6	16.6	10.2	7.6	8.2		
8	16.6	11.7	11.8	11.3	14.1	25.6	20.6	17.5	17.5	10.5	12.9	12.9	25.6	35.2	32.6	16.4	21.6	16.6	13.4	13.4		
9	17.9	6.4	5.6	8.9	10	10	9.9	10.7	10.4	10.9	12.4	12.4	15.6	34.6	32.6	19.2	23.9	19.6	12.2			
10	3.2	6.6	5.2	6.4	6.3	6.8	6.4	6.5	8.5	8.4	7.5	7.9	11.6	11.6	20.9	22.2						
11	3.2	11.2	5.2	6.4	6.5	6.8	6.4	6.5	8.5	8.4	7.5	7.9	11.6	6.9	20.9	22.2						
12		1.8	4.9	3.6	5.9	6.5	7	7.5	8.3	8.4	7.8	5	1.6	3	19.6	24.2	18.1					
13			0.3	2.7	13.7	10.2	7	9.4	9.5	10.1	12.6	16.6	6.6	2.6	9.6	15.8	17.5					
14					6.6	5.8	5.8	5.8	9.3	11.9	20	20.6	13.6	10.6	1.5	2.9	9.7	10.7	7.9			
15					-2	6	6	6.4	5.7	9.3	10.7	16.6	15.1	14.6	5.6	-4.6	3.5	16.6	14.4	18.5	11.6	
16				-4.5	2.2	11.3	7.2	8.4	22.6	17.6	6.7	6.6	5.2	6.5	5.7	-0.6	4.9	5.7	5.8	6.6	6.1	8.7
17					6.1	6.2	7.4	8.4	22.6	22.6	11.1	3	5.1	5.2	5	4.1	5.9	5.3	5.6	5.8	7.3	11.6
18				-5	5.6	7.4	8.2	8.2	8.4	14	14	6.2	5.8	11.6	16.6	13.1	6.9	6.6	6	6.1	6.2	5.9
19			-5.3	5.1	7.5	7.3	8	7.8	8.9	8.2	10.6	7.2	6.4	11.8	5.4	6.5	6.6	6.6	1.9	1.4	6.2	5.8
20			-5.5	4.7	7.4	6.9	7	7.7	24.6	7.4	6.1	4.7	4	3.2	1.5	1.8	1.8	1.7	1.4	1.4	7.2	6.1
21			-5.8	4	4.9	7.1	7	6.6	25.6	10.3	5.8	9.6	1.8	0.6	1.3	1.6	1.6	1.6	1.4	1.4	7.1	1.3
22			-6.1	3.5	4.1	4.3	4.6	4.9	1.9	5	9.8	15.1	15.1	1.7	0.4	1	1	1.2	6.9	7.4	6.6	-3.4
23			-6.9	2.6	2.8	4	4.1	1.2	1.7	1.3	4.7	15.1	15.1	0.5	0	-0.3	-0.8	0.6	3.2	4.7	-1.1	2.7
24			-7.9	1.6	1.8	1.4	0.7	0.7	0.1	0.6	0.7	11.6	0.5	1.4	1.5	0.7	1.4	0.7	-0.4	-0.6	-6	-11.5
25			-9.4	0.3	1.9	0.5	0.4	0.2	0.2	◎	0.5	0.5	-1	-1.4	0.1	-0.2	0.5	0	0.3	-0.1	-0.7	-0.2
26			-10.9	-0.3	-0.7	0.9	0.3	-0.1	-0.6	-0.3	0.5	-0.1	-1.1	-0.3	-0.8	-1.1	0.4	-0.5	0.2	0.2	0.2	-0.8
27			-12.4	-2.2	0	1.9	1.7	0.3	-0.2	-0.2	-0.2	-0.2	-0.2	-0.3	-1.8						-0.6	-1.4
28								0.3	0.2	-0.1	-0.2	-0.1	-0.3	-2.5								
29									-0.2	0.5	-0.2	-0.2	-3.4									
30											3.1	-3.3										

Table 1. Elevation differences between the location of the marker and grid points

The experiment was performed by two students (Figure 9). One student wore the HMD and video camera and looked at the buildings the scales. The other held and operated the AR system and the PC, and captured images. A sample captured image is shown in Figure 10. From the captured image, the maximum invisible height for each rectangular solid scale was measured. They also walked around the square and confirmed that it was possible to view both the real video image and virtual scales, while walking.

Based on the invisible height measured from the captured images, a sample of height regulation plan was made. Then, all the scales were arranged so that each height was the same as the regulated height and linked to the marker (Figure 11). The experiment showed that the virtual shortened scales looked shorter than the target buildings from the viewpoint field (Figure 12).

Fig. 9. Photographs taken during the experiments at Osaka University

Fig. 10. 3D CG scales in the 16th row registered using AR

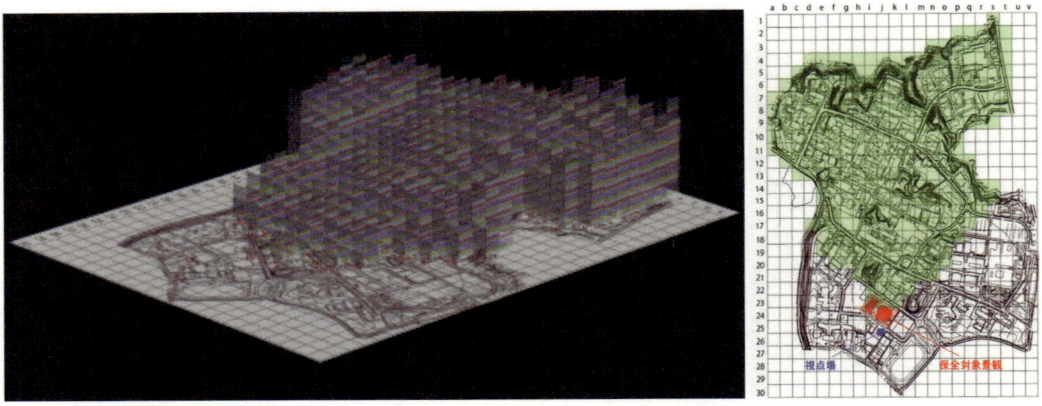

Fig. 11. 3D CG scales which conform to the height regulation placed on the gridded map

Fig. 12. A screen shot of the video image of the real buildings and marker with 3D CG scales of the 16th row, of which height are shortened so that they comply with the proposed regulation plan

	a	b	c	d	e	f	g	h	i	j	k	l	m	n	o	p	q	r	s	t	u	v
1																			235			
2																260	230	210	210	215		
3														240	255	235	230	220	210	210		
4				175	160	155	160	165	175	200	200	200	200	205	215	225	215	195	190	180		
5			205	195	160	150	160	175	195	200	205	210	220	225	225	215	220	205	190	180		
6		205	195	200	160	150	160	160	170	180	200	190	190	200	220	190	190	180	180	180		
7	220	215	200	200	170	140	145	150	175	195	200	185	185	205	210	195	180	175	165	175		
8	210	210	210	200	190	140	135	155	170	190	195	200	185	175	185	185	170	160	175	200		
9	200	210	200	185	175	140	145	155	165	175	175	175	175	165	145	150	125	125	170			
10	200	200	195	185	175	140	145	155	165	175	180	180	180	190	175	160						
11	190	185	185	175	160	135	135	145	155	165	175	175	175	150	140	125						
12		175	180	175	160	135	125	130	145	155	160	165	170	160	130	110	100					
13			160	160	140	130	110	115	125	135	140	140	150	140	120	105	125					
14					140	130	110	110	120	125	125	125	115	110	105	100	110	60	90			
15					140	120	95	95	105	115	115	115	110	100	95	105	60	70	75	—	—	
16				120	120	105	100	80	70	90	105	110	100	85	85	65	80	85	—	—	—	—
17					105	105	90	75	65	75	90	95	75	75	50	55	45	—	—	—	—	—
18				—	90	90	80	65	65	70	75	80	65	55	15	40	—	—	—	—	—	—
19			—	—	65	70	70	60	50	60	65	65	55	45	40	—	—	—	—	—	—	—
20			—	—	—	55	60	50	25	50	55	45	40	30	35	—	—	—	—	—	—	—
21			—	—	—	—	—	40	10	30	40	30	25	30	—	—	—	—	—	—	—	—
22			—	—	—	—	—	—	25	25	25	10	—	—	—	—	—	—	—	—	—	—
23			—	—	—	—	—	—	15	15	15	—	—	—	—	—	—	—	—	—	—	—
24			—	—	—	—	—	—	0	0	0	—	—	—	—	—	—	—	—	—	—	—
25			—	—	—	—	—	—	—	◎	—	—	—	—	—	—	—	—	—	—	—	—
26			—	—	—	—	—	—	—	—	—	—	—	—	—	—	—	—	—	—	—	—
27			—	—	—	—	—	—	—	—	—	—	—	—	—						—	—
28								—	—	—	—	—	—	—								
29									—	—	—	—	—	—								
30											—	—										

Table 2. A hypothetical regulation plan of height of buildings and structures to preserve the landscape

5. Experiment for assessment of accuracy

5.1 Accuracy and errors

Since ARToolKit is based on the computer vision technique which depends on the image of a physical marker on the video display, errors are inevitable. The factors of accuracy include precision of the camera, form of the marker, tilt angles of the marker, camera's angle against the marker, the number of pixels reprenting each edge of the marker on the computer display, computer programs and hardware, etc.

Each camera has its own camera parameters such as coordinates of the center of the camera, focal length, lenz distortion, etc. The default values of the camera parameters of ARToolKit must be adjusted to the camera used. This process is called "camera calibration." As all lenzes have distortion, correction of distorted images is very important.

Markers must be made as precise as possible and must be placed accurately because tilt angles of the marker have impact on the errors. Camera's angle against the marker is also an important factor. It is widely known that ARToolKit tends to become unstabel and have large error values if the camera is at the front of the marker, which will be described in the discussion section.

Markers should be displayed large enough relative to the video image because the precision depends on the number of pixels representing each edge of the marker. Thus, the size of the marker should be large enough, and the marker should not be placed far from the video camera. Since the captured video camera image is binarized and the marker is detected, the error is generated by whether the edge pixel is included or not. ARToolKit refers to the pixels on the computer display instead of the video camera's CCD pixels. Therefore, the user should use a computer with a large and high density display.

5.2 Experiment of measuring errors

An experiment was executed to measure the errors prone to the marker orientation and the distance between the marker and the virtual object. The marker was set at the distance of 7m from the video camera.

Four existing real buildings which are visible from the experiment site and of which precise location and dimension data can be obtained were selected. Then, virtual 3D wireframe rectangular solid models representing the edges of those buildings were made using OpenGL and linked to the marker. Three node points, A, B, and C, were marked for each virtual model. The distance between the marker and each building was 124 m, 428 m, 964 m and 2,851 m (Figure 13). The orientation from the marker to the video camera varied 0, 15, 30, 45, 60 degrees. The 0 degree case means that the camera was just in front of the marker. A photograph of the site for the case of 964 m is shown in Figure 14.

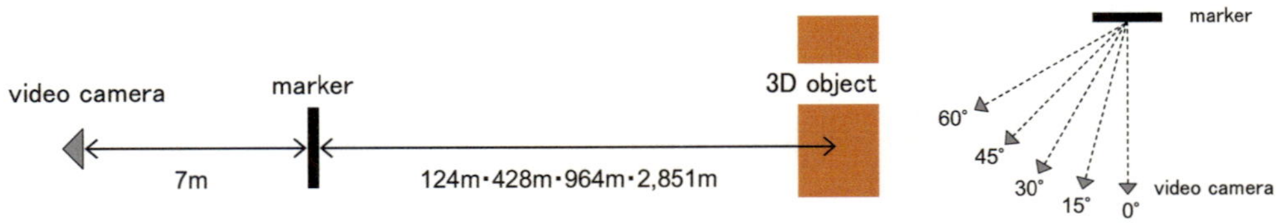

Fig. 13. Layout of video camera, marker and 3D objects (actual buildings)

Fig. 14. The marker, actual building, and virtual 3D CG object. Distance between the marker and the building = 964m.

For each angle of each case, the error of each node between the actual video image of the existing building and the wireframe virtual CG model located at the building place was observed in terms of the number of pixels. Then, the error in pixel was converted to height error in meter. Figure 15 shows the relationship between the average height errors in meter and the distance between the marker and the existing buildings for 5 different angle cases. Apparently, the cases of 0 degree indicated large errors of over 15m for the cases of 964m and 2,851m, which suggests the inability. However, for other cases, including the farthest building, the average errors were less than 7m. Especially, for the cases where the camera-marker angle is larger than 15 degrees and the distance between the marker and 3DCG object is less than 1km, the average errors were less than 3m.

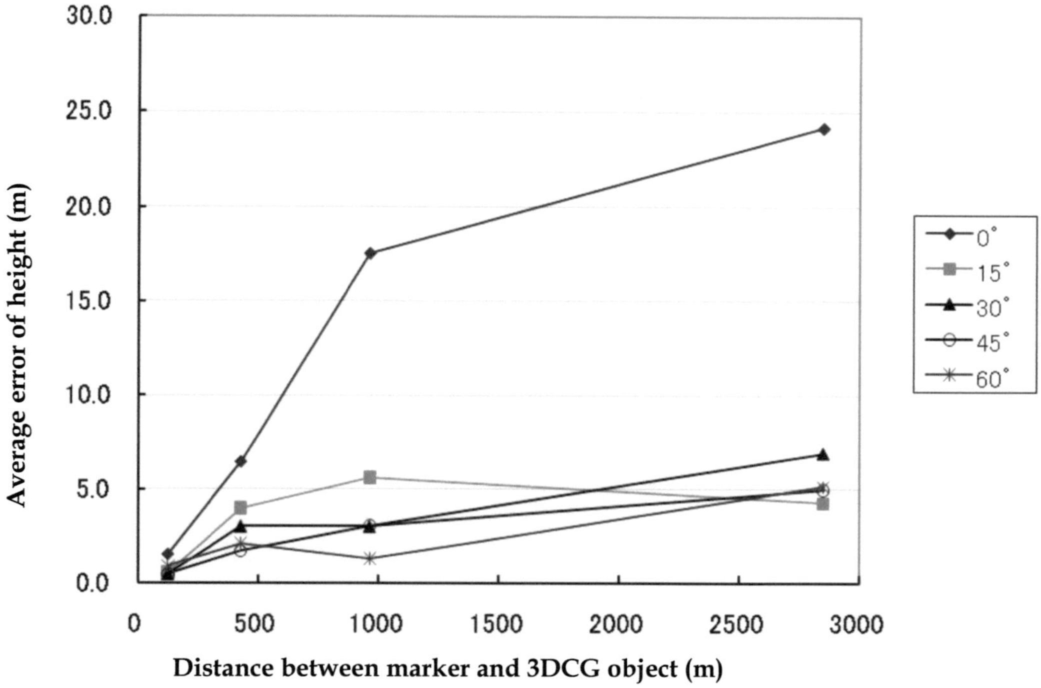

Fig. 15. The relationship between the average height errors and the distance between the marker and the buildings for 5 different marker-camera angle cases.

6. Discussion

The demonstration experiment result at Osaka University showed that the AR-based method proposed in this research was feasible and practical for determining invisible height from viewpoints to preserve good landscape. On the other hand, problems of accuracy and stability particularly related to ARToolKit have been identified.

The camera-marker angle of 0 degrees often produces unstable state or inability to identify the marker. It was reported the result of extensive accuracy experiments and concluded that the camera-marker angle between 0 and 30 degrees had low accuracy (Abawi et al., 2004). This problem has been identified by many AR researchers and is related to the reflection of light.

The size of the marker should be shown large enough on the computer display. However, if the marker becomes farther, the marker becomes smaller and thus, the error would become larger. To solve this problem, the author proposed a new method of using a set of four markers as a very large marker (Ota et al., 2010). In this method, the size of each marker is 400mm x 400mm. However, the four markers shown in Figure 16 work together as a single large marker of which edge length is equivalent to 2,000mm. As shown in Figure 17, the new method showed higher accuracy than the single marker method.

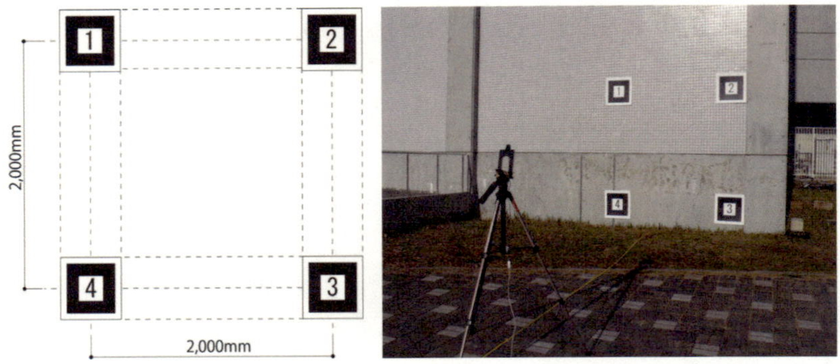

Fig. 16. A drawing of the four marker set (left) and a photograph showing the set of four markers placed on the wall

(a) (b)

Fig. 17. (a) Captured image of the wall and virtual CG structural blue lines in a single marker usage. Although four markers exist, only one marker was recognized. (b) When the four-marker method was used, the red lines had good agreement.

In the demonstration experiment at Osaka University, all the invisible heights were measured manually by reading the vertical scales with the interested structures on the captured images. Apparently, it takes much time and this process should be automated by making a program based on the image processing. In this research, translucent color-coded cubes were employed for representing height scales. If thin color-coded lines had been used instead, more rows could have been shown on the screen rather than just one row of scales.

7. Conclusion

Good landscape is often a symbol or treasure for the people living in the region. Such good landscape could be destroyed by constructing a new tall structures. In order to preserve good landscape, regulation of height of newly designed buildings is necessary. However, it would take a long time and much cost to evaluate invisible height of the background area from multiple viewpoint fields of the interested structure which makes a good landscape. Thus, in this research, a new methodology was proposed for evaluating the invisible height of virtual buildings that may be designed in the future from the multiple viewpoint fields using AR technology. Then, the prototype system was developed and applied to a sample good landscape site at Osaka University. To reduce errors, a large marker was made. Based on the maximum invisible height from the viewpoint field, a sample regulation plan was produced. The experiments showed the feasibility and practicality of the proposed methodology.

In order to evaluate the errors of the proposed method, an experiment was executed at Osaka University. Although when the marker-camera angle was 0 degrees the system showed some inability, it showed that necessary accuracy could be obtained through the proposed method, especially when the marker-camera angle ranges from 15 to 60 degrees.

Currently, more accurate and stable methods are being pursued. One of them is to use a set of four markers for representing a virtual very large marker. The result of this new method recently obtained was briefly introduced in the discussion. Future research includes using point cloud data which can be obtained using laser scanners for the registration of the camera in the 3D world in order to improve the accuracy and efficiency.

8. References

Abawi, D. F.; Bienwald, J. & Dorner, R. (2004). Accuracy in Optical Tracking with Fiducial Markers: An Accuracy Function for ARToolKit, *Proceedings of the Third IEEE and ACM International symposium on Mixed and Augmented Reality*, 2p

Azuma, R. (1997). A Survey of Augmented Reality, Presence: Teleoperators and Virtual Environments 6, 4, pp. 355-385

Dawood, N.; Benghi, C.; Lorenzen, T. & Pencreach, Y. (2009). Integration of Urban Development and 5D Planning, *Proceedings of the 9th International Conference on Construction Applications of Virtual Reality*, pp. 217-228, ISBN 978-1-74210-145-3, Sydney, Australia, The University of Sydney

Feiner, S.; MacIntyre, B. & Hollerer, T. (1997). A Touring Machine: Prototype 3D Mobile Augmented Reality System for Exploring the Urban Environment, *ISWC97*, 1, 4, pp. 208-217

Golparvar-Fard, M.; Pena-Mora, F. & Savarese, S. (2009). Monitoring of Construction Performance Using Daily Progress Photograph Logs and 4D As-planned Models, *Journal of Computing in Civil Engineering*, ASCE, 346 (6), pp. 53-63

Higuchi, T. (1988). *The Visual and Spatial Structure of Landscapes*, MIT Press.

Jiang, B. & Neumann, U. (2001). Extendible Tracking by Line Auto-Calibration, *International Symposium on Augmented Reality*, IEEE and ACM, pp. 97-103

Kameda, Y.; Takemasa, T. & Ohta, Y. (2004). Outdoor See-Through Vision Utilizing Surveillance Cameras, *Proceedings of the Third IEEE and ACM International Symposium on Mixed and Augmented Reality*, 10p

Kato, H. & Billinghurst, M. (1999). Marker Tracking and HMD Calibration for a Video-Based Augmented Reality Conferencing System, *Proceedings of the 2nd International Workshop on Augmented Reality*, pp. 85-94, San Francisco, CA, USA, <http://www.hitl.washington.edu/ artoolkit/>

Lin, Z.; Zhu, Q. & Gold, C. (2005). *Digital Terrain Modeling: Principles and Methodology*, CRC Press

Ota, N.; Yabuki, N. & Fukuda, T. (2010). Development of an Accurate Positioning Method for Augmented Reality Using Multiple Markers, *Proceedings of the International Conference on Computing in Civil and Building Engineering - 2010,* Nottingham, UK, Paper 4, 7p

Reitmayr, G. & Drummond, T. W. (2006). Going out: Robust Model-based Tracking for Outdoor Augmented Reality, *Proceedings of the IEEE International Symposium on Mixed and Augmented Reality,* pp. 109-118

Shin, D. & Dunston, P. (2009). Evaluation of Augmented Reality in Steel Column Inspection, *Automation in Construction,* Vol. 18, No. 2, pp.118-129

Soubra, S. (2008). Combining Virtual Environments and Simulations to Meet Sustainability Challenges of the Construction Sector, *Proceedings of the 8th International Conference on Construction Applications of Virtual Reality,* pp. 42-57, Kuala Lumpur, Malaysia

Steinbis, J.; Hoff, W. & Vincent, T. L. (2008). 3D Fiducials for Scalable AR Visual Tracking, *Proceedings of the IEEE International Symposium on Mixed and Augmented Reality,* pp. 183-184

Thomas, B.; Demezuk, V.; Piekarski, W.; Hepworth, D. & Bunther, B. (1998). A Wearable Computer System with Augmented Reality to Support Terrestrial Navigation, *Proceedings of the 2nd International Symposium on Wearable Computers,* pp. 166-167.

Wang, R. & Wang, X. (2009). Experimental Investigation of Co-Presence Factors in a Mixed Reality-Mediated Collaborative Design System, *Proceedings of the 6th International Conference on Cooperative Design, Visualization, and Engineering,* pp. 333-340, Luxembourg, Springer, Berlin

Yabuki, N. & Li, Z. (2007). Cooperative Reinforcing Bar Arrangement and Checking by Using Augmented Reality, *Proceedings of the 4th International Conference on Cooperative Design, Visualization, and Engineering,* pp. 50-57, ISBN 978-3-54-74779-6, Shanghai, China, September 2007, Springer, Berlin

Yabuki, N; Kawaguchi, T. & Fukuda, T. (2009). A Development Methodology of Virtual Reality Models for Urban Light Rail Transit Projects, *Proceedings of the 2009 International Workshop on Computing in Civil Engineering,* pp. 495-502, ISBN 978-0-7844-1052-3, Austin, TX, USA, ASCE, Reston

You, S.; Neumann, U. & Azuma, R. (1999). Orientation Tracking for Outdoor Augmented Reality Registration, *IEEE Computer Graphics and Applications,* November/ December, pp. 36-42

30

Virtual Reality Simulation System for Underground Mining Project

Keping Zhou and Mingming Guo
Central South University,
China

1. Introduction

Underground mining has the characteristics such as complex mining technology, poor visibility and sightlines, bad work condition and frequent geological disasters. It is the inevitable trend for the development of mining to innovate traditional mining industry by using modern high technologies to mitigate the deficiency. Virtual mine is the main part of digital mine, it is a new expression of mine and plays an important role in the construction of mine informatization. Virtual reality (VR for short) technology is considered as one of the three most promising technologies in the 21st century, and it has three characteristics: immersion, interactivity and imagination. Virtual reality technology can provide users with lively virtual mining environment in three-dimension, allowing users to not only immerse in the virtual mine scene but also interact with the mining equipment real-timely, which the traditional CAD design and pre-rendering three-dimensional animation can't achieve. Virtual reality technology has been got a wild range of applications and made remarkable achievements in many areas, such as virtual city, military simulation, aerospace simulation etc. It is a kind of innovation to support mine planning, mining design, disaster warning and disaster inversion by using VR technology in the field of mine.

Currently, the application research of mine VR simulation system has got rapid development at home and abroad, but only has little research on underground mining project VR simulation system. VR simulation system for underground mining project will enable users to get all-around perspective and real–time activity interaction in a virtual mine. At the main time, it has a positive meaning for virtual mining design, mine safety education and training, mining technology projects demonstration, mine production visualization management, disaster simulation and inversion etc. In this paper, Kafang polymetallic ore deposit in YunNan province of china was taken as the research object, the development process of VR simulation system for underground mining project was discussed in detail.

2. System general design

2.1 System analysis

According to the characteristics of virtual reality technology and currently needs of Kafang polymetallic ore deposit, the VR simulation system is used to realize deep immersion and achieve real-time interaction with objects in virtual mine, allowing users to roam arbitrary in the virtual scene and interact with the mining equipments. So, VR simulation system is designed for two parts.

1. Construct virtual mine scene

Virtual scene is the core of the whole virtual reality simulation system. So, not only the terrain and surface industry field but also the orebody, development and transportation system under the surface should be displayed. According to the development system form and mining method of Kafang polymetallic ore deposit, the virtual mine scene must have mine's terrain, mining equipments, orebody, shaft, tunnel, adit, ramp and other objects. The virtual scene should be lively, and users can feel that they are just like in the real mine. Virtual scene of Kafang mine is shown in fig.1.

2. Simulate mining process

The mining method of Kafang mine is "reconstruct mining environment and continuous caving afterwards filling mining method". It is a new continuous caving method by reconstructing the mining environment. That is, using high efficiency, high recovery rate mining technology, and high performance for trackless mining equipments. The procedure is to construct new mining environment using backfill body framework constructed by cemented stone by grouting since the stope is finished for the purpose of the creation of mining technology on continuous mining. The process of drilling, blasting, ore removal and filling should be displayed, and the most important is that users can interact with mining equipments real-timely.

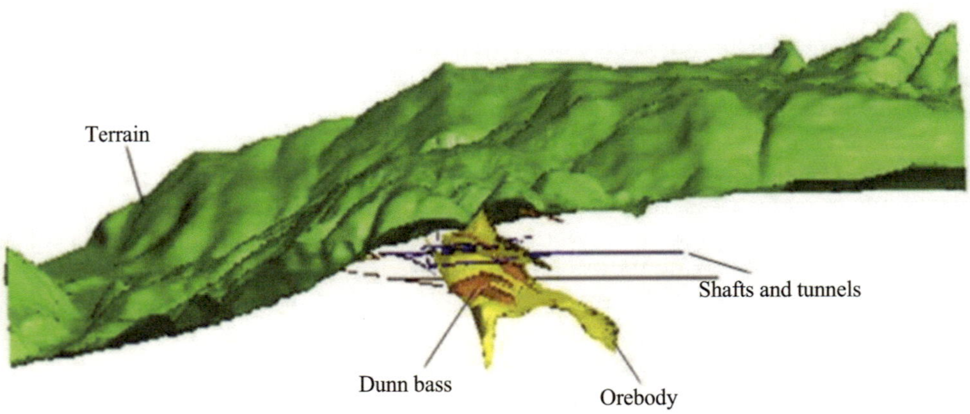

Fig. 1. Virtual scene of Kafang mine

2.2 System development environment

1. Hardware environment : Graphics workstations, three-channel 120 degree passive 3D display system, single-channel active 3D display system and stereos.
2. Software environment : Windows XP Professional sp2, 3DMine, Surpac Vision V5.2, OpenSceneGraph (OSG for short) and VS 2005.

   OSG is a cross-platform C++ API built on OpenGL for scene management and graphics rendering optimization, and most important is that it is open source multi-threaded and multi-display. However, OSG has nothing to do with the window system, providing no interaction way and interface management, so, the VR simulation system is take the VS

2005 as the development platform, and call the OSG library functions to realize the system function.
3. Network environment: Gigabit LAN.

2.3 System module analysis

Mining project VR simulation system is divided into five modules:
1. Display modes module: it is used to control the model's appearance. For example, to clearly see the polygonal structure of a model, go to wireframe mode, and disable texture mapping and lighting. Some of the commonly used commands are listed below:
   - Polygon mode—cycle between wireframe, point, and filled polygon rendering mode.
   - Texture mapping—toggle between textured and nontextured.
   - Lighting—disable and enable lighting.
   - Backface culling—toggle backface culling.
   - Fullscreen mode—toggle between fullscreen and windowed rendering.
2. Special effect module: it is used to enhance the 3D virtual scene realism and simulate rain, fog, snow and storm by using particle system of OSG platform
3. Roaming module: it includes manual roaming and automatic roaming. Manual roaming means that users can use mouth and keyboard to adjust the location and direction of viewpoint. Automatic roaming supplies the function of recording and replaying men-roaming paths.
4. Mining process simulation module: it is used to simulate the Kafang polymetallic ore deposit mining process which consists of development, cutting, stoping, filling and ventilation.
5. Stereoscopic display module: this module is to display the mine scene in 3D way, inputting it with "three-channel passive 3D display +3D stereo" mode and "single-channel active 3D display +3D stereo" mode. At the mean time, it can be used to increase or decrease the parallax to ensure the visual comfort of roaming process.

3. System development process

The development process of mining project VR simulation system in underground mine is shown in Fig.2.

3.1 Data management

Data management which is prepared for the total virtual scene is the foundation of VR simulation system. There are many kinds of data, terrain data, geological data, shaft and tunnel data, equipment data are prepared to model terrain, orebody, shaft, tunnel and mining equipment. They are from CAD design paper, including contour maps, orebody section line drawings, development system blueprints, equipment structure diagrams etc.
Image data taken by digital camera and high resolution satellite is used to map the texture on mine 3D geometric model. The texture include of terrain photographs, rocks and mining equipment pictures, these pictures should be corrected by picture processing software and converted into .JPEG and .RGBA format. In order to make the virtual mine scene be more believable, it is necessary to add audio data such as mine environment stereo sound and mining equipments working sound to virtual mine scene. The sounds are recorded by

recording equipment and clipped by professional software. Attribute data includes name and geographical coordinates of development project, ore grade, location of mining equipment, size and shape of tunnel cross-section.

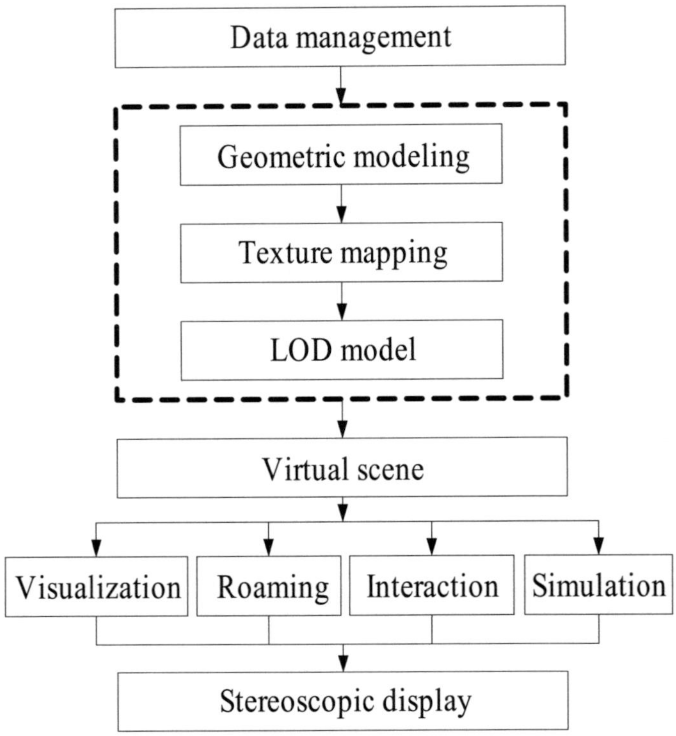

Fig. 2. The development process of VR simulation system

3.2 Scene modeling

Scene modelling is used to construct various models for VR simulation system. It is the key step in the establishment of the whole system and control the success of VR simulation system or not.

The characteristics of Underground mining scene modelling are in following three aspects: (a) shapes and types of the models for underground mining scene are different and opulent, and most of them are irregular. So, plenty of complex and completely different models need to be constructed. (b) The objects of virtual mine scene are divided into two categories: static objects and dynamic objects. In underground mining project VR simulation system, there are terrain models, orebody models, shaft models, tunnel models and ramp models etc, these irregular models belong to static objects. The main dynamic objects are mining equipment models such as tramcars models, LHD models and jumbo models. (c) The data of terrain model and shaft, tunnel models are too big. So, under the premise of meeting the requirements of project and visual sense, models should to be simplified properly to increase models display speed in VR system.

Scene modelling process contains three steps of geometric modelling, texture mapping and LOD models. The modelling process of VR simulation system is shown in fig.3.

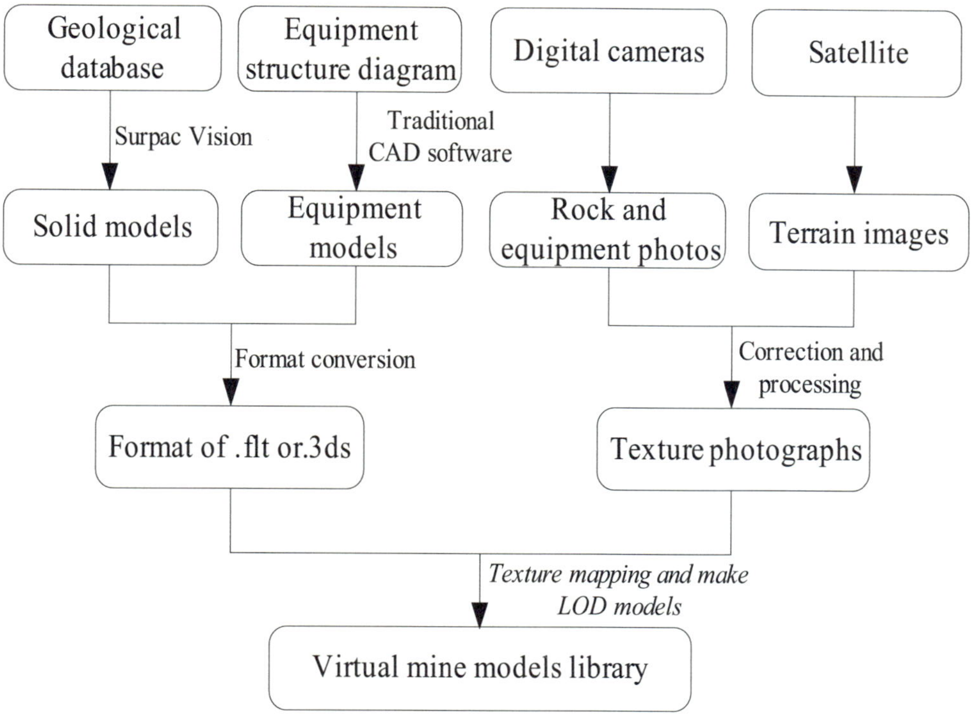

Fig. 3. The modelling process of VR simulation system

3.2.1 Geometric modelling

At present, many kinds of commercial software can meet the requirements of modeling mine models. Mine large project software (such as Surpac Vision, DataMine, Mircomine, 3DMine and DiMine) provides powerful modeling tools and modules based on geological database in the deposit modeling area. In Surpac Vision software, DTM model of terrain can be generated directly by contour, orebody model can be formed by connecting orebody section line, shaft models, tunnel models and ramp models are created by the central line and section of roadway. Fig.4 shows some solid models of Kafang polymetallic ore deposit which are created by CAD design paper.

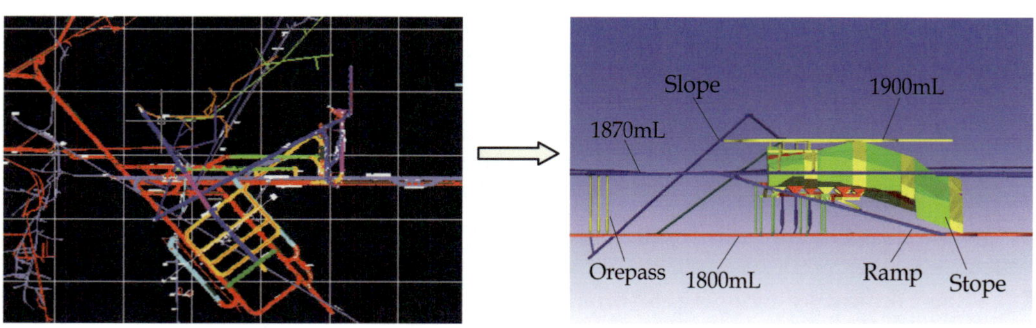

a) CAD design paper b) solid models

Fig. 4. Some solid models of Kafang polymetallic ore deposit

The traditional CAD software (such as AutoCAD, 3DMax and Maya) has the characteristics that are easy to operate, intuitive, easy to learn, make models realistic and so on. So, it was used to produce mining equipment models which need to be sophisticated and realistic. At last, all the models should be converted into .3ds or .flt or .x data format for texture mapping and LOD models production in professional virtual reality software (such as Multigen Creator). Note that: the format should be to minimize the conversion between models so that model will have a serious distortion. Table 1 lists the common VR software and platform and the data format they support.

Sort	Name	Data format	
		Input data format	Export data format
Mine large project software	Surpac	.dwg, .dxf, .dtm, .dm	dwg, .dxf, .dm, .dtm, .wrl
	3DMine	.dwg, .dxf, .dtm, .dm, 3dm, .shp	.dwg, .dxf, .dm, 3dm, .stl
Traditional CAD software	AutoCAD	.dwg, .dxf	.dwg, .dxf
	3DMax	.3ds, .dwg, .dxf, .obj, .stl , .shp, .wrl	.3ds, .dwg, .dxf, .obj, .stl., .wrl
Professional VR software	MultiGen Creator	.3ds, .dxf, .obj, .stl	.flt, .dxf, .obj, .stl, .wrl
3D model conversion software	Deep Exploration	.3ds, .obj, .geo, .flt, .x, .stl, .wrl, .ma, .mb, .dwg, .dxf	
VR system	InTouch	.dwg, .dxf, .dtm, .dm, .x, .shp	
	CyberMaker	.3ds, .obj, .geo, .flt, .osg, .ive	
VR development platform	OSG	.3ds, .obj, .geo, .dae, .shp, .flt, .osg, .ive	

Table 1. The common VR software and platform and the data format they support

3.2.2 Texture mapping

Texture mapping is a technology that maps the pixel value of 2D image bitmaps to the corresponding peak of 3D solid models. It is used to enhance the realistic and reduce the complexity of solid models. Three kinds of texture mapping technology are used in this system.

1. Projection texture mapping: texture image is projected directly onto three-dimensional geometric model to obtain surface texture coordinates of models, mining equipment models are mapped by using this technology, texture mapping of tramcars models is shown in fig.5.

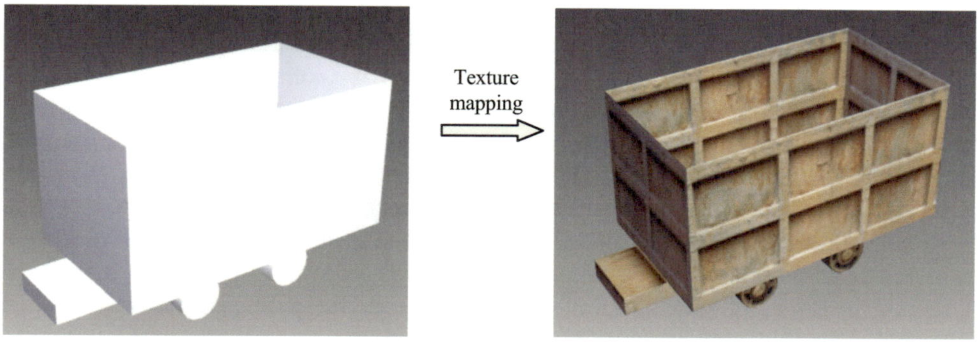

Fig. 5. Texture mapping of tramcars models

2. Transparent texture mapping: It is achieved by texture technology and integration technology. For example, the simulation of trees needs only one face. The advantage of this technology is that speed is fast and visual effects are good when you observe in the plains. Drawback is that if the rapid rotation around the bulletin board area, the surface can be seen in turn, and visual effects look bad from the high altitude. Through the bulletin board technology, roaming system allows users to add plants data in interactive way. At the main time, based on this idea, you can also increase the figure as well as that figure pictures are handled by transparent air technology and replaced by plants texture images.
3. Opaque one-sided texture mapping: it is simple and convenient, the sky ball and terrain are mainly used this method to map textures. By using satellite picture, texture mapping of Kafang polymetallic ore deposit terrain is showed in fig.6.

Fig. 6. Texture mapping of Kafang polymetallic ore deposit terrain

4. Texture splicing: texture is spliced continuously and repeatedly by a fundamental element splicing unit which is a small piece of representative and re-splicing texture unit. Shaft models, tunnel models and ramp models are taken in this way.

3.2.3 LOD model

LOD (level of detail) technology can not only ensure the visual effect of virtual scene, but also increase the frame rendering speed of scene and change the complexity of scene real-timely. When the viewpoint comes closer to objects, the object models are changed from simple to complex. At the main time, it is important to join the smoothing technology to reduce the mutation of level of detail. There are two main methods to produce LOD model in mining project virtual reality simulation system development, and one is making continuous approximation similar geometric models, and the other is reducing texture resolution. The mining equipment models and the terrain model (as the following fig.7 shows) are taken the first method, the orebody, shaft and tunnel models are used the second method.

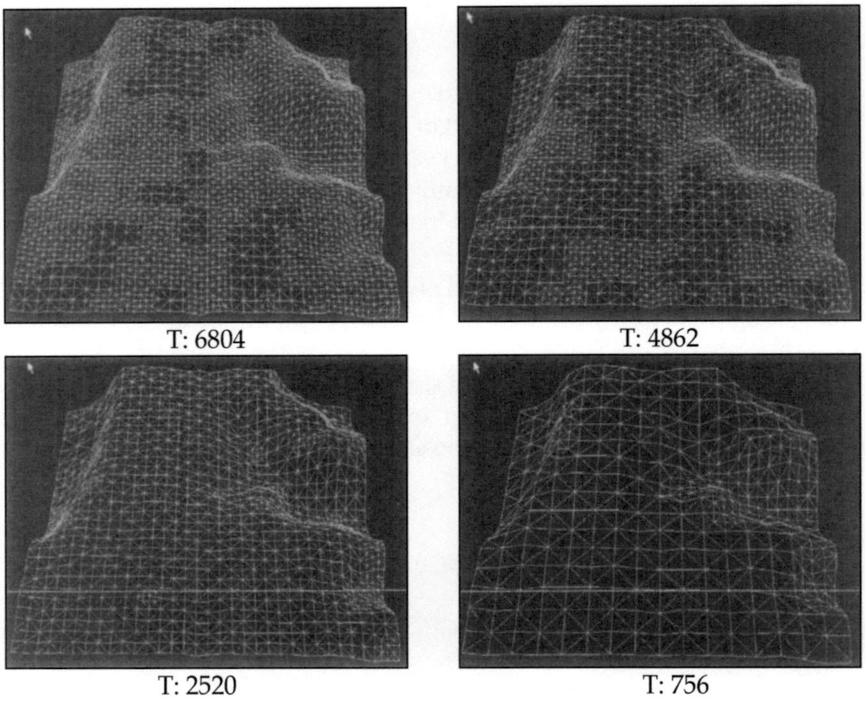

Fig. 7. LOD model of terrain ("T" means the number of the triangle)

3.3 Virtual scene

Virtual scene is the core of the whole virtual reality simulation system and collection of all visual objects in system. Under the support of virtual reality technology, scene visualization and interaction are used to build the virtual mine scene which has deep immersion and high interaction, Virtual mine is a complex system definitely, so the virtual reality simulation system is developed by object-oriented programming method based OSG and VS 2008 platform.

3.3.1 Visualization

Visualization is responsible for building a virtual mine environment of deep immersion. It is used to realize the functions, such as light, materials, geometry changes, transparent display and viewpoint attachment. Virtual scene should be set light and materials correctly.

Geometry change includes translation, rotation, scaling and other geometric operations. Transparent display can offer a way to users to observe a number of objects at the same time. For example, if the tunnels are semi-transparent, on one hand, it shows that tunnels are existent; on the other hand, it also represents the transport scheduling of mining equipments. Viewpoint attachment can make users have the feeling of driving car in the real mine when users roam in the tunnels (fig.8).

3.3.2 Scene roaming

Scene roaming can allow users to observe in virtual mine scene freely. Roaming is a process of moving viewpoints or changing sight line direction continuously to produce three-dimensional animation.

Fig. 8. Roaming in the tunnel

There are two kinds of roaming way in the virtual reality simulation.

1. Manual roaming: The location and direction of viewpoint are controlled by using the mouse and keyboard. In this virtual reality simulation, the operation "Ctrl+ left mouse button" controls the viewpoint movement of left or right, the operation "Ctrl+ right mouse button" controls the viewpoint movement of up or down, the operation "Ctrl+ middle mouse button" controls the viewpoint rotation.
2. Automatic roaming: Automatic roaming supplies a fixed roaming path to display virtual mine scene for users. The path is recorded in a notepad file where path information is interpolated, and then the path is played back. First of all, it is essential to record the initial viewpoint, rotation angle and elevation of sight line around the Z axis and so on; then, each continuous keyboard operation command is recorded with the format of "movement type, initial position, incremental movement, duration, and movement acceleration" for the purpose of interpreting the whole manual roaming process as the roaming command sequence; Thirdly, read the initial parameters from notepad files and set the system by using these parameters; At last, read the manual roaming operation command sequence and call the corresponding command processing functions for processing.

3.3.3 Interaction operation

In the system, interaction operation is mainly controlled by using the mouse for the scheduling of mining equipments. In mining equipments models management module, the car can be selected out of right-mouse menu and interacted with suspension, opening and reverse operation. At the same time, the car objects can added in the virtual mine scene.

In addition, it is important to develop a friendly man-machine interface (fig.9). System is divided into system control program interface and mine virtual reality simulation program interface. System control program interface is used to set up single-channel and multi-channel mode, and parameters of parallax, window size, render nodes and three-dimensional mode. Mine virtual reality simulation program interface is consisted of menu

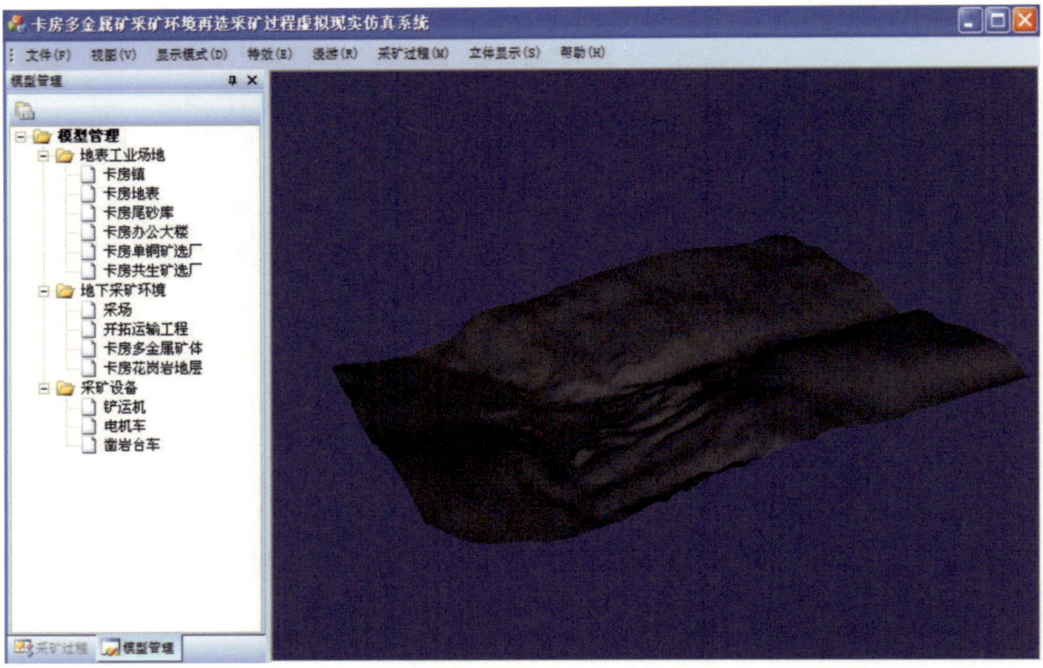

Fig. 9. One running window of VR simulation for underground mining project

and panel. Menu simulation running, roaming management, view, and help menu; panel which has the main operation function of the simulation program includes model management, viewpoint management and safety administration.

3.3.4 Simulation

Mining project simulation is not only a static scene simulation, but also a dynamic mining working environment for reproduction. There are four steps for mining technology in underground mine, such as: drilling, blasting, ore loading, ore removal and filling, so mining project simulation is mainly including the drilling simulation of drilling jumbo, the blasting simulation of rock, the ore loading process of tramcars, ore removal process of LHD, and grouting filling simulation. There are two ways to simulate the mining process, one is manual simulation, and the other is automatic demonstration. Users can drive the mining machines to control the process of drilling and ore removal in the virtual scene through manual simulation way. Automatic demonstration use the double buffer technology of OSG to set system clock, then order the animation together in accordance with the time to form the whole mining process. Besides, collision detection system is based on the level of AABB bounding box and blasting simulation is based on the osgParticle namespace of OSG platform. The result of mining process simulation is shown in fig.10 and explosion implementation procedures are as follows:

```
osg::Group *root= new osg::Group();
//set the speed of wind
osg::Vec3 position(0, 0, 0);
// application of  explosive
osgParticle::ExplosionEffect*explosion = new osgParticle::ExplosionEffect(position, 1.0f);
// application of explosion debris
osgParticle::ExplosionDebrisEffect*explosionDebri=new
osgParticle::ExplosionDebrisEffect(position, 1.0f);
//set smoke model
osgParticle::SmokeEffect* smoke = new osgParticle::SmokeEffect(position, 0.5f);
//set  fire model
osgParticle::FireEffect* fire = new osgParticle::FireEffect (position, 1.0f,5.0);
//set the wind effect
explosion->setWind(wind);
explosionDebri->setWind(wind);
smoke->setWind(wind);
fire->setWind(wind);
//join in scene node
root->addChild(explosion);
root->addChild(explosionDebri);
root->addChild(smoke);
root->addChild(fire);
```

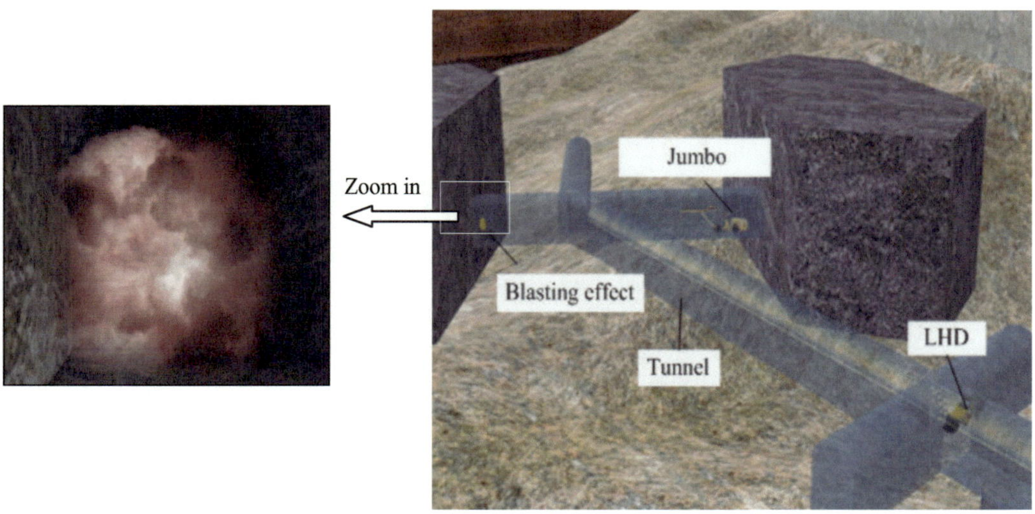

Fig. 10. Mining process simulation

3.4 Stereoscopic display

Stereoscopic display is divided into stereoscopic visual performance and stereoscopic sound performance. Stereoscopic visual performance can supply two view scenes for left eye and right eye separately by using virtual reality equipments firstly, such as professional DLP projector, receive the left eye and right eye video images through left eye and right eye respectively by drawing on three-dimensional glasses and form three-dimensional scene in users' brains finally. Stereoscopic sound performance can output stereo sound and video image through three-dimensional sound machine synchronously. In this VR simulation system, stereoscopic sound is realized by using OpenAL API in OSG platform. First of all, create a buffer. Second, load WAV data. "CreateBufferAndLoadWav" member function calls "COpenALBuffer" instance member function to create a buffer and load WAV data. In of "CreateSource"member function, source is created and buffer area is associated by calling "COpenALSource" instance member function.

The combine of stereoscopic visual performance and stereoscopic sound performance support very important deep information for virtual mine scene, and thus to improve its fidelity, reality and immersion. Three-channel passive 3D display is shown in fig.11 and single-channel active 3D display is shown in fig.12 and its implementation procedures are as follows:

```
osg::Group *root= new osg::Group();
//add model nodes
root->addChild( osgDB::readNodeFile("terrain.3ds"));
root->addChild( osgDB::readNodeFile("orebody.3ds"));
root->addChild ( osgDB::readNodeFile ("development. 3ds"));
viewer.setSceneData(root);
//set stereo
osg::DisplaySettings::instance()->setStereo(true);
//set eye separation
osg::DisplaySettings::instance()->setEyeSeparation (0.08);
viewer.realize();
viewer.run();
```

4. Conclusion

The virtual reality simulation system represents the mine's terrain, development and transportation system, orebody occurrence condition and underground mining process successful in 3D model, and then it can work well in three-channel passive 3D display mode and single-channel active 3D display mode. The virtual mine scene provide user with a very lively sense of immersion, and users can roam freely in the scene. At the same time, the system has a friendly man-machine interface, and users can interact with the mining equipments. All in all, the system basically meets the requirements of mining management expectation. Through the development of underground mining project VR simulation system, the system implementation method and process are studied and the result shows that this idea is reasonable and feasible.

Nevertheless, the VR simulation system still has the following disadvantages for future study: firstly, the tool for human-computer interaction which merely using keyboard and mouse is not enough, further research is necessary to develop professional virtual reality

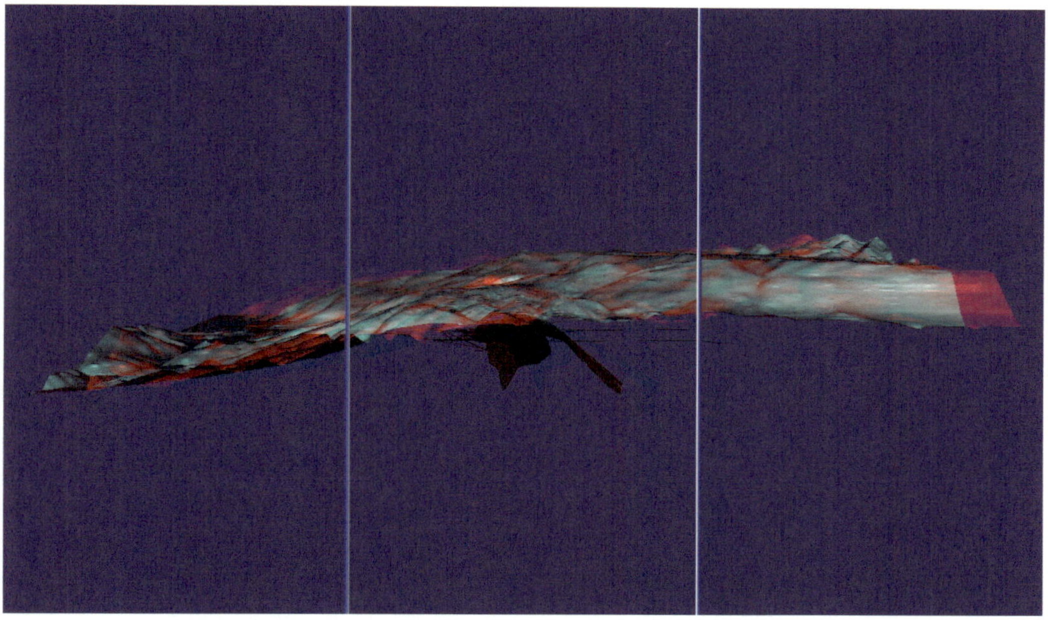

Fig. 11. Three-channel passive 3D display

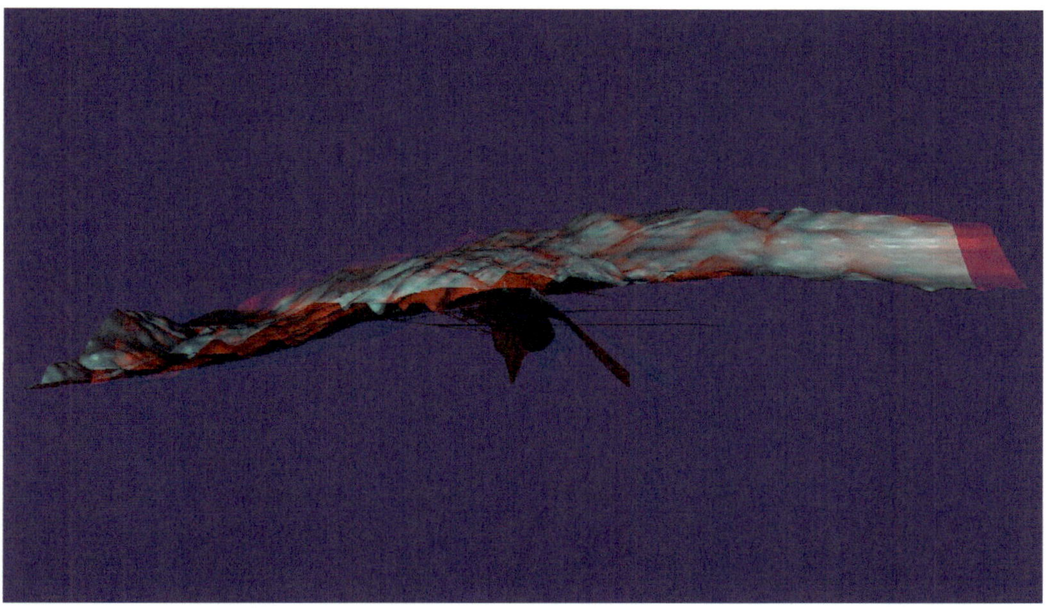

Fig. 12. Single-channel active 3D display

input device (3D mouse, Steering wheel, and data gloves, etc.) interface to enhance the interaction with the virtual mine scene; Secondly, the system don't have the function for data query and analysis module for 3D objects to realize the VR GIS function etc. At main time, virtual reality technology will play a greater advantage and role in mine ventilation simulation, numerical simulation and mine fire simulation etc. With the continuous development of virtual reality technology, VR is bound to have far-reaching effect to the mine future modernization.

5. References

Wu Lixin (2008), Progress of Digital Mine in China, *GEOMATICS WORLD,* 10(5), 6-13

Gu Desheng, Li Xibing (2006). *Modern metal deposits science and technology Exploitation*, Bei Jing, Metallurgy industry Press

Wang Deyong, Wu Zilian and Du Weixin (2006), Application of virtual reality technology in mine production simulation system, *Coal Mine Machinery*,27, 172-173

Hong Bingrong, Cai Zesu and Tang Haoxuan (2005). *Virtual reality and Its Application,* Bei Jing, National defense industry Press

Wu Lixin, Zhang Ruixin (2002), 3D Geoscience Modelling and Virtual Mine System, *Acta Geodaetica et Vartographica SiniCa,* 31(1), 28-32

HOLLAND R, DENBY B, et al. SAFE2VR(1999), A Virtual Reality Safety Training System, *Golden Computer Application in the Minerals Industry, Colorado : Colorado School of Mines* , 787

Li Jiangzhong, Chen Hongzhang and Sui Gang (2007), Study on Simulation System of Fully Mechanized Mining Face Based on Virtual Reality, *Journal of System Simulation*,19, 4164-4167

Wu Di, and Huang WenQian (2002), The development process and research of virtual reality technology, *Hydrographic surveying and charting,* 22, 15-17

Hua Zhen, Fan Hui, Li Jinjiang and so on (2003). Virtual reality-based study on the controll ability and visibility of mine ventilation system, *Metal Mine,* 325, 53-56

Zhao Jianzhong, Duan Kanglian and Hu Yaoqing (2003). Application of OpenGL in virtual reality system, *Journal of TaiYuan University of Technology,* 34, 39-42.

Yu Yan, Zhang Jinshan and Zheng Bangdong (2006). Simulation system based on VR for training technicians and workers in surface mining, *Express information of Mining Industry,* 442, 31-33

Wang Yongtian (2006). Augmented Reality-based digital reconstruction of Yuanmingyuan site, *Technology Review,* 24(3), 36-40

Li Lijun, Guan Tao and Wang Cheng(2006). Augmented Reality-based Virtual Town Planning Key Technology, *Computer Engineering and Design*,27(19), 3604-3608

Zhong Huijuan, Liu Xiaolin and Wu Xiaoli(2008). Augmented reality system and its key technology, *Computer Simulation,* 25(1), 252-255

P. J. Foster and A. Burton (2006). Modelling potential sightline improvements to underground mining vehicles using virtual reality, *Mining Technology,* 115, 85-90

Zhou Keping, Zhu Heling, Xiao Xiong and Chen Qingfa (2008). Control and simulation of ground pressure evolutional process based on reconstructed mining environment and continuous caving method, *Journal of Central South University (Science and Technology)* ,39, 417-422

Yu Yan, Zhang Jinshan and Zheng Bangdong (2006), Simulation System Based on VR for Training Technicians and Workers in Surface Mining, *EXPRESS INFORMATION OF MINING INDUSTRY*, 442,31-33

Li JianZhong, Nie Qisheng and Ma Baoming (2002), Application of Virtual Reality on mine industry, *Coal*, 11(5),33-34

Zhang Ruixin, Ren Tingxiang, Schofield D, Denby B, Williams M (1998), Virtual Reality and Its Application on Mining, *Journal of China University of Mining & Technology*, 27(3), 230-234

Gao Zhiwu, Qin Dexian, Deng Mingguo (2004). Application of virtual reality in Mineral Deposit, *Metal Mine*, 1, 287-289

Song Shucai, Yang Kejian, Wen Xiumei and so on (2005). Virtual Reality Technology and Its Application in teaching, *FU Jian Computer*, 5, 39-40

Hua Zhen, Fan Hui, Li Jinjiang and so on (2004), Application of virtual reality technology in mine ventilation system, *Coal Science and technoloty*, 32(3), 44-48

Liu Xiaoyan, Lin Hui, Zhang Hong (2003). *Virtual city construction principles and methods*, Bei Jing, Science Press

M. KIZIL (2003). Virtual reality applications in the Australian minerals industry, *South African Institute of Mining and Metallurgy*

P. Foster and A. Burton (2004). Virtual reality in improving mining ergonomics, *The Journal of The South African Institute of Mining and Metallurgy*, 3,129-133

Zhou Zhiyong, Chen Jianhong and Zhou Keping (2004). Application of Surpac Vision software in deposit modeling, *Mining Enginerring*, 2, 31-33

Zhou Keping, Guo Mingming, Yang Niange and Chen Qingfa (2008). Study on VR Simulation System of Development and Transportation for Underground Mine, *Computer system & application*, 17, 6-10

Wang Ruiling, Chen Zhengming and Li Jiejun (2006). A virtual navigating system based on 3D scene model, *Computer Applications and Software*, 18, 427-429

Guan Wei, Cai Xiaoling and Chen Hai (2007), Application of Level of Detail Technique in Scene Modeling, *Journal of System Simulation*, 19, 4164-4167

Seng Dengwen and Wang Hongxia (2005). Study and implementation of real time navigation system based on OpenGL, *J . Zhejiang Wat. Cons & Hydr. College*, 19, 63-65

Jia Huizhu (2002), *The research and implementation of virtual reality Three-dimensional display technology*, Da Qing(China), Da qing oil colleage, 22-31

Grigore C.Burdea and Philippe Coiffet (2005). *Virtual Reality Technology*, Bei Jing, electrciy industry Press

Gillies A.D.S., Wu H.W., Wala A.M. (2005). Australian Mine Emergency Exercises Aided by Fire Simulation, *Archives of Mining Sciences*, 50(1)

William R.Sherman, Alan B.Craig(2004). *Understanding Virtual Reality-Interface, Application, and Design*, Bei Jing, electrciy industry Press

A.P. Squelch (2001). Virtual reality for mine safety training in South Africa, *The Journal of The South African Institute of Mining and Metallurgy*, 7, 209-216

Vega LynX User's Guide(Version 3. 6). *Multigen-Paradigm*, Inc.2005

Li, Qing Han, Ke Qi.Shen and Yan Chun (2002). Research on controllable Visualization of mine surface Plant and development of virtual environment, *Journal of China University of Mining & Technology,* 1,27-29

Cullen, ET; Camm, TW; Jenkins, FM; and Mallett, LG(2006), Getting to zero: the human side of mining, *NIOSH Information Circular 9484,* 14-16.

KIZIL M.S., HANCOCK M.G., and EDMUNDS O.T (2001). Virtual Reality as a Training Tool, *Proceedings of the Australian Institute of Mining and Metallurgy Youth Congress,* Brisbane, Queensland, 2(6), 9–12

Guo Mingming, Zhou Keping (2009); Virtual Reality Simulation System for Underground Mining Process, *2009 4th International Conference on Computer Science & Education,* 1013-1017

Lu Hao, Luo Zhouquan and Yang Biao (2007), On Virtual Reality Technology and its Application in Mining, *China Tungsten Industry,* 22(4),22-25

Zhao Fezhi and Yu Lianlian (2006). Designing and implementing of Oil Field Security Operation Simulation System Based on Virtual Reality technology, *Computer system & application,* 11, 6-9

Wei Jing (2008), *Research on Virtual Mining System based on VR, Wu Han(China),* Wu Han Science and Technology University

Wu Qidi (2002), *System Simulation and Virtual Reality,* Bei Jing, Chemisitry industry Press

Mao Shanjun, Xiong Wei (2005), Design and primary implementation of coal mine virtual environment system, *Journal of China Coal Society,* 30(5), 571-575

Zhao Jianzhong, Chen Hongzhang and Sui Gang (2007). Study on Simulation System of Fully Mechanized Mining Face Based on Virtual Reality, *Journal of System Simulation,* 9(18), 4164-4167

Zhou Zhiyong, Chen Jianhong and Yang Libing (2008). 3D visualization modeling on geological and mining engineering in a large-sized mine, *J. Cent. South Univ. (Science and Technology),* 39(3), 423-426

Rao Hongliang (2004), *Study and Implement of Open Pit GIS System Based on Virtual Reality Technique,* Wu Han (China), Wu Han Science and Technology University

Zhao Jianzhong, Chen Hongzhang (2006). Study on Virtual Scene's Modeling of Fully Mechanized Mining Face, *Journal of System Simulation,* 8, 274-279

Luo Zhouquan, Liu Xiaoming and Su Jiahong (2006). Building of Three-Dimensional Models of Deposit Based on Surpac, *Metal Mine,* 358(4:33-36

Chen Wei, Xue Qingpo and Zhao Yang (2007). The current international evaluation of the more popular mining software, *Non-ferrous metals,* 59(4), 22-25

Wang Yongtao (2008). *Reserch and Realization on the visualization Technology in DaXin Manganese Mine,* Nan Ning(China), Guang Xi University

Gao Wenshu, Gao Xuan and Wang Lili (2008), The Application of solid mineral reserve estimation Based on 3D geological modelling and visualization of technology Micromine software, *Land & Resource,* 32 (6), 28-31

Fang Zhiheng, Wang Liguan and Feng Xinglong (2008). The Research and Practice of True Three-Dimensional Mining Method Design On DiMine Software, *China Molybdenum Industry,* 136-137

Wang Ruiling, Chen Zhengming and Li Jijun (2007). A Virtual Navigating System Based On 3D Scene Model, *Computer Application and Software*,24(7), 123-125

Liu Huanming (2005). *Research on Technology of Level of Detail Model Simplification,* Wu Han (China), Wu Han University of Technology

Xu Miaozhong (2003). *Research on Multi-resolution Representation and Visualization for Terrain Model in Virtual Reality,* Wu Han (China), Wu Han University

Zeng Qintian (2007). *Study of Poly-metallic Complex Deposit Visual Simulation and Technology of Three- dimensional Mining Design,* Chang Sha (China), Central South University

Cao ChuanFen (2004). *Study of Three- dimensional Method and Theory of Virtual City,* Chang Sha (China), Central South University

Zeng Wei (2005). *Delaunay Triangulation and Application Study of Polygonal Domains,* Ji Nan (China), Shan Dong University

Tao Songlin (1995). *Drilling and Blasting,* Metallurgy Industry Press

Liu Xiaoming (2007). *The Research and Application of Relevance Technology Based on the Cavity Monitoring System,* Chang Sha (China), Central South University

Li Qing, Han Keqi and Shen Yan (2002). Research on Controllable Visualization of Mine Surface Plant and Development of Virtual Environment, *Journal of China University of Mining & Technology,* 31(1), 27-29

Hou Xiang (2006). *Research of Visual Reality 3D modeling Technology,* Chong qing (China), Chong Qing University

Fu Yongming, Wang Yunjia (2004). Mine three-dimensional scene Navigation System Design and Implementation, *Modern Surveying,* 27(5), 11-14

Wan Gang, Xia Qing, Chen Gang and Wu Zhigang (2001). The Technique of Terrain Features' Geometry Modelling Used in Virtual Terrain Environment, *Journal of System Simulation,* 13, 73-76

Shang Jianga, Liu Xiuguo and Zheng Kun (2003). Research and Implementation of Interactive Walkthrough in 3D Scene, *Computer Engineering,* 29(2), 61-62

Jia Huizhu (2002). *The Research and realization of Three-dimensional virtual reality display technology,* Da Qing (China), Da Qing Petroleum Institute

Zhang Zhaoyan, Duan Xinhui and Wang Xinwu (2008). Application of Visual Simulation System in Simulation of Substation, *Computer Simulation*,25(2), 252-255

Shen Yanchun, Zhu Youhong and Caoli (2007). Design and Implementation of 3D Simulation Platform Based on OSG, *Computer Simulation,* 24(6), 207-211

Wen Zhuanping, Shen Yanchun(2009). Design and Implementation of Visual Campus Ramble System Based on OSG, *Computer Technology and Development,* 9(1), 217-220

Paul Martz (2008). *OpenSceneGraph Quick Start guide*

Yang Shixing, Cao Mingliang(2007). *Step Into OpenSceneGraph,* Zheng Zhou University Virtual Reality Laboratory.

Xu Ling (2008). Wu Han (China), *Research and Implementation of Roaming System Based on OpenSceneGraph Engine,* Wu Han (China), Wu Han University of Technology

FreeSouth (2008). *OpenSceneGraph Program Design,* www.osgChina.org

Tomas Akenine-Moller, Eric Haines (2004). *Real-time computer graphics,* Beijing, Beijing University Press

Liu Hongyu (2005). *Application Research on Virtual Reality System of Fully Mechanized Coalface, Su Zhao (China),* Su Zhou University

Part 8

Virtual Worlds and Human Society

31

The Otherness of Cyberspace, Virtual Reality and Hypertext[1]

Tuğrul İlter
Eastern Mediterranean University, North Cyprus

1. Introduction

The techno-cultural developments that are globally re-weaving us within satellite communication networks, the Internet, and the world wide web have also given us cyberspace, virtual reality, and hyper-text as new fabrics of culture-space-reality interaction. Coupled with an exponential growth in technological advances has been a similar mushrooming of cultural fantasies about altogether different futures.

The adjectives cyber, virtual, and hyper are meant to serve as the markers of this altogether different future, its different and other space/reality/textile. Even a traditional, calendarical distinction like a "new" millennium is infused with a magical substance by such references. We were excited about, and also scared from, the new millennium because it was supposed to mark the passage from the repetitive and familiar traditions and constraints or securities of the "old" to the "new" of this altogether different future. The reactions engendered by this excitement are Janus-faced, or, for those who are more familiar with the Batman mythology, two-faced, like the character played by Tommy Lee Jones who is called, simply, Two-Face, in the movie *Batman Forever*. Like another famous literary character, Robert Louis Stevenson's Dr. Jeykll and Mr. Hyde, Two-Face has both an evil and a good "face," and decides to do good or bad based upon the result of a coin flip. Similarly, our reactions to these developments are two-faced and contradictory in that we are both excited and scared, we lay out the welcome mat and start building and reinforcing the retaining wall, we feel both attracted and repulsed towards these developments. In the vast orientalist literature, for instance, the Orient is depicted both as an uncivilized, backward place ruled by despotic rulers, lacking freedom, and whose characteristics are the very opposite of what "we" in the West value and uphold, and yet also as an exotic place of attraction, attractive in its exoticism, both sexualized and found sexually attractive, where one can indulge beyond the reach of the restraints back "home" (See Fig. 1).

There is something of the unknown about them which triggers these reactions. Like the *terra incognita* of the Europeans during the "Age of Conquest and Discovery," cyberspace, virtual reality, and hypertext represent, in one of their guises, the freedom to break from the restraints of "our" known world, the source of much excitement. I find it significant that a very important US "civil liberties group defending [our] rights in the digital world" is called the "Electronic Frontier Foundation." The reference here is, of course, to the rapidly expanding

---

[1] A shorter, earlier version of this chapter was published in *Open House International* V32, N1, 83-88, 0168-2601.

frontier separating the young United States from "the Wild West," which was indeed a source of excitement, and represented boundless freedom to those who were part of this Westward expansion. By partaking in this boundless freedom, they were doing good, naturally, or so they thought. But to the natives, this exercise of freedom was sheer hell, wiping their land, their culture, and their freedom to write their own destiny as peoples with distinct identities—and not just as the exotic backdrop of Wild West shows, and later, movies—out of existence.

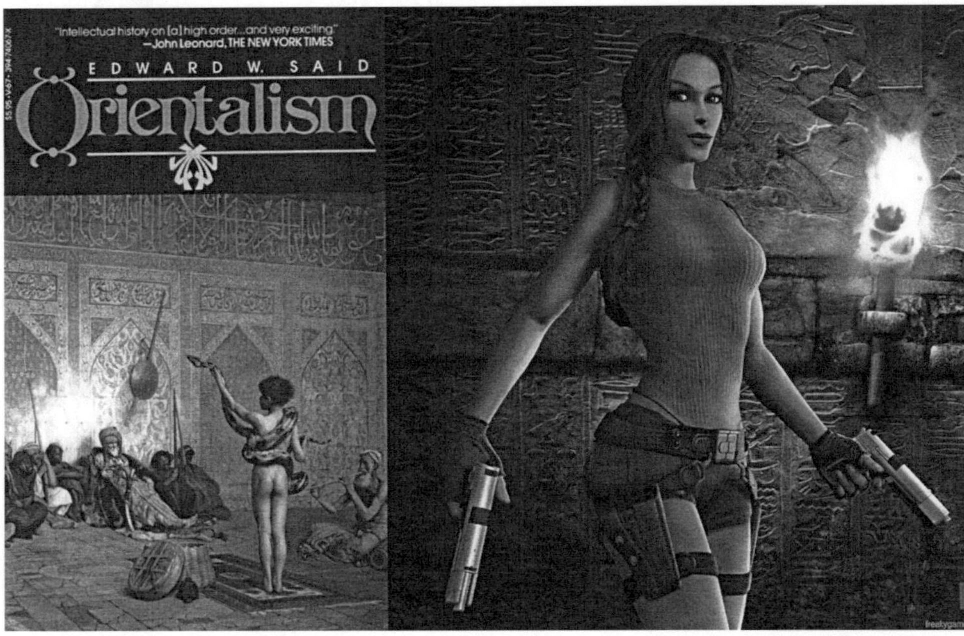

Fig. 1. The "Orient"—old and new—as an exotic place of attraction, both sexualized and and found sexually attractive.

Just as the Age of Conquest and Discovery had ushered in the age of colonialism and (capitalist) imperialism, bringing told and untold misery, including slavery, to many peoples around the world who were deemed inferior, less than human, and uncivilized with the help of highly cultivated Eurocentric lenses, this "old" story was repeated in the expansion of the "new" frontier in the US. And in these cases, we don't even have to wait for the delay of a coin-flip, or the nightfall after the day ends, for the evil "face" to show up. The "good" characters can, it seems, do evil in the very act of doing good. The evil other is not only there lurking in the shadows waiting for his/her turn after the good one, but is there at the same time. The self is thus divided both spatially and temporally, and cannot become self-identical in any fully final sense. So maybe, what we are led to see as our opposite other over there, may turn out to be mixed up with what is in us here, with what is familiar. We may recall, in this regard, a slogan from the anti-Vietnam war struggles in the US, which said, "we have seen the enemy, and it is us." In fact, is not "the external other over there" one such familiar story, but a story with a strange unfamiliarity, which we cannot quite place, within it? In the early European maps of the world, drawn during the age of discovery, their *terra incognita*, the undiscovered and unknown land, was depicted as populated by supposedly unfamiliar monster creatures, such as dragons, feeding into the peoples' fear of the unknown. However, these creatures drawn at the edges of their known world on those maps were not creatures emanating from the unknown, but they were, rather, the fantastic creations of the Europeans themselves. Thus, their very recognizability as monsters made these creatures familiar and homely. As the critique of orientalism made abundantly clear (Said, 1979), these fantastic European creations were subsequently projected onto the "lands of discovery."

In this chapter, taking the above observations as my lead, I engage with the question of the otherness of cyberspace, virtual reality, and hypertext, and how they are distinguished as "new" and altogether different. I pose the question: Are cyberspace/virtual reality/hypertext the opposite others of space/reality/text or are they, rather, the latter's iterable and itered rearticulation and retranscription?

2. The Modernist othering of cyberspace, virtual reality and hypertext

It is the novelty of cyberspace, virtual reality, and hypertext that feeds both the idolatry and the demonization or the excitement and the fear we feel towards them. They are new and modern (some would say postmodern) creations. Modern, as it is commonly construed, is a culturally biased, more specifically Euro- or West-centric, teleological concept, representing the telos of History understood as an unstoppable progressive movement from the old of the past to the new of the now, as commonly depicted in the replacement of the old year by the new on the eve of the new year. For the new to be new, it must be radically different from the old, giving it the aura of the unknown, and it is this aspect that feeds all the cultural fantasies, both anticipatory and fearful, about cyberspace, virtual reality, and hypertext.

We could begin by noting how this "new" future is distinguished by familiar binary oppositions like future vs. past and modern vs. traditional. They rely on the notion of a new that is uncontaminated by the old. Indeed, that is what the designation "modern" stands for. It is the modernist imaginary of a unilinear time, animated by a Eurocentric telos, that defines our opposites of the (advanced) modern and the (backward) traditional. Jacques Derrida (1982) refers to this mode of thought as a logocentric metaphysics of presence, which, in trying to banish its own difference or otherness inside, projects it onto a binary oppositional outside; he further specifies it as „Western" metaphysics, referring to „the activation of what is called Western thought, the thought whose destiny is to extend its domains while the boundaries of the West are drawn back" (1978, p.4), and as „the white mythology which reassembles and reflects the culture of the West" (1982, p. 213). Hence, its structure and operations are familiar. As Edward Said (1979) and others after him have shown, positioning oneself as an Oriental does not overcome the sovereignty of this Western metaphysics, since the founding reference of the Orient, the reference by which it is identified, *is* the Occident. Its binary oppositional makeup means that it cannot be opposed by a binary opposition, which rather sustains it. Derrida poses the problem of the ethnocentrism of this „Western metaphysics" from some of his earliest writings (1978, pp. 278-293, 1976 p. 4, 101-140). Much of postcolonial theory is informed by this critique.

As the modernist imaginary led to and was shaped historically by a series of revolutions in Europe, the notion of "revolution" is used as the exemplary marker of a clean break from the pre-modern past. Thus, the French Revolution of 1789 was supposed to mark a clean break with the absolutism of the *Anciént Regime*; similarly, the Turkish Republic, representing such a revolutionary break, was supposed to have nothing to do with its less-than-civilized Ottoman past; we even talked and wrote about "epistemological breaks" that marked the leaving behind of old problematics or paradigms. Louis Althusser and Etienne Balibar (1970), for instance, argue that Karl Marx's thought is fundamentally incompatible with its antecedents because of its ground-breaking epistemology. Likewise, Thomas Kuhn (1970) theorizes scientific advancement not in terms of a cumulative acquisition of knowledge, but in terms of intellectually violent revolutions in which one paradigm, a conceptual worldview, is left behind and is replaced by another. The primary reason for these intellectual revolutions is that paradigms are conceptualized as incompatible, or rather as „incommensurable" with each other.

In the orientalist mapping of the modernist imaginary, the Occident and the Orient were likewise defined in terms of an (external) ontological difference: as Rudyard Kipling put it in British colonial India, "O, East is East, and West is West, and never the twain shall meet" (quoted in Harlow & Carter, 1999, p. 207). Yet, this is precisely what is problematized in recent postcolonial and postmodern theory. Gayatri Spivak, for example, reminds us that such a categorical distinction ignores or tries to forget their inter-implicational existence throughout the past and ongoing history of imperialism, colonialism and neo-colonialism. Emphasizing the "international division of labor," Spivak (1988) draws our attention to the epistemic violence involved in the constitution of "the colonial subject as Other," and warns us against buying into "a self contained representation of Europe," as this ignores "its production by the imperialist project" (pp. 272, 280-281, 291). Elsewhere Spivak (1993) notes, "Europe's 'memory' as itself has colonialism inscribed in it; keeping contemporary Europe 'pure' cannot escape that memory" (p. 113). Hence, the production and sustenance of both the sovereign-self and its other is dependent on their respective other. Their very being is inter-implicational, making them hybrid and excessive to any identification identified in terms of a binary opposition.

In the modernist imaginary, however, the oppositions are seen as safely external to each other. The outside does not contaminate and creolize the imagined purity of the inside. Their identity as, for example, distinct periods or styles, is uncontaminated by internal difference, by hybridity, by alterity, by otherness, by each one's other. This imaginary is what leads us to write about unified and distinct periods, spaced and following each other, along a unilinear time scale. We read and write about the "Middle Ages" as a unified period that is characteristically, uniformly, categorically and thus totally in the "dark" compared to the "Enlightenment" yet to come, the handmaiden of modernity. The modern period is similarly imagined as a totalized unity in its characterization. This is in defiance of the very obvious presence of different others, styles, characteristics, figures, who do not properly "belong" in "our" modern period but whom we designate as belonging to a different period that then needs to be located in the temporal past of that unilinear, oppositional scale.

Take the designation "backward" that is used routinely to characterize individuals, peoples, nations around the world. Those characterized as backward, are then seen and understood as belonging not to the present time but to the past—as measured on the modernist unilinear, oppositional scale, they are "back" in time—and thus, the past becomes their proper place and time of existence. They become like ghosts visiting from another time, which makes their presence in the present time of the modern a virtual one. As they are also actually existing, we could perhaps say that they are actu-virtual. Their actu-virtuality, their existence in "our" time, and not in "their" time, then becomes a problem, which is to say, *they* become a problem, to be dealt with by modern means and solutions ranging from expulsion from the ranks of humanity-proper to outright elimination.[2] Let us not forget that the Nazi concentration camps

[2] As an example of the rising tide of reactionary sentiments against immigrants and refugees around Europe, it was reported in the news recently that the French President Nicolas Sarkozy proposed to strip French nationality from those who commit certain crimes, particularly targeting foreign born nationals (Reuters 30 July 2010).

and the Holocaust are examples of "modern" solutions to this "problem." Zygmunt Bauman (1996), for example, argues that the Holocaust is not exceptional, representing the acts of a madman, but that it is the logical outcome of modernist thinking. Similarly, Giorgio Agamben discusses "the Camp" as "the biopolitical paradigm of the modern" in his *Homo Sacer: Sovereign Power and Bare Life* (1988), and draws our attention to how the unusual extension of power under the pretext of "a state of emergency" or a "state of exception"—a notion whose main reference continues to be Carl Schmitt, who has been called the "the crown jurist of the Third Reich"—among Western powers after the attacks of 9/11, has the potential to transform democracies into totalitarian states in his *State of Exception* (2005).

As the word modern means contemporary, those who claim modernity for themselves claim the present for themselves as well. It is their way of making themselves present—through such culturally specific representations involving an epistemic violence toward others. Thus, those who are deemed categorically different from "us" lose their claim to the present, and become essentially and epistemologically absent in the teleologically pre-sent time, despite their physical, material, and contemporary presence. That is why it is important to highlight the ethnocentrism, or more specifically the Euro- or West-centrism of the modernist imaginary and the epistemic violence that its ethnocentrism requires (Ilter, 1994). The history of colonialism and imperialism, and its neo- variants, is also the history of the attempt to "world" the world, that is to say, to reshape and reconfigure the world according to the dictates of this modernist imaginary.[3]

In dealing with this epistemic violence, the least we can do is to note that these different others did not come to be in our present by traveling in a time machine from the past. Rather, they are our contemporaries who are epistemologically and representationally projected to the past by the modernist imaginary, by the modernist worlding of the world. They represent a difference within that does not add up to complete the full presence of the modern. On the contrary, their presence in the modern troubles our traditional and conventional conception of the modern as purely and fully self-present. Ironically, it is to save this traditional conception that the excessive difference of the modern, its difference-within, is projected to the modern's outside by means of an ethnocentric and epistemic violence. In other words, what is thereby represented as new and modern turns out to be traditional itself. The recognition of this difference-within without recourse to an epistemic violence—a prejudicial way of knowing that erases it from the inside of the present and projects it to the outside—requires a deconstructive, post-modern rearticulation of the modern. Provided we rethink the word "new," we could say that it requires a new way of understanding the modern. The "post" of this post-modern rearticulation, therefore, does not and cannot refer to another indifferent period following the modern one, for this vision of successive periods along a unilinear path is informed precisely by the modernist imaginary. If we recall that the word modern means contemporary, it becomes clear that one cannot post the modern that way, or to say it differently, posting the modern that way is perfectly modernist.[4] Rather the post of post-

[3] I owe the phrase „worlding of the world" to Gayatri Spivak (1988) who uses it in, among other places, „Can the Subaltern Speak?"

4 Hal Foster distinguishes between "a postmodernism that deconstructs modernism" and "a postmodernism which repudiates the former to celebrate the latter: a postmodernism of resistance and a postmodernism of reaction" (Foster, 1983, p. xi-xii). I am highlighting the modernist architecture of this latter "postmodernism of reaction." See also Jean-François Lyotard who writes: "This idea of a linear chronology...in the sense of a simple succession, a diachronic sequence of periods in which each one is clearly identifiable...is itself perfectly 'modern'" (Lyotard, 1992, p. 76).

modern refers us to the modern's excessive difference within that prevents its closure onto itself and which opens it to further becoming (Ilter, 1994, p. 57-58). This is necessary to prevent the canonization of modernism's own rebellion and thus the closure of its nascent incompleteness. As we shall see, this notion of openness, to becoming other and different, is precisely what is meant by virtuality.

3. Binary oppositional reaction to cyberspace, virtual reality and hypertext

The modernist worlding of the world leaves us with two opposing possibilities in greeting cyberspace, virtual reality, and hypertext. As cybertechnophile handmaidens of the future, we greet them as harbingers of a future that will singularly liberate us from the limits and constraints of our traditional past, so that our present will cease to be constrained by the past and will, instead, be shaped and guided by this new, after-the-break future. Accordingly, they represent "the technology of miracles and dreams," allowing us to "play God," in virtual reality where "we can make water solid, and solids fluid; we can imbue inanimate objects (chairs, lamps, engines) with an intelligent life of their own. We can invent animals, singing textures, clever colors or fairies." Virtual reality alone is greeted as "the hope for the next century" with the ability to "afford glimpses of heaven" (Sherman & Judkins, 1992, p. 126-7, 134).

The euphoria afforded by this other, virtual existence rests on the promise of transcendence and liberation from our material and embodied existence in the here-and-now, providing access to an infinite, transcendent, and perfect other world. In Michael Benedict's words, "cyberspace is nothing more, or less, than the latest stage in [what Karl Popper designates as] World 3 [the world of objective, real and public structures which are the not-necessarily-intentional products of the minds of living creatures] with the ballast of materiality cast away—cast away again, and perhaps finally" (Benedict, 2000, p. 31). This notion of freedom based on the transcendence of material and corporeal "constraints" conceives the relation between virtual- or cyberspace and real space as a relation of mind to body, and rests on the patriarchal, hierarchical privilege accorded to the mind in Western thought. The often heard sexist mantra, "women are emotional, men are rational," is but one expression of this view which holds that women are trapped in their bodies and their sensual experience, whereas men are able to transcend it in the ideal world of thought. Plato held that material, embodied forms are flawed, and that truth was to be found in the realm of disembodied *Ideas*. Here the mental and the physical are clearly separated, and the above mentioned representation of cyberspace as "the intentional products of the minds of living creatures with the ballast of materiality cast away" follows this line of thought. This is ironic, in that what is touted as new, finally enabling us to cast materiality away, turns out to be not new but old. It repeats a very old understanding of the relation between mind and body, which construes that relationship as mind over body, and recycles it as new.

What is also striking is that the projection of such utopian possibilities is not at all unique to cyberspace, virtual reality, and hypertext. Similar utopian promises and aspirations, as well as the fears, anxieties, and panics that I will discuss further down, have accompanied every major technological innovation since the Renaissance, and, perhaps more markedly, since the industrial revolution. Johan Gutenberg's printing press, James Watt's steam engine, the railway and its "iron horse", and assembly line production based on Taylorist "scientific management" principles were all idolized—promising a wonderful new world full of possibilities not possible before—and demonized—fearful of the dangerous consequences—at the same time, eliciting reactions of both kinds. The industrial revolution, and the techno-cultural innovations that brought it about, was welcomed by the capitalists as a fabulous means of gaining wealth. This was aided by ideologies of utilitarianism that called for the capitalists' unimpeded pursuit of profit. This, however, brought about the deterioration of the working people's lifestyles and standards of living. A number of Charles Dickens' novels, including *Oliver Twist,* depict the horrible working conditions in the factories in Britain at the time. Thus, it is not surprising that to many working people, the machine symbolized submission to a regime that exploited and oppressed them. A well-known example of workers' resistance to such exploitation comes from the so-called Luddites, who took their name from a Ned Ludd, and took to destroying mechanized looms used in the British textile industry in the early eighteen hundreds. The movement had grown so strong for a while that the Luddites clashed in battles with the British army.

When we consider how similarly these earlier techno-cultural innovations were received compared with the contemporary examples discussed above, and further in this text, these make—in an ironical twist—the newness of the new computer-based technologies in question a part of a long-standing tradition.

Regarding hypertext, for example, George Landow, writes, in a typically modernist fashion, of "a paradigm shift" that "marks a revolution in human thought" providing us with "a way into the contemporary episteme in the midst of major changes" (Landow, 1997, p. 2). Articulating the insights of designers of computer software like Theodor Nelson, who coined the word hypertext, and Andries van Dam with those of critical theorists like Roland Barthes and Jacques Derrida, Landow reaches the following understanding of their work: "All four...argue that we must abandon conceptual systems founded upon ideas of center, margin, hierarchy, and linearity and replace them with ones of multi-linearity, nodes, links, and networks" (Landow, 1997, p. 2). And yet, the commonality of their relationship is misconstrued here. These related notions of a revolution in human thought, involving a paradigm shift where old concepts are abandoned and left behind, and are replaced by new ones, are precisely what are put in question and not warranted in the works of Barthes and, especially, of Derrida—but they do fit the modernist framework outlined earlier. Derrida's deconstruction is not destruction (of the old, or of what is criticized). The critic is not located in some metaphysical outside, like God is supposed to be, but is rather located within, and as part of the very textile weave that s/he is critical of. All her critical resources, including the language of her criticism, are inheritances that s/he borrows from the very textile that is put in question. However, as Derrida puts it, inheritance is not a given but a task. In what he refers to as "iterability" (repeatability with a difference), what is repeated, the old, changes and becomes different than what it was previous to the repetition. Everything harbors an unconditional secret that can never be fully and completely revealed, and is open to its own becoming different and other. This openness to a different future, always yet to come, this irreducible potential or secret, is what virtuality is about. By the same token deconstruction draws it power from the fact that things are always-already in deconstruction. Therefore, deconstruction is not an operation done by force on things from the outside. Hence, what is deconstructed is not erased or abandoned and replaced by something else entirely, in an operation of erasure or destruction, but is, rather, displaced from its privileged hierarchical position in the binary opposition by showing how it is indeed dependent and founded upon what it allegedly excludes and does not need.

Continuing with the opposite end of the spectrum of responses to cyberspace, virtual reality, and hypertext, we see various nostalgic Luddite reactions against their growing influence and power, a growth that is seen today as threatening our humanity, liberty, and reason.

According to Arthur and Marilouise Kroker, "we are living in a decisive historical time: the era of the post-human" where "virtualization in the cyber- hands of the new technological class is all about our being dumbed down," thus preventing "a critical analysis of the public situation" whereby the human species is "humiliated" as the subject of digital culture; indeed, what "we are talking about [is] a systematic assault against the human species" involving "the harvesting of human flesh as (our) bodies and minds are reduced to a database for imaging systems" (Kroker & Kroker, 2000, p. 97- 98, 101-103). The Krokers' attempt to introduce ethical concerns regarding technological innovation is thus based on an apocalyptic vision of cyber or virtual reality. Similarly, Kevin Robins quotes approvingly Peter Weibel who describes virtuality and cyberspace as psychotic, "where the boundaries between wish and reality are blurred," and continues to mourn how in this "psychotic" space "the reality of the real world is disavowed; the coherence of the self deconstructed into fragments; and the quality of experience reduced to sensation and intoxication" (Robins, 1995, p. 143-144). Although not specifically about cyberspace, Stanley Aronowitz's discussion of computer mediated work points out how "many corporations have used [computers] to extend their panoptic worldview" and how "they have deployed the computer as a means of employee surveillance that far exceeds the most imperious dreams of the panopticon's inventor Jeremy Bentham" (Aronowitz, 1994, p. 27). And indeed, we see many such examples around us.

A friend and colleague who teaches there informs me that the mayor of Balçova, who placed surveillance cameras in this town near İzmir, Turkey, put up bilboards in the city a while ago, which said the Balçova residents need not worry (for their safety), for they are watched over round the clock. In the UK, there are reportedly more surveillance cameras per person than in any other country in the world (Lewis, 2009). In London alone there are reportedly more than 500 000 cameras at work (Wall Street Journal, July 8, 2005). We could perhaps understand the appeal of a remarkable movie like *V for Vendetta* with this background of a trend towards a panoptic social order. Based on the graphic novel by Alan Moore and David Lloyd, and directed by James McTeigue, the movie takes place in London in a near future dystopian, completely authoritarian and panoptic society. The movie tells the story of a masked and costumed freedom fighter in this police state, whose attire commemorates Guy Fawkes, who attempted to destroy the Houses of Parliament in London with a group of Catholic conspirators in 1605.

4. Common root of the opposing reactions

These two reactions at odds with each other nevertheless share a common outlook. Both their enthusiasm for the singularly liberating nature of this new future as cyber technophiles, and their Luddite resistance to its singularly fascistic and panoptic encirclement are similarly informed by the modernist worlding of the world and the binary opposition between (advanced) modern and (backward) traditional or simply between future/present and past. Whether seen as good or bad, it is agreed that cyberspace, virtual reality, and hypertext herald an otherness defined in terms of an altogether different and new future to be distinguished categorically from the existing space/reality/textuality.

Within this framework, cyberspace, virtual reality, and hypertext are portrayed as signifiers of an altogether different and new future, and yet their otherness in a binary opposition is always and necessarily a "domestic other" whose otherness is not other to the binary structure of our knowledge, but one that is defined in its terms. Thus we always-already know what the other is all about. It is the binary opposite of what we know our world, and ourselves, to be. Indeed we rely on this supplementary other to define our world and ourselves. For example, "they are traditional and backward, we are modern and advanced." Backwardness of the other, then is not an unknown that is then discovered, but it is projected from within the binary oppositional structure of what we already know. Similarly, virtual reality becomes a make-believe simulation, such as when student pilots "fly" on the ground, and not the "actual" reality of flying. It is by reference to this "real" reality that "virtual" reality assumes its immediately recognizable, hence domestic, identity as make-believe, as not-quite- real. It is significant, I think, to recall at this point that Baudrillard's definition of simulacrum as a copy without an original, together with his depiction of the real as "not only what can be reproduced, but [as] that which is always already reproduced," is undermining precisely this binary opposition: "Whereas representation tries to absorb simulation by interpreting it as false representation, simulation envelops the whole edifice of representation as itself a simulacrum" (Baudrillard, 1983, p. 11).

5. The difference that does not add-up

If the otherness of cyberspace, virtual reality, and hypertext were radically other, on the other hand, if it were "wild," so to speak, and not "domesticated," I could not give a recognizable and familiar account of it in the given terms of the binary structure of my thinking. In that case, the other exceeds my thinking. The otherness of the other is other to my domesticated, oppositional other. Such alterity then requires another kind of response. It requires a rethinking, a transformation, a further becoming of how I know the other. Only then could we speak of "new paradigms" and "new concepts and theories," and not when we embrace the domestic "new" of the modernist binary.

Furthermore, the difference between this "wild" other and the "domestic" other is not an external difference but a difference within the same word/term/concept: the other. Similarly, the differences between cyber and normal (?) space, virtual and actual (?) reality, hyper and ordinary (?) text also refer to a difference within. This difference does not refer us to the outside but is radical; it is at the root. This difference-within corresponds to the becoming of their being: to their becoming different and other to themselves. Hence, they do not have a complete, final, finished once-and-for-all being either as origin or as telos. The full presence of their being is always deferred in a ceaseless, an-archic becoming without an origin or telos. Hence, there is no original and stable reality, space, or text, to be nostalgic for, and to return to, after the "detour" of their alienation from their "real" selves. That "detour" is no detour with its sights set on a final return home to satisfy the second reaction, but, rather, a re-turn, that is, another change in direction, and another future.[5] Therefore, our notions of space, reality, and text need to be complicated and rethought to accommodate what they seem to oppose: cyberspace, virtual reality, and hypertext. To put it differently, the attributes that we project onto cyberspace, virtual reality, and hypertext are already at work in conventional space, reality, and text.

The latency and potentiality that excites us about cyberspace, virtual reality and hypertext are not their exclusive characteristics. At least since phenomenology, structuralism and poststructuralism, as well as psychoanalysis, we know that things are not self-identical and

[5] In discussing metaphor, which "is determined by philosophy as a provisional loss of meaning...a certainly inevitable detour...with its sights set on...the circular reappropriation of literal, proper meaning," Jacques Derrida argues that "de-tour is a re-turn" (Derrida, 1982, p. 270).

self-coincident, and that there is a generative, irreducible difference within them. This difference assures that things always differ from, and defer, who or what they are. Who or what they are is never complete in any final sense, but always provisional, in becoming or in process, and always to-come, always to be completed. To indicate both the spatial and temporal aspect of this difference, Derrida (1982) has coined the term *differance*, spelled with an *a* (p. 1-27). This differance is what opens things to the non-determinability of the future and gives us hope as to the coming of the new. The new is thus based on a repetition, or rather iteration, that is repetition with difference: New and repetition together. New is never altogether new, but resides or comes out in/from the old. What ties repetition to the new is the incalculable excess that Derrida (2001) also calls the absolute and unconditional secret that can never be fully and finally revealed because it is always to-come (p. 57-59).

Cyberspace, virtual reality, hypertext are not self- sufficient, self-referential entities. Rather, they are relative and differential concepts that owe their status as cyber-, virtual-, and hyper- to a reference to and a comparison with the unqualified space, reality, and text. The qualifying adjectives cyber, virtual, and hyper define them clearly as the products of a technological intervention involving miniaturized computer chips, digitalization of media products, computer hardware and software, fiber optic and other cables, satellite communication networks, Internet, the world wide web, and the like. However, it would be misleading to think that the unqualified space, reality, and text are not the products of technological interventions. The ones we designate as traditional space, reality, and text are, indeed, the outcome of older technological interventions that we have grown accustomed to, ones that we no longer see as technological, but as given conditions of everyday operations of the real (Grosz, 1997, p. 109). The border between the two is not sustainable but porous and mobile. This does not mean that they are not different, but that their difference is not external and categorical but inter-implicational.

6. Conclusion

What excites and scares us about cyberspace, virtual reality, and hypertext is their obvious incompleteness. This makes them prone to imaginary and projected futures, and suitable for dreams, hopes, and fears regarding what is yet to come. Our excitement, for instance, comes from the idea of an indeterminate, unspecifiable, and open-ended future, and the precedence of futurity over past and present. But, as Elizabeth Grosz points out, we did not have to wait for the computer screen, the Internet, and the web to enter virtual space and its domain of latency and potentiality. "We live in its shadow more or less constantly" (Grosz, 1997, p. 111). As the oxymorons virtual reality, cyberspace, and hypertext imply, virtuality already resides in reality, and space, and the characteristics attributed to hypertext are already at work in the ordinary, unqualified text.

The real/space/text are always open to the future, that is to say, open to potentialities and (re)articulations or (re)inscriptions other than those that are realized at the present, and the non-sequential, non-hierarchical attributes of hypertext are already found in the unqualified text. We could say that virtual reality/cyberspace/hypertext derive their seductive power from this possibility of the real/space/text becoming other than themselves. Therefore, it should not surprise us too much that even after introducing hypertext in terms of a "paradigm shift," a "revolution in human thought," and a "new episteme abandoning the old," that George Landow should refer to the traditional "scholarly article" in the humanities or physical sciences as the perfect embodiment of hypertext (1997, p. 4) (Fig. 2).

Social Identities 267

which is then to be fulfilled by a return to one's origin before diasporic displacement, that is to say, by a return to the mother.

And yet, the multiple and shifting determinations of the home-to-return-to, force us to recognize that this supposedly arch-original home is reinvented anew at every cultural and historical turn, for example, as Greece or Turkey in the official Motherland discourses of Greek and Turkish Cypriots, as the Cyprus of differing memories in the similarly nostalgic constructions of Turkish-Cypriot or Greek-Cypriot communities abroad, as Europe in the oppositional discourse of the Turkish Cypriot 'This Homeland is Ours' movement, and so on. The multiplicity of these more or less hegemonic identities are further multiplied and complicated by the existence of other Cypriots such as Maronites, Latin Catholics, Armenians, Arabs, Britons, as well as more recent 'postmodern' migrants with or without, and more or less, proper IDs. The crowded spectacle of Cyprus indicates that no single explanation of Cypriot identity sending one back immediately to a single arch-origin is adequate. Rather, it implies that we – living in Cyprus, studying Cyprus, and anyone dealing with identity issues – are on the in-between, liminal[10] terrain of cultural difference, hybridity, and alterity, where the addition of the differences does not make a singular whole but which exceeds all such claims to wholeness at either the communal or national, or even international, regional levels. And once the liminality of Cyprus-space is established, the threat of cultural difference is no longer a threat posed by 'other' people, strangers or 'enemies' outside the territorial borders established to separate 'them' from 'us', and to keep 'them' from harming or otherwise contaminating the purity and unity of 'us'. Rather, it becomes a question of the otherness of that very 'people-as-one' (Bhabha, 1990, p. 301). Cultural difference resides in, nay, houses the people-as-one; it is, indeed, constitutive of the people-as-one. Hence, people-as-one is always already hybrid and 'contaminated' by otherness; hybridity is *not* the result of the mixture of two distinct identities that are themselves devoid of difference and alterity.

Both the Greek Cypriots in the internationally recognized Republic of Cyprus and the Turkish Cypriots in the internationally unrecognized Turkish Republic of Northern Cyprus affirm their national identity in diasporic terms by reference to a 'real' mother elsewhere, identified as Greece in the former and as Turkey in the latter (Figure 1).[11] Both republics put up the flags of their respective mothers alongside their own and sing the national anthem of their 'proper' mothers as their own. In his

Figure 1. Phallic mothers or 'Mine is bigger than yours'. William Elias Papas, 15 February 1964. © Guardian News & Media Ltd 1964.

Fig. 2. Landow upholds the traditional scholarly article (example on right) as the perfect embodiment of hypertext.

The interimplication of both sides of our opposition virtual reality/cyberspace/hypertext versus reality/space/text calls on us not to be content with, say, the domesticated otherness of the former as the representative of the emergent future as opposed to the latter's stagnant traditionality, but rather to rethink the latter to accommodate the excluded features attributed to the former. In an example of such rethinking, Donna Haraway argues that the figure of the cyborg is our ontology, that is to say, it does not belong to a future-yet-to-come, but to the always-already here and now (Haraway, 2000, p. 292). Her thesis, thus, involves a rethinking, a retranscription, and a reformulation of our ontology. Moreover, the deconstruction of the modernist teleology means that there is no predetermined teleological destiny inscribed in these new technologies either as a powerful force of liberation or as fascistic and panoptic encirclement, but, rather, that they imply the possibility of both—which is to say that they are like the old technologies in this respect as well. Therefore, our active participation in the orientation and reweaving of the textile fabric of the cyberspace could mean the difference between one or the other.

7. References

Agamben, G. (2005). *State of Exception* (K. Attell, Trans.), The University of Chicago Press, 0-226-00925-4, Chigaco and London.

Agamben, G. (1998). *Homo Sacer: Sovereign Power and Bare Life* (D. Heller-Roazen, Trans.), Stanford University Press, 0-8047-3218-3, Stanford California.

Althusser, L. & E. Balibar (2009). *Reading Capital,* (B. Brewster, Trans.), Verso, 978-1-84467-347-6, London and New York.

Aronowitz, S. (1994). Technology and the Future of Work. In: *Culture on the Brink*, G. Bender & T. Druckrey (Eds.), 15-29, Bay Press, 0-941920-28-3, Seattle.

Baudrillard, J. (1983). *Simulations* (P Foss, P. Patton, and P. Beitchman, Trans.), Semiotext(e), 0-936756-02-0, New York.

Bauman, Z. (1996). *Modernity and the Holocaust.* Cornell University Press, Ithaca, New York. 0-8014-8032-9

Benedict, M. (2000). Cyberspace: First Steps. In: *The Cybercultures Reader*, D. Bell & B. M. Kennedy (Eds.), 29-44, Routledge, 0-415-18379-0, London and New York.

Derrida, J. and M. Ferraris (2001). *A Taste For the Secret*, (G. Donis, Trans.), Polity, 0-7456-2334-4, Cambridge.

Derrida, J. (1982). *Margins of Philosophy* (A. Bass, Trans.), The University of Chicago Press, 0-226-14325-2, Chicago.

Derrida, J. (1978) *Writing and Difference*, (A. Bass, Trans.), The University of Chicago Press, 0-226-14329-5, Chicago and London.

Derrida, J. (1976). *Of Grammatology*, (G. C. Spivak, Trans.), The Johns Hopkins University Press, 0-8018-1879-6, Baltimore and London.

Foster, H. (1983). Postmodernism: A Preface. In: *The Anti-Aesthetic: Essays on Postmodern Culture*, H. Foster (Ed.), ix-xvi, Bay Press, 0941920-01, Port Townsend, Washington.

Grosz, E. (1997). Cyberspace, Virtuality, and the Real: Some Architectural Reflections. In: *Anybody*, C. C. Davidson (Ed.), 109-117, The MIT Press, 0262540886, Cambridge, Massachusetts.

Haraway, D. (2000). A Cyborg Manifesto: Science, Technology and Socialist Feminism in the Late Twentieth Century. In: *The Cybercultures Reader*, D. Bell & B. M. Kennedy (Eds.), 29-44, Routledge, 0-415-18379-0, London and New York.

Harlow, B. & Carter, M. (Eds.) (1999). *Imperialism & Orientalism: A Documentary Sourcebook*, Blackwell Publishers, 1-55786-711-9, Oxford.

Kroker, A. & Kroker, M. (2000). Code Warriors: Bunkering In and Dumbing Down. In: *The Cybercultures Reader*, D. Bell & B. M. Kennedy (Eds.), 96-103, Routledge, 0-415-18379-0, London and New York.

Kuhn, T. S. (1970). *The Structure of Scientific Revolutions* (Second edition, enlarged), The University of Chicago Press, 0-226-45804-0, Chicago and London.

Landow, G. P. (1997). *Hypertext 2.0: The Convergence of Contemporary Critical Theory and Technology*, The Johns Hopkins University, 0-8018-5586-1, Baltimore and London.

Ilter, T. (1994). The Unassimilable Otherness of the "Post" of Post-modern and the Radicality of Radical Sociology. In: *Critical Sociology* V20, N2, 51-80, 0896-9205.

Lewis, P. (2009). Every Step You Take: UK Underground Centre that is Spy Capital of the World. The Guardian, March 2, 2009.

Lyotard, J. (1992). *The Postmodern Explained: Correspondence 1982-1985* (Don Barry, Bernadette Maher, Julian Pefanis, Virginia Spate, and Morgan Thomas, Trans.), University of Minnesota Press, 0-8166-2211-6, Minneapolis and London.

Robins, K. (1995). Cyberspace and the World We Live In. *Body & Society*, V1, N3-4, 135-155.

Said, E. W. (1979). *Orientalism*, Vintage Books, 0-394-74067-X, New York.

Sherman, B. & Judkins, P. (1992). *Glimpses of Heaven, Visions of Hell: Virtual Reality and Its Implications*, Hodder and Stoughton, London. 0340569050

Spivak, G.C. (1993). Outside in the Teaching Machine. Routledge, New York and London. 0415964822

Spivak, G.C. (1988). Can the subaltern speak? In C. Nelson & L. Grossberg (Eds.), *Marxism and the Interpretation of Culture* (pp. 271-313). University of Illinois Press, 0252014014, Urbana and Chicago.

32

Actual Policing in Virtual Reality – A Cause of Moral Panic or a Justified Need?

Katalin Parti
National Institute of Criminology, Hungary

1. Introduction

This study aims to describe those aspects that qualify a form of behaviour as a crime in the virtual communities, these highly organised societies of the Internet. But the image of deviances may not be complete without entities watching over them. It is an interesting question, who could lay down and enforce virtual norms, if not the community itself. Today, organised crime, drug trafficking, money laundering, trafficking in human beings, and sexual exploitation of children are such focal issues of criminal law, whose prosecution does not stop at the boundaries of virtual communities, or the Internet. But what justification does the real world's jurisdiction have to intervene in the everyday life of independent virtual communities? If they have the right, who decides on the involvement of real authorities? What legal regulations does real-life law enforcement apply in a virtual space? Is there an appropriate response to crimes committed in the virtual world by real-life jurisdiction, and can different forms of virtual deviance be prevented with the tools of real-life crime prevention? These are the questions that I wish to answer in the followings.

2. Types of virtual communities

There are several attempts at classifying *online* communities. Williams believes that online communities are defined by technical development.[1] (Williams, 2010) The first phase of development is web 1.0, where users communicate with each other using electronic mailing systems, newsgroups and instant messages (e.g. MSN messenger). These platforms are static websites whose aim is forwarding textual information. Web 2.0 technology goes a little further than that, involves real-time interpersonal interaction and web content generation appears. Users may edit the contents of a webpage themselves. The more content there is, the greater the demand for the democratisation of content (e.g. wikis, blogs, social networking sites such as Facebook, MySpace, eBay, Bebo). The next step, web 3.0 technology is just taking shape today. This technology makes online interactivity more realistic, life-like and direct with its 3D graphic surfaces (e.g. Second Life, Habbo Hotel, Active Worlds). Users may enter these online surfaces represented by their virtual alteregos, the avatars. Most of these worlds allow their users several activities mimicking reality, such as for

[1] "*Web is increasingly socialized*" - notes Williams.

example buying a real estate or building a house in the virtual space, and having virtual movables. (Williams, 2010)
Reynolds classifies today's virtual realities as follows (*Four World Theory)*. There are online realities whose essence lies in playing together (ludic worlds), based on the rules set by the maker of the game. These communities can not change their rules, and those who do not like the given world may leave (e.g. World of Warcraft). But 'games' in a less traditional sense have also appeared. These communities copy the social order of the real world (social or civic worlds; e.g. Habbo Hotel, Second Life). The rules in these virtual worlds are laid down by the operator of the platform, but the users may have a much greater influence on the rules of civic worlds, and therefore they have more independence. Civic worlds are the closest copies of the geographical world. (Reynolds, 2005)
Groups of people, who not only support their current offline lives with new technological developments, but go a step further, and use thechnology to create and live a new life, are called virtual realities (VR) in Williams' theory. (Williams, 2006) VR is a graphically developed, virtual online social space created in a 3D environment.
In my interpretation, all users of the Internet are part of some online community. These may be e-mailing communities, but also websites, forums, chatrooms and online games or virtual communities modelled on reality (social or civic communities). Online communities, just as offline (geographical) communities are held together by shared interests, sociability, dialogue and the continuity and regularity of joint action. All Internet users belong to one or another community at their level, and all users of the Internet have the opportunity to overstep the limits of communities of various organisational levels, and join new communities. (For instance, users of Second Life[2] regularly keep contact with each other and other communities on other platforms – forums, chatrooms, websites and e-mails. Boellstorff, 2008)
In the following, I wish to discuss those online forms of deviance that occur in highly organised **civic** and **social worlds.** These well-developed online communities are modelled on reality, both in their technical realisation (3D visualisation), and objectives (making contact, the experience of being part of a community, and the recreation of the rules of traditional community life). I will attempt to describe the forms of deviance, the reasons of crime, the nature of harm, and the legality and effectiveness of the intervention of geographic jurisdiction.

3. Where does virtual harm begin?

3.1 The concept of harm in virtual worlds

Williams classifies harms occuring in online communities. (Williams, 2006) According to him, there are **1. cybercrimes, 2. cyber deviances, and 3. cyber harms.** While a cybercrime is a black letter crime procesuted by geographical criminal law and authorities, cyber deviances and cyber harms are harms caused in VR. Cyber harm is an activity which damages or offends one particular member of the community, but does not obviously violate everybody's idea of morals in general. In contrast, cyber deviance is a harmful act which the whole or the majority of the community but at least its leading personalities

[2] Second Life invented and created by Linden Laboratory Inc. California is a 3D social/civic space on the Internet. As its name implies, it is a virtual world in which members create an avatar and then use that character to live out a separate existence.

consider to be subversive for the community and as such, intolerable. We can also see that acts of one category sometimes turn into another. In relation to the spread of all annoying acts, it is more common for cyber harms to turn into deviances, and deviances into cybercrimes, than the other way round. The case of online harassment is a good example. Offline legal regulations already foresee punishment for the online forms of hate speech. Or let us take ageplay, the sexual exploitation of children[3] in the virtual world which used to be an isolated phenomenon with fews cases, but these days acts committed in VR are prosecuted in line with geographical legal regulations. These responses are justified by political, legal and social pressure, when the state is of the opinion that they have to do something against the situation considered to be 'unbearable' by certain interest groups. More 'esoteric' (not tangible, less clearly outlined) and less grave acts are left to the judgement of online communities. (Williams, 2006) These are the acts that later turn into offline criminal acts, which are grave enough to go beyond the limitations of response of online communites. (Williams, 2006)

The problem is that in many cases it is impossible to decide, whether cyber harm and cyber deviance qualify as cybercrime, and as such whether it is subject to the state's obligation to enforce criminal law, for the protection of its citizens. To give you a better idea of the confusion, let us see first what kind of deviances may occur in VR and what sets them apart from geographical crimes.

There have been many and varied attempts to classify cyber deviances. (See for instance Williams, 2006; 2010; Wykes, 2010) One of the better known classifications is given by Wall. (Wall, 2001) According to him, the first group is **cyber trespass** (information warfare: invasion of private space on the Internet by a hacker causing data loss and possibly economic standstill). The second group is **cyber theft** (spoofing, phishing, pharming, identity theft, cyber copyright infringement), where the user poses as an avatar of someone else which is achieved by hacking a user's account. (Williams, 2010) The third group is **cyber obscenity** (legal pornography and sexual misuse of children). (Rimm, 1995; Mehta & Plaza, 1997; Harmon & Boeringer, 1997) The fourth group is **cyber violence** (manifests in textual, visual and audio forms) which can be further divided as follows.

1. Flaming: debates on message boards and e-mails, containing text messages about others to a humiliating and libeleous effect. (Joinson, 2003)
2. Hate speech digital performances: digital performances inciting hatred, e.g. racist, homophobic or extremist websites. (Mann et al., 2003)
3. Online stalking: harassment through computer mediated communication (CMC) for the purpose of gaining information, intimidation, or simply contact with a non-consenting person. (Reno, 1999; Bocij, 2004; Meloy, 1998)
4. Virtual rape: while the stalker only sends messages, the virtual rapist brings the victim to act against his or her will.[4] (MacKinnon, 1997; Reid, 1999; Dibbel, 1998)

In my interpretation, there are **two underlying deviances in the virtual world**, depending on whether the actual (psychological or physical) damage is to the affected person or the

[3] The politically correct name of the phenomenon known from the media as 'child pornography'is 'child sexual abuse'. 'Pornography' assumes that the parties involved are equal, while a contact of sexual nature with a child is always abuse.

[4] One form of virtual rape is when the offender animates avatars against the wishes of their owners, and controls them to do humiliating things, e.g. entering a sexual relationship with another avatar against their will.

property created/represented by him/her. In that sense, slander, defamation, contribution to suicide, bodily harm, manslaughter, or crimes against sexual morals, among others, are forms of deviance against persons. Deviances against property are mainly causing financial damage, e.g. theft, copying without permission, damaging and destruction of objects created by avatars. Vandalism can belong to any of the two, depending on the nature of the damage caused.

3.1.1 Deviances against the person in virtual worlds

Judging **virtual deviances against persons** on the basis of geographical law is complicated, since the 'person' is missing, and the user is only present and contacting others in VR through his/her virtual alterego, but not in person. (Wall bases his opposites, cybercrime and meatcrime, on the same logic. Wall, 2010) For this reason, we could possibly treat crimes in the virtual world as attempts perpetrated on an unsuitable subject or with an unsuitable instrument. Practice, however, shows that this approach is misleading.

Deviances against persons are particularly dangerous, because the individual may sustain serious **psychological scars** even during textual communication. In the virtual world, textual communication is the substitute of verbal self-expression. Communication plays a role in identifying a person's place in social hierarchy. Hate speech can be especially destructive. (Becker et al., 2000; Matsuda et al., 1993; Butler, 1997) Hate speech, slander and defamation appear in online communities both as illocutionary and perlocutionary acts. (Austin, 1975) It is possible that a verbal (textual) insult only achieves its effect, when the addressee reads it. This may be immediate - typically in 3D social/civic community spaces - , or delayed, - e.g. when the addressee opens the message sent in an e-mail or posted on a message board. In CMC, real time conversation means that the addressee receives the message immediately, at the same time as it was written, which has an immediate effect. This is characteristic of most interactions in online communities. The text is however supplemented with emoticons, and phatic communication (e.g. using capitals for shouting). Because online communication is so expressive, it is no coincidence, that terrestrial law has conquered the online world with a ban on hate speech. The reason for this is that online texts may cause greater damage than spoken words. Online texts are written, can be re-read, and therefore get more deeply imprinted on the mind of the victim, moreover they invariably leave a trace on the Internet. At the same time, it is possible that the defamatory message is read by others which may unstabilise the individual's position and reputation in the community. (Markham, 1998; Turkle, 1995; MacKinnon, 1997) The offensive remarks put the opportunity of change and the control into the hands of the offender, who becomes a person of authority. (Delgado, 1993)

3.1.2 Deviances against property (of financial nature) in virtual worlds

Users may not only suffer psychological, but also actual **financial damage** in virtual worlds. Residents of virtual communities are often looking for opportunities to create themselves. (Oldenburg, 1999, quoted by Williams, 2006) In the virtual space, residents are free to create. They may pursue any creative, and at the same time lucrative business activity, like building houses, writing scripts for furniture, other pieces of home equipment and decorations, and for the appearance of avatars (scripting, fashion designing, motion design for avatars). Just like in the geographical world, residents of virtual communities can live on their takings from services sold. (Boellstorff, 2008) As residents may also trade their goods and services, the creation of goods is not merely a channel for self-expression, but also a job, as it represents financial value. Residents have no limitations in 'building', there is no central power that would limit creative self-expression for political or economic reasons. Virtual space is therefore also called **creationist capitalism**, where work is not compulsory, but a leasure activity, or even the primary form of self expression. This is why Boellstorff calls the internal structure of online communities playful capitalism, or ludocapitalism, where "production is melting into play". (Boellstorff, 2008: 206) Hence, in virtual worlds, the development of skills corresponds to the production of goods. This was the ideology that lead the creators of several virtual spaces to enable users to convert their income from virtual goods into an offline currency.[5] The creationist capitalism aspect of virtual worlds is further strengthened by the migration of business activities into the realm of the Internet. This is what Yar calls informational economy. (Yar, 2010, referring post-industrial capitalism at Bell, 1999, and Castells, 2002)

As we can see, virtual space is a free space which enables users to express themselves while generating financial profit. The larger the profit generated, the higher the risk of the creator. Financial gain gives a basis to possibly damaging actions. It is therefore indubitable that one may suffer damage in the virtual space, just as in the real world, through the loss, damage or destruction of goods created.

3.1.3 Cyber vandalism

The above classification should be completed with **cyber vandalism which neither fits into the category of deviances purely against property, nor those purely against persons**. Virtual vandalism means that the offender damages or destroys objects created and/or possessed by avatars, but this may cause psychological damage as well. When virtual objects are vandalised, they are not destroyed for good, as the scripts and codes can be restored, but there is damage done, of a material or psychological nature, if objects of sentimental value, such as gravestones, religious artefacts, devotional articles, or souvenirs are destroyed. (Williams, 2004)

In VR, constructions are a symbol of affiliation, as the act of building is also a symbol of belonging to the community. The vandalisation of institutions symbolising the community (buildings, memorial sites or tablets) is a means of renouncing community existance and breaking down community cohesion. (Williams, 2010) The more such attacks there are, the more fragmented the community becomes, as people are less happy to participate in community activities if the symbols of belonging are regularly vandalised. (For 'avoidance behaviour' of community members see Williams, 2006: 81, 83) If the community is weakened, online friendships will also weaken, and these are the essence of an online community. If we accept that online friendships are just as important as offline ones, then any harm done to online friendships may be just as painful a loss as losing a friend or the entire community in the offline world. Similarly, if a formal police building is created in the online world, it reassures the community, can be a means of prevention, and also strengthens ties to the community.

The umbrella term for the different forms of cyber vandalism that is **virtual violence against persons and objects** – or put simply 'causing disturbance to others' – is **griefing.**

[5] Sims Online was the first virtual space based on creationist capitalism. In 2004, 99% of objects were created by residents. (Ondrejka, 2004) Inspired by that, Second Life, launched in 2003, follows the strategy of a user-created inworld exclusively.

(Boellstorff, 2008; Williams, 2010) This may be a criminal or sub-criminal act, that is a crime or a deviance. For example, sending unsolicited e-mails with obscene, intimidating, or abusive content, or the publication of the personal data of an individual on a message board (data theft), which may lead to unsolicited contact, or libel and defamation (personal harm). But it may also involve the commission of deviant activities under the name of the assumed personality, and pretended friendships and business relations.[6] **Boellstorff believes that griefing** is 1. an intentional action 2. which is aimed at disturbing others, 3. that the griefer enjoys. (Boellstorff, 2008; Foo, 2004; Mulligan & Patrovsky, 2003) This stems in the fact that in online communities people are freed of their inhibitions (disinhibition). A positive manifestation of this is when people are altruistic, kind, and a negative one if "people think they can shoot and run", they can not be identified anyway. Anonymity makes offenders unscrupulous, and this also helps them to keep the victim depersonalised, and neutralise their deeds. (Curtis, 1992) Griefing never harms the victim in his actual physical form, it is therefore less frightening, less grave than its offline counterpart. The harasser and the harassed do not meet in person, and in most cases the harassment is in written form, and not in person. Other senses are not involved (such as smell, touch, vision and hearing). (Williams, 2010) So people can not be harmed physically by greifing, but on the other hand, it may cause serious financial damage, if for example griefing is used in business activities.

3.2 Contact points of virtual and geographical deviances

As we see, the concept of harm is somewhat different from the usual norms of the geographical world. In the VR, the concept of damage and harm is to be viewed in an abstract sense. There is for example no damage done if a suicide bomber blows himself up, as it does not endanger the lives of other avatars. It is another question that the users created the objects destroyed or damaged in such an attack with actual financial investments, and therefore there may be material damage. The users themselves behind the avatars, however, do not suffer any personal damage.

According to some research, cyber deviances do not always remain within the realm of online worlds, but can **migrate** to offline environments. (Quayle, 2010; Williams, 2006) A real world manifestation of griefing may be offline bullying, or teasing. (Schechner, 1988) Online stalking may give rise to offline stalking. John Robinson, who became known in the online community Cyberworld as Slavemaster was arrested in June 2000 by Kansas State police. He had several victims offline. The last of them was Susette Trouten, a member on Cyberworlds. Both of them participated in sado-masochistic rituals in the online community. Suzette also met the offender, who later killed him, offline. (ABCNews.com, 2000) Cyberworlds created a whole philosophy and phantasy world around sado-maso games, whose believers also realised their acts offline. Suzette Trouten fell victim to these. Reno believes that online stalking can be especially dangerous, as it may be a prelude to its physical manifestation. (Reno, 1999)

[6] Boellstorff presents a whole array of griefing. The amassing of junk in the online community space is a form of griefing, just like placing provocative objects (e.g. giant dildos) in central community spaces, but the mobbing of an avatar and talking to him abusively, or sending abusive, threatening, or intimidating instant messages to several residents are also forms of mobbing. It is particularly disturbing if the avatars are animated against the wishes of their owners, and are made to perform humiliating things. (Boellstorff, 2008)

According to research, it is not advisable to play down virtual harms. In 3D virtual communities **stronger bonds** may develop **than in earlier online communities** only based on textual communication (message boards, bulletin boards, etc.) as the virtual representation of the self appears here, which, together with emote commands deepens feelings and interactivity. (Bocij, 2004) Other research go even further than that, and claim that in the virtual world, **stronger community bonds than in the geographical world** may develop. In real life, we are constantly busy working and taking care of other important things, and we are performance oriented. As opposed to that, in the virtual world, we are more free, have more time, also to pay attention to others, as we are spending our leasure time at the online community. This makes people in the VR more open, more accepting, friendly, and even altruistic. (Boellstorff, 2008) An alternative social arena serves the very purpose of preventing and replacing the dysfunctional social relationships in the offline world. (Oldenburg, 1999) The bond has a significance in defining the **degree of harm**. The stronger the bond to the community, the greater the harm suffered.

We saw now that **virtual and actual are not clearly separated**. Either because online deeds may lead to offline ones, or because the online acts may cause actual psychological or financial damage in the real world. But it is impossible to establish the extent of the harm done in a virtual world. One of the reasons for this is that geographical harm-conception is not taken over one-to-one and also due to statistical problems.

4. Legislative trend – a shift to the virtual

4.1 The actors of moral panic

There are **no reliable statistics** for virtual crimes due to their complexity and their judgement varying from country to country. There are records available, but these mainly contain data collected primarily for financial and less for criminal law reasons, their data fields are not always compatible which makes comparisons impossible. (Wall, 2001) Damage suffered in an online environment very often does not materialise, and if there is material damage, it is very difficult to assess. (Wall, 2008; Moitra, 2003)

There may be no reporting if the victims are not aware of the attack, (Murff, 2007; Moitra, 2003) or perhaps the given country is not yet prepared for registering attacks carried out in computer systems, or the given act is not punishable under applicable law, or there is no forum (administrator or VR community arbitration) where the victim could report to. It is also possible that the victim has reported an offence, but the party entitled to judge the complaint believes there is no need for further measures in the case. Cybercrimes are defined in different ways in the criminal codes of different countries, even though the Council of Europe and the European Union made considerable efforts to unify legislation for laying the foundations of international criminal cooperation and the more effective prosecution of crimes.[7] The development of technology, however, is far more progressing than legislation, so acts may occur which have not been defined properly by law. (Lacey, 2002) Such is for example harassment in a virtual environment which according to

[7] The Council of Europe's treaty on cybercrimes adopted in Budapest on November 23, 2001 can be regarded as the first significant global unification agreement. (Convention on Cybercime, CETS. No. 185 - 23.XI.2001.) At European Union level, Council Framework Decision 2004/68/JHA of 22 December 2003 on combating the sexual exploitation of children and child pornography is the most significant effort. (OJ L 13/44-8)

geographical law, is not obviously classified as a crime. (Online harassment is very often only meant to disturb, and does not always contain an intimidation element. Geographical law, however, almost always demands an emotional effect for the act to qualify as harassment. See Bocij, 2004) The fact that there is no exact statistical data on the volume of deviances occurring in virtual spaces, only further increases the panic, as it may give the impression that virtual deviances are not transparent and uncontrollable. (Wall, 2008)

Overemphasising the negative effects of the Internet and its virtual communities is basically generating moral panic. This is where the responsibility of **traditional media** shows (I refer to the press, radio, and television as traditional media, offering pre-filtered contents to the audiences). Traditional media are true catalyst of moral panic, because by the very principles of their operation, it enhances the panic effect. Only shocking, scandalous or scary information has any newsworthiness. These media present such information in a pre-filtered manner, lifted out of the original context. Programmes that expressly emphasise the *fact* of downfall of morals, of the crisis of values and of the moral crisis further add to this. (Parti, 2010)

However, not only media news trigger panic. **Scientific research** on changes of behaviour in relation to the new medium, the Internet, can also fuel moral panic. Science may be objective in its principles, but it still can not explain a lot of phenomena, or predict their effects (see e.g. what an effect the presence in a VR community may have on the personality), and in such cases resorts to guesswork when looking for arguments and consequences.

Aversions towards cyber-communities are born out of the threat of emerging cyber-deviances. A cyber-deviance in general means the adjustment to the online environment coupled with double moral standards. Double moral standard (Michelet, 2003) means that the majority of users traditionally respects accepted norms, but in VR communities they live by different standards (e.g. they would not steal a mobile phone or a bag, but they have no qualms about downloading copyrighted software which is also illegal). These double moral standards are nourished by people's faith in anonymity that is the belief that the parties communicating online are unidentifiable.

Some social scientists even claim that the spread of online communication leads to the complete decline of existing moral values. The reason for this is the mass appearance of harmful contents on the Internet and their availability to anyone, especially youngsters. Such contents – like pornography, xenophobia, incitement to hatred or extremist ideas – were not available to anyone before the Internet age and were very difficult to spread. As by now everybody can potentially access these materials, they are becoming increasingly extreme due to the competition.

Moral panic is not only society's spontaneous reaction to the spread of a disturbing activity (deviance) or a new phenomenon. Such are for example today's moral panic reactions to the Internet as new technology, and the media. Some believe that causing panic is a means of governments in general to manage new, earlier unknown social symptoms. Panic can therefore also be an artificially generated balancing power, and as such, a means of prevention. (Parti, 2009) Moral panic, whatever triggers it, is suitable for repeatedly developing people's self-control.

Causing panic at government level can be justified less with the publication of perceived or actual facts or suppositions, than with intentions of prevention. Frank Füredi in his book on risk society (Füredi, 1997) elaborates that in a 'culture of fear' our interpersonal relations become dangerous. Above all, we have to concentrate on maintaining our private sphere, as that is the most likely to be affected. Füredi says that hysterisation keeps appearing in new areas.[8] This is, however, primarily not related to the dissemination of knowledge and information, but prevention. For example, The US government did not tell the truth, when they labelled AIDS as the greatest risk of homosexuals. (Füredi, 1997) Looking back, however, society tolerates this 'benign lie', because the government could only move people to practice self-moderation and self-control with this exaggerated prevention campaign. With this purpose in mind, it is not so obvious anymore whether in a similar situation we should tell the truth, or make use of a white lie as a means of prevention. According to another branch of the consciously caused panic theory which in many respects is similar to panic triggered by the media, moral panic is a means to maintain political power. This is similar to panic caused by the media in that both use panic as a means to achieve their own goals. (Korinek, 2006)

Garland and Simon (Garland, 2001; Simon, 2007) believe that politicians and crime prevention policy makers use this panic for tactical purposes, for crime prevention and risk control. They use the same tactics for cybercrime which is not surprising at all. Taipale calls the fear of technology FrankenTech. (Taipale, 2006) The developers of technology are often involved in crime prevention policies (including activists and the media), and it is in their interest to exaggerate the threat of cybercrime, as it sells their products. The gap between the expected (perceived) threat and the security-measures corresponds to the gap lying between the numerous cybercrime cases reported by media and the few actually solved by law enforcement. This is a so called 'reassurance gap' that needs to be bridged. (Innes 2004) A typical example for the need for reassurance is the public's need for stricter and more detailed legal regulations and police action. This is obviously impossible to realise, because it is not only the supposedly large number of crime and their wide-spread nature that is missing, but also the police forces are more prepared for mass response to crimes already committed than prevention and monitoring of those in the grey zone. (Wall, 2007)

Legislation on the new medium - even though only indirectly - also contributes to the deepening of the moral panic. Legislation is always based on scientific research and consultation with experts, but it can not shake off the effect of politics either. **Political interests** always try to ensure that public opinion prevails, and are certainly under pressure from the public opinion. For this reason, legislation also can not remain completely unaffected by the moral trends triggered by the feeling of panic. (Parti, 2010)

Legislation trends in recent times point to the penalisation of an ever wider circle of acts, the criminalisation of preparatory acts, and the exaggerated regulation of details.

4.2 The reverberations of moral panic in legislation – through the example of child sexual abuse

Of all waves of panic, perhaps the most pervasive is related to the sexual exploitation of children. (Jenkins, 1998). A research of Carnegie Mellon Univesity (Rimm, 1995) found in the early 1990s, that about half of all Internet content is of pornographic nature. Even though since then, this research has been proven to be methodologically flawed, it is still regarded

[8] Such is for example the sincerety of romantic relationships - can we believe it will last?; the safety of single women - will men really protect them, or rather bring more danger?; genetic engineering - what effects do genetically modified foods have on our body and environment?; state-of-the-art technologies - is it safe to use air conditioners in the office, or on an airplane?; Internet communication - is it safe, or does it lead to the abuse of our data?

as the moral panic genesis of the Internet. The moral panic is, however, not entirely unfounded, as with the advent of the Internet the online sex industry started to develop explosively and still has a huge financial potential. (Wall, 2001; Casey, 2004) This created a never-before-seen competition situation online, so that the pornography industry is forced to make its products more extreme, just to maintain demand. This extremisation mainly shows in the increasingly lower age of the actors. (Parti, 2010) Another element of the pornography panic is that consumers may become immune or indifferent to traditional pornography. The usual contents are not enough for old consumers, they always want something new and more exciting. Also, Internet users not consuming pornography are involuntarily faced with it online with increasing regularity which leads to a gradual desensitisation towards extreme contents. The following table shows how the nature of pornography has developed as a cause of the rise of the Internet.

When?	The audience of pornography	General opinion on pornography	Social attitude
Before the Internet	Targeted groups: marketeers, black market, news agents, buyers of erotic literature, visitors of video rental shops	'Extreme'	Excluding, rejecting
After the appearance and spread of the Internet	Groups are not specifically targeted: everybody with an Internet connection	'Ordinary'	Tolerant, accepting

Table: The transformation of pornography with the appearance of the Internet (Parti, 2010)

Panic also shows in legislation. The most recent examples for these are the European Council's Convention on Cybercrime adopted on 23 November 2001 (hereinafter Cybercrime Convention), Council Framework Decision 2004/68/JHA of 22 December 2003 on combating the sexual exploitation of children and child pornography (hereinafter Framework Decision), the Council of Europe Convention on the Protection of children against sexual exploitation and sexual abuse adopted on 25 October 2007 in Lanzarote[9] (hereinafter Lanzarote Convention), and the recommendation of the Committee on Civil Liberties, Justice and Home Affairs to the EP (hereinafter 2009 proposal for a EP recommendation).[10]

[9] Council of Europe Convention on the protection of children against sexual exploitation and sexual abuse (CETS. No. 201 – 25. X. 2007)

[10] Committee on Civil Liberties, Justice and Home Affairs' report with a proposal for a European Parliament recommendation to the Council on combating the sexual exploitation of children and child pornography (2008/2144(INI)) 26.01.2009; See also: European Parliament recommendation of 3 February 2009 to the Council on combating the sexual exploitation of children and child pornography (2008/2144(INI)) On 29 March 2010 the European Commission adopted a proposal for a new Directive on combating sexual abuse, sexual exploitation of children and child pornography. It follows up a previous proposal tabled in 2009. The Directive, if approved, will replace the Framework Decision 2004/68/JHA.

The Cybercrime Convention, the Framework Decision and the Lanzarote Convention regard all depictions of child sexual abuse as criminal. The objects of commission do not only include depictions of existing minors, but realistic images representing a minor, and also depictions of persons appearing to be a minor engaged in sexually explicit conduct.[11] Despite the above, the applicable law of different countries is not unified: not only visual or **graphic depictions**, but textual descriptions (Germany, see Sieber 1999), and voice recordings (answering machines) can be an act of commission too (Switzerland, see Suter-Zürcher, 2003). Hungary, where the act of commission of child pornography has a narrow definition only punishes the pornographic depiction of *existing* minors. At the same time, mainly in the youngest member states of the EU, such as Slovenia, Romania or Bulgaria, there is no clearly delineated legal practice concerning the acts of commission. (Parti, 2009)

In the past years, law enforcers have become increasingly interested in **virtual child sexual abuse,** the more spectacular, more interactive manifestation of the online sexual exploitation of children. Virtual child sexual abuse, also called ageplay is a sexual service which is - probably - offered by adult users to adult users. Virtual child prostitutes are available in virtual brothels, where there are playgrounds and children's rooms in place for the purpose. The perpetrators, behind whom there are real adults, may enter into a sexual relationship with virtual children with the help of action balls. The client pays for the virtual sexual intercourse to the provider of the services (a kind of madam operating a brothel) in virtual money. The virtual currency is quoted in the stock exchanges of the real world, and it can be converted to real money. The fact that there are often other avatars present and watching the virtual act, shows how popular these ageplays are.

In relation to crimes and deviances against persons in the virtual world, the underlying question is, who and how is **harmed** by these acts, if the physical body is not hurt, and not even in any danger? If we apply this question to virtual child sexual abuse, we may ask what role does the fight against ageplay, if there is no contact crime, and even the user posing as a child is actually an adult?

The debate is ongoing on what effect exactly the ageplay may have on the participants. According to some, the participants act out their desires through the game, and would never touch real children, while others say that it only promotes habituation.[12] (Clark & Scott, 2009) Quayle & Taylor write that the use of online images of children has several functions. It is a means of justifying behaviour, a way of making children compliant by blackmailing them, as trophies, or even as a form of currency for exchange with other paedophiles. (Quayle & Taylor, 2002; Sullivan, 2007) There is no proof that behaviours practiced in the virtual world will ever manifest in the real world. On the other hand there is no guarantee that virtual contact really keeps participants back from committing the same in the geographical world. The contact between the virtual and real world, however, is shown undeniably by the fact that ageplay is not an isolated phenomenon. There are also identified paedophile rings present in virtual communities (e.g. Boy Love Online in Second Life) which are trading images of real children.

[11] Art. 9 § 2 of the Cybercrime Convention; Art. 1 § b./ of the Framework Decision, Art. 20 § 3 of the Lanzarote Convention

[12] Psychologist and psychotherapist Lutz-Ulrich Besser said about ageplay that it breaks down inhibitions, therefore gets the person closer to an offline act, that is a contact crime. Besser believes that ageplay is a playful preparation of the contact with a real child and the commission of an offline crime.

There are also problems surrounding the definition of child sexual abuse in practice. Neither the Framework Decision, nor the Lanzarote Convention gives a definition of images that '**visually depict**' children.[13] Member states prosecuting realistic depictions of non-existent children could not come at an agreement so far regarding the extent to which the realistic images should be recognisable. For example, does a hand drawing of a child qualify? To what an extent should the children in a hand drawing be recognisable? To what an extent should a computer-generated image be recognisable (e.g. computer animations, child characters in computer games or avatars appearing in virtual communities)? The question may be rephrased as 'where exactly do the boundaries of a **virtual child** lie'. (Parti, 2009) A German public prosecutor (Peter Vogt, Oberstaatsanwalt, Halle) says that if the action and the age of the characters intended to be depicted are both clearly recognisable (e.g. in the computer-animated world of Second Life), then a crime is committed, independent of the virtual space and the actual age of the users behind the child-avatars. (Second Life Insider, 2007) The reason why virtual depictions are criminalised is that online and offline forms of abuse can not be separated, since not only the depicted child, but any child can be a victim. The necessary steps must be taken for the protection of children's human dignity, and against the popularisation of sexual exploitation of children. (Quayle, 2010; Williams, 2010) From the point of view of the criminal theory, criminalisation of depictions of non-existent children involves anticipatory criminal liability to an early endangering of goods as a means of prevention. Anticipatory criminal liability is abstract regulation of a societal process, hence, it is already a risk management tool, because it punishes the possible future transformation of an act based on a weak causal interdependence. (Zavrsnik, 2007)

The Lanzarote Convention and the 2009 proposal for an EP recommendation would not only regard the actual sexual abuse, but also its related **preparatory behaviours as sui generis criminal acts.** Such behaviour is for example an online chat session with the intention of sexual exploitation, or any other forms of contacting children online with the aim of the child's sexual abuse.[14] The question is, how it can be evidenced that the child was contacted online in preparation of an actual act of abuse offline, if the actual abuse does not take place (at least it is not attempted). In some countries – for example the United Kingdom (2004)[15], Austria (2006)[16] and Bulgaria (2007)[17] – such acts are punishable as sui generis crimes. In other countries, legal regulations on online child grooming are in preparation. (For an overview of countries see ICMEC annual reports on Child Pornography: Model Legislation and Global Review)

There is no general legal practice as regards regulating the possession of images of child sexual abuse. The Cybercrime Convention does give member states the opportunity to leave the act of possession unpunished, and therefore fails to create unified conditions for the prosecution of international child sexual abuse networks. At the same time, it is not clear

---

[13] Art. 1, b./ of the Framework Decision; Art. 20 § 2 of the Lanzarote Convention

[14] Art. 23 of the Lanzarote Convention

[15] The Sexual Offences Act (2003, Section 15) introduced the punishemnt of meeting children online (not in person, but by mobile phone, chatrooms or similar), if such happens with the intention of offline (physical) sexual abuse. Offenders face up to 10 years of inprisonment. See online at: http://www.opsi.gov.uk/acts/acts2003/en/ukpgaen_20030042_en_1.htm

16 The Austrian anti-stalking law (§107a StGB) punishes grooming with inprisonment of up to one year. See online at: http://www.internet4jurists.at/gesetze/bg_stgb01.htm#%A7_105

17 Section 155a Subsection (1) Criminal Code of the Republic of Bulgaria (State Gazette 38/2007) See online at: http://www.legislationline.org/documents/section/criminal-codes

whether the temporary storage of data such as *cookies, cache* or *temporary files* directory qualifies as a means of intentionally acquiring the depictions. A further question is, whether the establishment of criminal liability may be technically dependent on restorability. Acquiring and possession are also behaviours, whose criminalisation is aimed at the prevention of an event (sexual abuse) that may occur in the future, which is, in practice, not always causally linked to acquisition and possession. (Zavrsnik, 2010)

The Lanzarote Convention extends the scope of punishable preparatory behaviours, e.g. the **access** - without downloading - of websites containing child sexual abusive images.[18] Here, however, a question of proof arises, namely how to distinguish technically between intentional downloading and unintentional access. At the moment, whether the perpetrator **'accessed'** the child sexual abuse contents out of negligence or intentionally, can only be proven with indirect evidence. Such indirect evidence may be for instance the magnitude of further child sexual abuse images recovered from the computer of the accusee, their classification into galleries, or whether the accusee visited websites containing child sexual abusive material regularly or not. (Krone, 2004; 2005) By any means, a proof of intentional access beyond any doubt is at the moment technically not feasible.[19]

Abstract endangering delicts are very **difficult to prove**. While the abuse is not in at least an attemptual phase, we can not prove the causal link to online contact. In relation to the abstract endangering delicts, the danger of a thought police or an authoritarian state which passes judgement over people's activities not on the basis of actions, but thoughts, is very real. A wide array of online surveillance technologies are available today for the control of criminality, but only at the detriment of private life and human rights. (Wykes & Harcus, 2010) This is why the authors Wykes and Harcus remark that if governments continue this surveillance, they themselves will become terror governments, and the countries they govern become terror states.

In recent times, the sphere of persons or institutions that can be made liable in relation to virtual child sexual abuse has been extended. The liability of not only those making depictions available, but also that of the Internet service providers arises. The 2009 proposal for an EP recommendation would regard all persons 'serving' Internet users showing an interest in child abuse as criminal, among them also those **operating online chatrooms and forums** dealing with sexual exploitation of children. The question remains, however, which chatrooms can be proven to be aimed at the sexual exploitation of children. Is it sufficient for example for someone to initiate such a conversation in a chatroom and not to be expelled from the chatroom, or will it be only chatrooms with conversations exlusively of such nature that meet the criteria, or will there have to be such a chatroom service affiliated with a website containing child sexual expoitation content?

In the recent years, solutions for the blocking and filtering of illegal content on the Internet appeared one after the other. These also represent a rather controversial area of **crime**

---

[18] Art. 20 § 1.f/ of the Lanzarote Convention

[19] The Lanzarote Convention entered into force in July 2010. Countries who adopted the regulations of the convention into their national law include Denmark, the Netherlands, Greece, and the signatories include member states of the European Union such as France, Germany and the United Kingdom. These states support the ideas of the Convention on symbolic legislation. For the list of ratifications and signatories see:
http://conventions.coe.int/Treaty/Commun/ChercheSig.asp?NT=201&CM=8&DF=26/07/2010&CL=ENG

prevention. (See e.g. Sieber, 2009 on the debate surrounding German Internet-blocking efforts.) The government level control of the Internet is usually introduced under the aegis of the fight against online child sexual abuse, but it may be based on other delicts considered to be dangerous to the self or the public. The tools of content blocking on the Internet are not yet really effective, and can be by-passed with basic technical skills. On the other hand, the danger of overfiltering/overblocking is also realistic. This means that also some legal content is kept from the Internet users which infringes on such civic liberties as the freedom of access to information and fundamental rights such as the freedom of expression.

There are also moral, constitutional, debates, reconnaissance, and evidence difficulties related to **abstract endangering** crimes committed in an online environment. If the right to freedom of expression is a fundamental constitutional right, then on what grounds could the expression of an opinion be restricted which does not, only *may* pose a direct threat? What communication of how many users should be recorded for us to be able to prove the future intentional commission of the crime? If it is difficult to prove the intentional nature of the acquisition of illegal contents, than how will we prove that the attempts to groom a child had the final aim of sexual abuse – before any actual sexual abuse was attempted?

The international documents on the sexual exploitation of children clearly indicate legislative trends. They use criminal law to prevent the possible threat preceding the abstract threat – that is the anticipatory act of the crime. Criminal law may be a quick and simple response to a mass threat posing a great danger to certain layers of society (here minors) and can therefore be suitable to reassure society. It is another matter, whether this psychological tool achieves the goal of prevention in practice. Is it a necessary and proportionate tool for the prevention of such an abstract threat, and is criminal law really the most suitable means to reduce the threat?

The above mentioned legislative trends are influenced by the concerns communicated by the traditional media, the need for the protection of citizens (especially children), and the findings of scientific research. Therefore, legislation is shifting towards a detailed regulation which carries a couple of risks. Namely, there is a trap of overregulation, casuistic decisions, redundancy, and lack of transparency. There is also a troubling tendency of criminalising preparatory behaviours, due to the the fact that these are difficult to prove, and it is difficult to separate intentionality from negligence. Furthermore, due to overcriminalisation, criminal law becomes *prima ratio* instead of *ultima ratio*. Criminal law becomes the tool of primary reaction to milder deviances as well. This is a dangerous trend, especially if it is not coupled with other preventive tools, as information on safe Internet-use is scarce, and even parents are unaware of how they could prepare their children for the dangers of Internet-use. (Michelet, 2003; Mitchell et al., 2003; Kiesler et al., 2000; Turow & Nir, 2000)

5. Actual policing in virtual reality

Since in an ideal case, criminal law is only the last resort of regulators, let us see first what other means there are to fight harm and deviances in VR communities.

5.1 Self-regulation of virtual communities

The regulatory methods and bodies of virtual communities can be summarised as follows.

1. The community itself passes unwritten rules (informal rules: local 'customary law' that is written law in the making).

2. The community itself introduces written regulations (formal rules, such as conduct and content guidelines, e.g. Terms of Service, End User Licence Agreement).
3. A few members of the community decide on the rules based on authority bestowed on them by the community (case-by-case judgement, establishment and execution of sanctions e.g. expulsion from the community).
4. Internet Service Provider (ISP): the user accepts (registration) and regards as binding to himself the rules of the ISP when joining the community (when these rules are breached, the ISP may suspend or block the IP-address belonging to the given account, and in more severe cases may report to the authorities).
5. In the case of the gravest deviances (which cause great harm and are inevitably punishable under offline legal regulations), an external authority (investigative authority, jurisdiction) has competence on a national level.
6. Supranational level: the foundations of international cooperation are laid by international conventions and other documents. (For a general overview see Wall, 2001)

Virtual communities regulate primarily themselves with a set of regulations created from the bottom up (self-regulation**). Self-regulation** is a form of **informal social control** which the members of the community practice over rule-breakers. In the early stages of virtual worlds, the only regulator was the **system administrator**, who suspended or expelled members with technical means. This rather oligarchic system of regulation did not observe the interests of the community or the opinion of the community members, and could only work in smaller communities, where the control through the administrator was still effective. However, the continuous growth, democratic nature and zero-tolerance approach towards deviances of virtual communities lead to more mature regulations. This then resulted in the appearance of self-regulation and vigilante groups. The increasingly widespread organised activities of vandalistic groups demand a more serious defence and preparation from the community. One of the possible means of action against such organised attacks can be the vigilante groups, consisting of volunteering, independent 'policemen' (such a vigilante group in the virtual space Cyberworlds is Peacekeepers, see Williams, 2006). The tasks of vigilantes include the qualification of acts, sanctioning, the temporary ejection from the world, and account suspension or ultimate cancellation. The vigilantes' sheer presence has a preventive role, and increases the sense of security in the residents. (Crawford & Lister, 2004) If the vigilantes fail to reach their goal, the victim may report the attack at the ISP, who will warn the attacker to put an end to his behaviour, and suspend or block him from further participation. Users may also take action against the attacker individually by reporting him to the service provider (by sending an abuse report).[20] **If there is a more serious breach of rules,** the community may vote the attacker off from among the residents (ostracism). (Talin, 2003) Voting off from the community is based on the principle of shaming. Shaming functions as a punishment, and relies on the principle of conditioning which we learn at a young age. (Braithwaite, 1989) It teaches people to tell apart good and bad, and to feel guilty, if we think we have done something wrong. As the feeling of shame is an internal reaction (and not an external command), it has an immediate, and therefore educational effect. (Hirschi, 1969) Braithwaite says that the

[20] E.g. the Second Life Terms of Service says that 'big six transgressions', that is intolerance, harassment, assault, disclosure (of personal information), indecency and disturbing the peace may prompt an abuse report to Linden.

individual usually has the impulse to commit the crimes, but the stronger his ties to the (virtual) community, the greater the restraining effect. (Braithwaite, 1989)

The system of rules of virtual communities always corresponds to the needs of residents and is heterogenous. The governing is namely not practiced by a higher body, but the community based on organic rules, or a by a group of residents appointed by the community. Boellstorff calls this governance system 'grassroot governance'. (Boellstorff, 2008) Belonging to a virtual community may already in itself have a preventive function. The humiliation used by virtual communities may have a stronger restraining effect than the sanctions of geographical communities, since the bonds within a virtual community, as we have seen, may be stronger. However, community governance is also criticised.

The **administrator** represents his own selfish interests and not the community by setting the rules of joining the community, and judging the breaches of rules alone (dictatorship). (Doctorow, 2007; Chun, 2006) **Vigilantes** are effective in repelling systematic attacks destructive for the community, but are less effective in fighting sporadic, ad-hoc individual actions. The vigilantes are unable to act directly on the scene of the crime which means that action and sanction are separated in time. (Williams, 2010) **Abuse reports** sent by residents to the administrator carry the risk of another abuse, as they may contain false accusations which may lead to a tarnished reputation, account suspension, or financial losses even if the accusations are proven to be unfounded. If the reputation is tarnished disproportionately by the abuse report as compared to the damage caused, the abuse report is deviant, independent of whether it was at least partly justified or not. (Boellstorff, 2008)

Lessig says that **technology** is a more effective means of governance than legal regulations, norms or even community tools. (Lessig, 1999) This is the essence of the Internet, and regulation should also be based on this. The key to its effectiveness is that it can change the 'behaviour of avatars', can stop them from continuing their subversive behaviour, can be easily adjusted to the community's needs, can be a means of prevention and more than just a response to deviances (e.g. if the platform developer does not make certain behaviours possible). As it is automated, it is an invisible means of control, and does not give residents the feeling of being constantly watched and controlled. (Williams, 2006) Besides that, only technology makes immediate response possible. Lessig's main argument, however, is that technology does not rely on individual judgement, and there are no abuses of power. Technology is the most effective means of regulation, since it is liberal, equal and can be developed. Some critics say however, that even technical regulation can not be objective, as the system's crack-proofness always depends on the creativity of the code writers. Therefore technical design is also permeated by subjectivity. (Hosein et al., 2003)

5.2 Formal control of virtual communities – police presence

Eventhough there are only guesses as to the nature of threats, and estimates for their volume, and the criminal law assessment of preparatory acts is much debated, the presence of the police forces in VR communities is very real. While virtual communities solve the problem of crime prevention with their own internal control (**informal control**), geographical authorities carry out their criminal prosecution and preventive activities in a form approved by the state (**formal control**).

The presence of police organs in virtual communities on the one hand can raise the sense of security in virtual citizens, and on the other it is suitable for the surveillance of the life of virtual alteregos, and thereby for the discovery of crimes in an early stage through covert investigative measures.

Several countries maintain a police unit in virtual communities. One of the biggest both in terms of scope of action and the number of cooperating partners, is the London-based Child Exploitation and Online Protection Centre (CEOP)[21] which also carries out investigations in online environments to uncover child sexual abuse. CEOP cooperates with several police units and foreign police forces in the UK and abroad, because transnational crimes committed on the Internet demand international cooperation. CEOP has a central role in receiving and forwarding information. CEOP has the responsibility in the UK for receiving intelligence and information from overseas on child sexual abuse crimes. CEOP's Intelligence Faculty analyses and develops the material that they receive from other organisations and forwards details of individual suspects to local police forces, who in turn initiate their own investigations. CEOP's officers are technically the officers of the Serious Organized Crime Agency (SOCA). SOCA also has a Paedophilia Unit, but CEOP is an independent coordinator of online investigations into paedophilia cases.

CEOP does not only act as an investigative authority, but also makes considerable efforts in the fields of primary prevention, and informing the population about threats[22]. It also maintains a reporting centre, and keeps the knowledge of experts up-to-date with continuous trainings.

Other countries' police authorities are not directly present in virtual communities, that is they do not monitor communities directly, but may initiate criminal proceedings, if they acquire information on crimes committed in a virtual space. The German investigative television channel ReportMainz looked into the child sexual abuse scandal around Second Life. They found that the German Federal Criminal Police Office (Bundeskriminalamt) was informed by CEOP in early 2007 that in the virtual world of Second Life sexual services of child avatars are sold at brothels (that is children are forced into prostitution). There were German citizens among the offenders, who accessed the virtual community through German servers. The detectives of the Federal Criminal Police Office entered the virtual community, and together with the undercover detectives of CEOP uncovered the criminal ring. (Report Mainz, 2007; see also CEOP Center film, 2009) The administrator of Second Life, Linden Lab agrees to cooperation with investigative authorities, but the users' statement accepted when entering also stipulates that no acts may be committed in Second Life that would constitute crimes in the geographical world, and they expressly refer to the ban on abuse against children. What is more, they also ask users to report any such abuse they encounter to the International Centre for Missing and Exploited Children (ICMEC). They have also announced that they intend to develop a system that would prevent such abuse. How they would do it, remains a question.

The government bodies and the military of the US are also present in Second Life, where they possess islands. (Au, 2005) With the spread of the trade with virtual goods, there has been an extension of state power to virtual communities in recent times. The European Union levied a tax on its citizens who are residents in Second Life, and have an account in the virtual world. The residents pay tax after real and movable estate that they directly buy from the developer of the platform, Linden Lab.[23] The US Congress discussed a possible tax

[21] CEOP also maintains a website, http://www.ceop.gov.uk

[22] For CEOP's awareness-raising campaign see http://www.thinkuknow.co.uk

[23] Anything that a resident pays for to Linden Lab has VAT added. This includes premium account registration, purchases from the Land Store, land use fees (tier), Private Region fees, land auctions, LindeX transaction fees. (WikiSecondlife on VAT, 2010)

on Second Life residents after their income and property there, and also a possible intervention of the US authorities in the regulation of contents. (NeoWin, 2009) Boellstorff believes that this is bound to be the most debated issue in relation to VR communities in the future.

Eventhough most police organs are not directly present in virtual communities, they are carrying out investigations in relation to crimes in virtual worlds within the framework of international cooperation. Therefore Europol, the police cooperation organisation of the European Union, and the coordinator of international cooperation, Eurojust both have a significant role in uncovering crimes committed online. (See for example Operation Koala: CEOP press release, 2007)

5.3 Outsourcing of formal control

In recent times, there is a visible trend for state crime prevention activities (**formal control**) to be outsourced. More and more, the state's crime prevention role is taken over by NGOs, and the police also involve NGOs in their criminal prosecution activities (thereby strengthening informal control).

The reason for the outsourcing of state criminal prosecution activities is on the one hand the continuous specialisation of technical skills related to the Internet, and on the other the decentralisation of the state. (Yar, 2010) The concept of the traditional economic and social welfare state failed in the second half of the 20th century. The state is trying to perform these tasks traditionally in its own sphere of responsibility in that it hires NGOs for the purpose. Such tasks include containing crime, and also prevention. The decentralisation of the state is based on a neoliberal philosophy which gradually liberalises and deregulates markets, and privatises the public sphere. This has the advantage that costs are shared among those in charge of different tasks, and it also frees public agencies - such as the police force - from the burden of responsibility and the tasks in the ever expanding field of crime prevention. The growing rate of privatisation of the control of online crimes and its acquisition of economic players is a result of this neoliberal process. It was high time, as the police are not achieving any apparent results in the field of investigations into and the procesution of Internet crime against significant financial investments. (Wall, 2001)

Decentralisation not only shows in the outsourcing of criminal prosecution, but also that of crime prevention activities. The moral panic that the state made good use of and in certain cases artificially generated to shape the self-protection mechanisms of citizens has backfired. Citizens' fear of crime has become irrational. Füredi even speaks of a fear of fear itself (Füredi, 1997) which manifests in that citizens are overly afraid, and even panic when it comes to crimes, irrespective of whether there is an actual threat. (Wall, 2010) This is also mentioned in Garland's crime complex, where he says that we expect crime on a large scale, and go into a state of shock if we do not encounter it. (Garland, 2001) The fulfilment of crime prevention tasks - awareness raising, crime and subcrime reporting, victim assisting - is transferred more and more to user communities. User communities are self-regulating communities, hence they decide themselves what needs protecting and how, and what the means of protection should be.

According to Yar's classification, there are criminal prosecution organs participating in the regulation of the Internet which belong to the non-governmental area. On the other hand, commercial players carrying out profit-oriented policing activities have a great role to play in regulation. (Yar, 2010) Such is for example the awareness-raising activity of software manufacturers, or their contribution to containing online crime. An example for this is the Child Exploitation Tracking System (CETS) developed by Microsoft Corporations in 2005 for the tracking of online child sexual abuse offenders. The application based on Microsoft's technology is used by investigative authorities across the world to track the online movements of suspected offenders and to collect evidence without accidentally performing the same work twice.[24] This example shows well that external players are needed in criminal prosecution not only due to the growing number of tasks, and the insufficiency of state competencies, but also rapid technical development. The more the investigative authorities are unable to keep pace with technical development, the greater and more important the role of business organisations in the field of criminal prosecution.

For investigations in virtual worlds, the cooperation of the platform operator or the Internet service provider with investigative authorities is very often necessary for technical reasons. The platform operator, who is actually the system administrator, is the lord over virtual worlds. He has the log-in and other personal data of the suspected offender, without which the investigative authorities could never track down the offenders. (In the case of Second Life, Linden Lab cooperates with the authorities of the geographical world in reconnaisance activities. They establish who are behind the avatars committing crimes in the sense of geographical law, and put the user accounts at the disposal of investigative authorities.) A good example for the cooperation of Internet service providers is the application of solutions developed for the filtering and blocking of illegal and harmful online content. (Sieber & Nolde, 2008; Tous, 2009) Governments have the option of several different solutions for filtering illegal or harmful content. All of them are based on the principle that the main ISPs active in the given country should filter the content passing through their servers based on certain considerations, so that these do not get to the users. ISPs however also have an obligation to report to investigative authorities if they encounter illegal content. The Cybercrime Convention and the Data Retention Directive of the European Union prescribe a similar obligation for the ISPs in relation to the storage and forwarding to the investigative authority of traffic data.[25] Service provider cooperation plays an important part in each document, as data from ISPs serve as evidence in criminal proceedings.

The need for the private regulation of the Internet is natural. It is the interest of users and user communities to protect what they consider valuable and threatened, independent of priorities defined by the state. (For more on top-down initiative and consensus based processes see Castells, 2002) Several such citizens' initiatives of crime prevention developed in relation to the fight against online child abuse. Such is for example Internet Watch Foundation (IWF)[26] which was established in 1996 in the United Kingdom. IWF is a self-regulating system consisting of the representatives of content providers and telecommunication companies. Its method is the monitoring of online content. They are

---

[24] For more see: http://www.microsoft.com/industry/publicsector/government/cetsnews.mspx

[25] Directive 2006/24/EC of the European Parliament and of the Council of 15 March 2006 on the retention of data generated or processed in connection with the provision of publicly available electronic communications services or of public communications and the modification of directive 2002/58/EC (Data Retention Directive) (OJ L 105/54-63)

[26] IWF: http://www.iwf.org.uk

primarily fighting online child abuse, hate speech and racist content, and maintain a hotline for reports by the public. They compile a blacklist of non-desirable contents which several ISPs have adopted, and on the basis of which they remove content. Working To Halt Online Abuse (WHOA)[27] is a similar initiative started in 1997, and fighting against Internet harassment and assault. The International Association of Internet Hotlines (INHOPE)[28] was established in 1999, and defines and unifies the description of illegal and harmful online content, maintains reporting hotlines in 42 countries around the world, and also provides the public with advice adjusted to local conditions (helpline and awareness raising) on safe surfing. The organisation Cyberangels, mainly involved in awareness raising, was established in 1995, based on the example of Guardian Angels started in the US to fight street crime.[29] Cyberangels draws attention to the latest online crime trends, offers protection solutions to users in the case of online stalking, helps avoid identity theft and maintain online privacy. The Association of Sites Advocating Child Protection (ASACP)[30] is a certification association of pornographic websites registered in the US, and has been watching over the legality and compliance of pornographic content using the labelling technology since 1996. This organisation also has a hotline to promote the legal awareness of users.

The investigative authorities also cooperate with several service providers of online platforms to detect crimes. A recent example to this is a statement made by Facebook in July 2010 that they would add a Facebook Panic Button to the website. Facebook already allows its users to report online attacks against them, but the Panic Button would expressly be dedicated to reporting child sex abuse. The user would be able to send his report directly to CEOP by klicking the Panic Button. (CEOP press release, 2010) Besides child protection, there are a number of non-governmental organisations working in other fields, such as the freedom of speech and expression, privacy protection, and the free movement of information.

A virtual community is ideally regulated and governed from within, by itself (informal control). Formal (geographical) control is for many reasons not desirable. If the state once starts to restrict the freedom of speech – first only for reasons of fighting illegal and harmful content –, there is no guarantee that the restriction of civic liberties will stop at that. The state's demand for exerting criminal law clashes with civic liberties.

Virtual communities have grassroot governance, and no external, formal control fits into this system either from a technical, or a social structure point of view. Formal control has an effect that evolves towards the restriction of members' rights and is disruptive of the community. The rules of geographical authorities do not fit into the decentralised system of virtual communities. The Internet is transnational, and its nature does not allow any independent power to impose dedicated rules on it. What is more, the assessment of contents can be different in different jurisdictions, but the Internet does not distinguish between users on the grounds of their nationality, or what geographical law is applicable to any given user. (Williams, 2010; Boyle, 1997)

[27] WHOA: http://www.haltabuse.org/
[28] INHOPE: https://www.inhope.org/
[29] Cyberangels: http://www.cyberangels.org/security/index.php
[30] ASACP: http://www.asacp.org/

There may be concerns in relation to the activities of 'external', non-police organisations that they represent their own interests better, than those of the community. So for example manufacturers of content filter software have less interest in protecting consumers than in generating profit, and responding to the requirements of the marketplace. (Yar calls this democratic deficit: Yar, 2010)

6. Conclusion

In the 1990s, computer-mediated communication was judged without empirical research. But even today, we know relatively little about crimes and deviance occuring in the virtual world. (Williams, 2010)

Virtual worlds are not merely copies of the geographical world. Actual world computers and flesh and blood bodies are needed for their existence, and they possess a lot of elements of actual society. Through technology, residents can recreate their world in a way that nobody today can predict, since it is the first time in history this is happening. (Boellstorff, 2008)

There is need for research on the validity of criminological theories online (Williams, 2006) and how these communities could be regulated more effectively. Further concepts should be elaborated on what combination of formal, informal and technical control can effectively curb and give a response to offences.

Moral panic which only intensifies with the development of online communities, has an effect both on the degree of detail of legislation and the intensity of police intervention. The action of the authorities of the geographical world is absolutely necessary in relation to the gravest and most widespread acts. However, imposing rules on the communities is mainly the task of the comminities themselves. The decentralised technical structures of the Internet do not make it possible for an external entity to shape the rules to be followed. Attempts should be appreciated of course, and the state's efforts to exert criminal law are also understandable, as their aim is the protection of national security and the citizens. We should, however, concentrate on three important expectations.

The first one is that legal **regulations should be transparent and easy to follow**. In virtual communities, some activities are not realised as in real space, and the harm or actual threat they pose are not direct counterparts of geographical harms and threats, for which reason the prosecution of these acts in the virtual world is questionnable.

The second requirement is that criminal law should remain in its traditional role as **ultima ratio**. Criminal law should not be the primary means to curb virtual deviances. Legal regulations should be supplemented with preventive measures at government level, such as for example raising awareness of threats, school education, and public information campaigns.

The third very important criterion is **adjusting the approach of law enforcement to the virtual space**. This does not only mean the continuous technical training of law enforcement officers, but also the learning of an analytical approach which would help law enforcement understand the events of virtual communities, namely who does what and why in the virtual world. Knowledge of the virtual community teaches us to identify in what situations there is a real threat, and identify the preparatory behaviours of actual cimes. We should however also remember that correlation between events does not equal causality.

7. References

ABCNews.com, 2000: 'Barrel Killings Suspect Charged Again' 28 July 2000 *ABCNews.com* Available at: http://abcnews.go.com/US/story?id=96339&page=1; [15/05/2010]

Au, W.J. (2005). 'The Tragic of Tringo' *New World Notes'* 8 March, 2005 Available at: http://nwn.blogs.com/nwn/2005/03/the_tragics_of_.html [30/07/2010]

Austin, J.L. (1975). *How To Do Things With Words: [2nd ed.]* Harvard University Press ISBN 978-0-674-41152-4 Cambridge, MA

Becker, P.J., Byers, B. & Jipson, A. (2000). The contentuous American debate: the first Amendment and Internet-based hate speech. *International Review of Law, Computers, and Technology,* Vol. 14, No. 1: 33-41 ISSN 1364-6885

Bell, D. (1999) [1993]. *The Coming of Post-Industrial Society [3rd ed.]* Basic Books ISBN 0-465-01281 New York

Bocij, P. (2004). *Cyberstaling: Harassment in the Internet age and how to protect your family.* Praeger ISBN 0-275-98118-5 Westport, Connecticut, London

Boellstorff, T. (2008). *Coming of Age in Second Life.* Princeton University Press ISBN 978-0-691-13528-1 Princeton & Oxford

Boyle, J. (1997). Foucault in Cyberspace: surveillance, sovereignty and hard-wired censors. *University of Cincinnati Law Review,* Vol. 66 No. 2: 177-205 Available at: http://www.law.duke.edu/boylesite/foucault.htm [30/07/2010] ISSN 0009-6881

Braithwaite, J. (1989). *Crime, Shame and Reintegration,* Cambridge University Press ISBN 0-521-35668-7 Cambridge

Butler, J. (1997). *Excitable Speech:: A Politics of the Performative.,* Routledge ISBN 0-415-91587-2 London

Casey, E. (Ed.) (2004). *Digital evidence and computer crime. Forensic science, computers and the Internet [2nd ed.]* Elsevier Academic Press ISBN 0-12-163104-4 San Diego, CA

Castells, M. (2002). *The Internet Galaxy: Reflection on the Internet, Business and Society,* Oxford Univesrity Press ISBN 3-8100-3593-9 Oxford

CEOP Center film, 2009: *'Victim Identification'* Available at: http://www.youtube.com/watch?v=CTvufchSYMs [30/07/2010]

CEOP press release, 2007: *'46 Arrests in UK as international child sex offender network smashed'* 5 November 2007 Available at: http://www.ceop.police.uk/mediacentre/pressreleases/2007/ceop_05112007.asp; [27/07/2010]

CEOP press release, 2010: *'Facebook and CEOP get 'appy. Facebook and CEOP join forces to deliver internet safety to young internet users'* 12 July 2010 Available at: http://www.ceop.police.uk/mediacentre/pressreleases/2010/ceop_12072010fb.asp; [28/07/2010]

Chun, W. (2006). *Control and Freedom: Power and Paranoia in the Age of Fiber Optics,* MIT Press ISBN 978-0-262-03332-9 Cambridge, MA

Clark, N. & Scott, P.S. (2009). *Game addiction: The experience and the effects,* McFarland & Co. ISBN 978-0-7864-4364-2 North Carolina, US

Curtis, P. (1992). Mudding: Social Phenomena in Text-Based Virtual Realities, In: *Culture of the Internet.* Kiesler, S. (Ed.) 121-42 Lawrence Erlbaum Associates. ISBN 0-8058-1635-6 Mahwah, NJ

Delgado, R. (1993). Words that wound: A tort action for racial insults, In: *Words That Wound: Critical Race Theory, Assaultive Speech, And The First Amendment.* Matsuda, M.J.,

Lawrence, C.R., Delgado, R. & Crenshaw, K.W. (Eds.): 131-40 Westview Press ISBN 978-0-813-38428-3 Boulder, CO

Dibbel, J. (1998). *'A Rape in Cyberspace'* Available at: http://www.juliandibbell.com/articles/a-rape-in-cyberspace/; [02/05/2010]

Doctorow, C. (2007). 'Why Online Games are Dictatorship?' *Information Week* 16 April, 2007 Available at: http://informationweek.com/internet/showArticle.jhtml?articleID=199100026&pgno=1&queryText=; [01/05/2010]

Foo, C.Y. (2004). Redefining Grief Play. *Proceedings of the Other Players conference,* Copenhagen, Denmark. Available at: http://www.itu.dk/op/papers/yang_foo.pdf [27/10/2006]

Füredi, F. (1997). *Culture of Fear,* Continuum ISBN 0-304-3375-1 London

Garland, D. (2001). *The Culture of Control,* Oxford University Press ISBN 0-19-829937-0 Oxford

Harmon, D. & Boeringer, S.B. (1997). A content analysis of internet-accessible written pornographic depictions, *Electronic Journal of Sociology,* Available at: http://www.sociology.org/content/vol003.001/boeringer.html [18/07/2010] ISSN 1198-3655

Hirschi, T. (1969). *Causes of delinquency.* University of California Press ISBN 978-0-765-80900-1 Berkeley, LA

Hosein, G., Tsavios, P. & Whitley, E. (2003). Regulating architecture and architectures of regulation: Contributions from information systems, *International Review of Law, Computers and Techology,* Vol. 17 No. 1: 85-97 ISSN 1360-0869

ICMEC annual reports on Child Pornography: Model Legislation and Global Review, 2008, Alexandria, Virginia: USA, Available at: http://www.icmec.org/en_X1/English__5th_Edition_.pdf; [19/06/2010]

Innes, M. (2004). Reinventing tradition? Reassurance, neighbourhood security and policing, *Criminology and Criminal Justice* Vol. 4 No. 2: 151-71 ISSN 1748-8966

Jenkins, P. (1998). *Moral Panic. Changing concepts of the child molester in modern America.* Yale University Press ISBN 0-300-07387-9 New Haven & London

Joinson, A.N. (2003). *Understanding the Psychology of Internet Behaviour,* Palgrave Macmillan ISBN 0-333-98467-6 London

Kiesler, S., Zdaniuk, B., Lundmark, V. & Kraut, R. (2000). Troubles with the Internet: The dynamics of help at home, *Human-Computer Interaction,* Vol. 15 No. 4: 323-51 ISSN 1532-7051

Korinek L. (2006). *Bűnözési elméletek. [Theories on Offending]* Duna Palota és Kiadó ISBN 963-8036-97-4 Budapest

Krone, T. (2004). A Typology of Online Child Pornography Offending. Trends and Issues in Crime and Criminal Justice, *Leaflet of Australian Institute of Criminology,* No. 279 (June 2004) ISSN 1836-2206 Canberra

Krone, T. (2005). Does Thinking Make it so? Defining Online Child Pornography Possession Offences. Trends and Issues in Crime and Criminal Justice, *Leaflet of Australian High Tech Crime Centre,* No. 299 (April 2005) ISSN 1836-2206 Canberra

Lessig, L. (1999). *Code and Other laws of Cyberspace.* Basic Books 978-0-465-03913-5 New York

MacKinnon, C.A. (Ed.) (1997). *In Harm's Way: The Pornography Civil Rights Hearings,* Harvard University Press, ISBN 0-674-44578-3 Cambridge, Mass.

MacKinnon, R.C. (1997). Virtual rape, *Journal of Computer-Mediated Communication*, Vol. 2 No. 4, Available at: http://www3.interscience.wiley.com/cgi-bin/fulltext/120837717/HTMLSTART [16/08/2009] ISSN 1083-6101

Mann, D., Sutton, M. & Tuffin, R. (2003). The evolution of hate: social dynamics in white racist newsgroups, *Internet Journal of Criminology*, Available at: http://www.flashmousepublishing.com [21/06/2009] ISSN 1198-3655

Matsuda, M.J., Lawrence, C.R., Delgado, R. & Crenshaw, K.W. (1993). *Words That Wound: Critical Race Theory, Assaultive Speech, and The First Amendment*, Westview Press ISBN 978-0-813-38428-3 Boulder, CO

Markham, A.N. (1998). *Life Online: Researching Real Experience in Virtual Space*, Altamira Press ISBN 978-0-761-99030-7 Walnut Creek, CA

Mehta, M. D., & Plaza, D. E. (1997). Pornography in cyberspace: An exploration of what's in Usenet, In: *Culture of the Internet*, Kiesler, S. (Ed.): 53-67 Lawrence Erlbaum ISBN 0-8058-1635-6 Mahwah, NJ

Meloy, J. (1998). The psychology of stalking In: *The psychology of stalking: Clinical and forensic perspectives*, J. Meloy (Ed.):. 2-21 Academic Press ISBN: 0-12-490560-9 San Diego, CA

Michelet, I. (2003). *Our Children at Risk Online: The Example of Thailand.* A Survey Report. ECPAT International & UNICEF: 7-43 Available at: http://vac.wvasiapacific.org/downloads/ecpat2.pdf; [12/02/2008]

Mitchell, K.J., Finkelhor, D. & Wolak, J. (2003). The exposure of youth to unwanted sexual material on the internet. A national survey of risk, impact, and prevention, *Youth & Society*, Vol. 34, No. 3: 330-58 ISSN 1552-8499

Moitra, S.D. (2003). *Analysis and Modelling of Cybercrime: Prospects and Potential*, Research in Brief, Max Planck Institute for Foreign and International Criminal Law ISBN 3-86113-145-5 Freiburg

Mulligan, J. & Patrovsky, B. (2003). *Developing Online Games: An Insiders Guide*, New Riders ISBN 978-1-592-73000-1 Indianapolis

Murff, K. N. (2007). *Digital Crime Investigation Trends in State and Local Law Enfircement*, UMI Dissertation Services, UMI Number: 3294390 (No ISSN) Ann Arbor, Michigan, USA

NeoWin, 2009: 'IRS to tax Second Life/World of Warcraft earnings' 14 January 2009 *NeoWin* Available at: http://www.neowin.net/news/irs-to-tax-second-lifeworld-of-warcraft-earnings-3; [30/07/2010]

Oldenburg, R. (1999). *The Great Good Place*, Marlowe & Co. ISBN 1-6924-681-5 New York

Ondrejka, C.R. (2004). Escaping the Guilded Cage: User Created Content and Building the Metaverse, *Social Science Reserach Network Online* Available at: http://papers.ssrn.com/sol3/papers.cfm?abstract_id=538362; [12/07/2010]

Parti, K. (2009). *Gyermekpornográfia az interneten [Child pornography on the Internet]* Bíbor Kiadó ISBN 978-963-9634-92-3 Miskolc

Parti, K. (2010). Alterations in danger-awareness due to the infocommunication revolution and its effect on legislation, In: *Current Issues in IT Security. Proceedings of the interdisciplinary conference 12-14 May, 2009* Bellini, M., Brunst, P. & Jähnke, J. (Eds.): 91-105 Duncker & Humblot ISSN 1860-0093 Berlin

Quayle, E. (2010). Child pornography. In: *Handbook of Internet Crime*, Yar, J. & Jewkes, Y. (Eds.): 343-68 Willan Publishing ISBN 978-1-84392-524-8 USA & Canada

Quayle, E. & Taylor, M. (2002). Paedophiles, pornography and the Internet: Assessment issues *British Journal of Social Work*, Vol. 32 No. 7: 863-75 ISSN 0045-3102

Reid, E.M. (1999). Hierarchy and power: Social control in cyberspace, In: *Communities in Cyberspace*, Smith, M.A. & Kollock, P. (Eds.): 107-33 Routledge ISBN 0-415-19139-4 London

Reno, J. (1999). Cyberstalking: *A new challenge for law enforcement and industry*, U.S. Department of Justice: Washington, DC, Available at: http://www.justice.gov/criminal/cybercrime/cyberstalking.htm [01/12/2009]

Report Mainz, 2007: '*Kinderpornographie in Second Life*' Available at: http://www.youtube.com/watch?v=dynfVtC8Gt4; [27/07/2010]

Reynolds, R. (2005). '*The Four Worlds Theory*' Available at: http://terranova.blogs.com/terra_nova/2005/08/the_four_worlds.html; [13/07/2010]

Rimm, M. (1995). Marketing pornography on the information superhighway: a survey of 917,410 images, descriptions, short stories and animations downloaded 8.5 million times by consumers in over 2,000 cities in forty countries, provinces and territories, *The Georgetown Law Journal*, Vol. 83 No. 5: 1849-934 ISSN 0016-8092

Schechner, R. (1988). Playing, *Play and Culture*, Vol. 1, No. 1: 3-20 ISSN 0894-4253

Second Life Insider, 2007: 'Transcript of the German piece about age play' *Second Life Insider*, 11 May 2007, Available at: http://www.secondlifeinsider.com/2007/05/11/transcript-of-the-german-piece-about-age-play/; [21/07/2010]

Sieber, U. (2009). Sperrverpflichtungen gegen Kinderpornografie im Internet, *Juristen Zeitung* Vol. 64 No. 13: 653-62 ISSN 0022-6882

Sieber, U. & Nolde, M. (2008). *Sperrverfügungen im Internet*, Dunkel & Humblot ISBN 978-3-86113-861-7 Berlin

Simon, J. (2007). *Governing Through Crime: How the War on Crime Transformed American Democracy and Created a Culture of Fear*, Oxford University Press ISBN 0-19-518108-5 New York

Sullivan, J. (2007). Abuse spiral. *Presentation, proceeded at the Child Exploitation and Online Protection Centre Training*, Bucharest, 11-17 November 2007

Suter-Zürcher, S. (2003). *Die Strafbarkeit der sexuellen Handlungen mit Kindern nach Art. 187 StGB*. Universität Zürich ISBN 3-7255-4640-1 Basel-Genf

Taipale, K. (2006). Why can't we all get along: how technology, security and privacy can coexist in the digital age, In: *Cybercrime: Digital Cops in a Networked Environment*, Balkin, J., Grimmelmann, J., Katz, E., Kozlovski, N., Wagman, S. & Zarsky, T. (Eds.): 151-83: New York University Press ISBN 0-8147-9983-3 New York

Talin (2003). Managing Deviant Behaviour in Online Worlds, In: *Developing Online Games: An Insider's Guide*, Mulligan, J. & Partovsky, B. (Eds.): 347-60 New Riders ISBN 978-1-592-73000-1 Indianapolis

Tous, J. (2009). Government filtering of online content, *E-Newsletter on the Fight Against Cybercrime (enac)*, Vol. 1 No. 2: 14-20 ISSN 2013-5327

Turkle, S. (1995). *Life on Screen: Identity in the Age of the Internet*, Weidenfeld & Nicolson ISBN 0-684-80353-4 London

Turow, J. & Nir, L. (2000). *The Internet and the family 2000: The view from parents, the view from kids*, University of Pennsylvania, Annenberg Public Policy Center: Philadelphia, Available at: http://www.eric.ed.gov/PDFS/ED448874.pdf; [23/02/2008]

Wall, D.S. (2001). Maintaining order and law on the Internet, In: *Crime and the Internet,* Wall, D.S. (Ed.): 167-83 Routledge ISBN 0-415-24429-3 London

Wall, S.D. (2007). *Cybercrime: The Transformation of Crime in the Information Age,* Polity Press ISBN 978-0-7456-2735-9 Cambridge

Wall, D.S. (2008). Cybercrime, media and insecurity: The shaping of public perceptions of cybercrime, *International Review of Law Computers & Technology* Vol. 22 Nos. 1–2: 45–63 ISSN 1610-7608

Wall, D.S. (2010). Criminalising cyberspace: The rise of the Internet as a 'crime problem', In: *Handbook of Internet Crime* (op.cit.): 88-102

WikiSecondlife on VAT, 2010: http://wiki.secondlife.com/wiki/Linden_Lab_Official:Value_Added_Tax_(VAT)_Frequently_Asked_Questions#In_general.2C_who_should_be_charged_VAT.3F; [12/07/2010]

Williams, M. (2004). Understanding King Punisher and his order: Vandalism in a virtual reality community - motives, meanings and possible solutions, *Internet Journal of Criminology,* No ISSN, Available at: http://www.internetjournalofcriminology.com/Williams%20-%20Understanding%20King%20Punisher%20and%20his%20Order.pdf; [12/07/2010]

Williams, M. (2006). *Virtually Criminal. Crime, Deviance and Regulation Online,* Routledge ISBN 978-0-415-36404-1 London & New York

Williams, M. (2010). The virtual neighbourhood watch: Netizens in action, In: *Handbook of Internet Crime* (op.cit.): 562-80

Wykes, M. (2010). Harm, suicide and homicide in cyberspace: Assessing causuality and control, In: *Handbook of Internet Crime* (op.cit.): 369-94

Wykes, M. & Harcus, D. (2010). Cyber-terror: construction, criminalisation and control, In: *Handbook of Internet Crime* (op.cit.): 214-29

Yar, M. (2010). Private policing of Internet crime, In: *Handbook of Internet Crime,* Yar, J. & Jewkes, Y. (Eds.): 546-60 Willan Publishing ISBN 978-1-84392-524-8 USA & Canada

Zavrsnik, A. (2007). Virtual child pornography: The concept of a pseudo-photograph. *Presentation proceeded at 7th Annual Conference of the European Society of Criminology,* Bologna, 26-29 Sept, 2007

Zavrsnik, A. (2010). Criminal Justice Systems' (Over)Reactions to IT Security Threats, In: *Current Issues in IT Security. Proceedings of the interdisciplinary conference 12-14 May, 2009* (op.cit.): 117-40